THE SCOUTING NOTEBOOK 2002

Produced by STATS, Inc.
(Sports Team Analysis and Tracking Systems, Inc.)

John Dewan, Editor
Tony Nistler, Associate Editor
Marc Carl, Thom Henninger & Jim Henzler,
Assistant Editors

Statistics by STATS, Inc.

STATS INC.
PUBLISHING

**I dedicate this book to my daughter, Emily, and my wife, Kathy.
I cherish every day that I get to spend with you. You both can make me
laugh on the worst of days. Kathy, thanks for being a great mom and
wife. I appreciate everything you do for us. Emily, you'll never know
how much I love being your dad. Your smile melts my heart.
I love you both more than I can put into words.**

—Jeff Smith

The photographs which appear in *The Scouting Notebook 2002* were furnished individually by the following Major League Baseball teams, whose cooperation is gratefully acknowledged: Anaheim Angels, Baltimore Orioles, Boston Red Sox, Chicago White Sox/Ron Vesely, Cleveland Indians, Detroit Tigers, Kansas City Royals, Minnesota Twins, New York Yankees, Oakland Athletics, Seattle Mariners, Tampa Bay Devil Rays, Texas Rangers, Toronto Blue Jays, Arizona Diamondbacks, Atlanta Braves, Chicago Cubs, Cincinnati Reds, Colorado Rockies, Florida Marlins, Houston Astros, Los Angeles Dodgers, Montreal Expos, New York Mets, Philadelphia Phillies, Pittsburgh Pirates, St. Louis Cardinals, San Diego Padres and San Francisco Giants/Kuno. Thanks also to Brian Bahr, Tom Hauck and Matthew Stockman/Allsport for providing the Milwaukee Brewers photos.

Cover by Ryan Balock

Cover photos by David Durochick (Roger Clemens) and Tom Hauck/Allsport (Jason Giambi)

First Edition: January, 2002

Printed in the United States of America.

ISBN 1-884064-99-X

Notice To Our Loyal Readers:

Beginning with our 2002 editions, many of your favorite STATS annuals will only be available directly from STATS, Inc. We are reducing the number of our titles to be sold in bookstores nationwide, but are not reducing the number of titles we publish.

You can visit our online bookstore at www.stats.com and order a *free STATS Product Guide/Sports Calendar* to be sent directly to you. This will allow us to include you in future product availability announcements.

If you would like to be added to our mailing list in order to be informed about releases of titles and special offers, please fill out the form below and return by mail to:

STATS, Inc.
8130 Lehigh Avenue
Morton Grove, IL 60053
ATTN: Pubs Mailing Request

Or, you may fax this page to (847) 470-9140. Please direct the fax to the attention of "Pubs Mailing Request."

Name_____

Address_____

City_____ State_____ Zip_____

Phone (____)_____ Ext._____ Fax (____)_____

E-mail_____

For more information regarding the mailing list, please call **1-800-63-STATS**.

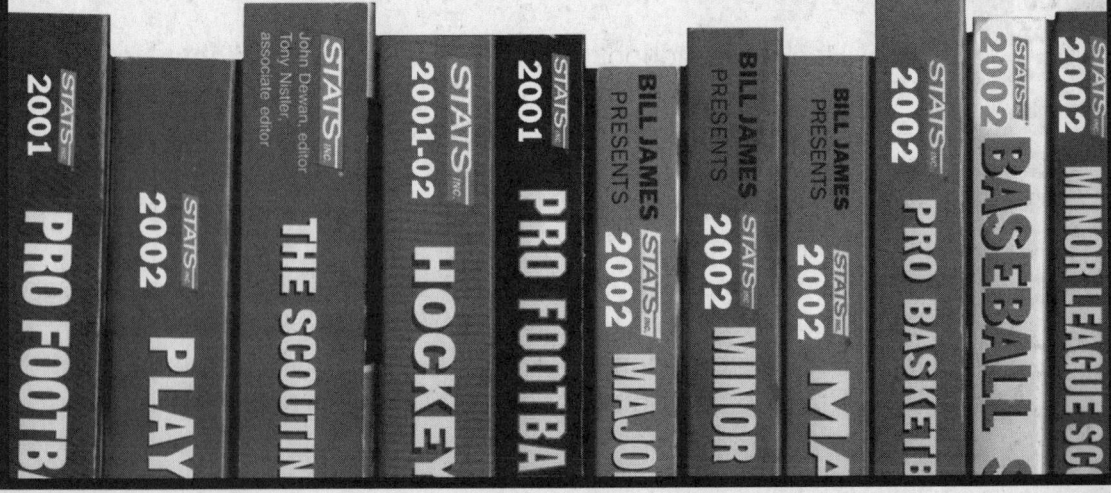

Acknowledgments

The largest and most labor-intensive annual published by STATS, Inc. is *The Scouting Notebook*. The countless hours invested during the fall and winter months produce a volume of work of which we all are proud. Thanks to all who had a hand in our efforts.

The STATS team is successfully anchored by President Alan Leib. Senior Vice President Steve Byrd steers our consumer and TV divisions, while Vice President Robert Schur directs our commercial divisions.

Tony Nistler manages the publications unit that produces this book and all of our other sports titles. Tony, Thom Henninger and Jim Henzler oversaw editorial responsibilities, with help from Taylor Bechtold, Norm DeNosaquo and Corey Roberts. Special thanks go to STATS co-founder John Dewan, who lent his expertise to this project by editing each and every page you now hold in your hands. Getting the numbers programmed appropriately was the responsibility of Tim Coletta. Marc Carl manipulated the many columns and tables that are key to the book's design. Getting the word out about and fulfulling orders for *The Scouting Notebook* and other STATS publications require the hard work of Mike Dreckmann, Walter Lis, Ryan Balock, Andy Degnan and Marc Moeller. Ryan designed this book's cover.

We couldn't get the book out without our Data Collection Department. Managing the collection of all the numbers you'll find on these pages is Allan Spear. Special thanks to Jeff Chernow, who oversees the accuracy of our MLB data. Thanks also to the vast network of reporters who cover each and every major league game.

Keeping STATS at the forefront of the sports information business on a daily basis are Jim Capuano, our Senior Vice President of Sales; Jeff Smith, who manages our technical operations; and Howard Lanin, who oversees our financial and administration areas.

The STATS Research Department for Fox Sports in Los Angeles is headed by Don Zminda, with help from Director of Operations Steve Vanderpool. Their team of sports researchers and technical staff provides many of the stats that are broadcast daily from the Fox Sports studios, as well as from remote pregame, postgame and live game telecasts on Fox and Fox Sports Net.

The Scouting Staff

The scouting reports on each team's ballpark, manager and significant players were written by the following people, in conjunction with our editors:

Anaheim Angels	Bill Shaikin *Los Angeles Times/* *Baseball America*
Baltimore Orioles	Rick Wilton *www.rototimes.com/* *hotsheet*
Boston Red Sox	Mat Olkin *Baseball Weekly*
Chicago White Sox	Phil Rogers *Chicago Tribune/* *Baseball America*
Cleveland Indians	Paul Hoynes *Cleveland Plain Dealer*
Detroit Tigers	Pat Caputo *Oakland (Mich.) Press/* *Baseball America*
Kansas City Royals	Marc Bowman *STATS, Inc.*
Minnesota Twins	John Sickels *STATS, Inc./ESPN.com*
New York Yankees	Mike Morrissey *New York Post*
Oakland Athletics	Lawr Michaels *www.creativesports.com*
Seattle Mariners	Mat Olkin *Baseball Weekly*
Tampa Bay Devil Rays	Marc Topkin *St. Petersburg Times/* *Baseball America*
Texas Rangers	Gerry Fraley *Dallas Morning News/* *Baseball America*
Toronto Blue Jays	Tom Maloney *STATS, Inc.*
Arizona Diamondbacks	Ed Price *East Valley Tribune* *(Mesa, Ariz.)*
Atlanta Braves	Bill Ballew *Baseball America*
Chicago Cubs	Mat Olkin *Baseball Weekly*

Cincinnati Reds	Peter Pascarelli *ESPN*
Colorado Rockies	Tracy Ringolsby *Rocky Mountain News* *(Denver)/Baseball America*
Florida Marlins	Mike Berardino *(South Florida) Sun-Sentinel/* *Baseball America*
Houston Astros	Chris Haft *Cincinnati Enquirer/* *Baseball America*
Los Angeles Dodgers	Don Hartack *STATS, Inc.*
Milwaukee Brewers	Mat Olkin *Baseball Weekly*
Montreal Expos	Mat Olkin *Baseball Weekly*
New York Mets	Bill Ballew *Baseball America*
Philadelphia Phillies	Tony Blengino *Diamond Library* *(Future Stars)*
Pittsburgh Pirates	John Perrotto *Beaver County (Pa.) Times/* *Baseball America*
St. Louis Cardinals	Peter Pascarelli *ESPN*
San Diego Padres	Trace Wood *longgandhi.com*
San Francisco Giants	Chris Haft *Cincinnati Enquirer/* *Baseball America*

The minor league prospect reports were written by Thom Henninger (AL) and Jim Henzler (NL), and we'd like to thank the player-development personnel who were willing to discuss their teams' farm systems. *Baseball America's* Jim Callis was a big help when it came to filling in blanks. The "Other Anaheim Angels," etc., were written by the STATS publications staff. I'd also like to thank Ryan Balock, Marc Carl and Tim Coletta for their integral roles in helping to get this edition to print. Finally, I would like to thank editor John Dewan, who pored over every scouting report with an unwavering eye for detail.

—Tony Nistler

Table of Contents

Foreword

by Josh Lewin
Broadcaster, FOX Sports Net/Texas Rangers

"Knowledge is good."

That quote is stolen straight from the fictional Faber College in "Animal House," but here's the tie-in—that movie was shot at the University of Oregon, arch-rival of Oregon State, which is where Fox' own resident Blutarski, Steve "Psycho" Lyons, spent his college days. Thus, I can sneak it into the foreword with both confidence and pride.

Between the Texas Rangers' TV schedule and the FOX Saturday Game of the Week, I'm scheduled to announce 160 games this spring and summer. At every one of them, you will find the following items in the broadcast booth: a scorebook, a couple of black-ink pens, each team's game notes, each team's media guide, diet soda and *The Scouting Notebook*.

Much as we announcers may like to pretend that we know it all, it's impossible to know every trend and talent of every current big leaguer and up-and-coming prospect. You can't talk to every manager, every pitching coach, and every scout. . . there just aren't enough hours in the day.

That's why *The Scouting Notebook* is an invaluable resource and security blanket. Truth be told, it's a resource that no baseball scout, executive, broadcaster or die-hard fan should walk the planet without.

Whether you're in or out of the baseball business, if you appreciate sharp analysis, thoughtful presentation and provocative commentary, flip to the next page, and then dig in. I trust you'll find *The Scouting Notebook* to be a remarkably helpful tool towards a greater insight of the players, the managers and ballparks around Major League Baseball.

And I know I'm not the lone Ranger on this one. All around both leagues, in every broadcast booth (and I would assume, in every front office) the green binding of *The Scouting Notebook* shines like a beacon. Of knowledge. Which, to review, is good.

Introduction

Welcome to the eighth edition of *The Scouting Notebook*. This is the 13th annual book of scouting reports that STATS, Inc. has created. We get several prominent baseball analysts and have them give us detailed reports on every major league player who saw significant action last season. We think you'll agree that our scouting staff features some of the top baseball minds around. Special thanks to Marc Bowman, Paul Hoynes and John Perrotto, who have contributed to all 13 books.

This is an encyclopedia of contemporary major league baseball. We tell you about the strengths and weaknesses of hundreds of players. Our analysis extends beyond major league players, too, covering each club's top minor league prospects. We study the statistics and we talk to the scouts. We look for the true ability that may have been exaggerated or obscured by the hype.

The Ballparks

We report on each club's ballpark. We detail how each stadium affects hitters, pitchers and fielders in general, as well as which players it helps and hurts the most. We also project what the park will do to rookies and other newcomers in 2002. We provide vital statistics for each park, such as its dimensions, capacity, elevation, playing surface and the amount of foul territory.

We also present our trademark park indexes, with which readers of our *Major League Handbook* are familiar. In a variety of statistical categories, we show how the home team and its opponents performed at the park and on the road. Interleague games aren't included. By comparing the overall totals at the park and on the road, we get a measure of the stadium's impact. We divide the home totals by the road totals and multiply by 100 to get the park index. An index of greater than 100 shows that the park favors a particular statistic, while an index of less than 100 means the opposite.

Most of the indexes are calculated on a per at-bat basis. Runs, hits, errors and infield errors are figured on a per-game basis. For most parks, we present data for both 2001 and the last three years overall. If the park's configuration has changed since the end of the 1999 season, we present the data for the different setups separately.

Most of the abbreviations are common, with these exceptions:

E-Infield: Infield errors.

LHB-Avg: Batting average by lefthanded hitters.

LHB-HR: Home runs by lefthanded hitters.

RHB-Avg: Batting average by righthanded hitters.

RHB-HR: Home runs by righthanded hitters.

We also list any indexes in which the park ranked in the top or bottom three in its league in 2001.

The Managers

On these pages, we analyze each manager's strengths and weaknesses, style and strategy, and outlook for 2002. We present his 2001 and career managerial record, and we also show how often he used starting pitchers on various days of rest. We compare his use and the performance of his starters to the league average.

We also provide statistical breakdowns detailing his handling of his pitching staff and his use of strategies like the sacrifice, the hit-and-run and defensive substitutions. To qualify for the rankings, a manager had to have his team for at least 100 games in 2001. Some of the terms listed in the statistics and rankings sections may be unfamiliar.

They include:

Hit & Run Success %: The percentage of hit-and-runs resulting in baserunner advancement with no double play.

Platoon Pct.: Frequency that the manager gets his hitters the platoon advantage (lefty vs. righty and vice versa). Switch-hitters always are considered to have the advantage.

Defensive Subs: The number of straight defensive substitutions with the team leading by four runs or fewer.

High-Pitch Outings: The number of times a manager's starting pitchers threw more than 120 pitches in a ballgame.

Quick/Slow Hooks: A Quick Hook occurs when a pitcher is removed after having pitched less than six innings and given up three runs or fewer. A Slow Hook occurs when a pitcher works more than nine innings, allows seven or more runs, or his total innings and runs equal 13 or more.

First-Batter Platoon Percentage: The percentage of times the managers' relievers had a platoon advantage over the first hitter they faced (lefty vs. lefty, righty vs. righty).

Mid-Inning Changes: The number of times the manager changed pitchers in the middle of an inning.

Pitchouts with a Runner Moving: The number of times the opposition was running when the manager called a pitchout.

Sacrifice Bunt Percentage: The percentage of bunts resulting in sacrifices or hits with runners on.

Starting Lineups Used: Based on batting order, 1-8 for National Leaguers, 1-9 for American Leaguers.

2+ Pitching Changes in Low-Scoring Games: The number of times a manager used at least three pitchers in a game in which his team allowed two runs or fewer.

The Players

For each major league team, we give extensive reports on 22 players. Twelve of them get a full page of scouting information, while 10 receive half-page reports. Because we like to get this book into your hands as soon as possible, players are listed with their 2001 clubs. We keep abreast of postseason transactions, and all player moves that took place through December 16, 2001 are noted. If you can't find a particular player, check the detailed index in the back.

Pages for primary players have two columns. The left column provides an in-depth report by an analyst. The right column contains statistical information:

Position: The first position shown is the player's most common position in 2001. Positions at which he played 10 or more games also are shown. For pitchers, SP stands for starting pitcher and RP for relief pitcher.

Bats and Throws: L stands for lefthanded, R stands for righthanded, and B stands for both (switch-hitter).

Ht: Height.

Wt: Weight.

Opening Day Age: This is the player's age on April 1, 2002.

Born: Birthdate and birthplace.

ML Seasons: This number indicates the number of different major league seasons in which the player has appeared. For example, if a player was called up to play in September in each of the last three seasons, the number shown would be 3. This is different from major league service, which is used to determine arbitration and free-agency eligibility.

Overall Statistics: These are traditional major league statistics for the player's 2001 season and his career. The one non-traditional stat that appears here is ratio, which is the number of baserunners allowed by a pitcher per inning: ((hits + walks)/IP).

Where He Hits The Ball

For every major league game in 2001, STATS reporters entered into our computers every ball hit into play. They kept track of the type of batted balls—grounders, flyballs, popups, line drives and bunts—as well as the distance each ball traveled. Direction was tracked by dividing the field into 26 "wedges" projecting out from home plate. Distance was measured in 10-foot increments outward from home plate.

Below are the hitting diagrams for lefthanded-hitting Ryan Klesko of the San Diego Padres. The chart on the left shows where Klesko hit the ball against lefthanders, while the chart on the right shows what he did against righties.

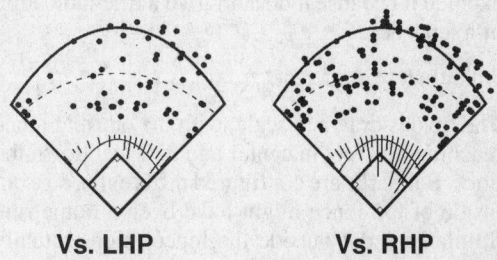

Vs. LHP   **Vs. RHP**

In the diagrams, groundballs and short line drives are shown by the lines of various lengths in the infield. The longer the line, the more groundballs and line drives were hit in that direction. As you can see from the charts on page 3, Klesko was able to pull the ball effectively and show power against lefties, but that wasn't always the case. The Atlanta product fared poorly against southpaws in his early days with the Braves, and manager Bobby Cox never gave him many at-bats against them.

Klesko's hit charts versus lefthanded pitching often looked like a spray hitter without power. After he was dealt to San Diego prior to the 2000 campaign, he played regularly against southpaws for the first time, and his terrific bat speed allowed him to hit a decent .256 with a .344 on-base percentage versus lefties over the last two seasons. For the first time in his career last year, he posted a slugging percentage above .400 facing southpaws, and his success is reflected in his hit chart.

A lot of experimentation went into producing the hitting diagrams. When we first started, we tried to show every single batted ball that was put into play by each player. We found that the charts became very cluttered for everyday players, so we began experimenting with trying to show only the most meaningful information. When all was said and done, here's what we ended up with:

a. Popups and bunts are excluded. We excluded popups because 95 percent of these are caught regardless of how fielders are positioned. We excluded bunts because defensing a bunt is an entirely different strategy primarily used against a select number of players or in specific situations.

b. For groundballs and short line drives, we include all batted balls.

c. For balls hit to the outfield, we excluded isolated points only if the chart contains more than 125 batted balls to the outfield. In such cases, if a player hits only one ball to a given area and had no other batted balls in the vicinity all season, we exclude it because it doesn't give a true indication of a tendency.

Other notes of interest:

The field is drawn to scale, with the outfield fence reaching 400 feet in center and 330 feet down the lines. Ballparks are configured differently, so a dot inside of the fence might have been a home run. Similarly, a dot outside the fence might actually have been in play.

Line drives under 170 feet are part of the infield.

We give responsibility for short liners to the infielders.

No distinction is made between hits and outs.

How Often He Throws Strikes

Our STATS reporters also tracked every pitch thrown in a major league game in 2001. The pitching graphs show how often the hurler throws strikes in different situations. Our data shows most pitchers will toss a strike between 40 and 80 percent of the time. Therefore we've constructed the chart to represent the 40-80 percent range.

The strike count includes swinging strikes, taken strikes, foul balls and balls put in play. Though not all batted balls come on pitches thrown within the strike zone, our theory is that most are and the ones that aren't would be difficult to judge. Our charts reflect these assumptions.

The charts are broken into four categories. *All Pitches* is straightforward, as is *First Pitch*. We define *Ahead* as counts with more strikes than balls. *Behind* includes counts with more balls than strikes. The appropriate league average is shown in each chart.

Below are the 2001 league averages. The National League threw a slightly higher percentage of strikes than the American League, as it has in all 13 years we have tracked this.

Strike Percentage by League — 2001		
	American	National
All Pitches	62.9%	63.1%
First Pitch	58.6%	59.2%
Ahead in the Count	60.7%	60.9%
Behind in the Count	67.8%	67.5%

2001 Situational Stats

There are eight situational breakdowns for every primary player. *Home* and *Road* show performance in his home ballpark and on the road. *First Half* and *Scnd Half* show performance before and after the 2001 All-Star break. For hitters, *LHP* and *RHP* show how the player hit against lefthanders and righthanders. For pitchers, *LHB* and *RHB* show how the opposition lefthanders and righthanders hit against the pitcher. *Sc Pos* shows batting or pitching performance with runners in scoring position. *Clutch* shows batting or pitching performance in clutch situations, defined as the seventh inning or later with the batting team ahead by one run, tied or with the tying run on base, at bat or on deck. Our definition is consistent with save situations.

2001 Rankings

This section shows how the player ranked in his league and among his teammates. Because of space considerations, we omitted some of the less interesting rankings when a player placed high in numerous categories.

We include many less traditional categories. The Definitions and Qualifications section below provides details for these statistics.

Definitions and Qualifications

The following are definitions and qualifications for the Major League Leaders and Rankings.

Definitions:

Times on Base — Hits plus walks plus hit-by-pitch.

Groundball-Flyball Ratio — Groundballs hit divided by the total of flyballs and popups hit. Bunts and line drives are excluded.

Runs/Times on Base — Runs scored divided by times on base.

Clutch — A player's batting average in the late innings of close games, defined as the seventh inning or later with the batting team ahead by one run, tied or with the tying run on base, at bat or on deck.

Bases Loaded — A player's batting average in bases-loaded situations.

GDP per GDP situation — Groundball double plays divided by groundball double-play situations, defined as a man on first base with less than two out.

Percentage of Pitches Taken — The percentage of pitches a player lets go by without swinging.

Percentage Swings Put In Play — The percentage of swings resulting in a batted ball into fair territory or a foul-ball out.

Run Support per Nine Innings — The number of runs scored for a pitcher while he was pitching, scaled to a nine-inning figure.

Baserunners per Nine Innings — The total of hits, walks and hit batsmen allowed per nine innings.

Strikeout-Walk Ratio — Strikeouts divided by walks.

Stolen-Base Percentage Allowed — Stolen bases divided by stolen-base attempts.

Save Percentage — Saves divided by save opportunities. Save opportunities include saves plus blown saves.

Blown Saves — A blown save is charged any time a pitcher enters a game in a save situation and loses the lead. A save situation is defined as any time a reliever enters the game with a lead, isn't the pitcher of record and either a) pitches at least one inning with a lead of no more than three runs; b) enters the game with the potential tying run on base, at bat or on deck; or c) pitches effectively for at least three innings.

Holds — A hold is given to a pitcher when he enters a game in a save situation and is removed before the end of the game while maintaining his team's lead. The pitcher must retire at least one batter to get a hold.

Percentage of Inherited Runners Scored — Percentage of runners already on base when a pitcher enters a game that he allows to score.

First Batter Efficiency — The batting average allowed by a reliever to the first batter he faces in a game.

Qualifications:

In order to be ranked, a player had to qualify with a minimum number of opportunities, as follows:

Batters

Batting average, slugging percentage, on-base percentage, home run frequency, groundball-flyball ratio, runs scored per time reached base and pitches seen per plate appearance — 3.1 plate appearances per team game

Percentage of pitches taken, lowest percentage of swings that missed and percentage of swings put into play — 9.26 pitches seen per team game

Percentage of extra bases taken as a runner — .09 opportunities to advance per team game

Stolen-base percentage — .12 stolen-base attempts per team game

Runners in scoring position — .62 plate appearances with runners in scoring position per team game

Clutch — .31 plate appearances in the clutch per team game

Bases loaded — .06 plate appearances with the bases loaded per team game

GDP per GDP situation — .31 plate appearances in GDP situations per team game

BA vs. LHP — .77 plate appearances against lefthanders per team game

BA vs. RHP — 2.33 plate appearances against righthanders per team game

BA at home — 1.55 plate appearances at home per team game

BA on the road — 1.55 plate appearances on the road per team game

Leadoff on-base percentage — .93 plate appearances in the No. 1 lineup spot per team game

Cleanup slugging percentage — .93 plate appearances in the No. 4 lineup spot per team game

BA on 3-1 count — .06 plate appearances with a 3-1 count per team game

BA with 2 strikes — .62 plate appearances with two strikes per team game

BA on 0-2 count — .12 plate appearances with an 0-2 count per team game

BA on 3-2 count — .12 plate appearances with a 3-2 count per team game

Pitchers

Earned run average, run support per nine innings, baserunners per nine innings, batting average allowed, slugging percentage allowed, on-base percentage allowed, home runs per nine innings, strikeouts per nine innings, strikeout-walk ratio, stolen-base percentage allowed, GDPs per nine innings, pitches thrown per batter and groundball-flyball ratio against — one inning per team game

Winning percentage — .09 decisions per team game

GDPs induced per GDP situation — .19 batters faced in GDP situations per team game

BA allowed, runners in scoring position — .77 batters faced with runners in scoring position per team game

ERA at home — .5 innings at home per team game

ERA on the road — .5 innings on the road per team game

BA vs. LHB — .77 lefthanders faced per team game

BA vs. RHB — 1.39 righthanders faced per team game

Relievers

ERA, batting average allowed, baserunners per nine innings, strikeouts per nine innings — .31 relief innings per team game

Save percentage — .12 save opportunities per team game

Percentage of inherited runners scoring — .19 inherited runners per team game

First batter efficiency — .25 games in relief per team game

Fielders

Percentage caught stealing by catchers — .43 stolen-base attempts per team game

Fielding percentage — .62 games at a position per team game (.19 chances per team game for pitchers)

Other Players

Some players didn't play enough to merit a full- or half-page essay, and aren't young enough or good enough to deserve a prospect report. But they did play in the majors last year, so we give them a brief evaluation. Following the half-page reports for each team, you'll find a page devoted to these part-timers under the heading "Other Anaheim Angels," etc. Each player gets a short summary and his 2002 Outlook is graded as follows:

A — Should be an important contributor.
B — Should play most of the season in the majors and contribute.
C — Unlikely to play much in the majors or contribute much if he does.
D — Unlikely to play in the majors.

Minor League Prospects

We present two pages of minor league prospects for each team. Thom Henninger and Jim Henzler spoke directly to major league player-development personnel and also looked beyond athletic tools by analyzing statistics. Each club has seven or eight featured prospects. We try to include most of the top phenoms, but our primary emphasis is on advanced players with the best chance of contributing in the majors in 2002.

For featured prospects who are hitters and played in Double-A or Triple-A in 2001, we include major league equivalencies. Developed by Bill James, the MLE translates minor league statistics into major league numbers. It does this by making a series of adjustments for a player's home ballpark, his league, his level of competition and his future major league home park.

We also include an organizational overview for each team, which gives you a glimpse into the current state of each club's minor league system. In addition, we summarize a few more notable prospects per team in a section called "Others to Watch."

Where we mention that managers voted a player as the best in a specific category in his league, our source is *Baseball America*.

Major League Leaders

After the team sections, we provide a complete listing of Major League leaders. The top three players in each category are shown for the American and National Leagues. You'll notice a STATS flavor to these leaders. Not only do we show the leaders for the common categories such as batting average, home runs and ERA, but you'll also find less traditional categories like steals of third and total pitches thrown.

Stars, Bums and Sleepers

This section tells you what to expect from each player in 2002: whether he'll improve, decline, remain consistent or emerge and surprise.

STATS' Top 50 Prospects

The book closes with STATS' ranking of the top 50 prospects in the game, based on the individual lists of the STATS editorial department. All players who haven't exceeded the rookie limits of 130 at-bats or 50 innings pitched in the major leagues are eligible.

American League Players

Edison International Field

Offense

Edison Field boosted scoring last year, but over the past two seasons it has proven to be a pretty fair park for both pitchers and hitters, much to the dismay of Mo Vaughn, who sorely misses the Green Monster at Fenway Park. The 18-foot wall in right field turns homers into doubles—and sometimes singles for slow lefthanded sluggers. The Angels' offensive woes in 2001 had little to do with the ballpark and plenty to do with the absence of Vaughn, as well as the poor seasons of Darin Erstad and Tim Salmon.

Defense

The infield surface has improved dramatically since Disney hired groundskeeper Barney Lopas away from the Marlins. Still, hot summer days make for dry infield dirt, which makes for an inordinate number of tricky hops. The asymmetrical outfield is difficult for visiting outfielders, but Salmon and Garret Anderson have worked hard to learn how the ball caroms in the corners and off the scoreboard in right.

Who It Helps the Most

Anderson, Adam Kennedy and even the retired Wally Joyner, all lefthanded batters, hit significantly better at home than on the road. The right-center field fence is closer to home plate than the left-center field fence, so flyballs and line drives that might otherwise be caught clank against that 18-foot wall for base hits.

Who It Hurts the Most

This isn't a ballpark factor so much as a climate factor, but the ball absolutely flies out of the park on warm summer afternoons. But the Angels rarely schedule games before 5 p.m., so power hitters such as Salmon and Troy Glaus lose a few home runs each year to the damp evening air.

Rookies & Newcomers

The newest Angels always need time to adjust to the home fans, who tend to sit quietly. Jarrod Washburn, whose ERA was 3.02 on the road and 4.65 at home, once chided the fans for cheering more for the rally monkey on the scoreboard than for the humans in Angels uniforms.

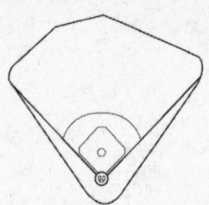

Dimensions: LF-330, LCF-387, CF-400, RCF-370, RF-330

Capacity: 45,050

Elevation: 160 feet

Surface: Grass

Foul Territory: Average

Park Factors

2001 Season

	Home Games			Away Games			
	Angels	Opp	Total	Angels	Opp	Total	Index
G	72	72	144	72	72	144	—
Avg	.265	.267	.266	.251	.258	.254	105
AB	2431	2564	4995	2491	2361	4852	103
R	319	353	672	290	299	589	114
H	645	685	1330	626	608	1234	108
2B	108	151	259	139	108	247	102
3B	11	6	17	14	11	25	66
HR	78	75	153	57	73	130	114
BB	229	230	459	211	234	445	100
SO	413	437	850	468	408	876	94
E	53	49	102	41	55	96	106
E-Infield	49	38	87	37	46	83	105
LHB-Avg	.275	.262	.269	.241	.256	.248	108
LHB-HR	29	30	59	26	28	54	105
RHB-Avg	.256	.271	.264	.261	.258	.260	102
RHB-HR	49	45	94	31	45	76	121

2000-2001

	Home Games			Away Games			
	Angels	Opp	Total	Angels	Opp	Total	Index
G	144	144	288	144	144	288	—
Avg	.272	.273	.273	.263	.267	.265	103
AB	4849	5106	9955	5057	4806	9863	101
R	697	735	1432	667	708	1375	104
H	1320	1394	2714	1330	1281	2611	104
2B	231	277	508	282	227	509	99
3B	21	12	33	34	22	56	58
HR	193	174	367	150	175	325	112
BB	500	515	1015	481	542	1023	98
SO	837	812	1649	939	771	1710	96
E	117	91	208	99	90	189	110
E-Infield	106	71	177	86	73	159	111
LHB-Avg	.281	.264	.273	.256	.270	.262	104
LHB-HR	86	66	152	78	76	154	98
RHB-Avg	.262	.280	.272	.271	.264	.267	102
RHB-HR	107	108	215	72	99	171	124

2001 Rankings (American League)
- Highest run factor
- Second-highest batting-average factor
- Second-highest hit factor
- Second-highest LHB batting-average factor
- Third-highest RHB home-run factor
- Third-lowest strikeout factor

Mike Scioscia

2001 Season

From Mike Scioscia, never is heard a discouraging word. Not until the end of the season was he willing to say his offense was bad. Scioscia was upbeat if the Angels won 10-0 or blew a late lead and lost in the most wrenching of ways. He has presided over the development of a group of young starting pitchers who must succeed for the team to have any chance of winning. But, even with a team that has made a September collapse an art form, he also presided over the ugliest final month in club history, as the Angels lost 19 of their final 21 games.

Offense

Neither Scioscia nor his hitting coach, Mickey Hatcher, could right an offense that scored 173 fewer runs from 2000 to 2001, hit 78 fewer homers and dropped 25 points in on-base percentage and 67 points in slugging. Even on a team with average speed, Scioscia tried to manufacture runs, often bunting, playing for one run and calling for steals and hit-and-run plays. Scioscia also juggled his batting order, at times irritating his players, though he prefers a set lineup if hitters are productive.

Pitching & Defense

Scioscia and pitching coach Bud Black deserve high marks for pushing young starters Ramon Ortiz, Scott Schoeneweis and Jarrod Washburn deep into games while protecting them by keeping their pitch counts between 90 and 110. Scioscia and Black also have developed one of the best bullpens in the league, even though no reliever besides closer Troy Percival has great stuff. The defense improved dramatically last year, with errors down 23 percent, in part because of the improvement of Glaus at third base and the stability of David Eckstein at shortstop.

2002 Outlook

Last August, with the Angels a season-high eight games over .500, they signed Scioscia to a three-year contract extension through 2005. The team responded by losing 26 of its final 34 games. The players respect Scioscia, and he generally communicates well with them. However, if the Angels again finish 27 games out of a playoff spot, Scioscia's optimism will be sorely tested.

Born: 11/27/58 in Upper Darby, PA

Playing Experience: 1980-1992, LA

Managerial Experience: 2 seasons

Manager Statistics

Year	Team, Lg	W	L	Pct	GB	Finish
2001	Anaheim, AL	75	87	.463	41.0	3rd West
2 Seasons		157	167	.485	—	—

2001 Starting Pitchers by Days Rest

	<=3	4	5	6+
Angels Starts	0	74	51	27
Angels ERA	—	4.19	4.47	5.36
AL Avg Starts	1	78	48	24
AL ERA	5.92	4.69	4.58	4.58

2001 Situational Stats

	Mike Scioscia	AL Average
Hit & Run Success %	36.2	35.0
Stolen Base Success %	69.0	71.0
Platoon Pct.	62.1	59.1
Defensive Subs	8	26
High-Pitch Outings	5	6
Quick/Slow Hooks	18/12	19/16
Sacrifice Attempts	66	54

2001 Rankings (American League)

- 2nd in hit-and-run attempts (116) and starting lineups used (130)
- 3rd in steals of home plate (1), fewest caught stealings of third base (3), sacrifice bunt attempts and pitchouts (50)

Garret Anderson

2001 Season

Garret Anderson wasn't happy about moving from center field back to left field, but he had his say and then had another typically solid season. Manager Mike Scioscia bounced him up and down the heart of the batting order, in response to the struggles of other hitters, but Anderson just kept pounding out the hits. He set career highs with 194 hits and 123 RBI, playing every day and playing consistently well and hard, especially notable traits given his team's September collapse and his acknowledged lapses in intensity earlier in his career.

Hitting

Anderson has evolved into a power threat without sacrificing his ability to make contact. He hits lefthanders and righthanders equally well, and he hit .296 with runners in scoring position in 2001. He was one of just two Angels (along with Orlando Palmeiro) who played in more than 100 games last year while hitting better than .270 in that situation. He now pulls pitches he used to be happy slapping the opposite way, and his 63 home runs the past two seasons reflect a hitter blossoming in his late 20s. He'll seldom take walks, and he'll hit into a fair number of double plays, but the Angels are satisfied with the combination of power and average.

Baserunning & Defense

Anderson has worked hard on his defense and become a good outfielder, capable of playing well at all three outfield positions. He rarely dives, so you seldom see him on TV. Despite having an average arm, he is adept at holding runners to singles on balls down the line. He stole a career-high 13 bases last year and will run if you're not paying attention to him.

2002 Outlook

The Angels believe Anderson could play long enough and well enough to collect 3,000 hits. While 3,000 eventually may be a reachable goal, he's another decade away from flirting with *that* milestone. If the Angels could bat him fifth, however, and if the hitters above him return to form, he could be a good bet to reach the 120-RBI milestone again in '02. If Anaheim moves Darin Erstad to first base, Anderson could be back in center.

Position: LF/CF/DH
Bats: L **Throws:** L
Ht: 6' 3"   **Wt:** 228

Opening Day Age: 29
Born: 6/30/72 in Los Angeles, CA
ML Seasons: 8

Overall Statistics

	G	AB	R	H	D	T	HR	RBI	SB	BB	SO	Avg	OBP	Slg
2001	161	672	83	194	39	2	28	123	13	27	100	.289	.314	.478
Career	1048	4179	530	1237	244	20	135	633	54	190	569	.296	.325	.461

Where He Hits the Ball

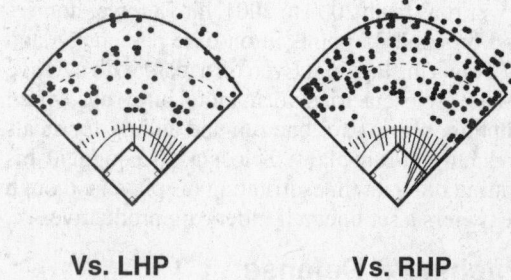

Vs. LHP   **Vs. RHP**

2001 Situational Stats

	AB	H	HR	RBI	Avg		AB	H	HR	RBI	Avg
Home	336	106	13	73	.315	LHP	208	60	6	34	.288
Road	336	88	15	50	.262	RHP	464	134	22	89	.289
First Half	362	101	15	62	.279	Sc Pos	199	59	5	88	.296
Scnd Half	310	93	13	61	.300	Clutch	100	31	5	22	.310

2001 Rankings (American League)

- 1st in fielding percentage in left field (.993) and lowest cleanup slugging percentage (.418)
- 2nd in at-bats, assists in left field (9) and fewest pitches seen per plate appearance (3.37)
- 5th in hits and games played
- 6th in RBI, steals of third (6) and lowest percentage of pitches taken (46.8)
- Led the Angels in batting average, at-bats, hits, doubles, total bases (321), RBI, games played, steals of third (6), batting average vs. righthanded pitchers and batting average at home
- Led AL left fielders in home runs and RBI

David Eckstein

Great Bunter

Position: SS/2B/DH
Bats: R **Throws:** R
Ht: 5' 8" **Wt:** 170

Opening Day Age: 27
Born: 1/20/75 in Sanford, FL
ML Seasons: 1
Pronunciation: eck-STEEN

2001 Season

David Eckstein wasn't considered much of a prospect, but he regularly produced averages in the .300s and on-base percentages in the .400s in the Red Sox' system. When Eckstein struggled in his first exposure to Triple-A ball in 2000, Boston put him on waivers and the Angels claimed him. He surprised Anaheim by claiming the shortstop job this spring and producing a .355 on-base percentage as a rookie. Not surprisingly, Eckstein slumped in July and September, but in between he batted .360 in a red-hot August.

Hitting

Eckstein is an ideal leadoff hitter, and not just because his generously listed 5-foot-8 frame shrinks the strike zone. He takes pitches and fouls off pitches, tiring opposing pitchers and providing teammates with a solid look at a pitcher's repertoire. He sprays the ball around the field, he's a terrific bunter and he also got on base 21 times last year after being hit by a pitch. Eckstein hit .239 in July, and the Angels were concerned opponents had figured the rookie out, but he rebounded to generate his highest monthly average in August.

Baserunning & Defense

Eckstein is adequate at shortstop, making up for limited range and arm strength with smart positioning and throwing mechanics that look awkward—almost as if he is a shot-putter—but produce remarkably accurate throws. His natural position is second base. Eckstein led the Angels with 29 stolen bases, getting caught just four times. He is fast enough and smart enough to take the extra base at every opportunity.

2002 Outlook

Ideally, Eckstein is the leadoff hitter and second baseman for Anaheim in 2002. But top shortstop prospect Alfredo Amezaga might not be ready to hit major league pitching, and manager Mike Scioscia might return Darin Erstad to the leadoff spot. The Angels won't hesitate to return Eckstein to shortstop, at least for this year. With experience, he should draw more walks; with a resurgent offense, he should score 100 runs.

Overall Statistics

	G	AB	R	H	D	T	HR	RBI	SB	BB	SO	Avg	OBP	Slg
2001	153	582	82	166	26	2	4	41	29	43	60	.285	.355	.357
Career	153	582	82	166	26	2	4	41	29	43	60	.285	.355	.357

Where He Hits the Ball

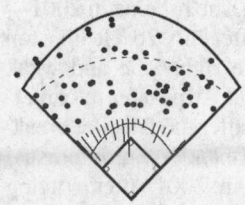
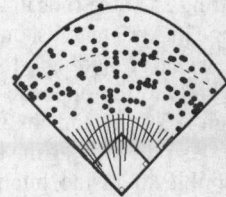

Vs. LHP   Vs. RHP

2001 Situational Stats

	AB	H	HR	RBI	Avg		AB	H	HR	RBI	Avg
Home	287	76	3	20	.265	LHP	165	50	3	15	.303
Road	295	90	1	21	.305	RHP	417	116	1	26	.278
First Half	307	85	3	22	.277	Sc Pos	122	31	1	36	.254
Scnd Half	275	81	1	19	.295	Clutch	76	28	0	11	.368

2001 Rankings (American League)

- 1st in sacrifice bunts (16), hit by pitch (21), lowest percentage of swings that missed (8.1) and batting average on an 0-2 count (.351)
- Led the Angels in singles, stolen bases, stolen-base percentage (87.9), bunts in play (33), highest percentage of swings put into play (51.9), steals of third (6), batting average vs. lefthanded pitchers, batting average on a 3-1 count (.750), on-base percentage for a leadoff hitter (.357), highest percentage of extra bases taken as a runner (72.4), batting average on the road and lowest percentage of swings on the first pitch (13.6)

Darin Erstad

2001 Season

At the start of the season, fans wondered whether the Angels would sign Darin Erstad to an extension of a contract that ended with the 2001 season. By the end of the summer, even Erstad said he wasn't sure if the Angels would bother to make an offer. His batting average plummeted almost 100 points (.355 to .258) and his slugging percentage plummeted almost 200 points (.541 to .360), leaving Erstad and the Angels hoping back and knee injuries were the explanation.

Hitting

An offseason knee injury, and the mechanical funk that resulted when Erstad tried to compensate for the injury, deprived him of his power stroke. After hitting 25 home runs in 2000, he hit nine in 2001—none in April and just one after July 26. He hit a ton of weak groundballs to the right side and weak flyballs to the opposite field, struck out a career-high 113 times and hit .233 after the All-Star break. He also hit .204 against lefthanders, proving susceptible to inside pitches in 2001 after solving them in 2000.

Baserunning & Defense

Erstad stole 24 bases last summer, the fourth time in five full major league seasons he has stolen at least 20. He is the fastest player on the team, and the Angels believe he could steal 30 to 40 bases if he were more aggressive. After Erstad won a Gold Glove in left field in 2000, the Angels moved him to center field in 2001. His arm is average but accurate. He plays balls side-to-side as well as anyone in the league, but could be better going back on balls. He never gives up on a play and dives without regard to his body.

2002 Outlook

The Angels could move Erstad to first base this year, where they believe he would be less susceptible to injury. Erstad refuses to accept mediocrity and figures to rebound after a winter of rehabilitation and intensive workouts. He is the clubhouse leader, but his batting average curve the past three seasons—.253 to .355 to .258—demands that a strong season precede any long-term contract.

Position: CF/1B
Bats: L **Throws:** L
Ht: 6' 2" **Wt:** 220

Opening Day Age: 27
Born: 6/4/74 in Jamestown, ND
ML Seasons: 6
Pronunciation: ER-stad

Overall Statistics

	G	AB	R	H	D	T	HR	RBI	SB	BB	SO	Avg	OBP	Slg
2001	157	631	89	163	35	1	9	63	24	62	113	.258	.331	.360
Career	785	3176	511	930	174	20	86	395	111	284	488	.293	.352	.441

Where He Hits the Ball

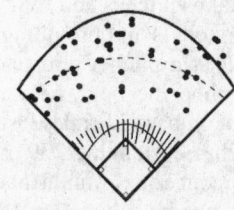 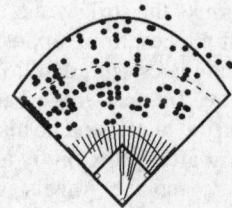

Vs. LHP **Vs. RHP**

2001 Situational Stats

	AB	H	HR	RBI	Avg		AB	H	HR	RBI	Avg
Home	323	89	3	30	.276	LHP	196	40	2	20	.204
Road	308	74	6	33	.240	RHP	435	123	7	43	.283
First Half	344	96	7	43	.279	Sc Pos	156	35	4	53	.224
Scnd Half	287	67	2	20	.233	Clutch	89	27	2	15	.303

2001 Rankings (American League)

- 1st in fielding percentage in center field (.998)
- 3rd in assists in center field (10) and lowest slugging percentage vs. lefthanded pitchers (.291)
- 4th in plate appearances (716)
- 5th in highest percentage of extra bases taken as a runner (60.0), lowest percentage of swings on the first pitch (16.5) and lowest batting average with the bases loaded (.100)
- Led the Angels in caught stealing (10), intentional walks (7), plate appearances (716), highest groundball-flyball ratio (1.7), fewest GDPs per GDP situation (5.3%) and on-base percentage vs. righthanded pitchers (.359)

Troy Glaus

2001 Season

The torch was passed at the 2001 All-Star Game, when Cal Ripken came out of the game, shaking hands with his replacement and heir apparent as the American League's starting third baseman for years to come, Troy Glaus. After leading the league with 47 home runs in 2000, Glaus followed with a 41-homer encore in 2001, and at 25 his power still is developing. He was not altogether consistent, batting .189 in June and .194 in August, but he persevered to bat .365 in September, at a time when his team was crumbling around him.

Hitting

Glaus ranked among the top four in the league in home runs, walks and strikeouts. He has unusually keen plate discipline for such a young player. If he can develop his ability to make contact with runners in scoring position—he struck out nearly once in every three at-bats in that situation in 2001—by using more of the field and pulling less, the Angels believe he can drive in 130 to 140 runs. He hit with extra pressure all season, with Mo Vaughn out for the season and Tim Salmon struggling terribly. Glaus dropped from .369 against lefthanders in 2000 to .252 last year.

Baserunning & Defense

A converted shortstop in the Ripken mold, Glaus has an exceptionally strong, though sometimes inaccurate, throwing arm. He reduced his errors from 33 in 2000 to 19 in 2001, while showing tremendous ability to make plays to his left and to charge slow rollers and bunts. Glaus, who stole 10 bases in 2001, has good baserunning instincts and surprisingly good speed considering his 6-foot-5, 230-pound frame.

2002 Outlook

Never had an Angel hit 40 home runs in a season until Glaus did it in 2000; now you almost can chalk him up for it. He plays nearly every day, and another 40-homer season would put him third or fourth in franchise history, behind Salmon, Brian Downing and maybe Garret Anderson. Glaus' career on-base percentage is .361, so the Angels' offense could be devastating if a consistent RBI threat emerges behind him in the lineup.

Position: 3B
Bats: R **Throws:** R
Ht: 6' 5" **Wt:** 245

Opening Day Age: 25
Born: 8/3/76 in Tarzana, CA
ML Seasons: 4
Pronunciation: GLOSS

Overall Statistics

	G	AB	R	H	D	T	HR	RBI	SB	BB	SO	Avg	OBP	Slg
2001	161	588	100	147	38	2	41	108	10	107	158	.250	.367	.531
Career	522	1867	324	475	113	3	118	312	30	305	515	.254	.361	.508

Where He Hits the Ball

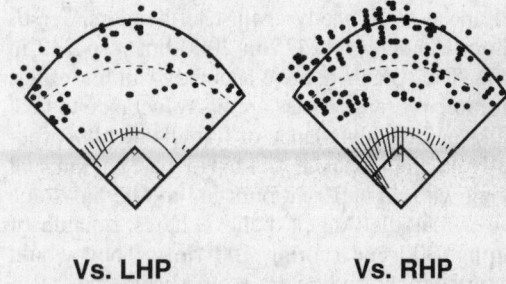

Vs. LHP   **Vs. RHP**

2001 Situational Stats

	AB	H	HR	RBI	Avg		AB	H	HR	RBI	Avg
Home	281	71	22	62	.253	LHP	151	38	9	25	.252
Road	307	76	19	46	.248	RHP	437	109	32	83	.249
First Half	320	79	22	54	.247	Sc Pos	158	40	10	62	.253
Scnd Half	268	68	19	54	.254	Clutch	94	22	6	16	.234

2001 Rankings (American League)

- 2nd in pitches seen (2,853) and errors at third base (19)
- 3rd in strikeouts and lowest cleanup slugging percentage (.449)
- Led the Angels in home runs, runs scored, walks, intentional walks (7), times on base (260), strikeouts, GDPs (16), pitches seen (2,853), games played, slugging percentage, on-base percentage, HR frequency (14.3 ABs per HR), highest percentage of pitches taken (59.6), cleanup slugging percentage (.449), slugging percentage vs. lefthanded pitchers (.517), slugging percentage vs. righthanded pitchers (.535) and on-base percentage vs. lefthanded pitchers (.407)
- Led AL third basemen in home runs

Adam Kennedy

2001 Season

No Angels player's stock fell as much as Adam Kennedy's during the season. He opened the year anchored at second base after a solid rookie season in 2000, but closed the year splitting time with Benji Gil and Jose Nieves and hearing the Angels discuss moving David Eckstein to second in 2002. If the Angels replace Kennedy, they would have nothing to show for the trade that sent All-Star outfielder Jim Edmonds to St. Louis for Kennedy and pitcher Kent Bottenfield.

Hitting

It wasn't Kennedy's fault that Gil hit so well that manager Mike Scioscia felt compelled to find spots for Gil in the lineup. Most often, Scioscia played Gil ahead of Kennedy against lefthanders, versus whom Kennedy hit .275 in 2000 but just .242 in 2001. The Angels believe Kennedy can hit lefties, but more pressing issues are his reluctance to take walks and the abundance of flyballs he hits, especially to the opposite field. He has an unusual swing with an uppercut built in, and he has some power, but the Angels believe he is capable of batting .300 and scoring 100 runs. They would prefer he focus on line drives and walks.

Baserunning & Defense

A converted shortstop, Kennedy still is learning second base. For now he must be considered below average. His hands are sure, but his range is average. His arm strength and accuracy could be better, and he needs work on turning the double play. He is an aggressive if not overly speedy baserunner, and he gets to second in a hurry on his doubles. Kennedy could steal 30 bases if he got on base more often.

2002 Outlook

The Angels desperately need more offense out of their middle infielders and would love for Kennedy to provide it. His defense is competent, but his offense is his ticket to the major leagues. He'll simply have to improve such statistics as his .190 average with runners in scoring position and his .318 on-base percentage.

Position: 2B
Bats: L **Throws:** R
Ht: 6' 1" **Wt:** 192

Opening Day Age: 26
Born: 1/10/76 in Riverside, CA
ML Seasons: 3

Overall Statistics

	G	AB	R	H	D	T	HR	RBI	SB	BB	SO	Avg	OBP	Slg
2001	137	478	48	129	25	3	6	40	12	27	71	.270	.318	.372
Career	326	1178	142	314	68	15	16	128	34	58	152	.267	.306	.390

Where He Hits the Ball

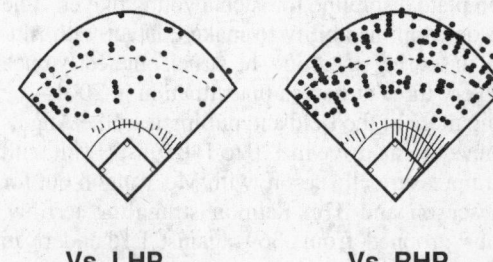

Vs. LHP   Vs. RHP

2001 Situational Stats

	AB	H	HR	RBI	Avg		AB	H	HR	RBI	Avg
Home	233	70	4	21	.300	LHP	99	24	0	5	.242
Road	245	59	2	19	.241	RHP	379	105	6	35	.277
First Half	260	79	4	22	.304	Sc Pos	100	19	2	32	.190
Scnd Half	218	50	2	18	.229	Clutch	84	20	0	6	.238

2001 Rankings (American League)

- 2nd in lowest batting average with runners in scoring position
- 4th in fielding percentage at second base (.984)
- 6th in sacrifice flies (9)
- Led the Angels in sacrifice flies (9), batting average on a 3-2 count (.273) and batting average with two strikes (.244)

Ramon Ortiz

2001 Season

Ramon Ortiz was dominant in spring training, so much so that it appeared the Angels might have developed their long-missing ace after all. No Angel has won 20 games since Nolan Ryan in 1974; no Angel has won 15 since Chuck Finley in 1996. Ortiz struck out a career-high 10 in his first start of the season, beating Texas, but he never struck out as many again all season. He was inconsistent at times but led the staff in innings pitched (208.2) and strikeouts (135) in his first full season in the majors. His two complete games came against the powerful offenses of Seattle and Cleveland.

Pitching

Ortiz has been tagged for potential dominance since 1997, when he led the minor leagues with 225 strikeouts in 181 innings. His pure stuff is the best of any Angels starter, and he can maintain velocity on his mid-90s fastball deep into a game. His slider and changeup are good, too. To remove the "potential" from his label as potential ace, Ortiz needs to develop the ability and confidence to pitch inside whatever the count.

Defense

As a highly emotional pitcher, Ortiz sometimes is too wound up to make the calm, routine defensive play. He committed six errors, more than all but infielders David Eckstein, Benji Gil, Troy Glaus and Adam Kennedy. He is average at best in holding runners on base, again sometimes complicated by his emotional nature.

2002 Outlook

After catcher Ben Molina injured his hamstring in May—he missed nearly two months—it took Ortiz six starts before he won. Ortiz trusts Molina, who can relax Ortiz at times and get in his face at other times. Manager Mike Scioscia treated Ortiz well, never asking him to make more than 116 pitches in any given start, and almost always keeping him between 90 and 110, but a healthy Molina might be the major factor in Ortiz developing into an ace.

Position: SP
Bats: R **Throws:** R
Ht: 6' 0" **Wt:** 170

Opening Day Age: 26
Born: 3/23/76 in Las Matas Cotui, DR
ML Seasons: 3
Pronunciation: or-TEEZ

Overall Statistics

	W	L	Pct.	ERA	G	GS	Sv	IP	H	BB	SO	HR	Ratio
2001	13	11	.542	4.36	32	32	0	208.2	223	76	135	25	1.43
Career	23	20	.535	4.86	59	59	0	368.1	369	156	252	50	1.43

How Often He Throws Strikes

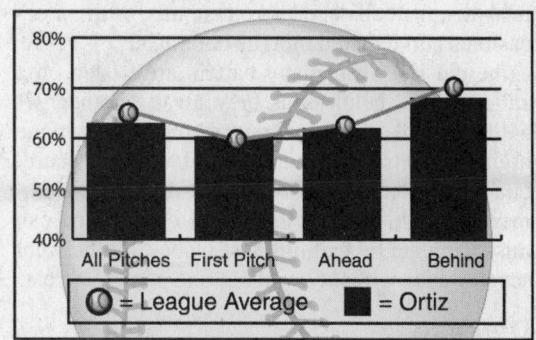

2001 Situational Stats

	W	L	ERA	Sv	IP		AB	H	HR	RBI	Avg
Home	6	6	4.66	0	100.1	LHB	425	121	11	54	.285
Road	7	5	4.07	0	108.1	RHB	388	102	14	45	.263
First Half	7	6	4.14	0	111.0	Sc Pos	211	49	3	68	.232
Scnd Half	6	5	4.61	0	97.2	Clutch	41	16	3	8	.390

2001 Rankings (American League)

- 1st in errors at pitcher (6)
- 2nd in fewest pitches thrown per batter (3.46) and lowest fielding percentage at pitcher (.864)
- 7th in highest slugging percentage allowed (.443)
- 8th in highest ERA at home
- 9th in hit batsmen (12), lowest strikeout-walk ratio (1.8), highest batting average allowed (.274) and highest on-base percentage allowed (.343)
- Led the Angels in wins, games started, complete games (2), innings pitched, batters faced (916), home runs allowed, strikeouts, wild pitches (7), winning percentage, fewest pitches thrown per batter (3.46), most run support per nine innings (5.1) and lowest batting average allowed with runners in scoring position

Troy Percival

2001 Season

Troy Percival pitched at less than his best in 2000, struggling to command his fastball and find any semblance of his curve after offseason shoulder surgery. He blew a league-leading 10 saves and finally yielded to the disabled list in August due to tendinitis in his elbow. He returned with a vengeance in 2001, converting 39 of 42 saves to break his own club record for save percentage. His ERA, which had risen in five consecutive seasons, fell to 2.65, his lowest since 1996. He walked 18, a career low, and made the All-Star team for the fourth time.

Pitching

There is no mystery to Percival's game. He throws fastballs, fastballs and more fastballs, with an occasional curve mixed in. If he commands his curve, as he did last year, many batters are frozen on a called strike, helpless as they await another 97-MPH fastball. His velocity was consistently in the high-90s all season, and several stadium scoreboards clocked him at 100 MPH during the summer. When his delivery gets out of sync, he can miss the plate by feet, not just inches, but he went seven weeks without a walk at one point last year.

Defense

Percival is so tough to hit—and so easy to run on—that most opponents will attempt to steal second. Percival's high leg kick prevents Angels catchers from throwing out many runners. Percival pays some attention to a runner if he represents the tying run, and he has experimented with a slide step, but he doesn't care if a runner steals so long as he preserves the victory. His wild delivery does not leave him in good position to field groundballs.

2002 Outlook

After Percival said a club official publicly disclosed details about failed negotiations for a contract extension, he asked to be traded and said he would not sign with the Angels after his contract expires this year. Even if the two sides reconcile, Percival already has outlasted the typical career span of a power closer, so the Angels must consider whether they would be better served renewing negotiations or trading him for prospects.

Position: RP
Bats: R **Throws:** R
Ht: 6' 3" **Wt:** 235

Opening Day Age: 32
Born: 8/9/69 in Fontana, CA
ML Seasons: 7
Pronunciation: PURR-si-vul
Nickname: Percy

Overall Statistics

	W	L	Pct.	ERA	G	GS	Sv	IP	H	BB	SO	HR	Ratio
2001	4	2	.667	2.65	57	0	39	57.2	39	18	71	3	0.99
Career	23	29	.442	3.09	417	0	210	431.1	279	186	531	44	1.08

How Often He Throws Strikes

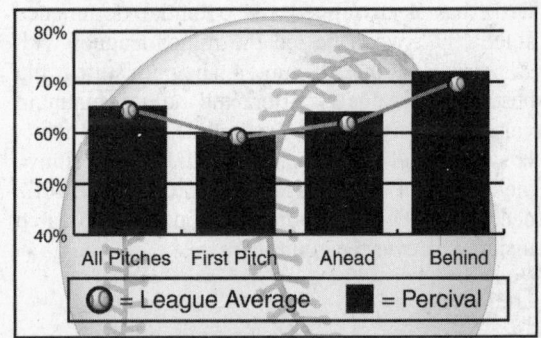

2001 Situational Stats

	W	L	ERA	Sv	IP		AB	H	HR	RBI	Avg
Home	3	2	3.64	18	29.2	LHB	125	22	2	10	.176
Road	1	0	1.61	21	28.0	RHB	84	17	1	8	.202
First Half	3	1	0.84	21	32.0	Sc Pos	49	12	2	15	.245
Scnd Half	1	1	4.91	18	25.2	Clutch	176	33	3	18	.188

2001 Rankings (American League)

- 2nd in lowest batting average allowed vs. lefthanded batters, save percentage (92.9) and lowest batting average allowed in relief (.187)
- 3rd in most strikeouts per nine innings in relief (11.1)
- 4th in saves
- Led the Angels in saves, games finished (50), save opportunities (42), lowest batting average allowed vs. lefthanded batters, save percentage (92.9), first batter efficiency (.173), lowest batting average allowed in relief (.187), most strikeouts per nine innings in relief (11.1) and fewest baserunners allowed per nine innings in relief (9.2)

Tim Salmon

2001 Season

No one gave it too much thought when Tim Salmon got off to a slow start. After all, he almost always starts slowly. But a .233 batting average in April gave way to sub-.200 averages in May, June and July, and manager Mike Scioscia dropped the perennial cleanup hitter as low as seventh in the lineup before the Angels finally placed Salmon on the disabled list because of nagging neck and shoulder injuries. When he returned, his play was better, but still a far cry from his usual excellence.

Hitting

Salmon posted career lows in batting average (.227), home runs (17) and runs batted in (49), all confounding given his proven consistency in producing typical seasons of .290 with 30 homers and 90 RBI. Foot and shoulder surgery limited his offseason work before the 2001 season, and the lingering effects of the shoulder injury affected his swing and strength. His .171 batting average with runners in scoring position was the worst of any American League regular. Amazingly, he nearly led the team in on-base percentage, contributing to the offense via the walk.

Baserunning & Defense

Salmon no longer is considered one of the elite outfielders in the league. His arm remains powerful and accurate—only Toronto's Raul Mondesi threw out more runners in 2001—but his range has diminished slightly, and he sometimes fails to take the most direct route to a flyball. He tied a career high with nine stolen bases. He is deceptively fast for his 6-foot-3, 225-pound frame, and the Angels believe he could succeed in taking the extra base more often.

2002 Outlook

The Angels signed Salmon to a four-year, $40-million contract extension in the spring of 2001, then gulped hard as he endured by far the worst season of his career. No one works harder, though, and the Angels have to believe that a return to good health will allow Salmon to return to his traditional role as an anchor in the lineup.

Position: RF/DH
Bats: R **Throws:** R
Ht: 6' 3" **Wt:** 225

Opening Day Age: 33
Born: 8/24/68 in Long Beach, CA
ML Seasons: 10
Pronunciation: SAM-en

Overall Statistics

	G	AB	R	H	D	T	HR	RBI	SB	BB	SO	Avg	OBP	Slg
2001	137	475	63	108	21	1	17	49	9	96	121	.227	.365	.383
Career	1250	4526	779	1288	252	17	247	806	38	779	1080	.285	.391	.511

Where He Hits the Ball

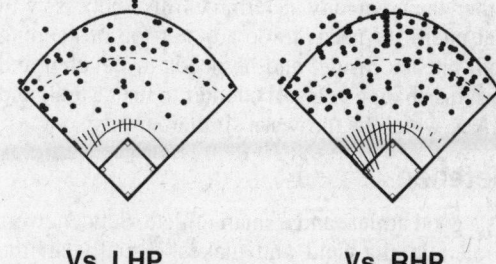

Vs. LHP   **Vs. RHP**

2001 Situational Stats

	AB	H	HR	RBI	Avg		AB	H	HR	RBI	Avg
Home	224	48	11	25	.214	LHP	125	29	4	15	.232
Road	251	60	6	24	.239	RHP	350	79	13	34	.226
First Half	252	52	9	26	.206	Sc Pos	129	22	5	30	.171
Scnd Half	223	56	8	23	.251	Clutch	73	17	2	4	.233

2001 Rankings (American League)

- 1st in lowest batting average, lowest batting average with runners in scoring position, lowest batting average with the bases loaded (0.000) and lowest batting average at home
- 2nd in fielding percentage in right field (.989) and assists in right field (13)
- 5th in lowest groundball-flyball ratio (0.7) and lowest batting average vs. righthanded pitchers
- 6th in walks, most pitches seen per plate appearance (4.09) and lowest percentage of swings put into play (35.4)
- Led the Angels in most pitches seen per plate appearance (4.09)

Scott Schoeneweis

2001 Season

In each of his two seasons in the starting rotation, Scott Schoeneweis has dazzled in April and disappointed the rest of the summer. In 2000, he went 4-0 with a 3.15 ERA in April and 3-10 with a 6.04 ERA the rest of the season. In 2001, he went 2-2 with a 2.91 ERA in April and 8-9 with a 5.67 ERA the rest of the season, and did not win in his final eight starts. He proved himself durable by pitching 205.1 innings.

Pitching

Schoeneweis relies on an outstanding sinker to induce a high number of groundballs, particularly for double plays. His fastball has satisfactory velocity, reaching 91 MPH at times, but movement rather than velocity determines his success with that pitch. He needs to do a better job of keeping both pitches inside, and he needs to develop and trust his change as a soft counter to his fastball and sinker, which he throws at similar speeds.

Defense

As a good athlete and a smart athlete, Schoeneweis is alert in the field and makes virtually all the routine plays. He continues to work on holding runners on base. Although he is lefthanded, that advantage in holding runners is negated because he lacks a sharp move to first base.

2002 Outlook

This season is critical for Schoeneweis. He walks far too many batters and throws far too many pitches. Because Schoenweis is a lefthanded sinkerballer, defense on the left side of the infield is crucial to his success. The continued improvement of third baseman Troy Glaus and the arrival of a shortstop with superior range, possibly top prospect Alfredo Amezaga in the not-too-distant future, would help immensely. If Schoeneweis cannot sustain success throughout the summer, the Angels might convert him to a bullpen specialist—lefties hit .209 with no home runs off him last season, righties batted .304 with 21 home runs—or they simply may let him go rather than face him in salary arbitration.

Position: SP
Bats: L **Throws:** L
Ht: 6' 0" **Wt:** 185

Opening Day Age: 28
Born: 10/2/73 in Long Branch, NJ
ML Seasons: 3
Pronunciation: SHOW-en-WEISS

Overall Statistics

	W	L	Pct.	ERA	G	GS	Sv	IP	H	BB	SO	HR	Ratio
2001	10	11	.476	5.08	32	32	0	205.1	227	77	104	21	1.48
Career	18	22	.450	5.27	90	59	0	414.2	457	158	204	46	1.48

How Often He Throws Strikes

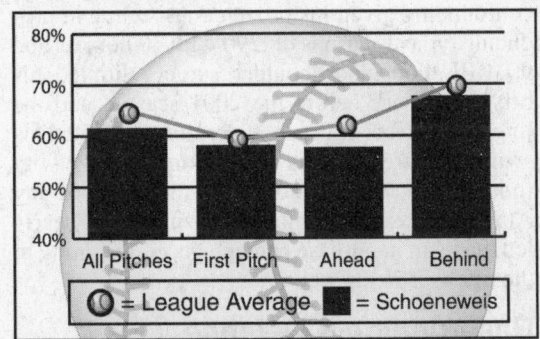

= League Average ■ = Schoeneweis

2001 Situational Stats

	W	L	ERA	Sv	IP		AB	H	HR	RBI	Avg
Home	5	3	5.40	0	105.0	LHB	196	41	0	18	.209
Road	5	8	4.75	0	100.1	RHB	612	186	21	87	.304
First Half	6	8	4.95	0	111.0	Sc Pos	199	59	4	78	.296
Scnd Half	4	3	5.25	0	94.1	Clutch	76	21	2	10	.276

2001 Rankings (American League)

- 1st in fielding percentage at pitcher (1.000)
- 2nd in GDPs induced (25), most GDPs induced per nine innings (1.1) and lowest strikeout-walk ratio (1.4)
- Led the Angels in games started, hits allowed, walks allowed, hit batsmen (14), pitches thrown (3,178), stolen bases allowed (20), GDPs induced (25), highest groundball-flyball ratio allowed (1.8), fewest home runs allowed per nine innings (.92), and most GDPs induced per nine innings (1.1)

Ismael Valdes

2001 Season

Ismael Valdes and the Angels took a chance on each other last year: Valdes needed somewhere to pitch, and the Angels needed someone to pitch. Valdes needed to re-establish himself as a competent major league starter after the Dodgers dumped him twice and the Cubs once within 12 months. He did a decent job filling a hole in the Angels' rotation, and he was 8-6 with a 3.48 ERA on August 15. He collapsed along with the rest of the team, however, losing seven of his final eight starts.

Pitching

Valdes recovered some of the velocity in his fastball, occasionally topping 90 MPH, but he did not recover all of the command he needs to succeed. His curve is good, although he lost his feel for the pitch toward the end of the season, and his change and slider are strictly complementary pitches. If, on any given day, he can put his fastball where he wants, he can keep his team in the game.

Defense

Valdes can make the routine plays to help himself in the field, but his defense is nothing spectacular. He holds runners on base well, and does a nice job of speeding his delivery with runners on base. Valdez picked off four opponents, and basestealers were successful just 50 percent of the time on his watch (9 of 18).

2002 Outlook

After posting an ERA below 4.00 in each of his first five major league seasons, Valdes put up a 5.64 ERA in 2000 and a 4.45 mark in 2001. Blister problems still nag him, but at 28 he's still young and otherwise healthy enough to regain his status as a quality starter. He credits much of his success last year to being reunited with manager Mike Scioscia, the former Dodgers bench coach, but Scioscia's Angels won't bring Valdes back if the expense is not minimal.

Position: SP
Bats: R **Throws:** R
Ht: 6' 4" **Wt:** 225

Opening Day Age: 28
Born: 8/21/73 in Ciudad Victoria, Mexico
ML Seasons: 8
Pronunciation: EES-mah-ALE val-DEZ
Nickname: Rocket

Overall Statistics

	W	L	Pct.	ERA	G	GS	Sv	IP	H	BB	SO	HR	Ratio
2001	9	13	.409	4.45	27	27	0	163.2	177	50	100	20	1.39
Career	72	74	.493	3.70	224	197	1	1295.2	1264	376	930	146	1.27

How Often He Throws Strikes

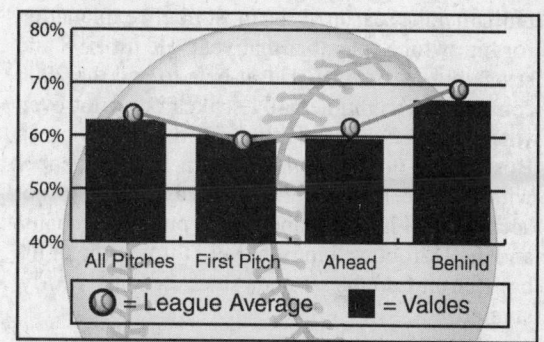

2001 Situational Stats

	W	L	ERA	Sv	IP		AB	H	HR	RBI	Avg
Home	4	9	4.48	0	88.1	LHB	320	94	9	35	.294
Road	5	4	4.42	0	75.1	RHB	318	83	11	35	.261
First Half	5	4	4.32	0	75.0	Sc Pos	141	35	1	46	.248
Scnd Half	4	9	4.57	0	88.2	Clutch	39	11	0	1	.282

2001 Rankings (American League)

- 1st in fielding percentage at pitcher (1.000) and least run support per nine innings (3.4)
- 5th in losses and lowest stolen-base percentage allowed (50.0)
- 8th in highest ERA and highest batting average allowed (.277)
- 10th in lowest winning percentage and highest slugging percentage allowed (.431)
- Led the Angels in losses, lowest stolen-base percentage allowed (50.0) and most GDPs induced per GDP situation (14.4%)

Mo Vaughn

2001 Season

For Mo Vaughn, there wasn't a 2001 season. In February, he underwent surgery to repair a torn biceps tendon in his left arm, and he spent the season in rehabilitation. The Angels sorely missed his bat in the middle of the lineup during a season in which they hit 78 fewer home runs and scored 173 fewer runs than in 2000. Vaughn has yet to play a full season in Anaheim while completely healthy, and yet he hit 36 home runs and drove in 117 runs in 2000.

Hitting

Vaughn suggests the biceps injury, apparently suffered on a swing in August 2000 but not diagnosed until after the season, is the most likely explanation for his awful September that year. He hit .198 and struck out 39 times in 111 at-bats to end the 2000 campaign. Vaughn actually strikes out a lot even when healthy. His beautiful inside-out swing in Boston, the one that enabled him to play pepper with the Green Monster in Fenway Park, did not accompany him to Anaheim. He pulls more balls, and the 18-foot wall in right field turns some of his homers into doubles—and, since he runs poorly, singles.

Baserunning & Defense

The Angels believe Vaughn must lose weight—he is listed at 275 pounds—to be effective defensively. He can scoop a throw from the dirt, but he has little range, and he led American League first basemen in errors in 2000. The Angels moved Darin Erstad back to first base—a position he played earlier in his career—towards the end of last season and might move Vaughn to DH in spring training, which he doesn't want to do. Vaughn seldom takes the extra base.

2002 Outlook

Vaughn appeared on a Boston radio station in October and asked the Red Sox to trade for him. The Angels would be happy to shed the remaining three years and $50 million of his contract. They need his bat, however, as there are no power hitters at the higher levels of their system.

Position: 1B/DH
Bats: L **Throws:** R
Ht: 6' 1" **Wt:** 275

Opening Day Age: 34
Born: 12/15/67 in Norwalk, CT
ML Seasons: 10
Nickname: The Hit Dog

Overall Statistics

	G	AB	R	H	D	T	HR	RBI	SB	BB	SO	Avg	OBP	Slg
2001						Did Not Play								
Career	1346	4966	784	1479	250	10	299	977	30	652	1262	.298	.387	.533

Where He Hits the Ball

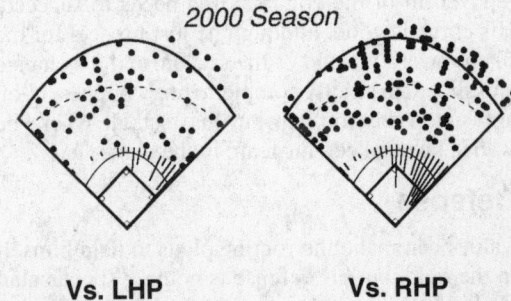

2000 Season

Vs. LHP   **Vs. RHP**

2001 Situational Stats

	AB	H	HR	RBI	Avg		AB	H	HR	RBI	Avg
Home	—	—	—	—	—	LHP	—	—	—	—	—
Road	—	—	—	—	—	RHP	—	—	—	—	—
First Half	—	—	—	—	—	Sc Pos	—	—	—	—	—
Scnd Half	—	—	—	—	—	Clutch	—	—	—	—	—

2001 Rankings (American League)

- Did not rank near the top or bottom in any category

Jarrod Washburn

2001 Season

After serving three stints on the disabled list in 2000, Jarrod Washburn was healthy and successful in 2001, winning 11 games and pitching 193 innings in his first full major league season. Ramon Ortiz has better stuff, but Washburn emerged as the better pitcher last year, coupling intense determination with a lively fastball. At one point, he started 14 consecutive games without a loss. In the past 10 years, the only Angels pitchers to start 30 games and post a lower ERA than Washburn are Chuck Finley and Mark Langston.

Pitching

Washburn relies on his fastball—he throws it three out of every four pitches—because of its late movement and because he can vary its speed between 83-92 MPH without losing the strike zone. His slider and change, decent now, should get better. He is not afraid to pitch behind in the count, but the Angels want him to concentrate on getting ahead of hitters so he can last longer in games. His only complete game in 65 major league starts was an eight-inning loss last year.

Defense

Washburn is a fine athlete who fields his position well. The lefthander neutralizes opposing running games with outstanding deception in his leg kick and an excellent slide step, and he ranked among league leaders in pickoff throws. He also nabbed 11 baserunners on his own.

2002 Outlook

Washburn is a winner, and the Angels need more of those. He missed his scheduled Opening Day start last year while recovering from strep throat, but he ought to get another chance in 2002. The Angels haven't sent a starting pitcher to the All-Star Game since 1997; Washburn could be the next one.

Position: SP
Bats: L **Throws:** L
Ht: 6' 1" **Wt:** 187

Opening Day Age: 27
Born: 8/13/74 in LaCrosse, WI
ML Seasons: 4

Overall Statistics

	W	L	Pct.	ERA	G	GS	Sv	IP	H	BB	SO	HR	Ratio
2001	11	10	.524	3.77	30	30	0	193.1	196	54	126	25	1.29
Career	28	20	.583	4.14	75	65	0	413.1	391	144	262	58	1.29

How Often He Throws Strikes

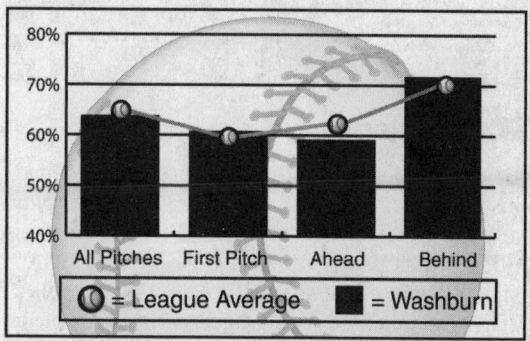

◯ = League Average   ■ = Washburn

2001 Situational Stats

	W	L	ERA	Sv	IP		AB	H	HR	RBI	Avg
Home	4	5	4.65	0	89.0	LHB	157	45	6	18	.287
Road	7	5	3.02	0	104.1	RHB	587	151	19	66	.257
First Half	7	4	3.52	0	107.1	Sc Pos	155	45	6	59	.290
Scnd Half	4	6	4.08	0	86.0	Clutch	36	11	3	8	.306

2001 Rankings (American League)

- 2nd in lowest ERA on the road and lowest groundball-flyball ratio allowed (0.7)
- 5th in runners caught stealing (12)
- 6th in fewest GDPs induced per nine innings (0.5) and lowest fielding percentage at pitcher (.941)
- 7th in pickoff throws (145)
- Led the Angels in ERA, home runs allowed, pickoff throws (145), runners caught stealing (12), highest strikeout-walk ratio (2.3), lowest on-base percentage allowed (.318), lowest ERA on the road, most strikeouts per nine innings (5.9), and fewest walks per nine innings (2.5)

Benji Gil

Position: SS/2B/1B/DH
Bats: R **Throws:** R
Ht: 6' 2" **Wt:** 210

Opening Day Age: 29
Born: 10/6/72 in Tijuana, Mexico
ML Seasons: 6
Pronunciation: GILL

Overall Statistics

	G	AB	R	H	D	T	HR	RBI	SB	BB	SO	Avg	OBP	Slg
2001	104	260	33	77	15	4	8	39	3	14	57	.296	.330	.477
Career	481	1355	135	320	62	10	28	142	17	93	382	.236	.287	.359

2001 Situational Stats

	AB	H	HR	RBI	Avg		AB	H	HR	RBI	Avg
Home	122	30	6	20	.246	LHP	143	42	4	15	.294
Road	138	47	2	19	.341	RHP	117	35	4	24	.299
First Half	151	50	5	23	.331	Sc Pos	67	18	1	28	.269
Scnd Half	109	27	3	16	.248	Clutch	38	6	1	3	.158

2001 Season

Benji Gil, a former first-round draft pick who made his major league debut at 20, appears to have found a niche as a utility player at 29. He honed his offensive skills at Triple-A Calgary in 1998-99, signed a minor league contract with the Angels in 2000 and emerged as a valued component of the team. He hit a career-high .296, 60 points above his career average, but batted .248 after the All-Star break and did not hit a home run after July 18.

Hitting, Baserunning & Defense

Gil is maturing as a hitter, not chasing as many of the bad pitches that used to tempt him. He has good power for a middle infielder (his slugging percentage was .477 in 2001; Garret Anderson's was .478) and good speed. His arm strength is terrific, and for a natural shortstop he has adapted nicely to second base. He also played first base and the outfield last summer.

2002 Outlook

Gil would like to play every day, but the Angels consider him strictly a utility player and wonder whether his second-half fade reflected an overexposed player. Still, Anaheim values his versatility and adaptability, and he values his major league job after two years without one. The Angels picked up their 2002 option on Gil.

Shigetoshi Hasegawa

Position: RP
Bats: R **Throws:** R
Ht: 5'11" **Wt:** 178

Opening Day Age: 33
Born: 8/1/68 in Kobe, Japan
ML Seasons: 5
Pronunciation:
shig-eh-toe-shi
HOSS-eh-gawa
Nickname: Shiggy

Overall Statistics

	W	L	Pct.	ERA	G	GS	Sv	IP	H	BB	SO	HR	Ratio
2001	5	6	.455	4.04	46	0	0	55.2	52	20	41	5	1.29
Career	30	27	.526	3.85	287	8	16	442.1	436	170	300	58	1.37

2001 Situational Stats

	W	L	ERA	Sv	IP		AB	H	HR	RBI	Avg
Home	3	2	3.33	0	27.0	LHB	95	21	1	9	.221
Road	2	4	4.71	0	28.2	RHB	115	31	4	19	.270
First Half	2	4	4.32	0	25.0	Sc Pos	56	13	0	21	.232
Scnd Half	3	2	3.82	0	30.2	Clutch	126	31	3	23	.246

2001 Season

Did the workload finally catch up to Shigetoshi Hasegawa, who had been virtually indestructible since joining the Angels in 1997? After six seasons as a starting pitcher in Japan, Hasegawa led American League relievers in innings pitched in 1998 and 2000 before doctors diagnosed a partially torn rotator cuff last May. He did not require surgery and said he did not believe overuse was a contributing factor. Hasegawa returned after six weeks to pitch 35 innings over the final four months (including October), with a 3.60 ERA.

Pitching & Defense

Hasegawa lives along the corners of the plate, using three pitches—fastball, forkball and slider—to induce groundballs. His fastball rarely exceeds the high 80s, and the Angels would not bring him into a game when they needed a strikeout. He is very good as a fielder and has a very quick move to home plate, preventing potential basestealers from getting a good jump.

2002 Outlook

Hasegawa is especially versatile, able to pitch three innings one day and work to one batter the next, as he's experienced in starting and closing. So long as Hasegawa maintains the ability to hit his spots, the Angels will be happy to keep him on their staff.

Mike Holtz

Position: RP
Bats: L **Throws:** L
Ht: 5' 9" **Wt:** 185

Opening Day Age: 29
Born: 10/10/72 in
Arlington, VA
ML Seasons: 6

Overall Statistics

	W	L	Pct.	ERA	G	GS	Sv	IP	H	BB	SO	HR	Ratio
2001	1	2	.333	4.86	63	0	0	37.0	40	15	38	5	1.49
Career	14	18	.438	4.56	301	0	3	203.1	200	97	195	20	1.46

2001 Situational Stats

	W	L	ERA	Sv	IP		AB	H	HR	RBI	Avg
Home	1	0	4.19	0	19.1	LHB	80	25	2	15	.313
Road	0	2	5.60	0	17.2	RHB	66	15	3	12	.227
First Half	0	0	3.98	0	20.1	Sc Pos	54	15	1	20	.278
Scnd Half	1	2	5.94	0	16.2	Clutch	52	13	3	7	.250

2001 Season

Manager Mike Scioscia appeared to lose confidence in Mike Holtz at times during the season, failing to summon his only lefthanded reliever in several games when the occasion demanded one. For a pitcher whose primary role is to get lefthanded hitters out, his opposing batting average against lefties was .313 last year, .213 in 2000. More baffling, his opposing batting average against righties was .227 last year, .300 in 2000.

Pitching & Defense

Holtz neutralizes lefthanded hitters with a sweeping curve, which is very slow and very good when it crosses the whole of the plate and finishes down and away. His fastball tops out at 89 MPH, but that's enough to keep lefthanded hitters honest if Holtz can locate the fastball inside, as hitters expecting the curve lean across the plate. His defense is good, but his delivery isn't quick enough to deter baserunners.

2002 Outlook

With a 5.65 ERA over the past three years, Holtz is hardly indispensable. If the Angels can't agree on a contract, they might let him go rather than risk an arbitration hearing. But good lefty relievers are hard to find, and Anaheim would prefer to give Holtz another chance to find his curve.

Al Levine

Position: RP
Bats: L **Throws:** R
Ht: 6' 3" **Wt:** 190

Opening Day Age: 33
Born: 5/22/68 in Park
Ridge, IL
ML Seasons: 6
Pronunciation: le-VINE

Overall Statistics

	W	L	Pct.	ERA	G	GS	Sv	IP	H	BB	SO	HR	Ratio
2001	8	10	.444	2.38	64	1	2	75.2	71	28	40	7	1.31
Career	14	19	.424	3.85	236	7	4	359.2	370	145	172	41	1.43

2001 Situational Stats

	W	L	ERA	Sv	IP		AB	H	HR	RBI	Avg
Home	6	4	1.88	1	43.0	LHB	132	38	5	16	.288
Road	2	6	3.03	1	32.2	RHB	144	33	2	22	.229
First Half	4	4	2.15	0	46.0	Sc Pos	83	23	2	32	.277
Scnd Half	4	6	2.73	2	29.2	Clutch	187	52	5	27	.278

2001 Season

In three seasons in Anaheim, Al Levine has emerged as a dependable and versatile reliever. He'll start if needed, and he'll finish when Troy Percival is unavailable. In 2001 he made his mark by replacing the injured Shigetoshi Hasegawa as Percival's setup man and remaining in that role after Hasegawa returned. He allowed one earned run in his first 11 appearances combined, and just one earned run in 20 outings in June and July.

Pitching & Defense

Levine worked hard on offseason conditioning and picked up a modest boost on his velocity, though he cannot live on a 90-MPH fastball alone. He gets better results with a sinking 85-MPH fastball than a straight 90-MPH fastball, but his slider is his best pitch. The Angels believe he is useful against all hitters, but his statistics were much better against righthanders (.229 opposing batting average, .299 opposing slugging percentage) than against lefthanders (.288, .470). He is adequate at holding runners on base and is below average as a fielder.

2002 Outlook

The bullpen is one of Anaheim's few strengths, and Levine's ability to pitch effectively, whether for three innings one day or for three consecutive days, makes him a valued member of that bullpen.

Ben Molina

Position: C
Bats: R **Throws:** R
Ht: 5'11" **Wt:** 210

Opening Day Age: 27
Born: 7/20/74 in Rio Piedras, PR
ML Seasons: 4

Overall Statistics

	G	AB	R	H	D	T	HR	RBI	SB	BB	SO	Avg	OBP	Slg
2001	96	325	31	85	11	0	6	40	0	16	51	.262	.309	.351
Career	259	900	98	244	36	2	21	121	1	45	90	.271	.314	.386

2001 Situational Stats

	AB	H	HR	RBI	Avg		AB	H	HR	RBI	Avg
Home	162	51	6	21	.315	LHP	101	22	3	14	.218
Road	163	34	0	19	.209	RHP	224	63	3	26	.281
First Half	118	29	0	12	.246	Sc Pos	90	27	0	30	.300
Scnd Half	207	56	6	28	.271	Clutch	62	24	2	12	.387

2001 Season

In explaining their offensive failures, the Angels often bemoaned the injuries and ineffectiveness of Darin Erstad, Mo Vaughn and Tim Salmon. But the loss of Ben Molina to a hamstring injury deprived them of one of their best clutch hitters for the better part of two months. The injury also deprived them of their starting catcher, who also is a calming influence for emotional righthander Ramon Ortiz.

Hitting, Baserunning & Defense

Molina has developed power he never showed in his seven minor league seasons, and he hit .300 with runners in scoring position in 2001. He rarely walks, but he puts the ball in play all over the field and can volley a bad ball over an infielder's head for a single. His defense is strong, but his throwing mechanics regressed last summer, probably a lingering effect of his injury. He is not a factor on the bases.

2002 Outlook

Molina was injury-prone in the minor leagues and needs to stay healthy this season to ease the concerns of the Angels. If he is injury-free, he will play every day and give the Angels a solid defensive catcher and a decent offensive threat near the bottom of the batting order.

Orlando Palmeiro

Position: DH/RF/LF
Bats: L **Throws:** L
Ht: 5'11" **Wt:** 180

Opening Day Age: 33
Born: 1/19/69 in Hoboken, NJ
ML Seasons: 7
Pronunciation: PALL-mare-oh

Overall Statistics

	G	AB	R	H	D	T	HR	RBI	SB	BB	SO	Avg	OBP	Slg
2001	104	230	29	56	10	1	2	23	6	25	24	.243	.319	.322
Career	535	1196	169	331	57	9	3	107	22	148	110	.277	.360	.347

2001 Situational Stats

	AB	H	HR	RBI	Avg		AB	H	HR	RBI	Avg
Home	107	22	0	10	.206	LHP	15	1	0	0	.067
Road	123	34	2	13	.276	RHP	215	55	2	23	.256
First Half	111	32	2	13	.288	Sc Pos	49	16	1	22	.327
Scnd Half	119	24	0	10	.202	Clutch	44	11	0	2	.250

2001 Season

Orlando Palmeiro has developed into a solid player. He lacks the power to play a corner outfield spot regularly and isn't gifted enough defensively to play center field every day. Yet he is a great role player, capable of spelling any outfielder when necessary and pestering any pitcher with his ability to foul off pitches, extend at-bats and reach base.

Hitting, Baserunning & Defense

Palmeiro is a slap hitter, often to the opposite field, but he has just enough power to keep opposing defenses honest, turning on the occasional pitch and muscling up to hit a sacrifice fly when necessary. He is not afraid to take pitches and hit with two strikes, and he is a good bunter. Palmeiro is adequate at all three outfield positions, with an acceptable arm. He does not utilize his speed with good jumps or superb instincts, so the Angels do not maximize their usage of him as a pinch-runner.

2002 Outlook

Palmeiro is an ideal pinch-hitter leading off an inning, someone who can start a rally with a single or walk. He's also an ideal pinch-hitter when a strikeout simply won't do; he makes terrific contact. He hit .327 last season with runners in scoring position. The Angels again will look to Palmeiro to approach .300 off the bench.

Lou Pote

Position: RP
Bats: R **Throws:** R
Ht: 6' 3" **Wt:** 200

Opening Day Age: 30
Born: 8/21/71 in
Evergreen Park, IL
ML Seasons: 3

Overall Statistics

	W	L	Pct.	ERA	G	GS	Sv	IP	H	BB	SO	HR	Ratio
2001	2	0	1.000	4.15	44	1	2	86.2	88	32	66	11	1.38
Career	4	2	.667	3.57	96	2	6	166.1	163	61	130	16	1.35

2001 Situational Stats

	W	L	ERA	Sv	IP		AB	H	HR	RBI	Avg
Home	1	0	4.82	0	46.2	LHB	157	42	7	23	.268
Road	1	0	3.38	2	40.0	RHB	184	46	4	26	.250
First Half	1	0	3.57	1	45.1	Sc Pos	105	24	1	36	.229
Scnd Half	1	0	4.79	1	41.1	Clutch	23	8	1	3	.348

2001 Season

For the first time in 11 pro seasons, Lou Pote spent the entire summer in the major leagues. He emerged from the depths of the bullpen and developed into a reliable middle reliever. His ERA was a bit misleading. The season lasted a few too many days, as his ERA jumped from 2.81 on September 26 to 4.15 after he gave up 14 runs in his final 3.1 innings.

Pitching & Defense

Pote might have the best curve on the team, and he trusts it enough to throw it in any situation. He can control his curve better than his fastball, which can make his fastball hittable since it tops out at 90-92 MPH. His split-finger pitch is sometimes useful. Pote is durable, and manager Mike Scioscia relies on him to eat innings when a starter gets knocked out early. He does not help himself as a fielder or with his slow delivery with runners on base.

2002 Outlook

After Pote held the Yankees to one run over five innings in an emergency start, the coaching staff discussed the possibility of using him as a fifth starter. If he can improve the command of his fastball, he might get that chance. If not, he has carved himself a niche in the middle innings.

Pat Rapp

Position: SP
Bats: R **Throws:** R
Ht: 6' 3" **Wt:** 230

Opening Day Age: 34
Born: 7/13/67 in
Jennings, LA
ML Seasons: 10

Overall Statistics

	W	L	Pct.	ERA	G	GS	Sv	IP	H	BB	SO	HR	Ratio
2001	5	12	.294	4.76	31	28	0	170.0	169	71	82	20	1.41
Career	70	91	.435	4.68	259	239	0	1387.1	1468	683	825	133	1.55

2001 Situational Stats

	W	L	ERA	Sv	IP		AB	H	HR	RBI	Avg
Home	2	6	4.45	0	89.0	LHB	344	92	9	46	.267
Road	3	6	5.11	0	81.0	RHB	303	77	11	44	.254
First Half	3	9	4.62	0	109.0	Sc Pos	151	46	6	71	.305
Scnd Half	2	3	5.02	0	61.0	Clutch	15	7	0	2	.467

2001 Season

The Angels asked Pat Rapp to eat innings and keep his team in the game. He performed as asked, pitching 170 innings but winning only five games due to a lack of run support. In September, after he was replaced in the starting rotation with youngster Matt Wise, Rapp revealed he had pitched most of the season with a partially torn labrum in his right shoulder. Perhaps that explains why manager Mike Scioscia never let him make more than 109 pitches.

Pitching & Defense

Rapp uses an assortment of pitches but lacks any one very good pitch. His fastball is below average, as is his change, but his curve and cut fastball are not bad. If he can put those two pitches where he wants to, he can win. He walks too many batters and pitches deep into too many counts, which prevents him from developing beyond a six-inning pitcher. He neither hurts nor helps himself defensively, and his pickoff move is above average for a righthander.

2002 Outlook

The Angels are not expected to invite Rapp back. He'll probably have to find another team in search of a veteran to plug a one-year hole in its starting rotation, which allows a youngster to develop and then take Rapp's job.

Scott Spiezio

Position: 1B/DH/3B/LF
Bats: B **Throws:** R
Ht: 6' 2" **Wt:** 225

Opening Day Age: 29
Born: 9/21/72 in Joliet, IL
ML Seasons: 6
Pronunciation: SPEE-zio

Overall Statistics

	G	AB	R	H	D	T	HR	RBI	SB	BB	SO	Avg	OBP	Slg
2001	139	457	57	124	29	4	13	54	5	34	65	.271	.326	.438
Career	621	1974	253	501	113	11	63	259	16	195	292	.254	.322	.418

2001 Situational Stats

	AB	H	HR	RBI	Avg		AB	H	HR	RBI	Avg
Home	224	64	8	29	.286	LHP	109	26	0	6	.239
Road	233	60	5	25	.258	RHP	348	98	13	48	.282
First Half	187	44	4	21	.235	Sc Pos	102	25	2	40	.245
Scnd Half	270	80	9	33	.296	Clutch	73	22	2	9	.301

2001 Season

The season was a frustrating one for Scott Spiezio, who watched from the bench as the Angels tried Wally Joyner and then rookie Larry Barnes at first base. After Joyner retired and Anaheim sent Barnes back to the minor leagues, Spiezio got his chance. In his 10-week run as the regular first baseman from July 8 to September 22, he fielded well and hit .319 with 11 home runs and 35 RBI. Then the Angels tried Darin Erstad at first base, a sign they believe they are a stronger club with Erstad or Mo Vaughn at first and Spiezio on the bench.

Hitting, Baserunning & Defense

A switch-hitter, Spiezio hits significantly better from the left side. He has patience at the plate and some pop, trailing only Troy Glaus, Garret Anderson and Tim Salmon on the team in home runs. His infield range is not great, but he plays first and third base very well and held his own in occasional outfield appearances. He'll run if you're not paying attention.

2002 Outlook

The Angels would oblige Spiezio and trade him to any team wishing to make him a starter, but until then they're happy to keep their bench stocked with a switch-hitter with pop in his bat and versatility afield.

Shawn Wooten

Position: DH/C/1B
Bats: R **Throws:** R
Ht: 5'10" **Wt:** 225

Opening Day Age: 29
Born: 7/24/72 in Glendora, CA
ML Seasons: 2

Overall Statistics

	G	AB	R	H	D	T	HR	RBI	SB	BB	SO	Avg	OBP	Slg
2001	79	221	24	69	8	1	8	32	2	5	42	.312	.332	.466
Career	86	230	26	74	9	1	8	33	2	5	42	.322	.340	.474

2001 Situational Stats

	AB	H	HR	RBI	Avg		AB	H	HR	RBI	Avg
Home	116	40	3	15	.345	LHP	115	35	6	18	.304
Road	105	29	5	17	.276	RHP	106	34	2	14	.321
First Half	128	42	7	23	.328	Sc Pos	54	18	0	21	.333
Scnd Half	93	27	1	9	.290	Clutch	27	11	1	4	.407

2001 Season

After an eight-year minor league odyssey that included two summers of independent league ball in Moose Jaw, Saskatchewan, Shawn Wooten made the Angels' roster in spring training. He stuck around all season too, hitting from day one and waiting for the Jose Canseco and Glenallen Hill experiments to flop before getting his chance at designated hitter. Although his season ended with September wrist surgery, he hit .312 in 221 at-bats, the only Angel to finish above .300.

Hitting, Baserunning & Defense

Wooten is here for his hitting, period. He has impressive power and bat speed, and he can pick a pitch and drive it against lefties or righties. He'll need to make better contact and, if possible, take more walks. He can play first base, third base and catcher, but he is best suited to DH. He is not a factor on the bases.

2002 Outlook

If Mo Vaughn becomes the DH, Wooten is on the bench. If Vaughn plays first base or changes teams, Wooten and Scott Spiezio figure to compete for or share the DH role. Wooten's hitting ability and humble attitude could keep him in the majors, if on the bench, for a few years.

Other Anaheim Angels

Larry Barnes (Pos: 1B, Age: 27, Bats: L)

	G	AB	R	H	D	T	HR	RBI	SB	BB	SO	Avg	OBP	Slg
2001	16	40	2	4	0	0	1	2	0	1	9	.100	.122	.175
Career	16	40	2	4	0	0	1	2	0	1	9	.100	.122	.175

Barnes enjoyed a solid season in Triple-A, where he hit .290 and slugged .515. He was called up to Anaheim twice to audition at first base and did not impress. His AVG, OBP and SLG all were below the Mendoza Line. 2002 Outlook: C

Toby Borland (Pos: RHP, Age: 32)

	W	L	Pct.	ERA	G	GS	Sv	IP	H	BB	SO	HR	Ratio
2001	0	1	.000	10.80	2	0	0	3.1	8	1	0	1	2.70
Career	9	8	.529	4.11	167	0	8	228.0	228	121	178	17	1.53

Borland's 13th minor league season was one of his best, as he posted a 2.30 ERA in 74 innings. However, his first appearance in the majors since 1998 was only a four-day stay. 2002 Outlook: C

Jamie Burke (Pos: C, Age: 30, Bats: R)

	G	AB	R	H	D	T	HR	RBI	SB	BB	SO	Avg	OBP	Slg
2001	9	5	1	1	0	0	0	0	0	0	2	.200	.200	.200
Career	9	5	1	1	0	0	0	0	0	0	2	.200	.200	.200

A rash of injuries to its catchers forced Anaheim to call up Burke three times last year. He batted only .219 in Triple-A, where he was splitting time as a backup at catcher and third base. 2002 Outlook: C

Brian Cooper (Pos: RHP, Age: 27)

	W	L	Pct.	ERA	G	GS	Sv	IP	H	BB	SO	HR	Ratio
2001	0	1	.000	2.63	7	1	0	13.2	10	4	7	2	1.02
Career	5	10	.333	5.33	27	21	0	128.1	138	57	58	23	1.52

Cooper spent the majority of his season as a Triple-A starter and improved in every category from the year before. He was called up in September and did a commendable job out of the pen and during his one start. 2002 Outlook: C

Jeff DaVanon (Pos: RF/CF, Age: 28, Bats: B)

	G	AB	R	H	D	T	HR	RBI	SB	BB	SO	Avg	OBP	Slg
2001	40	88	7	17	2	1	5	9	1	11	29	.193	.280	.409
Career	47	108	11	21	2	2	6	13	1	13	36	.194	.279	.417

After missing the 2000 season with a torn left labrum, DaVanon returned with mixed results. In the minors he batted .313 and slugged .566, but in the majors he hit .193 and struck out in nearly a third of his at-bats. 2002 Outlook: C

Jorge Fabregas (Pos: C, Age: 32, Bats: L)

	G	AB	R	H	D	T	HR	RBI	SB	BB	SO	Avg	OBP	Slg
2001	53	148	9	33	4	2	2	16	0	3	15	.223	.235	.318
Career	581	1672	140	413	52	5	20	189	4	106	204	.247	.290	.320

Signed as a backup catcher a year ago, Fabregas replaced an injured Ben Molina in May after overcoming an inflamed right elbow. He demonstrated he is at his best as a backup, and that's his role in Anaheim in 2002. 2002 Outlook: C

Jose Fernandez (Pos: DH, Age: 27, Bats: R)

	G	AB	R	H	D	T	HR	RBI	SB	BB	SO	Avg	OBP	Slg
2001	13	25	1	2	1	0	0	0	0	2	10	.080	.148	.120
Career	21	49	1	7	3	0	1	0	1	3	17	.143	.192	.204

Despite being named the Angels' Minor League Player of the Year while batting .338 with 30 HR and 114 RBI, Fernandez was placed on waivers in October and was claimed by the Cubs. 2002 Outlook: C

Steve Green (Pos: RHP, Age: 24)

	W	L	Pct.	ERA	G	GS	Sv	IP	H	BB	SO	HR	Ratio
2001	0	0	-	3.00	1	1	0	6.0	4	6	4	0	1.67
Career	0	0	-	3.00	1	1	0	6.0	4	6	4	0	1.67

Green had another solid season in the minors. The promising young starter went 6-2 with a 3.66 ERA in 10 games. His season came to an abrupt finish in June when he had surgery on a torn muscle in his right forearm. 2002 Outlook: D

Glenallen Hill (Pos: DH, Age: 37, Bats: R)

	G	AB	R	H	D	T	HR	RBI	SB	BB	SO	Avg	OBP	Slg
2001	16	66	4	9	0	0	1	2	0	0	20	.136	.136	.182
Career	1162	3715	528	1005	187	21	186	586	96	270	845	.271	.321	.482

Hill was acquired from the Yankees in March, with the hope that he could duplicate his 2000 AL performance, when he had a homer every 8.25 at-bats. He spent the majority of his time on the DL and was let go on June 1. 2002 Outlook: D.

Wally Joyner (Pos: 1B, Age: 39, Bats: L)

	G	AB	R	H	D	T	HR	RBI	SB	BB	SO	Avg	OBP	Slg
2001	53	148	14	36	5	1	3	14	1	13	18	.243	.304	.351
Career	2033	7127	973	2060	409	26	204	1106	60	833	825	.289	.362	.440

By retiring on June 14, his 39th birthday, Joyner finished his 16-year career back with his original team. Although he had a 22-game stretch in which he batted .366, he decided that he wasn't contributing enough and hung up the cleats. 2002 Outlook: D

Mark Lukasiewicz (Pos: LHP, Age: 29)

	W	L	Pct.	ERA	G	GS	Sv	IP	H	BB	SO	HR	Ratio
2001	0	2	.000	6.04	24	0	0	22.1	21	9	25	6	1.34
Career	0	2	.000	6.04	24	0	0	22.1	21	9	25	6	1.34

Last season was very encouraging for Lukasiewicz. In Triple-A, he had a 1.48 ERA and only walked two batters while striking out 41. His major league numbers were skewed by a six-run, one-out appearance, though. 2002 Outlook: C

Jose Molina (Pos: C, Age: 26, Bats: R)

	G	AB	R	H	D	T	HR	RBI	SB	BB	SO	Avg	OBP	Slg
2001	15	37	8	10	3	0	2	4	0	3	8	.270	.325	.514
Career	25	56	11	15	4	0	2	5	0	5	12	.268	.328	.446

In May, Molina, a defensive specialist, was called up from Triple-A to replace his injured brother, Ben, on the roster. After two weeks, he fractured a thumb and joined his brother on the DL. 2002 Outlook: C

Jose Nieves (**Pos**: 2B, **Age**: 26, **Bats**: R)

	G	AB	R	H	D	T	HR	RBI	SB	BB	SO	Avg	OBP	Slg
2001	29	53	5	13	3	1	2	3	0	2	20	.245	.298	.453
Career	167	433	38	100	18	5	9	45	1	21	88	.231	.273	.358

Nieves was recalled three times last season from Triple-A Salt Lake City. He played at every infield position and had only one error. However, he has not hit well enough to overcome his "utility" label. 2002 Outlook: C

Scot Shields (**Pos**: RHP, **Age**: 26)

	W	L	Pct.	ERA	G	GS	Sv	IP	H	BB	SO	HR	Ratio
2001	0	0	-	0.00	8	0	0	11.0	8	7	7	0	1.36
Career	0	0	-	0.00	8	0	0	11.0	8	7	7	0	1.36

Shields spent his second consecutive season in Triple-A, and lowered his ERA by almost half a run. Despite being a starter in the minors, he was impressive in two brief stints out of the Angels' bullpen. 2002 Outlook: C

Ben Weber (**Pos**: RHP, **Age**: 32)

	W	L	Pct.	ERA	G	GS	Sv	IP	H	BB	SO	HR	Ratio
2001	6	2	.750	3.42	56	0	0	68.1	66	31	40	4	1.42
Career	7	3	.700	4.15	75	0	0	91.0	94	37	54	4	1.44

For the first time in his career, Weber spent a full season on a major league roster. When his season ended in September with a broken ankle, he was leading AL rookie pitchers in appearances. 2002 Outlook: B

Matt Wise (**Pos**: RHP, **Age**: 26)

	W	L	Pct.	ERA	G	GS	Sv	IP	H	BB	SO	HR	Ratio
2001	1	4	.200	4.38	11	9	0	49.1	47	18	50	11	1.32
Career	4	7	.364	4.88	19	15	0	86.2	87	31	70	18	1.36

Wise did a lot of traveling between the majors and minors last season. Although mainly a starter, he was unscored upon in four innings of relief work for the Angels. 2002 Outlook: B

Anaheim Angels Minor League Prospects

Organization Overview:

The Angels have nurtured the arrival of hitting prospects Troy Glaus, Adam Kennedy and Shawn Wooten in recent seasons. The organization could use more pop from its young talent, but for the moment there isn't a power source in the high minors who is ready to step into the Anaheim lineup. The Angels are more likely to get pitching help from their farm system, as several righthanders are on the cusp of joining youngsters Ramon Ortiz, Jarrod Washburn and Scott Schoeneweis in Anaheim. The new regime under Bill Stoneman still has plenty of talent on hand—from Alfredo Amezaga and Elpidio Guzman to John Lackey, Francisco Rodriguez and Joe Torres—but it isn't likely to help much in 2002.

Alfredo Amezaga

Position: SS
Bats: B **Throws:** R
Ht: 5' 10" **Wt:** 165

Opening Day Age: 24
Born: 1/16/78 in Obregon, Sonora, Mexico

Recent Statistics

	G	AB	R	H	D	THR	RBI	SB	BB	SO	Avg
2000 A Lk Elsinore	108	420	90	117	13	4	4	44	73	63	70	.279
2001 AA Arkansas	70	285	50	89	10	5	4	21	24	22	55	.312
2001 AAA Salt Lake	49	200	28	50	5	4	1	16	9	14	45	.250
2001 MLE	119	462	57	116	12	4	3	26	21	23	101	.251

This junior college vet, drafted in 1999, is a polished player with impressive makeup and leadership skills. Amezaga makes good contact and controls the strike zone, and his plate discipline didn't suffer when he took up switch-hitting during the 2000 season. He split time between second base and shortstop in 2000, but he's the shortstop of the future after impressing Angels coaches in spring training and being named the Double-A Texas League's best defensive shortstop by the league's managers. They also named the potential leadoff man the circuit's most exciting player. With good hands, speed and instincts, Amezaga's defensive game is nearly ready, and the Angels believe his bat will follow. His numbers at Triple-A Salt Lake weren't pretty, but they come just two years after his debut in rookie ball.

Chris Bootcheck

Position: P
Bats: R **Throws:** R
Ht: 6' 5" **Wt:** 205

Opening Day Age: 23
Born: 10/24/78 in La Porte, IN

Recent Statistics

	W	L	ERA	G	GS	Sv	IP	H	R	BB	SO	HR
2001 A Rancho Cuca	8	4	3.93	15	14	0	87.0	84	45	23	86	11
2001 AA Arkansas	3	3	5.45	6	6	0	36.1	39	25	11	22	3

One of the Angels' two first-round picks in 2000, Bootcheck signed too late to play until 2001. He struggled early on, and one month into the season at high Class-A Rancho Cucamonga, Bootcheck went on the disabled list and missed more than a month with shoulder

tendinitis. He heated up and generated a 1.63 ERA in July that led to a promotion to Double-A Arkansas. His changeup needed work at the start of the season, but he has a good feel for the pitch and it's coming along well. He also throws a 92-93 MPH fastball and a slider, and the location and movement of his offerings were impressive in his debut season. Learning to adjust quickly to better hitters will speed up his ascent to Anaheim.

Elpidio Guzman

Position: OF
Bats: L **Throws:** L
Ht: 6' 2" **Wt:** 165

Opening Day Age: 23
Born: 2/24/79 in Santo Domingo, DR

Recent Statistics

	G	AB	R	H	D	THR	RBI	SB	BB	SO	Avg
2000 A Lk Elsinore	135	532	96	150	20	16	9	72	53	61	116	.282
2001 AA Arkansas	117	459	58	112	21	8	7	46	18	17	89	.244
2001 MLE	117	444	45	97	18	5	5	35	12	11	93	.218

Signed in 1995, Guzman has made steady progress since emerging with a solid season at Rookie-level Butte in '98. Improved plate discipline was a key component in his breakout 2000 campaign at high Class-A Lake Elsinore, where Guzman solidified his status as a budding five-tool prospect. While his walk rate and hitting percentages took a plunge in his first taste of Double-A ball, Guzman overcame a slow start and improved all season long. Breaking stuff at the higher level gave him trouble, but Guzman took instruction and put in extra work. Despite some rough spots, he is an exciting player with power potential. Already Guzman is a very polished center fielder with excellent speed and a solid arm.

Nathan Haynes

Position: OF
Bats: L **Throws:** L
Ht: 5' 9" **Wt:** 170

Opening Day Age: 22
Born: 9/7/79 in Oakland, CA

Recent Statistics

	G	AB	R	H	D	THR	RBI	SB	BB	SO	Avg
2000 AA Erie	118	457	56	116	16	4	6	43	37	33	107	.254
2001 AA Arkansas	79	316	49	98	11	5	5	23	33	32	65	.310
2001 MLE	79	303	38	85	9	3	3	17	22	20	68	.281

A supplemental first-round pick in 1997, Haynes maximized his above-average speed in the high Class-A California League in '99 by shortening his swing, hitting the ball on the ground more and drawing more walks. In 2000, in his first Double-A test, Haynes abandoned his plate patience and little-ball skills in the early going, and battled an assortment of injuries, but the Angels were pleased with a second-half rebound. After minor knee surgery before the 2001 campaign, Haynes fared better with the little-ball skills he must utilize to have a major league career, and his athletic ability began taking over in his second stint at the Double-A level. Defensively, Haynes combines his speed and good instincts to show terrific range. His arm is average.

John Lackey

Position: P **Opening Day Age:** 23
Bats: R **Throws:** R **Born:** 10/23/78 in
Ht: 6' 6" **Wt:** 200 Abilene, TX

Recent Statistics

	W	L	ERA	G	GS	Sv	IP	H	R	BB	SO	HR
2000 A Cedar Rapds	3	2	2.08	5	5	0	30.1	20	7	5	21	1
2000 A Lk Elsinore	6	6	3.40	15	15	0	100.2	94	56	42	74	9
2000 AA Erie	6	1	3.30	8	8	0	57.1	58	23	9	43	6
2001 AA Arkansas	9	7	3.46	18	18	0	127.1	106	55	29	94	11
2001 AAA Salt Lake	3	4	6.71	10	10	0	57.2	75	44	16	42	5

A second-round pick in 1999, Lackey showed good stuff in his pro debut at short-season Boise and climbed all the way to Double-A Erie in his second season. The Angels like his upside. Lackey throws a plus-fastball that can put hitters away, and he has a good feel for an average curveball and changeup. More than anything, though, the Angels like Lackey's smarts, toughness and competitive makeup. He may have struggled in his first exposure to Triple-A ball, but he knows how to use his three quality pitches and doesn't give in to hitters. He only needs to fine-tune the location of his stuff.

Bart Miadich

Position: P **Opening Day Age:** 26
Bats: R **Throws:** R **Born:** 2/3/76 in Torrence,
Ht: 6' 4" **Wt:** 205 CA

Recent Statistics

	W	L	ERA	G	GS	Sv	IP	H	R	BB	SO	HR
2001 AAA Salt Lake	4	4	2.44	55	0	27	59.0	40	20	29	73	4
2001 AL Anaheim	0	0	4.50	11	0	0	10.0	6	5	8	11	2

Originally signed by Boston in 1997, Miadich spent time in the Arizona system before he was released during spring training in 2000. The Angels signed him on the recommendation of Don Wakamatsu, Anaheim's Double-A Erie manager who had held the Double-A post in the Arizona system the year before. Coming off a lackluster season as a starter, Miadich was converted to relief, refined his mechanics with Wakamatsu's help and turned his career around. Using a low to mid-90s fastball and late-breaking slider, Miadich has learned to challenge hitters effectively and dominated them at Triple-A Salt Lake in 2001. He's also benefited from a changeup he learned with the Angels. His future progress will determine if he's better suited to setting up or finishing games.

Francisco Rodriguez

Position: P **Opening Day Age:** 20
Bats: R **Throws:** R **Born:** 1/7/82 in Caracas,
Ht: 6' 0" **Wt:** 165 VZ

Recent Statistics

	W	L	ERA	G	GS	Sv	IP	H	R	BB	SO	HR
2000 A Lk Elsinore	4	4	2.81	13	12	0	64.0	43	29	32	79	2
2001 A Rancho Cuca	5	7	5.38	20	20	0	113.2	127	72	55	147	13

The Angels outbid several clubs for Rodriguez in 1998, and *Baseball America* named him the best prospect in the Rookie-level Pioneer League in '99. He was solid again in the high Class-A California League in 2000 at age 18.

Shoulder and elbow tendinitis pushed back his season by six weeks that year, and he remained in extended spring training again in 2001 with elbow tendinitis. Rodriguez showed greater maturity in his approach and game preparation last summer. While he wasn't as dominant, he was better at taking his bullpen work onto the mound and at the mental aspects of setting up hitters and executing a game plan. That should make his power stuff—mid-90s fastball, nearly unhittable sharp-breaking slurve and decent changeup—more effective.

Joe Torres

Position: P **Opening Day Age:** 19
Bats: L **Throws:** L **Born:** 9/3/82 in Bronx,
Ht: 6' 2" **Wt:** 175 NY

Recent Statistics

	W	L	ERA	G	GS	Sv	IP	H	R	BB	SO	HR
2000 A Boise	4	1	2.54	11	10	0	46.0	27	17	23	52	0
2001 A Cedar Rapds	0	3	5.82	4	4	0	17.0	16	12	14	14	0
2001 R Provo	2	2	4.02	9	8	0	31.1	32	20	15	39	2

The 10th overall pick in the 2000 draft, Torres debuted in the short-season Northwest League and showed his good stuff as the youngest player in the circuit. He throws a 90-MPH fastball and has decent command of a big curve and slider that are advanced pitches. Plus, he's smart and poised. Last spring, Torres remained in extended spring training for seven weeks with what was called shoulder fatigue. He made four starts at Class-A Cedar Rapids before he was shut down at midseason. An MRI revealed no structural damage, but Torres took several weeks off before pitching at Rookie-level Provo in August. He mostly worked on mechanical adjustments to his delivery, which continued in instructional league. Torres should be ready for spring training.

Others to Watch

One of the top high school players in the 2001 draft, first-round pick **Casey Kotchman** (19) had little trouble adjusting to the wood bat and hit .541 in 37 Rookie-level at-bats before hyperextending his right forearm on a backswing. The 6-foot-3, 190-pound lefthander is a good athlete with tremendous makeup. He could come on quickly. . . Selected in the 1999 draft, **Brian Specht** (21) debuted in the high Class-A California League in 2000 and displayed good strike-zone judgment and speed. A pure shortstop, Specht has a terrific arm and a defensive game that is further along than his bat. Still, he reached Double-A Erie near midseason last summer and batted .265 in 155 at-bats. . . **Derrick Turnbow** (24) was with Anaheim for all of 2000 after being taken in the Rule 5 draft. The Angels like his low-90s sinker with late movement and a promising curveball with good depth and break. Turnbow started 2001 at Double-A Arkansas, where he posted a 2.57 ERA before breaking his arm pitching in April. He had surgical pins for a non-displaced fracture of the ulna bone removed in October, and he'll start getting his career back on track in the spring.

Oriole Park at Camden Yards

Offense

Mike Hargrove continued to run his team, more because of a lack of power than because of overwhelming speed. Oriole Park at Camden Yards was slightly below average in yielding home runs. Lefthanded hitters hit below the league norm at Camden Yards, due to the 25-foot wall in right field and the deep gap in right-center field that measures 391 feet. Last year, the home-run indexes for both righthanded (100) and lefthanded (96) hitters were either neutral, or very close to neutral. Camden Yards continues to yield fewer runs than the league average. Doubles and triples were noticeably below the league average.

Defense

The Orioles' defensive range is average at best, and the infield grass was kept higher than normal to help slow down the ball, which assisted the pitching staff. Camden Yards has its share of odd angles, but allows an unusually low number of doubles and triples.

Who It Helps the Most

Jeff Conine and Jerry Hairston Jr. hit slightly better at home than on the road. Both Jason Johnson and Josh Towers pitched much better at home, as did reliever Buddy Groom. Veteran Tony Batista hit much better at Camden yards after being acquired by the O's at midseason.

Who It Hurts the Most

Key younger players—Chris Richard, Larry Bigbie, Melvin Mora and Jay Gibbons—all hit much better on the road than at Camden Yards. As expected, the inexperienced pitching staff struggled as a group on the road. Cal Ripken hit 11 of his 14 home runs on the road.

Rookies & Newcomers

The Orioles now are entering a full-fledged rebuilding mode with the retirement of Cal Ripken, but most of the prospects who are expected to contribute in the near term are on the major league roster. Not surprising, lefthanded hitters Chris Richard and Jay Gibbons were hurt by the dimensions of Camden Yards, a park that clearly favored righthanded batters.

Dimensions: LF-337, LCF-376, CF-406, RCF-391, RF-320

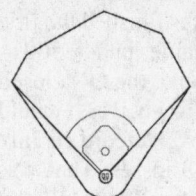

Capacity: 48,190

Elevation: 20 feet

Surface: Grass

Foul Territory: Average

Park Factors

2001 Season

	Home Games			Away Games			
	Orioles	Opp	Total	Orioles	Opp	Total	Index
G	71	71	142	73	73	146	—
Avg	.242	.260	.252	.257	.272	.265	95
AB	2306	2505	4811	2567	2464	5031	98
R	267	351	618	349	373	722	88
H	558	652	1210	661	671	1332	93
2B	104	128	232	139	152	291	83
3B	11	10	21	10	17	27	81
HR	50	87	137	63	83	146	98
BB	217	221	438	239	233	472	97
SO	421	432	853	451	409	860	104
E	47	48	95	56	52	108	90
E-Infield	45	42	87	50	43	93	96
LHB-Avg	.213	.259	.239	.256	.283	.271	88
LHB-HR	24	40	64	23	46	69	96
RHB-Avg	.259	.262	.260	.259	.263	.260	100
RHB-HR	26	47	73	40	37	77	100

1999-2000

	Home Games			Away Games			
	Orioles	Opp	Total	Orioles	Opp	Total	Index
G	144	144	288	144	144	288	—
Avg	.273	.262	.268	.272	.284	.278	96
AB	4777	5026	9803	5145	4854	9999	98
R	715	731	1446	748	830	1578	92
H	1306	1318	2624	1400	1377	2777	94
2B	244	198	442	300	297	597	76
3B	16	27	43	25	36	61	72
HR	161	188	349	177	182	359	99
BB	548	584	1132	496	595	1091	106
SO	786	933	1719	819	842	1661	106
E	94	83	177	95	98	193	92
E-Infield	82	73	155	84	81	165	94
LHB-Avg	.273	.250	.261	.280	.290	.285	91
LHB-HR	65	72	137	87	80	167	87
RHB-Avg	.274	.273	.273	.266	.278	.272	101
RHB-HR	96	116	212	90	102	192	109

2001 Rankings (American League)

- Lowest run factor
- Lowest double factor
- Lowest LHB batting-average factor
- Third-lowest batting-average factor
- Third-lowest hit factor

Mike Hargrove

2001 Season

Under Mike Hargrove, the Orioles finished the first two months of the season four games under .500 as they played competitively. In June, the O's closed the month at 14-14, but that was as good as it would get. Baltimore struggled to a 6-21 record in July and finished the season with 98 losses. That was the most losses ever by a Hargrove-led team, and the most by an Orioles team since losing 107 in 1988. Even though his team was undermanned, Hargrove played aggressively all season.

Offense

When Albert Belle was lost for the season in March, Hargrove's style went from more of a power-hitting approach to that of a running team. The Orioles tied for fifth in the league in stolen bases with 133, as they ran at every opportunity. He used the hit-and-run more than the average American League manager in an attempt to jump-start the offense. He avoided using the sacrifice bunt on most occasions, preferring to hit behind the runner. Because of an unsettled roster, Hargrove led the American League with 139 different lineup used in 2001. He prefers not to pinch hit, as the Orioles finished near the bottom of the American League in pinch-hitters used. Hargrove is not reluctant to use young and unproven players, such as Larry Bigbie, Jay Gibbons, Luis Matos and Josh Towers.

Pitching & Defense

Hargrove continued his practice of leaving his starters in the game, preferring to go with them than to turning the game over to an unsettled bullpen. He also struggled to find a closer most of the season, adding to the burden on the starting pitching. His team played sound but unspectacular team defense the entire season.

2002 Outlook

One would think that the Orioles have hit bottom and have only one way to go. . . and that's up. If Scott Erickson can return to the rotation and several of the young starters continue to develop, the pitching will improve. Several of the younger players must become more productive if the offense is going to score more runs. Baltimore will be improved, but won't reach the .500 mark this season.

Born: 10/26/49 in Perryton, TX

Playing Experience: 1974-1985, Tex, Cle, SD

Managerial Experience: 11 seasons

Manager Statistics

Year	Team, Lg	W	L	Pct	GB	Finish
2001	Baltimore, AL	63	98	.391	32.5	4th East
11 Seasons		858	777	.524	—	—

2001 Starting Pitchers by Days Rest

	<=3	4	5	6+
Orioles Starts	0	71	56	23
Orioles ERA	—	4.58	5.38	5.01
AL Avg Starts	1	78	48	24
AL ERA	5.92	4.69	4.58	4.58

2001 Situational Stats

	Mike Hargrove	AL Average
Hit & Run Success %	30.4	35.0
Stolen Base Success %	71.5	71.0
Platoon Pct.	52.5	59.1
Defensive Subs	20	26
High-Pitch Outings	3	6
Quick/Slow Hooks	13/17	19/16
Sacrifice Attempts	57	54

2001 Rankings (American League)

- 1st in starting lineups used (139)
- 2nd in pitchouts (71) and pitchouts with a runner moving (19)
- 3rd in steals of home plate (1)

Brady Anderson

Signed By
INDIANS

2001 Season

The signs of age caught up with Brady Anderson as he posted his worst season of the last ten years across the board. Anderson failed to reach double digits in home runs and he stole fewer than 15 bases for the first time since 1991, when he was a platoon player. He opened the season with a .194 average in April and struggled to reach the .200 plateau all season. Anderson's play in the field suffered, too, as he spent more time in right and left field than in center for much of the season.

Hitting

Anderson's power never surfaced last year, as his bat speed slowed to the point that he struggled to catch up to inside fastballs and pitches up in the zone. Anderson's lack of offensive punch even showed up against righthanders, pitchers he used to thrive off of. He hasn't completely lost the ability to pull the ball but the majority of his hits are to center and left field. For the second straight season, Anderson stood off the plate and was hit by a pitch only eight times.

Baserunning & Defense

Anderson no longer is a major threat on the bases. He struggled to steal 12 bases in 2001. Because he labored to get on base and lacked aggressiveness when aboard, Anderson attempted to steal only 16 times all year. His ability to go from first to third still is above average, but he no longer is a sure bet to score from first on a double. His fielding has declined the past two seasons and he is now better suited for right field, where his decreasing range can be disguised. Anderson registered eight outfield assists, seven from right field as a result of an accurate but weak arm.

2002 Outlook

Anderson's days in Baltimore are over, as the Orioles released him in November with a year still remaining on his contract. If he's able to regain the ability to hit righthanders in 2002, he'll have some value. Cleveland decided to take that risk, inking Anderson to a contract for around the minimum. He is expected to bat leadoff and start in left field for the Indians, filling the No. 1 spot vacated by Kenny Lofton.

Position: RF/LF
Bats: L **Throws:** L
Ht: 6' 1" **Wt:** 202

Opening Day Age: 38
Born: 1/18/64 in Silver Spring, MD
ML Seasons: 14

Overall Statistics

	G	AB	R	H	D	T	HR	RBI	SB	BB	SO	Avg	OBP	Slg
2001	131	430	50	87	12	3	8	45	12	60	77	.202	.311	.300
Career	1800	6419	1058	1648	334	67	209	756	311	942	1167	.257	.363	.427

Where He Hits the Ball

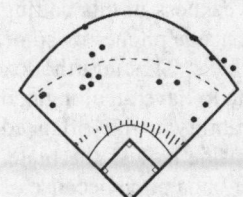
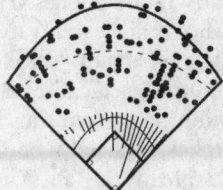

Vs. LHP   **Vs. RHP**

2001 Situational Stats

	AB	H	HR	RBI	Avg		AB	H	HR	RBI	Avg
Home	211	45	4	19	.213	LHP	81	15	2	11	.185
Road	219	42	4	26	.192	RHP	349	72	6	34	.206
First Half	254	52	6	29	.205	Sc Pos	82	22	3	39	.268
Scnd Half	176	35	2	16	.199	Clutch	63	12	0	6	.190

2001 Rankings (American League)

- 1st in lowest slugging percentage vs. righthanded pitchers (.301)
- 2nd in lowest batting average vs. righthanded pitchers and lowest batting average on the road
- 5th in fewest GDPs per GDP situation (4.3%)
- 6th in lowest on-base percentage for a leadoff hitter (.307)
- 8th in assists in right field (7), lowest batting average in the clutch and lowest on-base percentage vs. righthanded pitchers (.310)
- 10th in errors in right field (3)
- Led the Orioles in highest percentage of pitches taken (58.9), fewest GDPs per GDP situation (4.3%) and on-base percentage for a leadoff hitter (.307)

Tony Batista

2001 Season

In an apparent waiver blunder in June, Tony Batista was placed on waivers by Toronto and scooped up by the Orioles, who were in need of infield help. After posting career highs in home runs and RBI in 2000, Batista struggled to make consistent contact during the first half of the season. After he was claimed by Baltimore, Batista made better contact, but his power never returned to 1999-2000 levels. He finished the season hitting .313 in September and October combined, lending hope that he'll be an improved hitter in 2002.

Hitting

Batista continues to use an exaggerated open stance that allows him to see the ball better, especially inside pitches. The weakness in this batting stance is his inability to hit outside pitches by some pitchers, notably breaking balls. This unorthodox batting stance causes Batista to have an elongated swing, compromising his ability to hit offspeed pitches, especially on the inside half of the plate. It's rare to see Batista inside-out a pitch because of his stance and long swing. Lefthanded pitchers now give him the most trouble because he struggles with inside breaking pitches, and that has caused some of the loss in power.

Baserunning & Defense

Batista isn't known for great speed, but he remains one of the tougher hitters to retire on a double play. He's average going from first to third or attempting to score from second on a base hit to the outfield. Batista can play second, short or third, but has settled in at third base the past two seasons. He has a quick first step that allows him to get to balls hit to both his left and right sides on a consistent basis. His weakness is an arching throw to first base, making plays at first closer than they should be.

2002 Outlook

Batista is penciled in as the starting third baseman in Baltimore now that Cal Ripken has retired. He has two years remaining on a four-year, $16 million contract that he signed with Toronto. He'll bat fifth or sixth for the Orioles this season, but it remains to be seen if he can regain the power he lost last year.

Position: 3B/DH/SS
Bats: R **Throws:** R
Ht: 6' 0" **Wt:** 185

Opening Day Age: 28
Born: 12/9/73 in Puerto Plata, DR
ML Seasons: 6
Pronunciation: bah-TEESE-tah

Overall Statistics

	G	AB	R	H	D	T	HR	RBI	SB	BB	SO	Avg	OBP	Slg
2001	156	579	70	138	27	6	25	87	5	32	113	.238	.280	.435
Career	700	2437	349	634	125	13	125	385	24	156	462	.260	.308	.476

Where He Hits the Ball

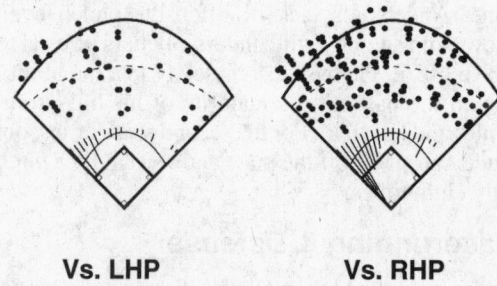

Vs. LHP	Vs. RHP

2001 Situational Stats

	AB	H	HR	RBI	Avg		AB	H	HR	RBI	Avg
Home	293	72	14	46	.246	LHP	128	26	5	22	.203
Road	286	66	11	41	.231	RHP	451	112	20	65	.248
First Half	314	66	14	50	.210	Sc Pos	153	35	5	58	.229
Scnd Half	265	72	11	37	.272	Clutch	98	19	4	14	.194

2001 Rankings (American League)

- 2nd in lowest on-base percentage (.280)
- 3rd in lowest on-base percentage vs. lefthanded pitchers (.257) and lowest on-base percentage vs. righthanded pitchers (.286)
- 4th in lowest batting average (.238)
- 5th in lowest batting average vs. lefthanded pitchers (.203)
- 6th in errors at third base (15) and lowest batting average on the road (.231)
- 7th in lowest batting average at home (.246)
- 9th in lowest batting average in the clutch (.194)
- Led the Orioles in triples (5) and batting average in the clutch (.275)

Mike Bordick

2001 Season

Mike Bordick returned to the Orioles last winter after being dealt to the Mets for the stretch run in 2000. He suffered a right shoulder injury in mid-June and never returned to the lineup. The injury required surgery in August to repair a tear in his right labrum. Before he was hurt, he was on pace to match his 1999 production and return to double digits in stolen bases.

Hitting

While his power has returned to his 1998 level, he continues to hit the ball to all fields. Still, his ability to get on base dropped off last year. Righthanded pitchers gave him trouble in 2001, as he was unable to make consistent contact with pitches near the outer half of the plate. Bordick continues to be one the American League's better bunters and an effective hit-and-run guy, which allows him to remain in the No. 2 spot in the batting order. He maintains the ability to work the count, making him one of the tougher outs in the junior circuit.

Baserunning & Defense

Bordick continues to take advantage of his baserunning savvy and first-step quickness. He was on pace to steal more than 20 bases before his shoulder injury last year. He is an intelligent though not very fast baserunner who rarely makes a mistake on the bases. Bordick's arm remains strong and he still is able to make the long throw from the shortstop hole. His ability to cover groundballs hit up the middle remains among the best in the American League, thanks to his quickness in getting to the ball. Bordick also continues to make the plays charging slow rollers hit his way.

2002 Outlook

Considering how well Bordick takes care of himself, he's expected to make a complete recovery from surgery on his right shoulder, and should be ready for the start of spring training. The Orioles will look to Bordick to provide leadership in the infield now that Cal Ripken has retired. He will continue to provide above-average defense at short and a steady bat at the top of the order.

Position: SS
Bats: R **Throws:** R
Ht: 5'11" **Wt:** 175

Opening Day Age: 36
Born: 7/21/65 in Marquette, MI
ML Seasons: 12
Pronunciation: BOR-dick

Overall Statistics

	G	AB	R	H	D	T	HR	RBI	SB	BB	SO	Avg	OBP	Slg
2001	58	229	32	57	13	0	7	30	9	17	36	.249	.314	.397
Career	1501	5060	600	1321	220	25	78	536	86	432	677	.261	.323	.361

Where He Hits the Ball

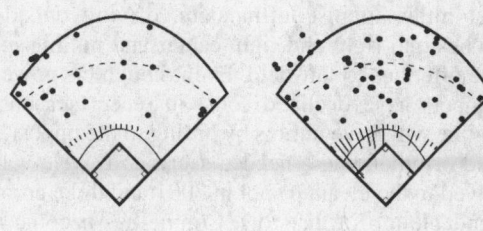

Vs. LHP   **Vs. RHP**

2001 Situational Stats

	AB	H	HR	RBI	Avg		AB	H	HR	RBI	Avg
Home	116	24	2	15	.207	LHP	63	21	3	10	.333
Road	113	33	5	15	.292	RHP	166	36	4	20	.217
First Half	229	57	7	30	.249	Sc Pos	51	13	0	21	.255
Scnd Half	0	0	0	0	-	Clutch	29	9	1	2	.310

2001 Rankings (American League)

- 1st in batting average on a 3-2 count (.429) and lowest batting average on a 3-1 count (0.000)
- 5th in batting average with two strikes (.269)

Jeff Conine

2001 Season

Jeff Conine showed why he's considered a valuable veteran both at the plate and in the field. He drove in 97 runs, the second-highest total in his career, even though the Orioles as a team struggled to score runs. In May and June he drove in 39 runs in one of the best two-month stretches in his career. His 12 stolen bases and 20 attempts both were career highs. In the field, Conine spent most of his time at first base, but also saw action at third and both outfield corner spots. His dependability in the field resulted in only four errors all season, all at first base.

Hitting

Conine has matured at the plate and is the Orioles' best hitter against lefthanders, driving outside pitches into right and right-center and pulling inside offerings to left field. Even though his power numbers have declined some in recent seasons, Conine will drive in runs by hitting to the opposite field or producing a needed sacrifice fly. He was moved to the cleanup spot in 2001 and did a commendable job in that role. Conine has become a tough out because he hits the pitch where it is thrown, rather than trying to pull outside offerings.

Baserunning & Defense

Conine's career high in stolen bases was a result of being an opportunistic runner and the aggressive approach of new manager Mike Hargrove. When he's on base, he's an intelligent runner, rarely making a mental mistake. He'll take an extra base when the opportunity warrants, but he rarely can go from second to home on a single to right field. His play around first is solid and his range is adequate. He also can play third and the outfield corners, but his range is limited. His outfield throws are accurate but only average in strength.

2002 Outlook

Because the Orioles do not have a viable replacement for the cleanup spot, Conine will return for another season in that role. His versatility in the field will allow Baltimore to use him where he is needed, whether that is at first, at DH or in the outfield. We should see another solid campaign from Conine in 2002.

Position:
1B/LF/3B/RF/DH
Bats: R **Throws:** R
Ht: 6' 1" **Wt:** 220

Opening Day Age: 35
Born: 6/27/66 in Tacoma, WA
ML Seasons: 11
Pronunciation:
COH-nine

Overall Statistics

	G	AB	R	H	D	T	HR	RBI	SB	BB	SO	Avg	OBP	Slg
2001	139	524	75	163	23	2	14	97	12	64	75	.311	.386	.443
Career	1245	4328	562	1252	229	21	146	694	27	443	795	.289	.354	.453

Where He Hits the Ball

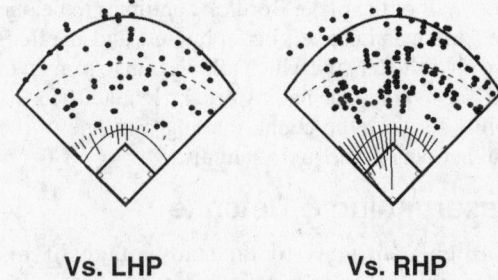

Vs. LHP   **Vs. RHP**

2001 Situational Stats

	AB	H	HR	RBI	Avg		AB	H	HR	RBI	Avg
Home	229	74	5	43	.323	LHP	125	47	4	31	.376
Road	295	89	9	54	.302	RHP	399	116	10	66	.291
First Half	242	76	9	48	.314	Sc Pos	140	56	9	87	.400
Scnd Half	282	87	5	49	.309	Clutch	71	18	1	8	.254

2001 Rankings (American League)

- 1st in highest percentage of swings on the first pitch (44.6)
- Led the Orioles in batting average, runs scored, hits, singles, total bases (232), RBI, walks, times on base (232), slugging percentage, on-base percentage, batting average with runners in scoring position, batting average vs. lefthanded pitchers, batting average vs. righthanded pitchers, batting average on an 0-2 count (.310), cleanup slugging percentage (.457), slugging percentage vs. lefthanded pitchers (.544), on-base percentage vs. lefthanded pitchers (.451), on-base percentage vs. righthanded pitchers (.365), batting average at home and batting average with two strikes (.222)

Jerry Hairston Jr.

Position: 2B
Bats: R **Throws:** R
Ht: 5'10" **Wt:** 175

Opening Day Age: 25
Born: 5/29/76 in Naperville, IL
ML Seasons: 4

2001 Season

Even though Delino DeShields was on the Orioles' roster at the start of last season, the second-base job was Jerry Hairston's. After a slow start in April when he hit only .190, he caught fire in May and June, hitting .312 and .310, respectively. From early July on, he labored to get on base as American League pitchers adjusted to his hitting style. Hairston's 29 stolen bases were a team high last year.

Hitting

Hairston's ability to hit righthanders did not carry over into his first full season in the majors. He struggled to hit the outside pitch, preferring to pull outside breaking balls rather than going with the pitch to right field. His short, compact swing became more of an upper cut later in the season, when he struggled at the plate. The larger strike zone also is causing him more problems, as he struggles with the high strike at times.

Baserunning & Defense

Hairston steals bases more from his quick first step and ability to get a good lead than pure speed. Still, he's one of the fastest players on the team going from first to third and can score from second on most hits to the outfield. Hairston covers more ground at second base for Baltimore than anyone since Robbie Alomar. He has a quick first step to the ball and has very good range to his left. His quickness comes from his days as a shortstop, as he handles slowly hit groundballs in front of him without a problem. Hairston is solid around the bag and when turning the double play.

2002 Outlook

Now that he has his first full season in the majors under his belt, he needs to improve his plate discipline and stamina to survive the second half of the season. If Hairston improves his approach at the plate and returns to a more level compact swing, he will be a much more productive leadoff hitter in 2002. The Orioles are expected to give him more at-bats in the leadoff spot this year.

Overall Statistics

	G	AB	R	H	D	T	HR	RBI	SB	BB	SO	Avg	OBP	Slg
2001	159	532	63	124	25	5	8	47	29	44	73	.233	.305	.344
Career	264	894	118	217	42	6	17	83	46	76	120	.243	.316	.360

Where He Hits the Ball

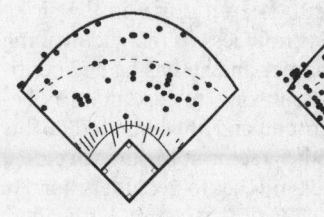

Vs. LHP

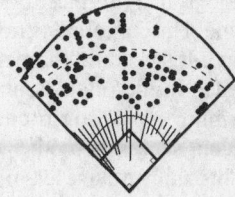

Vs. RHP

2001 Situational Stats

	AB	H	HR	RBI	Avg		AB	H	HR	RBI	Avg
Home	244	71	5	28	.291	LHP	124	36	2	14	.290
Road	288	53	3	19	.184	RHP	408	88	6	33	.216
First Half	301	80	4	33	.266	Sc Pos	118	27	2	38	.229
Scnd Half	231	44	4	14	.190	Clutch	83	20	3	11	.241

2001 Rankings (American League)

- 1st in errors at second base (19) and lowest batting average on the road
- 2nd in lowest slugging percentage and lowest slugging percentage vs. righthanded pitchers (.309)
- Led the Orioles in at-bats, triples, sacrifice bunts (9), stolen bases, caught stealing (11), pitches seen (2,327), plate appearances (602), games played, stolen-base percentage (72.5), most pitches seen per plate appearance (3.87), lowest percentage of swings that missed (11.5), highest percentage of swings put into play (47.6), steals of third (6) and lowest percentage of swings on the first pitch (17.9)

Jason Johnson

2001 Season

Jason Johnson never had major success in the minor leagues, but the Orioles have always felt he could be a frontline starter. They were rewarded for their patience last season when Johnson posted career highs in wins (10), strikeouts (114), quality starts (15) and innings (196). During the month of July, Johnson was among the American League's elite, winning three times and posting a superb 1.91 ERA. He faded after the All-Star break as his workload approached 200 innings.

Pitching

Johnson's four-seem fastball continues to improve and he can dominate when he has complete command of the pitch. His offspeed pitch is improving, though he struggles to keep it down in the strike zone. His curveball is now less of the wide-rolling type. It's become sharper and he has gained confidence in the pitch. Johnson's release point is becoming more consistent and that has led to his recent success. Another factor in his improvement is his ability to use less pitches to get hitters out. He has improved his capacity to retire lefthanders mainly by using the fastball on the inside part of the plate to setup his other pitches. When he tired late in the season, Johnson was less able to keep the ball in the park.

Defense

His move to first is slow and deliberate and baserunners take advantage of that weakness, successfully stealing 34 out of 53 times against him in 2001. Johnson misses not having Charles Johnson around to help keep the running game in check. Because of his large frame, the righthander struggles to field his position, especially when there is a play to his right. When he gets to the ball his throws are strong and accurate.

2002 Outlook

Based on his 2001 performance, Johnson will be the leader of the Orioles' rotation this year. If he can improve his stamina in the second half of the season, he'll improve even more and might approach 14-15 wins and 220 innings of work.

Position: SP
Bats: R   **Throws:** R
Ht: 6' 6"   **Wt:** 235

Opening Day Age: 28
Born: 10/27/73 in Santa Barbara, CA
ML Seasons: 5

Overall Statistics

	W	L	Pct.	ERA	G	GS	Sv	IP	H	BB	SO	HR	Ratio
2001	10	12	.455	4.09	32	32	0	196.0	194	77	114	28	1.38
Career	21	34	.382	5.29	95	79	0	485.0	517	221	303	76	1.52

How Often He Throws Strikes

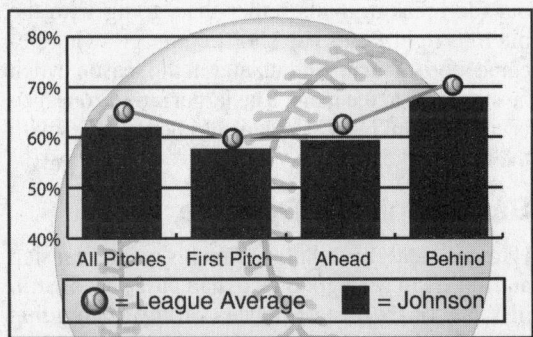

2001 Situational Stats

	W	L	ERA	Sv	IP		AB	H	HR	RBI	Avg
Home	7	4	2.97	0	103.0	LHB	373	98	16	46	.263
Road	3	8	5.32	0	93.0	RHB	381	96	12	51	.252
First Half	8	5	3.22	0	111.2	Sc Pos	190	42	3	62	.221
Scnd Half	2	7	5.23	0	84.1	Clutch	35	10	2	5	.286

2001 Rankings (American League)

- 1st in runners caught stealing (19) and lowest fielding percentage at pitcher (.833)
- 2nd in stolen bases allowed (34)
- 3rd in lowest ERA at home, errors at pitcher (4) and highest ERA on the road
- Led the Orioles in ERA, wins, games started, innings pitched, batters faced (856), home runs allowed, walks allowed, pitches thrown (3,257), lowest batting average allowed (.257), lowest slugging percentage allowed (.440), lowest on-base percentage allowed (.334), highest ground-ball-flyball ratio allowed (1.1), lowest ERA at home, lowest batting average allowed vs. righthanded batters and most GDPs induced per nine innings (0.7)

Jose Mercedes

2001 Season

The good news for Jose Mercedes was that he stayed healthy all season, which had been a career-long problem. He posted career highs in starts (31), innings pitched (184) and quality starts (13). On the negative side, Mercedes lost 17 times and never was able to get his ERA below 5.55. His best month was May, when he posted a 4.15 ERA, but he never approached that level of performance again.

Pitching

In the past, he has shown flashes of major league ability to locate his pitches where he wants in the strike zone. That command and control has all but disappeared, and he struggles to get ahead in the count. His fastball reaches 90 MPH on occasion, but late in games it rarely surpasses 88-89 MPH. He uses a cut fastball to help keep hitters off stride, but it flattens out at times. While Mercedes can change speeds to be effective, his breaking ball is average at best and isn't an out pitch. He's able to garner strikeouts when he mixes his pitches well and throws them for strikes.

Defense

Mercedes is an average fielder on the mound, but covers both sides of it well enough that bunters can't take advantage of his average fielding ability. His move to first base is considered so-so, but runners run on him more now that Charles Johnson isn't behind the plate. His throws to other bases tend to sail, but he doesn't make errors when fielding his position.

2002 Outlook

Due to his struggles as a starter, Mercedes was demoted to the bullpen and saw only two games in a relief role during the season. Unless he can develop better command of his pitches, he'll remain a borderline major league starter. He's eligible for arbitration and might not be back with Baltimore in 2002. Mercedes remained healthy for all of 2001 and that fact alone will help him find another job.

Position: SP
Bats: R **Throws:** R
Ht: 6' 1" **Wt:** 180

Opening Day Age: 31
Born: 3/5/71 in El Seibo, DR
ML Seasons: 7
Pronunciation: mer-SAY-deez

Overall Statistics

	W	L	Pct.	ERA	G	GS	Sv	IP	H	BB	SO	HR	Ratio
2001	8	17	.320	5.82	33	31	0	184.0	219	63	123	20	1.53
Career	33	39	.458	4.82	140	79	0	575.2	611	218	307	75	1.44

How Often He Throws Strikes

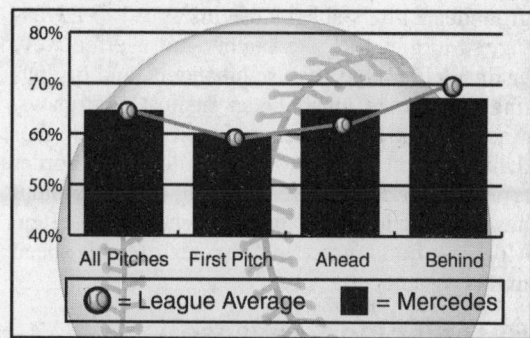

2001 Situational Stats

	W	L	ERA	Sv	IP		AB	H	HR	RBI	Avg
Home	3	7	6.72	0	72.1	LHB	374	112	10	58	.299
Road	5	10	5.24	0	111.2	RHB	371	107	10	53	.288
First Half	4	9	5.65	0	113.0	Sc Pos	190	58	4	83	.305
Scnd Half	4	8	6.08	0	71.0	Clutch	39	13	1	3	.333

2001 Rankings (American League)

- 1st in losses, fielding percentage at pitcher (1.000) and highest ERA
- 2nd in highest on-base percentage allowed (.354) and highest stolen-base percentage allowed (87.5)
- 4th in highest batting average allowed (.294) and highest slugging percentage allowed (.450)
- Led the Orioles in hits allowed, strikeouts, balks (2), highest strikeout-walk ratio (2.0), fewest pitches thrown per batter (3.64), lowest ERA on the road, most run support per nine innings (5.1), fewest home runs allowed per nine innings (.98), most strikeouts per nine innings (6.0) and fewest walks per nine innings (3.1)

Melvin Mora

2001 Season

Melvin Mora began the season as the starting center fielder. He got off to a slow start before catching fire in May and June, getting on base at a .418 and .404 clip, respectively. Then he went into a slump in early July and never recovered. However, his versatility again was a plus, as he shared shortstop duties with Brian Roberts after Mike Bordick went down with a season-ending shoulder injury.

Hitting

Mora doesn't utilize his speed enough and continues to hit more flyballs than groundballs. His swing has a slight upper-cut motion, resulting in too many popups and flyballs. When he hits line drives and groundballs, he's able to use his speed to advantage. Mora works the counts more effectively against lefthanders than righthanders, and his batting average is much better against southpaws. Another problem that he must overcome is a higher than expected strikeout rate for a top-of-the-order type of hitter. He's moved closer to the plate, and it has resulted in being hit by pitches more often. Mora is a fine bunter, and he often uses his speed in this capacity.

Baserunning & Defense

While Mora improved his stolen-base percentage in 2001, he still isn't that aggressive in attempting to steal bases. He is the Orioles' best player in going from first to third, and can score from first on any ball hit into the gap. Occasionally, he makes mental mistakes on the bases that get him thrown out. His success rate at stealing a base has improved as he's learned major league pitchers. His range continues to be average while playing shortstop, but his throws now are more accurate, reducing the number of errors he makes. When playing center field, he performed well but his throwing arm is just average.

2002 Outlook

As long as Mike Bordick is in Baltimore, Mora won't be the starting shortstop. He'll continue in a utility role this season, with the majority of his playing time coming in center field. Mora should benefit from another full season in the majors, but he's not ready to be a leadoff hitter.

Position: CF/SS
Bats: R **Throws:** R
Ht: 5'11" **Wt:** 180

Opening Day Age: 30
Born: 2/2/72 in Agua Negra, VZ
ML Seasons: 3
Pronunciation: MORE-a

Overall Statistics

	G	AB	R	H	D	T	HR	RBI	SB	BB	SO	Avg	OBP	Slg
2001	128	436	49	109	28	0	7	48	11	41	91	.250	.329	.362
Career	326	881	115	228	50	5	15	96	25	80	178	.259	.331	.378

Where He Hits the Ball

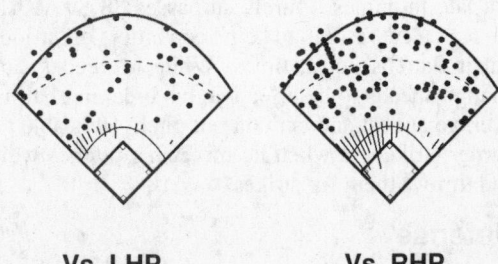

Vs. LHP   **Vs. RHP**

2001 Situational Stats

	AB	H	HR	RBI	Avg		AB	H	HR	RBI	Avg
Home	217	45	6	26	.207	LHP	107	33	1	16	.308
Road	219	64	1	22	.292	RHP	329	76	6	32	.231
First Half	260	72	5	30	.277	Sc Pos	103	24	0	38	.233
Scnd Half	176	37	2	18	.210	Clutch	65	12	1	6	.185

2001 Rankings (American League)

- 2nd in bunts in play (33)
- 6th in hit by pitch (14), lowest batting average vs. righthanded pitchers and lowest slugging percentage vs. righthanded pitchers (.340)
- 7th in lowest batting average in the clutch and lowest on-base percentage vs. righthanded pitchers (.307)
- 8th in errors in center field (3)
- 9th in assists in center field (4), lowest batting average and lowest slugging percentage
- Led the Orioles in hit by pitch (14) and bunts in play (33)

Chris Richard

Position: RF/CF/DH/1B
Bats: L **Throws:** L
Ht: 6' 2" **Wt:** 190

Opening Day Age: 27
Born: 6/7/74 in San Diego, CA
ML Seasons: 2

Baltimore

2001 Season

When the Orioles acquired Chris Richard from the Cardinals in 2000, they believed he was a first baseman and DH only. But last year he also showed an ability to play right field, and when called upon to play center, he handled it adequately. Consistency best describes Richard at the plate. He was steady every month and never suffered a slump. He more than doubled his at-bats in 2001, and he came come close to doubling his output from the 2000 season in many other offensive categories.

Hitting

Richard has a solid, level swing that prevents him from being tied up inside. He struggles mightily against lefthanders, generating very little power against southpaws. Inside fastballs continue to tie him up, and Richard also struggled to make consistent contact with outside pitches. Against righthanders, he generates power to all fields, though he prefers to pull anything thrown on the inside half of the plate. Richard continues to make progress hitting offspeed pitches, which no longer are a major problem. He's a below-average hitter with runners in scoring position, hitting much better when the bases are empty.

Baserunning & Defense

He's not blessed with blazing speed, but Richard does use his quickness in stealing a base and running the bases. He's an average runner moving from first to third, but can score from second on most hits to the outfield. First base is his natural position and he is more at ease there than in the outfield. His glove work in digging balls out of the dirt is solid, and he works well with pitchers covering first base. In the outfield, especially center, his overall range is limited, but he rarely makes an error on anything he can get to. His throws to the infield are fairly accurate but not that strong.

2002 Outlook

If Richard doesn't want to be labeled a platoon player, he needs to improve his hitting against southpaws. His chance to escape the label begins near midseason, as Richard underwent rotator cuff surgery in November and will miss the first half of the 2002 campaign.

Overall Statistics

	G	AB	R	H	D	T	HR	RBI	SB	BB	SO	Avg	OBP	Slg
2001	136	483	74	128	31	3	15	61	11	45	100	.265	.335	.435
Career	198	698	113	185	45	5	29	98	18	62	140	.265	.332	.468

Where He Hits the Ball

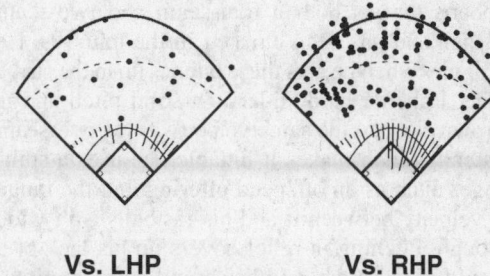

Vs. LHP   **Vs. RHP**

2001 Situational Stats

	AB	H	HR	RBI	Avg		AB	H	HR	RBI	Avg
Home	237	53	6	20	.224	LHP	106	22	1	8	.208
Road	246	75	9	41	.305	RHP	377	106	14	53	.281
First Half	215	59	10	28	.274	Sc Pos	113	27	2	41	.239
Scnd Half	268	69	5	33	.257	Clutch	69	14	1	7	.203

2001 Rankings (American League)

- 3rd in lowest stolen-base percentage (55.0) and lowest batting average at home
- 10th in assists in right field (5)
- Led the Orioles in home runs, doubles, strikeouts, GDPs (15), HR frequency (32.2 ABs per HR), slugging percentage vs. righthanded pitchers (.488) and batting average on the road

Willis Roberts

2001 Season

Willis Roberts took eight years to get to the major leagues, but it finally happened last season when he was signed as a minor league free agent by the Orioles. He opened the season as a reliever but quickly was moved to the rotation in mid-April, where he won four times and posted a 1.95 ERA. His command deserted him at times starting in May, and he struggled for nearly two months before rebounding in July. The Orioles then elected to move Roberts back to the bullpen because he struggled getting through a lineup the third time around. He was groomed as a closer, a role he assumed in August.

Pitching

Roberts throws both a four-seam and two-seam fastball and has been clocked in the mid-90s. He struggles when he gets these pitches up in the strike zone. Roberts' hard slider is a solid pitch and is thrown close to the same velocity as his two-seam fastball, which makes it hittable. He uses a split-finger pitch as an offspeed offering, but the range of velocity between it and his fastballs isn't wide enough. Pitching in relief covers up his lack of a true offspeed pitch, and he should be more effective coming out of the pen.

Defense

Because of his large frame, Roberts can be slow getting off the mound to field balls hit in front or to either side of him. This caused him to occasionally rush his throws to first base. His pickoff move to first is deliberate, but he compensates with velocity to keep runners close. He can be caught out of position at times when the first baseman needs to go wide of first to field his position.

2002 Outlook

The Orioles are convinced that he showed enough as the closer the last few weeks of the season to save games in 2002. Because Roberts doesn't have a changeup, this new role will allow him to use his most effective pitches to get the job done. He lacks experience as a stopper and will struggle at times. Talent-wise he has enough skills to be an effective closer immediately.

Position: RP/SP
Bats: R **Throws:** R
Ht: 6' 3" **Wt:** 175

Opening Day Age: 26
Born: 6/19/75 in San Cristobal, DR
ML Seasons: 2

Overall Statistics

	W	L	Pct.	ERA	G	GS	Sv	IP	H	BB	SO	HR	Ratio
2001	9	10	.474	4.91	46	18	6	132.0	142	55	95	15	1.49
Career	9	10	.474	5.00	47	18	6	133.1	145	55	95	15	1.50

How Often He Throws Strikes

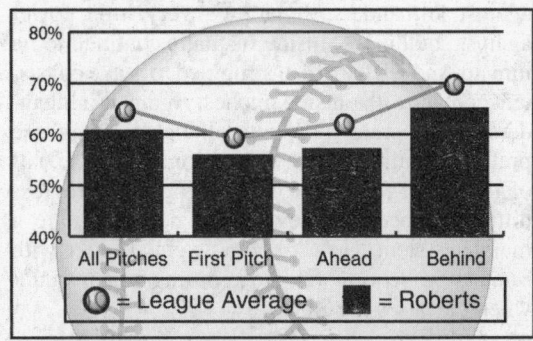

= League Average   = Roberts

2001 Situational Stats

	W	L	ERA	Sv	IP			AB	H	HR	RBI	Avg
Home	4	4	5.09	3	63.2	LHB		261	69	9	35	.264
Road	5	6	4.74	3	68.1	RHB		257	73	6	34	.284
First Half	6	7	5.24	0	92.2	Sc Pos		144	34	2	50	.236
Scnd Half	3	3	4.12	6	39.1	Clutch		82	23	5	14	.280

2001 Rankings (American League)

- 1st in losses among rookies
- 2nd in wins among rookies
- 6th in balks (2)
- Led the Orioles in balks (2), winning percentage, blown saves (4) and relief wins (3)

David Segui

Position: 1B/DH
Bats: B **Throws:** L
Ht: 6' 1" **Wt:** 202

Opening Day Age: 35
Born: 7/19/66 in
Kansas City, KS
ML Seasons: 12
Pronunciation:
seh-GHEE

2001 Season

Chronic soreness in his left knee finally caught up with David Segui in the middle of the season. He never completely returned to full-time status and managed only 292 at-bats. When he was in the lineup, he was a steady No. 3 hitter, batting around .300 and providing occasional power. His best month was June, when he hit .321 and slugged .509. It was then that Segui showed flashes of his 2000 form.

Hitting

Segui continues to be a productive switch-hitter, taking advantage of what the pitcher allows, which typically is a hit to the opposite field. While Segui takes the outside pitch, including breaking balls, to the opposite field, he rarely is overmatched with an inside fastball. As his knee troubles mounted, his strikeout rate increased as he struggled more. Last season, he hit a higher than usual number of fly-balls, largely because of his ailing knee. Segui continues to be one the American League's better hitters with an 0-1 count.

Baserunning & Defense

He rarely steals and has become almost a station-to-station runner because of injuries, struggling to score from second base on a single to center field. Segui has lost some of his agility and leg problems have reduced his range around the first-base bag. Segui still is able to charge in on bunts and slow rollers, but it no longer is an automatic out. His range toward second base has decreased, putting more responsibility on the second baseman. Segui's nine errors in 2001, a career high, may have had more to do with his injury than a loss of ability.

2002 Outlook

The outlook for Segui is cloudy due to the chronic nature of his left knee. He had surgery at the end of the season to remove some bone chips in the knee capsule. The prognosis is for a healthy Segui by the time spring training rolls around, but that remains to be seen. The Orioles would like him to return for one more season as they ease younger players into the everyday lineup.

Overall Statistics

	G	AB	R	H	D	T	HR	RBI	SB	BB	SO	Avg	OBP	Slg
2001	82	292	48	88	18	1	10	46	1	49	61	.301	.406	.473
Career	1345	4469	639	1308	267	15	131	636	16	482	605	.293	.360	.447

Where He Hits the Ball

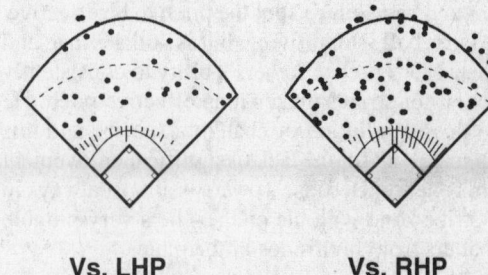

Vs. LHP   **Vs. RHP**

2001 Situational Stats

	AB	H	HR	RBI	Avg		AB	H	HR	RBI	Avg
Home	126	34	5	23	.270	LHP	77	26	2	14	.338
Road	166	54	5	23	.325	RHP	215	62	8	32	.288
First Half	226	67	8	36	.296	Sc Pos	67	25	2	35	.373
Scnd Half	66	21	2	10	.318	Clutch	34	7	0	3	.206

2001 Rankings (American League)

- 2nd in batting average on a 3-1 count (.750)
- 5th in errors at first base (9)
- Led the Orioles in batting average on a 3-1 count (.750) and highest percentage of extra bases taken as a runner (46.3)

Josh Towers

2001 Season

After getting his feet wet in May working in relief, Josh Towers burst onto the scene with five wins and a 1.49 ERA in June. During the second half of the season, Towers struggled as hitters adapted to his pitching style. His control and command already are impressive, as seen in his 16 walks in 140.1 innings. He finished the season with only eight wins after a promising start. Towers' season ended when he broke a finger on his pitching hand while taking out his frustrations after a poor outing.

Pitching

Towers' fastball can reach 91-92 MPH, but later in the game his velocity usually settles in around 88 MPH. His fastball doesn't have dramatic movement and he needs to spot the pitch to be effective. His curveball is improving, but is still average and lacks a sharp break. Towers' ability to consistently throw it for strikes makes it an effective pitch. He also does a solid job of changing speeds, and this skill makes up for the lack of significant movement on his pitches. Because Towers is almost always in the strike zone with his pitches, he's very hittable to batters from both sides of the plate.

Defense

Towers has a pretty good move to first that keeps runners honest. He charges bunts and groundballs hit to his left and right equally well, and makes solid throws to first. Occasionally, he's slow getting over to cover first base, a problem that he corrected by the second half of the season.

2002 Outlook

Towers throws so many strikes that major league hitters know he'll be around the plate, and that makes him very hittable. If he's going to make improvements this season, Towers will need to pitch off the plate more to be effective. Baltimore will give him the ball every fifth day in 2002, and he should surpass 200 innings and collect 12-13 wins. Towers is an intense pitcher. When he gets better control of his temper, he'll be more effective.

Position: SP
Bats: R **Throws:** R
Ht: 6' 1" **Wt:** 165

Opening Day Age: 25
Born: 2/26/77 in Port Hueneme, CA
ML Seasons: 1

Overall Statistics

	W	L	Pct.	ERA	G	GS	Sv	IP	H	BB	SO	HR	Ratio
2001	8	10	.444	4.49	24	20	0	140.1	165	16	58	21	1.29
Career	8	10	.444	4.49	24	20	0	140.1	165	16	58	21	1.29

How Often He Throws Strikes

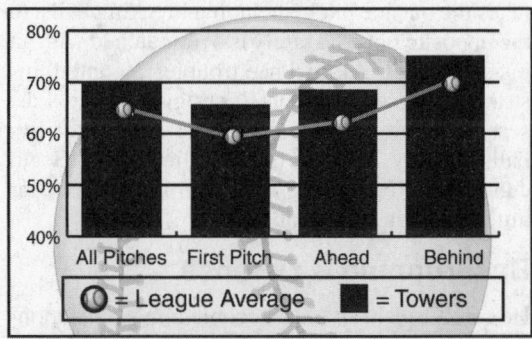

2001 Situational Stats

	W	L	ERA	Sv	IP		AB	H	HR	RBI	Avg
Home	4	4	3.28	0	71.1	LHB	257	79	9	30	.307
Road	4	6	5.74	0	69.0	RHB	299	86	12	37	.288
First Half	6	3	2.22	0	65.0	Sc Pos	114	32	5	44	.281
Scnd Half	2	7	6.45	0	75.1	Clutch	37	16	5	11	.432

2001 Rankings (American League)

- 1st in losses among rookies
- 3rd in wins among rookies
- Led the Orioles in GDPs induced (16) and most GDPs induced per GDP situation (16.7%)

Scott Erickson

Position: SP
Bats: R **Throws:** R
Ht: 6' 4" **Wt:** 230

Opening Day Age: 34
Born: 2/2/68 in Long Beach, CA
ML Seasons: 11

Overall Statistics

	W	L	Pct.	ERA	G	GS	Sv	IP	H	BB	SO	HR	Ratio
2001					Did Not Play								
Career	135	116	.538	4.43	326	322	0	2106.1	2281	745	1152	191	1.44

2001 Situational Stats

	W	L	ERA	Sv	IP		AB	H	HR	RBI	Avg
Home	—	—	—	—	—	LHB	—	—	—	—	—
Road	—	—	—	—	—	RHB	—	—	—	—	—
First Half	—	—	—	—	—	Sc Pos	—	—	—	—	—
Scnd Half	—	—	—	—	—	Clutch	—	—	—	—	—

2001 Season

Scott Erickson had Tommy John surgery in August of 2000 and missed the entire 2001 season. Erickson was throwing in September and there were rumors that he might pitch in one or two games when the roster expanded. It didn't happen but he's expected to be 100 percent for spring training.

Pitching & Defense

Erickson's trademark sharp-breaking slider is believed to be the cause of his elbow problems, and he has talked of scrapping the pitch. His fastball reaches 89 MPH when he's healthy. Erickson's sinker, one of the better ones in the American League before the injury, might be his out pitch this season. He's never had a traditional changeup but has tinkered with the pitch in recent seasons. His curveball is more of the flat variety, a possible result of his elbow woes. Because of his big frame, Erickson struggles to get off the mound and field bunts hit in front of him. His pickoff move to first base is average.

2002 Outlook

When he returns this spring, he'll be the veteran of the staff and expected to work with a very young rotation. Typically, pitchers who have Tommy John surgery need a full season to completely recover and regain their prior form.

Brook Fordyce

Position: C
Bats: R **Throws:** R
Ht: 6' 0" **Wt:** 190

Opening Day Age: 31
Born: 5/7/70 in New London, CT
ML Seasons: 7
Pronunciation: four-DICE

Overall Statistics

	G	AB	R	H	D	T	HR	RBI	SB	BB	SO	Avg	OBP	Slg
2001	95	292	30	61	18	0	5	19	1	21	56	.209	.268	.322
Career	405	1178	123	311	77	2	32	140	5	82	198	.264	.315	.414

2001 Situational Stats

	AB	H	HR	RBI	Avg		AB	H	HR	RBI	Avg
Home	139	25	0	2	.180	LHP	71	20	1	7	.282
Road	153	36	5	17	.235	RHP	221	41	4	12	.186
First Half	194	40	3	10	.206	Sc Pos	68	6	0	9	.088
Scnd Half	98	21	2	9	.214	Clutch	41	9	0	1	.220

2001 Season

Brook Fordyce entered spring training as the starter, based on his .300 average and 14 home runs in 2000. It became apparent early on that Fordyce was not going to repeat his offensive success of the two previous seasons. His struggles to shut down the opponent's running game also contributed to decreased playing time later in the summer.

Hitting, Baserunning & Defense

The long swing that plagued Fordyce earlier in his career returned last season, and he became very unproductive at the plate. He hit significantly more groundballs than flyballs in 2001, suggesting he is hitting on top of the ball and trying to pull pitches that he hit to the opposite field the year before. He was very ineffective with runners on base, causing his manager to remove him in key situations. Fordyce is below average in running the bases. Behind the plate, he throws out less than 20 percent of opposing thieves. Fordyce continues to struggle with blocking pitches in the dirt.

2002 Outlook

Because his offensive production has dropped dramatically, he enters the 2002 season battling for playing time at catcher rather than being the starter. Unless his bat rebounds early next season, Fordyce will be labeled a platoon player once again.

Jay Gibbons

Position: LF/DH
Bats: L **Throws:** L
Ht: 6' 0" **Wt:** 200

Opening Day Age: 25
Born: 3/2/77 in Rochester, MI
ML Seasons: 1

Overall Statistics

	G	AB	R	H	D	T	HR	RBI	SB	BB	SO	Avg	OBP	Slg
2001	73	225	27	53	10	0	15	36	0	17	39	.236	.301	.480
Career	73	225	27	53	10	0	15	36	0	17	39	.236	.301	.480

2001 Situational Stats

	AB	H	HR	RBI	Avg		AB	H	HR	RBI	Avg
Home	106	23	9	15	.217	LHP	27	10	2	5	.370
Road	119	30	6	21	.252	RHP	198	43	13	31	.217
First Half	166	39	11	27	.235	Sc Pos	68	12	4	22	.176
Scnd Half	59	14	4	9	.237	Clutch	30	6	1	3	.200

2001 Season

Originally a Toronto prospect, Jay Gibbons was selected by the Orioles in the Rule 5 draft in December 2000. When Albert Belle was forced to retire in March, Gibbons was given a lot more at-bats than originally planned. His season was cut short in early August when he suffered a broken hamate bone in his right wrist.

Hitting, Baserunning & Defense

Gibbons generates most of his power against righthanders by going the other way and driving the ball to the left-center field gap. His swing is short and quick for a player of his size, but he struggles with hard sliders and fastballs that tie him up when he's pitched inside. He is a natural first baseman with average range around the bag, yet he played left field for most of his rookie season. His throws from the outfield are weak but accurate. His range is limited, but he rarely makes a mistake in the field. Gibbons is a slow, prodding runner who struggles running from first to third.

2002 Outlook

The Orioles like Gibbons' power potential. With a full season under the youngster's belt, they believe he'll improve all of his offensive numbers across the board. If David Segui doesn't return to play first, he'll see increased playing time there.

Buddy Groom

Position: RP
Bats: L **Throws:** L
Ht: 6' 2" **Wt:** 207

Opening Day Age: 36
Born: 7/10/65 in Dallas, TX
ML Seasons: 10

Overall Statistics

	W	L	Pct.	ERA	G	GS	Sv	IP	H	BB	SO	HR	Ratio
2001	1	4	.200	3.55	70	0	11	66.0	64	9	54	4	1.11
Career	22	25	.468	4.91	549	15	23	533.2	605	206	360	51	1.52

2001 Situational Stats

	W	L	ERA	Sv	IP		AB	H	HR	RBI	Avg
Home	1	3	2.83	6	35.0	LHB	103	20	3	12	.194
Road	0	1	4.35	5	31.0	RHB	151	44	1	15	.291
First Half	1	3	3.48	6	33.2	Sc Pos	76	17	1	23	.224
Scnd Half	0	1	3.62	5	32.1	Clutch	141	36	2	17	.255

2001 Season

Durability is a word that fits Buddy Groom, as he set an American League record last season by appearing in 70 games for a sixth straight seasons. Groom posted career bests in ERA (3.55) and saves (11) in his second campaign in Baltimore.

Pitching & Defense

The improvement in his cut fastball this past season helped him become a bit more effective against righthanded hitters. His trademark pitch is a very sharp curveball that is almost unhittable for lefthanders when Groom has complete command of the pitch. His changeup is a work in progress and he uses it just to give hitters a different look, rather than to get them out. At times he struggles to get off the mound and field his position. His pickoff move to first is solid and it helps keep baserunners close to the bag.

2002 Outlook

The Orioles exercised their option to keep Groom in 2002. He is coming off an 11-save season, but it is unlikely he'll see as many save opportunities in 2002. His struggles against righthanded batters will prevent him from earning more chances. Groom is one of the better lefthanded specialists in the majors and he'll continue to be successful in that role.

Mike Kinkade

Position: LF/3B/DH
Bats: R **Throws:** R
Ht: 6' 1" **Wt:** 210

Opening Day Age: 28
Born: 5/6/73 in Livonia, MI
ML Seasons: 4
Pronunciation: kin-KADE

Ryan Kohlmeier

Position: RP
Bats: R **Throws:** R
Ht: 6' 2" **Wt:** 223

Opening Day Age: 24
Born: 6/25/77 in Salina, KS
ML Seasons: 2
Pronunciation: COAL-my-er

Overall Statistics

	G	AB	R	H	D	T	HR	RBI	SB	BB	SO	Avg	OBP	Slg
2001	61	160	19	44	5	0	4	16	2	14	31	.275	.345	.381
Career	97	217	24	56	8	1	6	23	3	17	41	.258	.329	.387

2001 Situational Stats

	AB	H	HR	RBI	Avg		AB	H	HR	RBI	Avg
Home	69	18	2	10	.261	LHP	88	25	3	11	.284
Road	91	26	2	6	.286	RHP	72	19	1	5	.264
First Half	110	30	4	13	.273	Sc Pos	46	9	0	11	.196
Scnd Half	50	14	0	3	.280	Clutch	23	4	0	1	.174

Overall Statistics

	W	L	Pct.	ERA	G	GS	Sv	IP	H	BB	SO	HR	Ratio
2001	1	2	.333	7.30	34	1	6	40.2	48	19	29	13	1.65
Career	1	3	.250	5.37	59	1	19	67.0	78	34	46	14	1.67

2001 Situational Stats

	W	L	ERA	Sv	IP		AB	H	HR	RBI	Avg
Home	1	1	4.64	3	21.1	LHB	81	32	8	18	.395
Road	0	1	10.24	3	19.1	RHB	84	16	5	13	.190
First Half	1	0	8.37	6	23.2	Sc Pos	40	13	4	19	.325
Scnd Half	0	2	5.82	0	17.0	Clutch	71	17	6	11	.239

2001 Season

Mike Kinkade has value for his ability to play multiple positions for Baltimore in a pinch. A third baseman by trade, he played first, third, left and right field, plus he caught in two games. He went on the disabled list in late August with a left shoulder contusion, and then suffered a right wrist injury in early October that ended his season.

Hitting, Baserunning & Defense

He hits pitchers from both sides of the rubber equally well, though not for power. Low and outside breaking balls tend to give him trouble. Kinkade is well below average when hitting with runners in scoring position, and that makes him a poor choice as a pinch-hitter. His baserunning speed is just a little bit above average, so he rarely attempts to steal a base. Except for second base, shortstop and center field, Kinkade can fill in at any position and hold his own defensively.

2002 Outlook

Kinkade's versatility will keep him in an Orioles' uniform in 2002, though it's unlikely he'll ever earn a full-time job in the majors. However, the O's acquisition of Marty Cordova likely means Kinkade won't see a marked increase in his playing time.

2001 Season

Ryan Kohlmeier began last season as the Orioles' closer, but his ineffectiveness cost him the closer role by early May. He spent the remainder of the season tinkering with his pitching motion, attempting to regain the command of his pitches. His final numbers were ugly across the board.

Pitching & Defense

When he is on, Kohlmeier relies on mixing his pitches and spotting an average fastball on the outside corner of the plate. He doesn't have an out pitch, but tends to rely heavily on a quick-breaking slider to get him out of jams. His four-seam fastball has solid movement, but his lack of command of the pitch can get him into trouble. Kohlmeier struggles to get lefthanders out, which limits his effectiveness. He fields his position adequately, but struggles at times to cover first base when needed. His pickoff move to first base is average.

2002 Outlook

Kohlmeier's arguably had only two productive months out of eight in his major league career, and he's close to returning to the minors for good if he doesn't take his game to the next level in 2002. His chance to stay comes in Chicago, as the White Sox claimed him off waivers in November.

Fernando Lunar

Position: C
Bats: R **Throws:** R
Ht: 6' 1" **Wt:** 190

Opening Day Age: 24
Born: 5/25/77 in Cantaura, VZ
ML Seasons: 2
Pronunciation: LOO-nar

Overall Statistics

	G	AB	R	H	D	T	HR	RBI	SB	BB	SO	Avg	OBP	Slg
2001	64	167	8	41	7	0	0	16	0	7	32	.246	.287	.287
Career	95	237	13	53	8	0	0	22	0	10	51	.224	.275	.257

2001 Situational Stats

	AB	H	HR	RBI	Avg		AB	H	HR	RBI	Avg
Home	82	21	0	4	.256	LHP	52	10	0	3	.192
Road	85	20	0	12	.235	RHP	115	31	0	13	.270
First Half	77	22	0	11	.286	Sc Pos	47	9	0	16	.191
Scnd Half	90	19	0	5	.211	Clutch	23	5	0	5	.217

2001 Season

Fernando Lunar came over to the Orioles from the Braves during the 2000 season. He's a borderline catching prospect who provided limited help last season when the Orioles struggled with injuries and ineffectiveness behind the plate.

Hitting, Baserunning & Defense

Lunar's career minor league batting average is .222 because he struggles to make consistent contact. He does not generate any power to the gaps because he is a defensive hitter at the plate. He is a below-average runner and almost never steals a base. Defensively, he is above average in all of his skills behind the plate. Lunar has a reputation as a defensive specialist and it is well deserved. His release on throws to second base is quick and he throws accurately. Lunar's mechanics in blocking pitches in the dirt are solid and he rarely allows a passed ball.

2002 Outlook

Unless he develops his offensive skills, Lunar will be considered a defensive replacement only as a major leaguer. He will be back with the Orioles on a limited basis as insurance this season, until they acquire a better hitting catcher.

Calvin Maduro

Position: SP/RP
Bats: R **Throws:** R
Ht: 6' 0" **Wt:** 180

Opening Day Age: 27
Born: 9/5/74 in Santa Cruz, Aruba
ML Seasons: 4
Pronunciation: mah-DUR-oh

Overall Statistics

	W	L	Pct.	ERA	G	GS	Sv	IP	H	BB	SO	HR	Ratio
2001	5	6	.455	4.23	22	12	0	93.2	83	36	51	10	1.27
Career	8	14	.364	5.84	56	29	0	203.1	208	96	111	31	1.50

2001 Situational Stats

	W	L	ERA	Sv	IP		AB	H	HR	RBI	Avg
Home	2	3	3.48	0	44.0	LHB	180	47	5	22	.261
Road	3	3	4.89	0	49.2	RHB	166	36	5	19	.217
First Half	0	2	4.58	0	17.2	Sc Pos	74	21	2	29	.284
Scnd Half	5	4	4.14	0	76.0	Clutch	17	4	0	3	.235

2001 Season

Calvin Maduro worked both as a starter and reliever for the Orioles last season and was effective at times. He showed promise, including a seven-inning scoreless effort against Seattle on August 31. Maduro was more effective as a reliever than a starter in 2001.

Pitching & Defense

Maduro's fastball rarely arrives faster than 86-87 MPH, and he needs good command of the pitch to stay out of trouble. His curveball and changeup are average but can be effective when he mixes them well with his fastball. Maduro is at his best when he uses his fastball to keep hitters off the plate, then drops his curveball over the outside corner. He has experimented with other pitches to give hitters a different look, but hasn't found one that is close to major league quality. Maduro has some quickness and gets off the mound to field his position well. His move to first base is about average.

2002 Outlook

Baltimore would like to keep Maduro in the bullpen where he is more effective, but that depends on if the O's can fill out the rotation next spring. If he pitches in relief next year, he's expected to have a solid season.

Sidney Ponson

Position: SP
Bats: R **Throws:** R
Ht: 6' 1" **Wt:** 225

Opening Day Age: 25
Born: 11/2/76 in Noord, Aruba
ML Seasons: 4
Pronunciation: pon-SONE

Overall Statistics

	W	L	Pct.	ERA	G	GS	Sv	IP	H	BB	SO	HR	Ratio
2001	5	10	.333	4.94	23	23	0	138.1	161	37	84	21	1.43
Career	34	44	.436	4.90	118	107	1	705.1	768	242	433	105	1.43

2001 Situational Stats

	W	L	ERA	Sv	IP		AB	H	HR	RBI	Avg
Home	3	5	4.60	0	72.1	LHB	274	88	14	43	.321
Road	2	5	5.32	0	66.0	RHB	283	73	7	33	.258
First Half	5	5	3.93	0	84.2	Sc Pos	141	39	6	54	.277
Scnd Half	0	5	6.54	0	53.2	Clutch	31	10	1	7	.323

2001 Season

In mid-April, Sidney Ponson battled tendinitis in his right forearm. The condition, described by some as "tennis elbow," plagued him off and on all season, and he finally was shut down at the end of August. Surprisingly, he was effective in May and June before the ailment took its toll on his pitching.

Pitching & Defense

Ponson's slider has improved and he is more comfortable using it in tight situations. His changeup was his most improved pitch two seasons ago, but he doesn't use it enough to set up his fastball and slider, which would give the hitter a different speed to look at. His fastball is clocked at 92-94 MPH on a regular basis and he has good control of the pitch. He gets in trouble when he relies on one pitch too much, or when he loses command of his breaking pitches. Ponson's size slows him down when he is fielding, and his move to first is average.

2002 Outlook

Baltimore is counting on Ponson to make a full recovery and anchor a young starting rotation. But until he improves his physical conditioning, he won't be more than a .500 pitcher. Even though Ponson's only 25-years-old, this season might be a make-or-break year in Baltimore.

B.J. Ryan

Position: RP
Bats: L **Throws:** L
Ht: 6' 6" **Wt:** 230

Opening Day Age: 26
Born: 12/28/75 in Bossier City, LA
ML Seasons: 3

Overall Statistics

	W	L	Pct.	ERA	G	GS	Sv	IP	H	BB	SO	HR	Ratio
2001	2	4	.333	4.25	61	0	2	53.0	47	30	54	6	1.45
Career	5	7	.417	4.66	117	0	2	116.0	96	74	124	13	1.47

2001 Situational Stats

	W	L	ERA	Sv	IP		AB	H	HR	RBI	Avg
Home	0	2	5.00	2	27.0	LHB	91	18	2	14	.198
Road	2	2	3.46	0	26.0	RHB	111	29	4	14	.261
First Half	2	3	5.57	2	32.1	Sc Pos	58	18	1	23	.310
Scnd Half	0	1	2.18	0	20.2	Clutch	83	18	0	9	.217

2001 Season

B.J. Ryan began the season as the Orioles' lefthanded specialist. A lack of depth in the bullpen forced manager Mike Hargrove to use him against righthanders, too, and he struggled in that role at times. Overall, last summer was a productive first full season in the majors for Ryan.

Pitching & Defense

Hitters have trouble picking up his release point because of his deceptive pitching motion. Ryan's slider is slightly above major league average, but he has a tendency to leave it over the plate against righthanders. His two-seam fastball is regularly clocked between 90-91 MPH. Ryan does have a changeup and curveball that he'll throw occasionally, but he has yet to fully develop these pitches. The command of his fastball and slider is improving, making him much more effective at the major league level. His move to first base is average for a lefthander and he fields his position adequately.

2002 Outlook

Ryan already has established himself against lefthanders. If he can develop an outpitch to use against righthanders, his role will increase with the Orioles. He pitched very well after the All-Star break, and that momentum should carry over into this season.

Other Baltimore Orioles

John Bale (**Pos**: LHP, **Age**: 27)

	W	L	Pct.	ERA	G	GS	Sv	IP	H	BB	SO	HR	Ratio
2001	1	0	1.000	3.04	14	0	0	26.2	18	17	21	2	1.31
Career	1	0	1.000	5.01	17	0	0	32.1	25	22	31	4	1.45

Bale had a chance to earn a spot in the rotation in 2001, but injuries prevented him from taking a step further in his development. He'll probably get another chance in 2002. 2002 Outlook: B

Casey Blake (**Pos**: 1B, **Age**: 28, **Bats**: R)

	G	AB	R	H	D	T	HR	RBI	SB	BB	SO	Avg	OBP	Slg
2001	19	37	3	9	1	0	1	4	3	4	12	.243	.317	.351
Career	40	92	10	22	5	0	2	6	3	9	26	.239	.311	.359

The 28-year-old Blake is no longer a prospect, but he did a nice job for the Twins in 2001. The Orioles claimed him off waivers on September 21, and the Twins claimed him back three weeks later. 2002 Outlook: C

Leslie Brea (**Pos**: RHP, **Age**: 23)

	W	L	Pct.	ERA	G	GS	Sv	IP	H	BB	SO	HR	Ratio
2001	0	0	-	18.00	2	0	0	2.0	6	3	0	2	4.50
Career	0	1	.000	12.27	8	1	0	11.0	18	13	5	3	2.82

Brea was not among the O's candidates for a spot in the rotation and spent 2001 as a reliever. He was in Baltimore for three ugly days in June. 2002 Outlook: C

Kris Foster (**Pos**: RHP, **Age**: 27)

	W	L	Pct.	ERA	G	GS	Sv	IP	H	BB	SO	HR	Ratio
2001	0	0	-	2.70	7	0	0	10.0	9	8	8	1	1.70
Career	0	0	-	2.70	7	0	0	10.0	9	8	8	1	1.70

Baltimore acquired Foster at the trade deadline from the Dodgers. He showed flashes that he could have a future as a reliever. 2002 Outlook: C

Geronimo Gil (**Pos**: C, **Age**: 26, **Bats**: R)

	G	AB	R	H	D	T	HR	RBI	SB	BB	SO	Avg	OBP	Slg
2001	17	58	3	17	2	0	0	6	0	5	7	.293	.369	.328
Career	17	58	3	17	2	0	0	6	0	5	7	.293	.369	.328

The Orioles acquired Gil at the trade deadline from the Dodgers. He came to Baltimore with a reputation for his defense, but he also hit pretty well. 2002 Outlook: C

Pat Hentgen (**Pos**: RHP, **Age**: 33)

	W	L	Pct.	ERA	G	GS	Sv	IP	H	BB	SO	HR	Ratio
2001	2	3	.400	3.47	9	9	0	62.1	51	19	33	7	1.12
Career	122	91	.573	4.18	294	264	0	1812.1	1840	665	1146	222	1.38

After finishing with 10 or more wins in eight consecutive seasons, Hentgen only lasted nine starts in 2001 due to injuries. He had Tommy John surgery in August and likely will miss most of 2002. 2002 Outlook: D

Jorge Julio (**Pos**: RHP, **Age**: 23)

	W	L	Pct.	ERA	G	GS	Sv	IP	H	BB	SO	HR	Ratio
2001	1	1	.500	3.80	18	0	0	21.1	25	9	22	2	1.59
Career	1	1	.500	3.80	18	0	0	21.1	25	9	22	2	1.59

Julio had a chance to take over the Orioles' closer job in early May but faltered. He came back to pitch decently at the end of the year. 2002 Outlook: C

Luis Matos (**Pos**: CF, **Age**: 23, **Bats**: R)

	G	AB	R	H	D	T	HR	RBI	SB	BB	SO	Avg	OBP	Slg
2001	31	98	16	21	7	0	4	12	7	11	30	.214	.300	.408
Career	103	280	37	62	13	3	5	29	20	23	60	.221	.288	.343

Matos, a decent prospect in the Orioles' farm system, underwent shoulder surgery March 13 and missed most of the 2001 campaign. A solid September put him back on the map. 2002 Outlook: B

Alan Mills (**Pos**: RHP, **Age**: 35)

	W	L	Pct.	ERA	G	GS	Sv	IP	H	BB	SO	HR	Ratio
2001	1	1	.500	9.64	15	0	0	14.0	20	11	9	6	2.21
Career	39	32	.549	4.12	474	5	15	636.0	577	395	456	83	1.53

Mills has been troubled by injuries recently. He spent the first half of 2001 rehabbing from shoulder surgery and almost retired in September. 2002 Outlook: C

Chad Paronto (**Pos**: RHP, **Age**: 26)

	W	L	Pct.	ERA	G	GS	Sv	IP	H	BB	SO	HR	Ratio
2001	1	3	.250	5.00	24	0	0	27.0	33	11	16	5	1.63
Career	1	3	.250	5.00	24	0	0	27.0	33	11	16	5	1.63

Paronto had a 5.60 ERA in his first callup, but improved to a 3.86 ERA the next time around. He was claimed off waivers by Cleveland in November. 2002 Outlook: C

John Parrish (**Pos**: LHP, **Age**: 24)

	W	L	Pct.	ERA	G	GS	Sv	IP	H	BB	SO	HR	Ratio
2001	1	2	.333	6.14	16	1	0	22.0	22	17	20	5	1.77
Career	3	6	.333	6.79	24	9	0	58.1	62	52	48	11	1.95

The Orioles have bounced Parrish between starting and relieving. Despite having good stuff, Parrish has had trouble with his control. 2002 Outlook: C

Tim Raines (**Pos**: LF, **Age**: 42, **Bats**: B)

	G	AB	R	H	D	T	HR	RBI	SB	BB	SO	Avg	OBP	Slg
2001	51	89	14	27	8	1	1	9	1	18	9	.303	.413	.449
Career	2404	8783	1562	2588	427	113	169	973	808	1308	947	.295	.386	.427

Montreal traded Raines Sr. to Baltimore at the end of the year so he could play with his son. He's a free agent and hopes to play another season. 2002 Outlook: C

Cal Ripken Jr. (**Pos**: 3B/DH, **Age**: 41, **Bats**: R)

	G	AB	R	H	D	T	HR	RBI	SB	BB	SO	Avg	OBP	Slg
2001	128	477	43	114	16	0	14	68	0	26	63	.239	.276	.361
Career	3001	11551	1647	3184	603	44	431	1695	36	1129	1305	.276	.340	.447

Ripken Jr.'s illustrious career came to an end October 6. The future Hall of Famer highlighted his farewell tour with a dramatic home run in the All-Star Game. He finished with 3,184 hits in 3001 games. 2002 Outlook: D

John Wasdin (**Pos**: RHP, **Age**: 29)

	W	L	Pct.	ERA	G	GS	Sv	IP	H	BB	SO	HR	Ratio
2001	3	2	.600	5.11	44	0	0	74.0	86	24	64	11	1.49
Career	31	29	.517	5.07	258	42	3	598.0	633	184	416	99	1.37

The O's signed Wasdin on June 8 after he was released by the Rockies. He pitched decently in his 26-game stint with Baltimore and was traded to Philadelphia in mid-December for RHP Chris Brock. 2002 Outlook: C

Baltimore Orioles Minor League Prospects

Organization Overview:

It had to be frustrating for the Orioles, having high-ceiling prospects Matt Riley, Luis Rivera and Richard Stahl miss all or most of the 2001 season. Still, there was plenty of good news, as a number of pitchers with less tools shined last summer. Riley, Rivera and Stahl didn't make much progress developmentally, but Rick Bauer, Erik Bedard, Sean Douglass, Beau Hale and John Stephens sure did. That's good news for an organization that doesn't have a lot of premium talent. No top-flight hitting prospect emerged in 2001, but that's not to say that the aging Orioles won't get some help soon from the likes of Larry Bigbie, Willie Harris, Tim Raines Jr., Keith Reed and Ed Rogers. These guys aren't quite ready, but they're in line to fill the holes left by the retired Cal Ripken and other aging veterans.

Rick Bauer

Position: P   **Opening Day Age:** 25
Bats: R **Throws:** R   **Born:** 1/10/77 in Garden
Ht: 6' 6" **Wt:** 212   Grove, CA

Recent Statistics

	W	L	ERA	G	GS	Sv	IP	H	R	BB	SO	HR
2001 AA Bowie	2	6	3.54	9	9	0	61.0	52	27	10	34	8
2001 AAA Rochester	10	4	3.89	19	18	0	113.1	119	63	28	89	10
2001 AL Baltimore	0	5	4.64	6	6	0	33.0	35	22	9	16	7

A fifth-round pick in 1997, Bauer debuted with a solid season at Rookie-level Bluefield in the Appy League. He spent most of the next three seasons getting through A-ball, as his control wavered and he struggled with being a consistent performer. Bauer turned a corner in his first full season in the high minors in 2001, going 12-10 (3.77) between Double-A Bowie and Triple-A Rochester. Bauer reached Baltimore in early September, and debuted by blanking the Mariners for six innings until a Bret Boone homer in the seventh stuck him with a 1-0 loss. A fastball-slider pitcher who has good life on his heater, Bauer produced three quality starts in six outings with the O's. To stick in Baltimore, he needs to consistently work lower in the strike zone and show better command of his pitches.

Larry Bigbie

Position: OF   **Opening Day Age:** 24
Bats: L **Throws:** L   **Born:** 11/4/77 in Hobart,
Ht: 6' 4" **Wt:** 190   IN

Recent Statistics

	G	AB	R	H	D	T	HR	RBI	SB	BB	SO	Avg
2001 AA Bowie	71	262	41	77	13	3	8	33	10	40	54	.294
2001 AAA Rochester	10	42	5	13	4	0	1	2	1	3	8	.310
2001 AL Baltimore	47	131	15	30	6	0	2	11	4	17	42	.229
2001 MLE	81	292	40	78	14	2	6	29	7	31	66	.267

The 21st overall pick in 1999, Bigbie is a natural hitter who is expected to show more pop as he fills out. He showed a little more in his first full season in the high minors in 2001, after adding 20 pounds to his frame during the offseason. His actually posted his best batting average after he reached Triple-A Rochester, but in Baltimore, the offspeed stuff from better pitchers found holes against Bigbie. His bat may need most of a year of Triple-A seasoning, but the O's like his power potential and versatility, as Bigbie has just enough speed and arm to handle all three outfield slots. The O's would be pleased to see Bigbie tack on another 20 pounds this offseason.

Sean Douglass

Position: P   **Opening Day Age:** 22
Bats: R **Throws:** R   **Born:** 4/28/79 in
Ht: 6' 6" **Wt:** 200   Lancaster, CA

Recent Statistics

	W	L	ERA	G	GS	Sv	IP	H	R	BB	SO	HR
2001 AAA Rochester	8	9	3.49	27	27	0	162.1	160	79	61	156	13
2001 AL Baltimore	2	1	5.31	4	4	0	20.1	21	12	11	17	3

A second-round pick in 1997, Douglass has made steady, dependable progress playing a full season at each level in the system. The end result is a seasoned minor leaguer who has learned how to pitch. Douglass has good life on his 90-MPH fastball and a decent changeup. His slurve needs to be more consistent, particularly in terms of location. An aggressive pitcher, Douglass was recalled to make an emergency start against Texas in July. That didn't go well, but in his three other starts in September, Douglass beat the Yankees and Red Sox, fanned 15 in 16 innings and posted a 3.24 ERA. The O's expect he will continue to pitch and learn in the major leagues in 2002.

Beau Hale

Position: P   **Opening Day Age:** 23
Bats: R **Throws:** R   **Born:** 12/1/78 in
Ht: 6' 2" **Wt:** 220   Mauriceville, TX

Recent Statistics

	W	L	ERA	G	GS	Sv	IP	H	R	BB	SO	HR
2001 A Frederick	1	2	1.32	5	5	0	34.0	30	8	4	30	1
2001 AA Bowie	1	5	5.11	12	12	0	61.2	74	39	15	40	8

The 14th overall pick in 2000, Hale is a bulldog with a terrific arm. He was a key player in Texas reaching the College World Series in his swan song, and he did it as a two-pitch pitcher. He's a fastball-slider power guy who temporarily lost some velocity off his mid-90s fastball last spring because of a pinched nerve in his shoulder. Still, he dominated at high Class-A Frederick in his first exposure to the pro game, and earned a promotion to Double-A Bowie. He made progress on his changeup at Frederick, but his struggles at Bowie are a reminder that changing speeds and deception will make his power stuff more effective. Hale is likely to start his second pro season at Bowie.

Keith Reed

Position: OF   **Opening Day Age:** 23
Bats: R **Throws:** R   **Born:** 10/8/78 in
Ht: 6' 4" **Wt:** 215   Yarmouth Port, MA

Recent Statistics

	G	AB	R	H	D	THR	RBI	SB	BB	SO	Avg
2000 A Delmarva	70	269	43	78	16	1	11	59	20	25	56	.290
2000 A Frederick	65	243	33	57	10	1	8	31	9	21	58	.235
2001 A Frederick	72	267	28	72	14	0	7	29	8	13	57	.270
2001 AA Bowie	18	67	7	17	3	0	1	8	2	6	10	.254
2001 AAA Rochester	20	74	11	23	7	1	2	11	1	5	14	.311

A basketball player from Massachusetts, Reed went to Providence College, where he was recruited to play baseball. Only after a big junior year in 1999 did scouts take notice. Reed has five-tool talent and has showed a little more power the last two seasons. It may have been compromised in 2001 by a lingering hand injury and minor hamstring troubles. He missed some time, but played through the hand ailment en route to Triple-A Rochester, where he did some of his better hitting late in the year. He's more of a gap-to-gap hitter, but more power may develop as he plays more and matures. He has very good speed and a terrific arm.

Brian Roberts

Position: SS   **Opening Day Age:** 24
Bats: B **Throws:** R   **Born:** 10/9/77 in
Ht: 5' 9" **Wt:** 170   Durham, NC

Recent Statistics

	G	AB	R	H	D	THR	RBI	SB	BB	SO	Avg
2001 AA Bowie	22	81	12	24	7	0	1	7	10	9	12	.296
2001 AAA Rochester	44	161	16	43	4	1	1	12	23	28	22	.267
2001 AL Baltimore	75	273	42	69	12	3	2	17	12	13	36	.253
2001 MLE	66	235	24	60	8	0	0	16	24	31	36	.255

Drafted in 1999, Roberts is more about instincts and desire, as his tools aren't special. Though a bit error-prone, he's a sound fielder with questions mostly about his arm. He had elbow surgery to remove bone chips early in 2000, but shows no lingering effects and may be fine on either side of second base. Roberts excels more at getting on base than driving the ball, but the O's want him to get stronger and show more pop as he fills out. They believe he may develop into a leadoff hitter or a decent No. 2 man with speed. Roberts was just two years removed from his draft day when he was recalled to fill in for an injured Mike Bordick.

Rich Stahl

Position: P   **Opening Day Age:** 20
Bats: R **Throws:** L   **Born:** 4/11/81 in
Ht: 6' 7" **Wt:** 185   Covington, GA

Recent Statistics

	W	L	ERA	G	GS	Sv	IP	H	R	BB	SO	HR
2000 A Delmarva	5	6	3.34	20	20	0	89.0	97	47	51	83	3
2001 A Delmarva	2	3	2.67	6	6	0	33.2	24	15	15	31	3
2001 A Frederick	1	1	1.95	6	6	0	32.1	26	13	15	24	1
2001 R Orioles	0	0	0.00	1	1	0	2.0	1	0	1	1	0

Selected 18th overall in 1999, Stahl signed too late to play until 2000. The 6-foot-7 lefty has the loose delivery and mid-90s heat of a future No. 1 starter, but shoulder discomfort led the Orioles to shut down Stahl after just 68 innings in 2001. He should be ready for spring training. Stahl throws across his body as many young pitchers his age do, and coaches are working on that and other mechanical components that can give big men trouble. His fastball is solid and likely to become more explosive, and his changeup is very good. A more consistent curveball, which may rival his fastball, will take more time. A return to high Class-A Frederick is likely.

John Stephens

Position: P   **Opening Day Age:** 22
Bats: R **Throws:** R   **Born:** 11/15/79 in
Ht: 6' 1" **Wt:** 200   Sydney, Australia

Recent Statistics

	W	L	ERA	G	GS	Sv	IP	H	R	BB	SO	HR
2000 A Frederick	7	6	3.05	20	20	0	118.0	119	45	22	121	5
2001 AA Bowie	11	4	1.84	18	17	0	132.0	95	32	21	130	10
2001 AAA Rochester	2	5	4.03	9	9	0	58.0	52	31	19	61	5

An Australian signed in 1996, Stephens has stellar command of three pitches and has learned to adjust to hitters at each level of development. In the Class-A Sally League in 1998, Stephens suffered an injury similar to whiplash while diving for a bunt. When he returned in '99, Stephens' fastball had dropped from the high 80s to the low 80s, although it's slowly inching back into the high 80s. Stephens also lost the break on his curve, yet he doiminated at Class-A Delmarva in '99. A smart pitcher, he's made steady progress and went 13-9 between Double-A Bowie and Triple-A Rochester in 2001, throwing a no-hitter and posting a 1.84 ERA at Bowie. Stephens succeeds using the same motion and arm action on his three pitches, which include a solid changeup.

Others to Watch

Lefty **Erik Bedard** (23) was a pleasant surprise in 2001, following up a solid 2000 season at Class-A Delmarva with a 9-2 (2.15) performance at high-A Frederick last summer. Bedard succeeded using a fastball, curve and change. . . Lefthanded-hitting **Willie Harris** (23) may become a valuable utilityman. He has the hands and arm to handle the middle infield or center field, and he batted a respectable .305-9-49 at Double-A Bowie after jumping from low-A ball in 2000. He also shows some plate patience. . . Outfielder **Tim Raines Jr.** (22) batted .274 at three levels in 2001 including Triple-A Rochester. He draws walks, but his strikeouts are high and righthanders give him trouble. His first-step quickness and speed helped him average 61 steals over the last three seasons. . . With five-tool potential, Dominican **Ed Rogers** (20) may develop the complete game of some of today's elite shortstops. He has it defensively—great arm, speed and impressive range—and the slight Rogers has held his own with the bat. He added 15-20 pounds before the 2001 season and showed more extra-base pop. He needs to learn better plate discipline.

Fenway Park

Offense

Fenway still is a hitters' park, but no longer is it the home-run haven it was before the roof box seats were added in the early 1980s. Now, it boosts scoring with a good hitters' background and, of course, the Green Monster, which turns potential outs into singles and doubles. It favors the hitters most during the hot midsummer months.

Defense

Right field here is the biggest, and—between the sun and the caroms—the trickiest in the majors. Of course, playing the Monster can be a challenge for the outfielder in the opposite corner, and a skilled defender can hold a not insignificant number of potential doubles to one base only. A catcher's arm isn't as important since the percentages often make basestealing a bad gamble.

Who It Helps the Most

Year in and year out, Troy O'Leary has had the widest home-road splits among Boston's hitters. Jason Varitek generally has traded homers for singles and doubles here, and has come out ahead. Among the newcomers, Chris Stynes has hit well there so far, and Carl Everett batted 114 points higher and produced twice as many doubles at Fenway in 2001. Rich Garces is hailed by the Fenway faithful as a cult hero, and he's pitched well at home. Derek Lowe also has done well at Fenway in three out of four seasons.

Who It Hurts the Most

Manny Ramirez produced slightly better road numbers, but still hit well at home. Trying to serve the ball into short left field didn't work very well here for Shea Hillenbrand. Frank Castillo, a control pitcher who allows the ball to be put into play, didn't pitch well in his first season at Fenway.

Rookies & Newcomers

New first baseman Tony Clark had a 27-game hitting streak at Fenway, which ended late in September. Casey Fossum already has won a few starts here and won't necessarily be hurt just because he's a southpaw. Ugueth Urbina keeps the ball out of play and shouldn't have any park-induced problems in his first full season in Boston.

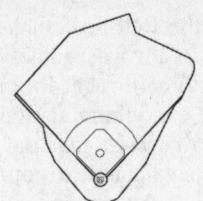

Dimensions: LF-310, LCF-379, CF-420, RCF-380, RF-302

Capacity: 33,993

Elevation: 21 feet

Surface: Grass

Foul Territory: Small

Boston

Park Factors

2001 Season

	Home Games			Away Games			
	Red Sox	Opp	Total	Red Sox	Opp	Total	Index
G	72	72	144	71	71	142	—
Avg	.277	.254	.265	.260	.255	.258	103
AB	2484	2542	5026	2524	2401	4925	101
R	361	342	703	342	323	665	104
H	687	645	1332	657	612	1269	104
2B	150	138	288	135	114	249	113
3B	18	9	27	8	16	24	110
HR	87	66	153	93	61	154	97
BB	246	233	479	223	243	466	101
SO	495	601	1096	503	535	1038	103
E	48	39	87	51	46	97	88
E-Infield	40	37	77	42	42	84	90
LHB-Avg	.280	.257	.268	.256	.241	.248	108
LHB-HR	42	28	70	46	32	78	90
RHB-Avg	.274	.251	.262	.264	.268	.266	99
RHB-HR	45	38	83	47	29	76	105

1999-2001

	Home Games			Away Games			
	Red Sox	Opp	Total	Red Sox	Opp	Total	Index
G	216	216	432	215	215	430	—
Avg	.281	.260	.270	.266	.248	.257	105
AB	7342	7612	14954	7656	7184	14840	100
R	1118	1002	2120	1076	951	2027	104
H	2062	1976	4038	2036	1781	3817	105
2B	461	393	854	415	353	768	110
3B	53	34	87	39	34	73	118
HR	214	196	410	277	220	497	82
BB	789	637	1426	769	697	1466	97
SO	1323	1653	2976	1390	1507	2897	102
E	175	141	316	132	123	255	123
E-Infield	150	119	269	113	97	210	128
LHB-Avg	.281	.263	.272	.259	.245	.252	108
LHB-HR	112	72	184	150	101	251	75
RHB-Avg	.281	.256	.268	.272	.251	.262	102
RHB-HR	102	124	226	127	119	246	89

2001 Rankings (American League)

- Second-highest double factor
- Third-highest batting-average factor
- Third-highest LHB batting-average factor
- Third-lowest infield-error factor

Joe Kerrigan

2001 Season

Joe Kerrigan was installed as the Red Sox' manager in mid-August while the team was gamely struggling to remain in the wild-card race. From the moment he took the reins, everything started going wrong. Nomar Garciaparra's wrist gave out, Pedro Martinez returned but proved unable to contribute, Jason Varitek's rehab was shut down, and the club completely fell apart. It was hard to get a read on his managerial style since circumstances prevented him from doing what he wanted.

Offense

Kerrigan came in with a mandate from above to bring stability to the lineup, and said he would, but he experimented anyway. He already has shown a preference for National League-style ball, trying to combat the running game by reversing Jimy Williams' ban on the use of the slide-step, and asking players to be prepared to run more often next season. All indications are that he will make more extensive use of the hit-and-run and the sacrifice than Williams did.

Pitching & Defense

Since Kerrigan's only major league coaching experience is as a pitching coach, it's hoped that handling the staff will be one of his strengths. One of his first moves as manager was to settle the closer situation by giving Derek Lowe's job to Ugueth Urbina. As Williams' pitching coach, Kerrigan was careful to monitor starters' pitch counts and get them out of the game too soon rather than too late.

2002 Outlook

If healthy, the BoSox have considerable talent, but it may be a challenge for Kerrigan to shape that talent into a winning ballclub. He has brought on board former Boston slugger Dwight Evans as the hitting coach to assist with that effort. Kerrigan will have some important decisions to make over several players' roles, including Jose Offerman and Derek Lowe. Yet, his biggest challenge may be to win the respect of the veterans, to convince them that he is not merely a pawn of the front office. The organization already may have solved another of Kerrigan's potential challenges when it shipped malcontent outfielder Carl Everett to Texas.

Born: 1/30/54 in Philadelphia, PA

Playing Experience: No major league experience

Managerial Experience: 1 season

Manager Statistics

Year	Team, Lg	W	L	Pct	GB	Finish
2001	Boston, AL	17	26	.395	13.5	2nd East
1 Season		17	26	.395	—	—

2001 Starting Pitchers by Days Rest

	<=3	4	5	6+
Red Sox Starts	0	20	11	9
Red Sox ERA	—	4.30	4.55	5.89
AL Avg Starts	1	78	48	24
AL ERA	5.92	4.69	4.58	4.58

2001 Situational Stats

	Joe Kerrigan*	AL Average
Hit & Run Success %	18.8	35.0
Stolen Base Success %	48.5	71.0
Platoon Pct.	54.3	59.1
Defensive Subs	6	26
High-Pitch Outings	0	6
Quick/Slow Hooks	10/2	19/16
Sacrifice Attempts	9	54

* Kerrigan managed the Red Sox for 43 games

2001 Rankings (American League)

- Did not rank near the top in any category

Dante Bichette

2001 Season

Last season probably is one Dante Bichette would like to forget. He had expected to play every day, but just before Opening Day he was informed that his role would be limited to serving as the designated hitter against lefthanders. By June, injuries had allowed him to get back into the regular lineup, usually in left field or at DH. He kept his average over .300 for much the year, albeit without his usual power or run production, before a sore elbow slowed him in the second half and forced him out of action for most of September. After having driven in 90 runs for seven straight seasons, he drove in only 49 in 2001.

Hitting

Bichette had been more of a gap hitter in the past, but he pulled the ball more often last year in an effort to adapt to his new home park. The effort yielded more doubles but no additional home runs. He likes to swing the bat and rarely takes a walk. He waited out just 20 free passes in 415 plate appearances in 2001. He may be reaching the point in his career where he no longer deserves to play regularly or hit in an RBI spot in the lineup, as he hit just .255 last year with men in scoring position.

Baserunning & Defense

Though he played the Wall adequately in left field, Bichette let a lot of balls fall in the few times he was asked to cover Fenway's spacious right field. His once-fearsome throwing arm no longer is much of a weapon. He hasn't stolen bases effectively in a few years and rarely runs any more.

2002 Outlook

Bichette was fairly productive when healthy last year, especially against lefties, but at his age, that may not be the case much longer. He became a free agent over the winter and probably will need to accept a more limited role wherever he lands. As his days in the outfield are numbered, he likely will stick in the American League if he sticks at all.

Position: DH/LF/RF
Bats: R **Throws:** R
Ht: 6' 2" **Wt:** 235

Opening Day Age: 38
Born: 11/18/63 in West Palm Beach, FL
ML Seasons: 14
Pronunciation: DAHN-tay bih-SHET

Overall Statistics

	G	AB	R	H	D	T	HR	RBI	SB	BB	SO	Avg	OBP	Slg
2001	107	391	45	112	30	1	12	49	2	20	76	.286	.325	.460
Career	1704	6381	934	1906	401	27	274	1141	152	355	1078	.299	.336	.499

Where He Hits the Ball

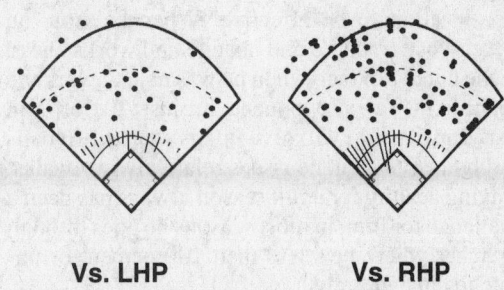

Vs. LHP   **Vs. RHP**

2001 Situational Stats

	AB	H	HR	RBI	Avg		AB	H	HR	RBI	Avg
Home	189	53	7	25	.280	LHP	112	38	2	12	.339
Road	202	59	5	24	.292	RHP	279	74	10	37	.265
First Half	204	68	8	33	.333	Sc Pos	110	28	4	38	.255
Scnd Half	187	44	4	16	.235	Clutch	67	15	1	7	.224

2001 Rankings (American League)

- 9th in assists in left field (4)
- Led the Red Sox in GDPs (13)

Frank Castillo

2001 Season

The Red Sox signed Frank Castillo as a free agent last winter, giving him a two-year, $4.5 million deal. They didn't expect him to overachieve as he had the year before, but they at the very least expected him to be a solid middle-of-the-rotation starter. For the most part, he was. He pitched well for them over the first couple of months of the season, going 7-4 with a 3.45 ERA in his first 14 starts. A strained back muscle in June sidelined him for six weeks, but he came back to pitch decently in August and September.

Pitching

Castillo has a varied repertoire, but he doesn't throw hard and relies on changing speeds and precise location to be effective. When he's on, he mixes a cutter, curve and change and works ahead of the hitters. In fact, when he was able to work the count in his favor, opponents hit just .201 off him last year. Castillo will give up his share of flyballs and home runs, but he issues relatively few walks. Staying healthy for a full season always has been a challenge for him; in most seasons he goes through stretches where he's less than 100 percent or unable to pitch entirely.

Defense

Since Castillo is slow to the plate, runners often take advantage. Despite the fact that he worked just 136.2 innings last year, he faced 33 stolen-base attempts, and only six of those attempts were thwarted. He's quick off the mound and handles himself well in the field, though. He gets to his share of groundballs by finishing his delivery in good position to field.

2002 Outlook

It's never easy to know what to expect from Castillo, who's inconsistent both from season to season and from month to month. He's capable of putting together a solid campaign, but as always, his health will be a constant concern.

Position: SP
Bats: R **Throws:** R
Ht: 6' 1" **Wt:** 200

Opening Day Age: 33
Born: 4/1/69 in El Paso, TX
ML Seasons: 10
Pronunciation: cas-TEE-oh

Overall Statistics

	W	L	Pct.	ERA	G	GS	Sv	IP	H	BB	SO	HR	Ratio
2001	10	9	.526	4.21	26	26	0	136.2	138	35	89	14	1.27
Career	76	88	.463	4.49	258	244	1	1426.2	1481	442	985	171	1.35

How Often He Throws Strikes

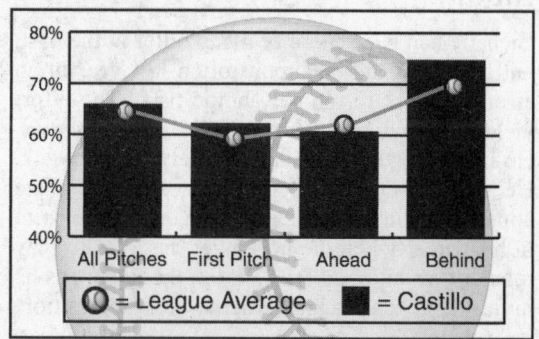

= League Average   ■ = Castillo

2001 Situational Stats

	W	L	ERA	Sv	IP		AB	H	HR	RBI	Avg
Home	3	7	5.01	0	70.0	LHB	257	64	7	28	.249
Road	7	2	3.38	0	66.2	RHB	274	74	7	35	.270
First Half	7	5	4.35	0	78.2	Sc Pos	124	32	4	48	.258
Scnd Half	3	4	4.03	0	58.0	Clutch	9	3	0	0	.333

2001 Rankings (American League)

- 5th in stolen bases allowed (27)
- 8th in fewest GDPs induced per GDP situation (3.2%)

Brian Daubach

2001 Season

The return to a platoon role seemed to benefit Brian Daubach last year. In 2000, the Red Sox decided to see if he could play every day, but he did little against the southpaws he was allowed to face. In 2001, he gave Boston steady production against righthanders all year, except when he was sidelined for three weeks in August with a staph infection in his ankle. Despite the cut in playing time, he set a new career mark with 22 homers.

Hitting

There's little subtlety to Daubach's approach. He sits on fastballs and will go after the first good one he sees, especially if it's down in the zone. He's not much for working the count or looking for anything in particular if he gets ahead. Not strictly a pull hitter, he has good power to all fields. He hasn't done much in the limited at-bats he's had against lefties. He improved his strike zone judgement in 2001, but he can be made to chase bad balls.

Baserunning & Defense

An adequate first baseman, Daubach knows his limits and plays within himself. Still, his .988 fielding percentage at first base in 2001 was one of the lowest in the majors among regulars. He logged a handful of games in the outfield last year, showing exceptionally limited range but catching what he got to. He also stole a base in 2001, and it could well be his last, even if he plays for another decade.

2002 Outlook

Despite Daubach's creditable performance the last three years, the Red Sox couldn't resist picking up Tony Clark with a simple waiver claim. A fast start in the spring by either Daubach or Clark could mean fewer at-bats for the other in 2002. Clark will pick up the at-bats against southpaws, but playing time versus righthanders is up for grabs. Both veterans have Boston's first-base prospects trying to catch them from behind.

Position: 1B
Bats: L **Throws:** R
Ht: 6' 1" **Wt:** 201

Opening Day Age: 30
Born: 2/11/72 in Belleville, IL
ML Seasons: 4
Pronunciation: DAW-back
Nickname: The Belleville Basher

Overall Statistics

	G	AB	R	H	D	T	HR	RBI	SB	BB	SO	Avg	OBP	Slg
2001	122	407	54	107	28	3	22	71	1	53	108	.263	.350	.509
Career	384	1298	170	345	94	8	64	223	2	134	335	.266	.339	.498

Where He Hits the Ball

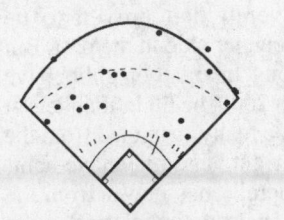
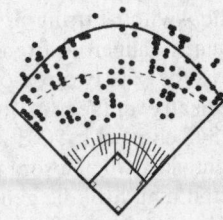

Vs. LHP   **Vs. RHP**

2001 Situational Stats

	AB	H	HR	RBI	Avg		AB	H	HR	RBI	Avg
Home	199	50	11	34	.251	LHP	59	10	3	9	.169
Road	208	57	11	37	.274	RHP	348	97	19	62	.279
First Half	238	65	14	45	.273	Sc Pos	107	24	5	44	.224
Scnd Half	169	42	8	26	.249	Clutch	57	16	2	8	.281

2001 Rankings (American League)

- 2nd in errors at first base (11)
- 4th in lowest percentage of swings put into play (34.7)
- 8th in assists at first base (75)
- 10th in lowest batting average with runners in scoring position
- Led the Red Sox in sacrifice flies (6) and batting average on a 3-2 count (.293)

Boston

Carl Everett

Position: CF
Bats: B **Throws:** R
Ht: 6' 0" **Wt:** 215

Opening Day Age: 30
Born: 6/3/71 in Tampa, FL
ML Seasons: 9

2001 Season

The Red Sox finally reached their breaking point with Carl Everett last season. The same could have been said a year ago, but the volatile outfielder was able to reach a fragile truce with then-manager Jimy Williams. That all seemed to end in spring training, when the Red Sox hit Everett with a hefty fine after he missed a team bus and skipped a workout. He got off to a good start though, before hurting his knee in June. He returned in late July, hit poorly the rest of the way, and was sent home in September after showing up late for a workout and getting into a confrontation with new manager Joe Kerrigan.

Hitting

The switch-hitting Everett had proven to be equally dangerous from either side in the past. But over the past two seasons, his platoon splits have been all over the map. In 2000, he hit lefthanders at a .348 clip, but in 2001 he really struggled from the right side, when a sore right hand may have hampered him. Still, he generally has power from the left side, where he crowds the plate and golfs pitches. He's aggressive and murders first-pitch fastballs, yet swings through a lot of pitches.

Baserunning & Defense

Everett likes to play shallow, which suited him well at Fenway Park. He has good range and covers the gaps well, and his good throwing arm is a weapon. Although he didn't run as often with Boston, he's picked his spots well and generally runs the bases aggressively.

2002 Outlook

Everett's repeated disciplinary problems led to the Red Sox making a trade with the Rangers in mid-December. Boston sent Everett to Texas for lefthanded pitcher Darren Oliver, who has a 13-20 record over the past two years. The Red Sox also reportedly agreed to pick up some of Everett's hefty salary. The talented outfielder moves from a good hitters' park to an even better hitters' park, but no matter how well he performs, he likely will remain something of a time bomb.

Overall Statistics

	G	AB	R	H	D	T	HR	RBI	SB	BB	SO	Avg	OBP	Slg
2001	102	409	61	105	24	4	14	58	9	27	104	.257	.323	.438
Career	844	2830	443	787	173	20	117	483	91	269	659	.278	.349	.477

Where He Hits the Ball

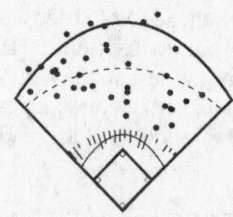

Vs. LHP

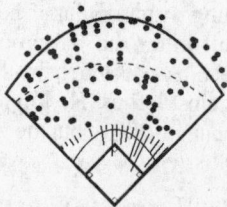

Vs. RHP

2001 Situational Stats

	AB	H	HR	RBI	Avg		AB	H	HR	RBI	Avg
Home	204	64	6	38	.314	LHP	132	26	3	12	.197
Road	205	41	8	20	.200	RHP	277	79	11	46	.285
First Half	282	80	9	42	.284	Sc Pos	98	28	5	43	.286
Scnd Half	127	25	5	16	.197	Clutch	66	16	2	7	.242

2001 Rankings (American League)

- 1st in lowest batting average on a 3-1 count (0.000)
- 2nd in fewest GDPs per GDP situation (2.7%), highest percentage of swings that missed (29.4), lowest batting average vs. lefthanded pitchers and lowest on-base percentage vs. lefthanded pitchers (.237)
- 3rd in errors in center field (5)
- 5th in lowest percentage of swings put into play (34.7)
- 6th in lowest slugging percentage vs. lefthanded pitchers (.318)
- 8th in lowest percentage of pitches taken (47.5)
- Led the Red Sox in stolen bases, hit by pitch (13) and fewest GDPs per GDP situation (2.7%)

Nomar Garciaparra

2001 Season

For most of last season, the biggest daily story in Boston was the latest word on Nomar Garciaparra's troublesome right wrist. The tendon problem developed early in spring training and required surgery in April. The club doggedly hung in the race, waiting for him to return, which he did—with a homer—on July 29. He hit well for the next three weeks, but his wrist wasn't up to the demands, and he went back on the disabled list for good in late August. In the 21 games in which he played, the Red Sox managed just a 10-11 record.

Hitting

A healthy Garciaparra is a deadly fastball hitter and perhaps the most dangerous first-pitch hitter in baseball. Over the past five years, he has batted .411 when he has put that first pitch into play. He has tremendously quick wrists and seemingly can hit any pitch hard to any part of the park. Garciaparra isn't afraid to go after a bad pitch if it's what he's looking for; he is one of the few hitters in the game who can succeed with that approach. Even with two strikes he remains dangerous.

Baserunning & Defense

It's easy to forget that in the minors, Garciaparra was known more for his glove than his bat. A terrific athlete with a strong arm, Garciaparra is especially strong making stops in the hole and throwing on the run. He has above-average speed and runs the bases aggressively, though he hasn't tried to steal as often in the last two years.

2002 Outlook

Even if Garciaparra's surgery has corrected the problem, wrist injuries sometimes take a long time to fully heal. So there's a possibility that he'll get off to a slow start. Of course, he's in such fine shape that he just as easily could put together a season that will erase memories of 2001. Heart-of-the-order mate Manny Ramirez certainly is hoping for the latter.

Position: SS
Bats: R **Throws:** R
Ht: 6' 0" **Wt:** 180

Opening Day Age: 28
Born: 7/23/73 in Whittier, CA
ML Seasons: 6
Pronunciation: no-mar GARCIA-par-uh

Overall Statistics

	G	AB	R	H	D	T	HR	RBI	SB	BB	SO	Avg	OBP	Slg
2001	21	83	13	24	3	0	4	8	0	7	9	.289	.352	.470
Career	616	2519	464	836	179	29	121	444	58	191	266	.332	.381	.570

Where He Hits the Ball

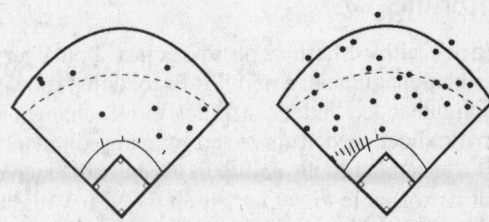

Vs. LHP	Vs. RHP

2001 Situational Stats

	AB	H	HR	RBI	Avg		AB	H	HR	RBI	Avg
Home	46	15	3	7	.326	LHP	16	5	0	0	.313
Road	37	9	1	1	.243	RHP	67	19	4	8	.284
First Half	0	0	0	0	-	Sc Pos	12	6	0	4	.500
Scnd Half	83	24	4	8	.289	Clutch	10	3	0	2	.300

2001 Rankings (American League)

- Did not rank near the top or bottom in any category

Boston

Pedro Martinez

2001 Season

Pedro Martinez came into last season as the game's premier starting pitcher and began the year in typical fashion, taking a 7-1 record and 1.44 ERA into June. That's when everything started to unravel. After several spotty performances, he went on the disabled list with a sore shoulder. There were conflicting reports over the nature and severity of the injury, and there was pressure for him to return and help keep the undermanned Red Sox in contention. It eventually came out that a small tear in his rotator cuff had been detected. He returned in late August, lacking his normal velocity. Three starts later, with the Red Sox out of the hunt, Martinez hung it up for good.

Pitching

When healthy, Martinez possesses just about every weapon imaginable: a mid-90s fastball that runs in on righthanded hitters, a killer circle change, a terrific slider, a good curve and amazing command. It's a testament to his ability to use his full arsenal that he was able to get by late in the year without being able to throw any harder than the mid-80s. The only thing he lacks is a bigger man's tirelessness, and the Red Sox try hard to give him extra rest whenever possible. Despite his maladies, he still managed to hold righthanded hitters to an otherworldly .176 batting average last season.

Defense

A terrific all-around athlete, Martinez has the agility to field his position and the quick feet to spin and throw to first. He prefers to look the runner back, though. He knows what to do with the ball in all situations. He has cut down on his miscues, and has just one error in the last three years combined.

2002 Outlook

Was 2001 Pedro Martinez' last dominant season? Only time will tell. A similar—though more severe—injury drastically shortened the career of his older brother Ramon. Pedro almost certainly will come back and pitch effectively, but there's no guarantee he'll be the Pedro of old. . . or that he even will last the full season in 2002.

Position: SP
Bats: R **Throws:** R
Ht: 5'11" **Wt:** 170

Opening Day Age: 30
Born: 10/25/71 in Manoguayabo, DR
ML Seasons: 10

Overall Statistics

	W	L	Pct.	ERA	G	GS	Sv	IP	H	BB	SO	HR	Ratio
2001	7	3	.700	2.39	18	18	0	116.2	84	25	163	5	0.93
Career	132	59	.691	2.66	296	229	3	1693.0	1262	467	1981	129	1.02

How Often He Throws Strikes

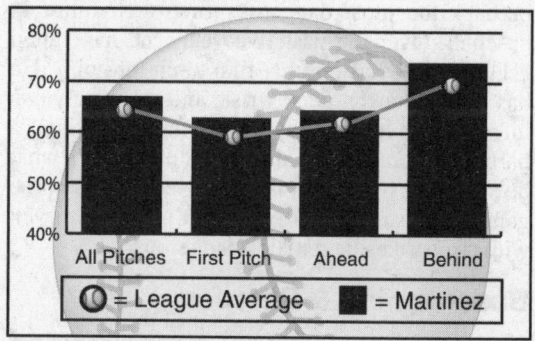

= League Average   = Martinez

2001 Situational Stats

	W	L	ERA	Sv	IP		AB	H	HR	RBI	Avg
Home	3	1	2.63	0	54.2	LHB	236	51	4	19	.216
Road	4	2	2.18	0	62.0	RHB	187	33	1	6	.176
First Half	7	2	2.26	0	103.2	Sc Pos	68	17	1	20	.250
Scnd Half	0	1	3.46	0	13.0	Clutch	38	7	0	2	.184

2001 Rankings (American League)

- 9th in strikeouts

Trot Nixon

2001 Season

The Red Sox' tumultuous 2001 season largely obscured the breakthrough year of Trot Nixon. The offseason signing of Manny Ramirez had threatened to eat into Nixon's playing time, but the third-year outfielder not only held his platoon role, but graduated to everyday play over the second half. When Carl Everett went down, Nixon even shifted from right field to center without missing a beat. He finished second on the team to Ramirez in hits, doubles, homers, RBI and walks.

Hitting

Nixon is an exceptionally patient hitter who almost always looks over a pitch or two before offering. Since he winds up in so many two-strike counts, it was an important development last season when he learned to protect the plate without sacrificing power. Though he gets good lift and hits the ball hard to all parts of the field, his home-run power runs from dead center to the right-field line. He finally got a chance to face southpaws during the second half of 2001, but still hasn't proven he can hit them.

Baserunning & Defense

Playing Fenway's right field requires a center fielder's range, and that's why Nixon is so valuable there and wasn't overextended when moved to center. Though his foot speed is average, he gets good jumps, runs good routes and always hustles. His strong arm and ability to play the caroms are assets in right. He's an alert, aggressive baserunner who rarely makes bad decisions.

2002 Outlook

Nixon has proven he can be a key part of the Red Sox' attack and defensive unit. This looks like the year he'll play regularly from the start and get the chance to learn to hit lefthanders. The departure of Carl Everett obviously opens up a lot of playing time in center field, and Nixon could find himself filling much of that void.

Position: RF/CF
Bats: L **Throws:** L
Ht: 6' 2" **Wt:** 200

Opening Day Age: 27
Born: 4/11/74 in Durham, NC
ML Seasons: 5

Overall Statistics

	G	AB	R	H	D	T	HR	RBI	SB	BB	SO	Avg	OBP	Slg
2001	148	535	100	150	31	4	27	88	7	79	113	.280	.376	.505
Career	410	1374	238	380	82	17	54	200	19	196	277	.277	.367	.479

Where He Hits the Ball

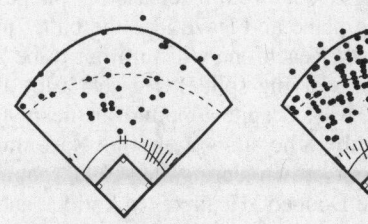

Vs. LHP   **Vs. RHP**

2001 Situational Stats

	AB	H	HR	RBI	Avg		AB	H	HR	RBI	Avg
Home	268	80	14	45	.299	LHP	105	22	1	14	.210
Road	267	70	13	43	.262	RHP	430	128	26	74	.298
First Half	266	72	15	46	.271	Sc Pos	124	32	5	58	.258
Scnd Half	269	78	12	42	.290	Clutch	78	21	7	24	.269

2001 Rankings (American League)

- 1st in lowest percentage of swings on the first pitch (9.0)
- 3rd in most pitches seen per plate appearance (4.14)
- 4th in errors in right field (5) and lowest slugging percentage vs. lefthanded pitchers (.295)
- Led the Red Sox in at-bats, runs scored, sacrifice bunts (6), sacrifice flies (6), pitches seen (2,620), plate appearances (633), games played, most pitches seen per plate appearance (4.14), bunts in play (9), highest percentage of pitches taken (63.7), batting average vs. righthanded pitchers, on-base percentage vs. righthanded pitchers (.393), batting average at home and lowest percentage of swings on the first pitch (9.0)

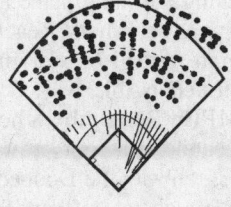

Boston

Hideo Nomo

2001 Season

The signing of Hideo Nomo understandably was overshadowed by the inking of Manny Ramirez, but the Japanese hurler proved to be a key acquisition as well. He became an immediate favorite by no-hitting Baltimore in his first start in a Red Sox uniform, and took an 11-4 record into August. Like the rest of the club, he floundered over the last third of the season, but he filled the role as the No. 2 starter, which is what he was signed to do. He fell just two frames short of reaching 200 innings for the year, and his 220 strikeouts paced the American League.

Pitching

Nomo's modus operandi is to release his pitches along the same plane and leave it to the batter to figure out whether each one will turn out to be a high fastball or a diving splitter. He gets a lot of strikeouts this way, despite topping out near 90 MPH. Remember, he also won the National League strikeout crown during his 1995 rookie season with the Dodgers. He mixes in a slider, and is tough on lefthanded and righthanded hitters alike. In the past, he's had problems after reaching the 75-pitch mark, but the Red Sox kept him under a tighter rein last year, and as a result, he maintained his stamina a lot better.

Defense

Nomo's coil-and-uncoil delivery leaves him vulnerable to basestealers, and when his team lacks a strong-armed catcher, as the Red Sox often did last year, he can be hurt badly by the stolen base. His delivery leaves him in poor position to field, and he doesn't get to many balls hit through the box.

2002 Outlook

Nomo became a free agent over the winter, and it isn't likely that the Red Sox will be able to entice him to return. Now 33, Nomo has yielded little to age and ought to remain a useful contributor as a No. 2, 3 or 4 starter wherever he ends up in 2002.

Position: SP
Bats: R **Throws:** R
Ht: 6' 2" **Wt:** 210

Opening Day Age: 33
Born: 8/31/68 in Osaka, Japan
ML Seasons: 7
Pronunciation:
hih-DAY-oh NO-mo

Overall Statistics

	W	L	Pct.	ERA	G	GS	Sv	IP	H	BB	SO	HR	Ratio
2001	13	10	.565	4.50	33	33	0	198.0	171	96	220	26	1.35
Career	82	71	.536	4.05	216	214	0	1348.2	1162	612	1432	163	1.32

How Often He Throws Strikes

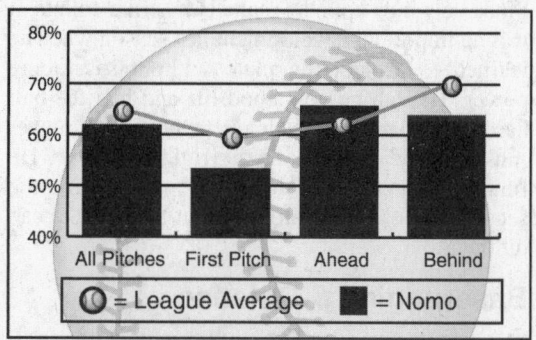

◯ = League Average   ■ = Nomo

2001 Situational Stats

	W	L	ERA	Sv	IP		AB	H	HR	RBI	Avg
Home	8	3	4.38	0	115.0	LHB	388	86	13	47	.222
Road	5	7	4.66	0	83.0	RHB	351	85	13	41	.242
First Half	8	4	3.83	0	110.1	Sc Pos	187	42	6	60	.225
Scnd Half	5	6	5.34	0	87.2	Clutch	35	8	0	2	.229

2001 Rankings (American League)

- 1st in walks allowed, strikeouts, stolen bases allowed (52) and most strikeouts per nine innings (10.0)
- 3rd in highest walks per nine innings (4.4)
- Led the Red Sox in wins, games started, complete games (2), shutouts (2), innings pitched, hits allowed, batters faced (849), home runs allowed, pitches thrown (3,238), pickoff throws (100), runners caught stealing (11), GDPs induced (13), winning percentage, highest strikeout-walk ratio (2.3), lowest batting average allowed (.231), lowest on-base percentage allowed (.320), lowest ERA at home, lowest batting average allowed vs. righthanded batters and most run support per nine innings (5.3)

Jose Offerman

2001 Season

Jose Offerman's 2000 season was ruined by a gimpy knee; he had no such excuse for his poor showing last year. Manager Jimy Williams was unhappy that Offerman came to camp carrying so much weight, and threatened to relegate him to a platoon role at first base. Williams declined to follow through on the threat, though, and Offerman saved his job by hitting well over the first two months. He suffered through a prolonged slump at midseason, however, and came out of it only after the Red Sox had fallen out of contention in September.

Hitting

Offerman once was a top-flight leadoff man, and he remains patient enough to draw a good number of walks. He no longer hits for a high enough average to be much of an asset at the top of the order. His on-base percentage while hitting No. 1 last year was a very pedestrian .322, and he showed almost no pop from the top spot. From either side of the plate, he's a line-drive hitter who hits to all fields. He's at his best when he gets ahead in the count and makes the pitcher come in to him.

Baserunning & Defense

Offerman has put on weight in recent years, and it's showed, both on the bases and in the field. He still has above-average speed but no longer possesses the quickness to be a basestealing threat. At second base, his good range used to make up for his weak double-play pivot, but he no longer moves well enough to have any redeeming defensive value anywhere except first base.

2002 Outlook

Offerman demanded a trade over the winter, but it may be hard to find a market for his services. With one year left on his hefty contract, Offerman probably will get his share of playing time. Whether it comes at second base or DH will depend largely upon the makeup of this year's Red Sox ballclub. The acquisition of Tony Clark off waivers, along with the presence of Brian Daubach in the lineup, means that Offerman likely won't see any time at first base in 2002.

Position: 2B/1B
Bats: B **Throws:** R
Ht: 6' 0" **Wt:** 190

Opening Day Age: 33
Born: 11/11/68 in San Pedro de Macoris, DR
ML Seasons: 12

Overall Statistics

	G	AB	R	H	D	T	HR	RBI	SB	BB	SO	Avg	OBP	Slg
2001	128	524	76	140	23	3	9	49	5	61	97	.267	.342	.374
Career	1387	5120	759	1417	223	68	48	471	162	695	828	.277	.363	.375

Where He Hits the Ball

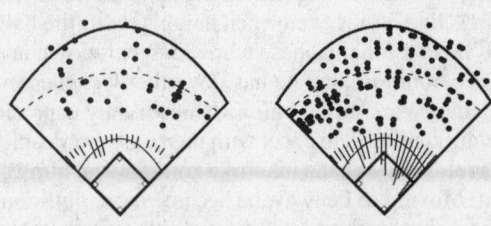

Vs. LHP   **Vs. RHP**

2001 Situational Stats

	AB	H	HR	RBI	Avg		AB	H	HR	RBI	Avg
Home	253	67	4	18	.265	LHP	129	28	1	12	.217
Road	271	73	5	31	.269	RHP	395	112	8	37	.284
First Half	313	85	4	25	.272	Sc Pos	108	30	3	40	.278
Scnd Half	211	55	5	24	.261	Clutch	64	13	0	6	.203

2001 Rankings (American League)

- 7th in errors at second base (11)
- 8th in lowest batting average vs. lefthanded pitchers and lowest slugging percentage vs. lefthanded pitchers (.326)
- 9th in batting average with the bases loaded (.500)
- 10th in lowest on-base percentage for a leadoff hitter (.322)
- Led the Red Sox in singles, highest groundball-flyball ratio (1.2), lowest percentage of swings that missed (11.9), batting average with the bases loaded (.500), on-base percentage for a leadoff hitter (.322), and highest percentage of extra bases taken as a runner (53.7)

Manny Ramirez

2001 Season

The Red Sox signed Manny Ramirez to a huge contract before the 2001 season, and for the most part, they got their money's worth last year. He initially balked at being moved from right field to left, but a hamstring injury limited him to designated-hitter duties for much of the season. Ramirez later played left without complaint. He carried the club's offense over the first half, driving in nearly a run per game, and his numbers would have been even better if he hadn't sat out with a minor injury after the club fell out of contention.

Hitting

Simply put, Ramirez arguably is the best hitter in the game. He has frightening power to all fields and stings line drives even when he fails to lift the ball. He'll occasionally chase a breaking ball down and away from him, but he has few other weaknesses. Pitchers work around him whenever they can, and yet he continues to excel with men on base, despite his refusal to expand his strike zone and get himself out. Moving to Fenway, he became more pull-conscious, but remained willing and able to go with the pitch when necessary.

Baserunning & Defense

Ramirez ran tentatively on the bases and in the field in 2001 due to recurring hamstring problems. Able to pick his spots earlier in his career, he has just three stolen bases in nine attempts over the past three years. Left field was a new position for him, but he generally played the Wall at Fenway adequately. His throwing arm is adequate for left field, though he pocketed just one assist in 482 innings at the position in 2001.

2002 Outlook

Ramirez' enthusiasm seemed to flag late last year, as the club disintegrated and fell into turmoil. If the Red Sox rebound in 2002, Ramirez could put together an even more impressive season. He'll need a lot more support around him on offense, however. Former Tiger Tony Clark might be able to supply a bit of that support if he can bounce back after two subpar seasons.

Position: DH/LF
Bats: R **Throws:** R
Ht: 6' 0" **Wt:** 205

Opening Day Age: 29
Born: 5/30/72 in Santo Domingo, DR
ML Seasons: 9
Pronunciation: ruh-MEER-ez

Overall Statistics

	G	AB	R	H	D	T	HR	RBI	SB	BB	SO	Avg	OBP	Slg
2001	142	529	93	162	33	2	41	125	0	81	147	.306	.405	.609
Career	1109	3999	758	1248	270	13	277	929	28	622	927	.312	.406	.594

Where He Hits the Ball

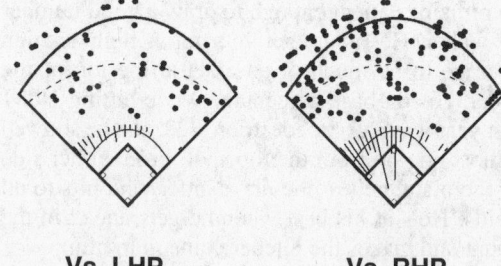

Vs. LHP   **Vs. RHP**

2001 Situational Stats

	AB	H	HR	RBI	Avg		AB	H	HR	RBI	Avg
Home	281	83	21	73	.295	LHP	117	40	10	25	.342
Road	248	79	20	52	.319	RHP	412	122	31	100	.296
First Half	328	110	26	84	.335	Sc Pos	159	50	8	77	.314
Scnd Half	201	52	15	41	.259	Clutch	78	25	5	23	.321

2001 Rankings (American League)

- 1st in intentional walks (25) and cleanup slugging percentage (.607)
- Led the Red Sox in batting average, home runs, hits, doubles, total bases (322), RBI, walks, times on base (251), strikeouts, slugging percentage, on-base percentage, HR frequency (12.9 ABs per HR), batting average with runners in scoring position, batting average vs. lefthanded pitchers, batting average on an 0-2 count (.310), slugging percentage vs. lefthanded pitchers (.650), slugging percentage vs. righthanded pitchers (.597), on-base percentage vs. lefthanded pitchers (.462), batting average on the road and batting average with two strikes (.231)

Ugueth Urbina

2001 Season

After having most of 2000 wiped out by a pair of surgeries to remove bone chips from his elbow, Ugueth Urbina rebounded with a quality season in 2001. His best work came after being dealt from Montreal to Boston at the trade deadline for To-mokazu Ohka and Richard Rundles. Urbina displaced Derek Lowe as the Red Sox' closer and converted nine of his 10 save opportunities in Boston. Ironically, an earlier trade to the Yankees reportedly had been scotched after a physical revealed bone chips in Urbina's elbow.

Pitching

Primarily a fastball/slider pitcher, Urbina lives on hard stuff and rarely needs to make use of his splitter and changeup. One troubling sign last year was that he struggled with lefthanded hitters; he had the same problem in 1996 and '97 and became a premier closer only after seemingly conquering it. Despite his injury-ravaged 2000, he seemed to regain his old velocity last summer and proved he still could pitch on consecutive days. He showed pinpoint control after joining the Red Sox, walking just three batters in 19 appearances after the trade.

Defense

Urbina gets mostly strikeouts and flyballs, so he fields only a handful of chances each season. When he's called on to handle a defensive play, he usually gets the job done. He pays no attention to baserunners and hardly shortens his high-effort delivery with men on base. So baserunners run on him even when representing the tying run.

2002 Outlook

With Derek Lowe expected to make a permanent move back into the starting rotation, Urbina goes into 2002 as the Red Sox' uncontested closer. It has to raise concern that the Yankees reportedly backed off a trade after examining his elbow. On the other hand, the Red Sox must have been satisfied with his condition, enough so to deal for him and move their old closer out of the bullpen entirely. Urbina ought to have another good year if healthy.

Position: RP
Bats: R **Throws:** R
Ht: 6' 2" **Wt:** 205

Opening Day Age: 28
Born: 2/15/74 in Caracas, VZ
ML Seasons: 7
Pronunciation: ooo-GETT ooor-bee-NAH
Nickname: Oogy

Overall Statistics

	W	L	Pct.	ERA	G	GS	Sv	IP	H	BB	SO	HR	Ratio
2001	2	2	.500	3.65	64	0	24	66.2	58	24	89	9	1.23
Career	31	27	.534	3.46	315	21	134	426.2	345	185	512	51	1.24

How Often He Throws Strikes

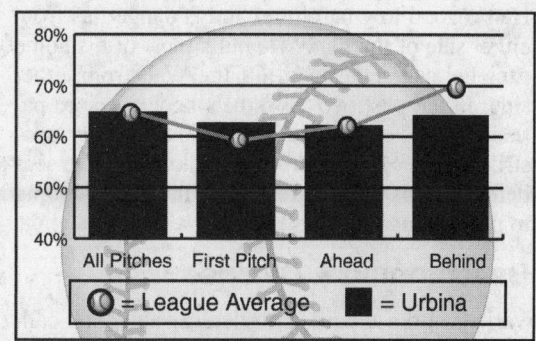

O = League Average   ■ = Urbina

2001 Situational Stats

	W	L	ERA	Sv	IP		AB	H	HR	RBI	Avg
Home	2	1	3.25	12	36.0	LHB	108	30	5	20	.278
Road	0	1	4.11	12	30.2	RHB	143	28	4	13	.196
First Half	0	1	3.72	13	38.2	Sc Pos	74	19	2	25	.257
Scnd Half	2	1	3.54	11	28.0	Clutch	128	30	3	22	.234

2001 Rankings (American League)

- Did not rank near the top or bottom in any category

Jason Varitek

2001 Season

Catcher Jason Varitek was on the way to perhaps his best season yet when he broke his elbow in June. Prior to the injury, he was hitting .293 and anchoring a pitching staff that had the Red Sox 10 games over .500. At first, it was hoped that he'd be able to return before the end of the year, but he suffered complications during rehab and had to be shelved for good late in the year. The blow was yet another setback to a club that had hoped to have him back for the stretch run.

Hitting

The switch-hitting Varitek recovered his old stroke last year after a bad wrist hampered him in 2000. He's a good low-ball hitter and is dangerous from either side of the plate. He pulls most of his home runs but can send liners off the Wall from either side. In the past two years he's become more patient and has steadily developed into a better two-strike hitter. He tends to be streaky, since he sees defense as his primary responsibility and is willing to play through injuries that only affect his swing.

Baserunning & Defense

Varitek works as hard at his defense and pitch-calling as any catcher in the game, and the Red Sox have had a much lower ERA with him behind the plate in each of the last two years. The club's disdain of the slide-step has hurt his caught-stealing numbers, but he's an above-average thrower, especially when compared to his replacement, Scott Hatteberg. Varitek's heavy legs are no asset on the basepaths.

2002 Outlook

Hopefully a winter's rest will allow Varitek's elbow to heal. There's a chance the nerve irritation in his elbow that flared up during rehab will recur, but he's expected to be ready to go this spring. If so, he'll be back behind the plate on a regular basis.

Position: C
Bats: B **Throws:** R
Ht: 6' 2" **Wt:** 220

Opening Day Age: 29
Born: 4/11/72 in Rochester, MI
ML Seasons: 5
Pronunciation: VARE-ih-tek

Overall Statistics

	G	AB	R	H	D	T	HR	RBI	SB	BB	SO	Avg	OBP	Slg
2001	51	174	19	51	11	1	7	25	0	21	35	.293	.371	.489
Career	421	1327	175	349	94	4	44	199	4	144	249	.263	.336	.439

Where He Hits the Ball

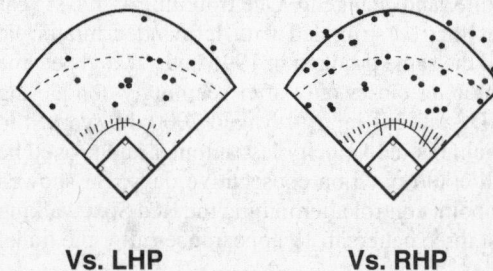

Vs. LHP   **Vs. RHP**

2001 Situational Stats

	AB	H	HR	RBI	Avg		AB	H	HR	RBI	Avg
Home	87	24	2	8	.276	LHP	53	15	1	4	.283
Road	87	27	5	17	.310	RHP	121	36	6	21	.298
First Half	174	51	7	25	.293	Sc Pos	38	11	2	19	.289
Scnd Half	0	0	0	0	-	Clutch	33	12	1	6	.364

2001 Rankings (American League)

- 1st in lowest batting average on a 3-1 count (0.000)
- 6th in batting average with two strikes (.268)
- 10th in batting average on a 3-2 count (.348)

Rolando Arrojo

Position: RP
Bats: R **Throws:** R
Ht: 6' 4" **Wt:** 220

Opening Day Age: 33
Born: 7/18/68 in
Havana, Cuba
ML Seasons: 4
Pronunciation:
ah-ROW-ho

Overall Statistics

	W	L	Pct.	ERA	G	GS	Sv	IP	H	BB	SO	HR	Ratio
2001	5	4	.556	3.48	41	9	5	103.1	88	35	78	8	1.19
Career	36	39	.480	4.50	129	97	5	618.2	632	228	461	76	1.39

2001 Situational Stats

	W	L	ERA	Sv	IP		AB	H	HR	RBI	Avg
Home	3	2	2.90	4	62.0	LHB	202	48	4	27	.238
Road	2	2	4.35	1	41.1	RHB	181	40	4	29	.221
First Half	2	2	3.56	5	65.2	Sc Pos	102	26	3	48	.255
Scnd Half	3	2	3.35	0	37.2	Clutch	75	24	2	16	.320

2001 Season

Rolando Arrojo pitched so poorly during spring training that the Red Sox put him in the bullpen. He made the move look like a stroke of genius by opening the year with 10 straight scoreless relief appearances. He cooled off in May and June, but joined the rotation in July and pitched brilliantly before coming down with a sore shoulder in August. He mixed five wins, five saves and three holds among his 41 appearances.

Pitching & Defense

The time in the bullpen seemed to rejuvenate Arrojo, who's always had trouble maintaining his effectiveness over the course of a game or a season. He throws all sorts of pitches from all different angles, something that's always worked well against righthanded hitters but never seemed to fool lefties until last year. He mostly relies on a sinker that runs in to righthanded hitters. He cuts off the running game well by varying his delivery, and he fields his position acceptably.

2002 Outlook

Arrojo came back to make a few relief appearances in September, but clearly things still were not right with his shoulder. If Arrojo can prove he's healthy this spring, then he can be a valuable contributor while wearing a number of different hats in Boston.

Rod Beck

Position: RP
Bats: R **Throws:** R
Ht: 6' 1" **Wt:** 235

Opening Day Age: 33
Born: 8/3/68 in
Burbank, CA
ML Seasons: 11
Nickname: Shooter

Overall Statistics

	W	L	Pct.	ERA	G	GS	Sv	IP	H	BB	SO	HR	Ratio
2001	6	4	.600	3.90	68	0	6	80.2	77	28	63	15	1.30
Career	35	41	.461	3.28	642	0	266	708.2	651	171	597	85	1.16

2001 Situational Stats

	W	L	ERA	Sv	IP		AB	H	HR	RBI	Avg
Home	2	3	4.43	4	40.2	LHB	141	30	7	16	.213
Road	4	1	3.38	2	40.0	RHB	165	47	8	26	.285
First Half	4	3	2.76	4	49.0	Sc Pos	81	18	3	26	.222
Scnd Half	2	1	5.68	2	31.2	Clutch	182	46	9	27	.253

2001 Season

The old soupbone finally went out on Rod Beck last year. After 11 largely injury-free seasons in the majors, Beck blew out his elbow in September and had Tommy John surgery soon afterward. He'd pitched very well in a setup role for the Red Sox over the first half, but struggled down the stretch. After allowing nine home runs in 31 innings during July and August, Beck worked only five innings in September.

Pitching & Defense

In recent seasons, as his fastball no longer hit 90 MPH consistently, Beck made his living more and more by changing speeds with his forkball and changeup. He would use his slider mostly for show. He's actually been tougher on lefthanded hitters than righthanders throughout his career, and he held lefties to a .213 clip last year. He seems to save his best stuff for tight spots. He knows what to do with the ball when he executes a play, and combats the running game as well as the average righty.

2002 Outlook

Beck, a free agent, isn't expected to pitch at all in 2002. As hard as it is to believe (as it seems like he's been in the league forever), he's only 33, so he could become a Norm Charlton-type mercenary if he's able to make it back.

Rich Garces

Position: RP
Bats: R **Throws:** R
Ht: 6' 0" **Wt:** 245

Opening Day Age: 30
Born: 5/18/71 in Maracay, VZ
ML Seasons: 9
Pronunciation: gar-SEZ
Nickname: El Guapo

Overall Statistics

	W	L	Pct.	ERA	G	GS	Sv	IP	H	BB	SO	HR	Ratio
2001	6	1	.857	3.90	62	0	1	67.0	55	25	51	6	1.19
Career	23	9	.719	3.49	261	0	7	320.0	269	152	280	28	1.32

2001 Situational Stats

	W	L	ERA	Sv	IP		AB	H	HR	RBI	Avg
Home	3	1	3.86	0	35.0	LHB	101	19	1	10	.188
Road	3	0	3.94	1	32.0	RHB	150	36	5	26	.240
First Half	2	0	3.03	0	35.2	Sc Pos	79	19	1	28	.241
Scnd Half	4	1	4.88	1	31.1	Clutch	105	20	3	9	.190

2001 Season

Last year Rich Garces dealt another blow to those who feel physical fitness is required of a professional athlete. He had his fourth straight solid season out of the Boston bullpen, pitching very well in a setup role for most of the year before having a few bad outings in September. He posted 17 holds for the second consecutive campaign and owns a sparkling 19-3 record over the past three years.

Pitching & Defense

With a low-90s fastball, a curve and a splitter, Garces is one of the rare righthanders who's consistently tougher against lefties. He's often brought in to pitch out of jams, and doesn't get rattled. He fields his position better than one would expect from a man of his stature, and he hasn't erred in five years. He isn't quick to the plate, however, and baserunners run on him at will. All 13 stolen-base attempts on his watch were successful in 2001.

2002 Outlook

Garces said he plans to come to camp in better shape this year—a sign that he's serious about landing a nice free-agent deal at the end of the 2002 season. Expect another good year from him. With Derek Lowe possibly headed for the Boston rotation and Rod Beck departing via free agency, the Red Sox need his solid work more than ever.

Scott Hatteberg

Position: C
Bats: L **Throws:** R
Ht: 6' 1" **Wt:** 205

Opening Day Age: 32
Born: 12/14/69 in Salem, OR
ML Seasons: 7
Pronunciation: hatt-EH-berg

Overall Statistics

	G	AB	R	H	D	T	HR	RBI	SB	BB	SO	Avg	OBP	Slg
2001	94	278	34	68	19	0	3	25	1	33	26	.245	.332	.345
Career	454	1310	163	350	86	2	34	159	1	175	209	.267	.357	.414

2001 Situational Stats

	AB	H	HR	RBI	Avg		AB	H	HR	RBI	Avg
Home	136	32	2	12	.235	LHP	51	9	1	4	.176
Road	142	36	1	13	.254	RHP	227	59	2	21	.260
First Half	139	32	1	13	.230	Sc Pos	56	14	2	21	.250
Scnd Half	139	36	2	12	.259	Clutch	50	11	1	5	.220

2001 Season

No one was more a victim of Boston's roster chaos last year than Scott Hatteberg. He was named the regular designated hitter at the start of the season, but sat in favor of the hobbled Manny Ramirez for most of April and May. Following Jason Varitek's injury in June, Hatteberg was pressed into everyday duty behind the plate for two months. His bat perked up, but his inability to stop the running game prompted a trade for Doug Mirabelli, and Hatteberg's role then became more limited.

Hitting, Baserunning & Defense

Hatteberg is a patient hitter who makes good contact, working deep counts but rarely striking out. He has decent power and takes good advantage of Fenway by hitting the ball hard to left field. He's been platooned throughout his career and hasn't proven he can hit southpaws. With a slow release and questionable accuracy, his arm is a problem, although he's a sound defensive catcher otherwise. He has little speed and runs conservatively.

2002 Outlook

If Jason Varitek returns to health, Hatteberg should assume his customary backup role and enjoy a better year. That is bad news for opposing basestealers, who likely won't be successful 81 percent of the time against the Red Sox in 2002.

Shea Hillenbrand

Position: 3B
Bats: R **Throws:** R
Ht: 6' 1" **Wt:** 200

Opening Day Age: 26
Born: 7/27/75 in Mesa, AZ
ML Seasons: 1
Pronunciation: SHAY

Overall Statistics

	G	AB	R	H	D	T	HR	RBI	SB	BB	SO	Avg	OBP	Slg
2001	139	468	52	123	20	2	12	49	3	13	61	.263	.291	.391
Career	139	468	52	123	20	2	12	49	3	13	61	.263	.291	.391

2001 Situational Stats

	AB	H	HR	RBI	Avg		AB	H	HR	RBI	Avg
Home	244	60	5	26	.246	LHP	132	30	2	13	.227
Road	224	63	7	23	.281	RHP	336	93	10	36	.277
First Half	279	73	7	29	.262	Sc Pos	127	28	0	33	.220
Scnd Half	189	50	5	20	.265	Clutch	76	22	2	10	.289

2001 Season

Rookie Shea Hillenbrand was the Red Sox' early surprise last year, though he soon came back to earth. Despite never having played above Double-A or as a full-time third baseman, injuries enabled him to open the year as the club's starter at that spot. He broke from the gate with a red-hot April, but cooled off and split time there over the second half.

Hitting, Baserunning & Defense

Hillenbrand is one of the most impatient hitters around, drawing few walks and rarely even getting to a three-ball count. A defensive hitter who hits the ball where it's pitched, he seldom strikes out, but he often gets himself out by putting a pitcher's pitch in play. He had a rough go of it against southpaws, despite having hit them very well the year before. He did a decent job at the hot corner, showing average range and a sometimes-erratic but strong enough arm. A former catcher, he's an average runner at best.

2002 Outlook

The pitchers seemed to figure out Hillenbrand after his first time around. Unless he makes some adjustments, he could be facing a much more limited role in 2002.

Mike Lansing

Position: SS/2B
Bats: R **Throws:** R
Ht: 6' 0" **Wt:** 195

Opening Day Age: 33
Born: 4/3/68 in Rawlins, WY
ML Seasons: 9
Nickname: Laser

Overall Statistics

	G	AB	R	H	D	T	HR	RBI	SB	BB	SO	Avg	OBP	Slg
2001	106	352	45	88	23	0	8	34	3	22	50	.250	.294	.384
Career	1110	4150	554	1124	254	17	84	440	119	299	570	.271	.324	.401

2001 Situational Stats

	AB	H	HR	RBI	Avg		AB	H	HR	RBI	Avg
Home	182	49	5	22	.269	LHP	107	29	2	6	.271
Road	170	39	3	12	.229	RHP	245	59	6	28	.241
First Half	183	40	1	11	.219	Sc Pos	86	17	1	24	.198
Scnd Half	169	48	7	23	.284	Clutch	59	15	0	5	.254

2001 Season

Mike Lansing wasn't expected to contribute much last year, but in May, out of sheer desperation, the Red Sox put him at shortstop. He hadn't played at short on a regular basis since the early 1990s with Montreal, but he was more or less the regular there in 2001 and proved to be surprisingly adequate. He even enjoyed a hot streak at the plate in July before hurting his knee in September.

Hitting, Baserunning & Defense

Lansing hits liners to all fields and generally makes decent contact, but at this point in his career he doesn't have the power or on-base skills to hit anywhere but at the bottom of the order. His on-base percentage has been below the .300 mark for two straight seasons. Age and injuries have left Lansing with below-average range at second and worse than that at short. He has a decent arm, but it barely was adequate from the left side of the diamond. He no longer is a running threat and hasn't reached double digits in stolen bases since 1998.

2002 Outlook

The Red Sox declined to pick up the $6 million option on Lansing's contract for 2002, making him a free agent. It may be hard for him to land a bench job after his performance the last two seasons.

Derek Lowe

Position: RP
Bats: R **Throws:** R
Ht: 6' 6" **Wt:** 200

Opening Day Age: 28
Born: 6/1/73 in
Dearborn, MI
ML Seasons: 5

Overall Statistics

	W	L	Pct.	ERA	G	GS	Sv	IP	H	BB	SO	HR	Ratio
2001	5	10	.333	3.53	67	3	24	91.2	103	29	82	7	1.44
Career	20	32	.385	3.64	298	22	85	484.1	477	141	370	36	1.28

2001 Situational Stats

	W	L	ERA	Sv	IP		AB	H	HR	RBI	Avg
Home	2	4	2.79	14	51.2	LHB	180	57	3	20	.317
Road	3	6	4.50	10	40.0	RHB	184	46	4	19	.250
First Half	4	6	3.71	15	51.0	Sc Pos	118	30	1	32	.254
Scnd Half	1	4	3.32	9	40.2	Clutch	213	66	6	31	.310

2001 Season

Derek Lowe fell about as far as one can possibly fall last year. He took the loss in five of his first 11 appearances and was dispatched to middle relief by early May. He pitched well enough to reclaim the closer role a few weeks later, but when he struggled in late July, the Red Sox dealt for Ugueth Urbina, who soon bumped Lowe back to middle relief. In late September, he joined the rotation and made three good starts.

Pitching & Defense

With a hard, running sinker, Lowe is the most extreme groundballer in the game today. In order to succeed as a starter, he'll need to develop more consistency with his curve and changeup, especially to lefthanded hitters. Lefties now own a .288 career mark against Lowe. As a reliever, his ability to work day after day is an asset. His nasty arsenal makes it very tough for catchers to throw out basestealers. He fields his position adequately.

2002 Outlook

Lowe's a quality pitcher, but it's far from automatic that he'll succeed as a starter this year, considering his earlier washouts as a starter in Boston and Seattle. If the conversion doesn't take, Lowe could find himself back in the pen trying to keep the score close for Urbina.

Troy O'Leary

Position: LF/RF
Bats: L **Throws:** L
Ht: 6' 0" **Wt:** 200

Opening Day Age: 32
Born: 8/4/69 in
Compton, CA
ML Seasons: 9
Nickname: Yum-Yum

Overall Statistics

	G	AB	R	H	D	T	HR	RBI	SB	BB	SO	Avg	OBP	Slg
2001	104	341	50	82	16	6	13	50	1	25	73	.240	.298	.437
Career	1008	3563	502	984	213	38	119	526	13	286	583	.276	.332	.457

2001 Situational Stats

	AB	H	HR	RBI	Avg		AB	H	HR	RBI	Avg
Home	171	46	9	27	.269	LHP	65	10	0	6	.154
Road	170	36	4	23	.212	RHP	276	72	13	44	.261
First Half	207	53	7	32	.256	Sc Pos	95	23	2	32	.242
Scnd Half	134	29	6	18	.216	Clutch	59	12	1	5	.203

2001 Season

Troy O'Leary looked to rebound last year after a trying 2000 season, but he found himself being squeezed out of the picture in Boston. The signing of Manny Ramirez helped produce a glut of outfielder/DH candidates, and O'Leary often found himself sitting against lefties. After Jimy Williams was fired, O'Leary was all but buried on the bench. O'Leary logged only 39 plate appearances after September 1, and he hit just .118 during that span.

Hitting, Baserunning & Defense

O'Leary uses Fenway well, taking outside pitches to left and pulling offspeed pitches into the open space in right field. He hit lefties well a few years ago when he was seeing them regularly, but has struggled against them lately in his more limited role. His range and arm in left field are only adequate, and he can be pressed to cover more territory in other parks. He's not well suited to right field but has been used there. He runs with intensity and smarts, but lacks good speed.

2002 Outlook

Boston declined the 2002 option on O'Leary's contract, but GM Dan Duquette says he is open to bringing O'Leary back. The departure of Carl Everett could make O'Leary's return more likely, but if O'Leary leaves, he may miss hitting in Fenway.

Chris Stynes

Position: 3B/2B
Bats: R **Throws:** R
Ht: 5'10" **Wt:** 185

Opening Day Age: 29
Born: 1/19/73 in
Queens, NY
ML Seasons: 7

Overall Statistics

	G	AB	R	H	D	T	HR	RBI	SB	BB	SO	Avg	OBP	Slg
2001	96	361	52	101	19	2	8	33	4	20	56	.280	.322	.410
Career	518	1526	239	445	68	5	34	150	45	113	180	.292	.344	.410

2001 Situational Stats

	AB	H	HR	RBI	Avg		AB	H	HR	RBI	Avg
Home	156	51	3	14	.327	LHP	106	37	3	8	.349
Road	205	50	5	19	.244	RHP	255	64	5	25	.251
First Half	149	46	4	14	.309	Sc Pos	81	25	2	25	.309
Scnd Half	212	55	4	19	.259	Clutch	55	18	2	10	.327

2001 Season

Chris Stynes missed his chances last year. He appeared to win at least a share of the second-base job to start the season, but he missed most of April with a strained hamstring. Then a beaning knocked him out of action until June. From then on, Stynes played fairly regularly and contributed with the bat while splitting time between second and third base. But he failed to lock down a full-time job at either spot.

Hitting, Baserunning & Defense

Stynes makes good contact and hits line drives to all fields. Though he hits for a good average, his lack of patience prevents him from being an ideal top-of-the-order hitter. His on-base percentage languished at .322 last year, though he has had that mark up to as high as .394 in 1997 and .386 in 2000. He has sure hands and average range at second or third, but his arm is sometimes stretched at third. Despite average speed, he runs the bases aggressively, although he hasn't been much of a basestealer the past couple of years.

2002 Outlook

Only at shortstop is there a starting infielder's name written in stone. Stynes could see extensive action in the Boston infield in 2002, either at second or third. He could enjoy his best season yet.

Tim Wakefield

Position: RP/SP
Bats: R **Throws:** R
Ht: 6'2" **Wt:** 210

Opening Day Age: 35
Born: 8/2/66 in
Melbourne, FL
ML Seasons: 9

Overall Statistics

	W	L	Pct.	ERA	G	GS	Sv	IP	H	BB	SO	HR	Ratio
2001	9	12	.429	3.90	45	17	3	168.2	156	73	148	13	1.36
Career	94	89	.514	4.41	312	205	18	1512.2	1498	644	1020	194	1.42

2001 Situational Stats

	W	L	ERA	Sv	IP		AB	H	HR	RBI	Avg
Home	5	6	3.63	2	79.1	LHB	262	59	5	30	.225
Road	4	6	4.13	1	89.1	RHB	367	97	8	50	.264
First Half	6	2	2.58	2	94.1	Sc Pos	181	43	2	63	.238
Scnd Half	3	10	5.57	1	74.1	Clutch	61	19	1	9	.311

2001 Season

Once again, Tim Wakefield's versatility was his curse last season. He re-upped with Boston for two years and $6.5 million in December 2000 with the hope that he would be a starter. But for the second straight year, the Red Sox sent him to the pen. He pitched very well in middle relief in April and May, earning a promotion back to the rotation in June, where he continued to excel before slumping in July and returning to the bullpen in late August.

Pitching & Defense

While Wakefield still relies primarily upon the knuckleball, he used his curveball a lot more last year, both early and late in the count. He also mixes in a low-80s fastball that understandably looks a lot faster. Like many knuckleballers, he runs hot and cold. He has a good move and a compact stretch delivery, although basestealers still are able to outrun his pitches. He was signed as a first baseman, so he fields his position well.

2002 Outlook

This season, as always, the Red Sox will be tempted to slot Wakefield into whatever role they need at a given moment. As a full-time starter, he could win 15 games. As a full-time reliever, he could work 80 games and throw 120 innings. He'll probably do a little of both.

Boston

Other Boston Red Sox

Israel Alcantara (**Pos**: LF, **Age**: 28, **Bats**: R)

	G	AB	R	H	D	T	HR	RBI	SB	BB	SO	Avg	OBP	Slg
2001	14	38	3	10	1	0	0	3	1	3	13	.263	.317	.289
Career	35	83	12	23	2	0	4	10	1	6	20	.277	.326	.446

Although he's a power hitter, Alcantara didn't homer in 38 at-bats last year with the Red Sox. He also whiffed 13 times and was benched for not running out a popup. It was a tough summer for Izzy. 2002 Outlook: C

Willie Banks (**Pos**: RHP, **Age**: 33)

	W	L	Pct.	ERA	G	GS	Sv	IP	H	BB	SO	HR	Ratio
2001	0	0	-	0.84	5	0	0	10.2	5	4	10	0	0.84
Career	31	38	.449	4.85	152	84	1	571.1	600	288	402	60	1.55

Banks made his first appearance in the big leagues since 1998 during a late-season callup from Triple-A Pawtucket. He made the most of his opportunity and impressed the Red Sox enough to be invited back in 2002. 2002 Outlook: C

Morgan Burkhart (**Pos**: DH, **Age**: 30, **Bats**: B)

	G	AB	R	H	D	T	HR	RBI	SB	BB	SO	Avg	OBP	Slg
2001	11	33	3	6	1	0	1	4	0	1	11	.182	.206	.303
Career	36	106	19	27	4	0	5	22	0	18	36	.255	.380	.434

Burkhart is a one-dimensional player who basically does almost nothing but hit. He did not even do that well in his short time with Boston in 2001. The Red Sox released him in early October. 2002 Outlook: C

Carlos Castillo (**Pos**: RHP, **Age**: 26)

	W	L	Pct.	ERA	G	GS	Sv	IP	H	BB	SO	HR	Ratio
2001	0	0	-	6.00	2	0	0	3.0	3	0	0	1	1.00
Career	10	7	.588	5.04	111	6	1	210.2	210	82	130	37	1.39

Castillo did not get much of a chance in 2001, only appearing in two games while jumping between Pawtucket and Boston. The Red Sox released Castillo at the end of September. 2002 Outlook: C

David Cone (**Pos**: RHP, **Age**: 39)

	W	L	Pct.	ERA	G	GS	Sv	IP	H	BB	SO	HR	Ratio
2001	9	7	.563	4.31	25	25	0	135.2	148	57	115	17	1.51
Career	193	123	.611	3.44	445	415	1	2880.2	2484	1124	2655	254	1.25

After a disappointing 2000 season in New York, Cone signed with the rival Red Sox and rebounded to have a decent 2001. He thought about retiring, but chances are he'll be back for at least one more year. He became a free agent in November, so his return likely won't be in Boston. 2002 Outlook: C

Paxton Crawford (**Pos**: RHP, **Age**: 24)

	W	L	Pct.	ERA	G	GS	Sv	IP	H	BB	SO	HR	Ratio
2001	3	0	1.000	4.75	8	7	0	36.0	40	13	25	3	1.47
Career	5	1	.833	4.15	15	11	0	65.0	65	26	42	3	1.40

Crawford performed well to start the season, but eventually was sent to the minors in mid-May. He was called up for one game in June but did not pitch particularly well. His disappointing first half took a turn for the worse after he hurt his back in June. 2002 Outlook: C

Todd Erdos (**Pos**: RHP, **Age**: 28)

	W	L	Pct.	ERA	G	GS	Sv	IP	H	BB	SO	HR	Ratio
2001	0	0	-	4.96	10	0	0	16.1	15	8	7	2	1.41
Career	2	0	1.000	5.57	63	0	2	93.2	105	45	58	12	1.60

Erdos was a Boston spring-training invitee after pitching for the Yankees and Padres in 2000. He had a rough first stint with the Red Sox in August but pitched decently in his second stint in September. 2002 Outlook: C

Bryce Florie (**Pos**: RHP, **Age**: 31)

	W	L	Pct.	ERA	G	GS	Sv	IP	H	BB	SO	HR	Ratio
2001	1	0	1.000	11.42	7	0	0	8.2	12	7	7	1	2.19
Career	20	24	.455	4.47	261	29	2	493.2	500	243	395	46	1.51

Florie made an amazing return to the big leagues after his orbital socket was shattered by a line drive in September of 2000. The Tigers picked him up after he was released by Boston at the end of July. 2002 Outlook: C

Craig Grebeck (**Pos**: SS, **Age**: 37, **Bats**: R)

	G	AB	R	H	D	T	HR	RBI	SB	BB	SO	Avg	OBP	Slg
2001	23	41	1	2	1	0	0	2	0	2	9	.049	.093	.073
Career	752	1988	239	518	116	8	19	187	4	228	274	.261	.340	.356

Grebeck was released by the Red Sox after the season. Injuries and a 2-for-41 showing at the plate led to his dismissal after one season in Boston. 2002 Outlook: D

Darren Lewis (**Pos**: RF/LF/CF, **Age**: 34, **Bats**: R)

	G	AB	R	H	D	T	HR	RBI	SB	BB	SO	Avg	OBP	Slg
2001	82	164	18	46	9	1	1	12	5	8	25	.280	.326	.366
Career	1296	4002	600	1002	134	36	27	335	246	396	503	.250	.323	.322

Lewis played in only 82 games in 2001, his lowest total since 1991. He became a free agent in November and will help a team with his defense in the outfield. 2002 Outlook: B

James Lofton (**Pos**: SS, **Age**: 28, **Bats**: B)

	G	AB	R	H	D	T	HR	RBI	SB	BB	SO	Avg	OBP	Slg
2001	8	26	1	5	1	0	0	1	2	1	4	.192	.214	.231
Career	8	26	1	5	1	0	0	1	2	1	4	.192	.214	.231

Boston recalled Lofton after injuries had depleted the team at shortstop in September. He saw time in eight big league games down the stretch, and signed a minor league contract to stay. 2002 Outlook: C

Allen McDill (**Pos**: LHP, **Age**: 30)

	W	L	Pct.	ERA	G	GS	Sv	IP	H	BB	SO	HR	Ratio
2001	0	0	-	5.52	15	0	0	14.2	13	7	16	2	1.36
Career	0	0	-	7.79	38	0	0	34.2	38	18	28	8	1.62

Time is running out for this 30-year-old lefty specialist. In four seasons in the majors, McDill has pitched in just 38 games with three different clubs. 2002 Outlook: C

Lou Merloni (**Pos**: SS, **Age**: 30, **Bats**: R)

	G	AB	R	H	D	T	HR	RBI	SB	BB	SO	Avg	OBP	Slg
2001	52	146	21	39	10	0	3	13	2	6	31	.267	.306	.397
Career	174	496	59	139	34	2	5	59	4	25	89	.280	.322	.387

Merloni was part of the committee the Red Sox used to fill in for the injured Nomar Garciaparra. His versatility and .280 career batting average make him valuable. 2002 Outlook: C

Doug Mirabelli (Pos: C, Age: 31, Bats: R)

	G	AB	R	H	D	T	HR	RBI	SB	BB	SO	Avg	OBP	Slg
2001	77	190	20	43	10	0	11	29	0	27	57	.226	.332	.453
Career	217	549	57	127	29	2	19	72	1	78	152	.231	.332	.395

The Red Sox acquired Mirabelli in mid-June from the Rangers. He filled in pretty nicely for injured starter Jason Varitek with four homers, 17 RBI and a .304 average in the month of August. 2002 Outlook: B

Joe Oliver (Pos: C, Age: 36, Bats: R)

	G	AB	R	H	D	T	HR	RBI	SB	BB	SO	Avg	OBP	Slg
2001	17	48	4	12	2	0	1	3	0	2	15	.250	.275	.354
Career	1076	3367	320	831	174	3	102	476	13	248	637	.247	.299	.391

Oliver changed teams for the seventh time in seven seasons when the Red Sox signed him near midseason. He is a veteran presence and third catcher at this point in his career. 2002 Outlook: C

Hipolito Pichardo (Pos: RHP, Age: 32)

	W	L	Pct.	ERA	G	GS	Sv	IP	H	BB	SO	HR	Ratio
2001	2	1	.667	4.93	30	0	0	34.2	42	10	17	3	1.50
Career	50	43	.538	4.41	349	68	20	769.1	835	285	394	54	1.46

Pichardo battled Red Sox management over playing time in between his two stints on the disabled list. The veteran quit the team in late August and filed for free agency. 2002 Outlook: C

Calvin Pickering (Pos: 1B, Age: 25, Bats: L)

	G	AB	R	H	D	T	HR	RBI	SB	BB	SO	Avg	OBP	Slg
2001	21	54	4	15	1	0	3	8	0	8	15	.278	.371	.463
Career	53	115	12	25	2	0	6	16	1	22	35	.217	.343	.391

As a one-time top Orioles prospect, Pickering never got a chance in the majors in Baltimore. He was traded to Cincinnati at the end of August, and then was acquired off waivers a week later by Boston. If he can get a chance with the Red Sox, he may be able to put up nice numbers. 2002 Outlook: C

Bret Saberhagen (Pos: RHP, Age: 37)

	W	L	Pct.	ERA	G	GS	Sv	IP	H	BB	SO	HR	Ratio
2001	1	2	.333	6.00	3	3	0	15.0	19	0	10	3	1.27
Career	167	117	.588	3.34	399	371	1	2562.2	2452	471	1715	218	1.14

Saberhagen fought off an ailing shoulder just long enough to pitch in three games for the Red Sox before going back on the shelf. He became a free agent in November, but he may retire. 2002 Outlook: C

Angel Santos (Pos: 2B, Age: 22, Bats: B)

	G	AB	R	H	D	T	HR	RBI	SB	BB	SO	Avg	OBP	Slg
2001	9	16	2	2	1	0	0	1	0	2	7	.125	.211	.188
Career	9	16	2	2	1	0	0	1	0	2	7	.125	.211	.188

The Red Sox seem to like the switch-hitting Santos. He was a September callup and went 2-for-16 with the big club. He may have a future as a utility man. 2002 Outlook: C

Pete Schourek (Pos: LHP, Age: 32)

	W	L	Pct.	ERA	G	GS	Sv	IP	H	BB	SO	HR	Ratio
2001	1	5	.167	4.45	33	0	0	30.1	35	15	20	4	1.65
Career	66	77	.462	4.59	288	176	2	1149.0	1198	420	813	140	1.41

After another stretch of injuries and ineffectiveness, Schourek was released in early August. He was not picked up by another club and remained a free agent in limbo at the end of the season. 2002 Outlook: C

John Valentin (Pos: SS, Age: 35, Bats: R)

	G	AB	R	H	D	T	HR	RBI	SB	BB	SO	Avg	OBP	Slg
2001	20	60	8	12	2	0	1	5	0	9	8	.200	.314	.283
Career	991	3709	596	1043	266	17	121	528	47	441	487	.281	.361	.460

Valentin returned from knee surgery in May and made his first appearance at shortstop since 1996. He was out for good a month later with a heel injury. Boston declined to pick up his option for 2002. 2002 Outlook: C

Boston Red Sox Minor League Prospects

Organization Overview:

After trading tons of talent to keep pace with the New York Yankees in the American League East in recent seasons, the Red Sox have very little in the high minors that can help them anytime soon. Those who were expected to help the team in the near future—Dernell Stenson, Wilton Veras, Morgan Burkhart, Paxton Crawford and Asian imports Jin Ho Cho, Sang-Hoon Lee and Sun-Woo Kim—haven't been able to get over the hump and make an impact in Boston. A couple of them still may emerge, but it's safe to say that the team's best prospects now are playing in the low minors. The Red Sox, facing the unknowns of a change of ownership, will have to spend money in the free-agent market to stay competitive until some help arrives from way down below.

Casey Fossum

Position: P   **Opening Day Age:** 24
Bats: B **Throws:** L   **Born:** 1/9/78 in Cherry
Ht: 6' 1" **Wt:** 160   Hill, NJ

Recent Statistics

	W	L	ERA	G	GS	Sv	IP	H	R	BB	SO	HR
2001 AA Trenton	3	7	2.83	20	20	0	117.2	102	47	28	130	5
2001 AL Boston	3	2	4.87	13	7	0	44.1	44	26	20	26	4

A supplemental first-round pick in 1999, Fossum enjoyed a solid debut at short-season Class-A Lowell before putting together back-to-back impressive seasons at high Class-A Sarasota and Double-A Trenton. Somehow he was 3-7 at Trenton, but he posted a 2.83 ERA while fanning 130 and walking just 28 in 117.2 innings there before the Red Sox called in late July. He pitched very well in relief with Boston before struggling in a few late-season starts. Fossum throws a hard slider that is his best pitch, as well as an average fastball with good downward movement and an OK changeup. He's a thin lefthander, and there's concern how well he will withstand heavy use. His future may be in relief, possibly as a situational lefty.

Sun-Woo Kim

Position: P   **Opening Day Age:** 24
Bats: R **Throws:** R   **Born:** 9/4/77 in Inchon,
Ht: 6' 2" **Wt:** 180   South Korea

Recent Statistics

	W	L	ERA	G	GS	Sv	IP	H	R	BB	SO	HR
2001 AAA Pawtucket	6	7	5.36	19	14	0	89.0	93	55	27	79	10
2001 AL Boston	0	2	5.83	20	2	0	41.2	54	27	21	27	1

One of the earliest Asian signings by Boston in 1997, Kim has been slow to develop. He's tended to give up plenty of hits and homers, largely because his command within the strike zone isn't polished. He has a moving, 94-95 MPH fastball that he usually can pinpoint for strikes, plus a slider and changeup that slowly are coming around. He has decent command of the changeup, but sometimes he gets under the slider and it flattens on him. Kim likes to pitch high to hitters, but he works high too much. He throws inside well against righthanded batters, but is less effective inside against lefties. Fine-tuning the little things continues, but the Red Sox are thinking about converting Kim to relief work.

Steve Lomasney

Position: C   **Opening Day Age:** 24
Bats: R **Throws:** R   **Born:** 8/29/77 in
Ht: 6' 0" **Wt:** 195   Melrose, MA

Recent Statistics

	G	AB	R	H	D	T	HR	RBI	SB	BB	SO	Avg
2000 AA Trenton	66	233	30	57	16	1	8	27	4	24	81	.245
2000 R Red Sox	6	15	2	4	2	0	0	1	0	4	6	.267
2001 AA Trenton	58	209	24	52	14	2	10	29	0	23	76	.249
2001 AAA Pawtucket	17	63	10	18	4	0	2	9	2	4	21	.286
2001 MLE	75	264	27	62	16	1	8	30	1	18	104	.235

A 1995 pick, Lomasney has shown solid catching skills and a decent arm, although his throws aren't always accurate. Initial concerns focused on his bat, but Lomasney staved them off by driving the ball better at Class-A Michigan in 1997. Breaking stuff has given him trouble, and that's still the case after two-plus seasons at Double-A Trenton. He does hit the fastball with good power and draws some walks, so his .239 career average is offset by his .348 on-base percentage to some degree. Lomasney is a mentally tough kid, and he has needed to be. Over the last 18 months, he's been mugged in Florida, broken his thumb, nose and big toe, and had the orbital bone of his eye broken by a line drive last August.

Rene Miniel

Position: P   **Opening Day Age:** 20
Bats: R **Throws:** R   **Born:** 4/26/81 in Santo
Ht: 6' 2" **Wt:** 175   Domingo, DR

Recent Statistics

	W	L	ERA	G	GS	Sv	IP	H	R	BB	SO	HR
2000 R Red Sox	2	4	4.00	21	1	7	36.0	37	21	21	31	1
2001 A Augusta	8	4	2.73	27	23	0	122.0	93	49	38	114	1

Miniel signed with the Red Sox in 1998 before spending two seasons in the Rookie-level Gulf Coast League getting his feet wet working in relief. He jumped to Class-A Augusta in 2001 and enjoyed a solid season, working as a starter and allowing just 93 hits while fanning 114 in 122 innings. He called on two key weapons, a low to mid-90s fastball and a decent curve, to retire Sally League hitters. Despite his success last summer, Miniel still is more of a thrower than a pitcher. He struggles with a changeup and his hard curve is loopy at times. As his secondary pitches come around, Miniel could take off and move toward Boston more quickly. High Class-A Sarasota should be his 2002 destination.

Greg Montalbano

Position: P
Bats: L **Throws:** L
Ht: 6' 2" **Wt:** 185

Opening Day Age: 24
Born: 8/24/77 in
Worcester, MA

Recent Statistics

	W	L	ERA	G	GS	Sv	IP	H	R	BB	SO	HR
2000 R Red Sox	0	2	3.75	4	4	0	12.0	13	6	3	14	1
2000 A Lowell	0	1	1.74	2	2	0	10.1	4	3	4	15	0
2001 A Sarasota	9	3	2.96	17	15	0	91.1	66	36	25	77	11
2001 AA Trenton	3	3	4.50	10	10	0	48.0	50	25	14	45	8

Montalbano was a 1999 pick, but he didn't sign until May 2000. The college product has an advanced feel for pitching. He throws strikes and changes speeds effectively with a fastball that will range from 86-92 MPH and a good curveball that still is inconsistent. He's a fierce competitor who will work high and get a lot of flyball outs. Montalbano needs to work inside more. His mix of bulldog and savvy came through en route to a 9-3 (2.96) record at high Class-A Sarasota, and he finished the year with a respectable stint at Double-A Trenton in his first full pro season. If he stays a starter, Montalbano probably will work the latter half of a major league rotation.

Freddy Sanchez

Position: SS
Bats: R **Throws:** R
Ht: 5' 11" **Wt:** 185

Opening Day Age: 24
Born: 12/21/77 in
Hollywood, CA

Recent Statistics

	G	AB	R	H	D	T	HR	RBI	SB	BB	SO	Avg
2000 A Lowell	34	132	24	38	13	2	1	14	2	9	16	.288
2000 A Augusta	30	109	17	33	7	0	0	15	4	11	19	.303
2001 A Sarasota	69	280	40	95	19	4	1	24	5	22	30	.339
2001 AA Trenton	44	178	25	58	20	0	2	19	3	9	21	.326

An 11th-rounder in 2000, Sanchez was a college pick who made good contact instantly at two Class-A stops in his debut season. He did the same in 2001, advancing to Double-A Trenton on the strength of a .339 average and .388 on-base percentage at high Class-A Sarasota. Sanchez has a nice swing and recognizes pitches effectively. He lacks quickness and doesn't run that well, and he may not have enough arm to play short. Yet he's fairly dependable picking up the ball and has good instincts on the field, so he may be a useful second baseman or utility player if he gets on base successfully when he's at the plate. Learning to draw more walks would help, as Sanchez won't always hit well above .300.

Seung Song

Position: P
Bats: R **Throws:** R
Ht: 6' 1" **Wt:** 192

Opening Day Age: 21
Born: 6/29/80 in Pusan,
South Korea

Recent Statistics

	W	L	ERA	G	GS	Sv	IP	H	R	BB	SO	HR
2000 A Lowell	5	2	2.60	13	13	0	72.2	63	26	20	93	1
2001 A Augusta	3	2	2.04	14	14	0	75.0	56	24	18	79	3
2001 A Sarasota	5	2	1.68	8	8	0	48.1	28	11	18	56	1

As good as Song was a year ago, when he posted a 2.60 ERA and fanned 93 batters in 72.2 innings for short-season Lowell in 2000, Song was even better at two full-season A-ball stops in 2001. His fastball jumped from the high 80s into the low 90s, and he displayed remarkable command of the pitch. He pinpointed it effectively on the corners and successfully induced hitters to chase high heat. He also threw a sharp-breaking curve and changeup, and he mixed his pitches smartly. Song, who signed with Boston before the 1999 season, uses a deceptive Nomo-like delivery, which makes it harder to be ready for a well-placed fastball or unexpected curve.

Dernell Stenson

Position: OF
Bats: L **Throws:** L
Ht: 6' 1" **Wt:** 230

Opening Day Age: 23
Born: 6/17/78 in
LaGrange, GA

Recent Statistics

	G	AB	R	H	D	T	HR	RBI	SB	BB	SO	Avg
2000 AAA Pawtucket	98	380	59	102	14	0	23	71	0	45	99	.268
2001 AAA Pawtucket	122	464	53	110	18	1	16	69	0	43	116	.237
2001 MLE	122	454	43	100	17	0	12	57	0	35	123	.220

Boston's third-round pick in 1996, Stenson rode his quick bat and short stroke to a breakout 1998 season at Double-A Trenton. He looked like a professional hitter, and with his power potential, Stenson seemed to be a star on the rise at age 20. Since then, he's spent three years at Triple-A Pawtucket and doesn't look any closer to the majors. His drop-off in his third season there in 2001 suggests a change of scenery would help, but what's held him back in Boston is his lack of a defensive position. He can't play the outfield well enough to claim a job, and he's a below-average first baseman. Offensively, his key weakness is trying to make contact with breaking balls. A big offensive season might rekindle hope for a DH job.

Others to Watch

Third baseman **Tony Blanco** (20) has four-tool talent and a lightning-quick bat. He stroked 23 doubles and 17 homers in 370 at-bats in the Class-A Sally League in 2001 despite bursitis in his right shoulder, which led to arthroscopic surgery in August. He has a strong arm, but his defensive work needs refinement. . . Righthander **Manny Delcarmen** (20) rifled a mid-90s fastball and a good curve at Rookie-level Gulf Coast hitters in 2001. He fanned 62 batters in 46 innings while posting a 2.54 ERA. Boston's second-round pick in the 2000 draft didn't debut until 2001, but he showed he's got a live arm and a high ceiling. . . Shoulder tendinitis delayed his season until July, but southpaw **Phil Dumatrait** (20) still had time to display the 12-to-6 curveball that is his best pitch. He fanned 48 in 43 innings between Rookie ball in Florida and short-season Class-A Lowell. . . While many young pitchers have the mid-90s velocity of righthander **Anastacio Martinez** (21), few have the combination of velocity and command that Martinez is showing. He can work both sides of the plate effectively, and he has a nice feel for his changeup. Martinez is worth watching after going 9-12 (3.35) at high Class-A Sarasota in 2001.

Comiskey Park

Offense

It was no surprise that Comiskey Park became more of a hitters' park in 2001. The outfield fences had been moved in during an offseason renovation, with the biggest differences in the corners. The shortened distance to the wall seemed to make Sox hitters less willing to go the opposite way or shorten their swings. While it will take years to know the significance of the new dimensions, Comiskey is not the same pitcher-friendly park that Frank Thomas once claimed had cost him 100 homers.

Defense

With the outfield wall reduced from nine feet to eight feet, even the lumbering Carlos Lee is a threat to rob hitters of home runs. Comiskey Park also allows infielders to enjoy the grooming of groundskeeper Roger Bossard, who is one of baseball's most respected yard men.

Who It Helps the Most

Nobody liked the new dimensions better than first baseman Paul Konerko, who quickly mastered the art of pulling the ball down the line to left. Newcomer Royce Clayton also thrived in the redesigned park, hitting 108 points higher at Comiskey than on the road. Keith Foulke, a flyball pitcher, was successful at Comiskey last year, but that has not always been the case.

Who It Hurts the Most

You've got to wonder if this is still a good park to break in young pitchers. Many of them suffered last season, including Jon Garland and Gary Glover. Mark Buehrle allowed four more home runs at Comiskey than on the road. That being said, it appears hitters who are tempted to swing for the fences suffer, with Carlos Lee and Magglio Ordonez the prime examples.

Rookies & Newcomers

Senior scouting director Duane Shaffer has said that Joe Borchard is the best power hitter to come from the college ranks since Mark McGwire. He's due to arrive at Comiskey Park in the second half of 2002, and should feel right at home.

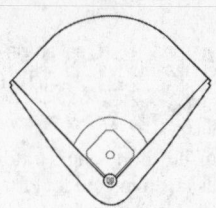

Dimensions: LF-330, LCF-377, CF-400, RCF-372, RF-335

Capacity: 44,321

Elevation: 595 feet

Surface: Grass

Foul Territory: Average

Park Factors

2001 Season

	Home Games			Away Games			
	White Sox	Opp	Total	White Sox	Opp	Total	Index
G	72	72	144	72	72	144	—
Avg	.268	.269	.269	.271	.269	.270	99
AB	2403	2534	4937	2472	2372	4844	102
R	366	377	743	347	345	692	107
H	645	681	1326	671	638	1309	101
2B	129	134	263	145	127	272	95
3B	12	10	22	13	17	30	72
HR	98	101	199	88	62	150	130
BB	261	232	493	205	218	423	114
SO	433	423	856	446	378	824	102
E	52	52	104	48	44	92	113
E-Infield	46	42	88	38	40	78	113
LHB-Avg	.270	.264	.266	.265	.276	.271	98
LHB-HR	31	48	79	32	27	59	135
RHB-Avg	.268	.273	.270	.275	.263	.269	100
RHB-HR	67	53	120	56	35	91	127

1999-2000

	Home Games			Away Games			
	White Sox	Opp	Total	White Sox	Opp	Total	Index
G	144	144	288	144	144	288	—
Avg	.281	.275	.278	.279	.279	.279	100
AB	4839	5100	9939	5148	4891	10039	99
R	789	752	1541	759	748	1507	102
H	1359	1403	2762	1437	1365	2802	99
2B	257	244	501	295	242	537	94
3B	36	17	53	25	30	55	97
HR	181	181	362	149	170	319	115
BB	500	500	1000	459	571	1030	98
SO	720	906	1626	840	828	1668	98
E	107	94	201	121	121	242	83
E-Infield	99	78	177	105	104	209	85
LHB-Avg	.261	.274	.268	.266	.290	.278	96
LHB-HR	39	83	122	55	77	132	94
RHB-Avg	.293	.276	.285	.288	.271	.280	102
RHB-HR	142	98	240	94	93	187	129

2001 Rankings (American League)

- Highest home-run factor
- Highest walk factor
- Second-highest LHB home-run factor
- Second-highest RHB home-run factor
- Third-highest error factor
- Third-highest infield-error factor

Jerry Manuel

2001 Season

With great expectations following a 95-win season in 2000, Jerry Manuel found himself facing the toughest test of his four-year managerial career. It appeared he had failed it miserably when the White Sox opened with a 14-29 record. But Manuel's steady style of leadership paid dividends the rest of the season, as the Sox rallied to post a winning season. They won without Frank Thomas and seven key pitchers, all of whom were lost to season-ending injuries before the All-Star break. Manuel dealt with difficult situations all year, beginning with Thomas' spring-training holdout.

Offense

Manuel sometimes is torn between his National League small-ball upbringing and the slug-it-out approach that wins in the American League. The Sox' awful start came when he was trying to put an emphasis on speed and defense, but it had more to do with poor contributions from Thomas, Magglio Ordonez and Ray Durham than force-feeding Royce Clayton and rookie center fielder Julio Ramirez into the lineup. While the Sox were second in the AL in home runs, they nevertheless led the league in sacrifice bunts.

Pitching & Defense

Every year we say that Manuel inherited an organization that had earned a reputation for poor fielding, and he has not found a way to significantly improve it. Despite an upgrade at shortstop, the White Sox still finished 10th in fielding percentage. Manuel is known for his quick hook, often pulling starters at the first hint of trouble, but had more patience with them last year. Perhaps the bullpen options weren't as inviting in 2000, when he led the AL in pitching changes. He does a good job working with young pitchers.

2002 Outlook

Owner Jerry Reinsdorf expects results from the arms buildup that commenced with the White Flag trade in 1997. So Manuel cannot afford to have the team stumble out of the gate. With Cleveland reducing its payroll and Thomas returning from injury, the Sox should be able to craft a 90-win team out of all the quality parts available to Manuel.

Born: 12/23/53 in Hahira, Georgia

Playing Experience: 1975-1982, Det, Mon, SD

Managerial Experience: 4 seasons

Manager Statistics

Year	Team, Lg	W	L	Pct	GB	Finish
2001	Chicago, AL	83	79	.512	8.0	3rd Central
4 Seasons		333	314	.513	—	—

2001 Starting Pitchers by Days Rest

	<=3	4	5	6+
White Sox Starts	3	73	51	24
White Sox ERA	6.19	4.71	4.49	4.34
AL Avg Starts	1	78	48	24
AL ERA	5.92	4.69	4.58	4.58

2001 Situational Stats

	Jerry Manuel	AL Average
Hit & Run Success %	35.5	35.0
Stolen Base Success %	67.6	71.0
Platoon Pct.	53.3	59.1
Defensive Subs	50	26
High-Pitch Outings	5	6
Quick/Slow Hooks	26/19	19/16
Sacrifice Attempts	95	54

2001 Rankings (American League)

- 1st in sacrifice bunt attempts
- 2nd in steals of third base (25), double steals (8), defensive substitutions, quick hooks, starts on three days rest and saves with over 1 inning pitched (16)
- 3rd in squeeze plays (4) and slow hooks

Mark Buehrle

2001 Season

Talk about taking advantage of an opportunity. Manager Jerry Manuel didn't put second-year lefty Mark Buehrle into his starting rotation until the end of spring training, yet he wound up as the White Sox ace and one of the American League's best lefthanded starters. Buehrle was leading the ERA race late in the season, but faded down the stretch to finish fourth. That probably was to be expected, as his 221-inning workload was 51 more than he had ever thrown in a season. He would have been named on many Rookie of the Year ballots, but threw 1.1 too many innings in 2000 to qualify.

Pitching

An otherworldly poise got this junior-college product to the big leagues after only 217 innings in the minors. He was mostly a two-pitch pitcher when he worked out of the Sox' bullpen down the stretch in 2000, relying on a fastball in the low-90s and a good curveball that he locates well. He had only dabbled with a changeup in the minors, but added it and a new cut fastball to his repertoire in 2001. He throws all four pitches in any count. Buehrle works fast and does a great job getting ahead of hitters. He ranked sixth in the American League with an average of 1.95 walks per nine innings in 2001, while holding hitters to a .230 batting average.

Defense

Only basestealers looking for a challenge try to run on Buehrle. He has one of the best pickoff moves in the majors and is quick to the plate. There were 12 stolen-base attempts against him in 2001, and only six succeeded. He is an aggressive fielder who sometimes tries to the force the action too much.

2002 Outlook

Buehrle credits David Wells for helping him develop so quickly. He learned his lessons well and will be counted on to become the bell cow of the White Sox' group of young starters. The one question about Buehrle is how well his arm will tolerate the workload it carried last season.

Position: SP
Bats: L **Throws:** L
Ht: 6' 2" **Wt:** 200

Opening Day Age: 23
Born: 3/23/79 in St. Charles, MO
ML Seasons: 2
Pronunciation: BURR-lee

Overall Statistics

	W	L	Pct.	ERA	G	GS	Sv	IP	H	BB	SO	HR	Ratio
2001	16	8	.667	3.29	32	32	0	221.1	188	48	126	24	1.07
Career	20	9	.690	3.47	60	35	0	272.2	243	67	163	29	1.14

How Often He Throws Strikes

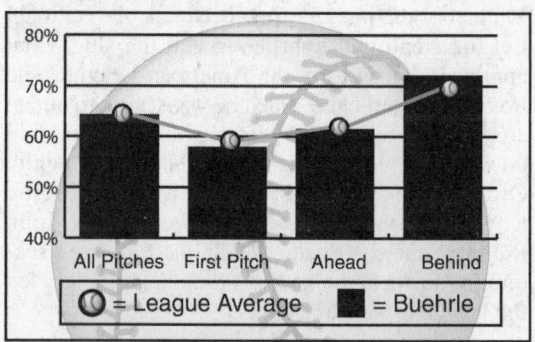

2001 Situational Stats

	W	L	ERA	Sv	IP		AB	H	HR	RBI	Avg
Home	7	5	3.43	0	112.2	LHB	154	32	5	23	.208
Road	9	3	3.15	0	108.2	RHB	662	156	19	54	.236
First Half	6	4	3.29	0	109.1	Sc Pos	155	34	3	50	.219
Scnd Half	10	4	3.29	0	112.0	Clutch	47	19	3	5	.404

2001 Rankings (American League)

- Led the White Sox in ERA, wins, complete games (4), shutouts (2), innings pitched, hits allowed, batters faced (885), home runs allowed, strikeouts, pitches thrown (3,324), GDPs induced (23), winning percentage, highest strikeout-walk ratio (2.6), lowest batting average allowed (.230), lowest slugging percentage allowed (.377), lowest on-base percentage allowed (.279), highest groundball-flyball ratio allowed (1.1), fewest pitches thrown per batter (3.76), lowest ERA at home, lowest ERA on the road, most run support per nine innings (5.6), lowest batting average allowed with runners in scoring position, most strikeouts per nine innings (5.1) and fewest walks per nine innings (2.0)

Royce Clayton

2001 Season

Two months into his first season in Chicago, Royce Clayton hung up a sign on his Comiskey Park locker that read, "In spite of." It was his vow to bounce back after falling deep into Jerry Manuel's doghouse, and he did it in a major way. Acquired from Texas to improve the Sox' weak fielding, Clayton was hitting .102 heading into play on May 29, but hit .310 the rest of the way to finish at .263, five points above his career average. He played well in the field, but saw his awful start at the plate magnified by the April struggles of others higher in the batting order.

Hitting

Clayton always has swung for the fences at the expense of his on-base percentage. He has a long swing that fails him against tough pitchers, especially righthanders. He's built his stats against lefthanders, and his batting average in 2001 was 91 points higher against lefties than righthanders. Clayton always seems to be behind in the count. But when he makes contact he can drive the ball to the gaps.

Baserunning & Defense

While other shortstops are flashier, few are as reliable as Clayton. He has good range and an accurate arm, and he committed only seven errors last season in 133 games. He takes offense to hard slides into second base, but otherwise does a good job turning double plays. Jerry Manuel was excited about Clayton's speed, yet he stole only 10 bases in 17 tries, which was a disappointment.

2002 Outlook

If the White Sox don't trade Clayton or Jose Valentin before camps open, they are likely to showcase them for scouts from other teams during spring training. The Sox want to go with a set lineup that doesn't leave Clayton or Valentin on the bench. This is the last year in Clayton's contract, so it will be a big season for him whether he's in Chicago or elsewhere. He's beginning to show age but there's no reason he shouldn't have a solid year.

Position: SS
Bats: R **Throws:** R
Ht: 6' 0" **Wt:** 185

Opening Day Age: 32
Born: 1/2/70 in Burbank, CA
ML Seasons: 11

Overall Statistics

	G	AB	R	H	D	T	HR	RBI	SB	BB	SO	Avg	OBP	Slg
2001	135	433	62	114	21	4	9	60	10	33	72	.263	.315	.393
Career	1347	4809	608	1242	225	43	79	499	182	366	888	.258	.312	.372

Where He Hits the Ball

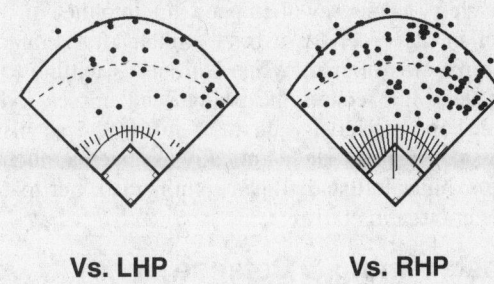

Vs. LHP   **Vs. RHP**

2001 Situational Stats

	AB	H	HR	RBI	Avg		AB	H	HR	RBI	Avg
Home	218	69	6	37	.317	LHP	102	34	2	12	.333
Road	215	45	3	23	.209	RHP	331	80	7	48	.242
First Half	207	41	3	25	.198	Sc Pos	106	32	2	53	.302
Scnd Half	226	73	6	35	.323	Clutch	61	13	1	3	.213

2001 Rankings (American League)

- 2nd in fielding percentage at shortstop (.988)
- 5th in sacrifice bunts (9) and most GDPs per GDP situation (18.4%)
- Led the White Sox in sacrifice flies (7) and batting average with the bases loaded (.400)

Ray Durham

2001 Season

Ray Durham gets older but not necessarily better. He remained too much of a streak hitter to thrive as a leadoff man, and a fielder whose range is surprisingly limited given his athleticism. While Durham did set a career high with 20 home runs and scored 100-plus runs for the fifth consecutive season, he was missing in action out of the chute. His .228 average and .314 on-base percentage in April contributed to the awful start that buried the White Sox.

Hitting

Durham has evolved as a power hitter, but not as a leadoff man. His .333 on-base percentage in the leadoff spot was a major disappointment, and manager Jerry Manuel even dropped him into the No. 3 spot in the order for a brief stretch after Frank Thomas was injured. While Durham is willing to get deep into counts, he swings and misses too often. His strikeout-walk ratio in 2001 was his worst since 1995. He historically has been a much better hitter lefthanded than righthanded, but that was not true in 2001.

Baserunning & Defense

Durham should make sure to send thank-you notices to the official scorers at Comiskey Park. His unusually high fielding percentage was in part the result of his getting the benefit of the doubt on many balls that bounced off his glove. He has never developed the range to his right that keeps him from becoming a top fielder. Most of his range comes on balls to his left. Durham has an average arm. He does a good job going back on popups. His stolen-base totals have dropped for three years in a row, but he has tremendous speed on the basepaths.

2002 Outlook

This is a big year for Durham, who is in the last year of a four-year contract. If he can raise his play from 2001 he will put himself in a strong negotiating position, but there is no guarantee that he will get another big deal from the White Sox. Second-base prospect Tim Hummel has climbed the minor league ranks in a short time and should be in the big league picture soon.

Position: 2B
Bats: B **Throws:** R
Ht: 5' 8" **Wt:** 180

Opening Day Age: 30
Born: 11/30/71 in Charlotte, NC
ML Seasons: 7

Overall Statistics

	G	AB	R	H	D	T	HR	RBI	SB	BB	SO	Avg	OBP	Slg
2001	152	611	104	163	42	10	20	65	23	64	110	.267	.337	.466
Career	1050	4134	713	1143	229	51	97	436	199	435	699	.276	.349	.427

Where He Hits the Ball

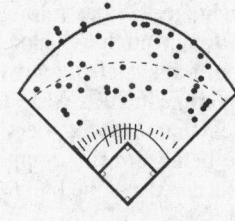

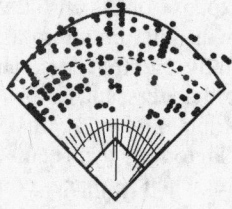

Vs. LHP   **Vs. RHP**

2001 Situational Stats

	AB	H	HR	RBI	Avg		AB	H	HR	RBI	Avg
Home	284	70	9	26	.246	LHP	143	37	6	19	.259
Road	327	93	11	39	.284	RHP	468	126	14	46	.269
First Half	319	80	11	34	.251	Sc Pos	115	30	4	41	.261
Scnd Half	292	83	9	31	.284	Clutch	82	17	1	9	.207

2001 Rankings (American League)

- 2nd in fielding percentage at second base (.986)
- 3rd in pitches seen (2,822) and highest percentage of extra bases taken as a runner (61.7)
- 5th in doubles and triples
- 6th in lowest batting average on an 0-2 count (.047)
- 7th in most pitches seen per plate appearance (4.08)
- Led the White Sox in at-bats, runs scored, doubles, triples, pitches seen (2,822), plate appearances (691), highest percentage of pitches taken (58.3), on-base percentage for a leadoff hitter (.333), highest percentage of extra bases taken as a runner (61.7) and lowest percentage of swings on the first pitch (17.3)

Keith Foulke

2001 Season

Keith Foulke was a rock for a pitching staff shattered by injury. He entered the season with a big responsibility and delivered everything anyone could have expected, setting a career high with 42 saves while compiling a 2.33 ERA. His season shouldn't be judged by his nine losses, as manager Jerry Manuel had to put him into tough situations to compensate for other breakdowns in the bullpen. He worked more than one inning to earn a save 10 times, and never once whined that his arm was sore.

Pitching

By now hitters know that Foulke is going to throw two changeups for every one fastball, but they still can't hit them. He never tips off his changeup with his delivery and constantly gets hitters to swing under it, hitting popups and flyballs. Foulke's fastball rarely exceeds 90 MPH, but it's good enough to jam hitters looking for the changeup. Hitters often attack his first pitch, knowing that they are in big trouble after an 0-1 count (.141 average). He held opponents to a .199 batting average overall last season. Foulke is especially effective at Comiskey Park, where he converted all 23 save situations and compiled a 1.24 ERA in 2001.

Defense

Foulke is tough to run on, allowing only three stolen bases last season. He is a fundamentally perfect fielder and is confident enough in his pitching to always get the easy out, rather than try to force the action. He has made only one error over the last three seasons. If there was a Gold Glove for closers, he would be a strong candidate.

2002 Outlook

As valuable as Foulke is to the White Sox, financial considerations were a threat to his future with the team. Foulke earned $3.1 million last summer and had turned down the organization's long-term offers. He easily could have asked for $6-8 million in a salary arbitration hearing this time around, which is more than Jerry Reinsdorf wants to pay any relief pitcher, but he signed a two-year, $10 million deal with Chicago in December.

Position: RP
Bats: R **Throws:** R
Ht: 6' 0" **Wt:** 210

Opening Day Age: 29
Born: 10/19/72 in Ellsworth AFB, SD
ML Seasons: 5
Pronunciation: FOLK

Overall Statistics

	W	L	Pct.	ERA	G	GS	Sv	IP	H	BB	SO	HR	Ratio
2001	4	9	.308	2.33	72	0	42	81.0	57	22	75	3	0.98
Career	17	20	.459	3.44	292	8	89	413.0	334	108	400	45	1.07

How Often He Throws Strikes

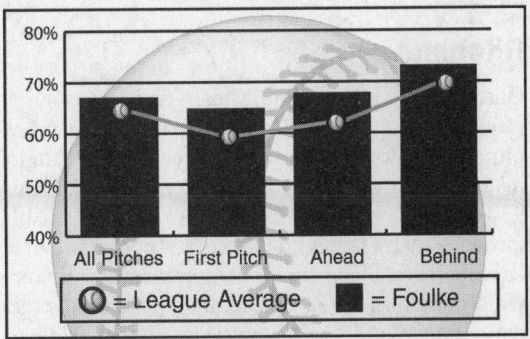

2001 Situational Stats

	W	L	ERA	Sv	IP		AB	H	HR	RBI	Avg
Home	4	5	1.24	23	43.2	LHB	156	33	3	18	.212
Road	0	4	3.62	19	37.1	RHB	131	24	0	13	.183
First Half	3	5	2.64	18	44.1	Sc Pos	73	17	1	28	.233
Scnd Half	1	4	1.96	24	36.2	Clutch	212	37	3	25	.175

2001 Rankings (American League)

- 1st in save percentage (93.3) and games finished (69)
- 3rd in save opportunities (45), first batter efficiency (.136), saves, relief ERA (2.33) and relief losses (9)
- 4th in games pitched
- 5th in relief innings (81.0)
- Led the White Sox in games pitched, saves, save opportunities (45), lowest batting average allowed vs. lefthanded batters, first batter efficiency (.136), relief losses (9), relief innings (81.0), relief ERA (2.33), lowest batting average allowed in relief (.199), most strikeouts per nine innings in relief (8.3) and fewest baserunners allowed per nine innings in relief (9.7)

Jon Garland

2001 Season

Experience is invaluable in a pitcher's development. Jon Garland got plenty of it, spending nearly a full season in the big leagues at age 21. His rapid rise and great expectations make it hard to remember that he is still just a colt. Garland seemed destined for Triple-A Charlotte with veterans like David Wells, Cal Eldred and Jim Parque in the season-opening rotation, but manager Jerry Manuel decided to keep him in the bullpen. He wasn't there long, however, as Eldred and Parque were quickly forced onto the disabled list. Garland wound up splitting the season between the rotation and bullpen, working five-plus innings in 13 of 16 starts. He asserted himself after the All-Star break but faded late.

Pitching

Garland has a great natural sinker, which was more effective after pitching coach Nardi Contreras got him to drop down to more of a three-quarters angle instead of an over-the-top delivery. He can throw 93-94 MPH, but gets more movement when he throws 90-91. He has not developed command of a curveball and changeup to complement the sinker, which produces lots of groundballs. He walks too many hitters and throws too many pitches. He has yet to make it past the seventh inning in any of his 29 career starts.

Defense

Garland stands 6-foot-6 and looks it on the mound. He gets to a lot of balls hit back towards the mound, but often sees them carom off him. He has made strides improving his fielding. He has an average move to first base and can be run on.

2002 Outlook

Garland failed to lock up a permanent rotation spot last season, so he'll have to earn it in spring training. He has pitched better in relief than as a starter, however, so he should have a job one way or another. There are lots of other pitching prospects on their way to Comiskey, though, so it is time for Garland to put his experience to use to make sure he's in the long-term plans.

Position: RP/SP
Bats: R **Throws:** R
Ht: 6' 6" **Wt:** 205

Opening Day Age: 22
Born: 9/27/79 in Valencia, CA
ML Seasons: 2

Overall Statistics

	W	L	Pct.	ERA	G	GS	Sv	IP	H	BB	SO	HR	Ratio
2001	6	7	.462	3.69	35	16	1	117.0	123	55	61	16	1.52
Career	10	15	.400	4.73	50	29	1	186.2	205	95	103	26	1.61

How Often He Throws Strikes

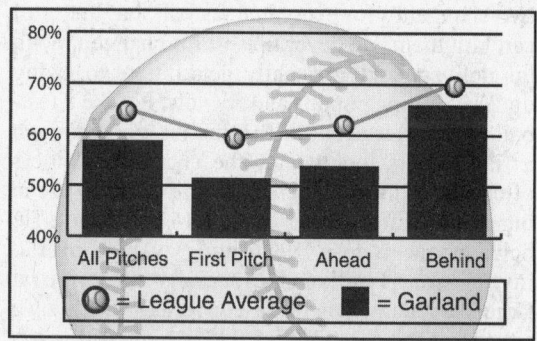

◯ = League Average   ■ = Garland

2001 Situational Stats

	W	L	ERA	Sv	IP		AB	H	HR	RBI	Avg
Home	3	3	4.28	0	54.2	LHB	217	60	6	21	.276
Road	3	4	3.18	1	62.1	RHB	227	63	10	32	.278
First Half	3	3	3.95	0	43.1	Sc Pos	118	27	3	34	.229
Scnd Half	3	4	3.54	1	73.2	Clutch	23	4	0	0	.174

2001 Rankings (American League)

- Led the White Sox in most GDPs induced per GDP situation (17.2%)

Paul Konerko

Position: 1B/DH
Bats: R **Throws:** R
Ht: 6' 2" **Wt:** 215

Opening Day Age: 26
Born: 3/5/76 in
Providence, RI
ML Seasons: 5
Pronunciation:
kone-err-coe

2001 Season

Day in and day out, Paul Konerko was among the White Sox' most consistent regulars. He continued the steady improvement that he's shown since getting the opportunity to play every day, while hitting fourth or fifth for most of the season. His playing time increased over 2000, when the late-season trade for Harold Baines cost him a 100-RBI season. He finished just short of triple figures again, this time due to hitting .152 during May. Konerko bounced back from that slump to put together four strong months. He also displayed strong leadership qualities and developed into a team spokesman in the clubhouse.

Hitting

Konerko is a big man who sometimes looks stiff at the plate. His bat might be only slider speed, but he compensates by seldom missing pitchers' mistakes. He is especially dangerous on pitches down in the strike zone and can fight off pitches up. His power is mostly to left field. Konerko has only a small platoon difference between lefthanders and righthanders. He defied a trend by hitting much better in day games than at night in 2001. The Sox will watch to see if it happens again this year.

Baserunning & Defense

Konerko probably will never win a Gold Glove, but he is becoming a better defensive first baseman. His first step has become quicker through hard work. He's got a good arm for a first baseman. He is a base-clogger despite an aggressive approach on the bases.

2002 Outlook

With Frank Thomas back in the lineup, Konerko will follow Thomas and Magglio Ordonez in what should be a very solid 3-4-5 punch. He signed a two-year, $6.1 million contract in January 2001, and he will be eligible for arbitration as a four-plus player following the season. It's unlikely the Sox would move him at some point, but not out of the question, especially if he has such a big season that his annual salary could jump well above the $5 million mark.

Overall Statistics

	G	AB	R	H	D	T	HR	RBI	SB	BB	SO	Avg	OBP	Slg
2001	156	582	92	164	35	0	32	99	1	54	89	.282	.349	.507
Career	522	1843	268	519	101	5	84	306	3	163	271	.282	.345	.479

Where He Hits the Ball

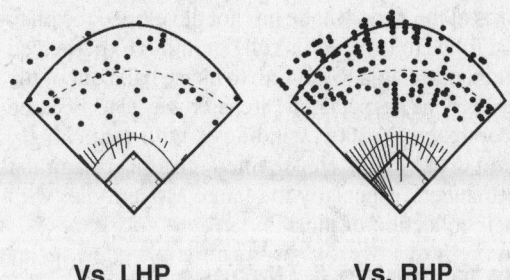

Vs. LHP   **Vs. RHP**

2001 Situational Stats

	AB	H	HR	RBI	Avg		AB	H	HR	RBI	Avg
Home	289	86	19	56	.298	LHP	111	33	5	21	.297
Road	293	78	13	43	.266	RHP	471	131	27	78	.278
First Half	295	83	17	47	.281	Sc Pos	150	40	8	67	.267
Scnd Half	287	81	15	52	.282	Clutch	79	23	3	12	.291

2001 Rankings (American League)

- 4th in fielding percentage at first base (.994) and assists at first base (90)
- 6th in GDPs (17)
- Led the White Sox in home runs, hit by pitch (9), GDPs (17), highest percentage of swings put into play (48.4) and batting average at home

Carlos Lee

2001 Season

More was expected of Carlos Lee than he could deliver in his second full season in the big leagues. The big man from Panama came out slugging, but finished with a whimper, hitting just .228 after the All-Star break to end the year far below projections. He had driven in 92 runs in his first full season and seemed poised for the first of many 100-RBI campaigns. Lee may have pressed when Frank Thomas was lost for the season, causing him to feel an increased responsibility.

Hitting

Lee is the type of hitter who causes opposing managers to pay attention during batting practice. He has a short, quick stroke that gives him power to all parts of the park. But he has not developed the plate discipline to use it to its full potential. Experienced pitchers are able to get him to chase balls out of the strike zone, especially pitches away. He became overanxious in 2001, winding up with a shockingly low walk total. He seemed confused against lefthanders, especially the Jamie Moyer types with their collection of junk.

Baserunning & Defense

Lee can catch opponents off guard with his speed, which he is learning to use. He stole 17 bases in 24 tries last season, and next year could match Magglio Ordonez' status as a 20-20 man. The converted third baseman seemed to regress in left field. He sometimes still struggles to make routine plays and almost never makes exceptional ones, although he did bring a home run back late in the season. Teams run on his throwing arm, which is below average.

2002 Outlook

Despite a slight drop-off in Lee's numbers, there's no reason he should not develop into a respected hitter. Look for him to bounce back. If he does, he will remain a key player in the White Sox' long-term plan. But if he does not have a solid first half, his playing time could suffer as players like Aaron Rowand, Jeff Liefer and Joe Borchard ascend to his level, if not pass him.

Position: LF/DH
Bats: R **Throws:** R
Ht: 6' 2" **Wt:** 235

Opening Day Age: 25
Born: 6/20/76 in Aguadulce, Panama
ML Seasons: 3

Overall Statistics

	G	AB	R	H	D	T	HR	RBI	SB	BB	SO	Avg	OBP	Slg
2001	150	558	75	150	33	3	24	84	17	38	85	.269	.321	.468
Career	429	1622	248	466	94	7	64	260	34	89	251	.287	.327	.472

Where He Hits the Ball

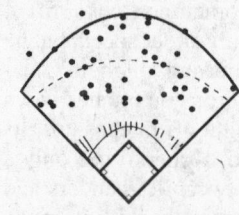 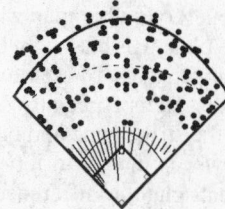

Vs. LHP   **Vs. RHP**

2001 Situational Stats

	AB	H	HR	RBI	Avg		AB	H	HR	RBI	Avg
Home	271	70	12	41	.258	LHP	115	28	2	12	.243
Road	287	80	12	43	.279	RHP	443	122	22	72	.275
First Half	291	89	15	52	.306	Sc Pos	146	41	8	58	.281
Scnd Half	267	61	9	32	.228	Clutch	84	27	5	22	.321

2001 Rankings (American League)

- 1st in errors in left field (8) and lowest fielding percentage in left field (.969)
- 2nd in assists in left field (9)
- Led the White Sox in lowest percentage of swings that missed (13.7), steals of third (5) and batting average in the clutch

Magglio Ordonez

2001 Season

They say all's well that ends well, but that wasn't quite true with Magglio Ordonez. His slow start was one of the reasons the White Sox went 14-29 to start the season. But once Ordonez was jump-started, it was hard to remember how the year had begun. He surpassed 100 RBI and made the American League All-Star team for the third year in a row. He also became only the second player in Sox history to have more than 20 home runs *and* more than 20 stolen bases in the same campaign. Tommie Agee managed that feat in 1966.

Hitting

Ordonez is a complete hitter with a compact swing that stays consistent. He has the ability to hit the ball hard to all fields and has shown increased discipline every year of his career. He managed as many walks as strikeouts last season, which should be a sign of good things to come. Ordonez swings at the first pitch often yet hangs in with two strikes, hitting .243 even in those situations in 2001. He is as good against righthanders as lefthanders, but last year he was better on the road than at the altered Comiskey Park.

Baserunning & Defense

Ordonez is a solid right fielder who seemed to have an off year in the field in 2001. He often was a tick short on the sliding—more like sitting—catches that have become his trademark. The stats showed he didn't get to as many balls as in previous seasons and he was charged with five errors. He is becoming an excellent baserunner, increasing his stolen-base total each of the last three years. He was 25-for-32 in stolen-base attempts last summer, a sign that he is reading pitchers well.

2002 Outlook

Rather than fight the Sox in arbitration every year, Ordonez signed a three-year contract extension in late July 2001. That should ensure that he will be the focal point of the lineup for years to come. He has averaged 119 RBI over the last three years, and Ordonez could blossom into an elite hitter if he keeps improving.

Position: RF
Bats: R **Throws:** R
Ht: 6' 0" **Wt:** 210

Opening Day Age: 28
Born: 1/28/74 in Caracas, VZ
ML Seasons: 5
Pronunciation: or-DOAN-yez
Nickname: Mags

Overall Statistics

	G	AB	R	H	D	T	HR	RBI	SB	BB	SO	Avg	OBP	Slg
2001	160	593	97	181	40	1	31	113	25	70	70	.305	.382	.533
Career	636	2409	381	727	139	9	111	432	66	207	259	.302	.358	.505

Where He Hits the Ball

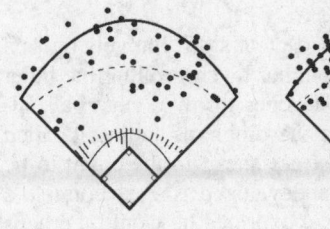
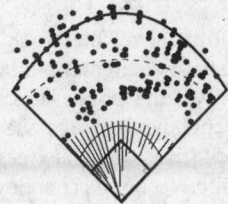

Vs. LHP   **Vs. RHP**

2001 Situational Stats

	AB	H	HR	RBI	Avg		AB	H	HR	RBI	Avg
Home	301	79	17	60	.262	LHP	117	38	12	32	.325
Road	292	102	14	53	.349	RHP	476	143	19	81	.300
First Half	306	91	19	54	.297	Sc Pos	154	49	7	79	.318
Scnd Half	287	90	12	59	.314	Clutch	81	23	1	17	.284

2001 Rankings (American League)

- 2nd in slugging percentage vs. lefthanded pitchers (.709) and batting average on the road
- Led the White Sox in batting average, hits, singles, total bases (316), RBI, stolen bases, walks, times on base (256), slugging percentage, on-base percentage, highest groundball-flyball ratio (1.4), batting average vs. lefthanded pitchers, batting average vs. righthanded pitchers, batting average on an 0-2 count (.205), cleanup slugging percentage (.509), slugging percentage vs. lefthanded pitchers (.709), on-base percentage vs. lefthanded pitchers (.403), on-base percentage vs. righthanded pitchers (.376) and batting average with two strikes (.243)
- Led AL right fielders in home runs and RBI

Jim Parque

2001 Season

Prior to the 2001 season, expectations had never been higher for Jim Parque, who didn't come close to fulfilling them. The White Sox were looking for Parque to step into Mike Sirotka's workhorse role after the David Wells trade, but may have miscast him. Parque has a 4.97 career ERA and a resume that shows he's never worked more than 187 innings in a season. He was off to a miserable start before shoulder pain surfaced and led to season-ending surgery to repair a torn labrum. It's unknown how long he pitched with the injury, but it was diagnosed only one start after a complete game against Minnesota on April 20, which was just his second in 88 career starts.

Pitching

Parque never has had great stuff, but gets by as a fastball-changeup pitcher by controlling the inner half of the plate. He does throw a curveball, although he's always had problems getting it called for strikes. He must get ahead in the count to be effective, but has not developed as much command as the White Sox had expected he would. Perhaps because his curveball never has been a plus pitch, lefthanded batters look forward to hitting against him.

Defense

Parque has an excellent pickoff move, which freezes most basestealers. He is not a good fielder, however. He moves well on the mound, but never has harnessed a tendency to try to do too much once he gets to a ball. He tends to work incredibly slowly with runners on base, which is most of the time he's pitching.

2002 Outlook

There's no guarantee that Parque will step back into the rotation spot he had held since 1998. While the White Sox expect him to be ready by spring training, how he will bounce back from surgery is a mystery. If Parque does not win a spot in the rotation, he probably will be used out of the bullpen, which is where some in the organization believe he is better suited. He has a lot to prove this season, especially since he figures to be a four-plus, arbitration-eligible player next winter.

Position: SP
Bats: L **Throws:** L
Ht: 5'11" **Wt:** 170

Opening Day Age: 26
Born: 2/8/76 in Norwalk, CA
ML Seasons: 4
Pronunciation: PAR-kay

Overall Statistics

	W	L	Pct.	ERA	G	GS	Sv	IP	H	BB	SO	HR	Ratio
2001	0	3	.000	8.04	5	5	0	28.0	36	10	15	7	1.64
Career	29	29	.500	4.97	90	88	0	501.2	589	209	314	65	1.59

How Often He Throws Strikes

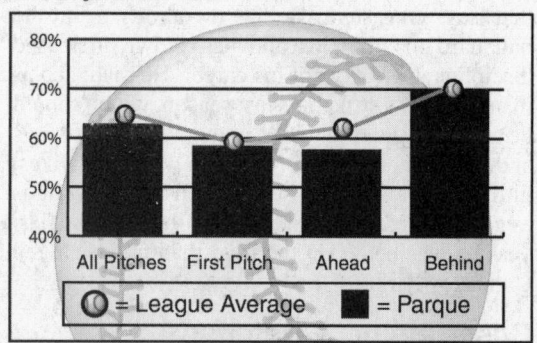

○ = League Average   ■ = Parque

2001 Situational Stats

	W	L	ERA	Sv	IP		AB	H	HR	RBI	Avg
Home	0	2	8.59	0	22.0	LHB	47	17	4	11	.362
Road	0	1	6.00	0	6.0	RHB	70	19	3	10	.271
First Half	0	3	8.04	0	28.0	Sc Pos	27	7	1	12	.259
Scnd Half	0	0	-	0	0.0	Clutch	2	2	0	0	1.000

2001 Rankings (American League)

- Did not rank near the top or bottom in any category

Frank Thomas

2001 Season

Finishing second to Jason Giambi in the MVP voting in 2000 didn't vanquish all of Frank Thomas' ghosts. All the goodwill went out the window when he followed an 0-for-9 performance in the postseason with a spring training walkout. Thomas set a bad tone for 2001 by leaving camp the day he arrived and staging a six-day holdout over his contract. He looked silly when he couldn't get his swing together during spring training or at the start of the season. Thomas didn't have the luxury of time because he was lost for the season with a torn tendon in his right arm on April 27.

Hitting

When Thomas is on his game, taking balls and pulverizing strikes, there are few more dangerous hitters in the game. He can smash pitches to left field or use an inside-out swing to fight off good pitches to right field. But he's been on a roller-coaster ride since winning a batting title in 1997. He never seemed to get comfortable at the plate in 2001. He was especially ineffective against righthanders, who worked the outside part of the plate to exploit his stance, which is generally far off the plate. Thomas seemed to press, expanding his strike zone to chase more pitches than usual.

Baserunning & Defense

Thomas hasn't been enthusiastic about playing first base since 1997, when he became the White Sox' primary designated hitter. He played only three games at first last year. When he does, he provides a large target for infielders and does a decent job of scooping throws, but his lack of range and arm strength are concerns. He is a below-average runner but will try to steal an occasional base.

2002 Outlook

Sox owner Jerry Reinsdorf could have invoked a "diminished skills" clause in Thomas' contract after 2001, deferring all but $250,000 per year, but decided not to exploit Thomas' injury. He's not likely to ignore back-to-back unproductive seasons, putting an onus on Thomas to have a big year. The clause cannot be invoked if Thomas is among the top 10 in MVP voting. But if he falls short of that standard, this could be his last year in Chicago.

Position: DH
Bats: R **Throws:** R
Ht: 6' 5" **Wt:** 275

Opening Day Age: 33
Born: 5/27/68 in Columbus, GA
ML Seasons: 12
Nickname: Big Hurt

Overall Statistics

	G	AB	R	H	D	T	HR	RBI	SB	BB	SO	Avg	OBP	Slg
2001	20	68	8	15	3	0	4	10	0	10	12	.221	.316	.441
Career	1550	5542	1091	1770	364	10	348	1193	29	1198	847	.319	.438	.577

Where He Hits the Ball

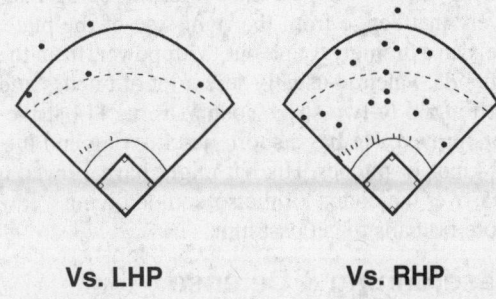

Vs. LHP   **Vs. RHP**

2001 Situational Stats

	AB	H	HR	RBI	Avg			AB	H	HR	RBI	Avg
Home	45	9	2	6	.200		LHP	16	5	2	4	.313
Road	23	6	2	4	.261		RHP	52	10	2	6	.192
First Half	68	15	4	10	.221		Sc Pos	18	3	1	5	.167
Scnd Half	0	0	0	0	-		Clutch	9	1	0	1	.111

2001 Rankings (American League)

- Did not rank near the top or bottom in any category

Jose Valentin

2001 Season

In the afterglow of a great 2000 season, Jose Valentin turned down more money from Baltimore and possibly a chance to join Seattle to remain with the White Sox. He might have wanted a mulligan on that decision after drifting through a frustrating year that wasn't salvaged with a career-high 28 homers. Valentin volunteered to change positions when the Sox pursued Alex Rodriguez, but in the end he moved to make room for Royce Clayton. He played center field but was haunted by leg problems that made life difficult in the outfield.

Hitting

The switch-hitting Valentin put together a career-best .509 slugging percentage despite being relatively ineffective from the right side of the plate. He's an extremely tough out, with power, from the left side. Valentin usually sees a lot of pitches and isn't afraid of two-strike counts, as his 114 strikeouts proved. He has a short, quick swing and hits all kinds of pitches. His bat might have slowed a tick over the course of the season, allowing a few more fastballs to get past him.

Baserunning & Defense

The jury is still out on where Valentin should be defensively. He started 18 games in center, 36 at shortstop and 57 at third base in 2001. His 36 errors in 2000 make it unlikely he will become a full-time shortstop again. He played well in the outfield and has the arm strength to stay there, but he believes that his chronic muscle pulls are aggravated by outfield play. He did not show a lot of range at third base, but he seldom played with two good wheels under him. He has a strong arm. Valentin has terrific instincts and is an excellent baserunner.

2002 Outlook

Jerry Manuel got tired of answering questions about how to fit Valentin and Clayton into the same lineup, making it likely that one of them or second baseman Ray Durham will be traded before Opening Day. Valentin would welcome one, as he did not seem to handle his uncertain role well. Still, his aggressive attitude and clubhouse leadership make him an important player for the White Sox.

Position: 3B/SS/CF
Bats: B **Throws:** R
Ht: 5'10" **Wt:** 185

Opening Day Age: 32
Born: 10/12/69 in Manati, PR
ML Seasons: 10
Pronunciation: VAL-en-teen

Overall Statistics

	G	AB	R	H	D	T	HR	RBI	SB	BB	SO	Avg	OBP	Slg
2001	124	438	74	113	22	2	28	68	9	50	114	.258	.336	.509
Career	1030	3415	559	845	191	26	143	503	106	407	805	.247	.328	.444

Where He Hits the Ball

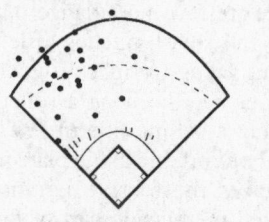 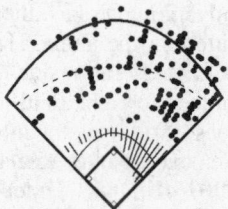

Vs. LHP   **Vs. RHP**

2001 Situational Stats

	AB	H	HR	RBI	Avg		AB	H	HR	RBI	Avg
Home	207	55	14	35	.266	LHP	64	13	3	7	.203
Road	231	58	14	33	.251	RHP	374	100	25	61	.267
First Half	238	67	14	36	.282	Sc Pos	86	26	5	39	.302
Scnd Half	200	46	14	32	.230	Clutch	72	20	4	13	.278

2001 Rankings (American League)

- 2nd in most pitches seen per plate appearance (4.14)
- 6th in lowest groundball-flyball ratio (0.7)
- 9th in HR frequency (15.6 ABs per HR) and lowest percentage of swings put into play (36.1)
- Led the White Sox in strikeouts, HR frequency (15.6 ABs per HR), most pitches seen per plate appearance (4.14) and slugging percentage vs. righthanded pitchers (.529)

David Wells

2001 Season

When the White Sox traded for David Wells, GM Ken Williams said it was because he wanted to know who would be starting Game 1 of the World Series. You had to admire the bold talk that followed a bold move, but in the end the Wells trade blew up like a trick cigar. Not only did Toronto complain that Williams had sent the Jays a package of damaged goods, but Wells turned out to be only slightly more healthy than Mike Sirotka, who was lost for the season with a torn labrum. Because of herniated discs in his back, Wells lasted only 16 starts before needing season-ending surgery. Wells caused his share of controversies along the way, the biggest coming when he questioned Frank Thomas' willingness to play hurt with an injury later diagnosed as a ruptured right triceps.

Pitching

There used to be two versions of Wells, both of which were equally effective. One featured a fastball in the 93-94 MPH range; the other used his pinpoint control to compensate for a fastball that peaked in the high-80s. It appears we've seen the last of the former version. Wells' sweeping curveball is a sight to see. He almost never threw harder than 91 MPH last season, but still used the curve to pitch some gems, including a win at Cleveland on Opening Day and three nine-inning gems. He works fast and gets a lot of groundballs.

Defense

Wells sometimes looks like a clown on the mound but don't be fooled. He's a better athlete than he looks. He has good reactions on comebackers and surprisingly quick feet. He is unusually easy to run against, mostly because of a slow delivery.

2002 Outlook

The White Sox rejected Wells' $9 million option for 2002, then lost interest in signing him to an incentive-laden contract because of questions about the diligence of his rehabilitation effort. Wells would love to make them regret their indifference. He would like to sign with one of the New York teams, but may wind up going to his eighth organization to extend his career. It will be a crapshoot for any team signing him.

Position: SP
Bats: L **Throws:** L
Ht: 6' 4" **Wt:** 235

Opening Day Age: 38
Born: 5/20/63 in Torrance, CA
ML Seasons: 15
Nickname: Boomer

Overall Statistics

	W	L	Pct.	ERA	G	GS	Sv	IP	H	BB	SO	HR	Ratio
2001	5	7	.417	4.47	16	16	0	100.2	120	21	59	12	1.40
Career	166	114	.593	4.08	495	325	13	2407.1	2462	559	1635	285	1.25

How Often He Throws Strikes

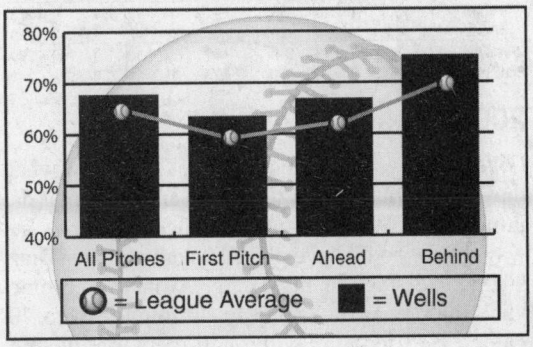

= League Average   ■ = Wells

2001 Situational Stats

	W	L	ERA	Sv	IP		AB	H	HR	RBI	Avg
Home	2	1	3.49	0	38.2	LHB	102	21	3	9	.206
Road	3	6	5.08	0	62.0	RHB	302	99	9	39	.328
First Half	5	7	4.47	0	100.2	Sc Pos	95	29	1	32	.305
Scnd Half	0	0	-	0	0.0	Clutch	41	12	1	6	.293

2001 Rankings (American League)

- 3rd in errors at pitcher (4) and highest batting average allowed vs. righthanded batters
- Led the White Sox in stolen bases allowed (17)

Chicago (AL)

Sandy Alomar Jr.

Position: C
Bats: R **Throws:** R
Ht: 6' 5" **Wt:** 235

Opening Day Age: 35
Born: 6/18/66 in Salinas, PR
ML Seasons: 14
Pronunciation: AL-uh-mar

Overall Statistics

	G	AB	R	H	D	T	HR	RBI	SB	BB	SO	Avg	OBP	Slg
2001	70	220	17	54	8	1	4	21	1	12	17	.245	.288	.345
Career	1063	3649	434	1002	203	9	97	480	25	180	407	.275	.313	.415

2001 Situational Stats

	AB	H	HR	RBI	Avg		AB	H	HR	RBI	Avg
Home	112	35	1	10	.313	LHP	44	12	2	7	.273
Road	108	19	3	11	.176	RHP	176	42	2	14	.239
First Half	185	45	2	17	.243	Sc Pos	52	13	1	15	.250
Scnd Half	35	9	2	4	.257	Clutch	41	14	1	5	.341

2001 Season

Give the Cleveland Indians credit. They knew what they were doing when they let Sandy Alomar Jr. jump to the White Sox as a free agent. There's no way that he could have played ahead of Einar Diaz at this late stage of his career. Alomar's chronic knee injuries again flared up, limiting him to 70 games. He tried to play through them, but wound up twice undergoing surgeries.

Hitting, Baserunning & Defense

Because of his knees, Alomar's best years as a hitter probably are past him. His bat has slowed so much that pitchers don't mess around with him, pumping in strikes. He seldom made them pay for this approach. Most of his hits are soft singles. He does a poor job working counts and rarely walks. He has a wealth of knowledge as a catcher, but moves poorly behind the plate. His arm remains decent, but his release is not as quick as it once was. He's a station-to-station runner.

2002 Outlook

Alomar returns for the final season on his two-year deal with the White Sox. The Sox need him to catch 100 games, but he hasn't done that since 1998. Manuel probably will take it easy on him early in the year, hoping that he can avoid the disabled list. Good luck.

Tony Graffanino

Position: 3B/2B
Bats: R **Throws:** R
Ht: 6' 1" **Wt:** 190

Opening Day Age: 29
Born: 6/6/72 in Amityville, NY
ML Seasons: 6
Pronunciation: graf-a-NEEN-oh

Overall Statistics

	G	AB	R	H	D	T	HR	RBI	SB	BB	SO	Avg	OBP	Slg
2001	74	145	23	44	9	0	2	15	4	16	29	.303	.370	.407
Career	414	964	148	248	48	8	19	95	21	101	205	.257	.329	.383

2001 Situational Stats

	AB	H	HR	RBI	Avg		AB	H	HR	RBI	Avg
Home	77	19	1	8	.247	LHP	47	15	1	6	.319
Road	68	25	1	7	.368	RHP	98	29	1	9	.296
First Half	84	22	2	6	.262	Sc Pos	35	7	0	12	.200
Scnd Half	61	22	0	9	.361	Clutch	31	8	1	5	.258

2001 Season

The rivalry being what it is, White Sox fans will never forgive Tony Graffanino for confusing a tag play for a force in a loss to the Cubs at Comiskey Park. It epitomized a season during which the heady Graffanino wasn't quite himself. He did some things well, but seldom made an impact late in a game. His playing time suffered with the arrival of Royce Clayton.

Hitting, Baserunning & Defense

Graffanino is aggressive in everything he does. He is the classic study of the guy who comes off the bench hacking at the first pitch. He is a fastball hitter with little power. He struggles deep in the count, when pitchers get him out with breaking pitches. He is a hard-nosed player, known for his hard slides into second. Unfortunately, he has little speed. He is a natural second baseman, yet does an adequate job at third base and even shortstop. He also played left field and first base last season.

2002 Outlook

There are no guarantees for Graffanino, but he's used to having to prove himself. On the strength of his good offense in 2001 and overall versatility, Graffanino goes to spring training with a leg up on a reserve's job. Manuel appreciates Graffanino's approach, but guys like him tend to come and go.

Bob Howry

Position: RP
Bats: L **Throws:** R
Ht: 6' 5" **Wt:** 220

Opening Day Age: 28
Born: 8/4/73 in Phoenix, AZ
ML Seasons: 4

Overall Statistics

	W	L	Pct.	ERA	G	GS	Sv	IP	H	BB	SO	HR	Ratio
2001	4	5	.444	4.69	69	0	5	78.2	85	30	64	11	1.46
Career	11	15	.423	3.71	247	0	49	271.2	234	116	255	32	1.29

2001 Situational Stats

	W	L	ERA	Sv	IP		AB	H	HR	RBI	Avg
Home	4	3	4.89	3	46.0	LHB	147	45	6	28	.306
Road	0	2	4.41	2	32.2	RHB	158	40	5	24	.253
First Half	3	3	4.58	3	39.1	Sc Pos	101	30	5	44	.297
Scnd Half	1	2	4.81	2	39.1	Clutch	178	56	5	35	.315

2001 Season

It was an up and down year for the quietly reliable Bob Howry, who bounced back from offseason shoulder surgery to work a full season and set a career high with 78.2 innings pitched. He often did not have his good stuff, though, and wound up with an ERA that was almost 1.4 runs higher than his career mark. He allowed 18 of 37 inherited runners to score.

Pitching & Defense

Howry always has gone right at hitters, challenging them to hit his fastball. That plan doesn't work, however, when your fastball struggles to hit 90 MPH after offseason surgery. He throws a curveball and a changeup when he's ahead in the count, but doesn't have the command to throw those pitches behind in the count. That makes his first pitch especially important. For a big man, Howry is an exceptional fielder who hasn't committed an error since 1998. He can be run on, however.

2002 Outlook

Howry signed a two-year contract extension with the Sox in late July. A return to form for Howry provides depth to the bullpen and a closer option other than Keith Foulke. If Howry struggles, he could wind up working the sixth and seventh innings instead of his customary slot in the eighth.

Mark Johnson

Position: C
Bats: L **Throws:** R
Ht: 6' 0" **Wt:** 185

Opening Day Age: 26
Born: 9/12/75 in Wheat Ridge, CO
ML Seasons: 4

Overall Statistics

	G	AB	R	H	D	T	HR	RBI	SB	BB	SO	Avg	OBP	Slg
2001	61	173	21	43	6	1	5	18	2	23	31	.249	.338	.382
Career	216	616	79	140	28	3	12	58	8	87	137	.227	.325	.341

2001 Situational Stats

	AB	H	HR	RBI	Avg		AB	H	HR	RBI	Avg
Home	85	21	2	9	.247	LHP	28	5	0	1	.179
Road	88	22	3	9	.250	RHP	145	38	5	17	.262
First Half	24	7	1	3	.292	Sc Pos	41	11	1	14	.268
Scnd Half	149	36	4	15	.242	Clutch	15	3	0	1	.200

2001 Season

Give Mark Johnson credit for mental toughness. He received back-to-back slaps from the organization in being dropped from the 2000 playoff roster and then losing his roster spot to rookie Josh Paul in the spring. Johnson did well playing regularly at Triple-A Charlotte, where he hit .270 with 24 RBI in 55 games before joining the Sox on June 19. Last year was his most productive season at the plate.

Hitting, Baserunning & Defense

Johnson is proof that no hitter is an easy out if he understands the strike zone. He seldom helps a pitcher out and twice led his minor leagues in walks. Johnson is developing some power, as he hit nine homers between Charlotte and Chicago last season. He is a major league-caliber receiver who knows the Sox' pitching staff better than any other catcher. He is a good athlete who could steal in double figures if he was on base more often.

2002 Outlook

Because he is a sound receiver and a lefty bat, Johnson could have a long career. Given concerns over Sandy Alomar's health and Josh Paul's abilities, this could be the first season that Johnson surpasses 250 at-bats. He needs to establish his presence quickly, however, because rising prospect Miguel Olivo figures to be in the mix in 2003.

Jeff Liefer

Position: LF/1B/3B/DH
Bats: L **Throws:** R
Ht: 6' 3" **Wt:** 210

Opening Day Age: 27
Born: 8/17/74 in Fontana, CA
ML Seasons: 3
Pronunciation: LEAF-er

Sean Lowe

Position: RP/SP
Bats: R **Throws:** R
Ht: 6' 2" **Wt:** 215

Opening Day Age: 31
Born: 3/29/71 in Dallas, TX
ML Seasons: 5

Overall Statistics

	G	AB	R	H	D	T	HR	RBI	SB	BB	SO	Avg	OBP	Slg
2001	83	254	36	65	13	0	18	39	0	20	69	.256	.313	.520
Career	133	378	44	95	20	1	18	53	2	28	101	.251	.304	.452

2001 Situational Stats

	AB	H	HR	RBI	Avg		AB	H	HR	RBI	Avg
Home	133	36	10	23	.271	LHP	19	2	0	0	.105
Road	121	29	8	16	.240	RHP	235	63	18	39	.268
First Half	138	35	9	17	.254	Sc Pos	63	15	3	20	.238
Scnd Half	116	30	9	22	.259	Clutch	33	7	2	5	.212

Overall Statistics

	W	L	Pct.	ERA	G	GS	Sv	IP	H	BB	SO	HR	Ratio
2001	9	4	.692	3.61	45	11	3	127.0	123	32	71	12	1.22
Career	17	11	.607	4.56	169	21	3	316.0	329	132	196	35	1.46

2001 Situational Stats

	W	L	ERA	Sv	IP		AB	H	HR	RBI	Avg
Home	5	2	4.26	2	61.1	LHB	235	66	5	26	.281
Road	4	2	3.02	2	65.2	RHB	245	57	7	27	.233
First Half	4	1	2.52	2	53.2	Sc Pos	120	28	1	39	.233
Scnd Half	5	3	4.42	1	73.1	Clutch	30	6	0	4	.200

2001 Season

If not for the White Sox's sentimental attachment to Harold Baines, Jeff Liefer would have spent a full season in the big leagues. Instead, he made the most of his opportunity when he was recalled on May 10, finally displaying his power potential in the majors. He lost playing time once Jose Canseco was signed, but still hit well enough to force the organization to keep playing him against righties.

Hitting, Baserunning & Defense

Liefer generates power from a swing that has been shortened in recent years. He homered once every 14 at-bats at Triple-A Charlotte in 2000, yet failed to homer in 124 at-bats with Chicago in 1999 and 2000. In his third try, he matched that ratio of one homer in every 14 at-bats. Liefer has hit lefties in the minors but was used almost exclusively as a platoon player. He's been a man without a position due to throwing problems. He started games at first base, third base, left field and right field last year. He is a slow runner who almost never steals a base.

2002 Outlook

Chicago wants to see more of Liefer, but isn't sure where he fits. A third-base platoon is possible if he fields adequately. A big spring could force manager Jerry Manuel to find him a spot. Otherwise he'll likely be an outfield reserve and bat off the bench.

2001 Season

For the second year in a row, the unsung Sean Lowe contributed a lot more than most of the White Sox' well-advertised pitching prospects. He helped manager Jerry Manuel keep his staff together by pitching well in a variety of roles. Lowe did this after an inauspicious beginning. After Manuel inexplicably didn't use him for a 14-day stretch in April, general manager Ken Williams sent him to Triple-A Charlotte for a refresher course. Lowe initially asked for a trade, but returned willing to let bygones be bygones. He has compiled a 17-6 record in three years with the Sox.

Pitching & Defense

Lowe comes at hitters with a fastball in the low-90s and a curveball that keeps hitters off balance. He is willing to work inside and thrives on the pressure of entering with runners on base. He is a groundball pitcher who can induce double plays when they are needed. He is most effective against righthanded hitters. Lowe is an average fielder.

2002 Outlook

Lowe has been Manuel's security blanket, but the righthander no longer is an option after he was traded to Pittsburgh in the Todd Ritchie deal. Lowe should get plenty of work.

Aaron Rowand

Position: LF/CF/RF
Bats: R **Throws:** R
Ht: 6' 1" **Wt:** 200

Opening Day Age: 24
Born: 8/29/77 in
Portland, OR
ML Seasons: 1

Chris Singleton

Great Range

Position: CF/LF
Bats: L **Throws:** L
Ht: 6' 2" **Wt:** 210

Opening Day Age: 29
Born: 8/15/72 in
Martinez, CA
ML Seasons: 3

Overall Statistics

	G	AB	R	H	D	T	HR	RBI	SB	BB	SO	Avg	OBP	Slg
2001	63	123	21	36	5	0	4	20	5	15	28	.293	.385	.431
Career	63	123	21	36	5	0	4	20	5	15	28	.293	.385	.431

2001 Situational Stats

	AB	H	HR	RBI	Avg		AB	H	HR	RBI	Avg
Home	68	20	3	15	.294	LHP	55	17	2	8	.309
Road	55	16	1	5	.291	RHP	68	19	2	12	.279
First Half	12	4	1	1	.333	Sc Pos	34	10	1	16	.294
Scnd Half	111	32	3	19	.288	Clutch	12	3	0	1	.250

2001 Season

While Aaron Rowand has never been one of Chicago's top prospects, he's been a productive player throughout his four-year pro career. When the Sox promoted Rowand from Triple-A Charlotte near midseason, he proved himself as a tough out, a clutch hitter and an in-your-face fielder, unafraid to run into outfield walls.

Hitting, Baserunning & Defense

With good upper-body strength, Rowand uses a short, quick swing to drive the ball all over the park. He has enough power to hit opposite-field homers. His plate discipline was a concern entering 2001, but he made tremendous strides at Charlotte that carried over to Chicago. His high on-base percentage wasn't projected. Usually a corner outfielder, Rowand played surprisingly well in center for Chicago. He has an average arm and throws accurately. He is not a burner, but can steal bases.

2002 Outlook

If the White Sox remain committed to Carlos Lee in left field, Rowand will have to win the everyday job in center to get 400-plus at-bats. He could wind up platooning with Chris Singleton. He could be an outstanding fourth outfielder, but it would be interesting to see what kind of numbers he could put up as a regular.

Overall Statistics

	G	AB	R	H	D	T	HR	RBI	SB	BB	SO	Avg	OBP	Slg
2001	140	392	57	117	21	5	7	45	12	20	61	.298	.331	.431
Career	420	1399	212	396	74	16	35	179	54	77	191	.283	.319	.434

2001 Situational Stats

	AB	H	HR	RBI	Avg		AB	H	HR	RBI	Avg
Home	187	59	4	21	.316	LHP	40	12	1	2	.300
Road	205	58	3	24	.283	RHP	352	105	6	43	.298
First Half	219	62	3	16	.283	Sc Pos	86	29	0	34	.337
Scnd Half	173	55	4	29	.318	Clutch	45	12	0	5	.267

2001 Season

Relegated to part-time status when Jose Valentin moved to center field, Chris Singleton worked hard with new batting coach Gary Ward and reclaimed his old job. He hit only .192 in April, but came on to hit .318 with surprisingly high .356 on-base and .491 slugging percentages after the All-Star break. He was as solid as ever defensively for a team that needs all the help it can get in the field.

Hitting, Baserunning & Defense

At times, it looks like pitchers can knock the bat out of Singleton's hands, but he was hitting the ball with authority late in the season. He shortened his swing and showed he could spray the ball into the gaps. The one thing he can't do is walk, a serious flaw for a guy with little power. Despite his speed, Singleton has trouble reading pitchers and was caught stealing on 11 out of 23 tries in 2001. He has excellent range and is an alert fielder. His arm is average, but he had nine assists last year.

2002 Outlook

Singleton always seems to be on the bubble and this year is no different. With Aaron Rowand and Joe Borchard in camp, Singleton will need a good spring to be the Opening Day center fielder. He seems destined for a career as a fourth or fifth outfielder, but has not accepted that viewpoint.

Chicago (AL)

Kip Wells

Traded To PIRATES

Position: SP/RP
Bats: R **Throws:** R
Ht: 6' 3" **Wt:** 195

Opening Day Age: 24
Born: 4/21/77 in Houston, TX
ML Seasons: 3

Overall Statistics

	W	L	Pct.	ERA	G	GS	Sv	IP	H	BB	SO	HR	Ratio
2001	10	11	.476	4.79	40	20	0	133.1	145	61	99	14	1.55
Career	20	21	.488	5.14	67	47	0	267.2	304	134	199	31	1.64

2001 Situational Stats

	W	L	ERA	Sv	IP		AB	H	HR	RBI	Avg
Home	5	3	3.63	0	57.0	LHB	247	66	7	29	.267
Road	5	8	5.66	0	76.1	RHB	269	79	7	41	.294
First Half	5	5	2.49	0	72.1	Sc Pos	157	41	2	55	.261
Scnd Half	5	6	7.52	0	61.0	Clutch	40	8	0	4	.200

2001 Season

While Kip Wells didn't do everything he had hoped, he did emerge as the only Wells to win 10 games for the White Sox. The former first-rounder avoided the run of injuries that jinxed Sox pitchers and split his season evenly between starting and relieving, making 20 appearances in both roles. He put up better numbers as a reliever after opening the season with four starts for Triple-A Charlotte.

Pitching & Defense

Former White Sox GM Ron Schueler once said Wells reminded him of a young Roger Clemens. While both are Texans, it is hard to see Wells developing into a dominant starter. His fastball is rarely above 93 MPH and he does not have an overwhelming breaking pitch. He's effective when he keeps the ball down in the strike zone, and he fared better against lefties than righties in 2001. Wells is a weak fielder who gets flustered when he is rushed. He has an average pickoff move.

2002 Outlook

Wells attacked hitters much better as a setup man last season, and could be valuable in that role. He wants to start, however, and his chance will come with the Pirates after he was moved in the December trade for Todd Ritchie.

Dan Wright

Position: SP
Bats: R **Throws:** R
Ht: 6' 5" **Wt:** 225

Opening Day Age: 24
Born: 12/14/77 in Longview, TX
ML Seasons: 1

Overall Statistics

	W	L	Pct.	ERA	G	GS	Sv	IP	H	BB	SO	HR	Ratio
2001	5	3	.625	5.70	13	12	0	66.1	78	39	36	12	1.76
Career	5	3	.625	5.70	13	12	0	66.1	78	39	36	12	1.76

2001 Situational Stats

	W	L	ERA	Sv	IP		AB	H	HR	RBI	Avg
Home	4	1	5.03	0	39.1	LHB	140	37	8	21	.264
Road	1	2	6.67	0	27.0	RHB	120	41	4	22	.342
First Half	0	0	-	0	0.0	Sc Pos	64	22	1	29	.344
Scnd Half	5	3	5.70	0	66.1	Clutch	10	2	0	0	.200

2001 Season

Dan Wright is a success story of the White Sox' arms buildup. He has been a double-digit winner in his two pro seasons, including 12 victories between Double-A Birmingham and Chicago in 2001. While he was wildly inconsistent with the Sox, he did not seem intimidated and had his best outings against Seattle and Cleveland.

Pitching & Defense

Before last season, both Wright's velocity and breaking pitch—a knuckle-curve—were rated as the best in the Sox' system. That says a lot, given how much talent the organization has stockpiled. Wright rarely showed the 95-MPH fastball that helped him reach the majors, as he generally topped out in the low 90s. He still was able to be effective because of his knuckle-curve, which freezes hitters. He was constantly behind in the count, however. He also must improve his fielding.

2002 Outlook

Had Wright finished strong in 2001, he could have locked up a spot in the 2002 rotation. Instead he will have to pitch well in spring training to earn it. It wouldn't hurt him to start in Triple-A, but there's an excellent chance that can be avoided. He enters the season with the same potential for upward mobility that Mark Buehrle displayed a year ago.

Other Chicago White Sox

Harold Baines (Pos: DH, **Age**: 43, **Bats**: L)

	G	AB	R	H	D	T	HR	RBI	SB	BB	SO	Avg	OBP	Slg
2001	32	84	3	11	1	0	0	6	0	8	16	.131	.202	.143
Career	2830	9908	1299	2866	488	49	384	1628	34	1062	1441	.289	.356	.465

Baines hit .133 in 83 at-bats before going on the DL with a strained hip flexor in mid-June. Chicago gave him one final at-bat in September, and he struck out. His career likely is over. 2002 Outlook: D

Rocky Biddle (Pos: RHP, **Age**: 25)

	W	L	Pct.	ERA	G	GS	Sv	IP	H	BB	SO	HR	Ratio
2001	7	8	.467	5.39	30	21	0	128.2	137	52	85	16	1.47
Career	8	10	.444	5.83	34	25	0	151.1	168	60	92	21	1.51

Biddle spent most of the year as a starter, but was inconsistent. His season ended a few weeks early when he had surgery to repair a small tear in his right labrum. He should be ready by spring training. 2002 Outlook: C

Jose Canseco (Pos: DH, **Age**: 37, **Bats**: R)

	G	AB	R	H	D	T	HR	RBI	SB	BB	SO	Avg	OBP	Slg
2001	76	256	46	66	8	0	16	49	2	45	75	.258	.366	.477
Career	1887	7057	1186	1877	340	14	462	1407	200	906	1942	.266	.353	.515

Canseco was playing for the independent Newark Bears before signing with Chicago in June. With Frank Thomas returning as the DH, Canseco will be looking for a new uniform. 2002 Outlook: C

Mark Dalesandro (Pos: C, **Age**: 33, **Bats**: R)

	G	AB	R	H	D	T	HR	RBI	SB	BB	SO	Avg	OBP	Slg
2001	1	0	0	0	0	0	0	0	0	0	0	-	-	-
Career	79	129	17	31	7	0	3	17	1	3	14	.240	.259	.364

Dalesandro was called up from Triple-A for a week due to injuries. He didn't have a plate appearance, and hasn't had one in the majors since 1999. 2002 Outlook: D

Cal Eldred (Pos: RHP, **Age**: 34)

	W	L	Pct.	ERA	G	GS	Sv	IP	H	BB	SO	HR	Ratio
2001	0	1	.000	13.50	2	2	0	6.0	12	3	6	1	2.50
Career	74	68	.521	4.57	196	191	0	1196.2	1172	510	789	150	1.41

Eldred had a five-inch screw inserted into his right elbow in 2000. He felt pain in that same elbow two innings into his second start of the season and did not pitch again. He is expected to retire. 2002 Outlook: D

Alan Embree (Pos: LHP, **Age**: 32)

	W	L	Pct.	ERA	G	GS	Sv	IP	H	BB	SO	HR	Ratio
2001	1	4	.200	7.33	61	0	0	54.0	65	17	59	14	1.52
Career	18	19	.486	4.86	364	4	4	346.0	333	156	317	47	1.41

Embree throws hard but has little movement. Chicago did not pick up his 2002 option, but as a lefty with a live arm, he'll find work somewhere. 2002 Outlook: C

Antonio Osuna (Pos: RHP, **Age**: 28)

	W	L	Pct.	ERA	G	GS	Sv	IP	H	BB	SO	HR	Ratio
2001	0	0	-	20.77	4	0	0	4.1	8	2	6	3	2.31
Career	24	21	.533	3.50	269	0	10	331.1	269	143	352	35	1.24

Osuna's season ended after 4.1 innings due to a torn labrum in his pitching shoulder. He had a strong 2000

campaign after surgery on his pitching elbow in 1999, so a successful 2002 season is possible. 2002 Outlook: B

Josh Paul (Pos: C, **Age**: 26, **Bats**: R)

	G	AB	R	H	D	T	HR	RBI	SB	BB	SO	Avg	OBP	Slg
2001	57	139	20	37	11	0	3	18	6	13	25	.266	.327	.410
Career	99	228	37	61	15	2	4	27	7	18	46	.268	.323	.404

Paul's receiving and leadership skills are advanced, but his bat has taken more time to develop. The Sox like him as a prospect, but he hasn't hit any better in Chicago than he has in the minors. 2002 Outlook: B

Herbert Perry (Pos: 3B/1B, **Age**: 32, **Bats**: R)

	G	AB	R	H	D	T	HR	RBI	SB	BB	SO	Avg	OBP	Slg
2001	92	285	38	73	21	1	7	32	2	23	55	.256	.326	.411
Career	337	1088	163	303	75	4	28	150	8	80	203	.278	.342	.432

Chicago moved Jose Valentin to third base for much of the season, which cut into Perry's playing time. He was traded to Texas in November and likely will have the same role as in Chicago last year. 2002 Outlook: C

Bill Pulsipher (Pos: LHP, **Age**: 28)

	W	L	Pct.	ERA	G	GS	Sv	IP	H	BB	SO	HR	Ratio
2001	0	0	-	6.00	37	0	0	30.0	36	21	20	5	1.90
Career	13	19	.406	5.13	101	46	0	323.0	356	139	201	44	1.53

Pulsipher's effectiveness in the majors has been minimal. He refused an assignment to Triple-A Charlotte in October, thus becoming a free agent. 2002 Outlook: C

Julio Ramirez (Pos: CF, **Age**: 24, **Bats**: R)

	G	AB	R	H	D	T	HR	RBI	SB	BB	SO	Avg	OBP	Slg
2001	22	37	2	3	0	0	0	1	2	2	15	.081	.128	.081
Career	37	58	5	6	1	0	0	3	2	3	21	.103	.148	.121

Ramirez is a tremendous fielder with a rocket arm and good speed. His lack of patience at the plate, however, keeps him from holding down a job as a reserve in the majors. He signed a minor league contract to stay with the White Sox. 2002 Outlook: C

Ken Vining (Pos: LHP, **Age**: 27)

	W	L	Pct.	ERA	G	GS	Sv	IP	H	BB	SO	HR	Ratio
2001	0	0	-	17.55	8	0	0	6.2	15	7	3	3	3.30
Career	0	0	-	17.55	8	0	0	6.2	15	7	3	3	3.30

Vining's last start was in 1999 before he underwent elbow surgery. He's pitched well in the minors since then, but with a plethora of young arms in the system, Vining won't have an easy path to the majors. 2002 Outlook: C

Kelly Wunsch (Pos: LHP, **Age**: 29)

	W	L	Pct.	ERA	G	GS	Sv	IP	H	BB	SO	HR	Ratio
2001	2	1	.667	7.66	33	0	0	22.1	21	9	16	4	1.34
Career	8	4	.667	4.20	116	0	1	83.2	71	38	67	8	1.30

Wunsch appeared in a league-high 83 games in 2000, and subsequently, had to undergo surgery for a torn left rotator cuff in June. He should return as the top lefty option in the Chicago bullpen in 2002. 2002 Outlook: B

Chicago (AL)

Chicago White Sox Minor League Prospects

Organization Overview:

Last summer, injuries created lost seasons for several young pitchers in the White Sox' system, including Jim Parque, Kelly Wunsch, Lorenzo Barcelo, Jason Stumm and Jon Rauch. The bad news may have slowed the progress of assembling the next stud rotation, but injuries heal and the Sox have tons of pitching talent ready to step up. The 2001 success of southpaw Mark Buehrle, who nearly won the American League ERA title, should provide inspiration to the likes of Jon Garland, Dan Wright, Jon Rauch, Gary Glover, Matt Ginter, Matt Guerrier, Corwin Malone and a host of other promising young pitchers who give the White Sox so much pitching depth in the minors. On top of that, a pair of Joes, Crede and Borchard, could break into the White Sox' lineup before the 2002 season is out.

Lorenzo Barcelo

Position: P
Bats: R **Throws:** R
Ht: 6' 4" **Wt:** 220
Opening Day Age: 24
Born: 8/10/77 in San Pedro de Macoris, DR

Recent Statistics

	W	L	ERA	G	GS	Sv	IP	H	R	BB	SO	HR
2001 AAA Charlotte	1	0	5.40	2	0	0	5.0	6	3	1	5	2
2001 AL Chicago	1	0	4.71	17	0	0	21.0	24	13	8	15	1

Signed by the Giants at age 16 in 1994, Barcelo perhaps had the highest ceiling of any of the talent acquired by the White Sox in the White Flag trade of '97. His career was slowed by Tommy John surgery the following year, but he enjoyed an impressive first full season back in 2000. After making 17 starts at Triple-A Charlotte that year, he joined the Sox' bullpen in July and posted a 3.69 ERA in 22 appearances. It seemed his mid-90s fastball and sharp-breaking curve were in the majors for good, but rotator cuff surgery last June set him back again. His rehab is progressing well and Barcelo should be ready to go when competition for jobs heats up in the spring.

Joe Borchard

Position: OF
Bats: B **Throws:** R
Ht: 6' 5" **Wt:** 220
Opening Day Age: 23
Born: 11/25/78 in Panorama City, CA

Recent Statistics

	G	AB	R	H	D	T	HR	RBI	SB	BB	SO	Avg
2000 R White Sox	7	29	3	12	4	0	0	8	0	4	4	.414
2000 A Winston-Sal	14	52	7	15	3	0	2	7	0	6	9	.288
2000 AA Birmingham	6	22	3	5	0	1	0	3	0	3	8	.227
2001 AA Birmingham	133	515	95	152	27	1	27	98	3	67	158	.295
2001 MLE	133	507	89	144	25	0	26	92	3	54	169	.284

After going 12th overall in 2000, Borchard split time between the Rookie-level team in Arizona and high Class-A Winston-Salem before finishing the season at Double-A Birmingham. Borchard, who comes equipped with power potential from both sides of the plate and an excellent arm, returned to Birmingham in 2001 and enjoyed a power explosion. He led the Southern League in RBI and finished second in homers. He also fared well in the White Sox' experiment to see if he can make it as a center fielder, and he'll play there until he shows he can't handle the job in the majors. Borchard, an aggressive player who wants to contribute, will swing at pitches he shouldn't. He needs to put in more work on his strike-zone discipline.

Joe Crede

Position: 3B
Bats: R **Throws:** R
Ht: 6' 3" **Wt:** 195
Opening Day Age: 23
Born: 4/26/78 in Jefferson City, MO

Recent Statistics

	G	AB	R	H	D	T	HR	RBI	SB	BB	SO	Avg
2001 AAA Charlotte	124	463	67	128	34	1	17	65	2	46	88	.276
2001 AL Chicago	17	50	1	11	1	1	0	7	1	3	11	.220
2001 MLE	124	460	66	125	33	0	17	64	1	46	92	.272

Drafted in 1996, Crede has made steady progress. He broke out in the high Class-A Carolina League in 1998, nearly claiming Triple Crown honors despite a painful bone spur in his right big toe. The injury lingered into 1999, forcing season-ending surgery that July. Crede was back on track at Double-A Birmingham in 2000, hitting for both average and power, and his numbers were nearly as good at Triple-A Charlotte last summer. Defensively, his running speed is below average, but he has plenty of arm and should be fine at third base. Dealing Herbert Perry opens the door for Crede, who seemed overmatched at times when he spent 12 days with the Sox last June. The Sox believe he was trying to do too much because he knew his opportunity was finite.

Matt Ginter

Position: P
Bats: R **Throws:** R
Ht: 6' 1" **Wt:** 215
Opening Day Age: 24
Born: 12/24/77 in Winchester, KY

Recent Statistics

	W	L	ERA	G	GS	Sv	IP	H	R	BB	SO	HR
2001 AAA Charlotte	2	3	2.59	22	1	0	76.1	62	26	24	67	3
2001 AL Chicago	1	0	5.22	20	0	0	39.2	34	23	14	24	2

The Sox' first-round pick in 1999, Ginter has risen rapidly, jumping from Class-A Burlington in '99 to Double-A Birmingham in 2000 to Triple-A Charlotte in 2001. He's been successful every step of the way, but so far hasn't been able to use his mid-90s fastball and nasty slider to produce similar results in Chicago. The quality of those two offerings make him a potential closer, but he hasn't trusted his stuff or used it effectively to get ahead of major league hitters. He's been working on a changeup, which he used a lot at Charlotte, but he didn't call on it much in Chicago. The Sox expect he'll show more at the major league level in 2002.

Gary Glover

Position: P
Bats: R **Throws:** R
Ht: 6' 5" **Wt:** 205

Opening Day Age: 25
Born: 12/3/76 in
Cleveland, OH

Recent Statistics

	W	L	ERA	G	GS	Sv	IP	H	R	BB	SO	HR
2001 AAA Charlotte	2	1	1.88	6	6	0	38.1	21	8	5	29	3
2001 AL Chicago	5	5	4.93	46	11	0	100.1	98	61	32	63	16

Glover, a Blue Jays pick in 1994, was dealt to Chicago in November 2000. He hadn't had much minor league success, except for a solid stint at Double-A Knoxville in 1999, yet the White Sox were impressed with his big body and great arm. Mechanical problems with his delivery had been known to take some velocity off an impressive fastball, but that wasn't an issue last spring, and his stuff and confidence were much better in 2001. He showed a mid-90s fastball and a hard-breaking slider in the spring, and he broke camp with the Sox. During the year, he improved his curveball and worked on a change, but remains a fastball-slider pitcher. He tired late in the season, but the Sox still view him as a starter.

Matt Guerrier

Position: P
Bats: R **Throws:** R
Ht: 6' 3" **Wt:** 190

Opening Day Age: 23
Born: 8/2/78 in
Cleveland, OH

Recent Statistics

	W	L	ERA	G	GS	Sv	IP	H	R	BB	SO	HR
2000 A Winston-Sal	0	3	1.30	30	0	19	34.2	25	13	12	35	0
2000 AA Birmingham	3	1	2.70	23	0	7	23.1	17	9	12	19	1
2001 AA Birmingham	11	3	3.10	15	15	0	98.2	85	42	32	75	8
2001 AAA Charlotte	7	1	3.54	12	12	0	81.1	75	33	18	43	7

A 10th-round pick in 1999, Guerrier is a sinker-slider pitcher with an outstanding changeup. While he's not overpowering, there's nothing straight in his arsenal, and he can paint the strike zone with all of his pitches. His fastball is in the 88-91 MPH range. Armed with the mentality of a closer, Guerrier is a consummate pitcher who doesn't make mistakes. He'll give up the occasional solo homer, but he bears down when runners are aboard. He didn't make the rotation of his first two clubs in 1999 and 2000, but through his bullpen success he emerged as a prospect and began starting in 2001. And Guerrier went 18-4 (3.30) between Double-A Birmingham and Triple-A Charlotte. He has a career ERA of 2.80.

Corwin Malone

Position: P
Bats: R **Throws:** L
Ht: 6' 3" **Wt:** 200

Opening Day Age: 21
Born: 7/3/80 in Grove
Hill, AL

Recent Statistics

	W	L	ERA	G	GS	Sv	IP	H	R	BB	SO	HR
2000 A Burlington	2	3	4.90	38	1	0	71.2	67	52	60	82	4
2001 A Kannapolis	11	4	2.00	18	18	0	112.1	83	30	44	119	2
2001 A Winston-Sal	0	1	1.72	5	5	0	36.2	25	10	10	38	1
2001 AA Birmingham	2	0	2.33	4	4	0	19.1	8	5	12	20	2

A high schooler drafted in 1999, Malone has the tools to succeed, but had been plagued by an erratic delivery that sent baseballs to the screen and produced a low percentage of effective pitches. During a breakout 2001 season, he learned to repeat his delivery consistently. He has good stuff, including a 92-93 MPH fastball, hard-breaking curve and an above-average changeup. Malone, a big kid who is an intense competitor, climbed through three levels in 2001 and was among the best on his team at each one. Suddenly he looks like a guy who could land near the top of a major league rotation.

Jon Rauch

Position: P
Bats: R **Throws:** R
Ht: 6' 11" **Wt:** 230

Opening Day Age: 23
Born: 9/27/78 in
Louisville, KY

Recent Statistics

	W	L	ERA	G	GS	Sv	IP	H	R	BB	SO	HR
2000 A Winston-Sal	11	3	2.86	18	18	0	110.0	102	49	33	124	10
2000 AA Birmingham	5	1	2.25	8	8	0	56.0	36	18	16	63	4
2001 AAA Charlotte	1	3	5.79	6	6	0	28.0	28	20	7	27	8

The 6-foot-11 Rauch, a third-round pick in 1999, took his 94-MPH fastball to the high Class-A Carolina League in his first full season as a pro, and dominated to the tune of 11-3 (2.86). He moved on to Double-A Birmingham in July, going 5-1 (2.25), and he closed out 2000 by fanning 21 batters in 11 innings for the gold-medal Olympic team. For someone his size, he showed a remarkable mix of power and control, thanks to a very good arm and superb mechanics. Unfortunately, his 2001 campaign was over after six Triple-A starts, as he needed surgery to repair a torn labrum in his pitching shoulder. His rehab in Arizona continues. He should be ready to go soon after camp breaks.

Others to Watch

Drafted in the fifth round last June, shortstop **Andy Gonzalez** (20) stands 6-foot-4 and should develop a power stroke as he matures. He debuted by batting .323 and slugging .508 in 189 at-bats in the Rookie-level Arizona League last summer. His defensive skills are raw, but he shows solid range and a good arm. . . The Sox made 6-foot-5 righthander **Kris Honel** (19) the 16th overall pick in the 2001 draft. Despite a mysterious wrist ailment that briefly dropped his velocity into the low 80s, Honel recorded a 2.89 ERA and fanned 53 in 56 innings between two Rookie-level stops. He has a great arm and a projectable body. He throws a knee-buckling curve and a 92-93 MPH fastball. . . Southpaw **Dennis Ulacia** (21), a heavy-legged high school kid drafted in 1999, was more committed to baseball in 2001, coming into camp lighter and more toned with a more serious approach. Ulacia won a game at four different levels, working at two Class-A stops at Kannapolis and Winston-Salem, as well as Double-A Birmingham, and pitching a gem in one start at Triple-A Charlotte. For the year, he was 15-5 with a 2.85 ERA. He throws a good slider, and his fastball and changeup are above-average pitches.

Chicago (AL)

Jacobs Field

Offense

The Indians hit .282 at home in 2001, their lowest batting average since Jacobs Field opened in 1994. It's still a great ballpark to hit in, especially for lefthanded sluggers. The wind usually blows from left to right field, making the power alley in right-center well within reach. The hitting background is good and there's not much foul territory. The bounces in the right-field corner are tricky enough that any ball hit down there is a potential triple.

Defense

The park is a breeding ground for errors. The infield grass is thick but short, and groundballs get through quickly. There were fewer bad hops on the infield in 2001, but because both teams put the ball in play so much at Jacobs Field, errors are bound to happen. The bounces off the 19-foot outfield wall that stretches from left to left-center field are tricky, and fielders must back each other up.

Who It Helps the Most

Lefty Jim Thome hit 30 of his 49 homers at home. He's good at pulling the ball down the 325-foot right-field line. Russell Branyan, another lefty, hit 11 of his 20 homers at home. Juan Gonzalez, in his only year as an Indian, hit 22 homers and drove in 74 runs at home. His righthanded swing with a slight uppercut was made to drive the ball into the left-field bleachers. Lefty Chuck Finley, no longer a power pitcher, went 4-0 in nine starts at home, compared to 4-7 on the road.

Who It Hurts the Most

Power pitchers like righthander Bartolo Colon can get stung. The opposition hit only .254 against him at home, but he gave up 19 homers and went 5-9. The entire staff gave up 20 more homers at home (84) than on the road (64).

Rookies & Newcomers

Matt Lawton has hit five homers and slugged .490 in 98 at-bats at Jacob Field. Milton Bradley hasn't played much there, but he's being counted on to replace Kenny Lofton. He'll have plenty of room to run and a good fence to climb in center field.

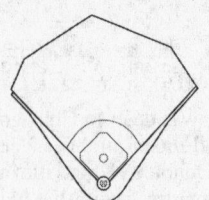

Dimensions: LF-325, LCF-370, CF-405, RCF-375, RF-325

Capacity: 43,368

Elevation: 660 feet

Surface: Grass

Foul Territory: Small

Park Factors

2001 Season

	Home Games			Away Games			
	Indians	Opp	Total	Indians	Opp	Total	Index
G	71	71	142	73	73	146	—
Avg	.281	.272	.276	.278	.269	.274	101
AB	2405	2518	4923	2563	2457	5020	101
R	390	371	761	410	366	776	101
H	675	684	1359	712	662	1374	102
2B	130	148	278	132	142	274	103
3B	10	8	18	23	17	40	46
HR	101	75	176	86	59	145	124
BB	255	254	509	252	259	511	102
SO	474	557	1031	481	522	1003	105
E	46	38	84	51	57	108	80
E-Infield	41	32	73	37	45	82	92
LHB-Avg	.281	.275	.278	.277	.295	.286	97
LHB-HR	50	29	79	40	24	64	118
RHB-Avg	.281	.269	.275	.278	.253	.265	103
RHB-HR	51	46	97	46	35	81	128

1999-2001

	Home Games			Away Games			
	Indians	Opp	Total	Indians	Opp	Total	Index
G	215	215	430	217	217	434	—
Avg	.292	.274	.283	.282	.268	.275	103
AB	7326	7671	14997	7721	7258	14979	101
R	1280	1142	2422	1293	1093	2386	102
H	2136	2101	4237	2181	1943	4124	104
2B	389	447	836	438	387	825	101
3B	40	37	77	50	43	93	83
HR	303	244	547	259	215	474	115
BB	885	827	1712	882	832	1714	100
SO	1386	1629	3015	1449	1518	2967	101
E	137	157	294	114	172	286	104
E-Infield	114	126	240	89	139	228	106
LHB-Avg	.293	.269	.281	.278	.278	.278	101
LHB-HR	152	115	267	121	93	214	120
RHB-Avg	.291	.278	.284	.287	.260	.273	104
RHB-HR	151	129	280	138	122	260	111

2001 Rankings (American League)

- Highest RHB home-run factor
- Second-highest strikeout factor
- Third-highest home-run factor
- Third-highest LHB home-run factor
- Lowest triple factor
- Lowest error factor

Charlie Manuel

2001 Season

Charlie Manuel won 91 games and led the Indians back to the postseason for the sixth time in seven years after falling short in 2000. Starting in late August, he was hospitalized three times for colon and gall bladder problems. He was a patient at the Cleveland Clinic when the Tribe clinched the American League Central on September 30, and didn't rejoin the team until the final weekend of the regular season. The Indians trailed the Twins at the All-Star break by five games, but rallied to win the division by six. They lost the Division Series to Seattle in five games.

Offense

Manuel saw the top of his veteran lineup age last year. With Kenny Lofton and Omar Vizquel not stealing as many bases as in the past, he had to wait for the big hit instead of trying to create runs. He made frequent use of the sacrifice bunt and sacrifice fly, but with a lineup of mostly power hitters, there weren't many opportunities to hit-and-run. He prefers a set lineup, but will ride the hot bat in platoon situations. He made better and more frequent use of pinch-hitters.

Pitching & Defense

Cleveland starters pitched the fewest innings in the AL last year, while the bullpen pitched the most. With the help of former pitching coach Dick Pole, Manuel protected rookie C.C. Sabathia, who won 17 games but was still fresh at the end of the year. Conversely, he had no problem letting Bartolo Colon throw 120 to 130 pitches a game. Manuel didn't demand a lot of extra defensive work from his fielders and pitchers during the season, and they could have used it. He made frequent use of defensive replacements, especially in left field.

2002 Outlook

Manuel's option for 2002 wasn't picked up until after the postseason. With new general manager Mark Shapiro in charge, the payroll getting cut and Manuel's health problems, it was significant that the manager didn't receive an option for 2003. Manuel is going to have to show he can manage a younger roster, with less offensive ability and more reliance on pitching.

Born: 1/04/44 in Northfork, WV

Playing Experience: 1969-1975, Min, LA

Managerial Experience: 2 seasons

Manager Statistics

Year	Team, Lg	W	L	Pct	GB	Finish
2001	Cleveland, AL	91	71	.562	—	1st Central
2 Seasons		181	143	.559	—	—

2001 Starting Pitchers by Days Rest

	<=3	4	5	6+
Indians Starts	3	76	47	26
Indians ERA	11.17	5.88	5.25	3.45
AL Avg Starts	1	78	48	24
AL ERA	5.92	4.69	4.58	4.58

2001 Situational Stats

	Charlie Manuel	AL Average
Hit & Run Success %	32.7	35.0
Stolen Base Success %	65.8	71.0
Platoon Pct.	60.7	59.1
Defensive Subs	49	26
High-Pitch Outings	10	6
Quick/Slow Hooks	28/17	19/16
Sacrifice Attempts	67	54

2001 Rankings (American League)

- 1st in sacrifice-bunt percentage (89.6%), quick hooks, starts with over 120 pitches (10) and relief appearances (484)
- 2nd in sacrifice bunt attempts, starts on three days rest and one-batter pitcher appearances (41)
- 3rd in intentional walks (34), defensive substitutions, mid-inning pitching changes (202) and first-batter platoon percentage

Cleveland

Roberto Alomar

2001 Season

Roberto Alomar put together his second MVP-caliber season in the last three years. He set a career high in batting average and tied his career mark in hits. He was in contention for the batting title until he hit .278 in August. He made his 12th trip to the All-Star Game and won his 10th Gold Glove, the most ever by a second baseman. Alomar, usually a good postseason hitter, batted .190 (4-for-21) in the Division Series against Seattle.

Hitting

A skilled switch-hitter who adjusts to the situation, Alomar will bunt one pitch and hit the next one out. He's a guess hitter who can be fooled on high fastballs and breaking balls down and away. He likes to bunt in the first inning to try to give his pitcher the early lead. Alomar works the count well from the No. 3 spot, and did a great job getting cleanup hitter Juan Gonzalez to the plate with runners on base. He hit .424 with runners in scoring position in 2001 after hitting .276 in those situations in 2000.

Baserunning & Defense

Alomar had 33 infield hits, while stealing 30 or more bases for the third straight year. He picks his spots on steals, with many coming late in one-sided games. He gets a good jump on pitchers, especially when it comes to stealing third. Defensively, he's earned every Gold Glove he's won. He's a second baseman with a shortstop's arm. His range going both left and right is still excellent, but hard slides can disrupt him from making the pivot.

2002 Outlook

The Indians were worried about Alomar's reaction to the payroll cuts and the team's decision to not bring Gonzalez back. Some felt he may have to be traded. But Alomar's initial response to the Tribe's new direction was positive. Yet he was dealt to the Mets in an eight-player trade on December 11. He moves Edgardo Alfonzo to third base, and the rock-solid Rey Ordonez works in the middle as Alomar's new pivot partner. He leaves behind Omar Vizquel, but joins a team more intent on winning now. He's signed through this year with an option for 2003.

Position: 2B
Bats: B **Throws:** R
Ht: 6' 0"   **Wt:** 185

Opening Day Age: 34
Born: 2/5/68 in Ponce, PR
ML Seasons: 14
Pronunciation: AL-uh-mar
Nickname: Robby

Overall Statistics

	G	AB	R	H	D	T	HR	RBI	SB	BB	SO	Avg	OBP	Slg
2001	157	575	113	193	34	12	20	100	30	80	71	.336	.415	.541
Career	2034	7796	1341	2389	446	72	190	1018	446	902	949	.306	.378	.455

Where He Hits the Ball

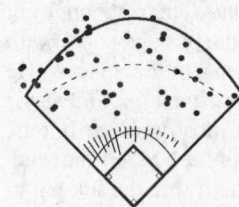
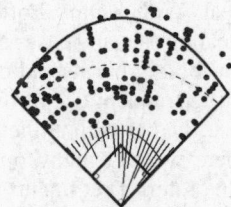

Vs. LHP   **Vs. RHP**

2001 Situational Stats

	AB	H	HR	RBI	Avg		AB	H	HR	RBI	Avg
Home	288	94	7	33	.326	LHP	154	43	7	23	.279
Road	287	99	13	67	.345	RHP	421	150	13	77	.356
First Half	310	111	9	52	.358	Sc Pos	132	56	3	68	.424
Scnd Half	265	82	11	48	.309	Clutch	80	22	2	17	.275

2001 Rankings (American League)

- 1st in fielding percentage at second base (.993)
- 2nd in triples, batting average with runners in scoring position and batting average vs. righthanded pitchers
- 3rd in batting average, on-base percentage vs. righthanded pitchers (.437), batting average on the road and steals of third (8)
- Led the Indians in batting average, runs scored, hits, singles, doubles, triples, stolen bases, times on base (277), games played, stolen-base percentage (83.3), steals of third (8), batting average with runners in scoring position, batting average vs. righthanded pitchers and batting average on the road
- Led AL second basemen in batting average

Dave Burba

Position: SP
Bats: R **Throws:** R
Ht: 6' 4" **Wt:** 240

Opening Day Age: 35
Born: 7/7/66 in Dayton, OH
ML Seasons: 12
Pronunciation: BUR-ba

2001 Season

Dave Burba never felt comfortable last season, even when he started the year at 8-2. His mechanics didn't feel right. He wasn't pitching like he was supposed to pitch and he was worried about the Indians picking up his $5 million option for 2002. He went 2-8 after his fast start, losing his spot in the starting rotation twice.

Pitching

The split-finger fastball gave Burba three good seasons in Cleveland. But by throwing it so much, he lost velocity on his fastball. When Burba went to throw his 88-92 MPH fastball last year, it wasn't there. Hitters stopped swinging at his 80-84 MPH splitter, which often dropped out of the strike zone, and that forced him to throw too many fat fastballs. Burba throws a curveball and changeup, with the curveball being the better of the two. He was moved to the bullpen in August and started using his legs more in his delivery. His velocity increased as a reliever, but his problems continued. He was convinced he was tipping his pitches, and that hurt his concentration.

Defense

Burba is an average fielder, but at times last year he was so frustrated that he'd forget to do fundamental things such as covering home on a wild pitch with a runner at third. He also got beat to first base a couple of times on bunts and infield grounders to the right side. Burba, who throws a lot of splitters in the dirt, doesn't hold baserunners well. In the last two years, the opposition has gone 40-for-46 in stolen bases when he's on the mound.

2002 Outlook

In the end, Burba was justified in worrying about his $5 million option, as the Indians didn't pick it up, making him a free agent. They did leave the door open for his return for less money, but that depends on what kind of market there is for him. He went 56-35 in four years with the Indians. For Burba to continue winning, the Indians believe he needs to pitch inside more.

Overall Statistics

	W	L	Pct.	ERA	G	GS	Sv	IP	H	BB	SO	HR	Ratio
2001	10	10	.500	6.21	32	27	0	150.2	188	54	118	16	1.61
Career	105	80	.568	4.46	408	211	1	1512.0	1510	660	1218	173	1.44

How Often He Throws Strikes

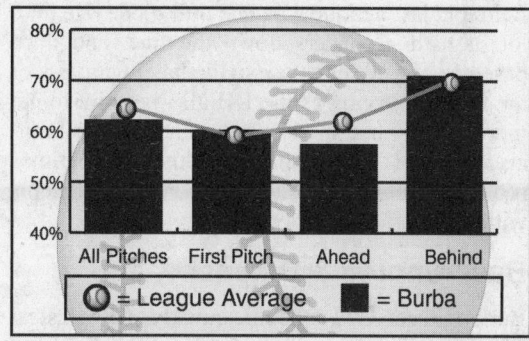

○ = League Average   ■ = Burba

2001 Situational Stats

	W	L	ERA	Sv	IP		AB	H	HR	RBI	Avg
Home	6	5	6.31	0	77.0	LHB	301	108	10	54	.359
Road	4	5	6.11	0	73.2	RHB	314	80	6	48	.255
First Half	8	6	6.45	0	90.2	Sc Pos	180	60	2	80	.333
Scnd Half	2	4	5.85	0	60.0	Clutch	15	2	0	0	.133

2001 Rankings (American League)
- 3rd in highest batting average allowed vs. lefthanded batters and highest batting average allowed with runners in scoring position

Ellis Burks

2001 Season

Ellis Burks signed a three-year, $20 million deal before last season with the idea of playing at least 100 games in the outfield. Sore knees limited him and he played all but 22 of his 124 games at DH. He was on the way to a strong offensive season when Houston's Octavio Dotel broke his right thumb with a pitch on July 15. Burks came back too soon and drove in just 19 runs in his final 46 games.

Hitting

He still has a short, quick swing at age 37. Burks looks for fastballs early in the count and isn't shy about swinging the bat. He can take pitches to right field, but last year he was in a pull mode. He hit a lot of hard grounders down the line, and third basemen played him close to the bag regardless of the inning. Serving as the DH allowed him to get more at-bats than his last two years in San Francisco, but his chronically sore knees sometimes robbed him of power and balance. He has problems with breaking balls away.

Baserunning & Defense

Burks still gets down the line quickly and will steal a base if a pitcher ignores him. He's old school and will go into second base hard to break up a double play. The Indians would have been better in 2001 if Burks could have played more left field, but his knees wouldn't cooperate. When he did play, he was aggressive and showed good speed going into the gap. He's not afraid of the wall and has a decent arm.

2002 Outlook

With Juan Gonzalez gone through free agency, the Indians need Burks or Jim Thome to move into the cleanup spot. Manager Charlie Manuel said he might even hit Burks leadoff against certain lefthanders. Burks came to the Indians with a reputation of being a positive influence in the clubhouse. The reputation held true, and the Indians will need more of his leadership as they begin to restructure.

Position: DH/LF
Bats: R **Throws:** R
Ht: 6' 2" **Wt:** 205

Opening Day Age: 37
Born: 9/11/64 in Vicksburg, MS
ML Seasons: 15

Overall Statistics

	G	AB	R	H	D	T	HR	RBI	SB	BB	SO	Avg	OBP	Slg
2001	124	439	83	123	29	1	28	74	5	62	85	.280	.369	.542
Career	1796	6483	1128	1893	363	62	313	1086	176	719	1178	.292	.364	.512

Where He Hits the Ball

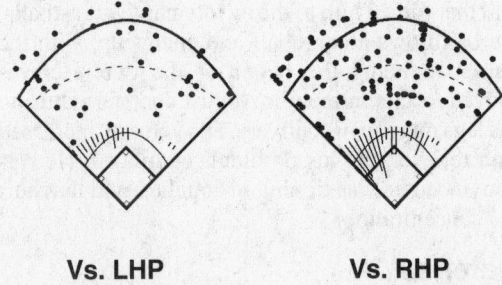

Vs. LHP   **Vs. RHP**

2001 Situational Stats

	AB	H	HR	RBI	Avg		AB	H	HR	RBI	Avg
Home	220	66	15	36	.300	LHP	110	27	9	17	.245
Road	219	57	13	38	.260	RHP	329	96	19	57	.292
First Half	279	79	21	54	.283	Sc Pos	106	27	6	45	.255
Scnd Half	160	44	7	20	.275	Clutch	61	15	2	4	.246

2001 Rankings (American League)

- 1st in lowest batting average with the bases loaded (0.000)
- 6th in sacrifice flies (9)
- 9th in slugging percentage
- 10th in HR frequency (15.7 ABs per HR) and GDPs (16)

Bartolo Colon

2001 Season

Bartolo Colon's 14 victories were his fewest since 1998, and his 12 losses were the most in his career. But he still looked like a No. 1 starter in spite of knee and elbow problems. In Game 1 of the Division Series against Seattle, he struck out 10 and threw eight scoreless innings in a 5-0 victory. He set a career high in innings pitched and struck out more than 200 batters for a second straight year. He went 5-9 at home, giving up an American League-high 19 longballs in his home park.

Pitching

Colon doesn't dance. He comes right at batters with two-seam and four-seam fastballs that range from 92-100 MPH. He throws his four-seamer consistently between 95-99 MPH. Tempo can be a problem. Colon always throws a lot of pitches—he threw the most in the AL in 2001—and if he takes a long time between pitches, it means bad things are about to happen. Colon has a 79-82 MPH changeup and a hard, 85-88 MPH curveball. But when he wants to change speeds, he often does it with his fastball, going from 88 to 97 MPH in the span of one pitch.

Defense

Colon has made 11 errors in five seasons, but last year fielded his position well. He gets off the mound quickly and his throws to first are strong and accurate. He started four double plays, a team high among pitchers. Few basestealers challenge him because he uses a slide step and is quick to the plate.

2002 Outlook

With Dave Burba a free agent and veterans Chuck Finley and Charles Nagy on the decline, Colon is the unquestioned leader of the rotation. The Indians want to build a rotation around him with young starters C.C. Sabathia, Ryan Drese and Jake Westbrook. What they need from Colon is a big season to lead the way.

Position: SP
Bats: R **Throws:** R
Ht: 6' 0" **Wt:** 230

Opening Day Age: 26
Born: 5/24/75 in Altamira, DR
ML Seasons: 5
Pronunciation: bar-TOE-loh ko-LONE

Overall Statistics

	W	L	Pct.	ERA	G	GS	Sv	IP	H	BB	SO	HR	Ratio
2001	14	12	.538	4.09	34	34	0	222.1	220	90	201	26	1.39
Career	65	41	.613	4.09	146	144	0	913.1	880	388	798	98	1.39

How Often He Throws Strikes

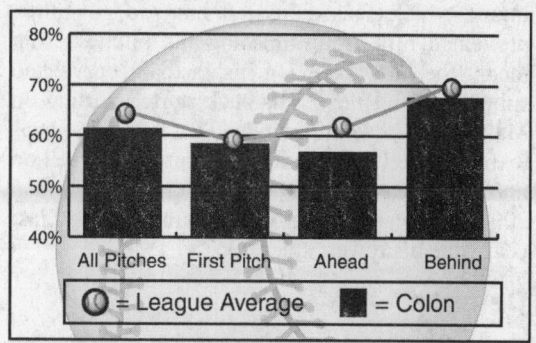

= League Average   = Colon

2001 Situational Stats

	W	L	ERA	Sv	IP		AB	H	HR	RBI	Avg
Home	5	9	4.27	0	137.0	LHB	446	124	17	58	.278
Road	9	3	3.80	0	85.1	RHB	397	96	9	37	.242
First Half	6	7	4.81	0	118.0	Sc Pos	191	49	6	65	.257
Scnd Half	8	5	3.28	0	104.1	Clutch	48	14	1	8	.292

2001 Rankings (American League)

- 1st in pitches thrown (3,650)
- 3rd in games started and walks allowed
- 5th in strikeouts and most pitches thrown per batter (3.85)
- Led the Indians in ERA, losses, games started, innings pitched, hits allowed, batters faced (947), home runs allowed, strikeouts, pickoff throws (141), GDPs induced (22), highest strikeout-walk ratio (2.2), highest groundball-flyball ratio allowed (1.2), lowest stolen-base percentage allowed (58.3), fewest pitches thrown per batter (3.85), lowest ERA at home, lowest ERA on the road, most GDPs induced per nine innings (0.9) and fewest walks per nine innings (3.6)

Cleveland

Chuck Finley

2001 Season

Chuck Finley came to Cleveland to reach the post-season. He made it for the first time since 1986, but things did not go as planned. In the least productive season of his long career, Finley went on the disabled list twice with an inflamed disc and nerve problems in his neck. Then he tore a rib-cage muscle and was still rounding into shape when the postseason began. Finley made two starts in the American League Division Series and lost them both.

Pitching

Finley still throws 90-92 MPH after almost 16 seasons and 3,000 innings. But the neck and nerve injury, which caused his left hand to go numb, prevented him from finishing his pitches. That meant the late action on his fastball, curve and splitter weren't there. His neck started hurting on May 11, but he kept pitching. That led to two trips to the disabled list in June. Finley prides himself on making at least 30 starts and pitching more than 200 innings a year. His 113.2 innings pitched last year were his fewest since 1987.

Defense

The 6-foot-6 Finley has an elegant, over-the-top delivery. It's a classic motion, but the way he fields resembles a car wreck. Once he gets off the mound, he has trouble getting his large body under control and anything can happen. He's made seven errors in the last two years. Finley does a good job of slowing the running game with pickoff moves, holding the ball and being quick to the plate. Seven of the 14 baserunners who tried to steal on him were thrown out in 2001.

2002 Outlook

If the Indians could trade Finley, they would. But he's in questionable health and is entering the third and final year of a $27 million contract. All the Indians can do is hope Finley stays healthy and pitches as he did in 2000, when he won 16 games. If that happens, Cleveland could have one of its best rotations in years.

Position: SP
Bats: L **Throws:** L
Ht: 6' 6" **Wt:** 225

Opening Day Age: 39
Born: 11/26/62 in Monroe, LA
ML Seasons: 16
Pronunciation: FIN-lee

Overall Statistics

	W	L	Pct.	ERA	G	GS	Sv	IP	H	BB	SO	HR	Ratio
2001	8	7	.533	5.54	22	22	0	113.2	131	35	96	14	1.46
Career	189	158	.545	3.83	492	435	0	3006.2	2886	1254	2436	291	1.38

How Often He Throws Strikes

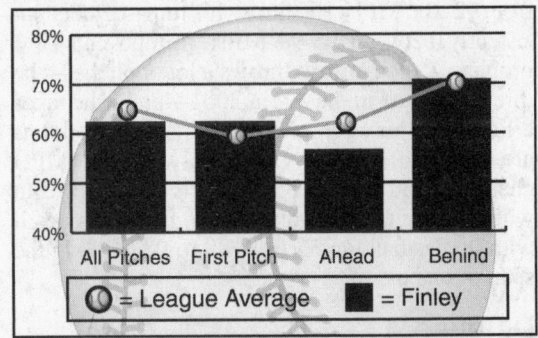

◯ = League Average ■ = Finley

2001 Situational Stats

	W	L	ERA	Sv	IP		AB	H	HR	RBI	Avg
Home	4	0	3.62	0	54.2	LHB	72	18	0	6	.250
Road	4	7	7.32	0	59.0	RHB	378	113	14	60	.299
First Half	4	4	6.45	0	67.0	Sc Pos	104	39	6	54	.375
Scnd Half	4	3	4.24	0	46.2	Clutch	23	7	0	2	.304

2001 Rankings (American League)

- 8th in errors at pitcher (3)

Travis Fryman

2001 Season

Travis Fryman followed his finest overall year in 2000 with his worst year in 2001. He missed the first two months with a strained ligament in his right elbow. When he returned, he couldn't find the swing that made him a consistent run producer throughout his career. He struggled offensively and defensively, going homerless in his first 166 at-bats, and making 12 errors in just 96 games at third base after a Gold Glove season there in 2000.

Hitting

When Fryman tried to change his throwing motion because of his sore elbow, he injured his right shoulder. With a bad elbow and shoulder, his bat speed and power vanished. When healthy, he's a good fastball hitter, especially fastballs up in the strike zone. But he was feeling for the ball last year, dumping flares and bloops into the outfield because he couldn't generate any pop with the bat. Pitchers who change speeds and move the ball around bother Fryman regardless of his physical condition. The injuries made him a more patient hitter, and he turned it up a notch with runners in scoring position.

Baserunning & Defense

It hurt to watch Fryman throw from third base. Every time he made a difficult one, his arm hung limp at his side. Gradually, his elbow improved and he worked his way around the pain. He still makes the play on the short hop well, and starts the 5-4-3 double play smoothly. Fryman knows how to run the bases, and always gives an honest effort. He slides hard into second base, but knee injuries have limited him to two steals in the last two years.

2002 Outlook

This is a big season for Fryman. He'll be 33 in the spring as he begins the final year of his current contract. He had arthroscopic surgery on his right shoulder in late November and was scheduled to spend much of the winter in Cleveland, rebuilding arm and shoulder strength. Fryman was expected to start throwing in January and be ready for spring training. The Indians need Fryman to rekindle his normal offensive productivity.

Position: 3B
Bats: R **Throws:** R
Ht: 6' 1" **Wt:** 205

Opening Day Age: 33
Born: 3/25/69 in Lexington, KY
ML Seasons: 12
Pronunciation: FRY-man

Overall Statistics

	G	AB	R	H	D	T	HR	RBI	SB	BB	SO	Avg	OBP	Slg
2001	98	334	34	88	15	0	3	38	1	30	63	.263	.327	.335
Career	1580	6084	853	1690	331	37	212	967	72	562	1287	.278	.339	.449

Where He Hits the Ball

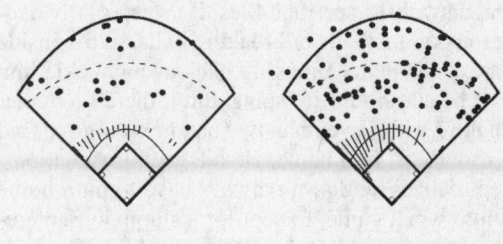

Vs. LHP   **Vs. RHP**

2001 Situational Stats

	AB	H	HR	RBI	Avg		AB	H	HR	RBI	Avg
Home	160	41	3	19	.256	LHP	74	19	0	3	.257
Road	174	47	0	19	.270	RHP	260	69	3	35	.265
First Half	103	28	0	6	.272	Sc Pos	85	26	1	36	.306
Scnd Half	231	60	3	32	.260	Clutch	52	8	0	4	.154

2001 Rankings (American League)

- 2nd in lowest batting average in the clutch
- 9th in batting average with the bases loaded (.500)

Juan Gonzalez

2001 Season

The one-year marriage of convenience between Juan Gonzalez and the Indians worked out well. Gonzalez, playing in a park he loves, withstood the nagging injuries that hindered him in Detroit and re-established himself as a high-priced, free-agent run producer. The Indians, meanwhile, found a talented, but temporary, cleanup hitter to drive their offense. Gonzalez finished second in the American League with 140 RBI and started the All-Star game in right field. He became the all-time home-run leader among Puerto Rican players when he hit No. 380 on June 22.

Hitting

Gonzalez is a master of the easy RBI. He led the league with 16 sacrifice flies. He's especially dangerous on fastballs or breaking balls on the inside part of the plate. Breaking balls away buckle him as if he doesn't have a spine. But if there's a runner on third with fewer than two out, he's going to find a way to get him home. He hits well in situations, and realizes he doesn't always have to hit a home run to win a game. Except for a slump in September, he produced in the clutch and hit better than .360 against lefties for a second straight year.

Baserunning & Defense

Manager Charlie Manuel couldn't believe the scope of Gonzalez' game. Before hamstring and knee problems slowed him, Gonzalez showed good speed going down the line, turning several singles into hustle doubles. In right field, he demonstrated above-average range, especially going into the gap. He had 10 assists, demonstrating a strong, accurate throwing arm. Diving is not part of his game.

2002 Outlook

Gonzalez went into the winter looking for a big-money deal. He turned down one from Detroit in 2000 because he didn't want to play for the Tigers. He would have liked to stay in Cleveland, but the Indians couldn't afford him. He's still fragile, missing 22 games with injury and illness in 2001, but he knows how to hit in the middle of the lineup.

Position: RF/DH
Bats: R **Throws:** R
Ht: 6' 3" **Wt:** 220

Opening Day Age: 32
Born: 10/16/69 in Vega Baja, PR
ML Seasons: 13
Nickname: Igor

Overall Statistics

	G	AB	R	H	D	T	HR	RBI	SB	BB	SO	Avg	OBP	Slg
2001	140	532	97	173	34	1	35	140	1	41	94	.325	.370	.590
Career	1503	5824	957	1727	346	22	397	1282	23	417	1125	.297	.345	.568

Where He Hits the Ball

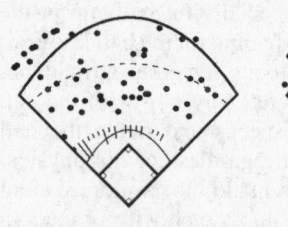 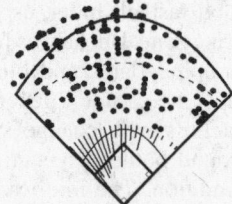

Vs. LHP   **Vs. RHP**

2001 Situational Stats

	AB	H	HR	RBI	Avg		AB	H	HR	RBI	Avg
Home	255	84	22	74	.329	LHP	117	43	10	35	.368
Road	277	89	13	66	.321	RHP	415	130	25	105	.313
First Half	308	107	23	83	.347	Sc Pos	158	53	8	100	.335
Scnd Half	224	66	12	57	.295	Clutch	70	19	5	21	.271

2001 Rankings (American League)

- 1st in sacrifice flies (16)
- 2nd in RBI and cleanup slugging percentage (.590)
- 3rd in batting average vs. lefthanded pitchers, slugging percentage vs. lefthanded pitchers (.675), fielding percentage in right field (.987) and GDPs (18)
- Led the Indians in doubles, RBI, GDPs (18), batting average with the bases loaded (.571), batting average vs. lefthanded pitchers, batting average on an 0-2 count (.234), cleanup slugging percentage (.590), slugging percentage vs. lefthanded pitchers (.675), on-base percentage vs. lefthanded pitchers (.417), batting average at home and batting average on a 3-2 count (.333)

Kenny Lofton

2001 Season

Kenny Lofton fought age, injury and the pressure of free agency for the second straight season. He saved face by hitting .299 (60-for-201) with 47 runs and 30 RBI from August 1 through October 7. However, he still finished with the lowest batting average of his career. His power and RBI numbers were good for a leadoff hitter, but the daring that made him the Indians' all-time leader in steals was missing. He stole a career-low 16 bases and was caught eight times. Lofton, who likes the big-game spotlight, hit .105 (2-for-19) in the American League Division Series.

Hitting

Lofton is a sucker for high fastballs and tries to hit them four miles. What he does is hit harmless flyballs to the warning track. He hit a lot of line drives that were caught in the first half, causing him to constantly change his stance. After the All-Star break, he went back to hitting fastballs and breaking balls up the middle and to left field. He hit well in the clutch, but defenses took away his bunting game by playing the third baseman in. Lofton can't drag bunt.

Baserunning & Defense

Lofton had the green light to steal all season, but rarely ran. Since dislocating his left shoulder in the 1999 postseason, he has been reluctant to use the headfirst slide. He gets from home to first in less than 3.8 seconds, but he no longer threatens pitchers by turning a walk into an automatic double by stealing a base. He can still make the flashy catch at the fence, but he gets bad jumps on balls hit in front of him. He's lost some arm strength because of his shoulder injury.

2002 Outlook

The Indians made it clear they would not pursue Lofton as a free agent. He'll find work because plenty of teams need a leadoff hitter, but his days of making $8 million a year are over. In fact, his days as a full-time player may be over unless he finds the desire to run again.

Position: CF
Bats: L **Throws:** L
Ht: 6' 0" **Wt:** 190

Opening Day Age: 34
Born: 5/31/67 in East Chicago, IN
ML Seasons: 11

Overall Statistics

	G	AB	R	H	D	T	HR	RBI	SB	BB	SO	Avg	OBP	Slg
2001	133	517	91	135	21	4	14	66	16	47	69	.261	.322	.398
Career	1366	5439	1050	1642	256	69	92	551	479	663	731	.302	.377	.425

Where He Hits the Ball

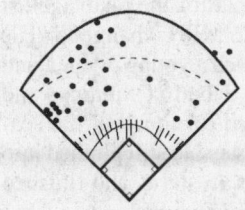 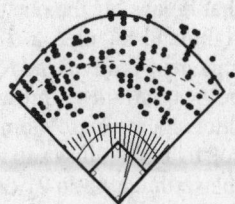

Vs. LHP   **Vs. RHP**

2001 Situational Stats

	AB	H	HR	RBI	Avg		AB	H	HR	RBI	Avg
Home	282	74	9	38	.262	LHP	118	29	2	13	.246
Road	235	61	5	28	.260	RHP	399	106	12	53	.266
First Half	241	57	5	28	.237	Sc Pos	103	32	2	47	.311
Scnd Half	276	78	9	38	.283	Clutch	62	21	1	12	.339

2001 Rankings (American League)

- 1st in errors in center field (6) and lowest fielding percentage in center field (.981)
- 4th in highest percentage of extra bases taken as a runner (60.8)
- 5th in lowest percentage of swings that missed (10.5)
- 7th in bunts in play (27)
- Led the Indians in batting average in the clutch, on-base percentage for a leadoff hitter (.321) and highest percentage of extra bases taken as a runner (60.8)

Cleveland

C.C. Sabathia

2001 Season

Manager Charlie Manuel fought the front office to get rookie C.C. Sabathia a spot in the Opening Day rotation. He won the fight and it's a good thing, because Sabathia went 17-5 and finished second to Seattle's Ichiro Suzuki in balloting for the Rookie of the Year Award. Sabathia's 17 wins were the most by a Tribe rookie lefthander since Gene Bearden won 20 in 1948. Sabathia led all rookie pitchers in victories, starts and strikeouts. In the Division Series, he beat Seattle in Game 3.

Pitching

The 6-foot-7 Sabathia has a smooth three-quarter delivery. He throws a 92-96 MPH fastball up in the strike zone. He throws an 83-86 MPH curveball that breaks off the outside part of the plate against righthanders, plus a 78-82 MPH changeup. His changeup is advanced for such a young pitcher, and he's not afraid to throw it. Sabathia's innings and pitch counts were monitored for much of the season to avoid injury and fatigue. He still pitched into the sixth inning in 21 of his 33 starts, and finished the regular season with 180.1 innings.

Defense

Sabathia is huge, weighing close to 270 pounds. He lumbers when he gets off the mound, but he's still agile and good at catching high choppers. Early in the season, teams rattled Sabathia by stealing off him. He didn't have a pickoff move, but former pitching coach Dick Pole showed him ways to slow the running game. Thirty-six percent (15 of 42) of the basestealers who tried to steal on him were thrown out.

2002 Outlook

For long stretches of the 2001 season, Sabathia was the Indians' best starter. They'd like that trend to continue, and look for him to pitch deeper into games. Hitters weren't familiar with him in 2001, but this year the league will adjust to him. He'll have to make his own adjustments to build on his rookie success.

Position: SP
Bats: L **Throws:** L
Ht: 6' 7" **Wt:** 250

Opening Day Age: 21
Born: 7/21/80 in Vallejo, CA
ML Seasons: 1

Overall Statistics

	W	L	Pct.	ERA	G	GS	Sv	IP	H	BB	SO	HR	Ratio
2001	17	5	.773	4.39	33	33	0	180.1	149	95	171	19	1.35
Career	17	5	.773	4.39	33	33	0	180.1	149	95	171	19	1.35

How Often He Throws Strikes

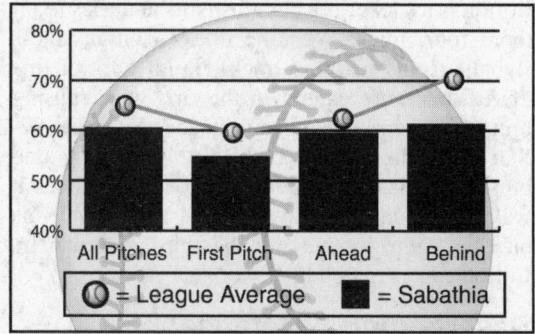

2001 Situational Stats

	W	L	ERA	Sv	IP		AB	H	HR	RBI	Avg
Home	4	3	4.30	0	73.1	LHB	114	29	1	12	.254
Road	13	2	4.46	0	107.0	RHB	539	120	18	67	.223
First Half	7	3	4.72	0	87.2	Sc Pos	149	38	7	64	.255
Scnd Half	10	2	4.08	0	92.2	Clutch	21	1	0	0	.048

2001 Rankings (American League)

- 1st in ERA among rookies, wins among rookies and most pitches thrown per batter (4.14)
- Led the Indians in wins, walks allowed, hit batsmen (7), wild pitches (7), balks (3), stolen bases allowed (27), runners caught stealing (15), winning percentage, lowest batting average allowed (.228), lowest slugging percentage allowed (.371), lowest on-base percentage allowed (.330), lowest batting average allowed vs. lefthanded batters, lowest batting average allowed vs. righthanded batters, most run support per nine innings (5.7), lowest batting average allowed with runners in scoring position, fewest home runs allowed per nine innings (.95) and most strikeouts per nine innings (8.5)

Jim Thome

2001 Season

The Indians were concerned that the enforcement of the high strike would hurt Jim Thome. But he adapted and hit career highs in homers and RBI. He became the Indians' all-time home-run leader by hitting No. 243 on May 29 in Detroit. In July, he was the American League Player of the Month, hitting .381 with 12 homers and 39 RBI. He hit 30 homers and 81 RBI at Jacobs Field, the best power numbers at home in the AL.

Hitting

Thome tried to reduce his strikeouts and raise his batting average by making more contact. He hit poorly until former hitting coach Clarence Jones suggested in May that he raise his hands so he would swing down on the ball. Thome's a patient hitter, who seemingly runs the count full on nearly every at-bat. But after he does, he takes far too many called third strikes, either on fastballs just off the plate or breaking balls down the middle. He gets power hungry sometimes and swings too hard at high fastballs. While he set a career high in strikeouts, Thome still hit well with runners in scoring position and raised his average after two straight years of decline.

Baserunning & Defense

For a man his size, Thome runs the bases well. He can score from second on a single to right field, and has a variety of slides he uses on close plays at the plate. Thome probably will never receive the credit he deserves for his play at first base, simply because it's overshadowed by his offense. But he handles balls to his left and right well and has a good arm on the 3-6-3 double play. His main problem is scooping low throws from other infielders.

2002 Outlook

On August 16, the Indians picked up their 2002 option on Thome for $7.5 million. He then celebrated by going out that night and hitting his 41st and 42nd homers. Look for him to replace Juan Gonzalez in the cleanup spot. Unless the Indians sign him to a multiyear deal, however, Thome becomes a free agent after the season. It will be interesting to see how he responds.

Position: 1B
Bats: L **Throws:** R
Ht: 6' 4" **Wt:** 240

Opening Day Age: 31
Born: 8/27/70 in Peoria, IL
ML Seasons: 11
Pronunciation: TOE-mee

Overall Statistics

	G	AB	R	H	D	T	HR	RBI	SB	BB	SO	Avg	OBP	Slg
2001	156	526	101	153	26	1	49	124	0	111	185	.291	.416	.624
Career	1230	4160	816	1186	240	18	282	809	17	875	1238	.285	.411	.555

Where He Hits the Ball

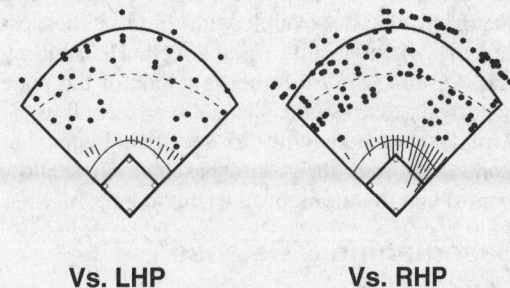

Vs. LHP   **Vs. RHP**

2001 Situational Stats

	AB	H	HR	RBI	Avg		AB	H	HR	RBI	Avg
Home	253	76	30	81	.300	LHP	142	33	4	22	.232
Road	273	77	19	43	.282	RHP	384	120	45	102	.313
First Half	272	79	26	64	.290	Sc Pos	148	49	13	77	.331
Scnd Half	254	74	23	60	.291	Clutch	87	28	8	19	.322

2001 Rankings (American League)

- 1st in strikeouts, HR frequency (10.7 ABs per HR), most pitches seen per plate appearance (4.16), slugging percentage vs. righthanded pitchers (.716), highest percentage of swings that missed (32.1), and lowest percentage of swings put into play (31.8)
- 2nd in home runs, walks, slugging percentage and on-base percentage vs. righthanded pitchers (.445)
- Led the Indians in home runs, total bases (328), walks, pitches seen (2,678), slugging percentage, on-base percentage, highest percentage of pitches taken (59.7) and on-base percentage vs. righthanded pitchers (.445)
- Led AL first basemen in home runs and RBI

Omar Vizquel

Position: SS
Bats: B **Throws:** R
Ht: 5' 9" **Wt:** 185

Opening Day Age: 34
Born: 4/24/67 in Caracas, VZ
ML Seasons: 13
Pronunciation: viz-KELL

2001 Season

Omar Vizquel won his ninth straight Gold Glove, but other than that, his game slipped in 2001. He stopped being a force at the top of the lineup, hitting for his lowest average since becoming an Indian in 1994 and stealing just 13 bases. He ended the season hitting .176 (16-for-91) over the final 25 games of the season. He rebounded in the Division Series, hitting .409 (9-for-22).

Hitting

As Kenny Lofton goes, so goes the man who hits behind him. That happens to be Vizquel, the Tribe's No. 2 hitter. Vizquel can hit a fastball and draw a walk, but when no one is on base in front of him, he sees a steady diet of sliders, curveballs and changeups. He has trouble with those pitches, especially when he hits righthanded. He's hitting .223 (73-for-327) from the right side of the plate over the last two years. Vizquel was second in the American League with 15 sacrifice bunts, but teams now play their third baseman so shallow against him that he stopped trying to bunt for hits.

Baserunning & Defense

Vizquel always has been a loose cannon on the bases when it comes to stealing. Last year he was thrown out in nine of 22 stolen-base attempts. That humbled him and he stole only one base after July 18. Vizquel's defense is still stunning. But a lack of arm strength surfaced last year. Several times he failed to throw out runners at first base on what used to be routine plays for him.

2002 Outlook

After extending Vizquel's contract through the 2004 season during spring training, the Indians went into the offseason looking to trade a veteran infielder to create salary room that would allow them to add an outfielder. They also faced having too many players getting old at the same time, and Vizquel looked like a guy who might go. His pivot partner, Roberto Alomar, was dealt to the Mets in a major surprise, so Vizquel *may* be staying. If he does, he works with a new second baseman in 2002. Newcomer Brady Anderson or Vizquel, who saw his on-base percentage plummet in 2001, could replace Lofton in the leadoff spot.

Overall Statistics

	G	AB	R	H	D	T	HR	RBI	SB	BB	SO	Avg	OBP	Slg
2001	155	611	84	156	26	8	2	50	13	61	72	.255	.323	.334
Career	1775	6420	919	1761	276	44	43	565	273	643	648	.274	.340	.351

Where He Hits the Ball

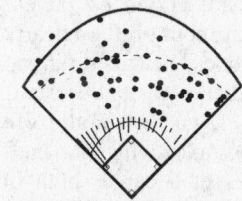
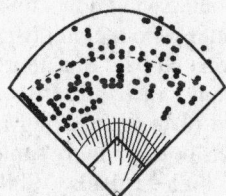

Vs. LHP   **Vs. RHP**

2001 Situational Stats

	AB	H	HR	RBI	Avg		AB	H	HR	RBI	Avg
Home	304	78	2	29	.257	LHP	171	39	1	11	.228
Road	307	78	0	21	.254	RHP	440	117	1	39	.266
First Half	324	88	1	22	.272	Sc Pos	126	32	0	44	.254
Scnd Half	287	68	1	28	.237	Clutch	80	17	2	10	.213

2001 Rankings (American League)

- 1st in fielding percentage at shortstop (.989), lowest slugging percentage, lowest HR frequency (305.5 ABs per HR) and lowest slugging percentage vs. lefthanded pitchers (.281)
- 2nd in sacrifice bunts (15)
- 3rd in lowest percentage of swings that missed (8.8)
- 4th in bunts in play (32) and highest percentage of swings put into play (52.7)
- Led the Indians in at-bats, sacrifice bunts (15), caught stealing (9), plate appearances (693), highest groundball-flyball ratio (1.3), bunts in play (32), lowest percentage of swings that missed (8.8) and lowest percentage of swings on the first pitch (18.7)

Bob Wickman

2001 Season

Bob Wickman didn't let a little thing like losing his job spoil his season. Wickman was replaced as Cleveland's closer by John Rocker on June 23. Wickman regained the closer's job on July 16 and never lost it again. He converted 32 of 35 save situations. In his last 18 appearances, he went 2-0 with 12 straight saves and a 0.49 ERA. He pitched with a sore right elbow for most of the second half, but it never kept him out of a save situation.

Pitching

Wickman is a sinker-slider pitcher. He's not a blow-'em-away closer, but he throws harder than people think. His fastball ranges from 90-93 MPH. His sinking fastball, which has good downward movement, is his outpitch. Wickman has a compact motion and he short-arms the ball. He can pitch more than one inning, but the Indians don't like to extend him past three outs. He's vulnerable to lefties, but not many hitters make good contact against him because he locates the ball well. Over the last two years, he's allowed just five homers in 140.1 innings.

Defense

On a pitching staff that made 22 errors last year, Wickman fielded his position cleanly. He handles balls back through the box and in front of the mound well, but a fast runner will test him if he has to cover first base on bunts and slow rollers. He's getting better at holding runners. Three of the five basestealers who ran on him in 2001 were thrown out.

2002 Outlook

At the end of last season, general manager Mark Shapiro said keeping Wickman was his No. 1 priority. Shapiro got his man, signing Wickman to a three-year, $16 million deal on November 5, the day he could have filed for free agency. Now the Indians' only concern is Wickman's physical condition. From spring training through the end of the season last year, he gained at least 20 pounds.

Position: RP
Bats: R **Throws:** R
Ht: 6' 1" **Wt:** 230

Opening Day Age: 33
Born: 2/6/69 in Green Bay, WI
ML Seasons: 10

Overall Statistics

	W	L	Pct.	ERA	G	GS	Sv	IP	H	BB	SO	HR	Ratio
2001	5	0	1.000	2.39	70	0	32	67.2	61	14	66	4	1.11
Career	58	42	.580	3.65	591	28	136	828.2	812	357	603	58	1.41

How Often He Throws Strikes

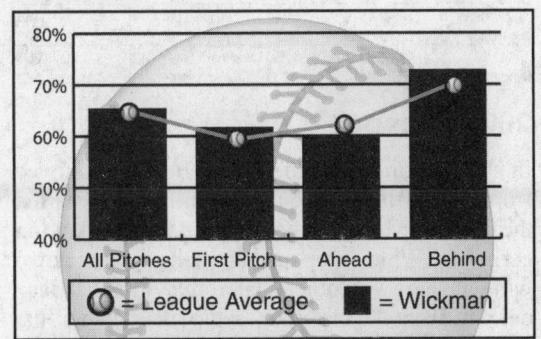

= League Average   = Wickman

2001 Situational Stats

	W	L	ERA	Sv	IP		AB	H	HR	RBI	Avg
Home	4	0	2.57	12	35.0	LHB	122	34	2	13	.279
Road	1	0	2.20	20	32.2	RHB	132	27	2	8	.205
First Half	3	0	2.75	15	36.0	Sc Pos	63	14	0	14	.222
Scnd Half	2	0	1.99	17	31.2	Clutch	163	39	3	16	.239

2001 Rankings (American League)

- 4th in save percentage (91.4) and games finished (56)
- 5th in relief ERA (2.39)
- 7th in saves
- 8th in games pitched and save opportunities (35)
- 10th in lowest batting average allowed in relief with runners on base (.206)
- Led the Indians in games pitched, saves, games finished (56), save opportunities (35), save percentage (91.4), blown saves (3), relief wins (5), relief innings (67.2) and relief ERA (2.39)

Danys Baez

Position: RP
Bats: R **Throws:** R
Ht: 6' 3" **Wt:** 225

Opening Day Age: 24
Born: 9/10/77 in Pinar Del Rio, Cuba
ML Seasons: 1
Pronunciation: DAN-ees BUY-ez

Overall Statistics

	W	L	Pct.	ERA	G	GS	Sv	IP	H	BB	SO	HR	Ratio
2001	5	3	.625	2.50	43	0	0	50.1	34	20	52	5	1.07
Career	5	3	.625	2.50	43	0	0	50.1	34	20	52	5	1.07

2001 Situational Stats

	W	L	ERA	Sv	IP		AB	H	HR	RBI	Avg
Home	3	3	2.45	0	22.0	LHB	69	13	1	6	.188
Road	2	0	2.54	0	28.1	RHB	109	21	4	16	.193
First Half	0	0	0.00	0	7.0	Sc Pos	47	12	3	20	.255
Scnd Half	5	3	2.91	0	43.1	Clutch	92	15	4	10	.163

2001 Season

In spring training, rookie Danys Baez was moved from the starting rotation to the bullpen. He started the year in the minors before joining Cleveland in early July. When setup man Paul Shuey went down with an elbow problem later that month, Baez quickly became the main setup man. After the All-Star break, he went 5-3 with a 2.91 ERA in 38 appearances, the most in the league after the break.

Pitching & Defense

Baez became much more aggressive and accurate with his pitches as a reliever. He throws a 94-97 MPH fastball with an 88-MPH curveball. When he became a reliever, the Indians replaced his changeup with a splitter, which became a good complement to his fastball. He's capable of pitching two innings at a time, but the Indians have to be careful not to overuse him because he thinks he can pitch every day. He's quick off the mound and fields his position well.

2002 Outlook

Despite Baez' success in the bullpen, new general manager Mark Shapiro spent the winter thinking about moving Baez back into the starting rotation. He loves Baez' arm and thinks he could help more as a starter. Baez is one of several young pitchers who the Indians are planning to rebuild around.

Russell Branyan

Position: 3B/LF
Bats: L **Throws:** R
Ht: 6' 3" **Wt:** 195

Opening Day Age: 26
Born: 12/19/75 in Warner Robins, GA
ML Seasons: 4
Pronunciation: BRAN-yen

Overall Statistics

	G	AB	R	H	D	T	HR	RBI	SB	BB	SO	Avg	OBP	Slg
2001	113	315	48	73	16	2	20	54	1	38	132	.232	.316	.486
Career	192	550	84	127	25	4	37	98	1	63	229	.231	.316	.493

2001 Situational Stats

	AB	H	HR	RBI	Avg		AB	H	HR	RBI	Avg
Home	157	43	11	29	.274	LHP	40	13	5	15	.325
Road	158	30	9	25	.190	RHP	275	60	15	39	.218
First Half	216	50	13	39	.231	Sc Pos	61	16	5	34	.262
Scnd Half	99	23	7	15	.232	Clutch	50	11	2	5	.220

2001 Season

Russell Branyan started the season at third base for an injured Travis Fryman. He was hitting .247 with 11 doubles, 12 homers and 33 RBI on June 2 when Fryman reclaimed his job. Branyan disappeared after that, hitting .216 (33-for-153) with eight homers and 71 strikeouts in his final 62 games. He hit his 20th homer on the last day of the season.

Hitting, Baserunning & Defense

It's going to take Branyan a long time to escape his reputation as the human strikeout machine. He has a long swing and is susceptible to breaking balls. He can hit a low fastball or hanging curve a mile, but he'll chase high heat. Branyan is better suited for left field than third base. He made 11 of his 14 errors at third. He runs decently and has a strong, but undisciplined arm.

2002 Outlook

Branyan was out of options last summer, and the Indians still face a decision on him. They need to play him everyday in the outfield or trade him. His kind of power needs to be developed, and he's shown that his swing will not survive a bench role. Since Cleveland traded away Brian Giles, Richie Sexson and Jeromy Burnitz, Branyan is the last hitter in the Tribe's pipeline with above-average power.

Jolbert Cabrera

Position:
LF/CF/2B/3B/RF/SS
Bats: R **Throws:** R
Ht: 6' 0" **Wt:** 177

Opening Day Age: 29
Born: 12/8/72 in
Cartagena, Colombia
ML Seasons: 4
Pronunciation:
HOLE-bert kah-brair-RAH

Overall Statistics

	G	AB	R	H	D	T	HR	RBI	SB	BB	SO	Avg	OBP	Slg
2001	141	287	50	75	16	3	1	38	10	16	41	.261	.312	.348
Career	272	501	83	126	20	4	3	53	19	25	65	.251	.297	.325

2001 Situational Stats

	AB	H	HR	RBI	Avg		AB	H	HR	RBI	Avg
Home	130	36	1	19	.277	LHP	109	28	0	17	.257
Road	157	39	0	19	.248	RHP	178	47	1	21	.264
First Half	141	39	0	17	.277	Sc Pos	83	26	0	37	.313
Scnd Half	146	36	1	21	.247	Clutch	50	12	1	6	.240

2001 Season

Jolbert Cabrera's goal is to be the best utility man in baseball. He helped his resume last year by playing six different positions, failing only to pitch, catch or play first base. He singled home the game-winning run on August 5, in the Indians' 15-14 victory over Seattle, which equaled the biggest comeback in big league history.

Hitting, Baserunning & Defense

Cabrera is a good fastball hitter who is dangerous with men on base. He makes contact and will work the count, but doesn't walk much. He tends to overswing and hits too many routine flyballs to the outfield. He's one of the fastest players on the Indians and runs the bases well. Center field and shortstop are his best positions. Left field is probably his worst. His arm is respectable.

2002 Outlook

Cabrera is young, versatile and doesn't draw a big paycheck. In other words, he's a perfect utility man. It looked like he would get a chance to start at second base immediately after the Roberto Alomar trade, but Cleveland since has signed Ricky Gutierrez with the intention of moving him to second base. Cabrera still may see more time there, but the Tribe's decision-makers think he may wear down as an everyday player.

Wil Cordero

Position: LF/1B/DH
Bats: R **Throws:** R
Ht: 6' 2" **Wt:** 210

Opening Day Age: 30
Born: 10/3/71 in
Mayaguez, PR
ML Seasons: 10
Pronunciation:
cor-DAIR-oh

Overall Statistics

	G	AB	R	H	D	T	HR	RBI	SB	BB	SO	Avg	OBP	Slg
2001	89	268	30	67	11	1	4	21	0	22	50	.250	.313	.343
Career	989	3597	500	995	220	19	99	457	45	253	623	.277	.331	.431

2001 Situational Stats

	AB	H	HR	RBI	Avg		AB	H	HR	RBI	Avg
Home	120	29	2	4	.242	LHP	84	25	1	5	.298
Road	148	38	2	17	.257	RHP	184	42	3	16	.228
First Half	146	43	3	13	.295	Sc Pos	67	11	1	17	.164
Scnd Half	122	24	1	8	.197	Clutch	37	8	1	5	.216

2001 Season

Wil Cordero had one of those missing-in-action seasons. He was in Cleveland, but no one could prove it. He lost playing time when Ellis Burks was confined to DH duties and Marty Cordova came out of nowhere to win the left-field job. Cordero endured a stretch of 257 at-bats, going back to 2000, without a homer, and a stretch of 86 at-bats without an RBI. He went 4-for-10 as a pinch-hitter.

Hitting, Baserunning & Defense

Cordero is in the big leagues because he can hit, but he didn't have much of an opportunity last year. When he did, he failed to show power or hit with runners in scoring position. He's a contact hitter who handles lefties well. Cordero won't scare anybody as a baserunner, but is an average defender at the outfield corners. He's better at first base, where he shows quickness and good hands.

2002 Outlook

If the Indians could, they'd drop Cordero in a heartbeat, but the chances of that happening are not good because of his $4 million salary for 2002. This year could be a springboard for Cordero. With Marty Cordova gone and so many changes in the outfield and the middle of the lineup, he could get more at-bats. If he does, his history says he'll hit.

Cleveland

Marty Cordova

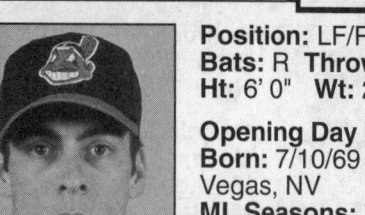

Position: LF/RF
Bats: R **Throws:** R
Ht: 6' 0" **Wt:** 206

Opening Day Age: 32
Born: 7/10/69 in Las Vegas, NV
ML Seasons: 7
Pronunciation: core-DOE-vuh

Overall Statistics

	G	AB	R	H	D	T	HR	RBI	SB	BB	SO	Avg	OBP	Slg
2001	122	409	61	123	20	2	20	69	0	23	81	.301	.348	.506
Career	812	2931	420	815	166	16	103	472	55	274	614	.278	.346	.451

2001 Situational Stats

	AB	H	HR	RBI	Avg		AB	H	HR	RBI	Avg
Home	190	56	9	25	.295	LHP	108	36	7	17	.333
Road	219	67	11	44	.306	RHP	301	87	13	52	.289
First Half	213	72	10	40	.338	Sc Pos	115	32	5	49	.278
Scnd Half	196	51	10	29	.260	Clutch	53	16	0	8	.302

2001 Season

Marty Cordova went to spring training on a make-good contract and made good. Not only did he make the Opening Day roster, he resurrected his career. He went on a 22-game hitting streak from April 22 through May 18, and then rode its momentum the rest of the season.

Hitting, Baserunning & Defense

After 2000, Cordova cut back on the weights, hit the speed bag, lost 20 pounds and opened his stance. With quicker hands and more flexibility, he generated more bat speed. He's aggressive at the plate and likes to swing early in the count. He'll take some bad hacks at breaking balls down and away, but will pull anything on the inside part of the plate. Cordova gives good effort on the bases. He plays deep in left or right field, and will dive for any ball he gets close to. He has trouble going back on balls and his arm is average.

2002 Outlook

Cordova was such a success story that he priced himself out of Cleveland. A year ago, the Indians signed him on the cheap for $650,000, but it took a three-year, $9.1 million deal from the Orioles to secure his services for 2002. Cordova shouldn't have trouble approaching 400 at-bats again.

Einar Diaz

Position: C
Bats: R **Throws:** R
Ht: 5'10" **Wt:** 185

Opening Day Age: 29
Born: 12/28/72 in Chiriqui, Panama
ML Seasons: 6
Nickname: The Dream

Overall Statistics

	G	AB	R	H	D	T	HR	RBI	SB	BB	SO	Avg	OBP	Slg
2001	134	437	54	121	34	1	4	56	1	17	44	.277	.328	.387
Career	354	1135	135	311	71	4	13	123	16	54	118	.274	.324	.378

2001 Situational Stats

	AB	H	HR	RBI	Avg		AB	H	HR	RBI	Avg
Home	206	59	0	27	.286	LHP	112	22	0	9	.196
Road	231	62	4	29	.268	RHP	325	99	4	47	.305
First Half	228	72	3	38	.316	Sc Pos	113	37	0	47	.327
Scnd Half	209	49	1	18	.234	Clutch	70	22	0	8	.314

2001 Season

Einar Diaz established himself as an everyday catcher after the Indians elected not to re-sign Sandy Alomar Jr. before the start of the 2001 season. Diaz caught 134 games, the most by a Tribe catcher since 1974. His 34 doubles led all American League catchers.

Hitting, Baserunning & Defense

Diaz is a dead-pull, contact hitter. He was hit 16 times by pitches because he dives across the plate trying to pull the ball to left field. He started to hit more to right field in the second half because he was always being pitched away. Diaz enjoyed a fine year hitting in the clutch, but lefties wore him out. The converted third baseman has a good arm, throwing out 35 percent (46-for-130) of the basestealers he faced. Diaz gets down the line well for a catcher, but doesn't run like he used to.

2002 Outlook

Diaz signed a four-year, $6.3 million contract in March 2001, making him the youngster in the Indians' aging lineup. At 29, he's emerging as one of best catchers in the league. The Indians would like to see him be more assertive in his game-calling. That may happen as they add more and more young arms to the staff this year.

Ricardo Rincon

Position: RP
Bats: L **Throws:** L
Ht: 5' 9" **Wt:** 190

Opening Day Age: 31
Born: 4/13/70 in
Veracruz, Mexico
ML Seasons: 5
Pronunciation:
rin-CONE

Overall Statistics

	W	L	Pct.	ERA	G	GS	Sv	IP	H	BB	SO	HR	Ratio
2001	2	1	.667	2.83	67	0	2	54.0	44	21	50	3	1.20
Career	10	14	.417	3.29	283	0	20	243.2	203	111	235	21	1.29

2001 Situational Stats

	W	L	ERA	Sv	IP			AB	H	HR	RBI	Avg
Home	1	0	2.56	1	31.2	LHB		94	20	2	12	.213
Road	1	1	3.22	1	22.1	RHB		103	24	1	9	.233
First Half	1	1	3.33	2	27.0	Sc Pos		55	10	1	18	.182
Scnd Half	1	0	2.33	0	27.0	Clutch		50	13	1	10	.260

2001 Season

Fully recovered from surgery on his left elbow in June 2000, Ricardo Rincon enjoyed his best season with the Indians. With John Rocker struggling, he became their most reliable lefty. He allowed just three runs in his last 23 appearances of the season. He kept his cool with runners on base, stranding 37 of his 45 inherited runners.

Pitching & Defense

Rincon's best pitch is an 83-88 MPH slider. What made it more effective last year is that he combined it with a 91-MPH sinking fastball. Used often as a matchup reliever against lefties since joining the Tribe, he did well when given the chance to face lefties *and* righties during the stretch run. Opposing batters hit just .174 against him in the second half. He showed durability by making a career-high 67 appearances. Rincon gets off the mound quickly to cover first or field balls in front of him.

2002 Outlook

Rincon figures to be a big part of the Indians' bullpen in 2002. Manager Charlie Manuel showed much more confidence in him last year, letting him stay in games longer. He could become the club's primary lefthanded setup man, and the Indians made sure to lock him up for this year and next by picking up his option for 2003 in late October.

John Rocker

Position: RP
Bats: R **Throws:** L
Ht: 6' 4" **Wt:** 225

Opening Day Age: 27
Born: 10/17/74 in
Statesboro, GA
ML Seasons: 4

Overall Statistics

	W	L	Pct.	ERA	G	GS	Sv	IP	H	BB	SO	HR	Ratio
2001	5	9	.357	4.32	68	0	23	66.2	58	41	79	4	1.49
Career	11	19	.367	3.05	248	0	87	230.0	169	148	302	18	1.38

2001 Situational Stats

	W	L	ERA	Sv	IP			AB	H	HR	RBI	Avg
Home	5	4	3.97	9	34.0	LHB		46	11	1	6	.239
Road	0	5	4.68	14	32.2	RHB		202	47	3	23	.233
First Half	4	4	3.23	21	39.0	Sc Pos		77	18	2	26	.234
Scnd Half	1	5	5.86	2	27.2	Clutch		166	41	4	27	.247

2001 Season

John Rocker's season hit rock bottom when he arrived in Cleveland from Atlanta on June 22. He had 19 saves with the Braves, but led Tribe relievers with seven losses and blew three of seven save opportunities. The Indians gave him the closer's job right after the trade, even though he had a tired arm. He quickly lost it and never accepted or adapted to being a setup man.

Pitching & Defense

Rocker throws a 94-97 MPH fastball and offsets it with a great curveball. For two weeks after the trade, he was throwing 90-93 MPH because of a tired arm. He has good stuff, but control problems and poor fielding on his part continually beat him. In nine total fielding chances with the Indians, he made three errors. Rocker went through his usual routine on the mound, snorting and gyrating, but there seemed to be a desperate quality to it. At least twice he wore earplugs to block out the crowd noise.

2002 Outlook

After the season, the Indians signed Bob Wickman to a three-year deal. It meant the end of Rocker's career as an Indian. Just how the Indians will get rid of Rocker remains to be seen. He is eligible for arbitration and due for a large raise.

Cleveland

Paul Shuey

Position: RP
Bats: R **Throws:** R
Ht: 6' 3" **Wt:** 215

Opening Day Age: 31
Born: 9/16/70 in Lima, OH
ML Seasons: 8
Pronunciation: SHOE-ee

Overall Statistics

	W	L	Pct.	ERA	G	GS	Sv	IP	H	BB	SO	HR	Ratio
2001	5	3	.625	2.82	47	0	2	54.1	53	26	70	1	1.45
Career	31	21	.596	3.72	322	0	21	367.1	332	192	411	31	1.43

2001 Situational Stats

	W	L	ERA	Sv	IP		AB	H	HR	RBI	Avg
Home	1	1	2.48		29.0	LHB	100	28	0	12	.280
Road	4	2	3.20	2	25.1	RHB	111	25	1	17	.225
First Half	5	3	2.20	2	41.0	Sc Pos	85	18	0	28	.212
Scnd Half	0	0	4.73	0	13.1	Clutch	118	28	0	17	.237

2001 Season

Paul Shuey lost a good part of the season because of two injuries to his right elbow that forced him to go on the disabled list. The second injury, a strain of the ulnar collateral ligament, idled him from July 22 until mid-September. Ligament transplant surgery seemed likely, but the nine appearances he made after September 18 apparently convinced the Indians otherwise.

Pitching & Defense

Shuey has three good pitches, a 92-97 MPH fastball, a 90-92 MPH splitter and a curveball. He's thrown the splitter too much the last two seasons, and the Indians felt that may have led to his elbow problems. The splitter is his strikeout pitch, but it can get hit a long way when he hangs one. Shuey has never been a great fielder, but he was especially bad in making four errors in nine chances in 2001. Basestealers were a near-perfect 12 for 13 off him.

2002 Outlook

The Indians are concerned about Shuey's elbow. He did not throw well when he came off the DL in September, so surgery still might be an option. If Shuey's healthy, he gives the Indians a veteran setup man for the bullpen. He signed a three-year $11 million deal just prior the start of the 2001 regular season.

Eddie Taubensee

Position: C
Bats: L **Throws:** R
Ht: 6' 3" **Wt:** 230

Opening Day Age: 33
Born: 10/31/68 in Beeville, TX
ML Seasons: 11
Pronunciation: TAU-bin-see

Overall Statistics

	G	AB	R	H	D	T	HR	RBI	SB	BB	SO	Avg	OBP	Slg
2001	52	116	16	29	2	1	3	11	0	10	19	.250	.315	.362
Career	975	2874	351	784	151	9	94	419	11	255	574	.273	.331	.430

2001 Situational Stats

	AB	H	HR	RBI	Avg		AB	H	HR	RBI	Avg
Home	65	19	2	7	.292	LHP	21	5	0	0	.238
Road	51	10	1	4	.196	RHP	95	24	3	11	.253
First Half	72	18	3	8	.250	Sc Pos	28	6	1	9	.214
Scnd Half	44	11	0	3	.250	Clutch	13	4	1	1	.308

2001 Season

Eddie Taubensee's first year with the Indians since 1991 did not go well. A viral infection that lodged in his liver put him on the disabled list from June 17 to July 27. He lost about 15 pounds and never regained his strength. Even before he was sick, he saw little playing time. The highlight of his season came when the Indians offered him a two-year contract extension in May. He quickly signed it.

Hitting, Baserunning & Defense

Taubensee can hit. He has power and can drive low fastballs on the inside part of the plate out of the park. He proved to be an excellent pinch-hitter, going 6-for-14 with two homers. Defensively, he's a liability. He threw out just one of 29 potential basestealers in 2001, and was charged with three errors and five passed balls. Taubensee runs hard on the bases, but isn't a threat to steal.

2002 Outlook

The Indians need a stronger, more defensive-minded Taubensee this year. If not, starter Einar Diaz may wear out by the All-Star break. The Indians were afraid to catch Taubensee after he came off the DL because it was a license to steal for the opposition. That's not a good situation for a backup catcher or a ballclub.

Mike Bacsik (Pos: LHP, **Age**: 24)

	W	L	Pct.	ERA	G	GS	Sv	IP	H	BB	SO	HR	Ratio
2001	0	0	-	9.00	3	0	0	9.0	13	3	4	0	1.78
Career	0	0	-	9.00	3	0	0	9.0	13	3	4	0	1.78

Bacsik once was rated with the best control of Cleveland's prospects. The soft-tossing lefty had a chance to help in Ohio, but he joined a more-established Mets staff in the Roberto Alomar trade. 2002 Outlook: C

Karim Garcia (Pos: RF, **Age**: 26, **Bats**: L)

	G	AB	R	H	D	T	HR	RBI	SB	BB	SO	Avg	OBP	Slg
2001	20	45	8	14	3	0	5	9	0	3	13	.311	.360	.711
Career	274	759	92	169	23	11	29	92	7	47	187	.223	.267	.397

Garcia clubbed 31 homers in Triple-A last year, and for the first time, had success in the majors. The Tribe re-signed him in mid-December. 2002 Outlook: B

Dave Hollins (Pos: DH, **Age**: 35, **Bats**: B)

	G	AB	R	H	D	T	HR	RBI	SB	BB	SO	Avg	OBP	Slg
2001	2	5	0	1	0	0	0	0	0	1	2	.200	.333	.200
Career	969	3329	577	868	166	17	112	482	47	464	684	.261	.359	.422

Hollins has moved between five organizations since 1999. The former All-Star spent most of that time injured or in the minors. His 2001 season also ended with an injury. 2002 Outlook: D

Tim Laker (Pos: C, **Age**: 32, **Bats**: R)

	G	AB	R	H	D	T	HR	RBI	SB	BB	SO	Avg	OBP	Slg
2001	16	33	5	6	0	0	1	5	0	6	8	.182	.308	.273
Career	181	358	36	79	14	2	5	39	3	28	91	.221	.278	.313

Laker was called up for six weeks while Eddie Taubensee was injured, and then later as a Setpember callup. He re-signed with Cleveland and will remain the third catcher unless someone is moved. 2002 Outlook: C

Mark Lewis (Pos: 3B, **Age**: 32, **Bats**: R)

	G	AB	R	H	D	T	HR	RBI	SB	BB	SO	Avg	OBP	Slg
2001	6	13	1	1	0	0	0	0	0	0	4	.077	.077	.077
Career	902	2795	320	736	155	13	48	306	29	196	511	.263	.312	.380

Lewis' days of being an everyday player are a distant memory. He declared for free agency in October and is hoping to find a job as a role player. 2002 Outlook: C

John McDonald (Pos: SS, **Age**: 27, **Bats**: R)

	G	AB	R	H	D	T	HR	RBI	SB	BB	SO	Avg	OBP	Slg
2001	17	22	1	2	1	0	0	0	0	1	7	.091	.167	.136
Career	44	52	3	13	1	0	0	0	0	1	11	.250	.278	.269

McDonald has a nice glove at shortstop but provides little with the bat. He's in line for some backup duty in the middle infield. 2002 Outlook: B

Charles Nagy (Pos: RHP, **Age**: 34)

	W	L	Pct.	ERA	G	GS	Sv	IP	H	BB	SO	HR	Ratio
2001	5	6	.455	6.40	15	13	0	70.1	102	20	29	10	1.73
Career	128	99	.564	4.40	294	290	0	1893.2	2097	570	1213	207	1.41

A variety of elbow ailments over the last few years have left Nagy with no cartilage in his pitching elbow. His recent stats prove the difficulty in being effective without cartilage. And it *sounds* painful. 2002 Outlook: C

Scott Radinsky (Pos: LHP, **Age**: 34)

	W	L	Pct.	ERA	G	GS	Sv	IP	H	BB	SO	HR	Ratio
2001	0	0	-	27.00	2	0	0	2.0	4	3	3	2	3.50
Career	42	25	.627	3.44	557	0	52	481.2	461	209	358	33	1.39

Radinsky missed the last halves of 1999 and 2000 with separate surgeries on his pitching elbow; he spent most of 2001 rehabbing in the minors. He re-signed in November, hoping to secure a lefty specialist role. 2002 Outlook: C

Dave Roberts (Pos: LF, **Age**: 29, **Bats**: L)

	G	AB	R	H	D	T	HR	RBI	SB	BB	SO	Avg	OBP	Slg
2001	15	12	3	4	1	0	0	2	0	1	2	.333	.385	.417
Career	75	165	30	40	5	0	2	14	12	12	20	.242	.292	.309

Roberts' speed and defense are the best things he has going for him. With the Indians trying to save some money, he might be able to snag a reserve spot in the outfield. 2002 Outlook: C

Rich Rodriguez (Pos: LHP, **Age**: 39)

	W	L	Pct.	ERA	G	GS	Sv	IP	H	BB	SO	HR	Ratio
2001	2	2	.500	4.15	53	0	0	39.0	41	17	31	2	1.49
Career	28	20	.583	3.77	570	2	7	620.1	624	249	381	61	1.41

Rodriguez had a nice season making brief appearances out of the bullpen. The lefty specialist filed for free agency in November and may change teams for the sixth time in his career. 2002 Outlook: B

Roy Smith (Pos: RHP, **Age**: 25)

	W	L	Pct.	ERA	G	GS	Sv	IP	H	BB	SO	HR	Ratio
2001	0	0	-	6.06	9	0	0	16.1	16	13	17	3	1.78
Career	0	0	-	6.06	9	0	0	16.1	16	13	17	3	1.78

Smith has had success in the minors over the last two years, but it did not translate in his major league debut last season. He likely will have another opportunity to gain a spot in the bullpen. 2002 Outlook: C

Steve Woodard (Pos: RHP, **Age**: 26)

	W	L	Pct.	ERA	G	GS	Sv	IP	H	BB	SO	HR	Ratio
2001	3	3	.500	5.20	29	10	0	97.0	129	17	52	10	1.51
Career	31	36	.463	4.88	141	94	0	632.0	739	136	438	83	1.38

Woodard's success has been as a reliever rather than as a starter. He complained when used as a long reliever, and the Tribe released him after a mediocre 2001 season. 2002 Outlook: C

Jaret Wright (Pos: RHP, **Age**: 26)

	W	L	Pct.	ERA	G	GS	Sv	IP	H	BB	SO	HR	Ratio
2001	2	2	.500	6.52	7	7	0	29.0	36	22	18	2	2.00
Career	33	29	.532	5.12	90	90	0	497.1	512	249	348	57	1.53

Wright's career has gone downhill since starting the seventh game of the World Series as a rookie. He's been busy with arm injuries, the latest being shoulder surgery. He should be ready by spring training. 2002 Outlook: C

Cleveland

Cleveland Indians Minor League Prospects

Organization Overview:

The cost of staying competitive over the last decade has been steep. The organization that has developed Albert Belle, Sean Casey, Bartolo Colon, Brian Giles, Danny Graves, Steve Kline, Charles Nagy, Manny Ramirez, Richie Sexson and Jim Thome isn't as deep in prospects now as it was several years ago. Russell Branyan is the only untapped power source who is on the cusp of helping in Cleveland, and Milton Bradley is the only other position player close to earning a regular job. The ownership has decided to cut back on spending, so the farm system once again becomes the primary source for talent in Cleveland. For now, the Indians hope a few of the young pitchers in the high minors will be ready to help a rebuilding pitching staff.

Milton Bradley

Position: OF   **Opening Day Age:** 23
Bats: B **Throws:** R   **Born:** 4/15/78 in Harbor
Ht: 6' 0" **Wt:** 190   City, CA

Recent Statistics

	G	AB	R	H	D	T	HR	RBI	SB	BB	SO	Avg
2001 AAA Ottawa	35	136	21	37	7	2	2	13	14	23	30	.272
2001 AAA Buffalo	30	114	18	29	3	0	5	15	9	19	31	.254
2001 NL Montreal	67	220	19	49	16	3	1	19	7	19	62	.223
2001 AL Cleveland	10	18	3	4	1	0	0	0	1	2	3	.222
2001 MLE	65	245	35	61	9	1	5	25	17	37	63	.249

Dealt to Cleveland last July, Bradley has escaped the pressures of being a top-flight Montreal prospect who must assume a major league job before he's ready. Already he is an outstanding center fielder with good speed and a strong arm. He's less polished as a hitter, but he strokes the ball well from both sides of the plate and has shown decent plate discipline in the minors. His patience has suffered in the majors, but the Indians are convinced he has too much ability to fail. Despite Kenny Lofton's departure, Cleveland isn't looking at Bradley as a leadoff hitter in 2002. He may take over Lofton's job, but would break into the lineup further down in the order.

Ryan Drese

Position: P   **Opening Day Age:** 25
Bats: R **Throws:** R   **Born:** 4/5/76 in San
Ht: 6' 3" **Wt:** 220   Francisco, CA

Recent Statistics

	W	L	ERA	G	GS	Sv	IP	H	R	BB	SO	HR
2001 AA Akron	5	7	3.35	14	13	0	86.0	64	34	29	73	4
2001 AAA Buffalo	5	1	4.01	11	10	0	60.2	60	28	17	52	7
2001 AL Cleveland	1	2	3.44	9	4	0	36.2	32	15	15	24	2

A fifth-round pick in 1998, Drese dominated in a brief stint at short-season Mahoning Valley in 1999 and climbed to high-A Kinston in his first full season as a pro. His progress slowed in 2000 when he tore a knee ligament in the offseason and re-injured the knee in a mid-April game with Kinston, this time requiring reconstructive surgery. Drese rebounded and split a productive 2001 season between Double-A Akron and Triple-A Buffalo before debuting effectively with Cleveland in the second half. His diverse repertoire includes a fastball, cutter, slider, curveball and changeup. His command of the fastball is less developed than for his other pitches, but he's effective when he has it. He'll compete for a job in Cleveland's rotation this spring.

Tim Drew

Position: P   **Opening Day Age:** 23
Bats: R **Throws:** R   **Born:** 8/31/78 in
Ht: 6' 1" **Wt:** 195   Valdosta, GA

Recent Statistics

	W	L	ERA	G	GS	Sv	IP	H	R	BB	SO	HR
2001 AAA Buffalo	8	6	3.92	18	18	0	108.0	115	54	27	75	13
2001 AL Cleveland	0	2	7.97	8	6	0	35.0	51	39	16	15	9

Drew joined brother J.D. as a first-round pick in 1997, and Tim went 13-5 (3.73) at high Class-A Kinston in '99 to lead the Carolina League in wins. Drew also pitched well at Double-A Akron to open 2000, but later struggled at Triple-A Buffalo. Drew added 15 pounds of muscle during the offseason and came into camp a different pitcher last spring. He impressed manager Charlie Manuel by pitching aggressively and secured the fifth-starter role. His spring success didn't carry over, though, as hitters adjusted to him and he wasn't able to counter quickly with his own adjustments. Drew calls on a fastball-changeup combo with his change as his out pitch. He tends to pound the strike zone, and he needs to better locate his pitches within it.

Alex Escobar

Position: OF   **Opening Day Age:** 23
Bats: R **Throws:** R   **Born:** 9/6/78 in Valencia,
Ht: 6' 1" **Wt:** 180   VZ

Recent Statistics

	G	AB	R	H	D	T	HR	RBI	SB	BB	SO	Avg
2001 AAA Norfolk	111	397	55	106	21	4	12	52	18	35	146	.267
2001 NL New York	18	50	3	10	1	0	3	8	1	3	19	.200
2001 MLE	111	384	46	93	18	3	9	44	13	29	154	.242

This top-flight Mets prospect struggled a bit last season and didn't make enough contact. Part of the problem was that he put too much pressure on himself to live up to expectations. He showed more success when he took things less seriously. He's a five-tool talent with the ability to hit for power and steal bases. While at Triple-A Norfolk last season, Escobar's batting average was nearly the same against lefthanded and righthanded pitchers. His walk rate declined at Norfolk, and he would progress rapidly if he improved his command of the strike zone. Traded to Cleveland in the Roberto Alomar deal, Escobar will continue to work on his plate discipline at Triple-A Buffalo in 2002.

Alex Herrera

Position: P
Bats: L **Throws:** L
Ht: 5' 11" **Wt:** 175

Opening Day Age: 22
Born: 11/5/79 in
Maracaibo, VZ

Recent Statistics

	W	L	ERA	G	GS	Sv	IP	H	R	BB	SO	HR
2000 A Columbus	4	3	3.43	20	0	0	42.0	41	25	21	41	1
2000 A Kinston	0	1	2.32	17	0	1	31.0	28	11	19	40	1
2000 AA Akron	0	0	0.00	2	0	0	1.1	2	1	1	1	0
2001 A Kinston	4	0	0.60	28	0	3	59.2	36	6	18	83	1
2001 AA Akron	3	0	2.83	15	0	2	28.2	24	9	9	22	1

After a solid North American debut split between Class-A Columbus and high-A Kinston in 2000, Herrera was even more unhittable at Kinston and Double-A Akron in 2001. A power pitcher signed in July 1997, he works effectively with a fastball-slider combo that is the best among all lefties in the system. He works in the low-90s with his fastball, and he puts hitters away with the slider. He showed signs of maturing in 2001, looking beyond his power approach to make quick adjustments to hitters, which he did effectively. Herrera's future is in the bullpen, and if he improves his command within the strike zone early in 2002, he may arrive quickly in Cleveland.

David Riske

Position: P
Bats: R **Throws:** R
Ht: 6' 2" **Wt:** 175

Opening Day Age: 25
Born: 10/23/76 in
Renton, WA

Recent Statistics

	W	L	ERA	G	GS	Sv	IP	H	R	BB	SO	HR
2001 AAA Buffalo	1	2	2.36	38	0	15	53.1	45	16	17	72	2
2001 AL Cleveland	2	0	1.98	26	0	1	27.1	20	7	18	29	3

Riske has overcome great odds as a 56th-round draft pick in 1996. And he has persevered through a bulging disk that required surgery in May 2000, and a labrum tear discovered that September ended his season after just seven innings of work. Riske bounced back and had a terrific season at Triple-A Buffalo in 2001. He earned a promotion to Cleveland, and quickly showed he has a future in the bullpen. He accumulates high strikeout totals for a guy who doesn't have great stuff. Riske calls on a solid fastball that is aided by impressive command and deception in his delivery. His secondary pitches are less effective, but work continues on an offspeed splitter and slurve. Sometimes he works with just his fastball.

Brian Tallet

Position: P
Bats: L **Throws:** L
Ht: 6' 7" **Wt:** 208

Opening Day Age: 24
Born: 9/21/77 in
Midwest City, OK

Recent Statistics

	W	L	ERA	G	GS	Sv	IP	H	R	BB	SO	HR
2000 A Mahoning Vy	0	0	1.15	6	6	0	15.2	10	2	3	20	0
2001 A Kinston	9	7	3.04	27	27	0	160.0	134	62	38	164	12

A second-round choice in 2000, Tallet went from starting the championship game of the 2000 College World Series for LSU to beginning a pro career at short-season Mahoning Valley. He proved difficult to hit in six starts and fanned better than a batter an inning there. Tallet maintained that strikeout rate despite jumping all the way to high Class-A Kinston in 2001, his first full season as a pro. The lefthander works with three solid offerings: a low-90s fastball, slider and changeup. His 6-foot-7 frame provides a nice downward angle for his pitches, and his mound presence is another plus that puts Tallet on the fast track to Cleveland.

Jake Westbrook

Position: P
Bats: R **Throws:** R
Ht: 6' 3" **Wt:** 185

Opening Day Age: 24
Born: 9/29/77 in Athens,
GA

Recent Statistics

	W	L	ERA	G	GS	Sv	IP	H	R	BB	SO	HR
2001 AAA Buffalo	8	1	3.20	12	12	0	64.2	60	27	23	45	2
2001 AL Cleveland	4	4	5.85	23	6	0	64.2	79	43	22	48	6

A Colorado first-round pick in 1996, Westbrook has pitched in four organizations because he's been moved in three major league trades. He posted double-digit wins in the final three seasons of the 1990s in the Montreal system, before moving from the Yankees to Cleveland for Dave Justice in July 2000. He was nursing a broken rib at the time, and debuted in the Indians' system with an 8-1 (3.20) performance at Triple-A Buffalo in 2001, his best showing in the high minors. In Cleveland, he struggled moving between the rotation and the bullpen before settling into the pen and pitching better there. He's smart on the mound, but has average stuff. He has a decent changeup that keeps hitters off his sinking fastball, but he must be more consistent with his slider.

Others to Watch

The 35th overall pick last June, **J.D. Martin** (19) set the Rookie-level Appy League on its ear by debuting with 22 scoreless innings. Showing remarkable poise and polish, he didn't allow a hit in three of his first six starts. His fastball is in the high 80s, but he has impressive command of a solid changeup and his breaking pitches, which overwhelmed hitters... Switch-hitting catcher **Vic Martinez** (23) is an excellent receiver who is advanced for his level at calling a game. His bat came around in 2001 at high Class-A Kinston, where he batted .329-10-57 and won the league's batting title and MVP award... An impressive athlete with size, speed and power potential, third baseman **Corey Smith** (19) has been challenged by his affiliation assignments, and his numbers don't really reflect his promise. Still, he had 18 homers and 85 RBI in 130 games in the Class-A Sally League in 2001... Another lefty who may be on the fast track is **Billy Traber** (22), the Mets' 2000 first-round pick who was dealt in the Roberto Alomar trade. He signed too late to play that year, but in 2001 he debuted in high Class-A ball and advanced to Triple-A Norfolk on the strength of a four-pitch arsenal that includes an 88-92 MPH fastball, curveball, changeup and splitter, which is his out pitch. He was 10-9 (3.09) in his pro debut.

Comerica Park

Offense

Comerica Park benefits line-drive hitters who stroke the ball into the gaps and lefthanded pull hitters. It is a nightmare for righthanded flyball hitters who count on towering drives over the left-field wall. It is extremely difficult to homer in left or center field. Because the park is so spacious, outfielders tend to play deeper and popfly base hits are common. Although the Tigers have only average speed, they led the American League and ranked second in the majors in triples in 2001. Of the 60 triples the Tigers hit last season, 44 were hit at home.

Defense

Comerica Park is good for pitchers because it is difficult to hit home runs there. It is bad for pitchers in that a lot of bloop hits fall in. Range in the outfield helps immensely to defuse potential problems defensively. The pace of the infield on groundballs is average.

Who It Helps the Most

Comerica Park is a good park for lefthanded hitters such as Robert Fick and Bobby Higginson, who pull the ball with power, yet are able to drive the ball up the gaps. It helps a pitcher such as Jose Lima, who yields a lot of flyballs. Balls that are home runs in virtually any other park in the major leagues are just long outs at Comerica Park.

Who It Hurts the Most

It is really tough on an outfielder who lacks instincts and range. Last season, Roger Cedeno was exposed badly at Comerica Park. His speed was not enough to make up for a poor jump. Conversely, left fielder Bobby Higginson, who does not have good speed, has performed well defensively at Comerica Park because he gets good jumps.

Rookies & Newcomers

Eric Munson should perform well at Comerica. He has a quick lefthanded bat. He pulls the ball with power, yet is capable of driving the ball into the gap. Pitcher Nate Cornejo also should do well at Comerica Park. He has extraordinary sinking action on his fastball and will yield a lot of groundballs.

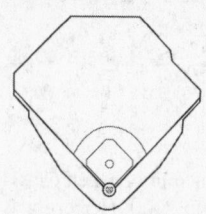

Dimensions: LF-345, LCF-395, CF-420, RCF-365, RF-330

Capacity: 40,120

Elevation: 585 feet

Surface: Grass

Foul Territory: Average

Park Factors

2001 Season

	Home Games			Away Games			
	Tigers	Opp	Total	Tigers	Opp	Total	Index
G	72	72	144	72	72	144	—
Avg	.263	.276	.270	.253	.296	.275	98
AB	2394	2503	4897	2520	2507	5027	97
R	309	357	666	324	414	738	90
H	629	692	1321	637	743	1380	96
2B	118	133	251	141	164	305	84
3B	40	27	67	15	18	33	208
HR	50	60	110	69	94	163	69
BB	210	255	465	201	234	435	110
SO	375	359	734	477	388	865	87
E	66	57	123	57	59	116	106
E-Infield	54	52	106	40	51	91	116
LHB-Avg	.279	.295	.287	.260	.284	.272	106
LHB-HR	27	43	70	30	44	74	96
RHB-Avg	.249	.261	.255	.247	.308	.276	92
RHB-HR	23	17	40	39	50	89	46

2000 Season

	Home Games			Away Games			
	Tigers	Opp	Total	Tigers	Opp	Total	Index
G	72	72	144	72	72	144	—
Avg	.280	.281	.280	.275	.281	.278	101
AB	2445	2572	5017	2573	2430	5003	100
R	350	358	708	396	401	797	89
H	684	723	1407	708	682	1390	101
2B	136	143	279	134	126	260	107
3B	20	19	39	16	21	37	105
HR	64	58	122	102	98	200	61
BB	273	203	476	233	250	483	98
SO	388	413	801	476	434	910	88
E	50	57	107	46	49	95	113
E-Infield	39	46	85	38	41	79	108
LHB-Avg	.291	.272	.280	.260	.261	.261	107
LHB-HR	27	37	64	33	56	89	72
RHB-Avg	.273	.289	.281	.282	.300	.290	97
RHB-HR	37	21	58	69	42	111	52

2001 Rankings (American League)

- Highest triple factor
- Second-highest walk factor
- Second-highest infield-error factor
- Lowest home-run factor
- Lowest strikeout factor
- Lowest RHB home-run factor
- Second-lowest double factor
- Second-lowest RHB batting-average factor

Phil Garner

Born: 4/30/49 in Jefferson City, TN

Playing Experience: 1973-1988, Oak, Pit, Hou, LA, SF

Managerial Experience: 10 seasons

2001 Season

Phil Garner called last season his most disappointing as a major league manager. Not only did the Tigers lose 13 more games than they did in 2000, but by the end of the season, the clubhouse was in disarray and it appeared as if the players had quit on Garner. At various points of the season, Garner was involved in shouting matches with Roger Cedeno and Robert Fick, and was criticized publicly by pitchers Jeff Weaver and C.J. Nitkowski. The young players the organization sent to him from the minor leagues did not make significant progress. And two players the organization had been hanging its collective hat on, shortstop Deivi Cruz and outfielder Juan Encarnacion, had dreadful seasons.

Offense

Garner pretty much plays it by the book. He bunts when it is traditionally called for, and he hits-and-runs when it is traditionally called for. Comerica Park is a spacious field and the Tigers lack power, so Garner tried to be more aggressive on the bases last season. Detroit attempted 194 steals compared to 121 in 2000, and the club was successful at the same rate, 69 percent. Because his team struggles so much to score runs, Garner is willing to give up a lot defensively to gain something offensively when he makes out the lineup card.

Pitching & Defense

The critisism that Garner received by some of his pitchers last year concerning overuse had some vailidity. He was one of the slowest managers in all of baseball when it came to taking his starters out of games in 2001. However, he is careful not to use his relievers on back-to-back days unless it is absolutely necessary. On defense, he was very conservative with his substitutions last year.

2002 Outlook

Garner is in the third year of a four-year contract. That makes this a make-or-break season for him in Detroit. Another season like 2001, and it will be unlikely that Garner will be around for the final year of his current pact.

Manager Statistics

Year	Team, Lg	W	L	Pct	GB	Finish
2001	Detroit, AL	66	96	.407	25.0	4th Central
10 Seasons		708	796	.478	—	

2001 Starting Pitchers by Days Rest

	<=3	4	5	6+
Tigers Starts	0	71	57	23
Tigers ERA	—	5.49	4.90	4.68
AL Avg Starts	1	78	48	24
AL ERA	5.92	4.69	4.58	4.58

2001 Situational Stats

	Phil Garner	AL Average
Hit & Run Success %	28.4	35.0
Stolen Base Success %	68.6	71.0
Platoon Pct.	64.2	59.1
Defensive Subs	14	26
High-Pitch Outings	9	6
Quick/Slow Hooks	12/23	19/16
Sacrifice Attempts	58	54

2001 Rankings (American League)

- 1st in squeeze plays (7)
- 2nd in slow hooks, mid-inning pitching changes (205) and one-batter pitcher appearances (41)
- 3rd in starts with over 120 pitches (9)

Matt Anderson

2001 Season

Matt Anderson emerged as a legitimate major league closer in 2001. The first overall choice in the 1997 draft, Anderson beat out Todd Jones to become the Tigers' bullpen stopper, and Jones was traded to Minnesota in late July. Anderson blew his first and last save opportunities, but converted 22 straight in between. He walked only 18 hitters in 56 innings, after walking 45 in 74.1 innings during 2000 and 35 in 38 innings during 1999. Over his career, Anderson had converted only one save in his first eight opportunities before he put together the 22-save stretch.

Pitching

Anderson is one of those rare pitchers who consistently registers 100 MPH or faster on the radar gun. But he also is living proof that it doesn't matter how hard a pitcher throws; major league hitters will catch up to anyone if they are allowed to sit on a fastball. Anderson's breaking ball, which is a knuckle curve, was much more effective last season because he was able to throw it for strikes consistently. He also added a split-finger pitch to his menu, giving him three vastly different levels of velocity with which to work. His fastball, which he is spotting better, arrives in the high 90s and sometimes tops 100 MPH. His breaking ball is in the high 80s and his splitter in the low 80s. Throw better poise into the mix, and out comes a big-time closer.

Defense

Anderson is an exceptional athlete. He runs well and reacts quickly on the mound. His pickoff move is average and sometimes he ignores baserunners. Anderson, however, has a relatively fast delivery to the plate. Coupled with his velocity, that does not make him easy to steal on.

2002 Outlook

For Anderson, comparing last season to the previous two was like night and day. The only reason he did not compile more saves in 2001 was his club's poor performance, which provided few leads to protect. He may be on the verge of becoming the game's next great closer.

Position: RP
Bats: R **Throws:** R
Ht: 6' 4" **Wt:** 200

Opening Day Age: 25
Born: 8/17/76 in Louisville, KY
ML Seasons: 4

Overall Statistics

	W	L	Pct.	ERA	G	GS	Sv	IP	H	BB	SO	HR	Ratio
2001	3	1	.750	4.82	62	0	22	56.0	56	18	52	2	1.32
Career	13	5	.722	4.62	210	0	23	212.1	188	129	199	21	1.49

How Often He Throws Strikes

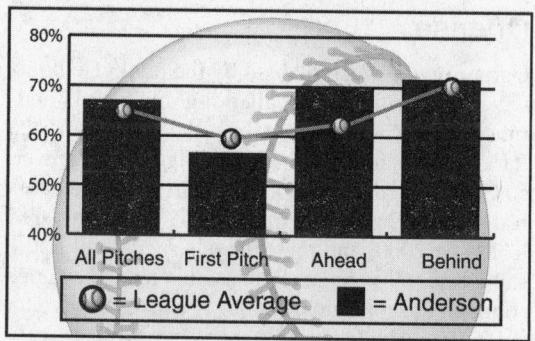

= League Average   = Anderson

2001 Situational Stats

	W	L	ERA	Sv	IP		AB	H	HR	RBI	Avg
Home	3	1	3.68	12	29.1	LHB	110	32	0	22	.291
Road	0	0	6.08	10	26.2	RHB	108	24	2	10	.222
First Half	3	0	5.45	8	34.2	Sc Pos	87	23	1	28	.264
Scnd Half	0	1	3.80	14	21.1	Clutch	108	25	1	19	.231

2001 Rankings (American League)

- 3rd in save percentage (91.7)
- 4th in highest relief ERA (4.82)
- 8th in wild pitches (9)
- Led the Tigers in games pitched, saves, games finished (41), wild pitches (9), save opportunities (24), save percentage (91.7), first batter efficiency (.236), lowest batting average allowed in relief (.257) and most strikeouts per nine innings in relief (8.4)

Roger Cedeno

Signed By
METS

2001 Season

With free agency pending for the first time following the 2001 season, Roger Cedeno was productive offensively. He set a career high with 48 RBI, 12 more than his previous best. He also was leading the American League in stolen bases with 55 when he was benched on September 10 by Detroit manager Phil Garner. He sat the rest of the year after a dispute with Garner during an intrasquad game, which took place while baseball was shut down because of the terrorist attacks.

Hitting

Cedeno does not have a smooth batting stroke. He chops at the ball and favors the high fastball. He does not hit low pitches nearly as well. A free swinger, Cedeno does not walk enough given his speed. He has limited power, but does drive the ball into the gaps. A switch-hitter, Cedeno hit much better from the left side early in his career, but he has closed the gap the past two seasons from the right side. He hit .282 righthanded last season and .313 in 2000, when he was with Houston.

Baserunning & Defense

Cedeno is an exceptional baserunner. He has excellent speed and good instincts, and he gets a good jump on basestealing attempts. If he has a weakness, it's that he occasionally gets too aggressive on the bases. Cedeno is not a good fielder. He is poor in center field and worse in right field. He made 12 errors last season, including seven in just 55 games in right. He cannot turn, run to a spot and wait for the ball. He has to watch it all way. He breaks slowly on the ball, especially on drives hit directly over his head. His arm is average.

2002 Outlook

The Tigers wanted to re-sign Cedeno, but he turned down a three-year, $13.5 million offer during the 2001 season. Any chance of returning ended with the blowup with Garner, although at the time the two sides still were at least $10 million apart and at odds over the length of the contract. In December, Cedeno agreed to a four-year, $18 million deal to play a corner-outfield slot with the Mets. He had his best big league season with them in 1999.

Position: CF/RF
Bats: B **Throws:** R
Ht: 6' 1" **Wt:** 205

Opening Day Age: 27
Born: 8/16/74 in Valencia Edo. Carabobo, Venezuela
ML Seasons: 7
Pronunciation: sid-AIN-yo

Overall Statistics

	G	AB	R	H	D	T	HR	RBI	SB	BB	SO	Avg	OBP	Slg
2001	131	523	79	153	14	11	6	48	55	36	83	.293	.337	.396
Career	671	1922	317	541	73	24	23	165	169	218	388	.281	.355	.380

Where He Hits the Ball

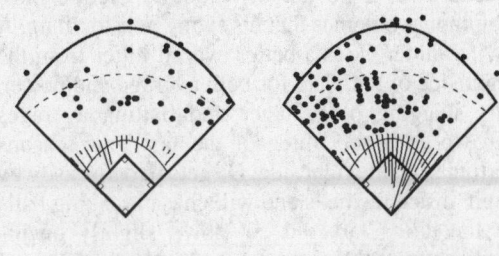

Vs. LHP   **Vs. RHP**

2001 Situational Stats

	AB	H	HR	RBI	Avg		AB	H	HR	RBI	Avg
Home	270	84	3	21	.311	LHP	142	40	3	14	.282
Road	253	69	3	27	.273	RHP	381	113	3	34	.297
First Half	305	84	1	21	.275	Sc Pos	110	35	2	43	.318
Scnd Half	218	69	5	27	.317	Clutch	68	22	0	10	.324

2001 Rankings (American League)

- 1st in caught stealing (15)
- 2nd in stolen bases, highest groundball/flyball ratio (2.5) and errors in right field (7)
- 3rd in errors in center field (5)
- 4th in triples and lowest HR frequency (87.2 ABs per HR)
- 5th in bunts in play (31)
- 6th in steals of third (6)
- Led the Tigers in batting average, hits, singles, triples, stolen bases, caught stealing (15), highest groundball-flyball ratio (2.5), stolen-base percentage (78.6), bunts in play (31), steals of third (6), batting average with runners in scoring position, batting average vs. righthanded pitchers and on-base percentage for a leadoff hitter (.338)

Tony Clark

2001 Season

For the first time since his first full season in the majors in 1997, Tony Clark got off to a good start. He was hitting .305 with 13 home runs and 51 RBI at the break and was the Tigers' lone representative at the All-Star game. After the break, Clark was hindered by a host of injuries. He was hampered by a stiff back, which has become a chronic problem. He also suffered from inflammation in his right wrist and a sore left shoulder. As a result, Clark collected just three home runs and 24 RBI following the All-Star break. He did not play after September 22 because of the wrist injury.

Hitting

Because he is so tall at 6-foot-7, Clark's most common problem is that his swing gets too long. A switch-hitter, he is a better overall hitter from the right side of the plate for both average and power. His slugging percentages and batting averages have been higher three of the last four seasons hitting from the right side. He gets tied up easily by high, inside fastballs and will chase breaking balls in the dirt. Clark did cut down slightly on his strikeouts in 2001.

Baserunning & Defense

Clark has no speed whatsoever. He has improved as a baserunner, finally ridding himself of a propensity to run into easy outs. Defensively, Clark has below-average range but usually will field grounders hit at him. A former outfielder, he does track popouts surprisingly well. He also is good at digging throws out of the dirt and presents a good throwing target.

2002 Outlook

His bat is live, but Clark's back ailment and his tendency to suffer other kinds of injuries have become a major concern. After numerous attempts to trade Clark, the Tigers put him on waivers in November and the Red Sox claimed him. He's hit .382-6-24 in 110 at-bats in his new home park. He had hit safely in all 27 games he had played at Fenway until he went 0-for-1 as a pinch-hitter in his last game there last September. Clark is eligible for free agency after the 2002 season.

Position: 1B/DH
Bats: B **Throws:** R
Ht: 6' 7" **Wt:** 245

Opening Day Age: 29
Born: 6/15/72 in Newton, KS
ML Seasons: 7

Overall Statistics

	G	AB	R	H	D	T	HR	RBI	SB	BB	SO	Avg	OBP	Slg
2001	126	428	67	123	29	3	16	75	0	62	108	.287	.374	.481
Career	772	2831	428	783	156	7	156	514	6	343	721	.277	.355	.502

Where He Hits the Ball

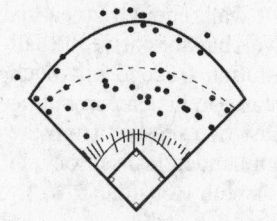 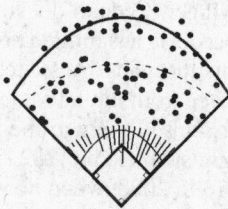

Vs. LHP   **Vs. RHP**

2001 Situational Stats

	AB	H	HR	RBI	Avg		AB	H	HR	RBI	Avg
Home	207	59	7	38	.285	LHP	140	45	7	28	.321
Road	221	64	9	37	.290	RHP	288	78	9	47	.271
First Half	269	82	13	51	.305	Sc Pos	116	35	6	59	.302
Scnd Half	159	41	3	24	.258	Clutch	56	14	3	6	.250

2001 Rankings (American League)

- 3rd in lowest percentage of swings put into play (33.5)
- 4th in lowest cleanup slugging percentage (.456)
- 6th in most GDPs per GDP situation (17.5%)
- 8th in intentional walks (10)
- 9th in slugging percentage vs. lefthanded pitchers (.557) and lowest batting average on a 3-1 count (.100)
- Led the Tigers in RBI, intentional walks (10), strikeouts, GDPs (14), slugging percentage, batting average vs. lefthanded pitchers, cleanup slugging percentage (.456), slugging percentage vs. lefthanded pitchers (.557) and batting average on the road

Deivi Cruz

2001 Season

Deivi Cruz took a step back in every aspect of his game last season. His batting average, doubles, RBI and slugging percentage all fell off dramatically. Even his on-base percentage, poor to begin with, went down. He missed six weeks of the season with a broken left foot and balked at the thought of playing third base, although he eventually did start seven straight games there. By the beginning of September, Cruz was a part-time player moving in and out of the lineup at shortstop, though he regained his starting job with a strong finish.

Hitting

Cruz swings at everything. High and wide. In the dirt. Breaking balls. Fastballs. It makes no difference. The end result is that Cruz seldom walks. The difference between last season and 2000, when Cruz ranked third in the American League with 46 doubles and drove in 82 runs, is that he missed on a lot of the good pitches that were served his way. In 2001, Cruz was not as good of a dead-fastball hitter, which had been his great strength. Also, pitchers adjusted to Cruz' success. Suddenly considered dangerous after posting surprising power numbers in 2000, he did not see as many good pitches to hit.

Baserunning & Defense

Cruz is amazingly slow for a middle infielder and is a poor baserunner. He shows bad instincts on the bases and is not a threat to steal. Defensively, Cruz' range is average. He does make the routine play well and has a strong, accurate arm. Cruz has exceptional ability making relay throws from the outfield.

2002 Outlook

The Tigers no longer look at Cruz as their shortstop of the future. They like Omar Infante, who starred as a 19-year-old for Double-A Erie in 2001, much better. In fact, Cruz was designated for assignment in December to make room on the 40-man roster for newly signed Craig Paquette. Cruz' days in Detroit appear to be over. If he has a long-range future in the major leagues, it could be at third base.

Position: SS
Bats: R **Throws:** R
Ht: 6' 0" **Wt:** 184

Opening Day Age: 26
Born: 11/6/75 in Nizao de Bani, Dominican Republic
ML Seasons: 5
Pronunciation: DAY-vee

Overall Statistics

	G	AB	R	H	D	T	HR	RBI	SB	BB	SO	Avg	OBP	Slg
2001	110	414	39	106	28	1	7	52	4	17	46	.256	.291	.379
Career	703	2405	258	652	157	9	37	277	12	69	256	.271	.293	.390

Where He Hits the Ball

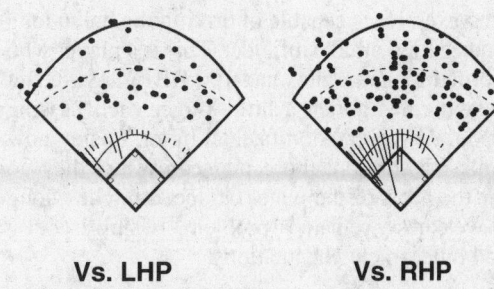

Vs. LHP   **Vs. RHP**

2001 Situational Stats

	AB	H	HR	RBI	Avg		AB	H	HR	RBI	Avg
Home	198	54	2	29	.273	LHP	112	25	2	14	.223
Road	216	52	5	23	.241	RHP	302	81	5	38	.268
First Half	210	52	2	24	.248	Sc Pos	102	30	3	44	.294
Scnd Half	204	54	5	28	.265	Clutch	68	15	1	8	.221

2001 Rankings (American League)

- 2nd in lowest fielding percentage at shortstop (.964)
- 4th in errors at shortstop (17)
- 8th in lowest batting average on a 3-2 count (.105)
- Led the Tigers in batting average on a 3-1 count (.500)

Damion Easley

2001 Season

Last season was another disappointing one for Damion Easley. His batting average continued to slide, reaching another low since he was acquired by Detroit from the Angels during the 1996 season. His on-base percentage, slugging percentage and stolen bases also continued to decline. Easley was hitting .289 entering July, but hit only .216 the remainder of the season. He did his best work hitting low in the batting order. In 167 at-bats hitting seventh or eighth, Easley batted .353. In the second spot, where he had 393 at-bats, Easley hit just .214.

Hitting

Easley trademarks are good balance in his stance and power. He is capable of driving the ball a long distance for a middle infielder. This is a player who recorded 27 home runs and 100 RBI in 1998. But his swing has gotten a little longer each passing season. Always a good fastball hitter, Easley now is missing some of those pitches even if they go near the heart of the plate. Offspeed pitches, long his weakness, remain a problem. Easley is not a good hitter in clutch situations.

Baserunning & Defense

At 32 with his frame filled out, Easley no longer is the above-average runner he used to be. He barely reached double figures in steals last season. He now is an average runner, at best. Easley is solid defensively. He makes the routine play and turns the double play well. His hands are good and his arm strength is above-average for the position. He makes excellent relay throws. He knows hitters well and reacts quickly to batted balls.

2002 Outlook

Easley has his shortcomings, not the least of which are the increasingly big holes in his swing. His production seems to fall each season, but he plays hard every day. Easley has been on a club devoid of leadership, especially last season, and has tried his best to lead in his own way, quietly and by example.

Position: 2B
Bats: R **Throws:** R
Ht: 5'11" **Wt:** 185

Opening Day Age: 32
Born: 11/11/69 in New York, NY
ML Seasons: 10

Overall Statistics

	G	AB	R	H	D	T	HR	RBI	SB	BB	SO	Avg	OBP	Slg
2001	154	585	77	146	27	7	11	65	10	52	90	.250	.323	.376
Career	1106	3885	554	998	209	20	111	476	104	372	688	.257	.334	.407

Where He Hits the Ball

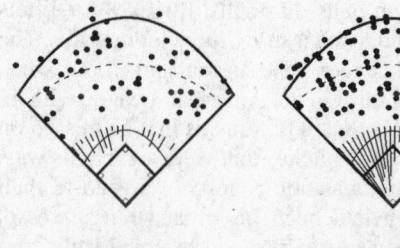

Vs. LHP   **Vs. RHP**

2001 Situational Stats

	AB	H	HR	RBI	Avg		AB	H	HR	RBI	Avg
Home	279	71	4	33	.254	LHP	148	35	2	17	.236
Road	306	75	7	32	.245	RHP	437	111	9	48	.254
First Half	299	84	6	33	.281	Sc Pos	155	39	2	50	.252
Scnd Half	286	62	5	32	.217	Clutch	75	18	1	6	.240

2001 Rankings (American League)

- 3rd in lowest percentage of extra bases taken as a runner (29.1)
- 5th in errors at second base (14) and fielding percentage at second base (.982)
- Led the Tigers in at-bats, hit by pitch (13), plate appearances (658), games played, highest percentage of swings put into play (49.9) and batting average on a 3-2 count (.292)

Juan Encarnacion

2001 Season

By the end of the 2001 season, Juan Encarnacion found himself entrenched in Detroit manager Phil Garner's doghouse. Although healthy, Encarnacion did not start a game after September 4, and did not play at all after September 10. He began the season in center field, but faltered defensively, misjudging several flyballs. Encarnacion was moved back to right field, the position he has played the best during his career. Although the move helped him defensively, Encarnacion continued to flounder at the plate. He hit 47 points lower than he did in 2000 and his on-base percentage was just .292.

Hitting

Encarnacion's obvious flaws as a hitter have become even more pronounced. He does not recognize pitches well and swings at too many offerings out of the strike zone. He does have raw power and has hit some tape-measure home runs. But such acts of power are few and far between. Mostly, he flails away aimlessly at breaking balls low and outside. Encarnacion has a 4.3-1 strikeout-walk ratio in his big league career, which says plenty about his lack of discipline at the plate.

Baserunning & Defense

Encarnacion has run the 60-yard dash in 6.4 seconds. Despite his excellent speed, he is not a good baserunner. He is a slow starter on batted balls while on the bases, and he does not get a good jump when attempting to steal. Encarnacion has a strong arm, but does not throw as well in games as he does during pregame work. He is far better in right field than he is in either center or left.

2002 Outlook

Encarnacion's instincts for the game are not good. He routinely hesitates before he reacts on the field and does not communicate well on or off the diamond. The Tigers cashed in on Encarnacion by trading him to the Reds for a more-productive Dmitri Young. Encarnacion joins a crowded outfield in Cincinnati and may not start. He better turn things around or he soon will be just another story of a five-tool player who wasted his considerable gifts.

Position: RF/CF
Bats: R **Throws:** R
Ht: 6' 3" **Wt:** 187

Opening Day Age: 26
Born: 3/8/76 in Las Matas de Faran, Dominican Republic
ML Seasons: 5
Pronunciation: en-car-NAH-see-own

Overall Statistics

	G	AB	R	H	D	T	HR	RBI	SB	BB	SO	Avg	OBP	Slg
2001	120	417	52	101	19	7	12	52	9	25	93	.242	.292	.408
Career	444	1670	222	450	84	24	53	224	68	78	339	.269	.310	.444

Where He Hits the Ball

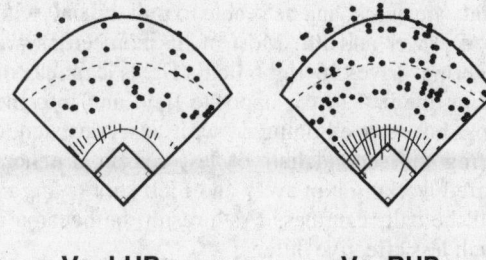

Vs. LHP   **Vs. RHP**

2001 Situational Stats

	AB	H	HR	RBI	Avg		AB	H	HR	RBI	Avg
Home	205	49	4	25	.239	LHP	116	30	4	14	.259
Road	212	52	8	27	.245	RHP	301	71	8	38	.236
First Half	271	70	10	44	.258	Sc Pos	110	21	2	40	.191
Scnd Half	146	31	2	8	.212	Clutch	64	25	3	14	.391

2001 Rankings (American League)

- 3rd in lowest batting average with runners in scoring position and lowest batting average on a 3-2 count (.088)
- 4th in batting average in the clutch
- 6th in errors in center field (4)
- 9th in triples
- Led the Tigers in batting average in the clutch

Robert Fick

Position: C/1B
Bats: L **Throws:** R
Ht: 6' 1" **Wt:** 189

Opening Day Age: 28
Born: 3/15/74 in Torrance, CA
ML Seasons: 4

2001 Season

During spring training, Robert Fick was told by Detroit manager Phil Garner that he would not be used as a catcher anymore. Then during the season, after Mitch Meluskey was lost to injury and rookie Brandon Inge struggled at the plate, Fick was made the club's everyday backstop. Fick led the Tigers in home runs with 19, but hit just two from July 25 until the end of the year. He did not perform well defensively. He allowed 12 passed balls in 78 games behind the plate, and threw out only 12 of 72 runners attempting to steal. By the end of the season, Fick no longer was starting at catcher.

Hitting

Fick has a smooth, compact lefthanded stroke. His hands are quick, and he is able to pull the ball with good power and lift. Most of his home runs are towering drives to right field. He is capable of hitting the ball to the opposite field and into the gaps, but stopped doing so with any consistency during the second half of last season. Pitchers started working him away and Fick kept trying to pull the ball regardless. As a result, he became a much less effective hitter.

Baserunning & Defense

Fick is not a good catcher. He does not receive the ball well, does not have a good feel for calling a game, and his throwing mechanics and arm strength are poor. He's also awkward at first base, especially when receiving throws. Fick took groundballs at third base during spring training, but that experiment was scrapped. Late in the season, he did play right field. He was not as bad as expected, given his lack of ability at other positions, but he didn't exactly remind anyone of Roberto Clemente.

2002 Outlook

Fick had a shouting match on the bench with Garner during a mid-July game in Cincinnati. And he got tossed around during a bench-clearing brawl in Kansas City and was suspended five games for his trouble. He is an emotional player, which is both a strength and a weakness, and a decent hitter. The Tigers will attempt to keep him in the lineup by trying him in right field in the spring.

Overall Statistics

	G	AB	R	H	D	T	HR	RBI	SB	BB	SO	Avg	OBP	Slg
2001	124	401	62	109	21	2	19	61	0	39	62	.272	.339	.476
Career	212	627	92	167	29	4	28	100	4	70	114	.266	.341	.459

Where He Hits the Ball

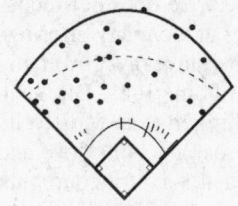 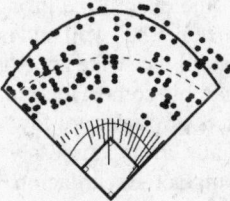

Vs. LHP   **Vs. RHP**

2001 Situational Stats

	AB	H	HR	RBI	Avg		AB	H	HR	RBI	Avg
Home	200	53	8	29	.265	LHP	76	18	2	9	.237
Road	201	56	11	32	.279	RHP	325	91	17	52	.280
First Half	205	63	14	39	.307	Sc Pos	124	29	3	39	.234
Scnd Half	196	46	5	22	.235	Clutch	66	19	1	7	.288

2001 Rankings (American League)

- 8th in errors at catcher (6)
- Led the Tigers in home runs and batting average with two strikes (.226)

Bobby Higginson

2001 Season

The dropoff was considerable. Bobby Higginson's batting average fell from .300 in 2000 to .277 last season. He also hit 13 fewer home runs, had 31 less RBI and his slugging percentage fell 93 points. It is hardly the stuff that earned Higginson a four-year, $34.5 million contract extension, which kicks in this season. As a topper, Higginson brooded in the clubhouse and became unpopular with some of his teammates.

Hitting

Higginson did not sting the ball last season like he has during most of his career. He still makes good contact and doesn't strike out much. In 2001, though, he missed having Dean Palmer in the lineup and Juan Gonzalez hitting behind him. Higginson has complained often about the distance of the fences at Comerica Park, but as a lefthanded pull hitter it should play to his strength. Right field is not ominous at Comerica. It is left field and center field that are unfair to hitters. When he is right, Higginson punishes a low, inside fastball and drives pitches from the middle half of the plate on out into the gaps. But Higginson wasn't right last season.

Baserunning & Defense

Higginson stole a career-best 20 bases last season, but also was caught stealing 12 times. He has average speed for a major league outfielder but is aggressive and smart on the bases. Defensively, he gets an excellent jump on the ball and generally has sure hands, although he did drop some flyballs in 2001, which was puzzling.

2002 Outlook

Amazingly, Higginson has not played a full season with a winning team since high school. At Temple University, in the minor leagues or in the major leagues, none of the teams he has played on has been above .500. All the losing seems to be wearing on him. Higginson presents the profile of a team leader in many ways and is popular with fans. Yet, he has not even come close to pulling off the leadership role. He probably would be best in a situation where he is just one of the main guys, not *the* main guy.

Position: LF
Bats: L **Throws:** R
Ht: 5'11"   **Wt:** 195

Opening Day Age: 31
Born: 8/18/70 in Philadelphia, PA
ML Seasons: 7

Overall Statistics

	G	AB	R	H	D	T	HR	RBI	SB	BB	SO	Avg	OBP	Slg
2001	147	541	84	150	28	6	17	71	20	80	65	.277	.367	.445
Career	972	3523	561	989	209	24	151	529	66	478	589	.281	.367	.482

Where He Hits the Ball

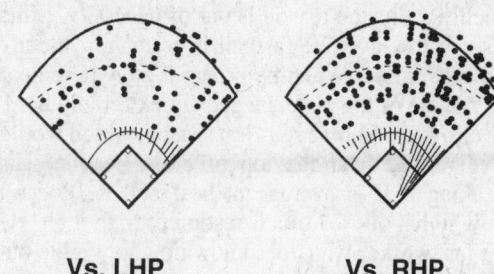

Vs. LHP   **Vs. RHP**

2001 Situational Stats

	AB	H	HR	RBI	Avg		AB	H	HR	RBI	Avg
Home	265	84	7	29	.317	LHP	164	48	8	25	.293
Road	276	66	10	42	.239	RHP	377	102	9	46	.271
First Half	259	74	9	39	.286	Sc Pos	142	40	4	57	.282
Scnd Half	282	76	8	32	.270	Clutch	69	20	3	9	.290

2001 Rankings (American League)

- 1st in errors (8) and assists in left field (10)
- 2nd in lowest fielding percentage in left field (.976)
- 4th in caught stealing (12)
- Led the Tigers in runs scored, total bases (241), sacrifice flies (9), walks, times on base (232), pitches seen (2,495), on-base percentage, HR frequency (31.8 ABs per HR), most pitches seen per plate appearance (3.94), highest percentage of pitches taken (60.2), lowest percentage of swings that missed (12.3), highest percentage of extra bases taken as a runner (37.5), on-base percentage vs. lefthanded (.396) and righthanded pitchers (.354), batting average at home and lowest percentage of swings on the first pitch (22.4)

Jose Lima

2001 Season

Jose Lima did not return to the form he displayed in 1998 and 1999, when he won 16 and 21 games in back-to-back seasons. He did, however, pitch much better after he was traded from Houston to Detroit on June 23 for pitcher Dave Mlicki and cash. Lima was 1-2 with a 7.30 ERA before the trade, and 5-10 with a 4.71 ERA after it. He won three of his first five decisions with Detroit, but didn't receive much hitting support from that point on.

Pitching

Lima's greatest strength also is his biggest weakness. It is his changeup, which is one of the best in the game. The problem is, he throws it way too much. Part of the reason is out of necessity. Lima has a below-average fastball in terms of velocity and movement. When he brings it anywhere near the middle of the plate, he gets hit extremely hard. He allowed 35 home runs last season, which would have ranked near the top of either league. His breaking ball is average at best and he doesn't show it that often. Lima is resourceful, though. He is a fast worker who does know how to wiggle out of jams. He averaged 6.1 innings in 18 starts after the trade.

Defense

Lima fields his position well. He is agile and quick on his feet, and shows decent range around the mound. He is, however, prone to making errors. He has averaged two per season the last four years. Lima is quick to home plate and has an average pickoff move.

2002 Outlook

In the final year of a three-year deal, Lima is not worth $6-plus million at this point of his career. He does, however, have value as a fourth or fifth starter. The Tigers are hoping his performance in 2002—when he will call spacious Comerica Park his home for an entire summer—will more closely resemble his better years in Houston than his dreadful 2000 campaign. He will eat up innings and bring a welcomed energy and frankness to the clubhouse.

Position: SP
Bats: R **Throws:** R
Ht: 6' 2" **Wt:** 205

Opening Day Age: 29
Born: 9/30/72 in Santiago, Dominican Republic
ML Seasons: 8
Pronunciation: LEE-mah

Overall Statistics

	W	L	Pct.	ERA	G	GS	Sv	IP	H	BB	SO	HR	Ratio
2001	6	12	.333	5.54	32	27	0	165.2	197	38	84	35	1.42
Career	59	68	.465	4.97	242	149	5	1069.2	1195	241	730	181	1.34

How Often He Throws Strikes

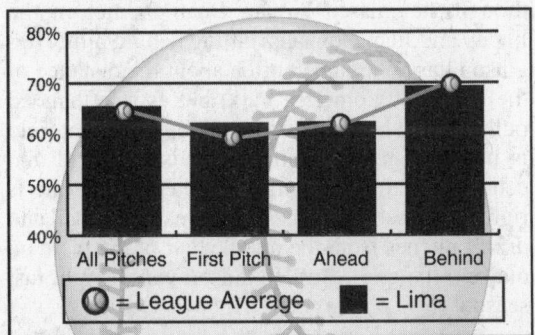

⊙ = League Average   ■ = Lima

2001 Situational Stats

	W	L	ERA	Sv	IP		AB	H	HR	RBI	Avg
Home	4	6	5.92	0	92.2	LHB	302	91	20	50	.301
Road	2	6	5.05	0	73.0	RHB	356	106	15	56	.298
First Half	2	2	6.91	0	70.1	Sc Pos	133	43	8	66	.323
Scnd Half	4	10	4.53	0	95.1	Clutch	44	14	3	7	.318

2001 Rankings (American League)

- 6th in lowest winning percentage (.333)
- Led the Tigers in home runs allowed (23)

Dean Palmer

2001 Season

Dean Palmer played his last game on July 1 because of an injury to his throwing shoulder, which required rotator cuff surgery later in the month. The same shoulder injury also hindered Palmer during the 2000 season, and surgery had been performed on it during the offseason. Palmer never fully recovered, though. When he played in 2001, he was used strictly as a designated hitter. At first, Palmer was able to hit despite the injury. He stroked six homers and knocked in 24 runs in May, but as the season wore on, he no longer was effective at the plate.

Hitting

Despite his injury woes, Palmer was a potent hitter against lefthanded pitching last season. He's always been successful versus lefthanders. It was against righthanders that he had problems, hitting just .184 and striking out 49 times in just 163 at-bats in 2001. Palmer still has excellent power but has been hurt to a degree by the spacious size of Comerica Park. He is capable of hitting home runs to left field, however, even though the stadium is much more conducive to lefthanded power hitters. Palmer struggles to make consistent contact and remains a streak hitter.

Baserunning & Defense

Will Palmer be able to play third base again? That will be the biggest question surrounding his future when spring training arrives. He was not a threat to win a Gold Glove to begin with, and now there are doubts as to whether he will be able to consistently make the long throw across the field. He did not adjust well while playing first base during the 2000 season. Palmer has below-average speed and rarely gambles on the bases.

2002 Outlook

At 33, Palmer still is capable of producing 100 or more RBI if his shoulder injuries are behind him. But his rehab may keep him out as much as half of the 2002 campaign. Although quiet by nature, Palmer is the consummate grinder. As such, he is a good leader in the Tigers' clubhouse. He was missed badly in that role after he was lost for the season in 2001.

Position: DH
Bats: R **Throws:** R
Ht: 6' 1" **Wt:** 210

Opening Day Age: 33
Born: 12/27/68 in Tallahassee, FL
ML Seasons: 12

Overall Statistics

	G	AB	R	H	D	T	HR	RBI	SB	BB	SO	Avg	OBP	Slg
2001	57	216	34	48	11	0	11	40	4	27	59	.222	.317	.426
Career	1327	4804	731	1217	229	15	275	843	48	492	1299	.253	.326	.479

Where He Hits the Ball

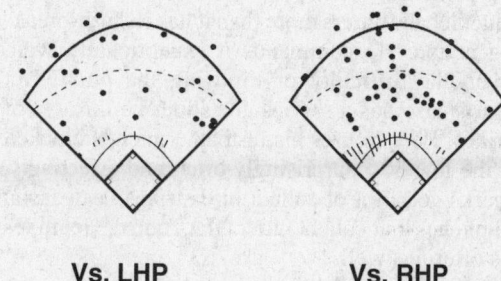

Vs. LHP   **Vs. RHP**

2001 Situational Stats

	AB	H	HR	RBI	Avg		AB	H	HR	RBI	Avg
Home	100	22	5	24	.220	LHP	53	18	6	14	.340
Road	116	26	6	16	.224	RHP	163	30	5	26	.184
First Half	216	48	11	40	.222	Sc Pos	62	15	4	28	.242
Scnd Half	0	0	0	0	-	Clutch	28	5	0	1	.179

2001 Rankings (American League)

- 4th in lowest batting average on a 3-2 count (.094)
- 6th in fewest GDPs per GDP situation (4.7%)
- 7th in lowest batting average with two strikes (.133)
- Led the Tigers in fewest GDPs per GDP situation (4.7%) and batting average on a 3-1 count (.500)

Steve Sparks

Position: SP
Bats: R **Throws:** R
Ht: 6' 0" **Wt:** 180

Opening Day Age: 36
Born: 7/2/65 in Tulsa, OK
ML Seasons: 6
Nickname: Sparky

2001 Season

At age 35, Steve Sparks had his best season in the major leagues, setting career bests in virtually every category. He also led the major leagues in complete games with eight, becoming the first Detroit pitcher to do so since Frank Lary in 1961. His 232 innings pitched were the most by a Tigers hurler since Jack Morris in 1990. Sparks was remarkably consistent throughout the year, not suffering any serious lulls.

Pitching

The key for Sparks in 2001 was that he threw strikes more consistently. He got ahead of the hitters by throwing a knuckleball for a strike on the first pitch. That sets up everything else he does. His knuckleball flutters more than it has a sharp-breaking action. He commands it exceptionally well, given the difficulty of throwing the pitch. But Sparks also has a serviceable slider he throws for strikes. He also uses his fastball, which is clocked in the low 80s, surprisingly often and effectively. Sparks got a lot of called third strikes last season on pitches that caught hitters flat-footed. He mixes his offerings well.

Defense

Sparks is an outstanding athlete who often is his own best friend in the field. He fields his position exceptionally well. He is quick, his hands are soft and he throws to bases accurately. Sparks' delivery to home plate is fast. He has an excellent move to first base, even though he is a knuckleballer, so he is not easy to steal on.

2002 Outlook

Sparks has established himself as a legitimate major league starter. In three of the last four years, he has pitched well in the role. In 1998, he helped Anaheim get back into contention with a string of several excellent starts. He did the same thing in 2000 with the Tigers after being called up from Triple-A Toledo. Last season, he easily was Detroit's best pitcher. With his stuff, age shouldn't be a factor in 2002. The Tigers agreed, signing him to a two-year, $8 million deal in November.

Overall Statistics

	W	L	Pct.	ERA	G	GS	Sv	IP	H	BB	SO	HR	Ratio
2001	14	9	.609	3.65	35	33	0	232.0	244	64	116	22	1.33
Career	48	47	.505	4.59	158	134	1	903.0	960	371	449	100	1.47

How Often He Throws Strikes

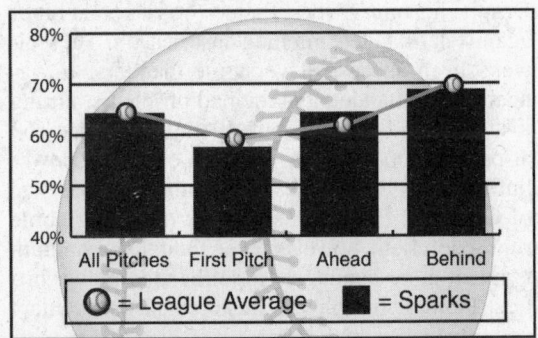

= League Average   = Sparks

2001 Situational Stats

	W	L	ERA	Sv	IP		AB	H	HR	RBI	Avg
Home	8	4	3.65	0	113.1	LHB	468	130	12	51	.278
Road	6	5	3.64	0	118.2	RHB	431	114	10	49	.265
First Half	6	3	3.77	0	114.2	Sc Pos	210	49	5	78	.233
Scnd Half	8	6	3.53	0	117.1	Clutch	75	19	2	4	.253

2001 Rankings (American League)

- 1st in complete games (8)
- 2nd in hits allowed, batters faced (982) and fewest strikeouts per nine innings (4.5)
- 4th in innings pitched
- Led the Tigers in ERA, wins, games started, complete games (8), innings pitched, hits allowed, balks (2), pickoff throws (110), runners caught stealing (8), GDPs induced (20), winning percentage, lowest on-base percentage allowed (.321), highest groundball-flyball ratio allowed (1.5), lowest stolen-base percentage allowed (52.9), lowest ERA at home, lowest ERA on the road, lowest batting average allowed with runners in scoring position, and fewest walks per nine innings (2.5)

Jeff Weaver

2001 Season

Jeff Weaver was up and down like a yo-yo in terms of performance and emotions in 2001. For May, his ERA was 1.64. In June, it was 6.81. In July, Weaver was 4-1. In August, he was 0-4. He also was involved in a brawl with Kansas City slugger Mike Sweeney on August 10. Weaver complained afterward that his teammates did not back him up when Sweeney charged the mound. He also griped about the way Detroit manager Phil Garner used him, sometimes saying Garner pulled him too soon from games, other times saying Garner left him in too long.

Pitching

Weaver cannot pitch up. When he does, he gets hurt. He is at his best when he gets on top of the ball and his fastball has a sinking action to it. He is at his worst when he rolls the ball toward the plate with his release and the ball stays up in the strike zone. A telltale sign Weaver is doing well is when he gets outs early in the count. Another sign: how he does against lefties. When Weaver struggles, generally it is because he is getting pounded by lefthanded hitters. He does throw hard, topping out at 94 MPH. He has a good feel on the mound and is one of those rare pitchers who can be effective using different arm angles.

Defense

Weaver is athletic. He runs well and fields his position well. His move to first is only average, though, and he often loses concentration and does not hold runners close.

2002 Outlook

Weaver has pitched seven complete games during his major league career, including five last season, and has lost them all. That sums up his career so far. He has been good, but not quite good enough to reach the higher tier of pitchers that his ability suggests he should be among. He lets his emotions get the better of him too often. Until he does a better job of controlling those emotions, Weaver will not reach his full potential.

Position: SP
Bats: R **Throws:** R
Ht: 6' 5" **Wt:** 200

Opening Day Age: 25
Born: 8/22/76 in Northridge, CA
ML Seasons: 3

Overall Statistics

	W	L	Pct.	ERA	G	GS	Sv	IP	H	BB	SO	HR	Ratio
2001	13	16	.448	4.08	33	33	0	229.1	235	68	152	19	1.32
Career	33	43	.434	4.57	94	92	0	593.0	616	176	402	72	1.34

How Often He Throws Strikes

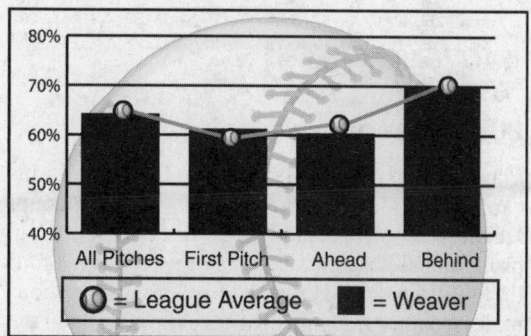

2001 Situational Stats

	W	L	ERA	Sv	IP		AB	H	HR	RBI	Avg
Home	6	8	4.03	0	120.2	LHB	472	131	13	58	.278
Road	7	8	4.14	0	108.2	RHB	411	104	6	48	.253
First Half	7	8	4.04	0	127.0	Sc Pos	216	59	3	80	.273
Scnd Half	6	8	4.13	0	102.1	Clutch	52	13	1	7	.250

2001 Rankings (American League)

- 1st in batters faced (985) and fielding percentage at pitcher (1.000)
- 2nd in losses and pitches thrown (3,619)
- 3rd in hit batsmen (14)
- 4th in complete games (5) and hits allowed
- 5th in innings pitched
- Led the Tigers in losses, games started, batters faced (985), walks allowed, hit batsmen (14), strikeouts, pitches thrown (3,619), stolen bases allowed (17), runners caught stealing (8), highest strikeout-walk ratio (2.2), lowest batting average allowed (.266), lowest slugging percentage allowed (.409), fewest home runs allowed per nine innings (.75) and most strikeouts per nine innings (6.0)

Shane Halter

Position: 3B/SS
Bats: R **Throws:** R
Ht: 6' 0" **Wt:** 180

Opening Day Age: 32
Born: 11/8/69 in LaPlata, MD
ML Seasons: 5

Overall Statistics

	G	AB	R	H	D	T	HR	RBI	SB	BB	SO	Avg	OBP	Slg
2001	136	450	53	128	32	7	12	65	3	37	100	.284	.344	.467
Career	408	1015	112	269	61	10	19	115	14	73	215	.265	.318	.401

2001 Situational Stats

	AB	H	HR	RBI	Avg		AB	H	HR	RBI	Avg
Home	226	67	4	37	.296	LHP	127	37	3	10	.291
Road	224	61	8	28	.272	RHP	323	91	9	55	.282
First Half	176	58	3	23	.330	Sc Pos	118	37	4	51	.314
Scnd Half	274	70	9	42	.255	Clutch	59	18	3	9	.305

2001 Season

Playing nearly every day for the first time in his career, Shane Halter had by far his best major league season. It actually was his best season in professional baseball. His 12 home runs were four times as many as Halter had hit in any previous major league campaign. The most he ever hit in the minor leagues was eight.

Hitting, Baserunning & Defense

While Halter tried to pull the ball too much in the past, he concentrated on driving it up the middle in 2001. He was much stronger because of his workout program, hence the improved power. First and foremost, he is good fastball hitter. Halter swings at too many bad pitches, however, and is not a good breaking-ball hitter. He played 74 games at third base and made 17 errors, as he struggles with the throw. He made just nine errors in 62 games at shortstop, and he executes the routine play better at short. Halter has below-average speed.

2002 Outlook

Halter should be a utility player as he is at his best when he plays for short stretches. Yet Halter may be the starting shortstop after the Tigers designated Deivi Cruz for assignment in December.

Chris Holt

Position: SP
Bats: R **Throws:** R
Ht: 6' 4" **Wt:** 205

Opening Day Age: 30
Born: 9/18/71 in Dallas, TX
ML Seasons: 5

Overall Statistics

	W	L	Pct.	ERA	G	GS	Sv	IP	H	BB	SO	HR	Ratio
2001	7	9	.438	5.77	30	22	0	151.1	197	57	80	18	1.68
Career	28	51	.354	4.76	133	112	1	736.2	853	253	426	69	1.50

2001 Situational Stats

	W	L	ERA	Sv	IP		AB	H	HR	RBI	Avg
Home	2	7	6.59	0	83.1	LHB	309	98	12	49	.317
Road	5	2	4.76	0	68.0	RHB	308	99	6	38	.321
First Half	6	7	5.84	0	103.1	Sc Pos	166	44	6	66	.265
Scnd Half	1	2	5.63	0	48.0	Clutch	16	3	0	1	.188

2001 Season

When Detroit general manager Randy Smith acquired Chris Holt from the Houston Astros prior to the start of the 2001 season, he declared that pitching in spacious Comerica Park would do wonders for him. It did not turn out that way. Holt was 2-7 with a 6.59 ERA at Comerica, and 7-9 (6.09) as a starter. He was pulled from the starting rotation in August and made his last seven appearances in relief. He still walked too many hitters, but he posted a 4.07 ERA as a reliever.

Pitching & Defense

Holt's fastball has neither velocity nor movement, and he pitches as if he knows it. He nibbles at the corners, falls behind often in the count and is hit hard when forced to throw the ball over the plate. Holt doesn't have an out pitch and it really hurts him. He isn't very athletic and rates as a poor fielder who does not hold runners particularly well.

2002 Outlook

Holt never has had a winning season in the major leagues and has nearly two losses for every victory during his career. The good sinking action his fastball featured when he was a rookie just isn't there any more. He won't last long in the major leagues unless it returns. The Tigers released him in November.

Jose Macias

Position: 3B/CF/2B
Bats: B **Throws:** R
Ht: 5'10" **Wt:** 173

Opening Day Age: 28
Born: 1/25/74 in Panama City, Panama
ML Seasons: 3
Pronunciation: muh-SEE-us

Overall Statistics

	G	AB	R	H	D	T	HR	RBI	SB	BB	SO	Avg	OBP	Slg
2001	137	488	62	131	24	6	8	51	21	32	54	.268	.316	.391
Career	215	665	89	176	27	11	11	77	23	50	79	.265	.319	.388

2001 Situational Stats

	AB	H	HR	RBI	Avg		AB	H	HR	RBI	Avg
Home	241	63	7	30	.261	LHP	126	30	0	4	.238
Road	247	68	1	21	.275	RHP	362	101	8	47	.279
First Half	267	79	5	28	.296	Sc Pos	121	32	1	39	.264
Scnd Half	221	52	3	23	.235	Clutch	67	15	1	5	.224

2001 Season

An everyday player for the first time in his career, Jose Macias held his own. His primary position was third base, where he started 83 games, but he also played second base and all three outfield positions. He started several times in center field in September and October, as Detroit manager Phil Garner wanted to take a look at him there as a possibility for the 2002 season.

Hitting, Baserunning & Defense

Macias makes consistent contact, a plus on a club that often does not collectively. A switch-hitter, he does have some power from the left side of the plate. He pulled all seven of his home runs at Comerica Park last season to right field, and hit all eight of his home runs lefthanded. His best position defensively is second base, though he also proved adequate in center field. He will make the routine play, but doesn't have the range at third base that he does at second. Macias has better than average speed and stole 21 bases last season.

2002 Outlook

In an ideal world, Macias is a utility player with the added value of playing respectably in the outfield. With Juan Encarnacion and Roger Cedeno out of the picture, Macias looks like the starting center fielder.

Wendell Magee

Position: CF/LF/RF/DH
Bats: R **Throws:** R
Ht: 6' 0" **Wt:** 220

Opening Day Age: 29
Born: 8/3/72 in Hattiesburg, MS
ML Seasons: 6
Pronunciation: muh-GHEE

Overall Statistics

	G	AB	R	H	D	T	HR	RBI	SB	BB	SO	Avg	OBP	Slg
2001	90	207	26	44	11	4	5	17	3	23	44	.213	.293	.377
Career	289	739	86	174	33	7	18	87	5	59	140	.235	.291	.372

2001 Situational Stats

	AB	H	HR	RBI	Avg		AB	H	HR	RBI	Avg
Home	114	31	3	12	.272	LHP	97	23	5	12	.237
Road	93	13	2	5	.140	RHP	110	21	0	5	.191
First Half	92	23	2	12	.250	Sc Pos	46	7	1	12	.152
Scnd Half	115	21	3	5	.183	Clutch	37	7	0	4	.189

2001 Season

Although he had 21 more at-bats than in 2000, Wendell Magee's production fell off last season. His average dropped 61 points to .213. His home runs fell from seven to five. He knocked in 17 runs compared to 31 in 2000.

Hitting, Baserunning & Defense

Magee does not hit righthanded pitching well. He hit just .191, fanned 27 times and showed virtually no power in 110 at-bats against righthanders. His on-base percentage versus righties was a dismal .268. He simply does not get good cuts against righthanders. He does much better against lefthanders, but still is not good. Magee is an average player in every way defensively. He does not run well, but he is capable of playing all three outfield positions adequately. His arm is average.

2002 Outlook

Magee had some good seasons in the minor leagues, but he hasn't been nearly as productive when given an opportunity in the majors. Still, he has some value as the last man on a roster. That's because he can play all three outfield positions and is a capable pinch-hitter against lefthanded pitching. He agreed to a one-year deal with Detroit in November. The changes in the Tigers' outfield may mean more playing time.

Detroit

Mitch Meluskey

Position: C
Bats: B **Throws:** R
Ht: 6' 0" **Wt:** 185

Opening Day Age: 28
Born: 9/18/73 in
Yakima, WA
ML Seasons: 3
Pronunciation:
mel-US-key

Overall Statistics

	G	AB	R	H	D	T	HR	RBI	SB	BB	SO	Avg	OBP	Slg
2001					Did Not Play									
Career	135	378	52	110	23	0	15	72	2	61	84	.291	.392	.471

2001 Situational Stats

	AB	H	HR	RBI	Avg		AB	H	HR	RBI	Avg
Home	—	—	—	—	—	LHP	—	—	—	—	—
Road	—	—	—	—	—	RHP	—	—	—	—	—
First Half	—	—	—	—	—	Sc Pos	—	—	—	—	—
Scnd Half	—	—	—	—	—	Clutch	—	—	—	—	—

2001 Season

Mitch Meluskey missed the entire season because of an injury to his throwing shoulder. It was diagnosed as looseness of the muscles and tendons around the capsule of the shoulder. He missed most of the 1999 season with a similar injury when he was with Houston. The Astros shipped Meluskey to the Tigers last winter in a six-player trade.

Hitting, Baserunning & Defense

Meluskey's strength is his hitting. He batted above .300 in every season he played in the high minors and displayed some power. He is a selective hitter who does not give in easily to the pitcher. He works deep into the count and does not strike out an exorbitant amount of the time. As a receiver, Meluskey is unrefined. He does not have the proper footwork on his throws. He also has a combative personality that often does not sit well with his teammates, limiting his leadership ability as a catcher.

2002 Outlook

Although he was able to play during spring training only, Meluskey already was in Detroit manager Phil Garner's doghouse. He needs to mature to reach his full potential as a hitter. Defensively, Meluskey has limited appeal as a catcher and his future may lie at first base or designated hitter.

Brian Moehler

Position: SP
Bats: R **Throws:** R
Ht: 6' 3" **Wt:** 235

Opening Day Age: 30
Born: 12/31/71 in
Rockingham, NC
ML Seasons: 6
Pronunciation:
MOLE-er

Overall Statistics

	W	L	Pct.	ERA	G	GS	Sv	IP	H	BB	SO	HR	Ratio
2001	0	0	-	3.38	1	1	0	8.0	6	1	2	0	0.88
Career	47	51	.480	4.49	128	128	0	789.1	886	225	433	95	1.41

2001 Situational Stats

	W	L	ERA	Sv	IP		AB	H	HR	RBI	Avg
Home	0	0	3.38	0	8.0	LHB	23	5	0	2	.217
Road	0	0	—	0	—	RHB	—	—	—	—	—
First Half	0	0	3.38	0	8.0	Sc Pos	6	2	0	3	.333
Scnd Half	0	0	—	0	0.0	Clutch	6	1	0	0	.167

2001 Season

Brian Moehler made his first start of the season against Minnesota at Comerica Park, pitched eight strong innings and did not pitch the remainder of the campaign. Moehler had a sore right shoulder. At first, it was diagnosed as tendinitis and then later inflammation. But during surgery in July, it was revealed that both his labrum and rotator cuff were torn.

Pitching & Defense

Moehler's fastball is in the 90-MPH range, and he works it around the strike zone effectively. It has good sinking movement. He also has a good cut fastball that he uses often against lefthanded hitters. Moehler has a good changeup and an average slider. He doesn't walk nor strikeout many hitters and allows a high ratio of hits per innings pitched. Moehler is not a good fielder and is average at holding runners.

2002 Outlook

Moehler is scheduled to start throwing off the mound again during spring training, but it probably would be optimistic to expect him to provide a major contribution this season. His surgery was far more extensive than had been expected. If the Tigers' medical staff is going to err during his rehabilitation process, it will be on the side of caution.

Danny Patterson

Position: RP
Bats: R **Throws:** R
Ht: 6' 0" **Wt:** 185

Opening Day Age: 31
Born: 2/17/71 in San Gabriel, CA
ML Seasons: 6

Overall Statistics

	W	L	Pct.	ERA	G	GS	Sv	IP	H	BB	SO	HR	Ratio
2001	5	4	.556	3.06	60	0	1	64.2	64	12	27	4	1.18
Career	24	16	.600	3.97	288	0	4	322.0	354	90	206	27	1.38

2001 Situational Stats

	W	L	ERA	Sv	IP		AB	H	HR	RBI	Avg
Home	2	3	4.76	0	34.0	LHB	104	34	3	19	.327
Road	3	1	1.17	1	30.2	RHB	130	30	1	10	.231
First Half	4	2	2.85	1	41.0	Sc Pos	79	21	2	26	.266
Scnd Half	1	2	3.42	0	23.2	Clutch	142	46	4	23	.324

2001 Season

Danny Patterson turned in his typically solid performance last season. He worked in a career-high 60 games and his ERA was a career-best 3.06. He pitched much better on the road, where his ERA was more than three-and-a-half runs better than at Comerica Park. Through May, Patterson's ERA was 1.08. He was hit harder after that.

Pitching & Defense

Patterson has three good pitches. He throws a sinking high-80s fastball, a sharp-breaking slider he commands well and a split-finger pitch. Durability is a question mark. Patterson doesn't pitch well when asked to work back-to-back days. The more limited his innings and appearances are, the more effective he is. Such limits help to keep him off the disabled list, where Patterson has landed frequently in the past. Patterson is not athletic and does not field his position well.

2002 Outlook

Patterson is a useful pitcher if deployed in a certain role. He is at his best when used for an inning or two in the middle of a ballgame. He also is capable of working as a setup man in a pinch. The 60 games and 64.2 innings he worked last season are the most that reasonably can be expected from Patterson, or he likely will break down physically.

Mark Redman

Position: SP
Bats: L **Throws:** L
Ht: 6' 5" **Wt:** 220

Opening Day Age: 28
Born: 1/5/74 in San Diego, CA
ML Seasons: 3

Overall Statistics

	W	L	Pct.	ERA	G	GS	Sv	IP	H	BB	SO	HR	Ratio
2001	2	6	.250	4.50	11	11	0	58.0	68	23	33	7	1.57
Career	15	15	.500	4.91	48	36	0	222.0	253	75	161	32	1.48

2001 Situational Stats

	W	L	ERA	Sv	IP		AB	H	HR	RBI	Avg
Home	1	3	4.55	0	29.2	LHB	21	7	0	1	.333
Road	1	3	4.45	0	28.1	RHB	214	61	7	27	.285
First Half	2	4	4.22	0	49.0	Sc Pos	64	17	2	20	.266
Scnd Half	0	2	6.00	0	9.0	Clutch	7	2	0	0	.286

2001 Season

Mark Redman made 11 starts last season, nine for the Twins in April and May, and two for Detroit in late August. He suffered a strained left triceps muscle, which sidelined him from late May until late August. In the meantime, he was traded to Detroit for reliever Todd Jones on July 28. After his two starts with the Tigers, Redman was put on the disabled list because of a small ligament tear in his right knee, which required arthroscopic surgery.

Pitching & Defense

Redman's top pitch is his changeup. There have been times when he has shown a good slider, too. Redman does not throw hard. He tops out at 90 MPH, but usually throws in the 80s without significant movement. He must spot his fastball effectively to have success. Redman is an average fielder.

2002 Outlook

There are two ways of looking at the Tigers' acquisition of Redman. One is that they got a bargain, a former first-round draft choice who won 12 games in 2000 and who could bounce back to form if he is healthy. The other is that the Tigers are getting a relatively young pitcher who doesn't throw hard, someone the Twins gave up on in a hurry for a reason.

Victor Santos

Position: RP
Bats: R **Throws:** R
Ht: 6' 3" **Wt:** 175

Opening Day Age: 25
Born: 10/2/76 in San Pedro de Macoris, Dominican Republic
ML Seasons: 1

Overall Statistics

	W	L	Pct.	ERA	G	GS	Sv	IP	H	BB	SO	HR	Ratio
2001	2	2	.500	3.30	33	7	0	76.1	62	49	52	9	1.45
Career	2	2	.500	3.30	33	7	0	76.1	62	49	52	9	1.45

2001 Situational Stats

	W	L	ERA	Sv	IP		AB	H	HR	RBI	Avg
Home	1	0	1.51	0	41.2	LHB	126	32	4	17	.254
Road	1	2	5.45	0	34.2	RHB	153	30	5	20	.196
First Half	1	2	3.92	0	43.2	Sc Pos	70	13	1	27	.186
Scnd Half	1	0	2.48	0	32.2	Clutch	15	4	0	0	.267

2001 Season

After missing most of the 2000 season because of an elbow injury that required arthroscopic surgery, Victor Santos came on quickly and reached the major leagues in 2001. He was called up on April 7 and expertly pitched 27.1 innings without allowing an earned run to begin his major league career. After finally surrendering his first earned runs of the season on May 18, Santos posted a 4.88 ERA the rest of the way and spent some time in the minors.

Pitching & Defense

Santos throws hard, in the low 90s, and his fastball has good life. He also has a respectable split-finger pitch. His command, however, is inconsistent. As a result, he tends to be either very good or very bad. There seems to be no in-between. Santos hides the ball well during his delivery and is much tougher against righthanded hitters than he is against lefthanders.

2002 Outlook

Santos was much better working in relief than he was as a starter. He has a good arm and a chance to stick in the major leagues for a long time, probably as a long reliever. But his control must be more consistent.

Randall Simon

Position: 1B/DH
Bats: L **Throws:** L
Ht: 6' 0" **Wt:** 180

Opening Day Age: 26
Born: 5/26/75 in Willemstad, Curacao
ML Seasons: 4

Overall Statistics

	G	AB	R	H	D	T	HR	RBI	SB	BB	SO	Avg	OBP	Slg
2001	81	256	28	78	14	2	6	37	0	15	28	.305	.341	.445
Career	191	504	58	156	31	2	11	67	2	33	56	.310	.351	.444

2001 Situational Stats

	AB	H	HR	RBI	Avg		AB	H	HR	RBI	Avg
Home	128	37	1	14	.289	LHP	43	10	2	9	.233
Road	128	41	5	23	.320	RHP	213	68	4	28	.319
First Half	38	13	0	4	.342	Sc Pos	58	23	1	31	.397
Scnd Half	218	65	6	33	.298	Clutch	30	5	1	9	.167

2001 Season

Signed as a minor league free agent, Randall Simon began last season at Triple-A Toledo. By the end of the year, he was Detroit's most consistent hitter. Called up to the majors on June 12, Simon gradually worked his way into the Tigers' everyday lineup at first base because of numerous injuries to Tony Clark.

Hitting, Baserunning & Defense

Simon is a free swinger who walked just 15 times in 256 at-bats in 2001. He hits the ball hard, but doesn't get a lot of lift on it. That is why he has hit relatively few home runs. For someone who takes a big hack, Simon hardly strikes out. He is a decent clutch hitter. Simon is short for a first baseman and doesn't present a good throwing target. Yet, he moves well around the bag. He is a slow runner who makes more than his share of mental errors on the bases.

2002 Outlook

In 504 major league at-bats, roughly the equivalent of one big league season, Simon has hit .310 with 11 home runs and 67 RBI. That may not be as much power as is expected from a first baseman, but the batting average is impressive. The Tigers are expected to start Dmitri Young at first, but Simon should make a good lefthanded bat off the bench.

Other Detroit Tigers

Willie Blair (Pos: RHP, Age: 36)

	W	L	Pct.	ERA	G	GS	Sv	IP	H	BB	SO	HR	Ratio
2001	1	4	.200	10.50	9	4	0	24.0	38	11	15	3	2.04
Career	60	86	.411	5.04	418	139	4	1274.0	1438	415	759	170	1.45

Blair was picked up by Detroit in June and lasted six weeks before being sent down. He will give free agency another try. 2002 Outlook: D

Dave Borkowski (Pos: RHP, Age: 25)

	W	L	Pct.	ERA	G	GS	Sv	IP	H	BB	SO	HR	Ratio
2001	0	2	.000	6.37	15	0	0	29.2	30	15	30	5	1.52
Career	2	9	.182	6.93	34	13	0	111.2	127	62	81	17	1.69

Borkowski missed time in 2000 and 2001 due to arm problems. He was signed to a minor league contract in November. 2002 Outlook: C

Javier Cardona (Pos: C, Age: 26, Bats: R)

	G	AB	R	H	D	T	HR	RBI	SB	BB	SO	Avg	OBP	Slg
2001	46	96	10	25	8	0	1	10	0	2	12	.260	.280	.375
Career	72	136	11	32	9	0	2	12	0	2	21	.235	.254	.346

Cardona was respectable offensively and defensively. However, with Mitch Meluskey expected back, Cardona likely won't play much in the majors. 2002 Outlook: C

Jermaine Clark (Pos: DH, Age: 25, Bats: L)

	G	AB	R	H	D	T	HR	RBI	SB	BB	SO	Avg	OBP	Slg
2001	3	0	1	0	0	0	0	0	0	0	0	-	-	-
Career	3	0	1	0	0	0	0	0	0	0	0	-	-	-

Clark was a Rule 5 draft pick from Seattle in 2000. When the Tigers wanted to send him to the minors, the Mariners acquired him back. Clark will find it tough to crack Seattle's roster. 2002 Outlook: C

Ryan Jackson (Pos: 1B/LF/RF, Age: 30, Bats: L)

	G	AB	R	H	D	T	HR	RBI	SB	BB	SO	Avg	OBP	Slg
2001	79	118	19	25	4	2	2	11	3	5	26	.212	.250	.331
Career	222	446	49	106	22	3	7	52	7	31	118	.238	.290	.348

Jackson hasn't duplicated his minor league success in the majors. He'll try again after signing a minor league deal with Detroit. 2002 Outlook: C

Matt Miller (Pos: LHP, Age: 27)

	W	L	Pct.	ERA	G	GS	Sv	IP	H	BB	SO	HR	Ratio
2001	0	0	-	7.45	13	0	0	9.2	16	4	6	0	2.07
Career	0	0	-	7.45	13	0	0	9.2	16	4	6	0	2.07

Miller was hit hard in May but didn't give up a run in 10 appearances in September and October. He might stay with Detroit as a lefty specialist out of the bullpen. 2002 Outlook: B

Heath Murray (Pos: LHP, Age: 28)

	W	L	Pct.	ERA	G	GS	Sv	IP	H	BB	SO	HR	Ratio
2001	1	7	.125	6.54	40	4	0	63.1	82	40	42	11	1.93
Career	2	13	.133	6.32	79	15	0	146.2	192	87	83	21	1.90

Murray has spent every other year in the majors since 1997. He allowed a .322 average in 2001, so this season looks to be spent in the minors. He has signed a minor league deal with Cleveland. 2002 Outlook: C

Jarrod Patterson (Pos: 3B, Age: 28, Bats: L)

	G	AB	R	H	D	T	HR	RBI	SB	BB	SO	Avg	OBP	Slg
2001	13	41	6	11	1	1	2	4	0	0	4	.268	.302	.488
Career	13	41	6	11	1	1	2	4	0	0	4	.268	.302	.488

Patterson had a taste of the majors while Deivi Cruz was on the disabled list. He could contribute as a bench player but likely won't see an open roster spot. 2002 Outlook: C

Matt Perisho (Pos: LHP, Age: 26)

	W	L	Pct.	ERA	G	GS	Sv	IP	H	BB	SO	HR	Ratio
2001	2	3	.400	5.72	30	4	0	39.1	54	14	19	5	1.73
Career	4	14	.222	6.99	81	28	0	204.2	272	119	147	33	1.91

Perisho had a 2.63 ERA in relief compared to a 10.57 ERA as a starter last year; his career ERA is nearly 3.5 runs lower when pitching out of the pen. If he stays in a reliever's role, he can be successful. 2002 Outlook: C

Luis Pineda (Pos: RHP, Age: 23)

	W	L	Pct.	ERA	G	GS	Sv	IP	H	BB	SO	HR	Ratio
2001	0	1	.000	4.91	16	0	0	18.1	16	14	13	2	1.64
Career	0	1	.000	4.91	16	0	0	18.1	16	14	13	2	1.64

Pineda has been brought along slowly due to injuries. The Reds like his promise and acquired him in the Dmitri Young trade. 2002 Outlook: B

Pedro Santana (Pos: 2B, Age: 25, Bats: R)

	G	AB	R	H	D	T	HR	RBI	SB	BB	SO	Avg	OBP	Slg
2001	1	0	0	0	0	0	0	0	0	0	0	-	-	-
Career	1	0	0	0	0	0	0	0	0	0	0	-	-	-

Santana has a ton of speed but only a .274 on-base percentage in Triple-A last year. His .317 career OBP doesn't bode well for him. 2002 Outlook: C

Kevin Tolar (Pos: LHP, Age: 31)

	W	L	Pct.	ERA	G	GS	Sv	IP	H	BB	SO	HR	Ratio
2001	0	0	-	6.75	9	0	0	10.2	7	13	11	0	1.88
Career	0	0	-	5.93	14	0	0	13.2	8	14	14	0	1.61

Tolar has a 3.50 ERA in 12 years in the minors, but the 31-year-old lefty has been unsuccessful in the big leagues. He should be back in the comfort of the minors. 2002 Outlook: C

Chris Wakeland (Pos: RF, Age: 27, Bats: L)

	G	AB	R	H	D	T	HR	RBI	SB	BB	SO	Avg	OBP	Slg
2001	10	36	5	9	2	0	2	6	0	0	13	.250	.250	.472
Career	10	36	5	9	2	0	2	6	0	0	13	.250	.250	.472

Wakeland has shown little understanding of the strike zone. He struck out 274 times in two years of Triple-A ball and didn't walk in 36 at-bats in the majors. 2002 Outlook: C

Detroit Tigers Minor League Prospects

Organization Overview:

The Tigers' farm system hasn't been much of a pipeline for most of the last decade, but it's improving under the regime of general manager Randy Smith. There are tons of promising young arms, ranging from righthanders Nate Cornejo, Adam Bernero, Fernando Rodney and Shane Loux to southpaws Adam Pettyjohn and Andy Van Hekken. And the middle infield at Comerica Park may shine with the not-too-distant arrival of youngsters Omar Infante and Ramon Santiago. Equally impressive is the talent that has come into the system more recently. Righthander Kenny Baugh went from Rice University to Double-A Erie in 2001, and five other prospects were ranked among the top 20 prospects in their Rookie and low Class-A leagues by *Baseball America*.

Kenny Baugh

Position: P   **Opening Day Age:** 23
Bats: R **Throws:** R   **Born:** 2/5/79 in
Ht: 6' 4" **Wt:** 185   Beaumont, TX

Recent Statistics

	W	L	ERA	G	GS	Sv	IP	H	R	BB	SO	HR
2001 A W Michigan	2	1	1.59	6	6	0	34.0	31	14	10	39	0
2001 AA Erie	1	3	2.97	5	5	0	30.1	23	16	6	30	5

Detroit's first-round pick out of Rice University last summer, Baugh enjoyed an impressive debut at Class-A West Michigan by effectively mixing his fastball and curveball. With velocity just a touch above 90 MPH, Baugh has impressive command and good life on his fastball. He also demonstrates good arm action on his changeup, but his curve needs to be more consistent. On the mound, Baugh is poised, smart and very competitive, and those traits were instrumental to his success in his pro debut. He earned a promotion to Double-A Erie and was just as impressive there. After surpassing 200 innings between Rice and the minors, the 22-year-old righthander tired at Erie and was shut down with three weeks left in the season as a precautionary measure.

Adam Bernero

Position: P   **Opening Day Age:** 25
Bats: R **Throws:** R   **Born:** 11/28/76 in Los
Ht: 6' 4" **Wt:** 205   Gatos, CA

Recent Statistics

	W	L	ERA	G	GS	Sv	IP	H	R	BB	SO	HR
2001 AAA Toledo	6	11	5.13	26	25	0	140.1	172	90	54	99	13
2001 AL Detroit	0	0	7.30	5	0	0	12.1	13	13	4	8	4

A polished pitcher from Armstrong Atlantic (Ga.) State, Bernero went undrafted but signed with the Tigers in 1999. He plowed through the system and made it to Detroit in 2000. He pitched respectably in three of his four Tigers starts that year, calling on a fastball with excellent sinking action and a very good changeup. He also throws a slider and split-finger pitch. Bernero experienced growing pains in his third pro season last summer. He settled back into a successful routine later in the year and returned to Detroit for five September relief appearances. Whether as a starter or a reliever, Bernero will compete for a job on the Tigers' staff in the spring.

Nate Cornejo

Position: P   **Opening Day Age:** 22
Bats: R **Throws:** R   **Born:** 9/24/79 in
Ht: 6' 5" **Wt:** 200   Wellington, KS

Recent Statistics

	W	L	ERA	G	GS	Sv	IP	H	R	BB	SO	HR
2001 AA Erie	12	3	2.68	19	19	0	124.1	107	47	41	105	12
2001 AAA Toledo	4	0	2.12	4	4	0	29.2	24	8	7	22	1
2001 AL Detroit	4	4	7.38	10	10	0	42.2	63	38	28	22	10

Detroit's first-round pick in 1998, Cornejo rose from high school ball to Double-A Jacksonville by the middle of the 2000 season. To get there, Cornejo exhibited good command of an 89-92 MPH sinker and mixed in a slider that was a major league-plus pitch at times. Both have good movement. His changeup needed more work, but that pitch and his late-breaking slider benefited from fine-tuning last summer. His consistency with both pitches made a big difference in his 2001 performance. Cornejo's sinker also picked up some steam and now comes in at 90-94 MPH. He wasn't ready for Detroit, but the Tigers like his chances because he's been a quick study at constantly making his own adjustments to hitters and situations, without guidance from his coaches.

Omar Infante

Position: SS   **Opening Day Age:** 20
Bats: R **Throws:** R   **Born:** 12/26/81 in Puerto
Ht: 6' 0" **Wt:** 150   La Cruz, VZ

Recent Statistics

	G	AB	R	H	D	T	HR	RBI	SB	BB	SO	Avg
2000 A Lakeland	79	259	35	71	11	0	2	24	11	20	29	.274
2000 A W Michigan	12	48	7	11	0	0	0	5	1	5	7	.229
2001 AA Erie	132	540	86	163	21	4	2	62	27	46	87	.302
2001 MLE	132	523	73	146	19	3	1	52	19	33	90	.279

Infante has impressed the Tigers with his passion to play and solid leadership skills. He isn't blessed with great speed for a shortstop, but he's very instinctive on the field and displays impressive range. Defensively, he is very advanced for his age. A more mature Infante in 2001 showed a better grasp of the game and more discipline as a hitter. It didn't matter that he was the youngest player in the Double-A Eastern League. He produced career highs in batting and on-base percentage, and he was effective at moving runners and executing the hit-and-run. Infante, who has started filling out and is getting stronger, sprays line drives and shows decent plate patience, which are good signs for a middle infielder who looks like he could be a frontline player someday.

Brandon Inge

Position: C
Bats: R **Throws:** R
Ht: 5' 11" **Wt:** 185

Opening Day Age: 24
Born: 5/19/77 in Lynchburg, VA

Recent Statistics

	G	AB	R	H	D	T	HR	RBI	SB	BB	SO	Avg
2001 R Tigers	3	10	1	1	0	0	1	2	0	2	2	.100
2001 A W Michigan	4	16	3	3	1	0	0	2	0	2	5	.188
2001 AAA Toledo	27	90	11	26	11	1	2	15	1	7	24	.289
2001 AL Detroit	79	189	13	34	11	0	0	15	1	9	41	.180

Drafted as a college shortstop in 1998, Inge immediately moved behind the plate and adjusted well. He's quick and athletic, with a strong arm and sound throwing mechanics. While Inge hasn't hit for average or power in the minors, the Tigers have challenged him by advancing him rapidly. That was true again in 2001, when the catcher of the future became the Opening Day backstop in Detroit. Inge's defensive game gave him the edge when Mitch Meluskey had season-ending shoulder surgery. Inge struggled at the plate while mainly focusing on catching duties and handling Detroit pitchers. Then he dislocated his shoulder in mid-June and missed several weeks. A year at Triple-A Toledo may provide a big boost to his confidence and development as a hitter.

Eric Munson

Position: 1B
Bats: L **Throws:** R
Ht: 6' 3" **Wt:** 220

Opening Day Age: 24
Born: 10/3/77 in San Diego, CA

Recent Statistics

	G	AB	R	H	D	T	HR	RBI	SB	BB	SO	Avg
2001 AA Erie	142	519	88	135	35	1	26	102	0	84	141	.260
2001 AL Detroit	17	66	4	10	3	1	1	6	0	3	21	.152
2001 MLE	142	506	75	122	32	0	21	87	0	61	146	.241

Drafted third overall in 1999, Munson's ticket to the bigs is his power potential, but a tendency to get pull-happy hurt him at Double-A Jacksonville in 2000. Munson returned to Double-A in 2001 and once again displayed the exceptionally quick bat that is capable of pulling nearly any fastball. The Tigers were pleased with his 2001 success following a stress fracture in his back that sidelined him in 2000. His ability to make contact and his power suffer against lefties, and learning to hit breaking pitches from southpaws will help. Focusing on hitting to all fields also is critical. His defensive game isn't as solid, but he should be adequate as a first baseman.

Adam Pettyjohn

Position: P
Bats: R **Throws:** L
Ht: 6' 3" **Wt:** 190

Opening Day Age: 24
Born: 6/11/77 in Phoenix, AZ

Recent Statistics

	W	L	ERA	G	GS	Sv	IP	H	R	BB	SO	HR
2001 AAA Toledo	5	8	3.44	17	17	0	107.1	107	51	26	78	9
2001 AL Detroit	1	6	5.82	16	9	0	65.0	81	48	21	40	10

Drafted in 1998, Pettyjohn has risen quickly through the system. What makes his climb impressive is that nothing about his game is overwhelming. He calls on a solid curveball and high-80s fastball. Both are thrown from a three-quarters delivery that makes his curve more of a slurve and the fastball tail away from righthanded hitters. His arm slot doesn't compromise his command, although he must keep working on pinpointing his fastball and changeup. Pettyjohn experienced minor shoulder trouble in 2000, but it didn't slow him down in his first full season of Triple-A ball. He simply kept getting better. The Tigers believe he also showed steady improvement in his major league starts.

Ramon Santiago

Position: DH
Bats: B **Throws:** R
Ht: 5' 11" **Wt:** 150

Opening Day Age: 20
Born: 8/31/81 in Las Matas De Farfan, DR

Recent Statistics

	G	AB	R	H	D	T	HR	RBI	SB	BB	SO	Avg
2000 A W Michigan	98	379	69	103	15	1	1	42	39	34	60	.272
2001 A Lakeland	120	429	64	115	15	3	2	46	34	54	60	.268

Blessed with great instincts, Santiago has been younger than the competition for most of his pro career. Yet he's often more polished defensively at short than his peers, thanks to his soft hands, quick feet and strong arm. He also bunts well and can steal a base, but drawing more walks and getting stronger were concerns when Santiago underwent labrum surgery during the 2000 season. Santiago spent all of 2001 as a designated hitter, as he continued to rehab his shoulder. He adjusted well to the role at high Class-A Lakeland, drawing more walks and fanning less often. His extensive rehab work also has eliminated concerns about Santiago getting stronger. To prepare for a return to short in 2002, he played second base in instructional league.

Others to Watch

The Tigers' second-round pick in 2000, lefthander **Chad Petty** (20), is a polished prospect with three budding pitches—a 90-MPH sinker, curve and moving changeup. He showed good command in the Rookie-level Gulf Coast League. . . Catcher **Mike Rivera** (25) always has hit, but he exploded for 33 homers and 101 RBI in just 112 games at Double-A Erie in 2001. His receiving skills are simply OK and his throwing needs work, but his bat is worth watching. . . Righthander **Fernando Rodney** (21) throws an explosive fastball in the high 90s. It doesn't have movement, but when he's on, that doesn't matter. With an improving slider, Rodney looks like closer material. . . When the Tigers unloaded speedster Brian Hunter on Seattle in 1999, they acquired **Andy Van Hekken** (22), a poised and intelligent lefty who is very effective with his high-80s fastball and curve. He commands the outer half of the plate successfully, and went 15-4 between high-A Lakeland and Double-A Erie. His changeup needs work but should be an effective weapon.

Ewing M. Kauffman Stadium

Offense

When they moved the outfield fences in 10 feet and lowered them from 12 to nine feet in 1995, club officials hoped to even out Kauffman Stadium's tendencies against home runs. Since then, it regularly has been one of the best hitters stadiums in the American League, promoting both runs and batting average. The good sight lines help reduce strikeout totals, while the summer heat helps the ball carry well, and homer rates increase from June through August. The symmetrical park assists lefthanders and righthanders equally, though the wind more often blows to left, further enhancing righties power totals.

Defense

A long-standing and well-earned reputation for groundskeeping excellence means immaculate fielding conditions for infielders. Corner outfielders should be cautious of the slight angles of the walls at the foul poles. Shots down the line often hug the wall and scoot by outfielders, turning singles into triples.

Who It Helps the Most

Righthanded power hitters have enjoyed Kauffman's dimensions, especially Mark Quinn. Contact hitters like Carlos Beltran have fared better in KC. Pitchers like Jeff Suppan and Cory Bailey who keep pitches down will succeed.

Who It Hurts the Most

Power pitchers like Blake Stein historically have trouble at Kauffman. Any pitcher who works high in the strike zone will be hurt by Kauffman's dimensions: Paul Byrd and Chad Durbin both permitted far more homers at home than elsewhere in 2001. Outfielders without great mobility will find the large outfield expanse wearing.

Rookies & Newcomers

Mike MacDougal will have to stay down in the zone to keep the ball in the park. Angel Berroa and Brandon Berger should see their power numbers increase at home. Endy Chavez will succeed in the outfield, though the stadium won't help his hitting. Neifi Perez' triples should increase.

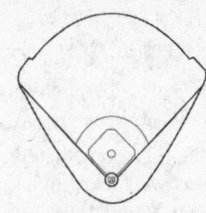

Dimensions: LF-330, LCF-375, CF-400, RCF-375, RF-330

Capacity: 40,793

Elevation: 750 feet

Surface: Grass

Foul Territory: Average

Park Factors

2001 Season

	Home Games Royals	Opp	Total	Away Games Royals	Opp	Total	Index
G	72	72	144	72	72	144	—
Avg	.272	.291	.282	.263	.262	.263	107
AB	2480	2588	5068	2547	2362	4909	103
R	340	421	761	321	347	668	114
H	675	752	1427	670	619	1289	111
2B	117	134	251	131	103	234	104
3B	20	22	42	16	15	31	131
HR	65	98	163	70	90	160	99
BB	180	243	423	179	275	454	90
SO	370	425	795	428	369	797	97
E	57	57	114	46	60	106	108
E-Infield	47	44	91	37	55	92	99
LHB-Avg	.273	.293	.285	.263	.263	.263	108
LHB-HR	13	49	62	32	46	78	78
RHB-Avg	.272	.288	.279	.263	.261	.262	106
RHB-HR	52	49	101	38	44	82	118

1999-2001

	Home Games Royals	Opp	Total	Away Games Royals	Opp	Total	Index
G	215	215	430	216	216	432	—
Avg	.288	.289	.288	.270	.271	.270	107
AB	7427	7701	15128	7630	7155	14785	103
R	1135	1236	2371	1050	1154	2204	108
H	2140	2224	4364	2057	1939	3996	110
2B	360	383	743	388	343	731	99
3B	65	53	118	41	38	79	146
HR	213	285	498	188	293	481	101
BB	623	821	1444	648	888	1536	92
SO	1087	1193	2280	1259	1143	2402	93
E	152	180	332	150	190	340	98
E-Infield	121	146	267	121	167	288	93
LHB-Avg	.287	.294	.291	.263	.271	.268	109
LHB-HR	44	139	183	56	141	197	89
RHB-Avg	.289	.284	.287	.273	.271	.272	105
RHB-HR	169	146	315	132	152	284	110

2001 Rankings (American League)
- Highest batting-average factor
- Highest hit factor
- Highest LHB batting-average factor
- Second-highest run factor
- Third-highest RHB batting-average factor
- Lowest LHB home-run factor
- Second-lowest walk factor

Tony Muser

2001 Season

After an encouraging 2000 season, many in the Royals' organization expected the club to be a playoff contender in 2001. Instead the season quickly deteriorated and Kansas City tied a franchise record with 97 losses. Despite the mounting failures, the Royals gave Tony Muser a vote of confidence, steadfastly refusing to replace the beleaguered manager. When winning, Muser played the role of calm mentor, but when things didn't go well he seemed more like a frustrated babysitter who couldn't get his young ballplayers to behave.

Offense

Muser's ability to work lineups was tested more severely than ever before when first Johnny Damon then Jermaine Dye and Rey Sanchez were traded. He likes a set lineup, usually tinkering only to move hot hitters into more prominent spots. Muser shuffles regulars through the DH spot to rest them and get at-bats for reserves. When feasible, Muser uses an aggressive running game. He has helped develop several good young position players, showing a lot of patience and helping them work through the inevitable rookie struggles.

Pitching & Defense

Lacking a true ace starter has handicapped Muser throughout his Royals tenure. He sometimes goes longer with starters, even youngsters, than he might otherwise because middle relief has been a serious problem for Kansas City in recent years. Development of stronger short relief was a plus in 2001, with each reliever having well-defined roles. Muser consistently has chosen hitters over fielders when making out a lineup card, instead challenging players to improve while playing more demanding positions on the field.

2002 Outlook

After surviving a late-season test of faith within the organization, Muser will be under pressure to win in 2002. The club's thin pocketbook can't afford the frontline starter it needs, so Muser's biggest test will be to develop consistent starting pitchers from within the organization—specifically youngsters such as Chad Durbin, Chris George and Dan Reichert.

Born: 8/01/47 in Van Nuys, California

Playing Experience: 1969-1978, Bos, CWS, Bal, Mil

Managerial Experience: 5 seasons

Manager Statistics

Year	Team, Lg	W	L	Pct	GB	Finish
2001	Kansas City, AL	65	97	.401	26.0	5th Central
5 Seasons		309	416	.426	—	—

2001 Starting Pitchers by Days Rest

	<=3	4	5	6+
Royals Starts	1	78	48	26
Royals ERA	6.35	5.25	4.32	4.90
AL Avg Starts	1	78	48	24
AL ERA	5.92	4.69	4.58	4.58

2001 Situational Stats

	Tony Muser	AL Average
Hit & Run Success %	33.0	35.0
Stolen Base Success %	70.4	71.0
Platoon Pct.	59.1	59.1
Defensive Subs	23	26
High-Pitch Outings	8	6
Quick/Slow Hooks	11/11	19/16
Sacrifice Attempts	50	54

2001 Rankings (American League)
- 2nd in starting lineups used (130)
- 3rd in pitchouts with a runner moving (16)

Carlos Beltran

2001 Season

Following a disappointing sophomore season full of distractions on and off the field, Carlos Beltran returned to the Royals' lineup in 2001 a focused player. He enjoyed excellent results, especially in the second half when he was one of the best hitters in the major leagues. He set new career bests in virtually all offensive categories, topping his 1999 Rookie of the Year performance. More importantly, Beltran settled comfortably into the No. 3 spot in the Kansas City batting order.

Hitting

The switch-hitting Beltran is a slightly better hitter against lefthanded pitchers, but overall he has only a small platoon differential. A smooth, easy swing belies his natural power. When making contact last year, Beltran slugged .638. He likes the ball up and primarily is a fastball hitter; he has trouble against finesse pitchers who can throw sharp breaking pitches down and away. Although Beltran has begun to curb his aggressive tendencies at the plate, he still strikes out quite a bit. If a pitcher can get ahead with a breaking pitch, he'll get Beltran to chase low pitches and hit grounders.

Baserunning & Defense

Beltran isn't just an outstanding basestealer (witness his 44 successful tries in 45 attempts the last two years), he is an outstanding baserunner. He runs the diamond smoothly and in a heads-up fashion that lets him take the extra base without unnecessary risk. He's very difficult to double up on grounders. Beltran also uses his speed in the outfield, where he demonstrates solid range. He owns an accurate arm and his throws are strong enough to catch baserunners unaware. He again was among major league leaders in outfield assists in 2001.

2002 Outlook

After getting his career back on track in 2001, Beltran is expected to produce big things over the next few years. He will be pressured to produce from the outset as a No. 3 hitter and to take his game to the next level. If he keeps his focus as he did in 2001, Beltran should meet those challenges and again reach new career bests.

Position: CF
Bats: B **Throws:** R
Ht: 6' 1" **Wt:** 190

Opening Day Age: 24
Born: 4/24/77 in Manati, PR
ML Seasons: 4
Pronunciation: BELL-tron

Overall Statistics

	G	AB	R	H	D	T	HR	RBI	SB	BB	SO	Avg	OBP	Slg
2001	155	617	106	189	32	12	24	101	31	52	120	.306	.362	.514
Career	423	1710	279	491	79	26	53	260	74	136	324	.287	.340	.457

Where He Hits the Ball

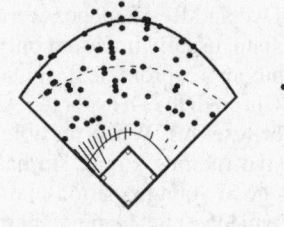 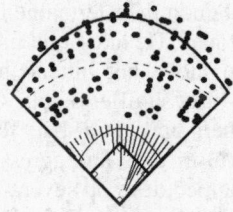

Vs. LHP   **Vs. RHP**

2001 Situational Stats

	AB	H	HR	RBI	Avg		AB	H	HR	RBI	Avg
Home	292	100	7	47	.342	LHP	168	53	4	17	.315
Road	325	89	17	54	.274	RHP	449	136	20	84	.303
First Half	335	88	12	44	.263	Sc Pos	142	55	7	79	.387
Scnd Half	282	101	12	57	.358	Clutch	86	23	5	17	.267

2001 Rankings (American League)

- 1st in stolen-base percentage (96.9) and assists in center field (14)
- 2nd in triples and lowest on-base percentage for a leadoff hitter (.278)
- Led the Royals in batting average, at-bats, runs scored, hits, singles, triples, total bases (317), RBI, stolen bases, times on base (246), strikeouts, pitches seen (2,477), plate appearances (680), games played, highest groundball-flyball ratio (1.4), batting average with runners in scoring position, batting average vs. lefthanded pitchers, batting average on a 3-1 count (.632), highest percentage of extra bases taken as a runner (50.0), on-base percentage vs. lefthanded pitchers (.372) and batting average at home

Dee Brown

Position: LF/DH
Bats: L **Throws:** R
Ht: 6' 0" **Wt:** 215

Opening Day Age: 24
Born: 3/27/78 in Bronx, NY
ML Seasons: 4

2001 Season

Dee Brown's rookie season was a mild disappointment. He shared outfield and DH duties early in the season, showing little power and streakiness borne of inexperience. Given a regular role in left field after Jermaine Dye was traded to Oakland late in July, Brown went into an extended slump. He hit .214 from then to the end of the season, with only 12 extra-base hits and 39 strikeouts. Brown sat on the bench as the Royals played other prospects for part of September.

Hitting

An impatient hitter, Brown will swing at the first pitch he likes. His plate judgment is not well refined; he lets too many good pitches go and is left flailing at poorer selections later in the at-bat. He has not yet developed his power potential and often is fooled on breaking pitches, hitting too many groundballs. Brown has superior upper-body strength and would do well to shorten his stroke in order to make better contact. A more compact swing also would help him pull the ball more with greater regularity, instead of hitting flies to leftfield as he often does now.

Baserunning & Defense

Brown has decent speed but has not used it well on the bases or in the outfield. In the majors, he has shown he can run the diamond effectively, taking advantage of opportunities to advance an extra base. In the outfield, Brown sometimes runs the wrong routes on flyballs, turning catchable balls into extra-base hits. His arm is average, at best, so he's limited to left field. Brown needs a lot of work to become just an average major league outfielder.

2002 Outlook

After a full season in the big leagues, Brown remains a work in progress. Although he didn't blossom as an everyday player as the Royals had hoped following the Dye trade, Brown again will be their everyday left fielder when the 2002 season begins. He will work in the lower part of the batting order. Because he still needs to work on several areas of his game, he is expected to have sporadic struggles even while he makes progress.

Overall Statistics

	G	AB	R	H	D	T	HR	RBI	SB	BB	SO	Avg	OBP	Slg
2001	106	380	39	93	19	0	7	40	5	22	81	.245	.286	.350
Career	138	433	46	99	20	0	7	44	5	27	98	.229	.274	.323

Where He Hits the Ball

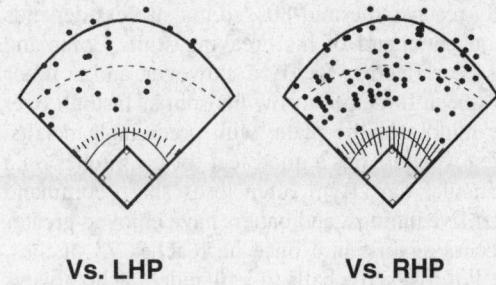

Vs. LHP   **Vs. RHP**

2001 Situational Stats

	AB	H	HR	RBI	Avg		AB	H	HR	RBI	Avg
Home	188	53	4	16	.282	LHP	89	23	3	11	.258
Road	192	40	3	24	.208	RHP	291	70	4	29	.241
First Half	184	51	5	27	.277	Sc Pos	105	31	2	32	.295
Scnd Half	196	42	2	13	.214	Clutch	61	8	1	4	.131

2001 Rankings (American League)

- 1st in lowest batting average in the clutch

Paul Byrd

2001 Season

Acquired at mid-season in a trade with the Phillies for reliever Jose Santiago, Paul Byrd stepped into the Kansas City rotation and became a sensation. He won five straight games on his way to being named Royals Pitcher of the Month for August before being shut down with a sore shoulder after just one start in September. Overall, it was a very successful campaign for Byrd, who had lost part of the 2000 season to arthroscopic shoulder surgery.

Pitching

Byrd works with a wide assortment of pitches, including a fastball, slider, screwball, curve and changeup. He has good control of all his offerings, working them to the edges of the plate. His fastball only reaches the mid-80s, so his success depends upon command of his breaking stuff. Command has been fleeting for Byrd, however, and at times he's been forced to throw his subpar fastball over the middle of the plate, with predictable results. Even when he has a good feel for his pitches on a particular day, Byrd often loses sharp command after five innings, and batters have enjoyed greater success against him once he reaches 75 pitches. He'll throw screwballs to lefthanders, who always have had an easier time against him. Staying healthy has been difficult for Byrd; he has lost significant time to injury during the last six years.

Defense

Because he relies so heavily on offspeed pitches, baserunners have an advantage against Byrd. He is not a good fielder, as his reaction on groundballs is slow and he doesn't have the quickness to grab bunts. Although he has improved with experience, Byrd remains a below-average glove man.

2002 Outlook

While Byrd would be hard-pressed to repeat his successful 1999 campaign with the Phillies, he can be a viable fourth or fifth starter in the majors, particularly if pitching for a team with a deep bullpen. For Byrd to enjoy sustained success, he will need to limit his pitch count to avoid overuse and find more consistent command of his offspeed stuff. If forced into a relief role, Byrd would be limited to middle-innings work only.

Position: SP
Bats: R **Throws:** R
Ht: 6' 1" **Wt:** 184

Opening Day Age: 31
Born: 12/3/70 in Louisville, KY
ML Seasons: 7

Overall Statistics

	W	L	Pct.	ERA	G	GS	Sv	IP	H	BB	SO	HR	Ratio
2001	6	7	.462	4.44	19	16	0	103.1	120	26	52	12	1.41
Career	35	35	.500	4.59	163	75	0	564.2	572	205	344	83	1.38

How Often He Throws Strikes

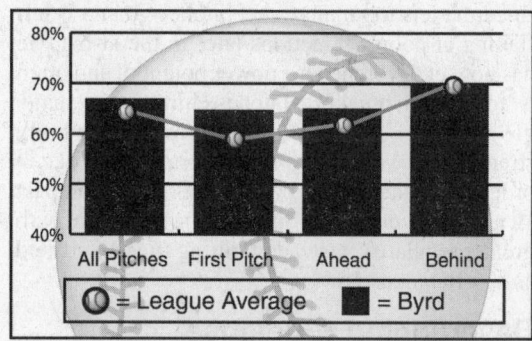

2001 Situational Stats

	W	L	ERA	Sv	IP		AB	H	HR	RBI	Avg
Home	1	6	6.89	0	47.0	LHB	210	74	7	25	.352
Road	5	1	2.40	0	56.1	RHB	195	46	5	19	.236
First Half	1	3	5.54	0	39.0	Sc Pos	101	23	5	37	.228
Scnd Half	5	4	3.78	0	64.1	Clutch	17	5	0	1	.294

2001 Rankings (American League)

- 10th in highest batting average allowed vs. lefthanded batters (.342)

Chad Durbin

Position: SP
Bats: R **Throws:** R
Ht: 6' 2" **Wt:** 200

Opening Day Age: 24
Born: 12/3/77 in Spring Valley, IL
ML Seasons: 3

2001 Season

Although they wanted to keep Chad Durbin in the rotation from the beginning of the season, the Royals instead sent him to Triple-A Omaha for five tune-up starts. Durbin was recalled at the beginning of May to take Blake Stein's spot in the Kansas City rotation and pitched fairly well, showing unusual poise for a young pitcher even while losing seven straight decisions in August and September. His poor record was more a reflection of the Royals' lack of run support than of Durbin's pitching.

Pitching

Durbin works mostly with a low-90s fastball, but his best pitch is an outstanding changeup. He has had inconsistent results with his curveball, sometimes finding it hard to throw the pitch for strikes or getting *too much* of the plate. Although he is not a power pitcher, Durbin can get a strikeout when he needs it. He will enjoy more success by keeping his offerings low and getting hitters to pound the ball into the turf. Improving command of his curveball could help Durbin make dramatic strides as a major league starter. He's unafraid to challenge hitters, in part accounting for his high number of homers allowed.

Defense

Durbin moves well coming off the mound to field his position. Still, he showed a bit of inexperience in 2001, making an occasional mental mistake on defense. He has not developed a consistent move to first base. He profited from baserunners' lack of knowledge about his delivery and from staying ahead in the count. Durbin will need to speed his delivery or develop a better pickoff move if he is to succeed against the running game.

2002 Outlook

Durbin has the makings of a durable seven-inning starter in the majors. The Royals are counting on him as a mid-rotation starter and expect him to build on his modest success from 2001. If he makes even half the progress in 2002 that he made in 2001, he will be a successful big league pitcher at a very young age.

Overall Statistics

	W	L	Pct.	ERA	G	GS	Sv	IP	H	BB	SO	HR	Ratio
2001	9	16	.360	4.93	29	29	0	179.0	201	58	95	26	1.45
Career	11	21	.344	5.82	46	45	0	253.2	293	102	135	40	1.56

How Often He Throws Strikes

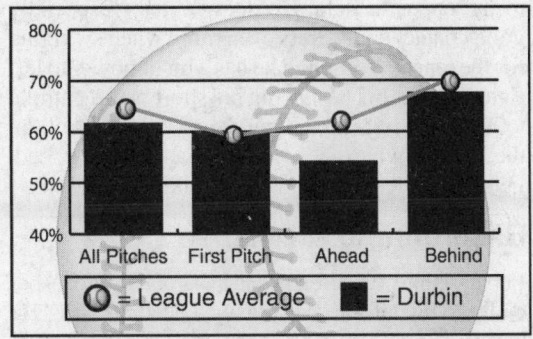

2001 Situational Stats

	W	L	ERA	Sv	IP		AB	H	HR	RBI	Avg
Home	7	8	4.27	0	109.2	LHB	366	102	7	38	.279
Road	2	8	5.97	0	69.1	RHB	332	99	19	59	.298
First Half	6	8	5.38	0	82.0	Sc Pos	156	51	8	71	.327
Scnd Half	3	8	4.55	0	97.0	Clutch	56	13	0	2	.232

2001 Rankings (American League)

- 1st in most GDPs induced per nine innings (1.2)
- 2nd in losses and least run support per nine innings (4.1)
- 3rd in highest slugging percentage allowed (.461) and most home runs allowed per nine innings (1.31)
- 4th in highest on-base percentage allowed (.349) and highest batting average allowed with runners in scoring position
- Led the Royals in losses, complete games (2), home runs allowed, pickoff throws (143), highest strikeout-walk ratio (1.6), lowest stolen-base percentage allowed (61.1), fewest pitches thrown per batter (3.75), lowest ERA at home and fewest walks per nine innings (2.9)

Carlos Febles

2001 Season

A dismal first half for Carlos Febles in which he missed six weeks due to a torn knee ligament ended when he was sent to Triple-A Omaha with a .200 batting average on July 1. When he returned in August, he was re-invigorated, showing a much more aggressive batting style. . . with much better results. Despite his struggles at the plate, Febles remained a defensive stalwart for Kansas City, helping the team set a club record for double plays.

Hitting

An increasingly more patient hitter who historically has hit lefthanders better, Febles is prone to chasing high fastballs, resulting in a lot of flyballs to the opposite field. He doesn't make especially good contact and suffers even more when swinging for the fences. Although he has a bit of power to left field, he is at his best using his short batting stroke to hit line drives up the middle or keep the ball on the ground where he can make use of his speed. Febles handles the bat well in bunting situations.

Baserunning & Defense

Febles shines on defense. He has good range, especially to his left, and displays an accurate arm. He has few equals at turning the double play. Febles sometimes plays too deep, permitting soft grounders to turn into hits. He doesn't compound his occasional errors, often rebounding with a spectacular play right after making a miscue. He has not yet developed his basestealing abilities and multiple injuries have diminished Febles' once above-average speed. He runs the bases aggressively enough to take an extra base on balls hit to the outfield.

2002 Outlook

If Febles could avoid injury in 2002, it would be a marked improvement over his first three major league seasons. Because he's such a fine fielder, he will stay in the Royals' lineup when healthy. However, until he shows more consistency at the plate—especially an improvement in making consistent contact—Febles will bat in the lower part of the KC batting order. He is expected to team with Neifi Perez again in 2002 to form one of the best defensive keystone combinations in the game.

Position: 2B
Bats: R **Throws:** R
Ht: 5'11" **Wt:** 185

Opening Day Age: 25
Born: 5/24/76 in El Seybo, DR
ML Seasons: 4
Pronunciation: FAY-bless

Overall Statistics

	G	AB	R	H	D	T	HR	RBI	SB	BB	SO	Avg	OBP	Slg
2001	79	292	45	69	9	2	8	25	5	22	58	.236	.291	.363
Career	313	1109	180	282	44	14	20	109	44	109	204	.254	.331	.373

Where He Hits the Ball

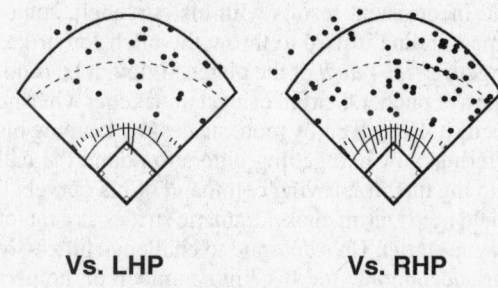

Vs. LHP   **Vs. RHP**

2001 Situational Stats

	AB	H	HR	RBI	Avg		AB	H	HR	RBI	Avg
Home	155	41	6	15	.265	LHP	93	21	2	6	.226
Road	137	28	2	10	.204	RHP	199	48	6	19	.241
First Half	80	16	0	5	.200	Sc Pos	59	15	2	15	.254
Scnd Half	212	53	8	20	.250	Clutch	35	4	1	2	.114

2001 Rankings (American League)

- 4th in lowest on-base percentage for a leadoff hitter (.302)
- Led the Royals in batting average on an 0-2 count (.261)

Roberto Hernandez

2001 Season

As Kansas City's primary offseason acquisition, Roberto Hernandez was expected to solve the Royals' bullpen problems. He was the proceeds of trading Johnny Damon to Oakland in a three-way deal with Tampa Bay. Despite a few early season stumbles, Hernandez did his part and finished with 28 saves. But Kansas City did not contend, making Hernandez' contributions seem less important. He performed as expected, giving manager Tony Muser confidence in his short-relief crew for the first time in years.

Pitching

Hernandez works primarily with an upper-90s fastball and also throws a splitter that can be difficult to hit, although he often has trouble controlling it. He's best used exclusively as a ninth-inning pitcher, and Hernandez occasionally makes trouble for himself as he has a poor record against first batters faced. Lefthanders have fared better against him. He loves the challenge of pitching out of trouble and thrives when he can challenge fastball hitters with his best heat. He has a bounce-back arm and is more than capable of working on consecutive days without showing any ill effects. One of the most durable relievers in the game, Hernandez has made at least 60 appearances every non-season for the last nine years.

Defense

With his focus on blowing fastballs past hitters, Hernandez often forgets about baserunners. He also gets so wrapped up with the man at the plate that he sometimes is caught out of position on groundballs, or makes mistakes going after a bunt. Hernandez tries to throw too hard to the bases, making for difficult chances for his infielders.

2002 Outlook

Advancing age hasn't slowed Hernandez much; he still throws hard and has the mentality of an ace closer. He should see more frequent use as a one-inning closer. That will help him forget about baserunners and let him focus on coming into the game to throw hard to a few batters. As long as he still has the good heater, Hernandez can be expected to succeed.

Position: RP
Bats: R **Throws:** R
Ht: 6' 4" **Wt:** 250

Opening Day Age: 37
Born: 11/11/64 in Santurce, PR
ML Seasons: 11
Pronunciation: her-NAN-dezz

Overall Statistics

	W	L	Pct.	ERA	G	GS	Sv	IP	H	BB	SO	HR	Ratio
2001	5	6	.455	4.12	63	0	28	67.2	69	26	46	7	1.40
Career	47	48	.495	3.14	643	3	294	723.0	636	293	677	56	1.28

How Often He Throws Strikes

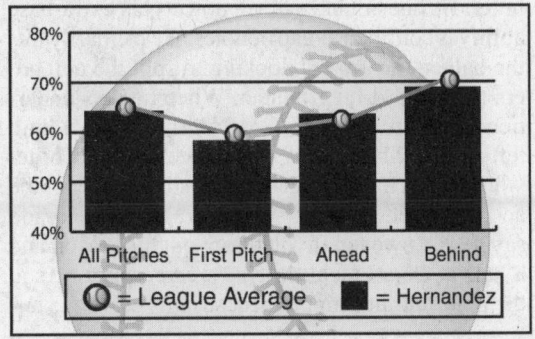

2001 Situational Stats

	W	L	ERA	Sv	IP		AB	H	HR	RBI	Avg
Home	5	2	3.79	14	40.1	LHB	137	41	4	17	.299
Road	0	4	4.61	14	27.1	RHB	122	28	3	16	.230
First Half	2	2	4.21	15	36.1	Sc Pos	76	19	1	25	.250
Scnd Half	3	4	4.02	13	31.1	Clutch	154	42	4	20	.273

2001 Rankings (American League)

- 5th in most GDPs induced per GDP situation (20.0%)
- 6th in relief losses (6) and games finished (55)
- 7th in lowest save percentage (82.4)
- 8th in saves
- Led the Royals in saves, games finished (55), save opportunities (34), save percentage (82.4), relief wins (5) and relief losses (6)

Brent Mayne

2001 Season

Returning to his original organization after more than five years away playing for four other teams, Brent Mayne gave the Royals exactly what they expected: steady defense and occasional offensive production. Mayne hit better than .300 while with the Rockies, then he made a big splash at the end of June by driving in four runs to win his first game after being traded back to Kansas City. Mayne and the Royals were such a good fit that he quickly signed a two-year, $5.25 million deal with an option for 2004 after the season ended.

Hitting

Mayne is patient at the plate and a good contact hitter. He doesn't have much power; his extra-base ability is confined to gap doubles. He primarily hits the ball on the ground, looking to split the defenders with a hard-hit grounder. When he gets underneath a pitch he generally hits to left and left-center. Mayne is a good breaking-ball hitter who can be challenged with hard stuff. He's not the accomplished hitter his .300 averages in Colorado say he is, however. If you throw out his season and a half at Coors Field, Mayne's career numbers at the plate are much more pedestrian.

Baserunning & Defense

Although Mayne merely is average behind the plate, he's prized as a good handler of young pitchers. His quick release and solid mechanics balance a slightly below-average arm, and his fairly good mobility helps him block errant pitches. Mayne is not a bad baserunner for a catcher. He doesn't steal bases, but he navigates the basepaths intelligently and with enough speed to occasionally take the extra sack when the opportunity presents itself.

2002 Outlook

Mayne's value to the Royals over the next two years will be gauged more by the development of young Royals hurlers than by how he hits or fields. He will be the club's regular backstop, usually hitting in the lower part of the order. If Mayne manages a few homers, hits for a decent average and especially helps Chris George, Mike MacDougal and others become viable big league pitchers, 2002 will be a successful season for him.

Position: C
Bats: L **Throws:** R
Ht: 6' 1" **Wt:** 191

Opening Day Age: 33
Born: 4/19/68 in Loma Linda, CA
ML Seasons: 12
Nickname: Mayner

Overall Statistics

	G	AB	R	H	D	T	HR	RBI	SB	BB	SO	Avg	OBP	Slg
2001	100	326	28	93	11	1	2	40	1	26	41	.285	.334	.344
Career	982	2726	271	741	147	4	28	322	13	277	426	.272	.339	.360

Where He Hits the Ball

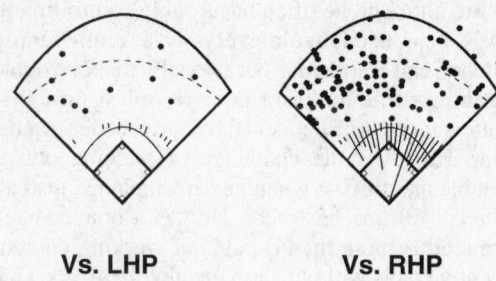

Vs. LHP   **Vs. RHP**

2001 Situational Stats

	AB	H	HR	RBI	Avg		AB	H	HR	RBI	Avg
Home	173	56	1	25	.324	LHP	34	7	0	6	.206
Road	153	37	1	15	.242	RHP	292	86	2	34	.295
First Half	198	65	2	28	.328	Sc Pos	94	32	0	37	.340
Scnd Half	128	28	0	12	.219	Clutch	50	16	0	5	.320

2001 Rankings (American League)

- Did not rank near the top or bottom in any category

Neifi Perez

2001 Season

Acquired from the Rockies in a three-team dead-line deal that saw Jermaine Dye dealt to Oakland, Neifi Perez took over the Royals' full-time short-stop duties from Rey Sanchez. Perez missed hit-ting-friendly Coors Field and took nearly a month to adjust to his new environs. He did team with Carlos Febles to give the Royals strong middle-in-field defense before his season ended a couple of weeks early due to thumb surgery.

Hitting

An impatient hitter who makes good contact, Perez looks to drive the first hittable offering through the infield. For a hitter with only modest power, he produces too many flyballs by trying to pull pitches on the outside part of the plate. He looks fastball on every pitch and has had trouble adjusting to good breaking stuff. The switch-hitting Perez shows lit-tle platoon differential, though he has more power as a righthanded hitter. He's a successful bunter who can slap the ball past the mound for a hit.

Baserunning & Defense

Perez excels with the glove. He's adept at charging softly-hit grounders and is equally skilled at going into the hole. He throws accurately and displays above-average range with fine double-play ability. His errors usually come on difficult throws that get past the first baseman, allowing a runner to ad-vance. Perez has above-average speed, but he isn't more than a modest basestealing threat. He's an assertive runner who usually will challenge for an extra base. Many of his extra-base hits happen when he legs out a double, and Perez often is among league leaders in triples.

2002 Outlook

The Royals would like to use Perez as a No. 2 hitter, taking advantage of his ability to make con-sistent contact and his moderate speed. He'd enjoy more success in that role if he would hit the ball on the ground more often. He's expected to again team with Febles in a fine keystone combination. Be-cause Kansas City views Angel Berroa as its future shortstop, Perez may not remain at short for long. He could shift to another position or move on to another organization before 2003.

Position: SS
Bats: B **Throws:** R
Ht: 6' 0" **Wt:** 177

Opening Day Age: 26
Born: 6/2/75 in Villa Mella, DR
ML Seasons: 6
Pronunciation: NAY-fee

Overall Statistics

	G	AB	R	H	D	T	HR	RBI	SB	BB	SO	Avg	OBP	Slg
2001	136	581	83	162	26	9	8	59	9	26	68	.279	.309	.396
Career	717	2927	413	817	132	50	44	293	36	143	306	.279	.311	.403

Where He Hits the Ball

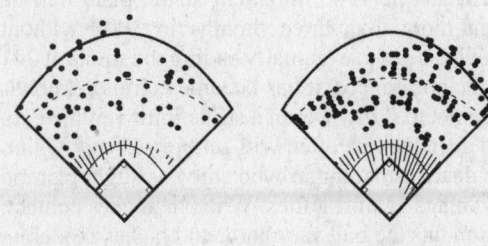

Vs. LHP   **Vs. RHP**

2001 Situational Stats

	AB	H	HR	RBI	Avg		AB	H	HR	RBI	Avg
Home	300	95	7	42	.317	LHP	169	45	3	18	.266
Road	281	67	1	17	.238	RHP	412	117	5	41	.284
First Half	330	102	6	41	.309	Sc Pos	124	39	1	48	.315
Scnd Half	251	60	2	18	.239	Clutch	74	20	0	7	.270

2001 Rankings (American League)

- Did not rank near the top or bottom in any cate-gory

Mark Quinn

2001 Season

Mark Quinn followed a strong second half in 2000 with a hot start in 2001, hitting nine homers and batting .324 in April. It was all downhill from there as he hit just .253 the rest of the way, losing playing time to a strained left hamstring and a September benching when he failed to back up center fielder Carlos Beltran. Quinn was a regular left fielder until he shifted to right field as a replacement for the traded Jermaine Dye. All in all, it was a very disappointing sophomore showing for Quinn.

Hitting

Quinn is one of the more aggressive hitters in the big leagues. He swings hard at virtually every pitch, and he is so impatient at the plate that he went more than three months in 2001 without drawing a walk, eventually ending the streak at 241 plate appearances. It has become common knowledge not to throw Quinn a strike until you have to, and even then he often will get himself out. Quinn is a dead fastball hitter who enjoys a slight platoon advantage against lefties. When he makes contact, Quinn hits the ball very hard, and he has moderate power to left field.

Baserunning & Defense

Quinn has above-average speed, although his hamstring strain slowed him in 2001. Situational baserunning, especially knowing when to take chances, is not a strength. Although his good speed helps in the outfield, Quinn too often runs poor routes on flyballs, making easy plays difficult and keeping him out of range on more difficult chances. Quinn has a good arm and is willing to use it. He likes to make the long throws home and to third base, sometimes missing the cutoff man.

2002 Outlook

Unless he shows more interest in listening to the coaching staff, Quinn is destined to remain a free-swinger who occasionally will hit a long home run, but more frequently underachieve. Conversely, with a more patient batting approach, Quinn could have a big year. He'll start the 2002 season as the incumbent right fielder, and the Royals are committed to developing his talents. If only Quinn now will heed the lessons.

Position: RF/LF/DH
Bats: R **Throws:** R
Ht: 6' 1" **Wt:** 195

Opening Day Age: 27
Born: 5/21/74 in La Miranda, CA
ML Seasons: 3

Overall Statistics

	G	AB	R	H	D	T	HR	RBI	SB	BB	SO	Avg	OBP	Slg
2001	118	453	57	122	31	2	17	60	9	12	69	.269	.298	.459
Career	270	1013	144	289	68	5	43	156	15	51	171	.285	.325	.490

Where He Hits the Ball

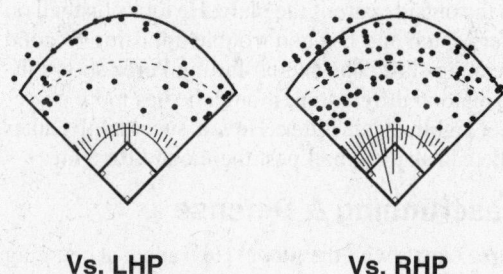

Vs. LHP   **Vs. RHP**

2001 Situational Stats

	AB	H	HR	RBI	Avg		AB	H	HR	RBI	Avg
Home	224	60	10	28	.268	LHP	125	36	6	11	.288
Road	229	62	7	32	.271	RHP	328	86	11	49	.262
First Half	200	60	11	31	.300	Sc Pos	108	26	1	35	.241
Scnd Half	253	62	6	29	.245	Clutch	75	18	1	10	.240

2001 Rankings (American League)

- 3rd in lowest percentage of pitches taken (44.5)
- 4th in most GDPs per GDP situation (18.8%)
- 9th in assists in left field (4)
- 10th in errors in right field (3) and GDPs (16)
- Led the Royals in hit by pitch (7), GDPs (16) and slugging percentage vs. lefthanded pitchers (.528)

Joe Randa

2001 Season

In most respects, the 2001 season was a repeat of the previous two campaigns for Joe Randa. While his batting average was down, his extra-base power and run production remained fairly consistent. He recovered from a poor start with a torrid May, then settled into a modest production level for the rest of the year. As the Royals pressed to score runs, Randa occasionally got into trouble by trying too hard to deliver a big hit. The result was a decent season overall, despite a disappointing average.

Hitting

A non-power hitter thrust into the role of a run producer, Randa has adjusted his batting style. He is less patient at the plate, but has developed into more of a flyball hitter than he was early in his career. His increasingly aggressive approach has made him an easier target for finesse pitchers who can get a first-pitch breaking ball over the plate to get ahead in the count. But he has become a more dangerous hitter for pitchers who must rely primarily on a fastball. Randa will hit the ball where it is pitched, though nearly all of his power is generated when he pulls the ball.

Baserunning & Defense

Randa is an above-average fielder who displays quickness at the hot corner and has enough range to fill in at second. He excels at starting around-the-horn double plays and owns a strong arm. Consistency is the key for Randa, as he tends to make his errors in bunches. He was once an above-average baserunner but has curtailed his basestealing since returning to Kansas City in 1999.

2002 Outlook

More than anyone, Randa personifies the current Royals' team as an adaptable player of multiple talents. He's a low-budget player forced into a starring role. Better suited to setting the table than driving in runs, Randa also has molded himself into a middle-of-the-order run producer. He does a lot of little things well and helps the team on both offense and defense, and he is a clubhouse leader. He never can be a big star, yet Randa can be a productive starter for a budget-conscious team like Kansas City.

Position: 3B/DH
Bats: R **Throws:** R
Ht: 5'11" **Wt:** 190

Opening Day Age: 32
Born: 12/18/69 in Milwaukee, WI
ML Seasons: 7
Nickname: The Joker

Kansas City

Overall Statistics

	G	AB	R	H	D	T	HR	RBI	SB	BB	SO	Avg	OBP	Slg
2001	151	581	59	147	34	2	13	83	3	42	80	.253	.307	.386
Career	873	3131	395	895	173	26	67	435	39	242	424	.286	.339	.422

Where He Hits the Ball

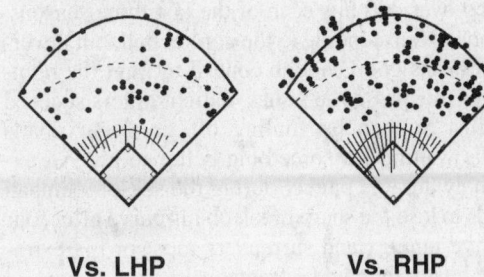

Vs. LHP   **Vs. RHP**

2001 Situational Stats

	AB	H	HR	RBI	Avg		AB	H	HR	RBI	Avg
Home	292	73	8	45	.250	LHP	161	42	2	23	.261
Road	289	74	5	38	.256	RHP	420	105	11	60	.250
First Half	324	82	6	51	.253	Sc Pos	168	53	6	72	.315
Scnd Half	257	65	7	32	.253	Clutch	80	18	3	14	.225

2001 Rankings (American League)

- 2nd in fielding percentage at third base (.966)
- Led the Royals in sacrifice flies (6), most pitches seen per plate appearance (3.70) and lowest percentage of swings on the first pitch (24.3)

Jeff Suppan

2001 Season

For the third straight season, Jeff Suppan was the Royals' winningest pitcher. As was the case in 2000, he started slowly and finished strong; he won six of his last eleven decisions after starting the year 4-9. Although again miscast as an ace, Suppan was the club's steadiest starter, nearly always pitching into the seventh inning while keeping the game under control. Opponents scored more than four earned runs in just five of Suppan's 34 starts.

Pitching

Suppan spots his low-90s fastball on the edges of the plate, then tries to get hitters to chase a sharp-breaking curve. He'll also use an occasional slider or changeup. He's very hittable, having surrendered over 200 hits each of the last three seasons. Suppan is susceptible to the gopher ball, but nevertheless has good enough control to limit the number of free passes he issues. Patient hitters succeed against Suppan by fouling off good curveballs while waiting for something better to hit. An extremely durable pitcher during the season, Suppan tends to lose the sharp break on his curve after four or five innings and surrenders most of his extra-base hits in the middle frames.

Defense

Because of a deliberate delivery and a heavy reliance upon an offspeed repertoire, Suppan is fairly easy to run against. Although he tries to wear opponents down with regular throws to first, baserunners have stolen 43 bases against him the last three seasons. Suppan is not an adept fielder. However, he has gotten better about fielding grounders through the box and has improved his ability to field bunts.

2002 Outlook

One of baseball's most consistent pitchers, Suppan is good for six innings before leaving while his team still has a chance to win. He almost never gets blown out of any game. Still, as long as he pitches in the No. 1 spot, Suppan won't be a big winner. He would suit a better team well as a fourth starter. Whether as a small-market ace or as a lower-rotation starter for a contender, Suppan will have an important role in 2002.

Position: SP
Bats: R **Throws:** R
Ht: 6' 2" **Wt:** 210

Opening Day Age: 27
Born: 1/2/75 in Oklahoma City, OK
ML Seasons: 7
Pronunciation: SUE-pon

Overall Statistics

	W	L	Pct.	ERA	G	GS	Sv	IP	H	BB	SO	HR	Ratio
2001	10	14	.417	4.37	34	34	0	218.1	227	74	120	26	1.38
Career	40	48	.455	4.96	157	142	0	880.1	978	296	501	122	1.45

How Often He Throws Strikes

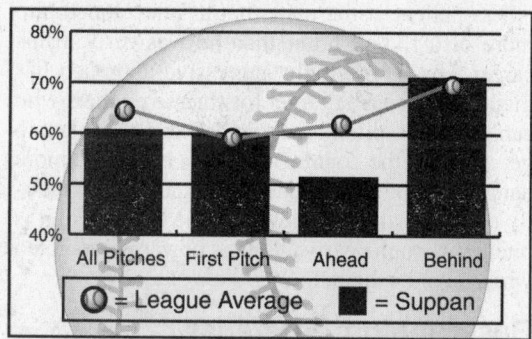

○ = League Average   ■ = Suppan

2001 Situational Stats

	W	L	ERA	Sv	IP		AB	H	HR	RBI	Avg
Home	4	6	4.80	0	95.2	LHB	460	108	13	45	.235
Road	6	8	4.04	0	122.2	RHB	389	119	13	60	.306
First Half	4	7	4.64	0	114.1	Sc Pos	191	43	5	66	.225
Scnd Half	6	7	4.07	0	104.0	Clutch	53	24	3	7	.453

2001 Rankings (American League)

- 3rd in games started
- 4th in losses
- Led the Royals in ERA, wins, games started, innings pitched, hits allowed, batters faced (946), home runs allowed, hit batsmen (12), strikeouts, pitches thrown (3,562), stolen bases allowed (15), lowest batting average allowed (.267), lowest slugging percentage allowed (.424), lowest on-base percentage allowed (.333), highest groundball-flyball ratio allowed (1.4), lowest ERA on the road, most run support per nine innings (4.7), lowest batting average allowed with runners in scoring position, fewest home runs allowed per nine innings (1.07) and most strikeouts per nine innings (4.9)

Mike Sweeney

Position: 1B/DH
Bats: R **Throws:** R
Ht: 6' 3" **Wt:** 225

Opening Day Age: 28
Born: 7/22/73 in Orange, CA
ML Seasons: 7

2001 Season

Although he just missed 100 RBI, which would have made him the first Royals player to crack the century mark in three straight years, Mike Sweeney still had a fine season in which he again hit for power and average. Despite not having Johnny Damon hitting in front of him and Jermaine Dye behind him for a full season, and despite battling a painful Achilles tendon injury all year, Sweeney remained an offensive force. He also grew in 2001, as a power hitter, as a first baseman and as a team leader.

Hitting

Sweeney's powerful swing distributes liners to all parts of the park. He doesn't swing for the fences, but his slight uppercut helped him reach the outfield seats 29 times last year. Sweeney has adjusted to pitching patterns and no longer is prone to chasing high pitches. It's still the best plan to work him in and out, up and down, but don't make a mistake by getting too much of the plate. He'll expand the strike zone to drive in runs and occasionally will overswing when trying to do too much. Finesse pitchers have had more success against him.

Baserunning & Defense

Even with a leg injury Sweeney showed he could run, reaching double digits in steals for the first time in 2001. He's still just an average baserunner who occasionally looks confused on the bases, but he has improved dramatically since his rookie season. Sweeney has shown even more improvement as a first baseman. His range is much better and he's making far better choices on grounders to the right side of the infield. Sweeney's throwing arm is below average, but he's an average fielder overall.

2002 Outlook

As the centerpiece to the Royals' offense, Sweeney will be the focus of opposing pitchers. If they can beat him, they have a good chance of limiting the entire offense. One of the league's best hitters, he's a modest star who won't let fame detract from his hard-nosed style of play. Sweeney works hard at all aspects of the game, and he's capable of continued high-average hitting with even more productive power numbers through his prime years.

Overall Statistics

	G	AB	R	H	D	T	HR	RBI	SB	BB	SO	Avg	OBP	Slg
2001	147	559	97	170	46	0	29	99	10	64	64	.304	.374	.542
Career	686	2443	389	739	156	2	99	435	30	248	271	.302	.372	.490

Where He Hits the Ball

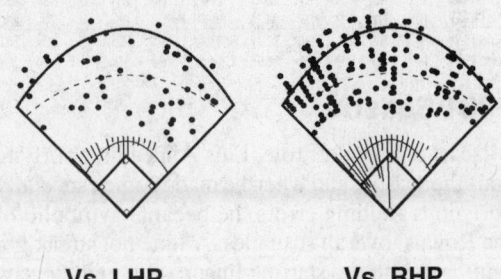

Vs. LHP   **Vs. RHP**

2001 Situational Stats

	AB	H	HR	RBI	Avg		AB	H	HR	RBI	Avg
Home	280	84	14	53	.300	LHP	142	38	6	24	.268
Road	279	86	15	46	.308	RHP	417	132	23	75	.317
First Half	342	114	21	65	.333	Sc Pos	149	46	9	71	.309
Scnd Half	217	56	8	34	.258	Clutch	72	18	4	13	.250

2001 Rankings (American League)

- 1st in errors at first base (12) and lowest fielding percentage at first base (.989)
- 2nd in doubles
- 5th in assists at first base (88)
- 6th in intentional walks (13)
- Led the Royals in home runs, doubles, sacrifice flies (6), walks, intentional walks (13), slugging percentage, on-base percentage, HR frequency (19.3 ABs per HR), steals of third (4), batting average vs. righthanded pitchers, cleanup slugging percentage (.520), slugging percentage vs. righthanded pitchers (.571), on-base percentage vs. righthanded pitchers (.386), batting average on the road and batting average with two strikes (.249)

Luis Alicea

Position: 2B/DH/3B
Bats: B **Throws:** R
Ht: 5' 9" **Wt:** 176

Opening Day Age: 36
Born: 7/29/65 in Santurce, PR
ML Seasons: 12
Pronunciation: al-a-SAY-a

Overall Statistics

	G	AB	R	H	D	T	HR	RBI	SB	BB	SO	Avg	OBP	Slg
2001	113	387	44	106	16	4	4	32	8	23	56	.274	.320	.367
Career	1247	3734	523	977	181	51	46	399	79	468	590	.262	.347	.374

2001 Situational Stats

	AB	H	HR	RBI	Avg		AB	H	HR	RBI	Avg
Home	192	45	1	19	.234	LHP	83	21	0	3	.253
Road	195	61	3	13	.313	RHP	304	85	4	29	.280
First Half	240	67	1	16	.279	Sc Pos	91	22	0	26	.242
Scnd Half	147	39	3	16	.265	Clutch	64	18	1	9	.281

2001 Season

Miscast in a leadoff role, Luis Alicea hit poorly to start the season, and when he made some especially egregious fielding errors, he became symbolic of the Royals' overall struggles. A June hot streak got him back into the starting lineup, although he saw more time in the lower part of the order and played less frequently at his accustomed second-base role. He saw more success when used as a designated hitter or third baseman and finished the year as a reserve when Kansas City turned to its youngsters.

Hitting, Baserunning & Defense

Reversing a career trend of better hitting from the right side, Alicea was a stronger lefthanded hitter in 2001. He doesn't have enough plate discipline to bat leadoff and is prone to chasing bad pitches, especially ones low and away. He's most successful using his decent speed as a slash-and-run hitter. Inconsistent glovework around second offsets his decent range. He's below average at the double-play pivot.

2002 Outlook

Although he still can play in the majors, Alicea's days as a starter are numbered. He re-signed with the Royals for 2002 and will be a bench player who can fill in briefly on the infield.

Jeff Austin

Position: RP
Bats: R **Throws:** R
Ht: 6' 0" **Wt:** 185

Opening Day Age: 25
Born: 10/19/76 in San Bernardino, CA
ML Seasons: 1

Overall Statistics

	W	L	Pct.	ERA	G	GS	Sv	IP	H	BB	SO	HR	Ratio
2001	0	0	-	5.54	21	0	0	26.0	27	14	27	4	1.58
Career	0	0	-	5.54	21	0	0	26.0	27	14	27	4	1.58

2001 Situational Stats

	W	L	ERA	Sv	IP		AB	H	HR	RBI	Avg
Home	0	0	6.06	0	16.1	LHB	44	12	1	4	.273
Road	0	0	4.66	0	9.2	RHB	55	15	3	15	.273
First Half	0	0	1.17	0	7.2	Sc Pos	31	8	2	15	.258
Scnd Half	0	0	7.36	0	18.1	Clutch	14	7	1	4	.500

2001 Season

The Royals may have been following a timetable when they promoted Jeff Austin to the majors, as he did little in a half-season at Triple-A Omaha to earn his first big league opportunity. Once in the majors, however, Austin pitched well enough, though he was used only in low impact situations. The luster clearly was off this former top prospect.

Pitching & Defense

Austin works primarily with a low-90s fastball, offset by an average changeup to set up his best pitch, a sharp curveball. He has been unable to develop a slider, and his changeup isn't different enough from his fastball to give him the kind of repertoire needed to be successful as a starter. Austin has fairly good control, and his strikeout ability could make him a viable reliever. He often was used for more than one inning at a time, without negative effect. Austin was a poor fielder in the majors last year, making two errors in six chances.

2002 Outlook

The Royals are not as committed to their highly-regarded prospect as they once were. Austin no longer is seen as a front-line starter and instead may settle in as a middle man in the majors. Still, because the Royals are desperate for starting pitching, Austin could get a shot at the rotation in 2002.

Cory Bailey

Position: RP
Bats: R **Throws:** R
Ht: 6' 1" **Wt:** 200

Opening Day Age: 31
Born: 1/24/71 in Herrin, IL
ML Seasons: 7

Overall Statistics

	W	L	Pct.	ERA	G	GS	Sv	IP	H	BB	SO	HR	Ratio
2001	1	1	.500	3.48	53	0	0	67.1	57	33	61	3	1.34
Career	6	6	.500	3.91	135	0	0	161.0	155	85	126	8	1.49

2001 Situational Stats

	W	L	ERA	Sv	IP		AB	H	HR	RBI	Avg
Home	1	0	3.20	0	39.1	LHB	116	19	0	9	.164
Road	0	1	3.86	0	28.0	RHB	128	38	3	21	.297
First Half	1	1	4.11	0	35.0	Sc Pos	80	19	0	26	.238
Scnd Half	0	0	2.78	0	32.1	Clutch	99	22	0	11	.222

2001 Season

A free-agent acquisition, Cory Bailey was recalled to the Royals at the end of April. He worked middle relief at first, then gradually moved into a more prominent setup position, often pitching an inning or less as a bridge to short-relievers Jason Grimsley and Roberto Hernandez. After a hiatus from the majors for more than two full years, Bailey had his best season ever in 2001.

Pitching & Defense

Bailey's best pitch is a sinking, low-90s fastball that he uses to get groundballs. He got into a groove with the pitch over the last half of the 2001 season, and he permitted just one home run over the last four months. When he buries the sinker in the dirt early in the count, however, Bailey has to come back with a less-effective straight fastball. Bailey can help himself in the field, which is important with the number of groundballs he produces. He also did a decent job of holding the running game in check in 2001.

2002 Outlook

Now that he has found a niche in middle relief, Bailey will have an opportunity to spend an entire season in the majors for the first time. His level of success will be dictated by how often he can get his sinker over for strike one.

Chris George

Position: SP
Bats: L **Throws:** L
Ht: 6' 1" **Wt:** 165

Opening Day Age: 22
Born: 9/16/79 in Houston, TX
ML Seasons: 1

Overall Statistics

	W	L	Pct.	ERA	G	GS	Sv	IP	H	BB	SO	HR	Ratio
2001	4	8	.333	5.59	13	13	0	74.0	83	18	32	14	1.36
Career	4	8	.333	5.59	13	13	0	74.0	83	18	32	14	1.36

2001 Situational Stats

	W	L	ERA	Sv	IP		AB	H	HR	RBI	Avg
Home	2	4	6.75	0	37.1	LHB	54	12	3	11	.222
Road	2	4	4.42	0	36.2	RHB	234	71	11	32	.303
First Half	0	0	-	0	0.0	Sc Pos	70	22	4	32	.314
Scnd Half	4	8	5.59	0	74.0	Clutch	15	2	0	1	.133

2001 Season

Easily the best pitcher at Triple-A Omaha, Chris George earned his first major league callup in July. After a few rough outings, George had increasingly better results and settled comfortably into the Royals' rotation by season's end. It was an encouraging debut for the former first-round draft pick.

Pitching & Defense

A moving, low-90s fastball is George's best pitch, and he supplements his heater with a deceptive changeup and average breaking stuff. He has fairly good control, though his command was somewhat lacking. He too often worked high in the strike zone last year, resulting in a lot of deep flyballs. George throws hard enough to be a strikeout pitcher, but he'll need more effective use of his offspeed stuff to keep hitters honest. The rookie's inexperience showed as he had difficulty holding baserunners. He is considered a good fielder who doesn't get rattled in pressure situations.

2002 Outlook

Reliable starting pitching is the Royals' greatest need, and George is their hope for the future. He'll be given every opportunity to succeed in the majors in 2002. The danger is that Kansas City's dearth of quality pitching will cause them to rely too heavily upon George too soon.

Jason Grimsley

Position: RP
Bats: R **Throws:** R
Ht: 6' 3" **Wt:** 205

Opening Day Age: 34
Born: 8/7/67 in Cleveland, TX
ML Seasons: 10

Overall Statistics

	W	L	Pct.	ERA	G	GS	Sv	IP	H	BB	SO	HR	Ratio
2001	1	5	.167	3.02	73	0	0	80.1	71	28	61	8	1.23
Career	29	34	.460	4.86	292	72	3	677.2	687	373	446	60	1.56

2001 Situational Stats

	W	L	ERA	Sv	IP		AB	H	HR	RBI	Avg
Home	1	1	1.58	0	40.0	LHB	161	42	4	15	.261
Road	0	4	4.46	0	40.1	RHB	133	29	4	20	.218
First Half	0	3	2.25	0	48.0	Sc Pos	78	17	3	26	.218
Scnd Half	1	2	4.18	0	32.1	Clutch	170	47	5	25	.276

2001 Season

Jason Grimsley recovered from offseason arthroscopic surgery on his right elbow and turned in an outstanding season as Roberto Hernandez' setup man. He often pitched in difficult circumstances and except for a short bad spell in July, he was excellent in that role. He led the club in holds, games pitched and ERA.

Pitching & Defense

Grimsley throws hard, mixing his mid-90s fastball with a sinker that he uses quite effectively to get groundballs. Getting the first pitch over for a strike has been his biggest challenge, and his success in that key area usually dictates how well he fares. He had unusual success against righthanders in 2001, reversing a trend from previous years. Grimsley has an average move to first; runners will take chances against him. He's not a good fielder and made four errors in just 80.1 innings in 2001.

2002 Outlook

Retaining Grimsley's services was a top priority for the Royals, so they inked him to a two-year, $3.9 million extension in early August. Following the best season of his career, he again will see duty as a short-relief specialist. He probably won't be tabbed as the closer any time in the foreseeable future, however.

Raul Ibanez

Position: DH/RF/LF/1B
Bats: L **Throws:** R
Ht: 6' 2" **Wt:** 200

Opening Day Age: 29
Born: 6/2/72 in Manhattan, NY
ML Seasons: 6
Pronunciation: e-BON-yez

Overall Statistics

	G	AB	R	H	D	T	HR	RBI	SB	BB	SO	Avg	OBP	Slg
2001	104	279	44	78	11	5	13	54	0	32	51	.280	.353	.495
Career	335	757	103	193	33	7	27	112	7	68	137	.255	.317	.424

2001 Situational Stats

	AB	H	HR	RBI	Avg		AB	H	HR	RBI	Avg
Home	138	36	5	24	.261	LHP	20	4	1	5	.200
Road	141	42	8	30	.298	RHP	259	74	12	49	.286
First Half	95	25	5	19	.263	Sc Pos	78	28	3	39	.359
Scnd Half	184	53	8	35	.288	Clutch	44	8	1	4	.182

2001 Season

The Royals version of "Survivor," Raul Ibanez was designated for assignment twice in 2001 before winning a platoon job as a DH and occasional outfielder. Playing regularly against righthanded pitchers, an inspired Ibanez raised his batting average from .150 in mid-June to above .300 by mid-August.

Hitting, Baserunning & Defense

A patient, fastball hitter who makes good contact, Ibanez often pulls the ball with a flyball swing. He occasionally will get caught up in trying to hit everything out of the park. He has more success when he can fight off breaking pitches until he gets a fastball to drive. Ibanez has some speed, though he rarely uses it to steal bases. He is not an accomplished fielder, but he did see action at all three outfield positions and at the corner infield spots in 2001. His arm is average and his lack of experience shows in the outfield.

2002 Outlook

After his breakout season in 2001, Ibanez has shown he belongs in the majors. Platooning still appears to be the best fit for the lefty hitter. If he can adjust to a fourth-outfielder role, he can be a productive player and should stay in the majors for an entire season for the first time in his career.

Dave McCarty

Position: 1B
Bats: R **Throws:** L
Ht: 6' 5" **Wt:** 215

Opening Day Age: 32
Born: 11/23/69 in Houston, TX
ML Seasons: 7

Overall Statistics

	G	AB	R	H	D	T	HR	RBI	SB	BB	SO	Avg	OBP	Slg
2001	98	200	26	50	10	0	7	26	0	24	45	.250	.328	.405
Career	479	1219	145	294	54	7	29	144	8	101	294	.241	.302	.368

2001 Situational Stats

	AB	H	HR	RBI	Avg		AB	H	HR	RBI	Avg
Home	116	31	5	16	.267	LHP	114	23	1	10	.202
Road	84	19	2	10	.226	RHP	86	27	6	16	.314
First Half	116	24	5	15	.207	Sc Pos	55	11	0	17	.200
Scnd Half	84	26	2	11	.310	Clutch	38	8	3	7	.211

2001 Season

Super-sub Dave McCarty failed to reprise his 2000 role as pinch-hitter extraordinaire in 2001. After hitting .381 off the bench in 2000, he managed just one pinch hit in 21 opportunities in 2001. When filling in for Mike Sweeney at first base, McCarty was merely a good fielder who didn't hit nearly enough for an American League first baseman.

Hitting, Baserunning & Defense

McCarty has a rigid, upright stance from which he tries to pull most pitches. He likes to swing at fastballs and doesn't adjust well to breaking pitches, especially breaking balls on the outside part of the plate. McCarty is an agile first baseman who fields his position well and shows good range. In fact, his defensive ability is the best part of his game. He reads flyballs well enough to handle a corner outfield spot adequately. McCarty is a slow baserunner who knows his limitations.

2002 Outlook

McCarty has found his niche as a reserve first baseman and pinch-hitter. His fielding ability and defensive versatility will help him keep a major league job, but he cannot produce enough at the plate to justify everyday use as a major league first baseman or designated hitter. He rates as strictly a solid bench player.

Jose Rosado

Position: SP
Bats: L **Throws:** L
Ht: 6' 0" **Wt:** 185

Opening Day Age: 27
Born: 11/9/74 in Jersey City, NJ
ML Seasons: 5
Pronunciation: ro-SAH-doh

Overall Statistics

	W	L	Pct.	ERA	G	GS	Sv	IP	H	BB	SO	HR	Ratio
2001					Did Not Play								
Career	37	45	.451	4.27	125	112	1	720.1	715	237	484	86	1.32

2001 Situational Stats

	W	L	ERA	Sv	IP		AB	H	HR	RBI	Avg
Home	—	—	—	—	—	LHB	—	—	—	—	—
Road	—	—	—	—	—	RHB	—	—	—	—	—
First Half	—	—	—	—	—	Sc Pos	—	—	—	—	—
Scnd Half	—	—	—	—	—	Clutch	—	—	—	—	—

2001 Season

For the second straight year, Jose Rosado had his season cut short by injury. After making just five starts in 2000 before losing the rest of the campaign to shoulder tendinitis and then surgery, Rosado had arm surgery and was lost for all of 2001. It was extremely disappointing for a team that was counting on Rosado to help ease its pitching woes.

Pitching & Defense

Before the injuries began to mount, Rosado had a low-90s fastball. He would throw curveballs for show and would get outs with an above-average changeup. He also threw cut fastballs to lefties. A very competitive individual, Rosado loves challenging hitters with heat. He also relies on changing speeds to keep hitters off balance. With runners on base, he becomes very deliberate, which has helped limit basestealing but also detracts from the focus of the fielders behind him. He is a below-average fielder in his own right.

2002 Outlook

Rosado has not pitched for almost two years. Even if he recovers the stuff he once had before the injuries, it will take him a while to reclaim his position as one of the league's better lefthanded starters. The Royals worry that he may never recover, and they will bring him along slowly.

Blake Stein

Position: RP/SP
Bats: R **Throws:** R
Ht: 6' 7" **Wt:** 240

Opening Day Age: 28
Born: 8/3/73 in McComb, MS
ML Seasons: 4
Pronunciation: STINE

Overall Statistics

	W	L	Pct.	ERA	G	GS	Sv	IP	H	BB	SO	HR	Ratio
2001	7	8	.467	4.74	36	15	1	131.0	112	79	113	20	1.46
Career	21	24	.467	5.14	90	64	1	429.0	392	254	327	72	1.51

2001 Situational Stats

	W	L	ERA	Sv	IP		AB	H	HR	RBI	Avg
Home	3	4	4.48	1	72.1	LHB	249	57	13	47	.229
Road	4	4	5.06	0	58.2	RHB	232	55	7	26	.237
First Half	4	6	5.78	0	71.2	Sc Pos	103	30	8	55	.291
Scnd Half	3	2	3.49	1	59.1	Clutch	15	4	1	3	.267

2001 Season

Inconsistent starts caused Blake Stein to lose his starting role by May. He had good results in long relief and also in a few spot starts and was re-inserted into the rotation by season's end. His struggles with control were not unexpected, as he has had this kind of problem before. He allowed 71 walks in just 131 innings pitched in 2001.

Pitching & Defense

Stein throws two-and four-seam fastballs in the low 90s and a hard slider. He has been far less consistent with offspeed stuff. Because he works high in the strike zone, Stein surrenders too many flyballs to go with his high strikeout rate. It's difficult for hitters to make contact with Stein's best stuff, but they don't have to when he struggles to find the plate. Because it takes time to unwind his 6-foot-7 frame, baserunners have found it relatively easy to steal against him. Stein sometimes has had problems fielding his position.

2002 Outlook

Stein owns major league stuff. The problem always has been a lack of consistency. Should he find the key to throwing strikes with some regularity, he quickly could become a successful middle-to end-of-the-rotation starter. Until then, he'll be limited to long relief and spot starts.

Gregg Zaun

Position: C
Bats: B **Throws:** R
Ht: 5'10" **Wt:** 190

Opening Day Age: 30
Born: 4/14/71 in Glendale, CA
ML Seasons: 7

Overall Statistics

	G	AB	R	H	D	T	HR	RBI	SB	BB	SO	Avg	OBP	Slg
2001	39	125	15	40	9	0	6	18	1	12	16	.320	.377	.536
Career	429	1136	141	287	58	6	26	141	17	156	161	.253	.345	.383

2001 Situational Stats

	AB	H	HR	RBI	Avg		AB	H	HR	RBI	Avg
Home	59	22	1	7	.373	LHP	53	14	2	6	.264
Road	66	18	5	11	.273	RHP	72	26	4	12	.361
First Half	0	0	0	0	-	Sc Pos	37	10	1	11	.270
Scnd Half	125	40	6	18	.320	Clutch	26	10	2	4	.385

2001 Season

Expected to capture the majority of Royals catching duties from the outset, Gregg Zaun instead was sidelined until the end of July with a torn calf muscle. When he returned, it was as a reserve behind Brent Mayne. Zaun thrived in that role, however, and a strong finish and some late-inning heroics helped him finish the season on a high note.

Hitting, Baserunning & Defense

Primarily a pull-hitter, Zaun looks fastball as he hits from a hunched stance. Although he's a switch-hitter, he's far more comfortable hitting against righthanded pitchers. Settling into a reserve role has helped him develop his situational hitting skills. Zaun can steal a few bases and always is looking to take an extra base, though he'll occasionally run into outs on the basepaths. He has decent arm strength and throws accurately. However, he gets rid of the ball late and basestealers have enjoyed success against him.

2002 Outlook

Zaun fits the reserve catching role well. While he lacks the defensive abilities to be an everyday backstop, Zaun won't hurt a club if used in the role briefly. He looks like Houston's backup after agreeing to a two-year, $2.35 million contract in December.

Other Kansas City Royals

Endy Chavez (**Pos**: LF, **Age**: 24, **Bats**: L)

	G	AB	R	H	D	T	HR	RBI	SB	BB	SO	Avg	OBP	Slg
2001	29	77	4	16	2	0	0	5	0	3	8	.208	.238	.234
Career	29	77	4	16	2	0	0	5	0	3	8	.208	.238	.234

Chavez saw his first action above Class-A ball last year. He hit well in the minors but was overmatched in the majors. The Royals like his speed and defense, but he needs more time in the high minors to become a better hitter. 2002 Outlook: C

Wilson Delgado (**Pos**: SS, **Age**: 26, **Bats**: B)

	G	AB	R	H	D	T	HR	RBI	SB	BB	SO	Avg	OBP	Slg
2001	14	25	1	3	0	0	0	1	0	3	10	.120	.214	.120
Career	137	265	34	65	6	1	1	18	4	21	55	.245	.306	.287

Delgado was called up in May when Joe Randa's back was bothering him. He lasted a month and made use of his 25 at-bats by looking up at the Mendoza Line. He opted for free agency in October. 2002 Outlook: C

Doug Henry (**Pos**: RHP, **Age**: 38)

	W	L	Pct.	ERA	G	GS	Sv	IP	H	BB	SO	HR	Ratio
2001	2	2	.500	6.07	53	0	0	75.2	75	45	57	14	1.59
Career	34	42	.447	4.19	582	0	82	665.2	611	341	541	83	1.43

Henry's first season back in the AL since 1994 was the worst of his career. The 38-year-old was equally bad throughout the season, posting a 6.07 ERA in the first and second half. 2002 Outlook: C

A.J. Hinch (**Pos**: C, **Age**: 27, **Bats**: R)

	G	AB	R	H	D	T	HR	RBI	SB	BB	SO	Avg	OBP	Slg
2001	45	121	10	19	3	0	6	15	1	8	26	.157	.226	.331
Career	247	671	71	143	17	1	22	74	10	50	157	.213	.273	.340

Hinch hit .160 in his stint as the backup catcher until he was sent down in July. If he can pass the Mendoza Line and put up decent numbers, he'll have another chance to stay in Kansas City. 2002 Outlook: C

Trenidad Hubbard (**Pos**: CF, **Age**: 35, **Bats**: R)

	G	AB	R	H	D	T	HR	RBI	SB	BB	SO	Avg	OBP	Slg
2001	5	12	2	3	0	1	0	0	0	0	2	.250	.250	.417
Career	377	617	106	165	27	7	15	63	23	65	135	.267	.340	.407

Hubbard has had more than 108 at-bats only once in his major league career. Last year he posted solid numbers in Triple-A, but only had 12 at-bats in the majors. Expect similar numbers wherever the free agent ends up. 2002 Outlook: C

Brian Meadows (**Pos**: RHP, **Age**: 26)

	W	L	Pct.	ERA	G	GS	Sv	IP	H	BB	SO	HR	Ratio
2001	1	6	.143	6.97	10	10	0	50.1	73	12	21	12	1.69
Career	36	44	.450	5.45	105	104	0	599.1	743	179	260	95	1.54

Meadows spent two months getting pounded in the majors. In 50.1 innings pitched, he allowed 73 hits, 12 homers and a .351 average. It was the first season in his career he did not post at least 11 wins. The 26-year-old became a free agent in October. 2002 Outlook: C

Luis Ordaz (**Pos**: 2B, **Age**: 26, **Bats**: R)

	G	AB	R	H	D	T	HR	RBI	SB	BB	SO	Avg	OBP	Slg
2001	28	56	8	14	3	0	0	4	0	3	8	.250	.295	.304
Career	172	344	40	75	11	0	0	26	10	22	40	.218	.266	.250

Ordaz started the season as the Royals' utitility infielder but eventually was designated for assignment. His .250 average, .295 OBP and .304 SLG last year were all well above his career averages. 2002 Outlook: C

Hector Ortiz (**Pos**: C, **Age**: 32, **Bats**: R)

	G	AB	R	H	D	T	HR	RBI	SB	BB	SO	Avg	OBP	Slg
2001	56	154	12	38	6	1	0	11	1	9	24	.247	.293	.299
Career	86	246	28	72	12	1	0	16	1	17	32	.293	.343	.350

Kansas City is loaded with bad backup catchers and Ortiz is no exception. He hit .247 with seven extra-base hits in 154 at-bats. He signed a minor league deal with the Royals in late November and will try to make the club. 2002 Outlook: C

Dan Reichert (**Pos**: RHP, **Age**: 25)

	W	L	Pct.	ERA	G	GS	Sv	IP	H	BB	SO	HR	Ratio
2001	8	8	.500	5.63	27	19	0	123.0	131	67	77	14	1.61
Career	18	20	.474	5.58	79	45	2	313.0	336	190	191	31	1.68

After a promising 2000, Reichert took a step backwards. The Royals questioned his durability as a starter and likely will want him to pitch out of the pen. His ERA is more than a run lower as a reliever. 2002 Outlook: B

Donnie Sadler (**Pos**: 2B/3B/SS/LF, **Age**: 26, **Bats**: R)

	G	AB	R	H	D	T	HR	RBI	SB	BB	SO	Avg	OBP	Slg
2001	93	185	28	30	6	0	1	5	7	18	37	.162	.243	.211
Career	249	515	81	110	20	5	5	34	16	34	103	.214	.268	.301

Sadler was acquired in June from the Reds and filled the utility role, playing three infield positions and all three outfield spots. He hit .129 in 101 at-bats and accumulated a grand total of two RBI with KC. 2002 Outlook: C

Brad Voyles (**Pos**: RHP, **Age**: 25)

	W	L	Pct.	ERA	G	GS	Sv	IP	H	BB	SO	HR	Ratio
2001	0	0	-	3.86	7	0	0	9.1	5	8	6	1	1.39
Career	0	0	-	3.86	7	0	0	9.1	5	8	6	1	1.39

Voyles was pitching in Double-A with Atlanta when he was acquired in the Rey Sanchez deal. For never pitching higher than Class-A ball, he had a successful year. He'll likely need more Triple-A seasoning. 2002 Outlook: C

Kris Wilson (**Pos**: RHP, **Age**: 25)

	W	L	Pct.	ERA	G	GS	Sv	IP	H	BB	SO	HR	Ratio
2001	6	5	.545	5.19	29	15	1	109.1	132	32	67	26	1.50
Career	6	6	.500	4.95	49	15	1	143.2	170	43	84	29	1.48

Wilson flashed potential in a two-month stretch, going 5-1 with a 2.97 ERA. He was 1-4 with an 8.28 ERA in his other appearances, though. Some of that can be blamed on a sore right elbow at the end of the year. 2002 Outlook: B

Kansas City Royals Minor League Prospects

Organization Overview:

The Royals' system has provided a steady supply of regulars over the last decade, including Johnny Damon, Mike Sweeney, Carlos Beltran, Carlos Febles, Mark Quinn and Dee Brown, who arrived in 2001. More noteworthy last summer were the debuts of pitching prospects Jeff Austin, Chris George and Mike MacDougal. Austin and George were first-round picks in 1998, and MacDougal was one of four first-round picks used on pitching in '99. Southpaw Jimmy Gobble and righthander Kyle Snyder were two others who now rank among the best of a crop of young pitchers whose success is critical to the small-market Royals. It's possible that hitting prospects Brandon Berger and Ken Harvey also could help out in 2002.

Brandon Berger

Position: OF
Opening Day Age: 27
Bats: R **Throws:** R
Born: 2/21/75 in
Ht: 5' 11" **Wt:** 200
Covington, KY

Recent Statistics

	G	AB	R	H	D	T	HR	RBI	SB	BB	SO	Avg
2001 AA Wichita	120	454	98	140	28	3	40	118	14	43	91	.308
2001 AL Kansas City	6	16	4	5	1	1	2	2	0	2	2	.313
2001 MLE	120	441	82	127	25	2	34	98	10	30	93	.288

In a 2001 season that he began as Double-A Wichita's fourth outfielder, Berger exploded to lead the Texas League in homers and finish second in RBI. While Berger never before had had a 20-homer season, the 1996 pick always has been a patient hitter with some pop. Last summer, however, he developed a better understanding of which pitches he can handle. He also has learned to go the other way with more power. His defensive game isn't as solid, but Berger is viewed as an average runner with good acceleration by the Royals. They want him to be more aggressive defensively. At the plate, Berger must continue working on his strike-zone judgment, going the other way and reducing his strikeouts.

Angel Berroa

Position: SS
Opening Day Age: 22
Bats: R **Throws:** R
Born: 1/27/80 in Santo
Ht: 6' 0" **Wt:** 175
Domingo, DR

Recent Statistics

	G	AB	R	H	D	T	HR	RBI	SB	BB	SO	Avg
2001 A Wilmington	51	199	43	63	18	4	6	25	10	9	41	.317
2001 AA Wichita	80	304	63	90	20	4	8	42	15	17	55	.296
2001 AL Kansas City	15	53	8	16	2	0	0	4	2	3	10	.302
2001 MLE	80	296	52	82	17	3	6	35	10	11	56	.277

Berroa, another promising shortstop prospect from the Dominican, was acquired from Oakland in the Johnny Damon deal in January 2001. A great athlete who has the speed, range and power arm to be a flashy fielder, Berroa was much less error-prone in 2001 and showed he can make any defensive play. He has a history as an effective bad-ball hitter, but Berroa was better at laying off pitches out of the strike zone last summer. After recording career highs in doubles (40) and homers (14) during the season, he showed power in instructional league that hadn't been seen before. The Royals are thinking about dealing Neifi Perez to make room for Berroa.

Tony Cogan

Position: P
Opening Day Age: 25
Bats: L **Throws:** L
Born: 12/21/76 in
Ht: 6' 2" **Wt:** 195
Chicago, IL

Recent Statistics

	W	L	ERA	G	GS	Sv	IP	H	R	BB	SO	HR
2001 AA Wichita	1	1	2.08	8	0	1	17.1	13	6	4	12	2
2001 AAA Omaha	1	1	2.79	9	0	2	9.2	14	3	3	8	1
2001 AL Kansas City	0	4	5.84	39	0	0	24.2	32	17	13	17	7

A 12th-round pick in 1999, Cogan was a polished college pitcher who enjoyed a strong pro debut as a reliever in the short-season Northwest League. The southpaw was converted back to a starter in 2000, and he showed promise making the move at Class-A Charleston in the Sally League. He returned to bullpen work in the high minors last summer, and showed significant improvement in his overall command. Cogan posted a 2.33 ERA in 27 innings between Double-A Wichita and Triple-A Omaha before earning time in the Royals' pen. Despite his minor league success in relief, the Royals expect to make a starter out of Cogan. A tough kid with great makeup, he throws a fastball, curveball and changeup with good movement against lefties and righties.

Jimmy Gobble

Position: P
Opening Day Age: 20
Bats: L **Throws:** L
Born: 7/19/81 in Bristol,
Ht: 6' 3" **Wt:** 175
TN

Recent Statistics

	W	L	ERA	G	GS	Sv	IP	H	R	BB	SO	HR
2000 A Chston-WV	12	10	3.66	25	25	0	145.0	144	75	34	115	10
2001 A Wilmington	10	6	2.55	27	27	0	162.1	134	58	33	154	8

A supplemental first-rounder in 1999, Gobble pitched just six innings of rookie ball in '99 before turning in a solid 12-10 (3.66) season in the Class-A Sally League as a teenager in 2000. He was even more effective at high-A Wilmington last summer, maintaining his rapid progress by working effectively and consistently within the strike zone. He showed much better command of his 90-MPH fastball and his curveball was better as well. It still needs some fine-tuning, and Gobble must develop enough confidence to throw it when he's behind in the count. He already has that confidence in his heater and changeup, giving Gobble the stuff to keep climbing. A little more polish and experience in the high minors and the lefty will be in Kansas City.

Alexis Gomez

Position: OF   **Opening Day Age:** 21
Bats: L **Throws:** L   **Born:** 8/6/80 in Loma De
Ht: 6' 2" **Wt:** 160   Cabrera, DR

Recent Statistics

	G	AB	R	H	D	T	HR	RBI	SB	BB	SO	Avg
2000 A Wilmington	121	461	63	117	13	4	1	33	21	45	121	.254
2001 A Wilmington	48	169	29	51	8	2	1	9	7	11	43	.302
2001 AA Wichita	83	342	55	96	15	6	4	34	16	27	70	.281
2001 MLE	83	334	46	88	13	5	3	28	11	18	71	.263

Signed in 1997, Gomez played two years in his homeland and one in rookie ball before jumping to high Class-A Wilmington as a teenager in 2000. Facing pitchers with college experience, he held his own with the bat. The Royals were equally impressed with how he handled the jump to Double-A in 2001. They see him as a potential All-Star with a nice blend of power and speed. Gomez has a great frame and is expected to get bigger and fill out. The Royals believe he simply needs to play to let his ability take over and become a consistent hitter. He's better defensively after making improvements to his throwing mechanics in 2001. He has learned to take better routes on balls and plays a solid center field.

Ken Harvey

Position: 1B   **Opening Day Age:** 24
Bats: R **Throws:** R   **Born:** 3/1/78 in Los
Ht: 6' 2" **Wt:** 240   Angeles, CA

Recent Statistics

	G	AB	R	H	D	T	HR	RBI	SB	BB	SO	Avg
2001 A Wilmington	35	137	22	52	9	1	6	27	3	13	21	.380
2001 AA Wichita	79	314	54	106	20	3	9	63	3	18	60	.338
2001 AL Kansas City	4	12	1	3	1	0	0	2	0	0	4	.250
2001 MLE	79	304	45	96	17	2	7	52	2	12	61	.316

There's been little doubt about Harvey's ability to make contact since he was the Royals' fifth-round pick in 1999. He hasn't hit below .335 in any of his three pro seasons, and his career on-base percentage is .421. He's a pure hitter who the Royals expect will hit for both power and average. He already has plus power, and he recorded career highs in doubles (30) and homers (15) in 2001. His defensive game must catch up to his bat. Harvey had surgery for bunions on his feet during 2000, which limited him to less than 200 at-bats that year. At the close of the 2001 season he had more surgery on the foot, which removed a bone spur and scar tissue.

Mike MacDougal

Position: P   **Opening Day Age:** 25
Bats: B **Throws:** R   **Born:** 3/5/77 in Las
Ht: 6' 4" **Wt:** 195   Vegas, NV

Recent Statistics

	W	L	ERA	G	GS	Sv	IP	H	R	BB	SO	HR
2001 AAA Omaha	8	8	4.68	28	27	0	144.1	144	90	76	110	13
2001 AL Kansas City	1	1	4.70	3	3	0	15.1	18	10	4	7	2

One of the early-round prizes of the 1999 draft, MacDougal quickly capitalized on his mid-90s heater, riding it to Double-A Wichita in 2000. His fastball has tremendous movement and sink, which has made it difficult to pinpoint in the strike zone. He went to instructional league a year ago to work on its location, and the payoff came during a solid second half of 2001, when MacDougal gained control of the pitch and showed consistent command of it. He didn't overthrow it as he had in the past, a sign of his conversion from thrower to pitcher. His slider is above average, too, but his changeup still needs work. He suffered a skull fracture when a bat hit him in the Royals' dugout during an October game.

Scott Mullen

Position: P   **Opening Day Age:** 27
Bats: R **Throws:** L   **Born:** 1/17/75 in San
Ht: 6' 2" **Wt:** 190   Benito, TX

Recent Statistics

	W	L	ERA	G	GS	Sv	IP	H	R	BB	SO	HR
2001 AAA Omaha	5	4	6.62	48	0	5	53.0	66	39	22	38	8
2001 AL Kansas City	0	0	4.50	17	0	0	10.0	13	6	9	3	0

Mullen has moved slowly since the Royals drafted him in 1996. He broke out with a 16-6 (3.06) season between high Class-A Wilmington and Double-A Wichita in 1998. Then he struggled in the high minors in '99 and was dumped from the 40-man roster. He began working out of the pen in 2000, which pushed his fastball near the mid-90s and helped his slurve. He was better in the minors that summer, putting him on the verge of helping the Royals in 2001. Cogan underwent surgery to clean out his shoulder after the 2000 season, and it took most of 2001 for his velocity to return. His changeup isn't quite ready for major league hitters.

Others to Watch

Jeremy Affeldt (22) is a 6-foot-4 lefty with good stuff and a fastball that is hard to pick up. He's stronger and more mature than a year ago, and it showed in his 10-6 (3.90) season at Double-A Wichita in 2001. He pitches inside better than anyone in the system. . . The Royals lost two young hurlers in the Rule 5 draft, but added one of their own in **Miguel Ascencio** (21) from the Phillies. The 6-foot-2, 160-pounder throws a low-90s fastball and offspeed stuff that still is inconsistent. Yet he came into his own in 2001, leading the high Class-A Florida State League with the only ERA under 3.00 among qualifiers. . . **Jeremy Hill** (24) was drafted as a catcher in 1996, but converted to pitching a year ago. His strong catching legs provide the thrust behind his fastball, and he takes a football mentality onto the mound. The first-year results were promising at two Class-A stops, where Hill allowed just 32 hits and fanned 79 in 60 innings. His secondary pitches need a lot of work. . . A second-rounder in 2000, catcher **Mike Tonis** (23) is a big guy with power potential. He made better contact and displayed more pop in 2001, batting .264-12-61 in 349 at-bats between high Class-A Wilmington and Double-A Wichita. As a catcher, he receives, throws and calls games well, but needs to work on trapping balls in the dirt.

Hubert H. Humphrey Metrodome

Offense

The advent of new "classic" parks makes the Metrodome an anachronism in more ways than one. It is no longer a big home-run park compared to its peers, and the bouncy artificial surface makes it a throwback to the speed-oriented baseball of the 1970s. The park is excellent for doubles, triples and line-drive hitting in general. Lefthanded batters can drive balls over the short right-field fence with ease, but righthanded hitters find the deep power alley to left field a hindrance.

Defense

The infield turf is quick but bounces are true, so fewer infield errors are generally made in the Metrodome than in other parks. The off-white roof is very hard on the outfielders, or on infielders tracking high popups. It seems as if at least one or two games a year are decided by fielders losing balls in the ceiling during critical situations.

Who It Helps the Most

Gap hitters with good speed, like Luis Rivas and Cristian Guzman, usually do well in the Metrodome. No pitcher is truly helped in the Dome, though Brad Radke and Joe Mays have adjusted very well to its conditions. LaTroy Hawkins fared much better at home than on the road in 2001, but that trend was not indicative of his career entering the season.

Who It Hurts the Most

Some hitters seem to have trouble with the visibility conditions, notably David Ortiz and Jacque Jones in 2001. Flyball pitchers like Eric Milton and Rick Reed can struggle here. Any fielder without Dome experience will have trouble, at least initially.

Rookies & Newcomers

Young outfielders Mike Cuddyer and Bobby Kielty will vie for an outfield spot, though neither seems likely to be helped by the Dome. The fifth spot in the rotation and numerous bullpen slots also are open. Young pitchers like Kyle Lohse, Brad Thomas, Juan Rincon and Adam Johnson will need to prove they can face the Metrodome challenge.

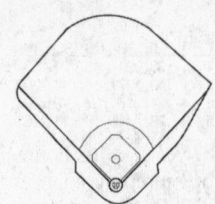

Dimensions: LF-343, LCF-385, CF-408, RCF-367, RF-327

Capacity: 48,678

Elevation: 815 feet

Surface: Turf

Foul Territory: Average

Park Factors

2001 Season

	Home Games			Away Games			
	Twins	Opp	Total	Twins	Opp	Total	Index
G	72	72	144	72	72	144	—
Avg	.269	.271	.270	.272	.263	.267	101
AB	2406	2548	4954	2549	2437	4986	99
R	342	344	686	340	335	675	102
H	648	691	1339	693	640	1333	100
2B	146	153	299	147	123	270	111
3B	14	20	34	20	11	31	110
HR	66	77	143	73	85	158	91
BB	230	183	413	223	217	440	94
SO	478	492	970	496	360	856	114
E	47	59	106	56	42	98	108
E-Infield	34	47	81	49	37	86	94
LHB-Avg	.275	.294	.282	.278	.261	.272	104
LHB-HR	39	35	74	47	34	81	93
RHB-Avg	.261	.257	.259	.262	.263	.263	98
RHB-HR	27	42	69	26	51	77	89

1999-2001

	Home Games			Away Games			
	Twins	Opp	Total	Twins	Opp	Total	Index
G	216	216	432	216	216	432	—
Avg	.271	.282	.277	.263	.275	.269	103
AB	7307	7805	15112	7557	7264	14821	102
R	1023	1166	2189	930	1063	1993	110
H	1980	2200	4180	1987	1996	3983	105
2B	451	474	925	397	370	767	118
3B	62	51	113	42	43	85	130
HR	152	271	423	179	261	440	94
BB	716	642	1358	677	667	1344	99
SO	1343	1443	2786	1411	1155	2566	106
E	139	160	299	145	157	302	99
E-Infield	109	137	246	124	141	265	93
LHB-Avg	.278	.290	.283	.265	.274	.269	105
LHB-HR	83	127	210	104	91	195	106
RHB-Avg	.262	.277	.271	.260	.276	.269	101
RHB-HR	69	144	213	75	170	245	85

2001 Rankings (American League)

- Highest strikeout factor
- Third-highest double factor
- Third-lowest walk factor
- Third-lowest RHB home-run factor

Minnesota Twins

2001 Season

After losing 93 times in 2000, the Twins won their first three games of 2001 and claimed 15 victories in their first 19 contests in April. By the end of May, they were 34-17 with a staff ERA of 3.79. An early lead in the American League Central slipped away when Cleveland took three of four from the Twins in Minnesota early in June, and a .500 record for the month was an omen for a second-half fade. After going 55-32 during the first half, the Twins were 30-45 the rest of the way. Still, the club produced its first winning record since 1992.

Offense

Manager Tom Kelly had the young Twins playing solid baseball from the start, but he couldn't do much about Doug Mientkiewicz' six-week swoon in late May and June. The Twins' first baseman was batting .403 on May 22, but he hit .212 from that point through the end of June and stroked just four homers after the All-Star break. The team slugged just .418 in the second half, leading to 129 fewer runs scored than in the first half. Only five AL teams hit fewer homers than the Metrodome-based Twins in 2001, and it's no accident that Kelly led all AL managers in hit-and-run attempts.

Pitching & Defense

Pitching is the strength of this young club, with the starting trio of Brad Radke, Eric Milton and Joe Mays leading the way. Each worked more than 220 innings and won at least 15 games, and Kelly rarely used a quick hook to remove one of his starters during a decent outing. Still, he frequently turned to his bullpen, which lacked a dominant closer. Kelly always has favored solid defensive players, often leaving better hitters on the bench.

2002 Outlook

Things are looking up for whomever replaces Kelly. His successor will have to find a leadoff hitter to replace the underrated Matt Lawton, and must try to locate more power and pitching help from the young players in the system. The contraction issue stalled the club's efforts to sign players for most of the offseason, and improving upon the Twins' 2001 record will require an improved performance from the talent already on board.

Last Five Seasons

Year	Team, Lg	W	L	Pct	GB	Finish
1997	Minnesota, AL	68	94	.420	18.5	4th Central
1998	Minnesota, AL	70	92	.401	24.0	4th Central
1999	Minnesota, AL	63	97	.394	33.0	5th Central
2000	Minnesota, AL	69	93	.426	26.0	5th Central
2001	Minnesota, AL	85	77	.525	6.0	2nd Central
Totals		355	453	.434	—	

Manager Statistics (Tom Kelly)

Year	Team, Lg	W	L	Pct	GB	Finish
2001	Minnesota, AL	85	77	.525	6.0	2nd Central
16 Seasons		1140	1244	.478	—	

2001 Starting Pitchers by Days Rest

	<=3	4	5	6+
Twins Starts	5	98	29	21
Twins ERA	5.46	4.18	4.77	4.35
AL Avg Starts	1	78	48	24
AL ERA	5.92	4.69	4.58	4.58

2001 Situational Stats

	Tom Kelly	AL Average
Hit & Run Success %	38.2	35.0
Stolen Base Success %	68.5	71.0
Platoon Pct.	68.6	59.1
Defensive Subs	6	26
High-Pitch Outings	4	6
Quick/Slow Hooks	10/5	19/16
Sacrifice Attempts	36	54

2001 Rankings—Tom Kelly (American Lg)

- 1st in steals of home plate (2), hit-and-run attempts (136) and starts on three days rest
- 2nd in double steals (8) and squeeze plays (5)
- 3rd in stolen-base attempts (213) and pinch-hitters used (128)

Cristian Guzman

2001 Season

Cristian Guzman was one of the most improved players in baseball in 2001. He showed month-to-month consistency for the first time in his career, boosted his on-base percentage and continued to wreck havoc on the basepaths. His .302 batting average was the second-highest figure among Twins regulars last season. A sour note was losing most of July and much of August with a shoulder injury. The Twins missed him greatly; his absence from the offense was a major factor in the team's midsummer fall from the top of the division.

Hitting

After two years of hard work, Guzman crafted a strong line-drive swing with good balance. He sprays hits to all fields but also is capable of pulling mediocre pitching for power. His blazing speed enables him to beat out many infield hits, and any ball hit into the gaps is a potential triple. He is dangerous against both lefthanders and righthanders. Guzman makes better contact than he used to, but still swings at bad pitches too often. He needs to boost his walk rate in order to be truly effective at the top of the batting order. He bunts very well.

Baserunning & Defense

The Twins consider Guzman a great tablesetter despite his mediocre on-base abilities. He has lightning speed and has refined his stealing technique considerably over the last two years to the point where he now is successful on three out of every four stolen-base attempts. Defensively, he shows good range and a powerful arm, though his shoulder problems robbed him of some arm strength last year. He still makes careless mistakes on routine plays, and his error rate remains too high.

2002 Outlook

Guzman will be just 24 on Opening Day of 2002, but he already has three seasons of experience with the Twins. He still has flaws in his game, though he already has made gigantic amounts of progress. If he settles down a bit with the glove and continues his offensive development, he'll be an All-Star.

Position: SS
Bats: B **Throws:** R
Ht: 6' 0" **Wt:** 195

Opening Day Age: 24
Born: 3/21/78 in Santo Domingo, DR
ML Seasons: 3
Pronunciation: GOOZ-mahn

Overall Statistics

	G	AB	R	H	D	T	HR	RBI	SB	BB	SO	Avg	OBP	Slg
2001	118	493	80	149	28	14	10	51	25	21	78	.302	.337	.477
Career	405	1544	216	400	65	37	19	131	62	89	269	.259	.302	.386

Where He Hits the Ball

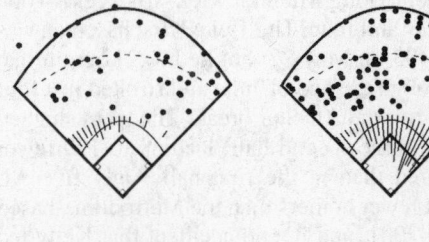

Vs. LHP   **Vs. RHP**

2001 Situational Stats

	AB	H	HR	RBI	Avg		AB	H	HR	RBI	Avg
Home	261	76	7	30	.291	LHP	125	39	2	9	.312
Road	232	73	3	21	.315	RHP	368	110	8	42	.299
First Half	347	107	7	34	.308	Sc Pos	119	35	2	42	.294
Scnd Half	146	42	3	17	.288	Clutch	75	35	0	8	.467

2001 Rankings (American League)

- 1st in triples, batting average in the clutch, errors at shortstop (21) and lowest fielding percentage at shortstop (.959)
- 5th in fewest pitches seen per plate appearance (3.43)
- 8th in highest groundball-flyball ratio (1.7)
- 9th in batting average on an 0-2 count (.290)
- Led the Twins in triples, sacrifice bunts (8), bunts in play (22), fewest GDPs per GDP situation (7.7%), batting average in the clutch and slugging percentage vs. lefthanded pitchers (.536)

Torii Hunter

2001 Season

Torii Hunter missed much of April with a pulled groin muscle, but he otherwise was more consistent and productive than in past seasons. He set career highs in runs, hits, doubles, home runs, RBI and slugging percentage, emerging as one of the major power threats in the Twins' lineup. He hit six homers in May, then five apiece in each of the following months. He also made numerous highlight-reel plays in center field, and was one of the many Minnesota fielders who seemed to be featured regularly on ESPN Baseball Tonight's "web gems" segment.

Hitting

Scouts always felt that Hunter could hit for power in the major leagues, but he didn't prove them right until last year. He learned how to drive pitches to the opposite field, particularly the good fastballs that would eat him up in the past. While his batting average fluctuated throughout the campaign, his power production remained steady. Hunter gets in trouble when he lengthens his swing, but he did a much better job of keeping it short and compact in 2001. His impatience is a serious problem, however, and better strike-zone judgment likely would help solve his remaining flaws at the plate.

Baserunning & Defense

Hunter is one of the fastest Twins, but he doesn't possess good basestealing technique. He performs other baserunning tasks very well and is aggressive about taking any base offered by the defense. The Twins think that Hunter is the best defensive outfielder in the American League, and opposing teams are starting to agree. He has tremendous range, a strong and accurate arm, and seldom makes a mistake. His awesome range in center field is a great asset, considering the large number of flyball pitchers on the staff.

2002 Outlook

Hunter made great progress in 2001, and he has his prime years ahead of him. His defense is terrific, and his bat is developing nicely. He still must continue to develop a sound eye at the plate, and if he can boost his on-base percentage, he could be a star.

Position: CF
Bats: R **Throws:** R
Ht: 6' 2" **Wt:** 205

Opening Day Age: 26
Born: 7/18/75 in Pine Bluff, AR
ML Seasons: 5

Overall Statistics

	G	AB	R	H	D	T	HR	RBI	SB	BB	SO	Avg	OBP	Slg
2001	148	564	82	147	32	5	27	92	9	29	125	.261	.306	.479
Career	389	1301	178	343	64	14	41	173	23	75	271	.264	.310	.429

Where He Hits the Ball

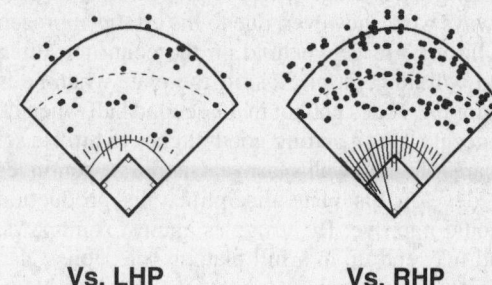

Vs. LHP   **Vs. RHP**

2001 Situational Stats

	AB	H	HR	RBI	Avg		AB	H	HR	RBI	Avg
Home	278	69	13	49	.248	LHP	125	32	6	19	.256
Road	286	78	14	43	.273	RHP	439	115	21	73	.262
First Half	288	73	13	48	.253	Sc Pos	166	44	6	65	.265
Scnd Half	276	74	14	44	.268	Clutch	85	22	6	15	.259

2001 Rankings (American League)

- 1st in assists in center field (14)
- 4th in fielding percentage in center field (.992) and highest percentage of swings that missed (26.7)
- 5th in lowest on-base percentage vs. righthanded pitchers (.303)
- 6th in errors in center field (4)
- Led the Twins in home runs, at-bats, strikeouts and HR frequency (20.9 ABs per HR)

Jacque Jones

2001 Season

Jacque Jones opened the season as Minnesota's regular left fielder, but he played poorly for much of the first half and was benched at times for lack of production. Poor patience at the plate was the main problem, but he worked hard at improving his strike-zone judgment in the second half, with positive results. He hit .307 after the All-Star break, and his on-base percentage after the break was 72 points higher than his mark before the All-Star game.

Hitting

Jones may have the quickest wrists on the club, and consequently he should be able to hit for a consistently good average with decent power. It doesn't always work, however, due to his erratic approach to hitting. He gets behind on the count too often and will lunge at pitches off the plate when he is slumping. Jones got hot in the second half when he concentrated on getting good pitches to hit. He set a career-high in walks last year, and if he continues to develop his plate discipline, his production should improve. He struggles against southpaws, and may end up in a full platoon role. Jones also presses with runners on base, making him better suited for the lower half of the batting order.

Baserunning & Defense

Jones runs well, but he doesn't read pitchers easily and won't be a major stolen-base threat unless he improves his approach. He otherwise is aggressive on the bases and will move up at any opportunity. Jones is a fine defensive outfielder, with above-average range, an accurate arm and good situational awareness. He has mastered the Metrodome, and combines with center fielder Torii Hunter to make a top-notch defensive unit.

2002 Outlook

Some within the organization are disappointed in Jones, and there is sentiment to seek another outfield option. But his strong second half should get him another opportunity to prove himself. He still has youth on his side, as well as a great deal of natural talent, and he could yet develop into a .300, 20-homer player.

Position: LF
Bats: L **Throws:** L
Ht: 5'10" **Wt:** 176

Opening Day Age: 26
Born: 4/25/75 in San Diego, CA
ML Seasons: 3

Overall Statistics

	G	AB	R	H	D	T	HR	RBI	SB	BB	SO	Avg	OBP	Slg
2001	149	475	57	131	25	0	14	49	12	39	92	.276	.335	.417
Career	398	1320	177	373	75	7	42	169	22	82	266	.283	.327	.445

Where He Hits the Ball

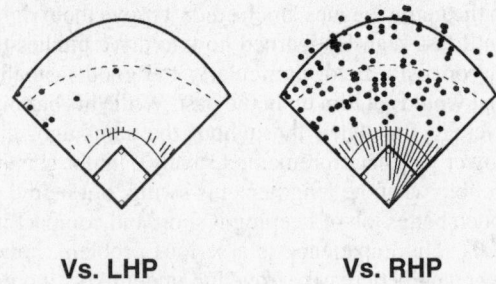

Vs. LHP　　　　**Vs. RHP**

2001 Situational Stats

	AB	H	HR	RBI	Avg		AB	H	HR	RBI	Avg
Home	226	58	5	17	.257	LHP	55	10	0	3	.182
Road	249	73	9	32	.293	RHP	420	121	14	46	.288
First Half	276	70	6	28	.254	Sc Pos	123	28	2	33	.228
Scnd Half	199	61	8	21	.307	Clutch	71	30	0	4	.423

2001 Rankings (American League)

- 2nd in batting average in the clutch
- 3rd in errors in left field (5) and fielding percentage in left field (.983)
- 4th in highest groundball-flyball ratio (2.1), assists in left field (8), lowest stolen-base percentage (57.1) and highest percentage of swings on the first pitch (39.5)
- Led the Twins in highest groundball-flyball ratio (2.1)

Corey Koskie

2001 Season

The Twins were counting on Corey Koskie to help a stagnant offense, and he certainly did his part. The fifth different player in the last five years to open the season in the cleanup spot for Minnesota, Koskie set career highs in runs, hits, doubles, homers, RBI, slugging percentage and stolen bases. The four-year veteran became the first Twin since Gary Gaetti in 1987 to have 25 homers and 100 RBI in a season. Koskie was especially impressive in July, hitting .351 with a .723 slugging percentage while swiping eight bases.

Hitting

Koskie is quite strong, but he didn't consistently loft the ball for power until 2001. He shows very good pull power but still takes pitches to the opposite field when necessary. Koskie slumps when he gets too passive against first-pitch fastballs, but overall his plate discipline is a great asset. He works very hard at improving his approach, frequently hitting off a batting tee with batting coach Scott Ullger to keep his wrists from rolling too much. He smashes righthanders and does enough against lefties to stay in the lineup every day.

Baserunning & Defense

Koskie doesn't have much raw speed, but he pays close attention to honing his baserunning skills. He stole 27 bases last year, but it was his 82-percent success rate that was even more surprising and impressive. That may not happen again, but he's proven that pitchers can't ignore him. He moves up aggressively on flyballs to the outfield. Twins officials are full of praise about Koskie's defense. He is alert, reliable, shows good range and has a strong and accurate arm. He ranks among the most underappreciated fielders in the league.

2002 Outlook

Expect Koskie back in the Twins' cleanup spot for 2002. He is signed through 2003 with an option for 2004. He's now one of the better third basemen in baseball, and the power core of Minnesota's offense. He is comfortable in a Twins uniform, and he will be the club's third baseman as long as they can afford him.

Position: 3B
Bats: L **Throws:** R
Ht: 6' 3" **Wt:** 217

Opening Day Age: 28
Born: 6/28/73 in Anola, MB, Canada
ML Seasons: 4
Pronunciation: KOSS-key

Minnesota

Overall Statistics

	G	AB	R	H	D	T	HR	RBI	SB	BB	SO	Avg	OBP	Slg
2001	153	562	100	155	37	2	26	103	27	68	118	.276	.362	.488
Career	427	1407	223	407	90	6	47	228	36	187	304	.289	.378	.462

Where He Hits the Ball

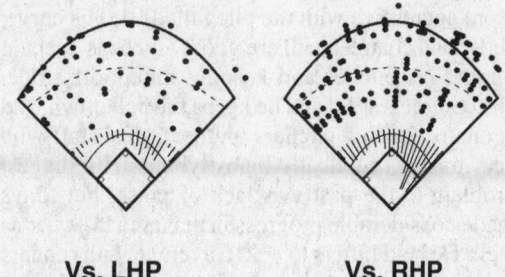

Vs. LHP   **Vs. RHP**

2001 Situational Stats

	AB	H	HR	RBI	Avg		AB	H	HR	RBI	Avg
Home	265	76	11	50	.287	LHP	165	40	6	25	.242
Road	297	79	15	53	.266	RHP	397	115	20	78	.290
First Half	293	76	12	55	.259	Sc Pos	177	46	7	75	.260
Scnd Half	269	79	14	48	.294	Clutch	79	22	4	17	.278

2001 Rankings (American League)

- 2nd in batting average with the bases loaded (.636)
- 3rd in fielding percentage at third base (.964)
- Led the Twins in runs scored, total bases (274), RBI, sacrifice flies (7), walks, intentional walks (9), hit by pitch (12), GDPs (16), pitches seen (2,461), plate appearances (649), games played, slugging percentage, stolen-base percentage (81.8), steals of third (6), batting average with the bases loaded (.636), cleanup slugging percentage (.498), highest percentage of extra bases taken as a runner (56.5), slugging percentage vs. righthanded pitchers (.519), and on-base percentage vs. righthanded pitchers (.382)

Joe Mays

2001 Season

After a rough sophomore campaign in 2000, Joe Mays had much to prove in 2001. He passed the test with flying colors. While Brad Radke and Eric Milton garnered the accolades as the anchors of the Twins' staff, it was Mays who led the team in wins, ERA and innings pitched. He ranked third in the American League ERA race, third in innings pitched, fifth in fewest baserunners allowed per nine innings (10.6) and sixth in opponents batting average (.235).

Pitching

Mays' velocity is average to slightly above average, ranging from 88-92 MPH. His fastball has very good sinking movement, and he was much more aggressive with the pitch in 2001. His curve, slider and changeup all are good, and he is adept at mixing his pitches and keeping hitters off stride. His control is solid and he keeps the ball down, and is one of the few pitchers on the Twins' staff who gets more groundballs than flyballs. His biggest problem in the past was lack of poise, but Mays made considerable progress in that area last year as well. He held hitters to a .216 average with runners on base and didn't let a bad performance in one start carry over to the next. He posted losses in back-to-back starts just twice last season.

Defense

Mays isn't a great athlete and won't be a terrific fielder, but he's improved his fundamentals and situational awareness—important for a groundball pitcher. He made just one error in 46 total chances in 2001. He works quickly when pitching well, which helps keep baserunners in check despite an average move to first base.

2002 Outlook

Twins coaches were full of praise for Mays throughout the 2001 season, focusing on his much-improved self-confidence. If he holds onto that, he will remain a very effective pitcher. Mays doesn't have the blazing stuff of a staff ace, but he has proven he can be a durable and consistent performer in the middle of the rotation.

Position: SP
Bats: B **Throws:** R
Ht: 6' 1" **Wt:** 185

Opening Day Age: 26
Born: 12/10/75 in Flint, MI
ML Seasons: 3

Overall Statistics

	W	L	Pct.	ERA	G	GS	Sv	IP	H	BB	SO	HR	Ratio
2001	17	13	.567	3.16	34	34	0	233.2	205	64	123	25	1.15
Career	30	39	.435	4.21	114	82	0	565.0	577	198	340	69	1.37

How Often He Throws Strikes

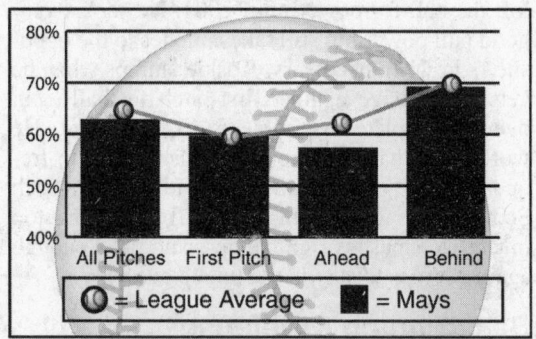

= League Average = Mays

2001 Situational Stats

	W	L	ERA	Sv	IP		AB	H	HR	RBI	Avg
Home	7	7	3.34	0	107.2	LHB	460	109	14	46	.237
Road	10	6	3.00	0	126.0	RHB	412	96	11	33	.233
First Half	11	5	3.02	0	122.1	Sc Pos	178	36	7	53	.202
Scnd Half	6	8	3.31	0	111.1	Clutch	55	12	3	6	.218

2001 Rankings (American League)

- 1st in lowest ERA on the road and lowest batting average allowed with runners in scoring position
- 3rd in ERA, games started and innings pitched
- Led the Twins in ERA, wins, losses, games started, shutouts (2), innings pitched, batters faced (957), walks allowed, wild pitches (11), pickoff throws (46), GDPs induced (19), lowest batting average allowed (.235), lowest slugging percentage allowed (.365), lowest on-base percentage allowed (.289), highest groundball-flyball ratio allowed (1.3), lowest ERA at home, lowest batting average allowed vs. lefthanded batters, lowest batting average allowed vs. righthanded batters and most GDPs induced per nine innings (0.7)

Doug Mientkiewicz

2001 Season

After posting a .414 batting average as a member of the gold-medal winning USA Olympic baseball team in Sydney in 2000, Doug Mientkiewicz won the Twins' first base job with a strong spring training in 2001. He quickly proved that the problems which had dogged him throughout his 1999 rookie campaign were a thing of the past. He hit over .300 in April, May, July and August, and provided steady offensive output and Gold Glove defense at first base. Mientkiewicz also showed some pop with 15 home runs, and Twins officials consistently praised his clubhouse leadership.

Hitting

Mientkiewicz is not a classic power-hitting first baseman; he is built more in the Mark Grace mode. He kept his swing short and compact in 2001, lashing line drives to all fields while occasionally pulling for power. He's strong enough to hit 20-plus homers in a season but is content to take pitches the opposite way for base hits and doubles more often than not. Mientkiewicz seldom swings at bad pitches, and his good walk rate helps boost his on-base percentage. He does well against lefthanders and doesn't need to be platooned.

Baserunning & Defense

Speed is not a plus for Mientkiewicz. His running speed is fair, but he'll never be a basestealing threat in the majors. He does know the fundamentals on the basepaths, however. Many observers consider Mientkiewicz to be the best defensive first baseman in the American League. He has excellent range, is very reliable, and has enough athletic ability to play third base, the outfield or even second base in an emergency. His diving stops at first saved plenty of earned runs for Twins' hurlers and frequently were featured on highlight reels.

2002 Outlook

Twins officials credit Mientkiewicz's improvement to a more relaxed attitude. He can be very hard on himself, but he showed much better confidence and poise last year, letting his talent shine through. He should remain productive for years to come, though it remains to be seen if he can be a consistent .300 threat.

Position: 1B
Bats: L **Throws:** R
Ht: 6' 2" **Wt:** 200

Opening Day Age: 27
Born: 6/19/74 in Toledo, OH
ML Seasons: 4
Pronunciation: mint-KAY-vich

Overall Statistics

	G	AB	R	H	D	T	HR	RBI	SB	BB	SO	Avg	OBP	Slg
2001	151	543	77	166	39	1	15	74	2	67	92	.306	.387	.464
Career	280	909	112	252	61	4	17	112	4	114	146	.277	.362	.409

Where He Hits the Ball

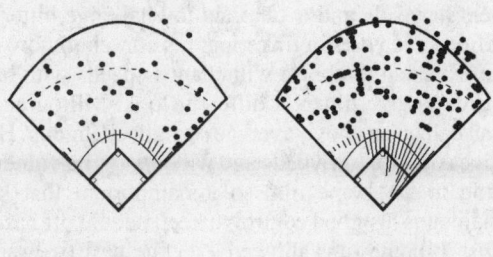

Vs. LHP   **Vs. RHP**

2001 Situational Stats

	AB	H	HR	RBI	Avg		AB	H	HR	RBI	Avg
Home	266	80	11	45	.301	LHP	143	46	3	20	.322
Road	277	86	4	29	.310	RHP	400	120	12	54	.300
First Half	307	97	11	54	.316	Sc Pos	140	33	3	55	.236
Scnd Half	236	69	4	20	.292	Clutch	86	27	3	14	.314

2001 Rankings (American League)

- 1st in fielding percentage at first base (.997)
- 8th in doubles
- 9th in on-base percentage vs. lefthanded pitchers (.409)
- Led the Twins in batting average, hits, doubles, sacrifice flies (7), times on base (242), on-base percentage, most pitches seen per plate appearance (3.88), batting average vs. lefthanded pitchers, batting average vs. righthanded pitchers, on-base percentage vs. lefthanded pitchers (.409), batting average at home, batting average on the road, lowest percentage of swings on the first pitch (20.3) and batting average on a 3-? count (.327)

Eric Milton

2001 Season

Eric Milton continues to tease the Twins with signs of greatness, being overpowering in one start, then mediocre—or worse—in the next one. His biggest rough stretch was in July (6.07 ERA), when he was bothered by a stiff back. He did best in April (2.73) and down the stretch in September (3.27). Despite his inconsistencies, the overall package makes him one of the most talented lefties in the league. He set career-best marks in wins, ERA and innings last year.

Pitching

Milton was clocked as high as 97 MPH in one start last year, but he works consistently in the 91-93 MPH range. He can throw the fastball on the corners or inside and is unafraid to challenge hitters. After three years of tinkering, his curveball now is an excellent pitch. He will change speeds with his curve to give hitters a different look. Milton also can call on an above-average straight changeup. He gives up a lot of flyballs and will always be vulnerable to the home run, so it's important that he maintains his good control to keep people off base. His 70 home runs allowed over the past two seasons is the second-highest total in the majors during that span. The Twins supervise his workload and pitch counts prudently, since he's been bothered by shoulder and elbow soreness throughout his career.

Defense

Milton is an above-average athlete, and he improved his fielding fundamentals in 2001. He has a fine move to first base and works quickly enough to control the running game. He was a good hitter in college, but he doesn't get to show that skill in the American League.

2002 Outlook

Milton's outlook for 2002 is the same as it was for 2001: he's immensely talented, and if he makes a few additional adjustments, he'll be one of the best pitchers in the game. Even if he doesn't improve, he's still very good, capable of winning 15-18 contests if he receives adequate run support.

Position: SP
Bats: L **Throws:** L
Ht: 6' 3" **Wt:** 220

Opening Day Age: 26
Born: 8/4/75 in State College, PA
ML Seasons: 4

Overall Statistics

	W	L	Pct.	ERA	G	GS	Sv	IP	H	BB	SO	HR	Ratio
2001	15	7	.682	4.32	35	34	0	220.2	222	61	157	35	1.28
Career	43	42	.506	4.79	134	133	0	799.1	812	238	587	123	1.31

How Often He Throws Strikes

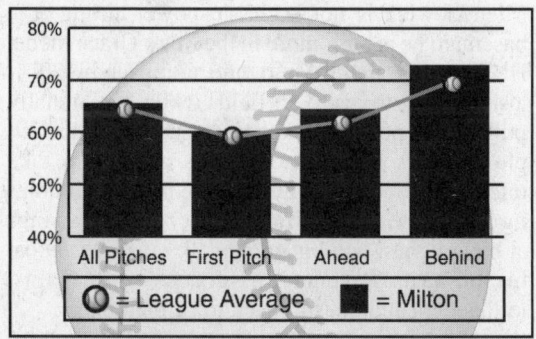

2001 Situational Stats

	W	L	ERA	Sv	IP		AB	H	HR	RBI	Avg
Home	8	4	4.63	0	101.0	LHB	142	35	11	21	.246
Road	7	3	4.06	0	119.2	RHB	722	187	24	84	.259
First Half	8	3	3.73	0	118.1	Sc Pos	190	45	5	59	.237
Scnd Half	7	4	5.01	0	102.1	Clutch	67	15	2	7	.224

2001 Rankings (American League)

- 1st in fielding percentage at pitcher (1.000), lowest groundball-flyball ratio allowed (0.6) and fewest GDPs induced per nine innings (0.3)
- 2nd in home runs allowed and most home runs allowed per nine innings (1.43)
- 3rd in games started
- 4th in lowest stolen-base percentage allowed (42.9)
- 6th in highest slugging percentage allowed (.446)
- 8th in batters faced (944)
- Led the Twins in games started, home runs allowed, strikeouts, pitches thrown (3,536), winning percentage, lowest stolen-base percentage allowed (42.9) and most strikeouts per nine innings (6.4)

David Ortiz

2001 Season

David Ortiz began the 2001 season on a tear, hitting .309 in April with five home runs and a .605 slugging percentage. All went awry on May 4, when he fractured his right wrist sliding into home plate in a game against the Royals. He rehabbed quickly and returned to action on July 21, but he wasn't the same after the injury. Ortiz batted just .202 after coming off the disabled list, and his post-injury slugging percentage plummeted to .418.

Hitting

Ortiz is undeniably strong, and he was pulling the ball with authority before the injury. He has made great strides learning the strike zone and no longer strikes out as frequently as he used to. Ortiz lowered his hands and shortened his leg kick in spring training, adjustments that helped him against fastballs. After the injury, his timing looked off, and he struggled through most of the second half. Many observers felt he returned to action before he was physically ready, a testament more to his work ethic and the Twins' desire to have him in a power-starved lineup than to his prudence.

Baserunning & Defense

Ortiz may be the slowest member of the Minnesota lineup, and he lacks good instincts on the bases. He *did* improve his running fundamentals, but he never will be a threat to steal. Ortiz is primarily a DH now, playing first base only when Doug Mientkiewicz needs a day off. He catches what he gets to, but has limited range and poor mobility.

2002 Outlook

The Twins' DH role belongs to Ortiz in 2002. Despite his injury problems, he did set a career high in home runs last season. Wrist injuries take up to a year to heal properly, so it is not a surprise that he played poorly when he came back. Ortiz is just entering his prime, and he is a good bet to rebound strongly. He has 30-homer potential given good health.

Position: DH
Bats: L **Throws:** L
Ht: 6' 4" **Wt:** 230

Opening Day Age: 26
Born: 11/18/75 in Santo Domingo, DR
ML Seasons: 5
Pronunciation: or-TEEZ

Minnesota

Overall Statistics

	G	AB	R	H	D	T	HR	RBI	SB	BB	SO	Avg	OBP	Slg
2001	89	303	46	71	17	1	18	48	1	40	68	.234	.324	.475
Career	330	1065	163	281	76	2	38	163	3	143	252	.264	.351	.446

Where He Hits the Ball

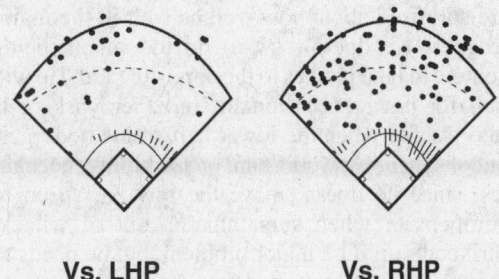

Vs. LHP   **Vs. RHP**

2001 Situational Stats

	AB	H	HR	RBI	Avg		AB	H	HR	RBI	Avg
Home	153	33	6	28	.216	LHP	86	19	4	12	.221
Road	150	38	12	20	.253	RHP	217	52	14	36	.240
First Half	90	28	6	18	.311	Sc Pos	93	22	5	33	.237
Scnd Half	213	43	12	30	.202	Clutch	35	8	3	7	.229

2001 Rankings (American League)

- Did not rank near the top or bottom in any category

A.J. Pierzynski

2001 Season

A.J. Pierzynski won a roster spot with a strong spring training, then spent the season in a platoon behind the plate with veteran Tom Prince. Pierzynski's forte is defense, but he provided surprising offense at times during the season. He hit .318 before the All-Star Break, thriving in June particularly (.372 batting, .538 slugging). His average dropped as the season progressed, but he maintained solid doubles power throughout the campaign. His 33 doubles were third most on the team behind Doug Mientkiewicz (39) and Corey Koskie (37).

Hitting

Scouts say that Pierzynski's bat is slow, and many are surprised about how well he's hit in the major leagues. He doesn't try to do too much, being content to take pitches to the opposite field. He will pull for power occasionally, but Pierzynski gets into trouble when the lower half of his body gets out of synch. He works hard on his hitting mechanics, since he doesn't have the raw bat speed to compensate when something is out of whack. Strikeouts aren't a major problem, but he needs to draw more walks in order to boost his on-base percentage and to get better pitches to hit. His high doubles total indicates a chance for more power to come.

Baserunning & Defense

Like most catchers, Pierzynski is a station-to-station runner who poses no basestealing threat. Twins coaches like his defense behind the plate; he is a bit error-prone but has good mobility and a quick release to second. Pierzynski puts down a good target for pitchers, and he does a fine job calling the game and handling the staff.

2002 Outlook

Barring a disaster or injury in spring training, Pierzynski will see a lot of action for the Twins in 2002. They like his glove, and his offensive game is turning out to be a real bonus for Minnesota. He likely won't be an everyday player, however, as long as he totes around a .159 average against big league lefties.

Position: C
Bats: L **Throws:** R
Ht: 6' 3" **Wt:** 220

Opening Day Age: 25
Born: 12/30/76 in Bridgehampton, NY
ML Seasons: 4
Pronunciation: PEER-zin-skee

Overall Statistics

	G	AB	R	H	D	T	HR	RBI	SB	BB	SO	Avg	OBP	Slg
2001	114	381	51	110	33	2	7	55	1	16	57	.289	.322	.441
Career	163	501	67	146	40	3	9	70	2	23	77	.291	.330	.437

Where He Hits the Ball

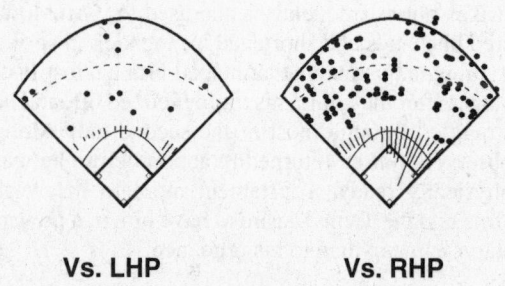

Vs. LHP   **Vs. RHP**

2001 Situational Stats

	AB	H	HR	RBI	Avg		AB	H	HR	RBI	Avg
Home	179	56	3	25	.313	LHP	60	10	0	4	.167
Road	202	54	4	30	.267	RHP	321	100	7	51	.312
First Half	211	67	2	31	.318	Sc Pos	111	34	3	46	.306
Scnd Half	170	43	5	24	.253	Clutch	61	19	0	10	.311

2001 Rankings (American League)

- 2nd in lowest fielding percentage at catcher (.985)
- 3rd in errors at catcher (10)
- Led the Twins in batting average with runners in scoring position

Brad Radke

Position: SP
Bats: R **Throws:** R
Ht: 6' 2" **Wt:** 188

Opening Day Age: 29
Born: 10/27/72 in Eau Claire, WI
ML Seasons: 7
Pronunciation: RAD-key

Minnesota

2001 Season

Brad Radke finally got to pitch for a contending club, and he received more than a pittance of run support for the first time in several years. He posted an ERA that was half a run better than league average, reduced his already low walk rate and kept his team in the game more often than not. Radke also set new career marks with six complete games and a pair of shutouts. But he missed much of August with a bruised thumb, and he struggled when the Twins needed him the most (5.96 ERA in September).

Pitching

When right, Radke runs his fastball to the plate at 89-92 MPH. The fastball has very good movement, especially when kept low in the strike zone. He complements his heater with a curve, slider and changeup, all of which rate as above-average. The changeup is his best pitch overall, and he isn't afraid to use it. Radke's command is outstanding. He also has been durable throughout his career, but there are concerns about his workload. For the second straight year, Radke's velocity dropped into the mid-80s at times in midsummer, due to fatigue and minor mechanical troubles. He left too many pitches out over the plate in September, resulting in poor numbers in that critical month.

Defense

Radke is one of the better defensive pitchers in the American League. He is quick off the mound, makes good decisions and holds runners well despite an average move. He works quickly, which helps keep his fielders alert and the runners anchored to first base.

2002 Outlook

Joe Mays won more games in 2001, and Eric Milton is more dominating, but Radke remains the Twins' ace. He had an offseason option to remain with the club or demand a trade heading into 2002, and he chose to stick around even with the brewing contraction issue. Despite his problems down the stretch, his numbers overall improved from his previous three seasons. The fact remains: give Radke some runs, and he will win.

Overall Statistics

	W	L	Pct.	ERA	G	GS	Sv	IP	H	BB	SO	HR	Ratio
2001	15	11	.577	3.94	33	33	0	226.0	235	26	137	24	1.15
Career	93	95	.495	4.27	231	230	0	1537.2	1637	316	942	202	1.27

How Often He Throws Strikes

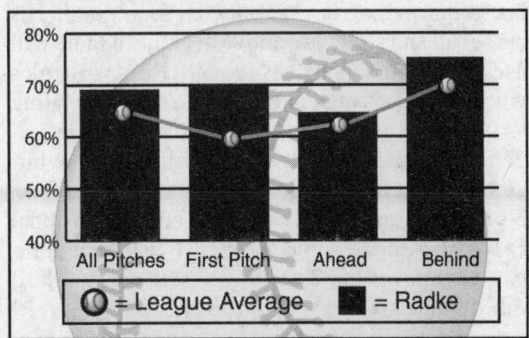

= League Average = Radke

2001 Situational Stats

	W	L	ERA	Sv	IP		AB	H	HR	RBI	Avg
Home	9	6	3.99	0	130.2	LHB	442	120	12	48	.271
Road	6	5	3.87	0	95.1	RHB	425	115	12	53	.271
First Half	10	4	3.58	0	138.1	Sc Pos	185	52	5	72	.281
Scnd Half	5	7	4.52	0	87.2	Clutch	83	23	1	4	.277

2001 Rankings (American League)

- 1st in highest strikeout-walk ratio (5.3), fewest pitches thrown per batter (3.45) and fewest walks per nine innings (1.0)
- 2nd in complete games (6)
- 4th in shutouts (2) and hits allowed
- 5th in fewest GDPs induced per nine innings (0.5)
- 6th in runners caught stealing (11)
- Led the Twins in complete games (6), shutouts (2), hits allowed, hit batsmen (10), stolen bases allowed (15), runners caught stealing (11), highest strikeout-walk ratio (5.3), most run support per nine innings (5.4), fewest home runs allowed per nine innings (.96) and fewest walks per nine innings (1.0)

Rick Reed

2001 Season

Seeking a veteran pitcher for the stretch run, the Twins took a huge gamble with the July 31 trade that sent outfielder Matt Lawton to the Mets for starter Rick Reed. Reed was 8-6 with a 3.48 ERA with New York prior to the swap, but he was very erratic after joining Minnesota. To make matters worse, the Twins' offense struggled with Lawton gone. Reed's 6.75 ERA in August was a big blow to the Twins' pennant hopes, and his overall 5.19 ERA for Minnesota was a major disappointment.

Pitching

When Reed is going well, he throws four pitches for quality strikes. His fastball lacks velocity, but his command of it generally is very good. His curveball and slider are above average, and he will use his changeup in any count. Reed struggles when he pitches high in the strike zone, generating too many extra-base hits and home runs. He seldom hands out free passes and will challenge hitters even when behind in the count. Coaches praise his intellect, and he has one of the best professional approaches in the game. Reed also has been durable, going over the 200-inning mark for the third time in the past five years in 2001.

Defense

Reed is a fine athlete, alert in the infield and adept at making the right decision in difficult situations. He controls the running game with a quick move to first base and a fast delivery. Reed is a good bunter.

2002 Outlook

Reed was dealt during a multiyear contract, and exercised his right to ask for another trade this offseason. Moving him may be a good idea, as Reed has been homer-prone since his most unhittable season in 1997. From 1998-2000, he allowed an ugly 1.7 homers per nine innings in games away from pitching-friendly Shea Stadium, compared to the overall National League average of 1.1. Bringing his homer-prone tendencies to Minnesota was a bad idea, as park indices from 1998-2001 conclude that among American League parks, few were more homer-friendly for lefthanded hitters than the Metrodome. His homer rate climbed substantially after moving to the American League.

Position: SP
Bats: R **Throws:** R
Ht: 6' 1"   **Wt:** 195

Opening Day Age: 36
Born: 8/16/65 in Huntington, WV
ML Seasons: 13

Overall Statistics

	W	L	Pct.	ERA	G	GS	Sv	IP	H	BB	SO	HR	Ratio
2001	12	12	.500	4.05	32	32	0	202.1	211	31	142	28	1.20
Career	72	57	.558	3.95	213	192	1	1222.2	1254	230	778	160	1.21

How Often He Throws Strikes

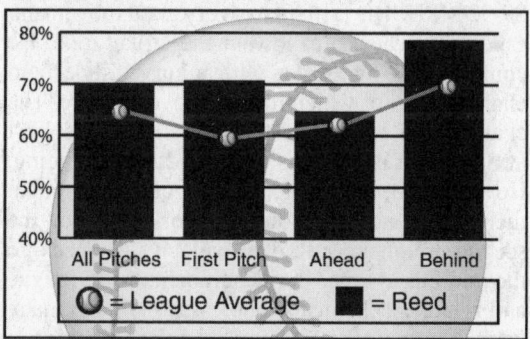

= League Average   = Reed

2001 Situational Stats

	W	L	ERA	Sv	IP		AB	H	HR	RBI	Avg
Home	6	8	3.86	0	126.0	LHB	398	110	15	47	.276
Road	6	4	4.36	0	76.1	RHB	389	101	13	43	.260
First Half	7	4	3.10	0	119.0	Sc Pos	163	43	7	63	.264
Scnd Half	5	8	5.40	0	83.1	Clutch	41	13	2	6	.317

2001 Rankings (American League)

- 5th in highest batting average allowed vs. lefthanded batters (.355)

Luis Rivas

2001 Season

Luis Rivas missed most of spring training with an abdominal strain, but the Twins were committed to him as their second baseman and he was handed the job anyway. The rust showed, as he hit just .200 in April and .231 in May. But Rivas played better as the season progressed, as he gained confidence and learned the pitchers. He finished his first full big league campaign with respectable totals of 70 runs scored and 31 stolen bases.

Hitting

Rivas uses a classic line-drive swing. He will pull the ball occasionally, but most of his success is found in the gaps. He'll never be a big power hitter, but he is strong enough to reach double-digits in home runs as he matures. Early in the season he was too anxious and easily could be overpowered with high fastballs or tricked with sliders away. When he relaxed he showed that he could put wood on quality pitching by hitting the ball on the ground and making good use of his above-average speed. Rivas hit .340 when used in the leadoff spot, but he needs to exhibit better plate discipline if he wants to retain the No. 1 role permanently. He can bunt if needed.

Baserunning & Defense

Speed is one of Rivas' best assets. He did a very good job reading pitchers and getting jumps on stolen-base attempts, and he should be good for 30-plus steals annually. Although his defensive stats were mediocre, Twins officials rave about Rivas' glove. They like his range, especially on artificial turf, as well as his soft hands and decent arm strength. He can be sloppy on routine plays, but he also will make spectacular stops.

2002 Outlook

Rivas has a lock on the second-base job in Minnesota, yet is at least five years from his prime. Given normal development, he should be a solid player, if not a special one. In the short-term, he needs to polish up his defense and improve his strike-zone judgment.

Position: 2B
Bats: R **Throws:** R
Ht: 5'11" **Wt:** 175

Opening Day Age: 22
Born: 8/30/79 in La Guaira, VZ
ML Seasons: 2
Pronunciation: REE-vas

Minnesota

Overall Statistics

	G	AB	R	H	D	T	HR	RBI	SB	BB	SO	Avg	OBP	Slg
2001	153	563	70	150	21	6	7	47	31	40	99	.266	.319	.362
Career	169	621	78	168	25	7	7	53	33	42	103	.271	.320	.367

Where He Hits the Ball

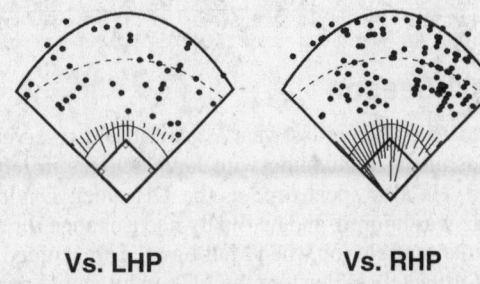

Vs. LHP   **Vs. RHP**

2001 Situational Stats

	AB	H	HR	RBI	Avg		AB	H	HR	RBI	Avg
Home	276	74	3	25	.268	LHP	137	33	2	7	.241
Road	287	76	4	22	.265	RHP	426	117	5	40	.275
First Half	279	69	4	29	.247	Sc Pos	132	35	0	39	.265
Scnd Half	284	81	3	18	.285	Clutch	80	24	1	7	.300

2001 Rankings (American League)

- 2nd in on-base percentage for a leadoff hitter (.392) and lowest fielding percentage at second base (.974)
- 3rd in errors at second base (15)
- 5th in batting average among rookies and RBI among rookies
- 6th in caught stealing (11), highest groundball-flyball ratio (1.9) and lowest HR frequency (80.4 ABs per HR)
- 8th in stolen bases
- Led the Twins in singles, stolen bases, caught stealing (11), games played and on-base percentage for a leadoff hitter (.392)

Chad Allen

Position: DH/LF/RF
Bats: R **Throws:** R
Ht: 6' 1" **Wt:** 195

Opening Day Age: 27
Born: 2/6/75 in Dallas, TX
ML Seasons: 3

Overall Statistics

	G	AB	R	H	D	T	HR	RBI	SB	BB	SO	Avg	OBP	Slg
2001	57	175	20	46	13	2	4	20	1	19	37	.263	.333	.429
Career	209	706	91	194	37	5	14	73	15	59	140	.275	.332	.401

2001 Situational Stats

	AB	H	HR	RBI	Avg		AB	H	HR	RBI	Avg
Home	75	20	1	7	.267	LHP	52	14	2	9	.269
Road	100	26	3	13	.260	RHP	123	32	2	11	.260
First Half	113	32	2	14	.283	Sc Pos	51	10	1	14	.196
Scnd Half	62	14	2	6	.226	Clutch	35	17	3	6	.486

2001 Season

Chad Allen began last year as an outfield reserve, occasionally platooning with Jacque Jones in left field. He also spent time as the DH when David Ortiz was injured, and he finally had a chance for a regular outfield job when Matt Lawton was traded. Unfortunately, Allen tore the ACL in his right knee on August 14, ending his season at just 175 at-bats.

Hitting, Baserunning & Defense

Allen is a line-drive hitter with fair power to all fields. He's strong but does not have a powerful enough swing to be considered a home-run threat. He kills cripple pitches but struggles when behind in the count, which he frequently is. Allen is best deployed in a reserve/platoon role, as he shows more pop against southpaws. He has decent speed but can be too aggressive on the bases. Allen is a good athlete with adequate range and arm strength. Twins coaches have criticized him for poor decision-making and lack of concentration on defense.

2002 Outlook

Allen needs a quick recovery from his knee injury after becoming a free agent in the fall. He doesn't have enough power or speed to earn a full-time job for a contending club, so he may try to catch on with a rebuilding club.

Brian Buchanan

Position: RF/DH
Bats: R **Throws:** R
Ht: 6' 4" **Wt:** 230

Opening Day Age: 28
Born: 7/21/73 in Miami, FL
ML Seasons: 2

Overall Statistics

	G	AB	R	H	D	T	HR	RBI	SB	BB	SO	Avg	OBP	Slg
2001	69	197	28	54	12	0	10	32	1	19	58	.274	.342	.487
Career	99	279	38	73	15	0	11	40	1	27	80	.262	.330	.434

2001 Situational Stats

	AB	H	HR	RBI	Avg		AB	H	HR	RBI	Avg
Home	95	33	7	21	.347	LHP	74	21	6	18	.284
Road	102	21	3	11	.206	RHP	123	33	4	14	.268
First Half	88	22	5	14	.250	Sc Pos	58	13	2	22	.224
Scnd Half	109	32	5	18	.294	Clutch	28	4	1	2	.143

2001 Season

After three seasons in Triple-A, Brian Buchanan was out of options. He made the club as a reserve outfielder and pinch-hitter, joining Eric Milton and Cristian Guzman on the roster to complete the trio of prospects acquired from the Yankees in the Chuck Knoblauch trade. Buchanan's problems on defense kept him from earning a regular job for manager Tom Kelly, but his bat proved quite effective against southpaws.

Hitting, Baserunning & Defense

Buchanan is very strong and has good pull power against mediocre pitching. He can be overpowered with strong fastballs, however, especially from righthanders. He swings at pitches off the plate too often. Buchanan destroys lefties and shows much more patience against southpaws, making him an ideal platoon candidate. He runs pretty well for a big guy but is not a basestealer. He has a right-field arm, but his range is limited, and Twins officials felt his glove wasn't good enough for him to play defense on a regular basis.

2002 Outlook

Buchanan has his limits, but his power against lefthanders makes him valuable on the bench. Expect him to be used as a pinch-hitter, outfield reserve and occasionally in the DH spot in 2002.

Jack Cressend

Position: RP
Bats: R **Throws:** R
Ht: 6' 1" **Wt:** 185

Opening Day Age: 26
Born: 5/13/75 in New Orleans, LA
ML Seasons: 2

Overall Statistics

	W	L	Pct.	ERA	G	GS	Sv	IP	H	BB	SO	HR	Ratio
2001	3	2	.600	3.67	44	0	0	56.1	50	16	40	6	1.17
Career	3	2	.600	3.99	55	0	0	70.0	70	22	46	6	1.31

2001 Situational Stats

	W	L	ERA	Sv	IP		AB	H	HR	RBI	Avg
Home	1	2	6.15	0	26.1	LHB	85	25	4	14	.294
Road	2	0	1.50	0	30.0	RHB	126	25	2	11	.198
First Half	2	1	3.70	0	24.1	Sc Pos	56	11	0	16	.196
Scnd Half	1	1	3.66	0	32.0	Clutch	29	8	0	8	.276

2001 Season

Jack Cressend was promoted to the Twins on May 5, replacing the injured David Ortiz. He began as the 12th man on the pitching staff, but as the season progressed he earned a larger share of the bullpen duties. He had five holds and three wins in 44 games, but he blew both of his save opportunities.

Pitching & Defense

Cressend's fastball is average, running 88-91 MPH. He owns a good curveball and has a better changeup than most relief pitchers, a byproduct of his background as a minor league starter. He mixes his pitches well, keeps the ball down, gets groundballs and pitched well with runners on base. He has proven to be much more useful against righties early on in his big league career, however. Cressend had problems in the Metrodome and is more effective on grass because of the high number of groundballs he generates. He is a good fielder and is decent at holding runners for a righthander.

2002 Outlook

The Twins project Cressend as an important member of their bullpen for 2002. He isn't likely to get many saves, but he will be relied on in the middle and late innings, bridging the gap to whoever closes. His effectiveness against lefties will be key to his development as a major league setup man.

Eddie Guardado

Position: RP
Bats: R **Throws:** L
Ht: 6' 0" **Wt:** 194

Opening Day Age: 31
Born: 10/2/70 in Stockton, CA
ML Seasons: 9
Pronunciation: gwar-DAH-doe

Overall Statistics

	W	L	Pct.	ERA	G	GS	Sv	IP	H	BB	SO	HR	Ratio
2001	7	1	.875	3.51	67	0	12	66.2	47	23	67	5	1.05
Career	32	39	.451	4.88	505	25	30	564.2	559	236	475	83	1.41

2001 Situational Stats

	W	L	ERA	Sv	IP		AB	H	HR	RBI	Avg
Home	5	0	3.90	4	30.0	LHB	90	15	1	8	.167
Road	2	1	3.19	8	36.2	RHB	148	32	4	19	.216
First Half	6	0	3.71	3	34.0	Sc Pos	83	12	2	22	.145
Scnd Half	1	1	3.31	9	32.2	Clutch	143	26	1	12	.182

2001 Season

Eddie Guardado opened 2001 just as he'd opened the previous six campaigns: as the main lefthanded option in the Twins' pen. But by the end of the year, he'd taken over as the closer from the disappointing LaTroy Hawkins. Guardado converted 12 of 14 save opportunities and recorded the best ERA in his career. Aside from missing two weeks in June with torn cartilage in his left knee, Guardado was effective throughout the season.

Pitching & Defense

Guardado's fastball is in the 90-92 MPH range, and occasionally rises a bit higher on the radar gun. His curveball is very good, and while he hangs it occasionally, it is very tough on lefthanded hitters. He was effective against both lefthanded and righthanded batters last year, showing the ability to spot his fastball inside against righties. He is a flyball pitcher and is somewhat more effective on the road than in the Metrodome. Guardado has a quick, compact delivery and is tough on runners attempting to steal. He is reliable with the glove.

2002 Outlook

Last year was the best season of Guardado's career. Considering Hawkins' recent struggles, Guardado may have the inside track on the closer's job for 2002, barring a trade or free-agent signing.

LaTroy Hawkins

Position: RP
Bats: R **Throws:** R
Ht: 6' 5" **Wt:** 204

Opening Day Age: 29
Born: 12/21/72 in Gary, IN
ML Seasons: 7

Overall Statistics

	W	L	Pct.	ERA	G	GS	Sv	IP	H	BB	SO	HR	Ratio
2001	1	5	.167	5.96	62	0	28	51.1	59	39	36	3	1.91
Career	29	54	.349	5.78	227	98	42	660.1	824	260	394	96	1.64

2001 Situational Stats

	W	L	ERA	Sv	IP		AB	H	HR	RBI	Avg
Home	1	1	4.70	17	30.2	LHB	98	27	1	17	.276
Road	0	4	7.84	11	20.2	RHB	105	32	2	26	.305
First Half	1	2	3.48	23	33.2	Sc Pos	70	23	1	39	.329
Scnd Half	0	3	10.70	5	17.2	Clutch	133	37	2	33	.278

2001 Season

LaTroy Hawkins converted 19 of his first 22 save opportunities, setting a big league record with 23 consecutive conversions carried over from 2000. After the All-Star Break, however, he posted a 10.70 ERA and was a major factor in the club's second-half swoon. The acquisition of Todd Jones seemed to unnerve him, and by the end of the year Hawkins lost the closer's job to Eddie Guardado.

Pitching & Defense

Hawkins' fastball hits 95 MPH, but it lacks movement, and his secondary pitches must be working for him to succeed. His slider and curve were strong at the beginning of the season, but as the campaign progressed he stopped throwing them for strikes. He tried adding a cut fastball, but it didn't help. By the end of the season, Hawkins was leaving everything up in the zone. He does have fine athletic ability and handled eight chances without error. His move to first is adequate.

2002 Outlook

There doesn't seem to be anything physically wrong with Hawkins, and by all accounts he works hard. But the league caught up with him last year, and he wasn't able to adjust. A change of scenery may be best, though he will be on the team's list of potential stoppers in 2002 if he stays in Minnesota.

Denny Hocking

Position: SS/2B/1B
Bats: B **Throws:** R
Ht: 5'10" **Wt:** 183

Opening Day Age: 31
Born: 4/2/70 in Torrance, CA
ML Seasons: 9
Pronunciation: HAWK-ing

Overall Statistics

	G	AB	R	H	D	T	HR	RBI	SB	BB	SO	Avg	OBP	Slg
2001	112	327	34	82	16	2	3	25	6	29	67	.251	.315	.339
Career	691	1756	223	446	86	15	20	168	36	149	331	.254	.312	.354

2001 Situational Stats

	AB	H	HR	RBI	Avg		AB	H	HR	RBI	Avg
Home	147	40	1	10	.272	LHP	81	18	0	3	.222
Road	180	42	2	15	.233	RHP	246	64	3	22	.260
First Half	153	40	1	17	.261	Sc Pos	71	14	0	19	.197
Scnd Half	174	42	2	8	.241	Clutch	65	16	1	12	.246

2001 Season

For the fifth year in a row, Denny Hocking was Minnesota's main utility player. The Twins love his defensive versatility and work ethic, but his bat is inconsistent. When he was needed the most, Hocking hit just .154 in July, getting the majority of time at shortstop when Cristian Guzman was injured.

Hitting, Baserunning & Defense

Hocking hits line drives from both sides of the plate, but he has marginal power at best. He is an effective gap hitter, more dangerous at home than on the road. His biggest flaw is lack of patience; his walk rate dropped compared to 2000, and not surprisingly his production was down across the board. He bunts well and is skilled at little ball. Hocking is fast enough to serve as a pinch-runner, though he's never been a big basestealer. What makes him so attractive to the Twins is his glove. He can play anywhere in the infield or outfield, and performs very well at second base and shortstop.

2002 Outlook

Hocking is a useful utility player who struggles when overexposed. His best efforts usually come as a defensive sub and emergency substitute, but he shouldn't be expected to play regularly, even for a couple of weeks. Don't expect his role to change much in '02, despite the new manager.

Todd Jones

Position: RP
Bats: L **Throws:** R
Ht: 6' 3" **Wt:** 230

Opening Day Age: 33
Born: 4/24/68 in
Marietta, GA
ML Seasons: 9

Overall Statistics

	W	L	Pct.	ERA	G	GS	Sv	IP	H	BB	SO	HR	Ratio
2001	5	5	.500	4.24	69	0	13	68.0	87	29	54	9	1.71
Career	35	33	.515	3.62	528	0	183	598.2	566	285	540	52	1.42

2001 Situational Stats

	W	L	ERA	Sv	IP		AB	H	HR	RBI	Avg
Home	5	2	4.25	7	36.0	LHB	123	40	5	24	.325
Road	0	3	4.22	6	32.0	RHB	156	47	4	19	.301
First Half	4	5	5.03	11	39.1	Sc Pos	86	29	3	36	.337
Scnd Half	1	0	3.14	2	28.2	Clutch	154	48	6	32	.312

2001 Season

Todd Jones came from Detroit to Minnesota on July 28, in exchange for injury-plagued starter Mark Redman. Jones' job was to stabilize the Twins' middle-relief corps behind closer LaTroy Hawkins. He posted a 2.08 ERA in August, but when Hawkins collapsed Jones didn't get a shot as the closer, being pushed aside in favor of Eddie Guardado. A year after tying for the American League lead with 42 saves, Jones notched just 13 saves in 2001—his lowest output since 1994.

Pitching & Defense

Jones' velocity gradually has declined. He no longer hits 95 MPH consistently, settling instead for a steady 91-92 MPH. His fastball does have good sink and running action, and he keeps the ball down. Jones' slider and curve aren't as sharp as they used to be, and he was hit hard by both lefthanders and righthanders at times last year. His fielding and ability to hold runners are adequate but not special.

2002 Outlook

Jones ended the season pitching poorly, and his status for 2002 is uncertain. If Jones returns to the Twins, it likely will be in a setup role. He no longer has the stuff or command to close, except in an emergency.

Kyle Lohse

Position: SP
Bats: R **Throws:** R
Ht: 6' 2" **Wt:** 190

Opening Day Age: 23
Born: 10/4/78 in Chico, CA
ML Seasons: 1
Pronunciation: loshe

Overall Statistics

	W	L	Pct.	ERA	G	GS	Sv	IP	H	BB	SO	HR	Ratio
2001	4	7	.364	5.68	19	16	0	90.1	102	29	64	16	1.45
Career	4	7	.364	5.68	19	16	0	90.1	102	29	64	16	1.45

2001 Situational Stats

	W	L	ERA	Sv	IP		AB	H	HR	RBI	Avg
Home	2	2	4.60	0	45.0	LHB	181	63	9	32	.348
Road	2	5	6.75	0	45.1	RHB	178	39	7	24	.219
First Half	2	0	4.74	0	24.2	Sc Pos	67	20	2	31	.299
Scnd Half	2	7	6.03	0	65.2	Clutch	6	4	1	2	.667

2001 Season

The Twins promoted Kyle Lohse to the majors on June 20, inserting him into the rotation immediately. He pitched well in June (3.38 ERA) and August (4.05), but struggled badly in July (7.52) and September (9.82). To put it another way, he was erratic. However, he did well enough in his strong outings to give hope for the future.

Pitching & Defense

The Twins never knew which Kyle Lohse would appear on the mound. Lohse's fastball was clocked as high as 93 MPH, but at times his heater would dip down to 88 MPH. His slider was sharp and overpowering on occasion, but he hung it high in the strike zone too often, resulting in too many hits and homers. Like the slider, his changeup alternated between very good and very mediocre. Righties have trouble against him, but lefties got good reads on his pitches and punished him. Lohse is a good athlete and is fundamentally sound.

2002 Outlook

Lohse will have a shot at the fifth spot in Minnesota's roation. If that doesn't work, he still could be useful in the bullpen, thanks to his ability to keep righties off base. The Twins like his potential, but he needs better consistency with all of his pitches and from outing-to-outing to earn a major role.

Travis Miller

Position: RP
Bats: R **Throws:** L
Ht: 6' 3" **Wt:** 215

Opening Day Age: 29
Born: 11/2/72 in Dayton, OH
ML Seasons: 6

Overall Statistics

	W	L	Pct.	ERA	G	GS	Sv	IP	H	BB	SO	HR	Ratio
2001	1	4	.200	4.81	45	0	0	48.2	54	20	30	5	1.52
Career	7	18	.280	5.06	198	14	1	263.1	326	111	196	27	1.66

2001 Situational Stats

	W	L	ERA	Sv	IP		AB	H	HR	RBI	Avg
Home	1	1	4.56	0	23.2	LHB	69	19	1	8	.275
Road	0	3	5.04	0	25.0	RHB	122	35	4	21	.287
First Half	1	2	4.28	0	27.1	Sc Pos	60	13	2	24	.217
Scnd Half	0	2	5.48	0	21.1	Clutch	52	11	2	6	.212

2001 Season

Travis Miller began the year as the second anti-lefty option in the Twins' pen, behind Eddie Guardado. He never moved beyond that role, and at times he was almost forgotten, pitching mostly in mopup situations or when the game was already out of control. He recorded just five holds after earning 10 in 2000, and he did not receive a single save opportunity.

Pitching & Defense

Miller is a big guy, but his fastball is average at best, hitting 91 MPH on a good day but often 2-3 MPH below that. His slider and changeup are decent, but he has trouble hitting his spots with those pitches. He can be tough on lefthanders and stifles their power, but righthanders clobber him, which limits his usefulness in anything but a spot-relief role. Miller made two errors last year, but he generally is regarded as a decent fielder with an adequate move to first base.

2002 Outlook

Like most Twins relievers, Miller pitched poorly in the second half, and his status is uncertain for 2002. He could end up with another club, or he once again could inhabit the back end of the Minnesota bullpen. Either way, it is hard to see him playing a key role in any bullpen.

Bob Wells

Position: RP
Bats: R **Throws:** R
Ht: 6' 0" **Wt:** 200

Opening Day Age: 35
Born: 11/1/66 in Yakima, WA
ML Seasons: 8

Overall Statistics

	W	L	Pct.	ERA	G	GS	Sv	IP	H	BB	SO	HR	Ratio
2001	8	5	.615	5.11	65	0	2	68.2	72	18	49	12	1.31
Career	38	27	.585	4.94	366	21	15	577.2	610	184	387	93	1.37

2001 Situational Stats

	W	L	ERA	Sv	IP		AB	H	HR	RBI	Avg
Home	5	2	6.25	0	31.2	LHB	87	23	4	18	.264
Road	3	3	4.14	2	37.0	RHB	177	49	8	20	.277
First Half	7	3	4.70	1	46.0	Sc Pos	60	16	1	25	.267
Scnd Half	1	2	5.96	1	22.2	Clutch	135	32	8	21	.237

2001 Season

For the third straight season, Bob Wells was the primary righthanded setup man in the Twins' bullpen. He pitched decently through most of the first half but performed poorly after the All-Star Break, with a dreadful 10.97 August ERA. Wells didn't get a chance to close when LaTroy Hawkins faltered, and at times he looked washed up.

Pitching & Defense

Wells never has commanded a good fastball, but his heater dropped as low as 85 MPH at times in the second half of last year. His slider lacked crispness, and he even had trouble locating his changeup during his August misery. His control remained strong, but his strikeout rate dropped sharply from his 2000 mark, a bad sign for the future. Wells is an extreme flyball pitcher who struggles in the Metrodome, especially when he gets his pitches up. He didn't make an error last year but is not considered to be a good fielder by scouts.

2002 Outlook

Wells will be 35 in 2002, and he clearly is on the downslope of his career. He's overcome the odds before, and may have another good season left in his bag of tricks. If he remains with the Twins, he'll have to earn his way back into the main setup role.

Other Minnesota Twins

John Barnes (Pos: RF, Age: 25, Bats: R)

	G	AB	R	H	D	T	HR	RBI	SB	BB	SO	Avg	OBP	Slg
2001	9	21	1	1	0	0	0	0	0	1	3	.048	.130	.048
Career	20	58	6	14	4	0	0	2	0	3	9	.241	.313	.310

Barnes was out until late May due to knee surgery. He bombed in Minnesota after rehab and was picked up on waivers by Colorado in September. He could do well as a backup if he gets to play in Coors. 2002 Outlook: C

Hector Carrasco (Pos: RHP, Age: 32)

	W	L	Pct.	ERA	G	GS	Sv	IP	H	BB	SO	HR	Ratio
2001	4	3	.571	4.64	56	0	1	73.2	77	30	70	8	1.45
Career	28	36	.438	4.17	458	1	15	567.0	556	279	455	40	1.47

Carrasco had a number of poor outings last season, and the Twins expressed their dismay by designating him for assignment in October. He is considering playing in Japan this season. 2002 Outlook: C

Mike Duvall (Pos: LHP, Age: 27)

	W	L	Pct.	ERA	G	GS	Sv	IP	H	BB	SO	HR	Ratio
2001	0	0	-	7.71	8	0	0	4.2	7	2	4	1	1.93
Career	1	1	.500	4.76	53	0	0	51.0	62	32	23	6	1.84

The most interesting part of Duvall's career is the 7.71 ERA he has fashioned in each of the last two years. He has surpassed five innings pitched only once in his four seasons in the majors. 2002 Outlook: C

Tony Fiore (Pos: RHP, Age: 30)

	W	L	Pct.	ERA	G	GS	Sv	IP	H	BB	SO	HR	Ratio
2001	0	1	.000	5.59	7	0	0	9.2	9	3	8	0	1.24
Career	1	2	.333	7.30	18	0	0	24.2	30	12	16	3	1.70

Fiore was signed as a minor league free agent in June. He has posted solid minor league numbers but his opportunities in the majors have been few and mostly unsuccessful. 2002 Outlook: C

Jason Maxwell (Pos: SS/3B, Age: 30, Bats: R)

	G	AB	R	H	D	T	HR	RBI	SB	BB	SO	Avg	OBP	Slg
2001	39	68	4	13	4	0	1	10	2	9	23	.191	.286	.294
Career	110	182	20	41	10	0	3	23	4	18	57	.225	.294	.330

Maxwell was the last man on the bench and rarely saw any playing time. He didn't help his cause by hitting below the Mendoza line. He opted for free agency in October and signed a minor league deal with Texas in mid-November. 2002 Outlook: C

Quinton McCracken (Pos: DH, Age: 31, Bats: B)

	G	AB	R	H	D	T	HR	RBI	SB	BB	SO	Avg	OBP	Slg
2001	24	64	7	14	2	2	0	3	0	5	13	.219	.275	.313
Career	508	1466	228	411	70	17	14	158	70	140	272	.280	.343	.380

McCracken is not the same player since tearing his ACL in 1999. Since then, he is hitting .189 in 95 at-bats in the majors. He's done well in the minors and looks destined to be there next year. 2002 Outlook: C

Dustan Mohr (Pos: RF, Age: 25, Bats: R)

	G	AB	R	H	D	T	HR	RBI	SB	BB	SO	Avg	OBP	Slg
2001	20	51	6	12	2	0	0	4	1	5	17	.235	.298	.275
Career	20	51	6	12	2	0	0	4	1	5	17	.235	.298	.275

Mohr put up surprising numbers in his first extended stay in Double-A. His performance in his brief callup won't inspire the Twins to let him skip Triple-A again. 2002 Outlook: C

Tom Prince (Pos: C, Age: 37, Bats: R)

	G	AB	R	H	D	T	HR	RBI	SB	BB	SO	Avg	OBP	Slg
2001	64	196	19	43	4	1	7	23	1	12	39	.219	.284	.357
Career	436	1017	94	210	57	3	18	118	7	86	219	.206	.281	.322

Prince is a career backup and reached the highest at-bat total of his career last season. He signed a one-year contract extension to remain the backup catcher for the Twins. 2002 Outlook: B

J.C. Romero (Pos: LHP, Age: 25)

	W	L	Pct.	ERA	G	GS	Sv	IP	H	BB	SO	HR	Ratio
2001	1	4	.200	6.23	14	11	0	65.0	71	24	39	10	1.46
Career	3	11	.214	6.39	31	22	0	132.1	156	54	93	18	1.59

Minnesota converted Romero to a starter in 2000, but his career ERA is nearly two runs lower as a reliever. He has a chance to stick with the Twins, but it is unclear in what capacity. 2002 Outlook: C

Johan Santana (Pos: LHP, Age: 23)

	W	L	Pct.	ERA	G	GS	Sv	IP	H	BB	SO	HR	Ratio
2001	1	0	1.000	4.74	15	4	0	43.2	50	16	28	6	1.51
Career	3	3	.500	5.90	45	9	0	129.2	152	70	92	17	1.71

Santana missed two months of the season with a partially torn muscle in his pitching elbow. One positive is that the Twins gave him a roster spot in late September, even though he pitched just one inning. 2002 Outlook: C

Minnesota Twins Minor League Prospects

Organization Overview:

The core of the current-day Twins came up from the farm system in waves. In 1999, Corey Koskie, Cristian Guzman, Torii Hunter, Jacque Jones and Joe Mays became fixtures in the Minnesota lineup. David Ortiz arrived for good in 2000, and Luis Rivas, A.J. Pierzynski and Doug Mientkiewicz came aboard during the club's promising 2001 campaign. The next wave of kids, who may arrive in 2002, features three key 1997 draft picks—Michael Cuddyer, Matthew LeCroy and Michael Restovich. This trio, along with Justin Morneau and 2001's first overall pick Joe Mauer, could team up with Koskie & Company to create a power-laden Twins lineup.

Mike Cuddyer

Position: 3B-1B   **Opening Day Age:** 23
Bats: R **Throws:** R   **Born:** 3/27/79 in Norfolk,
Ht: 6' 2" **Wt:** 202   VA

Recent Statistics

	G	AB	R	H	D	T	HR	RBI	SB	BB	SO	Avg
2001 AA New Britain	141	509	95	153	36	3	30	87	5	75	106	.301
2001 AL Minnesota	8	18	1	4	2	0	0	1	1	2	6	.222
2001 MLE	141	497	83	141	35	2	25	76	3	56	115	.284

A 1997 first-round pick, Cuddyer made a fairly smooth transition from shortstop to third base in 1999 in the high Class-A Florida State League. The move didn't hurt his bat, but his power dropped off at Double-A New Britain in 2000. A return to Double-A ball in 2001 restored Cuddyer's confidence, and an offseason strength program helped spark the best power surge of his pro career. With Corey Koskie lodged at third, Cuddyer played both first and third base last summer. He also spent 19 games in the outfield, and the Twins will explore his potential as a corner outfielder. He has an above-average arm and average speed. The Twins are looking for a righthanded power bat. Cuddyer could be the man.

Adam Johnson

Position: P   **Opening Day Age:** 22
Bats: R **Throws:** R   **Born:** 7/12/79 in San
Ht: 6' 2" **Wt:** 210   Jose, CA

Recent Statistics

	W	L	ERA	G	GS	Sv	IP	H	R	BB	SO	HR
2001 AA New Britain	5	6	3.82	18	18	0	113.0	105	53	39	110	10
2001 AAA Edmonton	1	1	5.70	4	4	0	23.2	19	15	10	25	0
2001 AL Minnesota	1	2	8.28	7	4	0	25.0	32	25	13	17	6

The Twins' first-round pick in 2000, Johnson left Cal State Fullerton as the school's strikeout king and debuted by fanning 92 batters in 69.1 innings at high Class-A Ft. Myers. He averaged a strikeout an inning as a second-year pro at Double-A New Britain and Triple-A Edmonton in 2001, calling on three solid pitches: a low-90s fastball, slider and a very good changeup. He reached Minnesota during the pennant chase, but struggled with location and often fell behind hitters. That kept him from setting up hitters for his changeup. The Twins believe he just needs more innings. He's a confident pitcher with a closer's mentality from his days as a finisher in college. Closing may be in his future, or he may mature into a solid middle-of-the-rotation performer.

Bobby Kielty

Position: OF   **Opening Day Age:** 25
Bats: B **Throws:** R   **Born:** 8/5/76 in Fontana,
Ht: 6' 1" **Wt:** 215   CA

Recent Statistics

	G	AB	R	H	D	T	HR	RBI	SB	BB	SO	Avg
2001 AAA Edmonton	94	341	58	98	25	2	12	50	5	53	76	.287
2001 AL Minnesota	37	104	8	26	8	0	2	14	3	8	25	.250
2001 MLE	94	328	44	85	23	1	9	38	3	40	82	.259

Kielty went undrafted, but signed with the Twins after leading the Cape Cod League in hitting in 1998. His 1999 season at Class-A Quad City was cut short by an allergic reaction to airborne oak pollen, which affected his use of eye contacts. Since undergoing laser surgery and abandoning contacts, Kielty has shown power from both sides of the plate and hit well in the high minors. Injuries and the Matt Lawton trade provided a big league opportunity for Kielty, who was recalled because he could switch-hit and cover all three outfield spots. He may need more Triple-A time to become more consistent at making contact, as better breaking pitches gave him trouble in the majors. When he has more success getting the bat on the ball, more power may follow.

Matt LeCroy

Position: DH   **Opening Day Age:** 26
Bats: R **Throws:** R   **Born:** 12/13/75 in
Ht: 6' 2" **Wt:** 225   Belton, SC

Recent Statistics

	G	AB	R	H	D	T	HR	RBI	SB	BB	SO	Avg
2001 AAA Edmonton	101	396	53	130	17	0	20	80	0	36	95	.328
2001 AL Minnesota	15	40	6	17	5	0	3	12	0	0	8	.425
2001 MLE	101	377	40	111	15	0	14	61	0	27	101	.294

Drafted in 1997, this power prospect emerged by leading all minor league catchers with 30 homers in 1999. With A.J. Pierzynski and Joe Mauer in the picture, LeCroy's future may be at first base or designated hitter. If he continues to make good contact, hit for power and draw walks, as he has in the minors, LeCroy should get ample opportunities to help the Twins with his bat. His 2001 campaign was compromised by a ribcage injury that cost him 30 games and a thigh bruise that limited his time behind the plate. Still, he led Triple-A Edmonton in homers, RBI and slugging. His catching skills aren't as promising as his power potential, but LeCroy will force his way into the Minnesota lineup if he hits for power against major league pitching.

Joe Mauer

Position: C-DH
Bats: L **Throws:** R
Ht: 6' 4" **Wt:** 215
Opening Day Age: 18
Born: 4/19/83 in St. Paul, MN

Recent Statistics

	G	AB	R	H	D	THR	RBI	SB	BB	SO	Avg
2001 R Elizabethtn	32	110	14	44	6	2	0	14	4	19	10	.400

Mauer adjusted quickly to the wood bat, batting .400 in his first exposure to pro ball. He displayed the impressive swing that led to his being drafted first overall in 2001, and he regularly put the ball in play with authority. He sprayed line drives all over the field and showed he knew a little about pulling the ball. The Twins are equally impressed with his makeup and maturity, as the high school product successfully handled the adversity and distractions of being the top pick. The Twins also are pleased with his receiving and throwing skills behind the plate, as he experienced no trouble with handling pitches thrown 10-15 MPH faster than he had seen in high school. He should start the 2002 season in A-ball.

Justin Morneau

Position: 1B
Bats: L **Throws:** R
Ht: 6' 4" **Wt:** 205
Opening Day Age: 20
Born: 5/15/81 in New Westminster, BC, Canada

Recent Statistics

	G	AB	R	H	D	THR	RBI	SB	BB	SO	Avg
2000 R Twins	52	194	47	78	21	0	10	58	3	30	18	.402
2000 R Elizabethtn	6	23	4	5	0	0	1	3	0	1	6	.217
2001 A Quad City	64	236	50	84	17	2	12	53	0	26	38	.356
2001 A Fort Myers	53	197	25	58	10	3	4	40	0	24	41	.294
2001 AA New Britain	10	38	3	6	1	0	0	4	0	3	8	.158

While Morneau struggled with a move behind the plate in his first full season as a pro in 2000, he still batted .402 in the Rookie-level Gulf Coast League. The Twins say they haven't written him off as a catcher, but he spent all of 2001 at first base and may work out in the outfield. Morneau is a big-bodied pull hitter with the potential to hit 30 homers in the majors. Despite losing time to shoulder troubles in 2001, Morneau cruised through the Class-A Midwest and Florida State leagues and struggled only at Double-A New Britain. His successful climb from low-A to Double-A ball, in just his second full season as a pro, suggests his rise may be rapid.

Mike Restovich

Position: OF
Bats: R **Throws:** R
Ht: 6' 4" **Wt:** 233
Opening Day Age: 23
Born: 1/3/79 in Rochester, MN

Recent Statistics

	G	AB	R	H	D	THR	RBI	SB	BB	SO	Avg
2000 A Fort Myers	135	475	73	125	27	9	8	64	19	61	100	.263
2001 AA New Britain	140	501	69	135	33	4	23	84	15	54	105	.269
2001 MLE	140	491	60	125	32	3	19	74	11	40	136	.255

Like Mike Cuddyer, Restovich is an impressive athlete with a great work ethic. He also shares Cuddyer's power potential as a hitter who may reach the 25-30 homer plateau as he matures into a major leaguer. Both are 1997 draft picks looking for work as corner outfielders with the Twins. Restovich runs well and has learned to take better paths to the ball. He has become a very good all-around outfielder. An advanced hitter with a good two-strike approach and an ability to pull the ball, Restovich was batting near .300 for most of the 2001 season. Then he was struck in the hand by a pitch in July, lost a week of playing time, and the injury affected his hitting the rest of the summer.

Juan Rincon

Position: P
Bats: R **Throws:** R
Ht: 5' 11" **Wt:** 190
Opening Day Age: 23
Born: 1/23/79 in Maracaibo, VZ

Recent Statistics

	W	L	ERA	G	GS	Sv	IP	H	R	BB	SO	HR
2001 AA New Britain	14	6	2.88	29	23	0	153.1	130	60	57	133	9
2001 AL Minnesota	0	0	6.35	4	0	0	5.2	7	5	5	4	1

One of Minnesota's best Latin American prospects of late is Rincon, a Venezuelan righthander who signed in 1996. Rincon has relied on a moving 91-92 MPH fastball and hard curveball to dominate hitters. He emerged with a 14-8 (2.92) season in the Class-A Midwest League in 1999, and led the circuit in strikeouts. Rincon's success continued until a midseason promotion to Double-A New Britain in 2000, when the lack of a polished changeup caught up with him. His changeup improved dramatically in Rincon's second go-round at New Britain in 2001, and he successfully set up hitters en route to a 14-6 (2.88) season. While his ceiling is as high as any Twins pitching prospect, there isn't much history of success for righthanded starters under six feet tall.

Others to Watch

Despite the forearm tendinitis that sidelined him until mid-April, righthanded reliever **Grant Balfour** (24) climbed from Double-A New Britain to Minnesota in 2001. He throws a low-90s fastball and a wicked slider that is his out pitch. He closed effectively at New Britain, but looks like a budding setup man. . . The hardest thrower in the Twins' system is righthander **Matt Kinney** (25), who calls on a mid-90s fastball, curve and changeup. He dominated hitters at Double-A New Britain early in 2000 and enjoyed five quality starts in eight outings in Minnesota. The top fifth-starter candidate last spring, Kinney struggled to throw strikes. He rebounded later in the year, but must fine-tune his pitch location to win the fifth-starter job in 2002. . . Pint-sized second baseman **Ruben Salazar** (24) shows a little pop and just keeps hitting. He needs to draw more walks, but hit .298 at Double-A New Britain in 2001. . . Australian lefty **Brad Thomas** (24) went 10-3 (1.96) at New Britain in 2001, setting up hitters effectively with fastball strikes early in the count. He learned the importance of getting ahead in Minnesota, where he struggled. He's at his best when he's calling on all of his pitches and not relying mostly on his above-average fastball.

Yankee Stadium

Offense

Once again, lefthanded hitters feasted at 161st and River Avenue in the Bronx. The House That Ruth Built continued to live up to its rep as a lefties' paradise, although righties also hit more homers in Yankee Stadium than in the average American League park. Over the past three years, the spacious outfield hasn't helped batting average and has yielded less than the AL average in runs scored.

Defense

The grass is grown high and all the way to the foul lines, unlike in some parks. The infield dirt is smooth and true. You can judge the wind by the weathervane bat above the outfield—whatever way the handle is pointing is where the wind is blowing. Death Valley in left-center field can be a nightmare for below-average left fielders. Errors are more plentiful in the South Bronx than in the average AL park.

Who It Helps the Most

Your average lefthanded pull hitter benefits from the Stadium. Tino Martinez hit 51 points higher and had 22 of his 34 homers there. Paul O'Neill hit 48 points higher at home, and Jorge Posada hit nearly two-thirds of his homers at the Stadium. Andy Pettitte went 10-3 (3.16) at home, while 5-7 (4.97) on the road. Mike Mussina was a .500 pitcher on the road and 11-5 at home.

Who It Hurts the Most

Alfonso Soriano had 15 fewer RBI in about the same number of at-bats home and away. Over the last three seasons, Orlando Hernandez is 21-14 (4.15) away from the Stadium and 12-15 (4.75) at home. Mariano Rivera's ERA over that span is twice as good on the road, 1.62 compared to 3.16.

Rookies & Newcomers

Jason Giambi should be the perfect hitter in the Stadium, because he is the prototypical lefthanded pull hitter who can use the right half of the park to his advantage. So could Nick Johnson, if the rookie first baseman gets extended playing time this season.

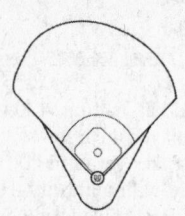

Dimensions: LF-318, LCF-399, CF-408, RCF-385, RF-314

Capacity: 57,545

Elevation: 55 feet

Surface: Grass

Foul Territory: Small

Park Factors

2001 Season

	Home Games			Away Games			
	Yankees	Opp	Total	Yankees	Opp	Total	Index
G	71	71	142	72	72	144	—
Avg	.276	.248	.262	.265	.265	.265	99
AB	2383	2468	4851	2565	2451	5016	98
R	378	295	673	345	332	677	101
H	657	612	1269	680	649	1329	97
2B	138	108	246	128	128	256	99
3B	6	6	12	10	16	26	48
HR	103	73	176	81	65	146	125
BB	217	208	425	226	204	430	102
SO	406	564	970	503	566	1069	94
E	49	61	110	48	47	95	117
E-Infield	43	42	85	44	45	89	97
LHB-Avg	.290	.242	.267	.254	.253	.254	105
LHB-HR	63	31	94	42	32	74	136
RHB-Avg	.265	.252	.258	.273	.273	.273	94
RHB-HR	40	42	82	39	33	72	115

1999-2001

	Home Games			Away Games			
	Yankees	Opp	Total	Yankees	Opp	Total	Index
G	215	215	430	216	216	432	—
Avg	.275	.250	.262	.277	.267	.273	96
AB	7192	7467	14659	7679	7298	14977	98
R	1140	936	2076	1155	1054	2209	94
H	1981	1864	3845	2130	1952	4082	95
2B	384	354	738	416	380	796	95
3B	29	25	54	42	47	89	62
HR	284	214	498	255	216	471	108
BB	845	713	1558	787	736	1523	105
SO	1278	1579	2857	1403	1493	2896	101
E	153	145	298	143	144	287	104
E-Infield	128	110	238	124	123	247	97
LHB-Avg	.273	.251	.262	.282	.264	.273	96
LHB-HR	157	100	257	128	105	233	113
RHB-Avg	.278	.249	.263	.274	.270	.272	97
RHB-HR	127	114	241	127	111	238	103

2001 Rankings (American League)

- Highest error factor
- Highest LHB home-run factor
- Second-highest home-run factor
- Second-lowest triple factor
- Second-lowest strikeout factor

Joe Torre

2001 Season

The Yankees failed to win their fourth world championship in a row last season, but it's hard to lay the blame at Joe Torre's feet. The Yankees' skipper continued to pull all the right strings, earning his fifth American League pennant in his six seasons in the Bronx. Torre knows how to take the heat and get the most out of his players, young and old.

Offense

Torre used 94 lineups in 2001, the fewest of any AL club. He believes in his hitters' ability to work counts, get on base and extend innings. His runners had better than a 75-percent success rate with stolen bases, including five double steals and a swipe of home. Torre sacrificed almost twice as much as in 2000, with an 80-percent success rate.

Pitching

Torre and pitching coach Mel Stottlemyre have been one of the best tandems in history based on win-loss results. Torre's relievers had 17 saves of more than one inning, the most any manager in baseball allowed. He manages his pitchers carefully, using at least three hurlers in 32 games where the Yankees allowed two runs or fewer.

Defense

Torre and Stottlemyre don't believe in the slide step, but have tried to make their pitchers better at holding runners on. Torre pitched out only 21 times last year, a paltry total for a team that caught only 22.6 percent of basestealers in non-pitchout situations in 2001. He didn't substitute for Chuck Knoblauch in left field as Knoblauch got more comfortable out there. Overall, his 14 defensive subs for the season were well below average.

2002 Outlook

Torre relies on his players more than his scouting reports or stats. He often lamented last year about the information overload that exists when some players try to use technology instead of common sense. Torre has as much sense as any manager in the game, and will continue to manage well as long as the Boss provides him with the horses. He signed a multiyear contract in December.

Born: 7/18/40 in Brooklyn, NY

Playing Experience: 1960-1977, Atl, StL, NYM

Managerial Experience: 20 seasons

Manager Statistics

Year	Team, Lg	W	L	Pct	GB	Finish
2001	New York, AL	95	65	.594	—	1st East
20 Seasons		1455	1375	.513	—	—

2001 Starting Pitchers by Days Rest

	<=3	4	5	6+
Yankees Starts	3	77	40	31
Yankees ERA	7.90	4.01	4.29	4.78
AL Avg Starts	1	78	48	24
AL ERA	5.92	4.69	4.58	4.58

2001 Situational Stats

	Joe Torre	AL Average
Hit & Run Success %	35.3	35.0
Stolen Base Success %	75.2	71.0
Platoon Pct.	56.0	59.1
Defensive Subs	14	26
High-Pitch Outings	10	6
Quick/Slow Hooks	16/13	19/16
Sacrifice Attempts	41	54

2001 Rankings (American League)

- 1st in steals of third base (28), starts with over 120 pitches (10), starts with over 140 pitches (1), saves with over 1 inning pitched (17) and first-batter platoon percentage
- 2nd in stolen base attempts (214) and starts on three days rest
- 3rd in stolen-base percentage, steals of second base (132), steals of home plate (1) and 2+ pitching changes in low-scoring games (32)

New York (AL)

Roger Clemens

2001 Season

Although he turned 39 during the season, Roger Clemens made history with his record sixth Cy Young Award. The hard-throwing righthander became the first pitcher to ever start a season 20-1 before he lost his final two decisions. The Yankees won 20 straight starts by Clemens from late May until mid-September, making him the surest bet in Las Vegas. Clemens' season was one long hot streak, although he aggravated his right hamstring during his first postseason appearance and lacked stamina until the World Series. He is within 20 victories of 300.

Pitching

Clemens is still a power pitcher, pure and simple. Even in late October he registered 97 MPH on radar guns. The Rocket relies on a four-seamer with hop that hitters chase high in the zone. His two-seam fastball runs in to righthanders. Clemens looks at the strike zone as nine quadrants, instead of the four quadrants that mediocre pitchers see. His forkball, affectionately known as "Mr. Splitty," continues to get hitters out, although he no longer was throwing it in the zone in October. He also throws a slider and changeup, but his command and velocity are what separate him from the pack.

Defense

Earlier in his career, Clemens looked inept in the field and unsure of himself in the stretch. Although he has suffered groin and hamstring injuries the past two years, he has worked hard at his pickoff move and defense. He won't win a Gold Glove, but he actually picked a runner off during the World Series. Baserunners ran easily and were 34 of 40 off Clemens last year.

2002 Outlook

With the Yankees failing to win the World Series for the first time in four years, some would say the franchise is in decline. That's the type of motivating force Clemens will use this season. Clemens has a contract through 2003 with an option for 2004, and he'll make a push for his 300th victory. He probably could pitch into his mid-40s because of his excellent conditioning, but will remain in the game only as long as the fire burns inside.

Position: SP
Bats: R **Throws:** R
Ht: 6' 4" **Wt:** 238

Opening Day Age: 39
Born: 8/4/62 in Dayton, OH
ML Seasons: 18
Nickname: Rocket

Overall Statistics

	W	L	Pct.	ERA	G	GS	Sv	IP	H	BB	SO	HR	Ratio
2001	20	3	.870	3.51	33	33	0	220.1	205	72	213	19	1.26
Career	280	145	.659	3.10	545	544	0	3887.0	3306	1258	3717	279	1.17

How Often He Throws Strikes

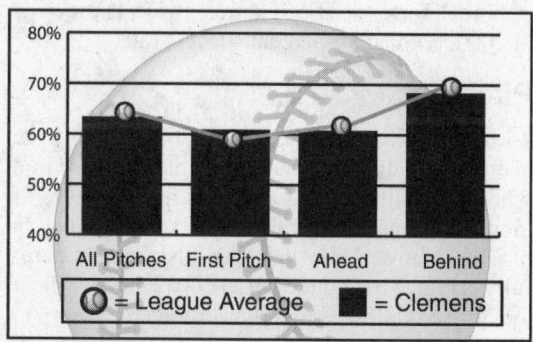

= League Average   = Clemens

2001 Situational Stats

	W	L	ERA	Sv	IP		AB	H	HR	RBI	Avg
Home	10	1	3.10	0	98.2	LHB	442	104	10	48	.235
Road	10	2	3.85	0	121.2	RHB	391	101	9	40	.258
First Half	12	1	3.55	0	124.1	Sc Pos	215	57	3	68	.265
Scnd Half	8	2	3.47	0	96.0	Clutch	38	11	1	4	.289

2001 Rankings (American League)

- 1st in wild pitches (14) and winning percentage
- 2nd in wins, stolen bases allowed (34), most run support per nine innings (6.6) and most strikeouts per nine innings (8.7)
- 3rd in strikeouts, pitches thrown (3,604), highest stolen-base percentage allowed (85.0) and most pitches thrown per batter (3.93)
- 5th in highest strikeout-walk ratio (3.0)
- Led the Yankees in wins, batters faced (918), walks allowed, pitches thrown (3,604), pickoff throws (147), stolen bases allowed (34), lowest ERA at home, most run support per nine innings (6.6), lowest batting average allowed with runners in scoring position and most strikeouts per nine innings (8.7)

Orlando Hernandez

2001 Season

It was a second straight subpar year for Orlando Hernandez, who missed much of the campaign with nagging injuries. The season began late for El Duque, who missed time in spring training because of inflammation in his right elbow. He had surgery on the second toe of his left foot in June and missed much of the year before returning in late August. Then, as the postseason neared, El Duque complained of a tired arm after a 4-7 regular season. His postseason was mediocre at best.

Pitching

At one point in the season, El Duque was reluctant to throw his patented curve and slider. At another point, he was unwilling to throw his fastball. It was a strange season for a righthander who relies on as much guile as command. El Duque has a great idea of the strike zone, but attempts to nibble or get hitters to chase. Lefties continued to solve the mystery of the Cuban mystery man, hitting him at a .278 clip. El Duque gave up 19 homers in 17 appearances in 2001, a troubling figure.

Defense

El Duque was bothered by his landing foot for much of the first half, which affected every aspect of his game. He has catlike reflexes and is very dutiful in throwing over to first, because his high leg kicks give baserunners a leg up on steals. Baserunners were 15 of 17 against him last summer.

2002 Outlook

The Yankees offered El Duque arbitration when his contract expired, but that in no way clarifies his long-term future. He was a disappointment on the field and his communication problems grew worse with manager Joe Torre and pitching coach Mel Stottlemyre. Also, he's rumored to be 36 instead of 32. It may be best at this point for the two sides to part ways amicably, instead of having the Yankees frustratingly watch El Duque decline again this year.

Position: SP
Bats: R **Throws:** R
Ht: 6' 2" **Wt:** 220

Opening Day Age: 32
Born: 10/11/69 in Villa Clara, Cuba
ML Seasons: 4
Pronunciation: her-NAN-dezz
Nickname: El Duque

Overall Statistics

	W	L	Pct.	ERA	G	GS	Sv	IP	H	BB	SO	HR	Ratio
2001	4	7	.364	4.85	17	16	0	94.2	90	42	77	19	1.39
Career	45	33	.577	4.13	100	99	0	645.2	576	232	506	88	1.25

How Often He Throws Strikes

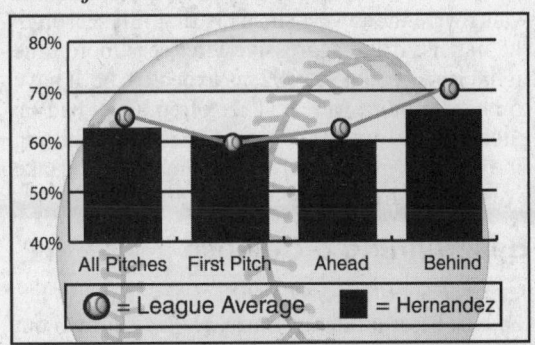

= League Average   = Hernandez

2001 Situational Stats

	W	L	ERA	Sv	IP		AB	H	HR	RBI	Avg
Home	1	3	5.06	0	32.0	LHB	194	54	12	28	.278
Road	3	4	4.74	0	62.2	RHB	169	36	7	18	.213
First Half	0	5	5.14	0	49.0	Sc Pos	76	13	2	19	.171
Scnd Half	4	2	4.53	0	45.2	Clutch	28	6	1	2	.214

2001 Rankings (American League)

- 3rd in fewest GDPs induced per GDP situation (1.5%)

Derek Jeter

Position: SS
Bats: R **Throws:** R
Ht: 6' 3" **Wt:** 195

Opening Day Age: 27
Born: 6/26/74 in Pequannock, NJ
ML Seasons: 7
Pronunciation: JEE-ter

2001 Season

Although he started 150 games at shortstop, Derek Jeter didn't seem entirely healthy for much of last season. His average was the lowest since 1997, and he committed most of his 15 errors in the first half of the year. Bothered by a strained left hamstring, a balky throwing shoulder and assorted bumps and bruises through much of the summer, Jeter showed both his steel will and vulnerability at the same time.

Hitting

Jeter is a tremendous first-pitch hitter who showed less patience than ever last year. He hit .437 with seven homers offering at the first pitch, but his walks were the fewest since his first full season in the majors. If the aggressive Jeter sees more time in the leadoff spot in 2002, as expected, he'll have to become more patient. Jeter often looks bad on pitches on the outside corner. He believes in hitting line drives or groundballs and letting his speed take over. He is a tremendous bunter.

Baserunning & Defense

Jeter is one of the speediest Yankees, and also has the best baserunning instincts. He was thrown out only three times in 30 attempts in 2001. Jeter runs hard out of the box and always attempts the extra base. Once again, Jeter's range factor (putouts plus assists per nine innings) ranked near the bottom of baseball. That either means Jeter's range is over-rated, or the opposition doesn't tend to hit in Jeter's direction. He made most of his errors early on after missing most of spring training due to injury. His shovel pass in the ALDS proves he's one of the best defenders when the game's on the line.

2002 Outlook

Knowing Jeter, he won't be satisfied until the Yankees are once again World Champions. Money and long-term security are not things he has to worry about since he signed his 10-year contract. The shortstop judges himself not on his past or present, but whether his team wins. Like the Yankees, Jeter has made winning easy, even if it's been a lot of hard work. He'll continue to work harder than ever.

Overall Statistics

	G	AB	R	H	D	T	HR	RBI	SB	BB	SO	Avg	OBP	Slg
2001	150	614	110	191	35	3	21	74	27	56	99	.311	.377	.480
Career	936	3744	715	1199	188	38	99	488	135	397	671	.320	.392	.470

Where He Hits the Ball

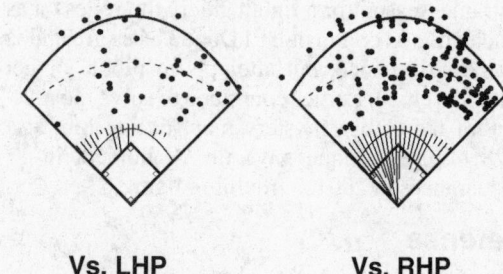

Vs. LHP   **Vs. RHP**

2001 Situational Stats

	AB	H	HR	RBI	Avg		AB	H	HR	RBI	Avg
Home	288	95	13	38	.330	LHP	123	41	5	14	.333
Road	326	96	8	36	.294	RHP	491	150	16	60	.305
First Half	343	101	8	42	.294	Sc Pos	132	43	1	48	.326
Scnd Half	271	90	13	32	.332	Clutch	99	27	1	14	.273

2001 Rankings (American League)

- 2nd in stolen-base percentage (90.0)
- 4th in singles
- 5th in runs scored, highest groundball-flyball ratio (2.0), errors at shortstop (15) and lowest fielding percentage at shortstop (.974)
- 6th in batting average vs. lefthanded pitchers
- Led the Yankees in batting average, at-bats, runs scored, hits, singles, triples, total bases (295), times on base (257), pitches seen (2,527), plate appearances (686), highest groundball-flyball ratio (2.0), stolen-base percentage (90.0), bunts in play (8), batting average vs. lefthanded pitchers, highest percentage of extra bases taken as a runner (59.7), slugging percentage vs. lefthanded pitchers (.528) and batting average at home

David Justice

2001 Season

As great as the 2000 season was for David Justice, that's how dismal last year became. Justice suffered the same groin injury twice and was a shell of his power-hitting self while simultaneously dealing with off-field problems that must have affected him. In his first full year in pinstripes, his average dropped 45 points and his power numbers were more than cut in half. And he scarcely played the outfield.

Hitting

Justice always looks fastball and adjusts accordingly. He was an automatic out when falling behind in the count, hitting just .158 in those situations in 2001. After a torrid 2000 campaign against southpaws, the lefthanded slugger managed just a .214 average against them and often was flailing miserably at breaking stuff. He never seemed locked in, hitting more groundballs than flyballs. That's never a good sign for a player with home-run power to all fields.

Baserunning & Defense

Never much of a basestealer, Justice attempted three swipes last year and was gunned down twice. He isn't tentative on the bases but knows his limitations. Justice likes to play the outfield and hit close to .300 in his limited stints in left and right, making only one error. He has bad knees but pretty good range and a deceptively strong arm. Of course, his drop in Game 1 of the World Series in Arizona was a lowlight.

2002 Outlook

In the final season of a contract that has a club option for 2003, Justice briefly moved to the other side of town after the Mets acquired him for Robin Ventura in mid-December. One week after that deal, the Mets traded Justice to the A's for reliever Mark Guthrie and minor league pitcher Tyler Yates. Justice is best suited for right field, but how he'll be used by the Athletics remains to be seen. Regardless, he needs to bounce back strong. Justice needs to regain the eye, swing and confidence that made him one of the game's best sluggers. The A's will be counting on his power to help take some of the sting out of the loss of Jason Giambi.

Position: DH/LF/RF
Bats: L **Throws:** L
Ht: 6' 3" **Wt:** 200

Opening Day Age: 35
Born: 4/14/66 in Cincinnati, OH
ML Seasons: 13

Overall Statistics

	G	AB	R	H	D	T	HR	RBI	SB	BB	SO	Avg	OBP	Slg
2001	111	381	58	92	16	1	18	51	1	54	83	.241	.333	.430
Career	1492	5227	875	1465	262	21	294	968	49	833	933	.280	.378	.507

Where He Hits the Ball

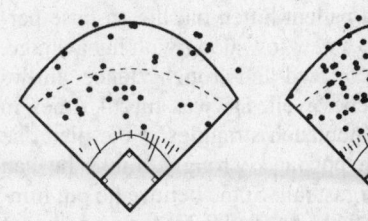

Vs. LHP   **Vs. RHP**

2001 Situational Stats

	AB	H	HR	RBI	Avg		AB	H	HR	RBI	Avg
Home	175	39	8	25	.223	LHP	112	24	7	17	.214
Road	206	53	10	26	.257	RHP	269	68	11	34	.253
First Half	224	55	10	30	.246	Sc Pos	93	18	4	32	.194
Scnd Half	157	37	8	21	.236	Clutch	62	10	1	1	.161

2001 Rankings (American League)
- 4th in lowest batting average with runners in scoring position and lowest batting average in the clutch
- 9th in assists in left field (4)

Chuck Knoblauch

2001 Season

In what certainly seems to be his final season in pinstripes, Chuck Knoblauch disappointed. He disappointed himself with a .250 average, disappointed the fans when he cooled off after a hot start, and disappointed the organization by not being the catalyst it could blindly depend on. One of the few Yankees to avoid the injury bug, Knoblauch moved from second base to left field in spring training. Although he naturally struggled at first, he seemed more confident and was not prone to the throwing problems that nearly ended his career. Plus, he added versatility to a very good major league pedigree. Now he inevitably moves on.

Hitting

Knoblauch is a patient hitter, but his on-base percentage sank to a new low along with his average. His distinctive crowd-and-crouch stance allows him to see pitches well. He was hit 14 times in 2001. When Knoblauch struggles at the plate, he gets too pull-happy and wrongly thinks he can handle the high fastball. Some believe he put himself into a funk when he tried to hit too many home runs.

Baserunning & Defense

Knoblauch is a tremendous baserunner, swiping 38 bags in 47 tries in 2001, a rate of 81 percent. For all the hullabaloo about moving to the outfield, Knoblauch made only two errors and collected eight assists. He did look shaky out there, however, having trouble coming in and going out on balls and possessing a below-average arm. Still, he probably would make a manager worry less out there than at second base, which he played in spring training and continued to make throwing errors.

2002 Outlook

It's hard to tell what the future holds for Knoblauch, an enigmatic player and teammate who will need to find the right fit for his talents. When he's on, Knoblauch is a terrifying leadoff man with a good batting eye and great wheels. When he's off, he looks like a below-average major leaguer, not the former Gold Glove second baseman or All-Star he used to be.

Position: LF/DH
Bats: R **Throws:** R
Ht: 5' 9" **Wt:** 175

Opening Day Age: 33
Born: 7/7/68 in Houston, TX
ML Seasons: 11
Pronunciation: NOB-lock
Nickname: Knobby

Overall Statistics

	G	AB	R	H	D	T	HR	RBI	SB	BB	SO	Avg	OBP	Slg
2001	137	521	66	130	20	3	9	44	38	58	73	.250	.339	.351
Career	1552	6066	1091	1776	313	64	92	593	388	776	698	.293	.382	.411

Where He Hits the Ball

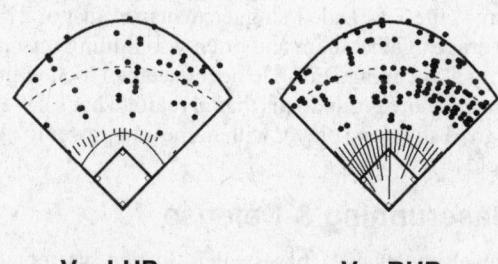

Vs. LHP   **Vs. RHP**

2001 Situational Stats

	AB	H	HR	RBI	Avg		AB	H	HR	RBI	Avg
Home	255	65	6	22	.255	LHP	99	25	3	11	.253
Road	266	65	3	22	.244	RHP	422	105	6	33	.249
First Half	333	84	4	29	.252	Sc Pos	96	25	1	31	.260
Scnd Half	188	46	5	15	.245	Clutch	82	22	1	8	.268

2001 Rankings (American League)

- 2nd in lowest percentage of swings that missed (8.2) and fielding percentage in left field (.989)
- 3rd in lowest slugging percentage
- 4th in assists in left field (8), steals of third (7) and lowest slugging percentage vs. righthanded pitchers (.336)
- 5th in stolen bases
- Led the Yankees in triples, hit by pitch (14), most pitches seen per plate appearance (3.95), highest percentage of pitches taken (59.1), lowest percentage of swings that missed (8.2), on-base percentage for a leadoff hitter (.336) and lowest percentage of swings on the first pitch (17.4)

Tino Martinez

2001 Season

Tino Martinez shook off doubts that he was on the downslope of his career, more than doubling his home-run total of 2000 and providing the Yankees with constant run production. He also added his typically stellar defense at first base and remained a leader in the clubhouse. Martinez' home run in Game 4 of the World Series epitomized his contributions to the Yankees: the club and its fans weren't sure he'd come through, but in the end he usually did.

Hitting

As streaky as ever, Martinez hit his home runs in bunches en route to his best season since 1997. When he was locked in, as he was when he hit 10 homers in July, he was as good as any power hitter in the American League. Martinez has trouble maintaining his stroke, however, and struggles to drive in runs when he's in a funk. He took advantage of the short porch in right and continued a recent trend of pulling the ball more. Martinez was busted inside late in the year and occasionally choked up against tough lefties.

Baserunning & Defense

Martinez was one of the slowest players on the team. He still hit into only 12 double plays in 2001, mostly because he elevates the ball rather than because he's discovered a fifth gear. If there's any fairness, Martinez should someday win a Gold Glove at first, as he possesses solid range and an accurate arm. He is much better defensively than Jason Giambi, and made only five errors last season.

2002 Outlook

The Hot Stove League is cooking in Martinez' kitchen, as the 34-year-old is likely to strike it rich in free agency and leave the Yankees behind after his former club inked Giambi to a megadeal. He was a valued cornerstone of the Yankees, albeit a quiet one who sometimes felt unappreciated by the front office. Some people in the organization wanted to keep him around to mentor Nick Johnson, but the writing was on the wall. It said, "Thanks for the memories."

Position: 1B
Bats: L **Throws:** R
Ht: 6' 2" **Wt:** 210

Opening Day Age: 34
Born: 12/7/67 in Tampa, FL
ML Seasons: 12

Overall Statistics

	G	AB	R	H	D	T	HR	RBI	SB	BB	SO	Avg	OBP	Slg
2001	154	589	89	165	24	2	34	113	1	42	89	.280	.329	.501
Career	1466	5363	773	1468	286	17	263	1002	18	565	801	.274	.343	.481

Where He Hits the Ball

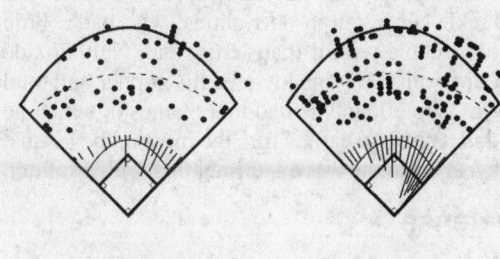

Vs. LHP   **Vs. RHP**

2001 Situational Stats

	AB	H	HR	RBI	Avg		AB	H	HR	RBI	Avg
Home	298	91	22	66	.305	LHP	175	45	10	32	.257
Road	291	74	12	47	.254	RHP	414	120	24	81	.290
First Half	332	87	17	63	.262	Sc Pos	179	49	15	88	.274
Scnd Half	257	78	17	50	.304	Clutch	104	35	7	22	.337

2001 Rankings (American League)

- 2nd in fielding percentage at first base (.996)
- 3rd in assists at first base (99)
- 8th in cleanup slugging percentage (.511)
- Led the Yankees in home runs, total bases (295), RBI, HR frequency (17.3 ABs per HR), batting average in the clutch and batting average with the bases loaded (.400)

2001 Season

On one September night in Boston, Mike Mussina was nearly perfect. The righthander, who had joined the Yankees after signing a six-year, $88.5 million contract, set down 26 Red Sox in a row. Carl Everett spoiled the perfect game bid, but he couldn't spoil Mussina's season: Moose was 17-11 and pitched great postseason games, including Game 3 of the ALDS against Oakland.

Pitching

Mussina, like other Yankees, has a full arsenal. He throws his fastball as hard as 93 MPH; from time to time, he will drop down a bit and throw it. Mussina also utilized his curveball, knuckle-curve and changeup extremely effectively in 2001. His knuckle-curve ran in on righties, who had a little more trouble with it than lefties did. Neither side hit him well. Mussina lowered his gopher ball total from 28 to 20, and he had nine games in which he did not allow an earned run, the most in the league. At year's end, he was experimenting with a splitter.

Defense

Mussina won his fifth Gold Glove in the past six seasons, taking home the Rawlings award after a year in which he made only one error. Moose won four straight awards from 1996-99 and continues to display his solid athleticism around the mound. His tendency to bend at the waist in the stretch didn't help baserunners, who were only 9-for-22 against him.

2002 Outlook

The only thing Mussina can improve upon this season is his dour personality. Moose may have made an impression on Yankees fans, but some media members were clearly slow to warm up to him, and vice versa. Mussina is reluctant to talk about himself, a trait the New York tabloid writers will be unable to break. But unless he injures himself, Moose will continue to be a frontline pitcher for the foreseeable future. A Cy Young Award this season is not out of the question.

Position: SP
Bats: B **Throws:** R
Ht: 6' 2" **Wt:** 185

Opening Day Age: 33
Born: 12/8/68 in Williamsport, PA
ML Seasons: 11
Pronunciation: myoo-SEE-nuh
Nickname: Moose

Overall Statistics

	W	L	Pct.	ERA	G	GS	Sv	IP	H	BB	SO	HR	Ratio
2001	17	11	.607	3.15	34	34	0	228.2	202	42	214	20	1.07
Career	164	92	.641	3.49	322	322	0	2238.1	2097	509	1749	230	1.16

How Often He Throws Strikes

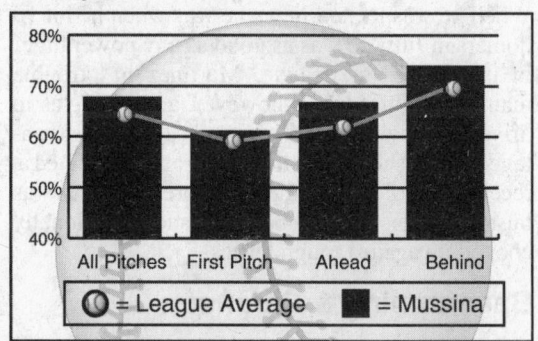

= League Average   = Mussina

2001 Situational Stats

	W	L	ERA	Sv	IP		AB	H	HR	RBI	Avg
Home	11	5	3.11	0	113.0	LHB	421	101	10	32	.240
Road	6	6	3.19	0	115.2	RHB	431	101	10	47	.234
First Half	9	7	3.35	0	123.2	Sc Pos	150	46	3	58	.307
Scnd Half	8	4	2.91	0	105.0	Clutch	70	19	0	3	.271

2001 Rankings (American League)

- 1st in lowest on-base percentage allowed (.274)
- 2nd in ERA, shutouts (3), strikeouts, highest strikeout-walk ratio (5.1) and fewest walks per nine innings (1.7)
- Led the Yankees in ERA, losses, games started, complete games (4), shutouts (3), innings pitched, home runs allowed, strikeouts, runners caught stealing (13), highest strikeout-walk ratio (5.1), lowest batting average allowed (.237), lowest slugging percentage allowed (.358), lowest stolen-base percentage allowed (40.9), lowest ERA on the road, lowest batting average allowed vs. righthanded batters, and fewest walks per nine innings (1.7)

Andy Pettitte

2001 Season

As late as mid-August, Andy Pettitte's season was stellar. He was 14-6 after a victory over the lowly Devil Rays on August 14, but went 1-4 over the next six weeks. Pettitte was injured when he was hit above the left elbow by a batted ball in late September, which didn't help him get back on track. The lefthander was uneven in the postseason, and his last World Series start left him with more questions than answers.

Pitching

Pettitte was among league leaders in fewest walks allowed, as he makes hitters earn their way on base. He no longer relies merely on inducing groundouts with a sinker; he also uses a cut fastball as well as a four-seamer with which he can blow hitters away. Pettitte also has a very good changeup. Two World Series losses, including a drubbing in Game 6, have led some to believe Pettitte may be tipping his pitches.

Defense

After an uncharacteristic 2000 season in which he made four errors, Pettitte was perfect in a staff-high 49 total chances last season. He fields bunts well and has an excellent move, picking off seven men in 2001. Pettitte holds runners on well, but will be called for the occasional balk. If teammate Mike Mussina regains his stranglehold on the Gold Glove in seasons to come, Pettitte's slim hopes to earn one will be dashed.

2002 Outlook

Pettitte's 103 victories over the past six seasons are the most by any American League pitcher, so he shouldn't have anything to prove. But the southpaw went 2-3 in the playoffs after the team had won his previous nine postseason starts. Pettitte's determination and desire to succeed and improve this season will be necessary if the Yankees are to return to dominance.

Position: SP
Bats: L **Throws:** L
Ht: 6' 5" **Wt:** 225

Opening Day Age: 29
Born: 6/15/72 in Baton Rouge, LA
ML Seasons: 7
Pronunciation: PET-it

Overall Statistics

	W	L	Pct.	ERA	G	GS	Sv	IP	H	BB	SO	HR	Ratio
2001	15	10	.600	3.99	31	31	0	200.2	224	41	164	14	1.32
Career	115	65	.639	3.99	228	221	0	1449.2	1530	497	998	116	1.40

How Often He Throws Strikes

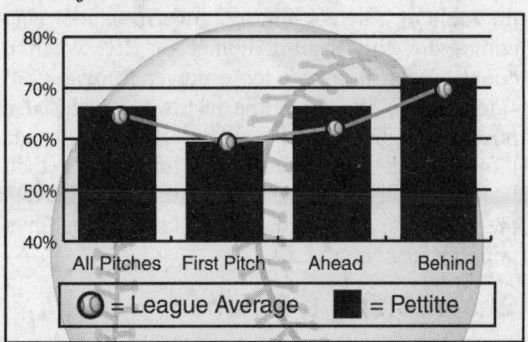

= League Average   = Pettitte

2001 Situational Stats

	W	L	ERA	Sv	IP		AB	H	HR	RBI	Avg
Home	10	3	3.16	0	108.1	LHB	167	42	3	22	.251
Road	5	7	4.97	0	92.1	RHB	629	182	11	69	.289
First Half	9	4	3.04	0	112.2	Sc Pos	206	60	2	73	.291
Scnd Half	6	6	5.22	0	88.0	Clutch	71	27	2	12	.380

2001 Rankings (American League)

- 1st in fielding percentage at pitcher (1.000)
- 2nd in fewest home runs allowed per nine innings (.63)
- 3rd in highest strikeout-walk ratio (4.0) and fewest walks per nine innings (1.8)
- 4th in most run support per nine innings (6.5)
- 6th in balks (2), most GDPs induced per nine innings (1.0) and highest batting average allowed (.281)
- Led the Yankees in hits allowed, balks (2), GDPs induced (22), highest groundball-flyball ratio allowed (1.5), fewest pitches thrown per batter (3.64), fewest home runs allowed per nine innings (.63) and most GDPs induced per nine innings (1.0)

Jorge Posada

2001 Season

Jorge Posada continues to improve his work with the Yankees' pitching staff while establishing himself as a clutch offensive threat. He nearly matched his career-best batting average and home-run numbers of 2000, while setting a new personal mark in RBI. Posada is the prime candidate to move up in the lineup with the exit of other longtime Yankees. Already one of the best catchers in the league, the two-time All-Star only needs to strengthen his defensive work.

Hitting

Earlier in his career, Posada was more of a threat to get on base and score. He seems to be working into the mold of a switch-hitting power producer who comes up with the big homer or RBI when it counts. He still enjoys more power from the left side, and for the first time in his career he also posted a higher average against righties. Posada looks for the ball down and can turn on a fastball from both sides. A tremendous hitter when ahead in the count, he still needs to cut down on his eye-popping strikeout total.

Baserunning & Defense

Posada won't try to stretch many gappers or steal many bases, but he is a converted second baseman with decent speed. What he needs to improve is his receiving. Posada could be an above-average defensive player, but he made a staggering 11 errors and allowed a major league-leading 18 passed balls. That's unacceptable, and although he only threw out 24 percent of runners, the Yankees' staff seems to enjoy working with him.

2002 Outlook

Although Posada mostly shifted between the fifth, sixth and seventh spots in the lineup last season, look for him to be in the fifth hole more in 2002. He needs to increase his discipline at the plate and his concentration behind it in order to reach the upper echelon of perennial All-Stars. He may be overlooked, but the Yankees realized last year how vital he is to the team when he was banged up or suspended.

Position: C
Bats: B **Throws:** R
Ht: 6' 2" **Wt:** 200

Opening Day Age: 30
Born: 8/17/71 in Santurce, PR
ML Seasons: 7
Pronunciation: hor-hay po-sa-da

Overall Statistics

	G	AB	R	H	D	T	HR	RBI	SB	BB	SO	Avg	OBP	Slg
2001	138	484	59	134	28	1	22	95	2	62	132	.277	.363	.475
Career	581	1928	287	516	117	4	85	326	6	300	505	.268	.369	.465

Where He Hits the Ball

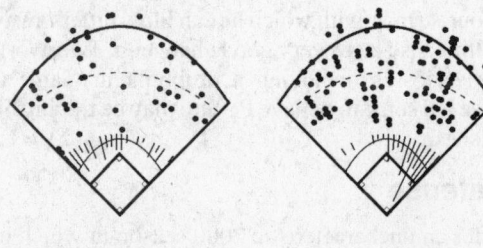

Vs. LHP   **Vs. RHP**

2001 Situational Stats

	AB	H	HR	RBI	Avg		AB	H	HR	RBI	Avg
Home	216	60	14	53	.278	LHP	147	40	5	26	.272
Road	268	74	8	42	.276	RHP	337	94	17	69	.279
First Half	260	79	13	62	.304	Sc Pos	132	45	7	74	.341
Scnd Half	224	55	9	33	.246	Clutch	86	23	4	18	.267

2001 Rankings (American League)

- 1st in errors at catcher (11)
- 4th in lowest fielding percentage at catcher (.990)
- Led the Yankees in strikeouts and batting average with runners in scoring position
- Led AL catchers in batting average and RBI

Mariano Rivera

2001 Season

It was all there for the taking: a fourth straight world championship and a ninth consecutive World Series save for Mariano Rivera. But in an ending we'll never forget, Luis Gonzalez and the Diamondbacks ruined what was a career year for the Yankees' closer, making him the losing pitcher in the last game of the season. For Rivera, who had 50 regular-season saves in 57 chances, it was his first blown save during the postseason since 1997.

Pitching

Teammate Mike Mussina marvels that Rivera does it with one pitch: the cut fastball. A few years ago, Rivera fooled around with his grip and began hurling a baseball that would break lefties' bats and veer away from righties as much as nine inches. Rivera also will throw a straight fastball away to lefties to keep them honest. Pitching coach Mel Stottlemyre believes Rivera gets much of his 97-MPH velocity from a strong lower body. He's an aggressive pitcher who hardly ever issues walks, allows home runs or bothers to pad strikeout totals. He also wants to pitch every day, and usually can go more than an inning.

Defense

In the heart-breaking Game 7 defeat, Rivera made a rare throwing error after fielding a bunt. That was unusual, because he's one of the best athletes on the team. He doesn't hold runners very well, because he usually retires the next man in the order. Covering first has been a sporadic problem over his career.

2002 Outlook

Around the All-Star break, Rivera revealed he had pain in back of his right ankle. He eventually took a cortisone shot to relieve the problem, and hoped offseason rest would cure the ache. The mental issue is making sure Rivera doesn't take his Game 7 loss too hard. Closers literally have been driven to their death after such defeats, but the devout and strong-minded Rivera should rebound.

Position: RP
Bats: R **Throws:** R
Ht: 6' 2" **Wt:** 185

Opening Day Age: 32
Born: 11/29/69 in Panama City, Panama
ML Seasons: 7

New York (AL)

Overall Statistics

	W	L	Pct.	ERA	G	GS	Sv	IP	H	BB	SO	HR	Ratio
2001	4	6	.400	2.34	71	0	50	80.2	61	12	83	5	0.90
Career	37	23	.617	2.58	403	10	215	533.0	419	156	478	31	1.08

How Often He Throws Strikes

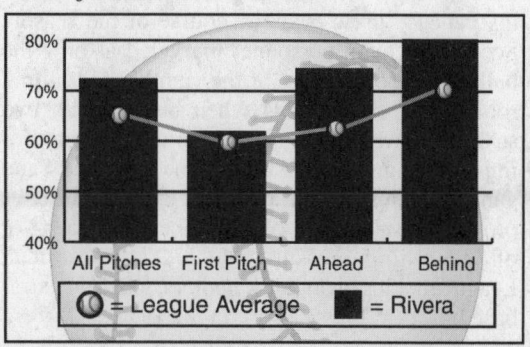

= League Average   = Rivera

2001 Situational Stats

	W	L	ERA	Sv	IP		AB	H	HR	RBI	Avg
Home	3	4	3.48	24	41.1	LHB	139	26	0	4	.187
Road	1	2	1.14	26	39.1	RHB	153	35	5	24	.229
First Half	2	4	2.66	29	47.1	Sc Pos	62	16	1	21	.258
Scnd Half	2	2	1.89	21	33.1	Clutch	238	48	4	24	.202

2001 Rankings (American League)

- 1st in save opportunities (57) and saves
- 2nd in fewest baserunners allowed per nine innings in relief (8.3) and games finished (66)
- 4th in lowest batting average allowed vs. lefthanded batters and relief ERA (2.34)
- 5th in games pitched
- 6th in blown saves (7) and relief innings (80.2)
- Led the Yankees in games finished (66), lowest batting average allowed vs. lefthanded batters, save percentage (87.7), first batter efficiency (.164), blown saves (7), relief losses (6), relief ERA (2.34), lowest batting average allowed in relief (.209), most strikeouts per nine innings in relief (9.3) and fewest baserunners allowed per nine innings in relief (8.3)

Alfonso Soriano

2001 Season

The rookie came on like gangbusters, easing Chuck Knoblauch's transition to the outfield while establishing a hint of things to come. Alfonso Soriano had a great season at second base, providing playoff heroics with his bat and spectacular, if unsteady, play in the field. He already is being touted as a 40-40 candidate and a great complement to shortstop Derek Jeter. Some say he should be moved to the outfield, but Soriano already has proved he can handle second base.

Hitting

Soriano came into the majors with a reputation as a free-swinger who was loath to draw a walk, but his patience grew over the course of the season. Scouts and team personnel marveled at how the ball jumped off the bat of the righthanded-hitting rookie. He still hit .194 when batting with two strikes and whiffed 125 times, so there's room for improvement. But his ALCS homer in Game 4 and game-winning hit in Game 5 of the World Series proved he isn't scared of going the other way—or of late-inning pressure. He led all American League rookies in doubles, homers, RBI and extra-base hits.

Baserunning & Defense

Soriano finished third in the American League with 43 steals in 57 attempts, including 11 swipes of third. That showed he had the guts of a cat burglar and an understanding of when to try for an extra base. Soriano made 19 errors, including way too many throwing errors. He had difficulty on the double-play pivot for a time because he was a natural shortstop.

2002 Outlook

The sky is the limit for Soriano, who finished third in voting for Rookie of the Year. He likely will get a crack at the top of the lineup this season unless manager Joe Torre decides the youngster strikes out too much. He should continue to grow in leaps and bounds.

Position: 2B
Bats: R **Throws:** R
Ht: 6' 1" **Wt:** 180

Opening Day Age: 24
Born: 1/7/78 in San Pedro de Macoris, DR
ML Seasons: 3
Pronunciation: soar-ee-ah-no

Overall Statistics

	G	AB	R	H	D	T	HR	RBI	SB	BB	SO	Avg	OBP	Slg
2001	158	574	77	154	34	3	18	73	43	29	125	.268	.304	.432
Career	189	632	84	164	37	3	21	77	45	30	143	.259	.294	.427

Where He Hits the Ball

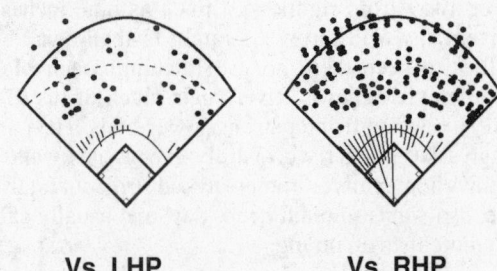

Vs. LHP   Vs. RHP

2001 Situational Stats

	AB	H	HR	RBI	Avg		AB	H	HR	RBI	Avg
Home	286	71	8	29	.248	LHP	98	25	3	11	.255
Road	288	83	10	44	.288	RHP	476	129	15	62	.271
First Half	313	82	6	33	.262	Sc Pos	133	30	3	49	.226
Scnd Half	261	72	12	40	.276	Clutch	94	22	3	11	.234

2001 Rankings (American League)

- 1st in home runs among rookies, RBI among rookies, errors at second base (19) and lowest fielding percentage at second base (.973)
- 2nd in caught stealing (14) and steals of third (11)
- 3rd in stolen bases
- 4th in batting average among rookies
- 5th in lowest on-base percentage
- 6th in lowest on-base percentage vs. righthanded pitchers (.303)
- 8th in batting average on a 3-1 count (.571)
- Led the Yankees in triples, stolen bases, caught stealing (14), games played, steals of third (11), fewest GDPs per GDP situation (6.3%), batting average on a 3-1 count (.571) and batting average on an 0-2 count (.239)

Bernie Williams

2001 Season

Bernie Williams was an All-Star for the fifth straight year, but that doesn't begin to tell his story. After a fairly consistent 2000 campaign, Williams was streaky over the course of the 2001 season, producing a torrid June between some other dismal months. He was one of the many Yankees who didn't hit much in the postseason, batting .235 in the ALCS and .208 in the World Series. Williams set a career high in doubles but saw his power numbers dip. This wasn't his best season.

Hitting

Williams moved out of his traditional cleanup spot for much of the year to accommodate a red-hot Tino Martinez. The switch-hitting center fielder continued to supply most of his power from the left side, although he hit lefties and righties equally well. Williams gets in trouble chasing breaking balls down and fastballs up. A patient hitter, he hit more flyballs than he has historically. His average dipped after the All-Star break, but his power was relatively consistent. He is still one of the best in close-and-late situations.

Baserunning & Defense

Ironically, Williams played some of his best center field ever and yet didn't win a Gold Glove for the first time in five years. He only made two errors while positioning himself about 20-30 feet closer to the infield to cut off bleeders and broken-bat base hits. Williams doesn't have a good arm and only had three assists in 2001. On the bases, he still seems unsure of himself despite good speed, and lacks natural instincts to know when to take the extra base.

2002 Outlook

Williams may well hit more than 30 homers and drive in 100 runs, but much of the pressure is off to do so. The Yankees added the likes of Robin Ventura and Jason Giambi in December. Still, it will be interesting to see how Williams adjusts to more of a leadership role. He is quiet and introspective, but may have to lead younger Yankees and newcomers—if only by example—if the club is to contend for another World Championship.

Position: CF
Bats: B **Throws:** R
Ht: 6' 2" **Wt:** 205

Opening Day Age: 33
Born: 9/13/68 in San Juan, PR
ML Seasons: 11

New York (AL)

Overall Statistics

	G	AB	R	H	D	T	HR	RBI	SB	BB	SO	Avg	OBP	Slg
2001	146	540	102	166	38	0	26	94	11	78	67	.307	.395	.522
Career	1383	5346	964	1629	316	50	207	896	130	744	830	.305	.389	.499

Where He Hits the Ball

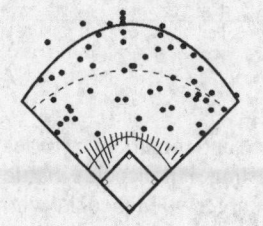
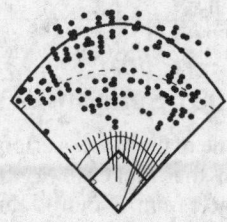

Vs. LHP   **Vs. RHP**

2001 Situational Stats

	AB	H	HR	RBI	Avg		AB	H	HR	RBI	Avg
Home	290	91	14	58	.314	LHP	151	47	5	22	.311
Road	250	75	12	36	.300	RHP	389	119	21	72	.306
First Half	268	86	15	50	.321	Sc Pos	142	35	1	54	.246
Scnd Half	272	80	11	44	.294	Clutch	75	25	3	12	.333

2001 Rankings (American League)

- 3rd in fielding percentage in center field (.994)
- 5th in cleanup slugging percentage (.528)
- 6th in sacrifice flies (9)
- 7th in intentional walks (11)
- Led the Yankees in doubles, sacrifice flies (9), walks, intentional walks (11), slugging percentage, on-base percentage, batting average vs. righthanded pitchers, cleanup slugging percentage (.528), slugging percentage vs. righthanded pitchers (.542), on-base percentage vs. lefthanded pitchers (.411), on-base percentage vs. righthanded pitchers (.389), batting average on the road, batting average on a 3-2 count (.340) and batting average with two strikes (.250)
- Led AL center fielders in batting average

Sterling Hitchcock

Position: SP
Bats: L **Throws:** L
Ht: 6' 0" **Wt:** 205

Opening Day Age: 30
Born: 4/29/71 in
Fayetteville, NC
ML Seasons: 10

Overall Statistics

	W	L	Pct.	ERA	G	GS	Sv	IP	H	BB	SO	HR	Ratio
2001	6	5	.545	5.63	13	12	0	70.1	89	21	43	6	1.56
Career	67	67	.500	4.75	222	187	3	1137.1	1204	416	884	158	1.42

2001 Situational Stats

	W	L	ERA	Sv	IP		AB	H	HR	RBI	Avg
Home	5	2	3.55	0	45.2	LHB	73	27	4	14	.370
Road	1	3	9.49	0	24.2	RHB	220	62	2	26	.282
First Half	1	0	1.29	0	7.0	Sc Pos	78	25	0	30	.321
Scnd Half	5	5	6.11	0	63.1	Clutch	9	3	0	0	.333

2001 Season

One of the more overlooked and remarkable stories on the Yankees was Sterling Hitchcock's battle back from Tommy John surgery. Hitchcock, who was dealt from San Diego to the Yankees on July 30, finished the year a gutsy 6-5. For Hitchcock, it was a homecoming to his first major league team.

Pitching & Defense

Despite lacking the velocity that allowed him to be MVP of the NLCS in 1998, Hitchcock pitched on guts and timing. Opponents batted .315 against him, and lefties hit .375, because Hitchcock's fastball barely registered above the mid-80s. Once he gets his fastball and splitter back to where they were, they will complement his changeup and breaking balls. Hitchcock was marvelous in the World Series, picking up a victory in Game 5. Defensively, he has a high leg kick but does not ignore baserunners, though they were perfect in 10 tries against him last year. He's an average fielder.

2002 Outlook

Hitchcock wants to stay with the Yankees, who acquired him at the end of a three-year contract. While the southpaw probably could earn more and be a No. 2 or No. 3 starter elsewhere, he may stay. The Yankees were pleased that "one of their own" returned to help the team during its postseason run.

Nick Johnson

Position: 1B
Bats: L **Throws:** L
Ht: 6' 3" **Wt:** 224

Opening Day Age: 23
Born: 9/19/78 in
Sacramento, CA
ML Seasons: 1

Overall Statistics

	G	AB	R	H	D	T	HR	RBI	SB	BB	SO	Avg	OBP	Slg
2001	23	67	6	13	2	0	2	8	0	7	15	.194	.308	.313
Career	23	67	6	13	2	0	2	8	0	7	15	.194	.308	.313

2001 Situational Stats

	AB	H	HR	RBI	Avg		AB	H	HR	RBI	Avg
Home	20	2	1	2	.100	LHP	18	7	0	4	.389
Road	47	11	1	6	.234	RHP	49	6	2	4	.122
First Half	0	0	0	0	-	Sc Pos	16	3	0	5	.188
Scnd Half	67	13	2	8	.194	Clutch	12	3	0	2	.250

2001 Season

Nick Johnson began last year as the Yankees' No. 1 prospect and ended it at the World Series. Although Johnson wasn't activated for the playoffs, he capped a successful season by watching what many think is his future: many trips to the postseason wearing pinstripes.

Hitting, Baserunning & Defense

Johnson looks like the total package as a hitter, and has a great eye for his age. Scouts say at worst he will be a great hitter for average like Mark Grace. After hitting .256-18-49 at Triple-A Columbus, the rookie struggled in his first cup of coffee with the Yankees after missing the 2000 season with a broken hand. He has added about 40 pounds over the last few years and should contribute power numbers in the future. Johnson is speedy for his frame and already is a good defensive first baseman.

2002 Outlook

Johnson would have had every opportunity to claim the first-base job if the Yankees' pursuit of Jason Giambi had come up empty. Johnson also worked out in the outfield while in the minors and lobbied to fill in there last summer. He could play left field, although some people believe that's a stretch. Making Johnson an everyday DH probably won't hurt him because of his solid makeup.

Ramiro Mendoza

Position: RP
Bats: R **Throws:** R
Ht: 6' 2" **Wt:** 195

Opening Day Age: 29
Born: 6/15/72 in Los Santos, Panama
ML Seasons: 6

Overall Statistics

	W	L	Pct.	ERA	G	GS	Sv	IP	H	BB	SO	HR	Ratio
2001	8	4	.667	3.75	56	2	6	100.2	89	23	70	9	1.11
Career	46	30	.605	4.18	215	57	12	607.0	664	138	352	60	1.32

2001 Situational Stats

	W	L	ERA	Sv	IP		AB	H	HR	RBI	Avg
Home	2	2	3.35	3	51.0	LHB	161	40	5	20	.248
Road	6	2	4.17	3	49.2	RHB	208	49	4	24	.236
First Half	6	2	4.08	3	57.1	Sc Pos	93	25	1	31	.269
Scnd Half	2	2	3.32	3	43.1	Clutch	125	20	2	7	.160

2001 Season

Although he missed time at the beginning and end of last season with a sore right shoulder, Ramiro Mendoza continued to build his reputation as an indispensable reliever. He could spot start, bridge the gap or set up games for Mariano Rivera, and he picked up six saves along the way. Mendoza, who also had 13 holds, wants to be a starter, but is too good in the pen.

Pitching & Defense

Mendoza is a classic groundball pitcher, seemingly able to induce double-play grounders at will with one sinker. He also has a nice fastball he isn't afraid of challenging hitters with, often to the detriment of remembering what got him in the big leagues. Mendoza's changeup is above average. He is a very good athlete, but he does not hold runners well.

2002 Outlook

Mendoza probably won't get his shot as a starter because he's too valuable as a reliever. He'll continue to work in the seventh and eighth innings and will inherit the setup job in 2003 if Mike Stanton moves on. Mendoza's health is always a mild concern, but he should be as fit as ever this season.

Shane Spencer

Position: LF/RF/DH
Bats: R **Throws:** R
Ht: 5'11" **Wt:** 225

Opening Day Age: 30
Born: 2/20/72 in Key West, FL
ML Seasons: 4

Overall Statistics

	G	AB	R	H	D	T	HR	RBI	SB	BB	SO	Avg	OBP	Slg
2001	80	283	40	73	14	2	10	46	4	21	58	.258	.315	.428
Career	251	803	116	216	39	5	37	133	5	63	166	.269	.324	.468

2001 Situational Stats

	AB	H	HR	RBI	Avg		AB	H	HR	RBI	Avg
Home	135	39	6	28	.289	LHP	64	20	4	19	.313
Road	148	34	4	18	.230	RHP	219	53	6	27	.242
First Half	78	16	4	12	.205	Sc Pos	79	20	1	30	.253
Scnd Half	205	57	6	34	.278	Clutch	37	9	0	1	.243

2001 Season

The year began with Shane Spencer as an afterthought in the Yankees' plans, and ended with him manning the outfield in Game 7 of the World Series. That's the result of a devoted work ethic and a determination to recover from a torn ACL in his right knee, which Spencer suffered in July 2000. For a time, he supplanted Chuck Knoblauch as the starting left fielder in 2001.

Hitting, Baserunning & Defense

It's very difficult to throw a fastball by Spencer. He tattoos lefties to the tune of a .330 career average. He does get anxious and jumpy because of his platoon role, often trying to do too much and swinging at balls out of the strike zone—especially high. Spencer is not much of a stolen-base threat, although he runs fairly well. He is a deceptively good outfielder, able to charge balls or go back on them and capable of making accurate throws.

2002 Outlook

Spencer was a candidate for a starting job this year, but the December acquisitions of Rondell White and John Vander Wal could reduce Spencer to a platoon role in right. He may see steady playing time, but it would behoove him to enter the spring in the best shape of his career.

New York (AL)

Mike Stanton

Position: RP
Bats: L **Throws:** L
Ht: 6' 1" **Wt:** 215

Opening Day Age: 34
Born: 6/2/67 in
Houston, TX
ML Seasons: 13

Overall Statistics

	W	L	Pct.	ERA	G	GS	Sv	IP	H	BB	SO	HR	Ratio
2001	9	4	.692	2.58	76	0	0	80.1	80	29	78	4	1.36
Career	46	36	.561	3.85	756	1	65	745.2	712	280	644	66	1.33

2001 Situational Stats

	W	L	ERA	Sv	IP		AB	H	HR	RBI	Avg
Home	3	1	0.89	0	40.2	LHB	113	32	2	15	.283
Road	6	3	4.31	0	39.2	RHB	191	48	2	14	.251
First Half	6	2	1.89	0	47.2	Sc Pos	70	20	0	22	.286
Scnd Half	3	2	3.58	0	32.2	Clutch	184	47	2	15	.255

2001 Season

Mike Stanton took over the setup role for the Yanks after Jeff Nelson moved on to Seattle. The lefty had a stellar first half, earning his first trip to the All-Star Game with a 6-2 record and a 1.89 ERA. After the break, he struggled a bit but reached a career high with nine wins. In the postseason, he was overpowering at times and vulnerable at others.

Pitching & Defense

Stanton lowered his ERA by more than a run and a half while working 12.1 more innings than in 2000. He was a workhorse who didn't walk many, but often left fat pitches over the plate. Stanton throws a fastball in the mid-90s and challenges hitters high with it. He complements it with a changeup, curve and slider. Stanton doesn't allow many stolen bases and is normally a good fielder, but made a rare throwing error in Game 3 of the ALCS against Seattle. He had a team-high 23 holds last year.

2002 Outlook

Stanton is in the final year of a three-year, $7.35 million contract. He'll be two months shy of his 35th birthday on Opening Day and begins his 14th season. As the saying goes, old lefties don't retire, they just keep going and going and going. Stanton needs to improve his efforts against lefties next season. They continue to hit him hard.

Randy Velarde

Position: 2B/3B/1B/DH
Bats: R **Throws:** R
Ht: 6' 0" **Wt:** 200

Opening Day Age: 39
Born: 11/24/62 in
Midland, TX
ML Seasons: 15
Pronunciation:
vuh-LAR-day

Overall Statistics

	G	AB	R	H	D	T	HR	RBI	SB	BB	SO	Avg	OBP	Slg
2001	93	342	50	95	19	2	9	32	6	34	86	.278	.356	.424
Career	1217	4111	611	1141	206	23	98	437	75	448	821	.278	.353	.410

2001 Situational Stats

	AB	H	HR	RBI	Avg		AB	H	HR	RBI	Avg
Home	160	48	3	15	.300	LHP	91	27	3	13	.297
Road	182	47	6	17	.258	RHP	251	68	6	19	.271
First Half	169	56	5	14	.331	Sc Pos	76	17	0	21	.224
Scnd Half	173	39	4	18	.225	Clutch	42	10	1	2	.238

2001 Season

A dream came true for Randy Velarde, who was acquired at the August 31 trade deadline and played in his first World Series. Unfortunately, the results weren't very good for Velarde, who originally reached the majors with New York. In limited action, he showed an ability to play many positions but didn't hit in any of them.

Hitting, Baserunning & Defense

Velarde is a patient hitter who has no problem going the opposite way or pulling the ball. He also has decent pop. In the last three years, though, he has gone from an everyday player to a utility man, and has had to adjust accordingly. Velarde is a savvy baserunner who is able to move from first to third with ease. He can play any infield position or a corner outfield spot, but is best suited for second or third base.

2002 Outlook

It's tough to say where on the field Velarde will land, or how much he'll play. The Yankees declined to pick up his option for 2002. With Robin Ventura now on board to play third base for New York, Velarde isn't likely to be brought back. He probably becomes a jack-of-all-trades type who gets used to life in a platoon role. He also can help any club as a teacher and mentor.

Gerald Williams

Position: CF/RF
Bats: R **Throws:** R
Ht: 6' 2"   **Wt:** 187

Opening Day Age: 35
Born: 8/10/66 in New Orleans, LA
ML Seasons: 10

Overall Statistics

	G	AB	R	H	D	T	HR	RBI	SB	BB	SO	Avg	OBP	Slg
2001	100	279	42	56	18	0	4	19	13	18	55	.201	.262	.308
Career	1012	2852	437	739	172	16	80	348	97	167	488	.259	.305	.415

2001 Situational Stats

	AB	H	HR	RBI	Avg		AB	H	HR	RBI	Avg
Home	131	24	3	10	.183	LHP	38	7	1	2	.184
Road	148	32	1	9	.216	RHP	241	49	3	17	.203
First Half	236	48	4	17	.203	Sc Pos	63	9	0	13	.143
Scnd Half	43	8	0	2	.186	Clutch	37	5	0	2	.135

2001 Season

It was a tough year for the man nicknamed Ice, who saw his playing time (if not his skills) melt and evaporate. Gerald Williams was released by Tampa Bay in late June, and didn't provide the offensive help the Yankees were looking for. While Williams is signed through 2002, the Yanks were not pleased with his 2001 output.

Hitting, Baserunning & Defense

Williams had dismal on-base and slugging percentages, which is what you get when you hit .201. He traditionally doesn't hit well against righties, a bad sign for someone looking for an everyday job. This came after a 2000 season during which he hit .274 with 21 homers and 89 RBI. Williams remains one of the fastest players in the game and stole 13 bases in 2001. He has an adequate arm for a center fielder, and can run down nearly every ball in sight.

2002 Outlook

The Yankees would like to be rid of Williams, preferring to give his spot to someone younger and cheaper. Williams most assuredly would prefer to be playing everyday, but a release by the Devil Rays is a black mark that's tough to overcome. If freed, Williams could find some kind of role elsewhere.

Enrique Wilson

Position: SS/3B/2B
Bats: B **Throws:** R
Ht: 5'11"   **Wt:** 180

Opening Day Age: 26
Born: 7/27/75 in Santo Domingo, DR
ML Seasons: 5

Overall Statistics

	G	AB	R	H	D	T	HR	RBI	SB	BB	SO	Avg	OBP	Slg
2001	94	228	17	48	8	1	2	20	0	9	37	.211	.238	.281
Career	324	904	100	239	51	3	11	84	9	56	112	.264	.305	.364

2001 Situational Stats

	AB	H	HR	RBI	Avg		AB	H	HR	RBI	Avg
Home	94	21	1	6	.223	LHP	48	9	0	2	.188
Road	134	27	1	14	.201	RHP	180	39	2	18	.217
First Half	137	25	1	9	.182	Sc Pos	65	12	1	19	.185
Scnd Half	91	23	1	11	.253	Clutch	48	11	1	5	.229

2001 Season

Even super-utility man Luis Sojo said it: Enrique Wilson is becoming what Sojo once was to the Yankees. The versatile infielder helped out at third base, shortstop and second after being acquired from Pittsburgh in June for a minor league pitcher. He hit 56 points better in New York and showed a good glove at the hot corner.

Hitting, Baserunning & Defense

The switch-hitting Wilson won't strike out much, but hardly ever draws a walk. He sprays line drives, much like Sojo, and doesn't hit home runs too often. He has some gap power. Wilson's most notorious run around the bases came in the 1998 ALCS between New York and Cleveland. He took advantage of Chuck Knoblauch's argument with an ump to score for the Indians. He's a heads-up player, and can fill in at just about any position.

2002 Outlook

Wilson is only 26 and it isn't too late to see him emerge as a full-time starter. The odds were in his favor before the Yankees acquired Robin Ventura in exchange for David Justice in December. Now he'll have to settle for a utility role in New York.

Jay Witasick

Traded To GIANTS

Position: RP
Bats: R **Throws:** R
Ht: 6' 4" **Wt:** 235

Opening Day Age: 29
Born: 8/28/72 in Baltimore, MD
ML Seasons: 6
Pronunciation: wi-TASS-ik

Overall Statistics

	W	L	Pct.	ERA	G	GS	Sv	IP	H	BB	SO	HR	Ratio
2001	8	2	.800	3.30	63	0	1	79.0	78	33	106	8	1.41
Career	25	28	.472	5.32	155	56	1	438.1	509	215	378	71	1.65

2001 Situational Stats

	W	L	ERA	Sv	IP		AB	H	HR	RBI	Avg
Home	5	1	2.82	1	38.1	LHB	111	32	3	22	.288
Road	3	1	3.76	1	40.2	RHB	197	46	5	29	.234
First Half	6	2	2.15	1	46.0	Sc Pos	106	29	6	48	.274
Scnd Half	2	0	4.91	0	33.0	Clutch	114	30	2	18	.263

2001 Season

From Day 1 as a Yankee, Jay Witasick had trouble blending in. The club acquired him from San Diego in late June and owner George Steinbrenner reportedly was upset it took Witasick a couple of days to make the cross-country trek to New York. Witasick had a 3-0 record with a 4.69 ERA in 32 relief appearances with the Yankees. He was used primarily as a setup man, but often was bypassed when manager Joe Torre needed sure outs.

Pitching & Defense

Witasick traditionally was best suited as a starter or for long relief, but the Yankees found he pitched best when given slivers of innings. A classic fastball-slider pitcher, Witasick doesn't even throw a changeup. At least he didn't until Game 6 of the World Series, when Arizona shelled him for 10 hits and nine runs in 1.1 innings. It was an outing so bad he decided to break out the changeup. Witasick is nothing to speak of as a fielder.

2002 Outlook

The Yankees did not want Witasick back because of his inability to pitch well in big games, which compromised Torre's confidence in him. He was traded to San Francisco in mid-December for John Vander Wal, and he now can resume starting or relieving with less scrutiny.

Mark Wohlers

Position: RP
Bats: R **Throws:** R
Ht: 6' 4" **Wt:** 207

Opening Day Age: 32
Born: 1/23/70 in Holyoke, MA
ML Seasons: 11
Pronunciation: WO-lers

Overall Statistics

	W	L	Pct.	ERA	G	GS	Sv	IP	H	BB	SO	HR	Ratio
2001	4	1	.800	4.26	61	0	0	67.2	69	25	54	8	1.39
Career	36	25	.590	3.85	469	0	112	482.0	419	246	511	31	1.38

2001 Situational Stats

	W	L	ERA	Sv	IP		AB	H	HR	RBI	Avg
Home	1	1	3.12	0	34.2	LHB	106	25	7	19	.236
Road	3	0	5.45	0	33.0	RHB	157	44	1	17	.280
First Half	3	1	4.11	0	35.0	Sc Pos	71	18	1	27	.254
Scnd Half	1	0	4.41	0	32.2	Clutch	82	21	1	11	.256

2001 Season

Mark Wohlers was psyched to get traded to the Yankees in the middle of the season, but his year ended with disappointment: he was left off the World Series roster, only to see the Yanks vanquished by Arizona. Wohlers was mediocre as a setup man and never fully earned manager Joe Torre's trust.

Pitching & Defense

Wohlers still can bring the heat, but his control problems and arm surgery leave him a far different pitcher than the one who dominated baseball in the mid-1990s. He was great against lefties, holding them to a .196 average while with New York in 2001. But he also threw a career-high 11 wild pitches. He can throw his fastball as hard as 100 MPH, but it doesn't move much and his splitter isn't very effective, either. Wohlers is nothing to speak of as a fielder and baserunners steal at will.

2002 Outlook

Wohlers was in the final year of a contract when he waived his no-trade clause last June and came to New York, but the Yankees declined his option for 2002 and almost certainly will let him go elsewhere. He wasn't the unhittable reliever of seasons past, and he'll likely fill a setup spot for a second-division team.

Other New York Yankees

Carlos Almanzar (Pos: RHP, Age: 28)

	W	L	Pct.	ERA	G	GS	Sv	IP	H	BB	SO	HR	Ratio
2001	0	1	.000	3.38	10	0	0	10.2	14	2	6	2	1.50
Career	6	9	.400	5.23	129	0	0	149.2	170	51	116	25	1.48

Almanzar spent a little over a month in the big leagues in parts of April, May and June. He only pitched in 10 games with the Yankees after pitching in a career-high 62 with the Padres in 2000. 2002 Outlook: C

Clay Bellinger (Pos: 3B/LF, Age: 33, Bats: R)

	G	AB	R	H	D	T	HR	RBI	SB	BB	SO	Avg	OBP	Slg
2001	51	81	12	13	1	1	5	12	1	4	23	.160	.207	.383
Career	181	310	57	60	11	3	12	35	7	22	81	.194	.258	.365

The Yankees like Bellinger because he has played at least five different positions in each of his three major league seasons. He does hit the occasional home run, but his bat has remained a weakness. 2002 Outlook: B

Darren Bragg (Pos: RF, Age: 32, Bats: L)

	G	AB	R	H	D	T	HR	RBI	SB	BB	SO	Avg	OBP	Slg
2001	23	61	5	16	7	0	0	5	3	4	24	.262	.318	.377
Career	656	1986	273	512	122	10	39	227	48	257	449	.258	.346	.388

The Yankees claimed Bragg off waivers from the Mets in June to backup Bernie Williams in center field. When the Yanks found a better option in Gerald Williams, Bragg was designated for assignment. 2002 Outlook: C

Scott Brosius (Pos: 3B, Age: 35, Bats: R)

	G	AB	R	H	D	T	HR	RBI	SB	BB	SO	Avg	OBP	Slg
2001	120	428	57	123	25	2	13	49	3	34	83	.287	.343	.446
Career	1146	3889	544	1001	200	8	141	531	57	348	699	.257	.323	.422

Brosius retired after playing in his fourth straight World Series. He goes out after hitting a dramatic, ninth-inning homer in the 2001 Series. 2002 Outlook: D

Randy Choate (Pos: LHP, Age: 26)

	W	L	Pct.	ERA	G	GS	Sv	IP	H	BB	SO	HR	Ratio
2001	3	1	.750	3.35	37	0	0	48.1	34	27	35	0	1.26
Career	3	2	.600	3.72	59	0	0	65.1	48	35	47	3	1.27

Choate has proven to be an asset for New York as a situational lefty out of the bullpen. The southpaw held lefties to a .183 batting average last season. He should have a job in 2002. 2002 Outlook: B

Michael Coleman (Pos: CF, Age: 26, Bats: R)

	G	AB	R	H	D	T	HR	RBI	SB	BB	SO	Avg	OBP	Slg
2001	12	38	5	8	0	0	1	7	0	0	15	.211	.205	.289
Career	22	67	8	13	1	0	1	9	1	1	26	.194	.203	.254

Coleman got a chance in the Yankees' outfield in early April. Injuries and poor play doomed his stay, and he signed with Boston in the fall. 2002 Outlook: C

Bobby Estalella (Pos: C, Age: 27, Bats: R)

	G	AB	R	H	D	T	HR	RBI	SB	BB	SO	Avg	OBP	Slg
2001	32	97	12	19	5	1	3	10	0	12	30	.196	.297	.361
Career	214	625	89	139	34	5	31	97	4	94	191	.222	.326	.442

The Giants gave up on Estalella and traded him and a minor league pitcher to the Yankees in early July for

Brian Boehringer. San Francisco's former catcher of the future only saw four at-bats in three games in New York. 2002 Outlook: C

Todd Greene (Pos: C, Age: 30, Bats: R)

	G	AB	R	H	D	T	HR	RBI	SB	BB	SO	Avg	OBP	Slg
2001	35	96	9	20	4	0	1	11	0	3	21	.208	.240	.281
Career	258	776	92	187	37	0	32	103	5	33	158	.241	.276	.412

New York picked up former prospect Greene after he was released by Toronto. He hit .294 in June and July while helping fill in for injured starter Jorge Posada, but faded in August and September. 2002 Outlook: C

Randy Keisler (Pos: LHP, Age: 26)

	W	L	Pct.	ERA	G	GS	Sv	IP	H	BB	SO	HR	Ratio
2001	1	2	.333	6.22	10	10	0	50.2	52	34	36	12	1.70
Career	2	2	.500	7.19	14	11	0	61.1	68	42	42	13	1.79

Keisler dominated Triple-A Columbus in 2000, but failed when he had an opportunity to be the fifth starter in New York. He underwent shoulder surgery in November and doesn't figure to be back until at least July. 2002 Outlook: C

Brandon Knight (Pos: RHP, Age: 26)

	W	L	Pct.	ERA	G	GS	Sv	IP	H	BB	SO	HR	Ratio
2001	0	0	-	10.13	4	0	0	10.2	18	3	7	5	1.97
Career	0	0	-	10.13	4	0	0	10.2	18	3	7	5	1.97

The Twins returned Knight, a Rule 5 draft pick, to the Yankees in late-March after he failed to make their 25-man roster. He didn't fair well with New York and was almost traded to Montreal. 2002 Outlook: C

Donzell McDonald (Pos: CF, Age: 27, Bats: B)

	G	AB	R	H	D	T	HR	RBI	SB	BB	SO	Avg	OBP	Slg
2001	5	3	0	1	0	0	0	0	0	0	2	.333	.333	.333
Career	5	3	0	1	0	0	0	0	0	0	2	.333	.333	.333

A groin injury kept McDonald from making New York's Opening Day roster in 2001. The Yanks recalled him in April as a reserve outfielder. He signed a minor league deal with Cleveland in November. 2002 Outlook: C

Paul O'Neill (Pos: RF, Age: 39, Bats: L)

	G	AB	R	H	D	T	HR	RBI	SB	BB	SO	Avg	OBP	Slg
2001	137	510	77	136	33	1	21	70	22	48	59	.267	.330	.459
Career	2053	7318	1041	2105	451	21	281	1269	141	892	1166	.288	.363	.470

O'Neill put together a nice 17-year career, totaling 2,105 hits and a .288 batting average. He retired after being a huge part of the Yankees' World Series run once again in 2001. 2002 Outlook: D

Christian Parker (Pos: RHP, Age: 26)

	W	L	Pct.	ERA	G	GS	Sv	IP	H	BB	SO	HR	Ratio
2001	0	1	.000	21.00	1	1	0	3.0	8	1	1	2	3.00
Career	0	1	.000	21.00	1	1	0	3.0	8	1	1	2	3.00

Despite winning a starting spot out of spring training, Parker suffered a lost season in 2001. He was shelled in his debut with New York, then battled shoulder problems the rest of the season. 2002 Outlook: C

Henry Rodriguez (Pos: DH, Age: 34, Bats: L)

	G	AB	R	H	D	T	HR	RBI	SB	BB	SO	Avg	OBP	Slg
2001	5	8	0	0	0	0	0	0	0	0	6	.000	.000	.000
Career	930	3011	388	783	176	9	160	520	10	272	795	.260	.321	.484

Rodriguez started the 2001 season on the disabled list with back trouble. When he was activated in May, he struck out six times in eight at-bats. New York released Rodriguez in mid-June. 2002 Outlook: C

Scott Seabol (Pos: DH, Age: 26, Bats: R)

	G	AB	R	H	D	T	HR	RBI	SB	BB	SO	Avg	OBP	Slg
2001	1	1	0	0	0	0	0	0	0	0	0	.000	.000	.000
Career	1	1	0	0	0	0	0	0	0	0	0	.000	.000	.000

Injuries gave Seabol a spot on the Yankees' Opening Day roster last summer. He got one at-bat with New York before he was sent down to Triple-A Columbus for good on April 20. 2002 Outlook: C

Luis Sojo (Pos: 3B, Age: 36, Bats: R)

	G	AB	R	H	D	T	HR	RBI	SB	BB	SO	Avg	OBP	Slg
2001	39	79	5	13	2	0	0	9	1	4	12	.165	.214	.190
Career	845	2567	300	671	103	12	36	261	28	124	198	.261	.298	.353

New York signed Sojo to a one-year deal in 2001 after he was a catalyst in its 2000 World Series run. He concluded a fine tenure with the Yankees by retiring in November. 2002 Outlook: D

Todd Williams (Pos: RHP, Age: 31)

	W	L	Pct.	ERA	G	GS	Sv	IP	H	BB	SO	HR	Ratio
2001	1	0	1.000	4.70	15	0	0	15.1	22	9	13	1	2.02
Career	3	3	.500	5.37	50	0	0	53.2	67	29	32	6	1.79

Williams appeared to have a bullpen spot secured in May until he went down with an abdominal strain. New York designated him for assignment shortly after he came off the injured list in July. 2002 Outlook: C

New York Yankees Minor League Prospects

Organization Overview:

Filling the fifth-starter job was a difficult task for the 2001 Yankees, who tried the likes of Adrian Hernandez, Brett Jodie, Randy Keisler, Ted Lilly and Christian Parker before dealing for Sterling Hitchcock in late July. New York, of course, has *traded* kids to fill holes, instead of *used* them to fill holes, and it still has a fairly deep system despite this tendency during its dynastic run. With so many guys departing after New York's loss to Arizona in the World Series, 2002 provides a test to the Yanks' approach. Will they give guys like Nick Johnson, Erick Almonte and Juan Rivera a chance to fill holes, or will they simply trade guys like them to fill the gaps?

Erick Almonte

Position: SS   **Opening Day Age:** 24
Bats: R **Throws:** R   **Born:** 2/1/78 in Santo
Ht: 6' 2" **Wt:** 180   Domingo, DR

Recent Statistics

	G	AB	R	H	D	THR	RBI	SB	BB	SO	Avg
2001 AA Norwich	3	12	2	3	0	0	0	1	1	6	.250
2001 AAA Columbus	97	345	55	99	19	3	12	55	4	44	90	.287
2001 AL New York	8	4	0	2	1	0	0	0	2	0	1	.500
2001 MLE	100	344	47	89	17	2	10	46	3	37	100	.259

Signed in 1996, Almonte ranked among the top prospects in the Rookie-level Gulf Coast League in '97. A free swinger, he struggled with making contact and plate discipline for most of the next two seasons, but hit for power at Double-A Norwich in 2000 and slugged a career-best .460 playing mostly at Triple-A Columbus last summer. It's equally impressive that his walk rate went up and his strikeout rate went down in 2001. Almonte runs and throws well, and has the instincts and quickness to make the move to second or third base. He mostly needs to continue working on his improved plate patience while waiting for his chance to play.

Brandon Claussen

Position: P   **Opening Day Age:** 22
Bats: L **Throws:** L   **Born:** 5/1/79 in Rapid
Ht: 6' 2" **Wt:** 175   City, SD

Recent Statistics

	W	L	ERA	G	GS	Sv	IP	H	R	BB	SO	HR
2000 A Greensboro	8	5	4.05	17	17	0	97.2	91	49	44	98	9
2000 A Tampa	2	5	3.10	9	9	0	52.1	49	24	17	44	1
2001 A Tampa	5	2	2.73	8	8	0	56.0	47	21	13	69	2
2001 AA Norwich	9	2	2.13	21	21	0	131.0	101	42	55	151	6

A 34th-round pick in 1998, Claussen was a draft-and-follow who had an impressive debut at short-season Staten Island in 1999. Then his progress in Class-A ball slowed until Claussen went 5-2 (2.73) in eight starts at high Class-A Tampa to open the 2001 season. He moved up to Double-A Norwich and won nine of 11 decisions to finish the season at 14-4 (2.31) with a minor league-best 220 strikeouts in 187 innings. Claussen bumped up the velocity a bit on his out pitch, an above-average cut fastball that has good action. He also added some bite to his curve, which he'll throw behind in the count. His overall command improved significantly, and that was key to Claussen's emergence as one of the Yankees' top pitching prospects in 2001.

Alex Graman

Position: P   **Opening Day Age:** 24
Bats: L **Throws:** L   **Born:** 11/17/77 in
Ht: 6' 4" **Wt:** 200   Huntingburg, IN

Recent Statistics

	W	L	ERA	G	GS	Sv	IP	H	R	BB	SO	HR
2000 A Tampa	8	9	3.65	28	28	0	143.0	120	64	58	111	6
2000 AA Norwich	0	1	11.81	1	1	0	5.1	6	7	4	3	3
2001 AA Norwich	12	9	3.52	28	28	0	166.1	174	83	60	138	10

A third-round pick in 1999, Graman enjoyed a strong debut at short-season Staten Island. Then he pitched well enough at high Class-A Tampa in 2000 to reach Double-A Norwich in his first full season as a pro. Graman made his rapid ascent on the strength of a polished four-pitch arsenal that includes a low-90s fastball, changeup, curve and splitter. His secondary pitches are especially solid. He might have been recalled last summer when the Yankees needed a fifth starter, but he had mechanical issues at the time. The southpaw's motor tends to run fast, and Yankees coaches were working with him to slow down his delivery and make it more fluid. By season's end, Graman was back on track at Norwich.

Drew Henson

Position: 3B   **Opening Day Age:** 22
Bats: R **Throws:** R   **Born:** 2/13/80 in San
Ht: 6' 5" **Wt:** 222   Diego, CA

Recent Statistics

	G	AB	R	H	D	THR	RBI	SB	BB	SO	Avg
2000 A Tampa	5	21	4	7	2	0	1	1	0	1	7	.333
2000 AA Norwich	59	223	39	64	9	2	7	39	0	20	75	.287
2000 AA Chattanooga	16	64	7	11	8	0	1	9	2	4	25	.172
2001 A Tampa	5	14	2	2	0	0	1	3	1	2	7	.143
2001 AA Norwich	5	19	2	7	1	0	0	2	0	1	4	.368
2001 AAA Columbus	71	270	29	60	6	0	11	38	2	10	85	.222
2001 MLE	76	281	25	59	5	0	9	33	1	8	93	.210

Henson simply wanted to be a Yankee. So when the Reds dealt Denny Neagle to New York for him and other prospects in July 2000, Henson returned to quarterbacking duties at Michigan that fall with pro football suddenly a more likely option. His baseball career was back on track last spring, when the Yankees re-acquired him and gave him a six-year, $17 million contract. He broke his left hand in April at high Class-A Tampa. When he returned, he played five games at Double-A Norwich before he moved up to Triple-A Columbus. He struggled at the plate, but his flashes of power and his strong arm were reminders of the tools he possesses. Neither his bat nor his defensive game are ready for New York.

Adrian Hernandez

Position: P **Opening Day Age:** 22
Bats: R **Throws:** R **Born:** 8/30/79 in
Ht: 6' 2" **Wt:** 185 Havana, Cuba

Recent Statistics

	W	L	ERA	G	GS	Sv	IP	H	R	BB	SO	HR
2001 AAA Columbus	8	7	5.51	21	21	0	117.2	116	75	60	97	13
2001 AL New York	0	3	3.68	6	3	0	22.0	15	10	10	10	7

As a Cuban defector who signed a four-year, $4 million contract in June 2000, Hernandez may have been saddled by expectations generated by the success of Orlando Hernandez, a fellow Cuban with whom he shares his surname. Adrian also is similar to El Duque as a pitcher, and for that Adrian has been dubbed "El Duquecito." His pitches—two fastballs (sinker and cutter), curve, changeup and a slider that humbles righthanders—come from several arm angles at varying speeds. His offerings are enhanced by good movement, and his delivery adds to the deception. Fine-tuning his changeup should help keep lefties at bay, and better command of his fastball will improve his game. He struggled as the Yankees' fifth starter, but 2002 presents new opportunities.

Ted Lilly

Position: P **Opening Day Age:** 26
Bats: L **Throws:** L **Born:** 1/4/76 in Lameta,
Ht: 6' 0" **Wt:** 185 CA

Recent Statistics

	W	L	ERA	G	GS	Sv	IP	H	R	BB	SO	HR
2001 AAA Columbus	0	0	2.84	5	5	0	25.1	16	10	8	30	2
2001 AL New York	5	6	5.37	26	21	0	120.2	126	81	51	112	20

The Dodgers under interim GM Tommy Lasorda gave away Lilly in a 1998 trade with Montreal. The Expos then shipped him and two others to the Yankees for Hideki Irabu in 1999. Lilly had a decent season at Triple-A Columbus in 2000, and was even better there during a brief stay in 2001. During his stints with the Yankees, Lilly has posted better numbers in relief, as he alternated quality starts and beatings as a starter. He throws an exceptional curveball and complements it with a low-90s four-seam fastball and a decent changeup. He's in the mix to earn a job with the Yankees in 2002.

Juan Rivera

Position: OF **Opening Day Age:** 23
Bats: R **Throws:** R **Born:** 7/3/78 in
Ht: 6' 2" **Wt:** 170 Guarenas, VZ

Recent Statistics

	G	AB	R	H	D	THR	RBI	SB	BB	SO	Avg
2001 AA Norwich	77	316	50	101	18	3	14	58	5	15	50	.320
2001 AAA Columbus	55	199	39	65	11	1	14	40	4	15	31	.327
2001 AL New York	3	4	0	0	0	0	0	0	0	0	0	.000
2001 MLE	132	498	77	149	25	2	23	85	6	23	85	.299

Signed in 1996, Rivera debuted in North America by leading the Rookie-level Gulf Coast League in homers (12) and RBI (45) in 1998. He spent most of the next two years at high Class-A Tampa, hitting .276-14-69 there in 2000 and closing the year by struggling in 62 at-bats at Double-A Norwich. Rivera returned to Norwich in 2001 and clobbered the ball. He continued his tear at Triple-A Columbus and finished the year at .322-28-98. Rivera, who now puts some lift on his drives, recognizes the breaking ball and handles offspeed stuff well with his quick bat. Defensively, he needs to improve his paths to the ball, but has a strong arm and throws accurately. New York's right fielder of the future needs more plate discipline and has some rough edges, but his time is coming.

Marcus Thames

Position: OF **Opening Day Age:** 25
Bats: R **Throws:** R **Born:** 3/6/77 in
Ht: 6' 2" **Wt:** 205 Louisville, MS

Recent Statistics

	G	AB	R	H	D	THR	RBI	SB	BB	SO	Avg
2000 AA Norwich	131	474	72	114	30	2	15	79	1	50	89	.241
2001 AA Norwich	139	520	114	167	43	4	31	97	10	73	101	.321
2001 MLE	139	505	102	152	39	2	27	87	7	55	108	.301

Thames hasn't batted .300 over a full summer since his pro debut in 1997, and this draft-and-follow pick from '96 never has shown the kind of power that generated 43 doubles and 31 homers in his third go-round at Double-A Norwich in 2001. He led the Eastern League in runs, doubles, on-base percentage (.410) and slugging (.598). Thames saw the ball well all summer and was far more selective at the plate. Swinging only at hittable pitches produced harder-hit balls. He not only improved at going the other way last season, he showed steady progress at driving the ball to the opposite field. He can play center field, although he may be better suited to a corner.

Others to Watch

The Yankees' first pick in 2001, outfielder **John-Ford Griffin** (22) was mature in his approach during his pro debut. He went to the plate with a plan and generated a .311 average and .413 OBP with his sweet lefthanded swing at short-season Staten Island in 2001. . . Venezuelan lefty **Dave Martinez** (21) made his North American debut in 1999. He posted ERAs below 3.00 in each of his first two seasons, and opened 2001 by going 6-0 (1.13) at Class-A Greensboro, baffling Sally League hitters with his command of his 91-92 MPH fastball and an improving curveball. . . Shortstop **Bronson Sardinha** (18) shows advanced instincts and plate discipline. Drafted in 2001, Sardinha batted .303 and posted a .398 OBP in the Rookie-level Gulf Coast League last summer. He also has plenty of raw power. . . A fourth-round pick in 2000, lefthander **Matt Smith** (22) went 5-4 (2.38) at short-season Staten Island in his debut, and followed up with an 11-5 (2.44) campaign between Class-A Greensboro and high Class-A Tampa in 2001. Smith was more dominant last summer, averaging more than a strikeout per inning. He reported to camp stronger and consistently worked in the 88-92 MPH range with his fastball. His breaking ball has sharp late-breaking movement.

Network Associates Coliseum

Offense

There certainly was no place like home for the Athletics. They boasted a 53-28 record at The Net last season, the third-best home mark in baseball. Since being enclosed to accommodate the football Raiders several years back, the ball carries more and becomes prone to swirling winds. Nevertheless, it takes some power to drive the ball out from gap to gap.

Defense

The park does favor pitchers. The turf is trimmed but thick, assisting groundball hurlers. The afternoon sun provides as high a sky as you will find, which can cause problems to the left side of the infield. Those shadows will fall across the infield, often leaving the mound and right-center field area in very bright sun. Pitchers throwing out of the light and into the shadow can take advantage, but the right side of the field sometimes pays a price.

Who It Helps the Most

Oakland plays in a spacious park that is non-discriminatory. For example, Eric Chavez is a lefty who hit better at home, while Jeremy Giambi and Terrence Long hit better on the road. Regardless, the A's scored enough to win their last 17 regular season home games in a row last year.

Who It Hurts the Most

Oakland hitters play a patience game. But with so much foul territory, fighting off a pitch into foul ground can spell an out because such popups are sometimes caught. Flyball hitters who overswing and hitters who have trouble taking the ball down the line also can have problems.

Rookies & Newcomers

In the bullpen, look for Chad Bradford and Luis Vizcaino to emerge. With the departure of Jason Giambi, there is a chance Olmedo Saenz will get the nod at first base. That is because Jason Hart, a top prospect, struggled at Triple-A last year. In the outfield, the loss of Johnny Damon could open a spot, and though Eric Byrnes looks like the obvious answer, Ryan Ludwick is a better bet. An even better scenario puts Adam Piatt in left field.

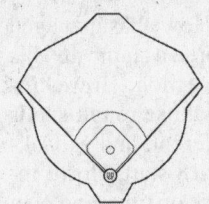

Dimensions: LF-330, LCF-362, CF-400, RCF-362, RF-330

Capacity: 43,662

Elevation: 25 feet

Surface: Grass

Foul Territory: Large

Park Factors

2001 Season

	Home Games Athletics	Opp	Total	Away Games Athletics	Opp	Total	Index
G	72	72	144	72	72	144	—
Avg	.257	.243	.250	.274	.268	.271	92
AB	2401	2533	4934	2563	2432	4995	99
R	376	284	660	434	315	749	88
H	618	615	1233	702	652	1354	91
2B	127	103	230	176	99	275	85
3B	7	9	16	12	11	23	70
HR	88	69	157	90	72	162	98
BB	303	184	487	284	209	493	100
SO	451	509	960	449	480	929	105
E	58	44	102	56	44	100	102
E-Infield	47	32	79	47	37	84	94
LHB-Avg	.274	.241	.259	.292	.260	.279	93
LHB-HR	48	22	70	51	29	80	91
RHB-Avg	.239	.244	.242	.250	.273	.263	92
RHB-HR	40	47	87	39	43	82	105

1999-2001

	Home Games Athletics	Opp	Total	Away Games Athletics	Opp	Total	Index
G	216	216	432	215	215	430	—
Avg	.263	.254	.258	.270	.282	.276	94
AB	7159	7583	14742	7670	7339	15009	98
R	1195	963	2158	1275	1111	2386	90
H	1880	1927	3807	2072	2072	4144	91
2B	360	376	736	443	389	832	90
3B	30	32	62	30	40	70	90
HR	290	192	482	304	228	532	92
BB	959	691	1650	971	749	1720	98
SO	1391	1379	2770	1530	1303	2833	100
E	172	145	317	162	146	308	102
E-Infield	135	116	251	133	122	255	98
LHB-Avg	.271	.258	.265	.282	.276	.280	95
LHB-HR	166	74	240	187	95	282	85
RHB-Avg	.253	.251	.252	.256	.287	.273	92
RHB-HR	124	118	242	117	133	250	100

2001 Rankings (American League)
- Third-highest strikeout factor
- Lowest batting-average factor
- Lowest RHB batting-average factor
- Second-lowest run factor
- Second-lowest hit factor
- Second-lowest LHB batting-average factor
- Third-lowest double factor

Oakland

Art Howe

2001 Season

It seems that every season Art Howe has managed the Athletics, the team has endured a slump and his tenure has been called into question. Howe, focused and low-key, has ridden those rough spells with aplomb. 2001 was no different, and as Oakland got off to a horrendous 8-18 start, Howe invoked two rules: come to the park on time, and play hard. His young team heard the words and proceeded to become the first club in history to log more than 100 wins after being 10 games under .500.

Offense

With names like Giambi, Tejada, Chavez, Damon and Dye gracing his lineup card, Howe hardly has to worry about his team's ability to produce runs. The biggest need is experience, and Howe and his brainy cluster of coaches are more than adept at helping the talented group along. Howe has been criticized for playing it too much by the book on offense, but if the results have been 193 wins over the past two seasons, what is there to complain about?

Pitching & Defense

As with the hitters, when a manager has talent in the forms of Barry Zito, Mark Mulder and Tim Hudson, it often seems like there is no need to coach. Call it only refinement, but the results speak for themselves. Athletics starters boasted a league-best 3.72 ERA in a major league-high 1,022 innings. On defense, the addition of Jermaine Dye in right field solidified the play of the outfield, while work with catcher Ramon Hernandez and third baseman Eric Chavez paid off handsomely.

2002 Outlook

The A's certainly have ability, which they hope to exploit in order to break through to the next level. Losing Jason Giambi and Johnny Damon will hurt, but Oakland has enough talent elsewhere that it would be a serious contender in any division of either league. Knowing the magic of general manager Billy Beane and his ability to fill spots and make deals, the 2002 A's should be up to the task of trying to fulfill all of their promise.

Born: 12/15/46 in Pittsburgh, PA

Playing Experience: 1974-1985, Pit, Hou, StL

Managerial Experience: 11 seasons

Manager Statistics

Year	Team, Lg	W	L	Pct	GB	Finish
2001	Oakland, AL	102	60	.630	14.0	2nd West
11 Seasons		889	892	.499	—	—

2001 Starting Pitchers by Days Rest

	<=3	4	5	6+
Athletics Starts	0	87	50	19
Athletics ERA	—	3.55	3.83	3.83
AL Avg Starts	1	78	48	24
AL ERA	5.92	4.69	4.58	4.58

2001 Situational Stats

	Art Howe	AL Average
Hit & Run Success %	27.9	35.0
Stolen Base Success %	70.1	71.0
Platoon Pct.	59.6	59.1
Defensive Subs	18	26
High-Pitch Outings	4	6
Quick/Slow Hooks	19/11	19/16
Sacrifice Attempts	40	54

2001 Rankings (American League)

- 1st in pinch-hitters used (131)
- 2nd in intentional walks (41), one-batter pitcher appearances (41) and 2+ pitching changes in low-scoring games (39)
- 3rd in fewest caught stealings of second base (24) and relief appearances (416)

Eric Chavez

2001 Season

After his fine 2001 campaign, there is little doubt that Eric Chavez not only has established himself as one of the elite third sackers in the game, but as one of its brightest rising stars as well. He cracked both the 30-homer and 100-RBI barriers for the first time last season. He and shortstop Miguel Tejada became the first third base-shortstop combo in history to top those totals in the same year. Chavez also set career highs in just about every offensive category. In the field, Chavez' defense was often spectacular.

Hitting

Chavez is a hitter who is just beginning to understand how good he is, let alone how good he can be. He is able to exploit the left-center and right-center field gaps, and as long as he stays on top of the ball, opposing pitchers should beware. The primary area he needs to work on is his concentration. Once Chavez learns to consistently focus and hit within himself, his numbers will take off even further.

Baserunning & Defense

An excellent baserunner with good speed, Chavez hits the field with "game" and takes advantage accordingly. He could steal 20 bases, even though his major league high to this point is a modest eight. He also could score 100 runs on a regular basis, possibly beginning this season. Chavez shined on defense last season, making the fewest errors of any American League third baseman who played in over 100 games. A converted shortstop, he has quick reflexes and a strong arm at the corner, and he won his first Gold Glove in 2001.

2002 Outlook

Following a tremendous second half last season, including a .379 average after August 31, look for Chavez to kick it up a notch—if that is possible—as confidence and experience meld with all that talent. A batting title looms, as do numbers consistently in the .300-30-100 range for a number of years to come.

Position: 3B
Bats: L **Throws:** R
Ht: 6' 0" **Wt:** 204

Opening Day Age: 24
Born: 12/7/77 in Los Angeles, CA
ML Seasons: 4
Pronunciation: shah-VEZ

Overall Statistics

	G	AB	R	H	D	T	HR	RBI	SB	BB	SO	Avg	OBP	Slg
2001	151	552	91	159	43	0	32	114	8	41	99	.288	.338	.540
Career	435	1454	233	400	91	7	71	256	12	152	254	.275	.343	.494

Where He Hits the Ball

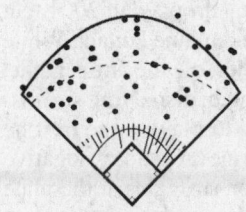
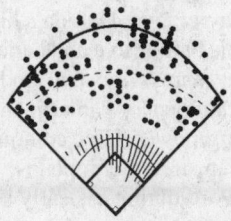

Vs. LHP   **Vs. RHP**

2001 Situational Stats

	AB	H	HR	RBI	Avg		AB	H	HR	RBI	Avg
Home	257	76	14	40	.296	LHP	183	47	7	35	.257
Road	295	83	18	74	.281	RHP	369	112	25	79	.304
First Half	302	74	11	46	.245	Sc Pos	149	45	10	82	.302
Scnd Half	250	85	21	68	.340	Clutch	87	29	5	17	.333

2001 Rankings (American League)

- 1st in fielding percentage at third base (.972)
- 4th in doubles and slugging percentage vs. righthanded pitchers (.602)
- Led AL third basemen in batting average and RBI

Johnny Damon

2001 Season

It seemed like a perfect merger when the Athletics acquired Johnny Damon in a three-team swap (that also netted Corey Lidle) last January. It was expected that Damon—who proved how well he fit into the mix by often skateboarding to the park—would excel perched atop Oakland's powerful lineup. Unfortunately, he opened the year in disappointing fashion. But Damon kept pushing, enjoyed a strong July and August, and finished the postseason with a flurry.

Hitting

A true professional in all aspects of his game, Damon is a dedicated worker who comes to play every day. As a leadoff hitter, getting on base is imperative. Damon's hit total dropped in 2001, but his batting eye and patience remained intact. While he sprays the ball and relies on the little game, Damon also can turn on a pitch, displaying surprising power. He's committed to playing the best he can, never complains, and never said a negative word during his early season struggles at the plate last year.

Baserunning & Defense

Speed is another important part of Damon's total package. He's a daring runner on the bases, able to steal a bag, take an extra one, and score lots of runs. Even though Damon's offensive numbers tailed in 2001, he still scored over 100 times. He is tremendous defensively and can make highlight plays as often as anyone. His return to center field after the A's acquired Jermaine Dye seemed to stabilize Damon's offense last season. While he batted .283 as a center fielder, his average fell to .222 otherwise.

2002 Outlook

Damon managed to surmount whatever struggles he had after going to Oakland. However, he's now a free agent, so Oakland certainly will have to spend some money to retain his services. He should be able to return to full form in 2002. The current economic picture, though, makes it all but certain that his resurgence will take place somewhere other than the Bay Area.

Position: CF/LF
Bats: L **Throws:** L
Ht: 6' 2" **Wt:** 190

Opening Day Age: 28
Born: 11/5/73 in Fort Riley, KS
ML Seasons: 7
Pronunciation: DAY-mun

Overall Statistics

	G	AB	R	H	D	T	HR	RBI	SB	BB	SO	Avg	OBP	Slg
2001	155	644	108	165	34	4	9	49	27	61	70	.256	.324	.363
Career	958	3701	612	1059	190	51	74	401	183	336	420	.286	.346	.425

Where He Hits the Ball

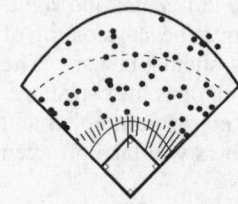 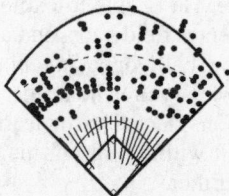

Vs. LHP   **Vs. RHP**

2001 Situational Stats

	AB	H	HR	RBI	Avg		AB	H	HR	RBI	Avg
Home	300	74	2	20	.247	LHP	211	56	3	21	.265
Road	344	91	7	29	.265	RHP	433	109	6	28	.252
First Half	356	85	7	35	.239	Sc Pos	136	38	4	41	.279
Scnd Half	288	80	2	14	.278	Clutch	83	18	1	11	.217

2001 Rankings (American League)

- 3rd in at-bats, plate appearances (719) and lowest percentage of swings on the first pitch (12.6)
- 4th in caught stealing (12) and pitches seen (2,801)
- Led the Athletics in at-bats, triples, stolen bases, caught stealing (12), pitches seen (2,801), plate appearances (719), stolen-base percentage (69.2), bunts in play (27), lowest percentage of swings that missed (12.4), highest percentage of swings put into play (50.9), fewest GDPs per GDP situation (6.4%), on-base percentage for a leadoff hitter (.324), highest percentage of extra bases taken as a runner (56.1) and lowest percentage of swings on the first pitch (12.6)

Jermaine Dye

2001 Season

It must have been deja vu all over again for Jermaine Dye last year. He began the season with a promising but untested Kansas City team that quickly fell out of the pennant chase. The Royals were missing tablesetter Johnny Damon, who had been dealt during the offseason. But by the trading deadline, Dye was reunited with Damon, this time in Oakland. Inserted into the No. 4 slot in the A's order, Dye played stellar defense and performed well with the bat.

Hitting

Although Dye had produced some good offensive stats in recent seasons, he was an aggressive and not always selective hitter with Kansas City. Knowing this, Oakland management wisely let Dye be himself. He responded by playing the A's kind of game, increasing his on-base percentage while maintaining good power. He turns on the ball quickly and supplies a presence that allows the rest of the lineup to relax at the plate. Dye's batting eye is solid and his on-base rate should continue to climb as he settles in with Oakland.

Baserunning & Defense

Dye possesses good speed and is a good and instinctive baserunner. However, stealing never has been a big part of his game. A Gold Glover, he ranks among the best defensive right fielders in baseball. He has an excellent arm, which the league knows and respects. As with the batting order, Dye's presence was the perfect fit that allowed Oakland's outfield to gel.

2002 Outlook

Pending a recovery from the horrific shin break he suffered in last fall's Division Series, Dye will play his first full season with Oakland this year. With Jason Giambi gone, the pressure mounts for Dye to help pick up some of the slack. If Dye could drive in 100 runs with Kansas City, he should be able to produce that and more for the A's.

Position: RF
Bats: R **Throws:** R
Ht: 6' 5" **Wt:** 220

Opening Day Age: 28
Born: 1/28/74 in Vacaville, CA
ML Seasons: 6

Overall Statistics

	G	AB	R	H	D	T	HR	RBI	SB	BB	SO	Avg	OBP	Slg
2001	158	599	91	169	31	1	26	106	9	57	112	.282	.346	.467
Career	706	2577	376	735	151	12	110	425	16	220	494	.285	.341	.481

Where He Hits the Ball

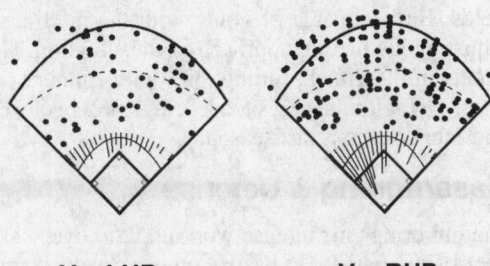

Vs. LHP   **Vs. RHP**

2001 Situational Stats

	AB	H	HR	RBI	Avg		AB	H	HR	RBI	Avg
Home	312	82	16	50	.263	LHP	164	48	4	28	.293
Road	287	87	10	56	.303	RHP	435	121	22	78	.278
First Half	321	90	12	42	.280	Sc Pos	177	49	9	84	.277
Scnd Half	278	79	14	64	.284	Clutch	70	11	1	5	.157

2001 Rankings (American League)

- 2nd in assists in right field (13) and lowest fielding percentage in right field (.979)
- 3rd in errors in right field (6) and lowest batting average in the clutch (.157)
- 4th in sacrifice flies (11)
- Led the Athletics in batting average on a 3-1 count (.545) and cleanup slugging percentage (.556)

Oakland

Jason Giambi

2001 Season

Do you think it's tough to produce an MVP season? Well if it is, Jason Giambi is making it look easy. On the heels of his great 2000, Giambi once again led the A's to postseason play. Though his home run and RBI totals dipped a tad, he slapped a career-high 47 doubles and raised his batting average for the sixth straight season, to .342. Giambi accomplished this with virtually no support from those hitting behind him for the first 90 games.

Hitting

Dedicated and professional, Giambi always wants to improve. He obviously knows how to work a count, but if he gets three hits in a game, he wants four. Giambi has power and can direct it to all fields. He is capable of going with the pitch and adjusting his batting approach to the situation. He excels in the clutch, hitting .397 with runners on base, .571 with the bases loaded, and .355 in close-and-late situations last season.

Baserunning & Defense

Giambi brings his intense work ethic to every aspect of the game. He has become a steady if unspectacular defensive player. He's the leader on the diamond, regularly facilitating communication, thoughtfully calling time and getting clear with his pitcher or fellow infielders to ensure that all are on the same page. He has no speed but succeeded on all four of his stolen base attempts the past two years. His bat and hustle ensure 100 runs or more.

2002 Outlook

Giambi read in these very pages in last year's edition of *The Scouting Notebook* that an MVP was suggested of him prior to his stunning 2000 season. When he saw us during spring training before the 2001 campaign, his first question was, "What did you write this year? Did you predict another MVP?" When we responded that we thought we would quit while we were ahead, Giambi smiled and said, "I can do it." His 2001 numbers prove it. Now, though, Giambi will take aim at the short porch in right field at Yankee Stadium, after signing a seven-year, $120 million deal with New York. Forty homers a year may become standard.

Position: 1B/DH
Bats: L **Throws:** R
Ht: 6' 3" **Wt:** 235

Opening Day Age: 31
Born: 1/8/71 in West Covina, CA
ML Seasons: 7
Pronunciation: gee-OM-bee

Overall Statistics

	G	AB	R	H	D	T	HR	RBI	SB	BB	SO	Avg	OBP	Slg
2001	154	520	109	178	47	2	38	120	2	129	83	.342	.477	.660
Career	953	3398	601	1048	228	7	187	675	9	586	602	.308	.412	.545

Where He Hits the Ball

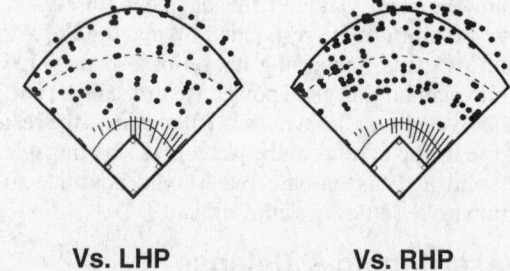

Vs. LHP   **Vs. RHP**

2001 Situational Stats

	AB	H	HR	RBI	Avg		AB	H	HR	RBI	Avg
Home	258	90	27	61	.349	LHP	189	63	11	40	.333
Road	262	88	11	59	.336	RHP	331	115	27	80	.347
First Half	283	91	19	60	.322	Sc Pos	113	40	7	72	.354
Scnd Half	237	87	19	60	.367	Clutch	76	27	5	15	.355

2001 Rankings (American League)

- 1st in doubles, walks, times on base (320), slugging percentage, on-base percentage and on-base percentage vs. righthanded pitchers (.491)
- Led the Athletics in batting average, home runs, runs scored, hits, total bases (343), RBI, walks, HR frequency (13.7 ABs per HR), batting average with runners in scoring position, batting average in the clutch, batting average vs. lefthanded pitchers, batting average vs. righthanded pitchers, slugging percentage vs. lefthanded pitchers (.577), slugging percentage vs. righthanded pitchers (.707), on-base percentage vs. lefthanded pitchers (.451) and batting average with two strikes (.271)
- Led AL first basemen in batting average

Jeremy Giambi

2001 Season

Entering last season, Jeremy Giambi looked like he would battle Adam Piatt for the chance to see considerable action in right field and at designated hitter. While Piatt fell by the wayside, the midseason acquisitions of Ron Gant and Jermaine Dye seemed to add new competition. But Giambi grabbed the DH spot with a tremendous July (.327 average and 18 RBI) and never looked back, establishing nice baseline totals in his first major league season with at least 400 plate appearances.

Hitting

Giambi is a very good hitter who uses all the fields to spray the ball. But he also can go deep without warning. He was effective in tough situations last year, batting .341 with runners in scoring position and two outs. He is still developing, and could increase all his numbers with a full season of play. He is capable of blasting 30 homers and sustaining a .300 average.

Baserunning & Defense

Leg injuries—particularly to his hamstrings and quads—have really hampered Giambi's running game. He did swipe 41 bases as a minor leaguer (in contrast, his brother Jason stole four), though only once did he steal more than nine in a season. But those quaky wheels have not allowed anyone to see what he can do with Oakland. He's attempted just two steals in the majors, getting nailed both times. Defensively, you'd like to keep him away from his glove, thus allowing him to commune with his bat as much as possible.

2002 Outlook

Now 27 years of age, Giambi has yet to crack 450 plate appearances in a big league season. But that threshold may fall in 2002, unless David Justice cuts into his at-bats too deeply. If he plays somewhere pretty much full-time, twenty homers and 35 doubles are reasonable power goals, and he could score close to 100 runs if he hits in the No. 2 slot. Should he bat lower in the order, the runs naturally would drop while his RBI might increase. The effect that the departure of big brother Jason has on "Little G" also should be monitored.

Position: DH/RF/LF/1B
Bats: L **Throws:** L
Ht: 6' 0" **Wt:** 200

Opening Day Age: 27
Born: 9/30/74 in San Jose, CA
ML Seasons: 4
Pronunciation: gee-OM-bee

Overall Statistics

	G	AB	R	H	D	T	HR	RBI	SB	BB	SO	Avg	OBP	Slg
2001	124	371	64	105	26	0	12	57	0	63	83	.283	.391	.450
Career	336	977	146	266	53	3	27	149	0	146	220	.272	.369	.416

Where He Hits the Ball

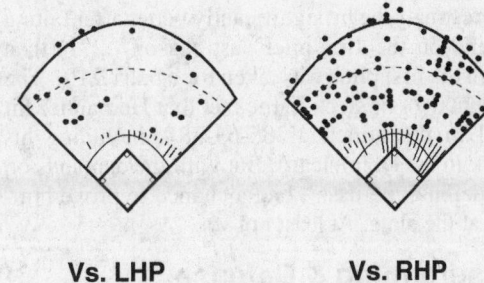

Vs. LHP   **Vs. RHP**

2001 Situational Stats

	AB	H	HR	RBI	Avg		AB	H	HR	RBI	Avg
Home	192	51	5	26	.266	LHP	72	18	3	10	.250
Road	179	54	7	31	.302	RHP	299	87	9	47	.291
First Half	165	48	4	19	.291	Sc Pos	100	29	0	40	.290
Scnd Half	206	57	8	38	.277	Clutch	60	16	1	10	.267

2001 Rankings (American League)

- 7th in errors in left field (3)
- 8th in lowest percentage of swings put into play (36.0)
- 10th in lowest batting average with the bases loaded (.118)
- Led the Athletics in batting average on an 0-2 count (.263)

Ramon Hernandez

2001 Season

If part of Oakland's success and mystique is the seemingly sudden appearance of young stars, Ramon Hernandez represents the model as well as anyone. Fast-tracked into a starting role in 2000, Hernandez' sophomore season included better defense, especially in holding baserunners and working with the young pitching staff. His offensive totals also improved, especially over the second half. After hitting just four home runs through July 15, he blasted 11 more the rest of the way.

Hitting

Hernandez is the best hitter on the team at going the opposite way, and the Athletics' inner circle maintains he is the best two-strike hitter in the league. Interestingly, he hit significantly better after falling behind on the first pitch last season (.271) than when the first pitch was taken for a ball (.219). The A's put a lot of stock in the fact that Hernandez hit well in the minors (.286-65-385, including his work in the Dominican). But with the demands on his defense, he hasn't had a chance to prove himself at the plate. At least not yet.

Baserunning & Defense

Defense was one of the knocks against Hernandez following the 2000 campaign. But he is a hard worker who listens to his coaches. And Ramon significantly improved his defensive play last season. He handled 168 more chances behind the dish, committing two fewer errors and participating in twice as many double plays (15). After spending much of spring training and the early season focusing on his footwork, Hernandez modestly improved his rate of runners caught stealing, from 22 percent in 2000 to 25 percent in 2001. Like most other backstops, he is not much of a threat on the bases.

2002 Outlook

Hernandez' future is as bright as he wants it to be. He's well thought of, possesses great tools, and has the good fortune of competing on a strong team. The young catcher is getting close to the 20-homer standard he should be able to reach on a regular basis over the next few years.

Position: C
Bats: R **Throws:** R
Ht: 6' 0" **Wt:** 227

Opening Day Age: 25
Born: 5/20/76 in Caracas, VZ
ML Seasons: 3
Pronunciation: ruh-MOWN

Overall Statistics

	G	AB	R	H	D	T	HR	RBI	SB	BB	SO	Avg	OBP	Slg
2001	136	453	55	115	25	0	15	60	1	37	68	.254	.316	.408
Career	319	1008	120	254	51	0	32	143	3	93	143	.252	.321	.398

Where He Hits the Ball

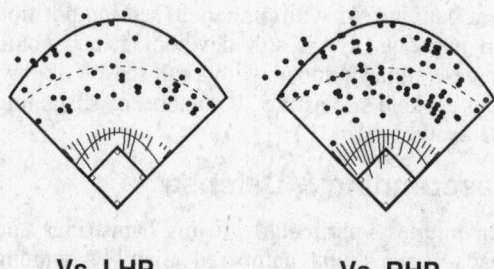

Vs. LHP   **Vs. RHP**

2001 Situational Stats

	AB	H	HR	RBI	Avg		AB	H	HR	RBI	Avg
Home	222	63	5	36	.284	LHP	162	39	5	16	.241
Road	231	52	10	24	.225	RHP	291	76	10	44	.261
First Half	250	56	4	26	.224	Sc Pos	116	28	3	42	.241
Scnd Half	203	59	11	34	.291	Clutch	69	15	3	6	.217

2001 Rankings (American League)

- 1st in errors at catcher (11)
- 3rd in highest percentage of runners caught stealing as a catcher (25.2)
- Led the Athletics in sacrifice bunts (9), highest groundball-flyball ratio (1.5) and batting average on a 3-2 count (.361)

Tim Hudson

2001 Season

Coming off a 20-win season in 2000, when he finished second in the American League Cy Young voting, Tim Hudson was clearly the ace of Oakland's staff. While the emergence of teammates Barry Zito and Mark Mulder last season may make some wonder, the reality is that Hudson took the ball for the third straight year in his cool, tough fashion. He refused to give way to hitters and tied for fourth in the league with 18 wins. His also performed well in the playoffs last fall, surrendering just one run over 9.2 innings versus the Yankees.

Pitching

The nicest of guys off the field, Hudson becomes Mr. Hyde once he hits the hill. And "hide" is exactly what most hitters did versus Hudson, as they had a difficult time reaching base. When Hudson gains command of his fastball—something that often takes three to four innings—the rest of his package falls into place. The fastball clocks in at around 93 MPH, and he works a wicked splitter, a changeup and a slider into the mix, effectively keeping hitters off balance. Part of this is due to his delivery, which has a similar arm action on all his pitches. When Hudson is on the mound, he's in charge.

Defense

Hudson threw 33 more innings in 2001 than the previous year, pushing up all of his totals. Though he did make one more error, he also handled 30 more chances and recorded 23 more assists. He does have a slow delivery which gives runners a chance to steal, but that too is improving. In 2000, only 11 percent of basestealers were erased on his watch, but last year his caught-stealing mark rose to 23 percent.

2002 Outlook

Hudson is clearly established as one of the best starters in the major leagues. He is tough, smart and knows how to win. Expect solid, consistent numbers in 2002 and beyond. He is the A's starter you probably want to hand the ball to when you most need a win.

Position: SP
Bats: R **Throws:** R
Ht: 6' 0" **Wt:** 160

Opening Day Age: 26
Born: 7/14/75 in Columbus, GA
ML Seasons: 3

Overall Statistics

	W	L	Pct.	ERA	G	GS	Sv	IP	H	BB	SO	HR	Ratio
2001	18	9	.667	3.37	35	35	0	235.0	216	71	181	20	1.22
Career	49	17	.742	3.61	88	88	0	573.2	506	215	482	52	1.26

How Often He Throws Strikes

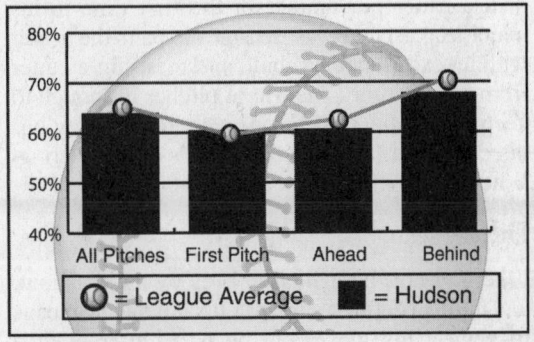

○ = League Average ■ = Hudson

2001 Situational Stats

	W	L	ERA	Sv	IP		AB	H	HR	RBI	Avg
Home	7	4	3.42	0	108.0	LHB	461	118	11	48	.256
Road	11	5	3.33	0	127.0	RHB	422	98	9	43	.232
First Half	9	5	3.02	0	131.0	Sc Pos	186	44	7	70	.237
Scnd Half	9	4	3.81	0	104.0	Clutch	78	16	0	2	.205

2001 Rankings (American League)

- 1st in games started and highest groundball-flyball ratio allowed (2.3)
- 2nd in innings pitched, pickoff throws (178) and errors at pitcher (5)
- 3rd in batters faced (980)
- 4th in wins, lowest slugging percentage allowed (.350) and lowest fielding percentage at pitcher (.928)
- 5th in ERA, pitches thrown (3,593) and highest stolen-base percentage allowed (77.4)
- Led the Athletics in ERA, losses, innings pitched, hits allowed, batters faced (980), wild pitches (9), pitches thrown (3,593), pickoff throws (178), stolen bases allowed (24) and lowest batting average allowed with runners in scoring position

Jason Isringhausen

2001 Season

Jason Isringhausen's struggles during the second half of the 2000 campaign returned in early 2001, when he blew six save opportunities in May and June. But "Izzy" got it back together and was deadly over the season's second half, converting 17 of 20 opportunities. He logged 43 save opportunities overall, a career high. He also registered a nice ratio of 74 strikeouts to 23 walks. He was dominating in postseason play, saving both Oakland victories.

Pitching

Depending heavily on his fastball, Isringhausen brings it at 96-97 MPH, helping him whiff more than a batter per inning for the first time in his major league career last season. He pairs the heater with an excellent curveball, and tosses in a cutter from time to time. The trio of pitches is enough to keep most hitters off balance, as long as Izzy has his command. When he does, he's overpowering. When he doesn't, leads can evaporate.

Defense

Like it or not, Isringhausen lives by the strikeout, and his own defense shows it. It's not that he means to neglect his glove, but he is a closer, with a closer's mentality. His focus is the hitter and not much else. That means he makes some errors and runners can take advantage of him on the bases. In his two years with Oakland, none of the 17 burglars who tried to steal have been pegged out. In fact, 27 of 28 have been successful over the past three seasons.

2002 Outlook

The Athletics liked Isringhausen, and he liked it in Oakland. But he could command a closer's salary, and Oakland management was reluctant to meet those demands. Isringhausen took a little less money to join the team near his hometown, the Cardinals, signing a four-year deal worth close to $30 million. With Izzy now pitching in a fastball league, look for his homers allowed and blown saves to increase while his save totals hold in the range of past seasons.

Position: RP
Bats: R **Throws:** R
Ht: 6' 3" **Wt:** 210

Opening Day Age: 29
Born: 9/7/72 in Brighton, IL
ML Seasons: 6
Pronunciation: IS-ring-how-zin
Nickname: Izzy

Overall Statistics

	W	L	Pct.	ERA	G	GS	Sv	IP	H	BB	SO	HR	Ratio
2001	4	3	.571	2.65	65	0	34	71.1	54	23	74	5	1.08
Career	28	29	.491	4.13	211	52	76	499.1	503	215	376	42	1.44

How Often He Throws Strikes

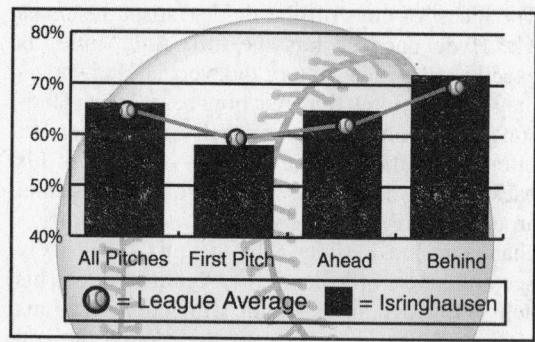

○ = League Average ■ = Isringhausen

2001 Situational Stats

	W	L	ERA	Sv	IP			AB	H	HR	RBI	Avg
Home	3	2	2.05	17	44.0	LHB		154	37	3	13	.240
Road	1	1	3.62	17	27.1	RHB		112	17	2	15	.152
First Half	2	2	2.63	17	37.2	Sc Pos		80	17	2	25	.213
Scnd Half	2	1	2.67	17	33.2	Clutch		180	39	4	26	.217

2001 Rankings (American League)

- 1st in blown saves (9)
- 4th in lowest save percentage (79.1)
- 5th in save opportunities (43)
- 6th in saves
- 7th in most strikeouts per nine innings in relief (9.3) and games finished (54)
- 9th in fewest baserunners allowed per nine innings in relief (9.7) and relief ERA (2.65)
- Led the Athletics in saves, games finished (54), save opportunities (43), save percentage (79.1), blown saves (9), relief ERA (2.65), lowest batting average allowed in relief (.203), most strikeouts per nine innings in relief (9.3) and fewest baserunners allowed per nine innings in relief (9.7)

Terrence Long

Position: CF/LF/RF
Bats: L **Throws:** L
Ht: 6' 1" **Wt:** 190

Opening Day Age: 26
Born: 2/29/76 in Montgomery, AL
ML Seasons: 3

2001 Season

Opening last season as Oakland's starting center fielder, Terrence Long picked right up where he left off at the end of 2000. He played in all 162 regular season games, before getting at least one hit in all five A's playoff games. His two-homer outburst in the Division Series opener helped keep the A's on what seemed an unstoppable path. Long did all that was asked during the campaign, changing defensive positions to accommodate trades and injuries, and pretty much improving all facets of his game.

Hitting

Long is an athlete with a huge upside. He was a highly regarded prospect and has delivered two solid offensive seasons. But he still is getting by on talent as he learns the finer aspects of the game. He has excellent gap power, and while his home run total dropped, Long is fully capable of a .300-30-100 season. Though his overall average dipped five points, his numbers against righthanded and lefthanded pitchers were more consistent. Over the course of the season he hit in almost every spot in the lineup.

Baserunning & Defense

Possessed with great speed, Long is a dangerous baserunner who has the ability to steal 20 bases and score 100 runs on a regular basis. He has a good glove and arm, and though he still is not a total left fielder, he improved dramatically over the 62 games he played there in 2001. He played at least 28 games in the other two outfield spots as well.

2002 Outlook

Long agreed to a four-year, $11.6 million contract extension last August. He has nowhere to go but up at this point, as he becomes an established outfielder on a veteran club. If Johnny Damon departs, Long is likely to reclaim the center-field job. If Damon re-signs, Long figures to produce equally well in left. The ante is in, and the 26-year-old should be able to not only belt 20-plus homers this season, but also steal 20 bases if the A's let him.

Overall Statistics

	G	AB	R	H	D	T	HR	RBI	SB	BB	SO	Avg	OBP	Slg
2001	162	629	90	178	37	4	12	85	9	52	103	.283	.335	.412
Career	303	1216	194	346	71	8	30	165	14	95	182	.285	.335	.430

Where He Hits the Ball

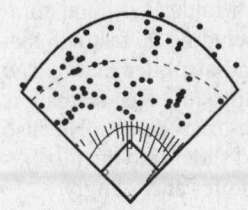
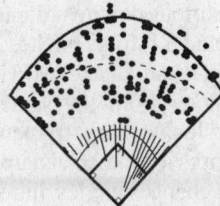

Vs. LHP   **Vs. RHP**

2001 Situational Stats

	AB	H	HR	RBI	Avg		AB	H	HR	RBI	Avg
Home	298	79	6	37	.265	LHP	227	63	4	30	.278
Road	331	99	6	48	.299	RHP	402	115	8	55	.286
First Half	338	92	9	44	.272	Sc Pos	167	48	1	63	.287
Scnd Half	291	86	3	41	.296	Clutch	87	26	0	12	.299

2001 Rankings (American League)

- 1st in games played
- 2nd in lowest cleanup slugging percentage (.423)
- 6th in GDPs (17)
- 7th in singles and errors in left field (3)
- 8th in at-bats and errors in center field (3)
- 10th in hits
- Led the Athletics in hits, singles, triples, strikeouts, GDPs (17) and games played

Mark Mulder

2001 Season

Mark Mulder enjoyed a breakthrough season in 2001. After his somewhat disappointing (9-10, 5.44) rookie campaign, the cool lefthander demonstrated why he had been the Athletics' first round pick (second overall) in 1998. While Mulder's 5-0, 2.27 May showed he was headed in the right direction, it was his three July shutouts that were pivotal in generating Oakland's spectacular second half. Mulder finished the season with totals that ranked among the elite in baseball, including an American League-high 21 victories.

Pitching

The lanky Mulder has a distinct advantage over hitters, with a height that forces hitters to confront a serious downward angle. Mulder has good command of four pitches, including a fastball that clocks around 93 MPH, and a splitter that he can deliver from the same arm slot. His fastball is explosive with tremendous movement. He also works a good changeup and slider into the mix. As he changes angles, hitters suffer accordingly.

Defense

While Mulder is quick to get to balls hit off the mound, he does boot one occasionally. A solid athlete, he holds runners reasonably well, with 18 of 26 would-be thieves succeeding against him. A quick lefty, Mulder's move to first base is good now, and will improve even further with experience.

2002 Outlook

Mulder signed a new four-year, $14.2 million deal near the end of the 2001 season. That, along with reaching 20 wins for the first time, solidifies his standing not only in the Athletics' rotation, but among the top starters in the American League as well. If Tim Hudson is the "gamer" on Oakland's staff and Barry Zito has the best stuff, Mulder is presently the most complete-looking pitcher of the three. Repeating a 20-win season is no easy task, but Mulder has a good chance. On the Athletics, his future Cy Young competition could come primarily from his teammates.

Position: SP
Bats: L **Throws:** L
Ht: 6' 6" **Wt:** 200

Opening Day Age: 24
Born: 8/5/77 in South Holland, IL
ML Seasons: 2

Overall Statistics

	W	L	Pct.	ERA	G	GS	Sv	IP	H	BB	SO	HR	Ratio
2001	21	8	.724	3.45	34	34	0	229.1	214	51	153	16	1.16
Career	30	18	.625	4.25	61	61	0	383.1	405	120	241	38	1.37

How Often He Throws Strikes

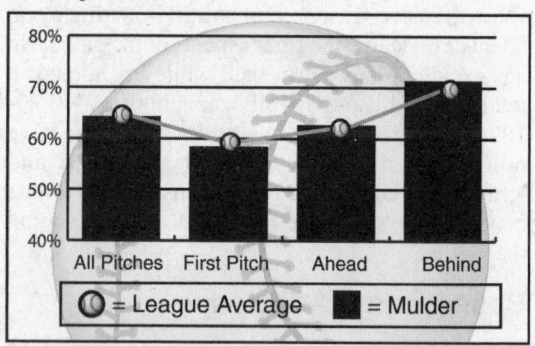

= League Average ■ = Mulder

2001 Situational Stats

	W	L	ERA	Sv	IP		AB	H	HR	RBI	Avg
Home	11	2	2.69	0	107.0	LHB	198	48	5	18	.242
Road	10	6	4.12	0	122.1	RHB	662	166	11	60	.251
First Half	9	6	3.77	0	119.1	Sc Pos	170	44	4	57	.259
Scnd Half	12	2	3.11	0	110.0	Clutch	64	17	2	7	.266

2001 Rankings (American League)

- 1st in wins, shutouts (4), GDPs induced (26) and lowest ERA at home
- 2nd in complete games (6), highest groundball-flyball ratio allowed (1.9) and fewest home runs allowed per nine innings (.63)
- 3rd in games started, pickoff throws (172) and lowest slugging percentage allowed (.349)
- 4th in highest strikeout-walk ratio (3.0)
- Led the Athletics in wins, complete games (6), winning percentage, highest strikeout-walk ratio (3.0), lowest on-base percentage allowed (.294), most run support per nine innings (5.8), fewest home runs allowed per nine innings (.63), most GDPs induced per nine innings (1.0) and fewest walks per nine innings (2.0)

Miguel Tejada

2001 Season

Miguel Tejada might not have been a household name when we entered the new century. But after back-to-back seasons of 30+ homers and 100+ RBI, he has demonstrated that he is indeed among the best middle infielders in the game. Tejada assembled fairly even halves last year, hitting for more power and average over the first half, but driving in more teammates after the All-Star break. Perhaps most importantly, he was always there, playing in all 162 games during the regular season.

Hitting

After improving his plate presence in each of his previous seasons in the majors, Tejada was more undisciplined in 2001. But while he walked less and reached base less often, he did improve his strikeout rate. He enjoyed some serious power streaks, such as the three-day run in May when he slammed three homers and drove in nine runs. While Tejada is capable of hitting the ball to all fields, most of his power appears to be down the left field line.

Baserunning & Defense

There is little on the diamond that Tejada can't do with evident ease, including playing defense and running the bases. With some experience under his belt, he makes the routine plays at shortstop. He also turns in his share of spectacular ones, showing good range. Tejada reached double digits in steals for the first time last season, and probably could steal 20 if afforded the opportunity. Scoring 100 runs is now normal for him.

2002 Outlook

Tejada has improved dramatically in three full-time seasons with Oakland. And he'll still be just 25 years of age on Opening Day. Any future strides may result in a more rounded game. Tejada could raise his average and improve his baserunning and defensive skills. He is a star in a key spot on a great team, with nowhere to go but up.

Position: SS
Bats: R **Throws:** R
Ht: 5' 9" **Wt:** 188

Opening Day Age: 25
Born: 5/25/76 in Bani, DR
ML Seasons: 5
Pronunciation:
mee-GHEL tay-HA-duh

Overall Statistics

	G	AB	R	H	D	T	HR	RBI	SB	BB	SO	Avg	OBP	Slg
2001	162	622	107	166	31	3	31	113	11	43	89	.267	.326	.476
Career	612	2286	368	587	119	11	95	367	32	196	393	.257	.324	.443

Where He Hits the Ball

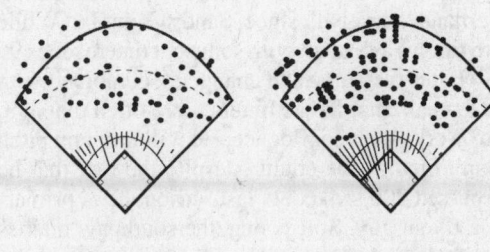

Vs. LHP   **Vs. RHP**

2001 Situational Stats

	AB	H	HR	RBI	Avg		AB	H	HR	RBI	Avg
Home	302	79	17	59	.262	LHP	187	51	8	35	.273
Road	320	87	14	54	.272	RHP	435	115	23	78	.264
First Half	340	92	19	55	.271	Sc Pos	164	50	11	83	.305
Scnd Half	282	74	12	58	.262	Clutch	90	24	1	6	.267

2001 Rankings (American League)

- 1st in games played
- 2nd in errors at shortstop (20)
- 4th in lowest fielding percentage at shortstop (.973)
- 6th in steals of third (6)
- Led the Athletics in games played and steals of third (6)

Oakland

Barry Zito

2001 Season

Paradoxically, the most free-spirited presence on the dynamite Athletics was also the major league's best pitcher over the final two months of last season. That would be Barry Zito, who was named the American League's Pitcher of the Month in both August and September, when he went 9-1 with a 1.14 ERA over 10 starts during that stretch. His brilliance continued into the postseason, when Zito held the Yankees to two hits and one run over eight innings. Sadly, his hitting mates ran into Mike Mussina and Mariano Rivera, who combined to allow six hits but no runs.

Pitching

Zito possesses what looks like the best lefthanded overhand curveball since Sandy Koufax. While Zito throws a fastball with some cut that reaches 90 MPH, it is the curve and changeup, combined with the fastball, that freeze hitters more often than not. Zito works with confidence. He will hurl any pitch at any time in the count. Despite the fact that he surpassed 200 strikeouts last season, he is primarily a flyout guy. Still young, the southpaw pitches best with the bags empty and in non-pressure situations. That figures to change as he gains more experience and related confidence.

Defense

Zito is generally quick to the plate, but he is still learning to hold baserunners. For a lefty, his move to first base isn't anything special. He is adequate off the mound, although he did commit a pair of miscues last season. Just like with the rest of his game, he'll become a more complete pitcher as his experience and knowledge begin to match his ability.

2002 Outlook

Zito was chosen with the ninth overall selection in the 1999 draft and was working in the big leagues about a year later. And one year after that, his 11 wins following the All-Star break ranked among the most in the majors. Expect that second-half surge to have a carryover effect in 2002. He boasts the best stuff on the Athletics' staff, and he should show it in the coming season.

Position: SP
Bats: L **Throws:** L
Ht: 6' 4" **Wt:** 205

Opening Day Age: 23
Born: 5/13/78 in Las Vegas, NV
ML Seasons: 2

Overall Statistics

	W	L	Pct.	ERA	G	GS	Sv	IP	H	BB	SO	HR	Ratio
2001	17	8	.680	3.49	35	35	0	214.1	184	80	205	18	1.23
Career	24	12	.667	3.25	49	49	0	307.0	248	125	283	24	1.21

How Often He Throws Strikes

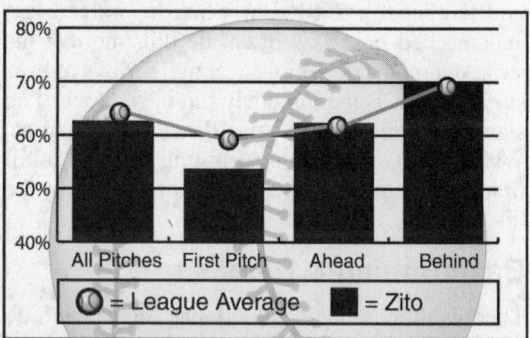

⊙ = League Average   ■ = Zito

2001 Situational Stats

	W	L	ERA	Sv	IP		AB	H	HR	RBI	Avg
Home	9	3	3.71	0	111.2	LHB	137	32	3	18	.234
Road	8	5	3.24	0	102.2	RHB	663	152	15	61	.229
First Half	6	6	4.58	0	112.0	Sc Pos	162	48	2	56	.296
Scnd Half	11	2	2.29	0	102.1	Clutch	23	7	2	5	.304

2001 Rankings (American League)

- 1st in games started
- 2nd in lowest slugging percentage allowed (.345) and most pitches thrown per batter (3.94)
- 3rd in lowest batting average allowed (.230), most strikeouts per nine innings (8.6) and fewest GDPs induced per nine innings (0.4)
- 4th in shutouts (2), strikeouts and lowest batting average allowed vs. righthanded batters
- Led the Athletics in walks allowed, hit batsmen (13), strikeouts, runners caught stealing (11), lowest batting average allowed (.230), lowest slugging percentage allowed (.345), lowest ERA on the road, lowest batting average allowed vs. righthanded batters and most strikeouts per nine innings (8.6)

Chad Bradford

Position: RP
Bats: R **Throws:** R
Ht: 6' 5" **Wt:** 205

Opening Day Age: 27
Born: 9/14/74 in
Jackson, MS
ML Seasons: 4

Overall Statistics

	W	L	Pct.	ERA	G	GS	Sv	IP	H	BB	SO	HR	Ratio
2001	2	1	.667	2.70	35	0	1	36.2	41	6	34	6	1.28
Career	5	2	.714	3.51	79	0	2	84.2	90	19	54	7	1.29

2001 Situational Stats

	W	L	ERA	Sv	IP		AB	H	HR	RBI	Avg
Home	2	0	2.41	1	18.2	LHB	40	12	3	6	.300
Road	0	1	3.00	0	18.0	RHB	106	29	3	15	.274
First Half	2	1	2.79	1	29.0	Sc Pos	43	14	2	16	.326
Scnd Half	0	0	2.35	0	7.2	Clutch	19	8	2	8	.421

2001 Season

Oakland acquired Chad Bradford from the White Sox last December for catcher Miguel Olivo. Bradford was limited during the spring but pitched well. He played musical chairs with Luis Vizcaino as they swapped roles between Oakland and Sacramento during the campaign. But by mid-August, Bradford had returned to stay. He wound up notching a solid season, making the playoff roster, and seeing limited action in the Division Series.

Pitching & Defense

A submariner, Bradford delivers his fastball at around 85-86 MPH. He balances a wide, sweeping curveball that points itself downward just enough to rattle hitters. He also has a changeup, but since inducing whiffs and grounders from righthanded batters is his current forte, there is little opportunity to use the offspeed pitch. Primarily a groundball hurler, Bradford fields his position well. However, he is slow to the plate, which baserunners exploit.

2002 Outlook

Some changes probably are due in Oakland's bullpen, and Bradford's role should broaden. Still, he will face lefties selectively until he shows he can get them out consistently. But Bradford should land a roster spot and log considerably more work, with results similar to those of last year.

Gil Heredia

Position: SP
Bats: R **Throws:** R
Ht: 6' 1" **Wt:** 221

Opening Day Age: 36
Born: 10/26/65 in
Nogales, AZ
ML Seasons: 10
Pronunciation:
her-RAY-dee-uh

Overall Statistics

	W	L	Pct.	ERA	G	GS	Sv	IP	H	BB	SO	HR	Ratio
2001	7	8	.467	5.58	24	18	0	109.2	144	29	48	27	1.58
Career	57	51	.528	4.46	267	128	4	954.0	1079	221	547	115	1.36

2001 Situational Stats

	W	L	ERA	Sv	IP		AB	H	HR	RBI	Avg
Home	4	5	5.04	0	64.1	LHB	234	68	8	23	.291
Road	3	3	6.35	0	45.1	RHB	221	76	19	43	.344
First Half	4	7	6.23	0	82.1	Sc Pos	98	26	5	36	.265
Scnd Half	3	1	3.62	0	27.1	Clutch	14	6	2	5	.429

2001 Season

While Gil Heredia was a pleasant surprise in 2000, perhaps fans and analysts should have paid more attention to his 0-2 record and 7.43 ERA in five August starts. In retrospect, his 2001 season looked a lot like August of 2000. Ineffective and overshadowed by Oakland's other stellar starters, Heredia was replaced in the rotation and made only six appearances over the final 10 weeks of the season.

Pitching & Defense

Control and the ability to change speeds are at the heart of Heredia's success. Topping out in the high 80s, he has to be around the plate with his cut fastball, sinking fastball and slider. One of his biggest problems has been righthanded hitters, who belted Heredia for a .344 average last year. Heredia holds runners well, but did make a career-high two errors in 2001.

2002 Outlook

Heredia's inability to make the postseason roster last fall speaks volumes. Odds are that the free agent will latch on elsewhere. In context, he did win 28 games over the previous two seasons, so the 36-year-old probably will get a few more chances in these pitching-desperate days. But wherever Heredia goes, he likely will not receive the kind of support he enjoyed during his Oakland tenure.

Oakland

Erik Hiljus

Position: SP
Bats: R **Throws:** R
Ht: 6' 5" **Wt:** 230

Opening Day Age: 29
Born: 12/25/72 in Panorama City, CA
ML Seasons: 3
Pronunciation: hill-yus

Overall Statistics

	W	L	Pct.	ERA	G	GS	Sv	IP	H	BB	SO	HR	Ratio
2001	5	0	1.000	3.41	16	11	0	66.0	70	21	67	7	1.38
Career	5	0	1.000	3.79	25	11	0	78.1	82	27	70	10	1.39

2001 Situational Stats

	W	L	ERA	Sv	IP		AB	H	HR	RBI	Avg
Home	2	0	3.00	0	30.0	LHB	145	36	3	15	.248
Road	3	0	3.75	0	36.0	RHB	121	34	4	17	.281
First Half	1	0	2.25	0	8.0	Sc Pos	70	21	2	25	.300
Scnd Half	4	0	3.57	0	58.0	Clutch	4	1	0	1	.250

2001 Season

At 28 years of age, but with nine minor league seasons and only 12 major league innings behind him, Erik Hiljus signed a free-agent contract with the Athletics last December. Oakland management knew what it was getting, as Hiljus went 8-5 with a 3.63 ERA at Triple-A before being summoned to The Net. There he replaced Gil Heredia in the rotation and responded with a 5-0 mark in eleven starts.

Pitching & Defense

Hiljus works hard at everything he does. A strike-out pitcher, he comes over the top with a fastball that touches 94 MPH. Command is an issue, though his fastball and slider make for an effective combination when he's on. Hiljus didn't commit an error last season, but then he had only five chances. His slide step move to first needs some work, as 12 of 13 basestealers were successful.

2002 Outlook

A late bloomer, Hiljus fits well within the mold of castaways from other organizations who succeed in Oakland. As part of one of the most vaunted rotations in baseball, he should do quite well. Sometimes success is being in the right place at the right time, and Hiljus proves the point. He could reach 10 wins as a full-time starter.

Cory Lidle

Position: SP
Bats: R **Throws:** R
Ht: 5'11" **Wt:** 180

Opening Day Age: 30
Born: 3/22/72 in Hollywood, CA
ML Seasons: 4
Pronunciation: LIE-dell

Overall Statistics

	W	L	Pct.	ERA	G	GS	Sv	IP	H	BB	SO	HR	Ratio
2001	13	6	.684	3.59	29	29	0	188.0	170	47	118	23	1.15
Career	25	14	.641	4.00	119	43	2	371.1	378	98	238	43	1.28

2001 Situational Stats

	W	L	ERA	Sv	IP		AB	H	HR	RBI	Avg
Home	8	5	4.03	0	114.0	LHB	380	81	14	32	.213
Road	5	1	2.92	0	74.0	RHB	322	89	9	42	.276
First Half	2	4	4.27	0	90.2	Sc Pos	139	39	5	49	.281
Scnd Half	11	2	2.96	0	97.1	Clutch	37	5	1	3	.135

2001 Season

A promising prospect plays well but languishes in the minor leagues, either because his team has no faith, or because a spot never opens. Enter Billy Beane, savior of the Cory Lidle's of the world, who snatched the righthander from Tampa Bay when the Rays weren't looking. Lidle rewarded the A's by becoming a solid No. 4 starter in 2001.

Pitching & Defense

A groundball pitcher, Lidle has a fastball in the low 90s that includes some sink. He also throws a good splitter that breaks downward effectively, and tosses in a curveball and changeup, all with good command. To be successful he must keep the ball down, something he managed last season. Lidle gets off the mound adequately and is the best on the club at holding baserunners.

2002 Outlook

Lidle established himself in 2001 as part of what may be the best rotation in baseball. He apparently has always had good stuff and just needed a chance, and he should continue to excel. Whatever natural talent Lidle possesses may be made even sharper by pitching on such a stellar staff. As is the case with the Braves' talented rotation, success and skill sometimes seem to breed themselves. The A's may have picked up the mantle.

Mike Magnante

Position: RP
Bats: L **Throws:** L
Ht: 6' 1" **Wt:** 185

Opening Day Age: 36
Born: 6/17/65 in Glendale, CA
ML Seasons: 11
Pronunciation: mag-nan-tee

Overall Statistics

	W	L	Pct.	ERA	G	GS	Sv	IP	H	BB	SO	HR	Ratio
2001	3	1	.750	2.77	65	0	0	55.1	50	13	23	7	1.14
Career	26	30	.464	3.99	452	19	3	589.0	628	223	336	43	1.44

2001 Situational Stats

	W	L	ERA	Sv	IP		AB	H	HR	RBI	Avg
Home	1	0	3.18	0	28.1	LHB	87	20	1	6	.230
Road	2	1	2.33	0	27.0	RHB	118	30	6	18	.254
First Half	0	1	2.76	0	29.1	Sc Pos	48	8	1	18	.167
Scnd Half	3	0	2.77	0	26.0	Clutch	80	14	0	6	.175

2001 Season

After a disappointing 2000, Mike Magnante last year logged his best numbers since 1997. He had surrendered more walks than strikeouts and a .311 opponents' batting average in 2000, but lowered his average allowed to .244 last season. With runners in scoring position, opponents mustered a meager .167 mark. Magnante's effectiveness earned him a spot on Oakland's postseason roster. He made one appearance in the playoffs.

Pitching & Defense

A southpaw, Magnante is good at retiring lefthanded batters. They averaged just .230 with one home run last season. And when his screwball is working, he is equally tough on righties. Magnante has a decent curve and a fastball in the mid-80's, both of which he uses to set up the screwball. He is adequate at best with the glove, but is very good at holding runners and possesses an excellent move to first base.

2002 Outlook

Oakland exercised its option on Magnante for 2002. He returned to form to fill a needed role in 2001. He also is a veteran voice on a club that is still very young, even with two years of postseason experience. Expect more of the same from Magnante in his 12th big league season.

Jim Mecir

Position: RP
Bats: B **Throws:** R
Ht: 6' 1" **Wt:** 210

Opening Day Age: 31
Born: 5/16/70 in Queens, NY
ML Seasons: 7
Pronunciation: meh-SEER

Overall Statistics

	W	L	Pct.	ERA	G	GS	Sv	IP	H	BB	SO	HR	Ratio
2001	2	8	.200	3.43	54	0	3	63.0	54	26	61	4	1.27
Career	20	19	.513	3.59	255	0	8	331.1	290	144	289	25	1.31

2001 Situational Stats

	W	L	ERA	Sv	IP		AB	H	HR	RBI	Avg
Home	0	3	3.73	2	31.1	LHB	118	23	0	3	.195
Road	2	5	3.13	1	31.2	RHB	116	31	4	25	.267
First Half	2	6	3.54	2	40.2	Sc Pos	67	16	1	23	.239
Scnd Half	0	2	3.22	1	22.1	Clutch	142	38	3	23	.268

2001 Season

Counted upon to lead Oakland's setup support in the late innings, Jim Mecir endured a lot of down time. He signed a three-year, $6.5 million contract extension a month before the season, but suffered two rough stretches involving injuries—a strained calf in June and an inflamed knee in August. He pitched well down the stretch, allowing just two earned runs in 12.1 innings after September 1.

Pitching & Defense

Mecir throws a screwball and is quite a card to play out of the bullpen. While he's good against righthanded batters, he can be devastating versus lefties. He owns a good fastball with movement in the low 90s, a slider, and is working on a splitter. A heady competitor on the mound, he covers his position adequately and is surehanded once he fields the ball. He is quick to the plate, but baserunners still can take advantage of him.

2002 Outlook

The A's already exercised their 2004 option on Mecir in November. He works in front of a new closer in 2002, after the A's parted ways with Jason Isringhausen and traded for Billy Koch. Pending good health, Mecir should pitch nearer his 2000 form in 2002.

Frank Menechino

Position: 2B
Bats: R **Throws:** R
Ht: 5' 9" **Wt:** 175

Opening Day Age: 31
Born: 1/7/71 in Staten Island, NY
ML Seasons: 3
Pronunciation: men-a-keen-o

Overall Statistics

	G	AB	R	H	D	T	HR	RBI	SB	BB	SO	Avg	OBP	Slg
2001	139	471	82	114	22	2	12	60	2	79	97	.242	.369	.374
Career	214	625	113	153	31	3	18	86	3	99	146	.245	.362	.390

2001 Situational Stats

	AB	H	HR	RBI	Avg		AB	H	HR	RBI	Avg
Home	237	55	4	31	.232	LHP	161	51	4	22	.317
Road	234	59	8	29	.252	RHP	310	63	8	38	.203
First Half	278	77	10	43	.277	Sc Pos	110	29	1	42	.264
Scnd Half	193	37	2	17	.192	Clutch	70	19	0	5	.271

2001 Season

Frankie Menechino's role in the Athletics' success last season was a revelation. The tough infielder was another astute Rule 5 selection by Oakland, snatched from the White Sox organization following the 1997 season. After a year and a half on Oakland's bench, he was pushed into an everyday role when Jose Ortiz lost the second base job. Menechino responded with punch and stability, particularly over the first half of the campaign.

Hitting, Baserunning & Defense

True to the A's mold of selectivity, Menechino is a patient hitter who focuses on getting on base. His .369 on-base percentage was the second highest on the club among qualifiers, while his 19 HBP ranked second in the league. The latter stat reveals that whatever Menechino lacks in natural ability, he more than makes up for in desire and intensity. His average speed is helped by good instincts. He has a steady but unspectacular glove and acceptable range. He is strong turning the double play.

2002 Outlook

Menechino probably is not a long-term solution, but he's the team's second sacker for now. Some of his second-half problems last year may have been rooted in fatigue. Expect a more even pace this season, with end results that are similar to 2000.

Olmedo Saenz

Position: DH/1B/3B
Bats: R **Throws:** R
Ht: 6' 0" **Wt:** 185

Opening Day Age: 31
Born: 10/8/70 in Chitre Herrera, Panama
ML Seasons: 4
Pronunciation: SIGNS

Overall Statistics

	G	AB	R	H	D	T	HR	RBI	SB	BB	SO	Avg	OBP	Slg
2001	106	305	33	67	21	1	9	32	0	19	64	.220	.291	.384
Career	284	788	116	206	51	4	29	106	2	66	156	.261	.343	.447

2001 Situational Stats

	AB	H	HR	RBI	Avg		AB	H	HR	RBI	Avg
Home	151	33	6	18	.219	LHP	139	33	4	17	.237
Road	154	34	3	14	.221	RHP	166	34	5	15	.205
First Half	192	44	4	14	.229	Sc Pos	73	8	0	18	.110
Scnd Half	113	23	5	18	.204	Clutch	50	12	4	9	.240

2001 Season

Plagued by injuries for much of the 2000 campaign, Olmedo Saenz arrived at spring training last season ready to claim a large share of Oakland's DH/utility role. He did log major league highs in games played and at-bats, but also endured lows in just about every offensive category in what proved to be a disappointing year.

Hitting, Baserunning & Defense

A valuable bat off the bench, Saenz can deliver a killer blow. He is a hard worker who takes the game seriously. He has a good eye, but doesn't always employ plate discipline. Although he can go with the pitch, he generates most of his power when pulling the ball. Saenz is not particularly fast on the bases, nor is he a threat to steal. He does have a solid arm and can play both corner infield spots, though not as well as either incumbent on the squad.

2002 Outlook

Saenz definitely can hit. The big questions surrounding him concern his ability to play an Oakland-style offense (that is, be more selective), and do so for a full season. With Jason Giambi moving on to New York, Saenz may have a chance to start. But he's more likely to continue his role off the bench.

Jeff Tam

Position: RP
Bats: R **Throws:** R
Ht: 6' 1" **Wt:** 202

Opening Day Age: 31
Born: 8/19/70 in
Fullerton, CA
ML Seasons: 4

Overall Statistics

	W	L	Pct.	ERA	G	GS	Sv	IP	H	BB	SO	HR	Ratio
2001	2	4	.333	3.01	70	0	3	74.2	68	29	44	3	1.30
Career	6	8	.429	3.24	167	0	6	186.1	175	60	106	11	1.26

2001 Situational Stats

	W	L	ERA	Sv	IP		AB	H	HR	RBI	Avg
Home	2	1	1.83	1	39.1	LHB	85	21	1	6	.247
Road	0	3	4.33	2	35.1	RHB	187	47	2	21	.251
First Half	1	3	3.74	3	43.1	Sc Pos	79	18	0	23	.228
Scnd Half	1	1	2.01	0	31.1	Clutch	128	30	3	12	.234

2001 Season

Returning from his surprising and impressive rookie season of 2000, Jeff Tam entered spring training with the setup job at hand. A terrible April (6.08 ERA) and sporadic arm issues resulted in a slight drop in many of his overall numbers. But he was particularly sharp during the months of July and August, when he compiled a 1.00 ERA over 26 games.

Pitching & Defense

Tam's strength is inducing groundballs, which he accomplishes with a good sinking fastball that arrives at around 91 MPH. He also throws a slider in the mid-to-high 80s, and is working on a splitter to increase his effectiveness against lefthanded hitters. Tam's defense is solid, but a deliberate delivery allows most base thieves to succeed.

2002 Outlook

Though Tam pitched well when it counted in 2001, he might be showing signs of a lot of work. While he did log 111.2 innings at Triple-A in 1997, he never had thrown 70-plus innings in consecutive seasons until now. Tam certainly goes into 2002 as a bullpen staple, but faltering will result in Luis Vizcaino or Chad Bradford usurping him.

Luis Vizcaino

Position: RP
Bats: R **Throws:** R
Ht: 5'11" **Wt:** 169

Opening Day Age: 24
Born: 6/1/77 in Bani, DR
ML Seasons: 3
Pronunciation:
VIS-ky-EE-no

Overall Statistics

	W	L	Pct.	ERA	G	GS	Sv	IP	H	BB	SO	HR	Ratio
2001	2	1	.667	4.66	36	0	1	36.2	38	12	31	8	1.36
Career	2	2	.500	5.61	49	0	1	59.1	66	26	51	11	1.55

2001 Situational Stats

	W	L	ERA	Sv	IP		AB	H	HR	RBI	Avg
Home	1	1	1.59	1	17.0	LHB	58	14	4	9	.241
Road	1	0	7.32	0	19.2	RHB	85	24	4	11	.282
First Half	0	0	6.00	0	6.0	Sc Pos	37	9	0	10	.243
Scnd Half	2	1	4.40	1	30.2	Clutch	19	4	1	2	.211

2001 Season

For the second straight year, Luis Vizcaino pitched for the big club in April only to struggle and subsequently get sent down. Effective at Triple-A (2-2, 2.14, seven saves over 27 games), he returned to Oakland after the All-Star break to help with the stretch run. He settled in, demonstrating much more consistency than he previously had at the major league level.

Pitching & Defense

Blessed with a great arm, Vizcaino can bring his fastball in the high 90s. When he's on and pairs the fastball with a splitter and slider, he is very tough to hit. Though his heat commands respect, Vizcaino's slider is his key to success. Getting a good angle and working the ball down is critical. But too often it floats and he pays the price. As a reliever, Vizcaino doesn't devote that much attention to baserunners, but he has a decent glove.

2002 Outlook

After getting settled in 2001, Vizcaino should establish himself as a setup man to begin this season. With Jason Isringhausen gone and the disposition of Billy Koch uncertain, Vizcaino is a key figure in the A's pen. Don't be surprised if he moves into the closer's role within the next year or so.

Oakland

Other Oakland Athletics

Andy Abad (**Pos**: 1B, **Age**: 29, **Bats**: L)

	G	AB	R	H	D	T	HR	RBI	SB	BB	SO	Avg	OBP	Slg
2001	1	1	0	0	0	0	0	0	0	0	0	.000	.000	.000
Career	1	1	0	0	0	0	0	0	0	0	0	.000	.000	.000

Abad produced again in the minors (.301-19-82). After making his major league debut in 2001, he inked a minor league deal with Florida for this year. 2002 Outlook: C

Mark Bellhorn (**Pos**: 2B, **Age**: 27, **Bats**: B)

	G	AB	R	H	D	T	HR	RBI	SB	BB	SO	Avg	OBP	Slg
2001	38	74	11	10	1	2	1	4	0	7	37	.135	.210	.243
Career	126	323	47	64	11	3	7	24	9	44	117	.198	.296	.316

Bellhorn debuted back in 1997, but has made only brief stops in Oakland since. He was traded to the Cubs in the offseason and could compete for an infield job, but he must work on his plate discipline. 2002 Outlook: C

Mike Fyhrie (**Pos**: RHP, **Age**: 32)

	W	L	Pct.	ERA	G	GS	Sv	IP	H	BB	SO	HR	Ratio
2001	0	2	.000	3.15	18	0	0	20.0	18	8	11	1	1.30
Career	0	7	.000	3.84	68	7	0	126.2	137	47	80	13	1.45

Fyhrie successfully began the season as a middle reliever for Chicago. He broke his left arm in May when he was struck by a broken bat. When he healed, he was traded to the A's and continued to succeed. 2002 Outlook: B

Ron Gant (**Pos**: LF/DH, **Age**: 37, **Bats**: R)

	G	AB	R	H	D	T	HR	RBI	SB	BB	SO	Avg	OBP	Slg
2001	93	252	46	65	13	3	10	35	5	35	80	.258	.345	.452
Career	1713	6099	1018	1564	288	49	302	945	239	732	1343	.256	.337	.468

Looking for righthanded power, Oakland traded for Gant on July 3. When he got off to a slow start, the A's decided to trade for Jermaine Dye. His option was declined in the fall and he became a free agent. 2002 Outlook: C

Mark Guthrie (**Pos**: LHP, **Age**: 36)

	W	L	Pct.	ERA	G	GS	Sv	IP	H	BB	SO	HR	Ratio
2001	6	2	.750	4.47	54	0	1	52.1	49	20	52	7	1.32
Career	44	48	.478	4.20	632	43	13	888.0	914	340	710	92	1.41

There was talk of Guthrie starting when he signed in Oakland, but he ended up in the pen as usual. He was traded to the Mets for David Justice. 2002 Outlook: B

John Jaha (**Pos**: DH, **Age**: 35, **Bats**: R)

	G	AB	R	H	D	T	HR	RBI	SB	BB	SO	Avg	OBP	Slg
2001	12	45	2	4	3	0	0	6	0	6	15	.089	.192	.156
Career	826	2775	470	730	126	5	141	490	36	430	686	.263	.369	.465

Jaha began the season recovering from shoulder surgery. He joined the team in May, only to return to the disabled list shortly thereafter. He returned to get one hit in his next 27 at-bats and decided to retire. 2002 Outlook: D

Billy McMillon (**Pos**: LF, **Age**: 30, **Bats**: L)

	G	AB	R	H	D	T	HR	RBI	SB	BB	SO	Avg	OBP	Slg
2001	40	92	7	20	8	1	1	14	1	7	25	.217	.284	.359
Career	151	356	41	91	20	3	7	56	4	37	82	.256	.324	.388

McMillon spent a full season in the majors for the first time. He was in danger of being demoted in June by

Detroit, but was claimed on waivers by Oakland. He had season-ending shoulder surgery in August, and then was released by the A's in November. 2002 Outlook: C

Greg Myers (**Pos**: C/DH, **Age**: 35, **Bats**: L)

	G	AB	R	H	D	T	HR	RBI	SB	BB	SO	Avg	OBP	Slg
2001	58	161	24	36	3	0	11	31	0	21	38	.224	.313	.447
Career	908	2539	267	638	124	7	66	321	3	202	441	.251	.305	.384

In need of a veteran backup, Oakland signed Myers when he was released in June by Baltimore. In games in which he caught, the majority of which were with the A's, pitchers had a combined ERA of 3.15. He re-signed with Oakland in November. 2002 Outlook: C

Adam Piatt (**Pos**: RF, **Age**: 26, **Bats**: R)

	G	AB	R	H	D	T	HR	RBI	SB	BB	SO	Avg	OBP	Slg
2001	36	95	9	20	5	1	0	6	0	13	26	.211	.300	.284
Career	96	252	33	67	10	6	5	29	0	36	70	.266	.357	.413

Platooning in right field, Piatt struggled to build on his 2000 debut. His efforts ended in June when he was diagnosed with viral meningitis. Since recovered, he will play winter ball to be ready for spring. 2002 Outlook: B

Rob Ryan (**Pos**: CF, **Age**: 28, **Bats**: L)

	G	AB	R	H	D	T	HR	RBI	SB	BB	SO	Avg	OBP	Slg
2001	8	8	0	0	0	0	0	0	0	0	6	.000	.000	.000
Career	55	64	8	15	2	1	2	7	0	5	21	.234	.300	.391

Ryan was acquired from Arizona in a midseason trade and batted only .225 for Oakland's Triple-A club. Nevertheless, he is a career .300 minor league hitter, and could be a decent reserve outfielder. 2002 Outlook: C

F.P. Santangelo (**Pos**: 2B, **Age**: 34, **Bats**: B)

	G	AB	R	H	D	T	HR	RBI	SB	BB	SO	Avg	OBP	Slg
2001	32	71	16	14	4	0	0	8	1	11	17	.197	.341	.254
Career	665	1691	258	415	87	14	21	162	37	240	319	.245	.364	.351

Santangelo has made a career out of versatility. He has played six positions for four organizations. He was released in November and will use his versatility to try to land a job. 2002 Outlook: C

Mario Valdez (**Pos**: DH, **Age**: 27, **Bats**: L)

	G	AB	R	H	D	T	HR	RBI	SB	BB	SO	Avg	OBP	Slg
2001	32	54	7	15	1	0	1	8	0	12	18	.278	.418	.352
Career	91	181	18	43	8	0	2	21	1	29	60	.238	.352	.315

Because of his ability to play multiple positions, Valdez made an Opening Day roster for the first time. He can hit for average and some power, but injuries limited his play and ended his season in June. 2002 Outlook: B

Tom Wilson (**Pos**: C, **Age**: 31, **Bats**: R)

	G	AB	R	H	D	T	HR	RBI	SB	BB	SO	Avg	OBP	Slg
2001	9	21	4	4	0	0	2	4	0	1	5	.190	.250	.476
Career	9	21	4	4	0	0	2	4	0	1	5	.190	.250	.476

After ten seasons of minor league catching, Wilson was finally called up to a major league club as an emergency backup. In his very first game with Oakland, he triumphantly hit a game-winning home run. 2002 Outlook: C

Oakland Athletics Minor League Prospects

Organization Overview:

Although trades for Johnny Damon and Jermaine Dye made a big splash, Oakland has become a serious contender through player development. The A's developed Jason Giambi, Miguel Tejada, Eric Chavez and Ramon Hernandez, as well as the core of their rotation, Tim Hudson, Barry Zito and Mark Mulder. As players have come and gone, the farm system has been there to inject new life into the Oakland roster, and it will be called upon again. Replacing Jason Giambi will be a monumental task, and losing Johnny Damon also would hurt. But the biggest losses may have been suffered in the front office. *Baseball America* regularly ranks the A's among the best organizations in baseball, and they will be hurt by losing Director of Player Personnel J.P. Ricciardi and Scouting Director Grady Fuson to other major league organizations.

Freddie Bynum

Position: SS-2B
Bats: L **Throws:** R
Ht: 6' 1" **Wt:** 180
Opening Day Age: 22
Born: 3/15/80 in Wilson, NC

Recent Statistics

	G	AB	R	H	D	THR	RBI	SB	BB	SO	Avg
2000 A Vancouver	72	281	52	72	10	1	1	26	22	31	58	.256
2001 A Modesto	120	440	59	115	19	7	2	46	28	41	95	.261

The A's second-round pick in 2000, Bynum is a shortstop with a great arm and a high ceiling defensively. He showed impressive tools in his debut at short-season Class-A Vancouver, and *Baseball America* named him the Northwest League's best prospect. Drafted out of a small community college, Bynum didn't play much as an amateur, so the jump to high Class-A Modesto in his first full season was a big one. The game was too fast for him at first, but he came on and gained confidence. He can run and he knows how to put the ball into play. Defensively, he has learned to position himself well, and he's very good at ranging and making the tough play. Mastering the routine stuff needs more work.

Eric Byrnes

Position: OF
Bats: R **Throws:** R
Ht: 6' 2" **Wt:** 210
Opening Day Age: 26
Born: 2/16/76 in Redwood City, CA

Recent Statistics

	G	AB	R	H	D	THR	RBI	SB	BB	SO	Avg
2001 AAA Sacramento	100	415	81	120	23	2	20	51	25	33	66	.289
2001 AL Oakland	19	38	9	9	1	0	3	5	1	4	6	.237
2001 MLE	100	397	64	102	19	1	15	40	18	25	68	.257

Scouts haven't been inclined to label Byrnes a prospect, but he's hard to ignore. Through hard work, Byrnes has managed to win a batting title in the high Class-A California League in 1999, develop some power as he's climbed through the A's system, and make himself a pretty solid all-around player. Byrnes doesn't have a picture-perfect swing, but he stroked 20 homers for the first time at Triple-A Sacramento in 2001. He's better suited to playing a corner outfield slot, but he keeps improving defensively. With a .391 career on-base percentage in the minors, he has shown some leadoff ability and could get some work at the top of the A's lineup.

Mark Ellis

Position: SS
Bats: R **Throws:** R
Ht: 5' 11" **Wt:** 180
Opening Day Age: 24
Born: 6/6/77 in Rapid City, SD

Recent Statistics

	G	AB	R	H	D	THR	RBI	SB	BB	SO	Avg
2000 A Wilmington	132	484	83	146	27	4	6	62	25	78	72	.302
2000 AA Wichita	7	22	4	7	1	0	0	4	1	5	5	.318
2001 AAA Sacramento	132	472	71	129	38	0	10	53	21	54	78	.273
2001 MLE	132	453	56	110	32	0	7	42	15	42	81	.243

Defensively, no one in the system is better than Ellis, a ninth-round pick in 1999 who came to Oakland in the Johnny Damon trade. His defensive acumen at short sparked the decision to skip Double-A and test him at Triple-A Sacramento in 2001. He was buried early on at the plate, but he impressed the A's by rebounding nicely to bat .273 and show more power than he had at high Class-A Wilmington the year before. His arm strength is not great, but the A's believe it's not a hindrance to playing short because he positions himself so well to get the ball to first base. A polished player on the left side, his opportunity with the A's may come at second base.

Esteban German

Position: 2B
Bats: R **Throws:** R
Ht: 5' 10" **Wt:** 180
Opening Day Age: 23
Born: 12/26/78 in Haina, Santo Domingo, DR

Recent Statistics

	G	AB	R	H	D	THR	RBI	SB	BB	SO	Avg
2000 AA Midland	24	75	13	16	1	0	1	6	5	18	21	.213
2000 A Visalia	109	428	82	113	14	10	2	35	78	61	86	.264
2001 AA Midland	92	335	79	95	20	3	6	30	31	63	66	.284
2001 AAA Sacramento	38	150	40	56	8	0	4	14	17	18	20	.373
2001 MLE	130	460	91	126	23	2	7	34	32	54	89	.274

German never has appeared on prospect lists, but he's steadily climbed through the Oakland system since he was signed in 1996. The pint-size German has made consistent contact, and his plate discipline has generated a .407 career on-base percentage. Last summer he eliminated a slight loop in his swing and learned to hit down on the ball more effectively. That bolsters the leadoff skills of a guy who has stolen at least 40 bases in each of his minor league seasons, including 48 between Double-A Midland and Triple-A Sacramento in 2001. German has improved on the double-play pivot and at going to his right for the ball, and more repetitions will help his overall defense and his consistency on routine plays.

Oakland

Jason Hart

Position: 1B
Bats: R **Throws:** R
Ht: 6' 4" **Wt:** 237
Opening Day Age: 24
Born: 9/5/77 in Walnut Creek, CA

Recent Statistics

	G	AB	R	H	D	T	HR	RBI	SB	BB	SO	Avg
2000 AA Midland	135	546	98	178	44	3	30	121	4	67	112	.326
2000 AAA Sacramento	5	18	4	5	1	0	1	4	0	3	7	.278
2001 AAA Sacramento	134	494	71	122	26	1	19	75	3	57	102	.247
2001 MLE	134	476	56	104	22	0	14	59	2	44	106	.218

The RBI king of the high Class-A California League in 1999, Hart was a Triple Crown threat in the Double-A Texas League in 2000. Playing at Midland's hitting-happy Christensen Stadium may send up a flag about Hart's prospect status, but he hit half of his 30 homers on the road, and his road slugging percentage nearly matched his home mark. Although Hart had a great spring training in 2001, he struggled mightily early on at Triple-A Sacramento and never enjoyed a red-hot stretch, even though hot streaks have been a trademark. Hart still needs to work on his defensive game, and the A's would like to see him go the other way more.

Chad Harville

Position: P
Bats: R **Throws:** R
Ht: 5' 9" **Wt:** 186
Opening Day Age: 25
Born: 9/16/76 in Selmer, TN

Recent Statistics

	W	L	ERA	G	GS	Sv	IP	H	R	BB	SO	HR
2001 A Visalia	0	0	0.00	1	1	0	3.0	3	0	0	3	0
2001 A Modesto	0	0	3.00	2	1	0	3.0	2	2	0	3	0
2001 AAA Sacramento	5	2	3.98	33	0	8	40.2	35	20	12	55	5
2001 AL Oakland	0	0	0.00	3	0	0	3.0	2	0	0	2	0

A second-rounder in 1997, Harville has relied heavily on a high-90s fastball. When he was touched for far more homers at Triple-A Sacramento in 2000 (eight) than in his three previous minor league seasons combined (three), it was apparent he needed more movement on his fastball. He suffered a strained rotator cuff last spring and didn't pitch until June, but he's been phenomenal since then. Harville no longer overthrows the ball, and he has transformed from a thrower to a pitcher. Once limited to mostly a straight fastball, he now throws a decent sinker that moves. He also uses a curveball effectively, and his changeup is coming on. His bolstered arsenal allows him to change planes and speeds on hitters.

Ryan Ludwick

Position: OF
Bats: R **Throws:** L
Ht: 6' 3" **Wt:** 203
Opening Day Age: 23
Born: 7/13/78 in Satellite Beach, FL

Recent Statistics

	G	AB	R	H	D	T	HR	RBI	SB	BB	SO	Avg
2000 A Modesto	129	493	86	130	26	3	29	102	10	68	128	.264
2001 AA Midland	119	443	82	119	23	3	25	96	9	56	113	.269
2001 AAA Sacramento	17	57	10	13	3	0	1	7	2	2	16	.228
2001 MLE	136	478	70	110	21	2	18	78	7	36	135	.230

A 1999 second-round pick, Ludwick has big-time power potential. In his first full pro season in 2000, he initially swung for the fences and struggled at high Class-A Modesto. He later tapped into his power by stroking the ball to all fields. While Ludwick was less pull-conscious at Double-A Midland in 2001, he still missed a lot of hittable pitches. He also needs to make little adjustments, such as improving his two-strike approach. Ludwick is a polished fielder with a strong arm, and he may have just enough speed to make it as a center fielder. He suffered a stress fracture in his back during the Arizona Fall League, but should be ready to go in the spring.

Mario Ramos

Position: P
Bats: L **Throws:** L
Ht: 5' 11" **Wt:** 165
Opening Day Age: 24
Born: 10/19/77 in Aurora, IL

Recent Statistics

	W	L	ERA	G	GS	Sv	IP	H	R	BB	SO	HR
2000 A Modesto	12	5	2.90	26	24	0	152.0	131	63	50	134	6
2000 AA Midland	2	0	1.32	4	4	0	27.1	24	6	6	19	0
2001 AA Midland	8	1	3.07	15	15	0	93.2	71	37	28	68	7
2001 AAA Sacramento	8	3	3.14	13	13	0	80.1	74	32	27	82	5

A 1999 pick, Ramos enjoyed a strong pro debut at high Class-A Modesto in 2000. His advanced fastball-changeup combo was as good as ever last summer, but a big difference in 2001 was the development of his curveball. It didn't show much action before the season, but came along nicely. His best tool is his mental approach and preparation. He's all business on the mound and learns hitters' weaknesses before he faces them. He throws a cut fastball that is hard for hitters to pick up, and his curve and change make him a solid three-pitch pitcher. Ramos projects as a middle-of-the-rotation guy.

Others to Watch

Oakland's first-round pick last summer out of Long Beach State, **Bobby Crosby** (22) is a natural baseball player with power potential. He's 6-foot-3, so he's one of the new, bigger shortstops coming into today's game. He stands a bit upright and rigid on the field, a little like Cal Ripken. Crosby debuted by batting .395 in 38 at-bats at high Class-A Modesto. . . Southpaw **Claudio Galva** (22) lacks a dominating pitch, but he successfully moved to the bullpen in 2001 and held his own at Double-A Midland and Triple-A Sacramento. Using a low-90s fastball, good slider and budding changeup, Galva posted a 2.88 ERA and saved 11 games between the two levels. . . Dominican lefthander **Juan Pena** (22) features a big-time changeup that has registered big-time strikeouts at lower levels. He's starting to show better command of his low-90s fastball and breaking pitch, and Pena was 11-9 (4.07) in his first exposure to hitting-friendly Double-A Midland. . . A 19th-round pick in 2000, outfielder **Chris Tritle** (19) got it right the second time in the Rookie-level Arizona League. He came from a small school in Iowa and took a while to adjust to professional life. He was ready in 2001, batting .336 and leading the circuit in homers (9), stolen bases (26) and slugging (.565).

Safeco Field

Offense

Parks often play differently from one season to the next, but Safeco Field has been perfectly consistent during its two-plus seasons. It cut scoring by a significant amount when the Mariners moved into it partway through the 1999 season, it hurt hitters to a similar extent in 2000, and it suppressed scoring by nearly the same amount last season. At this point, it seems safe to say it's one of the best pitchers' parks in baseball. Though it has a retractable roof, Safeco often is open to the cool sea air, which keeps the ball from carrying and limits home runs. Hitters also complain about the glare and shadows during day games, which helps explain why batting averages suffer there as well.

Defense

Since the power alleys are deep and many flyballs fall short of the seats, it pays to have outfielders who can cover a lot of ground. Pitchers can throw strikes with the confidence that the park will hold all but the hardest-hit drives. The outfield walls are only eight feet high, so having a player like Mike Cameron, who can climb the wall to take away an occasional home run, is a bonus.

Who It Helps the Most

It's hard to find a single pitcher who's been with Seattle for any length of time who *hasn't* benefited from Safeco. Pitchers who put the ball in play, such as Jamie Moyer, seem to gain more than power pitchers like Freddy Garcia. Extreme flyballers like Paul Abbott tend to be helped the most. The hitters that are hurt the least tend to be the ones with the least power, such as Carlos Guillen or Ichiro Suzuki.

Who It Hurts the Most

Power hitters who hit the ball from gap to gap seem to lose the most. Mike Cameron is the best example. Mike McLemore and Dan Wilson also suffer.

Rookies & Newcomers

Joel Pineiro pitched incredibly well in limited time there last year, and should continue to feel the wind at his back. Whichever players are brought in to fill second base and left field should be expected to perform below their customary levels.

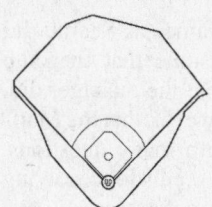

Dimensions: LF-331, LCF-390, CF-405, RCF-387, RF-327

Capacity: 47,116

Elevation: -2 feet

Surface: Grass

Foul Territory: Average

Park Factors

2001 Season

	Home Games Mariners	Opp	Total	Away Games Mariners	Opp	Total	Index
G	72	72	144	72	72	144	—
Avg	.286	.224	.255	.292	.249	.271	94
AB	2414	2451	4865	2639	2437	5076	96
R	395	253	648	421	311	732	89
H	690	550	1240	770	607	1377	90
2B	138	112	250	146	131	277	94
3B	13	6	19	19	16	35	57
HR	66	60	126	73	82	155	85
BB	277	192	469	277	223	500	98
SO	415	463	878	460	474	934	98
E	30	61	91	40	64	104	88
E-Infield	26	50	76	33	57	90	84
LHB-Avg	.298	.233	.265	.297	.264	.281	94
LHB-HR	22	31	53	16	37	53	104
RHB-Avg	.275	.218	.246	.288	.237	.263	94
RHB-HR	44	29	73	57	45	102	75

1999-2000 (post All-Star 1999)

	Home Games Mariners	Opp	Total	Away Games Mariners	Opp	Total	Index
G	108	108	216	105	105	210	—
Avg	.247	.248	.248	.280	.282	.281	88
AB	3496	3735	7231	3717	3519	7236	97
R	534	480	1014	599	568	1167	84
H	864	926	1790	1040	993	2033	86
2B	154	192	346	216	206	422	82
3B	13	9	22	17	26	43	51
HR	124	108	232	146	118	264	88
BB	509	413	922	440	426	866	107
SO	754	725	1479	726	560	1286	115
E	64	64	128	73	75	148	84
E-Infield	51	53	104	62	62	124	82
LHB-Avg	.238	.240	.239	.279	.285	.282	85
LHB-HR	43	38	81	27	60	87	97
RHB-Avg	.252	.254	.253	.280	.280	.280	90
RHB-HR	81	70	151	119	58	177	84

2001 Rankings (American League)
- Lowest hit factor
- Lowest infield-error factor
- Second-lowest batting-average factor
- Second-lowest home-run factor
- Second-lowest RHB home-run factor
- Third-lowest run factor
- Third-lowest triple factor
- Third-lowest error factor
- Third-lowest RHB batting-average factor

Seattle

Lou Piniella

2001 Season

When a team wins as many games as Seattle did last year, some inevitably assume that the club would have won no matter what the manager did. It's important to remember, however, that the Mariners came into the season with many questions. Lou Piniella deserves a lot of credit for resolving almost all of them to the club's advantage.

Offense

Piniella had hoped that Ichiro Suzuki would be able to replace the departed Alex Rodriguez in the No. 3 spot, but was forced to change his plans in the spring when Ichiro proved better suited to the top of the order. Though he would have preferred to have another power hitter, Piniella maximized what he had by stacking players with high on-base percentages in the top four spots in the lineup and following them with Bret Boone and Mike Cameron, two players who'd hit closer to the top of the order in other seasons. The results were that the Mariners not only led the majors in runs scored, but also scored more runs than the sum of their offensive accomplishments should have produced. With players like Ichiro and Mark McLemore, he was able to call for a lot of steals and hit-and-runs.

Pitching & Defense

With two Gold Glovers in the outfield, Piniella was able to get his pitchers to work up and exploit the new high strike to great effect. He made a gutsy move by replacing John Halama in the rotation with rookie Joel Pineiro in midseason, and the move worked wonderfully. He showed his appreciation for defense in Safeco Field by sticking with glove men David Bell and Dan Wilson, even when they weren't producing at the plate.

2002 Outlook

Piniella might need to pull another rabbit out of his hat if Bret Boone can't be re-signed. The rest of his lineup looks to be fairly set, though, after the Mariners acquired Jeff Cirillo. Piniella's two biggest challenges this year will be to live up to the expectations created by the team's major league record-tying victory total in 2001, and to bring along some of the system's young pitchers.

Born: 8/28/43 in Tampa, FL

Playing Experience: 1964-1984, Bal, Cle, KC, NYY

Managerial Experience: 15 seasons

Manager Statistics

Year	Team, Lg	W	L	Pct	GB	Finish
2001	Seattle, AL	116	46	.716	—	1st West
15 Seasons		1226	1066	.535	—	—

2001 Starting Pitchers by Days Rest

	<=3	4	5	6+
Mariners Starts	3	86	39	26
Mariners ERA	2.20	3.71	3.42	4.26
AL Avg Starts	1	78	48	24
AL ERA	5.92	4.69	4.58	4.58

2001 Situational Stats

	Lou Piniella	AL Average
Hit & Run Success %	41.9	35.0
Stolen Base Success %	80.6	71.0
Platoon Pct.	63.7	59.1
Defensive Subs	64	26
High-Pitch Outings	5	6
Quick/Slow Hooks	22/11	19/16
Sacrifice Attempts	62	54

2001 Rankings (American League)

- 1st in stolen-base attempts (216), stolen-base percentage, steals of second base (149), double steals (11), defensive substitutions and 2+ pitching changes in low-scoring games (44)
- 2nd in steals of third base (25), hit-and-run success percentage and starts on three days rest
- 3rd in squeeze plays (4)

Paul Abbott

2001 Season

A sore shoulder delayed the start of Paul Abbott's 2001 season, and it took him about a month to pitch his way into shape. But beginning with a complete-game victory over the Royals on May 28, and carrying through the end of the regular season, he pitched as well as he ever has, winning 15 of 17 decisions. Granted, his record had as much to do with the quality of the team behind him as the quality of his work, but Abbott pitched well and consistently gave the Mariners a chance to win.

Pitching

Abbott works primarily with a 90-MPH fastball and an excellent straight change. He'll mix in a slider, but his reliance on the changeup makes him one of the few pitchers who's equally effective against hitters from either side of the plate. He relies on his outfielders to chase down the flyballs he induces. His fastball is straight and hittable, so he tries to work off the corners. As a result, Abbott runs a lot of deep counts and frequently runs up high pitch counts before getting into the late innings. He also tends to lose effectiveness around the 100-pitch mark, so he's prone to early hooks.

Defense

Though he lacks a good pickoff move, Abbott makes things tough for basestealers by using the slide step and varying his delivery. Six of the 13 basestealing attempts against him were thwarted during the 2001 season. He's capable in the field and rarely hurts himself with the glove. He has just one error over the last two seasons.

2002 Outlook

Though no one expects him to go 17-4 again, Abbott is a solid middle-of-the-rotation starter who's been a valuable contributor when healthy. If he's able to start 30 games, he should be able to win a dozen of them, and possibly more if he gets anywhere near the type of run support he received in 2001.

Position: SP
Bats: R **Throws:** R
Ht: 6' 3" **Wt:** 195

Opening Day Age: 34
Born: 9/15/67 in Van Nuys, CA
ML Seasons: 8

Overall Statistics

	W	L	Pct.	ERA	G	GS	Sv	IP	H	BB	SO	HR	Ratio
2001	17	4	.810	4.25	28	27	0	163.0	145	87	118	21	1.42
Career	38	21	.644	4.28	125	80	0	550.2	489	289	396	66	1.41

How Often He Throws Strikes

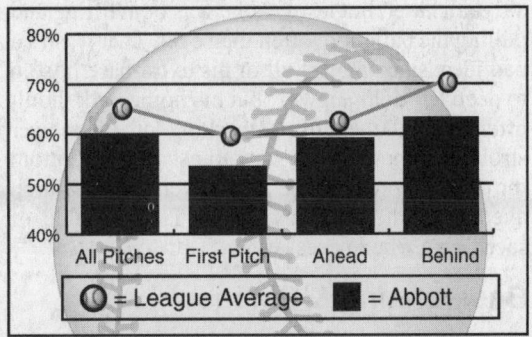

2001 Situational Stats

	W	L	ERA	Sv	IP			AB	H	HR	RBI	Avg
Home	8	1	2.90	0	71.1	LHB		341	83	8	38	.243
Road	9	3	5.30	0	91.2	RHB		267	62	13	35	.232
First Half	7	2	4.42	0	77.1	Sc Pos		151	34	4	48	.225
Scnd Half	10	2	4.10	0	85.2	Clutch		4	1	0	2	.250

2001 Rankings (American League)
- 1st in most run support per nine innings (7.8), fielding percentage at pitcher (1.000) and highest walks per nine innings (4.8)
- 2nd in winning percentage
- 3rd in lowest strikeout-walk ratio (1.4) and lowest groundball-flyball ratio allowed (0.8)
- 4th in walks allowed, wild pitches (11), most pitches thrown per batter (3.87) and highest ERA on the road
- 5th in lowest batting average allowed vs. righthanded batters
- Led the Mariners in walks allowed, wild pitches (11), winning percentage, lowest stolen-base percentage allowed (53.8) and most strikeouts per nine innings (6.5)

David Bell

2001 Season

David Bell's job seemed to be in jeopardy early in the season when he got off to a slow start and the team was looking to add a hitter. No deals came to fruition, though, and Bell was able to hold the third-base job all year. His most productive stretch of the season was an eight-week span from May 23 through July 18, during which he batted .327 with nine homers and 33 RBI. Though his bat wasn't much of an asset for most of the year, his glove certainly was.

Hitting

At times in 2001 it seemed that Bell was making more of an effort to hit for power. He's always been a flyball hitter, but last year he was both lifting and pulling the ball more often than ever. That wasn't a bad idea, since almost all of his extra-base hits go to deep left field anyway, but his home park didn't often reward the effort. Working on his power stroke may be his only way to escape the bottom third of the order, since he's never hit for a high average or drawn many walks. He's capable of sacrificing when necessary.

Baserunning & Defense

Bell inherited his father Buddy's soft hands and strong arm, and he makes all the plays at second or third (though he did not log any time at second base in 2001). His straight-ahead speed and his ability to take extra bases are barely average, but his first-step quickness and canny positioning give him good range in the field. He's skilled on the pivot and handles himself at second as well as he does at third when asked to play at the keystone.

2002 Outlook

Bell became a free agent at season's end. The Mariners upgraded their third-base production by trading for Jeff Cirillo, so Bell will land elsewhere. A change of scenery could mean a return to second base. It's likely he'll put up better numbers in just about any other home park.

Position: 3B
Bats: R **Throws:** R
Ht: 5'10" **Wt:** 190

Opening Day Age: 29
Born: 9/14/72 in Cincinnati, OH
ML Seasons: 7

Overall Statistics

	G	AB	R	H	D	T	HR	RBI	SB	BB	SO	Avg	OBP	Slg
2001	135	470	62	122	28	0	15	64	2	28	59	.260	.303	.415
Career	726	2383	293	608	133	10	61	278	14	179	355	.255	.309	.396

Where He Hits the Ball

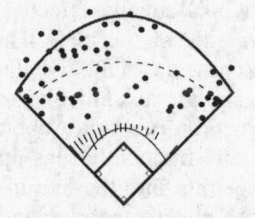 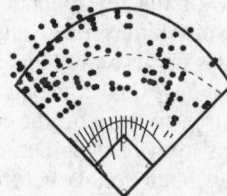

Vs. LHP   **Vs. RHP**

2001 Situational Stats

	AB	H	HR	RBI	Avg		AB	H	HR	RBI	Avg
Home	226	58	7	27	.257	LHP	125	32	4	17	.256
Road	244	64	8	37	.262	RHP	345	90	11	47	.261
First Half	268	70	9	44	.261	Sc Pos	128	39	2	47	.305
Scnd Half	202	52	6	20	.257	Clutch	76	24	5	12	.316

2001 Rankings (American League)

- 3rd in lowest on-base percentage
- 4th in fielding percentage at third base (.962) and lowest groundball-flyball ratio (0.7)
- Led the Mariners in batting average on a 3-2 count (.341)

Bret Boone

2001 Season

No one saw it coming. No one. Bret Boone, a nine-year veteran with decent power and few other offensive attributes, returned to Seattle and exploded with one of the better offensive seasons a second baseman ever has put together. Batting fifth in the order, he finished fourth in the league in hitting and drove in an American League-high 141 runs while maintaining his usual excellence in the field. His .444 batting average, .497 on-base percentage and .715 slugging percentage against southpaws all ranked first among AL hitters.

Hitting

How was Boone able to make such a remarkable breakthrough? Two things: plenty of added muscle, and a better approach at the plate whereby he focused on using the entire field. Formerly a pull hitter, he now was both willing and able to hit the ball hard—or out—to right field. Pitchers who used to simply keep the ball away from him were forced to adjust, and never did find a new way to keep him in check. Southpaws in particular had a terrible time, as Boone posted one of the highest averages against lefthanders in years.

Baserunning & Defense

Always a top defender, Boone's strong arm allows him to set up deep and cut off plenty of grounders other second basemen wave at. He also has soft hands and a smooth pivot. He never had displayed above-average foot speed and might have lost a step since bulking up. Still, he takes his share of extra bases and doesn't run into many outs.

2002 Outlook

A free agent, Boone is in good position to cash in on his monster season. The Mariners certainly want him back. If he signs elsewhere, his RBI count may suffer from no longer batting behind on-base machines John Olerud and Edgar Martinez, but there's no reason he can't keep his other numbers within reach of his 2001 levels.

Position: 2B
Bats: R **Throws:** R
Ht: 5'10" **Wt:** 180

Opening Day Age: 32
Born: 4/6/69 in El Cajon, CA
ML Seasons: 10

Overall Statistics

	G	AB	R	H	D	T	HR	RBI	SB	BB	SO	Avg	OBP	Slg
2001	158	623	118	206	37	3	37	141	5	40	110	.331	.372	.578
Career	1230	4534	621	1202	252	17	162	677	52	347	868	.265	.321	.435

Where He Hits the Ball

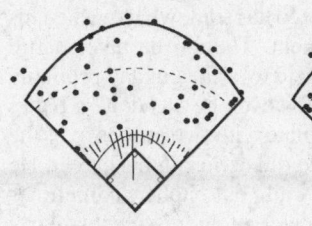 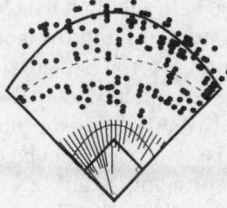

Vs. LHP   Vs. RHP

2001 Situational Stats

	AB	H	HR	RBI	Avg		AB	H	HR	RBI	Avg
Home	307	99	19	74	.322	LHP	144	64	9	29	.444
Road	316	107	18	67	.339	RHP	479	142	28	112	.296
First Half	340	110	22	84	.324	Sc Pos	202	61	8	102	.302
Scnd Half	283	96	15	57	.339	Clutch	75	26	4	18	.347

2001 Rankings (American League)

- 1st in RBI, batting average vs. lefthanded pitchers, slugging percentage vs. lefthanded pitchers (.715) and on-base percentage vs. lefthanded pitchers (.497)
- 2nd in hits, total bases (360), sacrifice flies (13) and batting average with two strikes (.271)
- 3rd in runs scored and fielding percentage at second base (.986)
- 4th in batting average and batting average on the road
- Led the Mariners in home runs, total bases (360), sacrifice flies (13), slugging percentage, HR frequency (16.8 ABs per HR) and batting average with two strikes (.271)
- Led AL second basemen in home runs and RBI

Mike Cameron

2001 Season

Multitalented Mike Cameron was one of the Mariners' key players last year, both offensively and defensively. Batting fifth or sixth for most of the summer, he hit a career-high 25 home runs and finished third on the club with a personal-best 110 RBI. Cameron was on fire in June, when he batted .311, scored 18 runs, drove in 23 and slugged .622. His blanket coverage of center field snuffed out many a rally, helped give Seattle pitchers the confidence to pitch up in the strike zone and earned him the first Gold Glove of his career.

Hitting

Cameron has very good power to all fields and still is learning to use it. He naturally gets good lift on the ball, although Safeco has somewhat masked his continuing improvement. Though he takes a full cut, Cameron isn't afraid to strike out and probably never will hit .300. However, he has done a better job of protecting the plate with two strikes over the past two years than he did earlier in his career. He knows how to take a walk, but pitchers sometimes take advantage of his lack of aggressiveness early in the count.

Baserunning & Defense

When it comes to center-field defense, there's Andruw Jones, Torii Hunter and Cameron, and then there's everyone else. Cameron has a good arm and excellent speed, and he is one of the best in the business at turning his back to the ball and running it down. His leaping catches at the wall are becoming a staple on sports highlight shows. He made six errors in center, but he also flagged down 411 balls. He puts his speed to excellent use on the bases, stealing plenty of bags while hardly ever getting caught.

2002 Outlook

After being bounced up and down the lineup in the past, Cameron found a home as a run producer last year. He's still in his prime at age 29, so look for his power to continue developing as he settles into the role.

Position: CF
Bats: R **Throws:** R
Ht: 6' 2" **Wt:** 190

Opening Day Age: 29
Born: 1/8/73 in LaGrange, GA
ML Seasons: 7

Overall Statistics

	G	AB	R	H	D	T	HR	RBI	SB	BB	SO	Avg	OBP	Slg
2001	150	540	99	144	30	5	25	110	34	69	155	.267	.353	.480
Career	747	2449	409	617	128	26	88	354	146	323	657	.252	.344	.433

Where He Hits the Ball

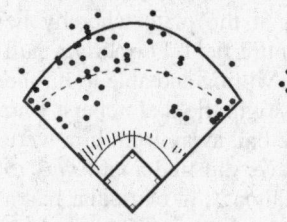 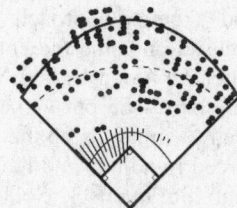

Vs. LHP **Vs. RHP**

2001 Situational Stats

	AB	H	HR	RBI	Avg		AB	H	HR	RBI	Avg
Home	259	57	7	36	.220	LHP	136	41	6	31	.301
Road	281	87	18	74	.310	RHP	404	103	19	79	.255
First Half	289	80	15	58	.277	Sc Pos	149	43	11	84	.289
Scnd Half	251	64	10	52	.255	Clutch	75	19	3	15	.253

2001 Rankings (American League)

- 1st in highest percentage of extra bases taken as a runner (77.4) and errors in center field (6)
- 2nd in sacrifice flies (13), lowest groundball-fly-ball ratio (0.6), lowest batting average at home and lowest fielding percentage in center field (.986)
- 4th in strikeouts and assists in center field (8)
- 5th in stolen-base percentage (87.2) and most pitches seen per plate appearance (4.09)
- 6th in stolen bases
- Led the Mariners in sacrifice flies (13), hit by pitch (10), strikeouts, pitches seen (2,591) and stolen-base percentage (87.2)
- Led AL center fielders in RBI

Freddy Garcia

Position: SP
Bats: R **Throws:** R
Ht: 6' 4" **Wt:** 235

Opening Day Age: 25
Born: 10/6/76 in Caracas, VZ
ML Seasons: 3

2001 Season

When the Mariners looked around for an ace starter last season, Freddy Garcia stepped up and answered the call. Displaying new maturity and focus, he pitched brilliantly from start to finish and became one of the top starters in the American League. He went 10-1 during the first half, and wrapped up the season by posting a 2.91 ERA in the second half, which was better than his first-half mark. Although Garcia didn't lead the team in victories, he clearly was the M's most effective starter.

Pitching

Garcia challenges hitters with a low-90s fastball, an excellent changeup and a curveball that he throws at two different speeds. He comes right after righthanded hitters, who are lucky even to reach base against him, but he works more carefully to lefties. With powerful legs and loose arm action, he has excellent stamina and gets tougher as the game goes on. He also worked more efficiently in 2001, which enhanced his staying power. In the past, he sometimes would get himself into a jam before he'd really start to bear down, but last year he remained focused throughout the entire game.

Defense

Garcia's newfound maturity was evident in his fielding as well. He was quick off the mound to cover first or grab a roller and start a double play, and he knocked down more than his share of balls back through the box. He pays little attention to baserunners and remains easy to run on, but that's less of a liability when he's ahead late in the game.

2002 Outlook

There's every reason to believe the 25-year-old righthander will be one of the top starters in baseball for years to come. He easily pitched well enough to win 20 games last year, and he is as good a bet as anyone to reach that plateau in 2002, perhaps picking up some personal hardware at the end of the campaign.

Overall Statistics

	W	L	Pct.	ERA	G	GS	Sv	IP	H	BB	SO	HR	Ratio
2001	18	6	.750	3.05	34	34	0	238.2	199	69	163	16	1.12
Career	44	19	.698	3.60	88	87	0	564.1	516	223	412	50	1.31

How Often He Throws Strikes

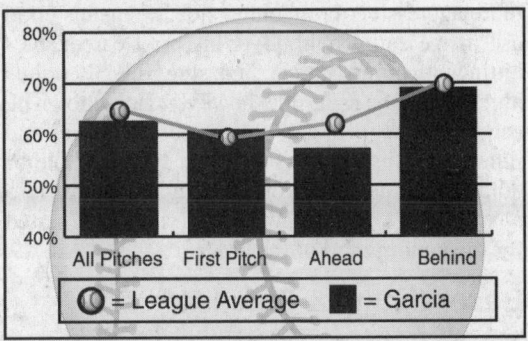

= League Average ■ = Garcia

2001 Situational Stats

	W	L	ERA	Sv	IP		AB	H	HR	RBI	Avg
Home	9	4	3.02	0	119.1	LHB	475	115	10	37	.242
Road	9	2	3.09	0	119.1	RHB	409	84	6	42	.205
First Half	10	1	3.18	0	124.1	Sc Pos	199	43	3	62	.216
Scnd Half	8	5	2.91	0	114.1	Clutch	59	15	0	3	.254

2001 Rankings (American League)

- 1st in ERA, innings pitched, lowest batting average allowed (.225), lowest slugging percentage allowed (.344), fewest home runs allowed per nine innings (.60), lowest batting average allowed vs. righthanded batters and highest stolen-base percentage allowed (90.0)
- Led the Mariners in games started, complete games (4), shutouts (3), batters faced (971), strikeouts, pitches thrown (3,521), stolen bases allowed (18), GDPs induced (23), lowest on-base percentage allowed (.283), highest groundball-flyball ratio allowed (1.5), most GDPs induced per GDP situation (14.6%), lowest ERA on the road and lowest batting average allowed with runners in scoring position

Carlos Guillen

2001 Season

Carlos Guillen's first season as a major league regular was anything but easy. Taking over at shortstop for departed superstar Alex Rodriguez, and eager to keep from being labeled injury-prone, Guillen played through several minor injuries before a serious case of tuberculosis drained him and eventually sidelined him late in the year. Despite all that, he played fine defense and fared acceptably at the plate, and even made an unexpected return for the second round of the playoffs.

Hitting

From the left side, the switch-hitting Guillen is a fairly patient hitter, while from the right side he's more aggressive. From either side, he makes good use of the entire field. Over his brief career, he's hitting 49 points higher and slugging 37 points higher from the right side, however. He's shown he can bunt runners along when needed. Injuries and illness hurt his numbers in 2001. He's capable of doing more and still is young enough to mature into a No. 2 hitter. Right now, though, he's best suited for the bottom third of the order.

Baserunning & Defense

After playing mainly third base in 2000, Guillen moved back to his natural position last season and made all the plays. He committed just 10 errors in 137 games at short in 2001. He's rangy and sure-handed, and his throws are crisp and accurate, even when he throws on the run. He has good speed but isn't much of a basestealer.

2002 Outlook

It was important to Guillen to establish himself last year, and he sometimes remained in the lineup when he probably shouldn't have. Better health, security and maturity likely will lead to a better offensive season in 2002. Even if Guillen doesn't produce more at the plate, his job may remain secure, since the Mariners seem quite pleased with his glovework.

Position: SS
Bats: B **Throws:** R
Ht: 6' 1" **Wt:** 180

Opening Day Age: 26
Born: 9/30/75 in Maracay, VZ
ML Seasons: 4
Pronunciation: GEY-un

Overall Statistics

	G	AB	R	H	D	T	HR	RBI	SB	BB	SO	Avg	OBP	Slg
2001	140	456	72	118	21	4	5	53	4	53	89	.259	.333	.355
Career	245	802	128	208	37	7	13	103	7	85	157	.259	.329	.372

Where He Hits the Ball

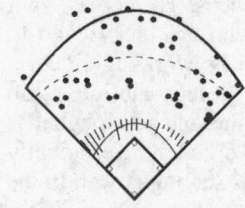 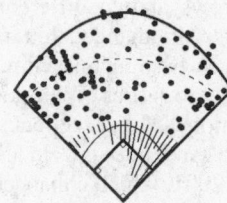

Vs. LHP   **Vs. RHP**

2001 Situational Stats

	AB	H	HR	RBI	Avg		AB	H	HR	RBI	Avg
Home	213	61	2	21	.286	LHP	139	41	3	16	.295
Road	243	57	3	32	.235	RHP	317	77	2	37	.243
First Half	278	68	4	38	.245	Sc Pos	117	31	2	46	.265
Scnd Half	178	50	1	15	.281	Clutch	66	13	1	4	.197

2001 Rankings (American League)

- 3rd in lowest HR frequency (91.2 ABs per HR)
- 4th in fielding percentage at shortstop (.980) and lowest slugging percentage
- 7th in lowest batting average on the road

Edgar Martinez

2001 Season

Sometimes it seems fate conspires to prevent Edgar Martinez from getting his due, no matter what he does. No sooner had he escaped from the long shadow of Alex Rodriguez when Bret Boone and Ichiro Suzuki joined the club and garnered the lion's share of the credit for the club's stellar season. It scarcely was mentioned that Martinez drove in nearly as many runs per game as Boone, got on base more regularly than Ichiro and drove in more runs—in only 132 games—than any 38-year-old ever had in any season.

Hitting

Few players in the game have better home-run power from foul pole to foul pole than Martinez. He always seems to have a plan, and when he hits one, he usually makes it look like he had been anticipating the pitch all along. He's one of the most patient hitters in the game, and occasionally lulls pitchers into laying the first one in there, only to make them pay immediately. Pitchers often try to move him off the plate early in the count, but it's a pattern he's grown used to seeing. He struggled at times against lefties last season, but that was not indicative of a career trend.

Baserunning & Defense

Since Martinez is unusually susceptible to muscle problems in his legs, baserunning and defense are hazards to be avoided whenever possible. In the occasional interleague game in a National League park, he gets by at first base. He steals a few bases a year to keep pitchers from ignoring him completely, but otherwise takes few risks.

2002 Outlook

Moving to a bigger ballpark and the expansion of the strike zone haven't slowed Martinez down, but age eventually will. He turns 39 in January. He probably will go out as John Kruk and Tony Gwynn did, dragged down by injuries but batting .300 until the end. The Mariners hope that won't be for several more years.

Position: DH
Bats: R **Throws:** R
Ht: 5'11" **Wt:** 200

Opening Day Age: 39
Born: 1/2/63 in New York, NY
ML Seasons: 15

Overall Statistics

	G	AB	R	H	D	T	HR	RBI	SB	BB	SO	Avg	OBP	Slg
2001	132	470	80	144	40	1	23	116	4	93	90	.306	.423	.543
Career	1672	5902	1060	1882	443	15	258	1041	47	1066	931	.319	.425	.530

Where He Hits the Ball

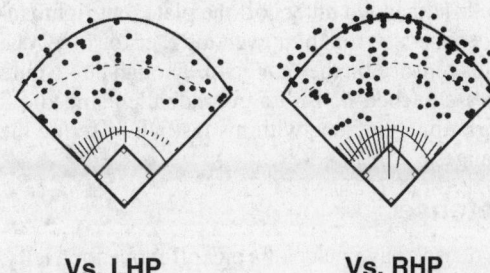

Vs. LHP   **Vs. RHP**

2001 Situational Stats

	AB	H	HR	RBI	Avg		AB	H	HR	RBI	Avg
Home	233	71	10	68	.305	LHP	126	31	5	25	.246
Road	237	73	13	48	.308	RHP	344	113	18	91	.328
First Half	278	84	13	67	.302	Sc Pos	152	46	8	93	.303
Scnd Half	192	60	10	49	.313	Clutch	68	18	1	19	.265

2001 Rankings (American League)

- 2nd in on-base percentage, lowest percentage of swings on the first pitch (12.5) and lowest percentage of extra bases taken as a runner (29.0)
- 3rd in highest percentage of pitches taken (65.3)
- 4th in most pitches seen per plate appearance (4.13)
- 5th in batting average vs. righthanded pitchers and on-base percentage vs. righthanded pitchers (.433)
- Led the Mariners in doubles, on-base percentage, most pitches seen per plate appearance (4.13), slugging percentage vs. righthanded pitchers (.573), on-base percentage vs. righthanded pitchers (.433) and lowest percentage of swings on the first pitch (12.5)

Jamie Moyer

Position: SP
Bats: L **Throws:** L
Ht: 6' 0" **Wt:** 175

Opening Day Age: 39
Born: 11/18/62 in
Sellersville, PA
ML Seasons: 15

2001 Season

Changeup artist Jamie Moyer rebounded from a difficult 2000 to enjoy his finest season last year. After a mediocre first half, the southpaw went 9-1 with a 2.30 ERA from August 1 through the end of the season. He enjoyed a stellar second half before sparkling in his three postseason starts, winning all three. At age 38, he became the oldest first-time 20-game winner in history.

Pitching

With Moyer, it's all about location and changing speeds. He succeeds with a mid-80s fastball because he's able to spot it on both sides of the plate while mixing it with a slow curve and one of the game's most deceptive changeups. He constantly backs lefthanded hitters off the plate, but righthanders generally find him even tougher to solve, due to his reliance on the changeup. Though he's a pure finesse pitcher, he isn't a groundballer, since he'll work up in the zone with his fastball to set up the change.

Defense

He doesn't have much of a pickoff move for a lefty, but Moyer is quick enough to the plate to keep the running game in check. In the field, he's his own fifth infielder. He's committed just one error over the last two seasons. He finishes his delivery in good position to field, and is unflappable in any situation.

2002 Outlook

Though Moyer is getting up there in years—he turns 40 in November 2002—there's no reason to expect him to suddenly grow old. He didn't miss a single start last year, and he actually threw fewer pitches per game over the course of a full season than he had since 1996. Having Mike Cameron and Ichiro Suzuki in the outfield to chase down his flyballs ought to keep him feeling young, too.

Overall Statistics

	W	L	Pct.	ERA	G	GS	Sv	IP	H	BB	SO	HR	Ratio
2001	20	6	.769	3.43	33	33	0	209.2	187	44	119	24	1.10
Career	151	117	.563	4.22	405	353	0	2292.0	2388	664	1381	267	1.33

How Often He Throws Strikes

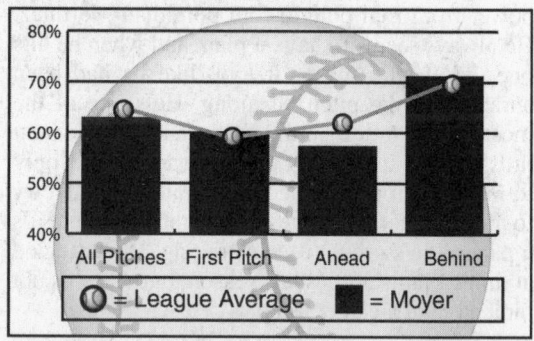

2001 Situational Stats

	W	L	ERA	Sv	IP		AB	H	HR	RBI	Avg
Home	11	3	2.77	0	107.1	LHB	214	54	9	24	.252
Road	9	3	4.13	0	102.1	RHB	567	133	15	54	.235
First Half	9	4	4.75	0	100.1	Sc Pos	133	31	2	44	.233
Scnd Half	11	2	2.22	0	109.1	Clutch	37	3	0	1	.081

2001 Rankings (American League)

- 1st in fielding percentage at pitcher (1.000)
- 2nd in wins and lowest ERA at home
- 4th in winning percentage, lowest on-base percentage allowed (.285) and fewest walks per nine innings (1.9)
- 6th in ERA
- 7th in highest strikeout-walk ratio (2.7), most run support per nine innings (6.0) and lowest ground-ball-flyball ratio allowed (0.9)
- 9th in lowest batting average allowed (.239) and fewest strikeouts per nine innings (5.1)
- Led the Mariners in wins, hit batsmen (10), runners caught stealing (7), highest strikeout-walk ratio (2.7), lowest ERA at home and fewest walks per nine innings (1.9)

John Olerud

2001 Season

Who was the cleanup hitter on the team that won the most games in American League history? Edgar Martinez? Wrong. Bret Boone? Wrong. It was John Olerud, who once again made important contributions to a winning team while largely escaping notice. He delivered what's become the standard John Olerud year, batting close to .300 with roughly 20 homers and 100 RBI, plus plenty of doubles and walks while playing solid defense at first base.

Hitting

Olerud's swing is like the man himself—smooth, efficient and productive. He hits the ball where it's pitched, and if he happens to pull it, he's quite capable of reaching the right-field fence. An excellent breaking-ball hitter with patience and discipline, he is good at both working himself into hitter's counts and protecting the plate if he gets to two strikes. Hard-throwing lefthanders sometimes give him problems. While he's batted just .245 against lefties over the last three seasons, he's posted a respectable .361 on-base percentage against them over that span. In the last three seasons he's reached base at a .423 clip against righthanders.

Baserunning & Defense

Olerud is so smooth around the bag that for a long time many failed to appreciate how gifted a fielder he is. Though his range is only average, he digs out low throws effortlessly, throws accurately and makes over-the-shoulder catches of popups look easy. Once again, he led American League first basemen in assists by a wide margin. On the bases, he's a plodder but knows his limitations.

2002 Outlook

If any major leaguer can be considered a sure thing, it's Olerud. He's durable and consistent, and at age 33, he's still young enough to have several good years left. He's going into the last year of his contract, but as a native of Seattle who attended Washington State University, he seems content to play in the Northwest.

Position: 1B
Bats: L **Throws:** L
Ht: 6' 5" **Wt:** 220

Opening Day Age: 33
Born: 8/5/68 in Seattle, WA
ML Seasons: 13
Pronunciation: OLE-le-RUDE

Overall Statistics

	G	AB	R	H	D	T	HR	RBI	SB	BB	SO	Avg	OBP	Slg
2001	159	572	91	173	32	1	21	95	3	94	70	.302	.401	.472
Career	1714	5902	927	1768	399	12	207	960	11	1016	802	.300	.404	.476

Where He Hits the Ball

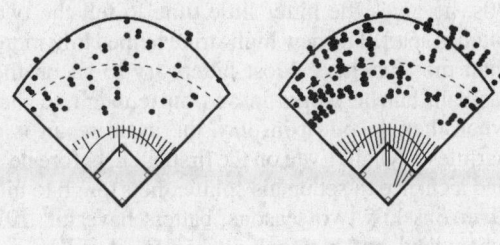

Vs. LHP   **Vs. RHP**

2001 Situational Stats

	AB	H	HR	RBI	Avg		AB	H	HR	RBI	Avg
Home	277	79	15	55	.285	LHP	142	35	3	23	.246
Road	295	94	6	40	.319	RHP	430	138	18	72	.321
First Half	304	96	11	58	.316	Sc Pos	183	48	6	73	.262
Scnd Half	268	77	10	37	.287	Clutch	75	21	1	13	.280

2001 Rankings (American League)

- 1st in assists at first base (121) and GDPs (21)
- 2nd in highest percentage of swings put into play (53.7)
- 4th in intentional walks (19)
- 5th in errors at first base (9) and fielding percentage at first base (.993)
- Led the Mariners in walks, intentional walks (19), GDPs (21), games played and cleanup slugging percentage (.460)

Kazuhiro Sasaki

2001 Season

Seattle closer Kazuhiro Sasaki followed up his Rookie of the Year season with a sophomore performance that was even better. The Mariners had a late-inning lead to protect almost daily—especially over the first few months of the season—and Sasaki regularly answered the call and came out no worse for the wear. He finished second to Mariano Rivera in the American League in saves, cut his walks by nearly two-thirds, and remained as tough to hit as any closer in the game.

Pitching

Sasaki uses the same approach to both lefthanded and righthanded hitters, mixing high fastballs and a devastating splitter. With a fastball in the mid-90s, he gives the hitter little time to tell the two pitches apart. The new high strike helped him more than most pitchers. Most hitters try to sit on the fastball, but he works in and out enough so that when they do put it in play, the usual result is a harmless flyball. Even on the first pitch, before he's had a chance to set up his splitter, he's tough to hit. Over Sasaki's two seasons, batters have hit .193 when they put his first pitch into play. He got burned on a few high fastballs as a rookie, but gave up almost half as many home runs last year.

Defense

Frankly, it's hard to tell how good a fielder Sasaki is, since he seems to get nothing but strikeouts and flyballs. He's gotten the job done when necessary, committing only one error in his first two major league seasons. His splitter is a tough pitch for a catcher to throw on, but Sasaki did a better job of cutting off the running game last season.

2002 Outlook

Though he's approaching his mid-30s, Sasaki has shown no signs of slipping. He is signed only through this season, so how much longer he pitches in a Mariners uniform remains to be seen. In any case, while Sasaki is in Seattle, he should be a top closer with 40-plus saves being a very reachable goal.

Position: RP
Bats: R **Throws:** R
Ht: 6' 4" **Wt:** 209

Opening Day Age: 34
Born: 2/22/68 in Sendai, Japan
ML Seasons: 2
Pronunciation: kaz-oo-hero sa-sa-key
Nickname: Daimajin

Overall Statistics

	W	L	Pct.	ERA	G	GS	Sv	IP	H	BB	SO	HR	Ratio
2001	0	4	.000	3.24	69	0	45	66.2	48	11	62	6	0.89
Career	2	9	.182	3.20	132	0	82	129.1	90	42	140	16	1.02

How Often He Throws Strikes

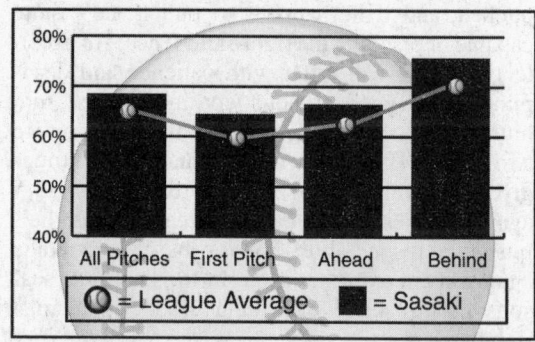

2001 Situational Stats

	W	L	ERA	Sv	IP			AB	H	HR	RBI	Avg
Home	0	2	3.26	16	30.1		LHB	133	29	4	17	.218
Road	0	2	3.22	29	36.1		RHB	113	19	2	10	.168
First Half	0	3	3.03	29	38.2		Sc Pos	63	13	2	11	.206
Scnd Half	0	1	3.54	16	28.0		Clutch	171	36	4	23	.211

2001 Rankings (American League)

- 2nd in save opportunities (52) and saves
- 3rd in fewest baserunners allowed per nine innings in relief (8.5) and games finished (63)
- 6th in blown saves (7)
- 7th in save percentage (86.5) and lowest batting average allowed in relief (.195)
- Led the Mariners in saves, games finished (63), save opportunities (52), save percentage (86.5), blown saves (7) and relief losses (4)

Aaron Sele

2001 Season

Like so many of his teammates, Aaron Sele put together his best season in 2001. He won 12 of his first 13 decisions, and only in June did he struggle, when he posted a 6.04 ERA in five starts. Otherwise, he was pretty solid from beginning to end, making at least 33 starts for the fifth straight season. He notched 21 quality starts, more than Mark Buehrle, Bartolo Colon or Joe Mays. The only letdown was that he performed poorly in his three postseason starts.

Pitching

When he was with Texas, Sele went for strikeouts and groundballs. But in his two years in more pitcher-friendly Safeco Field, he showed more willingness to let hitters put the ball in play and hit it into the air. He works the corners with a high-80s fastball to set up his excellent overhand curve, but he has little to fall back on when he can't get the curve over. Since his out pitch has so much drop, lefthanded hitters often find him tougher than righthanders. The Mariners' deep bullpen enabled them to pull Sele sooner last year than they had in the past, which seemed to help him stay sharp.

Defense

Sele throws to first a lot, but he doesn't have that good of a pickoff move. His slide step is a better deterrent and keeps runners close. Still, baserunners have stolen 22 bases in 34 tries during Sele's two seasons in Seattle. Sometimes erratic in the field in the past, he committed only one error last summer while showing decent mobility around the mound.

2002 Outlook

Sele is a free agent, and it remains to be seen whether the Mariners will be able to bring him back. The Washington State University alum is at his best in cool weather and has been helped by Safeco Field, so he might show signs of decline if he chooses to sign elsewhere.

Position: SP
Bats: R **Throws:** R
Ht: 6' 5" **Wt:** 215

Opening Day Age: 31
Born: 6/25/70 in Golden Valley, MN
ML Seasons: 9
Pronunciation: SEE-lee

Overall Statistics

	W	L	Pct.	ERA	G	GS	Sv	IP	H	BB	SO	HR	Ratio
2001	15	5	.750	3.60	34	33	0	215.0	216	51	114	25	1.24
Career	107	68	.611	4.33	242	241	0	1466.1	1580	548	1082	137	1.45

How Often He Throws Strikes

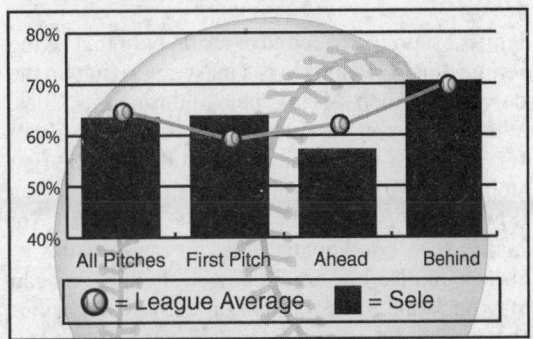

2001 Situational Stats

	W	L	ERA	Sv	IP		AB	H	HR	RBI	Avg
Home	8	2	3.37	0	123.0	LHB	438	101	15	50	.231
Road	7	3	3.91	0	92.0	RHB	389	115	10	40	.296
First Half	10	1	3.54	0	114.1	Sc Pos	159	47	4	62	.296
Scnd Half	5	4	3.67	0	100.2	Clutch	44	13	3	6	.295

2001 Rankings (American League)

- 3rd in most run support per nine innings (6.6)
- 5th in winning percentage and fewest strikeouts per nine innings (4.8)
- 8th in fewest walks per nine innings (2.1) and highest stolen-base percentage allowed (70.0)
- 9th in fewest pitches thrown per batter (3.62), lowest ERA at home and lowest groundball-fly-ball ratio allowed (1.0)
- 10th in lowest on-base percentage allowed (.306)
- Led the Mariners in hits allowed, home runs allowed, pickoff throws (137) and fewest pitches thrown per batter (3.62)

Ichiro Suzuki

2001 Season

Having lost Alex Rodriguez to free agency, the Mariners outbid all other major league teams for the exclusive rights to perennial Japanese League batting champ Ichiro Suzuki, and then spent millions more to sign him. With Ichiro being the first Japanese hitter to join the majors, there was some skepticism, and last spring some baseball observers warned that he couldn't get around on good fastballs and would disappoint. The gamble paid off, however, as Ichiro enjoyed one of the finest rookie seasons of all time. He captured the American League Rookie of the Year Award, the junior circuit's MVP honors *and* a Gold Glove.

Hitting

Ichiro's supreme bat control rivals only that of the retired Tony Gwynn. He is a master at sizing up the defense and then serving the ball through its holes. With runners on base, he has more holes to shoot for, and takes full advantage. His stride is the first step to a running start and he seems to get a step down the line before he even meets the ball. He makes such good contact that he rarely walks or strikes out. He has decent power, though, and can stay back and drive the ball on the rare occasions that he chooses to.

Baserunning & Defense

Ichiro's tremendous speed results in a lot of infield hits and hurried throws. On the bases, he's a catcher's nightmare, liable to run in any situation and always difficult to catch. On just about any other team, he would be a Gold Glove center fielder, but thanks to Mike Cameron, he's a Gold Glove right fielder with a center fielder's range. Early in the year, he made a now-legendary throw to cut down a runner at third, and no one ran on him after that.

2002 Outlook

Though he was the Rookie of the Year, Ichiro had been performing at the same level in Japan for years. He's now proven he can do it in America, and considering he just turned 28 years of age in October, he likely will be productive on this side of the pond for many seasons to come.

Position: RF
Bats: L **Throws:** R
Ht: 5'11" **Wt:** 157

Opening Day Age: 28
Born: 10/22/73 in Kasugai, Japan
ML Seasons: 1
Pronounciation: ee-chee-row

Overall Statistics

	G	AB	R	H	D	T	HR	RBI	SB	BB	SO	Avg	OBP	Slg
2001	157	692	127	242	34	8	8	69	56	30	53	.350	.381	.457
Career	157	692	127	242	34	8	8	69	56	30	53	.350	.381	.457

Where He Hits the Ball

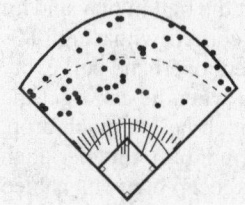
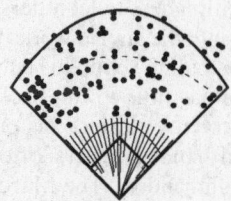

Vs. LHP   **Vs. RHP**

2001 Situational Stats

	AB	H	HR	RBI	Avg		AB	H	HR	RBI	Avg
Home	332	114	5	34	.343	LHP	192	61	1	23	.318
Road	360	128	3	35	.356	RHP	500	181	7	46	.362
First Half	386	133	5	41	.345	Sc Pos	137	61	1	55	.445
Scnd Half	306	109	3	28	.356	Clutch	95	38	2	12	.400

2001 Rankings (American League)

- 1st in batting average, at-bats, hits, singles, stolen bases, plate appearances (738), highest ground-ball-flyball ratio (2.6), highest percentage of swings put into play (54.8), batting average with runners in scoring position, batting average vs. righthanded pitchers, batting average on the road, batting average among rookies, fielding percentage in right field (.997) and steals of third (14)
- Led the Mariners in runs scored, times on base (280), bunts in play (17), lowest percentage of swings that missed (8.8), batting average in the clutch, batting average with the bases loaded (.545), on-base percentage for a leadoff hitter (.382) and batting average at home
- Led AL right fielders in batting average

Jay Buhner

Position: LF
Bats: R **Throws:** R
Ht: 6' 3" **Wt:** 210

Opening Day Age: 37
Born: 8/13/64 in
Louisville, KY
ML Seasons: 15
Pronunciation:
B-YOU-ner
Nickname: Bone

Overall Statistics

	G	AB	R	H	D	T	HR	RBI	SB	BB	SO	Avg	OBP	Slg
2001	19	45	4	10	2	0	2	5	0	8	9	.222	.340	.400
Career	1472	5013	798	1273	233	19	310	965	6	792	1406	.254	.359	.494

2001 Situational Stats

	AB	H	HR	RBI	Avg		AB	H	HR	RBI	Avg
Home	28	7	2	5	.250	LHP	22	3	1	1	.136
Road	17	3	0	0	.176	RHP	23	7	1	4	.304
First Half	0	0	0	0	-	Sc Pos	17	3	1	3	.176
Scnd Half	45	10	2	5	.222	Clutch	4	0	0	0	.000

2001 Season

For most of Seattle's 2001 season, longtime Mariner Jay Buhner could only sit and watch, sidelined by a sore arch in his left foot. By the time he returned in September, all he had time to do was try to tune up for a reserve role in the postseason. He hit his only two homers of the regular season during Seattle's last four games in October. In the postseason he went 2-for-9 with a homer.

Hitting, Baserunning & Defense

Buhner still has a good batting eye, but it's hard to say how much of his power remains. In the past, his extra-base pop and ability to draw walks made him valuable despite his low average and high strikeout totals. A dyed-in-the-wool power hitter, he aims to pull and loft the ball. Before his foot problems he had the range to cover either outfield corner, and threw well enough for right field, but had below-average speed on the bases.

2002 Outlook

The 37-year-old outfielder became a free agent after the season and hinted at retirement. Because Buhner missed significant time in each of the last four seasons with four separate injuries, teams might be reluctant to count on him for much.

Norm Charlton

Position: RP
Bats: B **Throws:** L
Ht: 6' 3" **Wt:** 205

Opening Day Age: 39
Born: 1/6/63 in Fort
Polk, LA
ML Seasons: 13
Nickname: The Sheriff

Overall Statistics

	W	L	Pct.	ERA	G	GS	Sv	IP	H	BB	SO	HR	Ratio
2001	4	2	.667	3.02	44	0	1	47.2	36	11	48	4	0.99
Career	51	54	.486	3.71	605	37	97	899.1	798	409	808	70	1.34

2001 Situational Stats

	W	L	ERA	Sv	IP		AB	H	HR	RBI	Avg
Home	1	1	1.90	1	23.2	LHB	71	12	2	9	.169
Road	3	1	4.13	0	24.0	RHB	99	24	2	9	.242
First Half	2	1	3.86	0	25.2	Sc Pos	45	10	1	14	.222
Scnd Half	2	1	2.05	1	22.0	Clutch	66	12	2	8	.182

2001 Season

Thirty-eight-year-old Norm Charlton, who had pitched a total of three innings in the major leagues in 2000 and hadn't thrown effectively in several years, returned with a flourish in 2001. He was especially effective while posting a 2.05 ERA in 22 innings during the second half. As Seattle's second lefty out of the pen, he struck out a batter an inning and held lefties to a .169 average.

Pitching & Defense

Though he isn't the horse he once was, Charlton was as effective as ever last year, at least for a few batters at a time. Having regained command of his low-90s fastball, he once again was able to set up hitters for hard splitters in the dirt. The specialist role seemed to keep him fresh. His delivery leaves him twisted around toward third, and he's no sure bet to handle the balls that find him.

2002 Outlook

Charlton's string of unlikely resurrections is enough to make a cat envious. After all, in 2001 he posted his first sub-4.00 ERA dating back to 1995. While it's impossible to say how close he is to the end of his last baseball life, Charlton returns for another season in Seattle after signing a one-year, $1.25 million contract in December.

Seattle

John Halama

Position: SP/RP
Bats: L **Throws:** L
Ht: 6' 5" **Wt:** 210

Opening Day Age: 30
Born: 2/22/72 in Brooklyn, NY
ML Seasons: 4
Pronunciation: ha-LA-ma

Overall Statistics

	W	L	Pct.	ERA	G	GS	Sv	IP	H	BB	SO	HR	Ratio
2001	10	7	.588	4.73	31	17	0	110.1	132	26	50	18	1.43
Career	36	27	.571	4.74	105	77	0	488.1	568	151	263	57	1.47

2001 Situational Stats

	W	L	ERA	Sv	IP		AB	H	HR	RBI	Avg
Home	6	7	4.50	0	68.0	LHB	129	46	7	17	.357
Road	4	0	5.10	0	42.1	RHB	317	86	11	42	.271
First Half	6	5	5.42	0	78.0	Sc Pos	75	25	3	36	.333
Scnd Half	4	2	3.06	0	32.1	Clutch	52	15	0	3	.288

2001 Season

The Mariners finally ran out of patience with John Halama last year. The lefthanded finesse pitcher pitched as decently as ever until late June, when a couple of poor starts resulted in a brief demotion to Triple-A Tacoma. Recalled after the All-Star break, he was given one more start, but blew it and was sent to the bullpen, where he soaked up mostly meaningless innings for the rest of the year.

Pitching & Defense

Halama lacks a major league fastball, so he offers an endless assortment of curves, sinkers and changeups at varying speeds and locations. He continually tries to get hitters to offer at something just off the plate. His lack of stamina is a major weakness. Oddly, lefthanded hitters give him trouble. He fields his position decently, and completely negates the running game with one of the best pickoff moves around.

2002 Outlook

Seattle's ample young pitching talent may make it tough for Halama to make the club in 2002. He could be moved in a trade, as the Mariners are trying to acquire a bat in exchange for some of the organization's pitching surplus. Even if Halama catches on elsewhere, it may be hard for him to find a role he can succeed in.

Al Martin

Position: LF/DH
Bats: L **Throws:** L
Ht: 6' 2" **Wt:** 214

Opening Day Age: 34
Born: 11/24/67 in West Covina, CA
ML Seasons: 10

Overall Statistics

	G	AB	R	H	D	T	HR	RBI	SB	BB	SO	Avg	OBP	Slg
2001	100	283	41	68	15	2	7	42	9	37	59	.240	.330	.382
Career	1132	4004	645	1112	208	46	129	459	171	373	828	.278	.341	.449

2001 Situational Stats

	AB	H	HR	RBI	Avg		AB	H	HR	RBI	Avg
Home	113	28	2	14	.248	LHP	10	1	0	1	.100
Road	170	40	5	28	.235	RHP	273	67	7	41	.245
First Half	155	33	4	25	.213	Sc Pos	88	22	3	36	.250
Scnd Half	128	35	3	17	.273	Clutch	31	3	0	2	.097

2001 Season

Things never worked out in Seattle for Al Martin. Last year he shared left field and got off to a brutal start, batting .151 in 93 at-bats during April and May. His struggles all but killed his chances of earning a larger role. His bat revived a bit in mid-season, but a torn muscle in his throwing elbow kept him out of the lineup for most of September and October.

Hitting, Baserunning & Defense

Lefthanders simply own Martin—he's batted just .203 against them over the last three years—and he's rarely allowed to face them. Even against righthanders, his willingness to chase bad pitches makes him liable to get himself out whenever he falls behind. He does his best hitting early in the count and always looks to pull. Despite decent speed, Martin gets poor jumps and isn't much of an outfielder. His weak arm limited him to left even before his elbow injury. He'll steal an occasional base and he is above average on the basepaths.

2002 Outlook

Martin became a free agent at season's end and his future is uncertain. He will have to take a big pay cut to catch on somewhere, and may have trouble finding anything more than a part-time role.

Mark McLemore

Position: LF/3B/SS
Bats: B **Throws:** R
Ht: 5'11" **Wt:** 207

Opening Day Age: 37
Born: 10/4/64 in San Diego, CA
ML Seasons: 16

Overall Statistics

	G	AB	R	H	D	T	HR	RBI	SB	BB	SO	Avg	OBP	Slg
2001	125	409	78	117	16	9	5	57	39	69	84	.286	.384	.406
Career	1552	5296	826	1377	209	43	42	516	249	735	816	.260	.349	.340

2001 Situational Stats

	AB	H	HR	RBI	Avg		AB	H	HR	RBI	Avg
Home	191	53	2	24	.277	LHP	71	12	1	9	.169
Road	218	64	3	33	.294	RHP	338	105	4	48	.311
First Half	193	56	4	26	.290	Sc Pos	103	28	1	47	.272
Scnd Half	216	61	1	31	.282	Clutch	56	19	2	11	.339

2001 Season

When Seattle signed Bret Boone, Mark McLemore, the incumbent second baseman, demanded to be traded. The Mariners kept him instead and found new ways to use him, and McLemore responded with one of his finest seasons. He served as Seattle's backup shortstop and third baseman, and saw plenty of time in left field. When he wasn't starting, he was the Mariners' most valuable bench player and pinch-hitter.

Hitting, Baserunning & Defense

The switch-hitting McLemore always has been more effective from the left side. A patient hitter who's adept at working a walk, he sprays line drives. With good speed and instincts, he runs the bases aggressively and always is a threat to steal against a righty. Though he hadn't played shortstop or third base in years, he showed adequate range at both spots, but his arm was a bit stretched at third. He remains a good second baseman and a rangy outfielder, capable of covering all three spots.

2002 Outlook

McLemore has generated the best on-base percentages of his career in recent seasons, and Seattle gave a two-year, $6 million deal to a valuable commodity who may never be a regular at any one position again. That is a compliment.

Jeff Nelson Unhittable

Position: RP
Bats: R **Throws:** R
Ht: 6' 8" **Wt:** 235

Opening Day Age: 35
Born: 11/17/66 in Baltimore, MD
ML Seasons: 10

Overall Statistics

	W	L	Pct.	ERA	G	GS	Sv	IP	H	BB	SO	HR	Ratio
2001	4	3	.571	2.76	69	0	4	65.1	30	44	88	3	1.13
Career	39	35	.527	3.23	603	0	21	620.2	494	331	648	40	1.33

2001 Situational Stats

	W	L	ERA	Sv	IP		AB	H	HR	RBI	Avg
Home	1	2	1.80	3	30.0	LHB	78	13	1	8	.167
Road	3	1	3.57	1	35.1	RHB	143	17	2	9	.119
First Half	3	1	2.19	4	37.0	Sc Pos	54	8	1	15	.148
Scnd Half	1	2	3.49	0	28.1	Clutch	109	15	2	9	.138

2001 Season

The signing of free-agent reliever Jeff Nelson to a three-year, $10.65 million deal in December 2000 turned out to be one of the Mariners' best moves last year. He arguably enjoyed his finest summer, and as their primary righthanded setup man, he enabled the Mariners to close out the vast majority of close games from the seventh inning on.

Pitching & Defense

One of the most unhittable pitches in the game is Nelson's big-breaking slider. Delivered with a funky sidearm motion, the pitch has spectacular lateral movement—it can start out aimed at a righthanded hitter's hip and still wind up completely out of his reach. Mixing it with his decent fastball is all he needs to do. He'll give up a walk or two when batters are able to lay off, but Nelson hardly ever gets hit hard. Lefthanded hitters have slightly better success against him. His slider is an easy pitch to run on, but those who are fortunate enough to reach base against him generally don't try to push their luck.

2002 Outlook

Nelson is well established as one of the top setup men around. With a stingy 2.60 ERA over the last two seasons, he shows no signs of slipping. Look for him to continue to excel.

Jose Paniagua

Traded To ROCKIES

Position: RP
Bats: R **Throws:** R
Ht: 6' 2" **Wt:** 190

Opening Day Age: 28
Born: 8/20/73 in San Jose de Ocoa, DR
ML Seasons: 6
Pronunciation: pahn-ee-AH-gwah

Overall Statistics

	W	L	Pct.	ERA	G	GS	Sv	IP	H	BB	SO	HR	Ratio
2001	4	3	.571	4.36	60	0	3	66.0	59	38	46	7	1.47
Career	18	20	.474	4.20	228	14	12	315.0	301	172	242	30	1.50

2001 Situational Stats

	W	L	ERA	Sv	IP		AB	H	HR	RBI	Avg
Home	1	0	6.83	2	29.0	LHB	105	27	0	15	.257
Road	3	3	2.43	1	37.0	RHB	148	32	7	26	.216
First Half	3	2	4.15	2	43.1	Sc Pos	70	19	1	32	.271
Scnd Half	1	1	4.76	1	22.2	Clutch	114	28	2	18	.246

2001 Season

Jose Paniagua picked the wrong time to go into a slump. After serving as the club's top righthanded setup man in 2000, he began the 2001 season sharing the role with Jeff Nelson, who'd been signed over the winter. The arrangement worked wonderfully at first, as each pitched well over the first two months. Paniagua suffered through several rough outings in June, though, and soon was demoted to middle relief. He never got back on track, and had a poor second half and postseason.

Pitching & Defense

Few pitchers pitch inside as effectively as Paniagua, who likes to work in on righthanded hitters' fists with his low-90s cut fastball. He makes better use of his forkball and slider when facing lefthanded hitters, who also find him very tough and have homered off him only once in the last two years. He's a competent fielder and pays enough attention to runners to keep them close.

2002 Outlook

Following Paniagua's down year, Seattle traded him and two minor league pitchers to Colorado in the Jeff Cirillo deal. He could become a fixture for the rebuilding Rockies.

Joel Pineiro

Position: SP
Bats: R **Throws:** R
Ht: 6' 1" **Wt:** 180

Opening Day Age: 23
Born: 9/25/78 in Rio Pedres, PR
ML Seasons: 2
Pronunciation: jo-EL pi-ne-ro

Overall Statistics

	W	L	Pct.	ERA	G	GS	Sv	IP	H	BB	SO	HR	Ratio
2001	6	2	.750	2.03	17	11	0	75.1	50	21	56	2	0.94
Career	7	2	.778	2.76	25	12	0	94.2	75	34	66	5	1.15

2001 Situational Stats

	W	L	ERA	Sv	IP		AB	H	HR	RBI	Avg
Home	4	0	0.64	0	42.0	LHB	135	31	1	13	.230
Road	2	2	3.78	0	33.1	RHB	127	19	1	6	.150
First Half	0	0	0.00	0	2.1	Sc Pos	42	13	0	16	.310
Scnd Half	6	2	2.10	0	73.0	Clutch	16	0	0	0	.000

2001 Season

One of the Mariners' biggest surprises last season was rookie righthander Joel Pineiro, who sparkled in the second half. He was called up in July, and after making several impressive relief appearances, he replaced John Halama in the starting rotation late in the month. He reeled off four straight brilliant starts before coming back to earth somewhat, and was moved to the bullpen in September as the club prepared for the playoffs.

Pitching & Defense

As young pitchers sometimes do, Pineiro showed improved velocity last season, throwing consistently in the low 90s. He also added a changeup, and with an already fine curveball, his once-borderline arsenal became rather impressive. His curve has been his best pitch, and his fastball shows good movement down in the strike zone. He handled all eight of his chances in the field in 2001.

2002 Outlook

Rumors swirled during the offseason that the Mariners would trade some of their young pitching for a potent bat. Pineiro would be a highly coveted commodity, so it's possible he could be moved. Still, Seattle might be better off with him in the mix, battling for a rotation spot in the spring.

Arthur Rhodes

Position: RP
Bats: L **Throws:** L
Ht: 6' 2" **Wt:** 205

Opening Day Age: 32
Born: 10/24/69 in Waco, TX
ML Seasons: 11

Overall Statistics

	W	L	Pct.	ERA	G	GS	Sv	IP	H	BB	SO	HR	Ratio
2001	8	0	1.000	1.72	71	0	3	68.0	46	12	83	5	0.85
Career	56	44	.560	4.53	381	61	12	759.2	672	357	739	90	1.35

2001 Situational Stats

	W	L	ERA	Sv	IP		AB	H	HR	RBI	Avg
Home	4	0	1.03	0	35.0	LHB	120	24	2	13	.200
Road	4	0	2.45	3	33.0	RHB	124	22	3	9	.177
First Half	5	0	1.95	2	37.0	Sc Pos	66	14	2	19	.212
Scnd Half	3	0	1.45	1	31.0	Clutch	136	26	2	14	.191

2001 Season

Arthur Rhodes was the American League's best lefthanded setup man last year, and frankly it wasn't even close. He easily led AL relievers in ERA and holds (32), stranded 58 of the 68 baserunners he inherited and was a key member of the major leagues' best bullpen. Taking advantage of the new expanded strike zone, he cut his walks by more than half and enjoyed his finest season.

Pitching & Defense

With mid-90s heat, Rhodes was well equipped to test the new upper limits of the strike zone, especially against righthanded hitters. He can get hitters out with sheer velocity, but he also can do it with movement or by changing speeds. He gets lefthanded hitters to chase his hard slider or hit his curveball or changeup on the ground. He has a poor move to first, but throws enough high fastballs to make basestealers wary.

2002 Outlook

Rhodes has held up fine despite frequent use the last two years. In his second straight season of 70-plus appearances in 2001, he posted his career-best ERA and limited opponents to exactly one baserunner per inning, the lowest mark of his career. Rhodes is in his prime and ought to remain one of the more feared southpaws in the game.

Dan Wilson

Position: C
Bats: R **Throws:** R
Ht: 6' 3" **Wt:** 202

Opening Day Age: 33
Born: 3/25/69 in Barrington, IL
ML Seasons: 10

Overall Statistics

	G	AB	R	H	D	T	HR	RBI	SB	BB	SO	Avg	OBP	Slg
2001	123	377	44	100	20	1	10	42	3	20	69	.265	.305	.403
Career	974	3165	349	830	167	10	76	397	22	221	563	.262	.312	.393

2001 Situational Stats

	AB	H	HR	RBI	Avg		AB	H	HR	RBI	Avg
Home	174	45	4	16	.259	LHP	131	38	8	18	.290
Road	203	55	6	26	.271	RHP	246	62	2	24	.252
First Half	193	53	6	24	.275	Sc Pos	101	30	2	32	.297
Scnd Half	184	47	4	18	.255	Clutch	44	9	2	4	.205

2001 Season

Coming off a subpar offensive season in 2000, Dan Wilson re-established himself as Seattle's No. 1 catcher last year. His production was inconsistent, as he batted .213 in April and July, and hit better than .300 in June and August. Still, as the starting catcher for most games against righties and nearly all games against southpaws, Wilson provided his usual mix of acceptable offense and fine defense.

Hitting, Baserunning & Defense

Even at the plate, Wilson is defensive. He's good at fighting off two-strike offerings, but rarely attacks a pitch, even when ahead in the count. He generates flyballs to all fields and occasionally reaches the fences when he gets something to pull. He is one of the better bunters in the league. A respected catch-and-throw guy, he has a strong, accurate arm and committed only one error last season. He runs fairly well for a catcher.

2002 Outlook

Wilson, a longtime favorite of manager Lou Piniella, fits in well with the club's new defense-first approach. However, his impending free agency after 2002 and lack of offense last year prompted the M's to trade for the Padres' Ben Davis. The two catchers will share time, so look for another 350-375 at-bat season from Wilson.

Seattle

Other Seattle Mariners

Pat Borders (Pos: C, Age: 38, Bats: R)

	G	AB	R	H	D	T	HR	RBI	SB	BB	SO	Avg	OBP	Slg
2001	5	6	1	3	0	0	0	0	0	0	1	.500	.500	.500
Career	1006	3052	267	782	155	12	67	327	6	149	507	.256	.291	.381

Borders, a 2000 Olympics gold medal winner, has had only 40 major league at-bats since 1998. He decided to file for free agency, hoping that some major league club is looking for a veteran backup. 2002 Outlook: D

Ryan Franklin (Pos: RHP, Age: 29)

	W	L	Pct.	ERA	G	GS	Sv	IP	H	BB	SO	HR	Ratio
2001	5	1	.833	3.56	38	0	0	78.1	76	24	60	13	1.28
Career	5	1	.833	3.71	44	0	0	89.2	86	32	66	15	1.32

Franklin, a flyball pitcher, led the Seattle bullpen in innings pitched last season. As a result, he also led in home runs allowed. He was able to limit the damage, though, as eight of his 13 homers allowed were of the solo variety. 2002 Outlook: B

Charles Gipson (Pos: LF/CF/RF, Age: 29, Bats: R)

	G	AB	R	H	D	T	HR	RBI	SB	BB	SO	Avg	OBP	Slg
2001	94	64	16	14	2	2	0	5	1	4	20	.219	.282	.313
Career	252	224	50	53	9	5	0	19	8	19	51	.237	.306	.321

Gipson played six positions during his first full season in the majors. In an almost equal number of at-bats, he hit much better against righthanders. He hit .310 against them, compared to .143 against lefties. 2002 Outlook: C

Stan Javier (Pos: LF/CF/RF, Age: 38, Bats: B)

	G	AB	R	H	D	T	HR	RBI	SB	BB	SO	Avg	OBP	Slg
2001	89	281	44	82	14	1	4	33	11	36	47	.292	.375	.391
Career	1763	5047	781	1358	225	40	57	503	246	578	839	.269	.345	.363

Javier served as an important utility guy, who for the second consecutive year played four different positions, plus DH. He retired after Seattle's loss to the Yankees in the ALCS, ending a solid career that lasted 17 years. 2002 Outlook: D

Gene Kingsale (Pos: LF, Age: 25, Bats: B)

	G	AB	R	H	D	T	HR	RBI	SB	BB	SO	Avg	OBP	Slg
2001	13	19	4	5	0	0	0	1	3	2	4	.263	.364	.263
Career	81	194	27	47	4	1	0	17	5	9	32	.242	.284	.273

A struggling Kingsale was claimed off waivers from Baltimore in July. He turned it around in the Seattle organization, producing better numbers in most offensive categories. The Mariners re-signed him for 2002, reaching an agreement on a minor league contract in mid-November. 2002 Outlook: C

Tom Lampkin (Pos: C, Age: 38, Bats: L)

	G	AB	R	H	D	T	HR	RBI	SB	BB	SO	Avg	OBP	Slg
2001	79	204	28	46	10	0	5	22	1	18	41	.225	.309	.348
Career	673	1515	192	361	68	7	46	199	19	155	227	.238	.320	.383

Seattle's backup catcher for a third straight season, Lampkin remained healthy after an injury-plagued 2000. Still solid defensively, his hitting has dropped off the last two seasons. Lampkin was traded to San Diego in December and may share catching duties with Wiki Gonzalez. 2002 Outlook: B

Scott Podsednik (Pos: LF, Age: 26, Bats: L)

	G	AB	R	H	D	T	HR	RBI	SB	BB	SO	Avg	OBP	Slg
2001	5	6	1	1	0	1	0	3	0	0	1	.167	.167	.500
Career	5	6	1	1	0	1	0	3	0	0	1	.167	.167	.500

A knee injury limited Podsednik's season to a total of 71 games, but he still had a promising season at Triple-A. He was sent to Puerto Rico to play winter ball, and continued to succeed. 2002 Outlook: C

Anthony Sanders (Pos: LF, Age: 28, Bats: R)

	G	AB	R	H	D	T	HR	RBI	SB	BB	SO	Avg	OBP	Slg
2001	9	17	1	3	0	0	0	2	0	2	3	.176	.263	.294
Career	13	25	3	6	3	0	0	4	0	2	5	.240	.296	.360

After appearing in nine out of Seattle's first 15 games, Sanders refused a demotion and declared free agency. Despite his reputation as an outstanding outfielder, no team signed him until he agreed to a minor league deal with the Reds in the fall. 2002 Outlook: C

Ed Sprague (Pos: 1B, Age: 34, Bats: R)

	G	AB	R	H	D	T	HR	RBI	SB	BB	SO	Avg	OBP	Slg
2001	45	94	9	28	7	0	2	16	0	11	18	.298	.374	.436
Career	1203	4095	506	1010	225	12	152	558	6	358	833	.247	.318	.419

Sprague was signed in May and went on to play a variety of positions while hitting well. He failed to finish over .300 when he went 0-1 in the final game. As a versatile part-timer, he declared free agency. 2002 Outlook: C

Brett Tomko (Pos: RHP, Age: 28)

	W	L	Pct.	ERA	G	GS	Sv	IP	H	BB	SO	HR	Ratio
2001	3	1	.750	5.19	11	4	0	34.2	42	15	22	9	1.64
Career	39	32	.549	4.45	132	91	1	635.2	613	226	470	88	1.32

Despite mostly starting at Triple-A Tacoma, Tomko was much better as a reliever while in the majors (2-0, 3.86). The San Diego native re-signed in November, only to be dealt to the Padres in a six-player trade in December. He looks like a starter again. 2002 Outlook: B

Seattle Mariners Minor League Prospects

Organization Overview:

The Pacific Rim has placed two key players in Seattle, 2001 American League MVP Ichiro Suzuki and closer Kazuhiro Sasaki, who was the AL Rookie of the Year in 2000. The farm system also has been busy there, as the Mariners have signed promising Koreans Cha Baek and Shin-Soo Choo. Meanwhile, scouting in Australia has unearthed the budding talents of Chris Snelling and Craig Anderson. Seattle's overseas efforts provide depth to an organization that has plenty of young talent. A few pitchers could step up at some point in 2002, including starters Ryan Anderson, Greg Wooten, Rafeal Soriano and Jeff Heaverlo. The one position prospect who could have started for the AL West champs in 2002 was unheralded shortstop Ramon Vazquez, but the M's traded him to the Padres in a six-player deal in mid-December.

Ryan Anderson

Position: P **Opening Day Age:** 22
Bats: L **Throws:** L **Born:** 7/12/79 in
Ht: 6' 10" **Wt:** 215 Southfield, MI

Recent Statistics

	W	L	ERA	G	GS	Sv	IP	H	R	BB	SO	HR
2000 AAA Tacoma	5	8	3.98	20	20	0	104.0	83	51	55	146	8

The imposing lefthander, a 1997 first-round pick, came into camp last spring with a chance to pitch in Seattle before the summer was over. But after having trouble getting loose early in spring training, Anderson was diagnosed with a torn labrum and had shoulder surgery that ended his season. Prior to his surgery, Anderson had fared well against older, more experienced hitters. In both 1999 and 2000, he led his entire classification in strikeouts per nine innings. Making that possible was a live mid-90s fastball, a respectable changeup and a curveball that was devastating when he had it under control. Anderson should be throwing early in spring training and may be close to 100 percent by the start of the season. The Mariners hope he is ready for game action in April.

Jeff Heaverlo

Position: P **Opening Day Age:** 24
Bats: R **Throws:** R **Born:** 1/13/78 in Palo
Ht: 6' 1" **Wt:** 185 Alto, CA

Recent Statistics

	W	L	ERA	G	GS	Sv	IP	H	R	BB	SO	HR
2000 AAA Tacoma	0	1	4.85	2	2	0	13.0	14	7	6	4	2
2000 A Lancaster	14	6	4.22	27	27	0	155.2	170	84	52	159	18
2001 AA San Antonio	11	6	3.12	27	27	0	178.2	164	75	40	173	12

A mature and polished college pitcher, this 1999 pick has come on quickly and turned in his finest season at Double-A San Antonio in 2001. He came to the pro game with a wicked slider—the best in the organization—and it was key to his fine performance at high Class-A Lan-

caster in 2000. Yet he had a tendency to rely too much on the pitch, which he used heavily in college to pitch away because of the aluminum bat. A big difference in 2001 was his improved confidence in his fastball. His fastball has good sink, but he's been prone to turn to the slider. That changed in 2001 and helped spark a very strong second half. His changeup is his third pitch, a solid offering that requires more consistency. Heaverlo is likely to start 2002 at Triple-A Tacoma.

Kenny Kelly

Position: OF **Opening Day Age:** 23
Bats: R **Throws:** R **Born:** 1/26/79 in Plant
Ht: 6' 3" **Wt:** 180 City, FL

Recent Statistics

	G	AB	R	H	D	T	HR	RBI	SB	BB	SO	Avg
2000 AA Orlando	124	489	73	123	17	8	3	29	31	59	119	.252
2001 AA San Antonio	121	478	72	125	20	5	11	46	18	45	111	.262
2001 MLE	121	463	63	110	18	3	9	40	13	34	120	.238

A Devil Rays 1997 second-rounder, Kelly played both pro baseball and college football at the University of Miami until he abandoned quarterbacking duties before the 2000 baseball season. He has fabulous tools—impressive bat speed, solid range and running ability, plus a strong and accurate arm—but playing baseball part-time has hindered his development. The Rays sold him to Seattle in April, simply to save the $1.25 million Kelly was owed for giving up football. It was Seattle's good fortune that Kelly started pounding the ball and showing more power in 2001. He displayed pop to all fields in the Arizona Fall League, suggesting that he's made adjustments. More at-bats and more plate discipline will help him after missing so much time to football.

Antonio Perez

Position: SS **Opening Day Age:** 20
Bats: R **Throws:** R **Born:** 7/26/81 in Bani,
Ht: 5' 11" **Wt:** 175 DR

Recent Statistics

	G	AB	R	H	D	T	HR	RBI	SB	BB	SO	Avg
2000 A Lancaster	98	395	90	109	36	6	17	63	28	58	99	.276
2001 AA San Antonio	5	21	3	3	0	0	0	0	0	0	7	.143

Signed by the Reds in 1998, Perez escaped a crowded middle-infield picture when he was dealt to Seattle in the Ken Griffey Jr. trade. Despite a move from second base to short, Perez took the high Class-A California League by storm in 2000, stroking 59 extra-base hits in just 395 at-bats. A quick, short stroke generates surprising pop for the slight middle infielder, and Perez someday may develop a bit more power. He also has shown good command of the strike zone. His defensive game features very good speed and hands, plus a strong arm. A broken navicular bone in his right wrist ended his season in April. Perez is hitting and throwing in the Dominican, and he may play in games before winter ball is over. He should be ready to go in the spring.

Chris Snelling

Position: OF   **Opening Day Age:** 20
Bats: L **Throws:** L   **Born:** 12/3/81 in North
Ht: 5' 10" **Wt:** 165   Miami, FL

Recent Statistics

	G	AB	R	H	D	THR	RBI	SB	BB	SO	Avg
2000 A Wisconsin	72	259	44	79	9	5	9	56	7	34	34	.305
2001 A San Berndno	114	450	90	151	29	10	7	73	12	45	63	.336

The Aussie outfielder, signed in 1999, has great makeup, phenomenal instincts and an all-out play-to-win approach. He also has plenty of talent, showing an advanced ability to make contact and hit for average, plus he draws walks, shows some pop, flashes some range and plays solid defense. He's batted better than .300 in each of his three pro seasons, and in 2001—at the age of 19—he won the batting title of the high Class-A California League. His hustling ways also may contribute to injuries, as Snelling broke his hand diving into an outfield wall in 2000 and suffered a season-ending stress fracture of his right ankle late in 2001. The M's see him as a high-average leadoff type with gap power.

Rafael Soriano

Position: P   **Opening Day Age:** 22
Bats: R **Throws:** R   **Born:** 12/19/79 in San
Ht: 6' 1" **Wt:** 175   Jose, DR

Recent Statistics

	W	L	ERA	G	GS	Sv	IP	H	R	BB	SO	HR
2000 A Wisconsin	8	4	2.87	21	21	0	122.1	97	41	50	90	3
2001 A San Berndno	6	3	2.53	15	15	0	89.0	49	28	39	98	4
2001 AA San Antonio	2	2	3.35	8	8	0	48.1	34	18	14	53	5

Once a light-hitting outfielder, Soriano was converted to pitching prior to the 1999 season. He not only has a better feel for pitching than one might expect, but also a moving mid-90s fastball that initially generated lots of strikeouts. He lacked secondary pitches then, but now he's a fastball-slider guy whose stuff gave hitters trouble at high Class-A San Bernardino and Double-A San Antonio in 2001. His changeup is a work in progress, but both the fastball and slider are major league pitches. Soriano also pitches inside and works both sides of the plate aggressively. He may get more Double-A seasoning early in 2002, but he's on track to becoming a top-flight pitcher.

Jamal Strong

Position: OF   **Opening Day Age:** 23
Bats: R **Throws:** R   **Born:** 8/5/78 in
Ht: 5' 10" **Wt:** 180   Pasadena, CA

Recent Statistics

	G	AB	R	H	D	THR	RBI	SB	BB	SO	Avg
2000 A Everett	75	296	63	93	7	3	1	28	60	52	29	.314
2001 A Wisconsin	51	184	41	65	12	1	0	19	35	40	27	.353
2001 A San Berndno	81	331	74	103	11	2	0	32	47	51	60	.311

A 2000 pick after four years of college ball, Strong lacks extra-base pop, but calls on impressive little-ball skills.

He's the fastest man in the system, a good center fielder who can run the ball down. He has a bit of an inside-out swing, and gets the barrel of the bat on the ball and hits it on the ground. Strong also knows how to draw walks, and his .431 on-base percentage over his two pro seasons opens the door for his speed. Strong stole 60 bases at short-season Everett in 2000, and he swiped 82 more between Class-A Wisconsin and high-A San Bernardino last summer. The Mariners would like to see him work on using his bunting skills more in game situations.

Matt Thornton

Position: P   **Opening Day Age:** 25
Bats: L **Throws:** L   **Born:** 9/15/76 in Three
Ht: 6' 6" **Wt:** 220   Rivers, MI

Recent Statistics

	W	L	ERA	G	GS	Sv	IP	H	R	BB	SO	HR
2000 A Wisconsin	6	9	4.01	26	17	0	103.1	94	59	72	88	2
2001 A San Berndno	14	7	2.52	27	27	0	157.0	126	56	60	192	9

A 1998 first-round pick, Thornton progressed slowly over his first three pro seasons, struggling with his control. The 6-foot-6 southpaw, who played more basketball as an amateur and took up baseball late, simply needed more time to develop. The pieces came together in 2001, when he improved the command of his fastball and made significant progress on a slider that is his out pitch. Thornton's 192 strikeouts ranked first in the high Class-A California League. He has a sound delivery and works inside effectively, but his changeup needs more fine-tuning. Gaining command of his offspeed pitch and simply working more innings could push Thornton onto the fast track to Seattle.

Others to Watch

Australian lefty **Craig Anderson** (21) throws three pitches he can get over the plate. He keeps hitters off balance by effectively mixing his fastball, curve and changeup, and demonstrating a solid feel for pitching. He was 11-8 (3.71) at Class-A Wisconsin in 2000 and 11-4 (2.26) at high-A San Bernardino last summer. . . A top-flight Korean prospect who signed a year ago, outfielder **Shin-Soo Choo** (19) has good tools. He shows a nice swing and power potential, and he runs and throws well. He pounded pitchers in the Rookie-level Arizona League last summer, batting .302 with a .420 on-base percentage. He stroked 10 doubles, 10 triples and four homers in 199 at-bats. . . **Ryan Christianson** (20) has the tools to be an above-average major league catcher. A bout with elbow tendinitis compromised his throwing in 2000, but he ranked third in the Class-A Midwest League by throwing out 38 percent of basestealers in 2001. He shows pop to all fields, but making contact and driving the ball doesn't come as easy as his defense. . . Righthander **Clint Nageotte** (21) has above-average pitches in his low-90s fastball and curve, and he went 11-8 (3.13) and led the Class-A Midwest League in strikeouts with 187 in 152.1 innings. His changeup is developing.

Tropicana Field

Offense

Tropicana Field apparently is not going to be the offensive playground that many expected. Part of the problem has been the Rays' poor offensive teams. They've been outhit, outhomered and out-scored at home in each of their four seasons. But the overall numbers, aside from an excessive amount of triples in 2001, are not out of the ordinary and rank in the middle of the league.

Defense

The unusual infield alignment, with the all-dirt basepaths and FieldTurf playing surface, does not appear to be an issue. The outfield setup, with the off-white roof, asymmetrical design and stadium catwalks, does create problems each season. The outfield is large and the Rays are trying to acquire the type of players needed to defend it properly.

Who It Helps the Most

Lefthanded slugger Ben Grieve should benefit from the cozy dimensions, but didn't really take advantage in terms of home runs last year. Catcher Toby Hall, called up in late July, likes to routinely pound the ball into the large gaps, hitting .344 at home as opposed to .250 on the road. Greg Vaughn also likes hitting at Tropicana, though more for average than power. Slap-hitting Jason Tyner figures to prosper as well.

Who It Hurts the Most

For some reason, Tanyon Sturtze compiled a 5.04 ERA at home compared to a mark of 3.84 on the road. Perhaps it was no more than a fluke. The same goes for second baseman Brent Abernathy, who hit 111 points better on the road than he did at the Trop. The tricky outfield dimensions make it tougher for Grieve defensively.

Rookies & Newcomers

Outfielders Carl Crawford and Josh Hamilton, who possess that special combination of speed and power, are the type of players who should prosper at Tropicana Field. Unfortunately, they may not get there until the end of 2002 or even 2003.

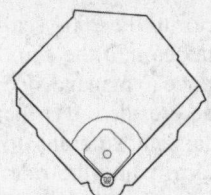

Dimensions: LF-315, LCF-370, CF-404, RCF-370, RF-322

Capacity: 44,445

Elevation: 15 feet

Surface: Turf

Foul Territory: Average

Park Factors

2001 Season

	Home Games Devil Rays	Opp	Total	Away Games Devil Rays	Opp	Total	Index
G	72	72	144	72	72	144	—
Avg	.267	.272	.269	.251	.275	.263	103
AB	2433	2548	4981	2480	2390	4870	102
R	306	388	694	287	408	695	100
H	649	693	1342	622	657	1279	105
2B	157	154	311	123	132	255	119
3B	12	15	27	4	10	14	189
HR	50	88	138	54	98	152	89
BB	206	236	442	198	286	484	89
SO	475	493	968	507	422	929	102
E	49	43	92	67	40	107	86
E-Infield	44	37	81	56	36	92	88
LHB-Avg	.268	.270	.269	.268	.281	.274	98
LHB-HR	20	36	56	24	38	62	86
RHB-Avg	.266	.273	.270	.236	.270	.254	106
RHB-HR	30	52	82	30	60	90	91

2000-2001

	Home Games Devil Rays	Opp	Total	Away Games Devil Rays	Opp	Total	Index
G	143	143	286	144	144	288	—
Avg	.258	.274	.266	.256	.278	.267	100
AB	4805	5123	9928	4991	4790	9781	102
R	612	773	1385	617	776	1393	100
H	1241	1403	2644	1276	1332	2608	102
2B	272	292	564	220	266	486	114
3B	21	32	53	11	25	36	145
HR	118	186	304	131	177	308	97
BB	467	462	929	417	531	948	97
SO	901	946	1847	981	802	1783	102
E	108	87	195	113	85	198	99
E-Infield	96	78	174	94	74	168	104
LHB-Avg	.262	.272	.268	.269	.294	.282	95
LHB-HR	40	78	118	46	74	120	95
RHB-Avg	.256	.276	.265	.247	.264	.255	104
RHB-HR	78	108	186	85	103	188	99

2001 Rankings (American League)
- Highest double factor
- Second-highest triple factor
- Second-highest RHB batting-average factor
- Third-highest hit factor
- Lowest walk factor
- Second-lowest error factor
- Second-lowest infield-error factor
- Second-lowest LHB home-run factor
- Third-lowest home-run factor

Hal McRae

2001 Season

Hal McRae joined the Rays prior to the 2001 season as bench coach. But 14 games into the campaign, he received a second chance to manage, one he didn't think he'd get. McRae presided over the Rays' transition from lackadaisical veterans to hungry youngsters and seemed to enjoy the ride. After a 27-61 first half (including a 4-10 record under Larry Rothschild), the Rays went 35-39 in the second half, producing a 27-29 mark after August 1.

Offense

McRae was one of the most hard-nosed and aggressive players of his era and the Rays (the McRays?) took on his personality. McRae would put even the most lead-footed players in motion, trying to create runs with singles, hit-and-runs and stolen bases and by forcing the defense to make mistakes. The players bought into the concept, honoring McRae's request to play without fear. In McRae's ideal design, Greg Vaughn and Ben Grieve will provide some power in the middle of an order that is otherwise built for speed.

Pitching & Defense

McRae also favors athletic and fast players on defense, especially up the middle, where he wants fielders to cover a lot of ground. He needs to improve his handling of the pitching staff, both in terms of removing starters and arranging the bullpen. He delegated much of the responsibility to pitching coach Bill Fischer, but then fired Fischer after the season and hired Jackie Brown.

2002 Outlook

McRae actually remade most of the coaching staff, hiring Lee May (first base) and Glenn Ezell (bullpen) during the season, then adding Brown, Tom Foley (third base) and Milt May (hitting) after the campaign. With the benefit of a full spring training, McRae should be able to share his strategies and spout his philosophies from the start. His low-key style was the perfect fit for the wave of young players. However, the intensity is likely to be turned up a notch this season, especially if the players aren't hustling as much as they did last year.

Born: 7/10/45 in Avon Park, Florida

Playing Experience: 1968-1987, Cin, KC

Managerial Experience: 5 seasons

Manager Statistics

Year	Team, Lg	W	L	Pct	GB	Finish
2001	Tampa Bay, AL	58	90	.392	34.0	5th East
5 Seasons		344	367	.484	—	—

2001 Starting Pitchers by Days Rest

	<=3	4	5	6+
Devil Rays Starts	0	73	40	29
Devil Rays ERA	—	5.84	4.97	4.09
AL Avg Starts	1	78	48	24
AL ERA	5.92	4.69	4.58	4.58

2001 Situational Stats

	Hal McRae*	AL Average
Hit & Run Success %	47.0	35.0
Stolen Base Success %	68.8	71.0
Platoon Pct.	54.8	59.1
Defensive Subs	15	26
High-Pitch Outings	5	6
Quick/Slow Hooks	16/28	19/16
Sacrifice Attempts	61	54

* McRae managed the Devil Rays for 148 games

2001 Rankings (American League)

- 1st in hit-and-run success percentage and slow hooks
- 3rd in fewest caught stealings of third base (3), sacrifice-bunt percentage (83.6%) and saves with over 1 inning pitched (12)

Brent Abernathy

2001 Season

Brent Abernathy seemed headed toward a wasted season when he lost a spring training battle with Bobby Smith, got off to a slow start at Triple-A and missed several weeks with an injury. But Abernathy refused to give up and was in the majors by June, quickly establishing himself as the Rays' starting second baseman. He homered at Fenway Park in his debut and hit safely in his first 10 games. He proved he had the offensive skills to go along with his defensive abilities and relentless hustle.

Hitting

Abernathy shows the makings of doing what good No. 2 hitters are supposed to do—make contact, move the ball around and get on base. The Rays hope he continues to improve in each area. Abernathy knows he doesn't have much power, but got into a few ruts where he was swinging for the fences. As with any young player, he will improve once he has a better grasp of the strike zone, which should allow him to boost his on-base percentage. He was vulnerable at times to high fastballs. Abernathy was impressive in the clutch, as his .351 average with runners in scoring position ranked second on the team.

Baserunning & Defense

Abernathy is one of those players who doesn't have any singularly outstanding skills but is successful because he incorporates a healthy dose of desire and hustle. He showed considerable improvement at hanging in when turning the double play, though some in the organization are concerned about his footwork. He tends to play deep to compensate for limited range, but has the arm to cover the added distance. He uses his knowledge and intuition on the bases, and could average 15-20 steals per season.

2002 Outlook

Abernathy did enough in three months to establish himself as the starter at second, though he likely will have to constantly prove himself. If he continues to develop, he could be a solid contributor, both in the No. 2 slot in the batting order and at second base.

Position: 2B
Bats: R **Throws:** R
Ht: 6' 1" **Wt:** 185

Opening Day Age: 24
Born: 9/23/77 in Atlanta, GA
ML Seasons: 1

Overall Statistics

	G	AB	R	H	D	T	HR	RBI	SB	BB	SO	Avg	OBP	Slg
2001	79	304	43	82	17	1	5	33	8	27	35	.270	.328	.382
Career	79	304	43	82	17	1	5	33	8	27	35	.270	.328	.382

Where He Hits the Ball

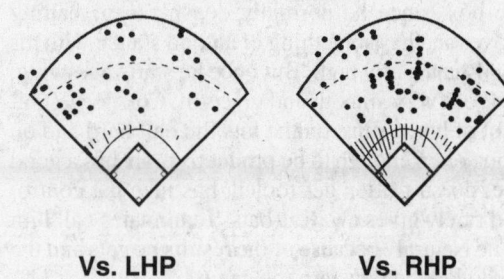

Vs. LHP   **Vs. RHP**

2001 Situational Stats

	AB	H	HR	RBI	Avg		AB	H	HR	RBI	Avg
Home	127	26	3	13	.205	LHP	75	24	2	7	.320
Road	177	56	2	20	.316	RHP	229	58	3	26	.253
First Half	45	13	1	3	.289	Sc Pos	77	27	0	26	.351
Scnd Half	259	69	4	30	.266	Clutch	43	10	1	5	.233

2001 Rankings (American League)

- 3rd in batting average among rookies
- 9th in fewest GDPs per GDP situation (5.5%)
- 10th in batting average with two strikes (.254)
- Led the Devil Rays in fewest GDPs per GDP situation (5.5%)

Steve Cox

2001 Season

Steve Cox' first battle last season was getting in the lineup consistently. That didn't happen until late July, when Fred McGriff accepted a trade to the Cubs. Cox' next biggest challenge was to perform consistently. He hit .273 once he inherited the starting first base job, a tad off his impressive rookie showing in 2000. But that was better than what he did in occasional duty during the first three and a half months, which included some awkward days in the outfield. He did improve his home run and RBI totals overall despite missing more than two weeks with a lower back strain.

Hitting

Cox can look a bit unorthodox when he steps into the box, since he normally doesn't wear batting gloves and has something of an odd stance with his hands unusually high. But once he starts his swing, he looks very smooth and graceful. Cox doesn't hit a lot of home runs, but he hits the ball hard and on a line often enough to be productive. He has a good eye, doesn't often get fooled, has nice bat control and rarely gives away at-bats. Teammates call him "The Natural" because of the results he gets and the hard work he puts into the game.

Baserunning & Defense

Cox isn't known for his speed, but he is sound fundamentally and does a decent job getting around the bases. Now that his outfield days appear behind him, he can concentrate on being an even better first baseman. He is very smooth around the bag and occasionally can make the outstanding play.

2002 Outlook

With McGriff out of the picture, Cox can come to spring training knowing the starting job is his. When he last did that at Triple-A in 1999, Cox was MVP of the International League. What remains to be seen is where he lands in the lineup. He hit in every slot in the batting order during the 2001 campaign, but seems suited for the middle of the lineup.

Position: 1B
Bats: L **Throws:** L
Ht: 6' 4" **Wt:** 222

Opening Day Age: 27
Born: 10/31/74 in Delano, CA
ML Seasons: 3

Overall Statistics

	G	AB	R	H	D	T	HR	RBI	SB	BB	SO	Avg	OBP	Slg
2001	108	342	37	88	22	0	12	51	2	24	75	.257	.323	.427
Career	230	679	81	182	42	1	23	86	3	70	124	.268	.347	.434

Where He Hits the Ball

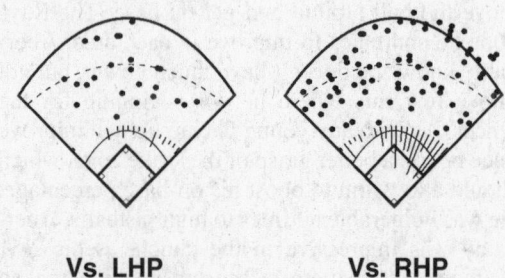

Vs. LHP   **Vs. RHP**

2001 Situational Stats

	AB	H	HR	RBI	Avg		AB	H	HR	RBI	Avg
Home	162	47	3	23	.290	LHP	69	16	0	10	.232
Road	180	41	9	28	.228	RHP	273	72	12	41	.264
First Half	169	41	6	26	.243	Sc Pos	97	21	3	36	.216
Scnd Half	173	47	6	25	.272	Clutch	61	13	0	3	.213

2001 Rankings (American League)

- 1st in lowest batting average on an 0-2 count (0.000)
- 7th in lowest batting average with runners in scoring position
- Led the Devil Rays in hit by pitch (10)

Chris Gomez

2001 Season

For an organization constantly reminded of its mistakes (Kevin Stocker, Wilson Alvarez, Vinny Castilla, Juan Guzman), the Rays made an excellent acquisition when they signed Chris Gomez after his release from the Padres last June. He spent a month at Triple-A before joining the Rays July 24, and immediately established himself as their starting shortstop. Gomez played steady defense and provided more offense—in terms of both average and power—than Tampa Bay expected. He also seemed to be over the knee problems that had slowed him the previous two seasons.

Hitting

For years, Gomez had been known as little more than a singles hitter. He felt his production was the result of being a No. 8 hitter in the National League. When he joined the Rays, he returned to a simpler, more aggressive batting style. The result was the rediscovery of some welcome power. Of his eight home runs, seven came in a span of 93 at-bats. The outburst occurred after he had hit only one in his previous 500 at-bats. Pitchers with overpowering fastballs still can get Gomez out, and the Rays protected him at times. But he showed the ability to put the ball in play and produce runs.

Baserunning & Defense

Gomez came to Tampa Bay labeled as a shortstop who makes all the routine plays, and he more or less lived up to the billing. He handled everything hit at him, but showed limited range when extended to either side. Gomez said his knees felt better as the season went on, so it's possible he will regain another step. He hasn't been much of a basestealer and the knee injuries haven't helped in that regard.

2002 Outlook

The Rays went into the offseason wanting to resign Gomez, and they got it done in December. The two sides agreed to a one-year deal that includes a club option for 2003. Getting Gomez under contract took the pressure off the Rays, who have no shortstop prospects in the system ready to take over.

Position: SS
Bats: R **Throws:** R
Ht: 6' 1" **Wt:** 195

Opening Day Age: 30
Born: 6/16/71 in Los Angeles, CA
ML Seasons: 9

Overall Statistics

	G	AB	R	H	D	T	HR	RBI	SB	BB	SO	Avg	OBP	Slg
2001	98	301	37	78	19	0	8	43	4	17	38	.259	.298	.402
Career	892	2871	323	722	145	10	41	313	25	295	554	.251	.325	.352

Where He Hits the Ball

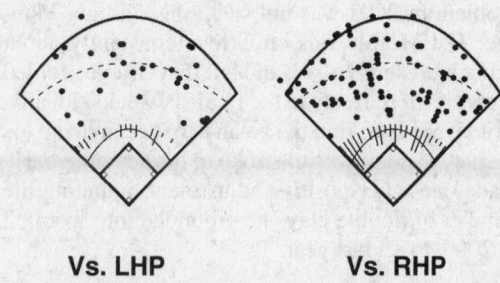

Vs. LHP   **Vs. RHP**

2001 Situational Stats

	AB	H	HR	RBI	Avg		AB	H	HR	RBI	Avg
Home	146	39	5	22	.267	LHP	74	18	1	5	.243
Road	155	39	3	21	.252	RHP	227	60	7	38	.264
First Half	112	21	0	7	.188	Sc Pos	71	16	3	34	.225
Scnd Half	189	57	8	36	.302	Clutch	53	16	2	9	.302

2001 Rankings (American League)

- Led the Devil Rays in sacrifice flies (3)

Tampa Bay

Ben Grieve

2001 Season

The Rays were expecting big numbers after acquiring Ben Grieve from Oakland in a three-team trade that cost them Roberto Hernandez and Cory Lidle. But Grieve's team-record 159 strikeouts weren't what they had in mind. Grieve's production, especially his lack of power, was disappointing. Critics point out that he needed a strong finish just to reach his meager totals; optimists say his solid September-October was a sign of things to come. Grieve was just happy the miserable season was over.

Hitting

Grieve has a sweet natural swing that makes it easy to see why greatness is expected. He can generate power and hit the ball to all fields. His biggest problem in 2001 was not swinging enough. Manager Hal McRae was on Grieve constantly about being more aggressive, and felt that Grieve seemed to swing more freely in the final six weeks. Ideally, Grieve needs to find the balance between using his keen eye and powerful stroke to his advantage. He made one other positive adjustment, reducing the number of double plays he grounded into from 32 in 2000, to 13 last year.

Baserunning & Defense

Simply put, Grieve is slow. That limits what he can do on the bases and in the outfield. In an effort to get him more into the game, McRae kept giving Grieve the green light. And Grieve stole a career-high seven bases, all after July 25. His outfield play can be an adventure, as Grieve has trouble tracking balls hit over his head and has a below-average arm.

2002 Outlook

The Rays had Grieve thinking he would be a lefthanded force in the middle of their lineup for years. They still hope that's the case. McRae talked about playing Grieve in right field every day this season, and Grieve planned to embark on an off-season conditioning program to make himself stronger. But there's a good chance that his future is going to be as a designated hitter.

Position: RF/LF/DH
Bats: L **Throws:** R
Ht: 6' 4" **Wt:** 230

Opening Day Age: 25
Born: 5/4/76 in Arlington, TX
ML Seasons: 5
Pronunciation: greev

Overall Statistics

	G	AB	R	H	D	T	HR	RBI	SB	BB	SO	Avg	OBP	Slg
2001	154	542	72	143	30	2	11	72	7	87	159	.264	.372	.387
Career	639	2298	350	635	138	5	87	375	16	321	545	.276	.371	.454

Where He Hits the Ball

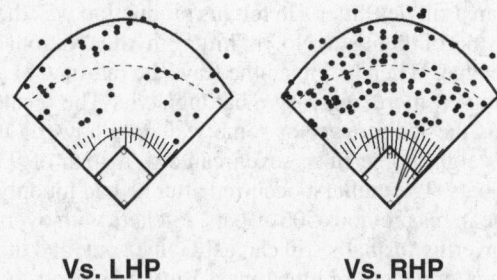

Vs. LHP **Vs. RHP**

2001 Situational Stats

	AB	H	HR	RBI	Avg		AB	H	HR	RBI	Avg
Home	253	68	5	30	.269	LHP	150	44	3	27	.293
Road	289	75	6	42	.260	RHP	392	99	8	45	.253
First Half	288	69	6	34	.240	Sc Pos	143	39	5	60	.273
Scnd Half	254	74	5	38	.291	Clutch	72	12	2	8	.167

2001 Rankings (American League)

- 2nd in strikeouts
- Led the Devil Rays in batting average, at-bats, hits, singles, doubles, total bases (210), walks, times on base (238), strikeouts, pitches seen (2,589), plate appearances (639), on-base percentage, highest groundball-flyball ratio (2.1), most pitches seen per plate appearance (4.05), highest percentage of pitches taken (62.9), batting average with the bases loaded (.583), batting average vs. righthanded pitchers, slugging percentage vs. lefthanded pitchers (.440), on-base percentage vs. lefthanded pitchers (.399), on-base percentage vs. righthanded pitchers (.362), batting average on the road and lowest percentage of swings on the first pitch (23.0)

Joe Kennedy

2001 Season

To understand how much progress Joe Kennedy made during the 2001 season, consider this: He went to spring training simply hoping to make the jump from low Class-A to Double-A. But by the first week of June he was starting in the major leagues. Kennedy opened strong, allowing three runs or less in five of his first six outings with Tampa Bay. He then rebounded from a seven-game losing streak to finish 7-8. He showed signs that he should be able to stick around for a long time.

Pitching

Kennedy has a strong arm and can deliver his fastball repeatedly in the 90-94 MPH range. Making it even more of a weapon is a funky delivery that allows him to sneak the fastball by some hitters. But what sets him apart is a nasty overhand curveball—a 12-to-6, falling-off-the-table type. The curve not only is a tremendous strikeout pitch for Kennedy, it makes his fastball and changeup even more effective. The change improved considerably by the end of 2001. He also is something of a control artist, allowing only 12 walks in 73 minor league innings last year before being promoted.

Defense

Kennedy was a catcher growing up and still has good all-around skills, giving him the opportunity to help himself defensively. With time he should learn to stay calm and not rush when he fields the ball. As he gets more comfortable on the mound, Kennedy also should be able to develop his pickoff move into a greater weapon.

2002 Outlook

Having given him a 20-start, no-pressure apprenticeship in 2001, the Rays will be expecting a lot from Kennedy in the future. They hope that he continues to refine his offspeed pitches, develop his confidence and not get caught up in the success he's had to date. If he continues to progress, he could be a front-of-the-rotation guy for a long time.

Position: SP
Bats: R **Throws:** L
Ht: 6' 4" **Wt:** 225

Opening Day Age: 22
Born: 5/24/79 in La Mesa, CA
ML Seasons: 1

Overall Statistics

	W	L	Pct.	ERA	G	GS	Sv	IP	H	BB	SO	HR	Ratio
2001	7	8	.467	4.44	20	20	0	117.2	122	34	78	16	1.33
Career	7	8	.467	4.44	20	20	0	117.2	122	34	78	16	1.33

How Often He Throws Strikes

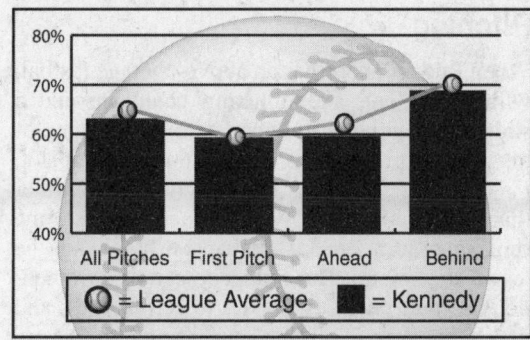

◉ = League Average ■ = Kennedy

2001 Situational Stats

	W	L	ERA	Sv	IP		AB	H	HR	RBI	Avg
Home	4	2	3.25	0	55.1	LHB	89	20	3	12	.225
Road	3	6	5.49	0	62.1	RHB	365	102	13	47	.279
First Half	3	2	3.98	0	40.2	Sc Pos	112	24	3	38	.214
Scnd Half	4	6	4.68	0	77.0	Clutch	2	0	0	0	.000

2001 Rankings (American League)

- 3rd in lowest batting average allowed with runners in scoring position
- 4th in losses among rookies
- 5th in wins among rookies

Ryan Rupe

2001 Season

In a season full of disappointments, Ryan Rupe was one of Tampa Bay's biggest. The 26-year-old righthander was unable to sustain success for any extended period. After winning back-to-back games in the first part of June, he won only once more the rest of the campaign. He put a whopping 220 men on base in 143 innings and allowed a team-record 30 home runs. Only a lack of innings kept him from qualifying for the worst ERA. The season included an ill-fated move to the bullpen and a demotion to Triple-A. By the end, there were questions if Rupe, who had surgery in 2000 to remove a blood clot, was completely healthy. But Rupe insisted he was.

Pitching

When Rupe is on, he has an above-average fastball with movement, a dominating changeup and a slider that can be nasty when he buries it. One of his primary problems is maintaining his arm slot. He too often seemed to be throwing uphill rather than on the downward plane he needs. The home runs show how quickly he can be hurt when he leaves the ball up. The changeup can be a tremendous second pitch, especially to lefthanders, and makes his fastball all that much better. He has to improve on throwing the slider to righthanders.

Defense

A classic power pitcher who is big, tall and gangly, Rupe is not much of a fielder. Adding to his defensive shortcomings, he gets so worked up that at times he borders on being out of control. He has worked on holding runners better.

2002 Outlook

Assuming Rupe is healthy, he will need a strong spring showing to reclaim a spot in the rotation. The Rays feel they have four solid starters in Nick Bierbrodt, Joe Kennedy, Tanyon Sturtze and Paul Wilson. There are two or three others with whom Rupe will compete for whatever spots remain. But some in the organization still feel Rupe can be a front-end starter.

Position: SP
Bats: R **Throws:** R
Ht: 6' 5" **Wt:** 230

Opening Day Age: 27
Born: 3/31/75 in Houston, TX
ML Seasons: 3
Pronunciation: roop

Overall Statistics

	W	L	Pct.	ERA	G	GS	Sv	IP	H	BB	SO	HR	Ratio
2001	5	12	.294	6.59	28	26	0	143.1	161	48	123	30	1.46
Career	18	27	.400	5.90	70	68	0	376.2	418	136	281	66	1.47

How Often He Throws Strikes

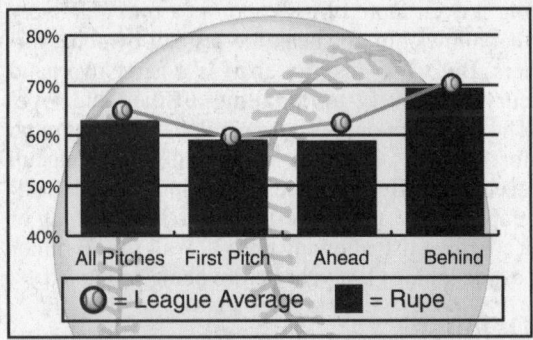

2001 Situational Stats

	W	L	ERA	Sv	IP		AB	H	HR	RBI	Avg
Home	4	5	5.14	0	77.0	LHB	289	85	17	55	.294
Road	1	7	8.28	0	66.1	RHB	279	76	13	48	.272
First Half	4	8	7.18	0	79.0	Sc Pos	125	44	6	73	.352
Scnd Half	1	4	5.88	0	64.1	Clutch	20	7	1	7	.350

2001 Rankings (American League)

- 1st in highest batting average allowed with runners in scoring position
- 2nd in lowest winning percentage
- 3rd in home runs allowed
- 8th in losses
- 10th in fewest GDPs induced per GDP situation (4.0%)
- Led the Devil Rays in home runs allowed and strikeouts

Tanyon Sturtze

2001 Season

Tanyon Sturtze was miscast as a setup man by former Tampa Bay manager Larry Rothschild in spring training. But Hal McRae moved Sturtze into the rotation in early May and the righthander flourished there. He became the Rays' most dependable and successful starter, going 11-10 with a 4.32 ERA in 27 starts. He also delivered 15 quality performances. By the end of the year, Sturtze was voted the team's Most Valuable Player by local writers. If the true test of a starter's ability is how he keeps his team in the game, Sturtze rated as a definite success. The Rays were 15-12 in his starts, compared to 47-88 in all other contests.

Pitching

Sturtze doesn't do anything fancy. He throws a fastball in the 93-94 MPH range, along with a splitter and a slider. His key to success is keeping the fastball down in the zone and burying the splitter when necessary. He'll need the occasional reminder to be aggressive in the strike zone, but showed considerable improvement and maturity as a starter. He finished strong, winning his last three starts (twice against the Yankees) despite throwing a career high 195.1 innings overall.

Defense

Sturtze is a tremendous athlete who can do a lot of things to help himself on the mound, such as fielding grounders in his area and covering bases well. He does need to do a better job of holding runners, however.

2002 Outlook

Having established himself as one of the Rays' top starters last season, Sturtze will have to keep working hard to maintain his position. He may head into spring training as arguably the No. 1 guy, but he'll need to continue to be on top of his game, as the Rays will be looking to set aside innings for their young pitchers. Now 31 years of age, Sturtze is one of the older hurlers on Tampa Bay's staff.

Position: SP/RP
Bats: R **Throws:** R
Ht: 6' 5" **Wt:** 205

Opening Day Age: 31
Born: 10/12/70 in Worcester, MA
ML Seasons: 6
Pronunciation: STURTS

Overall Statistics

	W	L	Pct.	ERA	G	GS	Sv	IP	H	BB	SO	HR	Ratio
2001	11	12	.478	4.42	39	27	1	195.1	200	79	110	23	1.43
Career	18	15	.545	4.99	86	39	1	315.1	339	134	181	41	1.50

How Often He Throws Strikes

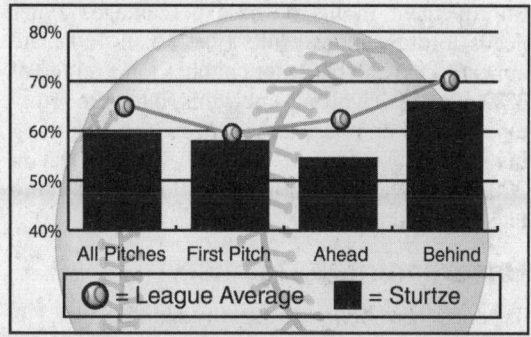

○ = League Average   ■ = Sturtze

2001 Situational Stats

	W	L	ERA	Sv	IP		AB	H	HR	RBI	Avg
Home	5	5	5.04	0	94.2	LHB	361	102	7	45	.283
Road	6	7	3.84	1	100.2	RHB	376	98	16	47	.261
First Half	3	7	5.24	1	92.2	Sc Pos	193	44	4	69	.228
Scnd Half	8	5	3.68	0	102.2	Clutch	69	14	3	11	.203

2001 Rankings (American League)

- Led the Devil Rays in ERA, wins, games started, innings pitched, hits allowed, batters faced (837), walks allowed, pitches thrown (3,206), winning percentage, highest strikeout-walk ratio (1.4), lowest batting average allowed (.271), lowest slugging percentage allowed (.419), lowest on-base percentage allowed (.345), highest ground-ball-flyball ratio allowed (1.0), fewest pitches thrown per batter (3.83), lowest ERA at home, lowest ERA on the road, most run support per nine innings (4.7), lowest batting average allowed with runners in scoring position, fewest home runs allowed per nine innings (1.06), most strikeouts per nine innings (5.1) and fewest walks per nine innings (3.6)

Jason Tyner

Position: LF/CF
Bats: L **Throws:** L
Ht: 6' 1" **Wt:** 170

Opening Day Age: 24
Born: 4/23/77 in
Beaumont, TX
ML Seasons: 2
Pronunciation: tie-ner

2001 Season

After spending the first six weeks of the 2001 season in the minor leagues, Jason Tyner proved himself to be a dynamic leadoff hitter with the potential to disrupt an inning. He set team records for infield hits, bunt singles and stolen bases while playing in just 105 games. He produced three hitting streaks of 10 games or more, as well as three four-hit games.

Hitting

Tyner is developing into the classic leadoff hitter, dropping bunts and slapping the ball where it's pitched while using his speed to his advantage. But to reach elite status, he will have to make a marked improvement in his on-base percentage. Tyner needs to draw more walks (just 15 in 420 plate appearances) and take more pitches (an average of 3.29 per PA). The Rays knew this, but were reluctant to dwell on it last season for fear of disturbing his overall progress. It will be a bigger deal in 2002. Improved conditioning would prevent future late-season slumps.

Baserunning & Defense

Tyner is a fast and fundamentally sound runner. His confidence grew enough last season that he was looking to steal second anytime he got on. The Rays were encouraging him to attempt stealing third more frequently as well. Tyner considers himself a center fielder, but manager Hal McRae seems to prefer him in left. To become the everyday center fielder, Tyner will have to be more aggressive chasing balls and take more direct routes. He has an average arm but compensates with positioning and anticipation.

2002 Outlook

As long as he continues to contribute offensively, Tyner is going to be in the lineup on a regular basis. He sets the tone and tempo for the Rays. If Greg Vaughn comes back to be the everyday left fielder, the Rays likely will make Tyner the everyday center fielder. If not, Tyner again could split time between those two spots.

Overall Statistics

	G	AB	R	H	D	T	HR	RBI	SB	BB	SO	Avg	OBP	Slg
2001	105	396	51	111	8	5	0	21	31	15	42	.280	.311	.326
Career	155	520	60	139	12	5	0	34	38	20	58	.267	.299	.310

Where He Hits the Ball

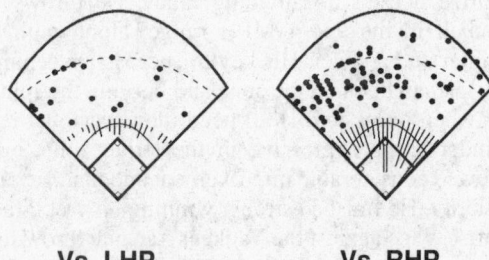

Vs. LHP   **Vs. RHP**

2001 Situational Stats

	AB	H	HR	RBI	Avg		AB	H	HR	RBI	Avg
Home	210	60	0	10	.286	LHP	81	26	0	4	.321
Road	186	51	0	11	.274	RHP	315	85	0	17	.270
First Half	125	41	0	5	.328	Sc Pos	87	24	0	18	.276
Scnd Half	271	70	0	16	.258	Clutch	64	24	0	7	.375

2001 Rankings (American League)

- 3rd in batting average on a 3-2 count (.400)
- 6th in bunts in play (29) and batting average in the clutch
- 7th in errors in left field (3) and lowest on-base percentage for a leadoff hitter (.315)
- 8th in stolen bases
- 9th in stolen-base percentage (83.8) and assists in center field (4)
- Led the Devil Rays in stolen bases, stolen-base percentage (83.8), bunts in play (29), batting average in the clutch, on-base percentage for a leadoff hitter (.315) and batting average with two strikes (.210)

Greg Vaughn

Position: DH/LF
Bats: R **Throws:** R
Ht: 6' 0" **Wt:** 202

Opening Day Age: 36
Born: 7/3/65 in
Sacramento, CA
ML Seasons: 13
Pronunciation: von

2001 Season

At first glance, it might appear that Greg Vaughn had a decent season that was only slightly below his usual production. But a closer look at the numbers reveals it actually was a pretty bad year. Vaughn was headed for the All-Star Game with a .244 average, 21 homers and 60 RBI when he injured his hamstring in the final game before the break. Slowed by assorted leg injuries, he never was the same player. He hit .213 with three homers and 22 RBI in the second half, missing most of the final month.

Hitting

For years, Vaughn has been considered an excellent fastball hitter, with the patience to wait for the right pitch and the strength to pull it. As a result, pitchers don't tend to give him too many, instead tormenting him with offspeed junk and sinkers. A series of shoulder injuries appeared to have slowed Vaughn's bat, and the leg injuries affected his drive and speed. He seemed to have difficulty with the new strike zone for much of the season, reflected by his 130 strikeouts in 136 games. He still can be good in the clutch, as he hit more than 50 points better with men in scoring position than he did overall.

Baserunning & Defense

Vaughn has surprising speed when his legs aren't sore, especially when going from home to first, which allows him to log a dozen or so infield hits every year. He considers himself a complete player, but his injuries have severely limited his defense. The sore shoulder prevents him from making strong throws, while the calf and hamstring strains limit his range. Despite hustle and dogged determination, he doesn't catch everything he gets to.

2002 Outlook

With two years and $18 million remaining on his contract, Vaughn probably is going to be around for a while, even though the salary-cutting Rays would love to move him. Vaughn insists he will be in shape to play left field every day.

Overall Statistics

	G	AB	R	H	D	T	HR	RBI	SB	BB	SO	Avg	OBP	Slg
2001	136	485	74	113	25	0	24	82	11	71	130	.233	.333	.433
Career	1640	5815	981	1427	271	21	344	1038	118	816	1418	.245	.339	.477

Where He Hits the Ball

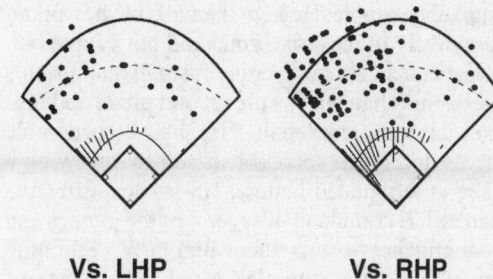

Vs. LHP   **Vs. RHP**

2001 Situational Stats

	AB	H	HR	RBI	Avg		AB	H	HR	RBI	Avg
Home	238	59	12	43	.248	LHP	104	20	3	12	.192
Road	247	54	12	39	.219	RHP	381	93	21	70	.244
First Half	316	77	21	60	.244	Sc Pos	143	41	10	62	.287
Scnd Half	169	36	3	22	.213	Clutch	67	15	4	11	.224

2001 Rankings (American League)

- 1st in lowest batting average vs. lefthanded pitchers
- 2nd in batting average on a 3-1 count (.750) and lowest batting average
- 3rd in highest percentage of swings that missed (29.2), lowest batting average on an 0-2 count (.033) and lowest batting average on the road
- Led the Devil Rays in home runs, runs scored, total bases (210), RBI, sacrifice flies (3), slugging percentage, HR frequency (20.2 ABs per HR), steals of third (3), batting average with runners in scoring position, batting average on a 3-1 count (.750), highest percentage of extra bases taken as a runner (53.1) and slugging percentage vs. righthanded pitchers (.457)

Paul Wilson

2001 Season

Paul Wilson's season really had four parts. He enjoyed a dazzling spring training that had some Rays officials suggesting he was one of the top starters in the entire league. But Wilson endured a miserable first two months when he couldn't seem to do anything right, going 2-7 with an 8.43 ERA. Exiled to the bullpen for two months, he was relegated mainly to mopup work but used the time to work some things out. He then followed with an impressive final two months, during which he went 6-2 with a 2.55 ERA in his last 12 starts and rekindled the hopes the Rays had in him.

Pitching

Wilson's turnaround was incredibly dramatic and remarkably simple. He kept the ball down, worked aggressively in the strike zone and got people out. He features an above-average fastball, can use his slider or his changeup as his second pitch, and also mixes in some curveballs. He had considerable success during his second-half run by throwing a sinker to lefthanded batters. He is most effective when he has command of several of the pitches and the confidence to mix them regularly, refraining from nibbling. His struggles raised some questions given his medical history, but the 151 innings he threw seemed to indicate all his arm trouble is behind him.

Defense

Having shed some weight since his days with the Mets, Wilson is a good athlete in decent shape. He comes off the mound well and is very determined and intense about doing everything he can to help his team win. Like many of the Rays pitchers, he needs to do a better job holding runners and going quicker to the plate.

2002 Outlook

With the promise he showed in the second half of 2001, Wilson is poised for a breakthrough performance where he wins big and establishes himself as a front-of-the-rotation starter. Unfortunately, the Rays thought the same thing a year ago.

Position: SP/RP
Bats: R **Throws:** R
Ht: 6' 5" **Wt:** 235

Opening Day Age: 29
Born: 3/28/73 in Orlando, FL
ML Seasons: 3

Overall Statistics

	W	L	Pct.	ERA	G	GS	Sv	IP	H	BB	SO	HR	Ratio
2001	8	9	.471	4.88	37	24	0	151.1	165	52	119	21	1.43
Career	14	25	.359	4.87	74	57	0	351.1	360	139	268	37	1.42

How Often He Throws Strikes

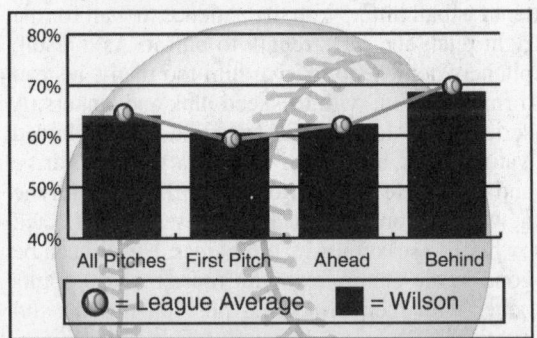

= League Average   = Wilson

2001 Situational Stats

	W	L	ERA	Sv	IP		AB	H	HR	RBI	Avg
Home	5	3	4.78	0	79.0	LHB	294	84	13	42	.286
Road	3	6	4.98	0	72.1	RHB	300	81	8	52	.270
First Half	2	7	7.59	0	72.1	Sc Pos	148	41	4	70	.277
Scnd Half	6	2	2.39	0	79.0	Clutch	17	7	0	2	.412

2001 Rankings (American League)

- 1st in pickoff throws (180)
- 5th in hit batsmen (13)
- Led the Devil Rays in hit batsmen (13) and pickoff throws (180)

Randy Winn

2001 Season

Randy Winn received the most extensive playing time of his four years with Tampa Bay. He took advantage by playing his best baseball and putting up the best numbers of his career. He showed more determination than he had in the past. Winn's 50 RBI nearly matched his previous total, while his six home runs exceeded what he had done before. Splitting time between center and right field, he ranked sixth in the American League with 12 outfield assists. The additional playing time took a toll, however. He endured two extended second-half slumps, forcing manager Hal McRae to rest Winn on a regular basis.

Hitting

Winn is a versatile and useful player who may not do anything extraordinary but can do a lot of things pretty well. He is a switch-hitter who not only can hit the ball out of the park or into the gaps, but also slap a single or drop a bunt. Although he hit nearly 50 points better while batting righthanded, he showed more power from the other side. However, he had hit a fewer points higher against righties over the previous three years combined.

Baserunning & Defense

Winn runs well and can steal a base when needed, even though his steal percentage in 2001 (55 percent) still was below the 68-percent mark he posted as a rookie in 1998. He is getting more confident on the bases. He can play all three outfield positions adequately, though he is most comfortable in center field. He makes up for the lack of a strong arm with good positioning and anticipation.

2002 Outlook

Although Tampa Bay used Winn extensively as a starter, his true value may be as a fourth outfielder. He has the potential to be a good one, along the lines of Dave Martinez. The Rays went into the offseason looking to solidify their outfield situation, but if Ben Grieve and/or Greg Vaughn can't play the field on a regular basis, Winn likely will play a key role again. If not, he could be an extra outfielder or trade bait.

Position: RF/CF
Bats: B **Throws:** R
Ht: 6' 2" **Wt:** 193

Opening Day Age: 27
Born: 6/9/74 in Los Angeles, CA
ML Seasons: 4

Overall Statistics

	G	AB	R	H	D	T	HR	RBI	SB	BB	SO	Avg	OBP	Slg
2001	128	429	54	117	25	6	6	50	12	38	81	.273	.339	.401
Career	367	1229	177	332	55	19	10	107	53	110	238	.270	.334	.370

Where He Hits the Ball

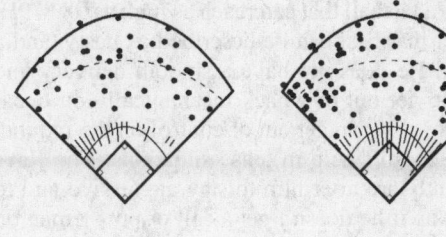

Vs. LHP　　　**Vs. RHP**

2001 Situational Stats

	AB	H	HR	RBI	Avg		AB	H	HR	RBI	Avg
Home	227	67	3	30	.295	LHP	124	38	0	13	.306
Road	202	50	3	20	.248	RHP	305	79	6	37	.259
First Half	179	52	4	25	.291	Sc Pos	112	32	0	39	.286
Scnd Half	250	65	2	25	.260	Clutch	59	16	1	8	.271

2001 Rankings (American League)

- 2nd in lowest stolen-base percentage (54.5)
- 6th in errors in right field (4) and assists in right field (8)
- 9th in assists in center field (4)
- Led the Devil Rays in triples, caught stealing (10), lowest percentage of swings that missed (18.6), highest percentage of swings put into play (44.1), batting average vs. lefthanded pitchers and batting average at home

Tampa Bay

Esteban Yan

Position: RP
Bats: R **Throws:** R
Ht: 6' 4" **Wt:** 230

Opening Day Age: 27
Born: 6/22/74 in
Campina del Seibo, DR
ML Seasons: 6
Pronunciation: YAHN

2001 Season

The conversion of Esteban Yan from pitching in the seventh and eighth innings to working in the ninth didn't go particularly well. In his first season as the Rays' closer, Yan blew nine saves, tying for the major league lead, and picked up six losses. He also allowed a .279 average to first batters and put 80 men on base in 62.1 innings. He was at his worst during a stretch in late July and early August when he blew four games in eight chances. For the second time in three seasons, he spent time on the disabled list because of shoulder problems, though he did finish strong.

Pitching

Yan has the physical abilities to succeed. He throws a fastball that can reach as high as 98 MPH, a slider that best can be described as nasty, and a splitter. He does not have a smooth delivery and tends to get out of whack mechanically on occasion. He also can get out of control on the mound, which doesn't help in tense situations. The Rays frequently are after him to stay aggressive and to not let up if he doesn't get a call or puts a man on base. A bigger question is whether he has the killer instinct and resiliency needed to succeed as a closer.

Defense

Yan is big and slow and not particularly athletic. He often is not in a good fielding position at the end of his violent delivery, making him vulnerable to bunts. Adding to the problem, he doesn't do much out of the ordinary to hold runners on.

2002 Outlook

Manager Hal McRae stayed with Yan through some very rough times in 2001, sticking to the belief that Yan would be better for it. Yan might not get the benefit of the doubt in 2002, especially as his salary goes up through the arbitration process and potential heirs Victor Zambrano and Jesus Colome continue to develop.

Overall Statistics

	W	L	Pct.	ERA	G	GS	Sv	IP	H	BB	SO	HR	Ratio
2001	4	6	.400	3.90	54	0	22	62.1	64	11	64	7	1.20
Career	19	23	.452	5.44	218	23	23	368.2	410	136	309	58	1.48

How Often He Throws Strikes

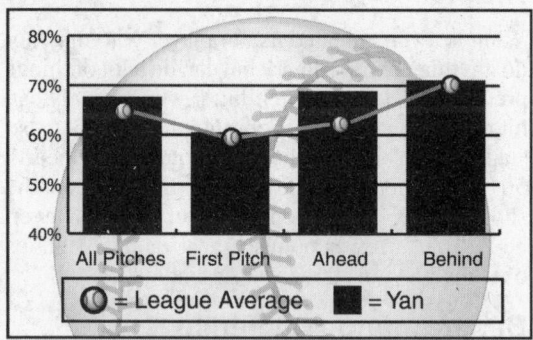

2001 Situational Stats

	W	L	ERA	Sv	IP		AB	H	HR	RBI	Avg
Home	2	3	3.53	15	35.2	LHB	125	34	2	15	.272
Road	2	3	4.39	7	26.2	RHB	119	30	5	20	.252
First Half	2	3	5.14	8	28.0	Sc Pos	66	16	1	26	.242
Scnd Half	2	3	2.88	14	34.1	Clutch	146	46	6	29	.315

2001 Rankings (American League)

- 1st in blown saves (9)
- 2nd in lowest save percentage (71.0)
- 6th in relief losses (6)
- 9th in most strikeouts per nine innings in relief (9.2) and games finished (51)
- 10th in save opportunities (31)
- Led the Devil Rays in saves, games finished (51), save opportunities (31), lowest batting average allowed vs. lefthanded batters, save percentage (71.0), blown saves (9) and relief losses (6)

Wilson Alvarez

Position: SP
Bats: L **Throws:** L
Ht: 6' 1" **Wt:** 245

Opening Day Age: 32
Born: 3/24/70 in
Maracaibo, VZ
ML Seasons: 10

Overall Statistics

	W	L	Pct.	ERA	G	GS	Sv	IP	H	BB	SO	HR	Ratio
2001					Did Not Play								
Career	86	77	.528	3.96	250	224	1	1433.0	1324	708	1074	153	1.42

2001 Situational Stats

	W	L	ERA	Sv	IP		AB	H	HR	RBI	Avg
Home	—	—	—	—	—	LHB	—	—	—	—	—
Road	—	—	—	—	—	RHB	—	—	—	—	—
First half	—	—	—	—	—	Sc Pos	—	—	—	—	—
Scnd Half	—	—	—	—	—	Clutch	—	—	—	—	—

2001 Season

In the first two seasons of his five-year, $35 million contract with the Rays, Wilson Alvarez went 15-23 with a 4.46 ERA. But those officially are the good old days. He has not pitched at all in the majors the past two years due to shoulder problems that included surgery in May of 2000. In 2001 he made nine minor league starts. He was close to returning to the majors on two occasions, but developed additional setbacks both times.

Pitching & Defense

Alvarez twice won 15 games in a season when working for the White Sox. He's been at his best when he's used his low-90s fastball to set up his offspeed stuff. His problems have come when he didn't have the confidence to throw the fastball, relied on his breaking ball and fell behind hitters. Alvarez is not very athletic on the mound and has to work hard to keep weight off.

2002 Outlook

The Rays are hoping to have a healthy Alvarez, who makes $8 million and has a complete no-trade clause, back in their rotation. But they're no longer counting on it. Alvarez likely won't regain the velocity he had before the shoulder injury, and that could lead to more problems with his confidence in throwing the fastball.

Nick Bierbrodt

Position: SP
Bats: L **Throws:** L
Ht: 6' 5" **Wt:** 185

Opening Day Age: 23
Born: 5/16/78 in
Tarzana, CA
ML Seasons: 1
Pronunciation:
BEER-braut

Overall Statistics

	W	L	Pct.	ERA	G	GS	Sv	IP	H	BB	SO	HR	Ratio
2001	5	6	.455	5.55	16	16	0	84.1	100	39	73	17	1.65
Career	5	6	.455	5.55	16	16	0	84.1	100	39	73	17	1.65

2001 Situational Stats

	W	L	ERA	Sv	IP		AB	H	HR	RBI	Avg
Home	4	3	5.58	0	50.0	LHB	64	19	4	13	.297
Road	1	3	5.50	0	34.1	RHB	280	81	13	41	.289
First Half	2	1	9.00	0	18.0	Sc Pos	94	27	6	37	.287
Scnd Half	3	5	4.61	0	66.1	Clutch	0	0	0	0	-

2001 Season

The Rays acquired Nick Bierbrodt, whose minor league career was slowed by injuries, from Arizona in late July and immediately moved him into their starting rotation. Although Bierbrodt said he welcomed the opportunity to pitch without the pressure of a pennant race, he was inconsistent. There were several games when he was impressive on the mound, but others when he wasn't.

Pitching & Defense

The lanky Bierbrodt has the physical tools to succeed, starting with a 90-94 MPH fastball that tends to sink. He also throws a curveball and at times a nasty slider. His changeup might be most effective. It's important for him to strike a balance in his pitch selection and to improve the command of all his offerings, since home runs hurt him. Bierbrodt seems to be fundamentally sound defensively.

2002 Outlook

There was some question whether the Rays would use Bierbrodt as a starter or a reliever, and if they would keep him in the majors. Manager Hal McRae needed about a month to say Bierbrodt not only would be in the rotation for the rest of last season but would be there in 2002 as well. The key for Bierbrodt will be to continue his progress and not be satisfied with reaching the big leagues.

Jesus Colome

Position: RP
Bats: R **Throws:** R
Ht: 6' 2" **Wt:** 170

Opening Day Age: 21
Born: 6/2/80 in San
Pedro de Macoris, DR
ML Seasons: 1
Pronunciation:
hay-soos cal-um-ay

Overall Statistics

	W	L	Pct.	ERA	G	GS	Sv	IP	H	BB	SO	HR	Ratio
2001	2	3	.400	3.33	30	0	0	48.2	37	25	31	8	1.27
Career	2	3	.400	3.33	30	0	0	48.2	37	25	31	8	1.27

2001 Situational Stats

	W	L	ERA	Sv	IP		AB	H	HR	RBI	Avg
Home	1	1	3.68	0	22.0	LHB	70	13	1	7	.186
Road	1	2	3.04	0	26.2	RHB	108	24	7	19	.222
First Half	1	0	3.00	0	9.0	Sc Pos	49	7	1	16	.143
Scnd Half	1	3	3.40	0	39.2	Clutch	59	8	3	4	.136

2001 Season

Jesus Colome was a prized acquisition during the 2000 season. He was disappointing at spring training and Triple-A, but the Rays promoted him to the big leagues anyway, and the results at times were impressive. But other times, especially when the Rays were behind, Colome seemed disinterested and was ineffective.

Pitching & Defense

Colome was billed as having an outstanding arm and he showed it, frequently reaching 99 MPH on the radar. Unfortunately, his fastball occasionally stays too straight. Another problem is that he doesn't yet have a dependable second pitch, so hitters can sit on the fastball. Until Colome refines his changeup and/or slider, it may be tough for him, particularly as batters see him more often. Colome is a casual fielder, though his arm can compensate. Opposing basestealers were successful on all six attempts last year.

2002 Outlook

The Rays have to decide how best to use Colome. He has the potential to be a dominating closer, but was inconsistent coming out of the bullpen. He seemed to do better in longer outings. There is some thought to returning him to a starter's role, which is how he was used in Oakland's system.

John Flaherty

Position: C
Bats: R **Throws:** R
Ht: 6' 1" **Wt:** 200

Opening Day Age: 34
Born: 10/21/67 in New
York, NY
ML Seasons: 10
Nickname: Flash

Overall Statistics

	G	AB	R	H	D	T	HR	RBI	SB	BB	SO	Avg	OBP	Slg
2001	78	248	20	59	17	1	4	29	1	10	33	.238	.269	.363
Career	837	2732	255	695	134	3	64	321	8	145	394	.254	.293	.376

2001 Situational Stats

	AB	H	HR	RBI	Avg		AB	H	HR	RBI	Avg
Home	109	27	3	15	.248	LHP	35	10	1	4	.286
Road	139	32	1	14	.230	RHP	213	49	3	25	.230
First Half	169	40	1	15	.237	Sc Pos	59	17	0	22	.288
Scnd Half	79	19	3	14	.241	Clutch	34	8	3	6	.235

2001 Season

It was a lost season for John Flaherty. He began the year as the Rays' starting catcher before being dropped into a part-time role with Mike DiFelice. Flaherty then was relegated to backup duty following the promotion of top prospect Toby Hall, and was sidelined for the final month with a herniated disk in his neck. When Flaherty did play, he didn't fare particularly well at the plate.

Hitting, Baserunning & Defense

Flaherty is most effective when he hits the ball where it's pitched and drives the ball to all fields. He tends to get away from that approach and attempts various adjustments to compensate. He has a decent arm and can throw with some of the best catchers in the game when his mechanics and footwork are good. Consistency is his problem. Like most catchers, Flaherty isn't much of a baserunner.

2002 Outlook

Flaherty received a series of cortisone shots at the end of the 2001 season, which was expected to alleviate the disk problem without the need for surgery. The Rays would like to move his $3.25 million salary. His injury makes that difficult, however, at least until the end of spring training. He most likely will return as the backup to and mentor for Hall, playing perhaps twice a week.

Toby Hall

Position: C
Bats: R **Throws:** R
Ht: 6' 3" **Wt:** 205

Opening Day Age: 26
Born: 10/21/75 in Tacoma, WA
ML Seasons: 2

Overall Statistics

	G	AB	R	H	D	T	HR	RBI	SB	BB	SO	Avg	OBP	Slg
2001	49	188	28	56	16	0	4	30	2	4	16	.298	.321	.447
Career	53	200	29	58	16	0	5	31	2	5	16	.290	.316	.445

2001 Situational Stats

	AB	H	HR	RBI	Avg		AB	H	HR	RBI	Avg
Home	96	33	1	17	.344	LHP	47	14	0	4	.298
Road	92	23	3	13	.250	RHP	141	42	4	26	.298
First Half	0	0	0	0	-	Sc Pos	66	20	2	27	.303
Scnd Half	188	56	4	30	.298	Clutch	30	8	0	7	.267

2001 Season

Toby Hall's development was one of the highlights of Tampa Bay's dismal season. He had a solid four months at Triple-A (.335-19-72), winning International League MVP honors despite playing only 94 games. Promoted in late July, he took over as the starting catcher and immediately showed the offensive and defensive skills that were expected of him.

Hitting, Baserunning & Defense

Hall made quick adjustments to major league pitching and proved himself a steady hitter and a dependable run producer. He especially was adept at hitting with two strikes, though he could do a better job at not getting into that hole. His 22-29 strikeout-walk ratio at Triple-A was impressive and gives reason to think he can be an even tougher out. A converted infielder, Hall has made a smooth transition to behind the plate. His arm strength and ability to stop runners are average. Like most catchers, he doesn't have much speed.

2002 Outlook

Hall is expected to be the starting catcher in 2002 and beyond. Many in the organization think he's a future All-Star. While Hall did well hitting and throwing in 2001, a key to his development and the team's success will be how he handles the pitching staff during good and bad times.

Aubrey Huff

Position: 3B/DH/1B
Bats: L **Throws:** R
Ht: 6' 4" **Wt:** 221

Opening Day Age: 25
Born: 12/20/76 in Marion, OH
ML Seasons: 2

Overall Statistics

	G	AB	R	H	D	T	HR	RBI	SB	BB	SO	Avg	OBP	Slg
2001	111	411	42	102	25	1	8	45	1	23	72	.248	.288	.372
Career	150	533	54	137	32	1	12	59	1	28	90	.257	.295	.388

2001 Situational Stats

	AB	H	HR	RBI	Avg		AB	H	HR	RBI	Avg
Home	192	38	5	16	.198	LHP	87	15	1	14	.172
Road	219	64	3	29	.292	RHP	324	87	7	31	.269
First Half	215	51	4	18	.237	Sc Pos	105	28	1	34	.267
Scnd Half	196	51	4	27	.260	Clutch	52	13	1	7	.250

2001 Season

Aubrey Huff got the chance he was waiting for when the Rays benched Vinny Castilla in mid-April. But Huff didn't do much to take advantage, struggling defensively at third base and at the plate. He eventually was sent back to Triple-A for a two-week refresher in late August, which he said helped his approach as much as his swing.

Hitting, Baserunning & Defense

Huff's struggles were comprehensive. He struggled against lefthanded pitchers, hit into a team-record 18 double plays and made 20 errors overall. There were times when he showed the smooth, powerful swing that made him a top hitting prospect, but too often he pressed and gave away at-bats. Despite having speed that is considerably below average, Huff did finish with 25 doubles.

2002 Outlook

Unless he shows dramatic improvement in spring training, Huff probably has played his way off of third base. He looked much more comfortable during an August stint at first, and he hit better during a September trial run as designated hitter. If Greg Vaughn can play left field full-time this year, Huff could be the everyday DH. More likely, Huff will fill in at first and perhaps third base, as well as take a turn at DH against some righthanded pitchers.

Russ Johnson

Position: 3B/2B
Bats: R **Throws:** R
Ht: 5'10" **Wt:** 180

Opening Day Age: 29
Born: 2/22/73 in Baton Rouge, LA
ML Seasons: 5

Overall Statistics

	G	AB	R	H	D	T	HR	RBI	SB	BB	SO	Avg	OBP	Slg
2001	85	248	32	73	19	2	4	33	2	34	57	.294	.380	.435
Career	297	707	97	193	39	2	13	85	11	88	147	.273	.354	.389

2001 Situational Stats

	AB	H	HR	RBI	Avg		AB	H	HR	RBI	Avg
Home	116	42	1	16	.362	LHP	69	18	1	6	.261
Road	132	31	3	17	.235	RHP	179	55	3	27	.307
First Half	167	46	3	22	.275	Sc Pos	59	22	1	27	.373
Scnd Half	81	27	1	11	.333	Clutch	44	14	1	9	.318

2001 Season

Russ Johnson spent five weeks in April and May as the starting second baseman. He played so well that manager Hal McRae said he probably was the team's MVP to that point. But a strained right quadriceps landed Johnson on the disabled list and he never got the chance to get back in the lineup on a regular basis. He instead had to settle for another solid year as one of the game's better utility infielders and solid pinch-hitters.

Hitting, Baserunning & Defense

Johnson is tough, gritty, determined and hard working. He has a good eye, more power than expected and decent speed. It's tough to throw a fastball by him, and he knows how to work a pitcher to prolong an at-bat. Johnson has an above-average arm and came up as a shortstop. But the rap is that he doesn't have enough range to play the position in the big leagues. He still can be a spot starter there and at second and third base.

2002 Outlook

Johnson's role isn't likely to change. He's good at what the Rays ask him to do, accepts the assignment without showing his frustration and works hard to be ready when called upon. He's a valuable guy to have around.

Travis Phelps

Position: RP
Bats: R **Throws:** R
Ht: 6' 2" **Wt:** 170

Opening Day Age: 24
Born: 7/25/77 in Rocky Comfort, MO
ML Seasons: 1

Overall Statistics

	W	L	Pct.	ERA	G	GS	Sv	IP	H	BB	SO	HR	Ratio
2001	2	2	.500	3.48	49	0	5	62.0	53	24	54	6	1.24
Career	2	2	.500	3.48	49	0	5	62.0	53	24	54	6	1.24

2001 Situational Stats

	W	L	ERA	Sv	IP		AB	H	HR	RBI	Avg
Home	2	0	2.64	4	30.2	LHB	103	23	1	13	.223
Road	0	2	4.31	1	31.1	RHB	132	30	5	20	.227
First Half	1	1	3.19	4	31.0	Sc Pos	59	14	3	28	.237
Scnd Half	1	1	3.77	1	31.0	Clutch	68	17	2	10	.250

2001 Season

Travis Phelps' story is an impressive one. As an 89th-round pick in the 1996 draft, he's the lowest-round draft pick to ever reach the majors. But what made the tale even better is that Phelps pitched well enough to stick around and earn a role in the bullpen as one of the Rays' top setup men. He appeared in 49 games, third most among American League rookies. He also held batters to an impressive .226 average.

Pitching & Defense

Phelps throws hard and is learning to throw without fear. He gets into the 90s with his fastball and is working to refine his breaking ball and changeup. The conversion to major league setup man is as much mental as anything, and Phelps has handled that well. He is particularly tough on first batters, allowing eight hits in 43 at-bats. The only concern with Phelps has been durability, and that should improve with experience.

2002 Outlook

With continued improvement and a stronger body, Phelps has a chance to emerge as an impressive young reliever. He has shown the ability to handle tight situations and to get tough outs, recording five saves last season. The Rays like what they've seen.

Bryan Rekar

Position: SP
Bats: R **Throws:** R
Ht: 6' 3" **Wt:** 220

Opening Day Age: 29
Born: 6/3/72 in Oaklawn, IL
ML Seasons: 7
Pronunciation: ree-car

Overall Statistics

	W	L	Pct.	ERA	G	GS	Sv	IP	H	BB	SO	HR	Ratio
2001	3	13	.188	5.89	25	25	0	140.2	167	45	87	21	1.51
Career	25	47	.347	5.51	129	106	0	648.0	776	202	381	98	1.51

2001 Situational Stats

	W	L	ERA	Sv	IP		AB	H	HR	RBI	Avg
Home	2	7	4.92	0	78.2	LHB	312	93	9	52	.298
Road	1	6	7.11	0	62.0	RHB	256	74	12	42	.289
First Half	1	10	5.53	0	107.1	Sc Pos	155	45	4	68	.290
Scnd Half	2	3	7.02	0	33.1	Clutch	29	9	1	4	.310

2001 Season

Bryan Rekar followed up his best major league season, when he worked 173.1 innings and earned a $1.4-million contract, with his worst campaign. He won just three games and lost 13 last year, enduring streaks of six and seven defeats in a row. He averaged less than six innings per start and missed five weeks with shoulder tendinitis. But he did come back to pitch the final six weeks with no apparent limitations.

Pitching & Defense

When Rekar is on, he has some of the best stuff on the Rays staff. He throws a low to mid-90s fastball with movement and a nasty slider. He has a Hideo Nomo like turn in his windup that can disrupt a hitter's timing. Unfortunately, Rekar isn't very consistent in his performances, and there is some question whether he takes the proper approach into each game. He is not a particularly adept fielder, but can make most plays and holds runners well.

2002 Outlook

The breakthrough Rekar made in 2000 shows there is a chance he can be a successful starter. But that likely will have to be for another team, since the Rays are committed to their young pitchers and Rekar probably has priced himself out of Tampa Bay's plans.

Victor Zambrano

Position: RP
Bats: R **Throws:** R
Ht: 6' 0" **Wt:** 190

Opening Day Age: 27
Born: 8/6/74 in Los Teques, VZ
ML Seasons: 1

Overall Statistics

	W	L	Pct.	ERA	G	GS	Sv	IP	H	BB	SO	HR	Ratio
2001	6	2	.750	3.16	36	0	2	51.1	38	18	58	6	1.09
Career	6	2	.750	3.16	36	0	2	51.1	38	18	58	6	1.09

2001 Situational Stats

	W	L	ERA	Sv	IP		AB	H	HR	RBI	Avg
Home	3	1	4.50	1	26.0	LHB	78	16	3	13	.205
Road	3	1	1.78	1	25.1	RHB	111	22	3	7	.198
First Half	1	1	5.19	0	8.2	Sc Pos	53	6	1	12	.113
Scnd Half	5	1	2.74	2	42.2	Clutch	107	22	4	14	.206

2001 Season

Victor Zambrano was one the biggest surprises of last season. He was having a nondescript year at Triple-A when the Rays summoned him in late June. He proved to be one of their most dependable setup men and flashed the promise of possibly developing into a closer. His scoreless streak of 17.2 innings was just shy of the team record.

Pitching & Defense

Zambrano has an above-average fastball-slider-changeup repertoire. He makes it work by mixing his pitches and locating them when it matters most. He doesn't throw extraordinarily hard (low 90s fastball), but can get the strikeout when he needs it. The changeup is a good out pitch. His durability is a plus, as is his calm presence on the mound. About the only thing he doesn't have is the experience of pitching with the game on the line. A converted infielder, Zambrano is very athletic and has the ability to help himself defensively. However, basestealers were perfect in eight tries last year.

2002 Outlook

Zambrano will go into the season as the Rays' top setup man, but there is some thought that he might someday—perhaps someday soon—supplant Esteban Yan as closer. Once he gets experience, the Rays will be inclined to see what he can do.

Other Tampa Bay Devil Rays

Mickey Callaway (Pos: RHP, Age: 26)

	W	L	Pct.	ERA	G	GS	Sv	IP	H	BB	SO	HR	Ratio
2001	0	0	-	7.20	2	0	0	5.0	3	2	2	2	1.00
Career	1	2	.333	7.40	7	4	0	24.1	33	16	13	4	2.01

Last year, Callaway, who used to be a starter, saw his first big league action since 1999. He was traded to Anaheim in mid-December. 2002 Outlook: C

Doug Creek (Pos: LHP, Age: 33)

	W	L	Pct.	ERA	G	GS	Sv	IP	H	BB	SO	HR	Ratio
2001	2	5	.286	4.31	66	0	0	62.2	51	49	66	7	1.60
Career	4	12	.250	5.15	186	3	1	197.2	165	145	207	30	1.57

Creek reached career highs in appearances, innings, wins and ERA with Tampa Bay in 2001. Lefties have hit .182 against him over the past four seasons. 2002 Outlook: B

Jose Guillen (Pos: RF, Age: 25, Bats: R)

	G	AB	R	H	D	T	HR	RBI	SB	BB	SO	Avg	OBP	Slg
2001	41	135	14	37	5	0	3	11	2	6	26	.274	.317	.378
Career	529	1810	214	476	95	12	44	237	10	82	336	.263	.307	.402

Guillen was playing himself out of a job when he suffered a knee injury in May, and the Rays released him in November. He signed with Arizona and could play some with Reggie Sanders out of the picture. 2002 Outlook: B

Ken Hill (Pos: RHP, Age: 36)

	W	L	Pct.	ERA	G	GS	Sv	IP	H	BB	SO	HR	Ratio
2001	0	1	.000	12.27	5	0	0	7.1	10	5	2	4	2.05
Career	117	109	.518	4.06	332	315	0	1973.0	1938	852	1181	162	1.41

Hill was released in April after a rough start. The 14-year veteran had a stint with the Reds before winding up in Boston. 2002 Outlook: C

Paul Hoover (Pos: C, Age: 25, Bats: R)

	G	AB	R	H	D	T	HR	RBI	SB	BB	SO	Avg	OBP	Slg
2001	3	4	1	1	0	0	0	0	0	0	1	.250	.250	.250
Career	3	4	1	1	0	0	0	0	0	0	1	.250	.250	.250

Hoover made three appearances and started one game at catcher for Tampa Bay during a September callup. He was sent back down at the end of the season and likely will spend most of 2002 at Triple-A. 2002 Outlook: C

Felix Martinez (Pos: SS, Age: 27, Bats: B)

	G	AB	R	H	D	T	HR	RBI	SB	BB	SO	Avg	OBP	Slg
2001	77	219	24	54	13	1	1	14	6	10	46	.247	.294	.329
Career	239	641	77	137	26	7	3	39	18	53	143	.214	.287	.290

After posting the top range factor at shortstop in 2000, Martinez lost his starting job in May due to errors. His erratic play leaves his future in doubt. 2002 Outlook: C

Rusty Meacham (Pos: RHP, Age: 34)

	W	L	Pct.	ERA	G	GS	Sv	IP	H	BB	SO	HR	Ratio
2001	1	3	.250	5.60	24	0	0	35.1	39	11	13	1	1.39
Career	23	17	.575	4.43	218	9	9	343.0	381	93	198	39	1.38

After a terrific spring by Meacham, the Rays called him up in early April. He accumulated a 5.60 ERA in 24 appearances before going back to Triple-A. He became a free agent in October. 2002 Outlook: C

Ariel Prieto (Pos: RHP, Age: 32)

	W	L	Pct.	ERA	G	GS	Sv	IP	H	BB	SO	HR	Ratio
2001	0	0	-	2.45	3	0	0	3.2	6	2	2	0	2.18
Career	15	24	.385	4.85	70	60	0	352.1	407	176	231	34	1.65

The Devil Rays signed Prieto in March after the Indians released him. He made three appearances during stints in April and May before shutting down with shoulder trouble. He was let go in October. 2002 Outlook: C

Damian Rolls (Pos: 2B/CF, Age: 24, Bats: R)

	G	AB	R	H	D	T	HR	RBI	SB	BB	SO	Avg	OBP	Slg
2001	81	237	33	62	11	1	2	12	12	10	47	.262	.291	.342
Career	85	240	33	63	11	1	2	12	12	10	48	.263	.292	.342

Rolls' speed enabled the Rays to move him to the outfield after Brent Abernathy took over at second in June. He still needs to find a spot. 2002 Outlook: C

Brian Rose (Pos: RHP, Age: 26)

	W	L	Pct.	ERA	G	GS	Sv	IP	H	BB	SO	HR	Ratio
2001	0	3	.000	7.45	10	3	0	29.0	41	14	15	7	1.90
Career	15	23	.395	5.86	68	54	0	284.1	331	110	151	56	1.55

The Devil Rays acquired Rose off waivers from the Mets in late April. He has yet to be a factor in the big leagues. 2002 Outlook: C

Andy Sheets (Pos: SS, Age: 30, Bats: R)

	G	AB	R	H	D	T	HR	RBI	SB	BB	SO	Avg	OBP	Slg
2001	49	153	10	30	8	0	1	14	2	12	35	.196	.251	.268
Career	315	811	100	170	34	3	15	91	14	64	234	.210	.266	.314

Sheets hit .196 during a two-month stay in Tampa. The utility man hasn't hit above the Mendoza line since 1998. He became a free agent in October. 2002 Outlook: C

Bobby Smith (Pos: 2B, Age: 27, Bats: R)

	G	AB	R	H	D	T	HR	RBI	SB	BB	SO	Avg	OBP	Slg
2001	6	19	1	2	0	0	0	1	0	3	10	.105	.227	.105
Career	240	763	84	181	27	4	20	101	11	67	243	.237	.303	.362

Smith won the starting job at second base last spring over Brent Abernathy. He held the job for a week as a 2-for-19 start sent him to Triple-A until October. 2002 Outlook: C

Jeff Wallace (Pos: LHP, Age: 25)

	W	L	Pct.	ERA	G	GS	Sv	IP	H	BB	SO	HR	Ratio
2001	0	3	.000	3.40	29	1	0	50.1	43	37	38	4	1.59
Career	3	3	.500	4.20	119	1	0	137.0	119	117	120	11	1.72

Wallace compiled a solid 2.31 ERA through July during two stints with Tampa Bay. However, he faltered down the stretch with a 7.15 mark the rest of the way. Boston claimed him off waivers in December. 2002 Outlook: C

Dan Wheeler (Pos: RHP, Age: 24)

	W	L	Pct.	ERA	G	GS	Sv	IP	H	BB	SO	HR	Ratio
2001	1	0	1.000	8.66	13	0	0	17.2	30	5	12	3	1.98
Career	2	5	.286	6.43	30	8	0	71.1	94	29	61	12	1.72

Wheeler had two stints with the Devil Rays last year. He gave up a run in four innings during a short April callup, but then had a 10.54 ERA during a May-June recall. He was released in December. 2002 Outlook: C

Tampa Bay Devil Rays Minor League Prospects

Organization Overview:

Tampa Bay had made a habit of drafting tools-rich but raw talent that required loads of development time, so few minor leaguers were having an impact. Recent trades, however, have netted guys who will come on more quickly, including Brent Abernathy, Jesus Colome, Jason Tyner, Jason Conti, Nick Bierbrodt and Paul Wilson. Now the farm system is catching up, as youngsters like Joe Kennedy, Jason Standridge, Travis Harper, Jared Sandberg and Delvin James also are knocking at the door. Josh Hamilton, Bobby Seay and Matt White endured setbacks in 2001, but they and 2001 first-round pick Dewon Brazleton may not be far behind, either. The Rays soon will experience a baby boom.

Jason Conti

Position: OF
Bats: L **Throws:** R
Ht: 5' 11" **Wt:** 180

Opening Day Age: 27
Born: 1/27/75 in
Pittsburgh, PA

Recent Statistics

	G	AB	R	H	D	T	HR	RBI	SB	BB	SO	Avg
2001 AAA Tucson	92	362	68	120	23	6	9	52	2	33	54	.331
2001 AAA Durham	38	157	24	48	12	0	5	18	3	9	31	.306
2001 NL Arizona	5	4	1	1	0	0	0	0	0	1	2	.250
2001 MLE	130	496	70	145	31	4	10	53	3	31	88	.292

A 32nd-rounder by Arizona in 1996, Conti was shipped to the Rays in last summer's Albie Lopez deal. He is a dependable outfielder who can play center field, and he has made decent contact and drawn walks in the minors. Conti has batted better than .300 in each of the last three seasons at the Triple-A level, and he has a career .315 average and .385 OBP. Whether he will be a regular with Tampa Bay remains unanswered, but he has competition in the system from guys with similar games in Jason Tyner and Randy Winn. Avoiding a tendency to be pull-happy, spraying the ball more effectively and gaining better command of the strike zone will help his cause.

Carl Crawford

Position: OF
Bats: L **Throws:** L
Ht: 6' 2" **Wt:** 203

Opening Day Age: 20
Born: 8/5/81 in Houston, TX

Recent Statistics

	G	AB	R	H	D	T	HR	RBI	SB	BB	SO	Avg
2000 A Chston-SC	135	564	99	170	21	11	6	57	55	32	102	.301
2001 AA Orlando	132	537	64	147	24	3	4	51	36	36	90	.274
2001 MLE	132	533	62	143	24	2	4	50	28	29	97	.268

A gifted athlete who could have played college football or basketball, this 1999 second-round pick opted for baseball. Speed is his game, and he led the Class-A Sally League in hits and steals in 2000. While he lacks baseball experience and great instincts, he's smart, determined and extremely coachable. Crawford skipped high-A ball in 2001 and jumped to the Double-A Southern League, where initially he struggled. He was too defensive as a hitter, but worked hard, took instruction and finally let it fly with the bat as one of the youngest players in the league. His little-ball skills are advancing, but he must spray the ball more and work on his plate patience to make the most of his impressive tools.

Josh Hamilton

Position: OF
Bats: L **Throws:** L
Ht: 6' 4" **Wt:** 209

Opening Day Age: 20
Born: 5/21/81 in
Raleigh, NC

Recent Statistics

	G	AB	R	H	D	T	HR	RBI	SB	BB	SO	Avg
2000 A Chston-SC	96	392	62	118	23	3	13	61	14	26	72	.301
2001 AA Orlando	23	89	5	16	5	0	0	4	2	5	22	.180
2001 A Chston-SC	4	11	3	4	1	0	1	2	0	2	3	.364

Selected first overall in the 1999 draft, Hamilton is a legitimate five-tool prospect with a knowledge of the game seldom seen in someone so young. Hamilton batted .347 and slugged .593 in the Rookie-level Appy League in '99, and continued to excel in the Class-A Sally League in 2000. He showed impressive speed and a terrific arm in center field, and league managers rated Hamilton the best batting and power prospect in the circuit. After flirting with a possible major league job last March, Hamilton bypassed high-A ball and jumped to Double-A Orlando. He was 16-for-89 (.180) with 22 strikeouts before going on the disabled list with lower back inflammation in mid-May. Then Hamilton suffered a quadriceps injury that he later re-aggravated. In all, he played just 27 games in a frustrating season.

Travis Harper

Position: P
Bats: L **Throws:** R
Ht: 6' 4" **Wt:** 193

Opening Day Age: 25
Born: 5/21/76 in
Harrisonburg, VA

Recent Statistics

	W	L	ERA	G	GS	Sv	IP	H	R	BB	SO	HR
2001 AAA Durham	12	6	3.70	25	25	0	155.2	140	70	38	115	25
2001 AL Tampa Bay	0	2	7.71	2	2	0	7.0	15	11	3	2	5

Harper's career started slowly as a 1997 third-round pick of the Red Sox who had his contract voided because he had elbow tendinitis. After signing with Tampa Bay in '98, he quickly made up for lost time by reaching Double-A Orlando in '99. After going 10-5 (3.71) between Orlando and Triple-A Durham in 2000, and closing with four decent starts for the Devil Rays, Harper may have had his best pro season with a 12-6 (3.70) performance at Durham in 2001. He effectively works the strike zone with a low-90s fastball, but the big difference last summer was his success at locating his curveball. His changeup also improved. If he continues to progress, he's on his way to Tampa Bay, where his smarts and intense makeup will aid his cause.

Jared Sandberg

Position: 3B
Bats: R **Throws:** R
Ht: 6' 3" **Wt:** 185

Opening Day Age: 24
Born: 3/2/78 in Olympia, WA

Recent Statistics

	G	AB	R	H	D	THR	RBI	SB	BB	SO	Avg
2001 AA Orlando	8	28	4	8	2	0 1	4	0	6	10	.286
2001 AAA Durham	93	322	39	77	16	0 16	50	0	38	81	.239
2001 AL Tampa Bay	39	136	13	28	7	0 1	15	1	10	45	.206
2001 MLE	101	341	35	76	17	0 13	44	0	35	95	.223

The nephew of former Cub Ryne Sandberg, Jared had a breakthrough season in 1999, finishing second in the high Class-A Florida State League in home runs with 22. A back injury hindered him early in 2000 at Double-A Orlando, and he lacked power even as he played better later in the year. The power resurfaced in 2001 at Triple-A Durham, where Sandberg was challenged by better pitching. He gets pull-happy, which leaves him exposed on the outer half of the plate. He needs to drive balls to the right side and not limit his ability to cover the outer half. Because of injuries, Sandberg was promoted to the Rays in August and impressed with his athleticism and his defense, which included good hands and range.

Bobby Seay

Position: P
Bats: L **Throws:** L
Ht: 6' 2" **Wt:** 221

Opening Day Age: 23
Born: 6/20/78 in Sarasota, FL

Recent Statistics

	W	L	ERA	G	GS	Sv	IP	H	R	BB	SO	HR
2001 AA Orlando	2	5	5.98	15	13	0	64.2	81	48	26	49	9
2001 AL Tampa Bay	1	1	6.23	12	0	0	13.0	13	11	5	12	3

One of two loophole free agents signed by Tampa Bay in 1996, Seay never has surpassed 100 innings in a season because of a series of relatively minor ailments. That changed in 2000, when Seay stayed healthy and turned in his best season. Last summer he was plagued by a strained index finger that would go numb on him. Healthy or not, Seay's overall command wasn't as good in 2001 as the year before. He has a moving low-90s fastball, but his secondary pitches must be better. He's shown an above-average curveball in the past, and he needs a good changeup against righthanded batters. Seay must stay away from a strikeout mentality and focus on making good pitches and working hitters effectively.

Jason Standridge

Position: P
Bats: R **Throws:** R
Ht: 6' 4" **Wt:** 217

Opening Day Age: 23
Born: 11/9/78 in Birmingham, AL

Recent Statistics

	W	L	ERA	G	GS	Sv	IP	H	R	BB	SO	HR
2001 AAA Durham	5	10	5.28	20	20	0	102.1	130	73	50	48	13
2001 AA Orlando	0	2	5.59	2	2	0	9.2	12	6	4	7	0
2001 AL Tampa Bay	0	0	4.66	9	1	0	19.1	19	10	14	9	5

The Rays' first-round pick in 1997, Standridge benefited from a switch to a lower arm slot after a disappointing '98 campaign. He responded with a 13-5 (2.57) season

for two Class-A clubs in 1999. The change gave his low-90s fastball better sink, and he improved its location during a solid 2000. Standridge was impressive in camp last spring, but things didn't go as well at Triple-A Durham. Yet the Rays called him up to give him a change of scenery, plus a chance to see that he has the stuff to do it in the majors. Despite his Triple-A troubles, his secondary pitches improved, including a sharp-breaking curve that is his out pitch, and a changeup that still needs work.

Matt White

Position: P
Bats: R **Throws:** R
Ht: 6' 5" **Wt:** 230

Opening Day Age: 23
Born: 8/13/78 in Waynesboro, PA

Recent Statistics

	W	L	ERA	G	GS	Sv	IP	H	R	BB	SO	HR
2000 AA Orlando	7	6	3.75	20	20	0	120.0	94	56	58	98	10
2000 AAA Durham	3	2	2.83	6	6	0	35.0	36	14	16	28	1
2001 AAA Durham	0	5	7.80	7	7	0	30.0	33	28	25	16	4

Another loophole free agent from 1996, White looked like a bust after suffering a cracked vertebra in his back in '97. But after his second go-round at high Class-A St. Petersburg in 1999, White had his best season in 2000, faring better at mixing his mid-90s fastball and power curve. While he is prone to mechanical troubles, White was more consistent in nearly every way in 2000. His luck seemed to be on the upswing until last spring, when he struggled to pitch effectively at Triple-A Durham before needing arthroscopic surgery to repair his rotator cuff on May 31. White has worked hard at his rehab, and he's on track to return during the first half of 2002.

Others to Watch

Rocco Baldelli (20) is a superb athlete who the Rays believe is a star in the making. He needs to make better contact and get stronger—his 6-foot-4 frame will fill out—but he already has good speed and the skills of an excellent center fielder. Baldelli probably plays at high Class-A Bakersfield in 2002. . . Last June's third overall pick, collegiate righthander **Dewon Brazelton** (21), signed in late August and immediately joined the Rays because his contract put him on the major league roster on September 1. He didn't pitch in a game, but used the time to clean up his mechanics, sharpen the break on his curveball and tinker with his changeup. Brazelton regularly threw 95 MPH in instructional league appearances, and the Rays also were happy with his media-friendly off-the-field demeanor. . . An 18th-round pick last June, outfielder **Jonny Gomes** (21) benefited from a quick bat and raw power in leading the Rookie-level Appalachian League in homers with 16. He had a solid debut, batting .291 and also leading the circuit in on-base percentage (.442) and slugging (.597). . . The Rays' bullpen may be getting help in 2002 from hard-throwing righthander **Delvin James** (24). With makeup off the charts, James has worked hard to improve, adding a slider, cutter and splitter to his mid-90s heat over the last two years.

The Ballpark in Arlington

Offense

Like all teams, Texas wants to improve its pitching. The problem for the Rangers is that their staff works in one of the American League's better parks for hitters. The park's dimensions are fair, but the yawning outfield gaps are breeding grounds for triples. The Rangers and opponents combined to hit .287 with 11.6 runs and 7.9 extra-base hits per game at The Ballpark last season. Two quirks favor hitters: a glassed-in club for wealthy patrons adds to the boost the wind gives balls hit from right-center to the foul line, and balls hit into the right-field corner can be difficult to play.

Defense

Outfield speed is essential to keep balls from getting through the vast gaps. The Ballpark also places a premium on playing shallow in the outfield. As at Colorado's Coors Field, outfielders tend to play deep at The Ballpark, allowing an inordinate amount of flyballs to drop. The grounds crew has a difficult job keeping the infield from turning into raceway speed in the summer heat.

Who It Helps the Most

Rafael Palmeiro has become a dead pull hitter. Why not? The Ballpark favors lefthanded hitters who lift the ball, and Palmeiro is one of the best in the game in that department. He had 23 homers in 296 at-bats at home last season and has averaged a homer every 10.9 at-bats lifetime at the park.

Who It Hurts the Most

Righthanded reliever Jeff Zimmerman faces a bundle of lefthanded hitters. If they get the ball into the air at The Ballpark, Zimmerman is in trouble. He allowed six homers in only 41.2 innings at home last season, and his ERA nearly doubled there.

Rookies & Newcomers

The Rangers expect to break in another position player during the season: third baseman Hank Blalock. Blalock is the same age as third baseman Mark Teixeira, whom the Rangers took in the first round of the 2001 draft, but more accomplished. Switch-hitting center fielder Carl Everett could find his new home even more inviting than his previous home at Fenway Park.

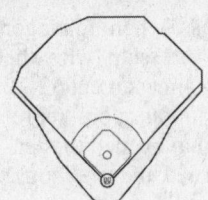

Dimensions: LF-332, LCF-390, CF-400, RCF-381, RF-325

Capacity: 49,115

Elevation: 551 feet

Surface: Grass

Foul Territory: Average

Park Factors

2001 Season

	Home Games			Away Games			
	Rangers	Opp	Total	Rangers	Opp	Total	Index
G	73	73	146	70	70	140	—
Avg	.281	.293	.287	.269	.292	.280	102
AB	2497	2683	5180	2513	2372	4885	102
R	396	442	838	393	415	808	99
H	701	787	1488	677	693	1370	104
2B	138	191	329	152	159	311	100
3B	15	24	39	4	17	21	175
HR	109	99	208	111	97	208	94
BB	255	262	517	240	262	502	97
SO	471	427	898	492	394	886	96
E	57	55	112	45	48	93	115
E-Infield	52	47	99	33	41	74	128
LHB-Avg	.279	.295	.287	.283	.304	.293	98
LHB-HR	44	50	94	46	40	86	98
RHB-Avg	.282	.292	.287	.261	.284	.272	106
RHB-HR	65	49	114	65	57	122	91

1999-2001

	Home Games			Away Games			
	Rangers	Opp	Total	Rangers	Opp	Total	Index
G	217	217	434	214	214	428	—
Avg	.294	.292	.293	.277	.292	.284	103
AB	7433	7929	15362	7620	7271	14891	102
R	1253	1290	2543	1151	1202	2353	107
H	2187	2313	4500	2108	2123	4231	105
2B	420	514	934	439	464	903	100
3B	48	54	102	27	50	77	128
HR	298	298	596	286	249	535	108
BB	820	766	1586	731	795	1526	101
SO	1208	1282	2490	1347	1216	2563	94
E	179	153	332	146	152	298	110
E-Infield	149	133	282	122	132	254	109
LHB-Avg	.288	.293	.290	.280	.295	.287	101
LHB-HR	141	137	278	126	108	234	116
RHB-Avg	.300	.291	.295	.273	.290	.282	105
RHB-HR	157	161	318	160	141	301	102

2001 Rankings (American League)

- Highest infield-error factor
- Second-highest error factor
- Third-highest triple factor

Jerry Narron

2001 Season

Jerry Narron inherited a mess when manager Johnny Oates resigned under pressure with the club at 11-17 last season. The Rangers went 62-72 under Narron, but they were a far more representative team than the bunch that opened the season in disarray. Narron lightened the clubhouse mood and argued the team should cut its losses with faded prospect Ruben Mateo. The Rangers had a winning record (38-37) after the All-Star break. No one in the organization can say how much weight that will carry with new general manager John Hart, who has the freedom to pick his own manager.

Offense

Narron tried to wean the Rangers from their dependence upon the home run with some National League-type strategy, but there was only so much he could do with the existing personnel. Texas struggled to create runs because of a lack of team speed and the general absence of the type of hitters who can put the ball in play on the hit-and-run. Texas hit 77 more homers than Seattle in 2001 but scored 37 fewer runs. If Narron gets the right roster, he will be an aggressive manager.

Pitching & Defense

Unlike Oates, who was uncomfortable with young players, Narron gave the ball to inexperienced starters Doug Davis, Aaron Myette and Rob Bell on a regular base. Davis showed significant improvement with regular work. Narron also stayed with Jeff Zimmerman as a closer, and Zimmerman converted his final 17 save chances. Narron wants more athletic outfielders who can play shallow. Last year's crop of outfielders were burned when playing shallow, so Narron had them returned to their usual depth: near the wall.

2002 Outlook

The late Birdie Tebbetts, one of the most respected minds in the game, said Narron came from the Walter Alston school of managing for his intelligence and quiet strength. Narron clearly became more comfortable with the job as the season progressed. The question is how long will the new general manger stick with him?

Born: 1/15/56 in Goldsboro, NC

Playing Experience: 1979-1987, NYY, Sea, Ana

Managerial Experience: 1 season

Manager Statistics

Year	Team, Lg	W	L	Pct	GB	Finish
2001	Texas, AL	62	72	.463	43.0	4th West
1 Season		62	72	.463	—	—

2001 Starting Pitchers by Days Rest

	<=3	4	5	6+
Rangers Starts	0	65	43	22
Rangers ERA	—	5.74	5.91	4.90
AL Avg Starts	1	78	48	24
AL ERA	5.92	4.69	4.58	4.58

2001 Situational Stats

	Jerry Narron*	AL Average
Hit & Run Success %	24.0	35.0
Stolen Base Success %	76.4	71.0
Platoon Pct.	58.7	59.1
Defensive Subs	19	26
High-Pitch Outings	6	6
Quick/Slow Hooks	9/18	19/16
Sacrifice Attempts	29	54

* Narron managed the Rangers for 134 games

2001 Rankings (American League)

- 1st in steals of home plate (2)
- 2nd in stolen-base percentage, fewest caught stealings of second base (22) and fewest caught stealings of third base (2)

Frank Catalanotto

2001 Season

When Jerry Narron took over as manager, he made getting more at-bats for Frank Catalanotto a prime objective. Narron succeeded by moving Catalanotto from the infield, where he had been a bat without a position, to the Rangers' injury-riddled outfield. Catalanotto hit a career-high .330 and competed for the American League batting title until the final week, when a 1-for-16 slump dropped him down the list. The Rangers turned down offers from several National League teams, most notably Houston and St. Louis, to keep Catalanotto. The NL clubs liked Catalanotto because of his versatility.

Hitting

Catalanotto understands the concept of letting the pitch come to him. He is patient and avoids getting too big with his swing by using the opposite field. He even shows some extra-base power when going the other way. Catalanotto had a major league-best .398 on-base percentage when batting leadoff. He also understands the strike zone and is willing to hit deep in a count. He batted .262 with two strikes last season, seventh-best average in the AL. He handled lefthanders when given the chance, hitting .326 in 46 at-bats against them.

Baserunning & Defense

Catalanotto's defense always will be a concern. His hands are marginal, and he has not thrown well since shoulder surgery in 1997. He made only one error in 92 games in the outfield last season, but that reflects his own limitations as much as his defensive play. Catalanotto dropped weight after being obtained from Detroit in the ill-fated Juan Gonzalez deal and runs better than expected. He has 21 steals in 28 tries in his two years with Texas and can get infield hits.

2002 Outlook

Where does Catalanotto play? Not second, where Michael Young is set. Possibly left field, where Rusty Greer has more injury problems. As long as Catalanotto hits at last year's pace, Texas will find swings for him. The acquisition of Carl Everett further crowds the Rangers' outfield, so Texas also could re-examine Catalanotto's trade value.

Position: LF/RF/2B/3B
Bats: L **Throws:** R
Ht: 5'11" **Wt:** 195

Opening Day Age: 27
Born: 4/27/74 in Smithtown, NY
ML Seasons: 5
Pronunciation: ca-tal-a-NAH-tow

Texas

Overall Statistics

	G	AB	R	H	D	T	HR	RBI	SB	BB	SO	Avg	OBP	Slg
2001	133	463	77	153	31	5	11	54	15	39	55	.330	.391	.490
Career	438	1270	198	382	78	9	38	159	27	102	186	.301	.362	.466

Where He Hits the Ball

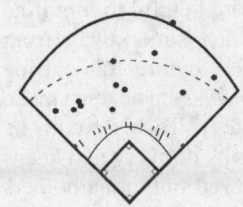 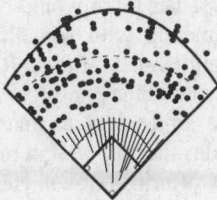

Vs. LHP   **Vs. RHP**

2001 Situational Stats

	AB	H	HR	RBI	Avg		AB	H	HR	RBI	Avg
Home	223	77	4	25	.345	LHP	46	15	0	4	.326
Road	240	76	7	29	.317	RHP	417	138	11	50	.331
First Half	209	62	6	30	.297	Sc Pos	107	34	1	40	.318
Scnd Half	254	91	5	24	.358	Clutch	71	18	1	5	.254

2001 Rankings (American League)

- 1st in on-base percentage for a leadoff hitter (.398)
- 3rd in batting average on a 3-2 count (.400)
- 4th in batting average vs. righthanded pitchers
- 5th in batting average
- 6th in lowest percentage of swings that missed (10.6)
- Led the Rangers in batting average, triples, highest groundball-flyball ratio (1.5), lowest percentage of swings that missed (10.6), batting average with runners in scoring position, batting average vs. righthanded pitchers, batting average on a 3-1 count (.571), batting average on the road, batting average on a 3-2 count (.400) and batting average with two strikes (.262)

Doug Davis

2001 Season

Doug Davis does not shrink from challenges. After giving up 10 runs in his major league debut in 1999, he returned to the minors and won his next four decisions. With Davis at 2-4 with a 7.00 ERA for seven starts last season, the Rangers demoted him to the minors. He returned to the big leagues on a mission. He was 9-6 with a 3.84 ERA in 23 starts after coming back. That stretch included 16 consecutive starts in which Davis worked at least six innings. He beat divisional foe Oakland in all three starts.

Pitching

Davis has one truly outstanding pitch: a cut fastball that he will throw at any time to righthanded hitters. The pitch would be more helpful to him if he came up with something that sinks away from righthanded hitters. Righties ignore the outside corner of the plate against Davis, and he must make the adjustment to that strategy. To his credit, he hides the ball well in his funky delivery and keeps his offerings down. He allowed only nine homers in his final 164.2 innings.

Defense

Davis comes off the mound at an awkward angle and is helpless at fielding his position. He had only two errors but could not help himself by making the play on numerous balls hit up the middle. The Rangers are reluctant to change Davis' follow-through to improve his defense, because that could affect his overall pitching. Davis slows running games with a very good pickoff move, and he nabbed 11 runners that way last season.

2002 Outlook

The Rangers believe Davis established himself as a starter last season. He does not have overpowering stuff, but he does have the intelligence and competitive streak to hold a middle-of-the-rotation spot. But will Davis again receive the six runs per game of support that he did last season? He ranked among the league leaders in that category in 2001.

Position: SP
Bats: R **Throws:** L
Ht: 6' 4" **Wt:** 190

Opening Day Age: 26
Born: 9/21/75 in Sacramento, CA
ML Seasons: 3

Overall Statistics

	W	L	Pct.	ERA	G	GS	Sv	IP	H	BB	SO	HR	Ratio
2001	11	10	.524	4.45	30	30	0	186.0	220	69	115	14	1.55
Career	18	16	.529	5.04	62	43	0	287.1	341	127	184	31	1.63

How Often He Throws Strikes

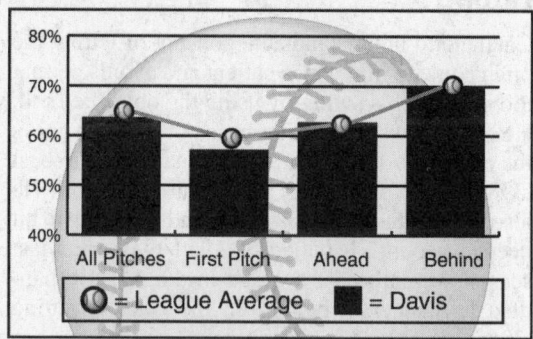

○ = League Average   ■ = Davis

2001 Situational Stats

	W	L	ERA	Sv	IP		AB	H	HR	RBI	Avg
Home	5	5	4.42	0	77.1	LHB	166	51	3	20	.307
Road	6	5	4.47	0	108.2	RHB	580	169	11	72	.291
First Half	4	6	4.98	0	86.2	Sc Pos	193	55	1	65	.285
Scnd Half	7	4	3.99	0	99.1	Clutch	50	19	1	7	.380

2001 Rankings (American League)

- 1st in highest on-base percentage allowed (.354)
- 2nd in lowest stolen-base percentage allowed (35.3)
- 3rd in highest batting average allowed (.295)
- 4th in fewest home runs allowed per nine innings (.68)
- Led the Rangers in ERA, walks allowed, pickoff throws (139), winning percentage, lowest batting average allowed (.295), lowest slugging percentage allowed (.429), highest groundball-flyball ratio allowed (1.3), fewest pitches thrown per batter (3.71), lowest ERA on the road, lowest batting average allowed vs. righthanded batters, fewest home runs allowed per nine innings (.68) and most GDPs induced per nine innings (0.8)

Rusty Greer

2001 Season

The Rangers gave Rusty Greer a three-year, $21.2 million contract extension during spring training last year, and he responded with another injury-plagued season. He underwent season-ending surgery in early August to repair a pinched nerve in his lower back. A few weeks later, Greer had another surgery, this time to remove bone chips from his left elbow. He seemed to be paying the price for years of all-out play with no regard for his body. Greer now has missed 172 games in the last three seasons.

Hitting

When healthy last year, Greer adapted to the lead-off spot. He had nearly as many walks as strikeouts and a .345 on-base percentage in the role. He still can hit for extra-bases with his opposite-field swing; he had 23 doubles in only 245 at-bats last season. Greer does not feel comfortable looking to pull pitches, so he is unlikely to again approach the 26 homers he hit in 1997. He has not handled lefthanded pitching as he did earlier in his career. He has batted only .241 against southpaws over the last two campaigns.

Baserunning & Defense

Greer played much of last season with a bad leg and did not run well. Never a major threat to steal, he ran only three times in 62 games. Greer's range in left field had begun shrinking before last year, making him less than the outfielder he was just a few seasons ago. His arm strength is below-average, making left field his only outfield spot.

2002 Outlook

The Rangers worry that Greer is on the far side of his career at age 33. Texas expects him to be ready for Opening Day, but there are no guarantees. The organization cannot commit to a position for Greer because of his recent inability to stay in the lineup. The Rangers liked Frank Catalanotto, especially his offense, in left field after Greer's season-ending surgery. There now is some talk of using Greer as a backup first baseman and part-time designated hitter in 2002, though he more likely will at least begin the season as the starting left fielder.

Position: LF
Bats: L **Throws:** L
Ht: 6' 0" **Wt:** 195

Opening Day Age: 33
Born: 1/21/69 in Fort Rucker, AL
ML Seasons: 8

Texas

Overall Statistics

	G	AB	R	H	D	T	HR	RBI	SB	BB	SO	Avg	OBP	Slg
2001	62	245	38	67	23	0	7	29	1	27	32	.273	.342	.453
Career	976	3630	619	1107	249	23	118	597	30	500	538	.305	.388	.484

Where He Hits the Ball

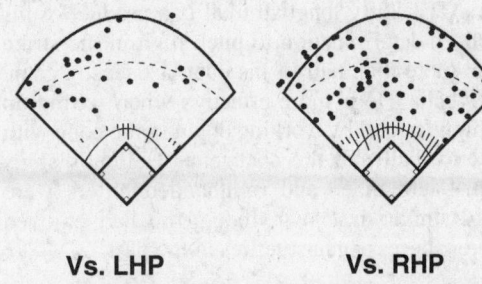

Vs. LHP　　　　　　**Vs. RHP**

2001 Situational Stats

	AB	H	HR	RBI	Avg		AB	H	HR	RBI	Avg
Home	114	28	2	15	.246	LHP	60	14	1	10	.233
Road	131	39	5	14	.298	RHP	185	53	6	19	.286
First Half	245	67	7	29	.273	Sc Pos	53	16	2	24	.302
Scnd Half	0	0	0	0	-	Clutch	38	7	0	3	.184

2001 Rankings (American League)

- 3rd in errors in left field (5)
- 6th in on-base percentage for a leadoff hitter (.345)

Rick Helling

2001 Season

Rick Helling recovered from a slow start and again served as the staff workhorse. He logged more than 215 innings for the fourth straight year and ranked among the American League's top 10 for pitches thrown for the fourth consecutive season. He also won in double figures for the fourth time in a row, though his 12 victories marked his lowest output since 1997. Helling and leads were not a good combination, however. He gave up a lead 15 times in the inning after going ahead in 2001, and the bullpen had six blown saves behind him.

Pitching

Helling led the majors in homers allowed (38 in 215.2 innings) for the second time in the last three years. That lofty longball total is a product of his stubborn determination to pitch high in the strike zone; more than half of his outs last season came on flyballs. He is more effective when setting up his high fastball by working down in the zone with the curveball and the changeup. Helling's splits against lefthanded and righthanded hitters were eerily similar last year, though he had enjoyed greater success against lefties in the past.

Defense

Helling is a good athlete with a fundamentally sound delivery that leaves him in good fielding position. He also shuts down running attacks by varying his delivery. Opponents had only seven steals in 20 tries with Helling on the mound last season, good for the lowest success rate against an AL starter.

2002 Outlook

If Helling wants a long career, he must cut the pitch load. The question is whether the Rangers have any other workhorses in their stable to lighten his load. He said last year's stunning early-season decline in velocity was not caused by all the pitches he has thrown, but others were not so certain.

Position: SP
Bats: R **Throws:** R
Ht: 6' 3" **Wt:** 220

Opening Day Age: 31
Born: 12/15/70 in Devils Lake, ND
ML Seasons: 8

Overall Statistics

	W	L	Pct.	ERA	G	GS	Sv	IP	H	BB	SO	HR	Ratio
2001	12	11	.522	5.17	34	34	0	215.2	256	63	154	38	1.48
Career	72	58	.554	4.75	201	171	0	1111.2	1129	436	766	177	1.41

How Often He Throws Strikes

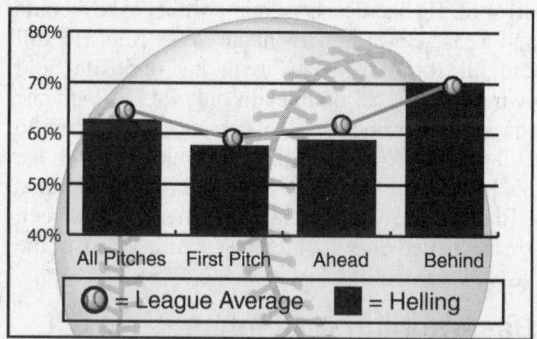

2001 Situational Stats

	W	L	ERA	Sv	IP		AB	H	HR	RBI	Avg
Home	9	2	3.78	0	116.2	LHB	469	139	19	64	.296
Road	3	9	6.82	0	99.0	RHB	392	117	19	58	.298
First Half	5	8	5.54	0	117.0	Sc Pos	187	51	8	74	.273
Scnd Half	7	3	4.74	0	98.2	Clutch	37	9	1	4	.243

2001 Rankings (American League)

- 1st in hits allowed, home runs allowed, lowest stolen-base percentage allowed (35.0), highest slugging percentage allowed (.532), highest ERA on the road and most home runs allowed per nine innings (1.59)
- Led the Rangers in wins, losses, games started, complete games (2), innings pitched, batters faced (941), strikeouts, pitches thrown (3,603), runners caught stealing (13), highest strikeout-walk ratio (2.4), lowest on-base percentage allowed (.344), lowest ERA at home, most run support per nine innings (6.1), lowest batting average allowed with runners in scoring position, most strikeouts per nine innings (6.4) and fewest walks per nine innings (2.6)

Gabe Kapler

2001 Season

Gabe Kapler singed a three-year, $5.6 million contract extension in February 2000, but he failed to build off his strong finish to the 2000 season. He began the 2001 campaign on the disabled list because of a torn quadriceps muscle in his right leg, and his average dropped below .250 for most of the second half after a hideous 18-for-118 slump. As he did in 2000, however, Kapler finished on the upswing. He hit .326 with four homers in his final 89 at-bats.

Hitting

Kapler's swing remains complicated and lacking in power. He has not hit more than 18 home runs in a season, and he had a career-low .437 slugging percentage last year. His swing can go haywire because of its many pieces, and Kapler tends to sweep the bat through the hitting zone rather than snap it. He twice went more than 70 at-bats without a homer last season. The swing makes him vulnerable to offspeed pitches away, and it gets him into big trouble when he falls behind in the count. When he got behind in the count last year, he hit just .191 with a .197 on-base percentage.

Baserunning & Defense

Though he may not have the power, Kapler has the speed to be a 30-30 performer. He had 23 steals but still is learning the running game, as evidenced by the fact that he ran into a team-high 11 outs on the bases. Kapler played the entire season in center field. He made better decisions, particularly on his throws, but may be better suited to a corner-outfield spot.

2002 Outlook

The Rangers traded for center fielder Carl Everett in mid-December. That means a switch to right field for Kapler, and questions as to whether he can hit for enough power to be a corner outfielder. Kapler has a strong enough arm to make the Rangers feel comfortable with the move, but they would love to see an increase in that slugging percentage.

Position: CF
Bats: R **Throws:** R
Ht: 6' 2" **Wt:** 208

Opening Day Age: 26
Born: 8/31/75 in Hollywood, CA
ML Seasons: 4
Pronunciation: CAP-ler

Overall Statistics

	G	AB	R	H	D	T	HR	RBI	SB	BB	SO	Avg	OBP	Slg
2001	134	483	77	129	29	1	17	72	23	61	70	.267	.348	.437
Career	387	1368	199	370	83	7	49	187	44	146	205	.270	.340	.449

Where He Hits the Ball

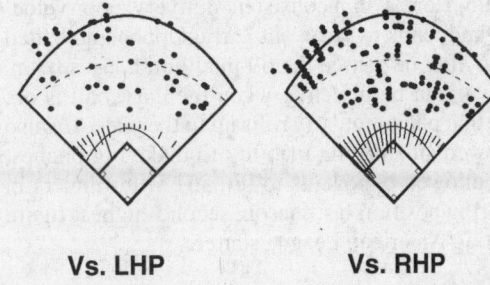

Vs. LHP   **Vs. RHP**

2001 Situational Stats

	AB	H	HR	RBI	Avg		AB	H	HR	RBI	Avg
Home	252	67	11	36	.266	LHP	119	32	7	18	.269
Road	231	62	6	36	.268	RHP	364	97	10	54	.266
First Half	237	59	10	37	.249	Sc Pos	130	35	3	52	.269
Scnd Half	246	70	7	35	.285	Clutch	73	24	3	13	.329

2001 Rankings (American League)

- 2nd in fielding percentage in center field (.997)
- 4th in assists in center field (8)
- 6th in lowest percentage of swings on the first pitch (17.0)
- 7th in batting average with the bases loaded (.556)
- 8th in highest percentage of swings put into play (50.5)
- Led the Rangers in stolen bases, caught stealing (6), highest percentage of pitches taken (61.2), highest percentage of swings put into play (50.5), batting average in the clutch, highest percentage of extra bases taken as a runner (51.0) and lowest percentage of swings on the first pitch (17.0)

Darren Oliver

2001 Season

High-profile agent Scott Boras' strange hold over Texas owner Tom Hicks first showed when the Rangers signed Darren Oliver as a free agent against the advice of their baseball operatives. Oliver, entering the final season of a three-year, $19-million deal, has been a huge bust. He is 13-20 in 49 starts and is the first pitcher in franchise history to have an ERA of more than 6.00 for at least 100 innings in consecutive seasons. He had only 10 quality starts in 28 tries. Mix in three stays on the disabled list since June 2000, and it is hard to see where Oliver has helped.

Pitching

Oliver pitches as if his left shoulder were injured again. He has an inconsistent delivery, poor velocity and tends to wear out early. Opponents batted .316 after he passed the 60-pitch mark last season. Oliver can be effective when the curveball is on, but that pitch regularly rolls up to the plate. He also showed an amazing inability to make big pitches. He allowed opponents to hit .351 with runners in scoring position last season, second-highest figure among American League starters.

Defense

Oliver picked off five runners last season, but he can be run against by teams that gamble on going with the first move. Opponents had 12 steals in 17 tries with Oliver pitching. Oliver is, at best, an average fielder who comes off the mound slowly.

2002 Outlook

The Rangers hoped someone would take the final year of Oliver's contract, and the Red Sox did in exchange for the privilege of sending Carl Everett to Texas. Boston gets a mediocre rotation candidate who doesn't pitch deep into games and has not pitched a nine-inning complete game in his last 58 starts. There is no reason to believe he will shake that streak in 2002.

Position: SP
Bats: R **Throws:** L
Ht: 6' 2" **Wt:** 220

Opening Day Age: 31
Born: 10/6/70 in Kansas City, MO
ML Seasons: 9

Overall Statistics

	W	L	Pct.	ERA	G	GS	Sv	IP	H	BB	SO	HR	Ratio
2001	11	11	.500	6.02	28	28	0	154.0	189	65	104	23	1.65
Career	67	60	.528	5.04	232	177	2	1096.0	1233	473	668	130	1.56

How Often He Throws Strikes

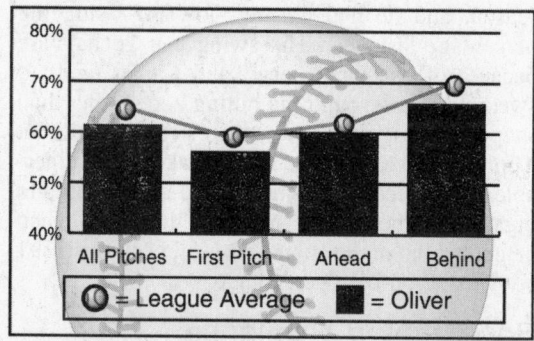

= League Average = Oliver

2001 Situational Stats

	W	L	ERA	Sv	IP		AB	H	HR	RBI	Avg
Home	4	5	6.59	0	56.0	LHB	162	51	4	24	.315
Road	7	6	5.69	0	98.0	RHB	456	138	19	71	.303
First Half	7	4	6.20	0	69.2	Sc Pos	154	54	3	67	.351
Scnd Half	4	7	5.87	0	84.1	Clutch	20	3	1	2	.150

2001 Rankings (American League)

- 2nd in highest ERA on the road and highest batting average allowed with runners in scoring position
- 6th in balks (2)
- 9th in highest batting average allowed vs. righthanded batters
- Led the Rangers in losses, wild pitches (8), stolen bases allowed (12) and GDPs induced (18)

Rafael Palmeiro

Position: 1B/DH
Bats: L **Throws:** L
Ht: 6' 0" **Wt:** 190

Opening Day Age: 37
Born: 9/24/64 in Havana, Cuba
ML Seasons: 16
Pronunciation: pahl-MARE-oh
Nickname: Raffy

Texas

2001 Season

Rafael Palmeiro made a conscious decision several years ago to sacrifice average for power. He had his seventh consecutive season of at least 38 homers but also hit below .300 for the fifth time in the last six years. Palmeiro's career average has dropped from .300 to .294 in that span, but the extra run production has been advantageous to his clubs. His knees continued to deteriorate, pushing him closer to becoming a full-time designated hitter.

Hitting

The switch to becoming a pull hitter made Palmeiro an ideal candidate to play in The Ballpark in Arlington. A lefthanded hitter who gets the ball in the air at the park will be rewarded with home runs, and few lefthanded hitters pull the ball in the air more often than Palmeiro. Since returning to the Rangers for the 1999 season, he has 77 homers and a .621 slugging percentage at home. The approach leaves Palmeiro vulnerable to offspeed pitches, but he remains one of the few power hitters who annually finishes with more walks than whiffs.

Baserunning & Defense

Less than a decade ago, Palmeiro stole 22 bases in 25 tries. He had double-figure steals as recently as 1998. Those days are gone. Palmeiro is 37, and his knees approach the Orlando Cepeda class. He rarely can take the extra base. The knees also have detracted from his Gold Glove-quality defense. He had eight errors last season, and his range decreased.

2002 Outlook

The Rangers have heralded prospect Carlos Pena ready to take over at first base, but would Palmeiro accept the move? Switching to full-time DH work essentially signals an advanced stage in a player's career. Palmeiro had a superb season as the full-time DH in 1999, but that was a one-time thing because of spring-training knee surgery. Before the Rangers and Palmeiro were forced to come to some kind of mutually acceptable arrangement, Texas decided to try Pena in the outfield. That scenario has been complicated by the acquisition of Carl Everett.

Overall Statistics

	G	AB	R	H	D	T	HR	RBI	SB	BB	SO	Avg	OBP	Slg
2001	160	600	98	164	33	0	47	123	1	101	90	.273	.381	.563
Career	2258	8446	1357	2485	488	36	447	1470	89	1036	1073	.294	.372	.519

Where He Hits the Ball

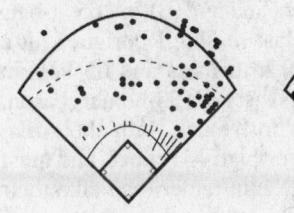
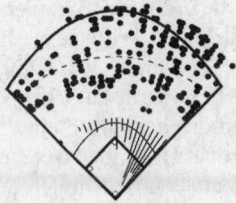

Vs. LHP   **Vs. RHP**

2001 Situational Stats

	AB	H	HR	RBI	Avg		AB	H	HR	RBI	Avg
Home	296	75	23	56	.253	LHP	151	41	12	32	.272
Road	304	89	24	67	.293	RHP	449	123	35	91	.274
First Half	319	86	25	67	.270	Sc Pos	161	44	8	69	.273
Scnd Half	281	78	22	56	.278	Clutch	86	19	5	20	.221

2001 Rankings (American League)

- 1st in lowest groundball-flyball ratio (0.6)
- 3rd in home runs, HR frequency (12.8 ABs per HR), batting average with the bases loaded (.583), cleanup slugging percentage (.568) and lowest fielding percentage at first base (.992)
- 4th in total bases (338)
- 5th in walks and plate appearances (714)
- 6th in RBI, times on base (272) and assists at first base (83)
- 7th in pitches seen (2,679), games played, slugging percentage and slugging percentage vs. lefthanded pitchers (.576)
- Led the Rangers in walks, intentional walks (8), batting average with the bases loaded (.583) and cleanup slugging percentage (.568)

Alex Rodriguez

2001 Season

If any player can be worth a record-setting $252 million contract, it just might be Alex Rodriguez. He led the American League in homers in 2001 with 52, finished among the top seven in the other Triple Crown categories and played in every game. All but one of his starts came at shortstop. A negative reaction to his April return to Seattle put Rodriguez into a brief funk, but otherwise the enormous expectations generated by his contract did not seem to faze him.

Hitting

The move out of the pitchers' paradise that is Seattle's Safeco Field turned Rodriguez into a Triple Crown candidate. In 2000 with Seattle, Rodriguez hit .272 with 13 homers and 51 RBI in 265 at-bats at home. With Texas last season, Rodriguez hit a league-high .361 with 26 homers and 65 RBI in 313 home at-bats. In his lust for a 50-homer season, Rodriguez sometimes lost touch with the strike zone. He fanned a career-high 131 times, and most teams chose to pitch to him rather than take their chances with Rafael Palmeiro or Ivan Rodriguez. A-Rod received only six intentional walks.

Baserunning & Defense

Rodriguez' baseball smarts shows on both the basepaths and in the field. He stole 18 bases in 21 tries and was tops on the team in terms of taking the extra base. Larger than most shortstops, Rodriguez bases his defensive work on positioning more than range, though his range also is well above average. He has plenty of arm but never shows more than is needed on a particular play. Rodriguez had some careless moments that contributed to 18 errors, third-most among AL shortstops.

2002 Outlook

Rodriguez said he came to Texas for the chance to win, an odd claim in light of the Rangers' struggles and Seattle's staggering success last season. He insisted he is with the club for the long haul, but frustration at more losing could show at some point. Playing in the heat for the first time in his career, Rodriguez appeared to hold up just fine during the second half of 2001. Still, it is unlikely that he will play every game again this season.

Position: SS
Bats: R **Throws:** R
Ht: 6' 3" **Wt:** 215

Opening Day Age: 26
Born: 7/27/75 in New York, NY
ML Seasons: 8
Pronunciation: rod-RI-guez
Nickname: A-Rod

Overall Statistics

	G	AB	R	H	D	T	HR	RBI	SB	BB	SO	Avg	OBP	Slg
2001	162	632	133	201	34	1	52	135	18	75	131	.318	.399	.622
Career	952	3758	760	1167	228	14	241	730	151	385	747	.311	.378	.571

Where He Hits the Ball

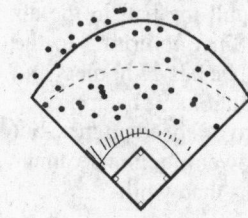

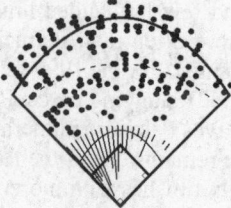

Vs. LHP   **Vs. RHP**

2001 Situational Stats

	AB	H	HR	RBI	Avg		AB	H	HR	RBI	Avg
Home	313	113	26	65	.361	LHP	132	39	12	31	.295
Road	319	88	26	70	.276	RHP	500	162	40	104	.324
First Half	339	105	25	73	.310	Sc Pos	150	46	15	82	.307
Scnd Half	293	96	27	62	.328	Clutch	90	26	4	19	.289

2001 Rankings (American League)

- 1st in home runs, runs scored, total bases (393), pitches seen (2,881), games played and batting average at home
- Led the Rangers in at-bats, hits, singles, doubles, RBI, times on base (292), strikeouts, slugging percentage, on-base percentage, HR frequency (12.2 ABs per HR), most pitches seen per plate appearance (3.94), batting average vs. lefthanded pitchers, slugging percentage vs. lefthanded pitchers (.606), slugging percentage vs. righthanded pitchers (.626), on-base percentage vs. lefthanded pitchers (.369) and on-base percentage vs. righthanded pitchers (.407)
- Led AL shortstops in batting average, home runs and RBI

Ivan Rodriguez

2001 Season

For the second consecutive year, Ivan Rodriguez' season ended early because of an injury. This injury was more chilling because it hinted at the beginning of the wearing-down process that levels most catchers. Rodriguez underwent surgery in September to repair a damaged patella tendon in the left knee. The repetitive stress of catching triggered the problem. Rodriguez showed some signs of slippage before the surgery. After improving his batting average in each of the four previous years, his mark dropped to .308 in 2001.

Hitting

Teams struggle to find a way to pitch Rodriguez because he swings at nearly every pitch—he took a major league-low 40.5 percent of pitches last season—and usually hits even pitches out of the strike zone hard. The good thing about that approach is that Pudge has a consistent .500 slugging percentage. The bad thing is that he's a double-play machine. He has grounded into 61 double plays in his last 346 games over the past three years.

Baserunning & Defense

Rodriguez won his 10th consecutive Gold Glove, tying Hall of Famer Johnny Bench for the most by a catcher. He won because of his arm. He threw out 23 of 46 runners, marking the fourth time in the last five seasons he had a caught-stealing rate of at least 50 percent. Rodriguez' arm obscures some other weaknesses in his defense, however. He tries to handle pitches in the dirt with quick hands rather than his body, and he continues to show little interest in the art of game management. He must share the blame for Texas' on-going pitching problems.

2002 Outlook

The big-ticket addition of shortstop Alex Rodriguez makes it possible that Ivan Rodriguez could be gone as soon as he proves his knee is sound. Pudge can become a free agent after this season, and he is in no mood to give a local discount again. Rather than tie up about $40 million in two players, new general manager John Hart could trade the All-Star catcher. Hart has taken such bold steps before. He let Albert Belle and Manny Ramirez walk out of Cleveland.

Position: C
Bats: R **Throws:** R
Ht: 5' 9" **Wt:** 205

Opening Day Age: 30
Born: 11/30/71 in Vega Baja, PR
ML Seasons: 11
Pronunciation: rod-RI-gez
Nickname: Pudge

Overall Statistics

	G	AB	R	H	D	T	HR	RBI	SB	BB	SO	Avg	OBP	Slg
2001	111	442	70	136	24	2	25	65	10	23	73	.308	.347	.541
Career	1371	5248	785	1595	312	26	196	769	75	279	692	.304	.341	.485

Where He Hits the Ball

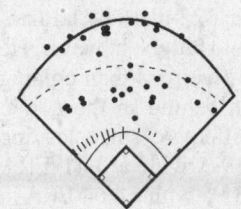
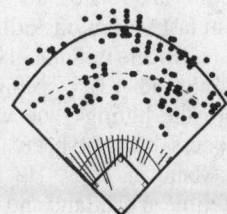

Vs. LHP   **Vs. RHP**

2001 Situational Stats

	AB	H	HR	RBI	Avg		AB	H	HR	RBI	Avg
Home	206	65	16	32	.316	LHP	83	24	5	11	.289
Road	236	71	9	33	.301	RHP	359	112	20	54	.312
First Half	283	84	17	42	.297	Sc Pos	112	32	4	42	.286
Scnd Half	159	52	8	23	.327	Clutch	63	19	5	12	.302

2001 Rankings (American League)

- 1st in lowest percentage of pitches taken (40.5)
- 5th in fielding percentage at catcher (.990)
- Led the Rangers in batting average on an 0-2 count (.297)
- Led AL catchers in home runs

Kenny Rogers

2001 Season

Kenny Rogers underwent season-ending surgery in July to correct a blockage that caused a circulation problem in his left shoulder. It was the latest sign that age is catching up to him. Rogers has had back problems for several years, and he had elbow surgery last winter. He did absorb innings while in the rotation, working at least six frames in his first 15 starts and 17 of 20 starts overall. At 5-7, Rogers had a losing record for only the second time in the last nine years.

Pitching

A hard-thrower as a kid, Rogers now gets by on guile and breaking pitches. That means lots of deep counts and lots of hits. Opponents hit .307 against him last season, including a .323 mark by lefthanders. Rogers will not give into hitters, however. He would rather risk issuing a free pass than coming into the hitting zone when behind in the count. Rogers has not been as effective since leaving Oakland in 1999. He is 19-3 with a 3.41 ERA lifetime at Oakland and 113-95 with a 4.64 ERA in all other parks. His changeup has not been good for nearly two years. Improvement on that pitch would help him considerably.

Defense

Rogers is an excellent fielder who functions as a fifth infielder, but that skill sometimes works against him. He will try a risky play rather than settle for the safe out. He holds runners well and has a clever pickoff move. He picked off a pair of baserunners last season, and has 10 pickoffs to his credit over the past three seasons.

2002 Outlook

The Rangers are not certain what to expect from Rogers after two offseasons of surgeries. This is the final year of Rogers' contract, and Texas is more likely to trade him than work out another deal.

Position: SP
Bats: L **Throws:** L
Ht: 6' 1" **Wt:** 217

Opening Day Age: 37
Born: 11/10/64 in Savannah, GA
ML Seasons: 13
Nickname: The Gambler

Overall Statistics

	W	L	Pct.	ERA	G	GS	Sv	IP	H	BB	SO	HR	Ratio
2001	5	7	.417	6.19	20	20	0	120.2	150	49	74	18	1.65
Career	132	98	.574	4.23	556	271	28	2049.1	2093	778	1315	204	1.40

How Often He Throws Strikes

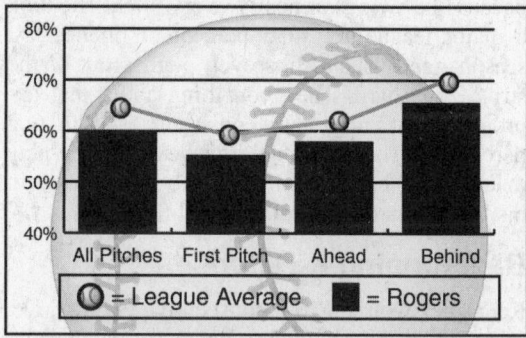

○ = League Average   ■ = Rogers

2001 Situational Stats

	W	L	ERA	Sv	IP		AB	H	HR	RBI	Avg
Home	4	5	5.97	0	78.1	LHB	124	40	6	26	.323
Road	1	2	6.59	0	42.1	RHB	364	110	12	46	.302
First Half	4	6	6.05	0	108.2	Sc Pos	128	39	7	57	.305
Scnd Half	1	1	7.50	0	12.0	Clutch	31	13	0	4	.419

2001 Rankings (American League)

- 9th in highest batting average allowed with runners in scoring position
- 10th in highest batting average allowed vs. righthanded batters
- Led the Rangers in most GDPs induced per GDP situation (15.5%)

Michael Young

Position: 2B
Bats: R **Throws:** R
Ht: 6' 1" **Wt:** 190

Opening Day Age: 25
Born: 10/19/76 in Covina, CA
ML Seasons: 2

2001 Season

The Texas organizational plan called for Michael Young to spend the entire season at Triple-A Oklahoma and focus on second base. He had split time between the middle-infield spots while in the Toronto organization. The plan changed because of an injury to Randy Velarde, but Young held together and improved as the season progressed. In fact, he played so well that the Rangers moved Jason Romano, a former darling of the organization, from second base to center field because Young blocked his path.

Hitting

Young became the first Texas second baseman since Julio Franco in 1991 to reach double-figures in homers. The drawback to that for the Rangers is Young forgets he is not a power hitter and gets too big with his swing. He has legitimate line-drive power, but he must learn to use his speed to be more than a .250 hitter. He simply gave away too many at-bats. His bunting ability and pitch selection also could be better. Young must do better than 26 walks and a .298 on-base percentage.

Baserunning & Defense

Young is the fastest player on the major league roster for the Rangers, but the makeup of the lineup limited his chances to run. He had three steals in only four tries. Young showed solid range at second, perhaps the best the Rangers have had from the position in more than a decade. He made at least one plus defensive play per game. He needs work on the double-play pivot but got better during the season.

2002 Outlook

Young is what a club looks for: young, athletic and on the low end of the salary pole. He played well at second, but that may not prove to be his position for the long haul. He manned center field in college, and some members of the Toronto organization believed that is his best position. The Rangers may have to consider that as they look to improve their center-field defense, though the acquisition of Carl Everett means Young won't see much time in center in the immediate future.

Overall Statistics

	G	AB	R	H	D	T	HR	RBI	SB	BB	SO	Avg	OBP	Slg
2001	106	386	57	96	18	4	11	49	3	26	91	.249	.298	.402
Career	108	388	57	96	18	4	11	49	3	26	92	.247	.296	.399

Where He Hits the Ball

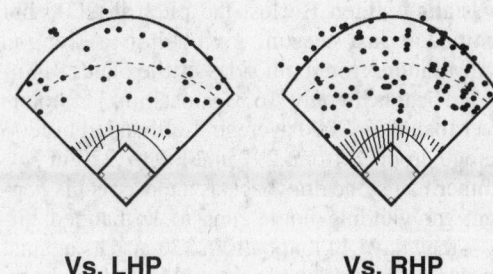

Vs. LHP   **Vs. RHP**

2001 Situational Stats

	AB	H	HR	RBI	Avg		AB	H	HR	RBI	Avg
Home	192	52	7	26	.271	LHP	98	25	5	14	.255
Road	194	44	4	23	.227	RHP	288	71	6	35	.247
First Half	125	28	2	14	.224	Sc Pos	95	25	1	35	.263
Scnd Half	261	68	9	35	.261	Clutch	58	12	1	3	.207

2001 Rankings (American League)

- 3rd in RBI among rookies
- 4th in home runs among rookies
- 5th in sacrifice bunts (9)
- Led the Rangers in sacrifice bunts (9) and bunts in play (10)

Jeff Zimmerman

2001 Season

When Tim Crabtree lost the closer's job in Texas last season, Jeff Zimmerman stepped in to fill the void and again defied expectations. He had 28 saves in 31 chances, good for the fifth-best success rate in the American League, and he also showed the mental toughness needed to handle the job. Zimmerman responded to a blown save against Seattle on July 2 by converting his final 17 chances of the year. He also had the fourth-lowest batting average against (.192) among AL relievers and averaged 9.1 strikeouts per nine innings.

Pitching

Zimmerman, an independent-league product, made the AL All-Star team in 1999 because of a devastating slider. He lost the pitch in 2000 but regained it last season, giving him a weapon against hitters from both sides of the plate. Right-handed batters hit only .163 against him, 115 points lower than their 2000 average. Lefthanded hitters' average dropped from .297 in 2000 to .220 in '01. Zimmerman's one drawback as a closer is his penchant for yielding home runs to lefthanded hitters—they have 14 longballs in 238 at-bats against him during the last two seasons. Most of the homers came when Zimmerman overthrew the slider, causing it to stay flat. He is better when pulling back on the velocity.

Defense

Zimmerman generally comes out of his delivery in good fielding position. Unlike most closers, he can be quick to the plate. Opponents had only four steals in 10 tries with Zimmerman on the mound last season. He does not have a threatening pickoff move and has yet to register a pickoff in the big leagues.

2002 Outlook

Zimmerman earned a chance to begin the 2002 season as the closer, but the decision hinges on general manager John Hart's willingness to constantly turn over the roster. Hart wants the same bullpen depth that his Cleveland teams had, and that could mean adding a reliever who would bump Zimmerman back into a setup role.

Position: RP
Bats: R **Throws:** R
Ht: 6' 1" **Wt:** 200

Opening Day Age: 29
Born: 8/9/72 in Kelowna, BC, Canada
ML Seasons: 3

Overall Statistics

	W	L	Pct.	ERA	G	GS	Sv	IP	H	BB	SO	HR	Ratio
2001	4	4	.500	2.40	66	0	28	71.1	48	16	72	10	0.90
Career	17	12	.586	3.27	196	0	32	228.2	178	73	213	29	1.10

How Often He Throws Strikes

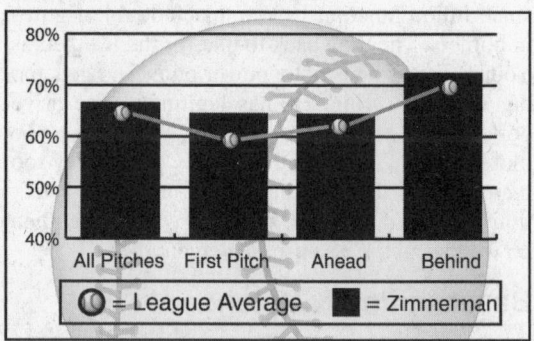

= League Average   = Zimmerman

2001 Situational Stats

	W	L	ERA	Sv	IP		AB	H	HR	RBI	Avg
Home	2	3	3.02	16	41.2	LHB	127	28	8	14	.220
Road	2	1	1.52	12	29.2	RHB	123	20	2	12	.163
First Half	3	4	3.38	12	42.2	Sc Pos	67	11	3	18	.164
Scnd Half	1	0	0.94	16	28.2	Clutch	167	33	6	17	.198

2001 Rankings (American League)

- 4th in fewest baserunners allowed per nine innings in relief (8.6)
- 5th in save percentage (90.3) and lowest batting average allowed in relief (.192)
- 6th in relief ERA (2.40)
- Led the Rangers in saves, games finished (53), save opportunities (31), lowest batting average allowed vs. lefthanded batters, save percentage (90.3), lowest percentage of inherited runners scored (21.6), relief ERA (2.40), lowest batting average allowed in relief (.192), most strikeouts per nine innings in relief (9.1) and fewest baserunners allowed per nine innings in relief (8.6)

Rob Bell

Position: SP
Bats: R **Throws:** R
Ht: 6' 5" **Wt:** 225

Opening Day Age: 25
Born: 1/17/77 in
Newburgh, NY
ML Seasons: 2

Overall Statistics

	W	L	Pct.	ERA	G	GS	Sv	IP	H	BB	SO	HR	Ratio
2001	5	10	.333	6.67	27	27	0	149.2	176	64	97	32	1.60
Career	12	18	.400	5.87	53	53	0	290.0	306	137	209	64	1.53

2001 Situational Stats

	W	L	ERA	Sv	IP		AB	H	HR	RBI	Avg
Home	4	5	5.87	0	92.0	LHB	315	97	18	58	.308
Road	1	5	7.96	0	57.2	RHB	272	79	14	48	.290
First Half	2	5	6.09	0	65.0	Sc Pos	138	45	4	66	.326
Scnd Half	3	5	7.12	0	84.2	Clutch	36	9	0	3	.250

2001 Season

In a swap of disappointing prospects, Texas sent Ruben Mateo to Cincinnati for Rob Bell in June. Bell excited the Rangers when he arrived, but then hit a long slump. He was 1-5 with a 8.09 ERA for his final 11 starts. He had the highest ERA (7.18) among American Leaguers with at least 100 innings. He also allowed at least five runs in 11 of his 19 starts with Texas, including a stretch of seven straight starts from late July to the end of August.

Pitching & Defense

The Rangers never saw Bell's heralded 12-to-6 curveball for more than a few pitches at a time. The inconsistency of the curve essentially reduced him to a fastball-only pitcher, as his changeup did not have enough separation from the fastball to be effective. Without a good curveball and changeup, Bell struggled against lefties. He also built up high pitch counts early in games, forcing the bullpen into play. Teams ran against Bell because of a high leg kick, but he didn't make an error in 23 chances.

2002 Outlook

Bell is only 25 and has a power arm. To be effective, he must become more consistent and improve pitches that complement the fastball. Texas will let him start, but his spot in the rotation isn't guaranteed. They need to see improvement. . . soon.

Chad Curtis

Position: CF/LF
Bats: R **Throws:** R
Ht: 5'10" **Wt:** 185

Opening Day Age: 33
Born: 11/6/68 in
Marion, IN
ML Seasons: 10

Overall Statistics

	G	AB	R	H	D	T	HR	RBI	SB	BB	SO	Avg	OBP	Slg
2001	38	115	24	29	3	0	3	10	7	14	21	.252	.338	.357
Career	1204	4017	648	1061	195	16	101	461	212	510	676	.264	.349	.396

2001 Situational Stats

	AB	H	HR	RBI	Avg		AB	H	HR	RBI	Avg
Home	59	17	1	6	.288	LHP	47	9	0	2	.191
Road	56	12	2	4	.214	RHP	68	20	3	8	.294
First Half	66	21	3	9	.318	Sc Pos	24	8	0	4	.333
Scnd Half	49	8	0	1	.163	Clutch	14	3	0	0	.214

2001 Season

The 2001 season may have been the end of the line for a gritty and sometimes misunderstood competitor who has played with six teams in the last eight years. Chad Curtis was the Rangers' starting center fielder before he endured a series of leg ailments that limited him to 115 at-bats. He talked at the end of the season of finishing his career in Japan to sample the culture. Curtis sometimes rubbed teammates the wrong way with his rigid standards, but he really does care about winning.

Hitting, Baserunning & Defense

As was the case at the start of his career, Curtis felt that there wasn't a high fastball he couldn't handle. Teams took advantage of that vanity, getting him to chase pitches out of the zone. The occasional home run hurt more than it helped, because it reinforced Curtis' belief that he was a power hitter. A bulked-up Curtis still can run, but not well enough to play center field for an extended period. He had seven steals in eight tries with the Rangers last season. His arm is average.

2002 Outlook

A contending team could use Curtis on its bench, but he may have lost his passion for the game. If the fire is out, he will go home rather than just hang around to pick up a paycheck.

Bill Haselman

Position: C
Bats: R **Throws:** R
Ht: 6' 3" **Wt:** 225

Opening Day Age: 35
Born: 5/25/66 in Long Branch, NJ
ML Seasons: 11
Pronunciation: HASS-el-man

Overall Statistics

	G	AB	R	H	D	T	HR	RBI	SB	BB	SO	Avg	OBP	Slg
2001	47	130	12	37	6	0	3	25	0	8	27	.285	.331	.400
Career	516	1424	169	372	87	3	44	192	9	103	274	.261	.313	.419

2001 Situational Stats

	AB	H	HR	RBI	Avg		AB	H	HR	RBI	Avg
Home	78	25	2	14	.321	LHP	44	14	2	7	.318
Road	52	12	1	11	.231	RHP	86	23	1	18	.267
First Half	14	4	0	3	.286	Sc Pos	45	16	1	22	.356
Scnd Half	116	33	3	22	.284	Clutch	13	3	0	1	.231

2001 Season

The quintessential backup catcher, Bill Haselman missed the first 12 weeks of the regular season while recovering from offseason right shoulder surgery, as well as the arthroscopic right elbow surgery he underwent prior to Opening Day. But he *still* played more than planned. A season-ending knee injury to Ivan Rodriguez forced the Rangers to give 130 at-bats and 35 starts to Haselman.

Hitting, Baserunning & Defense

Haselman still can hit a fastball, particularly from lefthanders. He certainly is no more than a station-to-station runner once he does get on base. His strength lies in his ability to work with pitchers. He helps set game plans and understands how to nurse young pitchers through difficult moments. He also had a higher degree of difficulty because he had to work with a young staff that collapsed in the final weeks. Haselman has not thrown well since his original shoulder surgery in 1987, but he handles other defensive demands of the position.

2002 Outlook

If the new administration trades Ivan Rodriguez, Haselman again could be pressed into front-line duty. He is signed through 2002, and there are no legitimate organizational catching prospects close to the majors.

Mike Lamb

Position: 3B
Bats: L **Throws:** R
Ht: 6' 1" **Wt:** 195

Opening Day Age: 26
Born: 8/9/75 in West Covina, CA
ML Seasons: 2

Overall Statistics

	G	AB	R	H	D	T	HR	RBI	SB	BB	SO	Avg	OBP	Slg
2001	76	284	42	87	18	0	4	35	2	14	27	.306	.348	.412
Career	214	777	107	224	43	2	10	82	2	48	87	.288	.335	.387

2001 Situational Stats

	AB	H	HR	RBI	Avg		AB	H	HR	RBI	Avg
Home	151	48	1	25	.318	LHP	50	15	2	5	.300
Road	133	39	3	10	.293	RHP	234	72	2	30	.308
First Half	69	22	1	8	.319	Sc Pos	66	24	1	27	.364
Scnd Half	215	65	3	27	.302	Clutch	47	12	0	4	.255

2001 Season

No one was helped more by Texas' in-season change of managers than Mike Lamb. Buried by Johnny Oates, Lamb got a second chance under Jerry Narron. The Rangers released veteran third baseman Ken Caminiti, so Lamb received another half-season trial. After a slow start, he kept his average above .300 for the club's final 65 games.

Hitting, Baserunning & Defense

Lamb has hit only 10 homers in 777 major league at-bats, not nearly enough power for a corner infielder. His swing is an odd creation. His lower body moves as if he wants to pull the ball, but his upper body goes to the opposite field. The result is a general lack of pop. Lamb is a below-average runner. His hands are good, but he again had defensive problems and tied for the third-most errors (18) among AL third basemen. Most of his errors come on throws doomed by poor footwork, a sign that he still is learning the position.

2002 Outlook

Texas is overloaded with young third basemen: Lamb, top prospect Hank Blalock and first-round draft choice Mark Teixeira. Lamb may have only spring training to hold off their charge. He could end up as a useful bench player because of his catching background.

Ricky Ledee

Position: RF/CF
Bats: L **Throws:** L
Ht: 6' 1" **Wt:** 190

Opening Day Age: 28
Born: 11/22/73 in
Ponce, PR
ML Seasons: 4
Pronunciation: la-DAY

Overall Statistics

	G	AB	R	H	D	T	HR	RBI	SB	BB	SO	Avg	OBP	Slg
2001	78	242	33	56	21	1	2	36	3	23	58	.231	.303	.351
Career	345	1038	150	254	58	13	25	165	23	117	258	.245	.322	.398

2001 Situational Stats

	AB	H	HR	RBI	Avg		AB	H	HR	RBI	Avg
Home	121	31	1	20	.256	LHP	30	8	0	10	.267
Road	121	25	1	16	.207	RHP	212	48	2	26	.226
First Half	70	15	0	10	.214	Sc Pos	74	21	1	33	.284
Scnd Half	172	41	2	26	.238	Clutch	40	9	0	5	.225

2001 Season

The prospect tag finally should have fallen off Ricky Ledee at age 27. He missed the first 10 weeks of the season because of a spring-training hamstring injury and showed little on his return. Ledee hit only .231 with minimal power and spent large portions of the final weeks on the bench. He knows how to play the game but never will meet the hype created during his time with the Yankees.

Hitting, Baserunning & Defense

Ledee has 1,038 career at-bats, which may be enough to say that his .245 average gives a true picture of his talent level. He tends to be passive at the plate, and that gets him into bad hitting situations. He had two strikes in the count during 128 of his 272 plate appearances last season and hit only .155 in those situations. The rest of Ledee's game reflected his struggles at the plate. Usually a solid baserunner and good corner outfielder, he had problems in both areas.

2002 Outlook

New general manager John Hart may not want Ledee around simply because he reminds him of a bad mistake. With Cleveland, Hart traded David Justice to the Yankees for Ledee. Justice helped the Yankees win the 2000 World Series, while Ledee hit .222 in a month with the Indians.

Chris Michalak

Position: SP/RP
Bats: L **Throws:** L
Ht: 6' 2" **Wt:** 195

Opening Day Age: 31
Born: 1/4/71 in Joliet, IL
ML Seasons: 2

Overall Statistics

	W	L	Pct.	ERA	G	GS	Sv	IP	H	BB	SO	HR	Ratio
2001	8	9	.471	4.41	35	18	1	136.2	157	55	67	19	1.55
Career	8	9	.471	4.69	40	18	1	142.0	166	59	72	20	1.58

2001 Situational Stats

	W	L	ERA	Sv	IP		AB	H	HR	RBI	Avg
Home	4	5	5.19	1	69.1	LHB	141	40	5	23	.284
Road	4	4	3.61	0	67.1	RHB	394	117	14	51	.297
First Half	6	6	4.25	0	95.1	Sc Pos	140	37	0	47	.264
Scnd Half	2	3	4.79	1	41.1	Clutch	28	9	2	2	.321

2001 Season

Chris Michalak went to the same Illinois high school as the Rudy of Notre Dame football fame, and he turned in a Rudy-like season. Michalak made an Opening Day roster (as a starter with Toronto) for the first time in his nine-year career. He beat the defending World Champion Yankees twice in April. He then pitched poorly after a good first two months and went to Texas in a waiver claim, where he was used exclusively as a reliever.

Pitching & Defense

Michalak relies on the classic lefthanders style of nibbling with offspeed pitches. Disciplined hitters can get favorable counts against him. Rather than give in, Michalak continued to nibble when behind in the count and allowed 55 walks in 136.2 innings. He had problems when some managers challenged his mesmerizing pickoff move. Michalak had a major league-high six balks and seemed flustered by the close inspection. He also picked off 10 runners with the move.

2002 Outlook

Michalak could be in the wrong place at the wrong time. New general manager John Hart likes power arms in the bullpen, and that is not Michalak's game. He does offer the appeal of being a lefty who can soak up a lot of innings out of the bullpen.

Juan Moreno

Position: RP
Bats: L **Throws:** L
Ht: 6' 1" **Wt:** 205

Opening Day Age: 27
Born: 2/28/75 in
Maiquetia, VZ
ML Seasons: 1

Overall Statistics

	W	L	Pct.	ERA	G	GS	Sv	IP	H	BB	SO	HR	Ratio
2001	3	3	.500	3.92	45	0	0	41.1	22	28	36	6	1.21
Career	3	3	.500	3.92	45	0	0	41.1	22	28	36	6	1.21

2001 Situational Stats

	W	L	ERA	Sv	IP		AB	H	HR	RBI	Avg
Home	1	1	2.19	0	24.2	LHB	70	12	3	10	.171
Road	2	2	6.48	0	16.2	RHB	74	10	3	6	.135
First Half	1	0	2.79	0	19.1	Sc Pos	30	5	2	11	.167
Scnd Half	2	3	4.91	0	22.0	Clutch	50	6	3	4	.120

2001 Season

Teams waste millions of dollars trying to find effective lefthanded relievers. The Rangers stumbled upon Juan Moreno in the Venezuelan Winter League as he was trying to revive his career after being released by Oakland. He received a chance because of the early-season bullpen fiasco and pitched well until showing signs of fatigue.

Pitching & Defense

Moreno has several variations of the slider and a live fastball that will touch 90 MPH. He had 36 strikeouts in 41.1 innings and was more than a one-hitter specialist. He held righthanded batters to a .135 average with 19 strikeouts in 74 at-bats. Moreno held the first batter faced to a .158 average—ninth-lowest average in the AL—but could improve on the seven walks in those situations. He had rotator cuff surgery in May 2000 and had not fully regained lost strength. He posted a 5.87 ERA for his final 27 appearances. Moreno is a below-average fielder, and he was called for three balks. One of those balks cost the Rangers a game.

2002 Outlook

If a pitcher needs 18 months to be completely healed from rotator cuff surgery, Moreno should be better in 2002. His anticipated role will keep him out of most decisions and save chances, however.

Aaron Myette

Position: SP
Bats: R **Throws:** R
Ht: 6' 4" **Wt:** 195

Opening Day Age: 24
Born: 9/26/77 in New
Westminster, BC,
Canada
ML Seasons: 3
Pronunciation: my-YET

Overall Statistics

	W	L	Pct.	ERA	G	GS	Sv	IP	H	BB	SO	HR	Ratio
2001	4	5	.444	7.14	19	15	0	80.2	94	37	67	12	1.62
Career	4	7	.364	6.82	25	18	0	99.0	111	55	79	14	1.68

2001 Situational Stats

	W	L	ERA	Sv	IP		AB	H	HR	RBI	Avg
Home	0	2	6.58	0	39.2	LHB	174	55	6	30	.316
Road	4	3	7.68	0	41.0	RHB	147	39	6	29	.265
First Half	0	1	9.00	0	18.0	Sc Pos	102	34	2	47	.333
Scnd Half	4	4	6.61	0	62.2	Clutch	10	2	1	1	.200

2001 Season

Aaron Myette shuttled between the majors and minors before returning to the parent club to stay in July. He teased the Rangers with an occasional good start but finished with the third-highest ERA (7.14) among American Leaguers with at least 75 innings. He did earn respect among teammates for his willingness to protect batters. In three instances, Myette responded to a knockdown pitch at a Texas hitter by drilling an opponent.

Pitching & Defense

Myette found the velocity he had lost during his final season with the White Sox and again had a consistent 93-MPH fastball. Texas believes he has a significant upside as a starter because he also commands a slider and changeup. He often gets too much of the plate, however, which explains why opponents had a .492 slugging percentage against him. Myette could help himself by fielding his position better. He also needs to develop a slide-step, as opponents ran freely against him.

2002 Outlook

Myette has one minor league option remaining, and the Rangers could use it at the start of the 2002 season. He has 30 career starts at Triple-A and could benefit from more grooming at that level. The arm is there, but he is raw.

Ruben Sierra

Position: DH/RF
Bats: B **Throws:** R
Ht: 6' 1" **Wt:** 215

Opening Day Age: 36
Born: 10/6/65 in Rio Piedras, PR
ML Seasons: 15

Overall Statistics

	G	AB	R	H	D	T	HR	RBI	SB	BB	SO	Avg	OBP	Slg
2001	94	344	55	100	22	1	23	67	2	19	52	.291	.322	.561
Career	1776	6813	947	1837	363	57	263	1121	135	514	1023	.270	.317	.455

2001 Situational Stats

	AB	H	HR	RBI	Avg		AB	H	HR	RBI	Avg
Home	187	58	13	35	.310	LHP	84	27	4	17	.321
Road	157	42	10	32	.268	RHP	260	73	19	50	.281
First Half	147	46	13	38	.313	Sc Pos	99	21	1	39	.212
Scnd Half	197	54	10	29	.274	Clutch	64	19	4	14	.297

2001 Season

Ruben Sierra spent 1999 in the Atlantic League and began 2000 with the Cancun Lobstermen of the Mexican League before Texas brought him back to stabilize its Triple-A team. He started 2001 in Oklahoma but made the most of a chance to return to the majors that came about because of an injury to Chad Curtis.

Hitting, Baserunning & Defense

Sierra defied nature and regained lost bat speed last season. He finally gave up a destructive taste for weight lifting, and his body became freer. As has been his career pattern, the switch-hitter posted a better average from the right side but showed more power from the left. He still is impatient and rarely walks. Sierra ran better and played the outfield better than expected, which is not to say he could handle the defensive demands of the position full time. He does not go back on balls well, and his arm is limited.

2002 Outlook

Sierra is 36 but has taken care of his body. If he keeps his newfound, upbeat attitude and stays away from the weights, he could play several more years. He is better suited as a designated hitter but could be used in the outfield. The problem is that Texas currently has a surplus of outfielders.

Mike Venafro

Position: RP
Bats: L **Throws:** L
Ht: 5'10" **Wt:** 180

Opening Day Age: 28
Born: 8/2/73 in Takoma Park, MD
ML Seasons: 3
Pronunciation:
VEN-ah-froh

Overall Statistics

	W	L	Pct.	ERA	G	GS	Sv	IP	H	BB	SO	HR	Ratio
2001	5	5	.500	4.80	70	0	4	60.0	54	28	29	2	1.37
Career	11	8	.579	3.95	212	0	5	184.2	181	71	98	8	1.36

2001 Situational Stats

	W	L	ERA	Sv	IP		AB	H	HR	RBI	Avg
Home	5	3	6.21	2	33.1	LHB	97	25	0	19	.258
Road	0	2	3.04	2	26.2	RHB	128	29	2	19	.227
First Half	2	2	2.76	3	32.2	Sc Pos	77	22	0	33	.286
Scnd Half	3	3	7.24	1	27.1	Clutch	125	35	2	21	.280

2001 Season

Mike Venafro was one of 11 American Leaguers with at least 70 relief appearances. The workload may have caught up to him, however. He had a 9.15 ERA in his last 21 outings, a stretch that included consecutive performances in which he allowed 10 runs without getting an out. He posted a career-worst 4.80 ERA overall. Still, Venafro understands the art of setting up a closer, and he had 21 holds, third-best among AL lefthanders.

Pitching & Defense

In the best of times for Venafro, the ball will be put in play against him; he averaged only 4.35 strikeout per nine innings. To be effective, he must be able to sink the fastball. That pitch stayed high and straight during the final two months of the season, causing many problems. His curveball has been effective against lefthanded hitters. Lefty batsmen did not have a homer in 97 at-bats against him in 2001. Venafro needs fielding practice this spring. He mishandled several bunt plays and had four errors in only 21 chances.

2002 Outlook

New manager Jerry Narron extended the length of Venafro's appearances. Narron must decide if that contributed to Venafro's poor finish. If so, he probably goes back to being a situational reliever.

Jeff Brantley (Pos: RHP, **Age**: 38)

	W	L	Pct.	ERA	G	GS	Sv	IP	H	BB	SO	HR	Ratio
2001	0	1	.000	5.14	18	0	0	21.0	26	9	11	5	1.67
Career	43	46	.483	3.39	615	18	172	859.1	754	366	728	105	1.30

Brantley was signed in January in order to provide some insurance in the bullpen. Despite struggling in the spring, he made the Opening Day roster. He continued to struggle and was released in May. 2002 Outlook: D

Francisco Cordero (Pos: RHP, **Age**: 24)

	W	L	Pct.	ERA	G	GS	Sv	IP	H	BB	SO	HR	Ratio
2001	0	1	.000	3.86	3	0	0	2.1	3	2	1	0	2.14
Career	3	5	.375	4.93	79	0	0	98.2	109	68	69	13	1.79

Cordero's season began on the DL with a stress fracture in the left side of his back, and it ended in June with a stress fracture in the right side. 2002 Outlook: C

Tim Crabtree (Pos: RHP, **Age**: 32)

	W	L	Pct.	ERA	G	GS	Sv	IP	H	BB	SO	HR	Ratio
2001	0	5	.000	6.56	21	0	4	23.1	37	14	16	3	2.19
Career	21	22	.488	4.20	342	0	9	394.0	434	150	288	29	1.48

Crabtree converted his first four save chances but landed on the DL in mid-April. He returned to lose his closer's job, and then in June he partially tore a rotator cuff. He became a free agent in November. 2002 Outlook: B

R.A. Dickey (Pos: RHP, **Age**: 27)

	W	L	Pct.	ERA	G	GS	Sv	IP	H	BB	SO	HR	Ratio
2001	0	1	.000	6.75	4	0	0	12.0	13	7	4	3	1.67
Career	0	1	.000	6.75	4	0	0	12.0	13	7	4	3	1.67

Dickey pitched three complete games as a full-time starter for Triple-A Oklahoma last season, while also setting career highs in innings pitched (163), wins (11) and strikeouts (120). 2002 Outlook: C

Kelly Dransfeldt (Pos: SS, **Age**: 26, **Bats**: R)

	G	AB	R	H	D	T	HR	RBI	SB	BB	SO	Avg	OBP	Slg
2001	4	3	0	0	0	0	0	0	0	0	0	.000	.000	.000
Career	36	82	5	13	3	0	1	7	0	4	26	.159	.198	.232

Dransfeldt again was unable to live up to his past success in the minor leagues. He's now a strong glove, no-hit utility infielder. 2002 Outlook: C

Kevin Foster (Pos: RHP, **Age**: 33)

	W	L	Pct.	ERA	G	GS	Sv	IP	H	BB	SO	HR	Ratio
2001	0	1	.000	6.62	9	0	0	17.2	21	10	16	2	1.75
Career	32	30	.516	4.86	100	83	0	509.2	500	220	417	88	1.41

Foster began the season pitching very well in Triple-A for Texas. He was called up in July and made his first appearances in the majors since 1998. He later refused an assignment and was released. 2002 Outlook: C

Ryan Glynn (Pos: RHP, **Age**: 27)

	W	L	Pct.	ERA	G	GS	Sv	IP	H	BB	SO	HR	Ratio
2001	1	5	.167	7.04	12	9	0	46.0	59	26	15	7	1.85
Career	8	16	.333	6.42	41	35	0	189.1	237	102	87	32	1.79

Glynn's career took a step backwards in 2001, as he coped with a variety of ailments during the first two months. He went on the DL in June with an injured back, and was demoted upon his return. 2002 Outlook: C

Mike Hubbard (Pos: C, **Age**: 31, **Bats**: R)

	G	AB	R	H	D	T	HR	RBI	SB	BB	SO	Avg	OBP	Slg
2001	5	11	1	3	1	0	1	1	0	0	4	.273	.273	.636
Career	104	192	11	32	2	0	4	11	0	4	60	.167	.187	.240

Hubbard had a successful season in the minors, batting .310 while slugging .527. He was called up twice to be the backup catcher and then refused a demotion and was signed by Baltimore in the fall. 2002 Outlook: C

Marcus Jensen (Pos: C, **Age**: 29, **Bats**: B)

	G	AB	R	H	D	T	HR	RBI	SB	BB	SO	Avg	OBP	Slg
2001	12	29	0	5	1	0	0	2	0	0	10	.172	.172	.207
Career	129	308	31	59	16	1	5	25	0	46	95	.192	.297	.299

After being claimed off waivers from Boston in June, Jensen regained his batting eye in the minors. He improved in every category, but his offense cooled in the majors as a backup. 2002 Outlook: C

Jonathan Johnson (Pos: RHP, **Age**: 27)

	W	L	Pct.	ERA	G	GS	Sv	IP	H	BB	SO	HR	Ratio
2001	0	0	-	9.58	5	0	0	10.1	13	7	11	2	1.94
Career	1	1	.500	7.71	22	1	0	46.2	61	33	40	5	2.01

Johnson was the seventh pick overall in the 1995 draft but has failed to live up to expectations. He did hold lefties to a .235 average in a brief stint in 2001. Arizona bought him from Texas in April. 2002 Outlook: C

Mike Judd (Pos: RHP, **Age**: 26)

	W	L	Pct.	ERA	G	GS	Sv	IP	H	BB	SO	HR	Ratio
2001	1	1	.500	5.28	12	3	0	29.0	34	15	16	4	1.69
Career	4	3	.571	7.20	28	8	0	75.0	91	39	61	14	1.73

Judd had a solid ERA of 4.05 for Tampa before he was disabled in May. He refused a demotion and was claimed off waivers by Texas. He pitched only six times for the organization, before landing back on the DL. 2002 Outlook: C

Chris Magruder (Pos: LF, **Age**: 24, **Bats**: B)

	G	AB	R	H	D	T	HR	RBI	SB	BB	SO	Avg	OBP	Slg
2001	17	29	3	5	0	0	0	1	0	1	5	.172	.226	.172
Career	17	29	3	5	0	0	0	1	0	1	5	.172	.226	.172

Texas was pleased to get Magruder in the Andres Galarraga trade last July. His tools aren't exciting, but he's a smart player who does most things well. He can play all three outfield positions and batted .294-17-62 between Double-A and Triple-A in 2001. 2002 Outlook: C

Pat Mahomes (Pos: RHP, **Age**: 31)

	W	L	Pct.	ERA	G	GS	Sv	IP	H	BB	SO	HR	Ratio
2001	7	6	.538	5.70	56	4	0	107.1	115	55	61	17	1.58
Career	41	37	.526	5.57	283	60	5	654.0	683	363	416	111	1.60

Mahomes was signed for his ability to start or relieve. Last season he was much better out of the bullpen, where he had 4.58 ERA but suffered from a lack of control. He opted for free agency in November. 2002 Outlook: B

Ruben Mateo (**Pos**: RF, **Age**: 24, **Bats**: R)

	G	AB	R	H	D	T	HR	RBI	SB	BB	SO	Avg	OBP	Slg
2001	40	129	18	32	5	2	1	13	1	9	28	.248	.322	.341
Career	124	457	66	121	25	3	13	50	10	23	90	.265	.316	.418

Mateo, once the top prospect in the Texas organization, struggled after breaking his leg in 2000. He was traded to Cincinnati in June, and he will have to fight for playing time. 2002 Outlook: B

Craig Monroe (**Pos**: RF, **Age**: 25, **Bats**: R)

	G	AB	R	H	D	T	HR	RBI	SB	BB	SO	Avg	OBP	Slg
2001	27	52	8	11	1	0	2	5	2	6	18	.212	.293	.346
Career	27	52	8	11	1	0	2	5	2	6	18	.212	.293	.346

Monroe's Triple-A stats last year (.280-20-75) mirrored his Double-A numbers from 2000. Once a threat to steal, he's swiped only 24 bases since 1999. 2002 Outlook: C

Mark Petkovsek (**Pos**: RHP, **Age**: 36)

	W	L	Pct.	ERA	G	GS	Sv	IP	H	BB	SO	HR	Ratio
2001	1	2	.333	6.69	55	0	0	76.2	103	28	42	14	1.71
Career	46	28	.622	4.74	390	41	5	710.0	797	222	358	82	1.44

Last season, Petkovsek was consistently terrible. He had four separate months with an ERA over 9.00 and allowed 30 of 53 inherited runners to score. 2002 Outlook: C

Bo Porter (**Pos**: LF/RF, **Age**: 29, **Bats**: R)

	G	AB	R	H	D	T	HR	RBI	SB	BB	SO	Avg	OBP	Slg
2001	48	87	18	20	4	2	1	6	3	9	34	.230	.296	.356
Career	89	126	23	27	5	2	2	8	3	13	52	.214	.284	.333

Despite shuffling between Texas and Triple-A last season, Porter actually had his best season in the majors. His numbers did not impress, however, and he was placed on waivers at the end of the season. 2002 Outlook: C

Scott Sheldon (**Pos**: 3B/SS, **Age**: 33, **Bats**: R)

	G	AB	R	H	D	T	HR	RBI	SB	BB	SO	Avg	OBP	Slg
2001	61	120	11	24	5	0	3	11	1	3	35	.200	.216	.317
Career	141	285	34	67	16	0	8	33	1	15	84	.235	.275	.375

Sheldon regressed offensively last season, after his promising first full major league season in 2000. Primarily a third baseman, he proved himself useful again as a versatile utility player. 2002 Outlook: C

J.D. Smart (**Pos**: RHP, **Age**: 28)

	W	L	Pct.	ERA	G	GS	Sv	IP	H	BB	SO	HR	Ratio
2001	1	2	.333	6.46	15	0	0	15.1	19	4	10	3	1.50
Career	1	3	.250	5.35	44	0	0	67.1	75	21	31	7	1.43

Smart was another Texas pitcher who excelled in the minors but struggled in the majors. He had season-ending rotator cuff surgery in July, and should be out for at least a year to rehab. 2002 Outlook: D

Brandon Villafuerte (**Pos**: RHP, **Age**: 26)

	W	L	Pct.	ERA	G	GS	Sv	IP	H	BB	SO	HR	Ratio
2001	0	0	-	14.29	6	0	0	5.2	12	4	4	3	2.82
Career	0	0	-	12.60	9	0	0	10.0	16	8	5	3	2.40

After lowering his ERA by almost four runs in his second full year at Triple-A, Villafuerte spent almost three weeks with Texas. He bombed in his final outing for the Rangers, getting one out while giving up seven runs. 2002 Outlook: C

Texas Rangers Minor League Prospects

Organization Overview:

Mentioning the Rangers is most likely to induce images of power hitters such as Pete Incaviglia, Juan Gonzalez, Rafael Palmeiro and Alex Rodriguez. A few years from now, the Rangers may have a new generation of power hitters to talk about, which could include Carlos Pena, Kevin Mench, Travis Hafner and Mark Teixeira. Texas pitching has been poor of late, but the farm system provides hope for the future. The Rangers acquired promising righthander Justin Duchscherer from Boston in June, and a homegrown crew that includes Joaquin Benoit, Danny Kolb, Colby Lewis, Spike Lundberg, Ryan Dittfurth, Jovanny Cedeno and Omar Beltre eventually may fill some big holes in the current rotation.

Joaquin Benoit

Position: P
Bats: R **Throws:** R
Ht: 6' 3" **Wt:** 205

Opening Day Age: 22
Born: 7/26/79 in Santiago, DR

Recent Statistics

	W	L	ERA	G	GS	Sv	IP	H	R	BB	SO	HR
2001 AA Tulsa	1	0	3.32	4	4	0	21.2	23	8	6	23	1
2001 AAA Oklahoma	9	5	4.19	24	24	0	131.0	113	63	73	142	14
2001 AL Texas	0	0	10.80	1	1	0	5.0	8	6	3	4	3

Signed in 1996, Benoit has incredible stuff, but he has battled injuries constantly before enjoying his first injury-free season in 2001. Working extensively at Triple-A Oklahoma with pitching coach Lee Tunnell, who focused on fundamentals, Benoit became a more complete pitcher last summer. His best pitches are an above-average fastball and sharp-breaking slider, and he made good progress with his changeup and all of his offerings in 2001. He struggled early on at Oklahoma, but got untracked and fanned more than a batter an inning for the first time in his career. Being consistent is critical to Benoit, who will be lights out for 6-7 innings, but finds trouble in one bad frame. He'll battle for a rotation spot with Texas in the spring.

Hank Blalock

Position: 3B
Bats: L **Throws:** L
Ht: 6' 1" **Wt:** 192

Opening Day Age: 21
Born: 11/21/80 in San Diego, CA

Recent Statistics

	G	AB	R	H	D	T	HR	RBI	SB	BB	SO	Avg
2000 A Savannah	139	512	66	153	32	2	10	77	31	62	53	.299
2001 A Charlotte	63	237	46	90	19	1	7	47	7	26	31	.380
2001 AA Tulsa	68	272	50	89	18	4	11	61	3	39	38	.327
2001 MLE	68	266	44	83	16	3	10	53	2	29	39	.312

A high school pick in 1999, Blalock exploded with a monster season between high Class-A Charlotte and Double-A Tulsa last summer, batting a combined .352-18-108. Then he tore up the Arizona Fall League as one of its youngest players. Blalock is a pure hitter with gap power, but he most impressed the Rangers with his ability to adjust from at-bat to at-bat and even between pitches. He should hit for both average and power as a major leaguer. Blalock is average defensively and will make the routine plays. His major league position may change, though, as Texas drafted coveted third sacker Mark Teixeira in the first round of the 2001 draft.

Justin Duchscherer

Position: P
Bats: R **Throws:** R
Ht: 6' 3" **Wt:** 164

Opening Day Age: 24
Born: 11/19/77 in Aberdeen, SD

Recent Statistics

	W	L	ERA	G	GS	Sv	IP	H	R	BB	SO	HR
2001 AA Trenton	6	3	2.44	12	12	0	73.2	49	25	14	69	6
2001 AA Tulsa	4	0	2.08	6	6	0	43.1	39	14	10	55	3
2001 AAA Oklahoma	3	3	2.84	7	7	0	50.2	48	20	10	52	6
2001 AL Texas	1	1	12.27	5	2	0	14.2	24	20	4	11	5

Acquired last June during his sixth season in the Boston system, the tall, wiry Duchscherer isn't overpowering and won't prosper based on pure stuff. He succeeds with solid command and an ability to change speeds effectively, and he fared well with Texas when he had both working for him. His velocity has shown a bit of a rise, but he isn't likely to get much faster than his current 86-88 MPH. As a pitcher, he's studious about working hitters and getting ahead. He uses his fastball to set up his other pitches, which include a sharp downward-breaking curve and changeup. A little fine-tuning with his overall command is his ticket to sticking in Texas.

Danny Kolb

Position: P
Bats: R **Throws:** R
Ht: 6' 4" **Wt:** 215

Opening Day Age: 27
Born: 3/29/75 in Sterling, IL

Recent Statistics

	W	L	ERA	G	GS	Sv	IP	H	R	BB	SO	HR
2001 A Charlotte	1	2	3.86	7	3	0	18.2	21	8	2	16	1
2001 AA Tulsa	1	0	0.00	1	0	0	2.0	0	0	1	0	0
2001 AAA Oklahoma	0	1	1.42	12	0	3	19.0	13	3	4	21	1
2001 AL Texas	0	0	4.70	17	0	0	15.1	15	8	10	15	2

A 1995 pick, Kolb established himself with a strong 1996 season in the Class-A Sally League. He struggled with his command for the next two years, but Kolb got back on track in 1999 at Double-A Tulsa. Elbow problems that flared up late in '99 led to elbow surgery to remove bone chips and repair a ligament in June 2000. Kolb still was rehabbing last spring and was brought along slowly. He returned in the second half and dominated hitters at Triple-A Oklahoma, calling on a mid-90s fastball that runs in on righthanders. To give hitters a different look, he once again throws the slider that led to his surgery. He closed out 2001 with the Rangers and showed he could handle setup duties. A solid spring should keep him in Texas.

Kevin Mench

Position: OF **Opening Day Age:** 24
Bats: R **Throws:** R **Born:** 1/7/78 in
Ht: 6' 0" **Wt:** 215 Wilmington, DE

Recent Statistics

	G	AB	R	H	D	THR	RBI	SB	BB	SO	Avg
2000 A Charlotte	132	491	118	164	39	9	27	121	19	78	72	.334
2001 AA Tulsa	120	475	78	126	34	2	26	83	4	34	76	.265
2001 MLE	120	466	68	117	31	1	22	73	2	25	79	.251

A 1999 pick, Mench jumped to high Class-A Charlotte in his second pro season, showed power to all fields and batted .334-27-121. He was just as dominant in the Arizona Fall League a year ago, but he suffered a wrist injury in spring training, which bothered him throughout 2001. Calling on his impressive bat speed, Mench still displayed power at Double-A Tulsa. Learning to make adjustments at the plate will be an ongoing process for Mench, who saw his walk rate drop in his first exposure to the high minors. He may not be Gold Glove material, but he's a good athlete who could be an adequate left fielder. He has an average arm and runs OK.

Carlos Pena

Position: 1B **Opening Day Age:** 23
Bats: L **Throws:** L **Born:** 5/17/78 in Santo
Ht: 6' 2" **Wt:** 210 Domingo, DR

Recent Statistics

	G	AB	R	H	D	THR	RBI	SB	BB	SO	Avg
2001 AAA Oklahoma	119	431	71	124	38	3	23	74	11	80	127	.288
2001 AL Texas	22	62	6	16	4	1	3	12	0	10	17	.258
2001 MLE	119	426	66	119	36	2	22	69	8	74	130	.279

A first-round pick in 1998, Pena has a fluid swing that produces power. He previewed his pop at high Class-A Charlotte in 1999, then broke out with a .299-28-105 season at Double-A Tulsa in 2000. The lefthanded hitter has developed a shortened stroke that doesn't hinder his power, and his plate patience is a big plus. Pena battled a few injuries in 2001, including hamstring troubles that hurt his hitting early at Triple-A Oklahoma. Still, he generated numbers similar to those of his breakout year. He debuted with Texas in September, showing the same plate discipline and power. Pena, who has soft hands and quick feet around the first-base bag, is playing right field in winter ball and may get a look there in the spring.

Jason Romano

Position: 2B **Opening Day Age:** 22
Bats: R **Throws:** R **Born:** 6/24/79 in Tampa,
Ht: 6' 0" **Wt:** 185 FL

Recent Statistics

	G	AB	R	H	D	THR	RBI	SB	BB	SO	Avg
2000 AA Tulsa	131	535	87	145	35	2	8	70	25	56	84	.271
2001 AA Tulsa	46	186	19	45	9	1	1	19	8	16	31	.242
2001 R Rangers	5	21	2	3	0	0	0	0	1	1	8	.143
2001 A Charlotte	3	10	3	4	2	0	0	1	1	4	1	.400
2001 AAA Oklahoma	41	149	32	47	6	1	4	13	3	20	28	.315
2001 MLE	87	330	45	87	13	0	3	28	7	30	60	.264

A 1997 pick, Romano immediately moved from third base to second. He worked hard on the move and emerged as a prospect by batting .312-13-71 as one of the youngest regulars in the high Class-A Florida State League in 1999. The power has dropped off in the high minors, but the Rangers expect him to control the strike zone effectively enough to become a leadoff man. When Romano broke his thumb and missed several weeks last summer, the Rangers used his rehab to work him in the outfield. When he returned, Romano tore it up at Triple-A Oklahoma. He has taken well to left field and polished his game during instructional league. He only needs to work on getting better reads and tracking balls better.

Mark Teixeira

Position: 3B **Opening Day Age:** 21
Bats: B **Throws:** R **Born:** 4/11/80 in
Ht: 6' 3" **Wt:** 225 Annapolis, MD

Recent Statistics

	G	AB	R	H	D	THR	RBI	SB	BB	SO	Avg
2001				Did Not Play								

Widely considered the top hitting prospect among college players, Teixeira was the fifth overall pick in the 2001 draft. A fractured ankle that required two surgical screws during his final season at Georgia Tech didn't hurt his draft status, but signing late kept him from playing minor league ball. The Rangers got their first glimpse of Teixeira during instructional league, where he demonstrated a great attitude and work ethic. He also handled the media pressure well, which has convinced the Rangers that all of the attention won't hinder his development. He has a premium bat and should hit for both average and power. Occasionally the ball jumps off a premier prospect's bat in a way seldom seen, and the Rangers saw that when Teixeira made good contact.

Others to Watch

A young bulldog on the mound, righty **Omar Beltre** (19) throws an above-average fastball that comes in at 92-94 MPH. He went 6-3 (3.38) at Rookie-level Pulaski in 2001 and now heads to A-ball. . . **Ryan Dittfurth** (22) is a classic strikeout pitcher, which often means a high walk rate. He impressed the Rangers by bringing his walk rate down while going 9-6 (3.48) at high Class-A Charlotte in 2001. Hard work with the major league staff in spring training produced better command of his above-average fastball and all of his pitches. . . Hamate-bone surgery a year ago and a follow-up procedure this fall have been bumps in the road for first baseman **Travis Hafner** (24), a power prospect who hit .346-22-109 at high Class-A Charlotte in 2000 and .282-20-74 in just 323 at-bats at Double-A Tulsa in 2001. The Rangers see the studious, hard-working Hafner hitting for average and power. . . For righthander **Spike Lundberg** (24), every step of the way is a challenge because he throws in the high 80s and depends on good command of a half-dozen pitches. He also studies hitters and keeps books on them. He stumbled at Triple-A Oklahoma in 2001, but a mix of smarts and command can work in his favor.

SkyDome

Offense

The character of SkyDome changes according to whether the retractable roof is open or closed. Immediately following the winter, batted balls fly with ease through stagnant air until the roof is opened. Under the open sky, wind currents tend to boost balls hit to right-center and down the right-field line, while making it more difficult to reach the stands to the left of center field. Long alleys and the bouncy artificial turf produce a high percentage of extra-base hits. There's ample foul ground.

Defense

The club has considered installing grass or a different form of turf. In the meantime, it is imperative the middle of the defense has outstanding range and defensive ability. For the World Series titles in 1992-93, the Blue Jays had Devon White in center, Roberto Alomar at second, and Manny Lee and Tony Fernandez at shortstop. Balls can scorch through the holes and easily elude outfielders to get into the alleys.

Who It Helps the Most

Line-drive gap hitters and contact-groundball hitters have advantages. Shannon Stewart averaged .351 last year, Homer Bush .378 and Fernandez .333. When the breeze is going to right, it aids lefthanded power hitters such as Carlos Delgado, who hit 30 homers at home in 2000.

Who It Hurts the Most

Pitchers inducing grounders can be hurt. At Sky-Dome, starter Chris Carpenter was 3-8 with a 4.83 ERA, while on the road he was 8-3 with a 3.26 ERA. Attendance has fallen and the crowd is quiet. The atmosphere may affect an emotional player such as Raul Mondesi (.245, 10 HR, 39 RBI). Delgado, who slumped to 13 homers last year, has tried to encourage more crowd noise.

Rookies & Newcomers

Vernon Wells hit .343 at home in limited action last year, and he covers a lot of ground in the outfield. Top prospect Felipe Lopez, who is in line for the shortstop job heading into spring training, will like hitting on the turf.

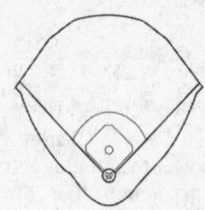

Dimensions: LF-328, LCF-375, CF-400, RCF-375, RF-328

Capacity: 50,516

Elevation: 300 feet

Surface: Turf

Foul Territory: Large

Park Factors

2001 Season

| | Home Games | | | Away Games | | | |
	Blue Jays	Opp	Total	Blue Jays	Opp	Total	Index
G	72	72	144	71	71	142	—
Avg	.265	.272	.268	.257	.276	.267	101
AB	2459	2552	5011	2544	2453	4997	99
R	348	358	706	333	310	643	108
H	652	693	1345	654	678	1332	100
2B	120	170	290	123	138	261	111
3B	10	14	24	18	7	25	96
HR	84	76	160	96	74	170	94
BB	218	222	440	197	207	404	109
SO	477	479	956	500	449	949	100
E	43	46	89	47	44	91	96
E-Infield	39	36	75	35	32	67	110
LHB-Avg	.246	.287	.268	.273	.295	.284	94
LHB-HR	38	37	75	54	33	87	88
RHB-Avg	.279	.259	.269	.245	.260	.252	107
RHB-HR	46	39	85	42	41	83	100

1999-2001

| | Home Games | | | Away Games | | | |
	Blue Jays	Opp	Total	Blue Jays	Opp	Total	Index
G	216	216	432	215	215	430	—
Avg	.274	.280	.277	.271	.280	.275	101
AB	7340	7716	15056	7716	7342	15058	100
R	1110	1184	2294	1110	1063	2173	105
H	2012	2157	4169	2088	2057	4145	100
2B	431	501	932	399	394	793	118
3B	24	33	57	37	37	74	77
HR	287	244	531	297	255	552	96
BB	681	731	1412	694	712	1406	100
SO	1364	1389	2753	1475	1294	2769	99
E	136	123	259	134	143	277	93
E-Infield	123	102	225	108	120	228	98
LHB-Avg	.275	.290	.283	.276	.283	.280	101
LHB-HR	160	115	275	166	112	278	97
RHB-Avg	.273	.271	.272	.266	.278	.272	100
RHB-HR	127	129	256	131	143	274	95

2001 Rankings (American League)
- Highest RHB batting-average factor
- Third-highest run factor
- Third-highest walk factor
- Third-lowest LHB batting-average factor
- Third-lowest LHB home-run factor

Buck Martinez

2001 Season

A major league catcher from 1969-1986, then a broadcast analyst for both TSN in Canada and ESPN, Buck Martinez did not enjoy nearly the same success of catcher/broadcaster counterpart Bob Brenly in Arizona. For that matter, his team under-performed the 1999-2000 Jays managed by veteran Jim Fregosi. While thought to be secure, Martinez' status could be affected by the appointment of new general manager J.P. Ricciardi.

Offense

Like Fregosi in his first season, Martinez began the job by motivating hitters to advance runners, encouraging them to cut down swings in run-scoring situations with two strikes, and preaching patience for better pitch selection. But this roster was built for the longball. At one point, six players were on pace for 100 strikeouts. Several prominent hitters slumped compared to their 2000 performances and runs decreased from 861 to 767. Hitting instructor Cito Gaston held to different philosophies, and the former manager was fired after the season.

Pitching & Defense

Martinez and pitching coach Mark Connor stressed aggressive, get-ahead-in-the-count pitching. They moved patiently with young pitchers Roy Halladay, Kelvim Escobar and Brandon Lyon, with promising results. Fifth-year starter Chris Carpenter began to realize his potential. The bullpen set a club record with 471 appearances, in part because Martinez didn't get the innings expected from veterans Steve Parris and Joey Hamilton. As a former catcher, Martinez believes firmly in strength up the middle, so expect him to improve that area in 2002. Among the possibilities are subbing more often for catcher Darrin Fletcher, establishing a regular second baseman and putting Vernon Wells in center.

2002 Outlook

Martinez admitted the mistake of straying from his convictions and failing to hold players accountable to his vision. Expect the club to energize the offense with more running and National League-style play. Refreshingly outspoken, he'll be better prepared to handle relationships with players. He's looking for a clubhouse leader to emerge.

Born: 11/07/48 in Redding, CA

Playing Experience: 1969-1986, KC, Mil, Tor

Managerial Experience: 1 season

Toronto

Manager Statistics

Year	Team, Lg	W	L	Pct	GB	Finish
2001	Toronto, AL	80	82	.494	16.0	3rd East
1 Season		80	82	.494	—	—

2001 Starting Pitchers by Days Rest

	<=3	4	5	6+
Blue Jays Starts	1	80	58	14
Blue Jays ERA	3.60	4.74	4.23	4.35
AL Avg Starts	1	78	48	24
AL ERA	5.92	4.69	4.58	4.58

2001 Situational Stats

	Buck Martinez	AL Average
Hit & Run Success %	34.5	35.0
Stolen Base Success %	73.9	71.0
Platoon Pct.	55.5	59.1
Defensive Subs	28	26
High-Pitch Outings	2	6
Quick/Slow Hooks	25/15	19/16
Sacrifice Attempts	47	54

2001 Rankings (American League)

- 1st in intentional walks (47), mid-inning pitching changes (221) and one-batter pitcher appearances (57)
- 2nd in steals of second base (135), pinch-hitters used (129), relief appearances (471) and first-batter platoon percentage
- 3rd in steals of home plate (1) and hit-and-run attempts (110)

Chris Carpenter

2001 Season

Fully recovered from elbow surgery in September 1999, Chris Carpenter rebounded from a horrid 2000 season to pass the 200-inning mark for the first time. He started promisingly but went into a mysterious seven-game losing streak from July 1 through August 19, when his ERA climbed from 3.67 to 4.59. He allowed two earned runs in 26.2 innings over his next four starts, getting three wins, and reached the .500 mark in his final outing against Cleveland.

Pitching

Carpenter works quickly, relying on a four-seam fastball that normally runs 92-93 MPH, a sinker or two-seamer, and a dropping curve that rates with the best. He also throws a below-average changeup and slider. Last year, he ranked among American League leaders in double-play grounders and groundball-flyball ratio. Inconsistent command inside the strike zone gets him into trouble occasionally. Opponents have batted .285 against him over his career, and have hit one homer for every eight innings. At his best against righthanded hitters, Carpenter either gets ahead in the count with the curve, or sets up the hitter to swing at the curve.

Defense

A good spin move to first base keeps runners close, and he works quickly to the plate with an efficient motion. Fifty percent of runners attempting to steal last year were caught. An accomplished high school hockey player, Carpenter is a steady and athletic fielder, so it could be just a matter of bad luck that he has been struck by so many liners on the mound.

2002 Outlook

With four years of major league service, Carpenter was eligible for arbitration a year ago. The Jays have dangled him in the trade market, but in 2001 he showed an ability to fulfill his potential as a steady 15-game winner and determined workhorse. Look for more of the same in 2002.

Position: SP
Bats: R **Throws:** R
Ht: 6' 6" **Wt:** 225

Opening Day Age: 26
Born: 4/27/75 in Exeter, NH
ML Seasons: 5

Overall Statistics

	W	L	Pct.	ERA	G	GS	Sv	IP	H	BB	SO	HR	Ratio
2001	11	11	.500	4.09	34	34	0	215.2	229	75	157	29	1.41
Career	45	45	.500	4.79	139	122	0	797.1	895	304	567	100	1.50

How Often He Throws Strikes

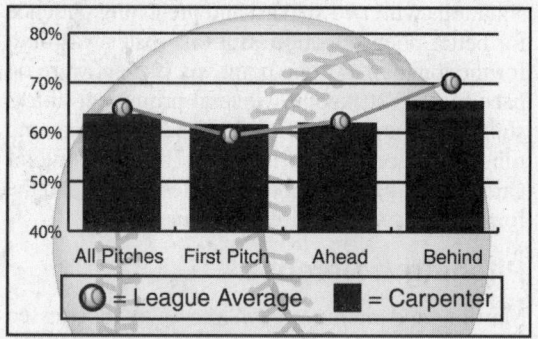

2001 Situational Stats

	W	L	ERA	Sv	IP		AB	H	HR	RBI	Avg
Home	3	8	4.83	0	113.2	LHB	400	115	13	45	.288
Road	8	3	3.26	0	102.0	RHB	435	114	16	49	.262
First Half	7	5	3.99	0	121.2	Sc Pos	192	44	4	57	.229
Scnd Half	4	6	4.21	0	94.0	Clutch	29	12	0	4	.414

2001 Rankings (American League)

- 1st in fielding percentage at pitcher (1.000)
- Led the Blue Jays in ERA, wins, losses, games started, complete games (3), shutouts (2), innings pitched, batters faced (930), home runs allowed, walks allowed, strikeouts, pitches thrown (3,299), GDPs induced (25), winning percentage, lowest batting average allowed (.274), lowest slugging percentage allowed (.449), lowest on-base percentage allowed (.345), highest groundball-flyball ratio allowed (1.7), fewest pitches thrown per batter (3.55), lowest ERA at home, lowest ERA on the road, lowest batting average allowed with runners in scoring position, fewest home runs allowed per nine innings (1.21) and most strikeouts per nine innings (6.6)

Jose Cruz

2001 Season

Jose Cruz improves both offensively and defensively on an annual basis. Last year he raised his batting average 32 points over his 2000 mark and established career highs in most major offensive categories. He joined Shawn Green as the only Blue Jays to join the 30-30 club (homers and steals) in spite of a 15-day stint on the disabled list. In the leadoff spot, he showed prodigious power with 16 homers in 229 at-bats, but averaged only .240 and struck out too frequently. Behind Carlos Delgado in the No. 5 slot, he hit .306 with 10 homers in 121 at-bats.

Hitting

A switch-hitter, Cruz has a quick bat and a slight upper cut. He generally hits for power lefthanded and for average righthanded, though the gap has lessened in the average department. Lefthanded, his strength is down and in. Righthanded, it's up and middle-out. He has the power to hit 40 homers and the ability to average .300. His at-bats have become more aggressive, resulting in fewer walks but better overall numbers. His weakness is outside pitching, notably breaking balls, and he is attempting to counter this by taking more pitches the other way. To boost his RBI total, he needs to make contact more consistently. Last year, Cruz averaged .219 with runners in scoring position.

Baserunning & Defense

Cruz has above-average speed and sharp instincts on the basepaths. Taking advantage of the green light last year, he was successful on 32 of 37 attempts. Having played consecutive years without a trip to the minors, he's more knowledgeable about the pitchers' moves. Defensively, Cruz is adept at tracking down balls hit into the gaps as well as those hit in front of him. He is willing to dive to make a play. He has an average but generally accurate arm and regularly hits the cutoff man.

2002 Outlook

Signed through 2002, he'll earn $3.7 million this season. Cruz could be moved to left or right to make way for top prospect Vernon Wells in center. Cruz' power and speed suit him ideally to the No. 3 slot in the order.

Position: CF/LF
Bats: B **Throws:** R
Ht: 6' 0" **Wt:** 200

Opening Day Age: 27
Born: 4/19/74 in Arroyo, PR
ML Seasons: 5

Overall Statistics

	G	AB	R	H	D	T	HR	RBI	SB	BB	SO	Avg	OBP	Slg
2001	146	577	92	158	38	4	34	88	32	45	138	.274	.326	.530
Career	623	2276	360	575	122	16	116	319	79	278	574	.253	.333	.473

Where He Hits the Ball

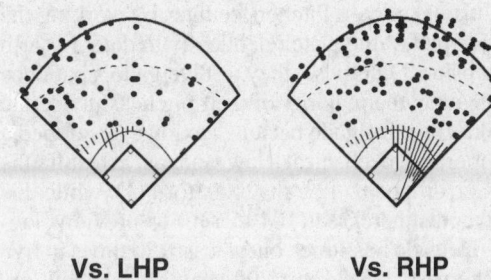

Vs. LHP   **Vs. RHP**

2001 Situational Stats

	AB	H	HR	RBI	Avg		AB	H	HR	RBI	Avg
Home	291	79	15	47	.271	LHP	138	40	8	23	.290
Road	286	79	19	41	.276	RHP	439	118	26	65	.269
First Half	278	82	11	44	.295	Sc Pos	128	28	4	46	.219
Scnd Half	299	76	23	44	.254	Clutch	97	28	6	14	.289

2001 Rankings (American League)

- 3rd in lowest on-base percentage for a leadoff hitter (.284)
- 4th in lowest fielding percentage in center field (.989)
- 5th in highest percentage of swings on the first pitch (38.7)
- 6th in stolen-base percentage (86.5)
- Led the Blue Jays in stolen bases, stolen-base percentage (86.5), batting average on a 3-1 count (.500) and slugging percentage vs. lefthanded pitchers (.543)
- Led AL center fielders in home runs

Carlos Delgado

2001 Season

For the second consecutive season, Carlos Delgado played all 162 games and reached the century mark in walks and runs. He got off to a good start with a pair of three-homer games in April. Overall, however, his season was disappointing. After making a run at the American League Triple Crown in 2000, Delgado's average dropped 65 points in 2001, his slugging percentage slid 124 points, his doubles fell from 57 to 31, and RBI from 137 to 102. He hit just .246 with 13 homers and 42 RBI at home.

Hitting

Delgado starts in a slightly open stance and closes quickly. An aggressive swinger with a good eye, he has tremendous power from left-center field to the right-field corner. Pitchers counter by working the inside part of the plate relentlessly to deter his arm extension. Otherwise, they test Delgado's patience by leaving the majority of their pitches outside the strike zone. Delgado became anxious, developed a temporary mechanical flaw and as a result, his walks dropped (123 in 2000 to 111) while his strikeouts increased (104 to 136) to previous levels. Delgado has struck out at least 130 times in five of the past six seasons, 2000 being the exception. After hitting effectively against lefthanders in consecutive seasons, he dropped to .246 last year.

Baserunning & Defense

Delgado reduced his errors to single figures (9) and increased his fielding percentage to .994, a personal high since taking over first base in 1997. On the flip side, in spite of his hard work, he continues to react slowly to hard-hit balls to his left and right. He digs out low throws from his infielders inconsistently. On the bases, he matched a career high with three steals. Once he gets going, Delgado has decent speed for his size.

2002 Outlook

Delgado signed a four-year, $68 million contract before the 2001 season. He was under pressure from the front office and media last year to exert more leadership on and off the field. In the second year of the contract, expect him to play more relaxed and elevate his offensive game closer to 2000 levels.

Position: 1B
Bats: L **Throws:** R
Ht: 6' 3"   **Wt:** 225

Opening Day Age: 29
Born: 6/25/72 in Aguadilla, PR
ML Seasons: 9
Pronunciation: del-GAH-doh

Overall Statistics

	G	AB	R	H	D	T	HR	RBI	SB	BB	SO	Avg	OBP	Slg
2001	162	574	102	160	31	1	39	102	3	111	136	.279	.408	.540
Career	991	3475	595	978	245	8	229	706	8	547	864	.281	.388	.554

Where He Hits the Ball

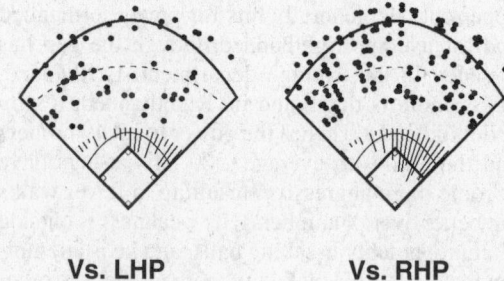

Vs. LHP   **Vs. RHP**

2001 Situational Stats

	AB	H	HR	RBI	Avg		AB	H	HR	RBI	Avg
Home	281	69	13	42	.246	LHP	171	42	8	31	.246
Road	293	91	26	60	.311	RHP	403	118	31	71	.293
First Half	308	78	24	59	.253	Sc Pos	150	41	9	62	.273
Scnd Half	266	82	15	43	.308	Clutch	100	25	6	15	.250

2001 Rankings (American League)

- 1st in games played and lowest percentage of extra bases taken as a runner (25.5)
- 2nd in walks and assists at first base (103)
- Led the Blue Jays in home runs, total bases (310), RBI, walks, intentional walks (22), hit by pitch (16), times on base (287), pitches seen (2,801), plate appearances (704), games played, slugging percentage, on-base percentage, HR frequency (14.7 ABs per HR), most pitches seen per plate appearance (3.98), highest percentage of pitches taken (59.9), cleanup slugging percentage (.567), slugging percentage vs. righthanded pitchers (.586), on-base percentage vs. righthanded pitchers (.435), batting average on the road and lowest percentage of swings on the first pitch (22.0)

Kelvim Escobar

2001 Season

Kelvim Escobar moved into the starting rotation on July 28 and pitched like an ace in August, going 4-0 with a 1.71 ERA. Ultimately, he finished 4-4 (3.18) in 11 starts after a mysterious numbing of his forearm affected him down the stretch. As a reliever, Escobar began the season by holding opponents scoreless in eight of his first nine, and 15 of 17 appearances. As veteran Paul Quantrill took over the setup role, Escobar's attitude deteriorated, resulting in a six-week slump. He rebounded in July to earn the starting berth.

Pitching

Escobar has moved in and out of the rotation since 1998, after breaking in as a closer in '97. He throws an overpowering four-seamer that reaches the plate at 93-97 MPH with good movement. A hard sinker and nasty forkball complement the fastball. Also in the repertoire are a changeup and an infrequently used curve. He has good control, though he'll make mistakes up in the zone. He has been equally effective against lefthanders and righthanders. His challenges are maintaining concentration through the duration of a start, and keeping his rhythm with runners on base. Confidence remains fragile, though he appears outwardly poised on the mound. Last year, he reduced his time between pitches to reverse the tendency of hypnotizing his fielders with his deliberate approach. Overall, his numbers suggested a breakout year. He held opponents to a .204 batting average, .287 on-base percentage and .314 slugging mark.

Defense

Escobar's ability to hold runners remains a primary weakness. Last year runners were successful stealing 18 out of 19 times. An athlete in excellent physical condition, he finishes his delivery in good position to field batted balls and cover first base.

2002 Outlook

Having worked as a closer during his rookie season in 1997, Escobar returns to the role in 2002. He has ideal stuff to finish games, but the mental makeup is debatable. With Billy Koch gone, a strong performance early in the season will be vital to Escobar's confidence.

Position: RP/SP
Bats: R   **Throws:** R
Ht: 6' 1"   **Wt:** 210

Opening Day Age: 25
Born: 4/11/76 in La Guaira, VZ
ML Seasons: 5

Toronto

Overall Statistics

	W	L	Pct.	ERA	G	GS	Sv	IP	H	BB	SO	HR	Ratio
2001	6	8	.429	3.50	59	11	0	126.0	93	52	121	8	1.15
Career	40	39	.506	4.71	184	75	16	590.2	582	272	500	59	1.45

How Often He Throws Strikes

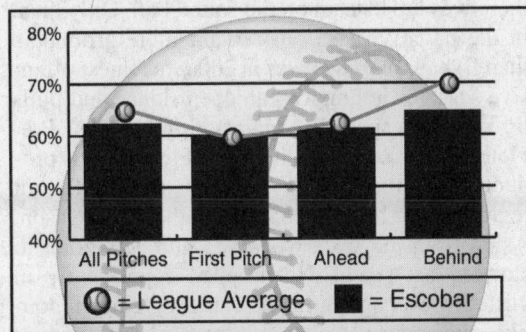

◯ = League Average   ■ = Escobar

2001 Situational Stats

	W	L	ERA	Sv	IP		AB	H	HR	RBI	Avg
Home	3	5	2.82	0	76.2	LHB	217	44	6	23	.203
Road	3	3	4.56	0	49.1	RHB	238	49	2	20	.206
First Half	0	4	4.89	0	46.0	Sc Pos	98	20	2	35	.204
Scnd Half	6	4	2.70	0	80.0	Clutch	88	19	0	9	.216

2001 Rankings (American League)

- 2nd in lowest batting average allowed vs. righthanded batters, lowest batting average allowed with runners in scoring position and lowest batting average allowed in relief with runners on base (.163)
- 5th in lowest batting average allowed in relief with runners in scoring position (.160)
- Led the Blue Jays in stolen bases allowed (18), lowest batting average allowed vs. lefthanded batters, lowest batting average allowed vs. righthanded batters, first batter efficiency (.182), lowest batting average allowed in relief (.193), most strikeouts per nine innings in relief (9.5) and fewest baserunners allowed per nine innings in relief (10.4)

Darrin Fletcher

Position: C
Bats: L **Throws:** R
Ht: 6' 2" **Wt:** 205

Opening Day Age: 35
Born: 10/3/66 in Elmhurst, IL
ML Seasons: 13

2001 Season

Toronto's No. 1 catcher strained his back in spring training and never fully found his rhythm at the plate. In an identical number of at-bats as 2000, Darrin Fletcher's home-run total was nearly cut in half from 20, and his slugging percentage declined a whopping 161 points from a career-best .514. His on-base percentage fell 81 points, and he lost 94 points from the .320 batting average that ranked second among AL catchers in 2000. Fletcher did bat .260 after the All-Star break, but fell off again in September/October with a .232 mark.

Hitting

Fletcher makes contact consistently, but last season there was little steam on the batted ball. Only once in the past five years has he hit more grounders than flyballs, and that was in 2000, his finest offensive season. He employs an open stance and pulls by routine, especially against righthanders. Previously used as a platoon player, Fletcher was productive against lefties in 1999 and 2000, but regressed and hit just .162 against them last season. Aside from the back woes, the numbers point to slowing bat speed. He dropped significantly in virtually every significant category except doubles, which were well down from his 1999 output (26).

Baserunning & Defense

Extremely slow afoot, Fletcher is vulnerable to the double play. He had 18 GIDP in 2001, including four in 15 at-bats with the bases loaded. Behind the plate, he is a quiet, solid receiver with a calming influence on pitchers. His career fielding percentage is a solid .993. Accurate throwing compensates for below-average arm strength. His caught-stealing percentage improved from 21.5 in 2000 to 24.2 last season.

2002 Outlook

Fletcher signed a two-year, $7.75 million contract prior to the 2001 season. Barring a strong rebound, he's likely to be subjected to strict platoon duty in the second year of his deal. If an exercise program for his back is successful, though, he again could top 400 at-bats.

Overall Statistics

	G	AB	R	H	D	T	HR	RBI	SB	BB	SO	Avg	OBP	Slg
2001	134	416	36	94	20	0	11	56	0	24	43	.226	.274	.353
Career	1200	3775	369	1020	208	8	121	561	2	251	386	.270	.320	.426

Where He Hits the Ball

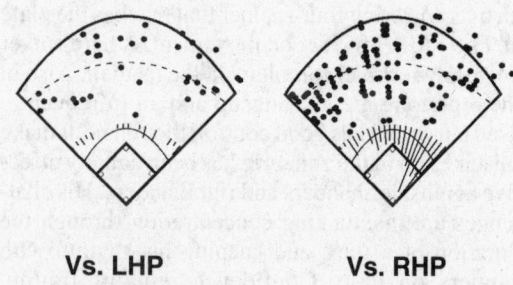

Vs. LHP   **Vs. RHP**

2001 Situational Stats

	AB	H	HR	RBI	Avg		AB	H	HR	RBI	Avg
Home	206	47	7	33	.228	LHP	74	12	3	8	.162
Road	210	47	4	23	.224	RHP	342	82	8	48	.240
First Half	235	47	5	33	.200	Sc Pos	96	25	2	41	.260
Scnd Half	181	47	6	23	.260	Clutch	75	23	2	10	.307

2001 Rankings (American League)

- 1st in most GDPs per GDP situation (26.1%)
- 2nd in fielding percentage at catcher (.995)
- 3rd in GDPs (18)
- Led the Blue Jays in GDPs (18), lowest percentage of swings that missed (11.7) and highest percentage of swings put into play (49.8)

Brad Fullmer

2001 Season

Brad Fullmer's numbers originally satisfied the Blue Jays, who acquired their designated hitter in a three-way trade with Texas and Montreal in March 2000. However, more was expected of Fullmer after he hit .295-32-104 over 133 games during his 2000 debut in the American League. Despite 40 more at-bats in 2001, most of his production dropped due to a June-July slump and his struggles against lefthanded pitching. Homers fell most dramatically, from 32 to 18. Fullmer played the field (first base) in only one of his 2001 appearances.

Hitting

Fullmer puts every ounce of his amply muscled frame into each swing and hits the ball extremely hard. He tries to pull relentlessly, but has the ability to go to the opposite field. He's tough to strike out when he resists high-fastball bait. He punishes low, middle-in fastballs and offspeed pitches alike. Pitchers attack the outside portion of the plate, and lefties especially enjoyed considerable success with their breaking stuff last year. Fullmer averaged .202 against southpaws with a .286 slugging percentage, down from .226 and .430 in 2000. Don't blame slumps on lack of work ethic; he puts a lot of time into the cage and weight room.

Baserunning & Defense

Fullmer is an excellent, instinctive baserunner with decent speed once he gets up a head of steam. He lacks the first-step quickness required of basestealers, though. His .987 fielding percentage stems from almost 2,000 career chances, almost entirely from National League experience with the Expos. The Jays used him at first base only twice in his first two AL seasons. He has decent range but struggles with footwork. His hands are the opposite of soft.

2002 Outlook

Signed through this season on the back end of a two-year contract, Fullmer is challenged to avoid platoon duty in the DH role. He may fill in at first base more often. The Jays dangled him for trade last July, and rumors persist that the Jays may deal one of their DH types.

Position: DH
Bats: L **Throws:** R
Ht: 6' 0" **Wt:** 215

Opening Day Age: 27
Born: 1/17/75 in Chatsworth, CA
ML Seasons: 5

Overall Statistics

	G	AB	R	H	D	T	HR	RBI	SB	BB	SO	Avg	OBP	Slg
2001	146	522	71	143	31	2	18	83	5	38	88	.274	.326	.444
Career	538	1896	247	531	140	7	75	315	16	131	268	.280	.329	.480

Where He Hits the Ball

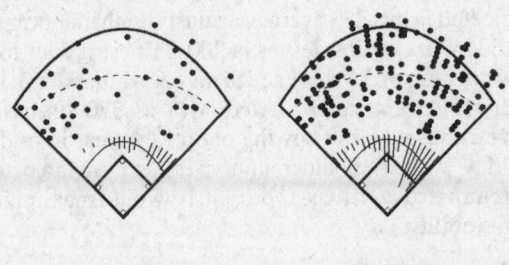

Vs. LHP   **Vs. RHP**

2001 Situational Stats

	AB	H	HR	RBI	Avg		AB	H	HR	RBI	Avg
Home	262	72	8	45	.275	LHP	119	24	2	18	.202
Road	260	71	10	38	.273	RHP	403	119	16	65	.295
First Half	316	87	10	53	.275	Sc Pos	146	40	6	68	.274
Scnd Half	206	56	8	30	.272	Clutch	87	17	1	5	.195

2001 Rankings (American League)

- 1st in fewest pitches seen per plate appearance (3.35) and lowest on-base percentage vs. lefthanded pitchers (.233)
- 2nd in lowest percentage of pitches taken (43.8) and lowest slugging percentage vs. lefthanded pitchers (.286)
- 3rd in lowest batting average vs. lefthanded pitchers and highest percentage of swings on the first pitch (40.0)
- 10th in lowest batting average in the clutch and lowest batting average on a 3-2 count (.111)
- Led the Blue Jays in highest percentage of extra bases taken as a runner (52.5)

Alex Gonzalez

Position: SS
Bats: R **Throws:** R
Ht: 6' 0" **Wt:** 200

Opening Day Age: 28
Born: 4/8/73 in Miami, FL
ML Seasons: 8

2001 Season

Alex Gonzalez hit primarily out of the two-hole to establish career highs in at-bats, runs, hits, homers, RBI and strikeouts. In the field, he reduced his errors to a total of just 10, for a .987 fielding percentage in 768 chances, both career bests.

Hitting

Every Toronto hitting coach believes "Gonzo" is capable of averaging at least .280. His hitting percentages over the last two years nearly matched his career numbers, suggesting he has plateaued as a hitter. Gonzalez has gap power to right-center field but often tries to pull, which partly explains his tendency to be a streaky hitter. He falls prey to breaking balls and outside fastballs, which is reflected in his .233 average against righthanders and .336 mark against lefties in 2001. His strikeout-to-walk ratio of 3.5:1 exceeded his career mark of 3:1. In 1999, Gonzalez started with a .370 on-base percentage before bowing out for the year in mid-May with a shoulder injury. If he were able to return to that patient approach, he would maximize his ability.

Baserunning & Defense

A Gold Glove-caliber shortstop, Gonzalez has outstanding range, turns the double play smoothly and makes the play from the hole routinely with a laser arm. His style reflects that used by Cal Ripken Jr. in his shortstop days: what he lacks in flash, he more than compensates for with anticipation and knowledge of the hitters. A good baserunner, Gonzalez stole 21 bases in 1998 and returned to that form last season, proving successful on 18 of 29 attempts.

2002 Outlook

Gonzalez signed a four-year, $20 million contract before the 2001 season. He may complete the contract in Chicago, as the Cubs acquired him in December for reliever Felix Heredia and minor league shortstop Jim Deschaine. The Cubs need to fill the top two spots in the batting order, but it's doubtful Gonzalez will be a candidate. He simply doesn't make enough contact or demonstrate enough patience at the plate.

Overall Statistics

	G	AB	R	H	D	T	HR	RBI	SB	BB	SO	Avg	OBP	Slg
2001	154	636	79	161	25	5	17	76	18	43	149	.253	.303	.388
Career	890	3258	407	798	172	20	83	350	85	257	758	.245	.304	.386

Where He Hits the Ball

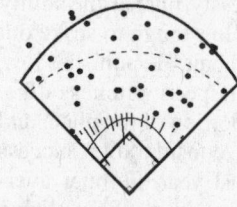

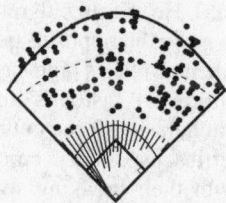

Vs. LHP   **Vs. RHP**

2001 Situational Stats

	AB	H	HR	RBI	Avg		AB	H	HR	RBI	Avg
Home	319	85	9	44	.266	LHP	122	41	4	13	.336
Road	317	76	8	32	.240	RHP	514	120	13	63	.233
First Half	348	88	7	47	.253	Sc Pos	170	43	5	60	.253
Scnd Half	288	73	10	29	.253	Clutch	100	22	3	12	.220

2001 Rankings (American League)

- 2nd in lowest on-base percentage vs. righthanded pitchers (.281)
- 3rd in fielding percentage at shortstop (.987)
- 4th in lowest on-base percentage
- 5th in at-bats, sacrifice flies (10), strikeouts and batting average vs. lefthanded pitchers
- 6th in caught stealing (11)
- 7th in lowest stolen-base percentage (62.1) and lowest batting average vs. righthanded pitchers
- Led the Blue Jays in sacrifice bunts (7), sacrifice flies (10), caught stealing (11), strikeouts, bunts in play (20) and batting average vs. lefthanded pitchers

Roy Halladay

Position: SP
Bats: R **Throws:** R
Ht: 6' 6" **Wt:** 225

Opening Day Age: 24
Born: 5/14/77 in
Denver, CO
ML Seasons: 4
Pronunciation:
HOWL-luh-day

2001 Season

Following an abysmal and confounding 2000 campaign, Roy Halladay lost the fifth-starter battle during spring training to 30-year-old rookie Chris Michalak. Halladay's route back to the majors started at high Class-A Dunedin with the installment of a consistent, three-quarter arm delivery. He found confidence at stops in Double-A and Triple-A ball before making his 2001 debut on July 2. By season's end, he was considered the top performer in Toronto's rotation, holding opponents to two runs or fewer in seven of his last eight outings.

Pitching

His four-seam fastball travels in the mid-90s range and enters the strike zone with late movement. His sinker breaks hard and late. A curve is above average, and a split-finger pitch is coming along. Stored away is a knuckle curve that goes back to his high school days in Colorado. Despite the overpowering arsenal, Halladay's strikeout-walk ratio barely exceeded 1:1 after his first three major league seasons. Anxious with runners on base, he tried to overpower hitters and lost command. Last year, he acquired composure while learning to trust his stuff. In his final half-dozen outings, the strikeout-walk ratio approached 8:1. The only issue was his durability. Hitters averaged .359 against him between pitches 61-75 of his starts.

Defense

Runners stole 14 bases against him in 17 games in 2001, as he focused his concentration on the plate. His pickoff move is average, but he could be quicker to the plate. Halladay is agile for his size. He easily fields balls hit to both sides of the mound, and he covers first base in plenty of time.

2002 Outlook

Halladay is earning $2.5 million at the back end of a contract. He's expected to build on his breakout 2001 season with a consistent 2002 campaign at the front of the Toronto rotation.

Overall Statistics

	W	L	Pct.	ERA	G	GS	Sv	IP	H	BB	SO	HR	Ratio
2001	5	3	.625	3.16	17	16	0	105.1	97	25	96	3	1.16
Career	18	17	.514	4.95	74	49	1	336.1	369	148	235	38	1.54

How Often He Throws Strikes

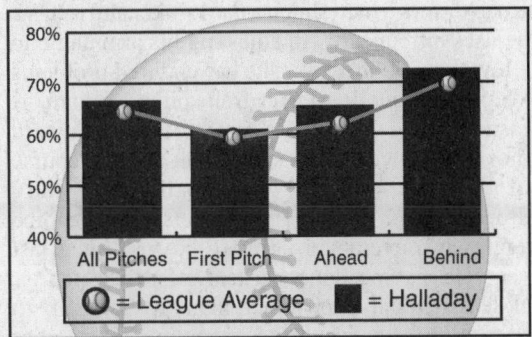

2001 Situational Stats

	W	L	ERA	Sv	IP		AB	H	HR	RBI	Avg
Home	3	0	3.15	0	45.2	LHB	202	46	2	23	.228
Road	2	3	3.17	0	59.2	RHB	200	51	1	13	.255
First Half	0	0	9.72	0	8.1	Sc Pos	92	26	0	28	.283
Scnd Half	5	3	2.60	0	97.0	Clutch	17	5	0	2	.294

2001 Rankings (American League)

- Did not rank near the top or bottom in any category

Billy Koch

2001 Season

Working as the Blue Jays' primary closer except for two brief stretches in May and June, Billy Koch converted 36 of 44 save opportunities. The eight blown saves nearly matched his total of nine from the two previous years. Koch's fastball frequently touched 100 MPH on the radar gun in 1999-2000, but last season it lost some velocity and movement. His lack of dominance is reflected in his weak 2001 numbers: a 2:1 strikeout-walk ratio, a .286 average and .460 slugging mark against first batters faced, and lefties hitting .289 against him.

Pitching

Besides the four-seamer that averages 95-97 MPH, Koch throws a hard slider, a hard sinker and a curve he uses infrequently. In adjusting his arm angle to a low three-quarters slot, he has endured problems keeping his motion intact from pitch to pitch. A fastball once known for its wicked downward movement has flattened somewhat; over the course of three seasons, his groundball-flyball ratio dropped from 1.94 to 1.36. Hitters have become aggressive, averaging .308 on the first pitch last year. He may need a consistent offspeed pitch, or at least an out pitch other than the fastball, to restore his effectiveness. His continuing inability to mix up his pitches has resulted in strikeout totals well below those expected of a power pitcher.

Defense

Koch's move to first is average. His motion to the plate was adjusted before the 2000 season to eliminate the high leg kick with runners aboard. Still, he's been run against successfully, with seven stolen bases in seven attempts in 2001, and runners stealing 18 of 21 over the past three seasons. Koch comes out of his delivery balanced, and he's extremely quick off the mound to field grounders or cover first base.

2002 Outlook

In the final year of a three-year contract, during which he'll make $2.35 million, Koch will want to establish himself as one of the game's premier closers. He now must try to regroup in Oakland, after the A's acquired him for two minor leaguers in December.

Position: RP
Bats: R **Throws:** R
Ht: 6' 3" **Wt:** 205

Opening Day Age: 27
Born: 12/14/74 in Rockville Center, NY
ML Seasons: 3
Pronunciation: KOTCH

Overall Statistics

	W	L	Pct.	ERA	G	GS	Sv	IP	H	BB	SO	HR	Ratio
2001	2	5	.286	4.80	69	0	36	69.1	69	33	55	7	1.47
Career	11	13	.458	3.57	193	0	100	211.2	202	81	172	18	1.34

How Often He Throws Strikes

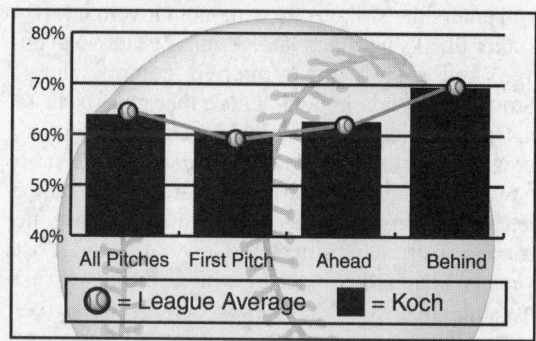

○ = League Average   ■ = Koch

2001 Situational Stats

	W	L	ERA	Sv	IP		AB	H	HR	RBI	Avg
Home	2	5	6.87	15	38.0	LHB	121	35	5	19	.289
Road	0	0	2.30	21	31.1	RHB	139	34	2	20	.245
First Half	1	2	4.86	16	37.0	Sc Pos	78	19	2	32	.244
Scnd Half	1	3	4.73	20	32.1	Clutch	180	49	6	31	.272

2001 Rankings (American League)

- 4th in save opportunities (44), blown saves (8) and games finished (56)
- 5th in saves and highest relief ERA (4.80)
- 6th in lowest save percentage (81.8) and most baserunners allowed per nine innings in relief (14.0)
- Led the Blue Jays in saves, games finished (56), wild pitches (5), save opportunities (44), save percentage (81.8), blown saves (8) and relief losses (5)

Raul Mondesi

2001 Season

Coming off elbow surgery, the right fielder was on pace for his third 30-30 performance (homers and stolen bases) in five years until skidding down the stretch. After the All-Star break, Raul Mondesi batted .207 with 11 homers and 31 RBI. His lack of offensive output generated questions about his motivation and physical conditioning.

Hitting

An aggressive pull hitter and free swinger, Mondesi goes for low fastballs, high fastballs and anything in between. He's still relying heavily on his abundance of natural talent. Though capable of hitting offspeed pitches, opponents have had success baiting him with out-of-the-zone breaking stuff. Since breaking in with the Dodgers in 1993, Mondesi has failed to reach the 100 RBI mark in every season, in part because he refuses to cut down his swing in run-scoring situations. Last season, his batting average with runners in scoring position and two out was .203.

Baserunning & Defense

Very aggressive with great instincts on the basepaths, Mondesi has stolen at least 25 bases four times in the past seven seasons. His speed is deceptive because of his tank-like build, and he can be an intimidating physical force on a close play at the plate. Mondesi constantly will look to take the extra base while getting caught a low percentage of times. He covers ground reasonably well in right field, and his cannon arm remains explosive after elbow surgery. He led the major leagues with 19 outfield assists in 2001.

2002 Outlook

The final two option years of Mondesi's contract were picked up when the Blue Jays traded Shawn Green and Jorge Nunez to the Dodgers for him and pitcher Pedro Borbon Jr. This is the first of those two seasons, and he's scheduled to make $11 million in 2002. However, the Jays are overloaded in the outfield. If they don't deal Mondesi away, he'll be playing every day in right field.

Position: RF
Bats: R **Throws:** R
Ht: 5'11" **Wt:** 215

Opening Day Age: 31
Born: 3/12/71 in San Cristobal, DR
ML Seasons: 9
Pronunciation: MON-de-see

Toronto

Overall Statistics

	G	AB	R	H	D	T	HR	RBI	SB	BB	SO	Avg	OBP	Slg
2001	149	572	88	144	26	4	27	84	30	73	128	.252	.342	.453
Career	1161	4447	709	1253	238	43	214	669	192	335	864	.282	.335	.499

Where He Hits the Ball

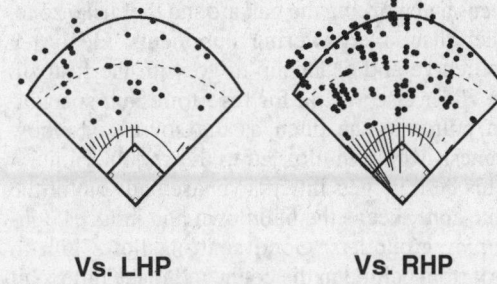

Vs. LHP   **Vs. RHP**

2001 Situational Stats

	AB	H	HR	RBI	Avg		AB	H	HR	RBI	Avg
Home	274	67	10	39	.245	LHP	107	32	7	19	.299
Road	298	77	17	45	.258	RHP	465	112	20	65	.241
First Half	340	96	16	53	.282	Sc Pos	170	43	10	60	.253
Scnd Half	232	48	11	31	.207	Clutch	88	27	3	15	.307

2001 Rankings (American League)

- 1st in errors in right field (8), assists in right field (19) and lowest fielding percentage in right field (.972)
- 3rd in on-base percentage vs. lefthanded pitchers (.453)
- 4th in steals of third (7)
- 5th in highest percentage of swings that missed (26.7) and lowest batting average at home
- 6th in caught stealing (11)
- Led the Blue Jays in caught stealing (11), steals of third (7), batting average in the clutch, batting average with the bases loaded (.455) and on-base percentage vs. lefthanded pitchers (.453)

Mike Sirotka

2001 Season

In 2000 with the White Sox, Mike Sirotka went 13-7 with a 3.40 ERA over his final 26 outings, won a career-high 15 games and trimmed his ERA for the second consecutive year to 3.79, best among American League lefties. The Blue Jays got him in exchange for ace lefty David Wells in a six-player trade on January 14, 2001. Sirotka reported a shoulder problem immediately. Following an investigation by the commissioner's office, Sirotka remained with Toronto and did not throw a pitch before undergoing season-ending surgery on his shoulder.

Pitching

Sirotka is a classic lefty who thrives by changing speeds and working the ball around the strike zone, rather than overpowering opponents. He has a good curve and changeup to go with the fastball. The slider also was in his repertoire, but speculation points to the pitch as the source of elbow soreness, which in turn led to the shoulder injury. At his best, he gets hitters to chase balls out of the strike zone, keeps the ball down and induces double-play grounders. Good control allows him to work from behind in the count and make hitters hit his pitch. His slugging percentage allowed in 2000 was .405, 10th lowest in the American League.

Defense

Sirotka is effective at holding runners with his move to first base. In 2000, he yielded only eight stolen bases in 197 innings. He's agile off the mound, solid with the glove and adept at starting double plays on comebackers. His instincts keep him from forcing action on tough plays.

2002 Outlook

Major surgery performed by Dr. James Andrews on April 24 repaired three labrum tears and fraying in the rotator cuff. Sirotka started a throwing program in late September. Barring a significant setback, he was expected to be ready by mid-May, although that timetable either could be advanced or delayed.

Position: SP
Bats: L **Throws:** L
Ht: 6' 1" **Wt:** 200

Opening Day Age: 30
Born: 5/13/71 in Chicago, IL
ML Seasons: 6
Pronunciation: sir-ROT-ka

Overall Statistics

	W	L	Pct.	ERA	G	GS	Sv	IP	H	BB	SO	HR	Ratio
2001					Did Not Play								
Career	45	42	.517	4.31	125	111	0	710.1	803	207	435	86	1.42

How Often He Throws Strikes

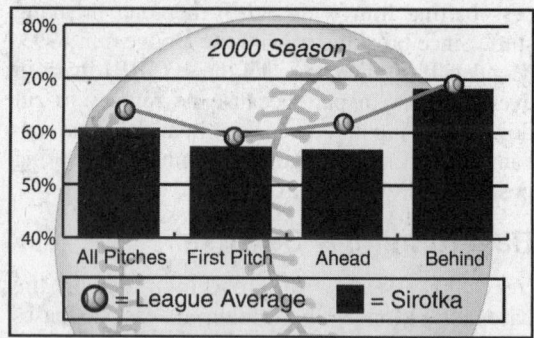

2000 Season

= League Average   = Sirotka

2001 Situational Stats

	W	L	ERA	Sv	IP		AB	H	HR	RBI	Avg
Home	—	—	—	—	—	LHB	—	—	—	—	—
Road	—	—	—	—	—	RHB	—	—	—	—	—
First Half	—	—	—	—	—	Sc Pos	—	—	—	—	—
Scnd Half	—	—	—	—	—	Clutch	—	—	—	—	—

2001 Rankings (American League)

- Did not rank near the top or bottom in any category

Shannon Stewart

2001 Season

Shannon Stewart became the fourth player in the 25-year history of the Blue Jays to achieve 200 hits in a single season. To reach .300 for a third staright year, Stewart averaged no worse than .277 in any month. The Blue Jays experimented by using their leadoff hitter in the No. 3 slot for 52 games. He maintained his batting average, but his run production amounted to just 22 RBI. Among American League leadoff hitters with at least 350 at-bats, only Seattle's Ichiro Suzuki had a better on-base percentage.

Hitting

Stewart has a very quick bat, 20-homer power and the ability to go to all fields for extra-base hits. While he doesn't draw the walks of a prototype leadoff hitter, he has a good eye and enough patience to work for his pitch. Having hammered inside fastballs since coming into the majors, Stewart over the past two seasons has improved his ability to take outside fastballs or breaking balls from righthanders to the opposite field. He has a steady demeanor, works hard on his game and stays in muscular shape, leaving some scouts to believe he has the potential to become a batting champion.

Baserunning & Defense

In 1998, Stewart stole 51 bases, then 37 the following year for a combined total of 88. In the past two seasons, he has accumulated just 47 bags. He still has the speed, but a fear of hamstring strains and Toronto's home-run-powered offense have limited his attempts. Defensively, Stewart shows excellent left-to-right range in left field, but sometimes struggles on balls hit in front of him or directly over his head. His throwing arm was weakened permanently by a high school football injury, permitting average runners to routinely take the extra base.

2002 Outlook

Stewart can become a free agent after the 2003 season, under terms of the basic agreement in force at the end of the 2001 campaign. Toronto probably will attempt to sign him long-term first, or trade him if an agreement appears unlikely.

Position: LF/DH
Bats: R **Throws:** R
Ht: 6' 1" **Wt:** 205

Opening Day Age: 28
Born: 2/25/74 in Cincinnati, OH
ML Seasons: 7

Overall Statistics

	G	AB	R	H	D	T	HR	RBI	SB	BB	SO	Avg	OBP	Slg
2001	155	640	103	202	44	7	12	60	27	46	72	.316	.371	.463
Career	643	2570	431	776	158	24	56	276	148	234	344	.302	.369	.447

Where He Hits the Ball

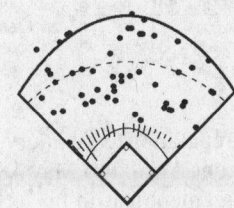
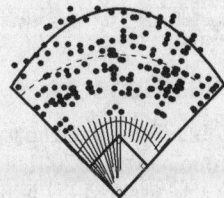

Vs. LHP   **Vs. RHP**

2001 Situational Stats

	AB	H	HR	RBI	Avg		AB	H	HR	RBI	Avg
Home	325	114	6	35	.351	LHP	117	39	1	9	.333
Road	315	88	6	25	.279	RHP	523	163	11	51	.312
First Half	365	118	6	35	.323	Sc Pos	139	40	1	46	.288
Scnd Half	275	84	6	25	.305	Clutch	94	27	1	14	.287

2001 Rankings (American League)

- 2nd in singles and batting average at home
- 3rd in hits, doubles, errors in left field (5) and lowest fielding percentage in left field (.981)
- 4th in at-bats, on-base percentage for a leadoff hitter (.370) and batting average with two strikes (.270)
- Led the Blue Jays in batting average, at-bats, runs scored, hits, singles, doubles, triples, highest groundball-flyball ratio (1.6), batting average with runners in scoring position, batting average vs. righthanded pitchers, batting average on an 0-2 count (.245), on-base percentage for a leadoff hitter (.370), batting average at home and batting average on a 3-2 count (.351)
- Led AL left fielders in batting average

Homer Bush

Position: 2B
Bats: R **Throws:** R
Ht: 5'10" **Wt:** 180

Opening Day Age: 29
Born: 11/12/72 in East St Louis, IL
ML Seasons: 5

Overall Statistics

	G	AB	R	H	D	T	HR	RBI	SB	BB	SO	Avg	OBP	Slg
2001	78	271	32	83	11	1	3	27	13	8	50	.306	.336	.387
Career	337	1135	158	333	48	5	10	108	60	52	211	.293	.332	.371

2001 Situational Stats

	AB	H	HR	RBI	Avg		AB	H	HR	RBI	Avg
Home	119	45	2	14	.378	LHP	60	17	0	3	.283
Road	152	38	1	13	.250	RHP	211	66	3	24	.313
First Half	121	45	2	15	.372	Sc Pos	73	21	0	23	.288
Scnd Half	150	38	1	12	.253	Clutch	39	12	0	3	.308

2001 Season

Homer Bush lived up to his reputation as an injury-prone player in 2001. He spent April 5 to May 18 on the disabled list with a ligament tear in his left thumb, and missed the stretch from June 26 to August 1 with a strained right hamstring. In 2000, he missed time early with a hip injury, and he missed the last two months with a hand fracture.

Hitting, Baserunning & Defense

Bush is an aggressive fastball hitter with doubles power and good bat control. A 42-for-109 stretch during last May and June boosted his batting average to .388, suggesting that his poor 2000 season was something of an aberration. In 1999, Bush hit .320 and stole 32 bases in 40 attempts, but over the past two seasons he has totaled just 22 steals. He grows more uncomfortable as the count deepens, which pretty much restricts him to the bottom of the order. He lost confidence trying to work the count as the No. 2 hitter in 2000. He has good range at second base, stands in on the double play and makes a smooth pivot. His arm is average.

2002 Outlook

Bush went into the offseason as the incumbent at second base. If he isn't traded, he will battle promising second-base prospect Orlando Hudson for the starting job.

Bob File

Position: RP
Bats: R **Throws:** R
Ht: 6' 4" **Wt:** 215

Opening Day Age: 25
Born: 1/28/77 in Philadelphia, PA
ML Seasons: 1

Overall Statistics

	W	L	Pct.	ERA	G	GS	Sv	IP	H	BB	SO	HR	Ratio
2001	5	3	.625	3.27	60	0	0	74.1	57	29	38	6	1.16
Career	5	3	.625	3.27	60	0	0	74.1	57	29	38	6	1.16

2001 Situational Stats

	W	L	ERA	Sv	IP		AB	H	HR	RBI	Avg
Home	3	2	3.38	0	34.2	LHB	95	23	3	12	.242
Road	2	1	3.18	0	39.2	RHB	164	34	3	21	.207
First Half	3	1	1.74	0	41.1	Sc Pos	74	20	2	28	.270
Scnd Half	2	2	5.18	0	33.0	Clutch	89	27	4	20	.303

2001 Season

In his fourth professional season and rookie year, Bob File easily established a personal high for innings pitched. The middle reliever went 3-1 with a 1.74 ERA in the first half, then 2-2 (5.18) in the second. He held opponents to a .220 batting average and .328 slugging percentage.

Pitching & Defense

An accomplished offensive player in college, File converted to pitching after being drafted as a 19th-round selection of the 1998 draft. He throws a 91-MPH fastball with above-average movement and good command, a late-breaking sinker that is effective against lefthanded hitters, plus a soft curve. Despite a good overall baserunners-inning ratio, the second half showed that a third pitch is required, and he's developing a splitter. He fields the position extremely well, and gets to first base quickly for coverage. Baserunners exploited his motion to the plate to steal nine of 11 successfully.

2002 Outlook

File should work in middle relief throughout the season. There is a possibility of converting him to starting duty down the road. If the Jays proved to be overloaded in the bullpen, that project could begin soon at Triple-A Syracuse.

Jeff Frye

Position: 2B/3B
Bats: R **Throws:** R
Ht: 5' 9" **Wt:** 170

Opening Day Age: 35
Born: 8/31/66 in Oakland, CA
ML Seasons: 8
Pronunciation: FRY

Overall Statistics

	G	AB	R	H	D	T	HR	RBI	SB	BB	SO	Avg	OBP	Slg
2001	74	175	24	43	6	1	2	15	2	12	18	.246	.305	.326
Career	667	2155	316	626	135	11	16	194	56	212	279	.290	.357	.386

2001 Situational Stats

	AB	H	HR	RBI	Avg		AB	H	HR	RBI	Avg
Home	101	28	2	10	.277	LHP	36	10	1	1	.278
Road	74	15	0	5	.203	RHP	139	33	1	14	.237
First Half	117	24	1	9	.205	Sc Pos	36	8	1	13	.222
Scnd Half	58	19	1	6	.328	Clutch	33	8	1	3	.242

2001 Season

The Blue Jays signed Jeff Frye as a utility infielder, but he underwent arthroscopic knee surgery in the spring. He struggled to find his rhythm at the plate despite some regular first-half playing time in place of injured second baseman Homer Bush. He did bat .349 after June and hit for only the second cycle in team history on August 17, but received just 61 at-bats over that span as the club phased in younger players.

Hitting, Baserunning & Defense

Frye is a smart contact hitter with little power. He shows excellent bat control and strike-zone discipline, bunts expertly and hits to all fields. He's more productive against lefties. Knee surgeries in the 1993 and 1998 seasons have slowed his running, but he still has decent defensive range. His throwing arm is suited best to second base, although he can handle third and short in a pinch. He has good hands, plays a solid second and hangs in well while making the pivot for a double play.

2002 Outlook

Frye is a solid fundamental player, but his utility value is limited by his lack of speed and flexibility in the field. His knees may not be able to handle regular duty. He does have the ability to sit for long periods of time, then produce at the plate.

Cesar Izturis

Traded To DODGERS

Position: 2B
Bats: B **Throws:** R
Ht: 5' 9" **Wt:** 155

Opening Day Age: 22
Born: 2/10/80 in Lara, VZ
ML Seasons: 1
Pronunciation: IS-turis

Overall Statistics

	G	AB	R	H	D	T	HR	RBI	SB	BB	SO	Avg	OBP	Slg
2001	46	134	19	36	6	2	2	9	8	2	15	.269	.279	.388
Career	46	134	19	36	6	2	2	9	8	2	15	.269	.279	.388

2001 Situational Stats

	AB	H	HR	RBI	Avg		AB	H	HR	RBI	Avg
Home	72	23	1	6	.319	LHP	30	6	0	2	.200
Road	62	13	1	3	.210	RHP	104	30	2	7	.288
First Half	48	15	1	4	.313	Sc Pos	26	8	1	6	.308
Scnd Half	86	21	1	5	.244	Clutch	15	1	0	0	.067

2001 Season

The Jays called up Cesar Izturis to sub for injured second baseman Homer Bush and injured shortstop Alex Gonzalez from June 23 through July 31 before he was sent back to Triple-A Syracuse in the midst of a 2-for-21 slump. As a late-season callup, he averaged .302 in September and October. He played 41 games at second base and six games at shortstop.

Hitting, Baserunning & Defense

Signed as a 16-year-old in 1996, Izturis moved quickly through the system as a contact hitter and top-notch defensive shortstop. In his second season at Syracuse last summer, he hit .292 with 24 stolen bases, and earned honors as the International League All-Star shortstop. To maximize his speed and baserunning ability, he needs to increase his walks and hit the ball on the ground more. Defensively, his quickness, soft hands and good arm remind scouts of fellow countryman Omar Vizquel.

2002 Outlook

There are openings in Toronto's infield, but Izturis will challenge Alex Cora for starting shortstop duties in Los Angeles after being dealt to the Dodgers in December.

Esteban Loaiza

Position: SP
Bats: R **Throws:** R
Ht: 6' 3" **Wt:** 210

Opening Day Age: 30
Born: 12/31/71 in Tijuana, Mexico
ML Seasons: 7
Pronunciation: s-TAY-bahn low-EYE-zah

Overall Statistics

	W	L	Pct.	ERA	G	GS	Sv	IP	H	BB	SO	HR	Ratio
2001	11	11	.500	5.02	36	30	0	190.0	239	40	110	27	1.47
Career	60	63	.488	4.77	210	177	1	1102.1	1278	319	671	143	1.45

2001 Situational Stats

	W	L	ERA	Sv	IP		AB	H	HR	RBI	Avg
Home	8	5	5.25	0	96.0	LHB	380	125	9	38	.329
Road	3	6	4.79	0	94.0	RHB	398	114	18	59	.286
First Half	5	9	5.60	0	107.2	Sc Pos	194	46	6	61	.237
Scnd Half	6	2	4.26	0	82.1	Clutch	35	12	0	1	.343

2001 Season

Named the No. 1 starter in spring training, Esteban Loaiza fit the bill well in April by winning four games. However, over the next two months, he went 1-7 with a 6.52 ERA. By the end of the season, he'd been relegated to swing man duty.

Pitching & Defense

Using a smooth and seemingly effortless delivery, Loaiza throws a flat fastball to a peak of 94 MPH, a slider in the mid-80s, a sinker and changeup. The action on his pitches and his inconsistent command in the strike zone can work against him. Loaiza's frustrating inconsistency sometimes can be traced to a lack of preparation in between starts, or his focus once on the mound. Overall last year, hitters averaged .307 with lefthanders hitting .329. He's an agile fielder who finishes his motion in good position to make plays, though he does have a propensity for the occasional error.

2002 Outlook

Loaiza signed a two-year contract prior to the 2001 season, a deal Toronto soon regretted making. He makes $5.8 million this year. The Jays almost traded him at the July deadline and were expected to try unloading his contract during the offseason. If he stays, he likely would pitch from the back of the rotation.

Felipe Lopez

Position: 3B
Bats: B **Throws:** R
Ht: 6' 1" **Wt:** 175

Opening Day Age: 21
Born: 5/12/80 in Bayamon, PR
ML Seasons: 1

Overall Statistics

	G	AB	R	H	D	T	HR	RBI	SB	BB	SO	Avg	OBP	Slg
2001	49	177	21	46	5	4	5	23	4	12	39	.260	.304	.418
Career	49	177	21	46	5	4	5	23	4	12	39	.260	.304	.418

2001 Situational Stats

	AB	H	HR	RBI	Avg		AB	H	HR	RBI	Avg
Home	71	21	3	10	.296	LHP	58	17	3	10	.293
Road	106	25	2	13	.236	RHP	119	29	2	13	.244
First Half	0	0	0	0	-	Sc Pos	45	16	1	17	.356
Scnd Half	177	46	5	23	.260	Clutch	30	6	0	3	.200

2001 Season

A top shortstop prospect, Felipe Lopez celebrated his 21st birthday in May as one of the youngest players in the Triple-A International League. Meanwhile, third baseman Tony Batista was playing his way out of the Toronto lineup and was waived in June. In early August, Lopez was moved to third base at Triple-A Syracuse, played just two games there and was recalled as Toronto's new third baseman. After batting .279-16-44 and slugging .506 in 89 games at Syracuse, the youngster held his own in 49 games with the Jays.

Hitting, Baserunning & Defense

Lopez is a budding five-tool prospect who already is a skilled defender with solid range and an impressive arm. At the plate, the 21-year-old has a quick bat and demonstrated more power in 2001. He struggled more in 2000, when he was adjusting to a jump from low-A to Double-A ball. The power resurfaced last summer, but Lopez needs to develop more plate discipline. He has excellent speed, but must learn the nuances of basestealing.

2002 Outlook

Over the winter, the Jays dealt shortstop Alex Gonzalez to the Cubs and acquired third-base prospect Eric Hinske. Suddenly Lopez is starting at a position he is prepared to play in the majors.

Brandon Lyon

Position: SP
Bats: R **Throws:** R
Ht: 6' 1" **Wt:** 170

Opening Day Age: 22
Born: 8/10/79 in Salt Lake City, UT
ML Seasons: 1

Overall Statistics

	W	L	Pct.	ERA	G	GS	Sv	IP	H	BB	SO	HR	Ratio
2001	5	4	.556	4.29	11	11	0	63.0	63	15	35	6	1.24
Career	5	4	.556	4.29	11	11	0	63.0	63	15	35	6	1.24

2001 Situational Stats

	W	L	ERA	Sv	IP		AB	H	HR	RBI	Avg
Home	2	3	4.15	0	30.1	LHB	128	37	1	12	.289
Road	3	1	4.41	0	32.2	RHB	109	26	5	15	.239
First Half	0	0	-	0	0.0	Sc Pos	57	14	1	22	.246
Scnd Half	5	4	4.29	0	63.0	Clutch	14	3	0	0	.214

2001 Season

Sharp control and uncanny poise added up to Brandon Lyon reaching the majors in just his second pro season out of Dixie Junior College in Utah. After beating Baltimore in his August 4 debut, Lyon was whacked around in three consecutive starts. In four of the next five, he held opponents to four runs on 19 hits in 26.1 innings. Between Double-A Tennessee and Triple-A Syracuse, he went 10-3 with a 3.69 ERA in 20 starts.

Pitching & Defense

Lyon throws an average four-seam fastball in the low 90s, uses the sinker as an out pitch, and mixes in an excellent changeup, slider and weak curve. He throws strikes with all of them, generally with solid command within the zone. He studies hitters, listens to coaching and makes quick adjustments. In his first exposure to big league hitting, he was a little too anxious to get ahead of the hitters; they averaged .395 on 0-0 counts. While his move to first may need work, he fields his position well.

2002 Outlook

Lyon is penciled into the Blue Jays' rotation as a fourth or fifth starter. Keeping his slot may depend upon Mike Sirotka's comeback, his early-season performance, or both.

Dan Plesac

Position: RP
Bats: L **Throws:** L
Ht: 6' 5" **Wt:** 217

Opening Day Age: 40
Born: 2/4/62 in Gary, IN
ML Seasons: 16
Pronunciation: PLEE-sac
Nickname: Sac, Sac-Man

Overall Statistics

	W	L	Pct.	ERA	G	GS	Sv	IP	H	BB	SO	HR	Ratio
2001	4	5	.444	3.57	62	0	1	45.1	34	24	68	4	1.28
Career	60	67	.472	3.65	946	14	155	1002.1	921	373	963	96	1.29

2001 Situational Stats

	W	L	ERA	Sv	IP		AB	H	HR	RBI	Avg
Home	2	1	3.09	1	23.1	LHB	87	16	3	10	.184
Road	2	4	4.09	0	22.0	RHB	77	18	1	9	.234
First Half	2	2	3.91	0	25.1	Sc Pos	43	9	0	13	.209
Scnd Half	2	3	3.15	1	20.0	Clutch	102	22	2	10	.216

2001 Season

Dan Plesac returned to Toronto as a free agent and turned in one of the most effective performances of his 16-year career, holding opponents to a career-best .207 batting average. His emphasis on leg conditioning paid off in the second half, as he held opponents to a .159 batting average in 26 games.

Pitching & Defense

Used as a specialist through much of the 1990s, Plesac revitalized his career by improving his changeup and sinking fastball to be tougher against righthanded hitters (.234). His four-seam fastball peaks at 93 MPH, and the big-breaking slider is his out pitch against lefthanders. A thorough knowledge of the hitters and constant adjustments to pitching patterns keep him a step ahead. Last year, he restricted opponents to a .209 batting average with runners in scoring position, and stranded 37 of 46 inherited runners. He holds runners decently (10 attempted steals, four caught) but can be slow getting to balls chopped to the right side.

2002 Outlook

Plesac was contemplating retirement, although it's obvious he has plenty of gas left in the tank. He decided in November to return to the Jays and will be used in the late innings as a setup man, primarily against lefties but frequently against righties.

Paul Quantrill

Traded To DODGERS

Position: RP
Bats: L **Throws:** R
Ht: 6' 1" **Wt:** 190

Opening Day Age: 33
Born: 11/3/68 in London, ON, Canada
ML Seasons: 10
Pronunciation: KWAN-trill

Vernon Wells

Top Prospect

Position: CF
Bats: R **Throws:** R
Ht: 6' 1" **Wt:** 210

Opening Day Age: 23
Born: 12/8/78 in Shreveport, LA
ML Seasons: 3

Overall Statistics

	W	L	Pct.	ERA	G	GS	Sv	IP	H	BB	SO	HR	Ratio
2001	11	2	.846	3.04	80	0	2	83.0	86	12	58	6	1.18
Career	52	64	.448	3.89	530	64	18	937.1	1084	262	555	96	1.44

2001 Situational Stats

	W	L	ERA	Sv	IP		AB	H	HR	RBI	Avg
Home	3	1	5.06	2	37.1	LHB	107	38	2	19	.355
Road	8	1	1.38	0	45.2	RHB	207	48	4	21	.232
First Half	7	2	2.13	1	50.2	Sc Pos	94	19	2	34	.202
Scnd Half	4	0	4.45	1	32.1	Clutch	174	46	3	25	.264

Overall Statistics

	G	AB	R	H	D	T	HR	RBI	SB	BB	SO	Avg	OBP	Slg
2001	30	96	14	30	8	0	1	6	5	5	15	.313	.350	.427
Career	57	186	22	53	13	0	2	14	6	9	33	.285	.320	.387

2001 Situational Stats

	AB	H	HR	RBI	Avg		AB	H	HR	RBI	Avg
Home	35	12	1	6	.343	LHP	43	16	1	6	.372
Road	61	18	0	0	.295	RHP	53	14	0	0	.264
First Half	30	8	1	2	.267	Sc Pos	16	3	0	4	.188
Scnd Half	66	22	0	4	.333	Clutch	16	3	0	0	.188

2001 Season

Having a surgical pin removed from his right femur before the season—a byproduct of a sledding accident three years ago—made a world of difference. Toronto's primary setup man, Paul Quantrill held opponents scoreless in 29 of his first 30 outings, shared the team lead in victories, led the American League in appearances and recorded a career-best strikeout-to-walk ratio.

Pitching & Defense

Excellent command allows Quantrill to rely almost exclusively on his sinker and fastball. He works aggressively, rarely giving in to a hitter. Very durable, Quantrill has reached the 80-inning mark four times in the past five seasons. Defensively he moves quickly off the mound in any direction, and keeps runners honest with a quick move. While the sinker makes him extremely tough on grass against all hitters, overall he's less effective against lefthanders and has to pitch out of trouble frequently on SkyDome's turf.

2002 Outlook

The Jays signed the Canadian to a three-year contract extension in early August. But he'll move to the Dodgers' bullpen after being dealt in a four-player trade between Toronto and Los Angeles in December.

2001 Season

Vernon Wells has spent the past two seasons at Triple-A Syracuse. He had two stints with the Jays, one as an injury replacement in May, followed by a season-ending callup on August 26. Wells had six multi-hit games down the stretch to push his batting average to .381 in mid-September. It was depressed by a 2-for-20 skid over the final eight days.

Hitting, Baserunning & Defense

A five-tool player, Wells is an aggressive, above-average contact hitter with a good eye. Extending his at-bats to draw more walks would make him an excellent leadoff candidate. The requisite speed and instincts are present to develop into a dangerous basestealer. In the minors, he concentrated on leveling and shortening his swing to drive the ball consistently. The jury remains out on his ability to deal with breaking balls. Defensively, he has great range and a strong, accurate arm. He makes the reads necessary to play a shallow center. He has the versatility to play left or right, as well.

2002 Outlook

The Jays patiently have allowed Wells to make adjustments to his hitting approach, and now he should be ready to start on an everyday basis in center or right. At the least, he should be the club's fourth outfielder coming out of spring training.

Kevin Beirne (Pos: RHP, Age: 28)

	W	L	Pct.	ERA	G	GS	Sv	IP	H	BB	SO	HR	Ratio
2001	0	0	-	12.86	5	0	0	7.0	13	6	5	1	2.71
Career	1	3	.250	7.46	34	1	0	56.2	63	26	46	10	1.57

The White Sox have a ton of young pitching and Beirne was stuck in the logjam when he was traded to the Blue Jays last offseason. He did not fair well during his time in Toronto last summer. 2002 Outlook: C

Pedro Borbon (Pos: LHP, Age: 34)

	W	L	Pct.	ERA	G	GS	Sv	IP	H	BB	SO	HR	Ratio
2001	2	4	.333	3.71	71	0	0	53.1	48	12	45	8	1.13
Career	12	11	.522	4.24	289	0	5	216.2	192	107	174	21	1.38

After being overused in 2000, Borbon had a strong year as a lefty specialist. He can pitch two or more innings but is best utilized in the specialist role. 2002 Outlook: B

Brian Bowles (Pos: RHP, Age: 25)

	W	L	Pct.	ERA	G	GS	Sv	IP	H	BB	SO	HR	Ratio
2001	0	0	-	0.00	2	0	0	3.2	4	1	4	0	1.36
Career	0	0	-	0.00	2	0	0	3.2	4	1	4	0	1.36

Bowles may get a look in Toronto's bullpen in 2002. He pitched well last year at Triple-A and didn't give up a run in a couple of outings in the majors. 2002 Outlook: C

Alberto Castillo (Pos: C, Age: 32, Bats: R)

	G	AB	R	H	D	T	HR	RBI	SB	BB	SO	Avg	OBP	Slg
2001	66	131	9	26	4	0	1	4	1	7	30	.198	.255	.252
Career	317	753	63	168	24	0	8	65	2	73	160	.223	.295	.287

Castillo mostly started against lefties and was Chris Michalak's personal catcher. His average plummeted from .271 on June 15 to its final mark of .198. He was released in mid-December. 2002 Outlook: C

Matt DeWitt (Pos: RHP, Age: 24)

	W	L	Pct.	ERA	G	GS	Sv	IP	H	BB	SO	HR	Ratio
2001	0	2	.000	3.79	16	0	0	19.0	22	10	13	2	1.68
Career	1	2	.333	5.79	24	0	0	32.2	42	19	19	6	1.87

DeWitt was with the ChiSox for about two months last winter, but was sent back to the Jays. He pitched well in Toronto, but was released in October. 2002 Outlook: C

Scott Eyre (Pos: LHP, Age: 29)

	W	L	Pct.	ERA	G	GS	Sv	IP	H	BB	SO	HR	Ratio
2001	1	2	.333	3.45	17	0	2	15.2	15	7	16	1	1.40
Career	10	16	.385	5.50	95	29	2	227.1	258	129	158	45	1.70

The Blue Jays acquired Eyre from the White Sox in November of 2000. He spent most of last summer at Triple-A stuck behind three lefties, but had a nice year at both Syracuse and Toronto. 2002 Outlook: C

Tony Fernandez (Pos: 3B/DH, Age: 39, Bats: B)

	G	AB	R	H	D	T	HR	RBI	SB	BB	SO	Avg	OBP	Slg
2001	76	123	11	36	4	0	2	15	1	8	17	.293	.338	.374
Career	2158	7911	1057	2276	414	92	94	844	246	690	784	.288	.347	.399

Toronto signed Fernandez to a minor league contract in early June after Milwaukee released him. He was a free agent and planned on retiring. 2002 Outlook: D

John Frascatore (Pos: RHP, Age: 32)

	W	L	Pct.	ERA	G	GS	Sv	IP	H	BB	SO	HR	Ratio
2001	1	0	1.000	2.20	12	0	0	16.1	16	4	9	4	1.22
Career	20	17	.541	4.00	274	5	1	371.0	391	145	206	50	1.44

Frascatore spent about a month with the Blue Jays last year. He had a decent ERA, but never fit into Toronto's plans and was released in August. 2002 Outlook: C

Ryan Freel (Pos: 2B, Age: 26, Bats: R)

	G	AB	R	H	D	T	HR	RBI	SB	BB	SO	Avg	OBP	Slg
2001	9	22	1	6	1	0	0	3	2	1	4	.273	.333	.318
Career	9	22	1	6	1	0	0	3	2	1	4	.273	.333	.318

Freel made the Jays out of spring training and played well during a string of starts in April. But he suffered an ankle injury and didn't return. He signed a minor league deal with Tampa Bay. 2002 Outlook: C

Chris Latham (Pos: LF/RF, Age: 28, Bats: B)

	G	AB	R	H	D	T	HR	RBI	SB	BB	SO	Avg	OBP	Slg
2001	43	73	12	20	3	1	2	10	4	10	28	.274	.369	.425
Career	106	211	31	41	5	1	3	19	8	23	85	.194	.274	.270

Latham saw his first action in the majors since '99 when he was called up in July. He hit .321 in July and August, but faded badly down the stretch. 2002 Outlook: C

Luis Lopez (Pos: 3B, Age: 28, Bats: R)

	G	AB	R	H	D	T	HR	RBI	SB	BB	SO	Avg	OBP	Slg
2001	41	119	10	29	4	0	3	10	0	8	16	.244	.291	.353
Career	41	119	10	29	4	0	3	10	0	8	16	.244	.291	.353

Lopez was inconsistent in 2001, hitting .266 in July but only .160 thereafter. He was just happy to be in the majors but was released in December. 2002 Outlook: C

Steve Parris (Pos: RHP, Age: 34)

	W	L	Pct.	ERA	G	GS	Sv	IP	H	BB	SO	HR	Ratio
2001	4	6	.400	4.60	19	19	0	105.2	126	41	49	18	1.58
Career	39	41	.488	4.51	115	108	0	634.1	690	240	417	89	1.47

Toronto placed Parris on waivers in June after he started 3-5 with a 5.43 ERA. He was not claimed and returned to the Jays to go 1-1 with a 3.52 ERA before needing shoulder surgery in September. 2002 Outlook: B

Brian Simmons (Pos: LF/CF, Age: 28, Bats: B)

	G	AB	R	H	D	T	HR	RBI	SB	BB	SO	Avg	OBP	Slg
2001	60	107	8	19	5	0	2	8	1	8	26	.178	.239	.280
Career	119	252	26	55	8	3	8	31	5	17	58	.218	.269	.369

Toronto acquired Simmons from the White Sox in the David Wells deal. The Jays thought he would be their fourth outfielder, but he struggled. The Sox got him back on waivers in November. 2002 Outlook: C

Chris Woodward (Pos: 2B, Age: 25, Bats: R)

	G	AB	R	H	D	T	HR	RBI	SB	BB	SO	Avg	OBP	Slg
2001	37	63	9	12	3	2	2	5	0	1	14	.190	.203	.397
Career	88	193	26	37	11	2	5	21	1	13	48	.192	.242	.347

The versatile Woodward can play all four infield spots. However, he was plagued by injuries and ineffectiveness last year and may not be back in 2002. 2002 Outlook: C

Toronto

Toronto Blue Jays Minor League Prospects

Organization Overview:

The big league club has endured budget cuts, but maybe the team's acquisition by Rogers Communications will mean more money for player development. That could bring back the glory days when the Blue Jays developed the likes of Carlos Delgado, Shawn Green, Shannon Stewart, Billy Koch, Steve Karsay, Vernon Wells and Chris Carpenter. The Jays already have depth at catcher and a ton of young arms to watch in the next few years. The major league club was helped by Brandon Lyon and Bob File in 2001, and there may be a 2002 breakout candidate among hurlers Pasqual Coco, Chris Baker, Mike Smith and Matt Ford. New general manager J.P. Ricciardi stepped in and traded shortstop Alex Gonzalez and acquired third-base prospect Eric Hinske, opening the door to a new infield built around second baseman Orlando Hudson, Felipe Lopez at short and Hinske.

Pasqual Coco

Position: P

Bats: R **Throws:** R

Ht: 6' 1" **Wt:** 180

Opening Day Age: 24

Born: 9/8/77 in Santo Domingo, DR

Recent Statistics

	W	L	ERA	G	GS	Sv	IP	H	R	BB	SO	HR
2001 AA Tennessee	0	1	3.94	3	3	0	16.0	13	7	5	13	3
2001 AAA Syracuse	8	6	4.66	22	22	0	121.2	128	67	50	82	11
2001 AL Toronto	1	0	4.40	7	1	0	14.1	12	8	6	9	0

Signed as a 16-year-old in 1994, Coco enjoyed two solid seasons in the Dominican Summer League before emerging as a prospect with 15 wins between Class-A Hagerstown and Dunedin in 1999. With good arm action on his fastball-changeup combo, he easily handled the jump to Double-A Tennessee in 2000. Coco returned to Tennessee last spring to make his initial starts in warmer weather, and he struggled early on in the cool spring temperatures at Triple-A Syracuse. He pitched much better later in the year, going 4-0 (2.83) in August, and closed out the season with Toronto. He throws a moving fastball in the low 90s, but Coco still must perfect a breaking pitch. He's working on both a slider and splitter.

Gabe Gross

Position: OF

Bats: L **Throws:** R

Ht: 6' 3" **Wt:** 205

Opening Day Age: 22

Born: 10/21/79 in Baltimore, MD

Recent Statistics

	G	AB	R	H	D	T	HR	RBI	SB	BB	SO	Avg
2001 A Dunedin	35	126	23	38	9	2	4	15	4	26	29	.302
2001 AA Tennessee	11	41	8	10	1	0	3	11	0	6	12	.244

A pure hitter with impressive power potential coming out of Auburn, Gross was the 15th overall pick of the 2001 draft. Clearly he had no trouble adjusting to the wood bat. He hit from the start and batted .302 with a .426 OBP in his first exposure to pro pitching at high Class-A

Dunedin. Gross was promoted to Double-A Tennessee late in the season, and he debuted with a pair of homers. Gross already is big, but he expects to bulk up to make his adjustment to higher levels easier. His outfield work isn't as refined as his bat, but he has an above-average arm. The Jays will explore whether Gross has enough arm to be a major league right fielder.

Eric Hinske

Position: 3B

Bats: L **Throws:** R

Ht: 6' 2" **Wt:** 225

Opening Day Age: 24

Born: 8/5/77 in Menasha, WI

Recent Statistics

	G	AB	R	H	D	T	HR	RBI	SB	BB	SO	Avg
2000 AA West Tenn	131	436	76	113	21	9	20	73	14	78	133	.259
2001 AAA Sacramento	121	436	71	123	27	1	25	79	20	54	113	.282
2001 MLE	121	417	56	104	23	0	18	62	14	42	117	.249

Hinske went from the Cubs to Oakland last spring in a trade that allowed Chicago to retain Rule 5 pickup Scott Chiasson. A 1998 pick, Hinske opened 2001 at Triple-A Sacramento, where he overcame a tendency to be pull-conscious and showed steady progress in displaying opposite-field power. His plate patience also is developing nicely. Working on going the opposite way remains a priority, as pitchers will change speeds on Hinske, using pitches that are more hittable to the opposite field. He plays first and third base equally well. He was in the mix to replace Jason Giambi in Oakland until he became Toronto's third baseman of the future in the Billy Koch trade. More Triple-A seasoning may be needed.

Orlando Hudson

Position: 2B

Bats: B **Throws:** R

Ht: 6' 0" **Wt:** 175

Opening Day Age: 24

Born: 12/12/77 in Darlington, SC

Recent Statistics

	G	AB	R	H	D	T	HR	RBI	SB	BB	SO	Avg
2000 A Dunedin	96	358	54	102	16	2	7	48	9	37	42	.285
2000 AA Tennessee	39	134	17	32	4	3	2	15	3	15	18	.239
2001 AA Tennessee	84	306	51	94	22	8	4	52	8	37	42	.307
2001 AAA Syracuse	55	194	31	59	14	3	4	27	11	23	34	.304
2001 MLE	139	490	73	143	36	8	6	71	16	49	79	.292

It takes incredible dedication and hard work to succeed as a 43rd-round pick, and Hudson shows plenty of both. Drafted in 1997 and signed the next year as a draft-and-follow, Hudson joined the Jays as a third baseman and climbed through the system rapidly. The Class-A Florida State League's All-Star third baseman in 2000, Hudson moved to second base last spring, transformed himself into a frontline second-base prospect, and still enjoyed a career year. He's a line-drive gap hitter from both sides of the plate and demonstrates decent patience. He hit better than .300 in 2001, the first time he has done so over a full season. The Jays believe he was their best player at Triple-A Syracuse at the end of the year.

Joe Lawrence

Position: C
Bats: R **Throws:** R
Ht: 6' 2" **Wt:** 190

Opening Day Age: 25
Born: 2/13/77 in Lake Charles, LA

Recent Statistics

	G	AB	R	H	D	T	HR	RBI	SB	BB	SO	Avg
2000 A Dunedin	101	375	69	113	32	1	13	67	21	69	74	.301
2000 AA Tennessee	39	133	22	35	9	0	0	9	7	30	27	.263
2001 AAA Syracuse	93	318	27	70	11	4	1	26	6	36	62	.220
2001 MLE	93	314	25	66	11	3	0	24	4	33	64	.210

A first-round pick drafted as an infielder in 1996, Lawrence successfully moved behind the plate during the 2000 season. The Jays lacked advanced catching prospects at the time, but have acquired Jayson Werth and have seen Josh Phelps emerge since then. His receiving skills need the most work, but a wrist injury that bothered him throughout the 2001 season slowed his progress and caused him great pain when he swung and missed. His hitting wasn't the same. Throughout his career he has made good contact and sprayed line drives all over the field. Eventually more power is expected, but the Jays aren't concerned about his bat. He needs more time behind the plate before he is ready for the majors.

Josh Phelps

Position: C-DH
Bats: R **Throws:** R
Ht: 6' 3" **Wt:** 215

Opening Day Age: 23
Born: 5/12/78 in Anchorage, AK

Recent Statistics

	G	AB	R	H	D	T	HR	RBI	SB	BB	SO	Avg
2001 AA Tennessee	136	486	95	142	36	1	31	97	3	80	127	.292
2001 AL Toronto	8	12	3	0	0	0	0	1	1	2	5	.000
2001 MLE	136	476	85	132	35	0	27	86	2	60	134	.277

A 10th-round pick in 1996, Phelps' emergence as one of the game's best catching prospects began with an All-Star season at high Class-A Dunedin in 1999. He slugged .562 based at a pitching-friendly park. Phelps was a dominant force against Double-A pitching in 2001, stroking 36 doubles and 31 homers to match his career-best .562 slugging mark. His quick bat has allowed him to adjust to breaking pitches in the minors, but his 0-for-12 stint in Toronto suggests he must make more adjustments to pitchers. Behind the plate, the 6-foot-3 Phelps is both strong and quick. His game-calling is solid, but his throwing and receiving need fine-tuning. Phelps will battle for starting catching duties in Toronto this spring.

Mike Smith

Position: P
Bats: R **Throws:** R
Ht: 5' 11" **Wt:** 195

Opening Day Age: 24
Born: 9/19/77 in Norwood, MA

Recent Statistics

	W	L	ERA	G	GS	Sv	IP	H	R	BB	SO	HR
2000 A Queens	2	2	2.29	14	12	0	51.0	41	18	17	55	1
2001 A Chston-WV	5	5	2.10	14	14	0	94.1	78	32	21	85	2
2001 AA Tennessee	6	2	2.42	14	14	0	93.0	80	32	26	77	7

Smith, a fifth-round pick out of the Univesity of Richmond in 2000, has made quite an impact by pitching successfully at Double-A Tennessee barely more than a year after signing. The Jays are impressed with his makeup and his polish. At 5-foot-11, Smith doesn't have the size of many pitching prospects, but he's a bulldog on the mound who pitches like a big man. He throws an above-average fastball in the low 90s, which he can jump to 93-94 MPH. He throws a four-seamer and a sinker, and mixes in a curveball and changeup. He consistently goes right after hitters with tenacity and a feel for pitching. His combination of smarts and guts has propelled Smith up the ladder, and he may be ready for Toronto soon.

Jayson Werth

Position: C
Bats: R **Throws:** R
Ht: 6' 5" **Wt:** 215

Opening Day Age: 22
Born: 5/20/79 in Springfield, IL

Recent Statistics

	G	AB	R	H	D	T	HR	RBI	SB	BB	SO	Avg
2000 A Frederick	24	83	16	23	3	0	2	18	5	10	15	.277
2000 AA Bowie	85	276	47	63	16	2	5	26	9	54	50	.228
2001 A Dunedin	21	70	9	14	3	0	2	14	1	17	19	.200
2001 AA Tennessee	104	369	51	105	23	1	18	69	12	63	93	.285
2001 MLE	104	362	45	98	22	0	15	61	8	47	98	.271

A first-round choice of the Orioles in 1997, Werth has been most successful as a contact hitter with solid plate discipline. He battled an ankle injury last spring, which caused him to get off to a very slow start, but he enjoyed a strong second half in which he found a power stroke. He produced career highs in doubles (26), homers (20), RBI (83) and slugging (.472), playing most of the season at Double-A Tennessee. He's also an above-average runner and a solid catching prospect. Defensively, his throwing needs the most work, but he's a solid receiver who is both quick and mobile. Continuing to develop his power is key for Werth, as Toronto also has catching prospects Josh Phelps and Joe Lawrence in its system.

Others to Watch

A 29th-round pick in 1999, righthander **Chris Baker** (24) showed promise in a swing role at high Class-A Dunedin in 2000. He was just as stingy with hits and walks in 2001, going 15-6 (3.37) as a full-time starter at Double-A Tennessee. He effectively mixes a low-90s fastball, curve and change, and doesn't beat himself. . . Maybe the third time is the charm. Outfielder **Tyrell Godwin** (22) has been a first-round pick twice before the Jays signed him as a third-rounder in 2001. He's blessed with all the tools, and he debuted by batting .368 and reaching base at a .464 clip at short-season Auburn. . . A southpaw from the Netherland Antilles, **Diegomar Markwell** (21) emerged as a pitching prospect in full-season Class-A leagues in 2001, going 8-8 (3.73) in 26 starts. Markwell's biggest gain was outstanding control that allowed him to work in and out successfully against hitters. Markwell, who works with a very good curve and an average fastball, changes speeds effectively with all of his pitches.

National League Players

Bank One Ballpark

Offense

"The BOB" generally helps hitters. The fence is reachable from the foul line to the gap in both left and right field. The ball seems to carry well, especially to left. The park is fair from gap to gap, even with the high wall and deep dimensions in center field. In past years, the roof has been open during games for about the first six weeks and perhaps the final week of the season. When the roof is closed, the park is air-conditioned, the temperature is lower and the ball doesn't carry as well.

Defense

A good center fielder is key at Bank One Ballpark, since there is plenty of ground to cover and some tricky angles. The ball can bounce around a bit in both oddly angled corners, so those outfielders have to stay alert. Some infielders complained during the World Series that the field was exceptionally hard. The grass always has been spotty because of the need to close the roof to cool the park and thus cut down on sunlight. The dirt path from home plate to first base never has been a factor in play.

Who It Helps the Most

Damian Miller and Luis Gonzalez had significantly higher batting averages at home last year, although Gonzalez had more extra-base hits on the road. Craig Counsell was much more productive at the BOB, slugging .434 in home games and just .280 on the road.

Who It Hurts the Most

Curt Schilling, who has a tendency to give up homers because he throws so many strikes, fares better on the road. The same factor also affects Brian Anderson. Matt Williams has been more productive away from home over the past four years.

Rookies & Newcomers

Jack Cust, a lefthanded hitter with power to all fields, could be helped by the reachable left-field fence if he makes the team. The Diamondbacks figure to remain a veteran team, so rookies may be fairly scarce.

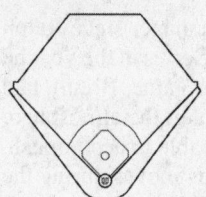

Dimensions: LF-330, LCF-374, CF-407, RCF-374, RF-334

Capacity: 48,500

Elevation: 1090 feet

Surface: Grass

Foul Territory: Average

Arizona

Park Factors

2001 Season

	Home Games			Away Games			
	D'backs	Opp	Total	D'backs	Opp	Total	Index
G	75	75	150	72	72	144	—
Avg	.283	.258	.270	.253	.233	.243	111
AB	2519	2605	5124	2578	2359	4937	100
R	408	349	757	350	269	619	117
H	713	672	1385	652	550	1202	111
2B	135	114	249	128	96	224	107
3B	17	14	31	17	6	23	130
HR	102	113	215	89	62	151	137
BB	268	211	479	274	222	496	93
SO	445	589	1034	505	593	1098	91
E	39	50	89	39	44	83	103
E-Infield	37	38	75	38	39	77	94
LHB-Avg	.303	.265	.288	.270	.253	.264	109
LHB-HR	51	47	98	51	25	76	128
RHB-Avg	.261	.255	.257	.234	.222	.227	113
RHB-HR	51	66	117	38	37	75	146

1999-2001

	Home Games			Away Games			
	D'backs	Opp	Total	D'backs	Opp	Total	Index
G	222	222	444	219	219	438	—
Avg	.281	.258	.269	.259	.248	.254	106
AB	7478	7715	15193	7745	7285	15030	100
R	1185	994	2179	1121	922	2043	105
H	2101	1987	4088	2007	1808	3815	106
2B	394	358	752	381	323	704	106
3B	68	52	120	48	28	76	156
HR	270	268	538	279	235	514	104
BB	778	658	1436	787	709	1496	95
SO	1303	1648	2951	1487	1724	3211	91
E	124	144	268	147	138	285	93
E-Infield	112	116	228	131	110	241	93
LHB-Avg	.292	.253	.277	.268	.259	.264	105
LHB-HR	137	91	228	145	75	220	105
RHB-Avg	.268	.260	.263	.250	.243	.246	107
RHB-HR	133	177	310	134	160	294	103

2001 Rankings (National League)

- Highest home-run factor
- Highest RHB home-run factor
- Second-highest batting-average factor
- Second-highest run factor
- Second-highest hit factor
- Second-highest RHB batting-average factor
- Third-highest LHB batting-average factor
- Third-highest LHB home-run factor
- Lowest walk factor

Bob Brenly

2001 Season

Bob Brenly became the first manager since Ralph Houk (1961) to win the World Series in the year he managed his first major league game. Brenly had been given the mandate to lighten the atmosphere in the clubhouse, a feat he was able to accomplish. He was heavily criticized for his moves during the World Series, but they actually were consistent with his managing style all season.

Offense

Although he likes to use aggressive baserunning to keep his players and the opponents on their toes, Brenly is somewhat limited by his slow roster. He tinkers with the lineup often, getting bench players some at-bats or moving hitters up and down the order depending on how they recently have fared. He studies statistical matchup histories but doesn't always go strictly by them.

Pitching & Defense

Brenly generally lets his starters work their way out of trouble. He often will try to get as much as possible out of the starter on a given night, especially when Randy Johnson and Curt Schilling are on the mound. On the other hand, Brenly will pull his aces in blowout games to try to save their arms for later in the season. In addition, he will not baby his relievers. He will ask pitchers to come out of the bullpen often, sometimes after a high pitch count only a day or two before. As he does with hitters, Brenly will ride the "hot hand" with relievers. The Diamondbacks ranked in the middle of the National League pack in calling for pitchouts, while they ranked near the bottom in number of intentional walks issued.

2002 Outlook

For the most part, Brenly's unorthodox moves worked out last year. But it still leaves open the question whether it was sound strategy or the team's talent that made more of a difference. As long as the Diamondbacks remain a veteran unit, Brenly's style probably will be generally effective.

Born: 2/25/54 in Coshocton, OH

Playing Experience: 1981-1989, SF, Tor

Managerial Experience: 1 season

Manager Statistics

Year	Team, Lg	W	L	Pct	GB	Finish
2001	Arizona, NL	92	70	.568	—	1st West
1 Season		92	70	.568	—	—

2001 Starting Pitchers by Days Rest

	<=3	4	5	6+
Diamondbacks Starts	4	96	20	32
Diamondbacks ERA	3.80	3.55	4.26	4.11
NL Avg Starts	1	80	47	24
NL ERA	5.03	4.43	4.53	4.28

2001 Situational Stats

	Bob Brenly	NL Average
Hit & Run Success %	43.9	35.1
Stolen Base Success %	65.1	66.5
Platoon Pct.	54.7	51.5
Defensive Subs	20	20
High-Pitch Outings	22	7
Quick/Slow Hooks	21/10	19/14
Sacrifice Attempts	89	87

2001 Rankings (National League)

- 1st in squeeze plays (12), pinch-hitters used (321), starts with over 120 pitches (22), starts with over 140 pitches (1) and starts on three days rest
- 3rd in hit-and-run success percentage and first-batter platoon percentage

Jay Bell

2001 Season

Jay Bell opened last year as Arizona's second baseman, but a midseason swoon cost him his job—first to Junior Spivey, then to Craig Counsell. Bell saw significant action at third base for the first time in his career, filling in at times for Matt Williams. But Bell's batting average was the lowest of his career for a full season, as he became an expensive bench player.

Hitting

A patient batter who likes to go deep in the count, Bell is primarily a fastball hitter. He prefers pitches away from him rather than in. But he'll chase pitches out of the strike zone with two strikes, particularly breaking balls. In addition, his power has dropped off significantly from his career-high home-run output of 38 in 1999. Bell is a good bunter, just as he was early in his career.

Baserunning & Defense

Bell has good hands in the field but not much range; balls others may reach get through the infield both to Bell's left and right. He does turn the double play fairly well, however. He played capably at third base last year, with good reactions and enough arm strength. That position doesn't test his lack of range as much. He has slowed down quite a bit, especially running to first base, and is not a threat to steal.

2002 Outlook

Counsell seems to have the edge for the second-base job, leaving Bell as a backup infielder. Bell has one year left on the five-year, $34 million contract he signed with Arizona on the eve of the expansion draft, and this could be the last season of his career. He has a full no-trade clause and thus it would be very difficult for Arizona to deal him, even if the Diamondbacks agreed to pick up most of his salary.

Position: 2B/3B
Bats: R **Throws:** R
Ht: 6' 0"   **Wt:** 184

Opening Day Age: 36
Born: 12/11/65 in Eglin AFB, FL
ML Seasons: 16

Overall Statistics

	G	AB	R	H	D	T	HR	RBI	SB	BB	SO	Avg	OBP	Slg
2001	129	428	59	106	24	1	13	46	0	65	79	.248	.349	.400
Career	1959	7233	1109	1934	392	67	193	846	91	826	1396	.267	.344	.420

Where He Hits the Ball

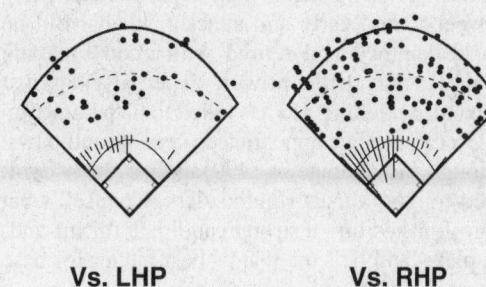

Vs. LHP   **Vs. RHP**

2001 Situational Stats

	AB	H	HR	RBI	Avg		AB	H	HR	RBI	Avg
Home	212	50	6	26	.236	LHP	116	26	3	12	.224
Road	216	56	7	20	.259	RHP	312	80	10	34	.256
First Half	294	79	11	37	.269	Sc Pos	80	21	3	31	.263
Scnd Half	134	27	2	9	.201	Clutch	61	17	2	6	.279

2001 Rankings (National League)
- 1st in most pitches seen per plate appearance (4.27)
- 4th in lowest batting average vs. lefthanded pitchers
- 5th in lowest slugging percentage vs. lefthanded pitchers (.353)
- 6th in lowest batting average on a 3-1 count (.077)
- 7th in highest percentage of pitches taken (61.3)
- 8th in lowest batting average
- Led the Diamondbacks in most pitches seen per plate appearance (4.27)

Craig Counsell

2001 Season

Craig Counsell opened last year as a utility in-fielder and wound up seeing substantial action at three positions. He filled in at third base while Matt Williams was injured, got playing time at shortstop while Tony Womack slumped and eventually settled in as the regular second baseman in place of Jay Bell. Counsell also played a couple games at first base in 2001. The only member of Arizona's postseason roster to have won a World Series previously (with the 1997 Marlins), Counsell was the Most Valuable Player of the National League Championship Series.

Hitting

Counsell holds his hands high in his stance to help him get started early and attack fastballs. But he can be jammed and retired with good breaking balls. He has little power, especially against lefthanded pitching. He has failed to hit a home run in 256 career plate appearances versus southpaws, although his average is .290 against them compared to .264 versus righthanders. Counsell's bat control makes him a strong candidate for hit-and-run plays, and he's the team's best bunter for base hits.

Baserunning & Defense

A heady baserunner, Counsell doesn't have out-standing speed but does have good instincts. In the field, he boasts very sure hands and an accurate arm. He has just enough arm strength to play on the left side of the infield, and good enough reactions to play third base. But he is best suited for second base, where he turns the double play well and has good range.

2002 Outlook

Based on his late-season play, Counsell seems to have the edge on Arizona's starting second-base job. With Junior Spivey available, Counsell could move to shortstop in the event Womack is traded, or to third base if Williams is again injured. But Arizona is ready to hand Counsell an everyday job and perhaps sign him to a multiyear deal. He will not be eligible for free agency until after the 2003 season.

Position: SS/2B/3B
Bats: L **Throws:** R
Ht: 6' 0" **Wt:** 175

Opening Day Age: 31
Born: 8/21/70 in South Bend, IN
ML Seasons: 6
Nickname: Rudy

Overall Statistics

	G	AB	R	H	D	T	HR	RBI	SB	BB	SO	Avg	OBP	Slg
2001	141	458	76	126	22	3	4	38	6	61	76	.275	.359	.362
Career	457	1284	186	345	65	11	11	116	14	165	182	.269	.354	.362

Where He Hits the Ball

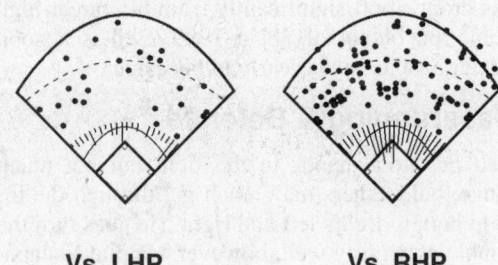

Vs. LHP   **Vs. RHP**

2001 Situational Stats

	AB	H	HR	RBI	Avg		AB	H	HR	RBI	Avg
Home	244	73	4	24	.299	LHP	101	34	0	5	.337
Road	214	53	0	14	.248	RHP	357	92	4	33	.258
First Half	220	58	4	17	.264	Sc Pos	88	26	0	33	.295
Scnd Half	238	68	0	21	.286	Clutch	68	17	1	6	.250

2001 Rankings (National League)

- 3rd in on-base percentage for a leadoff hitter (.377)
- 6th in lowest percentage of swings on the first pitch (16.9), highest percentage of pitches taken (61.7) and lowest HR frequency (114.5 ABs per HR)
- 7th in lowest slugging percentage
- 9th in lowest slugging percentage vs. righthanded pitchers (.350)
- 10th in highest groundball-flyball ratio (1.6)
- Led the Diamondbacks in sacrifice flies (6), highest percentage of pitches taken (61.7), on-base percentage for a leadoff hitter (.377) and lowest percentage of swings on the first pitch (16.9)

Steve Finley

2001 Season

Steve Finley got off to an atrocious start last season, collecting three hits in his first 41 at-bats. The streak included an 0-for-30 stretch and helped cripple his average at .207 in early June. But he batted .330 with 40 RBI after a five-game benching around the All-Star break. His final average was .275, which actually matched his career rate heading into the season. That mark was only five points below his excellent 2000 season.

Hitting

Finley is a deadly pull hitter, jumping on fastballs from the middle of the plate in and also down in the strike zone. He can be susceptible to breaking balls on the outside of the plate, however. After exceeding 30 homers in 1999 and 2000, his power dropped off last year. Finley is capable of great hot streaks; he has 18 career multihomer games, including three three-homer outbursts.

Baserunning & Defense

Although he did not win a third straight Gold Glove last year, Finley continues to excel in center field. He gets good jumps on flyballs, managing to run down balls in the gaps. He often makes catches on the run where others might be diving. He may be a little more tentative than in the past when charging and diving for balls in front of him, due to previous back problems. Finley does not have great arm strength but gets rid of the ball quickly and accurately.

2002 Outlook

At 36 years of age, Finley was the oldest player to play at least 100 games in center field last season. This will be the last season of the four-year contract he signed with Arizona after the 1998 campaign. Finley's commitment to physical conditioning and the motivation of free agency could push him to a big season. But other than his career year of 2000, he's been a notoriously slow starter.

Position: CF
Bats: L **Throws:** L
Ht: 6' 2"   **Wt:** 195

Opening Day Age: 37
Born: 3/12/65 in Union City, TN
ML Seasons: 13

Arizona

Overall Statistics

	G	AB	R	H	D	T	HR	RBI	SB	BB	SO	Avg	OBP	Slg
2001	140	495	66	136	27	4	14	73	11	47	67	.275	.337	.430
Career	1830	6822	1071	1873	329	94	202	818	265	581	920	.275	.332	.439

Where He Hits the Ball

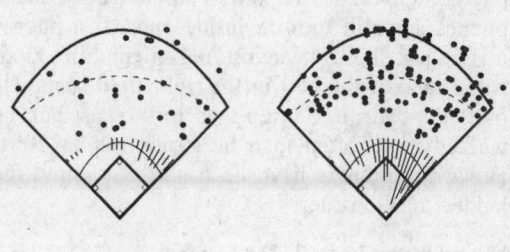

Vs. LHP   **Vs. RHP**

2001 Situational Stats

	AB	H	HR	RBI	Avg		AB	H	HR	RBI	Avg
Home	243	69	8	42	.284	LHP	102	24	2	18	.235
Road	252	67	6	31	.266	RHP	393	112	12	55	.285
First Half	283	66	5	33	.233	Sc Pos	133	37	5	58	.278
Scnd Half	212	70	9	40	.330	Clutch	84	20	1	6	.238

2001 Rankings (National League)

- 1st in fielding percentage in center field (.994)
- 4th in lowest batting average on an 0-2 count (.054)
- 6th in assists in center field (6)
- 7th in lowest percentage of swings on the first pitch (17.2)
- Led the Diamondbacks in highest percentage of extra bases taken as a runner (50.0)

Luis Gonzalez

2001 Season

After putting together the two best years of his career once he joined the Diamondbacks in 1999, Luis Gonzalez took his play to an MVP level last year. He set career highs in home runs and RBI and reached the rare levels of 100 extra-base hits and 400 total bases. He tied Ken Griffey Jr.'s record of 13 homers in April. Gonzalez also became the only player other than Babe Ruth in 1921 to exceed .320, 35 doubles, 50 homers, 120 runs, 130 RBI, 100 walks, 100 extra-base hits and 400 total bases.

Hitting

Although Gonzalez uses a wide-open stance, he stands very close to the plate and closes up as the pitch is delivered. That allows him to reach outside pitches and still turn on inside ones. If a pitcher misses just slightly when trying to jam him, Gonzalez can put the ball in the right field seats. He pulls the ball more often than in the past but, he walked more often than he struck out in 2001. However, pitchers have been able to "climb the ladder" on Gonzalez.

Baserunning & Defense

While Gonzalez has average speed, he's a good baserunner. He can leg out a triple or go first to third on a single to center or right field. He plays cautiously in left field. He will slide in to make a catch, but on plays to his left or right, he usually makes sure the ball doesn't get by him. Gonzalez has below-average arm strength but gets rid of the ball well and very accurately.

2002 Outlook

Although it's doubtful that Gonzalez can come close to the career year he enjoyed last season, he's established himself as a .300 hitter with 30-homer power. He has been extremely durable over the past three years. He enters 2002 with a streak of 348 consecutive games played (including the postseason).

Position: LF
Bats: L **Throws:** R
Ht: 6' 2" **Wt:** 195

Opening Day Age: 34
Born: 9/2/67 in Tampa, FL
ML Seasons: 12

Overall Statistics

	G	AB	R	H	D	T	HR	RBI	SB	BB	SO	Avg	OBP	Slg
2001	162	609	128	198	36	7	57	142	1	100	83	.325	.429	.688
Career	1599	5705	878	1632	365	51	221	917	101	652	770	.286	.363	.484

Where He Hits the Ball

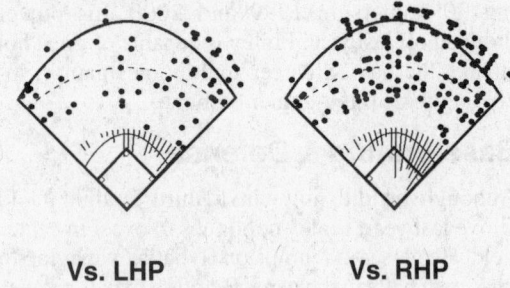

Vs. LHP   **Vs. RHP**

2001 Situational Stats

	AB	H	HR	RBI	Avg		AB	H	HR	RBI	Avg
Home	301	103	26	66	.342	LHP	186	58	15	42	.312
Road	308	95	31	76	.308	RHP	423	140	42	100	.331
First Half	330	117	35	86	.355	Sc Pos	136	47	15	80	.346
Scnd Half	279	81	22	56	.290	Clutch	80	22	5	10	.275

2001 Rankings (National League)

- 1st in plate appearances (728), games played and fielding percentage in left field (1.000)
- Led the Diamondbacks in batting average, home runs, at-bats, runs scored, hits, doubles, triples, total bases (419), RBI, walks, times on base (312), slugging percentage, on-base percentage, HR frequency (10.7 ABs per HR), batting average with runners in scoring position, batting average vs. lefthanded pitchers, batting average vs. righthanded pitchers, slugging percentage vs. righthanded pitchers (.716), on-base percentage vs. lefthanded pitchers (.414), on-base percentage vs. righthanded pitchers (.435), batting average at home and batting average on the road
- Led NL left fielders in RBI

Mark Grace

2001 Season

After 13 seasons with the Chicago Cubs, Mark Grace signed a two-year, $6 million deal with the Diamondbacks last offseason. The uniform may have changed, but he wound up having his typical year as Arizona's regular first baseman. He hit anywhere from second to ninth in the order and only rarely gave way to Greg Colbrunn or Erubiel Durazo in the lineup. Grace was particularly hot for a two-month stretch from April 24 to June 26, when he hit .382.

Hitting

Grace is an excellent contact hitter who sprays the ball to all fields, especially against righthanded pitching. He has a good eye for the strike zone, often holding up his swing at the last second. But he will jump on first-pitch fastballs. Although not much of a home-run threat, Grace should collect 30 or more doubles on balls to the gap and down the line. He is a good clutch hitter because of his ability to put the ball in play.

Baserunning & Defense

Defensively, Grace still ranks among the game's elite first basemen. He picks balls out of the dirt well and has good instincts in situations like bunt defenses and 3-6-3 double plays. He is not afraid to go for the force out at second base on balls hit to him. He is a slow runner and no threat to steal or bunt for a hit.

2002 Outlook

A good fit with Arizona's veteran group, Grace should continue to man first base for the Diamondbacks, even though it is their deepest position. His presence could cause Durazo to be traded or moved to the outfield. Grace's contract includes a mutual option for 2003, by which time Lyle Overbay might be ready to play first base.

Position: 1B
Bats: L **Throws:** L
Ht: 6' 2" **Wt:** 200

Opening Day Age: 37
Born: 6/28/64 in Winston-Salem, NC
ML Seasons: 14

Overall Statistics

	G	AB	R	H	D	T	HR	RBI	SB	BB	SO	Avg	OBP	Slg
2001	145	476	66	142	31	2	15	78	1	67	36	.298	.386	.466
Career	2055	7632	1123	2343	487	45	163	1082	68	1013	597	.307	.386	.447

Where He Hits the Ball

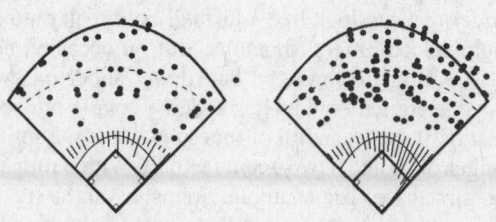

Vs. LHP   **Vs. RHP**

2001 Situational Stats

	AB	H	HR	RBI	Avg		AB	H	HR	RBI	Avg
Home	220	65	6	41	.295	LHP	149	44	2	26	.295
Road	256	77	9	37	.301	RHP	327	98	13	52	.300
First Half	248	79	9	46	.319	Sc Pos	129	40	5	62	.310
Scnd Half	228	63	6	32	.276	Clutch	82	23	3	16	.280

2001 Rankings (National League)

- 2nd in batting average with two strikes (.294)
- 4th in lowest percentage of swings that missed (8.0), highest percentage of swings put into play (56.0), batting average on an 0-2 count (.333) and fielding percentage at first base (.995)
- 6th in lowest cleanup slugging percentage (.466)
- 9th in batting average on a 3-2 count (.391) and highest percentage of pitches taken (60.4)
- Led the Diamondbacks in lowest percentage of swings that missed (8.0), highest percentage of swings put into play (56.0), cleanup slugging percentage (.466), batting average on a 3-2 count (.391) and batting average with two strikes (.294)

Randy Johnson

Position: SP
Bats: R **Throws:** L
Ht: 6'10" **Wt:** 232

Opening Day Age: 38
Born: 9/10/63 in Walnut Creek, CA
ML Seasons: 14
Nickname: Big Unit

2001 Season

Somehow, Randy Johnson exceeded the accomplishments of his first two seasons with Arizona and wound up winning his third straight National League Cy Young Award. He set a career high in wins and piled up the third highest strikeout total in modern major league history. He won 12 of his final 13 decisions in the regular season and became the first pitcher to win three games in a World Series since Mickey Lolich in 1968. Johnson also was the first to win Games 6 and 7 on consecutive days.

Pitching

Johnson's main weapons are a fastball that can reach triple digits on the radar gun and an 89 MPH slider that can look like a fastball but break onto a righthanded hitters' shoetops. But on occasion he also will try to throw a "backdoor" slider on the outside corner. And he has added a couple pitches that he'll use a handful of times per game—a split-finger pitch and a two-seam fastball. With a runner on first base, for example, Johnson might try a two-seamer to get a groundball instead of expending more pitches on a strikeout.

Defense & Hitting

The subject of a humorous commercial when he first came to Arizona, Johnson's hitting has improved. But he still managed just eight singles in 80 at-bats last season. His bunting ability is average. His fielding is poor; he has a tendency to hurry throws and also subject his defensive mates to the same type of movement he features on his pitches. While Johnson doesn't have a great pickoff move, he'll get some outs that way because of persistence.

2002 Outlook

Johnson keeps himself in excellent condition, and although he threw a high number of pitches in 2001, his innings total was down. Arizona picked up his 2003 option before last season began, expecting him to continue at his high level of performance for two more years. Despite being 38 years of age, Johnson has shown absolutely no signs of tailing off.

Overall Statistics

	W	L	Pct.	ERA	G	GS	Sv	IP	H	BB	SO	HR	Ratio
2001	21	6	.778	2.49	35	34	0	249.2	181	71	372	19	1.01
Career	200	101	.664	3.13	401	391	2	2748.1	2113	1160	3412	241	1.19

How Often He Throws Strikes

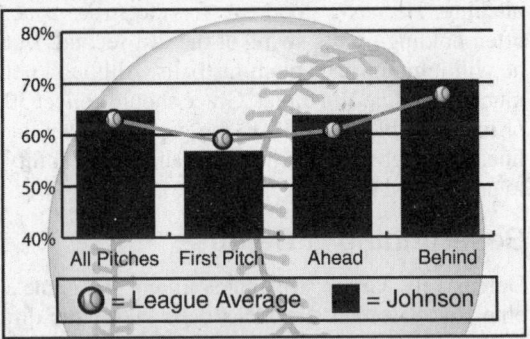

2001 Situational Stats

	W	L	ERA	Sv	IP		AB	H	HR	RBI	Avg
Home	12	3	2.54	0	131.1	LHB	107	21	1	13	.196
Road	9	3	2.43	0	118.1	RHB	783	160	18	51	.204
First Half	11	5	2.71	0	132.2	Sc Pos	180	32	2	43	.178
Scnd Half	10	1	2.23	0	117.0	Clutch	84	18	4	11	.214

2001 Rankings (National League)

- 1st in ERA, strikeouts, pitches thrown (4,076), runners caught stealing (15), lowest slugging percentage allowed (.309), lowest ERA on the road, most strikeouts per nine innings (13.4), errors at pitcher (4), lowest batting average allowed with runners in scoring position and most pitches thrown per batter (4.10)
- Led the Diamondbacks in shutouts (2), walks allowed, lowest batting average allowed (.203), highest groundball-flyball ratio allowed (1.2), lowest ERA at home, lowest batting average allowed vs. lefthanded batters, lowest batting average allowed vs. righthanded batters, fewest home runs allowed per nine innings (.68) and most GDPs induced per nine innings (0.6)

Byung-Hyun Kim

2001 Season

Byung-Hyun Kim's 2001 season may be remembered for his failures in Games 4 and 5 of the World Series. But for a two-month stretch in the middle of the year, he was one of the best closers in baseball. Kim began the season as a setup man and initially stayed in that role when Matt Mantei suffered an elbow injury. But Kim took over as closer when he proved he could throw strikes consistently. From June 9 to the end of August, he was 12-for-13 in save chances, with a 1.14 ERA, 23 hits allowed and 65 strikeouts in 47.1 innings. He experienced troubles with five home runs allowed in September, a problem that surfaced again in the World Series.

Pitching

Kim's hard sidearm stuff is unique in the major leagues. His fastball is 88-91 MPH, and he will vary speeds on his slider, sometimes throwing it as an "upshoot." When he tries to strike hitters out, he tends to nibble and get behind in the count. But when he focuses on throwing strikes, Kim's stuff is so hard to hit—especially for righthanders, but for lefties too—that he can whiff batters in bunches.

Defense & Hitting

Kim is a good athlete and a capable fielder, although he is very inexperienced as a hitter. He's managed one hit in 10 career at-bats. He worked hard last year on improving his delivery time to home plate, in an effort to give his catcher a better shot at throwing out basestealers.

2002 Outlook

Mantei is not expected to return for the beginning of the season and won't be able to pitch consecutive days for a while. That leaves Kim with at least a share of the closer's role. As he continues to mature, especially with his focus, and as he gets used to the transition from South Korea to the U.S., Kim could even improve.

Position: RP
Bats: R **Throws:** R
Ht: 5'11" **Wt:** 177

Opening Day Age: 23
Born: 1/19/79 in Kwangju, South Korea
ML Seasons: 3
Pronunciation: b-young h-yun

Overall Statistics

	W	L	Pct.	ERA	G	GS	Sv	IP	H	BB	SO	HR	Ratio
2001	5	6	.455	2.94	78	0	19	98.0	58	44	113	10	1.04
Career	12	14	.462	3.72	164	1	34	196.0	130	110	255	21	1.22

How Often He Throws Strikes

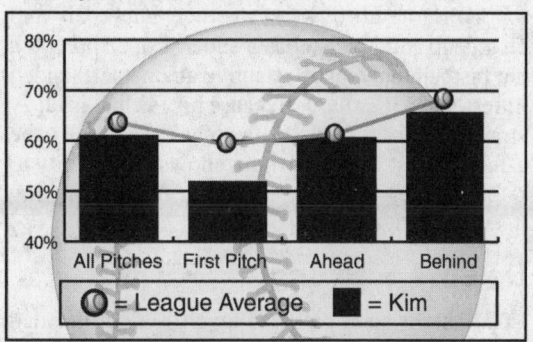

2001 Situational Stats

	W	L	ERA	Sv	IP		AB	H	HR	RBI	Avg
Home	2	2	3.55	12	50.2	LHB	156	31	8	15	.199
Road	3	4	2.28	7	47.1	RHB	179	27	2	15	.151
First Half	3	2	3.09	5	58.1	Sc Pos	69	12	1	16	.174
Scnd Half	2	4	2.72	14	39.2	Clutch	194	33	7	14	.170

2001 Rankings (National League)

- 1st in lowest batting average allowed in relief (.173)
- 3rd in relief innings (98.0)
- 4th in relief losses (6)
- 5th in lowest save percentage (82.6)
- 6th in fewest baserunners allowed per nine innings in relief (10.1) and lowest batting average allowed vs. lefthanded batters
- Led the Diamondbacks in games pitched, saves, games finished (44), save opportunities (23), holds (11), save percentage (82.6), first batter efficiency (.194), blown saves (4), relief wins (5), relief losses (6), relief innings (98.0), relief ERA (2.94) and most strikeouts per nine innings in relief (10.4)

Albie Lopez

2001 Season

Arizona acquired Albie Lopez near the trading deadline last season to fill out its rotation. He was obtained in a multi-player deal with Tampa Bay, where he had gone 5-12. Despite his 4-7 record with the Diamondbacks, Lopez pitched about as expected (4.00 ERA), with eight quality starts in 13 efforts. Two strong outings to end the season, when he allowed just six hits and one run over 17 innings, prevented Lopez from being the first 20-game loser in 21 years.

Pitching

Lopez has a good variety of pitches but needs to keep his approach simple. His fastball can get up to 95 MPH, he throws an average curveball and changeup and he also has a slider. Lopez prefers a cut fastball that can be effective against lefthanded hitters when it's sharp. Because his fastball is fairly straight, he must pitch down in the strike zone to be effective. But Lopez at times shows an inability to pitch to hitters' weaknesses rather than employing his usual pattern.

Defense & Hitting

Lopez has a good pickoff move for a righthanded pitcher. He also fields his position capably. While he was out of practice as a hitter because of his career in the American League, Lopez showed some improvement toward the end of last season. Nevertheless, he collected just one hit in 29 at-bats for the year.

2002 Outlook

Eligible for free agency after 2001, Lopez was not expected to re-sign with Arizona. There is no doubt that he has the above-average stuff to be a successful pitcher, as long as he maintains decent control and a good approach. Lopez also needs to improve his physical condition. He suffered a variety of nagging injuries last season, especially with the Devil Rays. He sometimes has problems with cramping calves and laxity (looseness) in his ankles.

Position: SP
Bats: R   **Throws:** R
Ht: 6' 2"   **Wt:** 240

Opening Day Age: 30
Born: 8/18/71 in Mesa, AZ
ML Seasons: 9
Pronunciation: LOE-pezz

Overall Statistics

	W	L	Pct.	ERA	G	GS	Sv	IP	H	BB	SO	HR	Ratio
2001	9	19	.321	4.81	33	33	0	205.2	226	75	136	26	1.46
Career	42	52	.447	4.75	252	88	4	763.0	831	308	504	104	1.49

How Often He Throws Strikes

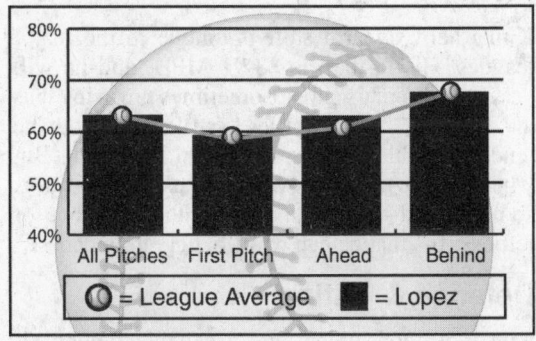

⊙ = League Average   ■ = Lopez

2001 Situational Stats

	W	L	ERA	Sv	IP		AB	H	HR	RBI	Avg
Home	4	9	4.49	0	102.1	LHB	365	109	13	44	.299
Road	5	10	5.14	0	103.1	RHB	439	117	13	69	.267
First Half	4	11	5.61	0	112.1	Sc Pos	205	58	5	83	.283
Scnd Half	5	8	3.86	0	93.1	Clutch	54	17	1	5	.315

2001 Rankings (National League)

- 1st in most GDPs induced per GDP situation (21.7%)
- 3rd in shutouts (2)
- Led the Diamondbacks in shutouts (2) and most GDPs induced per GDP situation (21.7%)

Reggie Sanders

2001 Season

After a poor 2000 season with Atlanta, Reggie Sanders took a one-year, $1.5 million deal with Arizona. He hoped to get playing time and revive his career before hitting the market again. He wound up starting 117 times in right field, setting a career high with 33 homers and driving in 90 runs, his most since 1995. He had various streaks of six homers in four games, four homers in three games and five homers in five games, accounting for almost half his final total.

Hitting

Sanders is a classic streak hitter and guess hitter. While capable of swatting home runs in four or five straight games, he also can go a week or two without hitting any. He feasts on middle and low fastballs but can be victimized by high fastballs, especially late in the count. He can look bad on breaking balls and changeups, unless he's specifically looking for the pitch. Sanders then has the power to hit it out. He will take outside pitches to right field.

Baserunning & Defense

Although he has good speed, Sanders doesn't try to steal bases as frequently as he did early in his career. And he didn't succeed at a high rate last season, falling to 58.3 percent from 84.0 the year before. He plays a solid right field, with good but not great range and an average arm. He may be able to play center field, but seems most comfortable in right.

2002 Outlook

Sanders is not expected to re-sign with Arizona, which has depth in its outfield and probably isn't willing to give the kind of salary nor length of deal that Sanders seeks. He was the Diamondbacks' No. 2 offensive weapon last year but probably is a No. 5 or 6 hitter on a good offensive team. Although he has worked hard on his fitness, he has made at least one trip to the disabled list in five of the past six seasons.

Position: RF
Bats: R **Throws:** R
Ht: 6' 1" **Wt:** 205

Opening Day Age: 34
Born: 12/1/67 in Florence, SC
ML Seasons: 11

Overall Statistics

	G	AB	R	H	D	T	HR	RBI	SB	BB	SO	Avg	OBP	Slg
2001	126	441	84	116	21	3	33	90	14	46	126	.263	.337	.549
Career	1167	4144	718	1112	220	44	195	630	229	489	1089	.268	.350	.484

Where He Hits the Ball

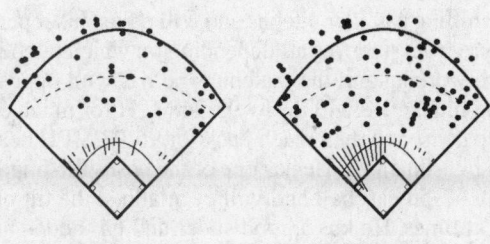

Vs. LHP   **Vs. RHP**

2001 Situational Stats

	AB	H	HR	RBI	Avg		AB	H	HR	RBI	Avg
Home	223	66	19	47	.296	LHP	129	33	14	25	.256
Road	218	50	14	43	.229	RHP	312	83	19	65	.266
First Half	237	61	19	57	.257	Sc Pos	136	30	8	54	.221
Scnd Half	204	55	14	33	.270	Clutch	71	16	8	15	.225

2001 Rankings (National League)

- 1st in fielding percentage in right field (.996)
- 2nd in fewest GDPs per GDP situation (1.9%)
- 4th in lowest batting average on the road
- 5th in lowest stolen-base percentage (58.3)
- 7th in highest percentage of swings that missed (29.8)
- 8th in slugging percentage vs. lefthanded pitchers (.643)
- Led the Diamondbacks in caught stealing (10), strikeouts and slugging percentage vs. lefthanded pitchers (.643)

Curt Schilling

2001 Season

Fully recovered from December 1999 shoulder surgery, Curt Schilling was the pitcher Arizona expected it was getting when the Diamondbacks obtained him for four players in July of 2000. Schilling enjoyed a career year, helping Arizona generate a 27-8 record in the games he started. He was especially clutch in two key areas. First, he went 13-1 with a 1.72 ERA in 17 starts following Diamondbacks losses. And second, he was tough against division opponents, going 11-1 with a 2.55 ERA versus National League West foes. Schilling finished second behind teammate Randy Johnson in the league's Cy Young voting.

Pitching

Schilling has four pitches and will adjust his repertoire from start to start depending on which pitches are working and the matchups he has with opposing hitters. He will throw 93-94 MPH for much of the game and then reach back for 96-97 MPH heat in big situations. He has one of the best split-finger pitches in baseball and will even adjust the tilt on it at times. He has a good slider and has added an overhand curve, which he uses early in the count just to keep hitters off balance. Because of his remarkable command, Schilling will allow a lot of home runs, but he's been able to limit the damage to mostly solo shots.

Defense & Hitting

While Schilling is improving as a hitter, he is still below average. Despite his good size, he has yet to hit a homer in the big leagues. He has become a good bunter, however. He fields his position capably and has a quick delivery to the plate, making it tough on basestealers.

2002 Outlook

This season marks the beginning of a three-year contract extension that Schilling signed after the 2000 campaign. The deal includes a full no-trade clause. With Schilling's commitment and extensive pregame preparation, there is no reason to believe that he can't maintain his high level of performance from last season.

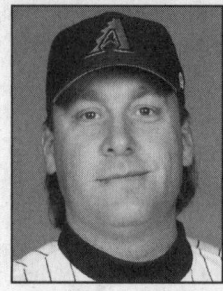

Position: SP
Bats: R **Throws:** R
Ht: 6' 4" **Wt:** 231

Opening Day Age: 35
Born: 11/14/66 in Anchorage, AK
ML Seasons: 14
Pronunciation: SHILL-ing

Overall Statistics

	W	L	Pct.	ERA	G	GS	Sv	IP	H	BB	SO	HR	Ratio
2001	22	6	.786	2.98	35	35	0	256.2	237	39	293	37	1.08
Career	132	101	.567	3.37	390	279	13	2158.2	1924	538	2032	217	1.14

How Often He Throws Strikes

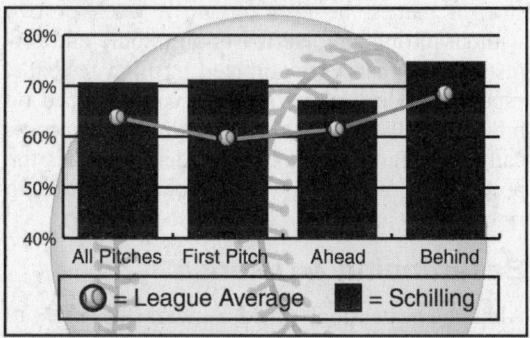

2001 Situational Stats

	W	L	ERA	Sv	IP		AB	H	HR	RBI	Avg
Home	11	4	3.13	0	132.1	LHB	448	111	20	42	.248
Road	11	2	2.82	0	124.1	RHB	520	126	17	42	.242
First Half	12	4	3.20	0	143.1	Sc Pos	156	37	3	44	.237
Scnd Half	10	2	2.70	0	113.1	Clutch	111	26	3	6	.234

2001 Rankings (National League)

- 1st in wins, games started, complete games (6), innings pitched, batters faced (1,021), home runs allowed, highest strikeout-walk ratio (7.5) and lowest on-base percentage allowed (.273)
- 2nd in ERA, strikeouts, pitches thrown (3,709), winning percentage and fewest walks per nine innings (1.4)
- 3rd in hits allowed, lowest ERA on the road and most strikeouts per nine innings (10.3)
- Led the Diamondbacks in sacrifice bunts (14), hits allowed, winning percentage, lowest stolen-base percentage allowed (30.8), fewest pitches thrown per batter (3.63), most run support per nine innings (5.4) and fewest walks per nine innings (1.4)

Matt Williams

2001 Season

A variety of leg injuries cost Matt Williams almost two months in the middle of last season. He endured a number of false starts before he actually came off the disabled list. And when he did return, Williams soon lost his job as Arizona's cleanup hitter. His power was well off his standards from previous years, although he did produce a respectable RBI total, given his playing time.

Hitting

Williams likes to swing early in the count, especially at fastballs. He still can make solid contact and drive the ball to all fields. But his leg problems over the past few years may be costing him home runs, as he isn't generating power with his lower body and hips. In addition, his bat speed is slowing. When Williams is on, he hits the ball from gap to gap instead of pulling it. Despite his size, he's actually a good drag bunter, although he rarely shows it.

Baserunning & Defense

No third baseman has better hands than Williams. He cleanly picks the short and difficult hops, and has an accurate arm with plenty of strength. He is a bit better on balls to his left, and his feet remain nimble enough to allow him to reach balls and get in good throwing position. Williams is a slow runner who has stolen just one base each of the past two seasons.

2002 Outlook

As long as he's healthy—which is never a given, as his legs have let him down the past two years—Williams is Arizona's third baseman. He has two seasons to go on the five-year extension he signed after coming to the Diamondbacks following the 1997 campaign. He also has a full no-trade clause. But Williams no longer is a cleanup-type hitter, even though he may be Arizona's best choice for the role.

Position: 3B
Bats: R **Throws:** R
Ht: 6' 2" **Wt:** 219

Opening Day Age: 36
Born: 11/28/65 in Bishop, CA
ML Seasons: 15

Overall Statistics

	G	AB	R	H	D	T	HR	RBI	SB	BB	SO	Avg	OBP	Slg
2001	106	408	58	112	30	0	16	65	1	22	70	.275	.314	.466
Career	1762	6651	951	1789	322	33	362	1162	50	432	1296	.269	.316	.491

Where He Hits the Ball

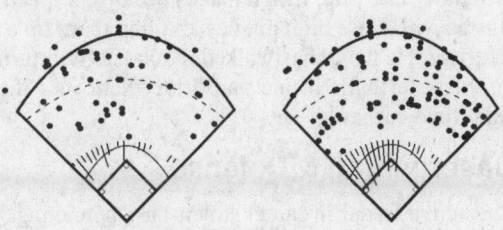

Vs. LHP   **Vs. RHP**

2001 Situational Stats

	AB	H	HR	RBI	Avg		AB	H	HR	RBI	Avg
Home	201	51	7	25	.254	LHP	115	36	8	28	.313
Road	207	61	9	40	.295	RHP	293	76	8	37	.259
First Half	143	38	5	21	.266	Sc Pos	109	31	5	44	.284
Scnd Half	265	74	11	44	.279	Clutch	62	26	2	9	.419

2001 Rankings (National League)

- 2nd in batting average in the clutch
- 4th in lowest cleanup slugging percentage (.429)
- 7th in lowest batting average on an 0-2 count (.071)
- Led the Diamondbacks in GDPs (15) and batting average in the clutch

Arizona

Tony Womack

2001 Season

Admittedly affected by the death of his father, Tony Womack began last season slowly. After two weeks on the disabled list with a right calf injury in late July and early August, he lost his starting spot down the stretch. But Womack recovered to bat .388 over his final 19 games, with 17 runs scored and 12 multihit games.

Hitting

Although his greatest asset is his speed, Womack bunts less often than might be expected. Of course, part of the reason is that teams defend against the bunt so consciously, bringing the third baseman in every time Womack bats. He became more of a slap hitter last year, which makes use of his speed. But he will chase high pitches and pop them up to left field. He never has walked much. He will turn on weak fastballs inside and drive them into the right field corner.

Baserunning & Defense

The active leader in career stolen-base percentage, Womack is successful because he picks his spots carefully. He will not just take off in obvious steal situations, usually waiting until late in the count. But he is as fast as any player in the game. Womack has shown decent range at shortstop but makes a large number of errors, both by fumbling balls and with inaccurate throws. He does not turn the double play well, a problem he also had when playing second base.

2002 Outlook

His strong finish seems to have the Diamondbacks committed to using Womack as their shortstop and leadoff man again this year. He has two seasons remaining on the four-year, $17 million contract he signed in late 1999. If Womack can hit the ball on the ground more often, use the bunt as a weapon and draw more walks, he has a chance to be a useful leadoff hitter.

Position: SS
Bats: L **Throws:** R
Ht: 5' 9" **Wt:** 170

Opening Day Age: 32
Born: 9/25/69 in Danville, VA
ML Seasons: 8
Pronunciation: WO-mack

Overall Statistics

	G	AB	R	H	D	T	HR	RBI	SB	BB	SO	Avg	OBP	Slg
2001	125	481	66	128	19	5	3	30	28	23	54	.266	.307	.345
Career	766	3074	462	844	120	46	23	231	267	197	406	.275	.320	.366

Where He Hits the Ball

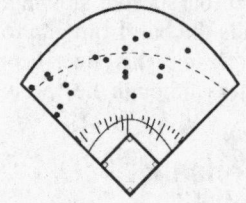
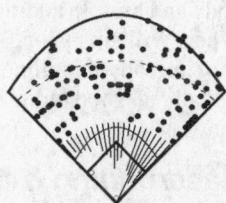

Vs. LHP   **Vs. RHP**

2001 Situational Stats

	AB	H	HR	RBI	Avg		AB	H	HR	RBI	Avg
Home	209	57	2	16	.273	LHP	96	18	0	2	.188
Road	272	71	1	14	.261	RHP	385	110	3	28	.286
First Half	310	72	1	17	.232	Sc Pos	93	24	1	28	.258
Scnd Half	171	56	2	13	.327	Clutch	78	26	0	5	.333

2001 Rankings (National League)

- 1st in lowest fielding percentage at shortstop (.955)
- 3rd in batting average on an 0-2 count (.342), errors at shortstop (22), lowest slugging percentage and lowest on-base percentage for a leadoff hitter (.297)
- 4th in lowest HR frequency (160.3 ABs per HR)
- 7th in stolen bases, batting average with the bases loaded (.500) and lowest on-base percentage
- Led the Diamondbacks in singles, stolen bases, highest groundball-flyball ratio (1.7), stolen-base percentage (80.0), bunts in play (21), steals of third (2), batting average with the bases loaded (.500) and batting average on an 0-2 count (.342)

Brian Anderson

Position: SP
Bats: R **Throws:** L
Ht: 6' 1" **Wt:** 183

Opening Day Age: 29
Born: 4/26/72 in Portsmouth, VA
ML Seasons: 9

Overall Statistics

	W	L	Pct.	ERA	G	GS	Sv	IP	H	BB	SO	HR	Ratio
2001	4	9	.308	5.20	29	22	0	133.1	156	30	55	25	1.40
Career	55	47	.539	4.70	183	158	1	996.2	1101	205	468	174	1.31

2001 Situational Stats

	W	L	ERA	Sv	IP		AB	H	HR	RBI	Avg
Home	2	4	6.65	0	65.0	LHB	147	40	4	19	.272
Road	2	5	3.82	0	68.1	RHB	382	116	21	60	.304
First Half	2	4	4.76	0	64.1	Sc Pos	104	38	4	52	.365
Scnd Half	2	5	5.61	0	69.0	Clutch	34	12	2	6	.353

2001 Season

Injuries—a bruised thumb, strained back and strained groin—hampered Brian Anderson through the first half of last season. But even when he was healthy, Anderson never returned to form. Although he was out of the rotation by September, he did pitch well in the postseason, including a start in Game 3 of the World Series.

Pitching, Defense & Hitting

Anderson's main pitches are a fastball and an above-average changeup. His third pitch is something between a cut fastball and a slider. To be successful, however, he has to rely on his two top pitches and be able to spot them on both sides of the plate. Anderson helps himself with good defense and an excellent pickoff move. He has given up switch-hitting, batting exclusively righthanded after May 22 last season. He is a good bunter.

2002 Outlook

Anderson has been the subject of trade speculation. But Arizona probably will hold on to him for the final year of his contract and depend on him for its rotation. If he can emulate the pitching pattern of Tom Glavine—fastballs and changeups, in and out with precision—Anderson can have success. But if he finds the middle of the plate too much, Anderson will have another difficult year.

Miguel Batista

Position: RP/SP
Bats: R **Throws:** R
Ht: 6' 2" **Wt:** 195

Opening Day Age: 31
Born: 2/19/71 in Santo Domingo, DR
ML Seasons: 7
Pronunciation: bah-TEESE-tah

Overall Statistics

	W	L	Pct.	ERA	G	GS	Sv	IP	H	BB	SO	HR	Ratio
2001	11	8	.579	3.36	48	18	0	139.1	113	60	90	13	1.24
Career	24	32	.429	4.74	182	63	1	524.0	534	254	348	59	1.50

2001 Situational Stats

	W	L	ERA	Sv	IP		AB	H	HR	RBI	Avg
Home	5	5	4.27	0	71.2	LHB	206	45	4	16	.218
Road	6	3	2.39	0	67.2	RHB	293	68	9	34	.232
First Half	4	5	3.56	0	73.1	Sc Pos	112	25	2	34	.223
Scnd Half	7	3	3.14	0	66.0	Clutch	76	17	3	8	.224

2001 Season

The Diamondbacks were impressed by Miguel Batista's work in the Dominican Winter League. And they were able to sign him, helped in large part by offering Batista a place on their 40-man roster. In spring training, he lost out to Bobby Witt in competition for the No. 5 starter spot. But by late April, injuries had required Batista to come out of the bullpen to start, and he shuttled between the two roles all year with ease. He set career bests in victories, games started, innings pitched and ERA.

Pitching, Defense & Hitting

Batista throws a variety of hard pitches with movement. He has a cut fastball to go along with a good slider, a split-finger, an occasional curve and a fastball that can reach 94 MPH. His command is not good and he will use the split-finger in tight spots. While Batista's delivery is slow, he will use a slide step to help cut down basestealers. His defense is shaky at times, and he's a poor hitter.

2002 Outlook

Believing Batista has figured out how to harness his live arm, Arizona will count on him as a starter this season. He could begin the year as the No. 3 man in the rotation, behind Randy Johnson and Curt Schilling.

Danny Bautista

Position: RF/CF
Bats: R **Throws:** R
Ht: 5'11" **Wt:** 204

Opening Day Age: 29
Born: 5/24/72 in Santo Domingo, DR
ML Seasons: 9
Pronunciation: BAW-tee-sta

Overall Statistics

	G	AB	R	H	D	T	HR	RBI	SB	BB	SO	Avg	OBP	Slg
2001	100	222	26	67	11	2	5	26	3	14	31	.302	.346	.437
Career	626	1540	202	403	73	13	41	195	24	82	272	.262	.300	.406

2001 Situational Stats

	AB	H	HR	RBI	Avg		AB	H	HR	RBI	Avg
Home	122	40	0	10	.328	LHP	88	21	0	8	.239
Road	100	27	5	16	.270	RHP	134	46	5	18	.343
First Half	107	32	1	9	.299	Sc Pos	56	20	0	18	.357
Scnd Half	115	35	4	17	.304	Clutch	44	11	1	6	.250

2001 Season

Danny Bautista played in 100 games as Arizona's fourth outfielder, spelling Steve Finley in center field and Reggie Sanders in right and batting .350 as a pinch-hitter. He hit .391 over his final 19 games with four homers and 14 RBI, and also played a key role in the postseason. He started the final games of both the NLCS and World Series, and hit .364 overall in the 2001 playoffs (8-for-22).

Hitting, Baserunning & Defense

Bautista is a good fastball hitter with good plate coverage. He can be fooled on high fastballs and good breaking pitches, however, and lefties gave him all kinds of troubles in 2001. Last season, he slugged 200 points higher against righthanded pitchers. He is a fast baserunner who can be over-aggressive at times. He plays similarly in the field, with good enough range to play center field and an above-average arm, but he often will overthrow his intended target.

2002 Outlook

Arizona is expected to make a strong effort to re-sign Bautista, who was a free agent after the season. With the anticipated departure of Reggie Sanders, Bautista could take over significant playing time in right field—at least as the righthanded half of a platoon.

David Dellucci

Position: RF/CF
Bats: L **Throws:** L
Ht: 5'10" **Wt:** 198

Opening Day Age: 28
Born: 10/31/73 in Baton Rouge, LA
ML Seasons: 5
Pronunciation: duh-LOO-chee

Overall Statistics

	G	AB	R	H	D	T	HR	RBI	SB	BB	SO	Avg	OBP	Slg
2001	115	217	28	60	10	2	10	40	2	22	52	.276	.349	.479
Career	353	819	103	232	40	15	17	111	7	74	195	.283	.349	.431

2001 Situational Stats

	AB	H	HR	RBI	Avg		AB	H	HR	RBI	Avg
Home	90	25	5	19	.278	LHP	26	6	0	4	.231
Road	127	35	5	21	.276	RHP	191	54	10	36	.283
First Half	128	38	7	25	.297	Sc Pos	57	17	4	30	.298
Scnd Half	89	22	3	15	.247	Clutch	53	17	5	15	.321

2001 Season

David Dellucci hit five home runs as a pinch-hitter last year. He and Erubiel Durazo, who also clubbed five, helped Arizona tie a record with 14 pinch-hit homers overall. Although Dellucci more than doubled his overall career total of longballs, which had been seven coming into last season, he never got much of a chance to play regularly. He started just 40 games, and only nine times after August 1.

Hitting, Baserunning & Defense

Like many lefthanded batters, Dellucci prefers the ball low, and he will hit pitches down and in a long way. He has good gap power and the speed to run out some triples. He is much more effective against righthanded pitching. Dellucci has the range to play center field but has a below-average throwing arm. He is a sub-.500 basestealer for his big league career.

2002 Outlook

With Reggie Sanders not expected to return, Dellucci should be in the mix for playing time in right field this season. Dellucci has not had a chance to be a regular since a 1999 career-threatening wrist injury. Even if he doesn't start, he could be a productive platoon player. The signing of Jose Guillen in mid-December further muddies the Arizona backup-outfielder situation, however.

Erubiel Durazo

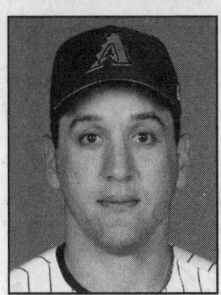

Position: 1B
Bats: L **Throws:** L
Ht: 6' 3" **Wt:** 240

Opening Day Age: 28
Born: 1/23/74 in Hermosillo, Mexico
ML Seasons: 3
Pronunciation: eh-ROO-bee-el du-RAH-zo

Overall Statistics

	G	AB	R	H	D	T	HR	RBI	SB	BB	SO	Avg	OBP	Slg
2001	92	175	34	47	11	0	12	38	0	28	49	.269	.372	.537
Career	211	526	100	150	26	2	31	101	2	88	135	.285	.387	.519

2001 Situational Stats

	AB	H	HR	RBI	Avg		AB	H	HR	RBI	Avg
Home	89	23	4	16	.258	LHP	32	6	0	2	.188
Road	86	24	8	22	.279	RHP	143	41	12	36	.287
First Half	121	33	10	32	.273	Sc Pos	54	14	3	22	.259
Scnd Half	54	14	2	6	.259	Clutch	50	11	2	9	.220

2001 Season

Erubiel Durazo was sent down in the final week of spring training because he was one of the few Diamondbacks who had minor league options. But he was back up before opening day due to an injury to Danny Klassen. Durazo wound up hitting five pinch-hit homers—all by May 20. However, he missed the second half of August with a lower back strain and at one point endured an 0-for-21 streak as a pinch-hitter.

Hitting, Baserunning & Defense

Durazo is a polished hitter for someone with so few big league at-bats. He has good strike-zone judgment and excellent power to the opposite field. He is aggressive on first-pitch fastballs. A slow runner with two career stolen bases, Durazo is not a standout first baseman. He struggles with throwing, especially while attempting the 3-6 play.

2002 Outlook

The Diamondbacks hoped to get Durazo some outfield work in the Mexican Pacific League, so he can compete for playing time in right field. He spent some time in right last spring, and was capable if not average. At this point in his career, Durazo needs to play. Teams have been interested in acquiring him for two years, but Arizona knows what it has and is hesitant to let him go.

Matt Mantei

Position: RP
Bats: R **Throws:** R
Ht: 6' 1" **Wt:** 200

Opening Day Age: 28
Born: 7/7/73 in Tampa, FL
ML Seasons: 6
Pronunciation: MAN-tie

Overall Statistics

	W	L	Pct.	ERA	G	GS	Sv	IP	H	BB	SO	HR	Ratio
2001	0	0	-	2.57	8	0	2	7.0	6	4	12	2	1.43
Career	6	9	.400	3.66	188	0	60	204.0	144	140	267	15	1.39

2001 Situational Stats

	W	L	ERA	Sv	IP		AB	H	HR	RBI	Avg
Home	0	0	2.45	0	3.2	LHB	11	5	2	4	.455
Road	0	0	2.70	2	3.1	RHB	16	1	0	0	.063
First Half	0	0	2.57	2	7.0	Sc Pos	8	2	1	3	.250
Scnd Half	0	0	-	0	0.0	Clutch	15	4	2	4	.267

2001 Season

Matt Mantei suffered an elbow injury while pitching against the Marlins on April 24. After a few weeks of trying to come back, a torn ligament was discovered in his elbow. He underwent elbow ligament replacement (Tommy John) surgery on June 19. By the end of the season, Mantei was ahead of schedule in his rehabilitation.

Pitching, Defense & Hitting

Mantei is most effective when he has confidence in his slider as his second pitch. While he throws 96-99 MPH, he needs another pitch to keep hitters off balance, and he's most likely to throw the slider for a strike. That pitch also comes from the same arm angle as his fastball. Mantei is a bit below average as a fielder and has little experience as a hitter, with one hit in five career at-bats. Opposing basestealers succeeded on eight of 10 attempts in 2000.

2002 Outlook

If he continues to progress, Mantei could be ready for the Opening Day roster. He is more likely to be activated a month into the season, although he may not be used on consecutive days for most or all of the campaign. Mantei is signed through 2003, with a player option for 2004.

Damian Miller

Position: C
Bats: R **Throws:** R
Ht: 6' 2" **Wt:** 218

Opening Day Age: 32
Born: 10/13/69 in
LaCrosse, WI
ML Seasons: 5

Overall Statistics

	G	AB	R	H	D	T	HR	RBI	SB	BB	SO	Avg	OBP	Slg
2001	123	380	45	103	19	0	13	47	0	35	80	.271	.337	.424
Career	391	1234	145	338	77	2	39	165	3	103	287	.274	.332	.434

2001 Situational Stats

	AB	H	HR	RBI	Avg		AB	H	HR	RBI	Avg
Home	174	53	9	31	.305	LHP	73	22	1	7	.301
Road	206	50	4	16	.243	RHP	307	81	12	40	.264
First Half	205	54	5	21	.263	Sc Pos	100	21	4	34	.210
Scnd Half	175	49	8	26	.280	Clutch	55	16	2	8	.291

2001 Season

Given a frontline job for the first time in his career, Damian Miller set personal highs in runs, hits and homers. His 123 games played were his most in professional baseball. But for the third straight year he suffered injuries down the stretch. He played much of the second half with a strained left Achilles' tendon and missed time the final two weeks with a right shoulder strain. He did recover in time to start 16 of 17 postseason games.

Hitting, Baserunning & Defense

With above-average arm strength and velocity, Miller has quick delivery times on throws to second base. He also has shown himself to be a fine receiver, able to catch the varied styles of Randy Johnson, Curt Schilling, Miguel Batista and Byung-Hyun Kim. Offensively, Miller is best when he's not trying to pull the ball too much and when he's taking pitches to right field. But he still prefers the fastball from the middle of the plate in, and can pull off breaking balls away.

2002 Outlook

Miller again will be Arizona's starting catcher, mainly because of his defense. The pitchers are comfortable with him, as is manager Bob Brenly. Miller likely will continue to hit eighth in the order. His durability, however, remains an issue.

Bret Prinz

Position: RP
Bats: R **Throws:** R
Ht: 6' 3" **Wt:** 185

Opening Day Age: 24
Born: 6/15/77 in
Chicago Heights, IL
ML Seasons: 1

Overall Statistics

	W	L	Pct.	ERA	G	GS	Sv	IP	H	BB	SO	HR	Ratio
2001	4	1	.800	2.63	46	0	9	41.0	33	19	27	4	1.27
Career	4	1	.800	2.63	46	0	9	41.0	33	19	27	4	1.27

2001 Situational Stats

	W	L	ERA	Sv	IP		AB	H	HR	RBI	Avg
Home	3	0	2.53	4	21.1	LHB	58	17	3	8	.293
Road	1	1	2.75	5	19.2	RHB	92	16	1	8	.174
First Half	3	0	1.13	8	24.0	Sc Pos	45	8	0	11	.178
Scnd Half	1	1	4.76	1	17.0	Clutch	83	20	3	10	.241

2001 Season

Called up early in the season, Bret Prinz took over as the Diamondbacks' closer when Matt Mantei suffered an elbow injury. He then moved to a setup role when Byung-Hyun Kim established himself as the closer. Prinz was very effective for three months, but then struggled a bit. After pitching in both ends of an August 31 doubleheader, he came down with rotator cuff tendinitis. He pitched just once more and missed the postseason.

Pitching, Defense & Hitting

Prinz throws 92-95 MPH from an almost sidearm angle, making him tough on righthanded hitters. He also throws a slider, which has some tilt but not much break, and is working on a changeup. Prinz will throw strikes and keep his fastball down, but misses spots at times. He can be affected defensively by falling off toward first base. He didn't make any plate appearances during his 46 games with Arizona last season.

2002 Outlook

Depending on Mantei's health, Prinz will be a middle reliever or the main setup man. Prinz impressed last year with his poise while breaking into the majors. He again should be trusted in late-game situations.

Todd Stottlemyre

Position: SP
Bats: L **Throws:** R
Ht: 6' 2" **Wt:** 210

Opening Day Age: 36
Born: 5/20/65 in
Yakima, WA
ML Seasons: 13
Pronunciation:
STOTT-ul-mire

Overall Statistics

	W	L	Pct.	ERA	G	GS	Sv	IP	H	BB	SO	HR	Ratio
2001							Did Not Play						
Career	138	119	.537	4.25	367	335	1	2171.1	2174	809	1575	242	1.37

2001 Situational Stats

	W	L	ERA	Sv	IP		AB	H	HR	RBI	Avg
Home	—	—	—	—	—	LHB	—	—	—	—	—
Road	—	—	—	—	—	RHB	—	—	—	—	—
First Half	—	—	—	—	—	Sc Pos	—	—	—	—	—
Scnd Half	—	—	—	—	—	Clutch	—	—	—	—	—

2001 Season

Todd Stottlemyre missed the entire 2001 season in an effort to make one more chance at a comeback. A dead nerve behind his right shoulder forced him to stop throwing during spring training. When the nerve still had not responded by midseason, he opted to have surgery to fix the torn rotator cuff and labrum he had injured in 1999. But by October, the nerve had regenerated and Stottlemyre was cleared to throw.

Pitching, Defense & Hitting

Always a fierce competitor, Stottlemyre is an aggressive pitcher with a basic fastball-slider approach. But he will throw a curveball and changeup as well. He is a decent hitter and bunter who fields his position well. Despite spending the first part of his career in the American League, Stottlemyre has managed to keep his average over .200. He also hit his first homer in 2000.

2002 Outlook

This is Stottlemyre's last shot. If his arm problems are worked out, and he doesn't suffer new injuries, he will fulfill the last season of his four-year contract. But if he has any problems in spring training, he likely will retire to allow Arizona to spend his salary on an acquisition or two.

Greg Swindell

Position: RP
Bats: R **Throws:** L
Ht: 6' 3" **Wt:** 230

Opening Day Age: 37
Born: 1/2/65 in Fort
Worth, TX
ML Seasons: 16
Pronunciation:
swin-DELL

Overall Statistics

	W	L	Pct.	ERA	G	GS	Sv	IP	H	BB	SO	HR	Ratio
2001	2	6	.250	4.53	64	0	2	53.2	51	8	42	12	1.10
Career	123	120	.506	3.82	630	269	7	2200.1	2275	496	1519	253	1.26

2001 Situational Stats

	W	L	ERA	Sv	IP		AB	H	HR	RBI	Avg
Home	0	3	5.00	1	27.0	LHB	81	21	6	11	.259
Road	2	3	4.05	1	26.2	RHB	123	30	6	19	.244
First Half	2	1	3.94	2	29.2	Sc Pos	40	12	2	18	.300
Scnd Half	0	5	5.25	0	24.0	Clutch	76	19	5	12	.250

2001 Season

Arizona signed Greg Swindell to a two-year contract extension prior to last season. But he wound up with less work than he had in his previous two years with the club. Swindell fell out of favor in the bullpen rotation for much of the campaign, mainly due to a propensity for giving up homers. He was used at times as a one-batter lefty, a role for which he is not particularly suited.

Pitching, Defense & Hitting

Swindell is primarily a two-pitch pitcher—a hard slider as his second pitch to lefthanded hitters and a forkball-type changeup to righthanders. But he is nonetheless durable and can be valuable. He has shown the ability to get both lefties and righties out and seems better with more frequent use. He rarely walks batters, but needs good location due to average velocity. He is an average fielder at best, but does keep runners at bay with a quick delivery. He rarely bats.

2002 Outlook

Swindell's contract status in relation to his spot in the bullpen pecking order could make Arizona try to trade him. But he showed before 2001 that he could pitch often and for multiple innings at a time. A veteran reliever like Swindell might be a good pickup for the right team.

Other Arizona Diamondbacks

Rod Barajas (**Pos**: C, **Age**: 26, **Bats**: R)

	G	AB	R	H	D	T	HR	RBI	SB	BB	SO	Avg	OBP	Slg
2001	51	106	9	17	3	0	3	9	0	4	26	.160	.191	.274
Career	61	135	13	24	4	0	5	15	0	5	31	.178	.207	.319

Barajas has solid catching skills and made the club last spring, but he struggled at the plate after hitting .261 as a part-time player in April. He ripped it up at Triple-A Tucson, so he may be ready in 2002. 2002 Outlook: B

Troy Brohawn (**Pos**: LHP, **Age**: 29)

	W	L	Pct.	ERA	G	GS	Sv	IP	H	BB	SO	HR	Ratio
2001	2	3	.400	4.93	59	0	1	49.1	55	23	30	5	1.58
Career	2	3	.400	4.93	59	0	1	49.1	55	23	30	5	1.58

The rookie lefthander got roughed up in three of his first four outings, but then posted a 2.08 ERA in 19 games between late April and mid-June. Despite his inconsistency, Brohawn managed to pitch in the World Series. 2002 Outlook: C

Ryan Christenson (**Pos**: LF, **Age**: 28, **Bats**: R)

	G	AB	R	H	D	T	HR	RBI	SB	BB	SO	Avg	OBP	Slg
2001	26	8	4	1	1	0	0	1	1	2	250	.125	.222	.250
Career	370	775	132	184	37	5	13	83	14	94	199	.237	.319	.348

After a poor start at Oakland's Triple-A Sacramento, Christenson was dealt in June to Arizona, where he produced his typically solid Triple-A numbers at Tucson. He was claimed by Milwaukee in the Rule 5 draft in December. 2002 Outlook: C

Greg Colbrunn (**Pos**: 1B, **Age**: 32, **Bats**: R)

	G	AB	R	H	D	T	HR	RBI	SB	BB	SO	Avg	OBP	Slg
2001	59	97	12	28	8	0	4	18	0	9	14	.289	.373	.495
Career	878	2513	299	725	138	9	85	387	29	152	404	.288	.338	.452

The righthanded hitter has made a career out of pounding southpaws, and Colbrunn's batted better than .300 in each of the three seasons before 2001 as a part-timer. A left knee sprain cost him two months last season. 2002 Outlook: B

Midre Cummings (**Pos**: LF, **Age**: 30, **Bats**: L)

	G	AB	R	H	D	T	HR	RBI	SB	BB	SO	Avg	OBP	Slg
2001	20	20	1	6	1	0	0	1	0	0	4	.300	.286	.350
Career	436	1057	126	271	56	8	20	117	8	89	187	.256	.316	.381

This former Minnesota hitting prospect still sits on the fringe of the majors by showing flashes of a good bat. Cummings needs to find the right situation to keep his major league career going as a fourth or fifth outfielder. 2002 Outlook: C

Mike DiFelice (**Pos**: C, **Age**: 32, **Bats**: R)

	G	AB	R	H	D	T	HR	RBI	SB	BB	SO	Avg	OBP	Slg
2001	60	170	14	32	5	1	2	10	1	8	49	.188	.239	.265
Career	352	1068	91	257	52	6	21	111	2	62	230	.241	.287	.360

DiFelice didn't make much contact last summer, except during a bar incident that led to his release in September. He signed with the Cards, who will use him to give Eli Marrero time at other positions. 2002 Outlook: B

Robert Ellis (**Pos**: RHP, **Age**: 31)

	W	L	Pct.	ERA	G	GS	Sv	IP	H	BB	SO	HR	Ratio
2001	6	5	.545	5.77	19	17	0	92.0	106	34	41	12	1.52
Career	6	5	.545	5.47	22	17	0	97.0	106	38	46	12	1.48

At age 30, this former White Sox prospect earned his first extended stay in the majors during spring training. He enjoyed eight quality starts, but later struggled and missed two months due to a badly bruised shin. 2002 Outlook: C

Geraldo Guzman (**Pos**: RHP, **Age**: 29)

	W	L	Pct.	ERA	G	GS	Sv	IP	H	BB	SO	HR	Ratio
2001	0	0	-	2.89	4	0	0	9.1	7	3	4	2	1.07
Career	5	4	.556	5.04	17	10	0	69.2	73	25	56	10	1.41

After most of a decade away from the game, Guzman signed with Arizona in 1999 and showed some promise as a starter when he reached the majors in 2000. He worked well as a reliever in 2001, but he was released by the Diamondbacks in November. 2002 Outlook: C

Ken Huckaby (**Pos**: C, **Age**: 31, **Bats**: R)

	G	AB	R	H	D	T	HR	RBI	SB	BB	SO	Avg	OBP	Slg
2001	1	1	0	0	0	0	0	0	0	0	1	.000	.000	.000
Career	1	1	0	0	0	0	0	0	0	0	1	.000	.000	.000

In his 11th pro season at age 30, Huckaby fanned in his first and only major league at-bat on the last Saturday of the season. He hit .306 in the minors in 2001, but he doesn't draw walks or show power. The catcher was released at the end of October. 2002 Outlook: C

Eric Knott (**Pos**: LHP, **Age**: 27)

	W	L	Pct.	ERA	G	GS	Sv	IP	H	BB	SO	HR	Ratio
2001	0	1	1.000	1.93	3	1	0	4.2	8	0	4	0	1.71
Career	0	1	1.000	1.93	3	1	0	4.2	8	0	4	0	1.71

The rookie lefthander hasn't dominated hitters in the minors, but he hasn't issued a lot of walks, either. He enjoyed a first taste of the majors during a September callup, and he wants more. 2002 Outlook: C

Mike Koplove (**Pos**: RHP, **Age**: 25)

	W	L	Pct.	ERA	G	GS	Sv	IP	H	BB	SO	HR	Ratio
2001	0	1	1.000	3.60	9	0	0	10.0	8	9	14	1	1.70
Career	0	1	1.000	3.60	9	0	0	10.0	8	9	14	1	1.70

The righthander has been effective in the high minors the last two years, and he saved 13 games and posted a 2.71 ERA between Double-A and Triple-A ball in 2001. Koplove's decent performance as a September callup helps his cause. 2002 Outlook: C

Chad Moeller (**Pos**: C, **Age**: 27, **Bats**: R)

	G	AB	R	H	D	T	HR	RBI	SB	BB	SO	Avg	OBP	Slg
2001	25	56	8	13	0	1	1	2	0	6	12	.232	.306	.321
Career	73	184	21	40	3	2	2	11	1	15	45	.217	.275	.288

For a second straight year Moeller got a chance to fill a hole on a major league roster, but he didn't do much with the bat during a six-week stay near midseason and as a September callup. 2002 Outlook: C

Mike Mohler (Pos: LHP, Age: 33)

	W	L	Pct.	ERA	G	GS	Sv	IP	H	BB	SO	HR	Ratio
2001	0	0	-	7.24	13	0	0	13.2	14	9	7	3	1.68
Career	14	27	.341	4.99	347	20	10	417.0	428	232	281	45	1.58

The veteran lefty has been up and down from the minors regularly in recent seasons, and the pattern continued with Arizona in 2001. He's been homer-prone and ineffective the last two years and became a free agent in November. 2002 Outlook: C

Mike Morgan (Pos: RHP, Age: 42)

	W	L	Pct.	ERA	G	GS	Sv	IP	H	BB	SO	HR	Ratio
2001	1	0	1.000	4.26	31	1	0	38.0	45	17	24	2	1.63
Career	140	185	.431	4.22	568	411	8	2738.1	2902	929	1390	263	1.40

Morgan just keeps on ticking, pitching in his 21st major league season and posting his best ERA since 1998. He pitched 4.2 scoreless innings in the World Series and won his first ring. Could lucky team No. 13 be ahead? 2002 Outlook: B

Armando Reynoso (Pos: RHP, Age: 35)

	W	L	Pct.	ERA	G	GS	Sv	IP	H	BB	SO	HR	Ratio
2001	1	6	.143	5.98	9	9	0	46.2	58	13	15	13	1.52
Career	68	62	.523	4.73	196	186	1	1078.0	1182	375	552	138	1.44

Reynoso won 10 games for Arizona in 1999 and 11 more in 2000, but it wasn't pretty. He started slowly in 2001 (1-4, 6.40) before a shoulder strain put him out for most of the rest of the year. 2002 Outlook: B

Erik Sabel (Pos: RHP, Age: 27)

	W	L	Pct.	ERA	G	GS	Sv	IP	H	BB	SO	HR	Ratio
2001	3	2	.600	4.38	42	0	0	51.1	57	12	25	8	1.34
Career	3	2	.600	4.72	49	0	0	61.0	69	18	31	9	1.43

Sabel had a decent season, and earned a longer look in Arizona with a 0.73 ERA in 12.1 innings in May. The 27-year-old was inconsistent after May, but was a solid performer and posted a 2.95 ERA at Triple-A Tucson. 2002 Outlook: C

Juan Sosa (Pos: 3B, Age: 26, Bats: R)

	G	AB	R	H	D	T	HR	RBI	SB	BB	SO	Avg	OBP	Slg
2001	2	1	0	0	0	0	0	0	0	0	1	.000	.000	.000
Career	13	10	3	2	0	0	0	0	0	2	3	.200	.333	.200

A light-hitting but speedy shortstop, Sosa came up to take the roster spot of an injured Matt Williams and fanned in his one at-bat. He inked a minor league deal with Detroit to pursue a longer-lasting cup of coffee. 2002 Outlook: C

Junior Spivey (Pos: 2B, Age: 27, Bats: R)

	G	AB	R	H	D	T	HR	RBI	SB	BB	SO	Avg	OBP	Slg
2001	72	163	33	42	6	3	5	21	3	23	47	.258	.354	.423
Career	72	163	33	42	6	3	5	21	3	23	47	.258	.354	.423

Spivey showed a propensity to get on base in the minors, and it carried over against major league lefties in 2001. He didn't fare so well against righthanders, but he's in line for a job in 2002. 2002 Outlook: B

Russ Springer (Pos: RHP, Age: 33)

	W	L	Pct.	ERA	G	GS	Sv	IP	H	BB	SO	HR	Ratio
2001	0	0	-	7.13	18	0	1	17.2	20	4	12	5	1.36
Career	19	32	.373	5.08	351	27	8	531.2	545	246	485	77	1.49

Springer showed promise a decade ago, but injuries have sidetracked his career the last few years. A shoulder sprain forced two stints on the DL in 2001, including a season-ending one on August 1. He opted for free agency in November. 2002 Outlook: C

Bobby Witt (Pos: RHP, Age: 37)

	W	L	Pct.	ERA	G	GS	Sv	IP	H	BB	SO	HR	Ratio
2001	4	1	.800	4.78	14	7	0	43.1	36	25	31	6	1.41
Career	142	157	.475	4.83	430	397	0	2465.0	2493	1375	1955	252	1.57

Witt staged a comeback of sorts, pitching effectively for Arizona after arriving in August. He was 3-0 in six starts beginning in late August and rode the tide to his first World Series title in 16 seasons. The 37-year-old is a free agent and may hang up the spikes. 2002 Outlook: C

Arizona

Arizona Diamondbacks Minor League Prospects

Organization Overview:

It's hard to argue about the success of a franchise that has just won the World Series in its fourth year of existence. But Arizona accomplished the feat with most of its best players on the wrong side of 30. And over the next few years, guys like Randy Johnson, Curt Schilling and Luis Gonzalez figure to suffer an inevitable decline. Fortunately for the Diamondbacks, their farm system may be ready to begin spitting out intriguing replacements as the veterans begin to fade. The D'Backs have done a decent job signing nondrafted players. And they're very happy with the drafts they've had the past two seasons. They say they've added 14 pitchers over the past couple years who can throw 95 MPH or better. Athleticism has been added to the system, and the organization appears stronger up the middle, though it might look for more depth at catcher. The Diamondbacks remain a veteran team, so the youngsters still may have to wait their turn.

Alex Cintron

Position: SS **Opening Day Age:** 23
Bats: B **Throws:** R **Born:** 12/17/78 in
Ht: 6' 2" **Wt:** 180 Humacao, PR

Recent Statistics

	G	AB	R	H	D	T	HR	RBI	SB	BB	SO	Avg
2001 AAA Tucson	107	425	53	124	24	3	3	35	9	15	48	.292
2001 NL Arizona	8	7	0	2	0	1	0	0	0	0	0	.286
2001 MLE	107	406	40	105	20	2	2	26	6	11	50	.259

Cintron has been highly touted and has hit in the .290-.310 range each of the past three seasons. He played at Triple-A at age 22 last year, and the Diamondbacks consider him an offensive middle infield prospect. However, they feel his stock has fallen and project him as no better than a utility player on a championship team or a starter on a second division club. Cintron can make the routine plays at shortstop, but lacks extreme range and quickness. He has hit for a good average in the past, but hasn't shown much power or the ability to draw walks. He played some games at second base last season, and it's possible Cintron will compete for a job with the Diamondbacks this spring.

Brad Cresse

Position: C **Opening Day Age:** 23
Bats: R **Throws:** R **Born:** 7/31/78 in Long
Ht: 6' 4" **Wt:** 215 Beach, CA

Recent Statistics

	G	AB	R	H	D	T	HR	RBI	SB	BB	SO	Avg
2000 A High Desert	48	173	35	56	7	0	17	56	0	17	50	.324
2000 AA El Paso	15	42	9	11	1	0	1	10	0	6	12	.262
2001 AA El Paso	118	429	55	124	39	1	14	81	0	44	116	.289
2001 MLE	118	409	40	104	33	0	10	59	0	27	124	.254

The Diamondbacks say Cresse is a catcher in the mold of Mike Piazza. That's obviously a high standard to live up to, but Cresse has shown big-time power potential ever since college. He led NCAA Division I with 30 homers and 106 RBI in 2000, capping the season by driving in the winning run in the title game of the College World Series. Arizona chose him in the fifth round of the draft, and he made it to Double-A in his first professional season. While there are few concerns about Cresse's offense, his work behind the plate hasn't been as highly regarded. It has gotten better, though. He needs to keep improving defensively, but has a chance to be a September callup this year.

Jack Cust

Position: OF **Opening Day Age:** 23
Bats: L **Throws:** R **Born:** 1/16/79 in
Ht: 6' 1" **Wt:** 205 Flemington, NJ

Recent Statistics

	G	AB	R	H	D	T	HR	RBI	SB	BB	SO	Avg
2001 AAA Tucson	135	442	81	123	24	2	27	79	6	102	160	.278
2001 NL Arizona	3	2	0	1	0	0	0	0	0	1	0	.500
2001 MLE	135	423	61	104	20	1	20	59	4	77	168	.246

Cust's ability to reach base has helped him make steady progress since being chosen in the first round of the 1997 draft. He made it to Triple-A last year, where he again demonstrated nice power potential. But while he topped 100 walks for the second straight season, he also topped 140 strikeouts for the third straight campaign. Nevertheless, his on-base percentage after five years of pro ball is a gaudy .445, and his slugging percentage is over .550. Those are the kinds of numbers that help put runs on the board. Cust probably is limited to left field, and he may return to Triple-A in 2002. But he could be called up at some point this season.

Scott Hairston

Position: 2B **Opening Day Age:** 21
Bats: R **Throws:** R **Born:** 5/25/80 in Fort
Ht: 6' 0" **Wt:** 190 Worth, TX

Recent Statistics

	G	AB	R	H	D	T	HR	RBI	SB	BB	SO	Avg
2001 R Missoula	74	291	81	101	16	6	14	65	2	38	50	.347

Hairston hails from a family that has produced three generations of major leaguers. And his father Jerry feels Scott will be better than all of them. It's hard to disagree with that comment after Scott's exceptional season in the Pioneer League, especially since the Diamondbacks say Missoula's park favors pitchers. Hairston's brother Jerry plays second base for the Orioles, and Scott knows the position. He has good range and can turn the double play, but he probably is just average defensively. The D'Backs like the big bat he brings to the park and say he reminds them of Bret Boone. Hairston has the potential to hit 25-30 homers. He likely will jump to high Class-A in 2002 and could reach Double-A if things go well.

Tim Olson

Position: SS
Bats: R **Throws:** R
Ht: 6' 2" **Wt:** 200

Opening Day Age: 23
Born: 8/1/78 in Grand Forks, ND

Recent Statistics

	G	AB	R	H	D	T	HR	RBI	SB	BB	SO	Avg
2000 A South Bend	68	261	37	57	14	2	2	26	15	15	49	.218
2001 A Lancaster	61	239	36	69	12	4	6	32	13	14	49	.289
2001 AA El Paso	46	167	29	53	13	0	2	24	4	11	36	.317

Olson may be the best athlete in the organization. The Diamondbacks claim he also could be their best minor league defender at three positions—third base, shortstop and center field. After getting taken in the seventh round of the 2000 draft, Olson split time between the outfield and third base in his professional debut. He then played shortstop and third base in the California League last year, before moving to shortstop full-time at Double-A. He has good quickness, a fine arm and has made great adjustments. He's an aggressive player who really seemed to take off at El Paso, where he hit over .300. The Diamondbacks feel he'll demonstrate power in the future, and have compared him to Rich Aurilia.

Lyle Overbay

Position: 1B
Bats: L **Throws:** L
Ht: 6' 2" **Wt:** 215

Opening Day Age: 25
Born: 1/28/77 in Centralia, WA

Recent Statistics

	G	AB	R	H	D	T	HR	RBI	SB	BB	SO	Avg
2001 AA El Paso	138	532	82	187	49	3	13	100	5	67	92	.352
2001 NL Arizona	2	2	0	1	0	0	0	0	0	0	1	.500
2001 MLE	138	502	60	157	42	2	9	73	3	41	98	.313

Although he led the Big West Conference with a .420 batting average in 1999, Overbay wasn't selected until the 18th round of that year's draft. But he hasn't stopped hitting since turning pro, batting .332 or better at each stop in the minor leagues. He's got a sweet lefty swing and sprays balls around the field. He lacks home run power at this point, but he did hit 49 doubles last season and the homers may come later. An outfielder in college, Overbay has been learning to play first base. He's reminiscent of Mark Grace, and if Overbay continues to produce, he might succeed Grace in Arizona's lineup.

Luis Terrero

Position: OF
Bats: R **Throws:** R
Ht: 6' 2" **Wt:** 193

Opening Day Age: 21
Born: 5/18/80 in Barahona, DR

Recent Statistics

	G	AB	R	H	D	T	HR	RBI	SB	BB	SO	Avg
2000 A High Desert	19	79	10	15	3	1	0	1	5	3	16	.190
2000 R Missoula	68	276	48	72	10	0	8	44	23	10	75	.261
2001 A South Bend	24	89	4	14	2	0	1	8	3	0	29	.157
2001 A Yakima	11	41	7	13	2	1	0	0	0	2	8	.317
2001 A Lancaster	19	71	16	32	9	1	4	11	5	1	14	.451
2001 AA El Paso	34	147	29	44	13	3	3	8	9	4	25	.299

Signed out of the Dominican Republic in 1997, Terrero made a grand tour of Arizona's system last season, peaking in Double-A. The Diamondbacks rave about the tools Terrero brings to the table. They say he has plus-plus speed, a plus-plus arm, good power and the ability to play center field and steal 25 bases. At the same time, there still are some things Terrero can work on, like playing under control, gaining consistency and avoiding breaking balls out of the strike zone. He's probably slated for El Paso in 2002. But he came on quite fast last year. He could remain a quick mover if he shows the kind of progress he made over the last few months of 2001.

Jose Valverde

Position: P
Bats: R **Throws:** R
Ht: 6' 4" **Wt:** 220

Opening Day Age: 22
Born: 7/24/79 in San Pedro De Macoris, DR

Recent Statistics

	W	L	ERA	G	GS	Sv	IP	H	R	BB	SO	HR
2000 A South Bend	0	5	5.40	31	0	14	31.2	31	20	25	39	1
2000 R Missoula	1	0	0.00	12	0	4	11.2	3	0	4	24	0
2001 AA El Paso	2	2	3.92	39	0	13	41.1	36	19	27	72	1

In terms of size and velocity, Valverde looks a lot like Armando Benitez, another hard-throwing reliever from the Dominican Republic. Valverde spent all of last season at Double-A, where he blew Texas League hitters away with 15.7 strikeouts per nine innings. He's always been a bullpen guy, where he can come hard at opposing batters in short spurts with his 95-96 MPH fastball. He also has a slider and changeup and is working on a splitter. He still walks a few batters, but has issued just three homers over the past three years. Considering his power arm, Valverde is a potential closer in the big leagues. But he may work as a setup man to Jeremy Ward at Triple-A this season, at least initially.

Others to Watch

Righthander **Jay Belflower** (22) struggled a bit as a starter at the University of Florida, but has taken to closing like a duck to water. He made it to Triple-A in his first pro season last year. He has great sink and command... **Chris Capuano** (23) is a lefthander with decent velocity. He has a 90-92 MPH go-to fastball and a pretty good slider. He needs to refine his pitches and may be back at Double-A this season. But he could skip a level if he has success. . . **Jesus Cota** (20) won the Triple Crown in the Pioneer League in 2001. He's a big, strong guy who has a compact stroke, puts his bat on the ball and has power to all fields. He could improve his footwork around first base... Righthander **Oscar Villarreal** (20) reached Double-A as a teenager last year. He's a Mexican with a good arm who knows how to pitch. The Diamondbacks call him a "spot pitcher"... Righthander **Jeremy Ward** (24) missed most of 2000 due to elbow surgery but has bounced back well. His slider is his out pitch and he'll likely close at Triple-A this year. . . Lefthander **Bill White** (23) led NCAA Division I with 16.0 strikeouts per nine innings in 2000. He features a power curveball and reached Double-A last season. He suffered a small tear in his labrum, but should be OK.

Ted Turner Field

Offense

The Braves did not hit well at Turner Field last year, resulting in a 40-41 record in Atlanta. They became the first team in major league history to reach the playoffs with a losing record at home. Chipper Jones and Brian Jordan were the only two regulars to hit above .300 at Turner. Always among the leaders in home runs while toiling at Atlanta-Fulton County Stadium, the Braves ranked 10th in the National League with 174 homers last year.

Defense

Atlanta's success for the past decade has centered on pitching. The Braves led the league with a 3.59 ERA in 2001 and have topped the majors in four of the last five campaigns. Turner Field, with its deep alleys and large outfield, as well as the ballhawking abilities of center fielder Andruw Jones, is considered a pitchers' park. Despite making 18 more infield errors at home than on the road during intraleague games, the Braves ranked fourth in the NL with a .983 fielding percentage.

Who It Helps the Most

Line-drive hitters do well due to the large amount of space in the outfield. Chipper Jones has learned how to benefit at home, and Marcus Giles should enjoy tremendous success in Atlanta.

Who It Hurts the Most

Andruw Jones has delivered more RBI during road games in every season since Turner Field opened in 1997. He's also hit 57 percent of his homers on the road (83 of 145) over the same span. Free agent John Burkett might welcome a move out of Atlanta. During his two seasons with the Braves, he compiled an ERA more than a run higher at home.

Rookies & Newcomers

Two players who received cups of coffee last September have the best chance of playing as rookies in 2002. Shortstop Wilson Betemit features a powerful right arm and the ability to drive the ball into the deep Turner Field gaps. Righthander Tim Spooneybarger figures to bolster the bullpen by forcing hitters to hit the ball on the ground. Vinny Castilla won't find Turner Field as home-run friendly as Enron Field.

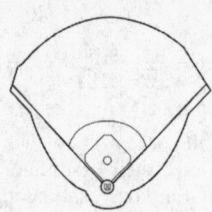

Dimensions: LF-335, LCF-380, CF-401, RCF-390, RF-330

Capacity: 49,714

Elevation: 1050 feet

Surface: Grass

Foul Territory: Average

Park Factors

2001 Season

| | Home Games | | | Away Games | | | |
	Braves	Opp	Total	Braves	Opp	Total	Index
G	72	72	144	72	72	144	—
Avg	.262	.256	.259	.255	.245	.250	104
AB	2384	2467	4851	2499	2376	4875	100
R	314	302	616	330	260	590	104
H	625	631	1256	637	582	1219	103
2B	117	94	211	117	99	216	98
3B	10	6	16	11	13	24	67
HR	79	68	147	77	67	144	103
BB	190	234	424	239	198	437	98
SO	441	501	942	501	496	997	95
E	51	49	100	37	45	82	122
E-Infield	47	40	87	29	37	66	132
LHB-Avg	.240	.279	.259	.264	.248	.257	101
LHB-HR	21	37	58	30	24	54	109
RHB-Avg	.279	.242	.259	.248	.243	.245	106
RHB-HR	58	31	89	47	43	90	99

1999-2001

| | Home Games | | | Away Games | | | |
	Braves	Opp	Total	Braves	Opp	Total	Index
G	216	216	432	216	216	432	—
Avg	.268	.248	.258	.263	.253	.258	100
AB	7104	7440	14544	7591	7246	14837	98
R	1033	848	1881	1074	898	1972	95
H	1904	1848	3752	1995	1836	3831	98
2B	367	295	662	384	327	711	95
3B	31	22	53	38	30	68	80
HR	232	201	433	261	199	460	96
BB	715	631	1346	786	660	1446	95
SO	1232	1550	2782	1453	1492	2945	96
E	163	198	361	145	166	311	116
E-Infield	145	162	307	123	143	266	115
LHB-Avg	.262	.262	.262	.263	.260	.261	100
LHB-HR	68	87	155	74	70	144	109
RHB-Avg	.272	.241	.255	.263	.250	.256	100
RHB-HR	164	114	278	187	129	316	90

2001 Rankings (National League)

- Highest error factor
- Highest infield-error factor
- Third-highest RHB batting-average factor

Bobby Cox

2001 Season

Last season may have been Bobby Cox' best effort at the Atlanta helm. He juggled a patchwork lineup that included a season-ending injury to Rafael Furcal, the release of Quilvio Veras and Rico Brogna, as well as disappointing showings by Javy Lopez and B.J. Surhoff, to win a major league record 10th straight division title. Cox also moved up to 12th on the all-time list with 1,704 managerial victories.

Offense

Cox does an excellent job of molding his strategy based on personnel. When Furcal and Veras were in the lineup early last season, the Braves were active on the basepaths. Afterwards, Atlanta was a station-to-station team that went the first three weeks of August without a stolen base. A conservative skipper, Cox realized his offense was not explosive, as evidenced by the fact that the Braves scored 81 fewer runs last year compared to 2000. So Atlanta fired hitting coach Merv Rettenmund in late October and hired former Braves third baseman and fan favorite Terry Pendleton to take over the post. Cox will continue to keep his players fresh by pinch-hitting liberally and employing double-switches as often as anyone in the game.

Pitching & Defense

The Braves have been playoff contenders for the past decade due to their exceptional pitching and defense. Cox trusts his veteran pitchers and allows them to provide input during the latter part of games. But he will not hesitate to pull a young hurler when the going gets tough. He believes in matchup situations and will employ as many as four relievers to get the final few outs. Cox also is not afraid to make defensive changes. A prime example came late last year when he moved Chipper Jones from third base to left field, even though Jones had not played the position since 1997.

2002 Outlook

Cox is among the biggest competitors in the game and is expected to remain at the Atlanta helm for another three seasons. He is a good motivator who treats players like professionals. With his leadership and input on roster decisions, Cox should have the Braves in playoff contention once again.

Born: 5/21/41 in Tulsa, OK

Playing Experience: 1968-1969, NYY

Managerial Experience: 20 seasons

Manager Statistics

Year	Team, Lg	W	L	Pct	GB	Finish
2001	Atlanta, NL	88	74	.543	—	1st East
20 Seasons		1704	1345	.559	—	—

2001 Starting Pitchers by Days Rest

	<=3	4	5	6+
Braves Starts	0	97	29	28
Braves ERA	—	3.45	3.10	4.23
NL Avg Starts	1	80	47	24
NL ERA	5.03	4.43	4.53	4.28

2001 Situational Stats

	Bobby Cox	NL Average
Hit & Run Success %	35.3	35.1
Stolen Base Success %	64.9	66.5
Platoon Pct.	57.0	51.5
Defensive Subs	23	20
High-Pitch Outings	4	7
Quick/Slow Hooks	12/9	19/14
Sacrifice Attempts	84	87

2001 Rankings (National League)
- 1st in pitchouts (90) and pitchouts with a runner moving (18)
- 2nd in intentional walks (55) and 2+ pitching changes in low-scoring games (39)
- 3rd in saves with over 1 inning pitched (8)

Rafael Furcal

2001 Season

Rafael Furcal's lingering shoulder problem grew more serious when he separated the joint on July 6 and subsequently underwent season-ending surgery. Earlier, the 2000 National League Rookie of the Year had gotten off to a sluggish start and was batting just .224 on May 13. He found his groove shortly thereafter and improved his average more than 50 points before going under the knife.

Hitting

Furcal is a switch-hitter with surprising power from the right side. But he tends to slap at the ball from the left side. Former Braves hitting coach Merv Rettenmund believes Furcal would be better served by batting exclusively righthanded, his natural side. The stats support Rettenmund's belief, as Furcal hit 100 points higher as a righty last year (.349 to .249). The 21-year-old is a patient hitter and Atlanta's best bunter. He also does a good job of keeping his hits on the ground in order to use his legs to get on base.

Baserunning & Defense

The Braves were concerned about Furcal's defense prior to his injury, but feel that his bothersome shoulder may have played a role in his 11 errors in 79 games. Furcal has a strong arm, good range and turns the double play well. He also possesses outstanding quickness and above-average speed, though some scouts thought he was a half step slower to first base last year. Furcal is an intelligent baserunner who ranked among the league leaders with 22 stolen bases at the time of his injury.

2002 Outlook

Atlanta is expecting Furcal to make a full recovery and return to shortstop. His days at the position could be numbered, however, with top prospect Wilson Betemit ascending the minor leagues. Furcal eventually could shift to second base, with Marcus Giles moving to third. Regardless of the defensive alignment, Furcal is the tablesetter for Atlanta's offense and a key component of the team's future success.

Position: SS
Bats: B **Throws:** R
Ht: 5'10" **Wt:** 165

Opening Day Age: 21
Born: 8/24/80 in Loma de Cabrera, Dominican Republic
ML Seasons: 2
Pronunciation: fur-CALL

Overall Statistics

	G	AB	R	H	D	T	HR	RBI	SB	BB	SO	Avg	OBP	Slg
2001	79	324	39	89	19	0	4	30	22	24	56	.275	.321	.370
Career	210	779	126	223	39	4	8	67	62	97	136	.286	.365	.377

Where He Hits the Ball

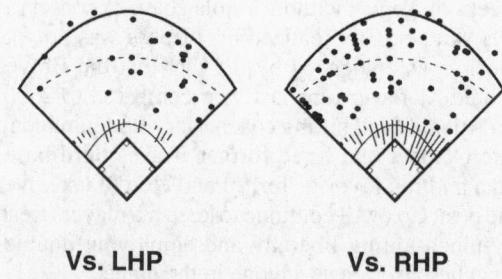

Vs. LHP   **Vs. RHP**

2001 Situational Stats

	AB	H	HR	RBI	Avg		AB	H	HR	RBI	Avg
Home	140	41	3	14	.293	LHP	83	29	2	9	.349
Road	184	48	1	16	.261	RHP	241	60	2	21	.249
First Half	324	89	4	30	.275	Scr Pos	67	20	0	24	.299
Scnd Half	0	0	0	0	-	Clutch	49	15	2	10	.306

2001 Rankings (National League)

- 1st in lowest batting average on a 3-1 count (0.000)
- 5th in bunts in play (25) and lowest on-base percentage for a leadoff hitter (.297)
- 9th in lowest batting average on an 0-2 count (.080)
- Led the Braves in stolen bases, stolen-base percentage (78.6), bunts in play (25), steals of third (3) and batting average on a 3-2 count (.250)

Marcus Giles

2002 Season

The number of Giles brothers in the major leagues doubled last year when Marcus Giles joined the Pirates' Brian at the game's top level. After an early-season promotion from Triple-A when he hit .308 with a grand slam, Marcus returned to Atlanta for good on July 20. Manager Bobby Cox handed Giles the starting job down the stretch and watched the rookie provide a spark at the top of the lineup.

Hitting

Although Giles is not a leadoff man, he was the best option Cox had at the end of last season. Giles is a line-drive hitter with above-average power. He makes hard, consistent contact with all types of pitches and uses the entire field. He also thrives on competition, excels in the clutch and was among the team leaders with a .352 average with runners in scoring position. His bat will keep him in the big leagues and could lead to his emergence as an All-Star.

Baserunning & Defense

The knock on Giles in the minors was his defense, but his glovework is much better than advertised. Through hard work, Giles has decent hands and decent range. He makes the occasional spectacular play while going to his left. His instincts for the position are not great, as evidenced by his tendency to be late covering the bag. While his speed is slightly better than average, he is a good and aggressive baserunner who has no qualms about dishing out some punishment when appropriate.

2001 Outlook

Giles draws numerous comparisons to Pete Rose with his stocky frame, all-out approach and infectious enthusiasm. He also might follow in Rose's footsteps by moving around the field during his career. While Giles currently holds the second-base job in Atlanta, he eventually could move to third base or left field to make room for prospect Wilson Betemit at shortstop, which would necessitate Rafael Furcal shifting to second. Regardless of which glove he wears, Giles' bat will land him in the lineup, hitting second behind Furcal.

Position: 2B
Bats: R **Throws:** R
Ht: 5' 8" **Wt:** 180

Opening Day Age: 23
Born: 5/18/78 in San Diego, CA
ML Seasons: 1

Overall Statistics

	G	AB	R	H	D	T	HR	RBI	SB	BB	SO	Avg	OBP	Slg
2001	68	244	36	64	10	2	9	31	2	28	37	.262	.338	.430
Career	68	244	36	64	10	2	9	31	2	28	37	.262	.338	.430

Where He Hits the Ball

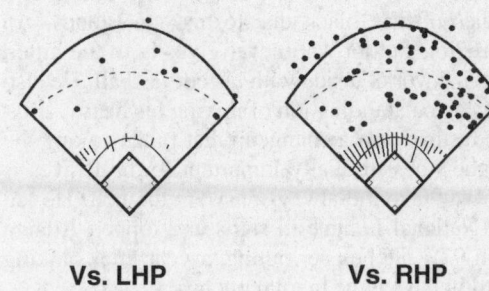

Vs. LHP   **Vs. RHP**

2001 Situational Stats

	AB	H	HR	RBI	Avg		AB	H	HR	RBI	Avg
Home	125	35	5	20	.280	LHP	49	14	2	8	.286
Road	119	29	4	11	.244	RHP	195	50	7	23	.256
First Half	13	4	1	4	.308	Sc Pos	54	19	4	24	.352
Scnd Half	231	60	8	27	.260	Clutch	37	7	1	7	.189

2001 Rankings (National League)

- 5th in batting average on a 3-2 count (.412)
- 8th in batting average on an 0-2 count (.304)
- Led the Braves in batting average on an 0-2 count (.304)

Atlanta

Tom Glavine

2001 Season

Tom Glavine would have won 20 games had he pitched for a better offensive team last season. The southpaw put together an outstanding July by going 4-0 with a 1.91 ERA over six starts. A sore left shoulder during the season's first two months and a bothersome blister on his left index finger for six weeks in late July and August led to the highest walk total of Glavine's career. Even so, he lost just two times in his last 21 starts.

Pitching

Some scouts thought the redefined strike zone would hurt Glavine more than most starters. But true to form, the lefthander made the necessary adjustments and continued to get the calls a few inches off the black due to his consistency. An incredible battler who never gives in to the hitter, Glavine works inside with his cut fastball. He also does an outstanding job of mixing his heavy, sinking fastball and a changeup that ranks among the league's best. Equally important to the Braves is the way Glavine always answers the bell. He led the National League in starts and topped Atlanta with 97.7 pitches per outing, a year after ranking third in the league in total pitches.

Defense & Hitting

Glavine may be the best all-around athlete among pitchers. His fielding is on the same level as Greg Maddux, who has dominated the Gold Glove Award for more than a decade. Glavine's move to first base is unexceptional yet effective. He was not called for a balk for the seventh consecutive season and allowed only 10 stolen bases last year. He also is an excellent hitter and finished tied for the major league lead in sacrifice bunts.

2002 Outlook

Glavine has won at least 13 games in each of the past 11 seasons, and he has reached 20 victories on five occasions. He owns 224 career wins and has a shot at attaining the magical 300 level for Hall of Fame entry. His chances of reaching that goal will increase if the Atlanta offense can give him better support in 2002.

Position: SP
Bats: L **Throws:** L
Ht: 6' 0"   **Wt:** 185

Opening Day Age: 36
Born: 3/25/66 in Concord, MA
ML Seasons: 15
Pronunciation: GLAV-in

Overall Statistics

	W	L	Pct.	ERA	G	GS	Sv	IP	H	BB	SO	HR	Ratio
2001	16	7	.696	3.57	35	35	0	219.1	213	97	116	24	1.41
Career	224	132	.629	3.40	469	469	0	3120.0	2964	1062	1927	226	1.29

How Often He Throws Strikes

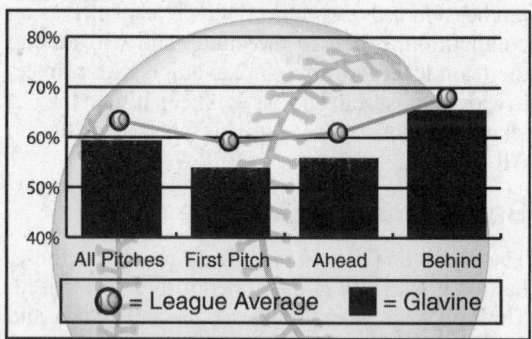

○ = League Average   ■ = Glavine

2001 Situational Stats

	W	L	ERA	Sv	IP		AB	H	HR	RBI	Avg
Home	6	3	3.46	0	104.0	LHB	182	46	5	20	.253
Road	10	4	3.67	0	115.1	RHB	635	167	19	61	.263
First Half	7	5	4.55	0	112.2	Sc Pos	171	37	4	55	.216
Scnd Half	9	2	2.53	0	106.2	Clutch	53	19	2	6	.358

2001 Rankings (National League)

- 1st in sacrifice bunts (17), games started and fielding percentage at pitcher (1.000)
- 2nd in lowest strikeout-walk ratio (1.2)
- 3rd in walks allowed
- 4th in fewest strikeouts per nine innings (4.8)
- 5th in runners caught stealing (11) and GDPs induced (24)
- Led the Braves in batters faced (929), home runs allowed, walks allowed, pitches thrown (3,397), GDPs induced (24), winning percentage, lowest stolen-base percentage allowed (47.6), most GDPs induced per GDP situation (13.5%), most run support per nine innings (4.9), lowest batting average allowed with runners in scoring position and most GDPs induced per nine innings (1.0)

Andruw Jones

2001 Season

Entering last season, Andruw Jones was on the verge of blossoming into one of the game's premier performers. But after playing decently the first three months, Jones struggled for most of the second half. Despite hitting just .221 after the All-Star break, Jones remained a solid run producer, equaling his career high in RBI and falling just two homers shy of his 2000 total. He remained durable and was the last player to play every inning in 2001 before resting on August 28 with a sore back.

Hitting

The Braves are concerned that Jones' plate discipline has not improved during his five seasons in the majors. He has outstanding power and can drive pitches off any hurler when he's seeing the ball well. But he can be an easy out when he falls into one of his funks. He came within four whiffs of equaling the Braves' single-season strikeout record due to his tendency to chase fastballs around his shoulders and breaking balls in the dirt.

Baserunning & Defense

Jones is the best defensive outfielder in the game and has as much natural ability as anyone who ever patrolled center field. He pocketed his fourth Gold Glove Award in 2001. Teams have quit running against his cannon for an arm, which limited him to 10 assists last year. Jones covers center from gap to gap and makes outstanding plays look routine. He gets incredible jumps, using a combination of speed and quickness. His speed has not been put to use on the basepaths consistently, as he stole just 11 bases in 15 attempts last season.

2002 Outlook

The Braves wasted little time in locking up one of their cornerstones when they signed Jones to a six-year, $75 million contract extension in mid-November. He won't celebrate his 25th birthday until the end of April. Given Jones' youth and unlimited potential, the Braves are unlikely to make any changes in center field now until 2008. In the meantime, Atlanta hopes that Jones regains his offensive consistency and hits closer to his .303 average of 2000, while maintaining his solid run production and Gold Glove defense.

Position: CF
Bats: R **Throws:** R
Ht: 6' 1" **Wt:** 210

Opening Day Age: 24
Born: 4/23/77 in Willemstad, Curacao
ML Seasons: 6

Overall Statistics

	G	AB	R	H	D	T	HR	RBI	SB	BB	SO	Avg	OBP	Slg
2001	161	625	104	157	25	2	34	104	11	56	142	.251	.312	.461
Career	827	2960	483	792	154	23	150	465	106	294	610	.268	.337	.487

Where He Hits the Ball

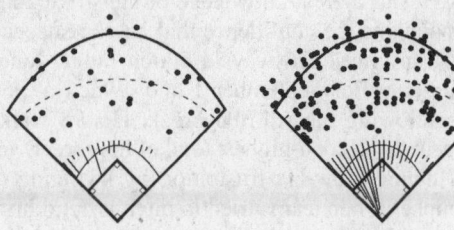

Vs. LHP   **Vs. RHP**

2001 Situational Stats

	AB	H	HR	RBI	Avg		AB	H	HR	RBI	Avg
Home	310	77	16	49	.248	LHP	111	28	5	16	.252
Road	315	80	18	55	.254	RHP	514	129	29	88	.251
First Half	349	96	19	58	.275	Sc Pos	147	42	5	66	.286
Scnd Half	276	61	15	46	.221	Clutch	93	24	4	14	.258

2001 Rankings (National League)

- 3rd in assists in center field (10)
- 4th in games played, highest percentage of extra bases taken as a runner (63.5), errors in center field (6) and lowest fielding percentage in center field (.987)
- Led the Braves in at-bats, RBI, sacrifice flies (9), strikeouts, pitches seen (2,666), plate appearances (693), games played, most pitches seen per plate appearance (3.85), steals of third (3) and batting average with the bases loaded (.500)
- Led NL center fielders in home runs

Chipper Jones

2001 Season

While the majority of Atlanta's offense sleep-walked through the 2001 campaign, Chipper Jones produced the best all-around performance of his career. Despite losing the speedy Rafael Furcal ahead of him in the lineup in early July, Jones became the first third baseman in major league history to register 100 RBI for six straight seasons. He also eclipsed his previous career high in batting average by 11 points, hit at least .320 from both sides of the plate and batted .310 or better both home and away.

Hitting

Jones has continued to mature and improve as a hitter. He has a great knowledge of the strike zone and maintains the confidence that he can succeed against any hurler. Always a clutch hitter, Jones batted .419 after September 1 and owned a .356 mark following the All-Star break. His 98 walks represent the second-highest total of his career, yet Jones didn't show his frustration by swinging at bad pitches when teams tried to pitch around him. A former Punch-and-Judy hitter when swinging righthanded, Jones now can drive the ball from either side due to a strenuous offseason conditioning program.

Baserunning & Defense

After struggling at third base in 2000, Jones was more consistent at the hot corner last year. Despite his improvement, he did see his first activity in left field since 1997 in order to give the lineup some added sock. Jones' excellent athleticism and strong arm enable him to play virtually anywhere. A smart baserunner who possessed above-average speed before a serious knee injury in 1995, he stole only nine bags and was caught 10 times last year.

2002 Outlook

Atlanta signed third baseman Vinny Castilla, which will force a move to left field for Jones. He is willing to play any position, but has said that he prefers to remain at one spot instead of moving around. No matter where he winds up, Jones is one of the game's premier hitters and an unheralded superstar on a national scale.

Position: 3B
Bats: B **Throws:** R
Ht: 6' 4" **Wt:** 210

Opening Day Age: 29
Born: 4/24/72 in DeLand, FL
ML Seasons: 8

Overall Statistics

	G	AB	R	H	D	T	HR	RBI	SB	BB	SO	Avg	OBP	Slg
2001	159	572	113	189	33	5	38	102	9	98	82	.330	.427	.605
Career	1094	4041	773	1240	237	23	227	737	106	652	609	.307	.400	.545

Where He Hits the Ball

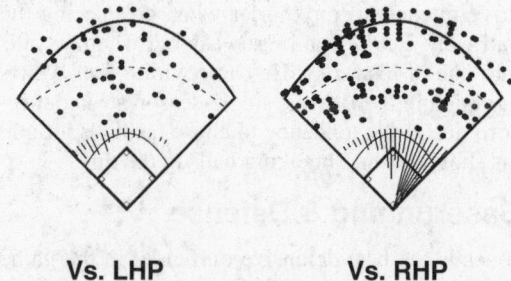

Vs. LHP   **Vs. RHP**

2001 Situational Stats

	AB	H	HR	RBI	Avg		AB	H	HR	RBI	Avg
Home	277	86	19	43	.310	LHP	109	41	8	27	.376
Road	295	103	19	59	.349	RHP	463	148	30	75	.320
First Half	305	94	25	65	.308	Sc Pos	113	36	7	61	.319
Scnd Half	267	95	13	37	.356	Clutch	84	26	4	10	.310

2001 Rankings (National League)

- 1st in batting average on the road
- Led the Braves in batting average, home runs, runs scored, hits, singles, doubles, triples, total bases (346), walks, intentional walks (20), times on base (289), slugging percentage, on-base percentage, HR frequency (15.1 ABs per HR), highest groundball-flyball ratio (1.3), highest percentage of pitches taken (55.1), batting average with runners in scoring position, batting average vs. lefthanded pitchers, batting average vs. righthanded pitchers, cleanup slugging percentage (.614) and batting average with two strikes (.217)
- Led NL third basemen in batting average

Brian Jordan

2001 Season

Brian Jordan provided leadership and steady contributions before coming through in several clutch situations down the stretch. His two home runs at Shea Stadium guided Atlanta to an improbable come-from-behind victory over the Mets on September 23. His ninth-inning grand slam six days later all but sealed the Braves' 10th consecutive division title. He equaled his career high for home runs and improved his batting average versus righthanders by 72 points over his 2000 mark.

Hitting

Jordan is the unquestioned spiritual leader of the Braves. He rises to the occasion and is capable of carrying the offensive load for an extended period. A former Pro Bowl safety with the Atlanta Falcons, Jordan plays the game with a football mentality and fights through injuries. He is one of the game's best fastball hitters and is strong enough to pull inside pitches. After constantly toying with his batting stance in 2000, Jordan returned to the basics and put together arguably his best all-around performance in 10 big league seasons.

Baserunning & Defense

Jordan blankets right field in a manner similar to the way he used to cover wide receivers. He uses his excellent speed to patrol the area between the gap and foul line, including the deep right-field alley at Turner Field, with relative ease. Jordan always is aggressive charging grounders and is not shy about trying to retire a pitcher at first base from right field. He committed just three errors in 2001 and led the Braves with 11 outfield assists—no easy task with Andruw Jones on the same club. Jordan also is an outstanding baserunner who puts constant pressure on the defense by taking the extra base every time the situation presents itself.

2002 Outlook

The Braves once wondered what to do with Jordan's hefty contract, but they now realize he's one of the game's best bargains when healthy. He avoided major injury last year and has averaged 146 games over the past four seasons. If the Braves are to win an 11th straight division title, Jordan once again will play a major role.

Position: RF
Bats: R **Throws:** R
Ht: 6' 1" **Wt:** 205

Opening Day Age: 35
Born: 3/29/67 in Baltimore, MD
ML Seasons: 10

Overall Statistics

	G	AB	R	H	D	T	HR	RBI	SB	BB	SO	Avg	OBP	Slg
2001	148	560	82	165	32	3	25	97	3	31	88	.295	.334	.496
Career	1077	3931	599	1128	208	31	149	656	112	259	622	.287	.337	.469

Where He Hits the Ball

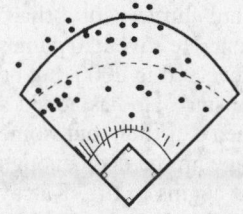
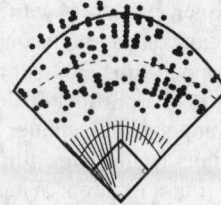

Vs. LHP   **Vs. RHP**

2001 Situational Stats

	AB	H	HR	RBI	Avg		AB	H	HR	RBI	Avg
Home	273	88	14	48	.322	LHP	113	33	8	31	.292
Road	287	77	11	49	.268	RHP	447	132	17	66	.295
First Half	299	85	11	50	.284	Sc Pos	153	44	9	71	.288
Scnd Half	261	80	14	47	.307	Clutch	82	25	5	19	.305

2001 Rankings (National League)

- 1st in highest percentage of extra bases taken as a runner (71.2)
- 2nd in fielding percentage in right field (.991)
- 3rd in assists in right field (11)
- 8th in lowest percentage of pitches taken (46.2)
- Led the Braves in GDPs (18), highest percentage of extra bases taken as a runner (71.2) and batting average at home

Steve Karsay

2001 Season

Steve Karsay experienced constant change last season. Expected to be a starter with Cleveland, he returned to the bullpen at the end of spring training. He then was traded with Steve Reed to Atlanta for John Rocker on June 22. Karsay was handed the closer's role with the Braves before losing the job to John Smoltz in late August. Karsay's best stretch came in his setup role with the Indians, where he posted a 1.25 ERA and allowed a .188 opponents batting average.

Pitching

Karsay owns one of the game's best arms but has had trouble keeping his right elbow healthy. He throws a 96-97 MPH fastball with above-average movement, along with a hard slurve with a sharp break that can be inconsistent. He saved 20 games as a part-time closer for Cleveland in 2000, but he harbors a burning desire to start. He has added a changeup and splitter when starting, but some scouts feel his repertoire may not be deep enough to join a rotation. When he begins to tire, Karsay leaves his pitches up in the strike zone, making him susceptible to the home-run ball.

Defense & Hitting

Karsay is a decent fielder with good hands who covers the area in front of the pitcher's mound from foul line to foul line. He also does a good job of covering first base. Runners can steal on the righthander, although his fastball enables catchers to nail many opposing basestealers. A career American Leaguer prior to joining Atlanta, Karsay's hitting abilities are untapped.

2002 Outlook

The Indians traded Karsay because of his pending free agency. The righthander had said that he wanted to sign with a team that will allow him to start. Yet he signed a four-year, $23 million deal with the Yankees, presumably to set up Mariano Rivera. The Flushing native still plays a key role for a talented team, and his incredible arm and intriguing potential may entice the Yankees to try him as a starter when Roger Clemens passes from the scene.

Position: RP
Bats: R **Throws:** R
Ht: 6' 3" **Wt:** 215

Opening Day Age: 30
Born: 3/24/72 in Flushing, NY
ML Seasons: 7
Pronunciation: CAR-say

Overall Statistics

	W	L	Pct.	ERA	G	GS	Sv	IP	H	BB	SO	HR	Ratio
2001	3	5	.375	2.35	74	0	8	88.0	73	25	83	5	1.11
Career	25	34	.424	4.00	243	40	29	477.1	495	157	370	44	1.37

How Often He Throws Strikes

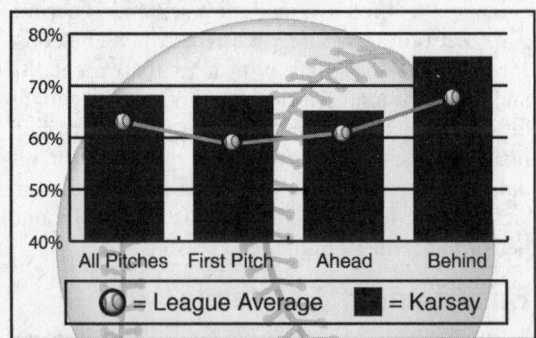

2001 Situational Stats

	W	L	ERA	Sv	IP		AB	H	HR	RBI	Avg
Home	0	2	1.52	3	41.1	LHB	148	38	2	8	.257
Road	3	3	3.09	5	46.2	RHB	172	35	3	18	.203
First Half	1	1	1.39	2	51.2	Sc Pos	64	14	0	18	.219
Scnd Half	2	4	3.72	6	36.1	Clutch	176	45	4	18	.256

2001 Rankings (National League)

- Led the Braves in first batter efficiency (.195) and relief losses (4)

Javy Lopez

2001 Season

Javy Lopez experienced numerous bumps and bruises throughout the season. He was hit in the head by Damian Jackson's bat in August before suffering a severely bruised toe in early September. He still managed to overcome a poor showing at the plate during the season's first five months to bat .377 in September. Lopez missed the last six games of the regular season as well as the Division Series due to a high left ankle sprain. But he showed his resiliency by hitting a two-run homer in the NLCS against Arizona.

Hitting

One of the game's best-hitting catchers, Lopez looked lost at the plate for much of last season. His .267 average was 23 points below his previous career norm, while his 82 strikeouts were three off his career high. He started chasing outside pitches in the dirt, a problem he had appeared to correct a few years ago. Lopez also displayed little patience and pressed when his average resided in the .245-.250 range at midseason. Despite showing a drop in home-run production, Lopez owns a potent bat and is capable of taking any pitcher deep, especially on low fastballs.

Baserunning & Defense

Criticized for his catching since arriving in the big leagues to stay in 1994, Lopez' work behind the plate regressed a bit last year. He retired less than 33 percent of opposing basestealers and committed 10 errors. He does a decent job of calling a game but is inconsistent with his footwork. Lopez has catcher's speed and a below-average baserunner. He did manage to steal his first base in three years last September.

2002 Outlook

Lopez has been a fixture in Atlanta's lineup for the past eight years. But he entered the offseason as a free agent looking for about $8 million per season. Atlanta appeared reluctant to reward Lopez with that type of deal, but the two sides finally agreed to a one-year, $6 million deal that gives Lopez a $7 million option for 2003. He'll be in Atlanta for at least one more season.

Position: C
Bats: R **Throws:** R
Ht: 6' 3" **Wt:** 200

Opening Day Age: 31
Born: 11/5/70 in Ponce, Puerto Rico
ML Seasons: 10
Pronunciation: HAH-vee LOE-pezz

Overall Statistics

	G	AB	R	H	D	T	HR	RBI	SB	BB	SO	Avg	OBP	Slg
2001	128	438	45	117	16	1	17	66	1	28	82	.267	.322	.425
Career	918	3199	388	917	146	11	160	533	8	212	575	.287	.335	.489

Where He Hits the Ball

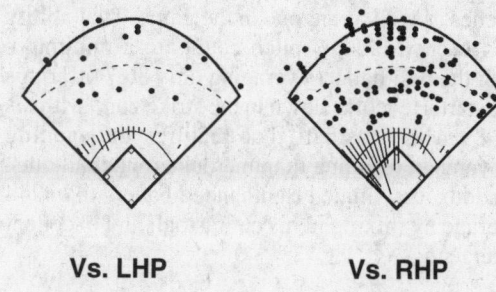

Vs. LHP   **Vs. RHP**

2001 Situational Stats

	AB	H	HR	RBI	Avg		AB	H	HR	RBI	Avg
Home	198	56	10	34	.283	LHP	85	18	5	11	.212
Road	240	61	7	32	.254	RHP	353	99	12	55	.280
First Half	263	66	9	35	.251	Sc Pos	119	33	5	49	.277
Scnd Half	175	51	8	31	.291	Clutch	71	22	4	13	.310

2001 Rankings (National League)

- 2nd in lowest fielding percentage at catcher (.989)
- 3rd in errors at catcher (10)
- Led the Braves in hit by pitch (10)

Greg Maddux

2001 Season

Greg Maddux was at his Cy Young Award-winning best during the first four months of the campaign. The righthander owned a 10-0 record and 2.45 ERA from June 5 to July 27, and went a record-breaking 72.1 innings without issuing a walk before finally relinquishing a free pass on August 12. However, Maddux didn't win a game after August 22. He failed to pick up a victory in his last 10 starts, including the playoffs.

Pitching

Maddux' approach to pitching has changed little in recent years. He continues to possess pinpoint control, allowing him to work ahead in the count on a constant basis. He confuses hitters by mixing his pitches as well as anyone in the game. That ability also keeps Maddux' pitch counts to a minimum, with the righthander averaging only 86.7 offerings per start. He works down in the strike zone with his 87-89 MPH fastball that features outstanding movement, resulting in numerous groundball outs. Maddux also limited righthanded batters to a .244 average by mixing in his cut fastball and excellent changeup.

Defense & Hitting

No pitcher has recorded more career putouts than Maddux, who swept the Gold Gloves for moundsmen throughout the 1990s. He picked up his 12th consecutive honor in 2001, joining just five other players in league history with a dozen or more Gold Glove Awards. The weakest aspect of his game always has been his ability to hold runners on base, a fact that led to a team-high 24 steals last year. Maddux helps himself at the plate as a capable bunter and adds the occasional hit.

2002 Outlook

Maddux no longer may be a perennial Cy Young candidate, but few pitchers are more consistent and productive than the Atlanta righthander. No one knows the game better than he does, and he can locate any of his pitches with uncanny accuracy at any time in the count. Since he has succeeded for several years without tremendous velocity, the 36-year-old Maddux should remain one of the game's better hurlers for the next few seasons.

Position: SP
Bats: R **Throws:** R
Ht: 6' 0" **Wt:** 185

Opening Day Age: 35
Born: 4/14/66 in San Angelo, TX
ML Seasons: 16
Pronunciation: MADD-ucks

Overall Statistics

	W	L	Pct.	ERA	G	GS	Sv	IP	H	BB	SO	HR	Ratio
2001	17	11	.607	3.05	34	34	0	233.0	220	27	173	20	1.06
Career	257	146	.638	2.84	505	501	0	3551.0	3206	760	2523	196	1.12

How Often He Throws Strikes

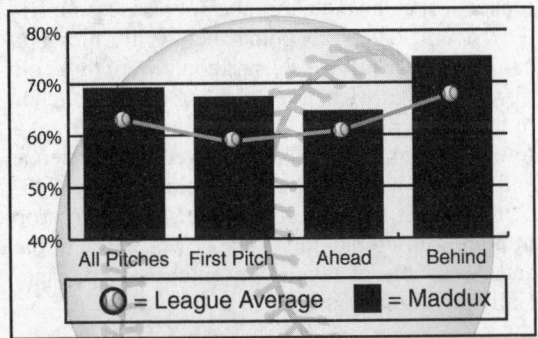

◐ = League Average   ■ = Maddux

2001 Situational Stats

	W	L	ERA	Sv	IP		AB	H	HR	RBI	Avg
Home	10	4	2.78	0	136.0	LHB	402	106	11	40	.264
Road	7	7	3.43	0	97.0	RHB	468	114	9	37	.244
First Half	10	5	2.41	0	127.0	Sc Pos	174	42	2	53	.241
Scnd Half	7	6	3.82	0	106.0	Clutch	67	11	1	3	.164

2001 Rankings (National League)

- 1st in shutouts (3), fewest pitches thrown per batter (3.18) and fewest walks per nine innings (1.0)
- 2nd in stolen bases allowed (24) and highest strikeout-walk ratio (6.4)
- 3rd in runners caught stealing (14)
- 4th in ERA, games started, innings pitched and lowest on-base percentage allowed (.278)
- Led the Braves in wins, complete games (3), innings pitched, hits allowed, hit batsmen (7), stolen bases allowed (24), runners caught stealing (14), highest strikeout-walk ratio (6.4), lowest on-base percentage allowed (.278), highest groundball-flyball ratio allowed (1.8) and lowest ERA at home

Kevin Millwood

2001 Season

Kevin Millwood had the heart cut out of his 2001 season when he spent 73 days on the disabled list with an inflamed right labrum in his shoulder. The injury prevented him from throwing the ball with any zip and led to 21 earned runs in his first 38.1 innings. He began to look stronger in mid-August. He won six of 10 decisions and posted a 4.03 ERA during the season's final two and a half months.

Pitching

For most of the campaign, Millwood didn't look like the power pitcher who had averaged 7.8 strikeouts per nine innings during his first four years in the majors. His shoulder ailment stole much of the heat from his mid-90s fastball and hard slider. It also hurt the consistency of his breaking ball and changeup. In addition, the injury and subsequent layoff affected his control. Millwood was on pace to eclipse his career high of 62 walks and wound up with five wild pitches. He continues to leave his pitches up in the strike zone, surrendering 20 home runs and producing a poor groundball-flyball ratio of 0.88.

Defense & Hitting

Millwood is one of the league's better fielders and did not commit an error last season. He does a decent job of holding runners on base but permitted 13 steals in 121 innings. He is a fair hitter who is capable of driving the ball when he manages to make contact.

2002 Outlook

A poor five-month stretch in 2000, followed by last year's injury-marred campaign, has led to back-to-back disappointing seasons for Millwood. Once considered a prime candidate to fill John Smoltz' power spot in the rotation, Millwood needs to prove his long-term worth this year. At age 27, he still has the ability to return to his 1999 form when he won 18 games with a 2.68 ERA. He must stay off the disabled list, however.

Position: SP
Bats: R **Throws:** R
Ht: 6' 4" **Wt:** 220

Opening Day Age: 27
Born: 12/24/74 in Gastonia, NC
ML Seasons: 5

Overall Statistics

	W	L	Pct.	ERA	G	GS	Sv	IP	H	BB	SO	HR	Ratio
2001	7	7	.500	4.31	21	21	0	121.0	121	40	84	20	1.33
Career	57	38	.600	3.86	133	126	0	787.1	732	238	662	89	1.23

How Often He Throws Strikes

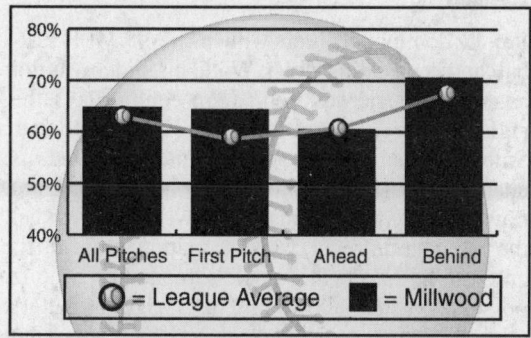

◎ = League Average   ■ = Millwood

2001 Situational Stats

	W	L	ERA	Sv	IP		AB	H	HR	RBI	Avg
Home	4	6	4.07	0	73.0	LHB	195	55	7	20	.282
Road	3	1	4.69	0	48.0	RHB	270	66	13	37	.244
First Half	1	3	4.93	0	38.1	Sc Pos	103	29	5	38	.282
Scnd Half	6	4	4.03	0	82.2	Clutch	9	2	0	1	.222

2001 Rankings (National League)
- Led the Braves in wild pitches (5)

John Smoltz

2001 Season

With the Braves' bullpen providing more questions than answers throughout most of the 1990s, there had been rumors for several seasons regarding the possibility of John Smoltz moving from the rotation to the closer's role. The shift finally became a reality during the second half of 2001. Battling back from Tommy John surgery that cost him all of 2000, the righthander went 2-2 with a 5.76 ERA in five starts and was on the disabled list with elbow and shoulder pain from June 10 to July 22. He moved to the bullpen upon his return and posted 10 saves in 11 opportunities while registering a 1.59 ERA during the season's final two months.

Pitching

Smoltz dominated hitters with his 97-98 MPH fastball and devastating slider. While his slider was not as sharp when he was used on consecutive days, the righthander's heater maintained its velocity. Smoltz picked up a knuckleball and improved his changeup in 1999 before undergoing surgery, but now he is focusing on his two power pitches to get the job done in relief. Making matters more difficult for hitters is the closer's mentality Smoltz possesses, which allows him to go right at batters with his impeccable control and overpowering stuff.

Defense & Hitting

Smoltz is an outstanding athlete who could have played college basketball. He has soft hands and good quickness off the mound and covers first base as well as any pitcher. He also takes considerable pride in his hitting, though that ability will not be called upon frequently in his new role.

2002 Outlook

Smoltz took himself off the free-agent market and signed a three-year, $30 million deal with Atlanta in early December. The Braves also have an option for 2005. Even though he would be an asset to most rotations, Smoltz instead will be a premier closer. He also becomes the highest-paid stopper in the game. The scary part is that most pitchers are much stronger in their second year after undergoing Tommy John surgery. The stage may be set for the second coming of Dennis Eckersley.

Position: RP
Bats: R **Throws:** R
Ht: 6' 3" **Wt:** 220

Opening Day Age: 34
Born: 5/15/67 in Warren, MI
ML Seasons: 13

Overall Statistics

	W	L	Pct.	ERA	G	GS	Sv	IP	H	BB	SO	HR	Ratio
2001	3	3	.500	3.36	36	5	10	59.0	53	10	57	7	1.07
Career	160	116	.580	3.35	392	361	10	2473.1	2145	784	2155	202	1.18

How Often He Throws Strikes

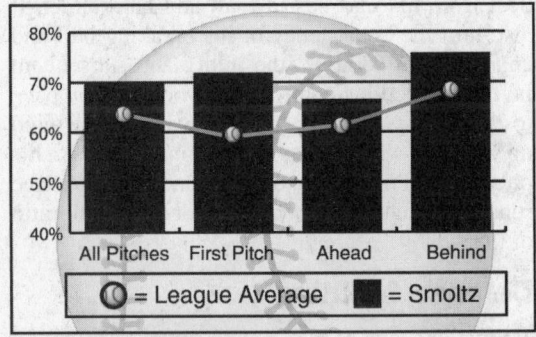

2001 Situational Stats

	W	L	ERA	Sv	IP		AB	H	HR	RBI	Avg
Home	1	1	3.80	4	23.2	LHB	114	30	4	12	.263
Road	2	2	3.06	6	35.1	RHB	109	23	3	12	.211
First Half	2	2	5.76	0	25.0	Sc Pos	48	11	1	16	.229
Scnd Half	1	1	1.59	10	34.0	Clutch	70	11	2	4	.157

2001 Rankings (National League)

- Did not rank near the top or bottom in any category

B.J. Surhoff

2001 Season

The Braves didn't get the offense they were hoping B.J. Surhoff would provide last year. The left fielder experienced a significant drop in production in the middle of Atlanta's lineup. His 10 homers and 58 RBI represented his lowest totals since 1994. He also batted .270 with runners in scoring position, 27 points below his career norm. After driving in at least 80 runs every year between 1996 and 1999, Surhoff has generated only 69 RBI in 612 at-bats with the Braves the past two seasons.

Hitting

Surhoff was a clutch hitter during his days in the American League. He knows how to coerce base hits out of pitchers by extending at-bats and hitting his pitch when he's in a groove. While his power is now below average for a corner outfielder, he remains capable of hitting the ball to all fields. His swing appears to have slowed over the past two years, though he still has quick wrists that allow him to pull righthanded pitchers. A career .289 hitter versus lefties entering last season, Surhoff batted a meager .219 against southpaws in 2001.

Baserunning & Defense

Surhoff is a mediocre outfielder whose range is overshadowed by Andruw Jones' gap-to-gap coverage in center field. Surhoff also has an accurate but below-average arm that is incapable of throwing out runners at home from anywhere but the shallowest part of left field. Years of catching are taking their toll on Surhoff's speed on the basepaths, but his intelligence makes him a slightly better than average baserunner.

2002 Outlook

It is no secret that the 37-year-old Surhoff is in the waning stages of his major league career. His production is to the point where he needs to sit at least once or twice per week. If he remains with the Braves, he probably will sit even more. Atlanta has signed Vinny Castilla to play third base, and Chipper Jones will take over in left. Surhoff never has seemed to enjoy playing in Atlanta since the Braves acquired him from Baltimore at the trade deadline in 2000. A new team might be the best scenario for everyone concerned.

Position: LF
Bats: L **Throws:** R
Ht: 6' 1" **Wt:** 200

Opening Day Age: 37
Born: 8/4/64 in Bronx, NY
ML Seasons: 15

Overall Statistics

	G	AB	R	H	D	T	HR	RBI	SB	BB	SO	Avg	OBP	Slg
2001	141	484	68	131	33	1	10	58	9	38	48	.271	.321	.405
Career	2004	7218	946	2026	392	39	170	1019	136	561	727	.281	.331	.416

Where He Hits the Ball

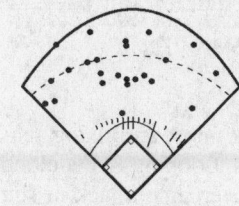 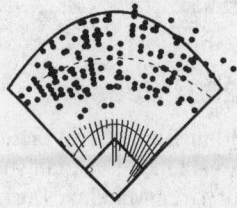

Vs. LHP   **Vs. RHP**

2001 Situational Stats

	AB	H	HR	RBI	Avg		AB	H	HR	RBI	Avg
Home	246	63	5	25	.256	LHP	73	16	0	10	.219
Road	238	68	5	33	.286	RHP	411	115	10	48	.280
First Half	253	71	5	38	.281	Sc Pos	115	31	1	43	.270
Scnd Half	231	60	5	20	.260	Clutch	71	19	0	13	.268

2001 Rankings (National League)
- 2nd in fielding percentage in left field (.986)
- 4th in assists in left field (8)
- Led the Braves in doubles, lowest percentage of swings that missed (10.3), highest percentage of swings put into play (49.9) and lowest percentage of swings on the first pitch (29.0)

Atlanta

John Burkett

Position: SP
Bats: R **Throws:** R
Ht: 6' 3" **Wt:** 215

Opening Day Age: 37
Born: 11/28/64 in New Brighton, PA
ML Seasons: 13
Pronunciation: BURK-it

Overall Statistics

	W	L	Pct.	ERA	G	GS	Sv	IP	H	BB	SO	HR	Ratio
2001	12	12	.500	3.04	34	34	0	219.1	187	70	187	17	1.17
Career	141	119	.542	4.23	384	364	1	2293.2	2465	603	1535	212	1.34

2001 Situational Stats

	W	L	ERA	Sv	IP		AB	H	HR	RBI	Avg
Home	4	6	3.58	0	100.2	LHB	367	82	9	32	.223
Road	8	6	2.58	0	118.2	RHB	446	105	8	44	.235
First Half	6	6	2.49	0	126.2	Sc Pos	166	36	2	50	.217
Scnd Half	6	6	3.79	0	92.2	Clutch	39	8	1	1	.205

2001 Season

John Burkett had one of the most surprising seasons among veteran starters. Looking like a clone of Greg Maddux, Burkett overcame a lack of run support to post his highest win total since 1995. The righthander did falter late in the year, going 0-4 with a 6.21 ERA over one five-game stretch.

Pitching, Defense & Hitting

The key to Burkett's success was improved conditioning that resulted in greater arm strength and allowed him to go deeper in games. He also emulated Maddux by throwing his two-seam fastball with excellent movement about 75 percent of the time, which enabled him to get ahead in counts. He kept hitters off-balance by mixing speeds with his solid cut fastball, mediocre curveball and four-seam fastball. Burkett led the NL in pickoff throws to first base. He didn't commit an error, but he is a marginal fielder who does not do a good job covering first base. He is nothing special as a hitter.

2002 Outlook

A free agent for the second time in as many seasons, Burkett should create significant demand this time. Still, while he turned his career around in 2001, Burkett is 37 years of age and rarely has been consistent for extended periods over his big league career.

Jose Cabrera

Position: RP
Bats: R **Throws:** R
Ht: 6' 0" **Wt:** 180

Opening Day Age: 30
Born: 3/24/72 in Santiago, Dominican Republic
ML Seasons: 5

Overall Statistics

	W	L	Pct.	ERA	G	GS	Sv	IP	H	BB	SO	HR	Ratio
2001	7	4	.636	2.88	55	0	2	59.1	52	25	43	5	1.30
Career	13	7	.650	3.81	148	0	4	167.2	160	58	131	19	1.30

2001 Situational Stats

	W	L	ERA	Sv	IP		AB	H	HR	RBI	Avg
Home	5	3	2.25	0	32.0	LHB	89	22	4	20	.247
Road	2	1	3.62	2	27.1	RHB	129	30	1	12	.233
First Half	5	2	1.10	2	32.2	Sc Pos	62	15	2	28	.242
Scnd Half	2	2	5.06	0	26.2	Clutch	84	24	2	13	.286

2001 Season

Jose Cabrera went from one extreme to the other in a couple of ways last year. Placed on waivers by Houston on April 2, he was picked up by Atlanta less than two weeks later and emerged as the Braves' top righthanded reliever by the second week of May. Cabrera tossed 13 straight scoreless innings from June 17 to July 16, but allowed 15 runs in 25.2 innings (5.26 ERA) the remainder of the season.

Pitching, Defense & Hitting

When in a groove, Cabrera has a 93-MPH fastball with a good splitter and decent changeup. He displays an aggressive attitude and is not afraid to challenge hitters, regardless of the situation. The righthander gets in trouble when he starts to be too fine with his heater, thereby reducing its velocity by 4-5 MPH while losing most of its movement. He is an average fielder and can be slow covering first base. Cabrera also has not recorded a hit in four major league at-bats.

2002 Outlook

Cabrera went from a key component in the bullpen to being left off Atlanta's playoff roster. He showed enough promise during his first three months with the Braves to earn another extended look in the bullpen.

Keith Lockhart

Position: 2B
Bats: L **Throws:** R
Ht: 5'10" **Wt:** 170

Opening Day Age: 37
Born: 11/10/64 in Whittier, CA
ML Seasons: 8

Overall Statistics

	G	AB	R	H	D	T	HR	RBI	SB	BB	SO	Avg	OBP	Slg
2001	104	178	17	39	6	0	3	12	1	16	22	.219	.289	.303
Career	789	1877	238	504	99	13	36	228	30	155	199	.269	.324	.393

2001 Situational Stats

	AB	H	HR	RBI	Avg		AB	H	HR	RBI	Avg
Home	99	21	0	3	.212	LHP	9	1	0	0	.111
Road	79	18	3	9	.228	RHP	169	38	3	12	.225
First Half	86	22	1	5	.256	Sc Pos	32	6	1	9	.188
Scnd Half	92	17	2	7	.185	Clutch	37	11	0	3	.297

2001 Season

Manager Bobby Cox turned to Keith Lockhart for much of August after Quilvio Veras was released and before rookie Marcus Giles got the nod down the stretch. Lockhart finished with a .219 batting average, easily his lowest mark since 1994. Nevertheless, the versatile utilityman led the Braves with 15 pinch-hits and did not commit an error in 319 innings split between second and third base.

Hitting, Baserunning & Defense

Lockhart is capable of hitting all kinds of pitching. He makes consistent contact, uses the entire field, and is equally effective as a starter or off the bench. He also drives the ball well from the left side, surprising more than a few pitchers with the occasional longball. Defensively, Lockhart has soft hands, a strong arm and decent range. The 37-year-old does not have great speed, but he almost never makes a mistake on the basepaths and is capable of taking the extra base due to his feel for the game.

2002 Outlook

Cox loves veteran players like Lockhart, who gives the manager a solid backup should something go wrong with a young starter like Giles. The Braves' roster will have a new look in 2002, but Lockhart should be a holdover due to his steadying influence and wide variety of contributions.

Jason Marquis

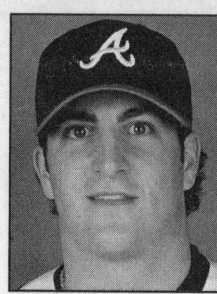

Position: RP/SP
Bats: L **Throws:** R
Ht: 6' 1" **Wt:** 185

Opening Day Age: 23
Born: 8/21/78 in Manhasset, NY
ML Seasons: 2
Pronunciation: mar-KEE

Overall Statistics

	W	L	Pct.	ERA	G	GS	Sv	IP	H	BB	SO	HR	Ratio
2001	5	6	.455	3.48	38	16	0	129.1	113	59	98	14	1.33
Career	6	6	.500	3.71	53	16	0	152.2	136	71	115	18	1.36

2001 Situational Stats

	W	L	ERA	Sv	IP		AB	H	HR	RBI	Avg
Home	1	5	4.66	0	56.0	LHB	186	41	8	23	.220
Road	4	1	2.58	0	73.1	RHB	296	72	6	32	.243
First Half	2	3	4.42	0	59.0	Sc Pos	111	27	2	39	.243
Scnd Half	3	3	2.69	0	70.1	Clutch	39	5	2	2	.128

2001 Season

Jason Marquis bounced between the rotation and bullpen in 2001, making 16 starts and 22 relief appearances. He was quite effective while replacing the injured Odalis Perez between late July and early September. Marquis allowed three earned runs or less in each of his last 10 starts.

Pitching, Defense & Hitting

Marquis' four-seam fastball resides in the mid-90s and has outstanding movement. The righthander's slider and changeup also are above-average, but his command of all his offerings leaves a lot to be desired. Some scouts are concerned about the way Marquis whips his pitches, a trait that could lead to shoulder problems. Others question his maturity and poise, though the Braves feel those traits will improve with experience. His hitting ability and glovework are not good. He committed three errors and posted a .909 fielding percentage last year.

2002 Outlook

Marquis has a great arm and exhibits aggressiveness on the mound, important ingredients to becoming a power pitcher. Atlanta is hoping this is the year Marquis steps up and claims either the fourth or fifth slot in its rotation. He has shown flashes of his considerable potential over the past two seasons and should be ready to make his move.

Atlanta

Dave Martinez

Position: RF/LF/1B
Bats: L **Throws:** L
Ht: 5'10" **Wt:** 175

Opening Day Age: 37
Born: 9/26/64 in New York, NY
ML Seasons: 16

Overall Statistics

	G	AB	R	H	D	T	HR	RBI	SB	BB	SO	Avg	OBP	Slg
2001	120	237	33	68	11	3	2	20	3	21	44	.287	.347	.384
Career	1919	5795	795	1599	238	72	91	580	183	567	893	.276	.341	.389

2001 Situational Stats

	AB	H	HR	RBI	Avg		AB	H	HR	RBI	Avg
Home	104	27	0	8	.260	LHP	35	9	0	3	.257
Road	133	41	2	12	.308	RHP	202	59	2	17	.292
First Half	134	44	0	11	.328	Sc Pos	59	12	1	18	.203
Scnd Half	103	24	2	9	.233	Clutch	64	25	0	1	.391

2001 Season

A bothersome right knee and a lack of production led to Dave Martinez getting his fewest at-bats in any full season since 1986. The veteran outfielder took two cortisone shots in his knee during the final two months, which contributed to a .233 batting average after the All-Star break. He still led Atlanta with 65 pinch-hit appearances, coming through with 13 hits. His .308 average on the road was second on the team to Chipper Jones' .349 mark.

Hitting, Baserunning & Defense

Martinez is a line-drive hitter who is a capable reserve at all three outfield positions. He has minimal power but can put the ball in play and will not hurt a team when one of the starters needs a night off. At age 37, Martinez no longer possesses plus speed, although he remains a good baserunner and can cover an adequate amount of real estate in the outfield. His arm remains one of his best tools, resulting in eight assists last year.

2002 Outlook

The Braves had coveted Martinez for several seasons and inked him to a two-year, $3 million deal prior to the 2001 campaign. He will return as Atlanta's fourth outfielder and be the top lefthanded hitter off manager Bobby Cox' bench.

Kevin McGlinchy

Position: RP
Bats: R **Throws:** R
Ht: 6'5" **Wt:** 220

Opening Day Age: 24
Born: 6/28/77 in Malden, MA
ML Seasons: 2

Overall Statistics

	W	L	Pct.	ERA	G	GS	Sv	IP	H	BB	SO	HR	Ratio
2001				Did Not Play									
Career	7	3	.700	2.75	74	0	0	78.2	77	36	76	7	1.44

2001 Situational Stats

	W	L	ERA	Sv	IP		AB	H	HR	RBI	Avg
Home	—	—	—	—	—	LHB	—	—	—	—	—
Road	—	—	—	—	—	RHB	—	—	—	—	—
First Half	—	—	—	—	—	Sc Pos	—	—	—	—	—
Scnd Half	—	—	—	—	—	Clutch	—	—	—	—	—

2001 Season

After battling shoulder tendinitis and pitching 8.1 major league innings in 2000, Kevin McGlinchy suffered a partial tear in his shoulder cartilage last spring and required surgery. Despite undergoing an arthroscopic procedure to repair the cartilage and shave a bone spur, McGlinchy made just two one-inning appearances in the Gulf Coast League.

Pitching, Defense & Hitting

McGlinchy throws two overpowering pitches that can overwhelm righthanders. Prior to undergoing surgery, his four-seam fastball was consistently in the mid-90s. His sharp-breaking slider looked eerily similar to his heater before diving into the dirt, usually too late for hitters who had committed to swinging at the fastball. A lack of concentration plagued McGlinchy as a starter but rarely affected him as a reliever. A good athlete, he fields his position well and was a decent hitter in the minors.

2002 Outlook

The Devil Rays selected McGlinchy in the Rule 5 draft in December. The righthander feels he has been jinxed since making the jump from the Class-A ranks to the majors three years ago. If healthy, he has the stuff and ability to make a strong impression on his new team.

Odalis Perez

Position: SP
Bats: L **Throws:** L
Ht: 6' 0" **Wt:** 150

Opening Day Age: 23
Born: 6/6/78 in La Matas de Farfan, Dominican Republic
ML Seasons: 3
Pronunciation: oh-DALL-iss

Overall Statistics

	W	L	Pct.	ERA	G	GS	Sv	IP	H	BB	SO	HR	Ratio
2001	7	8	.467	4.91	24	16	0	95.1	108	39	71	7	1.54
Career	11	15	.423	5.38	52	33	0	199.0	218	96	158	20	1.58

2001 Situational Stats

	W	L	ERA	Sv	IP		AB	H	HR	RBI	Avg
Home	3	4	5.15	0	50.2	LHB	73	25	5	14	.342
Road	4	4	4.63	0	44.2	RHB	299	83	2	30	.278
First Half	6	6	4.48	0	80.1	Sc Pos	89	28	2	34	.315
Scnd Half	1	2	7.20	0	15.0	Clutch	19	6	0	1	.316

2001 Season

Odalis Perez mixed poor appearances out of the bullpen with sometimes impressive stints as a starter. While the lefthander produced an 8.31 ERA as a reliever, he was 6-6 with a 4.57 ERA in 16 starts. He missed significant time in the season's second half with a cut on his pitching hand.

Pitching, Defense & Hitting

Perez possesses great talent, but he attracts criticism for his lackadaisical approach to the game. His best pitch is a 92-94 MPH four-seam fastball that moves down and in to righthanded hitters and down and away from lefthanders. Perez' slider also is a plus pitch, and his overall command is good. He struggles with his mechanics as well as his curveball, which was his best offering in the minors. Perez is a slow starter who experienced some trouble in the first inning last year. He is a good fielder and a respectable hitter for a pitcher.

2002 Outlook

With John Smoltz moving to the bullpen and the Braves looking to fill another spot in the rotation, Perez couldn't be in a better situation in 2002. Atlanta has been waiting for Perez to take his game to the next level, but inconsistency has been his albatross. Should he fail to grab the job once again, his days with the Braves could be numbered.

Steve Reed

Position: RP
Bats: R **Throws:** R
Ht: 6' 2" **Wt:** 212

Opening Day Age: 36
Born: 3/11/66 in Los Angeles, CA
ML Seasons: 10

Overall Statistics

	W	L	Pct.	ERA	G	GS	Sv	IP	H	BB	SO	HR	Ratio
2001	3	3	.500	3.55	70	0	1	58.1	52	23	46	6	1.29
Career	38	26	.594	3.67	607	0	17	641.2	583	217	488	84	1.25

2001 Situational Stats

	W	L	ERA	Sv	IP		AB	H	HR	RBI	Avg
Home	2	1	3.30	0	30.0	LHB	52	27	5	13	.519
Road	1	2	3.81	1	28.1	RHB	168	25	1	11	.149
First Half	3	1	2.80	0	35.1	Sc Pos	68	13	0	15	.191
Scnd Half	0	2	4.70	1	23.0	Clutch	43	13	0	5	.302

2001 Season

Steve Reed arrived with Steve Karsay from Cleveland on June 22 in exchange for John Rocker. Reed battled a strained right elbow in late August that may have contributed to his streakiness as a Brave. The righthander did not allow an earned run in his first eight games with Atlanta. He then surrendered seven earned runs over his next nine outings before putting together a 12-game scoreless stretch.

Pitching, Defense & Hitting

Reed used to be one of the premier middle relievers in the game. He now excels as a situational pitcher, which meshes perfectly with manager Bobby Cox' style. Reed held righthanded hitters to a .149 average last year by employing a sweeping slider with his near-submarine delivery. He also throws a mid-80s fastball and a changeup. He is not afraid to pitch inside. He is an excellent fielder and uses a quick delivery to throw off the timing of would-be basestealers.

2002 Outlook

The Braves gave opposing hitters completely different looks in the late innings with Reed and John Smoltz. At age 36, Reed is not as dominating as he used to be and has trouble getting lefthanded batters out. Still, the free agent fills an important role and should re-sign with the Braves.

Atlanta

Mike Remlinger

Position: RP
Bats: L **Throws:** L
Ht: 6' 1" **Wt:** 210

Opening Day Age: 36
Born: 3/23/66 in Middletown, NY
ML Seasons: 9
Pronunciation: rem-lin-JURR

Overall Statistics

	W	L	Pct.	ERA	G	GS	Sv	IP	H	BB	SO	HR	Ratio
2001	3	3	.500	2.76	74	0	1	75.0	67	23	93	9	1.20
Career	37	38	.493	3.99	366	59	16	643.1	576	321	613	77	1.39

2001 Situational Stats

	W	L	ERA	Sv	IP		AB	H	HR	RBI	Avg
Home	2	2	3.34	1	35.0	LHB	90	29	4	17	.322
Road	1	1	2.25	0	40.0	RHB	196	38	5	13	.194
First Half	3	1	2.88	0	50.0	Sc Pos	60	14	2	21	.233
Scnd Half	0	2	2.52	1	25.0	Clutch	173	40	4	17	.231

2001 Season

After two outstanding seasons in the Atlanta bullpen, Mike Remlinger experienced difficulty with his consistency and gave up nine home runs in 2001. The lefty took over the eighth-inning setup job from Kerry Ligtenberg in April and was leading the National League in holds before elbow tendinitis affected his performance the last two months. He still managed to lead the team with 74 appearances and limited opponents to a .234 average.

Pitching, Defense & Hitting

Remlinger is an unheralded hurler featuring a low-90s fastball, an effective changeup and a late-breaking slider. He goes right after hitters and uses his good control to work ahead in the count most of the time. He dominated righthanded hitters once again by constantly jamming them inside and holding them to a .194 average. Remlinger is an average fielder who quiets the running game. He allowed just one stolen base for the second straight season. Thankfully, as a career .075 hitter, he rarely steps into the batter's box.

2002 Outlook

The Braves picked up their $2 million option on Remlinger. He is one of the most important components of the team and should complement the team's closer, John Smoltz.

Rey Sanchez

Position: SS
Bats: R **Throws:** R
Ht: 5' 9" **Wt:** 175

Opening Day Age: 34
Born: 10/5/67 in Rio Piedras, Puerto Rico
ML Seasons: 11
Pronunciation: RAY SAN-chezz

Overall Statistics

	G	AB	R	H	D	T	HR	RBI	SB	BB	SO	Avg	OBP	Slg
2001	149	544	56	153	18	6	0	37	11	15	49	.281	.300	.336
Career	1167	3821	440	1047	158	24	12	300	51	182	407	.274	.311	.337

2001 Situational Stats

	AB	H	HR	RBI	Avg		AB	H	HR	RBI	Avg
Home	260	77	0	23	.296	LHP	133	34	0	9	.256
Road	284	76	0	14	.268	RHP	411	119	0	28	.290
First Half	331	96	0	22	.290	Sc Pos	114	31	0	34	.272
Scnd Half	213	57	0	15	.268	Clutch	76	15	0	5	.197

2001 Season

With Rafael Furcal lost for the season, the Braves acquired Rey Sanchez as an emergency replacement for the stretch drive. Sanchez had been a .303 hitter for Kansas City and had strung together a 21-game hitting streak during the first half. But he struggled against National League pitchers while committing only three errors in 48 games.

Hitting, Baserunning & Defense

Atlanta general manager John Schuerholz said before the playoffs that Sanchez had the best hands of any Braves shortstop he had seen. He makes most of the routine plays and turns the double play well, but his strong range is limited by an average arm. Sanchez is a free swinger at the plate with little power and discipline. He shined as the No. 2 hitter for Kansas City, but had difficulty finding success batting seventh and eighth for Atlanta. He is a decent bunter and can execute the hit-and-run. His baserunning skills are modest.

2002 Outlook

A free agent, Sanchez was looking to cash in on a big payday before he revealed his average hitting skills with the Braves. His days in Atlanta probably are over, but the 34-year-old should find a starting job for a non-contender looking to solidify its infield defense.

Other Atlanta Braves

Kurt Abbott (**Pos**: 2B, **Age**: 32, **Bats**: R)

	G	AB	R	H	D	T	HR	RBI	SB	BB	SO	Avg	OBP	Slg
2001	6	9	0	2	0	0	0	0	1	0	3	.222	.222	.222
Career	702	2044	273	523	109	23	62	242	22	133	571	.256	.305	.423

Abbott missed most of last season due to hernia surgery. If healthy, he has enough power and versatility to be an asset on some team's bench. 2002 Outlook: B

Cory Aldridge (**Pos**: RF, **Age**: 22, **Bats**: L)

	G	AB	R	H	D	T	HR	RBI	SB	BB	SO	Avg	OBP	Slg
2001	8	5	1	0	0	0	0	0	0	0	4	.000	.000	.000
Career	8	5	1	0	0	0	0	0	0	0	4	.000	.000	.000

In his five at-bats with the Braves, Aldridge took four strikes, swung and missed seven times, fouled off two pitches, put one pitch in play, and took no balls. Yikes. His average has been dropping. 2002 Outlook: C

Paul Bako (**Pos**: C, **Age**: 29, **Bats**: L)

	G	AB	R	H	D	T	HR	RBI	SB	BB	SO	Avg	OBP	Slg
2001	61	137	19	29	10	1	2	15	1	20	34	.212	.312	.343
Career	311	878	76	217	46	4	9	82	3	96	237	.247	.319	.339

Bako spent last year as Javy Lopez' backup. It could happen again, as both Lopez and Bako have re-signed. 2002 Outlook: B

Rico Brogna (**Pos**: 1B, **Age**: 31, **Bats**: L)

	G	AB	R	H	D	T	HR	RBI	SB	BB	SO	Avg	OBP	Slg
2001	72	206	15	51	9	0	3	21	3	14	46	.248	.297	.335
Career	848	2958	379	795	176	13	106	458	32	227	655	.269	.320	.445

Brogna's decline was swift and dramatic. After driving in more than 100 runs in 1998 and '99, his power evaporated the past two years. Though he said he retired last July, he didn't close the door entirely. 2002 Outlook: D

Ken Caminiti (**Pos**: 3B/1B, **Age**: 38, **Bats**: B)

	G	AB	R	H	D	T	HR	RBI	SB	BB	SO	Avg	OBP	Slg
2001	118	356	36	81	17	1	15	41	0	43	85	.228	.312	.407
Career	1760	6288	894	1710	348	17	239	983	88	727	1163	.272	.347	.447

Hampered by hamstring injuries, Caminiti was released by Texas in early July and did little after signing in Atlanta. The 38-year-old's future is in doubt after a November arrest for drug possession. 2002 Outlook: C

Mark DeRosa (**Pos**: SS, **Age**: 27, **Bats**: R)

	G	AB	R	H	D	T	HR	RBI	SB	BB	SO	Avg	OBP	Slg
2001	66	164	27	47	8	0	3	20	2	12	19	.287	.350	.390
Career	100	188	38	52	9	0	3	23	2	14	23	.277	.340	.372

With Rafael Furcal and Marcus Giles having shown what they can do, and with prospect Wilson Betemit headed for possible stardom, it'll be difficult for DeRosa to land more than a utility job. 2002 Outlook: B

Julio Franco (**Pos**: 1B, **Age**: 40, **Bats**: R)

	G	AB	R	H	D	T	HR	RBI	SB	BB	SO	Avg	OBP	Slg
2001	25	90	13	27	4	0	3	11	0	10	20	.300	.376	.444
Career	1916	7334	1117	2204	339	47	144	992	260	763	1026	.301	.366	.418

Franco had played in Japan and Mexico since 1998, but the Braves' problems at first base prompted them to sign him for their stretch drive. While he didn't fare all that poorly, Franco still is older than Methuselah. 2002 Outlook: B

Jesse Garcia (**Pos**: 2B, **Age**: 28, **Bats**: R)

	G	AB	R	H	D	T	HR	RBI	SB	BB	SO	Avg	OBP	Slg
2001	22	5	3	1	0	0	0	0	6	0	1	.200	.200	.200
Career	53	51	11	8	0	0	2	2	6	4	6	.157	.218	.275

Garcia came to the Braves in an offseason deal with the Orioles in December 2000. He doesn't do anything particularly well on offense and is no real prospect, but he does offer versatility. 2002 Outlook: C

Bernard Gilkey (**Pos**: LF, **Age**: 35, **Bats**: R)

	G	AB	R	H	D	T	HR	RBI	SB	BB	SO	Avg	OBP	Slg
2001	69	106	8	29	6	0	2	14	0	11	31	.274	.339	.387
Career	1239	4061	606	1115	244	24	118	546	115	466	708	.275	.352	.434

Gilkey endured personal problems and a strained quadriceps, but boosted his batting average nearly 100 points over a subpar 2000. However, his current legal troubles stemming from another DUI incident could carry over to this season. 2002 Outlook: C

Wes Helms (**Pos**: 1B/3B, **Age**: 25, **Bats**: R)

	G	AB	R	H	D	T	HR	RBI	SB	BB	SO	Avg	OBP	Slg
2001	100	216	28	48	10	3	10	36	1	21	56	.222	.293	.435
Career	113	234	30	53	11	3	11	38	1	21	62	.226	.292	.440

Helms had a chance to claim the Braves' first-base job last year but didn't seize it. He has decent power and can play a few positions, but may not possess the total offensive package to play every day. 2002 Outlook: B

Kerry Ligtenberg (**Pos**: RHP, **Age**: 30)

	W	L	Pct.	ERA	G	GS	Sv	IP	H	BB	SO	HR	Ratio
2001	3	3	.500	3.02	53	0	1	59.2	50	30	56	4	1.34
Career	9	8	.529	3.06	202	0	44	200.0	156	82	205	21	1.19

Two years removed from a torn ligament in his pitching elbow, Ligtenberg posted a 1.79 ERA after June 1. He no longer closes like he once did, but he can help in at least a middle-relief role. 2002 Outlook: A

Trey Moore (**Pos**: LHP, **Age**: 29)

	W	L	Pct.	ERA	G	GS	Sv	IP	H	BB	SO	HR	Ratio
2001	0	0	-	11.25	2	0	0	4.0	7	2	1	0	2.25
Career	3	10	.231	5.83	23	19	0	100.1	140	40	60	12	1.79

Moore worked his way back from rotator cuff surgery that sidelined him in 1999, but he was waived by the Expos after the 2000 season. He pitched well at Triple-A Richmond in 2001, but was sold to Japan's Hanshin Tigers during the offseason. 2002 Outlook: D

Damian Moss (**Pos**: LHP, **Age**: 25)

	W	L	Pct.	ERA	G	GS	Sv	IP	H	BB	SO	HR	Ratio
2001	0	0	-	3.00	5	1	0	9.0	3	9	8	1	1.33
Career	0	0	-	3.00	5	1	0	9.0	3	9	8	1	1.33

Moss was pitching in Double-A when he was a teenager. Unfortunately, that was six years ago. He still isn't old, but arm problems have plagued him. 2002 Outlook: C

Joe Nelson (**Pos**: RHP, **Age**: 27)

	W	L	Pct.	ERA	G	GS	Sv	IP	H	BB	SO	HR	Ratio
2001	0	0	-	36.00	2	0	0	2.0	7	2	0	1	4.50
Career	0	0	-	36.00	2	0	0	2.0	7	2	0	1	4.50

Nelson allowed more runs in two major league innings than he did in 39.2 innings at Triple-A. He figures to be swallowed up by a wave of good Braves pitching prospects over the next few years. 2002 Outlook: C

Eddie Perez (**Pos**: C, **Age**: 33, **Bats**: R)

	G	AB	R	H	D	T	HR	RBI	SB	BB	SO	Avg	OBP	Slg
2001	5	10	0	3	0	0	0	0	0	0	2	.300	.300	.300
Career	325	850	88	219	45	1	24	104	1	50	128	.258	.305	.398

Perez hasn't played much since tearing his rotator cuff early in 2000. But if his shoulder proves sturdy, he has a chance to regain a backup role. 2002 Outlook: C

Rudy Seanez (**Pos**: RHP, **Age**: 33)

	W	L	Pct.	ERA	G	GS	Sv	IP	H	BB	SO	HR	Ratio
2001	0	2	.000	2.75	38	0	1	36.0	23	19	41	4	1.17
Career	16	13	.552	4.32	242	0	11	245.2	214	130	238	24	1.40

After Seanez signed with the Padres before last season, San Diego returned him to Atlanta in August in a waiver trade. Though injuries continue to bite him, opposing hitters managed just a .178 average. 2002 Outlook: C

Chris Seelbach (**Pos**: RHP, **Age**: 29)

	W	L	Pct.	ERA	G	GS	Sv	IP	H	BB	SO	HR	Ratio
2001	0	0	-	7.88	5	0	0	8.0	9	5	8	3	1.75
Career	0	1	.000	8.38	7	0	0	9.2	12	5	9	3	1.76

The Braves drafted Seelbach in 1991, lost him to the Marlins in 1995 and re-signed him in 1999. He's perennially been stuck in Triple-A. 2002 Outlook: C

Scott Sobkowiak (**Pos**: RHP, **Age**: 24)

	W	L	Pct.	ERA	G	GS	Sv	IP	H	BB	SO	HR	Ratio
2001	0	0	-	9.00	1	0	0	1.0	2	0	0	0	2.00
Career	0	0	-	9.00	1	0	0	1.0	2	0	0	0	2.00

Sobkowiak missed most of 2000 and much of 2001 due to an elbow injury. Even though Sobkowiak has little

experience above Class-A, the Braves used him in the last game of the regular season. 2002 Outlook: C

Steve Torrealba (**Pos**: C, **Age**: 24, **Bats**: R)

	G	AB	R	H	D	T	HR	RBI	SB	BB	SO	Avg	OBP	Slg
2001	2	2	0	1	0	0	0	0	0	0	0	.500	.500	.500
Career	2	2	0	1	0	0	0	0	0	0	0	.500	.500	.500

Torrealba doubled in his only postseason at-bat last fall. He is an accomplished defensive catcher with a good arm. The Braves feel they can reach down and grab him if necessary this season. 2002 Outlook: C

Marc Valdes (**Pos**: RHP, **Age**: 30)

	W	L	Pct.	ERA	G	GS	Sv	IP	H	BB	SO	HR	Ratio
2001	1	0	1.000	7.71	9	0	0	7.0	7	1	3	4	1.14
Career	12	15	.444	4.95	144	22	4	250.2	281	118	135	21	1.59

Valdes set a record of sorts last season. He surrendered four homers, the most ever by anyone allowing seven or fewer total hits. He pitched OK at Triple-A but is a fringe candidate to stick on a staff. 2002 Outlook: C

Quilvio Veras (**Pos**: 2B, **Age**: 30, **Bats**: B)

	G	AB	R	H	D	T	HR	RBI	SB	BB	SO	Avg	OBP	Slg
2001	71	258	39	65	14	2	3	25	7	24	52	.252	.330	.357
Career	767	2780	469	750	129	15	32	239	183	427	462	.270	.372	.362

Veras' tenure in Atlanta was marred by knee, ankle and ribcage injuries. With other options, the Braves discarded Veras and he eventually signed with Boston. His leadoff skills still should be appealing. 2002 Outlook: B

Matt Whiteside (**Pos**: RHP, **Age**: 34)

	W	L	Pct.	ERA	G	GS	Sv	IP	H	BB	SO	HR	Ratio
2001	0	1	.000	7.16	13	0	0	16.1	23	7	10	5	1.84
Career	18	15	.545	5.10	284	1	9	402.1	449	152	254	49	1.49

Whiteside broke a bone in his pitching hand and was subsequently released in July. His 7.16 ERA, though awful, was not at all out of character from his overall mark of 7.00 in 61 games since 1998. 2002 Outlook: C

Atlanta Braves Minor League Prospects

Organization Overview:

The Braves deserve kudos for winning their division each of the past 10 non-strike seasons, the longest such streak in baseball history. But that sustained stretch of success has come with a price, limiting the impact Atlanta could make in the annual amateur draft. Since they haven't picked higher than 21st since 1992, the Braves say the top-notch position prospects are gone by the time their choice rolls around. Instead, the organization has focused on taking high-ceiling pitchers. The result of that drafting philosophy is evident in the list of the Braves' top prospects. The only position player who figures to make much of an impression over the next couple years is Wilson Betemit, and he was signed as an undrafted free agent out of the Dominican Republic. But Atlanta is knee-deep in talented pitchers. While many of the best prospects likely will reach Double-A this year, Tim Spooneybarger and Billy Sylvester could compete for bullpen spots in Atlanta in 2002.

Wilson Betemit

Position: SS
Bats: B **Throws:** R
Ht: 6' 2" **Wt:** 155

Opening Day Age: 20
Born: 11/2/81 in Santo Domingo, DR

Recent Statistics

	G	AB	R	H	D	T	HR	RBI	SB	BB	SO	Avg
2001 A Myrtle Bch	84	318	38	88	20	1	7	43	8	23	71	.277
2001 AA Greenville	47	183	22	65	14	0	5	19	6	12	36	.355
2001 NL Atlanta	8	3	1	0	0	0	0	0	1	2	3	.000

Betemit has been described in the past as a guy who can play shortstop in the big leagues and still bat third in the lineup. He is quite young, having signed with the Braves out of the Dominican Republic in 1996. He has all the tools you look for in a prospect, although his plate discipline isn't particularly strong. He has pop in his bat, and Atlanta compares him to Edgar Renteria defensively. Betemit could wind up at second or third base on the Braves, considering they already have Furcal and Giles in the mix. Betemit might force some shifting of the Braves' infield as early as this season.

Jung Bong

Position: P
Bats: L **Throws:** L
Ht: 6' 3" **Wt:** 175

Opening Day Age: 21
Born: 7/15/80 in Seoul, Korea

Recent Statistics

	W	L	ERA	G	GS	Sv	IP	H	R	BB	SO	HR
2000 A Macon	7	7	4.23	20	19	0	112.2	119	65	45	90	4
2000 A Myrtle Bch	3	1	2.18	7	6	0	41.1	33	14	7	37	1
2001 A Myrtle Bch	13	9	3.00	28	28	0	168.0	151	67	47	145	7

The Braves have been aggressive pursuers of talent worldwide, and Bong was signed out of Korea at age 17 in 1997. He is a 6-foot-3 lefthander with pretty good velocity for a southpaw. He improved by leaps and bounds last season, posting the fourth-best ERA in the Carolina League. It was his first year with a real effective breaking ball, which complemented a 90-91 MPH fastball and good changeup. He is a good athlete and his strikeout-walk ratio has exceeded 3:1 in his one and half seasons at Myrtle Beach. Since the Braves tend to move their pitchers one rung at a time, the next logical step for Bong is Double-A.

Brett Evert

Position: P
Bats: L **Throws:** R
Ht: 6' 6" **Wt:** 200

Opening Day Age: 21
Born: 10/23/80 in Salem, OR

Recent Statistics

	W	L	ERA	G	GS	Sv	IP	H	R	BB	SO	HR
2000 A Macon	1	4	4.64	7	7	0	42.2	53	27	9	29	7
2000 A Jamestown	8	3	3.38	15	15	0	77.1	92	52	19	64	6
2001 A Macon	1	0	0.74	6	6	0	36.1	25	5	3	34	0
2001 A Myrtle Bch	7	2	2.24	13	13	0	72.1	63	25	15	75	4

Despite suffering a bout of tendinitis, Evert overmatched two leagues last season. His strikeout totals exceeded his hits allowed at both stops in Class-A. He continued to display excellent control, particularly for a guy who's 6-foot-6 and fans so many opposing hitters. His fastball has improved considerably since he was drafted in the seventh round in 1999. Initially delivered at 86-87 MPH, the heater now touches 94 MPH. His secondary pitches also have improved, and Evert works with a curveball and changeup in addition to the fastball. He's a big, strong kid with great command, and the Braves say he has a chance to be a frontline starter in the big leagues.

Trey Hodges

Position: P
Bats: R **Throws:** R
Ht: 6' 3" **Wt:** 187

Opening Day Age: 23
Born: 6/29/78 in Houston, TX

Recent Statistics

	W	L	ERA	G	GS	Sv	IP	H	R	BB	SO	HR
2000 A Jamestown	0	2	5.95	13	2	0	19.2	22	14	12	13	3
2001 A Myrtle Bch	15	8	2.76	26	26	0	173.0	156	64	18	139	13

Hodges was named the Most Valuable Player of the 2000 College World Series, after he won two games and saved another in three appearances. His victory in the title game, when he provided four innings of solid relief, helped LSU post a dramatic comeback victory. The Braves grabbed him in the 17th round and took it slow with him due to injuries. He worked primarily out of the bullpen in his professional debut in 2000, but Atlanta moved him to the rotation last season. The results couldn't have been more dramatic, as he led the Carolina League with 15 wins. His fastball is 91-92 MPH, but he can throw it harder when necessary. He also works with a changeup and curveball, which serves as his strikeout pitch. Hodges keeps the ball down, throws strikes and has an impressive demeanor on the mound. He's probably headed for Double-A.

Kelly Johnson

Position: SS   **Opening Day Age:** 20
Bats: L **Throws:** R   **Born:** 2/22/82 in Austin,
Ht: 6' 1" **Wt:** 180   TX

Recent Statistics

	G	AB	R	H	D	T	HR	RBI	SB	BB	SO	Avg
2000 R Braves	53	193	27	52	12	3	4	29	6	24	45	.269
2001 A Macon	124	415	75	120	22	1	23	66	25	71	111	.289

Johnson played his first full professional season last year and was outstanding in the South Atlantic League, at least offensively. He has a strong arm and the Braves say he improved on defense, something that Johnson may have been more concerned about than anybody. Nevertheless, he committed 45 errors. It looks like his bat is good enough that he could move up even if forced to another position. He topped 20 homers and 20 stolen bases last year, demonstrating decent power to all fields. He struck out quite a bit, but his walk rate also was high. Behind Wilson Betemit, Johnson may be the Braves' second-best positional prospect.

Ben Kozlowski

Position: P   **Opening Day Age:** 21
Bats: L **Throws:** L   **Born:** 8/16/80 in St.
Ht: 6' 6" **Wt:** 220   Petersburg, FL

Recent Statistics

	W	L	ERA	G	GS	Sv	IP	H	R	BB	SO	HR
2000 A Macon	3	8	4.21	15	14	0	77.0	76	53	39	67	6
2001 A Macon	10	7	2.48	26	23	0	145.1	134	60	27	147	8
2001 A Myrtle Bch	0	2	3.77	2	2	0	14.1	15	7	3	13	1

The Braves' Class-A affiliates in the Carolina and South Atlantic Leagues both featured deep, talented pitching staffs loaded with prospects. And Kozlowski compiled the lowest ERA among those Braves hurlers who threw enough qualifying innings. It was quite an achievement for Kozlowski, who was selected in the 12th round out of a Florida community college in 1999. At 6-foot-6, he presents an imposing figure as a lefthander. He has command of the three basic pitches that every Atlanta farmhand seems to throw (fastball, curveball and changeup), with a fastball that travels around 91-92 MPH. Kozlowski could move fast if he's switched to situational relief.

Tim Spooneybarger

Position: P   **Opening Day Age:** 22
Bats: R **Throws:** R   **Born:** 10/21/79 in San
Ht: 6' 3" **Wt:** 190   Diego, CA

Recent Statistics

	W	L	ERA	G	GS	Sv	IP	H	R	BB	SO	HR
2001 AA Greenville	1	1	5.14	15	0	0	21.0	20	12	4	24	1
2001 AAA Richmond	3	0	0.71	42	0	5	50.2	33	5	21	58	1
2001 NL Atlanta	0	1	2.25	4	0	0	4.0	5	1	2	3	0

Spooneybarger has experienced nothing but success as an Atlanta farmhand. After permitting a ridiculously low 18 hits over 49.2 innings in 2000, he roared through two levels last season, pitching very well in Triple-A at age 21. His mid-90s fastball features good movement and life. His curveball is a nasty strikeout pitch. Opposing batters don't get good swings against Spooneybarger, as evidenced by his .185 batting average allowed at Triple-A Richmond last year. He's also surrendered just three home runs in 159.2 innings as a pro. He should get a shot at working in middle relief with Atlanta this season. The Braves say he eventually could close for them.

Adam Wainwright

Position: P   **Opening Day Age:** 20
Bats: R **Throws:** R   **Born:** 8/30/81 in
Ht: 6' 6" **Wt:** 190   Brunswick, GA

Recent Statistics

	W	L	ERA	G	GS	Sv	IP	H	R	BB	SO	HR
2000 R Braves	4	0	1.13	7	5	0	32.0	15	5	10	42	1
2000 R Danville	2	2	3.68	6	6	0	29.1	28	13	2	39	3
2001 A Macon	10	10	3.77	28	28	0	164.2	144	89	48	184	9

The Braves selected Wainwright with the 29th overall choice in 2000 out of a Georgia high school. Although he finished with a .500 record last season, his league-high 184 strikeouts confirmed his prospect status. He already throws strikes with his fastball, curveball and changeup. The breaking ball serves as a strikeout pitch. While Wainwright struggled at times and got tired near the end of last season, the Braves say that's OK. He was only a year removed from high school and simply may have worn down. They'd like him to work on staying strong in 2002 and feel he might be an eventual No. 1 starter in the big leagues.

Others to Watch

Righthander **Matt Belisle** (21) had surgery to repair a disk in his back and missed the entire season. He's been a prized jewel in the Braves' system for a couple of years and, when healthy, throws a 94-MPH fastball with life. . . . Atlanta signed shortstop **Ramon Castro** (22) when he was a 16-year-old in Venezuela in 1996. He showed more offensive ability at Double-A last year than he had before, and wound up at Triple-A. . . Injuries have contributed to **George Lombard's** (26) career stalling in Triple-A the past few years. He missed much of 2001 with foot problems. The Braves hope he can stay healthy and possibly help as an extra outfielder. . . Although they didn't choose righthander **Zach Miner** (20) until the fourth round of the 2000 draft, the Braves gave him first-round money to sign. He debuted strongly in the New York-Penn League last year. . . Righthander **Kenny Nelson** (20), a second-round pick in 2000, also is known as "Bubba." He went 12-8 with 154 strikeouts at Macon with a 94-MPH fastball, great breaking ball and good changeup. . . Righthander **Billy Sylvester** (25) is knocking on the door for a big league job. The Braves say he could pitch for a lot of clubs with his mid-90s fastball and big, hard breaking ball.

Wrigley Field

Offense

Few parks are as fickle as Wrigley Field. When a midsummer breeze is blowing out, ordinary fly-balls can carry into the bleachers—particularly in the short power alleys. But when the wind blows in or the cool lake air settles over it, the park can be a pitcher's best friend. It poses as the former more often than the latter, but its overall impact in a given season will depend upon which way the wind blows most often. Last season was one of the rare ones where the pitchers' winds were most prevalent.

Defense

The Cubs encourage their pitchers to keep the ball down to take advantage of the park's long grass and the all-too-convenient mud puddle in front of the plate. The grass slows grounders, so for infielders, a strong arm is relatively more important and great range is less so. The short power alleys lessen the center fielder's defensive responsibility.

Who It Helps the Most

In most seasons, Sammy Sosa gets enough flyballs up into the wind to take advantage of the park's influence. On the other hand, Bill Mueller, a hitter with a markedly different style, always has hit well here. Kerry Wood and Kyle Farnsworth succeed here by keeping the ball out of play.

Who It Hurts the Most

Matt Stairs and Rondell White didn't hit well here last year, although it wasn't a typical Wrigley season. Ron Coomer batted 29 points lower at home, but stroked nearly twice as many doubles at Wrigley.

Rookies & Newcomers

Fred McGriff has excellent straightaway power and should prosper if Wrigley's friendly winds return. Corey Patterson also should be able to find success here once he gets his feet on the ground. Juan Cruz seems to be a power pitcher in the mold of Wood and Farnsworth, so he should survive well enough.

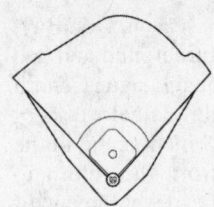

Dimensions: LF-355, LCF-368, CF-400, RCF-368, RF-353

Capacity: 39,059

Elevation: 595 feet

Surface: Grass

Foul Territory: Small

Park Factors

2001 Season

	Home Games			Away Games			Index
	Cubs	Opp	Total	Cubs	Opp	Total	
G	72	72	144	75	75	150	—
Avg	.268	.234	.251	.251	.262	.256	98
AB	2333	2432	4765	2573	2512	5085	98
R	353	288	641	345	345	690	97
H	626	568	1194	646	658	1304	95
2B	110	117	227	130	135	265	91
3B	15	7	22	15	17	32	73
HR	83	69	152	93	84	177	92
BB	265	246	511	257	257	514	106
SO	478	640	1118	503	596	1099	109
E	35	57	92	58	50	108	89
E-Infield	28	52	80	48	44	92	91
LHB-Avg	.261	.236	.248	.216	.289	.254	97
LHB-HR	30	26	56	36	43	79	71
RHB-Avg	.273	.232	.252	.270	.244	.258	98
RHB-HR	53	43	96	57	41	98	109

1999-2001

	Home Games			Away Games			Index
	Cubs	Opp	Total	Cubs	Opp	Total	
G	218	218	436	221	221	442	—
Avg	.265	.257	.261	.249	.277	.263	99
AB	7227	7608	14835	7623	7453	15076	100
R	1034	1081	2115	1021	1216	2237	96
H	1917	1956	3873	1901	2063	3964	99
2B	350	358	708	373	402	775	93
3B	44	26	70	38	62	100	71
HR	246	275	521	265	286	551	96
BB	826	784	1610	779	797	1576	104
SO	1477	1643	3120	1574	1511	3085	103
E	142	151	293	163	139	302	98
E-Infield	108	127	235	136	120	256	93
LHB-Avg	.256	.256	.256	.232	.279	.255	101
LHB-HR	71	96	167	99	118	217	78
RHB-Avg	.271	.258	.264	.261	.275	.268	99
RHB-HR	175	179	354	166	168	334	108

2001 Rankings (National League)

- Second-highest walk factor
- Third-highest strikeout factor
- Second-lowest LHB home-run factor

Don Baylor

2001 Season

Coming off a disastrous 97-loss season, Don Baylor led the Cubs to a 23-game turnaround and had them in contention for the National League Central flag and the wild-card spot until the final weeks of the season. Most of the improvement came in the club's pitching, specifically from the return to dominance of Kerry Wood, the development of Kyle Farnsworth and the addition of free agents Jeff Fassero, Jason Bere and Tom Gordon.

Offense

Baylor rarely had the luxury of a lead during 2000, so perhaps he might be forgiven for jumping at every opportunity to seize one in 2001. He's always been partial to one-run strategies, but he was even more extreme than ever last year, playing the infield in, sacrificing and moving runners with outs, even in the early innings. He showed an extraordinary amount of patience with non-hitting defensive whiz Gary Matthews Jr., as he had done the season before with Damon Buford.

Pitching & Defense

Baylor's emphasis on defense over offense was evident in his bench, where he carried defense-only types like Augie Ojeda and Robert Machado but couldn't always find room for the bats of Roosevelt Brown or Julio Zuleta. He was more careful with rookie Juan Cruz than he's been with young pitchers in the past, although he once again allowed Kerry Wood to pile up high pitch counts. He rides the hot hand in the bullpen and will work his top relievers hard while others collect dust.

2002 Outlook

It will be much harder for the Cubs to meet expectations this year, even having Fred McGriff in the lineup from the start. The club's improvement last year was mostly due to several key pitchers overachieving, something that probably won't happen again, especially with pitching coach Oscar Acosta gone to Texas after his late-season fallout in Chicago. Under pressure to contend, Baylor may find it hard to have patience with youngsters Corey Patterson and Juan Cruz.

Born: 6/28/49 in Austin, TX

Playing Experience: 1970-1988, Bal, Oak, Ana, NYY, Bos, Min

Managerial Experience: 8 seasons

Manager Statistics

Year	Team, Lg	W	L	Pct	GB	Finish
2001	Chicago, NL	88	74	.543	5.0	3rd Central
8 Seasons		593	640	.481	—	—

2001 Starting Pitchers by Days Rest

	<=3	4	5	6+
Cubs Starts	1	80	53	19
Cubs ERA	135.00	4.18	4.13	2.71
NL Avg Starts	1	80	47	24
NL ERA	5.03	4.43	4.53	4.28

2001 Situational Stats

	Don Baylor	NL Average
Hit & Run Success %	33.3	35.1
Stolen Base Success %	65.0	66.5
Platoon Pct.	51.3	51.5
Defensive Subs	42	20
High-Pitch Outings	5	7
Quick/Slow Hooks	22/12	19/14
Sacrifice Attempts	140	87

2001 Rankings (National League)

- 1st in sacrifice bunt attempts and defensive substitutions
- 2nd in steals of home plate (1), sacrifice-bunt percentage (89.3%) and starting lineups used (140)
- 3rd in fewest caught stealings of second base (31), pitchouts with a runner moving (14) and 2+ pitching changes in low-scoring games (36)

Jason Bere

2001 Season

The Cubs took a gamble by signing free agent Jason Bere to a two-year, $4.5 million deal in December 2000, and he turned out to be a pleasant surprise. In fact, he put together his best season since undergoing elbow surgery six years ago. He remained wildly inconsistent from start to start but was effective much more often than not. Bere allowed two earned runs or less in 16 of his 32 starts, and just as importantly, he stayed healthy all year. His 32 starts and 188 innings pitched were career highs.

Pitching

Since his surgery, Bere never has regained consistency with his curveball, the pitch that made him so effective in his first two years in the league. What made a big difference last year was his development of a fosh, a changeup that became his main offspeed pitch. When he was able to mix 90-MPH fastballs upstairs with foshes below the knees, he was tough on righthanded hitters, though lefthanded hitters weren't as easily fooled. Highly inefficient in the past, he went to three-ball counts less often last year. Manager Don Baylor handled him carefully, rarely allowing him to go much beyond 100 pitches, and Bere seemed stronger for it.

Defense & Hitting

An above-average fielder, Bere made just one error while handling 27 chances in 2001. He usually does a decent job holding runners but got little help from his catchers last year. For someone who came up through an American League club's system, he's proven to be surprisingly helpful at the plate. Bere contributed a .194 average, four doubles and seven sacrifices last season.

2002 Outlook

Bere is signed through 2002 and the Cubs are expecting another solid year out of him. It might be too late to expect him ever to get his curve back, but if he ever does, he could take another big step forward. Don't look for 200 innings out of his arm, but he should be a good bet to reach the 175-inning mark.

Position: SP
Bats: R **Throws:** R
Ht: 6' 3" **Wt:** 225

Opening Day Age: 30
Born: 5/26/71 in Cambridge, MA
ML Seasons: 9
Pronunciation: ber-AY

Overall Statistics

	W	L	Pct.	ERA	G	GS	Sv	IP	H	BB	SO	HR	Ratio
2001	11	11	.500	4.31	32	32	0	188.0	171	77	175	24	1.32
Career	70	55	.560	5.10	193	185	0	1018.2	992	596	854	132	1.56

How Often He Throws Strikes

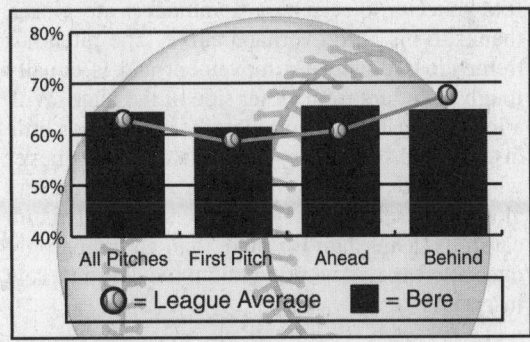

2001 Situational Stats

	W	L	ERA	Sv	IP		AB	H	HR	RBI	Avg
Home	5	5	4.27	0	92.2	LHB	280	81	11	47	.289
Road	6	6	4.34	0	95.1	RHB	430	90	13	41	.209
First Half	6	4	4.18	0	94.2	Sc Pos	159	37	6	60	.233
Scnd Half	5	7	4.44	0	93.1	Clutch	27	5	0	1	.185

2001 Rankings (National League)

- 4th in highest stolen-base percentage allowed (82.4)
- 5th in lowest groundball-flyball ratio allowed (1.0)
- 6th in most strikeouts per nine innings (8.4)
- 7th in lowest batting average allowed vs. righthanded batters
- Led the Cubs in pickoff throws (109)

Chicago (NL)

Flash Gordon

2001 Season

After missing a year and a half recovering from Tommy John surgery, Tom "Flash" Gordon made a triumphant return last year and helped unexpectedly propel the Cubs back into contention. The Cubs took a flier on him with a incentive-laden two-year, $5 million deal in December 2000, and for the most part the move paid off for both parties. Though he missed the month of April with strained triceps, and most of September with a sore elbow, in between he was one of the most effective closers in baseball.

Pitching

He may stand at just 5-foot-10, but don't let stature fool you. Gordon can be as dominant as any closer, thanks to his hard overhand curve. The pitch has tremendous downward movement and is equally tough on hitters from either side of the plate. With a low-90s fastball to complement it, he needs little else. Before his surgery he was a durable reliever who posted more multi-inning saves than any closer in baseball. Last year the Cubs handled him carefully, using him for more than an inning only once all year, and working him three days in a row just once.

Defense & Hitting

Though he handled only two chances all year, Gordon is an active and capable fielder. In fact, his last miscue in the field came in 1997. Basestealers find it easy to run on him because he throws so many curves. As a longtime American Leaguer, he came into 2001 having never swung a bat in a major league game, and he kept that part of his record intact.

2002 Outlook

The condition of Gordon's elbow is a cause for concern going into 2002. He wouldn't be the first pitcher to make it all the way back from Tommy John surgery only to suffer complications afterward. The Cubs will keep their fingers crossed and hope that a winter of rest cures the inflammation than bothered him late last year.

Position: RP
Bats: R **Throws:** R
Ht: 5'10" **Wt:** 190

Opening Day Age: 34
Born: 11/18/67 in Sebring, FL
ML Seasons: 13
Nickname: Flash

Overall Statistics

	W	L	Pct.	ERA	G	GS	Sv	IP	H	BB	SO	HR	Ratio
2001	1	2	.333	3.38	47	0	27	45.1	32	16	67	4	1.06
Career	105	98	.517	4.13	491	203	98	1690.1	1548	823	1498	137	1.40

How Often He Throws Strikes

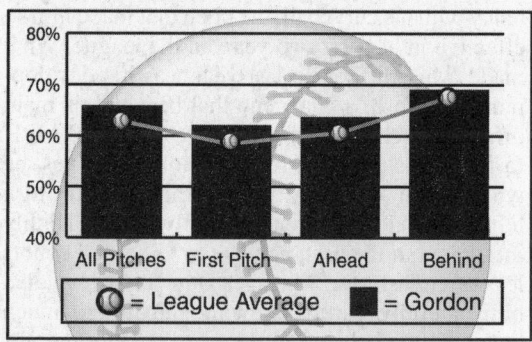

2001 Situational Stats

	W	L	ERA	Sv	IP		AB	H	HR	RBI	Avg
Home	1	0	2.93	15	27.2	LHB	69	13	1	5	.188
Road	0	2	4.08	12	17.2	RHB	101	19	3	13	.188
First Half	1	0	2.96	15	24.1	Sc Pos	24	10	1	14	.417
Scnd Half	0	2	3.86	12	21.0	Clutch	110	19	2	14	.173

2001 Rankings (National League)

- 6th in first batter efficiency (.159) and save percentage (87.1)
- 9th in save opportunities (31) and saves
- Led the Cubs in saves, games finished (40), save opportunities (31), save percentage (87.1) and first batter efficiency (.159)

Ricky Gutierrez

Position: SS
Bats: R **Throws:** R
Ht: 6' 1" **Wt:** 190

Opening Day Age: 31
Born: 5/23/70 in Miami, FL
ML Seasons: 9
Pronunciation: goo-tee-AIR-ez

2001 Season

Ricky Gutierrez had another solid season as the Cubs' shortstop last year. He was dropped from second to sixth in the lineup, but when the new No. 2 hitter, Bill Mueller, got hurt in midseason, Gutierrez was restored to his old spot and hit very well there. He played the most games and hit for the highest average of his career. He also reached double-digits in home runs for the second straight year.

Hitting

One of the most extreme groundball hitters in the game, Gutierrez tries to punch the ball through the infield. However, he also has been able to generated a bit more lift on occasion the past couple of seasons, resulting in those higher home-run totals. Since he, in effect, always takes a two-strike approach, he's a decent two-strike hitter but rarely drives the ball even when ahead in the count. He uses the opposite field well, especially against southpaws, who he'd always hit well until last year. He drew significantly fewer walks last year, but his ability to hit-and-run and sacrifice runners along remained valuable in the No. 2 spot.

Baserunning & Defense

Gutierrez is a solid shortstop, though he was less sure-handed last year than he had been the year before. His range is nothing special; he goes to his right better than to his left, so he plays closer to the second base bag than most shortstops. His hands and arm are fine, though. He has just enough speed to attempt an occasional steal, usually with a runner on third.

2002 Outlook

Gutierrez' chances of returning to Chicago all but vanished in December when the Cubs and Blue Jays made a deal for shortstop Alex Gonzalez. Gutierrez surfaced with a three-year deal from Cleveland, where he is expected to replace Roberto Alomar at second base. Gutierrez has played just 27 games at second—none since 1997—so there will be an adjustment period, particularly with the double play. Signing Gutierrez also leaves the door open to Cleveland trading shortstop Omar Vizquel.

Overall Statistics

	G	AB	R	H	D	T	HR	RBI	SB	BB	SO	Avg	OBP	Slg
2001	147	528	76	153	23	3	10	66	4	40	56	.290	.345	.402
Career	964	3126	423	835	122	25	34	308	49	333	519	.267	.342	.355

Where He Hits the Ball

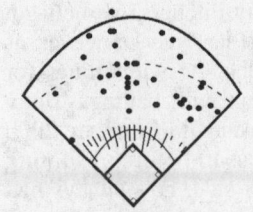 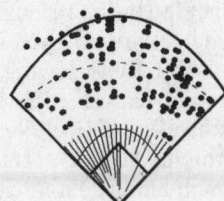

Vs. LHP   **Vs. RHP**

2001 Situational Stats

	AB	H	HR	RBI	Avg		AB	H	HR	RBI	Avg
Home	267	79	7	38	.296	LHP	124	32	2	10	.258
Road	261	74	3	28	.284	RHP	404	121	8	56	.300
First Half	268	75	8	34	.280	Sc Pos	130	38	4	57	.292
Scnd Half	260	78	2	32	.300	Clutch	78	24	2	15	.308

2001 Rankings (National League)

- 1st in sacrifice bunts (17)
- 4th in sacrifice flies (11) and lowest slugging percentage vs. lefthanded pitchers (.331)
- 5th in highest groundball-flyball ratio (2.1) and lowest on-base percentage vs. lefthanded pitchers (.306)
- 6th in fielding percentage at shortstop (.971)
- Led the Cubs in singles, sacrifice bunts (17), hit by pitch (10), highest groundball-flyball ratio (2.1) and highest percentage of extra bases taken as a runner (52.7)

Chicago (NL)

Todd Hundley

2001 Season

What was supposed to be a happy homecoming for Todd Hundley turned into a year-long nightmare. The Illinois native signed a four-year, $23.5 million deal with the Cubs in December 2000 and was expected to be their regular catcher and cleanup hitter. He was neither. Bothered by back problems and drained by the physical demands of day baseball, he struck out with alarming frequency, never got untracked and missed six weeks at midseason. He hit just .187 on the year, but what really irked Cubs fans was his .175 mark with runners in scoring position.

Hitting

A pull hitter with a pronounced uppercut, Hundley can ride a fastball a long way. Pitchers routinely got him out with offspeed stuff last year, however, as he had trouble staying back. A switch-hitter for most of his career, he went with batting strictly lefthanded late in 1999, and again from late 2000 through August of last year before resuming switch-hitting. From either side, he's always had trouble with southpaws. He still gets too pull-conscious against lefthanded hurlers.

Baserunning & Defense

There's no polite way to say it: Hundley is a liability behind the plate. Reconstructive elbow surgery has left him with a weak, erratic throwing arm, and basestealers test him at every opportunity. He nailed just 15 percent of would-be thieves in 2001. Powerfully built, he was less than agile at blocking pitches before his back problems handicapped him further. Few catchers have had their pitch-calling publicly questioned by their own manager and teammates more than Hundley. On the bases, he is slow even by catchers' standards.

2002 Outlook

Though he's been a quality hitter in the past, it's very much an open question whether Hundley will be able to help the Cubs. He'll need to hit to be valuable, but at such a demanding position, his physical condition very well could prevent him from ever being the offensive threat he once was.

Position: C
Bats: B **Throws:** R
Ht: 5'11" **Wt:** 195

Opening Day Age: 32
Born: 5/27/69 in Martinsville, VA
ML Seasons: 12

Overall Statistics

	G	AB	R	H	D	T	HR	RBI	SB	BB	SO	Avg	OBP	Slg
2001	79	246	23	46	10	0	12	31	0	25	89	.187	.268	.374
Career	1112	3470	461	821	158	7	184	553	14	413	895	.237	.321	.445

Where He Hits the Ball

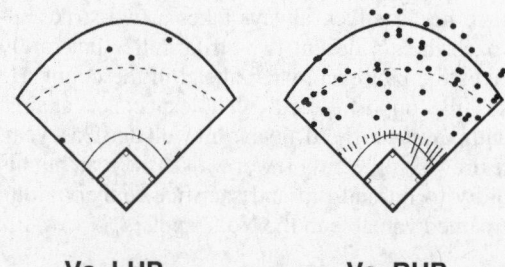

Vs. LHP　　　　　**Vs. RHP**

2001 Situational Stats

	AB	H	HR	RBI	Avg		AB	H	HR	RBI	Avg
Home	118	25	4	16	.212	LHP	24	7	0	5	.292
Road	128	21	8	15	.164	RHP	222	39	12	26	.176
First Half	156	28	4	19	.179	Sc Pos	63	11	2	18	.175
Scnd Half	90	18	8	12	.200	Clutch	40	11	4	9	.275

2001 Rankings (National League)
- 1st in lowest batting average on an 0-2 count (.037)
- 4th in lowest batting average with two strikes (.120)

Jon Lieber

2001 Season

Last year Jon Lieber made the All-Star team for the first time and was one of the best starters in the major leagues for much of the season. Though he staggered to the finish for the fourth straight year, he still managed to win 20 games for the first time in his career. Kerry Wood might have been more intimidating, but Lieber was the starter who gave the Cubs quality outings most consistently. He now has worked more than 200 innings in each of his three years in Chicago.

Pitching

Lieber always has dominated righthanded hitters while struggling to get lefthanded ones out, and that hasn't changed. His slider is one of the best in the game, and he uses his great command to set it up and make batters chase it out of the strike zone. He tries to work lefthanded hitters in and out with fastballs and changeups, without anywhere near the same success. He never misses a start but tends to wear down late in the year. This was the case again last year, even though manager Don Baylor made more of an effort to limit his pitch counts. His ERA in 2001 from September 1 on was 5.80.

Defense & Hitting

Lieber helps himself with the glove, handling plenty of balls hit back through the box. Last year he played errorless ball and was second among Cubs pitchers in chances (behind Julian Tavarez). His slide step makes him exceptionally tough to run on—nine runners tried to steal on him last year, and seven of them were thrown out. He's a fair hitter and a decent bunter.

2002 Outlook

Lieber is signed through 2002, with a club option for 2003. Though he probably didn't deserve to win 20 games, he certainly deserved to win 15, as he had for each of the previous four seasons. He is an excellent bet to keep on eating innings and pitching quality ball.

Position: SP
Bats: L **Throws:** R
Ht: 6' 2" **Wt:** 230

Opening Day Age: 31
Born: 4/2/70 in Council Bluffs, IA
ML Seasons: 8
Pronunciation: LEE-ber

Overall Statistics

	W	L	Pct.	ERA	G	GS	Sv	IP	H	BB	SO	HR	Ratio
2001	20	6	.769	3.80	34	34	0	232.1	226	41	148	25	1.15
Career	80	75	.516	4.23	251	204	2	1369.1	1450	299	1034	173	1.28

How Often He Throws Strikes

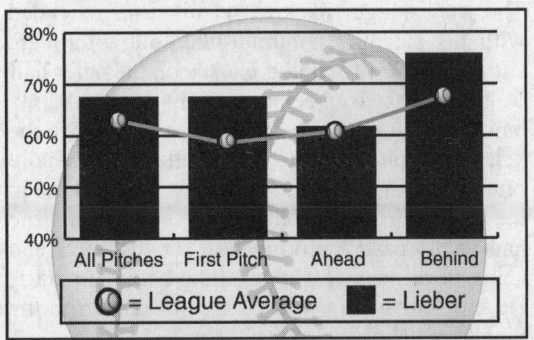

2001 Situational Stats

	W	L	ERA	Sv	IP		AB	H	HR	RBI	Avg
Home	12	1	3.39	0	122.0	LHB	403	120	15	52	.298
Road	8	5	4.24	0	110.1	RHB	485	106	10	45	.219
First Half	11	4	3.42	0	126.1	Sc Pos	166	37	7	69	.223
Scnd Half	9	2	4.25	0	106.0	Clutch	50	11	0	4	.220

2001 Rankings (National League)

- 1st in fielding percentage at pitcher (1.000)
- 2nd in complete games (5) and lowest stolen-base percentage allowed (22.2)
- 3rd in fewest walks per nine innings (1.6)
- Led the Cubs in wins, games started, complete games (5), innings pitched, hits allowed, batters faced (958), home runs allowed, pitches thrown (3,254), winning percentage, lowest on-base percentage allowed (.290), lowest stolen-base percentage allowed (22.2), fewest pitches thrown per batter (3.40), most run support per nine innings (5.8), lowest batting average allowed with runners in scoring position, most GDPs induced per nine innings (0.6), and fewest walks per nine innings (1.6)

Fred McGriff

2001 Season

It took Fred McGriff a few weeks to think it over, but once he decided to pull up his Florida roots in midseason and join the Cubs for their pennant push, he made his presence felt. Batting cleanup behind Sammy Sosa, he gave the Cubs much-needed protection for their big bopper and drove in 41 runs in 49 games for Chicago. Even at age 37, he showed few signs of slowing down, and reached his customary levels in all the major categories. After posting 31 home runs last year—the ninth time in he career he's reached that level—he now sits just 52 dingers shy of 500.

Hitting

The wiry slugger likes to get his arms extended with his patented windmill-like follow-through, and is capable of sending pitches on the outer half of the plate to deep center or right-center. A low-ball hitter, he generally lays off pitches above the belt. Those pitches were being called strikes more often last year, so as a result he hit from behind in the count more often and drew fewer walks than he had in the past. Unfortunately for the Rays and Cubs, he hit just .150 after falling behind in 2001. He hits lefthanders well enough to remain in the middle of the order against them.

Baserunning & Defense

With long, loping strides, McGriff probably wouldn't look fast even if he were. He'll run once in a blue moon but has the sense not to try it with anything real at stake. He's got acceptable range and pretty good hands at first base, and his below-average arm is more of an annoyance than a weakness.

2002 Outlook

McGriff ended up enjoying his time with the Cubs, and decided to exercise his one-year option and return in 2002. He hit well at Wrigley Field in his two months in a Cubs uniform and should continue to produce for them this year while batting behind Sosa.

Position: 1B/DH
Bats: L **Throws:** L
Ht: 6' 3" **Wt:** 215

Opening Day Age: 38
Born: 10/31/63 in Tampa, FL
ML Seasons: 16
Nickname: Crime Dog

Overall Statistics

	G	AB	R	H	D	T	HR	RBI	SB	BB	SO	Avg	OBP	Slg
2001	146	513	67	157	25	2	31	102	1	66	106	.306	.386	.544
Career	2201	7865	1243	2260	397	22	448	1400	71	1202	1698	.287	.381	.514

Where He Hits the Ball

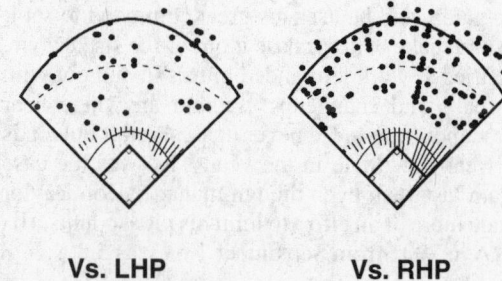

Vs. LHP	Vs. RHP

2001 Situational Stats

	AB	H	HR	RBI	Avg		AB	H	HR	RBI	Avg
Home	251	78	17	57	.311	LHP	149	44	11	37	.295
Road	262	79	14	45	.302	RHP	364	113	20	65	.310
First Half	294	97	15	53	.330	Sc Pos	136	42	8	39	.309
Scnd Half	219	60	16	49	.274	Clutch	59	19	4	10	.322

2001 Rankings (National League)

- 9th in cleanup slugging percentage (.559)
- Led the Cubs in cleanup slugging percentage (.559)

Bill Mueller

2001 Season

In his first season with the Cubs, Bill Mueller got off to an excellent start, playing great defense at third base and getting on base regularly from the second spot in the lineup. He hit .326 and crossed the plate 16 times in April. That ended suddenly in mid-May when he broke his left kneecap chasing a foul pop. After missing three months, he returned in August but wasn't able to play regularly or contribute much the rest of the way.

Hitting

The switch-hitting Mueller does almost everything expected of a No. 2 hitter: he makes good contact, hits for average, waits out walks and shoots the ball through the right side when a runner is on first. He struck out just 19 times in 2001, and now owns nearly as many career walks as strikeouts. An excellent hit-and-run man, he hits the ball where it's pitched and swings with equal skill from either side. He confirmed last year that his off year in 2000 was caused not by a decline in his skills but by the Giants' move to Pac Bell Park.

Baserunning & Defense

Cubs fans were pleasantly surprised with Mueller's glovework. Though his arm isn't a cannon, it's strong enough and quite accurate, and his hands are soft. His greatest asset is his mobility, including both his lateral range and his ability to charge bunts and squibbers. He's played some second base both in the minors and the majors and there have been occasional rumors that the Cubs will use him there if needed. He doesn't have much speed, however, and rarely tries to steal.

2002 Outlook

Mueller never hit well in either of his home parks in San Francisco, but seems to like the Friendly Confines just fine. He's on the Chicago payroll through 2002, and if his knee recovers fully, there's no reason Mueller can't produce his best work this season.

Position: 3B
Bats: B **Throws:** R
Ht: 5'10" **Wt:** 180

Opening Day Age: 31
Born: 3/17/71 in Maryland Heights, MO
ML Seasons: 6
Pronunciation: MILL-er
Nickname: Ferris, Muley

Overall Statistics

	G	AB	R	H	D	T	HR	RBI	SB	BB	SO	Avg	OBP	Slg
2001	70	210	38	62	12	1	6	23	1	37	19	.295	.403	.448
Career	667	2308	371	669	133	9	34	236	16	305	313	.290	.373	.399

Where He Hits the Ball

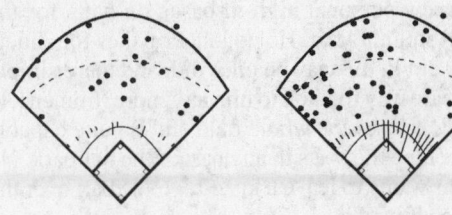

Vs. LHP   **Vs. RHP**

2001 Situational Stats

	AB	H	HR	RBI	Avg		AB	H	HR	RBI	Avg
Home	95	33	3	12	.347	LHP	46	18	2	8	.391
Road	115	29	3	11	.252	RHP	164	44	4	15	.268
First Half	126	40	5	16	.317	Sc Pos	49	12	0	14	.245
Scnd Half	84	22	1	7	.262	Clutch	31	11	1	2	.355

2001 Rankings (National League)

- Did not rank near the top or bottom in any category

Sammy Sosa

2001 Season

Sammy Sosa's unforgettable 1998 season was more memorable, but his 2001 campaign just might have been more valuable. In fact, if Barry Bonds hadn't simultaneously put together one of the greatest seasons of all time, Sosa might have captured another National League MVP award last year. Despite having little protection behind him for most of the season, he topped 60 homers for the third time in four years and led the majors in RBI while hitting for the best average of his career. His 160 RBI were 94 more than the next-highest total on the team.

Hitting

Sosa's patience continued to grow last year as he set a new personal high in bases on balls for the fourth straight year. He no longer fishes for sliders in the dirt in the way he once did, and there simply is no safe way to pitch to him any more. Immensely strong, he uses the whole field and is quite capable of reaching the seats in any part of the ballpark. No pitcher wants to leave a knee-high fastball over the plate to him.

Baserunning & Defense

Sosa carries a lot more weight—all muscle—than he did when he was young, and has all but stopped trying to steal bases. He still runs well, however, and takes extra bases without overreaching nearly as often as he did when he was young. It's similar in the outfield: he's a little less mobile, but he more than makes up for it by playing smarter. He's aggressive, and his range and arm still are above average.

2002 Outlook

It's natural to think Sosa could benefit from having Fred McGriff batting behind him for an entire season, but on the other hand it's hard to imagine how Sosa could improve on last year. Sosa signed a four-year, $72 million contract extension in March 2001, so there should be no financial distractions as he heads into the 2002 campaign.

Position: RF
Bats: R **Throws:** R
Ht: 6' 0" **Wt:** 225

Opening Day Age: 33
Born: 11/12/68 in San Pedro de Macoris, DR
ML Seasons: 13

Overall Statistics

	G	AB	R	H	D	T	HR	RBI	SB	BB	SO	Avg	OBP	Slg
2001	160	577	146	189	34	5	64	160	0	116	153	.328	.437	.737
Career	1725	6470	1093	1795	278	41	450	1239	231	635	1690	.277	.343	.542

Where He Hits the Ball

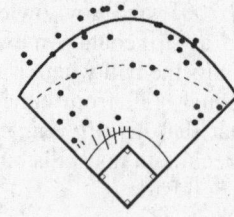 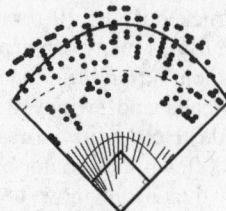

Vs. LHP　　　　　**Vs. RHP**

2001 Situational Stats

	AB	H	HR	RBI	Avg		AB	H	HR	RBI	Avg
Home	281	94	34	85	.335	LHP	93	36	13	30	.387
Road	296	95	30	75	.321	RHP	484	153	51	130	.316
First Half	298	93	29	83	.312	Sc Pos	139	45	14	89	.324
Scnd Half	279	96	35	77	.344	Clutch	85	27	8	21	.318

2001 Rankings (National League)

- 1st in runs scored, total bases (425), RBI, intentional walks (37), slugging percentage vs. lefthanded pitchers (.882) and on-base percentage vs. lefthanded pitchers (.569)
- Led the Cubs in batting average, home runs, hits, walks, times on base (311), strikeouts, pitches seen (2,732), plate appearances (711), slugging percentage, on-base percentage, HR frequency (9.0 ABs per HR), most pitches seen per plate appearance (3.84), fewest GDPs per GDP situation (3.8%), batting average with the bases loaded (.667), slugging percentage vs. righthanded pitchers (.709) and batting average with two strikes (.247)
- Led NL right fielders in home runs and RBI

Kevin Tapani

2001 Season

It was an up-and-down year for veteran Kevin Tapani. He had surgery on his right knee over the winter and battled soreness in it on and off all year. After winning eight of his first nine decisions, he slumped in June. He bounced back to pitch very well in July and August, but continued to lose as the club struggled to score runs for him and dropped nine straight at one point. He faded badly in September. All in all, he had an 8-1 start but a 1-13 finish, and didn't really deserve either mark.

Pitching

Doing more with less always has been Tapani's way. His fastball has good movement but unexceptional velocity, and his splitter and changeup are decent at best. What he has is excellent command and a great ability to change speeds. He'll often set up the hitter to look for an offspeed pitch and then throw a fastball by him. He's been much more effective against lefthanded hitters than righthanded ones in each of the last two years.

Defense & Hitting

Though not all that mobile, Tapani is highly reliable and committed only his first error in five years in 2001. His pickoff move is nothing special, but he gets the ball to the plate quickly. Opposing basestealers were successful less than 50 percent of the time with Tapani on the hill, and he also added one pickoff. A fair hitter, he had his best year with the stick, hitting .240. He also is a fairly good bunter.

2002 Outlook

The Cubs declined to pick up Tapani's $6.5 million option for 2002, and if they don't offer him enough to return, he may opt to retire. He's still an effective pitcher when healthy, and probably deserved a better record last year. He could be a solid middle-to-back-of-the-rotation starter for a club that needs one.

Position: SP
Bats: R **Throws:** R
Ht: 6' 0" **Wt:** 190

Opening Day Age: 38
Born: 2/18/64 in Des Moines, IA
ML Seasons: 13
Pronunciation: TAP-ah-nee
Nickname: Tap

Overall Statistics

	W	L	Pct.	ERA	G	GS	Sv	IP	H	BB	SO	HR	Ratio
2001	9	14	.391	4.49	29	29	0	168.1	186	40	149	24	1.34
Career	143	125	.534	4.35	361	354	0	2265.0	2407	554	1482	260	1.31

How Often He Throws Strikes

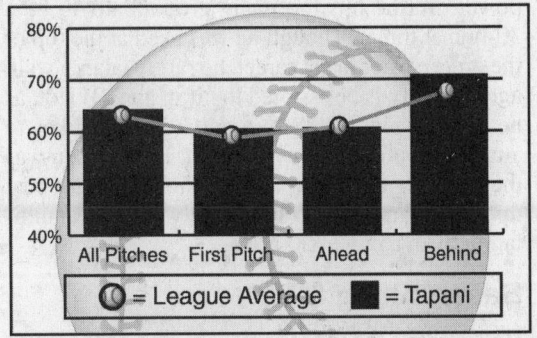

2001 Situational Stats

	W	L	ERA	Sv	IP		AB	H	HR	RBI	Avg
Home	6	6	3.06	0	100.0	LHB	266	61	9	36	.229
Road	3	8	6.59	0	68.1	RHB	401	125	15	49	.312
First Half	8	6	4.52	0	89.2	Sc Pos	154	40	8	63	.260
Scnd Half	1	8	4.46	0	78.2	Clutch	29	7	1	2	.241

2001 Rankings (National League)

- 4th in highest batting average allowed vs. righthanded batters
- 5th in highest strikeout-walk ratio (3.7)
- 6th in fewest GDPs induced per nine innings (0.4)
- 7th in losses and fewest walks per nine innings (2.1)
- 8th in lowest stolen-base percentage allowed (46.7)
- 9th in most strikeouts per nine innings (8.0)
- 10th in highest groundball-flyball ratio allowed (1.5) and lowest winning percentage
- Led the Cubs in losses, runners caught stealing (8), highest strikeout-walk ratio (3.7) and highest groundball-flyball ratio allowed (1.5)

Rondell White

Signed By YANKEES

Position: LF
Bats: R **Throws:** R
Ht: 6' 1" **Wt:** 215

Opening Day Age: 30
Born: 2/23/72 in Milledgeville, GA
ML Seasons: 9

2001 Season

Left fielder Rondell White got hurt soon after coming over in a trade from Montreal in 2000, and last year it was more of the same. Installed as the club's left fielder and No. 5 hitter, he was in the midst of a fine year in June when he went down with a strained groin muscle. He didn't get back into the lineup for good until September. Despite his two stints on the disabled list, he finished at .300 or better for the fourth consecutive year and set a new personal high with a .529 slugging percentage.

Hitting

White is an aggressive line-drive hitter who hits for a good average and is capable of pulling the ball for power. But he hits too many groundballs to be a 30-homer threat. Though he was used at the top of the order earlier in his career, he rarely takes a walk and probably is best-suited to hit in an RBI slot, as he did last year. He's got a quick bat and likes to attack fastballs early in the count. Last season was the first campaign in years in which he didn't beat up on lefthanders, and he'll likely resume annihilating them again in 2002.

Baserunning & Defense

He may have the speed to steal bases and the range to play center field, but White's repeated knee and leg injuries have convinced him to give up basestealing almost entirely. The Cubs steadfastly resisted the urge to move him from left field back to his old position. He's one of the rangiest left fielders around, but his very poor throwing arm is a liability.

2002 Outlook

White held a player option for 2002 but elected not to exercise it and filed for free agency. The Cubs still were hoping to re-sign him, but White agreed to a two-year, $10 million deal with the Yankees to play left field in the Bronx. As always, the key for White is to stay healthy. Unfortunately, his track record indicates that isn't all that likely.

Overall Statistics

	G	AB	R	H	D	T	HR	RBI	SB	BB	SO	Avg	OBP	Slg
2001	95	323	43	99	19	1	17	50	1	26	56	.307	.371	.529
Career	856	3146	470	929	186	24	120	441	89	231	562	.295	.351	.484

Where He Hits the Ball

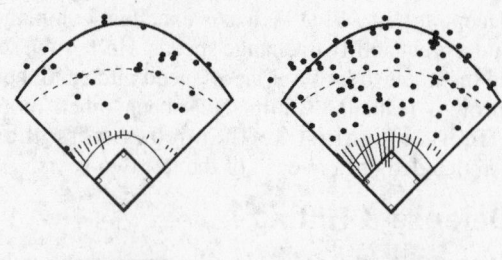

Vs. LHP   **Vs. RHP**

2001 Situational Stats

	AB	H	HR	RBI	Avg		AB	H	HR	RBI	Avg
Home	141	36	7	15	.255	LHP	71	19	1	8	.268
Road	182	63	10	35	.346	RHP	252	80	16	42	.317
First Half	255	77	13	36	.302	Sc Pos	81	29	3	34	.358
Scnd Half	68	22	4	14	.324	Clutch	46	16	2	10	.348

2001 Rankings (National League)

- 10th in errors in left field (3)
- Led the Cubs in batting average in the clutch and batting average on an 0-2 count (.286)

Kerry Wood

2001 Season

Though Kerry Wood returned from Tommy John surgery in 2000, it wasn't until last year that he made it all the way back. He showed his old command more often in 2001 than he had the previous year, and he went back to relying on the hard curve that had helped make him so overpowering as a rookie. Though a sore shoulder caused him to miss most of August, he returned in September and showed no lingering effects. He finished second in the National League among starters with 11.2 strikeouts per nine innings last year.

Pitching

With a mid-to upper-90s fastball, Wood throws just as hard as he did before surgery. His curve is hard to lay off, though he occasionally lacks command of it. When he's getting the pitch over, he'll rarely need to go to his slider. His third pitch is a cutter that he busts in on the hands of lefthanded hitters. In 2000, the Cubs had him lay off the curve and work on using a fosh as his second pitch, but he hasn't developed much confidence in it.

Defense & Hitting

Wood uses his legs to help generate velocity, so rather than abbreviate his stretch delivery, he has developed an excellent pickoff move. Baserunners still run on him, and many of them make it, but he picked off seven of them last year—the most of any righthanded pitcher in baseball. He's also a smooth fielder, making just one error in 33 chances in 2001. He's one of the better-hitting pitchers in the game, with respectable power and excellent bunting skills.

2002 Outlook

Wood's outlook is the same as it was following his rookie season, and the only thing that can keep him from stardom is a major arm injury. If he's able to make most of his starts in 2002, he's as good a bet to win 20 and strike out 225-plus batters as anyone. He'll have to work without his pitching coach of the last two years, Oscar Acosta, who has moved on to Texas after a late-season fallout with the Cubs and manager Don Baylor.

Position: SP
Bats: R **Throws:** R
Ht: 6' 5" **Wt:** 220

Opening Day Age: 24
Born: 6/16/77 in Irving, TX
ML Seasons: 3

Overall Statistics

	W	L	Pct.	ERA	G	GS	Sv	IP	H	BB	SO	HR	Ratio
2001	12	6	.667	3.36	28	28	0	174.1	127	92	217	16	1.26
Career	33	19	.635	3.78	77	77	0	478.0	356	264	582	47	1.30

How Often He Throws Strikes

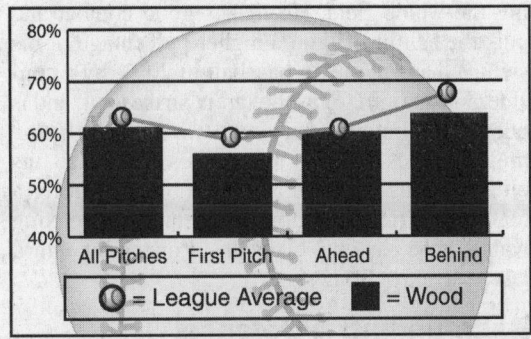

○ = League Average   ■ = Wood

2001 Situational Stats

	W	L	ERA	Sv	IP		AB	H	HR	RBI	Avg
Home	5	4	2.67	0	91.0	LHB	294	59	7	31	.201
Road	7	2	4.10	0	83.1	RHB	335	68	9	33	.203
First Half	8	5	3.61	0	112.1	Sc Pos	154	37	2	44	.240
Scnd Half	4	1	2.90	0	62.0	Clutch	42	12	2	4	.286

2001 Rankings (National League)

- 1st in lowest batting average allowed (.202)
- 2nd in lowest slugging percentage allowed (.315), most strikeouts per nine innings (11.2), most pitches thrown per batter (4.08), fewest GDPs induced per nine innings (0.3) and highest walks per nine innings (4.7)
- Led the Cubs in ERA, walks allowed, strikeouts, wild pitches (9), stolen bases allowed (22), lowest slugging percentage allowed (.315), lowest ERA at home, lowest ERA on the road, lowest batting average allowed vs. lefthanded batters, lowest batting average allowed vs. righthanded batters, fewest home runs allowed per nine innings (.83) and most strikeouts per nine innings (11.2)

Eric Young

2001 Season

Though it wasn't one of his best seasons, Eric Young had another fairly typical campaign as the Cubs' second baseman and leadoff hitter. He scored close to 100 runs, putting himself in scoring position often with doubles and stolen bases. He was a steady presence in a batting order that had few other constants, and manager Don Baylor valued his contributions to the Cubs' little-ball attack. Perhaps the only area that was a big disappointment in 2001 was his performance in the running game.

Hitting

Young consistently hits for a good average by using the whole field. He makes good contact and puts the ball in play on a higher percentage of his swings than anyone in baseball in 2001, by a considerable margin. Thus, he rarely strikes out, and is one of the better hitters with two strikes in the major leagues. He gets most of his extra-base hits on line drives to the gaps and is able to bunt for a hit or a sacrifice. He's done a decent job of coaxing walks in the past, but his walks dropped by a third last year, a troubling sign.

Baserunning & Defense

Though he remains one of the game's better basestealers, Young went through a couple of stretches last year when he wasn't able to steal effectively at all, possibly due to nagging leg and ankle injuries. His 31 swipes represented his lowest output since 1994, and he was successful just 69 percent of the time. Still, he reads righthanded pitchers' moves especially well. Far from a natural second baseman, his decent range somewhat offsets his weak arm, stiff hands and below-average pivot.

2002 Outlook

Young, a free agent, is unlikely to be brought back by the Cubs. Chicago re-signed Delino DeShields to man second base until young Bobby Hill is ready to take over the position. Coming off a less-than-stellar season, Young will need to show that he hasn't lost a step to age, wherever he signs.

Position: 2B
Bats: R **Throws:** R
Ht: 5' 8" **Wt:** 180

Opening Day Age: 34
Born: 5/18/67 in New Brunswick, NJ
ML Seasons: 10
Nickname: E.Y.

Overall Statistics

	G	AB	R	H	D	T	HR	RBI	SB	BB	SO	Avg	OBP	Slg
2001	149	603	98	168	43	4	6	42	31	42	45	.279	.333	.393
Career	1237	4524	.762	1307	238	39	55	427	377	489	323	.289	.365	.395

Where He Hits the Ball

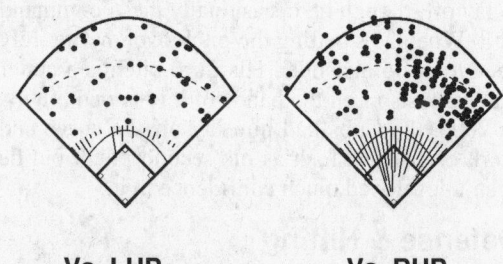

Vs. LHP　　　　**Vs. RHP**

2001 Situational Stats

	AB	H	HR	RBI	Avg		AB	H	HR	RBI	Avg
Home	278	86	4	19	.309	LHP	120	37	2	9	.308
Road	325	82	2	23	.252	RHP	483	131	4	33	.271
First Half	331	89	6	27	.269	Sc Pos	122	32	2	37	.262
Scnd Half	272	79	0	15	.290	Clutch	90	22	0	9	.244

2001 Rankings (National League)

- 1st in highest percentage of swings put into play (58.5)
- 2nd in errors at second base (12) and lowest fielding percentage at second base (.981)
- 3rd in bunts in play (32) and most GDPs per GDP situation (20.8%)
- 4th in caught stealing (14)
- Led the Cubs in at-bats, doubles, stolen bases, caught stealing (14), stolen-base percentage (68.9), bunts in play (32), lowest percentage of swings that missed (8.7), steals of third (4), on-base percentage for a leadoff hitter (.334), lowest percentage of swings on the first pitch (21.8) and batting average on a 3-2 count (.314)

Ron Coomer

Position: 3B/1B
Bats: R **Throws:** R
Ht: 6' 0" **Wt:** 215

Opening Day Age: 35
Born: 11/18/66 in
Chicago, IL
ML Seasons: 7

Overall Statistics

	G	AB	R	H	D	T	HR	RBI	SB	BB	SO	Avg	OBP	Slg
2001	111	349	25	91	19	1	8	53	0	29	70	.261	.316	.390
Career	787	2746	308	758	140	8	85	417	13	161	387	.276	.315	.426

2001 Situational Stats

	AB	H	HR	RBI	Avg		AB	H	HR	RBI	Avg
Home	163	40	3	25	.245	LHP	96	28	4	17	.292
Road	186	51	5	28	.274	RHP	253	63	4	36	.249
First Half	185	51	5	30	.276	Sc Pos	110	30	1	40	.273
Scnd Half	164	40	3	23	.244	Clutch	57	13	1	12	.228

2001 Season

Signed to a one-year, $1.2 million deal in January 2001 to back up the infield corners in Chicago, Ron Coomer missed most of April and September with knee problems. In between, he played more than the team would have liked. When Bill Mueller got hurt in May, Coomer took over as the full-time third baseman for three months, doing little more than plugging the hole. Once a cornerstone for the cash-strapped Twins, Coomer slugged a career-low .390 for the Cubs in 2001.

Hitting, Baserunning & Defense

Though he often batted in the middle of the order in Minnesota, Coomer has no major offensive strengths apart from an aptitude for hitting lefties reasonably well. He has moderate power and makes good contact, but draws few walks. In the field, he catches whatever he gets to at first or third; the problem is that he can't get to anything that's more than a few steps to either side. Even when healthy, he's among the slowest baserunners in the game and didn't even attempt a theft last year.

2002 Outlook

A free agent, Coomer might struggle to find work. Last season was not impressive, and there are few jobs for righthanded-hitting corner men with limited power and even more limited range.

Delino DeShields

Position: LF/2B
Bats: L **Throws:** R
Ht: 6' 1" **Wt:** 175

Opening Day Age: 33
Born: 1/15/69 in
Seaford, DE
ML Seasons: 12
Pronunciation:
duh-LINE-oh

Overall Statistics

	G	AB	R	H	D	T	HR	RBI	SB	BB	SO	Avg	OBP	Slg
2001	126	351	55	82	17	5	5	37	23	59	77	.234	.344	.353
Career	1548	5633	852	1520	238	73	77	551	453	733	1023	.270	.354	.379

2001 Situational Stats

	AB	H	HR	RBI	Avg		AB	H	HR	RBI	Avg
Home	183	41	3	19	.224	LHP	82	15	0	6	.183
Road	168	41	2	18	.244	RHP	269	67	5	31	.249
First Half	193	39	3	22	.202	Sc Pos	99	21	0	29	.212
Scnd Half	158	43	2	15	.272	Clutch	62	13	0	9	.210

2001 Season

Delino DeShields' had a fine year for Baltimore in 2000, though he'd been moved from second base to left field in midseason. Still, when he got off to a slow start in 2001, he found himself slowly being crowded out. The Orioles released him in late June, and the Cubs picked him up a week later. In Chicago he shared left field, filled in on the infield and served as the Cubs' top lefthanded pinch-hitter, and his bat came back to life.

Hitting, Baserunning & Defense

DeShields hits mostly line drives and groundballs, and he goes the other way more often than not. He didn't hit lefties well last year, but he's had no problems with them when he's played regularly. With great speed and acceleration, he's still one of the best percentage basestealers in the game when healthy. He has good mobility and a strong enough arm for left. He's a capable second baseman with decent range, but his arm is a bit weak.

2002 Outlook

DeShields will return to the Cubs in 2002 after signing a one-year, $1.25 million deal in early December. He is expected to keep second base warm for keystone prospect Bobby Hill, and also continue to fill in wherever needed in the field and pick up some pinch-hit at-bats.

Chicago (NL)

Kyle Farnsworth

Position: RP
Bats: R **Throws:** R
Ht: 6' 4" **Wt:** 220

Opening Day Age: 25
Born: 4/14/76 in Wichita, KS
ML Seasons: 3

Overall Statistics

	W	L	Pct.	ERA	G	GS	Sv	IP	H	BB	SO	HR	Ratio
2001	4	6	.400	2.74	76	0	2	82.0	65	29	107	8	1.15
Career	11	24	.314	4.76	149	26	3	289.0	295	131	251	50	1.47

2001 Situational Stats

	W	L	ERA	Sv	IP		AB	H	HR	RBI	Avg
Home	3	4	2.47	2	43.2	LHB	121	27	3	7	.223
Road	1	2	3.05	0	38.1	RHB	184	38	5	17	.207
First Half	0	3	3.00	0	42.0	Sc Pos	73	8	0	12	.110
Scnd Half	4	3	2.48	2	40.0	Clutch	194	44	6	20	.227

2001 Season

Before last year, Kyle Farnsworth had a closer's fastball but little else. Then he added a splitter and became—virtually overnight—one of the league's best setup men. He finished fourth in the National League with 24 holds, and allowed a major league-best .110 batting average with runners in scoring position (minimum 50 relief innings).

Pitching, Defense & Hitting

Farnsworth's splitter is one of the hardest around, and its combination of velocity and movement is deadly. With an upper-90s fastball to complement it, he doesn't need to do much more than mix the two. His command isn't great, but it's good enough to keep hitters swinging. Like many young smoke-throwing relievers, he ignores baserunners and goes for the out at the plate. A spectacularly erratic fielder during his first two seasons, he fielded all seven chances cleanly last year after being charged with four miscues in just 27 games in 1999. He's a hopeless hitter.

2002 Outlook

If Tom Gordon is unable to close for the Cubs this year, Farnsworth might be their best alternative. If Farnsworth is anywhere close to the pitcher he was last year, he'll do fine in either a setup or stopper role.

Jeff Fassero

Position: RP
Bats: L **Throws:** L
Ht: 6' 1" **Wt:** 200

Opening Day Age: 39
Born: 1/5/63 in Springfield, IL
ML Seasons: 11
Pronunciation: fuh-SAIR-oh

Overall Statistics

	W	L	Pct.	ERA	G	GS	Sv	IP	H	BB	SO	HR	Ratio
2001	4	4	.500	3.42	82	0	12	73.2	66	23	79	6	1.21
Career	104	95	.523	3.87	486	217	22	1669.0	1658	580	1405	168	1.34

2001 Situational Stats

	W	L	ERA	Sv	IP		AB	H	HR	RBI	Avg
Home	3	2	3.43	6	42.0	LHB	97	24	3	12	.247
Road	1	2	3.41	6	31.2	RHB	184	42	3	28	.228
First Half	1	2	2.48	11	40.0	Sc Pos	82	22	2	33	.268
Scnd Half	3	2	4.54	1	33.2	Clutch	160	43	5	31	.269

2001 Season

Coming off two poor seasons in a row, Jeff Fassero was signed to a two-year, $5.1 million deal by the Cubs in December 2000 and quickly made the signing look like a stroke of genius. The former starter returned to the bullpen and opened the season as Chicago's stand-in closer, converting nine of 11 saves before Tom Gordon returned. Bumped to a setup role, he was scored upon in only one of his next 42 appearances.

Pitching, Defense & Hitting

Fassero showed better velocity and command last year. When he's on, he's able to use his low-90s fastball to make hitters commit too early on his splitter and slider. Effective against hitters from either side of the plate, he showed that he's still able to work several days in a row. A reliable fielder, he doesn't have much of a move and never has picked off a runner, but he throws over to first a lot. He's as weak a hitter as you'll find.

2002 Outlook

Fassero seemed to be rejuvenated by his return to the bullpen. The Cubs and Fassero have a mutual option for 2003, so Chicago may end up being his fifth and final team, especially if he can continue to hold righthanded hitters to the .228 mark he posted against them last season.

Joe Girardi

Position: C
Bats: R **Throws:** R
Ht: 5'11" **Wt:** 200
Opening Day Age: 37
Born: 10/14/64 in Peoria, IL
ML Seasons: 13
Pronunciation: jer-AR-dee

Overall Statistics

	G	AB	R	H	D	T	HR	RBI	SB	BB	SO	Avg	OBP	Slg
2001	78	229	22	58	10	1	3	25	0	21	50	.253	.315	.345
Career	1171	3870	434	1044	176	25	35	408	43	260	568	.270	.318	.355

2001 Situational Stats

	AB	H	HR	RBI	Avg		AB	H	HR	RBI	Avg
Home	101	26	1	16	.257	LHP	57	15	1	6	.263
Road	128	32	2	9	.250	RHP	172	43	2	19	.250
First Half	132	28	1	10	.212	Sc Pos	49	18	0	19	.367
Scnd Half	97	30	2	15	.309	Clutch	48	9	0	3	.188

2001 Season

When the Cubs signed Todd Hundley to a rich free-agent deal over the winter, it looked like Joe Girardi's playing time would be slashed. It didn't quite work out that way, though. Hundley's playing time was limited by injuries and a deep slump, and Girardi—though playing less often—was able to continue to make valued contributions.

Hitting, Baserunning & Defense

Girardi's role at the plate is to avoid killing the offense. He's a groundball hitter who goes the other way a lot and rarely walks or hits for extra bases. He can bunt when asked. What he gives the club is a steady veteran behind the plate who can take charge and lead a young pitcher through a game. Still quick and light on his feet, he blocks balls well. His accurate throwing arm is a plus. He used to have above-average speed for a catcher, but knee problems slowed him considerably last year.

2002 Outlook

Girardi missed the final weekend of the 2001 campaign in order to undergo surgery to remove bone fragments from his left knee. He is expected to be ready to play by the start of training camp. If Hundley rebounds at all, Girardi's playing time could shrink. Still, if he's healthy, Girardi won't be allowed to rot on the bench.

Matt Stairs

Position: 1B/LF
Bats: L **Throws:** R
Ht: 5' 9" **Wt:** 225
Opening Day Age: 34
Born: 2/27/68 in Saint John, NB, Canada
ML Seasons: 9

Overall Statistics

	G	AB	R	H	D	T	HR	RBI	SB	BB	SO	Avg	OBP	Slg
2001	128	340	48	85	21	0	17	61	2	52	76	.250	.358	.462
Career	818	2485	398	658	140	6	140	470	21	358	520	.265	.359	.495

2001 Situational Stats

	AB	H	HR	RBI	Avg		AB	H	HR	RBI	Avg
Home	170	38	5	18	.224	LHP	29	5	0	7	.172
Road	170	47	12	43	.276	RHP	311	80	17	54	.257
First Half	200	52	10	37	.260	Sc Pos	92	23	5	43	.250
Scnd Half	140	33	7	24	.236	Clutch	44	6	0	3	.136

2001 Season

Acquired from Oakland before the season, Matt Stairs was asked to man first base—a position where he had logged just 16 games prior to 2001. He platooned there for most of the season and often batted cleanup, both with mixed results, before Fred McGriff was acquired from the Devil Rays at the trading deadline. After that, Stairs became a backup, part-time left fielder and pinch-hitter. He did manage to poke 17 homers in 340 at-bats.

Hitting, Baserunning & Defense

A pull hitter with an uppercut, Stairs is patient at the plate and shows good power against righthanders. Though he was platooned last year, he had fair success against southpaws as a full-timer in Oakland. He's built like a beer-league softball player (which probably is what endeared him to the Wrigley faithful), but he runs acceptably. He has the range and arm for either outfield corner and acquitted himself nicely at first base for someone who hadn't played the position before.

2002 Outlook

Stairs, a free agent, shouldn't be expected to land a full-time job. But he is a proven RBI producer with a bit of pop who should hook on somewhere as a part-timer or platoon player.

Chicago (NL)

Julian Tavarez

Position: SP
Bats: L **Throws:** R
Ht: 6' 2" **Wt:** 190

Opening Day Age: 28
Born: 5/22/73 in Santiago, DR
ML Seasons: 9
Pronunciation: JOOL-ee-en tah-VAR-rez

Overall Statistics

	W	L	Pct.	ERA	G	GS	Sv	IP	H	BB	SO	HR	Ratio
2001	10	9	.526	4.52	34	28	0	161.1	172	69	107	13	1.49
Career	50	33	.602	4.44	398	52	2	714.0	784	274	425	66	1.48

2001 Situational Stats

	W	L	ERA	Sv	IP		AB	H	HR	RBI	Avg
Home	6	4	4.40	0	73.2	LHB	250	80	6	47	.320
Road	4	5	4.62	0	87.2	RHB	370	92	7	40	.249
First Half	6	5	3.87	0	100.0	Sc Pos	161	46	3	70	.286
Scnd Half	4	4	5.58	0	61.1	Clutch	24	9	2	6	.375

2001 Season

In 2000, before becoming a free agent, Julian Tavarez moved from the Rockies' bullpen to the rotation and pitched well. The Cubs were convinced he could remain an effective starter and signed him to a two-year, $5 million deal in November 2000. He got off to a red-hot start and pitched decently for most of the year before running out of steam and losing his rotation spot in September.

Pitching, Defense & Hitting

With a sinker-slider repertoire, Tavarez gets more groundballs than just about any pitcher in baseball. He works in and out effectively to righthanded hitters but has trouble putting lefthanded batsmen away. He hadn't spent an entire season as a starter since 1994, and it showed, as he tended to wear out after about 75 pitches. He's an active fielder though he sometimes gets overanxious. His move to first is fairly good for a righthander. He can't hit but he is a good bunter.

2002 Outlook

The Cubs have Tavarez locked up through 2002 and could use him either in the rotation or the bullpen, depending upon their needs. He should be decent in either capacity, though he really struggled in his six relief appearances in 2001.

Michael Tucker

Position: CF/LF/RF
Bats: L **Throws:** R
Ht: 6' 2" **Wt:** 185

Opening Day Age: 30
Born: 6/25/71 in South Boston, VA
ML Seasons: 7

Overall Statistics

	G	AB	R	H	D	T	HR	RBI	SB	BB	SO	Avg	OBP	Slg
2001	149	436	62	110	19	8	12	61	16	46	102	.252	.322	.415
Career	868	2431	384	633	120	31	81	313	72	278	595	.260	.341	.435

2001 Situational Stats

	AB	H	HR	RBI	Avg		AB	H	HR	RBI	Avg
Home	214	47	4	24	.220	LHP	90	19	3	15	.211
Road	222	63	8	37	.284	RHP	346	91	9	46	.263
First Half	219	56	7	29	.256	Sc Pos	107	31	0	42	.290
Scnd Half	217	54	5	32	.249	Clutch	72	17	2	7	.236

2001 Season

The Cubs picked up Michael Tucker from Cincinnati in late July to add to their depth and flexibility in the outfield. He came through for Chicago in every way, hitting and fielding well while getting the majority of the playing time in center field. He hit 21 points higher with the Cubs than he did with the Reds in a similar number of at-bats.

Hitting, Baserunning & Defense

A streaky hitter with line-drive power, Tucker is useful against righthanders but always has struggled to hit lefties. Southpaws held him to a .211 batting average last year, and he's hit them at just a .234 clip for his career. He looks to pull the ball, but has trouble making contact and strikes out more than a hitter with his moderate power ought to. He's quick enough to steal a few bases and cover any of the three outfield positions well. His arm is strong enough for right field. He racked up nine outfield assists last year, four in just 112.1 innings in right.

2002 Outlook

Tucker picked up his two-year player option and elected to return to the Cubs through 2003. He'll provide an alternative in center field in case Corey Patterson isn't ready to take over. If Patterson plays, Tucker will make a nice fourth outfielder.

Todd Van Poppel

Signed By RANGERS

Position: RP
Bats: R **Throws:** R
Ht: 6' 5" **Wt:** 235

Opening Day Age: 30
Born: 12/9/71 in Hinsdale, IL
ML Seasons: 8

Overall Statistics

	W	L	Pct.	ERA	G	GS	Sv	IP	H	BB	SO	HR	Ratio
2001	4	1	.800	2.52	59	0	0	75.0	63	38	90	9	1.35
Career	30	43	.411	5.50	245	82	3	670.2	677	385	520	99	1.58

2001 Situational Stats

	W	L	ERA	Sv	IP		AB	H	HR	RBI	Avg
Home	2	1	1.60	0	39.1	LHB	96	27	4	11	.281
Road	2	0	3.53	0	35.2	RHB	186	36	5	15	.194
First Half	3	1	3.25	0	36.0	Sc Pos	88	10	2	15	.114
Scnd Half	1	0	1.85	0	39.0	Clutch	74	19	3	8	.257

2001 Season

Todd Van Poppel enjoyed his best season last year. The club's deep bullpen allowed Van Poppel to get the rest between appearances that he needed, and he responded with fine work in middle relief, pitching occasionally in a setup role. His 2.52 ERA in 2001 was more than three runs lower than the career mark he carried into the season.

Pitching, Defense & Hitting

Van Poppel works up in the zone with a 90-MPH fastball, a curve and a change. He sometimes fights his control, but not nearly as regularly as he used to. Lots of long counts still are his norm, however. He seems to work better with a day off between appearances. Generally a decent fielder, he had a poor year in the field, botching four of 14 chances. He does little to slow the running game, but has performed decently at the plate in limited trials.

2002 Outlook

Van Poppel signed a three-year, $7.5 million deal with the Rangers in late November. This will be his second stint with Texas. The good news is that his pitching coach in Chicago last year, Oscar Acosta, also will be working with the Rangers in 2002. The bad news is that Van Poppel could disappoint again, as he wasn't nearly as effective last year as his ERA would indicate.

David Weathers

Signed By METS

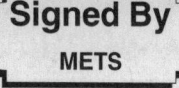

Position: RP
Bats: R **Throws:** R
Ht: 6' 3" **Wt:** 230

Opening Day Age: 32
Born: 9/25/69 in Lawrenceburg, TN
ML Seasons: 11

Overall Statistics

	W	L	Pct.	ERA	G	GS	Sv	IP	H	BB	SO	HR	Ratio
2001	4	5	.444	2.41	80	0	4	86.0	65	34	66	6	1.15
Career	38	46	.452	4.81	400	67	7	768.2	863	345	537	70	1.57

2001 Situational Stats

	W	L	ERA	Sv	IP		AB	H	HR	RBI	Avg
Home	2	2	3.24	2	50.0	LHB	108	23	4	7	.213
Road	2	3	1.25	2	36.0	RHB	193	42	2	19	.218
First Half	2	2	1.71	4	47.1	Sc Pos	87	14	1	20	.161
Scnd Half	2	3	3.26	0	38.2	Clutch	168	35	4	14	.208

2001 Season

David Weathers just keeps getting better. He had his best season in 2001, finishing among the National League leaders in appearances and relief ERA. The Brewers dealt him at the deadline to the Cubs along with minor league pitcher Roberto Miniel in exchange for highly-touted pitching prospect Ruben Quevedo and outfielder Peter Zoccolillo. In Chicago, Weathers continued to shine.

Pitching, Defense & Hitting

Weathers throws in the low 90s with a sinker and slider. His slider always has been tough on righthanded hitters, and over the last two years he's developed enough confidence in his sinker to use it effectively against lefties. He got into a good rhythm last year working every other day but has shown he's capable of pitching on consecutive days. Now that he's added a slide step, he's become much tougher to run on. Though he made a couple of errors last year, he's been a reliable fielder in the past. He's a non-factor at the plate.

2002 Outlook

A free agent, Weathers cashed in on a fine 2001 for a three-year, $9.4 million deal with the Mets. He might not duplicate last year's numbers, but he should remain an effective option to eat up the middle innings.

Chicago (NL)

Other Chicago Cubs

Manny Aybar (Pos: RHP, Age: 27)

	W	L	Pct.	ERA	G	GS	Sv	IP	H	BB	SO	HR	Ratio
2001	2	1	.667	6.35	17	1	0	22.2	28	17	16	5	1.99
Career	16	18	.471	5.14	168	28	3	348.1	362	159	233	43	1.50

Aybar was traded to the Cubs in March and later to Tampa in the McGriff deal. He stuggled with his control, but still has the arm to be in the majors. 2002 Outlook: B

Joe Borowski (Pos: RHP, Age: 30)

	W	L	Pct.	ERA	G	GS	Sv	IP	H	BB	SO	HR	Ratio
2001	0	1	.000	32.40	1	1	0	1.2	6	3	1	1	5.40
Career	5	8	.385	5.09	58	1	0	70.2	84	44	34	7	1.81

Borowski made his first start in the majors after 57 relief appearances with three other clubs. He served up Barry Bonds' 50th homer, and then was sent down to Iowa. He became a free agent after the season. 2002 Outlook: C

Roosevelt Brown (Pos: LF, Age: 26, Bats: L)

	G	AB	R	H	D	T	HR	RBI	SB	BB	SO	Avg	OBP	Slg
2001	39	83	13	22	6	1	4	22	0	7	12	.265	.326	.506
Career	117	238	30	68	20	2	8	46	1	13	48	.286	.323	.487

Last season Brown won the PCL batting title, and has batted .336 at Triple-A over the past three seasons. He needs to work on his center-field play to get some time in a crowded Cubs outfield. 2002 Outlook: B

Damon Buford (Pos: CF, Age: 31, Bats: R)

	G	AB	R	H	D	T	HR	RBI	SB	BB	SO	Avg	OBP	Slg
2001	35	85	11	15	2	0	3	8	0	4	23	.176	.213	.306
Career	699	1853	280	448	86	9	54	218	56	173	430	.242	.311	.385

The Cubs cut Buford in May due to his poor hitting. He spent time in the O's and Reds' systems, then signed a minor league deal with Boston for '02. 2002 Outlook: C

Courtney Duncan (Pos: RHP, Age: 27)

	W	L	Pct.	ERA	G	GS	Sv	IP	H	BB	SO	HR	Ratio
2001	3	3	.500	5.06	36	0	0	42.2	42	25	49	5	1.57
Career	3	3	.500	5.06	36	0	0	42.2	42	25	49	5	1.57

Duncan was an important part of the bullpen at the beginning of the season, as he posted a 2.22 ERA through May. Back and shoulder injuries limited his action and consistency thereafter. 2002 Outlook: B

Todd Dunwoody (Pos: LF, Age: 26, Bats: L)

	G	AB	R	H	D	T	HR	RBI	SB	BB	SO	Avg	OBP	Slg
2001	33	61	6	13	4	0	1	3	0	3	14	.213	.250	.328
Career	293	909	98	213	48	12	11	81	13	51	231	.234	.278	.350

Dunwoody hit .297 at Wrigley, but still strikes out too much to play every day. He signed a minor league contract with Cleveland in November. 2002 Outlook: C

Felix Heredia (Pos: LHP, Age: 25)

	W	L	Pct.	ERA	G	GS	Sv	IP	H	BB	SO	HR	Ratio
2001	2	2	.500	6.17	48	0	0	35.0	45	16	28	6	1.74
Career	21	13	.618	4.89	339	2	5	277.2	278	152	248	25	1.55

Coming off a poor season that ended early due to two stints on the DL, Heredia was traded to Toronto. Being a lefty, he has a good chance to stick. 2002 Outlook: B

Robert Machado (Pos: C, Age: 28, Bats: R)

	G	AB	R	H	D	T	HR	RBI	SB	BB	SO	Avg	OBP	Slg
2001	52	135	13	30	10	0	2	13	0	7	26	.222	.266	.341
Career	125	303	34	67	18	1	6	33	0	18	64	.221	.267	.347

Machado always has been known for his defensive prowess, but never could hit enough to earn a full-time position. After being called up in June, he had a few big hits, but not enough to win the job. 2002 Outlook: C

Ron Mahay (Pos: LHP, Age: 30)

	W	L	Pct.	ERA	G	GS	Sv	IP	H	BB	SO	HR	Ratio
2001	0	0	-	2.61	17	0	0	20.2	14	15	24	4	1.40
Career	7	2	.778	4.08	103	3	2	132.1	124	69	107	21	1.46

Mahay signed with the Cubs in May and was called up in August. He became the club's mid-inning lefty and may have found a home in Chicago. 2002 Outlook: B

Chad Meyers (Pos: 2B, Age: 26, Bats: R)

	G	AB	R	H	D	T	HR	RBI	SB	BB	SO	Avg	OBP	Slg
2001	18	17	1	2	0	0	0	0	0	2	5	.118	.348	.118
Career	97	211	26	44	11	0	0	9	5	14	43	.209	.282	.261

Meyers is a speedy guy, can play most any position and has had some success in the minors. The A's signed him to a minor league deal in November. 2002 Outlook: C

Will Ohman (Pos: LHP, Age: 24)

	W	L	Pct.	ERA	G	GS	Sv	IP	H	BB	SO	HR	Ratio
2001	0	1	.000	7.71	11	0	0	11.2	14	6	12	2	1.71
Career	1	1	.500	7.80	17	0	0	15.0	18	10	14	2	1.87

Ohman finished 2000 with Chicago, but did not make the 2001 Opening Day roster. He mixed success with failure between the Cubs and Triple-A Iowa. 2002 Outlook: C

Augie Ojeda (Pos: 3B/SS, Age: 27, Bats: B)

	G	AB	R	H	D	T	HR	RBI	SB	BB	SO	Avg	OBP	Slg
2001	78	144	16	29	5	1	1	12	1	12	20	.201	.269	.271
Career	106	221	26	46	8	2	3	20	1	22	29	.208	.282	.303

Ojeda can play three infield positions well. With Eric Young likely to move on, Ojeda needs to raise his average to have a shot at the open job. 2002 Outlook: C

Jason Smith (Pos: SS, Age: 24, Bats: L)

	G	AB	R	H	D	T	HR	RBI	SB	BB	SO	Avg	OBP	Slg
2001	2	1	0	0	0	0	0	0	0	0	1	.000	.000	.000
Career	2	1	0	0	0	0	0	0	0	0	1	.000	.000	.000

Smith was sent to Tampa as part of the McGriff deal. He is a steady infielder, who played mostly DH in a brief stint in this year's Arizona Fall League. He was batting .500 this fall before getting injured. 2002 Outlook: C

Julio Zuleta (Pos: 1B, Age: 27, Bats: R)

	G	AB	R	H	D	T	HR	RBI	SB	BB	SO	Avg	OBP	Slg
2001	49	106	11	23	3	0	6	24	0	8	32	.217	.288	.415
Career	79	174	24	43	11	0	9	36	0	10	51	.247	.309	.466

As a pinch-hitter last season Zuleta batted .318, had 13 RBI and slugged an awesome .818 in 22 at-bats. Those numbers should at least earn him a spot on the bench of some big league club. 2002 Outlook: C

Chicago Cubs Minor League Prospects

Organization Overview:

The perception of the Cubs as lovable losers might soon change, if it hasn't already. They improved by 23 wins between 2000 and 2001, the largest increase by any National League team. And the encouraging aspect of the Cubs' reversal of fortune is that it figures to be fortified by an impressive wave of reinforcements. Chicago's system is awash in good prospects at the upper levels who are just beginning their big league career or soon will be. Juan Cruz has a chance to stick in the rotation this season, while Mark Prior, last year's first-round pick, could be there by the end of the campaign. Other hurlers like Carlos Zambrano and Scott Chiasson also are close to contributing. And position players like Corey Patterson, Hee Seop Choi and Bobby Hill could be making impacts in the next year or two. The 2002 Cubs may only consolidate last year's sizable gains, but they look like they're on the brink of serious contention.

Scott Chiasson

Position: P
Opening Day Age: 24
Bats: R **Throws:** R
Born: 8/14/77 in
Ht: 6' 3" **Wt:** 200
Norwich, CT

Recent Statistics

	W	L	ERA	G	GS	Sv	IP	H	R	BB	SO	HR
2001 AA West Tenn	3	4	1.76	52	0	24	61.1	43	15	20	62	2
2001 AAA Iowa	0	0	2.25	11	0	10	12.0	11	3	0	14	1
2001 NL Chicago	1	1	2.70	6	0	0	6.2	5	2	2	6	2

The Cubs grabbed Chiasson with the first pick in the Rule 5 draft last offseason. He had been in Oakland's system, and the two teams eventually agreed to a trade that allowed Chiasson to be outrighted to the minors last March. Considering he hadn't yet pitched above Class-A, he probably needed the seasoning. The Cubs used him exclusively in relief, and he responded with a 1.84 ERA between two minor league levels. He's made a slight adjustment in his delivery that, along with the chance to go hard in shorter bursts out of the bullpen, helped increase his velocity into the 95-97 MPH range. He also throws a slider and has added a splitter. Chiasson can be expected to fight for a spot in the team's bullpen this year.

Hee Seop Choi

Position: 1B
Opening Day Age: 23
Bats: L **Throws:** L
Born: 3/16/79 in
Ht: 6' 5" **Wt:** 235
Chun-Nam, South Korea

Recent Statistics

	G	AB	R	H	D	T	HR	RBI	SB	BB	SO	Avg
2000 A Daytona	96	345	60	102	25	6	15	70	4	37	78	.296
2000 AA West Tenn	36	122	25	37	9	0	10	25	3	25	38	.303
2001 AAA Iowa	77	266	38	61	11	0	13	45	5	34	67	.229
2001 MLE	77	258	30	53	9	0	10	36	3	27	70	.205

When the Cubs allowed Mark Grace to sign as a free agent with Arizona after the 2000 season, many ob-servers expected Choi to eventually fill the vacuum at first base. That may still occur, but with Fred McGriff in the picture, Choi may have to wait another year or so. Although Choi hurt his hand and missed some time last season, he still managed to hit his share of home runs. His batting average dropped substantially from previous levels, however. A native of Korea, Choi is big man but fairly nimble in the field and on the bases. If healthy, his power stroke could merit a callup later this season.

Juan Cruz

Position: P
Opening Day Age: 21
Bats: R **Throws:** R
Born: 10/15/80 in
Ht: 6' 2" **Wt:** 155
Banao, DR

Recent Statistics

	W	L	ERA	G	GS	Sv	IP	H	R	BB	SO	HR
2001 AA West Tenn	9	6	4.01	23	23	0	121.1	107	56	60	137	6
2001 NL Chicago	3	1	3.22	8	8	0	44.2	40	16	17	39	4

Cruz signed out of the Dominican Republic in 1997. He shot through the Cubs' system, reaching Wrigley Field last August. Even though he's on the slight side, Cruz fires his fastball in the 94-97 MPH range. *Baseball America* last year called his breaking ball the best in the Cubs' minor leagues. It's a slider that darts and breaks late. He also throws a very good changeup. His assortment helped him make a pretty good impression in his eight starts for the Cubs, as he allowed three runs or less in seven of those outings. Some believe a spot in Chicago's rotation is Cruz' for the taking this spring. But he's been mentioned in trade possibilities, as well.

Bobby Hill

Position: 2B
Opening Day Age: 23
Bats: B **Throws:** R
Born: 4/3/78 in San
Ht: 5' 10" **Wt:** 180
Jose, CA

Recent Statistics

	G	AB	R	H	D	T	HR	RBI	SB	BB	SO	Avg
2000 IND Newark	132	481	109	157	22	9	13	82	81	101	57	.326
2001 R Cubs	3	9	1	2	0	0	0	1	1	2	3	.222
2001 AA West Tenn	57	209	30	63	8	1	3	21	20	32	39	.301
2001 MLE	57	205	27	59	7	0	2	19	15	25	41	.288

At times it seemed that Hill never would come to terms with a major league team. Drafted in the fifth round by the Angels in 1996, he instead opted for the University of Miami. Drafted in the second round by the White Sox in 1999, he instead played in an independent league the following season. Drafted in the second round by the Cubs in 2000, he finally signed that November. But the wait may be worthwhile. He possesses a leadoff man's skills, with the ability to hit for average, draw walks and steal bases. He played shortstop in college, but shifted to second base last year. Bothered by a groin injury for much of the season, he hit .345 in the Arizona Fall League. Despite his relative lack of professional experi-ence, he could reach Chicago sometime this year.

Chicago (NL)

Nic Jackson

Position: OF
Bats: L **Throws:** R
Ht: 6' 3" **Wt:** 205

Opening Day Age: 22
Born: 9/25/79 in
Richmond, VA

Recent Statistics

	G	AB	R	H	D	T	HR	RBI	SB	BB	SO	Avg
2000 A Eugene	74	294	39	75	12	7	6	47	25	22	64	.255
2001 A Daytona	131	503	87	149	30	6	19	85	24	39	96	.296

The Cubs selected Jackson in the third round of the 2000 draft with a pick they had acquired for losing Steve Trachsel. Jackson debuted with a fine performance in the Northwest League, ranking near the top in many offensive categories. And he emerged further in high Class-A last season, raising his average near .300 while continuing to show a nice package of power and speed. A *Baseball America* poll of Florida State League managers named him the most exciting player in the circuit. He led the league in total bases and finished second in RBI. Jackson has the ability to play center field, but might project better in a corner spot. He held his own in the Arizona Fall League and should be ready to move up to Double-A in 2002.

Dave Kelton

Position: 3B
Bats: R **Throws:** R
Ht: 6' 3" **Wt:** 205

Opening Day Age: 22
Born: 12/17/79 in
Dothan, AL

Recent Statistics

	G	AB	R	H	D	T	HR	RBI	SB	BB	SO	Avg
2000 A Daytona	132	523	75	140	30	7	18	84	7	38	120	.268
2001 AA West Tenn	58	224	33	70	9	4	12	45	1	24	55	.313
2001 MLE	58	220	30	66	8	3	11	41	0	19	58	.300

Kelton's 2001 season was similar to Hill's in a number of ways. Like Hill, Kelton played at Double-A and batted over .300. And like Hill, Kelton missed much of the campaign due to injury—in Kelton's case, a wrist ailment. Kelton also was going to try another position, left field, at the time of his physical problems. He's had troubles with throwing errors, so a shift to the outfield may be beneficial. A second-round pick in 1998, he shows nice power potential at the plate. He also produced a nice average in the Arizona Fall League, helping alleviate lingering health fears. He still strikes out quite a bit, and there may be questions about his best position, but Kelton's offense could carry him up the ladder.

Corey Patterson

Position: OF
Bats: L **Throws:** R
Ht: 5' 9" **Wt:** 180

Opening Day Age: 22
Born: 8/13/79 in Atlanta,
GA

Recent Statistics

	G	AB	R	H	D	T	HR	RBI	SB	BB	SO	Avg
2001 AAA Iowa	89	367	63	93	22	3	7	32	19	29	65	.253
2001 NL Chicago	59	131	26	29	3	0	4	14	4	6	33	.221
2001 MLE	89	355	50	81	19	2	5	25	14	23	68	.228

Patterson technically is not a rookie, having surpassed the maximum limit for at-bats. Still, he hasn't yet established himself in the big leagues. He also hasn't produced overwhelming numbers in the minors the past couple years, posting gradually declining batting averages and slugging percentages. But that doesn't mean Patterson isn't a good prospect or that he isn't the Cubs' center fielder of the (near) future. He continues to display fine speed, as well as nice power potential for a guy who can handle the center field chores. However, he's had problems against lefthanded pitching in the minors. And he doesn't draw as many walks as he could, though he can be a good "bad-ball" hitter. This could be the year Patterson grabs hold of a big league job.

Carlos Zambrano

Position: P
Bats: L **Throws:** R
Ht: 6' 4" **Wt:** 220

Opening Day Age: 20
Born: 6/1/81 in
Carabobo, VZ

Recent Statistics

	W	L	ERA	G	GS	Sv	IP	H	R	BB	SO	HR
2001 AAA Iowa	10	5	3.88	26	25	0	150.2	124	73	68	155	9
2001 NL Chicago	1	2	15.26	6	1	0	7.2	11	13	8	4	2

Zambrano was signed out of Venezuela in 1997. He's got good size and throws very hard, with a fastball that tops out at 99 MPH. He maintains his velocity deep into games, keeping it in the mid-90s even in the late innings. He can add movement to the heater by changing his arm slot, though the same tactic can cause his slider to flatten out. After working exclusively out of the bullpen at Triple-A in 2000, he returned to the rotation last year. He was very tough on righthanded batters while at Iowa, surrendering a puny .186 average. He didn't enjoy nearly the same kind of success during his trial with the Cubs, however. While his listed age is quite young, Zambrano might be able to crack Chicago's staff at some point this season, though his role isn't certain.

Others to Watch

Righthander **Ben Christensen** (24) had shoulder surgery and missed most of 2001. He's a sinker-slider guy and throws four pitches for strikes. . . Righthander **Jose Cueto** (23) has worked as both a starter and reliever and reached Double-A last year. His mid-90s fastball shows a bit more downward movement when he takes something off, and his slider may be even better. . . **Luis Montanez** (20) was the Cubs' first pick in the 2000 draft. He has a chance to be a decent offensive shortstop, but he strikes out a lot and may not be a terrific defender. . . Righthander **Mark Prior** (21) has been described by some as the best pitching prospect ever to come out of college. He has great command of his mid-90s fastball and it isn't inconceivable that he could make it to Chicago in his first pro season. . . Like Prior, lefthander **Steve Smyth** (23) is a product of USC. Smyth led the Southern League in ERA last season and throws four pretty good pitches. . . Righthander **Todd Wellemeyer** (23) struck out 167 batters in 147 innings at Lansing. His low-90s fastball has lots of life.

Cinergy Field

Offense

Modifications made due to ongoing construction of Cincinnati's new ballpark made a big difference at Cinergy Field. The ball carried well to both left- and right-center field. The opening of the outfield fence made wind much more of a factor. And installing a grass surface created a completely different feel to the whole stadium.

Defense

Though the elimination of artificial turf was a big change, Reds infielders adapted well to the natural surface. Outfield play was tougher than ever due to the wind conditions. As always, play along the foul lines was difficult due to the small amount of foul territory and the on-field bullpens that at times represent a hazard to outfielders.

Who It Helps the Most

Young sluggers like Adam Dunn have no trouble with the friendly power alleys at Cinergy Field. Cincinnati's batting order of line-drive hitters is helped by the gaps in right- and left-center. It also is a ballpark in which Ken Griffey Jr. can do a lot of damage if he's healthy for a full season. Aaron Boone enjoyed great success at Cinergy in 2001, batting .332 with 10 home runs, compared to a .255 average and four homers on the road.

Who It Hurts the Most

Ironically, the Reds played some of their worst baseball in Cincinnati, where they posted the lowest home winning percentage in the major leagues. With flyball pitchers lacking overpowering stuff, the Reds were vulnerable to the home run, which is one of the primary reasons for their struggles at home in 2001. Pete Harnisch surrendered seven home runs in only 15 home innings last season. Danny Graves sustained six of his seven blown saves at home.

Rookies & Newcomers

This is the last year for Cinergy Field, which means Cincinnati's many outstanding prospects likely will make their mark in the new ballpark. In the meantime, the key for 2002 will be to find pitchers who can keep flyballs to a minimum and take advantage of the solid team defense.

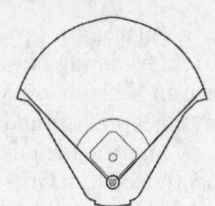

Dimensions: LF-325, LCF-370, CF-393, RCF-373, RF-325

Capacity: 39,800

Elevation: 550 feet

Surface: Grass

Foul Territory: Average

Park Factors

	Home Games			Away Games			Index
2001 Season							
	Reds	Opp	Total	Reds	Opp	Total	
G	75	75	150	72	72	144	—
Avg	.265	.280	.273	.263	.273	.268	102
AB	2560	2693	5253	2519	2431	4950	102
R	325	409	734	352	360	712	99
H	678	755	1433	663	663	1326	104
2B	153	171	324	124	139	263	116
3B	5	10	15	16	15	31	46
HR	76	98	174	87	76	163	101
BB	209	242	451	215	235	450	94
SO	499	450	949	568	422	990	90
E	64	59	123	64	56	120	98
E-Infield	53	49	102	52	50	102	96
LHB-Avg	.295	.280	.288	.288	.282	.285	101
LHB-HR	37	44	81	53	39	92	84
RHB-Avg	.242	.280	.262	.243	.267	.255	103
RHB-HR	39	54	93	34	37	71	123

	Home Games			Away Games			Index
1999-2000							
	Reds	Opp	Total	Reds	Opp	Total	
G	149	149	298	147	147	294	—
Avg	.274	.255	.265	.270	.243	.257	103
AB	4975	5152	10127	5243	4762	10005	100
R	758	711	1469	760	609	1369	106
H	1364	1315	2679	1415	1155	2570	103
2B	276	305	581	283	261	544	106
3B	29	27	56	41	27	68	81
HR	174	201	375	195	139	334	111
BB	542	590	1132	474	582	1056	106
SO	895	977	1872	1031	926	1957	95
E	97	83	180	97	115	212	84
E-Infield	77	70	147	77	93	170	85
LHB-Avg	.289	.263	.275	.286	.249	.267	103
LHB-HR	66	67	133	85	57	142	96
RHB-Avg	.266	.251	.259	.261	.239	.251	103
RHB-HR	108	134	242	110	82	192	122

2001 Rankings (National League)

- Third-highest double factor
- Second-lowest triple factor
- Second-lowest walk factor
- Third-lowest strikeout factor

Cincinnati

Bob Boone

2001 Season

It is impossible to fairly judge the managing performance of Bob Boone in 2001, considering how he went through the entire season without ever having his anticipated everyday lineup intact and healthy. The Reds sustained many injuries, including a serious hamstring pull that affected Ken Griffey Jr. and a groin pull and eventual hernia surgery that ruined Barry Larkin's season. In addition, Cincinnati endured year-long problems with starting pitching. It's no wonder then that Boone never had the Reds in contention.

Offense

Much of last season was spent experimenting or filling in at various positions. However, if everyone is healthy, Boone could go with a set lineup at most of the spots. With decent speed throughout the order, Boone likes to force the action with hit-and-run plays or steals. He also is not afraid to be unconventional when choosing the count or selecting the timing of his plays.

Pitching & Defense

With one of the worst starting rotations in baseball, Boone has had to lean on his bullpen out of necessity. He used his relievers early and often last year, as Scott Sullivan, Danny Graves and Jim Brower each topped 80 relief innings. However, Boone does a good job of keeping his bullpen as fresh as possible under the circumstances. He is very defense-oriented as a manager. He calls many of the pitches from the dugout and places great importance on his team making the fundamental plays in the field. Despite the team's injury woes in 2001, he made only an average number of defensive substitutions.

2002 Outlook

Boone has to have better luck with injuries than he did a year ago. Changes on the coaching staff (the Reds will not renew the contracts of third-base coach Ron Oester and first-base coach Bill Doran) also mean there should be much less tension around the team than there was in 2001. By leading a potentially dynamic everyday lineup and working with a lot of new players, Boone will have what amounts to a fresh start this season.

Born: 11/19/47 in San Diego, CA

Playing Experience: 1972-1990, Phi, Ana, KC

Managerial Experience: 4 seasons

Manager Statistics

Year	Team, Lg	W	L	Pct	GB	Finish
2001	Cincinnati, NL	66	96	.407	27.0	5th Central
4 Seasons		247	302	.450	—	—

2001 Starting Pitchers by Days Rest

	<=3	4	5	6+
Reds Starts	0	84	47	19
Reds ERA	—	6.18	4.90	4.57
NL Avg Starts	1	80	47	24
NL ERA	5.03	4.43	4.53	4.28

2001 Situational Stats

	Bob Boone	NL Average
Hit & Run Success %	31.9	35.1
Stolen Base Success %	65.6	66.5
Platoon Pct.	53.2	51.5
Defensive Subs	19	20
High-Pitch Outings	1	7
Quick/Slow Hooks	24/11	19/14
Sacrifice Attempts	88	87

2001 Rankings (National League)

- 1st in steals of home plate (2)
- 2nd in saves with over 1 inning pitched (9)
- 3rd in starting lineups used (132), pinch-hitters used (313) and quick hooks

Aaron Boone

2001 Season

Three different hand injuries helped limit Aaron Boone to just 103 games last season. Still, he produced decent power numbers when he was in the lineup. He slugged 14 homers and drove in 62 runs in only 381 at-bats, establishing himself as the Reds' front-line third baseman. He displayed significantly more power in home games last year. It was the fourth straight season in which he batted between .280 and .294 overall.

Hitting

Boone has greatly increased his strength over the past three years. He also has opened his stance slightly to allow him to handle balls on the inner half of the plate. He now is able to drive more balls away to right-center. Boone doesn't work deep counts and is prone to chase offspeed pitches out of the strike zone. He also must react more quickly to pitches that dive in at him. He can't afford to continue to miss large chunks of the season.

Baserunning & Defense

Though he possesses only average speed, Boone is a smart baserunner who doesn't make many mistakes and can't be ignored as an occasional basestealer. He remains inconsistent at third base, where he was on pace for more than 30 errors last season had he played in all 162 games. Boone's range is good and he has a solid, accurate arm. However, he is prone to mishandle balls in front of him and at times doesn't get himself in the best position to field grounders.

2002 Outlook

Boone has missed significant playing time during each of the past two seasons, hindering his development into a top-flight third baseman. He needs a full and healthy season to emerge into the 25-homer, 90-RBI player he seems capable of being. It may be worth remembering that his brother Bret enjoyed a banner year at age 32 in 2001. With so many other questions, the Reds are likely to bank on this being the year that Aaron rises to the next level.

Position: 3B
Bats: R **Throws:** R
Ht: 6' 2"   **Wt:** 200

Opening Day Age: 29
Born: 3/9/73 in La Mesa, CA
ML Seasons: 5

Overall Statistics

	G	AB	R	H	D	T	HR	RBI	SB	BB	SO	Avg	OBP	Slg
2001	103	381	54	112	26	2	14	62	6	29	71	.294	.351	.483
Career	400	1374	183	390	84	9	42	210	36	100	243	.284	.342	.450

Where He Hits the Ball

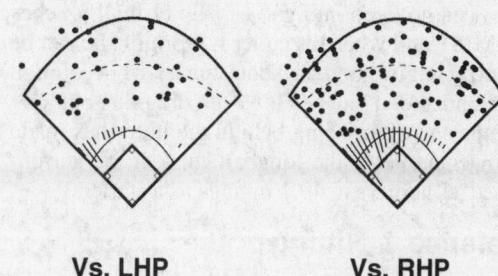

Vs. LHP   **Vs. RHP**

2001 Situational Stats

	AB	H	HR	RBI	Avg		AB	H	HR	RBI	Avg
Home	193	64	10	33	.332	LHP	98	30	5	16	.306
Road	188	48	4	29	.255	RHP	283	82	9	46	.290
First Half	220	64	8	33	.291	Sc Pos	95	27	1	38	.284
Scnd Half	161	48	6	29	.298	Clutch	52	17	2	7	.327

2001 Rankings (National League)
- 3rd in errors at third base (19)
- Led the Reds in sacrifice flies (6)

Jim Brower

Position: RP/SP
Bats: R **Throws:** R
Ht: 6' 2" **Wt:** 205

Opening Day Age: 29
Born: 12/29/72 in Edina, MN
ML Seasons: 3
Pronunciation: BROW-er

2001 Season

The Reds obtained Jim Brower in an offseason deal with the Indians that also involved Eddie Taubensee. Brower began the 2001 campaign by making four starts through the middle of May. He also had a five-start stretch after the All-Star break. Otherwise, he spent most of the year in long and middle relief. Overall, Brower ranked among Cincinnati's leaders in wins, innings pitched and strikeouts while also earning his first major league save.

Pitching

With a good sinker and slider, Brower can be a serviceable pitcher in either a starting or relief role. His arm is durable and reliable. However, he lacks the quality offspeed pitch to be a consistent starter who can go deep into games. His fastball touches 90 MPH, and when his cutter is working, he can be a surprisingly good strikeout hurler who is tough on righthanded hitters. However, dragging out long counts and often being behind the hitter has made Brower prone to the longball. In fact, he surrendered 11 homers in 49.1 innings as a starter.

Defense & Hitting

Brower doesn't get himself into good fielding position and can make mistakes with the glove, as his three errors over the past two seasons demonstrate. He does a decent job of holding runners, despite being fairly slow to the plate. Brower is a very good hitting pitcher who hit better than .300 last year. His eight hits ranked second among Reds hurlers.

2002 Outlook

On a Cincinnati pitching staff that has any number of questions, Brower's flexibility is a definite asset. While his ERA was a less-than-sparkling 6.02 in a starting role last year, it was an impressive 2.70 when coming on in relief. The Reds know Brower has the ability to do a passable job as a starter. However, it seems more likely that he will end up as a middle man in the bullpen, where he also can be available for spot starts.

Overall Statistics

	W	L	Pct.	ERA	G	GS	Sv	IP	H	BB	SO	HR	Ratio
2001	7	10	.412	3.97	46	10	1	129.1	119	60	94	17	1.38
Career	12	14	.462	4.69	72	23	1	217.0	226	101	144	36	1.51

How Often He Throws Strikes

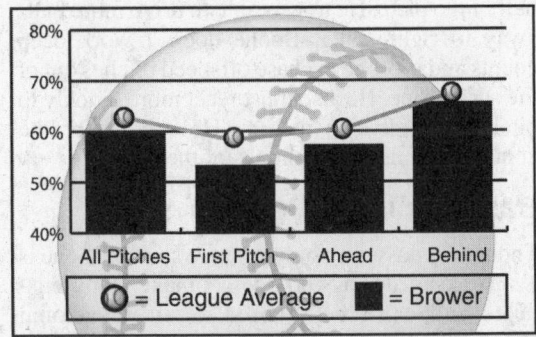

= League Average **= Brower**

2001 Situational Stats

	W	L	ERA	Sv	IP		AB	H	HR	RBI	Avg
Home	0	5	4.98	1	65.0	LHB	206	56	7	25	.272
Road	7	5	2.94	0	64.1	RHB	276	63	10	33	.228
First Half	4	6	3.62	1	69.2	Sc Pos	122	28	2	39	.230
Scnd Half	3	4	4.37	0	59.2	Clutch	39	11	2	4	.282

2001 Rankings (National League)

- 2nd in relief losses (7)
- 6th in lowest batting average allowed in relief (.202), lowest batting average allowed in relief with runners on base (.189) and lowest batting average allowed in relief with runners in scoring position (.171)
- 9th in relief ERA (2.70)
- Led the Reds in walks allowed, wild pitches (5), lowest batting average allowed vs. righthanded batters, lowest batting average allowed with runners in scoring position, relief losses (7), relief ERA (2.70), lowest batting average allowed in relief (.202) and fewest baserunners allowed per nine innings in relief (11.3)

Sean Casey

2001 Season

With injuries riddling the Reds all season, Sean Casey was the one constant in their lineup. He led Cincinnati in most major offensive categories, including games, hits, doubles, batting average and RBI. He batted over .300 for the third straight year and performed very well with runners in scoring position. However, he slumped badly in September, when he hit just .188.

Hitting

Casey's ability to develop more power remains in question. After clubbing 25 homers in 1999, his total dipped for the second straight year in 2001. He has the strength to hit the ball out anywhere, but he seems more comfortable driving the ball to the opposite field for singles and doubles. For a big man, he is tough to strike out. In addition, Casey always has handled himself against lefthanded pitching. Until he starts hitting more homers, the book on him will consist of crowding him inside with hard stuff and letting him have all the singles to left field that he's willing to take.

Baserunning & Defense

Despite the lack of great speed, Casey uses good judgment on the bases. Once in a great while, he can surprise opposing pitchers with a stolen base. He has improved every year as a first baseman. Though his range is limited, Casey has good hands, is solid at picking balls out of the dirt and has greatly smoothed out his footwork around the bag.

2002 Outlook

At first glance, you'd think the popular Casey would be a definite part of the Reds' future. However, he was unhappy with how general manager Jim Bowden floated his supposed contract demands. Although it would take a major deal, it is not out of the question that Cincinnati might use Casey to pare its payroll. If his power ever comes along, he would move into the top group of first basemen in the game.

Position: 1B
Bats: L **Throws:** R
Ht: 6' 4" **Wt:** 225

Opening Day Age: 27
Born: 7/2/74 in Willingboro, NJ
ML Seasons: 5
Pronunciation: KAY-see

Overall Statistics

	G	AB	R	H	D	T	HR	RBI	SB	BB	SO	Avg	OBP	Slg
2001	145	533	69	165	40	0	13	89	3	43	63	.310	.369	.458
Career	531	1919	286	597	136	6	65	326	5	200	278	.311	.382	.490

Where He Hits the Ball

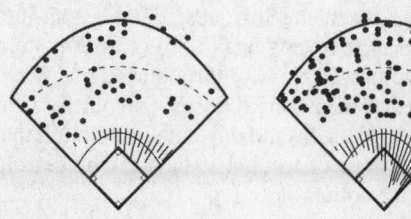

Vs. LHP   **Vs. RHP**

2001 Situational Stats

	AB	H	HR	RBI	Avg		AB	H	HR	RBI	Avg
Home	244	67	5	34	.275	LHP	156	43	2	22	.276
Road	289	98	8	55	.339	RHP	377	122	11	67	.324
First Half	301	99	10	61	.329	Sc Pos	146	52	3	72	.356
Scnd Half	232	66	3	28	.284	Clutch	75	27	1	14	.360

2001 Rankings (National League)

- 2nd in batting average on the road
- Led the Reds in batting average, runs scored, hits, singles, doubles, RBI, times on base (217), plate appearances (588), games played, on-base percentage, highest groundball-flyball ratio (1.8), most pitches seen per plate appearance (3.39), lowest percentage of swings that missed (14.3), highest percentage of swings put into play (46.2), batting average with runners in scoring position, batting average vs. righthanded pitchers, cleanup slugging percentage (.476), on-base percentage vs. lefthanded pitchers (.327), on-base percentage vs. righthanded pitchers (.386), batting average on the road and lowest percentage of swings on the first pitch (32.6)

Elmer Dessens

Position: SP
Bats: R **Throws:** R
Ht: 6' 0" **Wt:** 187

Opening Day Age: 30
Born: 1/13/72 in
Hermosillo, Mexico
ML Seasons: 5
Pronunciation:
dah-SENZ

2001 Season

Only two years removed from pitching in Japan, Elmer Dessens became the Reds' most reliable starting pitcher last season. Of course, that only may be a reflection of the Reds' current pitching problems. He led Cincinnati starters in all major categories and has won 21 games over the past two seasons, more than any Reds hurler.

Pitching

Dessens pitched more than 200 innings for the first time in his professional career. His success in 2001 can be attributed to his learning to more consistently change speeds, as well as his development of a good cutter and a two-seam sinking fastball, which led to an increase in groundballs. His four-seamer can reach the low 90s, but he gets into trouble when he reverts back to his earlier pattern of trying to power his way through hitters. When he's up in the strike zone, Dessens is vulnerable to the longball. He lacks the one consistent pitch that can get him out of trouble if he's pitching from behind in the count.

Defense & Hitting

Baserunners can have a tough time trying to steal on Dessens, though he lacks a quality pickoff move and at times gets distracted with men on base. Opposing thieves were successful on just 13 of 28 attempts in 2001. He is an adequate fielder of his position and gets off the mound fairly well to handle bunts. At the plate, Dessens is not an automatic out. He led all Reds pitchers with 11 hits last year and is capable of making fairly consistent contact.

2002 Outlook

In the muddled Cincinnati starting pitching situation, Dessens has emerged as one of the few givens entering this season. By no means does he possess top-of-the-rotation talent, and some might consider him no better than a journeyman. But he has proven himself capable of taking the ball every fifth day and keeping his club in the majority of games he starts. For better or worse, that ability makes him the Reds' ace heading into the spring .

Overall Statistics

	W	L	Pct.	ERA	G	GS	Sv	IP	H	BB	SO	HR	Ratio
2001	10	14	.417	4.48	34	34	0	205.0	221	56	128	32	1.35
Career	23	27	.460	4.78	135	58	1	455.1	523	128	271	54	1.43

How Often He Throws Strikes

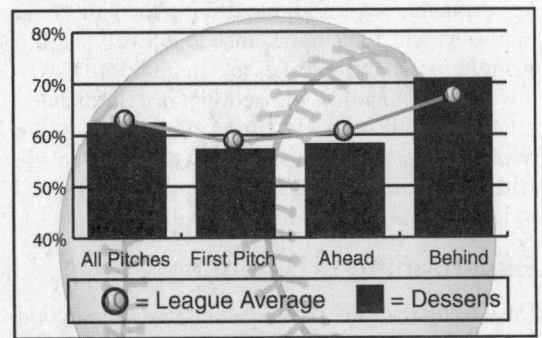

2001 Situational Stats

	W	L	ERA	Sv	IP		AB	H	HR	RBI	Avg
Home	6	8	3.74	0	120.1	LHB	369	120	18	43	.325
Road	4	6	5.53	0	84.2	RHB	422	101	14	49	.239
First Half	6	6	4.58	0	106.0	Sc Pos	152	49	4	56	.322
Scnd Half	4	8	4.36	0	99.0	Clutch	16	7	1	2	.438

2001 Rankings (National League)

- 1st in runners caught stealing (15) and fielding percentage at pitcher (1.000)
- 3rd in highest batting average allowed with runners in scoring position
- Led the Reds in ERA, sacrifice bunts (10), wins, games started, innings pitched, hits allowed, batters faced (862), home runs allowed, strikeouts, pitches thrown (3,181), stolen bases allowed (13), GDPs induced (15), winning percentage, highest strikeout-walk ratio (2.3), lowest batting average allowed (.279), lowest slugging percentage allowed (.442), lowest on-base percentage allowed (.325), highest groundball-flyball ratio allowed (1.3), lowest ERA at home and most strikeouts per nine innings (5.6)

Adam Dunn

2001 Season

In a Reds season fraught with so many disappointments, the arrival of Adam Dunn was certainly a bright spot. He had entered 2001 as one of baseball's best prospects, but hadn't yet played above Class-A. He blew through Double-A and Triple-A before arriving in the big leagues last July. The outfielder made an immediate impression, slugging nine home runs in his first month with the Reds. He finished with 19 homers in less than half a season in the majors. Combining that total with his minor league numbers, Dunn blasted 51 homers at all levels of play in 2001.

Hitting

The sky's the limit for Dunn, who is still developing physically and has only begun to learn to use his impressive strength, which is McGwire-esque. Dunn hangs in well against lefthanded pitching, and even with his limited professional experience, he has shown a promising knowledge of the strike zone. He is going to have his share of strikeouts because hard stuff up and in can tie him up. He is vulnerable to chasing offspeed stuff, too. However, he can hit the ball out to any field and has the kind of compact stroke that should help him eventually be something close to a .300 hitter.

Baserunning & Defense

Despite his size, Dunn is an above-average baserunner who is capable of stealing bases. He has improved significantly as an outfielder and has looked comfortable in right field. Dunn has average range and does not possess an exceptional throwing arm. He is the kind of athlete who continues to upgrade his release and footwork.

2002 Outlook

Dunn boasts all the characteristics of a star in the making. His physical ability is impressive and he also impressed the Reds with his work ethic and coachability. Possessing the tools to be an impact player, few observers would be surprised if Dunn begins fulfilling his immense potential this season.

Position: RF/LF
Bats: L **Throws:** R
Ht: 6' 6" **Wt:** 240

Opening Day Age: 22
Born: 11/9/79 in Houston, TX
ML Seasons: 1

Overall Statistics

	G	AB	R	H	D	T	HR	RBI	SB	BB	SO	Avg	OBP	Slg
2001	66	244	54	64	18	1	19	43	4	38	74	.262	.371	.578
Career	66	244	54	64	18	1	19	43	4	38	74	.262	.371	.578

Where He Hits the Ball

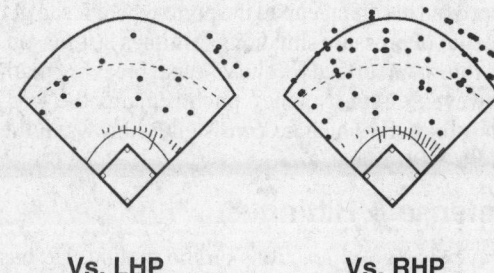

Vs. LHP   **Vs. RHP**

2001 Situational Stats

	AB	H	HR	RBI	Avg		AB	H	HR	RBI	Avg
Home	108	23	8	19	.213	LHP	71	20	6	14	.282
Road	136	41	11	24	.301	RHP	173	44	13	29	.254
First Half	0	0	0	0	-	Sc Pos	64	13	3	21	.203
Scnd Half	244	64	19	43	.262	Clutch	25	6	2	3	.240

2001 Rankings (National League)
- 2nd in home runs among rookies
- 5th in RBI among rookies

Danny Graves

Position: RP
Bats: R **Throws:** R
Ht: 5'11" **Wt:** 185

Opening Day Age: 28
Born: 8/7/73 in Saigon, Vietnam
ML Seasons: 6

2001 Season

Though both his earned run average and opponents' batting average rose considerably, Danny Graves again was one of the National League's top closers. He earned a career-high 32 saves, even though he often went several days between save opportunities. Only 10 of those 32 saves were recorded at home, where he compiled a 6.21 ERA. Opponents reached him for a .335 average at Cinergy Field, compared to a .197 mark on the road.

Pitching

Like many sinkerball pitchers, Graves' fastball often improves with the more work he gets. When he sits for several days, he often overthrows and tends to pitch from behind in the count. Graves has improved his changeup to the point where it can get him out of pressure situations. At times last season, he threw an effective slurve-type breaking ball. However, Graves' money pitch remains the two-seam fastball, which he consistently throws in the 92-96 MPH range.

Defense & Hitting

Graves has good reactions on the mound. He has worked on improving his move to first but still is vulnerable to stolen bases. He is also quickly developing a reputation as a dangerous hitter. Amazingly, he made his only hit of the year a home run—for the second straight season. Both homers occurred at Enron Field in Houston.

2002 Outlook

Graves has established his credentials as a top reliever by averaging 30 saves over the past three seasons. As a result, he is becoming a very expensive commodity. He also is eligible for arbitration. So the question now is whether he has become enough of a financial risk that the Reds feel the necessity to shop him. No matter where he pitches, Graves brings the competitive mentality of a closer just entering his prime.

Overall Statistics

	W	L	Pct.	ERA	G	GS	Sv	IP	H	BB	SO	HR	Ratio
2001	6	5	.545	4.15	66	0	32	80.1	83	18	49	7	1.26
Career	28	18	.609	3.47	299	0	97	419.2	400	167	248	35	1.35

How Often He Throws Strikes

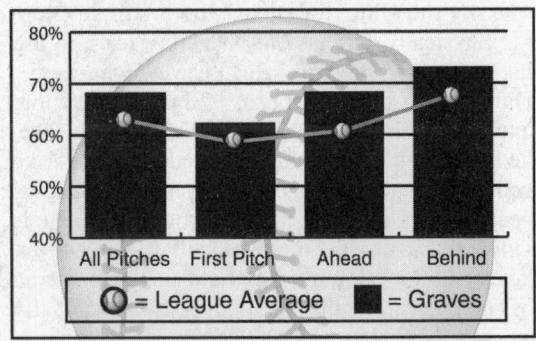

2001 Situational Stats

	W	L	ERA	Sv	IP		AB	H	HR	RBI	Avg
Home	3	4	6.21	10	37.2	LHB	133	40	5	27	.301
Road	3	1	2.32	22	42.2	RHB	177	43	2	19	.243
First Half	2	2	4.01	16	42.2	Sc Pos	97	27	4	41	.278
Scnd Half	4	3	4.30	16	37.2	Clutch	212	62	4	35	.292

2001 Rankings (National League)

- 2nd in blown saves (7) and fewest strikeouts per nine innings in relief (5.5)
- 3rd in lowest save percentage (82.1)
- 6th in relief wins (6)
- 7th in save opportunities (39) and saves
- 8th in games finished (54)
- 10th in relief losses (5), relief innings (80.1) and highest batting average allowed in relief (.268)
- Led the Reds in saves, games finished (54), save opportunities (39), most GDPs induced per GDP situation (18.5%), save percentage (82.1) and blown saves (7)

Ken Griffey Jr.

2001 Season

Ken Griffey Jr.'s season was seriously affected when he pulled up lame with a major hamstring injury in an exhibition game last spring. He was sidelined until June (he did have a handful of at-bats in April as a pinch-hitter) and hobbled for most of the campaign. Though he never completely recovered from the injury, Griffey was able to generate numbers that, when projected over a full season, would have been comparable to the superstar seasons he routinely has produced throughout his career.

Hitting

Griffey always is going to hit a lot of home runs. The question is whether he will make the necessary adjustments to again be the .300 hitter he hasn't been the last four seasons. He often has seemed to concentrate too much on lifting the ball, which can make him vulnerable to hard stuff up in the strike zone. Pitchers also can get him out with offspeed stuff off the outside corner. However, Griffey's bat speed is among the best in the game, and he doesn't miss many mistakes over the inner half of the plate.

Baserunning & Defense

Griffey's days as a basestealer may be behind him, especially if the hamstring trouble lingers. He remains an outstanding baserunner who rarely makes mistakes when trying for the extra base. While his range was affected somewhat by his leg troubles, even a subpar Griffey is one of baseball's best center fielders. He has unsurpassed instincts and aggressiveness in the field.

2002 Outlook

It would have been understandable had Griffey shut himself down for the season last year. Instead, he sent a positive message to the Reds when he worked hard to return and post a solid second half. Griffey has nearly 900 National League at-bats under his belt. If there are no lingering affects from his injury, virtually no power numbers are out of the question for him in 2002.

Position: CF
Bats: L **Throws:** L
Ht: 6' 3" **Wt:** 205

Opening Day Age: 32
Born: 11/21/69 in Donora, PA
ML Seasons: 13
Nickname: Junior, The Kid

Overall Statistics

	G	AB	R	H	D	T	HR	RBI	SB	BB	SO	Avg	OBP	Slg
2001	111	364	57	104	20	2	22	65	2	44	72	.286	.365	.533
Career	1791	6716	1220	1987	362	35	460	1335	175	885	1173	.296	.379	.566

Where He Hits the Ball

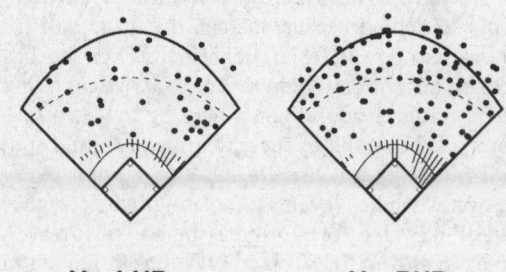

Vs. LHP   **Vs. RHP**

2001 Situational Stats

	AB	H	HR	RBI	Avg		AB	H	HR	RBI	Avg
Home	184	60	12	37	.326	LHP	126	32	5	22	.254
Road	180	44	10	28	.244	RHP	238	72	17	43	.303
First Half	88	20	4	12	.227	Sc Pos	87	27	3	40	.310
Scnd Half	276	84	18	53	.304	Clutch	68	21	2	14	.309

2001 Rankings (National League)
- 9th in lowest batting average vs. lefthanded pitchers
- 10th in errors in center field (3)
- Led the Reds in home runs, walks and slugging percentage vs. lefthanded pitchers (.437)

Barry Larkin

2001 Season

Injuries have played a big part in Barry Larkin's career, and the bug bit him again last year. He made two trips to the disabled list, beginning with a serious groin pull in late May and early June. He lasted only a couple of weeks after coming off the DL before hernia surgery ended his season. Limited to 45 total games, Larkin's injuries rendered meaningless whatever meager production he managed to provide. It was the second straight season where the Reds competed without their captain for significant periods of time.

Hitting

If Larkin is healthy, you can reasonably assume he'll wind up batting .300 or better. He is a difficult hitter to defend because he can drive the ball for extra-base power to all fields. However, he has looked uncomfortable in recent years when asked to bat in the leadoff spot, where he tends to lose some of the aggressiveness that makes him a special hitter. Larkin usually has one stretch every season when he elevates too many pitches or goes out of the strike zone for breaking balls. However, he has a proven track record of being a reliable run producer.

Baserunning & Defense

Larkin's recent groin troubles and prior knee problems have caused his stolen base totals to decline. But he remains a reliable basestealer who knows how to pick his spots. His physical troubles may have played a more significant role in the field, where his once magnificent range appeared to deteriorate last season. He has one of the better infield throwing arms in baseball.

2002 Outlook

Cincinnati gambled when it signed Larkin to a multiyear contract extension during the 2000 campaign. The Reds got burned when he was sidelined for three-fourths of last season. However, he was feeling close to 100 percent in October and ready for a rigorous offseason conditioning program. Don't bet against him coming back and being a major factor for the Reds once again.

Position: SS
Bats: R **Throws:** R
Ht: 6' 0" **Wt:** 185

Opening Day Age: 37
Born: 4/28/64 in Cincinnati, OH
ML Seasons: 16

Overall Statistics

	G	AB	R	H	D	T	HR	RBI	SB	BB	SO	Avg	OBP	Slg
2001	45	156	29	40	12	0	2	17	3	27	25	.256	.373	.372
Career	1854	6843	1163	2048	373	70	181	851	362	839	689	.299	.377	.454

Where He Hits the Ball

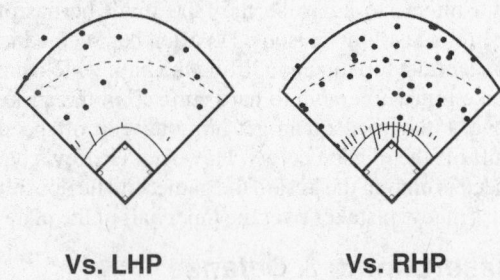

Vs. LHP   **Vs. RHP**

2001 Situational Stats

	AB	H	HR	RBI	Avg		AB	H	HR	RBI	Avg
Home	80	19	1	11	.238	LHP	39	13	1	6	.333
Road	76	21	1	6	.276	RHP	117	27	1	11	.231
First Half	156	40	2	17	.256	Sc Pos	29	8	1	14	.276
Scnd Half	0	0	0	0	-	Clutch	29	7	0	0	.241

2001 Rankings (National League)

- Did not rank near the top or bottom in any category

Pokey Reese

2001 Season

The future once was bright for Pokey Reese, but it turned cloudy after the worst season of his young career. He slipped in most offensive categories and batted just .188 in the top two spots in the lineup. Defensively, he was often shaky in an everyday role at shortstop following Barry Larkin's injury. Reese finished the year largely on the bench.

Hitting

After showing promising tools only a few years ago, Reese's stock as an offensive player has plummeted. The Reds have given up on Reese being a factor as a leadoff hitter, considering his worsening ability to draw walks or improve his on-base percentage. He is overmatched far too often by hard stuff. He also has not been able to apply suggestions to reduce his big swing. While his approach can produce the occasional extra-base hit, it easily can be handled by high fastballs, offspeed stuff and breaking balls out of the strike zone.

Baserunning & Defense

Reese is an excellent baserunner. Only his inability to get on base more consistently has kept him from swiping 40 bags. He gets as good a jump on steals as anyone in the National League and can turn doubles into triples with his great speed. Reese ranks among the best at second base with his good hands, outstanding range and ability to turn double plays. However, he was more erratic making the routine plays, particularly on throws from shortstop, the position at which he always had been projected.

2002 Outlook

When Reds general manager Jim Bowden went public with Reese's supposed contract demands, Reese's performance nose-dived to the point where he was openly asking out of Cincinnati by the end of last season. With the return to health of Larkin and the acquisition of Todd Walker, Reese has become a tradable item for the Reds. He is someone with the youth and ability to turn around his career, possibly in a new uniform.

Position: SS/2B
Bats: R **Throws:** R
Ht: 5'11" **Wt:** 180

Opening Day Age: 28
Born: 6/10/73 in Columbia, SC
ML Seasons: 5

Overall Statistics

	G	AB	R	H	D	T	HR	RBI	SB	BB	SO	Avg	OBP	Slg
2001	133	428	50	96	20	2	9	40	25	34	82	.224	.284	.343
Career	604	2061	279	516	94	15	36	180	120	159	359	.250	.308	.363

Where He Hits the Ball

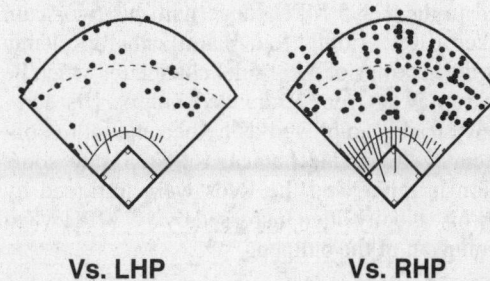

Vs. LHP   **Vs. RHP**

2001 Situational Stats

	AB	H	HR	RBI	Avg		AB	H	HR	RBI	Avg
Home	211	53	4	17	.251	LHP	93	21	3	11	.226
Road	217	43	5	23	.198	RHP	335	75	6	29	.224
First Half	255	57	6	24	.224	Sc Pos	85	18	3	33	.212
Scnd Half	173	39	3	16	.225	Clutch	75	16	0	0	.213

2001 Rankings (National League)

- 1st in stolen-base percentage (86.2)
- 5th in steals of third (6)
- 9th in stolen bases
- Led the Reds in stolen bases, stolen-base percentage (86.2), highest percentage of pitches taken (56.7) and steals of third (6)

Chris Reitsma

2001 Season

The Reds obtained Reitsma in exchange for Dante Bichette in August of 2000. Last year was Reitsma's first in the majors, and he endured some growing pains. Nevertheless, he convinced the Reds that he can be a part of their pitching future. He was among staff leaders in most categories and threw 182 innings, his high as a professional. He may have tired a bit late in the season, posting an 11.40 ERA after September 1.

Pitching

A fractured right elbow suffered in 1997 held Reitsma back early in his career, but he appears to have regained all of his arm strength. He averaged over 90 pitches per start and his velocity consistently held in the 92-95 MPH range with his two-seam sinker and his riding, four-seam fastball. Reitsma has the makings of a big time changeup, which he can run away from lefthanded hitters. His command steadily improved as he became more consistent with his mechanics. Reitsma saw some action in relief, and the Reds were intrigued by how his velocity often increased by 3-5 MPH when coming out of the bullpen.

Defense & Hitting

Reitsma is fairly slow coming home and is vulnerable to stolen bases, though he has a decent pickoff move. He has good athletic tools and can field his position. He struck out in half of his plate appearances, but handles the bat well enough to at least help out with sacrifices and occasional hits.

2002 Outlook

Barring trades, Reitsma would seem to be one of the few givens in the Reds' murky starting rotation. With a better team behind him, there is no reason why he can't be a 12-15 game winner. Some Reds people also view him as a possible option as a closer, because of his makeup and stuff. However, moving him to that role seems a long shot, at least for the immediate future.

Position: SP
Bats: R **Throws:** R
Ht: 6' 5" **Wt:** 214

Opening Day Age: 24
Born: 12/31/77 in Minneapolis, MN
ML Seasons: 1
Pronunciation: REETS-muh

Overall Statistics

	W	L	Pct.	ERA	G	GS	Sv	IP	H	BB	SO	HR	Ratio
2001	7	15	.318	5.29	36	29	0	182.0	209	49	96	23	1.42
Career	7	15	.318	5.29	36	29	0	182.0	209	49	96	23	1.42

How Often He Throws Strikes

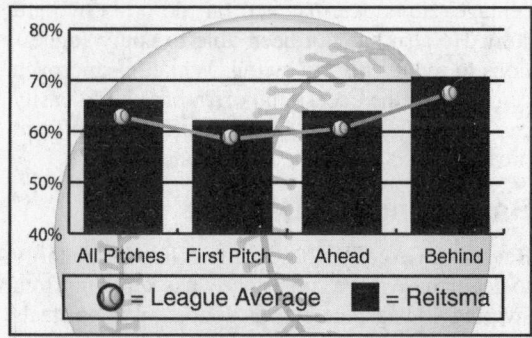

= League Average   = Reitsma

2001 Situational Stats

	W	L	ERA	Sv	IP		AB	H	HR	RBI	Avg
Home	3	10	5.15	0	94.1	LHB	330	92	10	45	.279
Road	4	5	5.44	0	87.2	RHB	395	117	13	65	.296
First Half	4	7	4.20	0	111.1	Sc Pos	179	59	6	84	.330
Scnd Half	3	8	7.00	0	70.2	Clutch	35	12	2	5	.343

2001 Rankings (National League)

- 1st in ERA among rookies, losses among rookies, fielding percentage at pitcher (1.000) and fewest GDPs induced per nine innings (0.2%)
- 2nd in lowest winning percentage and highest batting average allowed with runners in scoring position
- 3rd in highest ERA and fewest strikeouts per nine innings (4.7)
- 4th in losses
- Led the Reds in losses, wild pitches (5), fewest pitches thrown per batter (3.48), lowest ERA on the road, most run support per nine innings (5.1), fewest home runs allowed per nine innings (1.14) and fewest walks per nine innings (2.4)

Todd Walker

2001 Season

Cincinnati became the third stop in two years for Todd Walker, who was acquired from Colorado in a midseason deal. It was the second straight July that he had switched teams. He fit in well with the Reds as their regular second baseman. He batted .295 for them, much in line with the .297 average he produced for the Rockies before the trade. Overall, Walker reached career highs in home runs, runs scored and runs batted in.

Hitting

One concern about Walker always has been his ability to hit lefthanded pitching. He mustered a modest .178 average in 101 at-bats against them in 1999. However, last year he proved he could at least hold his own versus southpaws. He has begun to look for more pitches to drive for power, and last year he produced 54 extra-base hits. But Walker also has managed to maintain decent walk totals. He has become a legitimate extra-base hitter with his short stroke and ability to drive balls to the opposite field. He is a good breaking-ball hitter and stays back well on offspeed pitches.

Baserunning & Defense

Walker has good speed, but at times is guilty of being overly aggressive on the bases. He stole only one base in nine attempts last year. He has worked hard to improve his defensive play, which has been suspect in the past. Though he possesses average range, Walker has become more consistent in his ability to handle the routine plays and has upgraded his ability to turn the double play.

2002 Outlook

With Cincinnati likely to unload an unhappy Pokey Reese, Walker has a good chance of coming to spring training with the second-base job as his to lose. Walker could be poised to firmly establish himself as an everyday player with the ability to hit .300 and post good power numbers for the position. He might emerge as the Reds' best offensive second baseman since Joe Morgan.

Position: 2B
Bats: L **Throws:** R
Ht: 6' 0" **Wt:** 185

Opening Day Age: 28
Born: 5/25/73 in Bakersfield, CA
ML Seasons: 6

Overall Statistics

	G	AB	R	H	D	T	HR	RBI	SB	BB	SO	Avg	OBP	Slg
2001	151	551	93	163	35	2	17	75	1	51	82	.296	.355	.459
Career	594	2096	305	608	137	14	47	249	54	192	302	.290	.348	.436

Where He Hits the Ball

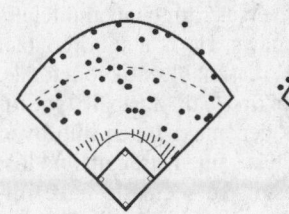 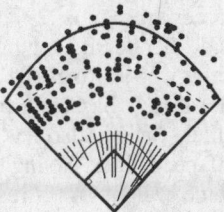

Vs. LHP   **Vs. RHP**

2001 Situational Stats

	AB	H	HR	RBI	Avg		AB	H	HR	RBI	Avg
Home	274	96	13	51	.350	LHP	108	29	2	12	.269
Road	277	67	4	24	.242	RHP	443	134	15	63	.302
First Half	275	83	11	42	.302	Sc Pos	128	35	2	56	.273
Scnd Half	276	80	6	33	.290	Clutch	76	15	2	9	.197

2001 Rankings (National League)

- 4th in errors at second base (11)
- 5th in on-base percentage for a leadoff hitter (.367) and lowest fielding percentage at second base (.984)
- 7th in batting average at home (.350)
- Led the Reds in on-base percentage for a leadoff hitter (.374) and batting average on a 3-2 count (.278)

Dmitri Young

2001 Season

Throughout the Reds' long lost season, no player was more valuable than Dmitri Young. The switch-hitter batted better than .300 for the fourth straight year, while swatting a career-high total of 21 home runs. Young also provided Cincinnati with great versatility by playing 38 games at first base and 36 more at third, in addition to his time in the outfield.

Hitting

Though he hit 31 points higher against righthanded pitchers in 2001, there is no significant career difference between Young's ability to hit from the right and left sides of the plate. That makes him a very tough out and can frustrate opposing managers as they try to gain a platoon advantage. Young's career average is .297 versus righthanded pitchers and .295 versus southpaws. He is a solid contact hitter who routinely has reasonable strikeout totals. He always has been a first-ball, fastball type of hitter. But he also has become a much improved offspeed hitter. Young has gained strength and lost some weight. As a result, he seems to have improved his bat speed, allowing him to turn on more pitches with home-run power.

Baserunning & Defense

Better conditioning helped Young become an improved and more aggressive baserunner. He stole eight bases last year, after stealing only 11 previously in his career. He probably is most comfortable in left field, where his range and arm are both average. However, he can be a capable first baseman, though one with limited range. Young also filled in last year at third base, where his hands were surprisingly good but his arm was a liability.

2002 Outlook

Young is just entering his prime as a proven .300 hitter with emerging power as he physically matures. He also was one of nine Reds players who were arbitration eligible at the end of the 2001 season, and in a salary dump he was traded to Detroit for outfielder Juan Encarnacion in December. Young said the Tigers told him he would spend most of his time at first base for the departed Tony Clark, but he also could play in the outfield.

Position: LF/1B/3B
Bats: B **Throws:** R
Ht: 6' 2" **Wt:** 235

Opening Day Age: 28
Born: 10/11/73 in Vicksburg, MS
ML Seasons: 6

Overall Statistics

	G	AB	R	H	D	T	HR	RBI	SB	BB	SO	Avg	OBP	Slg
2001	142	540	68	163	28	3	21	69	8	37	77	.302	.350	.481
Career	691	2359	321	700	157	15	72	332	19	192	390	.297	.351	.468

Where He Hits the Ball

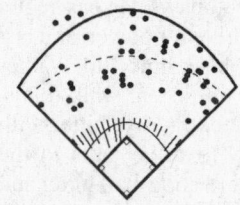 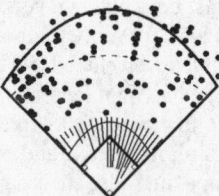

Vs. LHP   **Vs. RHP**

2001 Situational Stats

	AB	H	HR	RBI	Avg		AB	H	HR	RBI	Avg
Home	280	88	8	37	.314	LHP	157	44	3	17	.280
Road	260	75	13	32	.288	RHP	383	119	18	52	.311
First Half	296	97	8	32	.328	Sc Pos	125	34	3	45	.272
Scnd Half	244	66	13	37	.270	Clutch	83	24	4	15	.289

2001 Rankings (National League)

- 1st in lowest percentage of pitches taken (41.7)
- 2nd in errors in left field (7) and highest percentage of swings on the first pitch (46.8)
- 3rd in GDPs (22)
- 4th in assists in left field (8) and fewest pitches seen per plate appearance (3.19)
- Led the Reds in at-bats, total bases (260), intentional walks (10), GDPs (22), slugging percentage, HR frequency (25.7 ABs per HR), batting average vs. lefthanded pitchers, batting average on an 0-2 count (.279), highest percentage of extra bases taken as a runner (44.0), slugging percentage vs. righthanded pitchers (.520), batting average at home and batting average with two strikes (.233)

Brady Clark

Position: LF/RF
Bats: R **Throws:** R
Ht: 6' 2" **Wt:** 195

Opening Day Age: 28
Born: 4/18/73 in Portland, OR
ML Seasons: 2

Overall Statistics

	G	AB	R	H	D	T	HR	RBI	SB	BB	SO	Avg	OBP	Slg
2001	89	129	22	34	3	0	6	18	4	22	16	.264	.373	.426
Career	100	140	23	37	4	0	6	20	4	22	18	.264	.366	.421

2001 Situational Stats

	AB	H	HR	RBI	Avg		AB	H	HR	RBI	Avg
Home	64	15	4	13	.234	LHP	43	12	2	5	.279
Road	65	19	2	5	.292	RHP	86	22	4	13	.256
First Half	41	14	4	11	.341	Sc Pos	30	7	2	13	.233
Scnd Half	88	20	2	7	.227	Clutch	22	6	0	4	.273

2001 Season

Brady Clark has had to prove himself throughout his professional career. He wasn't drafted coming out of college, but hit .300 at three different stops in the minor leagues. As a 28-year-old rookie, he held his own last season as a pinch-hitter and spot starter in the outfield. He hit well in RBI situations and surprised with his occasional power.

Hitting, Baserunning & Defense

Clark has a good understanding of the strike zone and usually can be counted on to make contact. He can turn around good fastballs and is capable of hitting home runs if he gets an inside pitch he can drive. He has average speed and good instincts on the bases. His average arm and range seem to make him best suited to left field, though he can handle all three outfield positions.

2002 Outlook

A late bloomer who has succeeded at every level, Clark already has beaten long odds by getting to the majors. He will have to continue to fight for playing time, but his ability to reach base appears legitimate. He is likely to stick as an extra outfielder and be one of Bob Boone's busiest pinch-hitters off the bench.

Lance Davis

Position: SP
Bats: R **Throws:** L
Ht: 5'11" **Wt:** 165

Opening Day Age: 25
Born: 9/1/76 in Winter Haven, FL
ML Seasons: 1

Overall Statistics

	W	L	Pct.	ERA	G	GS	Sv	IP	H	BB	SO	HR	Ratio
2001	8	4	.667	4.74	20	20	0	106.1	124	34	53	12	1.49
Career	8	4	.667	4.74	20	20	0	106.1	124	34	53	12	1.49

2001 Situational Stats

	W	L	ERA	Sv	IP		AB	H	HR	RBI	Avg
Home	3	3	4.58	0	55.0	LHB	88	23	3	16	.261
Road	5	1	4.91	0	51.1	RHB	334	101	9	38	.302
First Half	1	1	9.30	0	20.1	Sc Pos	99	34	2	39	.343
Scnd Half	7	3	3.66	0	86.0	Clutch	21	4	0	0	.190

2001 Season

Recalled around midseason, Lance Davis made a solid major league debut. Overcoming a rough start, when he surrendered six homers in his first 20.1 innings, he settled down to go 7-3 with a 3.66 ERA after the All-Star break. In just 20 starts overall, he became the second biggest winner on the Reds' staff. He also threw the first complete game by a Reds rookie lefthander in 16 years.

Pitching, Defense & Hitting

Davis isn't very big, which may be one of the reasons he wasn't selected until the 16th round of the 1995 draft. He pitches in the style of a Tom Glavine-type lefty. His fastball has average velocity, and he tries to keep it away from most hitters. Davis gets many of his outs with an effective changeup, mixing in an occasional curveball and usually having good control. He has a deceptive pickoff move and fields his position well. At the plate, one of his four hits were doubles and he scored three runs.

2002 Outlook

Davis' ability to keep the Reds in most of his starts was a revelation in the second half. He holds one of the few certain spots in Cincinnati's rotation. He has the potential to be a consistent starter who can be counted on for double-digit wins.

Cincinnati

403

Pete Harnisch

Position: SP
Bats: R **Throws:** R
Ht: 6' 0" **Wt:** 228

Opening Day Age: 35
Born: 9/23/66 in Huntington, NY
ML Seasons: 14
Pronunciation: HAR-nish

Overall Statistics

	W	L	Pct.	ERA	G	GS	Sv	IP	H	BB	SO	HR	Ratio
2001	1	3	.250	6.37	7	7	0	35.1	48	17	17	9	1.84
Career	111	103	.519	3.89	321	318	0	1959.0	1822	716	1368	223	1.30

2001 Situational Stats

	W	L	ERA	Sv	IP		AB	H	HR	RBI	Avg
Home	0	2	7.80	0	15.0	LHB	66	15	2	12	.227
Road	1	1	5.31	0	20.1	RHB	85	33	7	16	.388
First Half	1	3	6.37	0	35.1	Sc Pos	43	14	2	19	.326
Scnd Half	0	0	-	0	0.0	Clutch	0	0	0	0	-

2001 Season

Pete Harnisch has battled arm troubles for years and missed much of the 2000 campaign due to weakness in his rotator cuff. Last year he couldn't make it through May before elbow problems ended his season. He made seven starts in all, averaging just five innings per outing. The Reds were expecting more from someone who was viewed as a staff leader.

Pitching, Defense & Hitting

Harnisch has never been a pitcher who wins with exceptional stuff. Instead, he has always been a great competitor who battles by changing speeds with his straight changeup and curveball, and by locating his average fastball. Physical troubles affect a pitcher's command as much as his stuff, and when Harnisch can't hit the corners and change speeds, he can't compete at the major league level. He is a good fielding pitcher who also pays close attention to baserunners. He handles the bat well and produced three runs in 11 at-bats last season.

2002 Outlook

Harnisch's future is unclear. He is a free agent without market value due to physical questions. He likely will need to sign an incentive-laden contract, thereby reducing the risk for the club while giving Harnisch a chance to revive his career.

Jason LaRue

Position: C
Bats: R **Throws:** R
Ht: 5'11" **Wt:** 200

Opening Day Age: 28
Born: 3/19/74 in Houston, TX
ML Seasons: 3
Pronunciation: la-RUE

Overall Statistics

	G	AB	R	H	D	T	HR	RBI	SB	BB	SO	Avg	OBP	Slg
2001	121	364	39	86	21	2	12	43	3	27	106	.236	.303	.404
Career	188	552	63	128	31	2	20	65	7	43	157	.232	.304	.404

2001 Situational Stats

	AB	H	HR	RBI	Avg		AB	H	HR	RBI	Avg
Home	177	38	3	16	.215	LHP	86	23	1	9	.267
Road	187	48	9	27	.257	RHP	278	63	11	34	.227
First Half	184	41	7	27	.223	Sc Pos	91	19	2	31	.209
Scnd Half	180	45	5	16	.250	Clutch	63	10	0	4	.159

2001 Season

Handed the starting catcher's job at age 27, Jason LaRue experienced an up and down year in his first full major league season. He began the campaign well, batting .333 in April, but dipped to .200 the next two months. Though he hit only .236 overall, LaRue demonstrated the ability to reach double digits in home runs. He also led National League backstops by throwing out 60 percent of opposing basestealers.

Hitting, Baserunning & Defense

LaRue can hit mistake pitches for power. However, he has trouble making consistent contact because of a big swing that can be exploited by hard stuff up and in and by offspeed pitches. LaRue has decent speed, considering he's a catcher. He has an average arm, good catching mechanics and he improved his release. But he often frustrated manager Bob Boone, an ex-receiver himself, with inconsistent pitch-blocking and pitch selection.

2002 Outlook

The Reds were disappointed by what they viewed as a lack of development by LaRue. He doesn't have any guarantees coming into this season. He could end up sharing time behind the plate with Kelly Stinnett. Corky Miller might enter into the mix as well.

Hector Mercado

Position: RP
Bats: L **Throws:** L
Ht: 6' 3" **Wt:** 235

Opening Day Age: 27
Born: 4/29/74 in
Catano, Puerto Rico
ML Seasons: 2
Pronunciation:
mur-CAH-do

Overall Statistics

	W	L	Pct.	ERA	G	GS	Sv	IP	H	BB	SO	HR	Ratio
2001	3	2	.600	4.08	56	0	0	53.0	55	30	59	6	1.60
Career	3	2	.600	4.16	68	0	0	67.0	67	38	72	8	1.57

2001 Situational Stats

	W	L	ERA	Sv	IP		AB	H	HR	RBI	Avg
Home	1	0	3.90	0	27.2	LHB	87	25	4	22	.287
Road	2	2	4.26	0	25.1	RHB	119	30	2	8	.252
First Half	2	2	3.73	0	31.1	Sc Pos	61	16	3	25	.262
Scnd Half	1	0	4.57	0	21.2	Clutch	31	10	1	5	.323

2001 Season

Fully healthy after a series of elbow and knee injuries, Hector Mercado was a durable and fairly reliable lefthander in the Reds' bullpen. Originally drafted by the Astros in 1992, Mercado worked most of the last decade in the minor leagues. But he managed to spend sizable portions of the 2001 campaign with Cincinnati. He finished third on the Reds with 56 appearances and earned the first three victories of his big league career.

Pitching, Defense & Hitting

Mercado has a sinking fastball in the low 90s and also throws a slider. However, his command often is erratic. He has been more effective against righthanded hitters because his sinker often runs away from them. He seems better suited to starting innings instead of trying to clean up other's messes, since he allowed more than 35 percent (12 of 34) of inherited runners to score. Mercado does not have a good move to first base and rarely bats.

2002 Outlook

Lefthanded relievers always are valuable and Mercado showed some consistency last season. He may not fill the typical role of a situational lefty, since he's performed better against righties at the major league level. Still, he is likely to remain in the Reds' bullpen mix as their busiest southpaw.

John Riedling

Position: RP
Bats: R **Throws:** R
Ht: 5'11" **Wt:** 190

Opening Day Age: 26
Born: 8/29/75 in Fort
Lauderdale, FL
ML Seasons: 2
Pronunciation:
READ-ling

Overall Statistics

	W	L	Pct.	ERA	G	GS	Sv	IP	H	BB	SO	HR	Ratio
2001	1	1	.500	2.41	29	0	1	33.2	22	14	23	1	1.07
Career	4	2	.667	2.39	42	0	2	49.0	33	22	41	2	1.12

2001 Situational Stats

	W	L	ERA	Sv	IP		AB	H	HR	RBI	Avg
Home	1	0	1.00	1	18.0	LHB	54	10	1	5	.185
Road	0	1	4.02	0	15.2	RHB	64	12	0	2	.188
First Half	0	1	2.89	1	28.0	Sc Pos	43	7	1	7	.163
Scnd Half	1	0	0.00	0	5.2	Clutch	34	7	1	5	.206

2001 Season

The Reds had hoped last year would be a breakout season for John Riedling. Instead, shoulder troubles ended his campaign prematurely. Before getting shelved with a right shoulder strain, Riedling offered glimpses of his potential by limiting opponents to a .186 batting average. He also allowed only three of 22 (13.6 percent) inherited runners to score.

Pitching, Defense & Hitting

Riedling's velocity reaches the mid 90s and he also has a hard splitter. His control remains uneven and he can be prone to wild pitches and pitching from behind in the count. He fired five wild pitches in his limited exposure last year. However, even when he fell behind in the count on the first pitch, Riedling surrendered a puny .193 average. He has good fielding mechanics and does a solid job of holding runners. He has little experience as a hitter.

2002 Outlook

In the cost-conscious world of the Reds, it is possible that some of their more expensive relievers could be traded. Riedling is viewed as a key option. Even though he doesn't have much experience saving games, he's being groomed to be a possible future closer.

Ruben Rivera

Position: CF/RF/LF
Bats: R **Throws:** R
Ht: 6' 3" **Wt:** 208

Opening Day Age: 28
Born: 11/14/73 in La Chorrera, Panama
ML Seasons: 7

Overall Statistics

	G	AB	R	H	D	T	HR	RBI	SB	BB	SO	Avg	OBP	Slg
2001	117	263	37	67	13	1	10	34	6	21	83	.255	.321	.426
Career	562	1378	214	301	61	11	58	185	45	163	451	.218	.310	.405

2001 Situational Stats

	AB	H	HR	RBI	Avg		AB	H	HR	RBI	Avg
Home	132	31	6	14	.235	LHP	79	19	4	11	.241
Road	131	36	4	20	.275	RHP	184	48	6	23	.261
First Half	173	45	7	24	.260	Sc Pos	78	17	0	20	.218
Scnd Half	90	22	3	10	.244	Clutch	56	11	3	10	.196

2001 Season

Ruben Rivera once ranked as one of baseball's most highly regarded prospects. But he landed with his third organization when the Padres released him and the Reds picked him up last March. While he teased the Reds with his athletic talents, he also enjoyed arguably his finest major league season. He clubbed 24 extra-base hits in only 263 at-bats and played well in all three outfield positions.

Hitting, Baserunning & Defense

While Rivera can hit the fastball with big-time power, he never has made the necessary adjustments to handle offspeed pitches and breaking balls. He is highly strikeout prone. Though he worked last year on cutting down his swing, he still fanned nearly four times as often as he drew a free pass. He remains a raw baserunner but has the ability to steal 20 bases. Rivera has outstanding defensive skills and can handle any of the three outfield positions.

2002 Outlook

The Reds are loaded with outfield prospects, and they allowed Rivera to escape via waivers to San Francisco in November. The Giants will be his third team in three seasons, and a solid spring will help keep his career alive.

Kelly Stinnett

Position: C
Bats: R **Throws:** R
Ht: 5'11" **Wt:** 225

Opening Day Age: 32
Born: 2/4/70 in Lawton, OK
ML Seasons: 8
Pronunciation: sti-NETT

Overall Statistics

	G	AB	R	H	D	T	HR	RBI	SB	BB	SO	Avg	OBP	Slg
2001	63	187	27	48	11	0	9	25	2	17	61	.257	.333	.460
Career	487	1393	166	329	63	4	48	165	8	140	387	.236	.320	.391

2001 Situational Stats

	AB	H	HR	RBI	Avg		AB	H	HR	RBI	Avg
Home	103	31	6	16	.301	LHP	40	13	1	6	.325
Road	84	17	3	9	.202	RHP	147	35	8	19	.238
First Half	140	37	6	17	.264	Sc Pos	44	10	1	16	.227
Scnd Half	47	11	3	8	.234	Clutch	38	7	2	4	.184

2001 Season

After three years with Arizona, Kelly Stinnett signed a free-agent deal with Cincinnati last offseason. His playing time decreased a bit with the Reds, though he became a valuable part of their catching corps. He hit more than 30 points higher than his previous career average, and topped .300 at Cinergy Field. He was on his way to career highs in many offensive categories before injuries sidelined him for much of the second half of the season.

Hitting, Baserunning & Defense

The burly Stinnett has exceptional power and can turn around some of the best fastballs in baseball. However, his vulnerability to breaking balls and offspeed pitches always has made him prone to strikeouts. Stinnett is an excellent receiver and handler of pitchers. While he has an above-average arm, his release is slow. He hasn't hit a triple since 1998, though he did match his career high with two stolen bases last season.

2002 Outlook

Impressed by his leadership skills and the way he worked with pitchers, the Reds signed Stinnett to a two-year contract extension in May that likely insures a significant role in 2002. He could approach 15-20 home runs if he gets the required at-bats and his patience at the plate continues to improve.

Scott Sullivan (Rubber Arm)

Position: RP
Bats: R **Throws:** R
Ht: 6' 3" **Wt:** 210

Opening Day Age: 31
Born: 3/13/71 in Carrollton, AL
ML Seasons: 7

Overall Statistics

	W	L	Pct.	ERA	G	GS	Sv	IP	H	BB	SO	HR	Ratio
2001	7	1	.875	3.31	79	0	0	103.1	94	36	82	10	1.26
Career	25	19	.568	3.62	373	0	8	534.1	457	194	443	60	1.22

2001 Situational Stats

	W	L	ERA	Sv	IP			AB	H	HR	RBI	Avg
Home	4	1	3.27	0	52.1	LHB		163	41	6	16	.252
Road	3	0	3.35	0	51.0	RHB		224	53	4	29	.237
First Half	2	1	3.29	0	54.2	Sc Pos		108	20	1	32	.185
Scnd Half	5	0	3.33	0	48.2	Clutch		191	43	5	20	.225

2001 Season

Scott Sullivan's durability has earned him a spot in the record books. Last year he became the first pitcher in history to lead the majors in relief innings for four straight seasons. He surpassed 100 innings each time, and missed by less than three innings the year before the streak began. The workload hasn't affected Sullivan's effectiveness. He earned a career-high seven wins in 2001.

Pitching, Defense & Hitting

Sullivan is more than just durable. He throws a sinking, sidearm, low-90s fastball that always has made him tough on righthanded hitters. He has improved his command of a cut fastball, which now is a good weapon against lefthanded batters. Sullivan is an adequate fielder, and while he lacks a good pickoff move, he holds runners well. He rarely hits in his setup role and struck out in all three at-bats last year.

2002 Outlook

Sullivan signed a three-year $6.95 million contract extension with a club option for 2004 in February 2000. He clearly figures into the Reds' rebuilding plans. Though not viewed as a closer, he ranks among the game's most valuable relievers. He figures to be either the Reds' busiest reliever or a very marketable trade commodity.

Scott Williamson

Position: RP
Bats: R **Throws:** R
Ht: 6' 0" **Wt:** 185

Opening Day Age: 26
Born: 2/17/76 in Fort Polk, LA
ML Seasons: 3

Overall Statistics

	W	L	Pct.	ERA	G	GS	Sv	IP	H	BB	SO	HR	Ratio
2001	0	0	-	0.00	2	0	0	0.2	1	2	0	0	4.50
Career	17	15	.531	2.88	112	10	25	206.0	147	120	243	15	1.30

2001 Situational Stats

	W	L	ERA	Sv	IP			AB	H	HR	RBI	Avg
Home	0	0	0.00	0	0.2	LHB		2	1	0	0	.500
Road	—	—	—	—	—	RHB		—	—	—	—	—
First Half	0	0	0.00	0	0.2	Sc Pos		2	0	0	1	.000
Scnd Half	0	0	—	0	0.0	Clutch		3	1	0	1	.333

2001 Season

Scott Williamson was an emerging star two years ago, when he was named the National League Rookie of the Year. But his career suddenly has reached a crossroads. He made 10 starts and threw 112 innings while going 5-8 in 2000. His 2001 season ended after just two appearances, when he was lost due to elbow surgery.

Pitching, Defense & Hitting

When healthy, Williamson throws in the upper 90s and has shown an overpowering slider. He's averaged more than 10 strikeouts per nine innings during his time with Cincinnati. However, Williamson must improve his command of the strike zone and the consistency of his offspeed pitch if he is to be a starting pitcher. He has a good pickoff move but otherwise is slow coming home. He is no factor as a batter, going 1-for-23 lifetime.

2002 Outlook

The main issue will be whether Williamson has recovered from his elbow surgery. If he is healthy enough to pitch, the Reds then must decide whether his future is in the bullpen or as a starter. The early signs point toward Cincinnati making him a candidate for its wide-open rotation.

Cincinnati

Other Cincinnati Reds

Jose Acevedo (**Pos**: RHP, **Age**: 24)

	W	L	Pct.	ERA	G	GS	Sv	IP	H	BB	SO	HR	Ratio
2001	5	7	.417	5.44	18	18	0	96.0	101	34	68	17	1.41
Career	5	7	.417	5.44	18	18	0	96.0	101	34	68	17	1.41

Although he may have needed another year in the minors, Acevedo made his major league debut with the Reds in 2001, making 18 starts. He owns an impressive 507-170 K-BB ratio in the minors. He may start to mimic those numbers in 2002. 2002 Outlook: B

Justin Atchley (**Pos**: LHP, **Age**: 28)

	W	L	Pct.	ERA	G	GS	Sv	IP	H	BB	SO	HR	Ratio
2001	0	0	-	6.10	15	0	0	10.1	12	5	8	4	1.65
Career	0	0	-	6.10	15	0	0	10.1	12	5	8	4	1.65

Atchley appeared in 15 games in 2001, lasting for a total of only 10.1 innings. The lefty needed surgery to repair a torn rotator cuff and labrum in his pitching shoulder in August. He is expected to be ready for spring training. 2002 Outlook: C

Juan Castro (**Pos**: SS/2B/3B, **Age**: 29, **Bats**: R)

	G	AB	R	H	D	T	HR	RBI	SB	BB	SO	Avg	OBP	Slg
2001	96	242	27	54	10	0	3	13	0	13	50	.223	.261	.302
Career	390	898	91	189	37	6	9	59	1	60	169	.210	.258	.295

Castro is solid defensively and can play any of the infield positions. The Reds were lucky to have him on the bench with last year's injuries to Barry Larkin and Pokey Reese. He has struggled at the plate in the majors. 2002 Outlook: B

D.T. Cromer (**Pos**: 1B, **Age**: 31, **Bats**: L)

	G	AB	R	H	D	T	HR	RBI	SB	BB	SO	Avg	OBP	Slg
2001	50	57	7	16	3	0	5	12	0	3	19	.281	.302	.596
Career	85	104	14	32	7	0	7	20	0	4	33	.308	.327	.577

Cromer's best years as a hitter may be behind him, even though he averaged a homer in every 11.4 at-bats in 2001. He needs to improve his hitting against lefties. He became a free agent in October. 2002 Outlook: C

Jared Fernandez (**Pos**: RHP, **Age**: 30)

	W	L	Pct.	ERA	G	GS	Sv	IP	H	BB	SO	HR	Ratio
2001	0	1	.000	4.38	5	2	0	12.1	13	6	5	1	1.54
Career	0	1	.000	4.38	5	2	0	12.1	13	6	5	1	1.54

Fernandez is a knuckleballer who still is developing. He also has a low-80s fastball and a slider. He made his major league debut this season, posting a 4.38 ERA in five appearances, including two starts. 2002 Outlook: C

Osvaldo Fernandez (**Pos**: RHP, **Age**: 33)

	W	L	Pct.	ERA	G	GS	Sv	IP	H	BB	SO	HR	Ratio
2001	5	6	.455	6.92	20	14	0	79.1	103	33	35	8	1.71
Career	19	26	.422	4.93	76	67	0	387.0	439	136	208	43	1.49

A control pitcher, Fernandez began the 2001 season as a starter but was moved to the bullpen after his ERA ballooned to a whopping 6.91. The Reds may choose to keep him in relief, as he has a history of arm problems. 2002 Outlook: C

Raul Gonzalez (**Pos**: LF, **Age**: 28, **Bats**: R)

	G	AB	R	H	D	T	HR	RBI	SB	BB	SO	Avg	OBP	Slg
2001	11	14	0	3	0	0	0	0	0	1	3	.214	.267	.214
Career	14	16	0	3	0	0	0	0	0	1	5	.188	.235	.188

Gonzalez improved his numbers at Triple-A in 2001 over the unimpressive stats he posted in 2000. The left fielder hit nearly .300 at Louisville with 11 homers in 2001. He walks often because of his discipline at the plate. 2002 Outlook: C

Wilton Guerrero (**Pos**: SS/2B, **Age**: 27, **Bats**: B)

	G	AB	R	H	D	T	HR	RBI	SB	BB	SO	Avg	OBP	Slg
2001	60	142	16	48	5	1	1	8	5	3	17	.338	.352	.408
Career	551	1506	178	435	51	28	11	121	34	57	213	.289	.315	.382

Guerrero is another Reds player who can play almost every position. He is a consistent hitter, batting .289 for his career. Unlike his younger brother Vladimir, he lacks pop and patience. The Reds exercised their 2002 option on Guerrero. 2002 Outlook: B

Joey Hamilton (**Pos**: RHP, **Age**: 31)

	W	L	Pct.	ERA	G	GS	Sv	IP	H	BB	SO	HR	Ratio
2001	6	10	.375	5.93	26	26	0	139.2	193	44	92	20	1.70
Career	70	63	.526	4.29	200	192	0	1205.1	1251	438	802	116	1.40

Hamilton, who was plagued by shoulder and hamstring problems in 1999 and 2000, was released by the Blue Jays after posting a 5.89 ERA in 22 starts. He didn't perform any better in four outings with the Reds. 2002 Outlook: C

Robin Jennings (**Pos**: RF/1B, **Age**: 29, **Bats**: L)

	G	AB	R	H	D	T	HR	RBI	SB	BB	SO	Avg	OBP	Slg
2001	48	132	14	35	8	2	3	18	0	7	18	.265	.300	.424
Career	93	213	22	52	14	2	3	24	1	10	31	.244	.279	.371

Jennings is a good hitter with some pop, but he never has had the opportunity to be an everyday player in the majors. He bounced between three different teams and their Triple-A affiliates in 2001. 2002 Outlook: C

Brandon Larson (**Pos**: 3B, **Age**: 25, **Bats**: R)

	G	AB	R	H	D	T	HR	RBI	SB	BB	SO	Avg	OBP	Slg
2001	14	33	2	4	2	0	0	1	0	2	10	.121	.171	.182
Career	14	33	2	4	2	0	0	1	0	2	10	.121	.171	.182

Larson is a former first-round pick who struggled with injuries early in his pro career. The third baseman has some power, but he needs to cut down on his strikeouts to make it at the major league level. 2002 Outlook: C

Scott MacRae (**Pos**: RHP, **Age**: 27)

	W	L	Pct.	ERA	G	GS	Sv	IP	H	BB	SO	HR	Ratio
2001	0	1	.000	4.02	24	0	0	31.1	33	8	18	0	1.31
Career	0	1	.000	4.02	24	0	0	31.1	33	8	18	0	1.31

Working primarily in relief over the last couple of seasons, MacRae is being considered for a starting spot in the Reds' rotation for 2002. He did not give up a home run in 31.1 innings of work for the Reds in 2001, but they released him in mid-November. 2002 Outlook: C

Corky Miller (Pos: C, Age: 26, Bats: R)

	G	AB	R	H	D	T	HR	RBI	SB	BB	SO	Avg	OBP	Slg
2001	17	49	5	9	2	0	3	7	1	4	16	.184	.263	.408
Career	17	49	5	9	2	0	3	7	1	4	16	.184	.263	.408

Miller has a chance to be the Reds' backup catcher in 2002. He hit .184 as a September callup, after batting .309 with 16 homers and 70 RBI in 103 games between Double-A and Triple-A last season. 2002 Outlook: B

Chris Piersoll (Pos: RHP, Age: 24)

	W	L	Pct.	ERA	G	GS	Sv	IP	H	BB	SO	HR	Ratio
2001	0	0	-	2.38	11	0	0	11.1	12	6	7	0	1.59
Career	0	0	-	2.38	11	0	0	11.1	12	6	7	0	1.59

After recording 19 saves with Double-A Chattanooga, Piersoll was impressive in 11 games with the Reds last season, posting a 2.38 ERA. With more work on his control, he could be a quality reliever in the majors. 2002 Outlook: C

Brian Reith (Pos: RHP, Age: 24)

	W	L	Pct.	ERA	G	GS	Sv	IP	H	BB	SO	HR	Ratio
2001	0	7	.000	7.81	9	8	0	40.1	56	16	22	13	1.79
Career	0	7	.000	7.81	9	8	0	40.1	56	16	22	13	1.79

Reith, who was working at the Double-A level, made his major league debut in 2001. He started eight games for the Reds, losing seven. He is young, has good stuff and may develop into a decent starter. 2002 Outlook: C

Dennys Reyes (Pos: LHP, Age: 24)

	W	L	Pct.	ERA	G	GS	Sv	IP	H	BB	SO	HR	Ratio
2001	2	6	.250	4.92	35	6	0	53.0	51	35	52	5	1.62
Career	11	17	.393	4.32	195	22	2	272.2	260	168	273	22	1.57

Reyes missed two months of the 2001 season with tendinitis in his elbow. The Reds decided to use him as a starter upon his return. He did not last more than 5.1 innings in six starts and was moved back to the bullpen. 2002 Outlook: B

Jose Rijo (Pos: RHP, Age: 36)

	W	L	Pct.	ERA	G	GS	Sv	IP	H	BB	SO	HR	Ratio
2001	0	0	-	2.12	13	0	0	17.0	19	9	12	1	1.65
Career	111	87	.561	3.15	345	260	3	1803.0	1621	643	1568	134	1.26

After six years away from the majors and numerous elbow operations, Rijo returned in 2001. Formerly a starter, he joined the Reds late in the season and was impressive in relief. He posted a 2.12 ERA in 13 games. 2002 Outlook: B

Frank Rodriguez (Pos: RHP, Age: 29)

	W	L	Pct.	ERA	G	GS	Sv	IP	H	BB	SO	HR	Ratio
2001	0	0	-	11.42	7	0	0	8.2	16	5	9	1	2.42
Career	29	39	.426	5.53	184	82	5	654.0	737	282	371	76	1.56

Rodriguez has a strong arm, but he does not have much variety in his pitching repertoire, making him predictable. Formerly a starter, he pitched well as a reliever at Triple-A in 2001, recording a 2.46 ERA in 43 appearances. 2002 Outlook: C

Deion Sanders (Pos: LF, Age: 34, Bats: L)

	G	AB	R	H	D	T	HR	RBI	SB	BB	SO	Avg	OBP	Slg
2001	32	75	6	13	2	0	1	4	3	4	10	.173	.235	.240
Career	641	2123	308	558	72	43	39	168	186	159	352	.263	.319	.392

Sanders had three hits in his first game with the Reds in 2001, but he totaled just 10 hits over his next 31 games before being released. He signed a minor league deal with the Blue Jays, but only appeared in 25 games in Triple-A. 2002 Outlook: D

Bill Selby (Pos: 2B, Age: 31, Bats: L)

	G	AB	R	H	D	T	HR	RBI	SB	BB	SO	Avg	OBP	Slg
2001	36	92	7	21	7	1	2	12	0	5	13	.228	.273	.391
Career	106	233	27	58	12	1	5	22	1	15	33	.249	.299	.373

Selby is a player who will jump in at any position if needed. In nine years in the minors, he has hit .276 with 133 homers. Despite his small stature, Selby possesses some pop in his bat. He signed a minor league contract with Cleveland in the fall. 2002 Outlook: C

Scott Winchester (Pos: RHP, Age: 28)

	W	L	Pct.	ERA	G	GS	Sv	IP	H	BB	SO	HR	Ratio
2001	0	2	.000	4.50	12	1	0	24.0	29	4	9	7	1.38
Career	3	8	.273	5.42	38	17	0	116.1	149	35	55	21	1.58

Winchester began his major league career in 1997 as a reliever. He flirted with starting the next year, but struggled and has since returned to the bullpen. He still will see an occasional spot start. 2002 Outlook: C

Cincinnati Reds Minor League Prospects

Organization Overview:

The Reds may have finished with their worst record since 1982 last season, but they could gain some solace from the success their minor league affiliates enjoyed. All six of their farm teams posted winning records. Their Triple-A club in Louisville was named the champion of the International League, while Billings captured the Pioneer League title. Even better, the organization produced Adam Dunn, who hit over 50 homers between the minors and Cincinnati and looks like a future All-Star. The Reds are happy with the depth of pitching in their system. But the top hurlers probably are a couple years away from contributing at the big league level. Cincinnati is not as deep in position players, and a couple of their best prospects, catcher Dane Sardinha and shortstop Rainer Olmedo, likely will have their gloves carry them. However, Austin Kearns has the potential to eventually join Dunn as an impact performer in the outfield.

Ben Broussard

Position: 1B
Bats: L **Throws:** L
Ht: 6' 2" **Wt:** 220
Opening Day Age: 25
Born: 9/24/76 in
Beaumont, TX

Recent Statistics

	G	AB	R	H	D	T	HR	RBI	SB	BB	SO	Avg
2000 AA Chattanooga	87	286	64	73	8	4	14	51	15	72	78	.255
2001 A Mudville	30	102	14	25	5	0	5	21	0	16	31	.245
2001 AA Chattanooga	100	353	81	113	27	0	23	69	10	61	69	.320
2001 MLE	100	343	68	103	26	0	19	58	7	44	73	.300

Broussard was chosen in the second round in 1999, after leading the Southland Conference with 27 home runs and a .427 batting average. His power has followed him as a professional. After starting slowly last year, he really took off after getting promoted to Double-A. He is a fairly decent athlete who has feasted on mistake pitches and hits both righthanded and lefthanded pitchers well. When pitchers started throwing around him last year, he continued to take walks at his usual high rate. His defense, once a liability, has improved. Still, his bat is his main weapon, and it is what will determine how far he can climb. He has made adjustments in the past and must continue to do so.

David Espinosa

Position: SS
Bats: B **Throws:** R
Ht: 6' 1" **Wt:** 200
Opening Day Age: 20
Born: 12/16/81 in
Caracas, VZ

Recent Statistics

	G	AB	R	H	D	T	HR	RBI	SB	BB	SO	Avg
2001 A Dayton	122	493	88	129	29	8	7	37	15	55	120	.262

While Espinosa was Cincinnati's first pick in the 2000 draft, he didn't make his professional debut until 2001. He had his problems defensively last year, committing 48 errors. But the Reds say he got through those difficul-

ties and made incredible improvement in the second half. His range is above average and his arm is strong though erratic. He needs to work on his footwork. A true switch-hitter, he held his own offensively in Class-A. He is a top-of-the-lineup sort, but could stand to reduce his strikeouts. He has gap power, can steal a base, and is learning to bunt more effectively.

Ty Howington

Position: P
Bats: B **Throws:** L
Ht: 6' 4" **Wt:** 225
Opening Day Age: 21
Born: 11/4/80 in
Vancouver, WA

Recent Statistics

	W	L	ERA	G	GS	Sv	IP	H	R	BB	SO	HR
2000 A Dayton	5	15	5.27	27	26	0	141.2	150	91	86	119	7
2001 A Dayton	4	0	1.15	6	6	0	39.0	15	7	9	47	0
2001 A Mudville	3	2	2.43	7	7	0	37.0	33	18	20	44	2
2001 AA Chattanooga	1	3	3.27	7	7	0	41.1	36	18	24	38	3

Howington's experience shows how misleading first-season stats can be. Chosen 14th overall in 1999, he debuted with a 5-15 record in the Midwest League. But when he returned to Dayton last season, he looked like the lights had clicked on. He dominated there before moving up and continuing his success in the California League. He finished at Double-A, where he wasn't quite as impressive, but still pretty darn good for a 20-year-old. One reason Howington was able to bounce back so well was that his velocity seemed to return. When he's on, he throws an 89-91 MPH fastball and a good breaking pitch. The Reds want him to get some innings and get stronger, but say he's on the fast track.

Austin Kearns

Position: OF
Bats: R **Throws:** R
Ht: 6' 3" **Wt:** 220
Opening Day Age: 21
Born: 5/20/80 in
Lexington, KY

Recent Statistics

	G	AB	R	H	D	T	HR	RBI	SB	BB	SO	Avg
2000 A Dayton	136	484	110	148	37	2	27	104	18	90	93	.306
2001 R Reds	6	17	2	3	2	0	0	4	0	2	7	.176
2001 AA Chattanooga	59	205	30	55	11	2	6	36	7	26	43	.268
2001 MLE	59	200	25	50	10	1	5	30	5	19	45	.250

Entering last season, many observers thought Kearns was a better prospect than Adam Dunn. But while Dunn shot to the majors and looks like a future star, Kearns endured a frustrating campaign. He hurt his thumb, tried to play through the injury and couldn't build upon his terrific 2000 season. He still has outstanding talent and the Reds say he's more polished than Dunn. Kearns has power, hits to all fields and shows good patience at the plate. He can play either corner outfield position and probably will wind up in right. The Reds were so impressed with Kearns' ability that they chose him with the seventh overall pick in 1998. And they continue to expect big things from him. It may not be long before he joins his good friend Dunn in Cincinnati.

Dustin Moseley

Position: P
Bats: R **Throws:** R
Ht: 6' 3" **Wt:** 190

Opening Day Age: 20
Born: 12/26/81 in Texarkana, AR

Recent Statistics

		W	L	ERA	G	GS	Sv	IP	H	R	BB	SO	HR
2001	A Dayton	10	8	4.20	25	25	0	148.0	158	83	42	108	10

Moseley was a supplemental first-round pick in 2000, the 34th choice overall. Drafted out of an Arkansas high school, he didn't sign until that November. Impressive in big league camp, Moseley made his professional debut last season, when he posted a winning record in the Midwest League. He has an above-average breaking ball and is dangerous when he can throw the curveball for strikes. His fastball is in the 90-92 MPH range and he throws a good changeup as his third pitch. Moseley will compete this season at age 20 and still is growing. He needs to get stronger and work on improving his command.

Ranier Olmedo

Position: SS
Bats: B **Throws:** R
Ht: 5' 11" **Wt:** 155

Opening Day Age: 20
Born: 5/31/81 in Maracay, VZ

Recent Statistics

		G	AB	R	H	D	THR	RBI	SB	BB	SO	Avg
2000	A Dayton	111	369	50	94	19	1	4	41	17	30	70	.255
2001	A Mudville	129	536	57	131	23	4	0	28	38	24	121	.244

Olmedo's fielding ability eventually may be his ticket to the big leagues. The Reds describe his hands and feet as gifted and say he has a strong arm. They also have mentioned him in the same breath with Omar Vizquel, another Venezuelan shortstop. But while Olmedo's defense draws raves, his offense has been slower to develop. He has spent only a year as a switch-hitter and is learning to bat from the left side. He hits well when going the other way, but must keep the ball out of the air and gets in trouble when he pulls pitches. He needs to improve his plate discipline, especially if he expects to be a leadoff hitter, where his speed could be of value. He struck out 121 times but led all Reds minor leaguers with 38 stolen bases last season.

Wily Mo Pena

Position: OF
Bats: R **Throws:** R
Ht: 6' 3" **Wt:** 215

Opening Day Age: 20
Born: 1/23/82 in Laguna Salada, DR

Recent Statistics

		G	AB	R	H	D	THR	RBI	SB	BB	SO	Avg
2000	A Greensboro	67	249	41	51	7	1	10	28	6	18	91	.205
2000	A Staten Ilnd	20	73	7	22	1	2	0	10	2	2	23	.301
2001	A Dayton	135	511	87	135	25	5	26	113	26	33	177	.264

The Reds acquired Pena from the Yankees in exchange for phenom Drew Henson last March. Pena then re-warded the Reds with a breakout year in the Midwest League. His impressive collection of tools had prompted a lot of interest before he signed a huge contract with the Yankees at age 16. He is a big, raw athlete who presents an awesome combination of power and speed. The Reds say he is an offensive production kind of guy, but he struck out in about one-third of his at-bats last season and needs to work on getting on base more often. He could improve his pitch selection and ability to recognize the breaking ball. Now out of his teens, Pena proved quite durable last season and might move up to Double-A in 2002.

Dane Sardinha

Position: C
Bats: R **Throws:** R
Ht: 5' 11" **Wt:** 205

Opening Day Age: 22
Born: 4/8/79 in Honolulu, HI

Recent Statistics

		G	AB	R	H	D	THR	RBI	SB	BB	SO	Avg
2001	A Mudville	109	422	45	99	24	2	9	55	0	12	97	.235

Sardinha is a tremendous defensive talent. The Reds say the catching game seems to come easy to him. He is quiet behind the plate, with hands and feet that are way above average. Sardinha also elicits praise for his arm and the way he blocks pitches and calls the game. On the other hand, he needs to improve offensively. While he possesses good power to the opposite field, the ball tends to get in on him when batting. He also doesn't recognize breaking pitches particularly well. A second-round pick in what looks like a bumper 2000 draft for Cincinnati, Sardinha has only one professional season under his belt. But he is said to be moving quickly. There is some feeling in the Reds organization that he's their top prospect.

Others to Watch

Cincinnati got righthander **Ricardo Aramboles** (20) in a deal for Mark Wohlers last summer. Aramboles has fanned about a man per inning as a pro. He doesn't have much experience above Class-A. . . The Reds acquired righthander **Chris Booker** (25) in the Michael Tucker deal last July. Booker has a live arm and a big time fastball that reaches 98 MPH, but his slider and splitter must develop. . . Lefty **Paul Darnell** (25) shifted from the starting rotation to relief at Double- and Triple-A last year. He's tough on lefthanded hitters and has a shot as a situational reliever. . . Bothered by injuries previously, righthander **Josh Hall** (21) posted the best ERA (2.65) in the Midwest League last season. He allowed only four home runs in 132.1 innings. . . Outfielder **Steve Smitherman** (23) is strong and athletic with a football-type body. He possesses easy power, can run, and hit 45 doubles and 20 homers at Dayton. . . Lefthander **Ryan Snare** (23) was drafted in the second round in 2000 and pitched well in the Midwest League. He has an 89-91 MPH fastball and a potential major league curveball, but must work on his changeup, strength and conditioning.

Cincinnati

Coors Field

Offense

Coors Field is a hitters' haven, and it's more than the way the ball carries in the dry, mile-high air. The outfield is the biggest in baseball, a concession former general manager Bob Gebhard made to have fences farther from home plate. The idea, however, has backfired. More than home runs, what hitters enjoy about Coors is that routine popups in other ballparks fall in for hits in the sizable gaps between the infielders and outfielders. Pitchers also tend to work defensively and wind up in hitters' counts because of a reluctance to throw strikes.

Defense

For the Rockies to be successful they have to become an elite defensive team, particularly in the outfield. Most outfielders play so deep because of the way the ball carries that it's become routine for baserunners to go first-to-third, even on balls hit to left field. There is no escape route for pitchers, which is why there is an annual effort to get the infield grass grown thicker and longer, a challenge given the desert climate of Denver.

Who It Helps the Most

Jeff Cirillo had been the poster boy for Coors Field, hitting 96 points higher at Coors Field than on the road. The park would seem suited for Juan Pierre to exploit his speed, but the center fielder hit only 13 points lower on the road than at Coors.

Who It Hurts the Most

Rookie Jason Jennings didn't give up a home run, but he allowed 11 runs in two home starts in 2001. Scott Elarton has a history of giving up longballs, and that was *before* he joined the Rockies. Mike Hampton gave up a career-high 31 home runs, and also showed the stress of Coors Field can carry over to the road.

Rookies & Newcomers

Pitchers Jason Young, Aaron Cook and Ryan Kibler figure to open the season at Double-A. But like Jennings in 2001, they won't surprise anybody if they finish the season in the big leagues and have to contend with the rare air and spacious confines.

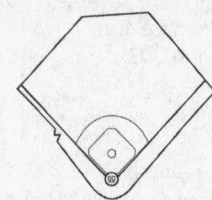

Dimensions: LF-347, LCF-390, CF-415, RCF-375, RF-350

Capacity: 50,449

Elevation: 5280 feet

Surface: Grass

Foul Territory: Average

Park Factors

	2001 Season						
	Home Games			Away Games			
	Rockies	Opp	Total	Rockies	Opp	Total	Index
G	75	75	150	75	75	150	—
Avg	.337	.287	.312	.255	.257	.256	122
AB	2668	2666	5334	2619	2456	5075	105
R	525	487	1012	347	343	690	147
H	898	766	1664	667	630	1297	128
2B	181	174	355	124	161	285	119
3B	38	16	54	16	17	33	156
HR	118	125	243	85	86	171	135
BB	224	305	529	252	252	504	100
SO	437	495	932	523	491	1014	87
E	48	55	103	43	51	94	110
E-Infield	33	42	75	35	49	84	89
LHB-Avg	.362	.280	.329	.274	.266	.271	122
LHB-HR	69	43	112	53	30	83	126
RHB-Avg	.308	.291	.298	.234	.252	.244	122
RHB-HR	49	82	131	32	56	88	143

	1999-2001						
	Home Games			Away Games			
	Rockies	Opp	Total	Rockies	Opp	Total	Index
G	225	225	450	225	225	450	—
Avg	.332	.307	.319	.252	.260	.256	125
AB	8053	8177	16230	7767	7331	15098	107
R	1628	1560	3188	973	1043	2016	158
H	2673	2509	5182	1955	1906	3861	134
2B	511	503	1014	375	427	802	118
3B	95	57	152	44	48	92	154
HR	355	392	747	205	229	434	160
BB	777	936	1713	725	840	1565	102
SO	1177	1449	2626	1429	1404	2833	86
E	149	205	354	145	162	307	115
E-Infield	112	165	277	122	151	273	101
LHB-Avg	.347	.299	.326	.269	.272	.270	121
LHB-HR	181	144	325	114	86	200	153
RHB-Avg	.317	.311	.314	.235	.253	.245	128
RHB-HR	174	248	422	91	143	234	166

2001 Rankings (National League)
- Highest batting-average factor
- Highest run factor
- Highest hit factor
- Highest LHB batting-average factor
- Highest RHB batting-average factor
- Second-highest double factor
- Second-highest triple factor
- Second-highest home-run factor
- Second-highest RHB home-run factor

Buddy Bell

2001 Season

Buddy Bell ran into what has become an annual problem for him as a manager, both in Detroit and now with the Rockies: a mid-season fade from contention. The Rockies were in the midst of the National League West and wild-card races in mid-June, but the club went into a 10-35 slide that sent it on its way to a second last-place finish in three years. Part of the challenge is keeping a feeling of unity on the team in light of all the roster shuffling Bell has been forced to deal with the last two seasons. Despite a lineup that often featured five of the eight regulars with less than a full year in the big leagues, the Rockies did win 14 of their final 27 games.

Offense

Bell had his challenges despite the offensive friendliness of Coors Field. He did not have a legitimate righthanded run-producer to protect the lefthanded bats of Larry Walker and Todd Helton, and as a result had to put Jeff Cirillo, his best No. 2 hitter, into the No. 5 slot. That left the Rockies without the bat-control player to slip between lead-off hitter Juan Pierre and No. 3 hitter Walker. With Pierre the only legitimate base-stealing threat, Bell was challenged to put the offense in motion.

Pitching & Defense

Bell likes to give his pitching coach freedom to run the staff and will face an adjustment period with Marcel Lachemann's decision to retire. Jim Wright will be making his debut as the pitching coach. Bell has realized that Coors is unique in its demands on a pitcher, particularly relievers, who respond better when called on often for short efforts. Bell stresses defensive fundamentals and will lean to defense in making out his lineup.

2002 Outlook

The Rockies are taking a low-key approach, finally. They would rather be a surprise than a disappointment. They are committed to giving young players an opportunity, but privately believe they have the makings of a quality pitching staff. They anticipate improved production from the righthanded bats of middle infielders Juan Uribe and Jose Ortiz.

Born: 8/27/51 in Pittsburgh, PA

Playing Experience: 1972-1989, Cle, Tex, Cin, Hou

Managerial Experience: 5 seasons

Manager Statistics

Year	Team, Lg	W	L	Pct	GB	Finish
2001	Colorado, NL	73	89	.451	19.0	5th West
5 Seasons		339	446	.432	—	—

2001 Starting Pitchers by Days Rest

	<=3	4	5	6+
Rockies Starts	1	63	59	31
Rockies ERA	11.12	5.54	5.44	5.40
NL Avg Starts	1	80	47	24
NL ERA	5.03	4.43	4.53	4.28

2001 Situational Stats

	Buddy Bell	NL Average
Hit & Run Success %	28.7	35.1
Stolen Base Success %	71.0	66.5
Platoon Pct.	60.9	51.5
Defensive Subs	14	20
High-Pitch Outings	8	7
Quick/Slow Hooks	18/30	19/14
Sacrifice Attempts	108	87

2001 Rankings (National League)

- 1st in slow hooks
- 2nd in stolen base attempts (186), steals of third base (25), steals of home plate (1), sacrifice bunt attempts and pinch-hitters used (314)
- 3rd in steals of second base (106), double steals (8), squeeze plays (9), relief appearances (476), mid-inning pitching changes (179) and one-batter pitcher appearances (49)

Shawn Chacon

2001 Season

Shawn Chacon was called up from Triple-A Colorado Springs to make an emergency start when Mike Hamtpon was sidelined by a stiff neck on April 29. The Rockies third-round draft choice in 1996 wound up sticking with the parent club, and became the most consistent member of the rotation. He was winless in his final 11 starts, but Colorado scored two or fewer runs when he was in the game in nine of those outings. He made 14 quality starts, and led the team with seven such efforts at Coors Field.

Pitching

Chacon is a power-type pitcher who struck out 134 in 160 innings in 2001. He has a quality fastball in the low 90s. His big pitch is a curveball. Having grown up in Greeley, Colo., he hasn't been affected by the mental block of using the pitch in Coors Field. He will throw a cut fastball and shows an offspeed pitch, but he needs to refine the latter to become a top-of-the-rotation pitcher.

Defense & Hitting

Chacon is athletic. He has simple mechanics and gets in good position to field. He will get into too much of a hurry in an effort to nab the lead man on a bunt play, but that should disappear with experience. Chacon needs to put in some extra time in the batting cage. He struggles to make contact—22 strikeouts in 47 at-bats—and he is not a proficient bunter, a skill that is a must for a pitcher to keep himself in games.

2002 Outlook

Chacon is one of the young arms that the Rockies feel gives them reason for long-range optimism. He goes into the season as a definite member of the rotation. Despite his so-so record as a rookie, he showed a toughness in tight games that could earn him a shot at the No. 3 spot as early as this season.

Position: SP
Bats: R **Throws:** R
Ht: 6' 3" **Wt:** 195

Opening Day Age: 24
Born: 12/23/77 in Anchorage, AK
ML Seasons: 1
Pronunciation: cha-CONE

Overall Statistics

	W	L	Pct.	ERA	G	GS	Sv	IP	H	BB	SO	HR	Ratio
2001	6	10	.375	5.06	27	27	0	160.0	157	87	134	26	1.53
Career	6	10	.375	5.06	27	27	0	160.0	157	87	134	26	1.53

How Often He Throws Strikes

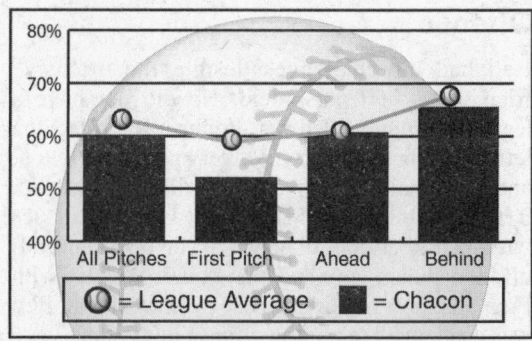

◎ = League Average ■ = Chacon

2001 Situational Stats

	W	L	ERA	Sv	IP		AB	H	HR	RBI	Avg
Home	4	5	5.27	0	80.1	LHB	253	66	9	38	.261
Road	2	5	4.86	0	79.2	RHB	352	91	17	51	.259
First Half	4	5	6.27	0	74.2	Sc Pos	156	43	4	58	.276
Scnd Half	2	5	4.01	0	85.1	Clutch	12	5	0	1	.417

2001 Rankings (National League)

- 3rd in losses among rookies
- 6th in lowest winning percentage
- 8th in walks allowed
- Led the Rockies in walks allowed, hit batsmen (10), wild pitches (6), pickoff throws (60), stolen bases allowed (14) and lowest batting average allowed vs. righthanded batters

Jeff Cirillo

Position: 3B
Bats: R **Throws:** R
Ht: 6' 1" **Wt:** 190

Opening Day Age: 32
Born: 9/23/69 in Pasadena, CA
ML Seasons: 8
Pronunciation: suh-RILL-o

2001 Season

Jeff Cirillo's final 2001 numbers were decent, but overall the season was a disappointment. He did hit .313, his fifth time in six years he's topped .300, and he set career highs with 17 home runs and 12 stolen bases. Cirillo, however, was being asked to assume a new role—providing protection for the lefthanded bats of Larry Walker and Todd Helton. And despite having three of the top 10 hitters in the National League ahead of him in the lineup (Walker, Helton and Juan Pierre), Cirillo drove in just 83 runs, 32 fewer than 2000. He also was on the disabled list for the first time in his eight-year career with a strained ribcage muscle.

Hitting

Cirillo changed his approach in 2001 and it didn't work. He tried to hit for power and became pull-conscious, which made him susceptible to pitches away. His style is to drive the ball into the alleys and pile up doubles, of which he had 53 in his Rockies debut in 2000 but only 26 last year. He is more suited for hitting second than fifth. His strength is working counts and fighting off pitches, then going the other way. He likes to bunt, but that doesn't work in a run-production role.

Baserunning & Defense

Cirillo became more aggressive on the bases. He has good speed and is alert at all times for the opposition to get lax when he is running the diamond. He doesn't make mistakes with the balls he gets to. He has good hands and a strong arm, and he is very good at charging the bunt play. His lateral movement is limited, however, particularly to the left.

2002 Outlook

Cirillo escapes another round of rebuilding in Colorado after the Rockies traded him for three young pitchers in December. He joins a Seattle club that won 116 games in 2001, and Cirillo will be in the lineup every day and will be expected to drive in runs. After last year's struggles in that role, he has a change of scenerey to help get his mental approach back in order. He should return to driving the ball into the alleys while racking up plenty of doubles.

Overall Statistics

	G	AB	R	H	D	T	HR	RBI	SB	BB	SO	Avg	OBP	Slg
2001	138	528	72	165	26	4	17	83	12	43	63	.313	.364	.473
Career	1084	3937	627	1224	265	19	94	570	47	440	507	.311	.383	.459

Where He Hits the Ball

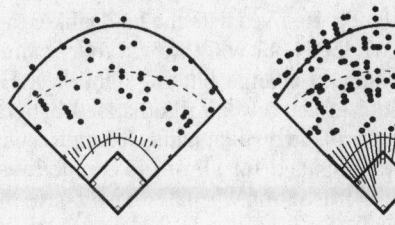

Vs. LHP   **Vs. RHP**

2001 Situational Stats

	AB	H	HR	RBI	Avg		AB	H	HR	RBI	Avg
Home	254	92	9	42	.362	LHP	121	32	0	13	.264
Road	274	73	8	41	.266	RHP	407	133	17	70	.327
First Half	266	82	11	47	.308	Sc Pos	146	46	4	61	.315
Scnd Half	262	83	6	36	.317	Clutch	78	24	3	13	.308

2001 Rankings (National League)

- 1st in fielding percentage at third base (.982)
- 2nd in highest percentage of extra bases taken as a runner (69.4) and lowest slugging percentage vs. lefthanded pitchers (.331)
- 3rd in batting average at home
- 6th in batting average on an 0-2 count (.316)
- 8th in batting average vs. righthanded pitchers
- 9th in singles, batting average with two strikes (.256), lowest cleanup slugging percentage (.490) and lowest on-base percentage vs. lefthanded pitchers (.324)
- Led the Rockies in sacrifice flies (9), GDPs (15), batting average on an 0-2 count (.316) and highest percentage of extra bases taken as a runner (69.4)

Mike Hampton

2001 Season

Mike Hampton, who signed an eight-year, $121 million deal with Colorado in December 2000, became the first Rockies pitcher to be selected to an All-Star team. He began the year by going 9-2 with a 2.98 ERA, but by season's end, Hampton showed the wear and tear of surviving in Coors Field. He continued to get groundballs—ranking third in the National League with 338 induced—but he also gave up a career-high 31 home runs. And he had a 5.10 ERA outside of Coors Field.

Pitching

Hampton has three quality pitches and an ability to change speeds off each one, particularly a fastball that in the same at-bat can have as much as a 6-MPH variance. He lives with the hard sinker that gets the groundballs but will throw a four-seamer up on occasion to change hitters' sightlines. He uses the slider effectively on righthanded batters, getting the offering in on their hands. Hampton will work pitch counts and for all of his competitiveness will show frustration when he doesn't have his best stuff.

Defense & Hitting

Hampton is as good an athlete as there is. He is spectacular in fielding his position, making it very difficult to bunt against him with his acrobatic endeavors. After struggling with the bat earlier in his career, he had made himself a tough out before coming to Colorado. Last year he began to swing for power instead of just trying to make contact. The result was seven home runs, equaling the NL record for a pitcher.

2002 Outlook

Hampton knew he had a challenge in Colorado. Now that he has experienced life in Coors Field for a full season, the expectation is that he will come back strong in 2002 to prove he can handle the demands of the hitter-friendly environment. He is expected to be fully recovered from late-November groin surgery by the time spring training opens, and he naturally will be counted on to be the ace of the rotation.

Position: SP
Bats: R **Throws:** L
Ht: 5'10" **Wt:** 180

Opening Day Age: 29
Born: 9/9/72 in Brooksville, FL
ML Seasons: 9

Overall Statistics

	W	L	Pct.	ERA	G	GS	Sv	IP	H	BB	SO	HR	Ratio
2001	14	13	.519	5.41	32	32	0	203.0	236	85	122	31	1.58
Career	99	66	.600	3.71	273	219	1	1463.2	1470	574	974	119	1.40

How Often He Throws Strikes

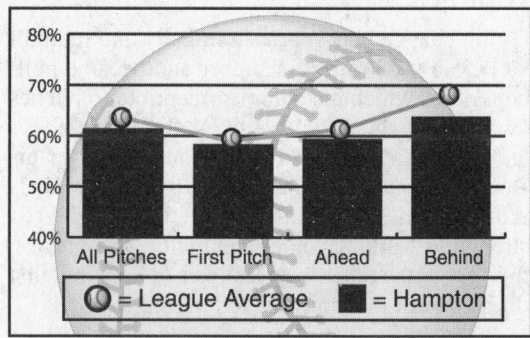

2001 Situational Stats

	W	L	ERA	Sv	IP		AB	H	HR	RBI	Avg
Home	8	6	5.77	0	93.2	LHB	159	55	8	35	.346
Road	6	7	5.10	0	109.1	RHB	638	181	23	86	.284
First Half	9	5	4.02	0	121.0	Sc Pos	199	49	3	76	.246
Scnd Half	5	8	7.46	0	82.0	Clutch	38	15	1	10	.395

2001 Rankings (National League)

- 1st in GDPs induced (29), lowest stolen-base percentage allowed (16.7), most run support per nine innings (7.1), fielding percentage at pitcher (1.000), highest ERA, highest ERA at home and highest batting average allowed vs. lefthanded batters
- Led the Rockies in wins, losses, games started, innings pitched, hits allowed, batters faced (904), home runs allowed, pitches thrown (3,295), lowest slugging percentage allowed (.486), highest groundball-flyball ratio allowed (1.8), fewest pitches thrown per batter (3.64), lowest ERA at home, lowest ERA on the road and fewest home runs allowed per nine innings (1.37)

Todd Helton

2001 Season

Todd Helton signed a new 11-year, $151 million contract with the Rockies just days before the start of the 2001 regular season. He then continued to establish himself as one of the game's premiere hitters. He became the first player in history to produce back-to-back seasons of 100 extra-base hits, finished second to teammate Larry Walker for the National League batting title and equaled the franchise record with 49 home runs. An All-Star selection for the second time, Helton also was awarded his first Gold Glove at first base, where he committed just two errors.

Hitting

Helton is a hitter's hitter. He uses the entire field and has the power to drive the ball out of the park to left field, as well as right. Asked to be a cleanup hitter, he showed the ability to expand the strike zone to enhance his run-production opportunities, and he can foul off pitches until he gets one he likes. With a maximum-effort swing, he has the hand-eye quickness and bat speed to wait before committing himself. He can handle the breaking ball, particularly from lefties who want to change speeds.

Baserunning & Defense

Helton is a below-average runner in terms of stealing bases, but once he gets going he is average. . . and aggressive. He always looks for the extra base, and over the last two years has matured into an intelligent baserunner who rarely misjudges his chances to advance. A former quarterback at Tennessee, where he was replaced by Peyton Manning, Helton has put in extra time learning to play defense. He is smooth on the 3-6-3 double play and relishes the opportunity to turn a sacrifice bunt into a fielder's choice.

2002 Outlook

At the age of 28, Helton is just coming into his prime. Given the benefit of Coors Field, where he has a .375 career batting average compared to .290 on the road, he has shown he is a player that can be counted on to hit 40-plus home runs, drive in 140-plus runs and score 110-plus runs.

Position: 1B
Bats: L **Throws:** L
Ht: 6' 2" **Wt:** 204

Opening Day Age: 28
Born: 8/20/73 in Knoxville, TN
ML Seasons: 5

Colorado

Overall Statistics

	G	AB	R	H	D	T	HR	RBI	SB	BB	SO	Avg	OBP	Slg
2001	159	587	132	197	54	2	49	146	7	98	104	.336	.432	.685
Career	665	2368	475	791	191	11	156	514	22	330	307	.334	.416	.622

Where He Hits the Ball

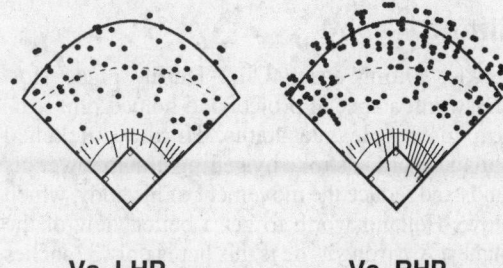

Vs. LHP **Vs. RHP**

2001 Situational Stats

	AB	H	HR	RBI	Avg		AB	H	HR	RBI	Avg
Home	297	114	27	84	.384	LHP	169	49	7	27	.290
Road	290	83	22	62	.286	RHP	418	148	42	119	.354
First Half	315	99	26	84	.314	Sc Pos	172	62	15	99	.360
Scnd Half	272	98	23	62	.360	Clutch	86	29	7	15	.337

2001 Rankings (National League)

- 1st in batting average vs. righthanded pitchers, cleanup slugging percentage (.722) and fielding percentage at first base (.999)
- Led the Rockies in home runs, runs scored, doubles, total bases (402), RBI, walks, times on base (300), strikeouts, pitches seen (2,824), plate appearances (697), slugging percentage, HR frequency (12.0 ABs per HR), most pitches seen per plate appearance (4.05), highest percentage of pitches taken (58.5), slugging percentage vs. righthanded pitchers (.758), on-base percentage vs. righthanded pitchers (.453) and lowest percentage of swings on the first pitch (26.8)
- Led NL first basemen in batting average, home runs and RBI

Todd Hollandsworth

2001 Season

After being acquired at the trading deadline in 2000 from Los Angeles, Todd Hollandsworth passed on the opportunity to become a free-agent after the 2000 campaign and signed a two-year, $5.5 million deal with the Rockies. What had the makings of a breakthrough season in 2001, however, went to pieces on May 11. He fouled a pitch off his right shin in the eighth inning and never returned to action, suffering severe nerve damage and a series of hairline fractures (although it took more than two months for doctors to properly diagnose the problems). Limited to 33 games, he did have a career-best 16-game hitting streak and hit three home runs against Arizona on April 15, including the three-run game-winner in the 10th.

Hitting

Rockies hitting coach Clint Hurdle made Hollandsworth a special project and helped him reaffirm his big league status. Hurdle quickened Hollandsworth's stroke by getting him to lower his hands and reduce the movement of his body, which allows Hollandsworth to get a better view of the pitches. As strong as he is, his bat is only 33 inches long, the shortest on the team, preventing him from having good plate coverage on pitches away.

Baserunning & Defense

Hollandsworth has plus-speed and is aggressive on the bases. He does get out of control at times, and can make ill-advised gambles trying to get the extra base. He has the potential to steal 30-plus bases, but he most likely will hit in the sixth spot of the lineup, thus limiting his opportunities to run. Hollandsworth is capable of playing all three outfield positions as well as first base, but his throws are only average. His speed is important in the vast expanse of left field at Coors.

2002 Outlook

Hollandsworth was showing signs of getting over his leg problems during the offseason and should be the Rockies' primary left fielder. However, the team's need for an extra righthanded bat in the lineup will put him on the bench more against lefthanded pitchers.

Position: LF/CF
Bats: L **Throws:** L
Ht: 6' 2" **Wt:** 207

Opening Day Age: 28
Born: 4/20/73 in Dayton, OH
ML Seasons: 7
Pronunciation: HAHL-enz-worth

Overall Statistics

	G	AB	R	H	D	T	HR	RBI	SB	BB	SO	Avg	OBP	Slg
2001	33	117	21	43	15	1	6	19	5	8	20	.368	.408	.667
Career	613	1858	283	515	101	13	58	221	60	150	404	.277	.332	.439

Where He Hits the Ball

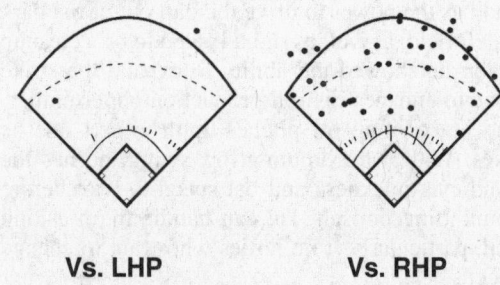

Vs. LHP   Vs. RHP

2001 Situational Stats

	AB	H	HR	RBI	Avg		AB	H	HR	RBI	Avg
Home	70	28	3	13	.400	LHP	19	3	1	3	.158
Road	47	15	3	6	.319	RHP	98	40	5	16	.408
First Half	117	43	6	19	.368	Sc Pos	30	6	1	11	.200
Scnd Half	0	0	0	0	-	Clutch	14	8	3	7	.571

2001 Rankings (National League)

- Did not rank near the top or bottom in any category

Jose Jimenez

2001 Season

Jose Jimenez continued his adjustment to a bullpen role in 2001, but two different stints on the disabled list kept him from enjoying his second year as a closer. He did lead the Rockies with 17 saves in 22 opportunities, making him 41-for-52 in two years as a reliever. He now sits third on the Rockies' all-time save list, five back of Darren Holmes and 19 behind Bruce Ruffin.

Pitching

Jimenez has mastered a sinking fastball and slider, but he shows no sign of an offspeed pitch, which is why he was moved out of a starting role. The fastball bores in at 92 MPH with severe sinking action, and is a big part of the reason that Jimenez gets so many groundballs. He also has a hard slider that he runs in on lefthanded hitters. A focus for the Rockies is keeping him in the flow of the game. When he starts to walk around the mound, he has trouble throwing the ball around the plate. He relies on his defense, having struck out only 81 batters in 125.2 innings during his two seasons as a reliever.

Defense & Hitting

Jimenez doesn't do much to help himself and seems oblivious to the details of defense. He doesn't face very many stolen-base attempts, and when they do run he has a quick delivery which gives his catcher a chance to throw out the average baserunner. Jimenez had only one at-bat last year and only 64 in his career, during which he has seven hits and 28 strikeouts.

2002 Outlook

The Rockies still are looking for a more typical closer, but the job is Jimenez' to lose. He has proven to be durable. He has appeared in 128 games during the last two years, with 56 of those appearances coming last year even though he was on the disabled list with tendinitis in his right shoulder for 32 contests.

Position: RP
Bats: R **Throws:** R
Ht: 6' 3" **Wt:** 228

Opening Day Age: 28
Born: 7/7/73 in San Pedro de Macoris, DR
ML Seasons: 4
Pronunciation: he-MEN-ez

Overall Statistics

	W	L	Pct.	ERA	G	GS	Sv	IP	H	BB	SO	HR	Ratio
2001	6	1	.857	4.09	56	0	17	55.0	56	22	37	6	1.42
Career	19	17	.528	4.73	161	31	41	310.0	314	129	206	26	1.43

How Often He Throws Strikes

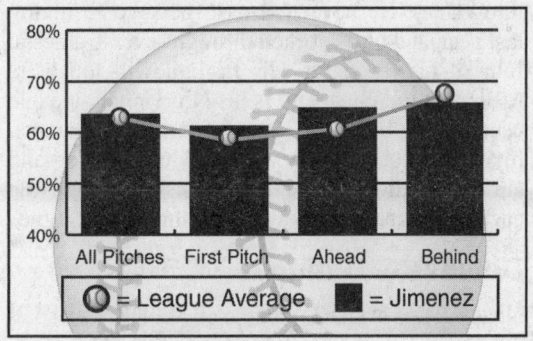

= League Average   ■ = Jimenez

2001 Situational Stats

	W	L	ERA	Sv	IP		AB	H	HR	RBI	Avg
Home	5	1	4.89	9	35.0	LHB	94	24	4	19	.255
Road	1	0	2.70	8	20.0	RHB	118	32	2	12	.271
First Half	4	1	4.14	12	37.0	Sc Pos	70	18	0	22	.257
Scnd Half	2	0	4.00	5	18.0	Clutch	107	25	3	20	.234

2001 Rankings (National League)

- 2nd in lowest save percentage (77.3)
- 6th in relief wins (6)
- 9th in fewest strikeouts per nine innings in relief (6.1)
- 10th in blown saves (5) and games finished (49)
- Led the Rockies in saves, games finished (49), save opportunities (22), save percentage (77.3), first batter efficiency (.204), blown saves (5) and relief wins (6)

Denny Neagle

2001 Season

After signing a five-year, $51 million deal with Colorado in December 2000, Denny Neagle proved a flyball pitcher actually could survive at Coors Field. He was 6-2 in 15 starts in the hitters' haven, and the Rockies were 11-4 in those contests. Neagle was only 3-6 with a 5.11 ERA in 15 starts on the road, however, and he continued to be haunted by second-half fades. He was 3-6 with a 6.56 ERA after the All-Star break.

Pitching

Neagle has a full assortment of pitches and uses them all, often using *too* many. He builds up high pitch counts, which keeps him from working deep into games. He never got past the seventh inning last year, and only worked through seven frames in four of his 30 starts. His fastball will touch 90 MPH, but the changeup is his No. 1 pitch. Neagle uses a cutter in on the hands to negate righthanded hitters and occasionally will break out an overhand curve. He didn't have the consistency with the curve last year and rarely would throw it at home.

Defense & Hitting

Neagle helps himself with the glove. He has a solid mechanical approach, which puts him in position to field balls up the middle. He breaks quickly on bunt plays and isn't afraid to go for the force. Neagle can handle the bat. He is a very good bunter and makes decent contact for a pitcher. He poked his second career grand slam last season.

2002 Outlook

Neagle will enter the second year of his mega-contract with the Rockies. He is a proven starter, most effective if he can be slotted into the No. 4 or 5 spot in a rotation, which is right where he should find himself in 2002. The Rockies expect Shawn Chacon and John Thomson to move in behind rotation ace Mike Hampton.

Position: SP
Bats: L **Throws:** L
Ht: 6' 3" **Wt:** 225

Opening Day Age: 33
Born: 9/13/68 in Annapolis, MD
ML Seasons: 11
Pronunciation: NAY-gull

Overall Statistics

	W	L	Pct.	ERA	G	GS	Sv	IP	H	BB	SO	HR	Ratio
2001	9	8	.529	5.38	30	30	0	170.2	192	60	139	29	1.48
Career	114	77	.597	4.07	350	251	3	1690.2	1670	519	1283	212	1.29

How Often He Throws Strikes

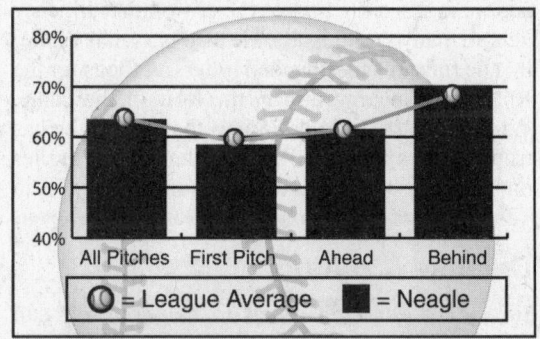

2001 Situational Stats

	W	L	ERA	Sv	IP		AB	H	HR	RBI	Avg
Home	6	2	5.70	0	79.0	LHB	170	51	5	21	.300
Road	3	6	5.11	0	91.2	RHB	506	141	24	74	.279
First Half	6	2	4.32	0	89.2	Sc Pos	164	49	5	61	.299
Scnd Half	3	6	6.56	0	81.0	Clutch	16	4	1	2	.250

2001 Rankings (National League)

- 2nd in most run support per nine innings (6.9), highest ERA, highest slugging percentage allowed (.503) and lowest groundball-flyball ratio allowed (0.6)
- 3rd in fewest GDPs induced per nine innings (0.4)
- 4th in most home runs allowed per nine innings (1.53)
- 6th in most pitches thrown per batter (3.90)
- Led the Rockies in ERA, strikeouts, winning percentage, highest strikeout-walk ratio (2.3), lowest batting average allowed (.284), lowest on-base percentage allowed (.344), most strikeouts per nine innings (7.3) and fewest walks per nine innings (3.2)

Jose Ortiz

2001 Season

Jose Ortiz came to the Rockies in a three-team deal on July 25 that sent Neifi Perez to Kansas City and Jermaine Dye to Oakland. Ortiz immediately assumed the starting second-base role for the Rockies. He spent only 53 games with Colorado, but still finished fourth among National League rookies with 13 home runs. He also drove in 35 runs, which was good enough for eighth among NL rookies.

Hitting

Ortiz is a legitimate power threat for a middle infielder. He's only 5-foot-9 but has the quick wrists to generate bat speed. He still is too pull conscious and is vulnerable to anything away, particularly breaking pitches. He opens up so quickly that he even has trouble handling strikes on the outer half of the plate. There isn't a fastball that is hard enough to sneak by him, however. He does have the strength and bat quickness to drive the ball to right field, and given his potential, he is expected to develop into a plus offensive middle infielder at Coors Field.

Baserunning & Defense

Ortiz did steal 22 bags three different times in the minor leagues, but he would not be considered a big-time stolen-base threat. He is a bit above average in speed, and that translates into the potential for extra-base hits at Coors. He tends to lose his concentration both on the bases and in the field. Ortiz has a strong arm for a second baseman, but his hands are hard and he is mechanical when turning the double play. If the power in his bat develops as expected, he could wind up a third baseman.

2002 Outlook

The Rockies are committed to Ortiz at second and Juan Uribe at shortstop as a middle infield to build around. Ortiz most likely will hit second in the order, though he doesn't have the type of plate discipline a manager wants out of that spot. Hitting behind Juan Pierre and ahead of Larry Walker and Todd Helton should allow Ortiz to see an abundance of fastballs.

Position: 2B
Bats: R **Throws:** R
Ht: 5' 9" **Wt:** 177

Opening Day Age: 24
Born: 6/13/77 in Santo Domingo, DR
ML Seasons: 2

Overall Statistics

	G	AB	R	H	D	T	HR	RBI	SB	BB	SO	Avg	OBP	Slg
2001	64	246	42	59	8	1	13	38	4	17	41	.240	.297	.439
Career	71	257	46	61	8	1	13	39	4	19	44	.237	.298	.428

Where He Hits the Ball

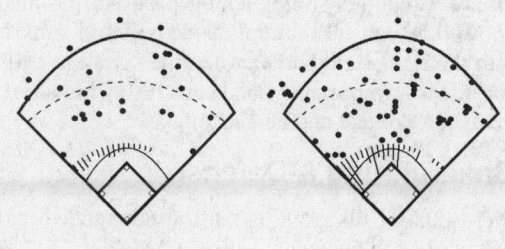

Vs. LHP   **Vs. RHP**

2001 Situational Stats

	AB	H	HR	RBI	Avg		AB	H	HR	RBI	Avg
Home	132	31	9	20	.235	LHP	71	16	4	10	.225
Road	114	28	4	18	.246	RHP	175	43	9	28	.246
First Half	42	7	0	3	.167	Sc Pos	68	17	3	25	.250
Scnd Half	204	52	13	35	.255	Clutch	42	10	3	8	.238

2001 Rankings (National League)

- 4th in home runs among rookies (13)

Juan Pierre

2001 Season

Juan Pierre answered all the questions in 2001, and did it emphatically. He proved he was durable. He proved he could hit for average. He showed he could handle lefthanded pitchers. He showed he could steal bases (46, tied for the National League lead). He also had 26 doubles, a club-record-tying 11 triples and two homers in his first full big league season.

Hitting

Pierre isn't pretty, but he is successful. He has an excellent understanding of what he has to do at the plate—put the ball on the ground and run. He slaps at pitches and gets a quick start out of the box. But after a strenuous strengthening program, he also showed he can turn on the inside ball and yank it into the right-field corner when the situation calls for it. Most importantly, he keeps his swing short, he makes contact and he gets on base.

Baserunning & Defense

Pierre knows his game is built around speed and has worked to become a better basestealer. He is a plus-runner and last year became only the second player in franchise history to steal more than 40 bases. He has been challenged defensively. After playing left field his first two pro seasons, he has had to do the bulk of his transition to center at Coors, which has the biggest center field in baseball. He has a below-average arm, but has worked to quicken his release.

2002 Outlook

Pierre will be counted on to build on his 2001 season, giving the Rockies a low-cost leadoff hitter who is among the best in the NL at getting on base. He will set the table for a lineup anchored by the big bats of Larry Walker and Todd Helton. With the confidence of a full big league season behind him, it is safe to assume Pierre will improve his basestealing in terms of both sheer numbers and success rate. He also figures to drive the ball more, thanks to his decision to continue to work on a conditioning program in the offseason.

Position: CF
Bats: L **Throws:** L
Ht: 6' 0" **Wt:** 180

Opening Day Age: 24
Born: 8/14/77 in Mobile, AL
ML Seasons: 2
Pronunciation: pee-AIR

Overall Statistics

	G	AB	R	H	D	T	HR	RBI	SB	BB	SO	Avg	OBP	Slg
2001	156	617	108	202	26	11	2	55	46	41	29	.327	.378	.415
Career	207	817	134	264	28	11	2	75	53	54	44	.323	.372	.392

Where He Hits the Ball

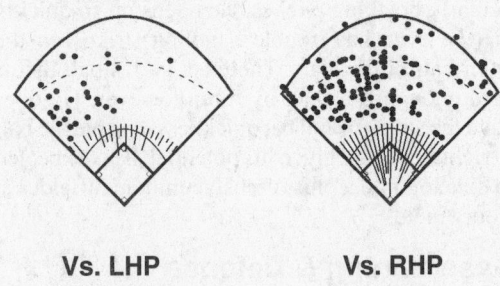

Vs. LHP   **Vs. RHP**

2001 Situational Stats

	AB	H	HR	RBI	Avg		AB	H	HR	RBI	Avg
Home	299	100	0	23	.334	LHP	121	35	0	9	.289
Road	318	102	2	32	.321	RHP	496	167	2	46	.337
First Half	313	102	1	24	.326	Sc Pos	136	47	2	53	.346
Scnd Half	304	100	1	31	.329	Clutch	79	29	0	7	.367

2001 Rankings (National League)

- 1st in singles, stolen bases, caught stealing (17), highest groundball-flyball ratio (2.8), bunts in play (55), lowest percentage of swings that missed (5.8), batting average with two strikes (.325), errors in center field (8), steals of third (14) and lowest HR frequency (308.5 ABs per HR)
- Led the Rockies in at-bats, hits, triples, sacrifice bunts (14), stolen-base percentage (73.0), bunts in play (55), highest percentage of swings put into play (56.3), steals of third (14), batting average in the clutch, on-base percentage for a leadoff hitter (.373), batting average on the road and batting average with two strikes (.325)
- Led NL center fielders in batting average

John Thomson

2001 Season

John Thomson missed the entire 2000 season and spent two stints on the disabled list during the 2001 campaign while recovering from surgery for a torn right labrum. He managed to put together a strong finish to last season, however, going 4-2 in 11 starts the final two months, with a 3.62 ERA. His 4.64 ERA at Coors Field was the best among Rockies starters. He also pitched the 12th complete-game shutout in Coors Field history against Milwaukee on September 30, 25 days after coming within two outs of a Coors Field shutout of Los Angeles.

Pitching

Thomson always has given the Rockies reason to feel he is something special because of a mid-90s sinker and his ability to throw strikes. His lengthy battle with injuries also may have given him time to think about what he needed to do to establish himself as a quality big league starter. After considering retirement in August 2000, Thomson returned last season and broke out a changeup to go with the sinker and fastball. More than that, he finally showed the ability to challenge Coors Field instead of being intimidated by it.

Defense & Hitting

With a simple delivery, Thomson should be a good fielder. Instead, he gets in a hurry when balls are hit in his direction and will have lapses on what to do with the ball. He has had enough work at the plate that he can give himself a lift now and then, but he has struck out 68 times in 144 big league at-bats, including 15 whiffs last year.

2002 Outlook

Thomson reaffirmed his status in the Colorado rotation last year, and he will go into the season most likely in the No. 2 slot behind Mike Hampton. His resiliency in the final two months of 2001 and his progress in an offseason conditioning program gives the Rockies every reason to believe that he will provide the consistent innings that they have envisioned for him ever since he broke into the big leagues in 1997.

Position: SP
Bats: R **Throws:** R
Ht: 6' 3" **Wt:** 190

Opening Day Age: 28
Born: 10/1/73 in Vicksburg, MS
ML Seasons: 4
Nickname: Red

Colorado

Overall Statistics

	W	L	Pct.	ERA	G	GS	Sv	IP	H	BB	SO	HR	Ratio
2001	4	5	.444	4.04	14	14	0	93.2	84	25	68	15	1.16
Career	20	35	.364	5.04	81	80	0	483.2	536	161	314	62	1.44

How Often He Throws Strikes

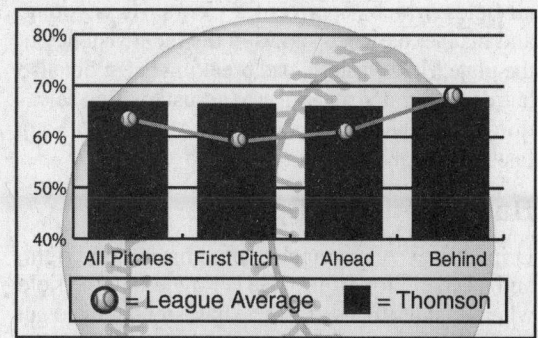

Legend: ◉ = League Average   ■ = Thomson

2001 Situational Stats

	W	L	ERA	Sv	IP		AB	H	HR	RBI	Avg
Home	2	2	4.64	0	54.1	LHB	164	29	7	19	.177
Road	2	3	3.20	0	39.1	RHB	187	55	8	22	.294
First Half	0	3	5.68	0	19.0	Sc Pos	68	18	3	25	.265
Scnd Half	4	2	3.62	0	74.2	Clutch	16	5	2	5	.313

2001 Rankings (National League)

- 3rd in lowest batting average allowed vs. lefthanded batters
- Led the Rockies in lowest batting average allowed vs. lefthanded batters

423

Juan Uribe

2001 Season

Juan Uribe, who played at the Class-A level in 2000, got his first big league exposure in 2001 after only three games at Double-A Carolina when Neifi Perez went on the disabled list. Uribe showed enough in his two-week audition that he initially was sent to Triple-A, and then in late July was recalled for good when Perez was traded to Kansas City. Uribe responded with the best offensive numbers of his pro career, equaling a club record with 11 triples in only 72 games (67 starts).

Hitting

Uribe has shown emerging power the last two seasons. He has a quick bat and can drive the ball to all fields, which is perfect for Coors. He is young, and his inexperience shows in his inconsistency at the plate. He will chase bad breaking balls, but also has demonstrated an ability to adjust to pitch selection during the course of a game. And there's not a fastball he can't handle.

Baserunning & Defense

Uribe has excellent range to both his left and right, and a cannon for an arm. He is flawless in the field when he stays focused, but he has a tendency to get lax which gets him in trouble. He can boot routine plays after making spectacular ones. Uribe is a plus-runner and is very aggressive out of the box. He will be a basestealing threat, but right now his chances are controlled from the bench while he gets a feel for the big league game.

2002 Outlook

Uribe will get an everyday opportunity from the start of the 2002 season. He doesn't like to sit out, and as long as he stays healthy and plays hard that won't be a problem. He did find himself on the bench for two games in late August last season when he got lackadaisical in the field. He will hit in the No. 8 slot, but figures to put up good numbers from that spot because he will expand his strike zone and likes the chance to drive in runs.

Position: SS
Bats: R **Throws:** R
Ht: 5'11" **Wt:** 173

Opening Day Age: 21
Born: 7/22/80 in Bani, DR
ML Seasons: 1
Pronunciation: ooh-REE-bay

Overall Statistics

	G	AB	R	H	D	T	HR	RBI	SB	BB	SO	Avg	OBP	Slg
2001	72	273	32	82	15	11	8	53	3	8	55	.300	.325	.524
Career	72	273	32	82	15	11	8	53	3	8	55	.300	.325	.524

Where He Hits the Ball

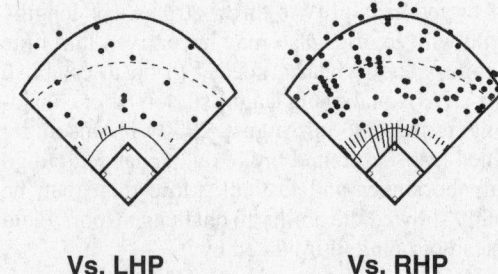

Vs. LHP   **Vs. RHP**

2001 Situational Stats

	AB	H	HR	RBI	Avg		AB	H	HR	RBI	Avg
Home	128	43	3	25	.336	LHP	45	14	2	14	.311
Road	145	39	5	28	.269	RHP	228	68	6	39	.298
First Half	40	11	0	6	.275	Sc Pos	82	27	2	41	.329
Scnd Half	233	71	8	47	.305	Clutch	43	11	0	3	.256

2001 Rankings (National League)

- 2nd in triples
- 4th in RBI among rookies
- Led the Rockies in triples and batting average with the bases loaded (.455)

Larry Walker

Position: RF
Bats: L **Throws:** R
Ht: 6' 3" **Wt:** 233

Opening Day Age: 35
Born: 12/1/66 in Maple Ridge, BC, Canada
ML Seasons: 13

Colorado

2001 Season

Larry Walker played through nagging injuries and logged 142 games. He also proved beyond a shadow of a doubt that if he is in the lineup, he will produce. In addition to winning his third batting title in four years, Walker drove in 123 runs and hit 38 homers, the second-best totals of his career. He also put to rest the questions about his ability to hit Randy Johnson, going 7-for-12 with the only home run by a lefthanded hitter off the Big Unit in 2001. On top of all that, Walker made his fifth All-Star appearance and won his sixth Gold Glove.

Hitting

Walker isn't a hitting video waiting to be filmed. He has a long swing, but he possesses enough strength and quickness to compensate. He uses the entire field, and has the power to hit the ball out of the park to left. He usually is patient, refusing to expand his strike zone, but he will get into ruts where he tries to force the issue and commits himself too quickly. He can be pounded inside, but it has to be off the plate. Randy Johnson aside, Walker did a number on *all* lefties last season.

Baserunning & Defense

Walker is slightly above average in terms of speed, but he is as good as there is in the game in terms of instincts on the bases. He doesn't run as often as he used to but will steal a critical base. He doesn't always run out groundballs, but when the ball goes into the outfield he usually pushes for the extra base. He has a center fielder's range, and an arm that isn't in the Valdimir Guerrero class for strength, but plays better because he never overthrows cutoff men or throws to the wrong base.

2002 Outlook

Even at age 35, Walker is one of the most talented players in the National League. He hired a personal trainer and personal dietician over the winter to help him stay healthy for the entire season. He still is maturing in his approach to the game and remains an MVP threat even if he does play half his games at Coors Field.

Overall Statistics

	G	AB	R	H	D	T	HR	RBI	SB	BB	SO	Avg	OBP	Slg
2001	142	497	107	174	35	3	38	123	14	82	103	.350	.449	.662
Career	1527	5403	1057	1702	370	46	309	1029	209	660	950	.315	.396	.572

Where He Hits the Ball

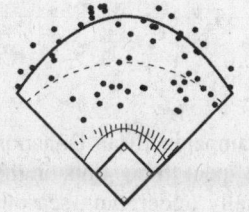

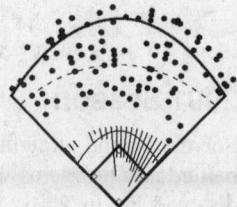

Vs. LHP   **Vs. RHP**

2001 Situational Stats

	AB	H	HR	RBI	Avg		AB	H	HR	RBI	Avg
Home	251	102	20	74	.406	LHP	148	56	14	52	.378
Road	246	72	18	49	.293	RHP	349	118	24	71	.338
First Half	297	102	27	83	.343	Sc Pos	124	47	11	85	.379
Scnd Half	200	72	11	40	.360	Clutch	66	21	6	15	.318

2001 Rankings (National League)

- 1st in batting average and batting average at home
- 2nd in on-base percentage
- 3rd in batting average vs. lefthanded pitchers and batting average vs. righthanded pitchers
- Led the Rockies in hit by pitch (14), on-base percentage, fewest GDPs per GDP situation (6.7%), batting average with runners in scoring position, batting average vs. lefthanded pitchers, slugging percentage vs. lefthanded pitchers (.750), on-base percentage vs. lefthanded pitchers (.443) and batting average on a 3-2 count (.304)
- Led NL right fielders in batting average

Brian Bohanon

Position: SP
Bats: L **Throws:** L
Ht: 6' 2" **Wt:** 250

Opening Day Age: 33
Born: 8/1/68 in Denton, TX
ML Seasons: 12
Pronunciation: bo-HAN-un

Overall Statistics

	W	L	Pct.	ERA	G	GS	Sv	IP	H	BB	SO	HR	Ratio
2001	5	8	.385	7.14	20	19	0	97.0	127	47	47	20	1.79
Career	54	60	.474	5.19	304	157	2	1116.0	1229	489	671	142	1.54

2001 Situational Stats

	W	L	ERA	Sv	IP		AB	H	HR	RBI	Avg
Home	2	6	9.00	0	61.0	LHB	108	32	7	23	.296
Road	3	2	4.00	0	36.0	RHB	285	95	13	48	.333
First Half	4	4	6.97	0	62.0	Sc Pos	102	39	5	53	.382
Scnd Half	1	4	7.46	0	35.0	Clutch	5	1	0	0	.200

2001 Season

For the second straight campaign Brian Bohanon battled arm problems. He spent three stints on the disabled list in 2001, finally undergoing season-ending surgery on his left elbow in late August. He came back strong after his first stint on the DL in May, winning three consecutive decisions, but the arm strength wasn't there. After his second disablement, he made seven starts and was just 1-4 with a 7.46 ERA.

Pitching, Defense & Hitting

Bohanon is proof that desire and experience can offset limited abilities. He was a solid 92-MPH hurler when he came out of high school, but he now relies on changing speeds and hitting spots. He often won't break the mid-80s with his fastball but has up to a 15-MPH differential in his pitches. He runs the cut fastball in on righties. When he doesn't have command of the strike zone, he is in trouble. Size limits his mobility, but he is an excellent athlete who can field his position and swing the bat.

2002 Outlook

Bohanon made major strides in his rehab from surgery, and by late October said his arm felt better than it had in years. However, his value lies more in his versatility than his stuff, and multiyear deals likely are a thing of the past for him.

Kane Davis

Position: RP
Bats: R **Throws:** R
Ht: 6' 3" **Wt:** 194

Opening Day Age: 26
Born: 6/25/75 in Ripley, WV
ML Seasons: 2

Overall Statistics

	W	L	Pct.	ERA	G	GS	Sv	IP	H	BB	SO	HR	Ratio
2001	2	4	.333	4.35	57	0	0	68.1	66	32	47	11	1.43
Career	2	7	.222	5.83	65	2	0	83.1	93	45	51	15	1.66

2001 Situational Stats

	W	L	ERA	Sv	IP		AB	H	HR	RBI	Avg
Home	0	2	5.12	0	38.2	LHB	95	32	7	15	.337
Road	2	2	3.34	0	29.2	RHB	167	34	4	18	.204
First Half	0	3	4.36	0	43.1	Sc Pos	68	14	3	24	.206
Scnd Half	2	1	4.32	0	25.0	Clutch	66	21	3	6	.318

2001 Season

A starting pitcher throughout his pro career, Kane Davis was moved into the bullpen after the Rockies acquired him from Milwaukee in the opening week of the 2001 season. He initially balked at the idea of working more than once every three days, but after being placed on the disabled list to build up endurance, he returned in the second half of the season to handle the longman duties for Colorado. He held righthanded hitters to a .204 average.

Pitching, Defense & Hitting

Davis has the mid-90s fastball and hard slider that should allow him to dominate in a relief role where he doesn't have to go through a lineup twice. He is not comfortable changing speeds, however, making it tough to think of him as a starting pitcher at Coors Field. He is athletic but can lose focus defensively and create problems for himself. He has six big league at-bats and has struck out each time.

2002 Outlook

Now that Davis has accepted the idea of pitching in relief, he can be expected to get plenty of work. Even with four weeks on the DL last year, he ranked fifth among National League rookies with 57 appearances, and his 68.1 innings were first among Rockies relievers. Both those numbers figure to increase this season.

Scott Elarton

Position: SP
Bats: R **Throws:** R
Ht: 6' 7" **Wt:** 240

Opening Day Age: 26
Born: 2/23/76 in Lamar, CO
ML Seasons: 4

Overall Statistics

	W	L	Pct.	ERA	G	GS	Sv	IP	H	BB	SO	HR	Ratio
2001	4	10	.286	7.06	24	24	0	132.2	146	59	87	34	1.55
Career	32	23	.582	4.91	124	71	3	506.1	495	206	395	76	1.38

2001 Situational Stats

	W	L	ERA	Sv	IP		AB	H	HR	RBI	Avg
Home	2	4	7.43	0	66.2	LHB	266	67	17	44	.252
Road	2	6	6.68	0	66.0	RHB	255	79	17	50	.310
First Half	4	8	6.92	0	105.1	Sc Pos	98	33	7	55	.337
Scnd Half	0	2	7.57	0	27.1	Clutch	11	4	1	3	.364

2001 Season

After winning 17 games with Houston in 2000, Scott Elarton battled injuries and inconsistency in 2001. He was on the disabled list with right biceps tendinitis when the Rockies acquired him for Pedro Astacio on July 31, and he wasn't activated until September. Elarton was given four starts in the final month in the hope that he would go into the offseason confident in his health.

Pitching, Defense & Hitting

Having grown up in Colorado, Elarton says he is looking forward to the opportunity with the Rockies. He has a solid, 90-plus MPH fastball that will peak at 95 MPH, and a sharp curveball. He has shown signs of a solid changeup and will need to refine that pitch to keep hitters off balance in Colorado. Elarton is agile despite his size. He can handle the bat, which will allow him to stay in games longer.

2002 Outlook

Elarton will get a shot at the fifth spot in the Colorado rotation, but he will have to prove that he is healthy and can cope with the way the ball carries in the thin air. The Rockies are banking on the fact that his 17 wins in 2000 came while calling hitter-friendly Enron Field home. If he struggles, he could wind up in a long-relief role.

Jason Jennings

Position: SP
Bats: R **Throws:** R
Ht: 6' 2" **Wt:** 242

Opening Day Age: 23
Born: 7/17/78 in Dallas, TX
ML Seasons: 1

Overall Statistics

	W	L	Pct.	ERA	G	GS	Sv	IP	H	BB	SO	HR	Ratio
2001	4	1	.800	4.58	7	7	0	39.1	42	19	26	2	1.55
Career	4	1	.800	4.58	7	7	0	39.1	42	19	26	2	1.55

2001 Situational Stats

	W	L	ERA	Sv	IP		AB	H	HR	RBI	Avg
Home	0	1	14.14	0	7.0	LHB	71	22	1	7	.310
Road	4	0	2.51	0	32.1	RHB	81	20	1	9	.247
First Half	0	0	-	0	0.0	Sc Pos	42	11	0	12	.262
Scnd Half	4	1	4.58	0	39.1	Clutch	3	0	0	0	.000

2001 Season

Jason Jennings made a big initial splash in the majors, becoming the first pitcher in history to toss a shutout and hit a home run in his big league debut. He opened the 2001 campaign at Double-A, and then spent the bulk of the year at Triple-A, where he was 2-1 with a 1.00 ERA in his final six starts before a mid-August callup by the Rockies. He won his first three big league starts but had trouble in two starts at Coors Field (0-1, 14.14).

Pitching, Defense & Hitting

Jennings has a hard sinker in the 92-94 MPH range, a quality changeup and a hard slider. He still works backwards in terms of his pitch selection, however, and needs to do a better job of establishing the fastball. He conjures up memories of Rick Rueschel with his sizable lower body but athletic quickness. He is an excellent fielder, who holds runners well, and he can hit. He was the DH at Baylor University when he wasn't pitching.

2002 Outlook

A catcher in high school, Jennings will get a solid shot to claim a spot in the Rockies' rotation. The team's first-round draft choice in 1999, he has shown a durability and competitiveness that can go a long way in securing a long-term role in Colorado's pitching plans.

Mike Myers

Position: RP
Bats: L **Throws:** L
Ht: 6' 4" **Wt:** 212

Opening Day Age: 32
Born: 6/26/69 in
Arlington Heights, IL
ML Seasons: 7

Overall Statistics

	W	L	Pct.	ERA	G	GS	Sv	IP	H	BB	SO	HR	Ratio
2001	2	3	.400	3.60	73	0	0	40.0	32	24	36	2	1.40
Career	8	16	.333	4.21	476	0	10	303.1	285	149	275	35	1.43

2001 Situational Stats

	W	L	ERA	Sv	IP		AB	H	HR	RBI	Avg
Home	2	3	3.65	0	24.2	LHB	91	21	2	12	.231
Road	0	0	3.52	0	15.1	RHB	51	11	0	4	.216
First Half	1	2	3.16	0	25.2	Sc Pos	44	9	0	12	.205
Scnd Half	1	1	4.40	0	14.1	Clutch	56	15	0	7	.268

2001 Season

Mike Myers became the first pitcher in history to make 70-plus appearances in six consecutive years. A situational lefthander, he stranded 51 of 65 inherited baserunners—the eighth-best percentage in the National League. Myers faced one batter in 28 of his 73 appearances. He wasn't bothered by Coors Field, where he had a 3.65 ERA compared to 3.52 on the road.

Pitching, Defense & Hitting

With a submarine style he adopted at the suggestion of Al Kaline when Myers was with Detroit, he is particularly difficult on lefthanded hitters. He uses a two-pitch mix of a sinking fastball and slider. He has made a conscious effort the last two years to work righthanders inside and has shown enough to get opportunities to stay in games against righties. Myers is athletic, but his sidearm delivery makes him vulnerable to the running game. Swinging a bat is not part of Myers' game.

2002 Outlook

Myers is signed through 2002 and will be a workhorse out of the Colorado pen. He will face the tough lefthanded hitter in the opposing lineup. He is resilient and effective enough that he won't be stretched out often because of the team's need to use him on consecutive days.

Alex Ochoa

Position: RF/LF
Bats: R **Throws:** R
Ht: 6' 0" **Wt:** 200

Opening Day Age: 29
Born: 3/29/72 in Miami
Lakes, FL
ML Seasons: 7
Pronunciation:
oh-CHO-ah

Overall Statistics

	G	AB	R	H	D	T	HR	RBI	SB	BB	SO	Avg	OBP	Slg
2001	148	536	73	148	30	7	8	52	17	45	76	.276	.334	.403
Career	685	1863	280	524	115	19	38	230	46	161	253	.281	.341	.425

2001 Situational Stats

	AB	H	HR	RBI	Avg		AB	H	HR	RBI	Avg
Home	282	76	5	22	.270	LHP	120	37	0	10	.308
Road	254	72	3	30	.283	RHP	416	111	8	42	.267
First Half	327	97	7	35	.297	Sc Pos	134	30	1	42	.224
Scnd Half	209	51	1	17	.244	Clutch	95	32	1	15	.337

2001 Season

Alex Ochoa came to the Rockies in a July 19 trade for Todd Walker and gave the team some stability in left field. Interestingly, Coors Field did little to help Ochoa. He hit .289 with seven home runs in 349 at-bats with Cincinnati, but only .251 with one homer and 17 RBI in 187 at-bats after the deal.

Hitting, Baserunning & Defense

Ochoa is a disciple of Jim Lefebrve and appeared to be taking his offensive game to a new level before coming to Colorado, where he became too power conscious and suffered for it. He began opening up too quickly, which led to chasing bad pitches. He has plus-speed and can steal a base or take an extra sack, an attribute that is ideal for Coors Field. He can play all three outfield positions, though he will get in trouble if he's asked to play too much center field. He has a strong, accurate arm.

2002 Outlook

Don't look for Ochoa to repeat last year's workload, which was the heaviest of his career. He is at his best when he gets regular rest, and he fits ideally into a platoon situation. He's an asset to a team because of his versatility and strong clubhouse presence, particularly with young Latin players.

Ben Petrick

Position: C
Bats: R **Throws:** R
Ht: 6' 0" **Wt:** 200

Opening Day Age: 24
Born: 4/7/77 in Salem, OR
ML Seasons: 3
Pronunciation: PEET-rick

Overall Statistics

	G	AB	R	H	D	T	HR	RBI	SB	BB	SO	Avg	OBP	Slg
2001	85	244	41	58	15	3	11	39	3	31	67	.238	.327	.459
Career	156	452	86	125	28	4	18	71	5	61	113	.277	.364	.476

2001 Situational Stats

	AB	H	HR	RBI	Avg		AB	H	HR	RBI	Avg
Home	127	31	7	23	.244	LHP	80	17	3	13	.213
Road	117	27	4	16	.231	RHP	164	41	8	26	.250
First Half	153	35	9	28	.229	Sc Pos	68	16	2	26	.235
Scnd Half	91	23	2	11	.253	Clutch	37	4	0	4	.108

2001 Season

Long considered the Rockies' long-term answer at catcher, Ben Petrick was given his chance to claim the job in late June when Brent Mayne was dealt to Kansas City, but he struggled. He spent a month at Triple-A Colorado Springs on what technically was an injury-rehab option. He provided another tease of what could be after rejoining the active roster September 1, hitting .356 in 16 games.

Hitting, Baserunning & Defense

Petrick has a compact swing and can drive the ball into the gaps. He has enough control to handle the breaking ball, but he can be overpowered inside. Petrick is a plus-runner and has the physical ability to steal 20 or more bases. He moves well behind the plate and blocks the ball well, but a hitch in his throw causes problems when he isn't mechanically perfect. Petrick was charged with eight errors and threw out only 11 of 57 baserunners in 2001.

2002 Outlook

Petrick will get another chance to prove he can handle big league receiving duties full-time, but the Rockies would like to add a solid veteran for protection. Colorado has toyed with the idea of having him play either second base or left field. He has the offensive potential to make the move, but it would be only as a last resort.

Jay Powell

Position: RP
Bats: R **Throws:** R
Ht: 6' 4" **Wt:** 225

Opening Day Age: 30
Born: 1/9/72 in Meridian, MS
ML Seasons: 7

Overall Statistics

	W	L	Pct.	ERA	G	GS	Sv	IP	H	BB	SO	HR	Ratio
2001	5	3	.625	3.24	74	0	7	75.0	75	31	54	9	1.41
Career	29	20	.592	3.81	382	0	22	406.2	393	199	330	27	1.46

2001 Situational Stats

	W	L	ERA	Sv	IP		AB	H	HR	RBI	Avg
Home	2	1	3.93	2	36.2	LHB	125	37	5	24	.296
Road	3	2	2.58	5	38.1	RHB	163	38	4	23	.233
First Half	2	2	3.67	0	41.2	Sc Pos	92	25	3	41	.272
Scnd Half	3	1	2.70	7	33.1	Clutch	137	38	2	29	.277

2001 Season

Jay Powell was acquired from Houston for lefty Ron Villone on June 27 and emerged as a critical member of the Rockies' bullpen. He converted seven of eight save opportunities for Colorado after failing in all five chances with the Astros. When closer Jose Jimenez was sidelined in midseason, Powell earned a save in six straight appearances.

Pitching, Defense & Hitting

Powell is a two-pitch pitcher. He has a fastball with good velocity, but it doesn't have much movement and he has to spot it to be successful. He can dominate hitters in short spurts with a hard slider. He gets flustered defensively but will hold runners well enough to give the catcher a chance. As a reliever, his opportunities at the plate are few and far between, which is just as well, as he has struck out eight times in 12 career at-bats.

2002 Outlook

Powell signed a three-year, $9 million deal with Texas, creating an impressive trio with Jeff Zimmerman and Todd Van Poppel in the Rangers' pen. Powell is best-suited for a setup role—and he looks like the bridge to Zimmerman—but he could assume at least part of the closing load. When he closes, he sometimes outthinks himself and also struggles with lefthanded hitters.

Colorado

Justin Speier

Position: RP
Bats: R **Throws:** R
Ht: 6' 4" **Wt:** 205

Opening Day Age: 28
Born: 11/6/73 in Walnut Creek, CA
ML Seasons: 4
Pronunciation: SPY-er

Overall Statistics

	W	L	Pct.	ERA	G	GS	Sv	IP	H	BB	SO	HR	Ratio
2001	6	3	.667	4.58	54	0	0	76.2	71	20	62	13	1.19
Career	11	8	.579	4.72	139	0	0	194.1	183	74	170	37	1.32

2001 Situational Stats

	W	L	ERA	Sv	IP		AB	H	HR	RBI	Avg
Home	4	1	4.34	0	45.2	LHB	93	23	4	18	.247
Road	2	2	4.94	0	31.0	RHB	194	48	9	29	.247
First Half	2	0	7.36	0	33.0	Sc Pos	73	18	5	36	.247
Scnd Half	4	3	2.47	0	43.2	Clutch	55	17	2	7	.309

2001 Season

After beginning the year with Cleveland, Justin Speier was claimed on waivers from the Mets on May 29. He took a couple of months to acclimate himself to the Rockies' organization. Once he got a feel in late July, however, he became a vital part of the Colorado bullpen. He had a 2.14 ERA in his final 25 appearances. He posted a ratio of 1.93 walks per nine innings in the National League—third best among NL relievers.

Pitching, Defense & Hitting

Speier is a three-pitch pitcher who regained confidence in his split-finger offering after joining the Rockies. With that pitch back to negate lefthanded hitters, he enjoyed renewed confidence in a fastball that comes in at 90-plus MPH. Speier is an average fielder at his position and tends to ignore baserunners. Having pitched exclusively in relief in his seven pro campaigns, his offensive abilities have eroded due to the lack of at-bats.

2002 Outlook

Speier has pitched himself into a key role in the Rockies' bullpen, most likely providing setup work for closer Jose Jimenez. His pitch selection allows him to go through a lineup more than once, which means he can be stretched out, and his resiliency allowed him to be called on often.

Gabe White

Position: RP
Bats: L **Throws:** L
Ht: 6' 2" **Wt:** 204

Opening Day Age: 30
Born: 11/20/71 in Sebring, FL
ML Seasons: 7

Overall Statistics

	W	L	Pct.	ERA	G	GS	Sv	IP	H	BB	SO	HR	Ratio
2001	1	7	.125	6.25	69	0	0	67.2	70	26	47	18	1.42
Career	22	21	.512	4.46	401.2	15	16	401.2	377	110	342	71	1.21

2001 Situational Stats

	W	L	ERA	Sv	IP		AB	H	HR	RBI	Avg
Home	1	2	7.43	0	36.1	LHB	93	25	6	20	.269
Road	0	5	4.88	0	31.1	RHB	166	45	12	23	.271
First Half	1	6	7.98	0	38.1	Sc Pos	48	17	5	27	.354
Scnd Half	0	1	3.99	0	29.1	Clutch	89	28	7	15	.315

2001 Season

The security of a three-year contract signed in February 2001 didn't pay off for Gabe White. He equaled a career-high with 69 appearances, but he got into such a first-half rut (7.98 ERA before the All-Star break) that even a solid finish (3.99 ERA after) couldn't obscure his struggles. He closed the campaign with his highest ERA since 1995.

Pitching, Defense & Hitting

White throws a steady 90-MPH fastball and a changeup. Those two pitches are enough for a reliever, but to be effective White has to have command, which was missing last year. He usually enjoys success against righthanded hitters because of his willingness to spot his fastball on their hands. However, he has a tendency to pitch behind in the count against lefthanders. White is quick off the mound and has a simple delivery that puts him in fielding position. He is sure handed, and has yet to commit a big-league error.

2002 Outlook

White's durability and the fact he has two more guaranteed seasons on his contract assures that he will get a chance to rebound from last year's disappointment. He is going to have to prove himself in a middle role, however, before he again will be entrusted with game situations in late innings.

Other Colorado Rockies

Kimera Bartee (Pos: LF, Age: 29, Bats: R)

	G	AB	R	H	D	T	HR	RBI	SB	BB	SO	Avg	OBP	Slg
2001	12	15	0	0	0	0	0	1	0	2	5	.000	.158	.000
Career	243	416	69	90	12	5	4	33	36	36	141	.216	.282	.298

Speed can keep you on the fringe of the majors, but Bartee was 0-for-15 with the Rockies and batted .192 at Triple-A Colorado Springs. If only he had learned to draw walks. The Cubs signed him to a minor league deal in December. 2002 Outlook: C

Todd Belitz (Pos: LHP, Age: 26)

	W	L	Pct.	ERA	G	GS	Sv	IP	H	BB	SO	HR	Ratio
2001	1	1	.500	7.71	8	0	0	9.1	9	3	5	2	1.29
Career	1	1	.500	6.39	13	0	0	12.2	13	7	8	2	1.58

Southpaw Belitz went from Oakland to Colorado in the midsummer Jermaine Dye deal. His 9.82 ERA at Triple-A Colorado Springs after the deal suggests he's learned the harsh realities of his new team. 2002 Outlook: C

Gary Bennett (Pos: C, Age: 29, Bats: R)

	G	AB	R	H	D	T	HR	RBI	SB	BB	SO	Avg	OBP	Slg
2001	46	131	15	32	6	1	2	10	0	12	24	.244	.308	.351
Career	129	341	34	87	15	1	5	40	0	36	62	.255	.327	.349

A veteran of 11-plus minor league seasons, Bennett enjoyed his longest stay in the majors in 2001. He was traded twice, from the first-place Phils to the Mets to Colorado. He must want to stay. 2002 Outlook: C

Cliff Brumbaugh (Pos: RF, Age: 27, Bats: R)

	G	AB	R	H	D	T	HR	RBI	SB	BB	SO	Avg	OBP	Slg
2001	21	46	6	10	2	0	1	4	0	3	14	.217	.265	.326
Career	21	46	6	10	2	0	1	4	0	3	14	.217	.265	.326

Brumbaugh was having a second straight solid season for the Rangers' Triple-A Oklahoma, but was waived after an 0-for-10 stint with Texas. He went to Triple-A Colorado Springs and posted a .419 OBP in 208 at-bats. 2002 Outlook: C

Brent Butler (Pos: 2B, Age: 24, Bats: R)

	G	AB	R	H	D	T	HR	RBI	SB	BB	SO	Avg	OBP	Slg
2001	53	119	17	29	7	1	1	14	1	7	7	.244	.287	.345
Career	53	119	17	29	7	1	1	14	1	7	7	.244	.287	.345

A Cardinals prospect dealt to Colorado, Butler has found Triple-A Colorado Springs to his liking the last two summers. He didn't do so well in his rookie debut, but he's in the mix for work in 2002. 2002 Outlook: B

Bobby Chouinard (Pos: RHP, Age: 29)

	W	L	Pct.	ERA	G	GS	Sv	IP	H	BB	SO	HR	Ratio
2001	0	0	-	8.22	8	0	0	7.2	10	1	5	4	1.43
Career	11	8	.579	4.57	111	13	1	181.0	197	65	110	26	1.45

Chouinard has had two decent seasons at Triple-A Colorado Springs and fared fine in Denver in 2000. It didn't go as well in 2001, and shoulder troubles led to labrum/rotator cuff surgery in September. He refused a minor league assignment in October and became a free agent. 2002 Outlook: B

Tim Christman (Pos: LHP, Age: 27)

	W	L	Pct.	ERA	G	GS	Sv	IP	H	BB	SO	HR	Ratio
2001	0	0	-	4.50	1	0	0	2.0	1	0	2	1	0.50
Career	0	0	-	4.50	1	0	0	2.0	1	0	2	1	0.50

Christman had surgery for a torn labrum in 2000. He had been an effective reliever in the minors until he worked at Triple-A Colorado Springs in 2001. 2002 Outlook: C

Jacob Cruz (Pos: LF/CF/RF, Age: 29, Bats: L)

	G	AB	R	H	D	T	HR	RBI	SB	BB	SO	Avg	OBP	Slg
2001	72	144	19	31	5	0	4	18	0	15	50	.215	.303	.333
Career	168	367	49	89	17	1	10	53	1	40	98	.243	.326	.376

Cruz makes contact, has some pop, draws walks and can play all three outfield spots. Colorado cut him in November without taking a long look. 2002 Outlook: C

Joe Davenport (Pos: RHP, Age: 26)

	W	L	Pct.	ERA	G	GS	Sv	IP	H	BB	SO	HR	Ratio
2001	0	0	-	3.48	7	0	0	10.1	8	7	8	1	1.45
Career	0	0	-	3.00	10	0	0	12.0	9	9	8	1	1.50

Davenport's Triple-A numbers haven't been pretty the last three years, especially in 2001. He did well in Colorado during his April stay, but that's not saying much. 2002 Outlook: C

Craig Dingman (Pos: RHP, Age: 28)

	W	L	Pct.	ERA	G	GS	Sv	IP	H	BB	SO	HR	Ratio
2001	0	0	-	13.50	7	0	1	7.1	11	3	2	4	1.91
Career	0	0	-	9.33	17	0	1	18.1	29	6	10	5	1.91

Dingman has been very solid in the high minors since 1999, but he's been dinged by the longball pretty hard in his short stays with the Yankees and Rockies. He signed a minor league deal with the Reds. 2002 Outlook: C

Mario Encarnacion (Pos: LF, Age: 24, Bats: R)

	G	AB	R	H	D	T	HR	RBI	SB	BB	SO	Avg	OBP	Slg
2001	20	62	3	14	1	0	0	3	2	5	14	.226	.284	.242
Career	20	62	3	14	1	0	0	3	2	5	14	.226	.284	.242

Encarnacion is a slow-developing prospect whose bat is coming around. He sure seemed to like hitting at Triple-A Colorado Springs (.378/.440/.622 in 45 AB) after the trade from Oakland. 2002 Outlook: C

Horacio Estrada (Pos: LHP, Age: 26)

	W	L	Pct.	ERA	G	GS	Sv	IP	H	BB	SO	HR	Ratio
2001	1	1	.500	14.54	4	0	0	4.1	8	1	4	1	2.08
Career	4	1	.800	7.50	15	4	0	36.0	48	25	22	10	2.03

Estrada has enjoyed some Triple-A success as a starter the last two seasons, but hasn't converted it into regular major league work when he's been given chances with Milwaukee and Colorado. 2002 Outlook: C

Sal Fasano (Pos: C, Age: 30, Bats: R)

	G	AB	R	H	D	T	HR	RBI	SB	BB	SO	Avg	OBP	Slg
2001	39	85	12	17	5	0	3	9	0	5	31	.200	.277	.365
Career	252	668	89	144	27	0	30	95	2	51	188	.216	.301	.391

Fasano was dealt twice in 2001, going from Oakland back to Kansas City and on to Colorado in June. Once again he didn't do much with the bat, doing his best hitting at Triple-A Colorado Springs. 2002 Outlook: C

Brooks Kieschnick (Pos: LF, Age: 29, Bats: L)

	G	AB	R	H	D	T	HR	RBI	SB	BB	SO	Avg	OBP	Slg
2001	35	42	5	10	2	1	3	9	0	3	13	.238	.289	.548
Career	113	173	20	38	6	1	8	27	1	19	47	.220	.297	.405

Kieschnick started well at Triple-A Colorado Springs, got called up in May and quickly injured a groin. He thought he might get a chance to play when the Rocks dealt Ron Gant, but he was demoted soon after. He opted for free agency in October. 2002 Outlook: C

Mark Little (Pos: LF/CF, Age: 29, Bats: R)

	G	AB	R	H	D	T	HR	RBI	SB	BB	SO	Avg	OBP	Slg
2001	51	85	18	29	6	0	3	13	5	1	20	.341	.378	.518
Career	58	97	18	30	6	0	3	13	6	3	25	.309	.356	.464

Little turns 30 this summer and had four years of Triple-A ball under his belt heading into the 2001 season. He got the call and hit well in stretches of May and August. He better hit well in March. 2002 Outlook: C

Adam Melhuse (Pos: C, Age: 30, Bats: B)

	G	AB	R	H	D	T	HR	RBI	SB	BB	SO	Avg	OBP	Slg
2001	40	71	5	13	2	0	1	8	1	6	18	.183	.241	.254
Career	64	95	8	17	2	1	1	12	1	9	24	.179	.245	.253

Melhuse has been playing Triple-A ball since 1997, and his .380 career OBP in the minors looks good. But his success getting on base hasn't carried over to the majors. He refused a minor league assignment in October and became a free agent. 2002 Outlook: C

Dan Miceli (Pos: RHP, Age: 31)

	W	L	Pct.	ERA	G	GS	Sv	IP	H	BB	SO	HR	Ratio
2001	2	5	.286	4.80	51	0	1	45.0	47	16	48	7	1.40
Career	33	36	.478	4.72	439	9	32	494.0	494	222	449	64	1.45

Miceli was a catalyst for the firing of Florida manager John Boles with his criticisms of Boles' decision-making. Miceli gets a failing grade in Florida, too, but later pitched very well for the Rocks. He opted for free agency in November. 2002 Outlook: B

Chris Nichting (Pos: RHP, Age: 35)

	W	L	Pct.	ERA	G	GS	Sv	IP	H	BB	SO	HR	Ratio
2001	0	3	.000	4.46	43	0	1	42.1	55	8	40	8	1.49
Career	0	3	.000	5.59	63	0	1	75.2	104	26	53	9	1.72

Mostly a Triple-A reliever since 1994, Nichting had a good season at Louisville and did well with Cincinnati in June. He was released in September, picked up by Colorado and then refused a minor league assignment in October and became a free agent. 2002 Outlook: C

Greg Norton (Pos: 3B/1B/LF, Age: 29, Bats: B)

	G	AB	R	H	D	T	HR	RBI	SB	BB	SO	Avg	OBP	Slg
2001	117	225	30	60	13	2	13	40	1	19	65	.267	.321	.516
Career	454	1218	164	305	64	7	46	158	9	146	296	.250	.332	.428

Norton probably won't be a regular, as the Rockies expect to acquire a replacement for Jeff Cirillo. Norton, who re-signed, batted .297 and slugged .571 in 91 at-bats during the second half. 2002 Outlook: B

Kevin Sefcik (Pos: LF/CF, Age: 31, Bats: R)

	G	AB	R	H	D	T	HR	RBI	SB	BB	SO	Avg	OBP	Slg
2001	1	1	0	0	0	0	0	0	0	0	0	.000	.000	.000
Career	425	771	92	212	36	10	6	56	21	80	102	.275	.351	.371

Sefcik hit .312 at Triple-A Colorado Springs and came up for one at-bat in June. He was claimed off waivers and batted .197 in Cleveland's system. The Rays signed him in November. 2002 Outlook: C

Terry Shumpert (Pos: 2B/3B/LF, Age: 35, Bats: R)

	G	AB	R	H	D	T	HR	RBI	SB	BB	SO	Avg	OBP	Slg
2001	114	242	37	70	14	5	4	24	14	15	44	.289	.337	.438
Career	689	1651	251	426	92	23	41	195	80	135	311	.258	.318	.416

Shumpert earned a utility role with the Rockies in 1999 with hitting percentages of .347/.413/.584. He hasn't been *that* good since, but still should get on base and play all over the diamond. The 35-year-old re-signed with Colorado for this season. 2002 Outlook: B

Colorado Rockies Minor League Prospects

Organization Overview:

The Rockies used their top selection on a pitcher in eight of the nine drafts between 1992 and 2000. Unfortunately, all Colorado has to show for those eight picks is a combined total of 33 wins and 40 losses in the big leagues. On a positive note, the Rockies took Todd Helton in the one year they opted for a position player with their first choice. They can only hope last year's top selection, shortstop Jason Nix, comes close to Helton's success. Nonetheless, Rockies rookies did make a pretty good impression in 2001. Juan Uribe looks like he could be a decent offensive shortstop. Shawn Chacon, a No. 3 pick in 1996, became only the second Rockies pitcher ever to allow less than a hit per inning (minimum 100 innings). And Jason Jennings, the top choice in 1999, compiled a 2.51 ERA in five road starts last year. He could turn out to be the first-round pitcher who proves the exception to the rule for Colorado.

Garrett Atkins

Position: 1B   **Opening Day Age:** 22
Bats: R **Throws:** R   **Born:** 12/12/79 in
Ht: 6' 3" **Wt:** 210   Orange, CA

Recent Statistics

	G	AB	R	H	D	T	HR	RBI	SB	BB	SO	Avg
2000 A Portland	69	251	34	76	12	0	7	47	2	45	48	.303
2001 A Salem	135	465	70	151	43	5	5	67	6	74	98	.325

Atkins was chosen in the fifth round of the 2000 draft and jumped to high Class-A last season, where his batting average ranked second in the Carolina League. He takes a solid approach to the plate, driving the ball to all fields and coaxing more than his share of walks. While he primarily has played first base in the Rockies' system, he's also spent some time at third. Colorado hopes he can move to the hot corner full-time. His arm has been tender, so he may need to build up his strength. Although Atkins has yet to hit a lot of home runs in the minors, he does produce other extra-base hits. He's a decent hitting prospect and should move up to Double-A in 2002.

Aaron Cook

Position: P   **Opening Day Age:** 23
Bats: R **Throws:** R   **Born:** 2/8/79 in Ft.
Ht: 6' 3" **Wt:** 175   Campbell, KY

Recent Statistics

	W	L	ERA	G	GS	Sv	IP	H	R	BB	SO	HR
2000 A Asheville	10	7	2.96	21	21	0	142.2	130	54	23	118	10
2000 A Salem	1	6	5.44	7	7	0	43.0	52	33	12	37	4
2001 A Salem	11	11	3.08	27	27	0	155.0	157	73	38	122	4

The Rockies took Cook in the second round of the 1997 draft out of an Ohio high school. He reached high Class-A in 2000 and competed there again last season. He was hot and cold in the first half of 2001 before locking in thereafter. Cook pitched very well in the Carolina

League playoffs, helping the Salem Avalanche win a pair of postseason series. He can be physically dominating, with a well above-average fastball in the low to mid-90s. He also has an average slider and is working on a changeup. He needs to continue developing his No. 3 pitch, probably in Double-A this year. A September call-up to Colorado is not out of the question.

Ryan Kibler

Position: P   **Opening Day Age:** 21
Bats: R **Throws:** R   **Born:** 9/17/80 in Tampa,
Ht: 6' 2" **Wt:** 185   FL

Recent Statistics

	W	L	ERA	G	GS	Sv	IP	H	R	BB	SO	HR
2000 A Asheville	10	14	4.41	26	26	0	155.0	173	107	67	110	9
2001 A Asheville	3	5	2.93	10	10	0	61.1	50	26	27	59	3
2001 A Salem	7	0	1.55	11	11	0	75.2	53	19	16	61	0
2001 AA Carolina	4	1	2.11	8	8	0	47.0	38	17	19	41	0

Kibler had a breakout season at age 21 last year. Selected in the second round of the 1999 draft, he opened 2001 in the South Atlantic League. Promoted to high Class-A, he went unbeaten in 11 starts and compiled a sparkling ERA. He then moved up to Double-A, where he again excelled. Part of his success stemmed from the fact that he didn't allow any homers in over 120 innings during his last two stops. Kibler works with an 88-92 MPH fastball that has above-average sink and life, as well as a slider and above-average changeup. He does a good job locating his pitches and is a tremendous competitor. He prepares and executes his gameplan as well as anyone in Colorado's system. Kibler could stand to put on a few pounds and to sharpen his slider.

Rene Reyes

Position: OF-1B   **Opening Day Age:** 24
Bats: B **Throws:** R   **Born:** 2/21/78 in
Ht: 5' 11" **Wt:** 202   Porlamar, Nueva
                                Esparta, VZ

Recent Statistics

	G	AB	R	H	D	T	HR	RBI	SB	BB	SO	Avg
2001 A Asheville	128	484	71	156	27	2	11	61	53	28	80	.322

Shoulder problems and knee surgery cost Reyes about a year-and-a-half between 1999 and 2000. But he showed few ill effects last season, when he led the Class-A South Atlantic League in batting average and stole more than 50 bases. A native of Venezuela, Reyes signed with the Rockies as a nondrafted free agent in 1996. He is a powerful athlete who hits from both sides of the plate. He has displayed the ability to drive the ball, and bat in the meat of the order. He split 2001 between first base and the outfield. The Rockies feel his arm is good enough to play any outfield position. They hope he can stay injury free and remain in the lineup this season, which figures to be spent in Double-A.

Denny Stark

Position: P **Opening Day Age:** 27
Bats: R **Throws:** R **Born:** 10/27/74 in
Ht: 6' 2" **Wt:** 210 Hicksville, OH

Recent Statistics

	W	L	ERA	G	GS	Sv	IP	H	R	BB	SO	HR
2001 AA San Antonio	1	0	0.00	1	1	0	6.0	2	0	3	7	0
2001 AAA Tacoma	14	2	2.37	24	24	0	151.2	124	52	41	130	12
2001 AL Seattle	1	1	9.20	4	3	0	14.2	21	15	4	12	5

For Stark, a 1996 draft pick, the injury bug hit in 1998, when an ankle injury altered his delivery and led to shoulder troubles. He finally was completely healthy in 2001 and finished first in wins and ERA in the Triple-A Pacific Coast League. Stark is an aggressive pitcher with a solid fastball and slider. He's working on his changeup, which looked much better in September during his major league stint with Seattle. Now 27 years of age, he may have a better chance of sticking in a big league rotation following a December trade to Colorado. However, he not only needs to build on his 2001 success in the spring, but he also must stay healthy.

Chin-Hui Tsao

Position: P **Opening Day Age:** 20
Bats: R **Throws:** R **Born:** 6/2/81 in Hualien,
Ht: 6' 2" **Wt:** 178 Taiwan

Recent Statistics

	W	L	ERA	G	GS	Sv	IP	H	R	BB	SO	HR
2000 A Asheville	11	8	2.73	24	24	0	145.0	119	54	40	187	8
2001 A Salem	0	4	4.67	4	4	0	17.1	23	11	5	18	1

Tsao managed to make just four starts last spring before undergoing Tommy John surgery and missing the rest of the campaign. Nevertheless, Tsao still is considered the top pitching prospect in Colorado's system. He was signed at age 18 out of Taiwan in 1999 and struck out more than 11 batters per nine innings in his American debut in 2000. When healthy, he features three above-average pitches—a 91-94 MPH fastball, slider and changeup—as well as fine command and an aggressive yet composed approach. While he could get by with blowing hitters away in Taiwan and showed the same ability in the Sally League, the Rockies feel Tsao may need a bit more experience facing American hitters. His rehab reportedly is going well, and Colorado hopes to have him back this April.

Cory Vance

Position: P **Opening Day Age:** 22
Bats: L **Throws:** L **Born:** 6/20/79 in Dayton,
Ht: 6' 1" **Wt:** 195 OH

Recent Statistics

	W	L	ERA	G	GS	Sv	IP	H	R	BB	SO	HR
2000 A Portland	0	2	1.11	7	3	0	24.1	11	5	8	26	1
2001 A Salem	10	8	3.10	26	26	0	154.0	129	65	65	142	9

Vance led the Atlantic Coast Conference with 13 wins in 2000, fanning more than a man per inning. He was chosen in the fourth round by the Rockies that June, and his strikeout rate has remained high as a pro. He debuted in the Northwest League the summer after getting drafted, and jumped up to high Class-A in 2001, where he posted the eighth best ERA in the Carolina League. His strikeout total exceeded his hits allowed, a good sign. Vance is a strong, durable southpaw who has a great feel for pitching. He features a three-pitch mix, including an 88-92 MPH fastball, solid average curveball and changeup. He needs to work on repeating and being consistent with his delivery. He likely is ticketed for Double-A in 2002.

Jason Young

Position: P **Opening Day Age:** 22
Bats: B **Throws:** R **Born:** 9/28/79 in
Ht: 6' 5" **Wt:** 205 Oakland, CA

Recent Statistics

	W	L	ERA	G	GS	Sv	IP	H	R	BB	SO	HR
2001 A Salem	6	7	3.44	17	17	0	104.2	104	47	28	91	8

While Young was slowed by injuries during his final season at Stanford, he was able to start the title game of the 2000 College World Series. The Rockies selected Young with their No. 2 pick in that year's draft, but he didn't make his professional debut until last season. He's a fairly polished hurler, with a fastball in the upper 80s to low 90s that's thrown along with a breaking ball and changeup. He also worked in the Arizona Fall League, where the Rockies wanted him to face a better level of competition. Other accomplished college pitchers in recent years, like Mark Mulder and Barry Zito, have made impacts in the big leagues fairly quickly. Colorado expects Young to enjoy the same kind of results.

Others to Watch

Righthanded reliever **Cam Esslinger** (25) has impressive stuff, including a 92-96 MPH fastball and above-average slider. He pitched well in the Arizona Fall League. . . Lefthander **Brian Fuentes** (26), already deceptive with a herky-jerky motion and late movement on his fastball, adapted a sidearm delivery halfway through the 2000 season. He was obtained from Seattle in the Jeff Cirillo deal and could see time in the bullpen. . . Catcher **Garett Gentry** (20) drove in more than 100 runs in the Astros' system last season. He then was included as part of the Pedro Astacio for Scott Elarton deal. . . **Matt Holliday** (22) is a big man with tremendous raw power and potential, though he hasn't yet put up outstanding home-run totals. He's played third base in the past, but the Rockies have tried moving him to the outfield. . . **Luke Hudson** (24) is a big, physical righthander with a low to mid-90s fastball. His 145 strikeouts ranked second in the Southern League in 2001. . . Lefthander **Josh Kalinowski** (25) struck out nearly 400 batters between 1998 and 1999, but battled nagging injuries in 2000. He seemed to turn a corner last year. His changeup is well above average and he pitched well in the Arizona Fall League.

Pro Player Stadium

Offense

After several years of trying, Marlins hitters overcame their phobias about batting at Pro Player Stadium. They hit 11 points higher and averaged 4.74 runs at home, compared with 4.43 on the road. They did this despite the poor lighting that leaves home plate in shadows and without an over-reliance on the running game, which characterized the reign of former manager John Boles, who was fired late last May. Better hitting was the main reason Florida went 46-34 at home, compared to a 30-52 mark in away games.

Defense

The biggest challenge remains the Teal Tower, a 26.5-foot high scoreboard in left-center field that causes some strange caroms. Cliff Floyd has become an expert at playing the wall, while Preston Wilson often outruns pitchers' mistakes that carry into the Bermuda Triangle in deep left-center. The infield and outfield grass is among the fastest in the league, which helps balls shoot through the gaps.

Who It Helps the Most

Pitchers in general and flyball pitchers in particular are aided, as the spacious dimensions and thick air keep balls in the park that easily would depart other venues. Among Marlins starters, A.J. Burnett and Ryan Dempster were more effective on the road than at home, while Brad Penny and Matt Clement experienced marked boosts at Pro Player. Mike Lowell hit 64 points higher at home, with two-thirds of his homers coming on familiar turf.

Who It Hurts the Most

Charles Johnson hit 40 points lower at home than on the road. Just five of his 18 homers came at Pro Player. Derrek Lee hit 30 points higher and slugged 13 of his 21 homers on the road. Preston Wilson hit 26 points higher with 14 of his 23 homers in away games.

Rookies & Newcomers

Josh Beckett allowed one earned run in 12 innings at home after a September callup. Fellow rookie Kevin Olsen thrived as well, making all four appearances at Pro Player. Florida won't hesitate to use rookies if financial concerns warrant it.

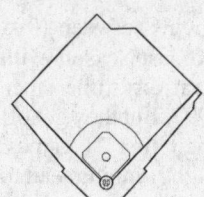

Dimensions: LF-330, LCF-385, CF-404, RCF-385, RF-345

Capacity: 36,331

Elevation: 10 feet

Surface: Grass

Foul Territory: Average

Florida

Park Factors

2001 Season

	Home Games Marlins	Opp	Total	Away Games Marlins	Opp	Total	Index
G	71	71	142	73	73	146	—
Avg	.261	.245	.253	.259	.275	.267	95
AB	2342	2419	4761	2570	2414	4984	98
R	312	304	616	321	387	708	89
H	612	592	1204	666	665	1331	93
2B	132	125	257	154	132	286	94
3B	18	24	42	6	20	26	169
HR	72	67	139	75	76	151	96
BB	220	276	496	197	299	496	105
SO	482	564	1046	540	427	967	113
E	41	39	80	55	42	97	85
E-Infield	34	32	66	44	31	75	90
LHB-Avg	.261	.253	.255	.267	.281	.276	92
LHB-HR	18	26	44	17	33	50	87
RHB-Avg	.261	.237	.252	.257	.271	.262	96
RHB-HR	54	41	95	58	43	101	102

1999-2001

	Home Games Marlins	Opp	Total	Away Games Marlins	Opp	Total	Index
G	214	214	428	218	218	436	—
Avg	.261	.255	.258	.258	.284	.271	95
AB	7182	7406	14588	7593	7243	14836	100
R	913	967	1880	944	1191	2135	90
H	1874	1886	3760	1957	2058	4015	95
2B	363	375	738	388	395	783	96
3B	56	68	124	33	51	84	150
HR	177	203	380	228	240	468	83
BB	712	848	1560	614	910	1524	104
SO	1483	1548	3031	1655	1223	2878	107
E	148	150	298	170	137	307	99
E-Infield	127	122	249	134	110	244	104
LHB-Avg	.272	.258	.264	.266	.289	.280	94
LHB-HR	46	74	120	50	109	159	74
RHB-Avg	.256	.252	.254	.254	.280	.266	96
RHB-HR	131	129	260	178	131	309	87

2001 Rankings (National League)

- Highest triple factor
- Highest strikeout factor
- Third-highest walk factor
- Third-lowest error factor

Florida Marlins

2001 Season

After improving from 54 to 79 wins between 1998 and 2000, the Marlins entered last season with arguably more optimism than at any time since their World Series triumph in 1997. But they got off to a slow start, losing 13 of their first 21 games. And after blowing a two-run, eighth-inning lead to the Mets on May 27, the Marlins had a new manager on Memorial Day, replacing John Boles with Tony Perez. The team responded to the change with a 19-10 spurt that put Florida five games over .500 and only two games out of first place on June 27. But a dreadful 9-20 record in August doomed the club to its fourth consecutive losing campaign.

Offense

The managerial switch from Boles to Perez had a dramatic effect on the Marlins' running game. Florida had led the majors with 168 stolen bases in 2000. The team swiped 42 bags in the 48 games with Boles at the helm last season, but after Perez took control, Florida stole just 47 bases in its final 114 contests. However, the Marlins still set a franchise record with 742 runs scored. The offense clubbed a franchise-high 166 home runs while leading the National League with 325 doubles, but the team ranked very low in drawing bases on balls.

Pitching & Defense

Perez wasn't as active as Boles in terms of calling for pitchouts or making defensive substitutions. Yet the team's defense showed marked improvement over 2000, committing 22 fewer errors while turning 30 more double plays. With Charles Johnson back behind the plate for Florida, opponents took fewer chances on the bases. The defense helped the pitching staff lower its ERA to 4.32.

2002 Outlook

Whoever takes over as Florida's manager will contend with one of the youngest rosters in baseball. But it's also very talented. A pitching staff boasting some of the finest arms in the game could be poised to upset the balance of power in the National League East, at least until financial considerations get in the way.

Last Five Seasons

Year	Team, Lg	W	L	Pct	GB	Finish
1997	Florida, NL	92	70	.568	9.0	2nd East*
1998	Florida, NL	54	108	.333	52.0	5th East
1999	Florida, NL	64	98	.395	39.0	5th East
2000	Florida, NL	79	82	.491	15.5	3rd East
2001	Florida, NL	76	86	.469	12.0	4th East
Totals		365	444	.451	—	—

* Won World Series

Manager Statistics (Tony Perez)

Year	Team, Lg	W	L	Pct	GB	Finish
2001	Florida, NL	54	60	.474	12.0	4th East
1 Season		54	60	.474	—	—

2001 Starting Pitchers by Days Rest

	<=3	4	5	6+
Marlins Starts	0	48	46	16
Marlins ERA	—	4.22	4.73	4.20
NL Avg Starts	1	80	47	24
NL ERA	5.03	4.43	4.53	4.28

2001 Situational Stats

	Tony Perez	NL Average
Hit & Run Success %	42.4	35.1
Stolen Base Success %	64.4	66.5
Platoon Pct.	40.2	51.5
Defensive Subs	8	20
High-Pitch Outings	5	7
Quick/Slow Hooks	7/8	19/14
Sacrifice Attempts	54	87

2001 Rankings—Tony Perez (National Lg)

- 1st in fewest caught stealings of second base (23)
- 3rd in fewest caught stealings of third base (3)

Antonio Alfonseca

2001 Season

Arbitration-eligible for the first time, Antonio Alfonseca signed a two-year, $6 million deal before last season that should have given him security and a free mind. Instead, he seemed to press at times, then gained an alarming amount of weight as the year progressed. Back problems ended his season with a week to go, and offseason surgery was likely. After matching the franchise mark with 45 saves the year before, he got just 34 opportunities as the Marlins suffered through a disappointing year. During one late-season stretch, Alfonseca had one save chance in a month-long span, and his command suffered from the rust.

Pitching

There isn't much finesse with Alfonseca. He pounds hitters with a wicked sinker that he regularly throws at 94-95 MPH. He also has touched 98 MPH with his four-seam fastball. Lefthanded batters continued to give him fits, so he started mixing in the occasional slider and changeup. But he remains essentially a one-pitch pitcher. Righthanded hitters accounted for only one of the six homers Alfonseca allowed. His groundball-flyball ratio climbed to 2.02, a career best. He inherited just five baserunners for the second straight year, as the Marlins continued to coddle him despite a .241 on-base percentage that he allowed to first batters.

Defense & Hitting

Alfonseca holds runners well enough and is quick enough to the plate. He does a decent job with the balls he gets to in the field, but when he gets heavy he's even more susceptible than normal to bunts and dribblers. He has not batted in more than two full seasons.

2002 Outlook

With the Marlins' future in doubt and austerity measures likely to be implemented, Alfonseca could be dealt. Braden Looper is coming along behind Alfonseca and already is locked up for two more years, so a $3.6 million closer could be deemed a luxury by this struggling franchise. However, Alfonseca's back condition could make him hard to trade until he shows he's healthy in the spring.

Position: RP
Bats: R **Throws:** R
Ht: 6' 5" **Wt:** 238

Opening Day Age: 29
Born: 4/16/72 in La Romana, DR
ML Seasons: 5
Pronunciation: AL-fon-say-ka
Nickname: Pulpo, Dragonslayer

Florida

Overall Statistics

	W	L	Pct.	ERA	G	GS	Sv	IP	H	BB	SO	HR	Ratio
2001	4	4	.500	3.06	58	0	28	61.2	68	15	40	6	1.35
Career	18	24	.429	3.77	274	0	102	305.2	340	111	198	30	1.48

How Often He Throws Strikes

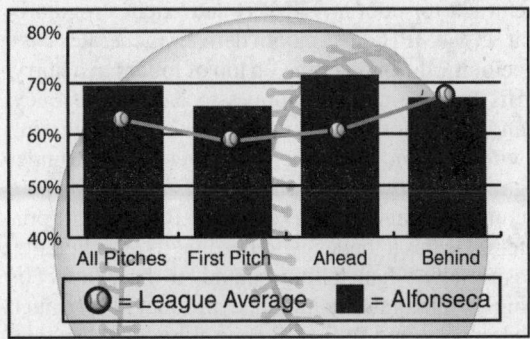

= League Average   ■ = Alfonseca

2001 Situational Stats

	W	L	ERA	Sv	IP		AB	H	HR	RBI	Avg
Home	2	3	3.34	17	32.1	LHB	126	38	5	16	.302
Road	2	1	2.76	11	29.1	RHB	116	30	1	9	.259
First Half	3	2	2.52	17	35.2	Sc Pos	50	14	2	20	.280
Scnd Half	1	2	3.81	11	26.0	Clutch	163	45	5	18	.276

2001 Rankings (National League)

- 4th in lowest save percentage (82.4) and highest batting average allowed in relief (.281)
- 6th in blown saves (6)
- 7th in fewest strikeouts per nine innings in relief (5.8)
- 8th in save opportunities (34) and saves
- 9th in games finished (52)
- Led the Marlins in saves, games finished (52), save opportunities (34), save percentage (82.4), first batter efficiency (.228), blown saves (6) and relief wins (4)

A.J. Burnett

2001 Season

It was another trip through Six Flags Over Pro Player Stadium for the Marlins' wild child of the rotation. A.J. Burnett missed the first five weeks with a broken right foot, suffered while running on a treadmill during offseason workouts. In his second start off the disabled list, Burnett threw a nine-walk no-hitter in San Diego. While some expected the no-no to elevate Burnett's focus and performance, there was little sign of that during a frustrating, uneven season. The low point came in early September, when he missed so badly with a warmup pitch that he nearly killed Billy the Marlin.

Pitching

Burnett tops out at 97 MPH and pitches regularly at 93-94 MPH. His smooth delivery generates easy velocity, the ball getting on top of hitters in a hurry. His knuckle-curve continues to lack consistency, and he spent the latter part of the season tinkering with a slider, which he hasn't yet debuted under game conditions. His changeup is solid and more consistent than the curve, which Burnett still prefers. He has a tendency to become too predictable, especially when falling behind in the count. His high walk totals are more a byproduct of too much adrenaline and failing to control his delivery than losing his arm slot.

Defense & Hitting

The former high school basketball star is a good fielder with quick feet. He has a good pickoff move, but opponents take advantage of his deliberate delivery, which can take upwards of 1.48 seconds to get the ball to the plate. He is one of the better bunters on the staff. However, he produced just four hits in 50 at-bats after batting .280 the year before.

2002 Outlook

Burnett is a year away from arbitration eligibility, which takes him out of danger in any Marlins rebuilding project. He should get another full year of starts, this time under a new pitching coach, in hopes that Burnett finally will find some consistency. He did finish 2001 with six quality starts in his last eight tries, so perhaps he can carry the momentum forward.

Position: SP
Bats: R **Throws:** R
Ht: 6' 5"   **Wt:** 205

Opening Day Age: 25
Born: 1/3/77 in North Little Rock, AR
ML Seasons: 3

Overall Statistics

	W	L	Pct.	ERA	G	GS	Sv	IP	H	BB	SO	HR	Ratio
2001	11	12	.478	4.05	27	27	0	173.1	145	83	128	20	1.32
Career	18	21	.462	4.18	47	47	0	297.1	262	152	218	31	1.39

How Often He Throws Strikes

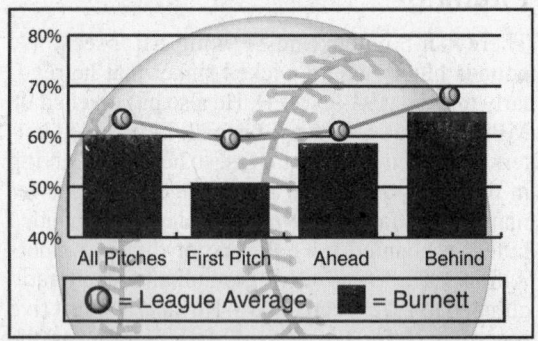

2001 Situational Stats

	W	L	ERA	Sv	IP		AB	H	HR	RBI	Avg
Home	7	5	4.52	0	83.2	LHB	324	80	5	26	.247
Road	4	7	3.61	0	89.2	RHB	305	65	15	45	.213
First Half	5	5	3.10	0	81.1	Sc Pos	137	29	4	44	.212
Scnd Half	6	7	4.89	0	92.0	Clutch	51	12	1	2	.235

2001 Rankings (National League)

- 5th in lowest batting average allowed (.231) and highest walks per nine innings (4.3)
- 6th in lowest batting average allowed with runners in scoring position
- 7th in runners caught stealing (9)
- 8th in lowest batting average allowed vs. righthanded batters, lowest strikeout-walk ratio (1.5) and highest ERA at home
- Led the Marlins in losses, complete games (2), pickoff throws (125), stolen bases allowed (16), runners caught stealing (9), lowest batting average allowed (.231), lowest ERA on the road, lowest batting average allowed vs. righthanded batters and lowest batting average allowed with runners in scoring position

Luis Castillo

Position: 2B
Bats: B **Throws:** R
Ht: 5'11" **Wt:** 175

Opening Day Age: 26
Born: 9/12/75 in San
Pedro de Macoris, DR
ML Seasons: 6
Pronunciation:
ca-STEE-yo

Florida

2001 Season

After avoiding arbitration by signing a one-year, $2.2 million deal in February 2001, Luis Castillo showed up 10 pounds overweight for spring training and never came close to matching his breakthrough campaign of 2000. He suffered through an injury-plagued season with recurring bouts of lower back and hamstring pain, which may or may not have been related. He tore ligaments in his left ankle at the end of the year, casting doubt on his ability to keep in shape through winter ball.

Hitting

Tired of hearing about his troubles with runners in scoring position, Castillo made that a focus and set a career high in RBI. But he went backward in just about every other significant offensive category. His strikeouts climbed dangerously high for a leadoff man with no power. Time and again he would look at quality strikes early in the count, then freeze on strike three. He lost some aggressiveness at the plate, seemed to outthink himself at times and got tied up all too often by fastballs on his hands. He capitalized when he saw mistakes out over the plate, showing good gap power to the opposite field.

Baserunning & Defense

Few infielders have a stronger arm or more range to their right than Castillo. While he is quick on the pivot and can make highlight plays up the middle, he remains wary of diving to his left. He still can't shake the memory of several injuries to his left shoulder, which was tightened up through surgery after the 1999 season. He didn't come close to defending his stolen-base crown, but that was due more to extra attention from pitchers and a loss of confidence than any real slowdown. His baserunning suffered as well last year, as he was gunned down seven times trying to take an extra base.

2002 Outlook

With highly rated prospect Pablo Ozuna coming off an injury-plagued season of his own, Castillo remains the Marlins' best and perhaps only option at second base. Another trip through arbitration will make him more expensive, and Florida can only hope he returns to his whirlwind form of 2000.

Overall Statistics

	G	AB	R	H	D	T	HR	RBI	SB	BB	SO	Avg	OBP	Slg
2001	134	537	76	141	16	10	2	45	33	67	90	.263	.344	.341
Career	558	2143	327	605	69	20	6	116	181	275	393	.282	.364	.342

Where He Hits the Ball

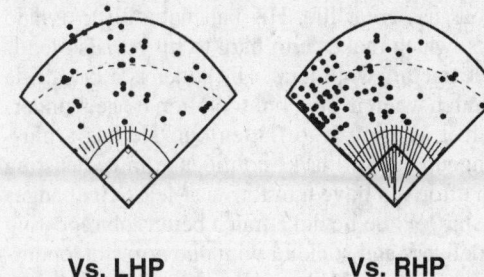

Vs. LHP   **Vs. RHP**

2001 Situational Stats

	AB	H	HR	RBI	Avg		AB	H	HR	RBI	Avg
Home	247	66	1	23	.267	LHP	128	36	2	16	.281
Road	290	75	1	22	.259	RHP	409	105	0	29	.257
First Half	316	84	1	20	.266	Sc Pos	98	32	0	43	.327
Scnd Half	221	57	1	25	.258	Clutch	76	13	0	5	.171

2001 Rankings (National League)

- 1st in errors at second base (13) and lowest fielding percentage at second base (.980)
- 2nd in caught stealing (16), highest groundball-flyball ratio (2.6), lowest percentage of swings that missed (6.5), lowest slugging percentage and lowest HR frequency (268.5 ABs per HR)
- Led the Marlins in singles, triples, stolen bases, walks, pitches seen (2,528), highest groundball-flyball ratio (2.6), most pitches seen per plate appearance (4.13), bunts in play (24), highest percentage of pitches taken (61.9), highest percentage of swings put into play (47.1), on-base percentage for a leadoff hitter (.347), lowest percentage of swings on the first pitch (20.1) and batting average on a 3-2 count (.312)

Matt Clement

2001 Season

Acquired from the Padres just five days before Opening Day, Matt Clement careened through another inconsistent season. Troubled by liver inflammation during spring training, he seemed to run out of steam in the middle innings on most nights. Pitching on the road remained his worst bugaboo, as his ERA was nearly two runs lower at home. He left two starts, 10 weeks apart, with tightness in his right forearm. But no time on the disabled list was required.

Pitching

Few pitchers are blessed with better raw stuff than Clement. His fastball tops out at 96 MPH and regularly clocks in at 92-93 MPH. Everything he throws has great life. His ball naturally cuts and sinks, which makes him hard to hit but also tends to elevate his walk total. His slider is a bona fide out pitch when it's on, but too often he gets underneath it, causing it to flatten out. He has a plus-changeup but still lacks confidence in it, resisting club efforts to have him throw at least 10 changes per start. While he did a much better job repeating his delivery and sticking with one arm slot, endurance remains a problem. He pitched past the sixth inning just 10 times and logged quality starts in only three of his last 11 tries.

Defense & Hitting

Although Clement is a very good bunter, he's otherwise hopeless at the plate. He is just an average fielder, despite being a good enough basketball player to field several Division I scholarship offers. He has an average pickoff move and hardly ever throws to first, but he compensates with an exceedingly quick delivery. His range of 1.1 to 1.2 seconds out of the stretch is the best on the team.

2002 Outlook

Still due around $7 million over the next two seasons (with an option for 2004), Clement could be dealt again this winter. Former general manager Dave Dombrowski was one of Clement's biggest supporters, but those who remain in the front office aren't sold.

Position: SP
Bats: R **Throws:** R
Ht: 6' 3"   **Wt:** 195

Opening Day Age: 27
Born: 8/12/74 in McCandless Township, PA
ML Seasons: 4
Pronunciation: clu-MENT

Overall Statistics

	W	L	Pct.	ERA	G	GS	Sv	IP	H	BB	SO	HR	Ratio
2001	9	10	.474	5.05	31	31	0	169.1	172	85	134	15	1.52
Career	34	39	.466	4.89	100	98	0	568.2	571	303	452	55	1.54

How Often He Throws Strikes

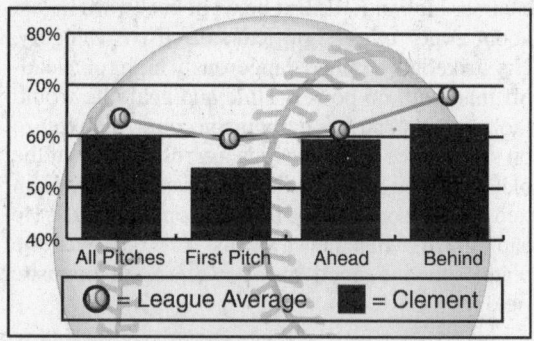

○ = League Average   ■ = Clement

2001 Situational Stats

	W	L	ERA	Sv		IP		AB	H	HR	RBI	Avg
Home	7	5	4.18	0		92.2	LHB	325	93	6	38	.286
Road	2	5	6.10	0		76.2	RHB	318	79	9	43	.248
First Half	4	6	5.47	0		98.2	Sc Pos	173	49	4	66	.283
Scnd Half	5	4	4.46	0		70.2	Clutch	29	11	0	2	.379

2001 Rankings (National League)

- 1st in wild pitches (15)
- 3rd in highest on-base percentage allowed (.365)
- 4th in highest walks per nine innings (4.5)
- 5th in hit batsmen (15)
- 8th in highest ERA
- 9th in walks allowed, fewest home runs allowed per nine innings (.80) and lowest strikeout-walk ratio (1.6)
- Led the Marlins in hit batsmen (15), wild pitches (15) and lowest stolen-base percentage allowed (54.5)

Ryan Dempster

Position: SP
Bats: R **Throws:** R
Ht: 6' 1" **Wt:** 201

Opening Day Age: 24
Born: 5/3/77 in Sechelt, BC, Canada
ML Seasons: 4

2001 Season

While many of his teammates eagerly accepted the first long-term security of their careers, Ryan Dempster last spring turned down an extension for a reported $14 million over four years. Extremely confident, he chose to try to build on a 14-win breakthrough campaign that had landed him in the All-Star Game the year before. Two ugly stretches in 2001 served to bookend a strong run in the middle. While he wound up with a career-best 15 wins, a 3-6 start and miserable finish were hardest to forget. Dempster posted a 10.80 ERA in his last five starts, failing to escape the first inning in his final appearance.

Pitching

After a second straight winter of intense workouts, Dempster was hitting 96 MPH with his fastball and pitching at 92-93 MPH. However, he never showed the knockout slider that carried him through previous seasons. His changeup has become a plus pitch as he's gained confidence with it. He was troubled throughout last season by stiffness in his back but still managed to work more than 200 innings for the second consecutive year. When his velocity dropped off to the high 80s late in the campaign, he adjusted by throwing more two-seamers. His command suffered again and his walk totals climbed. He allowed a .343 batting average on fresh counts and seemed to lose aggressiveness as that pattern became more obvious.

Defense & Hitting

No more than a decent fielder, Dempster has an average pickoff but struggles to control the running game. Because he's a bit predictable, opponents will run on the two-strike slider, for instance. He set a club record for pitchers with 16 sacrifice bunts but saw his career batting average drop to .070.

2002 Outlook

No longer lauded as the unchallenged ace of the staff, Dempster could share that distinction with rookie phenom Josh Beckett. A first-time arbitration eligible, Dempster will get a huge raise from the $400,000 he made last year. That could land him on the trading block this winter for a tight-fisted franchise.

Overall Statistics

	W	L	Pct.	ERA	G	GS	Sv	IP	H	BB	SO	HR	Ratio
2001	15	12	.556	4.94	34	34	0	211.1	218	112	171	21	1.56
Career	37	35	.514	4.62	106	103	0	639.1	646	340	541	78	1.54

How Often He Throws Strikes

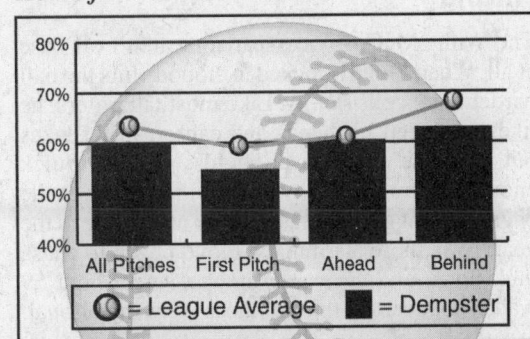

2001 Situational Stats

	W	L	ERA	Sv	IP		AB	H	HR	RBI	Avg
Home	7	4	5.24	0	89.1	LHB	382	103	11	51	.270
Road	8	8	4.72	0	122.0	RHB	428	115	10	57	.269
First Half	10	8	4.29	0	126.0	Sc Pos	227	63	3	84	.278
Scnd Half	5	4	5.91	0	85.1	Clutch	37	12	1	5	.324

2001 Rankings (National League)

- 1st in walks allowed and highest walks per nine innings (4.8)
- 4th in sacrifice bunts (16), games started, highest on-base percentage allowed (.362) and highest ERA at home
- 5th in pitches thrown (3,571), most run support per nine innings (5.9) and errors at pitcher (3)
- 7th in lowest strikeout-walk ratio (1.5)
- Led the Marlins in sacrifice bunts (16), wins, losses, games started, complete games (2), innings pitched, hits allowed, batters faced (954), home runs allowed, strikeouts, pitches thrown (3,571), winning percentage, most run support per nine innings (5.9) and most strikeouts per nine innings (7.3)

Cliff Floyd

2001 Season

For nearly four months, 2001 was Cliff Floyd's signature season. He crushed everything pitchers tried to run past him. He engaged in a public spat with Mets manager Bobby Valentine. He even made his first All-Star team as one of Valentine's at-large selections. With free agency looming after another season and some change, Floyd was setting himself up to become a very rich man. Then two lousy months may have cost him untold millions. Nagging injuries to his wrist and Achilles slowed him noticeably, both in the field and at the plate. He hit just three home runs after July 21, all on the road.

Hitting

The Willie McCovey comparisons aren't off base at all. When Floyd is locked in, nobody hits the ball harder more consistently. Like most tall hitters, he likes to extend his hands and can crush mistakes out over the plate to all fields. Usually quick enough to turn on quality pitches in his kitchen, he began to struggle with fastballs up and in late in the year. Even more alarmingly, Floyd began to chase junk down and away. He drew a career-high 59 walks, but nearly a third of those were intentional.

Baserunning & Defense

For a big man, Floyd is an aggressive and skillful baserunner. Only the heel injury kept him from posting his third season with at least 20 homers and 20 stolen bases. He is much improved in the field, particularly with his throwing, but he rarely went hard after balls once the Marlins fell out of the divisional race.

2002 Outlook

Due $6.5 million in the final season of a four-year, $19 million contract, Floyd appeared to be prime winter trade bait for the struggling Marlins. If he returns to South Florida, he again will bat third in the order and hold much of the team's hopes in his large hands. Even with a new club, he'll have to prove himself yet again if he hopes to climb into the sport's salary stratosphere.

Position: LF
Bats: L **Throws:** R
Ht: 6' 4" **Wt:** 235

Opening Day Age: 29
Born: 12/5/72 in Chicago, IL
ML Seasons: 9

Overall Statistics

	G	AB	R	H	D	T	HR	RBI	SB	BB	SO	Avg	OBP	Slg
2001	149	555	123	176	44	4	31	103	18	59	101	.317	.390	.578
Career	809	2612	424	741	182	17	104	429	100	271	521	.284	.355	.486

Where He Hits the Ball

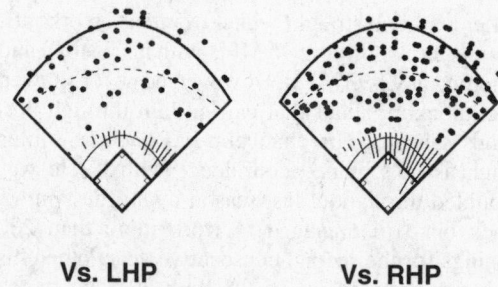

Vs. LHP   **Vs. RHP**

2001 Situational Stats

	AB	H	HR	RBI	Avg		AB	H	HR	RBI	Avg
Home	259	87	16	47	.336	LHP	148	46	9	34	.311
Road	296	89	15	56	.301	RHP	407	130	22	69	.319
First Half	313	107	21	70	.342	Sc Pos	142	46	14	79	.324
Scnd Half	242	69	10	33	.285	Clutch	84	28	4	14	.333

2001 Rankings (National League)

- 1st in errors in left field (8) and highest percentage of swings on the first pitch (50.3)
- 2nd in stolen-base percentage (85.7)
- Led the Marlins in batting average, home runs, runs scored, hits, doubles, total bases (321), RBI, intentional walks (19), times on base (245), plate appearances (629), slugging percentage, on-base percentage, HR frequency (17.9 ABs per HR), fewest GDPs per GDP situation (6.9%), batting average vs. lefthanded pitchers, batting average vs. righthanded pitchers, slugging percentage vs. lefthanded pitchers (.581), slugging percentage vs. righthanded pitchers (.577), on-base percentage vs. righthanded pitchers (.394) and batting average on the road

Alex Gonzalez

2001 Season

The Marlins' biggest enigma did little to rehabilitate his image. Alex Gonzalez remained moody and mercurial, although his attitude did improve for about a month after Tony Perez took over in late May. But when the club started losing again, Gonzalez started mailing it in. His lapses in concentration and judgment continue to anger Marlins officials and teammates alike. In his defense, he was bothered by a sore left elbow for much of the second half.

Hitting

After drawing 28 walks over his previous two seasons combined, Gonzalez doubled his career high with 30. A fifth of those were intentional, as he spent the bulk of the year batting eighth. His average with runners in scoring position was 40 points higher than his overall mark. That was about the extent of the positive news, however. He still has trouble with fastballs up in the zone, although he did a better job hitting breaking balls. Gonzalez can go to right-center with gap power and knows what to do with mistakes middle-in. But by and large, he's an easy out.

Baserunning & Defense

His thick calves and lack of instincts have kept Gonzalez from improving even moderately as a basestealer. His 12 career stolen bases in three-plus seasons are pathetic for a middle infielder. He is more aggressive taking extra bases on singles to the outfield. He led all major league shortstops with 26 errors, mainly because he gets lazy on throws, flipping the ball to first rather than staying on top. His range remains slightly above average, but he has terrible footwork, often failing to set himself for throws.

2002 Outlook

Now that he's eligible for arbitration for the first time, Gonzalez' act no longer may be as easy to swallow. He stands to be grossly overpaid as a sluggish player whose skills have shown little correlation to team success. The Marlins would love to upgrade at the most important defensive position on the field, but they could be hard-pressed to find a taker for Gonzalez.

Position: SS
Bats: R **Throws:** R
Ht: 6' 0" **Wt:** 170

Opening Day Age: 25
Born: 2/15/77 in Cagua, VZ
ML Seasons: 4

Overall Statistics

	G	AB	R	H	D	T	HR	RBI	SB	BB	SO	Avg	OBP	Slg
2001	145	515	57	129	36	1	9	48	2	30	107	.250	.303	.377
Career	415	1546	184	374	83	13	33	156	12	67	327	.242	.283	.376

Where He Hits the Ball

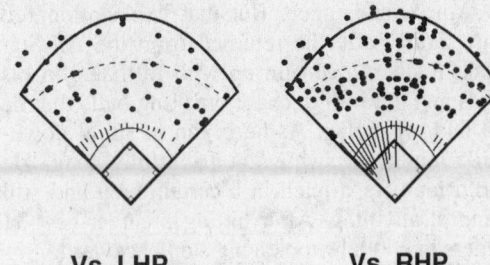

Vs. LHP   **Vs. RHP**

2001 Situational Stats

	AB	H	HR	RBI	Avg		AB	H	HR	RBI	Avg
Home	234	54	5	21	.231	LHP	115	27	2	11	.235
Road	281	75	4	27	.267	RHP	400	102	7	37	.255
First Half	289	71	4	26	.246	Sc Pos	107	31	2	40	.290
Scnd Half	226	58	5	22	.257	Clutch	86	18	1	8	.209

2001 Rankings (National League)

- 1st in errors at shortstop (26)
- 2nd in lowest fielding percentage at shortstop (.960)
- 3rd in lowest percentage of pitches taken (43.1)
- 5th in lowest batting average at home
- 6th in lowest on-base percentage
- 9th in highest percentage of swings on the first pitch (40.5)
- Led the Marlins in hit by pitch (10)

Charles Johnson

2001 Season

Brought back to a hero's welcome, Charles Johnson was supposed to lead a young Marlins club into the playoffs for the first time since he helped the 1997 team to a World Series title. For half a season, the plan worked beautifully. The beloved "C.J." was on pace for his best offensive year, made his second All-Star team and was playing his usual sterling defense. But after July 15, he hit just one home run, his offensive totals plummeted and he even got sloppy behind the plate.

Hitting

The party line during Johnson's big first half was that he had learned to stay back and go the other way with breaking balls during his two seasons in the American League. But that explanation fell apart shortly after he returned from the All-Star break. Pitchers tied him up with fastballs on his hands and got him to chase breaking balls that he had laid off earlier. As he began to spiral downward, Johnson's swing got frightfully long. He would look for a pitch in a certain area and still swing at anything. After hitting a career-best 31 homers in 2000, he took a big step backward.

Baserunning & Defense

While Johnson still can throw with the best, his game-calling and receiving skills have slipped. Few members of the Marlins' pitching staff posted significantly better numbers with Johnson behind the plate than backup Mike Redmond. Passed balls became a problem as Johnson struggled to handle an erratic, live-armed group. He is strictly a station-to-station runner on the bases.

2002 Outlook

Johnson's contract gave him the one-time right to elect free agency, but he decided in early December to play out the remainder of the five-year, $35 million deal he signed in December 2000. Considering the Marlins' financial troubles, as well as the uncertainty surrounding the ownership and location of the team, the decision had to have been a difficult one. In the end, he opted to stay close to his family and not test the shaky market. In the meantime, the Marlins hope his second-half swoon doesn't carry over into 2002.

Position: C
Bats: R **Throws:** R
Ht: 6' 2" **Wt:** 220

Opening Day Age: 30
Born: 7/20/71 in Fort Pierce, FL
ML Seasons: 8

Overall Statistics

	G	AB	R	H	D	T	HR	RBI	SB	BB	SO	Avg	OBP	Slg
2001	128	451	51	117	32	0	18	75	0	38	133	.259	.321	.450
Career	869	2885	351	724	148	4	128	421	3	337	750	.251	.331	.438

Where He Hits the Ball

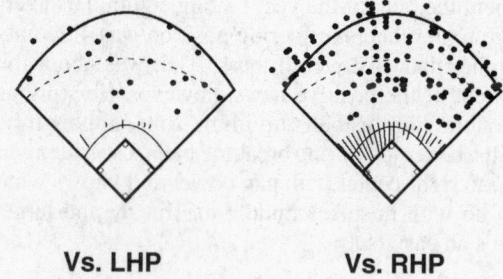

Vs. LHP   **Vs. RHP**

2001 Situational Stats

	AB	H	HR	RBI	Avg		AB	H	HR	RBI	Avg
Home	214	51	5	26	.238	LHP	53	13	1	3	.245
Road	237	66	13	49	.278	RHP	398	104	17	72	.261
First Half	256	73	16	56	.285	Sc Pos	116	36	4	53	.310
Scnd Half	195	44	2	19	.226	Clutch	87	22	4	14	.253

2001 Rankings (National League)

- 2nd in fielding percentage at catcher (.996)
- Led the Marlins in strikeouts

Derrek Lee

2001 Season

Derrek Lee's fourth full season in the majors started slowly, continuing a disturbing trend. Dropped to seventh in the order with the arrival of Charles Johnson, it took Lee until the middle of May to nose his batting average above the Mendoza Line for good. He had hit just five homers through mid-June. But once Tony Perez came down from the front office to manage the club on May 28, Lee seemed to relax. He finished with one of his better all-around seasons.

Hitting

A simple adjustment in Lee's stance keyed his late surge. Perez and batting coach Jack Maloof opened up Lee's front side, hoping to get him a longer look at the ball. It seemed to work, as Lee was able to avoid the prior bugaboo of inside fastballs that tied up his long arms. He was one of the club's better hitters with runners in scoring position and in late-and-close situations. He made lefties pay and again hit much better on the road, although with not nearly the home-road power disparity of the past. Anytime Lee can extend his arms, he can crush mistakes and hold his own against quality breaking balls.

Baserunning & Defense

Lee's height and tremendous wingspan have saved Marlins infielders dozens of errors each season. He's also one of the best at making the stretch-and-scoop play on balls in the dirt. His soft hands and quick reactions make him a first-rate weapon in the field, where he showed more aggressiveness than ever, often charging bunts and throwing to get the lead runner. Lee is no better than an average baserunner and is little threat to steal bases.

2002 Outlook

After just missing Super 2 arbitration status last winter, Lee finally gets to cash in, which could well make him expendable. The Marlins have Kevin Millar under contract for $900,000 this season and could move Millar back to first if another club would like to take a ride on the D-Lee Potential Bus.

Position: 1B
Bats: R **Throws:** R
Ht: 6' 5" **Wt:** 225

Opening Day Age: 26
Born: 9/6/75 in Sacramento, CA
ML Seasons: 5

Florida

Overall Statistics

	G	AB	R	H	D	T	HR	RBI	SB	BB	SO	Avg	OBP	Slg
2001	158	561	83	158	37	4	21	75	4	50	126	.282	.346	.474
Career	549	1764	245	457	96	9	72	243	11	186	463	.259	.335	.446

Where He Hits the Ball

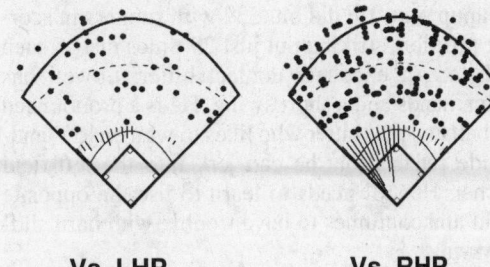

Vs. LHP   **Vs. RHP**

2001 Situational Stats

	AB	H	HR	RBI	Avg		AB	H	HR	RBI	Avg
Home	253	67	8	30	.265	LHP	116	36	6	14	.310
Road	308	91	13	45	.295	RHP	445	122	15	61	.274
First Half	290	72	11	39	.248	Sc Pos	134	40	4	47	.299
Scnd Half	271	86	10	36	.317	Clutch	96	33	5	11	.344

2001 Rankings (National League)

- 4th in assists at first base (115)
- 5th in errors at first base (8)
- 6th in lowest fielding percentage at first base (.994)
- Led the Marlins in at-bats, GDPs (18), games played, batting average in the clutch, highest percentage of extra bases taken as a runner (52.8) and on-base percentage vs. lefthanded pitchers (.394)

Mike Lowell

2001 Season

Signed to a three-year, $6.5 million extension before the 2001 season, Mike Lowell had another solid year in the middle of Florida's order. Though troubled at various times by thumb, wrist and hip problems, he managed to stay off the disabled list. Lowell isn't flashy and his power remains nothing special for third base, but he's so steady and such a positive force in the clubhouse that his employers don't quibble.

Hitting

Long praised as one of those hitters with a "nose for the RBI," Lowell reached triple digits in that category for the first time in 2001. Curiously, he failed to impress during an extended look in the cleanup spot. He did hit .339 with runners in scoring position, striking out just 25 times in 165 such at-bats. An excellent contact hitter, Lowell has quick hands and a short swing. He is a pronounced flyball and pull hitter who likes to wait on low-and-inside pitches that he can jerk into the left-field corner. He still needs to learn to use the opposite field and continues to have trouble with hard sliders away.

Baserunning & Defense

Once considered a step slow at third, Lowell has worked hard to improve his footwork and reaction time in the field. He now is considered perhaps the league's second-best defensive third baseman, although there's considerable room between him and Scott Rolen. Lowell moves equally well to either side. His throwing has become much more accurate and he has learned to come in on bunts and dribblers to his glove side. But his barehand play still needs work. Lowell is dreadfully slow on the bases, is no threat to steal and has a hard time scoring from first on all but the deepest doubles.

2002 Outlook

Lowell is due $6 million over the next two years, which could make him expendable in a full-scale salary dump. Barring that, he will remain a fixture at the hot corner for a club with precious little else it can count on from year to year.

Position: 3B
Bats: R **Throws:** R
Ht: 6' 4" **Wt:** 205

Opening Day Age: 28
Born: 2/24/74 in San Juan, PR
ML Seasons: 4

Overall Statistics

	G	AB	R	H	D	T	HR	RBI	SB	BB	SO	Avg	OBP	Slg
2001	146	551	65	156	37	0	18	100	1	43	79	.283	.340	.448
Career	391	1382	171	375	90	0	52	238	5	123	224	.271	.336	.449

Where He Hits the Ball

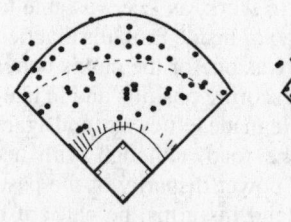 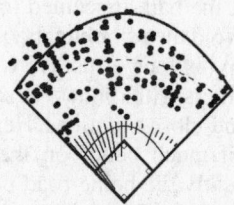

Vs. LHP   **Vs. RHP**

2001 Situational Stats

	AB	H	HR	RBI	Avg		AB	H	HR	RBI	Avg
Home	269	85	12	62	.316	LHP	127	36	4	18	.283
Road	282	71	6	38	.252	RHP	424	120	14	82	.283
First Half	281	80	11	62	.285	Sc Pos	165	56	6	84	.339
Scnd Half	270	76	7	38	.281	Clutch	90	22	2	8	.244

2001 Rankings (National League)

- 2nd in batting average on an 0-2 count (.343), fielding percentage at third base (.976), lowest cleanup slugging percentage (.406) and lowest percentage of extra bases taken as a runner (31.4)
- 3rd in lowest groundball-flyball ratio (0.6)
- 6th in sacrifice flies (10)
- 7th in lowest on-base percentage vs. lefthanded pitchers (.313)
- Led the Marlins in sacrifice flies (10), hit by pitch (10), batting average on an 0-2 count (.343) and batting average with two strikes (.243)

Brad Penny

2001 Season

After getting off to a 7-1 start, Brad Penny went nearly three months before notching his next win. Although he dropped eight straight decisions during that span, he didn't pitch poorly. Instead, he was a victim of the second-worst run support in the league. Some wondered if he wasn't adversely affected by the late-June release of controversial reliever Dan Miceli, who had been Penny's mentor and biggest supporter. Penny is a horse. He failed to last six innings just four times in 31 starts. He did miss two turns with a strained ribcage muscle in July but showed no ill effects upon his return.

Pitching

Penny throws hard, up to 98 MPH with his four-seam fastball. He relies mostly on a heavy sinker that he pounds into the zone at 93-94 MPH. As the year progressed, his curveball and changeup were much improved. At his best he was dominant, allowing just one hit over seven or more innings on three different occasions. He's around the plate more often than most young pitchers, issuing three or more walks in just six starts. Like several of his rotation mates, Penny struggled on the road, where he posted an ERA nearly three full runs higher than at home. He consistently has one of the highest groundball-flyball ratios on the team.

Defense & Hitting

Penny gets careless holding runners and needs to improve his pickoff move. Opposing basestealers took advantage of these weaknesses, making him susceptible to the big inning as he lost concentration and composure. At the plate, Penny swings like he knows what he's doing, though he could improve his bunting.

2002 Outlook

Depending on what happens with the rotation in front of him, Penny could open the year as Florida's No. 2 or 3 starter. Still another year from becoming eligible for arbitration, he is the perfect Marlin: young and cheap.

Position: SP
Bats: R **Throws:** R
Ht: 6' 4" **Wt:** 200

Opening Day Age: 23
Born: 5/24/78 in Broken Arrow, OK
ML Seasons: 2

Overall Statistics

	W	L	Pct.	ERA	G	GS	Sv	IP	H	BB	SO	HR	Ratio
2001	10	10	.500	3.69	31	31	0	205.0	183	54	154	15	1.16
Career	18	17	.514	4.10	54	53	0	324.2	303	114	234	28	1.28

How Often He Throws Strikes

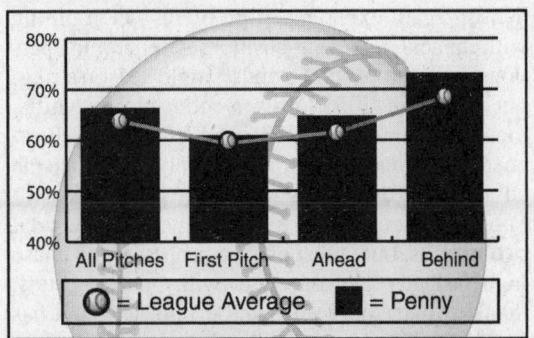

2001 Situational Stats

	W	L	ERA	Sv	IP		AB	H	HR	RBI	Avg
Home	6	5	2.27	0	107.0	LHB	369	87	5	34	.236
Road	4	5	5.23	0	98.0	RHB	393	96	10	49	.244
First Half	7	3	3.63	0	116.2	Sc Pos	148	46	5	67	.311
Scnd Half	3	7	3.77	0	88.1	Clutch	74	22	3	10	.297

2001 Rankings (National League)

- 1st in fielding percentage at pitcher (1.000)
- 2nd in least run support per nine innings (3.7)
- 3rd in lowest ERA at home
- 5th in GDPs induced (24) and fewest home runs allowed per nine innings (.66)
- 6th in most GDPs induced per nine innings (1.1)
- Led the Marlins in ERA, GDPs induced (24), highest strikeout-walk ratio (2.9), lowest slugging percentage allowed (.364), lowest on-base percentage allowed (.296), highest groundball-flyball ratio allowed (1.5), fewest pitches thrown per batter (3.51), lowest ERA at home, fewest home runs allowed per nine innings (.66), most GDPs induced per nine innings (1.1) and fewest walks per nine innings (2.4)

Preston Wilson

2001 Season

Preston Wilson endured his most challenging season, personally and professionally. He signed a five-year, $32 million contract extension during spring training that identified him as one of the Marlins' linchpins. He got off to a fast start, hitting .335 through the first two months. But June brought the longest slump of his career. He severely sprained his left thumb making a diving catch on July 1 and would not return until the middle of August. While he was out, his first child was born three months premature and died shortly thereafter.

Hitting

Wilson again experienced problems when hitting with runners in scoring position. After coming perilously close to Bobby Bonds' single-season strikeout record in 2000, Wilson reduced his whiffs, though at some cost to his productivity. He shortened his swing early in the year, relying on outside advice from former slugger George Foster, his godfather. Wilson regained his usual swing for the final two months, but still showed a propensity to chase high fastballs. He did better with breaking stuff, thanks to extremely quick and strong hands. He has power to all fields and still is learning how to use it.

Baserunning & Defense

Wilson is one of the fastest runners on the team. He failed to return to the 30-30 club, but that was more due to his prolonged absence than a decline in baserunning skill. He can go first to third and first to home with the best of them. A former high school running back, Wilson's speed enables him to outrun some bad jumps and questionable routes in the outfield. His arm remains lively but erratic.

2002 Outlook

Still due $31 million over the next four years, Wilson could well be moved over the winter. If he stays in South Florida, the Marlins would hope for much more consistency from a player who has shown he can hit both the high and low notes, but rarely spends much time in between.

Position: CF
Bats: R **Throws:** R
Ht: 6' 2" **Wt:** 193

Opening Day Age: 27
Born: 7/19/74 in Bamberg, SC
ML Seasons: 4

Overall Statistics

	G	AB	R	H	D	T	HR	RBI	SB	BB	SO	Avg	OBP	Slg
2001	123	468	70	128	30	2	23	71	20	36	107	.274	.331	.494
Career	455	1606	238	431	88	9	81	266	68	143	471	.268	.334	.486

Where He Hits the Ball

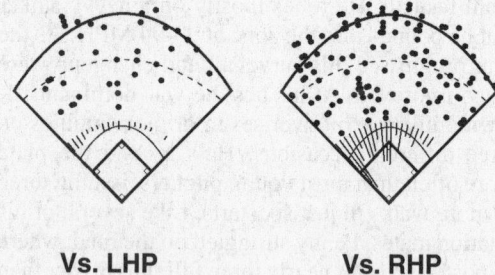

Vs. LHP   **Vs. RHP**

2001 Situational Stats

	AB	H	HR	RBI	Avg		AB	H	HR	RBI	Avg
Home	223	58	9	36	.260	LHP	106	22	5	11	.208
Road	245	70	14	35	.286	RHP	362	106	18	60	.293
First Half	287	77	9	40	.268	Sc Pos	139	29	4	45	.209
Scnd Half	181	51	14	31	.282	Clutch	76	15	3	9	.197

2001 Rankings (National League)

- 1st in assists in center field (12)
- 2nd in fielding percentage in center field (.993)
- 5th in lowest batting average with the bases loaded (.105) and highest percentage of swings on the first pitch (45.9)
- 6th in lowest batting average with runners in scoring position
- Led the Marlins in steals of third (4) and cleanup slugging percentage (.504)

Armando Almanza

Position: RP
Bats: L **Throws:** L
Ht: 6' 3" **Wt:** 220
Opening Day Age: 29
Born: 10/26/72 in El Paso, TX
ML Seasons: 3

Overall Statistics

	W	L	Pct.	ERA	G	GS	Sv	IP	H	BB	SO	HR	Ratio
2001	2	2	.500	4.83	52	0	0	41.0	34	26	45	8	1.46
Career	6	5	.545	4.37	133	0	0	103.0	80	78	111	12	1.53

2001 Situational Stats

	W	L	ERA	Sv	IP		AB	H	HR	RBI	Avg
Home	1	0	3.86	0	18.2	LHB	62	13	2	8	.210
Road	1	2	5.64	0	22.1	RHB	86	21	6	17	.244
First Half	0	1	3.04	0	26.2	Sc Pos	38	10	3	19	.263
Scnd Half	2	1	8.16	0	14.1	Clutch	58	18	3	12	.310

2001 Season

Armando Almanza began the year hot and posted a strong first half. But as he had the previous year, the lefty wore down after the All-Star break, a collapse blamed on bone chips in his throwing elbow. He was shut down with 10 days to go in the season and had arthroscopic elbow surgery.

Pitching, Defense & Hitting

Almanza's lively fastball can top out at 95 MPH. At his best, he complements it with a slow, biting curveball at 72-73 MPH. Perhaps because of the bone chips, he lost his feel for the curve in early August, allowing hitters to sit on his fastball with great success. Almanza has a solid changeup, which he uses to keep righthanders in check. The first batters he faced were able to reach base 42 percent of the time, a problem for someone often called on to face just one hitter. Almanza is a decent fielder who has improved against the running game. He had no plate appearances in 2001.

2002 Outlook

Still another year away from arbitration, Almanza must prove he can put a full season together before he'll earn a big payday. If Vic Darensbourg is moved to cut payroll, Almanza could inherit the role as the top situational lefty. He remains too inconsistent to be given any save opportunities.

Josh Beckett Top Prospect

Position: SP
Bats: R **Throws:** R
Ht: 6' 4" **Wt:** 190
Opening Day Age: 21
Born: 5/15/80 in Austin, TX
ML Seasons: 1

Overall Statistics

	W	L	Pct.	ERA	G	GS	Sv	IP	H	BB	SO	HR	Ratio
2001	2	2	.500	1.50	4	4	0	24.0	14	11	24	3	1.04
Career	2	2	.500	1.50	4	4	0	24.0	14	11	24	3	1.04

2001 Situational Stats

	W	L	ERA	Sv	IP		AB	H	HR	RBI	Avg
Home	2	0	0.75	0	12.0	LHB	48	5	1	2	.104
Road	0	2	2.25	0	12.0	RHB	39	9	2	7	.231
First Half	0	0	-	0	0.0	Sc Pos	15	5	2	8	.333
Scnd Half	2	2	1.50	0	24.0	Clutch	0	0	0	0	-

2001 Season

The No. 2 overall pick in 1999, Josh Beckett signed late and did two tours on the disabled list in 2000. Offseason tests detected a small tear in his labrum, fraying in his rotator cuff, biceps tendinitis and an impingement. He rehabbed his shoulder hard and came out firing, dominating Class-A and Double-A before making the most of a September callup.

Pitching, Defense & Hitting

Beckett is blessed with a true No. 1's repertoire and makeup. His four-seam fastball will hit 97 MPH, but he'd rather pitch at 93-94 and get easy outs with his sinker. He has a dazzling over-the-top curveball and a plus-changeup that is thrown with excellent arm speed and deception. His delivery is smooth, making the ball get on top of hitters in a hurry. He needs to get better at holding runners. Beckett is athletic but just an adequate fielder. He notched a double and single in only seven at-bats.

2002 Outlook

Barring a health setback, Beckett will open 2002 in Florida's rotation. While he still has two more minor league options remaining, club officials were ecstatic with his poise and performance in the majors last season. It won't be much longer before he rises to the top of the rotation and assumes the ace status scouts have predicted.

Vic Darensbourg

Position: RP
Bats: L **Throws:** L
Ht: 5'10" **Wt:** 165

Opening Day Age: 31
Born: 11/13/70 in Los
Angeles, CA
ML Seasons: 4
Pronunciation:
darens-berg

Overall Statistics

	W	L	Pct.	ERA	G	GS	Sv	IP	H	BB	SO	HR	Ratio
2001	1	2	.333	4.25	58	0	1	48.2	52	10	33	4	1.27
Career	6	13	.316	4.74	229	0	2	216.1	215	89	182	19	1.41

2001 Situational Stats

	W	L	ERA	Sv	IP		AB	H	HR	RBI	Avg
Home	1	1	2.63	1	24.0	LHB	85	25	3	23	.294
Road	0	1	5.84	0	24.2	RHB	103	27	1	7	.262
First Half	0	0	4.40	0	28.2	Sc Pos	55	16	1	23	.291
Scnd Half	1	2	4.05	1	20.0	Clutch	69	18	1	8	.261

2001 Season

Signed to three-year, $2.7 million extension in December 2000, Vic Darensbourg endured an inconsistent year. His season was marred by a late-August trip to the disabled list with shoulder inflammation and a small tear in his labrum. He later admitted pitching through nagging pain for several weeks before taking a nearly month-long break. Though it initially was feared he might have to undergo surgery, Darensbourg was able to return and pitched effectively down the stretch.

Pitching, Defense & Hitting

When he's on, Darensbourg puts hitters on their heels with a 91-94 MPH fastball and puts lefties away with a sharp slider. He struggled with his slider much of the season, one reason why lefthanders hit almost .300 against him. He was better against righthanded batters, mainly because his changeup was more consistent than the slider. A wiry athlete, Darensbourg fields his position and holds runners well, allowing just one stolen-base attempt. He had no plate appearances in 2001.

2002 Outlook

If the Marlins need to trim costs, they could try to move the remaining two years on Darensbourg's contract. Otherwise, he'll return as the club's top situational lefty.

Braden Looper

Position: RP
Bats: R **Throws:** R
Ht: 6' 5" **Wt:** 225

Opening Day Age: 27
Born: 10/28/74 in
Weatherford, OK
ML Seasons: 4

Overall Statistics

	W	L	Pct.	ERA	G	GS	Sv	IP	H	BB	SO	HR	Ratio
2001	3	3	.500	3.55	71	0	3	71.0	63	30	52	8	1.31
Career	11	8	.579	3.93	220	0	5	224.2	235	98	135	19	1.48

2001 Situational Stats

	W	L	ERA	Sv	IP		AB	H	HR	RBI	Avg
Home	1	1	4.98	1	34.1	LHB	112	28	6	15	.250
Road	2	2	2.21	2	36.2	RHB	148	35	2	19	.236
First Half	3	3	4.54	1	35.2	Sc Pos	67	14	2	25	.209
Scnd Half	0	0	2.55	2	35.1	Clutch	122	23	2	11	.189

2001 Season

Signed to a three-year, $2.6 million deal in early March 2001, Braden Looper struggled for much of last season before putting it together in the final two months. But he posted ERAs over 6.00 in both June and July, straining to assume the role of fallen setup man Dan Miceli.

Pitching, Defense & Hitting

Looper's fastball tops out at 98 MPH and regularly hits 94-95 MPH, but it tends to straighten out. The biggest difference, once he got rolling last year, was a more consistent slider. He also threw more changeups and four-seam fastballs to lefthanded hitters, who always had plagued him. Looper finally learned to bury those riding fastballs on lefties' fists. His sinker remained an effective weapon, garnering a 1.69 groundball-flyball ratio. He can be slow to the plate and easy to run on. He is a poor fielder because of a delivery that leaves him off balance and falling off toward the first-base side. He has struck out in all four career at-bats.

2002 Outlook

Looper has been groomed as a closer since he was drafted in 1996. Until the final two months of 2001, serious doubts remained about his ability to handle the role. His emergence could make high-priced stopper Antonio Alfonseca expendable.

Kevin Millar

Position: RF/LF/1B/3B
Bats: R **Throws:** R
Ht: 6' 0" **Wt:** 210

Opening Day Age: 30
Born: 9/24/71 in Los Angeles, CA
ML Seasons: 4
Pronunciation: mi-LAR

Overall Statistics

	G	AB	R	H	D	T	HR	RBI	SB	BB	SO	Avg	OBP	Slg
2001	144	449	62	141	39	5	20	85	0	39	70	.314	.374	.557
Career	374	1061	147	309	70	12	43	194	1	116	181	.291	.368	.501

2001 Situational Stats

	AB	H	HR	RBI	Avg		AB	H	HR	RBI	Avg
Home	228	81	13	57	.355	LHP	97	34	3	10	.351
Road	221	60	7	28	.271	RHP	352	107	17	75	.304
First Half	196	60	7	37	.306	Sc Pos	106	39	5	60	.368
Scnd Half	253	81	13	48	.320	Clutch	73	23	6	18	.315

2001 Season

Typecast for years as an extra man, Kevin Millar came into his own last season. But he didn't begin to see regular playing time until Tony Perez became Florida's manager. Perez took a chance and put Millar in right field, where his defensive deficiencies paled next to his nightly production in the middle of the lineup.

Hitting, Baserunning & Defense

Millar has the best idea on the team of situational hitting, especially with runners in scoring position. He thrives on mistakes, does his homework and thinks along with pitchers. Millar is a great guess hitter and knows how to set up pitchers. He is slow on the basepaths, but realizes his limitations and doesn't make dumb outs. He lacks the instincts and foot speed to be an above-average defender, despite his hard work. His arm is below average.

2002 Outlook

Millar will be in the lineup somewhere. He signed a two-year, $1.6 million deal before the 2001 season, making him a bargain on a team with financial concerns. Millar could stay in right field, move back to first base if Derrek Lee is dealt, or take over in left if Cliff Floyd is moved. Millar's productivity and price tag make him a perfect fit in Florida.

Vladimir Nunez

Position: RP
Bats: R **Throws:** R
Ht: 6' 4" **Wt:** 224

Opening Day Age: 27
Born: 3/15/75 in Havana, Cuba
ML Seasons: 4
Pronunciation: NOON-yez

Overall Statistics

	W	L	Pct.	ERA	G	GS	Sv	IP	H	BB	SO	HR	Ratio
2001	4	5	.444	2.74	52	3	0	92.0	79	30	64	9	1.18
Career	11	21	.344	4.69	117	27	1	274.1	269	120	197	32	1.42

2001 Situational Stats

	W	L	ERA	Sv	IP		AB	H	HR	RBI	Avg
Home	1	3	3.30	0	46.1	LHB	160	34	4	16	.213
Road	3	2	2.17	0	45.2	RHB	178	45	5	22	.253
First Half	2	2	2.91	0	52.2	Sc Pos	71	16	0	23	.225
Scnd Half	2	3	2.52	0	39.1	Clutch	84	16	2	9	.190

2001 Season

Injuries allowed Vladimir Nunez to spend part of May in the Marlins' starting rotation, where he never had seen much success. But after three decent starts he returned without complaint to the bullpen and contributed strongly as a long reliever. The Cuban defector went three or more innings five times. He finally seemed to warm to the role.

Pitching, Defense & Hitting

After years of hardheaded resistance, Nunez accepted the club's insistence he stick with one arm slot. Once he stopped dropping down, the movement on his pitches returned. Nunez neutralized lefthanded batters with a 91-94 MPH fastball and a nasty splitter. He wasn't as tough on righties but used both the slider and splitter to finish them off. He was more willing to pitch inside and threw more sinkers than in the past. Nunez is athletic and mobile, making him a good fielder. He has a quick move to the plate, which keeps baserunners from testing him. He is not much with the bat.

2002 Outlook

If he qualifies for Super 2 status, Nunez could be in line for a big raise through salary arbitration. Provided the Marlins hold on to him, the workhorse could move up a notch or two in the bullpen hierarchy. His days as a starter appear over.

Eric Owens

Position: RF/CF
Bats: R **Throws:** R
Ht: 6' 0" **Wt:** 198

Opening Day Age: 31
Born: 2/3/71 in Danville, VA
ML Seasons: 7

Overall Statistics

	G	AB	R	H	D	T	HR	RBI	SB	BB	SO	Avg	OBP	Slg
2001	119	400	51	101	16	1	5	28	8	29	59	.253	.302	.335
Career	564	1727	232	452	65	11	21	157	89	141	227	.262	.319	.349

2001 Situational Stats

	AB	H	HR	RBI	Avg		AB	H	HR	RBI	Avg
Home	190	50	4	17	.263	LHP	113	31	4	7	.274
Road	210	51	1	11	.243	RHP	287	70	1	21	.244
First Half	294	73	4	18	.248	Sc Pos	93	24	0	21	.258
Scnd Half	106	28	1	10	.264	Clutch	58	13	2	6	.224

2001 Season

Eric Owens was slowed by a quadriceps injury during spring training, got traded from his dream destination (San Diego) just before Opening Day and never really hit his stride. Handed the Marlins' right-field job and No. 2 spot in the order, he failed miserably on both accounts.

Hitting, Baserunning & Defense

Owens failed to get on base at a rate commensurate with his role. He has trouble catching up with high fastballs and will chase soft stuff down in the zone. He swings for the fences far too often for someone with warning-track power. In the outfield, his jumps, routes and arm left much to be desired. He spent the final two months either injured or sulking on the bench. Speed was supposed to be one of his best tools, but the Marlins never saw it. Owens put on 10-15 pounds during the season and the infield hits he beat out in San Diego turned into easy outs.

2002 Outlook

Still owed $2.4 million, including a pair of $200,000 roster bonuses the next two winters, Owens won't be easy to move, which the Marlins almost certainly will attempt to do. His stock has dropped markedly and it's doubtful many teams view him as an everyday player. His best chance is to hook on somewhere as a fourth outfielder.

Mike Redmond

Position: C
Bats: R **Throws:** R
Ht: 6' 1" **Wt:** 185

Opening Day Age: 30
Born: 5/5/71 in Seattle, WA
ML Seasons: 4

Overall Statistics

	G	AB	R	H	D	T	HR	RBI	SB	BB	SO	Avg	OBP	Slg
2001	48	141	19	44	4	0	4	14	0	13	13	.312	.376	.426
Career	256	711	68	209	30	1	7	68	0	57	82	.294	.359	.368

2001 Situational Stats

	AB	H	HR	RBI	Avg		AB	H	HR	RBI	Avg
Home	75	26	3	9	.347	LHP	56	21	3	7	.375
Road	66	18	1	5	.273	RHP	85	23	1	7	.271
First Half	69	25	3	9	.362	Sc Pos	29	9	1	9	.310
Scnd Half	72	19	1	5	.264	Clutch	13	5	0	1	.385

2001 Season

Mike Redmond was forced to assume the classic caddie's role when the Marlins signed All-Star Charles Johnson. Redmond accepted the demotion with typical grace. He remained a trusted confidante to a young pitching staff, particularly ace Ryan Dempster.

Hitting, Baserunning & Defense

Redmond has worked hard to improve his bat speed. He pulled more balls, forcing defenses to play him more straight up, but he was careful not to become too enamored of his new skill. He torments lefties, even those of quality. Redmond still gets overpowered at times, especially with hard stuff on the inner half. He is slow but dogged on the bases. Few catchers call a better game than Redmond, who has an encyclopedic knowledge of opposing hitters. His blocking skills are better than Johnson's and his arm is right there, as well.

2002 Outlook

Finally eligible for salary arbitration, Redmond again figures to fill a backup role for the Marlins. Johnson chose not to exercise an opt-out clause in the five-year contract he signed in December 2000, a move that all but eliminated Redmond's chances at a starting job. He is a solid citizen with no ego, and he remains valuable to a team in transition.

Jesus Sanchez

Traded To CUBS

Position: SP
Bats: L **Throws:** L
Ht: 5'10" **Wt:** 155

Opening Day Age: 27
Born: 10/11/74 in Bani, DR
ML Seasons: 4
Pronunciation: HAY-soos

Overall Statistics

	W	L	Pct.	ERA	G	GS	Sv	IP	H	BB	SO	HR	Ratio
2001	2	4	.333	4.74	16	9	0	62.2	61	31	46	7	1.47
Career	23	32	.418	5.06	142	80	0	494.0	520	258	368	73	1.57

2001 Situational Stats

	W	L	ERA	Sv	IP		AB	H	HR	RBI	Avg
Home	2	2	3.03	0	35.2	LHB	49	10	1	3	.204
Road	0	2	7.00	0	27.0	RHB	189	51	6	28	.270
First Half	1	0	1.32	0	13.2	Sc Pos	57	12	0	19	.211
Scnd Half	1	4	5.69	0	49.0	Clutch	3	1	0	1	.333

2001 Season

Jesus Sanchez got a salary bump to $1.425 million last winter, then lost his spot in the rotation with a horrific spring. He spent the first three months at Triple-A, where he worked as both a starter and situational reliever. Recalled to fill a spot in the bullpen, he moved into the rotation when Chuck Smith endured injury problems.

Pitching, Defense & Hitting

Sanchez' velocity has been down for several years. He'll top out at 93 MPH but generally pitches at 88-89 MPH. He has a tough time repeating his delivery, and location remains a constant bugaboo. He has a good changeup but doesn't throw it enough. He muscles up at inopportune times and his stuff will flatten out and elevate. Sanchez is an adequate fielder and has a first-rate pickoff move that opponents have learned to fear. He is an above-average hitter for a pitcher.

2002 Outlook

Sanchez showed flashes of brilliance last season, usually against lesser competition. That didn't discourage the Cubs, who traded a minor league pitcher to Florida for Sanchez. The hard-throwing lefty will work out of the pen unless he claims the fifth-starter role for Chicago.

Chuck Smith

Position: SP
Bats: R **Throws:** R
Ht: 6' 1" **Wt:** 185

Opening Day Age: 32
Born: 10/21/69 in Memphis, TN
ML Seasons: 2

Overall Statistics

	W	L	Pct.	ERA	G	GS	Sv	IP	H	BB	SO	HR	Ratio
2001	5	5	.500	4.70	15	15	0	88.0	89	35	71	10	1.41
Career	11	11	.500	3.84	34	34	0	210.2	200	89	189	16	1.37

2001 Situational Stats

	W	L	ERA	Sv	IP		AB	H	HR	RBI	Avg
Home	4	2	3.16	0	42.2	LHB	158	48	8	31	.304
Road	1	3	6.15	0	45.1	RHB	178	41	2	14	.230
First Half	4	5	5.20	0	71.0	Sc Pos	80	21	5	37	.263
Scnd Half	1	0	2.65	0	17.0	Clutch	8	2	0	2	.250

2001 Season

Voted the Marlins' top 2000 rookie after waiting nearly a decade for his chance, Chuck Smith entered last spring penciled in as the No. 2 starter. A freak baserunning injury just before Opening Day left him with a sprained pitching shoulder and landed him on the disabled list until early May. Smith then pitched erratically before going back on the DL in late July with shoulder and elbow woes. He later admitted concealing the pain in his arm.

Pitching, Defense & Hitting

Smith's stuff was electric at times as a rookie, but he took a step back in '01. He usually pitched at 88-90 MPH, several notches below the previous year. He also throws a curve, slider and changeup with split action. He had good life on his stuff, but his location suffered due to nagging pain. He had soreness in his arm even before the baserunning fall. Smith is an adequate fielder and holds runners well enough. He is not much with the bat.

2002 Outlook

Smith returns with no guarantees. Because he's two more years away from achieving arbitration status, he could serve as a low-price option if the Marlins dismantle. Failing that, he'll compete for a spot at the back of a crowded rotation, with a move to the bullpen possible.

Florida

Jeff Abbott (Pos: CF, **Age**: 29, **Bats**: R)

	G	AB	R	H	D	T	HR	RBI	SB	BB	SO	Avg	OBP	Slg
2001	28	42	5	11	3	0	0	5	0	3	7	.262	.326	.333
Career	233	596	82	157	33	2	18	83	6	38	91	.263	.307	.416

Abbott began the season with tendinitis in his knees and then spent most of 2001 at Triple-A. He'll likely never be more than a spare outfielder or pinch-hitter. 2002 Outlook: B

Juan Acevedo (Pos: RHP, **Age**: 31)

	W	L	Pct.	ERA	G	GS	Sv	IP	H	BB	SO	HR	Ratio
2001	2	5	.286	4.18	59	0	0	60.1	68	34	47	6	1.71
Career	26	30	.464	4.41	263	34	19	457.0	477	185	279	62	1.45

The Marlins acquired Acevedo from the Rockies in August in exchange for a minor league infielder. He sliced his ERA in half after leaving Colorado, in part because he pitched better with men on. He refused a minor league assignment and became a free agent. 2002 Outlook: B

Dave Berg (Pos: 2B/3B/SS, **Age**: 31, **Bats**: R)

	G	AB	R	H	D	T	HR	RBI	SB	BB	SO	Avg	OBP	Slg
2001	82	215	26	52	12	1	4	16	0	14	39	.242	.292	.363
Career	354	911	109	249	55	3	10	83	8	92	190	.273	.343	.373

Berg's ability to play three infield positions raises his value. However, his batting average has declined each of the past three seasons. 2001 Outlook: B

Ricky Bones (Pos: RHP, **Age**: 32)

	W	L	Pct.	ERA	G	GS	Sv	IP	H	BB	SO	HR	Ratio
2001	4	4	.500	5.06	61	0	0	64.0	71	33	41	7	1.63
Career	63	82	.434	4.85	375	164	1	1278.1	1422	464	564	167	1.48

After allowing no homers and a 2.38 ERA through the end of May, Bones returned to his usual self, permitting a 6.53 ERA thereafter. A veteran of seven teams, he'll be searching for yet another employer. 2002 Outlook: C

Ramon Castro (Pos: C, **Age**: 26, **Bats**: R)

	G	AB	R	H	D	T	HR	RBI	SB	BB	SO	Avg	OBP	Slg
2001	7	11	0	2	0	0	0	1	0	1	1	.182	.250	.182
Career	81	216	14	47	8	0	4	19	0	27	51	.218	.304	.310

Castro has crushed the ball in Triple-A the past two years and has little left to prove. He's still highly regarded, but Charles Johnson is in his way. 2002 Outlook: C

Alex Fernandez (Pos: RHP, **Age**: 32)

	W	L	Pct.	ERA	G	GS	Sv	IP	H	BB	SO	HR	Ratio
2001								, Did Not Play					
Career	107	87	.552	3.74	263	261	0	1760.1	1693	552	1252	190	1.28

Fernandez, who didn't pitch at all in 1998 and 2001 because of arm troubles, was forced to retire in September. 2002 Outlook: D

Andy Fox (Pos: SS, **Age**: 31, **Bats**: L)

	G	AB	R	H	D	T	HR	RBI	SB	BB	SO	Avg	OBP	Slg
2001	54	81	8	15	0	1	3	7	1	15	17	.185	.327	.321
Career	527	1327	177	326	46	11	25	118	42	140	265	.246	.332	.353

Fox broke a finger last April and required surgery. He didn't return until after the All-Star break, and didn't get his first hit until August. Florida extended his contract through this season. 2002 Outlook: B

Jason Grilli (Pos: RHP, **Age**: 25)

	W	L	Pct.	ERA	G	GS	Sv	IP	H	BB	SO	HR	Ratio
2001	2	2	.500	6.08	6	5	0	26.2	30	11	17	6	1.54
Career	3	2	.600	5.94	7	6	0	33.1	41	13	20	6	1.62

Grilli was part of the Livan Hernandez deal with the Giants in 1999. Once a highly regarded prospect, Grilli's career has stalled due to injuries and ineffectiveness. He needs to prove he's healthy. 2002 Outlook: C

Mike Gulan (Pos: 3B, **Age**: 31, **Bats**: R)

	G	AB	R	H	D	T	HR	RBI	SB	BB	SO	Avg	OBP	Slg
2001	6	6	1	0	0	0	0	0	0	2	2	.000	.250	.000
Career	11	15	3	0	0	0	0	1	0	3	7	.000	.167	.000

Gulan has been stuck in Triple-A since 1995. He has some power and became a .300 hitter at Triple-A Calgary the past two years, but the odds of him getting another chance to end his big league collar aren't great. He'll try elsewhere, as he's now a free agent. 2002 Outlook: C

John Mabry (Pos: RF, **Age**: 31, **Bats**: L)

	G	AB	R	H	D	T	HR	RBI	SB	BB	SO	Avg	OBP	Slg
2001	87	154	14	32	7	0	6	20	1	13	46	.208	.287	.370
Career	814	2361	264	640	129	3	55	285	6	180	461	.271	.325	.398

Mabry went 16-for-77 with 23 strikeouts in both the first and second halves of last year. He's good for an occasional home run, but his batting average has been on the decline since 1996. He's a free agent. 2002 Outlook: C

Ryan McGuire (Pos: RF, **Age**: 30, **Bats**: L)

	G	AB	R	H	D	T	HR	RBI	SB	BB	SO	Avg	OBP	Slg
2001	48	54	8	10	2	0	1	8	1	7	15	.185	.270	.278
Career	351	605	64	131	33	4	7	53	3	86	137	.217	.312	.319

McGuire did nothing with Florida to prove he deserved a job in the major leagues, though he did bat .301 at Triple-A. He signed a minor league contract with Baltimore in mid-November. 2002 Outlook: C

Chad Mottola (Pos: RF, **Age**: 30, **Bats**: R)

	G	AB	R	H	D	T	HR	RBI	SB	BB	SO	Avg	OBP	Slg
2001	5	7	1	0	0	0	0	1	0	2	2	.000	.200	.000
Career	43	95	12	19	3	0	3	9	2	8	22	.200	.267	.326

Mottola has been boucing around Triple-A since 1995. If 33 homers and 102 RBI for Syracuse in 2000 didn't earn him time in the majors, he may never get a shot. He became a free agent in October. 2002 Outlook: C

Lyle Mouton (Pos: LF, **Age**: 32, **Bats**: R)

	G	AB	R	H	D	T	HR	RBI	SB	BB	SO	Avg	OBP	Slg
2001	21	17	1	1	0	0	0	1	0	0	7	.059	.059	.059
Career	328	805	96	225	43	2	22	116	9	71	209	.280	.339	.420

After refusing a minor league assignment with the Marlins last May, Mouton accepted minor league deals with the Tigers and then the Astros. Considering his battting average with Florida, he can't afford to be choosy. 2002 Outlook: C

Johnny Ruffin (**Pos**: RHP, **Age**: 30)

	W	L	Pct.	ERA	G	GS	Sv	IP	H	BB	SO	HR	Ratio
2001	0	0	-	4.91	3	0	0	3.2	5	4	4	0	2.45
Career	10	6	.625	4.13	139	0	3	196.0	187	93	163	25	1.43

Once a top prospect with the White Sox, Ruffin signed a minor league deal with the Reds in August. He has logged a grand total of 12.2 big league innings during the past two seasons. 2002 Outlook: C

Joe Strong (**Pos**: RHP, **Age**: 39)

	W	L	Pct.	ERA	G	GS	Sv	IP	H	BB	SO	HR	Ratio
2001	0	0	-	1.35	5	0	0	6.2	3	3	4	1	0.90
Career	1	1	.500	5.81	23	0	1	26.1	29	15	22	4	1.67

Strong was a great story in 2000, when he made the Marlins as a 37-year-old rookie. But he appeared in only five games last year, none of which the Marlins trailed by fewer than four runs. He refused a minor league assignment and became a free agent. 2001 Outlook: C

Ryan Thompson (**Pos**: RF, **Age**: 34, **Bats**: R)

	G	AB	R	H	D	T	HR	RBI	SB	BB	SO	Avg	OBP	Slg
2001	18	31	6	9	5	0	0	2	0	1	8	.290	.313	.452
Career	354	1120	149	271	62	4	44	152	8	83	309	.242	.302	.422

Thompson hasn't gathered more than 50 major league at-bats in any season since 1995. But he's still trying. When the Marlins returned him to the minors last summer, he opted to sign with the Expos. He then signed with the Brewers in December. 2002 Outlook: C

Florida

455

Florida Marlins Minor League Prospects

Organization Overview:

If the talk about possible contraction doesn't involve them and they don't hold a major fire sale, the Marlins' future could be quite bright, at least on the field. That might sound strange, considering they haven't finished with a winning record since their World Championship in 1997. Perhaps worse, general manager Dave Dombrowski has left the franchise and joined Detroit. But any team with a nucleus of pitchers that includes Brad Penny, Ryan Dempster and A.J. Burnett has got to be taken seriously. And Josh Beckett has a chance to be better than any of them. He should be a frontrunner for Rookie of the Year consideration this season. In addition, virtually all of Florida's key offensive players are either in their prime or just entering it. But the question is whether the Marlins will be able to afford to keep all their talent as it reaches arbitration and free agency. Still, the system appears ready to keep churning out replacements. Florida's top four affiliates each finished above .500 last season, with its two full-season Class-A clubs posting the best records in their respective leagues.

Allen Baxter

Position: P   **Opening Day Age:** 18
Bats: R **Throws:** R   **Born:** 7/6/83 in
Ht: 6' 4" **Wt:** 215   Richmond, VA

Recent Statistics

	W	L	ERA	G	GS	Sv	IP	H	R	BB	SO	HR
2001 R Marlins	2	3	2.38	9	7	0	34.0	25	13	8	40	0
2001 A Utica	0	0	3.60	1	1	0	5.0	3	2	3	5	0

Florida liked Baxter's arm when it chose him out of a Virginia high school in the third round in 2001. He's already pretty big for a guy who didn't turn 18 years of age until after the draft. His fastball currently travels in the low 90s and can reach as high as 96 MPH. He also throws a slider and changeup. His stats would indicate he was more than ready for the challenge of the Rookie-level Gulf Coast League, where he recorded five strike-outs for every walk. His performance there helped earn him a start in the short-season New York-Penn League to close his year. Baxter has begun his professional career in impressive fashion.

Miguel Cabrera

Position: SS   **Opening Day Age:** 18
Bats: R **Throws:** R   **Born:** 4/18/83 in
Ht: 6' 2" **Wt:** 185   Maracay, Aragua, VZ

Recent Statistics

	G	AB	R	H	D	T	HR	RBI	SB	BB	SO	Avg
2000 R Marlins	57	219	38	57	10	2	2	22	1	23	46	.260
2000 A Utica	8	32	3	8	2	0	0	6	0	2	6	.250
2001 A Kane County	110	422	61	113	19	4	7	66	3	37	76	.268

The Marlins signed Cabrera when he was just 16 years of age in 1999. The Venezuelan shortstop already has

compiled an impressive resume for someone so young. He was playing in short-season Class-A in 2000, and moved up to the Midwest League last season. Clearly, Cabrera is an electric talent. He has all the tools and makes all the plays defensively. He features a plus arm, a quick first step, nice lateral movement and good instincts. He held his own offensively at Kane County at age 18. As he matures physically, he figures to add strength and power, with a corresponding increase in extra-base hits. He may be ticketed for high Class-A this season, though the Marlins won't discount a move to Double-A.

Adrian Gonzalez

Position: 1B   **Opening Day Age:** 19
Bats: L **Throws:** L   **Born:** 5/8/82 in San
Ht: 6' 2" **Wt:** 190   Diego, CA

Recent Statistics

	G	AB	R	H	D	T	HR	RBI	SB	BB	SO	Avg
2000 R Marlins	53	193	24	57	10	1	0	30	0	32	35	.295
2000 A Utica	8	29	7	9	3	0	0	3	0	7	6	.310
2001 A Kane County	127	516	86	161	37	1	17	103	5	57	83	.312

The Marlins made Gonzalez the top pick of the 2000 draft and signed him to a $3 million bonus. Although he hit .297 in his first professional season, he didn't manage any homers in 61 games. But the first baseman began to show more power as a 19-year-old in the Midwest League last year. Gonzalez is a line-drive hitter who sprays balls to all fields. As he gets stronger, he might develop a stroke that will deliver even more home runs. He's not a burner, but has good instincts on the basepaths and is a solid defender. The Marlins are impressed with his knowledge of the game and say he's been everything that they expected. He has a chance to play in Double-A before leaving his teens.

Blaine Neal

Position: P   **Opening Day Age:** 23
Bats: L **Throws:** R   **Born:** 4/6/78 in
Ht: 6' 5" **Wt:** 205   Maurelton, NJ

Recent Statistics

	W	L	ERA	G	GS	Sv	IP	H	R	BB	SO	HR
2001 AA Portland	2	3	2.36	54	0	21	53.1	43	17	21	45	1
2001 NL Florida	0	0	6.75	4	0	0	5.1	7	4	5	3	0

Florida drafted Neal in the fourth round in 1996 as a pitcher. But he suffered injuries and spent some time at first base in 1998 before returning to the mound the next season. He's shown enough ability since then that he's projected as a possible closer. Neal's velocity returned as he got healthy. His fastball is thrown in the 92-96 MPH range and he also has a hard slider. Those two offerings may be enough to allow him to work in a setup role, but he might need a third pitch in order to close. Neal made four late-season appearances with the Marlins in 2001.

After a successful stint in the Arizona Fall League, he's banging on the door for a big league job.

Abraham Nunez

Position: OF
Bats: B **Throws:** R
Ht: 6' 2" **Wt:** 186

Opening Day Age: 22
Born: 2/5/80 in Haina, DR

Recent Statistics

	G	AB	R	H	D	THR	RBI	SB	BB	SO	Avg
2000 A Brevard Cty	31	103	17	20	4	0	1	9	11	28	34	.194
2000 AA Portland	74	221	39	61	17	3	6	42	8	44	64	.276
2001 AA Portland	136	467	75	112	14	9	17	53	26	83	155	.240
2001 MLE	136	453	62	98	12	8	12	44	18	60	171	.216

Nunez, a native of the Dominican Republic, originally was signed by Arizona in 1996. The Marlins were able to land him in 1999 as part of the Matt Mantei trade. At this point in his career, Nunez' production hasn't quite caught up to his promise. Obviously, his ability to hit for power and steal bases is enticing to many scouts. Nunez has five-tool talent and is a plus defensive center fielder. Unlike many tools players, he has demonstrated a willingness to take walks, drawing 83 free passes last season. Unfortunately, Nunez' high strikeout rate threatens to swallow up his batting average. Reducing that total will be one key as he gets close to the majors.

Kevin Olsen

Position: P
Bats: R **Throws:** R
Ht: 6' 2" **Wt:** 200

Opening Day Age: 25
Born: 7/26/76 in Covina, CA

Recent Statistics

	W	L	ERA	G	GS	Sv	IP	H	R	BB	SO	HR
2001 AA Portland	10	3	2.68	26	26	0	154.2	123	56	21	144	11
2001 NL Florida	0	0	1.20	4	2	0	15.0	11	2	2	13	0

Olsen has been something of a surprise, considering he wasn't chosen until the 26th round of the 1998 draft. He hadn't done a whole lot to attract much attention until last season. But his performance in 2001, when his ERA ranked fourth in the Eastern League, deserves recognition. As his strikeout-walk ratio at Double-A would indicate, Olsen throws lots of strikes. He is deceptive and locates his pitches well. Although he isn't overpowering, his 88-92 MPH fastball, slider and changeup are enough to keep hitters honest. His stuff also was enough to help him make a nice impression in his four appearances with the Marlins last year. Florida says Olsen could emerge as a No. 4 or 5 starter in the majors.

Will Smith

Position: OF
Bats: L **Throws:** R
Ht: 6' 1" **Wt:** 185

Opening Day Age: 20
Born: 10/23/81 in Alexandria, LA

Recent Statistics

	G	AB	R	H	D	THR	RBI	SB	BB	SO	Avg
2000 R Marlins	54	204	37	75	21	2	2	34	7	26	24	.368
2001 A Kane County	125	535	92	150	26	2	16	91	4	32	74	.280

The Marlins' affiliate at Kane County featured a few intriguing outfield prospects. Chip Ambres was a No. 1 pick in 1998, while Jim Kavourias led the team with 23 home runs. But Smith is a couple years younger than either of them. He made an immediate impact after getting picked in the sixth round of the 2000 draft, ranking fourth in the Rookie-level Gulf Coast League with a .368 average. Smith continued to have success in the Class-A Midwest League last year, pacing the club in runs scored. The Marlins describe him as a pure hitter who finds a way to put the bat on the ball. He's adequate in left field and probably is confined to a corner position.

Claudio Vargas

Position: P
Bats: R **Throws:** R
Ht: 6' 3" **Wt:** 210

Opening Day Age: 22
Born: 5/19/79 in Valverde Mao, DR

Recent Statistics

	W	L	ERA	G	GS	Sv	IP	H	R	BB	SO	HR
2000 A Brevard Cty	10	5	3.28	24	23	0	145.1	126	64	44	143	10
2000 AA Portland	1	1	3.60	3	2	0	15.0	16	9	6	13	1
2001 AA Portland	8	9	4.19	27	27	0	159.0	122	77	67	151	25

Vargas is another example of the Marlins' efforts in mining talent from the Caribbean. He's from the Dominican Republic and signed with the organization at age 16. Although his record was under .500 at Double-A last year, his 151 strikeouts tied for second most in the Eastern League. And he was tough to hit, surrendering fewer than seven hits per nine innings. Vargas has three plus-pitches, including a low-90s fastball that can reach 95 MPH, a curveball and a changeup. He had a tendency to be hurt by the longball in 2001, as he shared the league lead with 25 home runs allowed. Nevertheless, the Marlins feel Vargas has a chance to be a front-end starter in the big leagues.

Others to Watch

Outfielder **Chris Aguila** (23), a third-round pick in 1997, made it to Double-A last season. He has decent tools, but the Marlins say he still needs experience. . . Righthander **Wes Anderson** (22), who has had injury problems in the past, underwent surgery on his labrum and may not be back until midseason of 2002. He went 1-6 in the Florida State League. . . **Benito Baez** (24) walked only seven batters while striking out 56 at Triple-A last year. He could see action as a lefty specialist with the Marlins. . . The Mets chose lefthander **Geoff Goetz** (22) with the sixth overall pick in 1997 and eventually traded him to the Marlins in the Mike Piazza deal. Goetz now pitches in relief and recorded a 1.53 ERA at Double-A in 2001. . . While righthander **Gary Knotts** (25) experienced shoulder problems near the end of last season, he reportedly will be ready to go by spring training. He's been a starter in the minors, but might be able to help in the Marlins' bullpen. . . Outfielder **Brett Roneberg** (23) was born in Australia and has spent six seasons in the Marlins' system. He does a nice job drawing walks and began showing more power last year, which he finished at Double-A Portland.

Enron Field

Offense

The offensive boost Enron Field provides is definite but not extreme. Yes, the average of 10.3 runs per game ranked fifth in the majors. But the Astros and their opponents combined to hit just .266 there. While the ball flies out to left field into the Crawford Boxes and beyond, right field plays even easier for power hitters. And long drives to center simply die.

Defense

It's a tricky outfield to play. Left field's challenges include the protrusion halfway up the line and the panels in the manual scoreboard, both of which can produce funny caroms. The columns and recesses in the wall extending from left to center also can generate unusual bounces, and the center-field flagpole is an obvious hazard. Right field looks relatively tame, but drives into the corner can scoot around for a while before being corralled.

Who It Helps the Most

Though most Astros thrived in Enron, the differences between their home and road performances weren't overly lopsided. After enduring perceived horrors in 2000, several Astros proved that you can pitch well in Enron if you. . . well, pitch well. Nelson Cruz, Octavio Dotel and Roy Oswalt had ERAs under 3.00 at home, while Billy Wagner limited opponents to a .205 batting average there.

Who It Hurts the Most

Pedro Astacio's ERA was a lofty 6.48 at Enron in 2001, compared to 3.99 away from his home park. Jose Lima's demons (10.08 ERA, .384 opponents' batting average at Enron) continued to haunt him, so he was sent to Detroit last June. Mike Jackson's ERA was significantly higher at home.

Rookies & Newcomers

The success of youngsters such as Wade Miller, Oswalt and Dotel should temper Enron's negative reputation among pitchers. But some reputations die hard, such as the park's knack for stimulating offense. Because it does happen, albeit not to the degree everybody thinks, hitters like potential new starters Morgan Ensberg and Adam Everett will continue to step eagerly into Enron's batter's box.

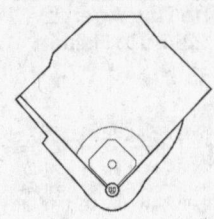

Dimensions: LF-315, LCF-362, CF-435, RCF-373, RF-326

Capacity: 40,950

Elevation: 22 feet

Surface: Grass

Foul Territory: Average

Park Factors

2001 Season

	Home Games			Away Games			
	Astros	Opp	Total	Astros	Opp	Total	Index
G	75	75	150	72	72	144	—
Avg	.276	.257	.266	.261	.260	.261	102
AB	2515	2624	5139	2494	2424	4918	100
R	408	366	774	351	309	660	113
H	694	674	1368	651	631	1282	102
2B	148	119	267	135	120	255	100
3B	19	13	32	10	11	21	146
HR	101	115	216	86	83	169	122
BB	264	219	483	269	217	486	95
SO	509	620	1129	506	511	1017	106
E	47	58	105	52	48	100	101
E-Infield	41	49	90	47	41	88	98
LHB-Avg	.312	.276	.287	.263	.258	.259	111
LHB-HR	20	55	75	22	30	52	146
RHB-Avg	.268	.243	.257	.261	.262	.261	98
RHB-HR	81	60	141	64	53	117	112

2000-2001

	Home Games			Away Games			
	Astros	Opp	Total	Astros	Opp	Total	Index
G	147	147	294	147	147	294	—
Avg	.279	.274	.276	.267	.266	.267	103
AB	4937	5241	10178	5138	4972	10110	101
R	871	828	1699	754	713	1467	116
H	1376	1434	2810	1373	1324	2697	104
2B	286	273	559	256	254	510	109
3B	43	40	83	20	27	47	175
HR	224	234	458	190	181	371	123
BB	577	492	1069	577	497	1074	99
SO	987	1112	2099	1053	974	2027	103
E	101	99	200	119	104	223	90
E-Infield	87	82	169	99	89	188	90
LHB-Avg	.295	.299	.298	.281	.273	.276	108
LHB-HR	59	113	172	48	76	124	144
RHB-Avg	.274	.255	.265	.262	.261	.262	101
RHB-HR	165	121	286	142	105	247	113

2001 Rankings (National League)

- Highest LHB home-run factor
- Second-highest LHB batting-average factor
- Third-highest triple factor
- Third-highest home-run factor
- Third-lowest walk factor

Jimy Williams

2001 Season

The fact that the Red Sox dismissed Jimy Williams as their manager came as no great shock. But he was let go on August 16, with the Red Sox only two games behind the wild-card leaders. Williams' ability to keep Boston in first place for over two months and build a 65-53 record despite numerous injuries struck many observers as remarkable.

Offense

Williams won't have trouble adjusting to the National League. He regularly used his entire 25-man roster, a common trait among NL skippers but less typical in the AL. Though he didn't always employ tactics such as the bunt or hit-and-run with the ponderous BoSox, he is willing to do so if his lineup warrants. Williams also likes to platoon, and he changes lineups more than any other manager. These tendencies could be tested in Houston, where entrenched veterans such as Craig Biggio and Jeff Bagwell might balk at frequent changes.

Pitching & Defense

It'll be just as intriguing to see how Williams' penchant for utilizing multiple pitchers meshes with the Astros' staff. His predecessor, Larry Dierker, allowed his starters to work out of trouble. By contrast, Williams tends to remove them at the first sign of duress. It should mean more work for Octavio Dotel, who emerged as a top setup man in 2001, and premier closer Billy Wagner. Williams wants to have his best defensive team on the field as much as possible, which prompts much platooning and dictates virtually all of his late-game substitutions. Good-hit, no-field Astros like Daryle Ward and Tony Eusebio could be in trouble.

2002 Outlook

Williams is no fool. He realizes he's taking over a team that has reached the playoffs four times in the previous five years. It also boasts legitimate Hall of Fame candidates in Bagwell and Biggio and some of the game's brightest young stars in Roy Oswalt, Wade Miller and Lance Berkman. Williams might be wise to strike a balance by leaving his top performers alone while devoting his energies to bolstering the team around them with his various devices.

Born: 10/04/43 in Santa Maria, CA

Playing Experience: 1966-1967, StL

Managerial Experience: 9 seasons

Manager Statistics

Year	Team, Lg	W	L	Pct	GB	Finish
2001	Boston, AL	65	53	.551	5.0	2nd East
9 Seasons		695	593	.539	—	—

2001 Starting Pitchers by Days Rest

	<=3	4	5	6+
Red Sox Starts	0	45	49	15
Red Sox ERA	—	4.72	3.59	4.38
AL Avg Starts	1	78	48	24
AL ERA	5.92	4.69	4.58	4.58

2001 Situational Stats

	Jimy Williams	AL Average
Hit & Run Success %	40.0	35.0
Stolen Base Success %	62.5	71.0
Platoon Pct.	64.5	59.1
Defensive Subs	26	26
High-Pitch Outings	5	6
Quick/Slow Hooks	26/4	19/16
Sacrifice Attempts	31	54

2001 Rankings (American League)

- 1st in fewest caught stealings of second base (16), fewest caught stealings of third base (1), pitchouts (106) and pitchouts with a runner moving (29)
- 2nd in sacrifice-bunt percentage (83.9%) and quick hooks
- 3rd in hit-and-run success percentage

Moises Alou

2001 Season

Surrounded by stellar teammates, Moises Alou nevertheless was called the Astros' most indispensable performer by many people who closely followed the team. He was Houston's most productive player in clutch situations, hitting .353 from the seventh inning on and .388 with runners in scoring position and two outs. Still prone to nagging injuries, Alou was bothered twice by a strained right calf, one of the ailments that plagued him in 2000.

Hitting

Alou has no glaring weaknesses at the plate, as his career statistics indicate. Renowned as one of the best fastball hitters around, he also victimizes pitchers who try to throw him repeated breaking pitches. He's a pull-oriented hitter at cozy Enron Field but remains more than capable of driving the ball to other fields at any park. Practically the only way to pitch Alou is to pound fastballs low and away or up and in under his hands—though tying him up with inside pitches is difficult.

Baserunning & Defense

Alou is a fundamentally sound baserunner who can take the extra base. However, with his history of leg injuries, he is less prone to gamble on the basepaths. He is not a true basestealing threat. Defensively, Alou has regressed due to his physical problems. His move to right field, a less tricky spot to play at Enron, has minimized his shortcomings. He's a little more adept at going back on balls than coming in on them. His arm, though strong, isn't accurate.

2002 Outlook

Alou was an intriguing player on the free-agent market. His bat could help make any team a contender. But age and physical erosion prevents him from being everybody's first or second choice. Alou wanted a three-year contract; the Astros were said to be willing to offer two years at a less-than-exorbitant amount. It was up to Alou to determine whether staying at Enron with a potent lineup was worth taking less money. Suitors had to notice his ability to hit away from Enron. He probably could thrive as a designated hitter for two or three years.

Position: RF
Bats: R **Throws:** R
Ht: 6' 3" **Wt:** 195

Opening Day Age: 35
Born: 7/3/66 in Atlanta, GA
ML Seasons: 10
Pronunciation: MOY-sezz ah-LOO

Overall Statistics

	G	AB	R	H	D	T	HR	RBI	SB	BB	SO	Avg	OBP	Slg
2001	136	513	79	170	31	1	27	108	5	57	57	.331	.396	.554
Career	1181	4238	696	1297	260	29	202	834	81	446	578	.306	.372	.524

Where He Hits the Ball

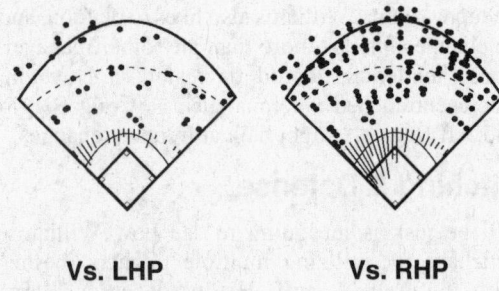

Vs. LHP   **Vs. RHP**

2001 Situational Stats

	AB	H	HR	RBI	Avg		AB	H	HR	RBI	Avg
Home	264	90	15	62	.341	LHP	99	42	5	21	.424
Road	249	80	12	46	.321	RHP	414	128	22	87	.309
First Half	287	104	18	65	.362	Sc Pos	158	51	5	80	.323
Scnd Half	226	66	9	43	.292	Clutch	76	30	6	20	.395

2001 Rankings (National League)

- 3rd in batting average, batting average in the clutch, fielding percentage in right field (.991) and highest percentage of swings on the first pitch (46.8)
- 5th in assists in right field (10)
- 7th in batting average on the road and fewest pitches seen per plate appearance (3.24)
- Led the Astros in batting average, intentional walks (14), batting average in the clutch and batting average at home

Pedro Astacio

Position: SP
Bats: R **Throws:** R
Ht: 6' 2" **Wt:** 210

Opening Day Age: 32
Born: 11/28/69 in Hato Mayor, Dominican Republic
ML Seasons: 10
Pronunciation: ah-STAH-see-oh

2001 Season

The strain of pitching at Coors Field may have finally beaten down Pedro Astacio last season. After finishing with a 47-35 record for the Rockies from 1997-2000, he posted a 6-13 record for them last year. In addition, he came down with inflammation in his throwing shoulder less than a month after being traded to Houston last July 31 for righthander Scott Elarton and a player to be named (Garett Gentry). The injury eventually was diagnosed as a torn labrum, and Astacio never pitched after August 21. Until then, he had managed to escape serious injury in his career.

Pitching

With his loose-limbed motion, Astacio had seemed impervious to injury. His ability to coax groundballs helped him succeed at Coors Field, where virtually every other pitcher has struggled. Astacio was capable of looking downright dominant on occasion, as long as he maintained command of his darting fastball, which travels in the range of 90 MPH. He also could summon a hard-breaking curveball, a decent sinker and an arresting changeup, which he'd use to neutralize lefthanded batters. Astacio's bugaboo often was one bad inning in which he'd implode without warning. If he could avoid or survive that, he had a good chance of proceeding to victory.

Defense & Hitting

A fluid athlete, Astacio performs all of a pitcher's defensive tasks with little trouble. The lapses that occasionally strike him on the mound also can hurt him in the field. He's quick with his pickoff move as well as with his delivery to the plate, which helps discourage basestealers. Astacio is a better hitter than he showed last year (.094), though his 11 sacrifice bunts reflected his ability with the bat.

2002 Outlook

The good news for Astacio is that he should recover in time to pitch this year. The bad news is that he was eligible for free agency this offseason, so his injury severely limited his earning potential. Nor were the Astros inclined to pick up his $9 million option. He will get a chance to pitch again, but his career is clearly at a crossroads.

Overall Statistics

	W	L	Pct.	ERA	G	GS	Sv	IP	H	BB	SO	HR	Ratio
2001	8	14	.364	5.09	26	26	0	169.2	181	54	144	22	1.39
Career	103	96	.518	4.50	308	265	0	1742.2	1798	572	1366	218	1.36

How Often He Throws Strikes

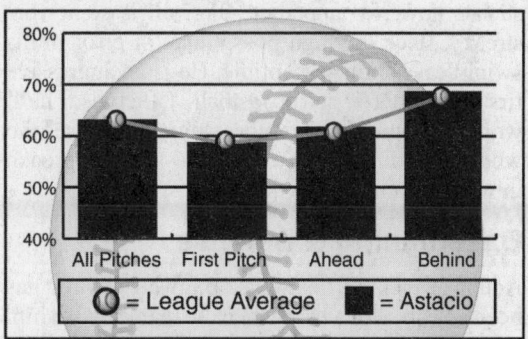

2001 Situational Stats

	W	L	ERA	Sv	IP		AB	H	HR	RBI	Avg
Home	3	6	6.48	0	75.0	LHB	304	87	10	43	.286
Road	5	8	3.99	0	94.2	RHB	351	94	12	49	.268
First Half	6	9	5.18	0	116.1	Sc Pos	157	45	5	66	.287
Scnd Half	2	5	4.89	0	53.1	Clutch	31	8	2	4	.258

2001 Rankings (National League)

- 4th in complete games (4)
- 5th in lowest winning percentage (.364)
- 6th in most run support per nine innings (5.9)
- 7th in losses (14), hit batsmen (13), runners caught stealing (9) and highest ERA (5.09)
- 9th in highest slugging percentage allowed (.461)

Houston

Jeff Bagwell

2001 Season

Though Jeff Bagwell's batting average dipped below .300 for the first time since 1997, he became the only player in history to collect 30 home runs, 100 runs scored, 100 RBI and 100 walks for six consecutive seasons. Still, he began absorbing barbs from Houston fans. They pointed out that Bagwell hit only .278 if you take away July, when he was named NL Player of the Month. They insisted he doesn't drive in enough clutch runs, and they decried his career-high 135 strikeouts.

Hitting

Bagwell's swing ought to be labeled, "Don't try this at home." Rare is the player who can control such a powerful uppercut. Bagwell is somewhat streaky, since the high possibility for error in his swing leaves him susceptible. He is an aggressive first-ball hitter if fed a fastball. Otherwise, he'll work the count. Unlike most sluggers, he uses the whole field and adapts a wise two-strike approach in which he cuts his swing a tad.

Baserunning & Defense

Adept at picking his spots, Bagwell always has been able to steal a base when the team needed him to get into scoring position. Last year he was successful on 11 of 14 attempts. He is a fundamentally sound baserunner, enabling him to break up double plays and take extra bases. Bagwell plays first base with the same intensity he brings to the plate. He won't hesitate to throw to any base on bunt plays or grounders, and he's constantly in proper position on popups.

2002 Outlook

Barring a cataclysmic transaction, Bagwell will finish his career in Houston since he's signed through 2006. He underwent offseason surgery to repair a torn labrum in his right shoulder, an injury he apparently played through for most of 2001. Despite that and last year's batting average, however, he shows no signs of slowing down. Bagwell never has dwelled on personal achievements, yet he can derive extra incentive from having 2,000 career hits and 400 home runs within his sights.

Position: 1B
Bats: R **Throws:** R
Ht: 6' 0" **Wt:** 195

Opening Day Age: 33
Born: 5/27/68 in Boston, MA
ML Seasons: 11
Pronunciation: BAG-well

Overall Statistics

	G	AB	R	H	D	T	HR	RBI	SB	BB	SO	Avg	OBP	Slg
2001	161	600	126	173	43	4	39	130	11	106	135	.288	.397	.568
Career	1637	5949	1199	1803	394	26	349	1223	178	1098	1157	.303	.415	.554

Where He Hits the Ball

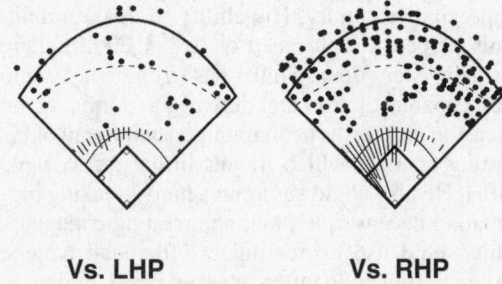

Vs. LHP   Vs. RHP

2001 Situational Stats

	AB	H	HR	RBI	Avg		AB	H	HR	RBI	Avg
Home	301	92	21	72	.306	LHP	98	29	5	22	.296
Road	299	81	18	58	.271	RHP	502	144	34	108	.287
First Half	327	88	21	68	.269	Sc Pos	151	52	14	95	.344
Scnd Half	273	85	18	62	.311	Clutch	83	16	1	8	.193

2001 Rankings (National League)

- 1st in assists at first base (143)
- 2nd in pitches seen (2,890) and errors at first base (12)
- 3rd in walks and plate appearances (717)
- 4th in games played and lowest fielding percentage at first base (.992)
- Led the Astros in home runs, runs scored, RBI, walks, strikeouts, GDPs (20), pitches seen (2,890), plate appearances (717), games played, HR frequency (15.4 ABs per HR), most pitches seen per plate appearance (4.03), highest percentage of pitches taken (59.0), steals of third (2), highest percentage of extra bases taken as a runner (61.3) and lowest percentage of swings on the first pitch (27.6)

Lance Berkman

2001 Season

The page devoted to Lance Berkman in this publication last year said he had "a chance to become a true multi-skilled offensive threat." Mission accomplished. His first full season in the majors was prodigious, as Berkman led the National League with 55 doubles and ranked among the top 10 in numerous other offensive categories. His doubles and extra-base hits (94) totals were the most ever by a switch-hitter. He also made his first of what could be many appearances on the All-Star team.

Hitting

Capable of batting anywhere from third through fifth in the lineup, Berkman settled into the cleanup spot. He combines the eagerness of a hitter who likes to swing at the first or second pitch with the patience of an artist who drew 92 walks last season. From the right side, Berkman likes the ball high; from the left, he's fairly relentless with the exception of a hole in his swing on pitches up and in. Berkman improved dramatically as a righthanded batter, hiking his average 90 points from that side. But he boasts substantially more power lefthanded. Any team hoping to neutralize him late in the game had better heat up its southpaw relievers.

Baserunning & Defense

Berkman has good first-step quickness breaking from the lefthanded batter's box. But his stolen-base success rate of 44 percent showed that he could stand to learn the element of surprise from teammate Jeff Bagwell. Berkman doesn't embarrass himself in the outfield. He appears to have found a home in left, which can be challenging at Enron due to its nooks and crannies. Though Berkman started 40 games in center field, he's not entirely a natural for that position.

2002 Outlook

Since Berkman barely has more than two years of service time, the Astros can lowball him for one more season before they have to start paying him what he's worth. They might find it economical to lock him up with a multiyear deal, similar to the four-year, $32 million agreement they reached with Richard Hidalgo before last season.

Position: LF/CF
Bats: B **Throws:** L
Ht: 6' 1" **Wt:** 205

Opening Day Age: 26
Born: 2/10/76 in Waco, TX
ML Seasons: 3

Overall Statistics

	G	AB	R	H	D	T	HR	RBI	SB	BB	SO	Avg	OBP	Slg
2001	156	577	110	191	55	5	34	126	7	92	121	.331	.430	.620
Career	304	1023	196	318	85	6	59	208	18	160	215	.311	.406	.579

Where He Hits the Ball

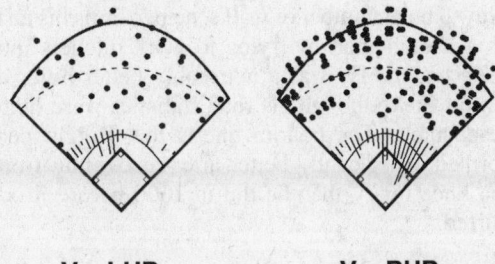

Vs. LHP   **Vs. RHP**

2001 Situational Stats

	AB	H	HR	RBI	Avg		AB	H	HR	RBI	Avg
Home	277	93	13	56	.336	LHP	120	37	2	13	.308
Road	300	98	21	70	.327	RHP	457	154	32	113	.337
First Half	315	115	25	79	.365	Sc Pos	167	52	7	84	.311
Scnd Half	262	76	9	47	.290	Clutch	91	28	7	21	.308

2001 Rankings (National League)

- 1st in doubles
- Led the Astros in hits, doubles, triples, total bases (358), times on base (296), slugging percentage, on-base percentage, fewest GDPs per GDP situation (5.7%), batting average with the bases loaded (.471), batting average vs. lefthanded pitchers, batting average vs. righthanded pitchers, cleanup slugging percentage (.598), slugging percentage vs. lefthanded pitchers (.467), slugging percentage vs. righthanded pitchers (.661), on-base percentage vs. lefthanded pitchers (.400), on-base percentage vs. righthanded pitchers (.438), batting average on the road and batting average on a 3-2 count (.296)

Houston

Craig Biggio

2001 Season

Craig Biggio made an admirable recovery from reconstructive knee surgery. He returned to the leadoff spot, flashed the power that has distinguished him from other hitters at the top of the order and lifted his batting average 24 points from 2000. The two tears he suffered in his left knee while trying to turn a double play affected him, but he managed to minimize their impact.

Hitting

A few years ago, it was impossible to jam Biggio. But his ability to turn on inside pitches was lacking when last season opened. However, he adjusted as the year progressed and resumed driving many of those pitches with authority. While Biggio doesn't draw a huge number of walks, he performs his task as a leadoff man by trying to work pitchers into deep counts. He was a noticeably better hitter at Enron Field, though his road statistics were quite respectable. The bottom line is that Biggio performed significantly better after recovering from his knee injury than he did in 2000 before it occurred.

Baserunning & Defense

These facets of Biggio's play have suffered the most. He took shorter leads from first base and his 11 steal attempts were a career low for a full season. This contrasted sharply with the period from 1994-99, when he never swiped fewer than 25 bases. Then again, some of Biggio's decreased mobility could have stemmed simply from age, not just the injury. His 35 doubles and three triples indicate he remained capable of taking the extra base. Although he committed only 11 errors, his range looked noticeably diminished. His arm never was remarkably strong, but he has compensated by getting rid of relays more quickly—an adjustment which partly masked his decline in the field.

2002 Outlook

Knee and all, Biggio remains an above-average performer who does things few other leadoff batters can. His contract runs through 2003, and with what he has endured (and achieved) he doesn't need to play his way into another multiyear deal. Nevertheless, he'll definitely continue to play hard.

Position: 2B
Bats: R **Throws:** R
Ht: 5'11" **Wt:** 180

Opening Day Age: 36
Born: 12/14/65 in Smithtown, NY
ML Seasons: 14
Pronunciation: BIDG-ee-oh

Overall Statistics

	G	AB	R	H	D	T	HR	RBI	SB	BB	SO	Avg	OBP	Slg
2001	155	617	118	180	35	3	20	70	7	66	100	.292	.382	.455
Career	1955	7383	1305	2149	437	46	180	811	365	913	1146	.291	.381	.436

Where He Hits the Ball

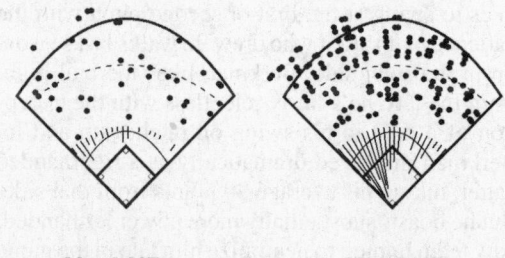

Vs. LHP	Vs. RHP

2001 Situational Stats

	AB	H	HR	RBI	Avg		AB	H	HR	RBI	Avg
Home	301	95	10	31	.316	LHP	108	24	6	13	.222
Road	316	85	10	39	.269	RHP	509	156	14	57	.306
First Half	332	100	14	38	.301	Sc Pos	98	38	2	47	.388
Scnd Half	285	80	6	32	.281	Clutch	77	18	2	12	.234

2001 Rankings (National League)

- 1st in hit by pitch (28), batting average with runners in scoring position and on-base percentage for a leadoff hitter (.378)
- 2nd in lowest batting average vs. lefthanded pitchers
- 3rd in plate appearances (717)
- 4th in errors at second base (11)
- 5th in fielding percentage at second base (.984)
- Led the Astros in at-bats, singles, hit by pitch (28), plate appearances (717), highest ground-ball-flyball ratio (1.3), batting average with runners in scoring position, batting average on an 0-2 count (.286), on-base percentage for a leadoff hitter (.378) and batting average with two strikes (.239)

Vinny Castilla

2001 Season

If the Comeback Player of the Year Award could be given to somebody overcoming adverse circumstances within a season instead of from one year to the next, Vinny Castilla would have been the runaway winner for 2001. Released by lowly Tampa Bay on May 10 after hitting .215 for the Devil Rays, Castilla signed with the Astros on May 15. He blasted the first of his 23 homers that night, a total that fell two shy of Doug Rader's single-season franchise record for third basemen set in 1970.

Hitting

Formerly one of the National League's best fastball hitters, Castilla has lost a little bat speed. He still has enough to get around on most pitches, but his strikeout rate in 2001 was the highest of his career. Scouts taking a hard look at Castilla thought he lost 10-12 pounds, which helped all facets of his game, including his swing. Pitchers try to get Castilla out by crowding him so that he'll look inside, before victimizing him with sliders away. Skeptics may want to dismiss his resurgence as a product of playing at Enron Field. But they need only check Castilla's home and road statistics to see he did much better elsewhere.

Baserunning & Defense

All those years playing in Coors Field taught Castilla to run the bases efficiently. Though he lacks impressive speed, he's fast enough to take an additional base. He still charges balls well, which, combined with his above-average arm, helps him thrive defensively. He seemed to improve in the field as the season progressed, a natural byproduct of staying healthy and playing daily.

2002 Outlook

If Castilla stays healthy and in decent physical condition, he should be able to duplicate his 2001 output for at least one more season. Atlanta, the organization that originally signed Castilla in 1990, inked him to a much larger two-year, $8 million deal in December. While Castilla pushes Chipper Jones into the outfield in Atlanta, the Astros probably turn to Chris Truby or prospect Morgan Ensberg at third base.

Position: 3B
Bats: R **Throws:** R
Ht: 6' 1" **Wt:** 205

Opening Day Age: 34
Born: 7/4/67 in Oaxaca, Mexico
ML Seasons: 11
Pronunciation: cas-TEE-yah

Overall Statistics

	G	AB	R	H	D	T	HR	RBI	SB	BB	SO	Avg	OBP	Slg
2001	146	538	69	140	34	1	25	91	1	35	108	.260	.308	.467
Career	1187	4385	609	1262	209	19	234	744	24	272	670	.288	.331	.504

Where He Hits the Ball

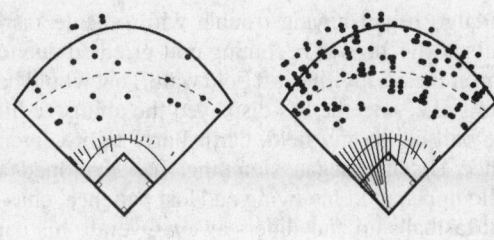

Vs. LHP   **Vs. RHP**

2001 Situational Stats

	AB	H	HR	RBI	Avg		AB	H	HR	RBI	Avg
Home	269	63	12	43	.234	LHP	79	20	4	9	.253
Road	269	77	13	48	.286	RHP	459	120	21	82	.261
First Half	265	70	9	38	.264	Sc Pos	163	47	7	69	.288
Scnd Half	273	70	16	53	.256	Clutch	83	16	1	8	.193

2001 Rankings (National League)
- 2nd in lowest percentage of pitches taken (42.0)
- 4th in fielding percentage at third base (.963)

Houston

Richard Hidalgo

2001 Season

There were times when Richard Hidalgo batted as low as seventh in the Astros lineup last season. That wasn't quite what he or the team had planned after his huge 2000 campaign (.314-44-122). It's easy to cite possible sources of Hidalgo's dropoff. He gained weight. He missed 11 games with a groin strain and acute tonsillitis. The Astros gave him a four-year, $32 million contract before last season, so perhaps he imperceptibly lost some of his drive or tried too hard to justify all that money. Then again, Hidalgo's only 26. Time will tell whether this was an isolated bad year or the start of a slide.

Hitting

Hidalgo began having trouble with outside fast-balls, a sign he was becoming pull-oriented due to Enron Field's inviting left field wall. That would be a mistake, since he has displayed the ability to hit the ball out to any field, particularly right-center. Once Hidalgo began slumping, he developed a mild uppercut in his swing and lost patience, chasing fastballs up and sliders away. Overall, his bat didn't look as quick as it did in 2000, helping pitchers discover a hole in his swing on deliveries up and in.

Baserunning & Defense

Hidalgo's weight gain shouldn't obscure the fact that he plays hard. But his groin problem and thicker body seemed to discourage him from running. His doubles total dropped from 42 to 29, and his steal attempts dipped from 19 to eight. Defensively, Hidalgo didn't show the range that a center fielder should, though he has decent instincts and a very strong arm. He may be better suited for right field.

2002 Outlook

Hidalgo isn't going anywhere. Not just because of his contract status, but also because he'll be needed to help shore up the offense if Moises Alou departs as a free agent. It's ridiculous to think Hidalgo can't bounce back and have a decent season. Perhaps expecting him to duplicate his 2000 numbers was unrealistic. His true level probably lies somewhere between the past two years.

Position: CF/RF/LF
Bats: R **Throws:** R
Ht: 6' 3"   **Wt:** 190

Opening Day Age: 26
Born: 7/2/75 in Caracas, Venezuela
ML Seasons: 5
Pronunciation: HUH-dahl-go

Overall Statistics

	G	AB	R	H	D	T	HR	RBI	SB	BB	SO	Avg	OBP	Slg
2001	146	512	70	141	29	3	19	80	3	54	107	.275	.356	.455
Career	500	1726	276	486	116	8	87	299	28	187	345	.282	.361	.509

Where He Hits the Ball

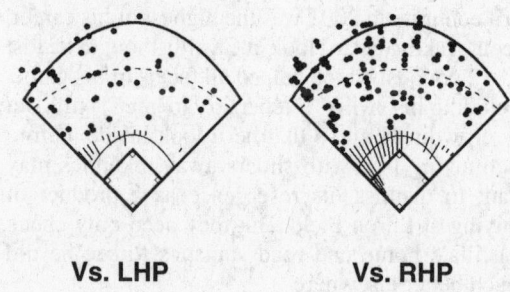

Vs. LHP   **Vs. RHP**

2001 Situational Stats

	AB	H	HR	RBI	Avg		AB	H	HR	RBI	Avg
Home	251	72	13	49	.287	LHP	105	30	3	18	.286
Road	261	69	6	31	.264	RHP	407	111	16	62	.273
First Half	272	73	13	49	.268	Sc Pos	148	37	3	54	.250
Scnd Half	240	68	6	31	.283	Clutch	93	18	4	16	.194

2001 Rankings (National League)

- 1st in lowest batting average with the bases loaded (0.000)
- 4th in sacrifice flies (11), hit by pitch (16), fielding percentage in center field (.990) and assists in center field (8)
- Led the Astros in sacrifice flies (11)

Julio Lugo

2001 Season

Julio Lugo continued to show signs of developing into a handy, heady player. Although his batting average dropped 20 points, his 15 sacrifice bunts and seven sacrifice flies—both sharp increases from 2000—indicate that he was focused on doing what he could to contribute. Lugo's power was streaky, as he homered eight times in his first 125 at-bats but only twice in 388 subsequent at-bats. Those last two homers happened to come off Arizona's Curt Schilling and Randy Johnson in a span of three at-bats.

Hitting

Lugo remains a work in progress. His selectivity is lacking, as shown by his tendency to swing at too many pitcher's pitches. He falls prey to the basic offensive antidote—he gets crowded up and in early in the count, then chases low-and-away sliders later in the at-bat once he expands his strike zone. All Lugo needs is a little plate discipline, because he has good bat speed. He'll occasionally try to capitalize on his speed by drag-bunting. His slight build belies his power, which can only be enhanced by playing at Enron Field.

Baserunning & Defense

Now that Craig Biggio has slowed down, Lugo is Houston's only "speed" player. Yet his stolen-base rate was subpar last year, revealing that he hasn't learned to read pitchers and consistently get a good jump. Consistency also is the key on defense. Lugo has OK range and a strong arm, but he is prone to committing errors on the most routine plays. He takes plenty of extra grounders, so he simply needs to relax and let his ability carry him.

2002 Outlook

Lugo may have to battle highly touted prospect Adam Everett for his position this spring, although serious doubts remain about Everett's offensive ability. Lugo underwent minor knee surgery in November, but should be OK when camp opens. The Astros likely will stick with Lugo at shortstop for the time being. He looked comfortable in 40 starts at second base in 2000, and he eventually could move there after Biggio retires.

Position: SS
Bats: R **Throws:** R
Ht: 5'10" **Wt:** 165

Opening Day Age: 26
Born: 11/16/75 in Barahona, Dominican Republic
ML Seasons: 2

Overall Statistics

	G	AB	R	H	D	T	HR	RBI	SB	BB	SO	Avg	OBP	Slg
2001	140	513	93	135	20	3	10	37	12	46	116	.263	.326	.372
Career	256	933	171	254	42	8	20	77	34	83	209	.272	.335	.399

Where He Hits the Ball

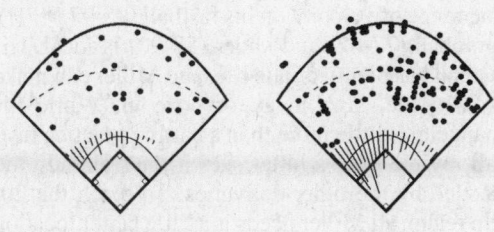

Vs. LHP   **Vs. RHP**

2001 Situational Stats

	AB	H	HR	RBI	Avg		AB	H	HR	RBI	Avg
Home	269	72	6	21	.268	LHP	107	32	1	3	.299
Road	244	63	4	16	.258	RHP	406	103	9	34	.254
First Half	287	81	10	25	.282	Sc Pos	94	19	1	25	.202
Scnd Half	226	54	0	12	.239	Clutch	65	11	0	1	.169

2001 Rankings (National League)

- 2nd in lowest stolen-base percentage (52.2)
- 3rd in bunts in play (32) and errors at shortstop (22)
- 4th in lowest batting average with runners in scoring position
- 5th in lowest fielding percentage at shortstop (.964)
- 6th in sacrifice bunts (15)
- Led the Astros in sacrifice bunts (15), stolen bases, caught stealing (11), stolen-base percentage (52.2) and bunts in play (32)

Wade Miller

2001 Season

Wade Miller developed into the ace of Houston's staff in his first full season in the big leagues. Examples of his consistency abounded: he pitched at least six innings in 28 of 32 starts, he allowed three earned runs or less 23 times, and the Astros were 22-10 when he pitched. He posted a .500 record after the All-Star break but improved both his ERA and opponents' batting average.

Pitching

Miller has a chance to become the National League's next great pitcher. All his deliveries—fastball, curveball, slider and changeup—are well above average, and he uses each of them aggressively and intelligently on both sides of the plate. The range of velocity on his fastball (95-97 MPH), curveball (77-82) and slider (88-90) is ideal. His fastball has plenty of late life, and Miller can make it tail, ride, sink away or bore in. While his changeup is little more than a batting practice fastball, by the time a hitter sees it, he's already too dazzled by the other deliveries. To reach the 20-win realm, all Miller needs is a little better location and increased knowledge of how to use his vast repertoire. The 31 homers he allowed last year shows a tendency to make mistakes in the heart of the strike zone.

Defense & Hitting

Miller isn't a completely polished defender yet, but is athletic enough to become one. His ability to hold runners should improve with experience. His .167 batting average was an upgrade over his rookie season, suggesting he might develop into the type of pitcher who can help himself with the bat. He and Shane Reynolds laid down the most sacrifice bunts among Astros pitchers, with 10 apiece.

2002 Outlook

Nothing should stop Miller from establishing himself further. He already has proven that he can survive at Enron Field and endure the pressure of a division race. The Astros would be wise to sign Miller to a long-term contract soon. If they don't, arbitration will drive his salary to the stratosphere once he becomes eligible for the process.

Position: SP
Bats: R **Throws:** R
Ht: 6' 2" **Wt:** 185

Opening Day Age: 25
Born: 9/13/76 in Reading, PA
ML Seasons: 3

Overall Statistics

	W	L	Pct.	ERA	G	GS	Sv	IP	H	BB	SO	HR	Ratio
2001	16	8	.667	3.40	32	32	0	212.0	183	76	183	31	1.22
Career	22	15	.595	4.15	53	49	0	327.1	304	123	280	49	1.30

How Often He Throws Strikes

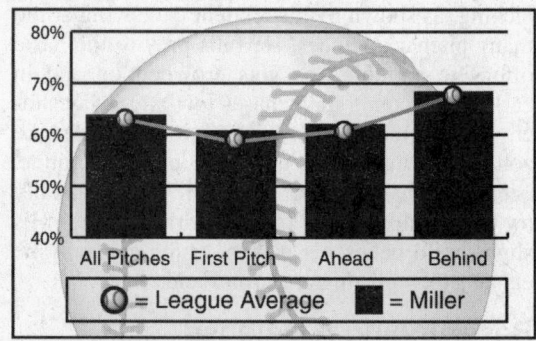

= League Average   = Miller

2001 Situational Stats

	W	L	ERA	Sv	IP		AB	H	HR	RBI	Avg
Home	8	3	4.08	0	90.1	LHB	365	79	14	42	.216
Road	8	5	2.88	0	121.2	RHB	416	104	17	44	.250
First Half	11	3	3.79	0	121.0	Sc Pos	147	35	5	52	.238
Scnd Half	5	5	2.87	0	91.0	Clutch	53	7	1	2	.132

2001 Rankings (National League)

- 4th in runners caught stealing (13)
- 5th in lowest ERA on the road
- Led the Astros in ERA, wins, games started, innings pitched, batters faced (873), home runs allowed, walks allowed, strikeouts, wild pitches (8), pitches thrown (3,338), pickoff throws (62), stolen bases allowed (10), runners caught stealing (13), lowest batting average allowed (.234), lowest slugging percentage allowed (.399), lowest on-base percentage allowed (.304), lowest stolen-base percentage allowed (43.5), lowest ERA on the road, lowest batting average allowed vs. lefthanded batters, lowest batting average allowed with runners in scoring position and most strikeouts per nine innings (7.8)

Roy Oswalt

2001 Season

Some might argue that Roy Oswalt, not Wade Miller, is the Astros' true ace. Oswalt's outstanding first-year performance included a 12-2 record as a starter, as he led major league rookies in ERA and winning percentage. A late-season groin injury prevented him from compiling even better numbers. He became the third pitcher in history whose team won his first eight starts; St. Louis' Allen Watson (1993) and Los Angeles' Fernando Valenzuela (1981) were the others. With all due respect to Watson, Oswalt's career seems poised to follow Valenzuela's impressive path more closely.

Pitching

It was impossible to tell Oswalt was a rookie last year, since his demeanor betrayed absolutely no fear. Oswalt's lively fastball often was clocked at 89-93 MPH, but occasionally reached as high as 95-96. Later in the season, his velocity decreased slightly when pitching out of the stretch, which might have been a symptom of his groin injury. Oswalt complements his fastball with a sharp-breaking curveball, a crisp slider (83-86 MPH) and a changeup that he used primarily against lefthanded batters. As his 6-to-1 strikeout-walk ratio demonstrated, he has solid command of all his pitches.

Defense & Hitting

You can bet that Oswalt's groin injury will lead the Astros to watch carefully when he dashes from the mound to field a bunt or cover first base. But Oswalt's spry athleticism should allow him to avoid any future difficulties. He can hit fastballs as well as throw them, batting .191 last year. His nine hits ranked second to Miller's 11 among Astros pitchers.

2002 Outlook

If Oswalt and Miller stay healthy and develop the sort of friendly rivalry in which they're continually trying to top each other, the National League is in huge trouble for a long time. Should Carlos Hernandez or Tim Redding develop into a capable pitcher, the Astros will have a starting trio that rivals Oakland's Tim Hudson, Mark Mulder and Barry Zito in its youth and accomplishment.

Position: SP
Bats: R **Throws:** R
Ht: 6' 0" **Wt:** 170

Opening Day Age: 24
Born: 8/29/77 in Kosciusko, MS
ML Seasons: 1
Pronunciation: OH-swalt

Overall Statistics

	W	L	Pct.	ERA	G	GS	Sv	IP	H	BB	SO	HR	Ratio
2001	14	3	.824	2.73	28	20	0	141.2	126	24	144	13	1.06
Career	14	3	.824	2.73	28	20	0	141.2	126	24	144	13	1.06

How Often He Throws Strikes

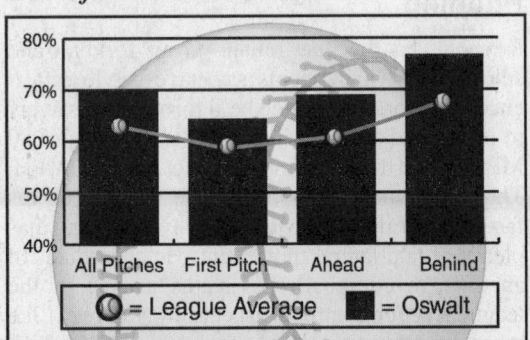

= League Average   = Oswalt

2001 Situational Stats

	W	L	ERA	Sv	IP		AB	H	HR	RBI	Avg
Home	8	1	2.15	0	83.2	LHB	274	66	5	18	.241
Road	6	2	3.57	0	58.0	RHB	263	60	8	27	.228
First Half	7	1	2.26	0	51.2	Sc Pos	100	20	3	29	.200
Scnd Half	7	2	3.00	0	90.0	Clutch	30	6	0	4	.200

2001 Rankings (National League)

- 1st in winning percentage and wins among rookies
- 2nd in lowest ERA at home
- 7th in complete games (3)
- Led the Astros in complete games (3), winning percentage and lowest ERA at home

Shane Reynolds

2001 Season

Overcoming a sequence of injuries, Shane Reynolds doubled his 2000 victory total. He had missed most of the second half of 2000 with a degenerative disk problem in his lower back. He then began last year on the disabled list with a torn lateral meniscus in his left knee, but recovered smoothly and launched a streak in May in which he worked seven-plus innings in nine of 10 starts. After returning to the DL in mid-August with a lower back strain, he remained healthy down the stretch. His win on the final day of the regular season was his 100th career victory and clinched the National League Central for the Astros.

Pitching

Reynolds has become reliant on his forkball and split-finger, which scouts say have subtle differences. His forkball, which he'll throw aggressively to lefthanded and righthanded hitters, averages 80 MPH, while the split-finger travels at 82-83 MPH. Though Reynolds has lost a little velocity on his fastball, it ranges between 87-91 MPH and has plenty of late lateral movement. He also mixes in an average curveball. His status as one of the league's better control artists hasn't suffered. Like most hurlers who rely on sinking deliveries, Reynolds primarily encounters trouble when his pitches stay up.

Defense & Hitting

Reynolds hit .077 last year, following a .225 average in 2000. He did manage to clobber his fifth career homer and garnished that with 10 sacrifice bunts, sharing the team lead among pitchers. Always fundamentally attentive, Reynolds recorded his third consecutive errorless season. Like most Houston pitchers, he holds runners on base well.

2002 Outlook

This is a year of decision for the Astros and Reynolds. His contract expires after the season, though the club holds an option on his services for 2003. If one or more of Houston's younger starters falters or if Reynolds wins 15-20 games, the Astros will have no choice but to keep him. But if his performance slips or the team goes on an austerity kick, he'll be bound for free agency.

Position: SP
Bats: R **Throws:** R
Ht: 6' 3" **Wt:** 210

Opening Day Age: 34
Born: 3/26/68 in Bastrop, LA
ML Seasons: 10

Overall Statistics

	W	L	Pct.	ERA	G	GS	Sv	IP	H	BB	SO	HR	Ratio
2001	14	11	.560	4.34	28	28	0	182.2	208	36	102	24	1.34
Career	100	80	.556	3.91	261	235	0	1548.1	1658	332	1262	158	1.29

How Often He Throws Strikes

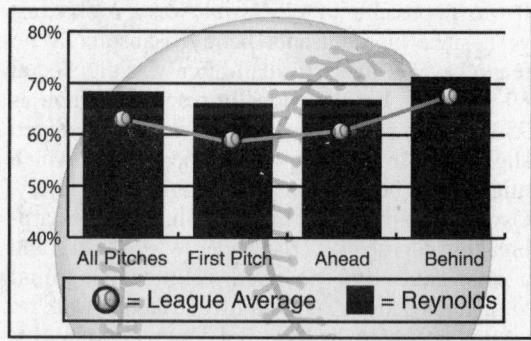

2001 Situational Stats

	W	L	ERA	Sv	IP		AB	H	HR	RBI	Avg
Home	7	6	5.44	0	89.1	LHB	327	99	11	40	.303
Road	7	5	3.28	0	93.1	RHB	390	109	13	45	.279
First Half	8	7	4.59	0	100.0	Sc Pos	151	48	3	57	.318
Scnd Half	6	4	4.03	0	82.2	Clutch	33	11	1	2	.333

2001 Rankings (National League)

- 1st in fielding percentage at pitcher (1.000)
- 2nd in fewest pitches thrown per batter (3.30)
- 3rd in highest ERA at home
- 4th in highest batting average allowed with runners in scoring position
- Led the Astros in losses, complete games (3), hits allowed, GDPs induced (19), highest strikeout-walk ratio (2.8), highest groundball-flyball ratio allowed (1.9), fewest pitches thrown per batter (3.30), most run support per nine innings (5.6), fewest home runs allowed per nine innings (1.18), most GDPs induced per nine innings (0.9) and fewest walks per nine innings (1.8)

Billy Wagner

Position: RP
Bats: L **Throws:** L
Ht: 5'11" **Wt:** 180

Opening Day Age: 30
Born: 7/25/71 in
Tannersville, VA
ML Seasons: 7

2001 Season

Billy Wagner suffered a partially torn flexor tendon that required surgery in June of 2000. But he showed no ill effects from the injury and re-established himself as one of baseball's top closers last season. The Astros received a scare last June when Wagner suffered a mild strain in his left forearm and landed on the 15-day disabled list. But he recovered smoothly, earned a save the day after he was activated from the DL and resumed a streak of 18 converted opportunities in a row.

Pitching

It's always startling when Wagner gets pounded, which does happen once in a while. It occurs simply because there's no mystery to what he does. His fastball regularly exceeds 95 MPH and often hits 98 MPH, and he throws it nearly 90 percent of the time. Even his slider travels in the 86-87 MPH range. Wagner always has defied the percentages by dominating righthanded hitters, mainly because he isn't afraid to pound his fastball inside against them. Though every closer must have a "gunslinger" approach, few wear that attitude as well as Wagner, who truly enjoys the challenge.

Defense & Hitting

Wagner is a non-factor as a hitter, not because he's incapable of swinging the bat, but because he hasn't been called upon to try. He never batted last year after having just two at-bats in 2000. Similarly, Wagner's defensive abilities, such as fielding and holding runners close, are rarely tested, since most of his outs come on strikeouts and flyballs and opponents only occasionally reach base.

2002 Outlook

While Wagner was eligible for salary arbitration, he and the Astros had discussed the framework for a multiyear contract. With the possible exception of Octavio Dotel, who has emerged as a competent late-inning reliever, the Astros have no obvious replacement for Wagner. With 146 career saves, Wagner will resume his pursuit of Dave Smith, Houston's all-time saves leader with 199.

Overall Statistics

	W	L	Pct.	ERA	G	GS	Sv	IP	H	BB	SO	HR	Ratio
2001	2	5	.286	2.73	64	0	39	62.2	44	20	79	5	1.02
Career	21	23	.477	2.73	316	0	146	343.1	230	146	501	33	1.10

How Often He Throws Strikes

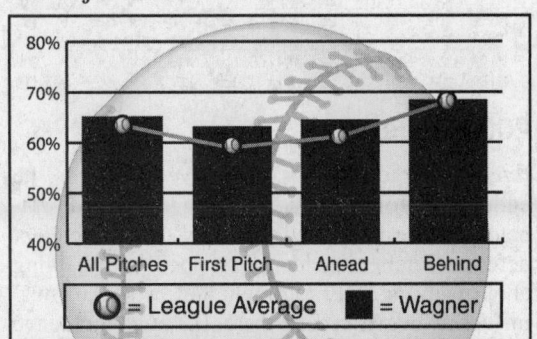

= League Average   = Wagner

2001 Situational Stats

	W	L	ERA	Sv	IP		AB	H	HR	RBI	Avg
Home	1	4	3.71	16	34.0	LHB	46	12	1	8	.261
Road	1	1	1.57	23	28.2	RHB	176	32	4	14	.182
First Half	2	3	3.00	19	33.0	Sc Pos	47	9	1	12	.191
Scnd Half	0	2	2.43	20	29.2	Clutch	162	30	3	16	.185

2001 Rankings (National League)

- 1st in save percentage (95.1)
- 3rd in first batter efficiency (.138) and most strikeouts per nine innings in relief (11.3)
- 4th in fewest baserunners allowed per nine innings in relief (9.9)
- 5th in games finished (58) and lowest batting average allowed in relief (.198)
- 6th in save opportunities (41) and saves
- 10th in relief ERA (2.73) and relief losses (5)
- Led the Astros in saves, games finished (58), save opportunities (41), save percentage (95.1), first batter efficiency (.138) and relief losses (5)

Houston

Brad Ausmus — Gold Glover

Position: C
Bats: R **Throws:** R
Ht: 5'11" **Wt:** 195

Opening Day Age: 32
Born: 4/14/69 in New Haven, CT
ML Seasons: 9
Pronunciation: AHHS-muss

Overall Statistics

	G	AB	R	H	D	T	HR	RBI	SB	BB	SO	Avg	OBP	Slg
2001	128	422	45	98	23	4	5	34	4	30	64	.232	.284	.341
Career	1041	3430	442	889	160	24	53	333	78	347	571	.259	.332	.366

2001 Situational Stats

	AB	H	HR	RBI	Avg		AB	H	HR	RBI	Avg
Home	212	48	4	20	.226	LHP	70	13	2	6	.186
Road	210	50	1	14	.238	RHP	352	85	3	28	.241
First Half	227	44	1	12	.194	Sc Pos	115	24	1	27	.209
Scnd Half	195	54	4	22	.277	Clutch	57	10	0	3	.175

2001 Season

Even by Brad Ausmus' offensive standards, he endured a poor season at the plate last year. Fortunately, he compensated with his usual excellent defense. Pitchers suddenly stopped complaining about working at Enron Field and, with Ausmus' influence, began to cope there. It's no coincidence that Houston's stretch of four postseason appearances in five years began during Ausmus' first tour of duty with the club and resumed upon his return.

Hitting, Baserunning & Defense

Ausmus shuts down an opponents' running game. His caught-stealing percentage (40%) ranked second in the majors last year. His footwork is nimble, he frames pitches deftly, and he has a strong arm and quick release. He received part of the credit for the accelerated development of young pitchers like Wade Miller and Roy Oswalt. Though Ausmus' offense suffered in 2001, he's capable of hitting the ball to the right side or laying down a bunt. He still has above-average speed for a catcher.

2002 Outlook

Ausmus will have a new backup in Gregg Zaun in 2002. Ausmus is signed through this year with a club option for 2003, so he isn't going anywhere immediately.

Kent Bottenfield

Position: SP
Bats: R **Throws:** R
Ht: 6' 3" **Wt:** 240

Opening Day Age: 33
Born: 11/14/68 in Portland, OR
ML Seasons: 9

Overall Statistics

	W	L	Pct.	ERA	G	GS	Sv	IP	H	BB	SO	HR	Ratio
2001	2	5	.286	6.40	13	9	1	52.0	61	16	39	16	1.48
Career	46	49	.484	4.54	292	116	10	911.2	950	385	566	123	1.46

2001 Situational Stats

	W	L	ERA	Sv	IP		AB	H	HR	RBI	Avg
Home	0	3	6.14	1	29.1	LHB	90	30	4	16	.333
Road	2	2	6.75	0	22.2	RHB	122	31	12	28	.254
First Half	2	5	6.40	1	52.0	Sc Pos	45	16	4	28	.356
Scnd Half	0	0	-	0	0.0	Clutch	3	0	0	0	.000

2001 Season

Kent Bottenfield's season ended in June due to inflammation in his throwing shoulder. Even before he was hurt, he didn't exactly distinguish himself. He began the year as Houston's fifth starter, moved to the bullpen in mid-April, and won only once after rejoining the rotation in early May.

Pitching, Defense & Hitting

Bottenfield compensates for his lack of velocity—his fastball doesn't exceed 88-89 MPH—with superior location. He likes to work the outer third of the plate, and he'll stay there if the umpire is giving him that pitch. That pitch is often a slider, which is probably his most effective delivery. He also tries to keep hitters off balance with a changeup and a curveball that he'll throw to either side of the plate. Bottenfield is a fair hitter (.162 lifetime) who usually bunts efficiently. Befitting his veteran's status, he has refined his pickoff move and slide step to allow him to control the running game.

2002 Outlook

Bottenfield was destined to go looking for a job as a bargain-basement free agent this offseason. Given the eternal hunger for pitching, he almost was guaranteed to get at least a spring training invitation from some team. At his best, he can contribute as a fourth or fifth starter.

Nelson Cruz

Position: RP
Bats: R **Throws:** R
Ht: 6' 1" **Wt:** 185

Opening Day Age: 29
Born: 9/13/72 in Puerta
Plaza, Dominican
Republic
ML Seasons: 4

Overall Statistics

	W	L	Pct.	ERA	G	GS	Sv	IP	H	BB	SO	HR	Ratio
2001	3	3	.500	4.15	66	0	2	82.1	72	24	75	11	1.17
Career	10	12	.455	4.70	141	6	2	216.1	214	69	178	32	1.31

2001 Situational Stats

	W	L	ERA	Sv	IP		AB	H	HR	RBI	Avg
Home	3	1	2.74	0	46.0	LHB	132	36	5	22	.273
Road	0	2	5.94	2	36.1	RHB	172	36	6	23	.209
First Half	1	1	3.94	2	48.0	Sc Pos	78	21	7	38	.269
Scnd Half	2	2	4.46	0	34.1	Clutch	63	15	2	9	.238

2001 Season

After bouncing between Triple-A and the majors for four years, Nelson Cruz finally stuck in the big leagues for a full season and showed he might stay for good. He proved adept in situational matchups against righthanded batters and as an innings-eater. Cruz combined with Mike Williams, Mike Jackson and Octavio Dotel to form one of the best corps of righthanded relievers in the league.

Pitching, Defense & Hitting

Once reliant on his sinker and slider, Cruz has leaned more heavily on a changeup that averages 81 MPH. He's confident enough to throw it to lefthanded and righthanded hitters regardless of the situation. His fastball occasionally can reach 92-93 MPH, though it averages 90. He has a curveball that he rarely throws. Cruz is more than adequate defensively. He managed his first major league hit last year and is now 1-for-7 lifetime.

2002 Outlook

Cruz is good enough to add real depth to a bullpen. His role could become more significant if the Astros don't retain the likes of Jackson or Williams, who are more experienced working near the end of a game. As his 2001 2.74 home ERA showed, Cruz' greatest value might be as a pitcher who doesn't mind performing at Enron Field.

Octavio Dotel

Position: RP
Bats: R **Throws:** R
Ht: 6' 0" **Wt:** 175

Opening Day Age: 26
Born: 11/25/75 in Santo
Domingo, Dominican
Republic
ML Seasons: 3
Pronunciation:
dough-TEL

Overall Statistics

	W	L	Pct.	ERA	G	GS	Sv	IP	H	BB	SO	HR	Ratio
2001	7	5	.583	2.66	61	4	2	105.0	79	47	145	5	1.20
Career	18	15	.545	4.48	130	34	18	315.1	275	157	372	43	1.37

2001 Situational Stats

	W	L	ERA	Sv	IP		AB	H	HR	RBI	Avg
Home	3	2	1.70	2	58.1	LHB	172	41	1	16	.238
Road	4	3	3.86	0	46.2	RHB	213	38	4	19	.178
First Half	5	4	3.22	1	64.1	Sc Pos	97	18	1	29	.186
Scnd Half	2	1	1.77	1	40.2	Clutch	159	30	1	9	.189

2001 Season

Success has helped Octavio Dotel adjust to life in the bullpen. The former starter emerged as a dominant reliever after leaving the rotation for good last May 1, compiling a 1.93 ERA in relief. He was particularly handy at Enron Field, where his ability to avoid home runs proved crucial.

Pitching, Defense & Hitting

Dotel always could throw hard. Once he went to the bullpen full-time, he no longer had to husband his energy, leaving him better able to feature his powerful pitching array. His fastball averages 95 MPH with lively movement. He also gets a lot of outs with an 85 MPH slider. If that weren't enough, he can call upon a sweeping curveball that freezes hitters. Though Dotel's a good athlete, he's an awful hitter. He's quick off the mound to cover first base and field bunts, but is prone to brief lapses.

2002 Outlook

It's safe to say that Dotel has started his last game for a long time. If Billy Wagner were injured, the Astros would immediately call upon Dotel as their emergency closer. They might even turn to Dotel if Wagner departs as a free agent after 2002. For now, Houston likes the idea of bringing out both relievers as a virtually unhittable righty-lefty tandem in the late innings.

Mike Jackson

Position: RP
Bats: R **Throws:** R
Ht: 6' 2" **Wt:** 225

Opening Day Age: 37
Born: 12/22/64 in Houston, TX
ML Seasons: 15

Overall Statistics

	W	L	Pct.	ERA	G	GS	Sv	IP	H	BB	SO	HR	Ratio
2001	5	3	.625	4.70	67	0	4	69.0	68	22	46	14	1.30
Career	58	64	.475	3.35	902	7	142	1086.2	869	436	951	115	1.20

2001 Situational Stats

	W	L	ERA	Sv	IP		AB	H	HR	RBI	Avg
Home	0	2	6.06	1	32.2	LHB	119	35	7	18	.294
Road	5	1	3.47	3	36.1	RHB	143	33	7	20	.231
First Half	2	1	3.62	4	37.1	Sc Pos	65	16	4	25	.246
Scnd Half	3	2	5.97	0	31.2	Clutch	140	35	5	17	.250

2001 Season

Mike Jackson became the 13th pitcher in history to make 900 appearances. His 67 outings proved the lesion in his throwing shoulder that sidelined him in 2000 had healed. While he didn't occupy the closer's role, he did perform that function when Billy Wagner went on the disabled list in June. Jackson usually bridged the gap between the starter and the Octavio Dotel-Wagner late-inning combo.

Pitching, Defense & Hitting

Sitting out 2000 didn't change Jackson's style. He resumed using his slider as his primary out pitch, though its previously nasty break deserted him at times. He complemented the slider with an 89-92 MPH fastball and a split-finger that reached 85-87 MPH. He probably wouldn't have lasted this long without his pinpoint control. He's a fair fielder and above average at keeping runners close. With 28 at-bats in his career, Jackson's hitting is irrelevant.

2002 Outlook

Jackson hoped to stay with the Astros. His future with the team might be tied to Doug Brocail, who suffered shoulder problems and missed the 2001 campaign. The Astros declined to pick up Brocail's option for 2002 but still re-signed him at a lesser price. If he were to return healthy, the Astros might be less inclined to retain Jackson.

Dave Mlicki

Position: SP
Bats: R **Throws:** R
Ht: 6' 4" **Wt:** 205

Opening Day Age: 33
Born: 6/8/68 in Cleveland, OH
ML Seasons: 9
Pronunciation: muh-LICK-ee

Overall Statistics

	W	L	Pct.	ERA	G	GS	Sv	IP	H	BB	SO	HR	Ratio
2001	11	11	.500	6.17	34	29	0	167.2	203	74	97	37	1.65
Career	62	70	.470	4.67	240	177	1	1146.2	1236	438	777	160	1.46

2001 Situational Stats

	W	L	ERA	Sv	IP		AB	H	HR	RBI	Avg
Home	5	3	4.50	0	68.0	LHB	305	98	19	54	.321
Road	6	8	7.31	0	99.2	RHB	361	105	18	56	.291
First Half	5	8	7.50	0	90.0	Sc Pos	161	47	4	65	.292
Scnd Half	6	3	4.64	0	77.2	Clutch	19	2	0	0	.105

2001 Season

Another member of the Detroit alumni club, Dave Mlicki came to Houston in the Jose Lima trade last June 23. Mlicki then replaced Scott Elarton in the Astros' starting rotation on July 21, and furthered the team's pennant drive by posting a 6-3 record and 4.91 ERA after that point.

Pitching, Defense & Hitting

As Mlicki's strikeout totals indicate, he lacks a dominant or overpowering pitch. He must mix his deliveries and pitch to spots to succeed. His slider, which travels at about 83 MPH and has a short, quick break, is his best pitch. He throws his 89 MPH fastball when he needs to hit a spot. He'll use a changeup, though he occasionally throws it too hard, and completes his assortment of pitches with a mediocre curveball. Mlicki's hitting (.116 lifetime) is nothing to brag about. While he's a decent athlete who moves well off the mound, his career total of nine errors is mildly alarming.

2002 Outlook

Mlicki can be a back-of-the-rotation starter for a lot of clubs. Signed through this season, he might return to that role for the Astros. Or Houston may elect to use him in middle relief, a role to which he's fairly accustomed. Either way, Mlicki's handy to have around.

Chris Truby

Position: 3B
Bats: R **Throws:** R
Ht: 6' 2" **Wt:** 190

Opening Day Age: 28
Born: 12/9/73 in Palm Springs, CA
ML Seasons: 2

Overall Statistics

	G	AB	R	H	D	T	HR	RBI	SB	BB	SO	Avg	OBP	Slg
2001	48	136	11	28	6	1	8	23	1	13	38	.206	.276	.441
Career	126	394	39	95	21	5	19	82	3	23	94	.241	.288	.464

2001 Situational Stats

	AB	H	HR	RBI	Avg		AB	H	HR	RBI	Avg
Home	60	12	4	10	.200	LHP	34	9	4	7	.265
Road	76	16	4	13	.211	RHP	102	19	4	16	.186
First Half	120	26	7	22	.217	Sc Pos	39	8	2	15	.205
Scnd Half	16	2	1	1	.125	Clutch	13	2	1	3	.154

2001 Season

Last season didn't work out as Chris Truby had planned. He was Houston's Opening Day third baseman but hit poorly (.217), prompting his demotion to Triple-A and the Astros' acquisition of Vinny Castilla. The boost Castilla provided virtually guaranteed that Truby would stay in the minors. He was recalled on August 19 but played sparingly and hit even worse than before (.125).

Hitting, Baserunning & Defense

For the second straight year, Truby struggled against righthanded pitchers, which is akin to a baker struggling with dough. But while Truby has several holes in his swing, his power should continue to earn chances. Defensively, he has quick feet, a strong arm and above-average hands. His speed is unimpressive, though his fundamentals on the bases help him survive.

2002 Outlook

One way or another, Truby will have to upgrade his play this year. He'll receive another opportunity to secure Houston's third-base job, and his chances obviously improve with Castilla gone. But Truby also has to look over his shoulder at the Astros' top third-base prospect, Morgan Ensberg, who has proven he can hit Triple-A pitching. If Ensberg keeps progressing, Truby could get squeezed out.

Jose Vizcaino

Position: SS/2B
Bats: B **Throws:** R
Ht: 6' 1" **Wt:** 180

Opening Day Age: 34
Born: 3/26/68 in San Cristobal, Dominican Republic
ML Seasons: 13
Pronunciation: vid-kie-ah-no

Overall Statistics

	G	AB	R	H	D	T	HR	RBI	SB	BB	SO	Avg	OBP	Slg
2001	107	256	38	71	8	3	1	14	3	15	33	.277	.322	.344
Career	1288	4097	498	1106	141	37	22	353	68	294	574	.270	.319	.339

2001 Situational Stats

	AB	H	HR	RBI	Avg		AB	H	HR	RBI	Avg
Home	111	33	1	6	.297	LHP	36	9	0	3	.250
Road	145	38	0	8	.262	RHP	220	62	1	11	.282
First Half	127	34	1	5	.268	Sc Pos	48	14	0	11	.292
Scnd Half	129	37	0	9	.287	Clutch	51	17	0	1	.333

2001 Season

Jose Vizcaino reinforced his reputation as a dependable utility infielder, posting his highest batting average since 1996. His hitting, which has been little more than adequate, got a boost from Enron Field. A key for Vizcaino was avoiding injuries for a second consecutive season.

Hitting, Baserunning & Defense

When Vizcaino goes to the plate, chances are he'll get his bat on the ball but not much else. His lifetime slugging percentage is a limp .339, and the home run he hit last year ended a streak of 542 at-bats without one. But Vizcaino is adept at playing the "little game"—bunting, hitting to the opposite field and running the bases well. He has average speed and never has been a basestealing threat. He's OK defensively, with fair hands and an average arm. He won't make many spectacular plays, but he'll execute most of the routine ones. However, his .937 fielding percentage as a shortstop last year bordered on unacceptable.

2002 Outlook

Overall, the Astros were happy with Vizcaino and re-signed him in the fall at one-year and $1.7 million. The feeling was mutual, particularly since Vizcaino realized playing in Enron could enhance his offensive production.

Daryle Ward

Position: LF/RF
Bats: L **Throws:** L
Ht: 6' 2" **Wt:** 230

Opening Day Age: 26
Born: 6/27/75 in
Lynwood, CA
ML Seasons: 4

Overall Statistics

	G	AB	R	H	D	T	HR	RBI	SB	BB	SO	Avg	OBP	Slg
2001	95	213	21	56	15	0	9	39	0	19	48	.263	.323	.460
Career	282	630	69	166	31	2	37	116	0	44	142	.263	.310	.495

2001 Situational Stats

	AB	H	HR	RBI	Avg		AB	H	HR	RBI	Avg
Home	99	30	5	22	.303	LHP	26	8	4	8	.308
Road	114	26	4	17	.228	RHP	187	48	5	31	.257
First Half	139	35	7	26	.252	Sc Pos	74	19	3	30	.257
Scnd Half	74	21	2	13	.284	Clutch	34	10	3	4	.294

2001 Season

Daryle Ward remained one of the most dangerous hitters kept under wraps in the major leagues. Reluctant to trade him and see him blossom elsewhere, yet not quite willing to hand him an everyday job, the Astros gave the slugger 51 fewer at-bats than the year before. In 630 career at-bats—roughly a full season—Ward has 37 homers and 116 RBI. The baseball world has noticed.

Hitting, Baserunning & Defense

Ward has outstanding power and, like a lot of lefties, likes to golf low pitches. Changing locations and speeds can frustrate him. Ward partly has himself to blame for his reserve status, because he's a below-average outfielder who lacks range and an accurate, strong arm. While he might be able to survive playing one of the corners at Enron, he may be best suited for first base. Ward's lack of speed makes him a liability running the bases.

2002 Outlook

Ward's fate is tied to Moises Alou. If Alou leaves as a free agent, as expected, Ward probably will receive a chance to start. If Alou stays, Ward likely will be buried again. Ward would be perfect for an American League team needing a first baseman-designated hitter. But so far, the Astros have resisted all trade proposals.

Mike Williams

Position: RP
Bats: R **Throws:** R
Ht: 6' 2" **Wt:** 204

Opening Day Age: 33
Born: 7/29/68 in
Radford, VA
ML Seasons: 10

Overall Statistics

	W	L	Pct.	ERA	G	GS	Sv	IP	H	BB	SO	HR	Ratio
2001	6	4	.600	3.80	65	0	22	64.0	60	35	59	9	1.48
Career	29	41	.414	4.43	341	55	70	644.0	644	281	502	78	1.44

2001 Situational Stats

	W	L	ERA	Sv	IP		AB	H	HR	RBI	Avg
Home	3	3	5.08	14	33.2	LHB	117	30	8	15	.256
Road	3	1	2.37	8	30.1	RHB	129	30	1	12	.233
First Half	2	3	3.86	17	35.0	Sc Pos	82	15	1	18	.183
Scnd Half	4	1	3.72	5	29.0	Clutch	156	41	5	18	.263

2001 Season

Obtained from Pittsburgh last July 31, Mike Williams added depth to Houston's bullpen. After serving as the Pirates' closer, Williams had to adjust to a subordinate role with the Astros and to pitching at Enron Field. He experienced more success with the former than the latter. As an Astro, Williams posted a 1.88 ERA and .189 opponents' batting average in 16 road outings, compared with 7.88 and .333 in nine Enron appearances.

Pitching, Defense & Hitting

Williams' fastball has average velocity (89 MPH) and must stay low to be effective. His slider is an extremely good pitch, with sharp, late movement. He has a hard, heavy sinker he likes to throw inside to righthanders. Williams will throw his changeup, which also has sinking action, to lefties and righties. Defensively, he rarely hurts himself, though his slower-than-average delivery invites stolen bases. He never batted for the Astros.

2002 Outlook

Pittsburgh traded Williams because he was eligible for free agency. That's also why the Astros were likely to let him go, since they're just as unwilling to accommodate his salary increase. Though Williams seems best suited as a setup man, his experience as a closer will enhance his marketability.

Other Houston Astros

Glen Barker (Pos: CF, Age: 30, Bats: B)

	G	AB	R	H	D	T	HR	RBI	SB	BB	SO	Avg	OBP	Slg
2001	70	24	12	2	0	0	0	1	4	3	6	.083	.233	.083
Career	235	164	53	38	4	1	3	18	30	21	48	.232	.330	.323

Barker's poor batting limited his opportunities to use his speed on the bases. He had surgery to repair a torn labrum but is expected to be okay. 2002 Outlook: C

Tony Eusebio (Pos: C, Age: 34, Bats: R)

	G	AB	R	H	D	T	HR	RBI	SB	BB	SO	Avg	OBP	Slg
2001	59	154	16	39	8	0	5	14	0	17	34	.253	.339	.403
Career	598	1739	179	479	87	5	30	241	1	182	324	.275	.346	.383

Eusebio has been a solid backup in Houston for eight years, and he holds the club record with a 24-game hitting streak. Gregg Zaun has been signed, so it's time to move on. 2002 Outlook: B

Wayne Franklin (Pos: LHP, Age: 28)

	W	L	Pct.	ERA	G	GS	Sv	IP	H	BB	SO	HR	Ratio
2001	0	0	-	6.75	11	0	0	12.0	17	9	9	4	2.17
Career	0	0	-	5.94	36	0	0	33.1	41	21	30	6	1.86

Franklin started the season in the Houston bullpen, but was demoted after posting a 6.94 ERA in April. He allowed four homers in just 11.2 innings of work. He must work on his control in the minors. 2002 Outlook: C

Charlie Hayes (Pos: 3B, Age: 36, Bats: R)

	G	AB	R	H	D	T	HR	RBI	SB	BB	SO	Avg	OBP	Slg
2001	31	50	4	10	2	0	0	4	0	7	16	.200	.293	.240
Career	1547	5262	580	1379	251	16	144	740	47	420	918	.262	.316	.398

A 14-year veteran, Hayes played just 31 games in 2001, the lowest total since joining the majors in 1988. He was released after hitting a lowly .200. It is doubtful that he'll catch on with another team in 2002. 2002 Outlook: D

Scott Linebrink (Pos: RHP, Age: 25)

	W	L	Pct.	ERA	G	GS	Sv	IP	H	BB	SO	HR	Ratio
2001	0	0	-	2.61	9	0	0	10.1	6	6	9	0	1.16
Career	0	0	-	4.43	20	0	0	22.1	24	14	15	4	1.70

Linebrink can overpower batters with a fastball in the mid-90s, but has also dramatically improved his change-up and split-finger. He looked solid in his nine appearances with Houston. 2002 Outlook: C

Jim Mann (Pos: RHP, Age: 27)

	W	L	Pct.	ERA	G	GS	Sv	IP	H	BB	SO	HR	Ratio
2001	0	0	-	3.38	4	0	0	5.1	3	4	5	0	1.31
Career	0	0	-	5.63	6	0	0	8.0	9	5	5	1	1.75

Mann spent last year as the closer in Triple-A. Despite a good year (6-3, 2.51 ERA, 27 saves), his best chance in the majors is likely as a setup man. 2002 Outlook: C

Orlando Merced (Pos: RF/LF, Age: 35, Bats: L)

	G	AB	R	H	D	T	HR	RBI	SB	BB	SO	Avg	OBP	Slg
2001	94	137	19	36	6	1	6	29	5	14	32	.263	.333	.453
Career	1145	3535	509	987	199	23	94	529	50	446	578	.279	.359	.428

Nearly 82 percent of Merced's career hits have come against righties. His playing time was curbed in 2001

because of the talent in the Astros' outfield. He was re-signed in December and will be used primarily as a pinch-hitter. 2002 Outlook: B

Brian Powell (Pos: RHP, Age: 28)

	W	L	Pct.	ERA	G	GS	Sv	IP	H	BB	SO	HR	Ratio
2001	0	1	.000	18.00	1	1	0	3.0	5	3	3	1	2.67
Career	5	10	.333	6.48	28	22	0	118.0	140	52	63	26	1.63

Powell won't overpower his opponent, but has improved his control enough to possibly earn a spot in the majors within the next year. He was 9-8 with a 3.17 ERA at Triple-A in 2001, including a no-hitter. 2002 Outlook: C

Scott Servais (Pos: C, Age: 34, Bats: R)

	G	AB	R	H	D	T	HR	RBI	SB	BB	SO	Avg	OBP	Slg
2001	11	16	1	6	0	0	0	0	0	2	3	.375	.444	.375
Career	820	2493	243	611	130	2	63	319	3	183	407	.245	.306	.375

With Brad Ausmus and Tony Eusebio splitting time in Houston, Servais spent most of 2001 with Triple-A New Orleans, where he hit .338. Yet he signed a new minor league pact with Houston. 2002 Outlook: C

Joe Slusarski (Pos: RHP, Age: 35)

	W	L	Pct.	ERA	G	GS	Sv	IP	H	BB	SO	HR	Ratio
2001	0	1	.000	9.00	12	0	0	16.0	25	4	11	4	1.81
Career	13	21	.382	5.18	118	34	3	305.2	342	125	173	45	1.53

Slusarski began as a starter, but since 1995 he's pitched primarily in relief. Cut by Atlanta early last season, Slusarski posted a 2.48 ERA in 31 relief appearances in Triple-A. He struggles with lefties. 2002 Outlook: C

Bill Spiers (Pos: C, Age: 35, Bats: L)

	G	AB	R	H	D	T	HR	RBI	SB	BB	SO	Avg	OBP	Slg
2001	4	3	0	1	0	0	0	0	0	1	0	.333	.500	.333
Career	1252	3408	477	922	158	35	37	388	97	355	496	.271	.341	.370

Spiers announced his retirement from baseball in October after being limited to just four games in 2001 due to back surgery. Spiers played every position but pitcher and catcher in his career. 2002 Outlook: D

Ricky Stone (Pos: RHP, Age: 27)

	W	L	Pct.	ERA	G	GS	Sv	IP	H	BB	SO	HR	Ratio
2001	0	0	-	2.35	6	0	0	7.2	8	2	4	1	1.30
Career	0	0	-	2.35	6	0	0	7.2	8	2	4	1	1.30

Stone made his major league debut this season after spending eight years on various teams in the minors. As a September call-up, he allowed two earned runs in 7.2 innings of work. 2002 Outlook: C

Ron Villone (Pos: LHP, Age: 32)

	W	L	Pct.	ERA	G	GS	Sv	IP	H	BB	SO	HR	Ratio
2001	6	10	.375	5.89	53	12	0	114.2	133	53	113	18	1.62
Career	29	31	.483	4.91	274	57	5	566.0	560	321	443	72	1.56

A reliever by trade, Villone also is used as a spot starter. The lefty boasts a 3.93 ERA in relief over the past three seasons, compared to 5.48 as a starter. He had knee surgery in October, but will be ready for 2002. 2002 Outlook: B

Houston Astros Minor League Prospects

Organization Overview:

The Astros are in an interesting position. They've captured four of the last five National League Central Division titles, and only the Braves, Yankees and Indians have won more games over the past decade. But the Astros have flopped in the playoffs, where they've lost 12 of 14 games since 1997. They've now changed managers, hiring Jimy Williams and possibly marking a transition. Nevertheless, Houston's future looks quite rosy, thanks in large measure to a farm system that rates among the best in baseball. All five of Houston's full-season affiliates qualified for the postseason after combining for a sparkling .613 (387-244) winning percentage during the regular season. The system recently has produced the likes of Lance Berkman and Roy Oswalt. And they figure to be joined by an impressive wave of prospects over the next year or so.

John Buck

Position: C
Bats: R **Throws:** R
Ht: 6' 3" **Wt:** 200

Opening Day Age: 21
Born: 7/7/80 in Kemmerer, WY

Recent Statistics

	G	AB	R	H	D	THR	RBI	SB	BB	SO	Avg
2000 A Michigan	109	390	57	110	33	0	10	71	2	55	81	.282
2001 A Lexington	122	443	72	122	24	1	22	73	4	37	84	.275

One veteran observer has called Buck the best catching prospect he's seen since Johnny Bench. Like Bench, Buck's defense draws raves, with the arm strength and quick release to get the ball to second base in 1.85 seconds. He probably could play defense in the majors right now, though his game-calling might need some work. Buck's offense isn't shabby, either. He's a big, strong, smart hitter who displayed a power surge in the South Atlantic League last season. The Astros say he projects as a .275 hitter with the potential for 35 homers. He needs to improve his plate discipline and making more contact. Buck's next logical stop is Double-A.

Morgan Ensberg

Position: 3B
Bats: R **Throws:** R
Ht: 6' 2" **Wt:** 210

Opening Day Age: 26
Born: 8/26/75 in Redondo Beach, CA

Recent Statistics

	G	AB	R	H	D	THR	RBI	SB	BB	SO	Avg
2000 AA Round Rock	137	483	95	145	34	0	28	90	9	92	107	.300
2001 AAA New Orleans	87	316	65	98	20	0	23	61	6	45	60	.310
2001 MLE	87	314	62	96	20	0	23	58	4	43	63	.306

Ensberg generated notice in 2000 when he batted .300 with 28 homers at Double-A. He then confirmed his status by his performance at Triple-A last year. A wrist injury suffered in midseason depressed his totals a bit. However, he was challenging for the Pacific Coast League home-run title before getting hurt. Ensberg is a

disciplined hitter who will take the ball the other way and drive in runs. In the field he's an above-average defender. Though no facet is exceptional, he possesses the range, arm and hands to handle third base. His wrist injury wasn't considered serious and the Astros had him playing winter ball this offseason. With Vinny Castilla out of the picture, Ensberg should compete with Chris Truby for a starting spot in Houston's lineup. At age 26, this may be the best chance he'll ever have to carve out significant playing time.

Adam Everett

Position: SS
Bats: R **Throws:** R
Ht: 6' 0" **Wt:** 156

Opening Day Age: 25
Born: 2/6/77 in Austell, GA

Recent Statistics

	G	AB	R	H	D	THR	RBI	SB	BB	SO	Avg
2001 AAA New Orleans	114	441	69	110	20	8	5	40	24	39	74	.249
2001 NL Houston	9	3	1	0	0	0	0	0	1	0	1	.000
2001 MLE	114	439	66	108	20	7	5	38	19	37	78	.246

We've heard about Everett for a while, but this may be the year that he makes an impact in the major leagues. The Red Sox chose Everett with the 12th overall selection in the 1998 draft, before trading him to the Astros in the deal involving Carl Everett following the 1999 season. Adam's fielding ability at shortstop is his calling card. He has a great arm, good range and he makes any club better defensively. But while the Astros claim he's making progress with the bat, his offense remains a project. Julio Lugo would seem to have the better offensive skills, but Everett's fielding prowess may be too enticing to overlook. The Astros say Everett could give Lugo a strong run for the money in 2002.

Carlos Hernandez

Position: P
Bats: L **Throws:** L
Ht: 5' 10" **Wt:** 145

Opening Day Age: 21
Born: 4/22/80 in Guacara, VZ

Recent Statistics

	W	L	ERA	G	GS	Sv	IP	H	R	BB	SO	HR
2001 AA Round Rock	12	3	3.69	24	23	0	139.0	115	60	69	167	11
2001 NL Houston	1	0	1.02	3	3	0	17.2	11	2	7	17	1

Hernandez' small size belies his amazing stuff. While his low-90s fastball is more than adequate for a southpaw, it's his curveball that serves as his out pitch. He can throw the breaking ball on any count whenever he needs an out, and he delivers it with complete command. In addition, his changeup is a straight, swing-and-miss kind of offering that can make opposing hitters look foolish. Because he has been so dominating in the minors, the Astros say he might have a learning curve as he progresses to higher levels. Even though he won't turn 22 until April, it's possible Hernandez will skip Triple-A and leap onto the Astros' staff this spring.

Jason Lane

Position: OF
Bats: R **Throws:** L
Ht: 6' 2" **Wt:** 220

Opening Day Age: 25
Born: 12/22/76 in Santa Rosa, CA

Recent Statistics

	G	AB	R	H	D	T	HR	RBI	SB	BB	SO	Avg.
2000 A Michigan	133	511	98	153	38	0	23	104	20	62	91	.299
2001 AA Round Rock	137	526	103	166	36	2	38	124	14	61	98	.316
2001 MLE	137	519	93	159	35	1	36	112	10	46	106	.306

Lane is one of those rare position players who throws lefthanded yet hits from the right side. And his talent with a bat in his hands isn't very common, either. His career path has mirrored Morgan Ensberg's in a couple of ways. First, he played collegiately at USC. Second, he's been so productive offensively since turning pro that he has demanded attention. Lane enjoyed a tremendous season at Double-A and was named the 2001 Texas League MVP. The Astros describe his power as "plus-plus," particularly for Enron Field. While he's improved defensively, he's best suited as a corner outfielder. Even though he already has turned 25, he could be headed to Triple-A for at least a chunk of the 2002 campaign.

Tony Pluta

Position: P
Bats: R **Throws:** R
Ht: 6' 2" **Wt:** 190

Opening Day Age: 19
Born: 10/28/82 in Visalia, CA

Recent Statistics

	W	L	ERA	G	GS	Sv	IP	H	R	BB	SO	HR
2001 A Lexington	12	4	3.20	26	26	0	132.1	107	52	86	138	7

The Lexington Legends, Houston's Sally League affiliate, boasted the best record in the circuit last season. Pluta arguably has the highest ceiling of anyone on the Legends' deep and talented pitching staff. Drafted at age 17 in 2000, he didn't sign until that August and saw some of his first professional action in the instructional league. That's where he impressed the Astros with a 98-MPH heater in stints that lasted no more than two innings. As an 18-year-old starter in Class-A, his fastball normally resided in the low 90s, teaming with a good curveball to form a mean combination. His changeup and command need work, but the Astros say Pluta is an A-1 citizen with lots of growth potential. This year, it's possible that Pluta will be bumped to Double-A while still a teenager.

Tim Redding

Position: P
Bats: R **Throws:** R
Ht: 6' 0" **Wt:** 180

Opening Day Age: 24
Born: 2/12/78 in Rochester, NY

Recent Statistics

	W	L	ERA	G	GS	Sv	IP	H	R	BB	SO	HR
2001 AA Round Rock	10	2	2.18	14	14	0	90.2	64	26	25	113	5
2001 AAA New Orleans	4	1	4.54	6	6	0	37.2	22	21	19	42	4
2001 NL Houston	3	1	5.50	13	9	0	55.2	62	38	24	55	11

Redding bears striking similarities to Roy Oswalt, the phenom who led National League rookies with 14 wins last season. Both are 6-foot righthanders who were cho-sen after the 19th round in their respective drafts. Most importantly, they've each enjoyed tremendous success professionally. Redding is aggressive on the mound, which isn't surprising considering his fastball sits between 93-95 MPH and will sometimes reach 98. He also throws an 80-82 MPH power curveball, as well as a slider that is something of a show pitch right now. He lacks feel for his changeup and the Astros say he needs more innings. It isn't out of the question that he could stick on their staff this season, possibly working out of the bullpen. He eventually could team with Oswalt and Wade Miller to form the heart of a rotation that would boast at least three No. 1-type righthanders.

Wilfredo Rodriguez

Position: P
Bats: L **Throws:** L
Ht: 6' 3" **Wt:** 180

Opening Day Age: 23
Born: 3/20/79 in Bolivar, VZ

Recent Statistics

	W	L	ERA	G	GS	Sv	IP	H	R	BB	SO	HR
2001 AA Round Rock	5	9	4.78	42	10	0	92.1	94	61	56	94	10
2001 NL Houston	0	0	15.00	2	0	0	3.0	6	5	1	3	2

Rodriguez will be remembered as the pitcher who served up Barry Bonds' record-tying 70th homer last season. Signed out of Venezuela in 1995, Rodriguez reached the majors at age 22. However, he may not be the prized prospect he once was. After breezing through the low minors, he has seemed to hit a wall the past couple of seasons. He worked mostly in relief in 2001, a sign that expectations may have lowered. Nevertheless, his fastball resides in the mid-90s, and lefties who throw that hard don't grow on trees. He also has a decent curveball, helping to make him simply dominant at times. At other times he's very hittable, which shouldn't happen. Command is the key issue for Rodriguez. He should compete for at least a spot in the Astros bullpen in 2002.

Others to Watch

Keith Ginter (25) has nice power for a second baseman, but faces a roadblock in Craig Biggio. Ginter's ability to also play third base and left field will help his chances of sticking in Houston. . . **Dave Matranga** (25) also plays second base, though he's probably a better defender than Ginter. His average jumped to .302 at Double-A last year. . . Righthander **Mike Nannini's** (21) changeup is his best pitch, and he throws a nice 12-6 curveball, helping him go 15-5 in the Sally League. His fastball straightens out at times, and he needs to improve the sink on his two-seamer. . . Righthander **Chad Qualls** (23), a No. 2 pick in 2000, went 15-6 in the Midwest League and has tremendous upside. He features a nasty arm angle that is tough for righthanded batters to pick up. . . Shortstop **Tom Whiteman** (22) burst into prospect status by ranking second in the Sally League with a .319 average. The Astros say he has the potential to hit 25 homers annually, and call him a fluid player for whom everything seems easy.

Dodger Stadium

Offense

Long regarded as one of the most pitcher-friendly stadiums in baseball, Dodger Stadium was next-to-lowest in runs per game last season. While the dimensions of the outfield wall seem average, the angle from the foul poles to the gaps is rather steep. The night air is rather heavy as it rolls from the Pacific into Chavez Ravine, knocking many fly-balls down before they can reach the seats. The wind almost always flows from left-to-right, so lefthanded hitters generally get a bit of a boost. Foul territory was huge before some expensive seats were added a few years back, but there still is plenty of foul ground to cover.

Defense

There are no surprises in most of the concentric outfield, but it can get a little tricky right near the poles where fans can reach over the low railing to battle for souvenirs. The warning track is made of a rubberized material that causes the ball to bounce like a golf ball, and the stuff tears uniforms and skin like paper. The infield gets harder and drier as the long hot summer progresses, making grounders faster and hops trickier.

Who It Helps the Most

Flyball pitchers like Jeff Shaw receive the most benefit from pitching half their games at Dodger Stadium. Chan Ho Park's home ERA is almost two full runs lower than his road total over the course of his career.

Who It Hurts the Most

All hitters lose something when playing at Dodger Stadium. Those who tend to elevate the ball, such as Eric Karros, Gary Sheffield, Shawn Green and Paul Lo Duca, will end up with fewer extra-base hits over the course of a season.

Rookies & Newcomers

Eric Gagne works up in the zone. He will have a better shot at sticking in the bigs thanks to his home park. Mike Trombley was horrible upon coming over from Baltimore, but he might settle in to give the club some innings in 2002.

Dimensions: LF-330, LCF-385, CF-395, RCF-385, RF-330

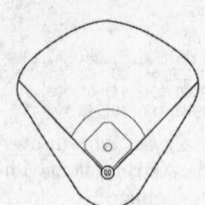

Capacity: 56,000

Elevation: 340 feet

Surface: Grass

Foul Territory: Large

Park Factors

2001 Season

	Home Games			Away Games			
	Dodgers	Opp	Total	Dodgers	Opp	Total	Index
G	72	72	144	75	75	150	—
Avg	.248	.239	.243	.264	.260	.262	93
AB	2346	2477	4823	2626	2469	5095	99
R	299	292	591	401	368	769	80
H	581	592	1173	692	643	1335	92
2B	112	107	219	130	135	265	87
3B	11	9	20	16	13	29	73
HR	86	75	161	104	89	193	88
BB	241	238	479	230	227	457	111
SO	474	562	1036	494	540	1034	106
E	51	43	94	56	55	111	88
E-Infield	41	33	74	49	46	95	81
LHB-Avg	.235	.243	.240	.265	.251	.257	93
LHB-HR	26	43	69	36	41	77	95
RHB-Avg	.254	.236	.245	.263	.268	.265	93
RHB-HR	60	32	92	68	48	116	84

1999-2001

	Home Games			Away Games			
	Dodgers	Opp	Total	Dodgers	Opp	Total	Index
G	219	219	438	222	222	444	—
Avg	.256	.241	.248	.262	.265	.264	94
AB	7187	7529	14716	7806	7428	15234	98
R	962	961	1923	1184	1076	2260	86
H	1837	1818	3655	2049	1969	4018	92
2B	314	331	645	396	408	804	83
3B	28	24	52	45	42	87	62
HR	269	249	518	286	256	542	99
BB	775	783	1558	839	755	1594	101
SO	1392	1593	2985	1489	1524	3013	103
E	189	151	340	170	182	352	98
E-Infield	157	116	273	146	155	301	92
LHB-Avg	.249	.241	.244	.251	.276	.265	92
LHB-HR	88	117	205	92	116	208	101
RHB-Avg	.259	.242	.251	.268	.257	.263	95
RHB-HR	181	132	313	194	140	334	98

2001 Rankings (National League)

- Highest walk factor
- Second-lowest run factor
- Second-lowest double factor
- Second-lowest infield-error factor
- Second-lowest RHB batting-average factor
- Third-lowest batting-average factor
- Third-lowest hit factor

Jim Tracy

2001 Season

Seen as a big gamble when the Dodgers hired Jim Tracy to be their new manager last offseason, the move turned out to be a good one. He remained upbeat despite a horrible rash of injuries and kept the club in contention until deep into September. He quickly gained the players' trust by not ripping them in the press and taking the pressure off of them with his level-headed commentary.

Offense

Having served as Davey Johnson's bench coach, Tracy had a good idea what his crew could and could not do. He tends to play the game by the book, and he studies matchups and statistical tendencies to try to get an edge whenever possible. When the sacrifice seemed appropriate, the rookie manager called for it. In fact, he is going to have to guard against becoming too predictable. On the other hand, he gambled with his lineup construction, using Paul Lo Duca almost equally between the leadoff and No. 5 spots.

Pitching & Defense

One of Tracy's more brilliant moves was to stretch Terry Adams out during spring training. When several of his starters went down, the skipper knew that the lifelong reliever could step into the role. He and pitching coach Jim Colburn appeared to be of one mind as they tried to nurse young pitchers Eric Gagne and Luke Prokopec along. Tracy's bullpen roles were very strict, and he stayed with Jeff Shaw and Matt Herges when the veteran closer and young middle man struggled. Tracy likes to use a set lineup for the most part, and he was very adept at saving primo pinch-hitter Dave Hansen for just the right spot.

2002 Outlook

While the Dodgers have severe payroll concerns, they now have a managerial team in place that is on the same page. Tracy will have some serious decisions to make in the spring regarding his starting rotation and his closer, as well as how to shore up center field and possibly shortstop. Other than perhaps Shawn Green, no one on the club has more job security than Tracy, who had options for 2003 and 2004 exercised by the Dodgers.

Born: 12/31/55 in Hamilton, OH

Playing Experience: 1980-1981, ChC

Managerial Experience: 1 season

Manager Statistics

Year	Team, Lg	W	L	Pct	GB	Finish
2001	Los Angeles, NL	86	76	.531	6.0	3rd West
1 Season		86	76	.531	—	—

2001 Starting Pitchers by Days Rest

	<=3	4	5	6+
Dodgers Starts	2	83	40	27
Dodgers ERA	14.09	3.72	4.92	3.32
NL Avg Starts	1	80	47	24
NL ERA	5.03	4.43	4.53	4.28

2001 Situational Stats

	Jim Tracy	NL Average
Hit & Run Success %	27.8	35.1
Stolen Base Success %	67.9	66.5
Platoon Pct.	50.3	51.5
Defensive Subs	20	20
High-Pitch Outings	8	7
Quick/Slow Hooks	15/13	19/14
Sacrifice Attempts	81	87

2001 Rankings (National League)

- 2nd in steals of home plate (1)
- 3rd in starts on three days rest

Terry Adams

2001 Season

When Jim Tracy talked of stretching Terry Adams out in spring training, it was regarded with bemused skepticism. And sure enough, once April came around the lifelong reliever was back in his usual setup role. Eventually, injuries and poor performances by the young starters forced Adams into the rotation and he took to it immediately. He actually got stronger as he became more accustomed to the role, and posted a 3.12 ERA in September before a tired arm forced him to miss his last two starts.

Pitching

No other Dodger throws harder than Adams. His fastball consistently reaches 95 MPH, though it lacks movement. He complements the heater with a hard slider, and both pitches are "heavy," so hitters tend to pound them into the ground. His 2.29 groundball-flyball ratio was the second-highest in baseball last year, and he allowed just nine balls to leave the yard. He can get into trouble by nibbling too much. If Adams is going to remain a starter, he will need to develop an offspeed pitch that will keep hitters honest.

Defense & Hitting

Adams is not a very good fielder, as he has some bulk to his lower body and does not get off the mound all that well. Neither does he possess a good pickoff move, and with his rather large leg kick, runners have an easy time of it with him on the mound. As might be expected from a converted reliever, Adams looked rather helpless at the plate last season. He is a pretty good bunter, however.

2002 Outlook

After 363 career relief appearances, Adams could not have picked a better time to make the transition to starting, as he enters a weak field of free agents. It would not be surprising to see him thrive in the new role. For one thing, he is built like a (work)horse and allowed just a .240 average after his 75th pitch in a given game last year. And he always has handled hitters on both sides of the plate. In fact, he has been more effective against lefties in his career, holding them to a .236 average.

Position: SP/RP
Bats: R **Throws:** R
Ht: 6' 3" **Wt:** 215

Opening Day Age: 29
Born: 3/6/73 in Mobile, AL
ML Seasons: 7

Overall Statistics

	W	L	Pct.	ERA	G	GS	Sv	IP	H	BB	SO	HR	Ratio
2001	12	8	.600	4.33	43	22	0	166.1	172	54	141	9	1.36
Career	37	43	.463	4.04	385	22	39	581.1	581	261	484	40	1.45

How Often He Throws Strikes

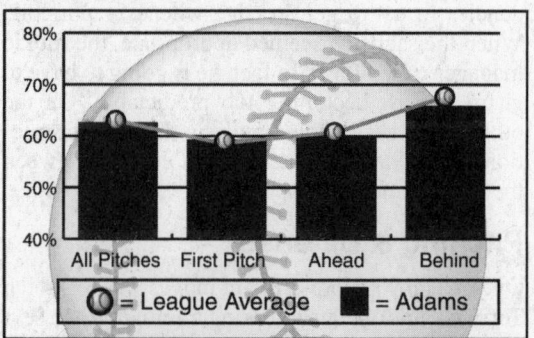

2001 Situational Stats

	W	L	ERA	Sv	IP		AB	H	HR	RBI	Avg
Home	6	3	3.46	0	78.0	LHB	289	67	3	30	.232
Road	6	5	5.09	0	88.1	RHB	356	105	6	43	.295
First Half	4	2	4.97	0	70.2	Sc Pos	165	52	2	60	.315
Scnd Half	8	6	3.86	0	95.2	Clutch	105	22	2	9	.210

2001 Rankings (National League)

- 1st in fewest home runs allowed per nine innings (.49)
- 2nd in highest groundball-flyball ratio allowed (2.3)
- 4th in balks (2)
- 5th in highest batting average allowed with runners in scoring position
- 7th in lowest slugging percentage allowed (.364)
- Led the Dodgers in stolen bases allowed (11), GDPs induced (17), winning percentage, highest strikeout-walk ratio (2.6), highest groundball-flyball ratio allowed (2.3), fewest pitches thrown per batter (3.71), most run support per nine innings (4.4), most GDPs induced per nine innings (0.9) and fewest walks per nine innings (2.9)

James Baldwin

2001 Season

James Baldwin spent the first three weeks of the 2001 campaign on the disabled list as he recovered from offseason shoulder surgery. Slowly working his way back into form, the seven-year veteran understandably was erratic and lasted four or fewer innings in four of his first 14 starts for the White Sox. Traded to the Dodgers a week before the deadline, Baldwin averaged almost 6.2 innings per start in the National League. His 3-6 record with the club was deceiving, as they scored just 3.9 runs per nine innings when he was on the hill.

Pitching

Though formerly a flamethrower, Baldwin tops out right around 90 MPH these days. While his fastball may not have great velocity, it has good tailing action. Baldwin has impeccable control and uses every last inch of the strike zone as he moves the ball up, down, in and out. He mixes in a cutter that slides away from the righthanders, and his curveball is good enough to lock guys up. Perhaps due to the damaged shoulder, he seems to take a while to loosen up, which may explain some of the abbreviated outings.

Defense & Hitting

Baldwin moves pretty well for a man of his size and gets off the mound in good shape. He keeps runners close by throwing to first rather frequently, and his delivery to the plate is relatively quick. For a lifetime American Leaguer, Baldwin takes a decent hack at the plate and made contact in more than half his plate appearances. Though he recorded just one sacrifice, that skill will no doubt evolve should he stay in the Senior Circuit.

2002 Outlook

Though shoulder problems are notoriously difficult to fully overcome, Baldwin has shown the guts and smarts it will take for him to last as a pitcher rather than simply a thrower. At season's end, the Dodgers already were talking up Baldwin as being part of the 2002 rotation. After all, new GM Dan Evans came over from the White Sox and was mostly responsible for bringing the competitive veteran out to Los Angeles.

Position: SP
Bats: R **Throws:** R
Ht: 6' 3" **Wt:** 235

Opening Day Age: 30
Born: 7/15/71 in Southern Pines, NC
ML Seasons: 7

Overall Statistics

	W	L	Pct.	ERA	G	GS	Sv	IP	H	BB	SO	HR	Ratio
2001	10	11	.476	4.42	29	28	0	175.0	191	63	95	25	1.45
Career	72	59	.550	4.98	196	177	0	1095.0	1176	412	719	160	1.45

How Often He Throws Strikes

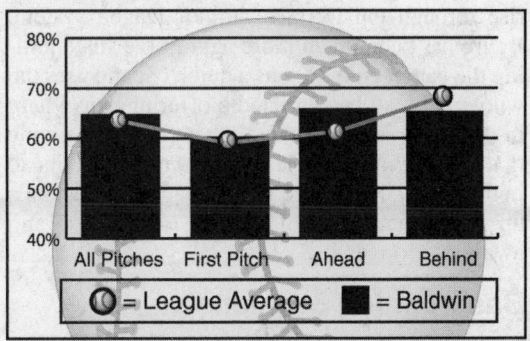

= League Average   = Baldwin

2001 Situational Stats

	W	L	ERA	Sv	IP		AB	H	HR	RBI	Avg
Home	6	4	3.76	0	105.1	LHB	320	83	14	49	.259
Road	4	7	5.43	0	69.2	RHB	360	108	11	40	.300
First Half	5	5	4.70	0	84.1	Sc Pos	159	43	2	57	.270
Scnd Half	5	6	4.17	0	90.2	Clutch	48	7	2	2	.146

2001 Rankings (National League)

- Did not rank near the top or bottom in any category

Adrian Beltre

2001 Season

Considering how his season began, Adrian Beltre ended up with some decent numbers. A botched appendectomy during the offseason still had not healed as spring training rolled around, and the young Dominican had to go back under the knife here in the States. He finally hit the diamond in mid-May, but even then, Beltre looked thin and out of playing shape. The spring had returned to his step by the second half, during which he hit .281, but he never found the consistent power stroke that the club expects him to develop.

Hitting

Though he had shown patience during his meteoric rise through the Dodgers' minor league system, Beltre has been much more aggressive since joining the parent club. He has a quick bat and uses the whole field, so he can handle offerings anywhere in the strike zone. It's the pitches outside the zone that get him into trouble. Pitchers try to get ahead in the count, then entice Beltre to go after fastballs up and in and/or hard breaking stuff down and away.

Baserunning & Defense

Beltre has good instincts on the basepaths, and while he is aggressive, he seldom runs himself into trouble. One gets the feeling that he could steal 30 bags were he ever turned loose. In the field, the third sacker is dynamite when charging bunts and slow rollers. He also has better-than-average range, especially to his glove side, but still has trouble on hoppers hit right at him. Beltre has a cannon, and many of his errors come on ill-advised throws.

2002 Outlook

Now that Beltre is healthy again, it would not be a surprise to see him make a quantum leap this year. The ball jumps off of his bat, so a 25-homer, 90-RBI season looks about right. As he puts some bulk on his young body, Beltre should develop more power and eventually should settle into one of the spots in the heart of the batting order. This kid is a rising star whose career just took a brief hiatus last season due to some weird circumstances.

Position: 3B
Bats: R **Throws:** R
Ht: 5'11" **Wt:** 170

Opening Day Age: 22
Born: 4/7/79 in Santo Domingo, DR
ML Seasons: 4
Pronunciation: BELL-tray

Overall Statistics

	G	AB	R	H	D	T	HR	RBI	SB	BB	SO	Avg	OBP	Slg
2001	126	475	59	126	22	4	13	60	13	28	82	.265	.310	.411
Career	493	1718	232	464	88	11	55	234	46	159	304	.270	.335	.430

Where He Hits the Ball

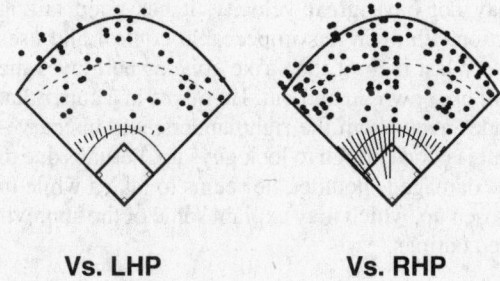

Vs. LHP   Vs. RHP

2001 Situational Stats

	AB	H	HR	RBI	Avg		AB	H	HR	RBI	Avg
Home	223	52	4	22	.233	LHP	98	26	3	15	.265
Road	252	74	9	38	.294	RHP	377	100	10	45	.265
First Half	190	46	7	24	.242	Sc Pos	123	33	1	46	.268
Scnd Half	285	80	6	36	.281	Clutch	90	19	2	13	.211

2001 Rankings (National League)

- 4th in lowest fielding percentage at third base (.952)
- 5th in lowest percentage of swings on the first pitch (16.2) and errors at third base (16)
- Led the Dodgers in most pitches seen per plate appearance (3.83) and lowest percentage of swings on the first pitch (16.2)

Kevin Brown

2001 Season

The 2001 season started and ended with Kevin Brown on the disabled list, and the injuries got progressively worse as the year wore on. Through all of the maladies, from a strained Achilles tendon to an irritated nerve in his neck and finally to a torn muscle in his right elbow, the ultimate warrior wanted to pitch. The fact that Brown performed as well as he did was nothing short of stunning.

Pitching

When healthy, Brown has as much movement on his pitches as anyone in baseball. He throws a live sinking fastball that bores down and in on righthanded hitters, then mixes in a four-seamer that tops out in the mid-90s. He also has a wicked slider and will change his release point from pitch to pitch. In fact, the various angles from which Brown releases the ball may have led to the torn muscle in his elbow. Then again, he averaged more than 240 innings from 1996 through the 2000 campaign, so that workload also may have contributed to the wear and tear. Brown never wants to leave a game and always believes that he can get the next guy out.

Defense & Hitting

While not the most talented glove man, Brown comes racing off the mound after every ball within reach and will take charge on popups until he virtually is pushed out of the way. His errors come from trying to do too much and from having too much movement on his throws to the bases. Though awkward with the stick, he is not an automatic out and can get the bunt down when asked.

2002 Outlook

Time is taking its toll on the 37-year-old, and he may have to learn how to put it into cruise control on occasion. According to team doctors, Brown did no further damage to his arm by pitching through what must have been some substantial pain, so he is expected to be starting on Opening Day. Only time will tell how much movement and velocity he has lost.

Position: SP
Bats: R **Throws:** R
Ht: 6' 4" **Wt:** 200

Opening Day Age: 37
Born: 3/14/65 in McIntyre, GA
ML Seasons: 15

Overall Statistics

	W	L	Pct.	ERA	G	GS	Sv	IP	H	BB	SO	HR	Ratio
2001	10	4	.714	2.65	20	19	0	115.2	94	38	104	8	1.14
Career	180	118	.604	3.18	402	399	0	2776.1	2588	768	2021	169	1.21

How Often He Throws Strikes

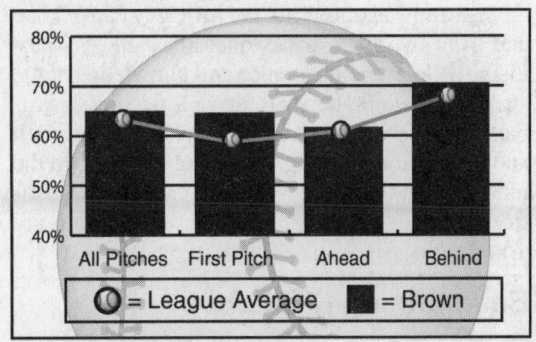

O = League Average   ■ = Brown

2001 Situational Stats

	W	L	ERA	Sv	IP		AB	H	HR	RBI	Avg
Home	4	2	2.43	0	63.0	LHB	213	56	6	22	.263
Road	6	2	2.91	0	52.2	RHB	207	38	2	10	.184
First Half	7	4	3.02	0	83.1	Sc Pos	84	20	1	23	.238
Scnd Half	3	0	1.67	0	32.1	Clutch	20	6	2	4	.300

2001 Rankings (National League)

- 2nd in lowest batting average allowed vs. righthanded batters
- 5th in most GDPs induced per GDP situation (20.3%)
- Led the Dodgers in most GDPs induced per GDP situation (20.3%) and lowest batting average allowed vs. righthanded batters

Alex Cora

2001 Season

Alex Cora was handed the starting shortstop position last season and proceeded to hit .194 over the first two months. While his principal value was expected to be as a solid glove man, the club wanted at least a little something offensively out of the spot and Cora quickly became part of a platoon with Jeff Reboulet. To his credit, the 26-year-old never let the plate struggles affect his play in the field and he hustled every step of the way.

Hitting

Though he occasionally will yank one over the closest right-field wall, Cora usually carries a pop-gun to the plate. However, since outfielders play quite shallow against him, the little guy can get one and even two extra bases once the ball gets past them. He lacks both patience and knowledge of the strike zone, so he hopes to drive a first-pitch fastball. Cora is clueless against any breaking pitch and takes some of the ugliest swings this side of the ninth spot in the order. While he can get the sacrifice down on occasion, No. 8 hitters seldom are asked to do so.

Baserunning & Defense

Cora is a good baserunner yet lacks the speed to do much damage on the diamond. The lack of foot speed really limits his game, as he really could use some infield hits and drag bunts to help inflate his batting average. On the defensive side, Cora is better than average. He has all the tools: soft hands, good range in both directions and a strong throwing arm. Like a lot of young shortstops, his errors come on the easier plays when he seems to lose concentration.

2002 Outlook

Cora's game is extremely limited and his future would seem to be as a utility infielder. He has played second and short during his tenure with the Dodgers and looks just as good at both positions. Cora will be challenged for playing time at shortstop, as the Dodgers traded for slick-fielding Cesar Izturis, a 22-year-old Toronto prospect whose bat also is a question mark. Cora must improve his hitting, because age works in Izturis' favor.

Position: SS
Bats: L **Throws:** R
Ht: 6' 0" **Wt:** 180

Opening Day Age: 26
Born: 10/18/75 in Caguas, PR
ML Seasons: 4

Overall Statistics

	G	AB	R	H	D	T	HR	RBI	SB	BB	SO	Avg	OBP	Slg
2001	134	405	38	88	18	3	4	29	0	31	58	.217	.285	.306
Career	283	821	80	181	37	10	8	64	4	59	123	.220	.285	.319

Where He Hits the Ball

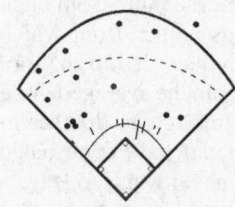 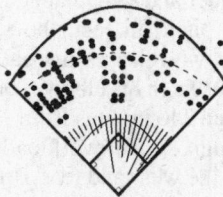

Vs. LHP   **Vs. RHP**

2001 Situational Stats

	AB	H	HR	RBI	Avg		AB	H	HR	RBI	Avg
Home	194	39	2	14	.201	LHP	41	12	1	6	.293
Road	211	49	2	15	.232	RHP	364	76	3	23	.209
First Half	230	48	4	21	.209	Scr Pos	78	20	1	24	.256
Scnd Half	175	40	0	8	.229	Clutch	72	15	0	2	.208

2001 Rankings (National League)

- 1st in lowest batting average vs. righthanded pitchers and lowest slugging percentage vs. righthanded pitchers (.294)
- 3rd in lowest on-base percentage vs. righthanded pitchers (.273)
- 4th in lowest batting average on an 0-2 count (.054) and lowest fielding percentage at shortstop (.962)
- 6th in errors at shortstop (20)
- Led the Dodgers in GDPs (16) and bunts in play (10)

Shawn Green

2001 Season

After taking a year to get acclimated to the new pitchers and parks, Shawn Green showed the National League what all the hubbub was about in Toronto. While his first half was solid, the right-fielder just exploded after the All-Star Game. He knocked in 20 runs in the first 17 games following the break and ended up with the third-most long-balls in baseball (29) after over the season's second half.

Hitting

Green's swing can get a bit long, so opposing pitchers try to tie him up underneath his hands. Their attempts better have some mustard on them, however, because he really can turn on the inside pitch. Teams have been employing the shift more and more against him; if nothing else, it should keep him from staying too pull-conscious. Green hangs in there against southpaws, who try to tempt him with breaking stuff away. When he is on, he will stay on those pitches on the outer half of the plate and drive them to left and left-center.

Baserunning & Defense

Green may be this generation's Joe DiMaggio, if only because he plays the game so elegantly. It never looks as though he is breaking a sweat, yet he really can chew up the turf with his long strides. He could easily steal 40 bases were it asked of him. When making the turn, Green hits each bag with utter precision. He looks the same in the outfield, where he gets quick jumps and seldom makes a bad decision. While his arm is not a gun, it has the accuracy of a laser, and he never misses the cutoff man.

2002 Outlook

Green is hugely popular in his home town, and now that he has had his breakthrough season in Los Angeles, he quickly should become the corner-stone of the team. He set new highs in both home runs and RBI last season, and it is not beyond the realm of possibility that he would leave those totals in the dust over the next few seasons. After all, Green is just 29 years old.

Position: RF
Bats: L **Throws:** L
Ht: 6' 4" **Wt:** 200

Opening Day Age: 29
Born: 11/10/72 in Des Plaines, IL
ML Seasons: 9

Overall Statistics

	G	AB	R	H	D	T	HR	RBI	SB	BB	SO	Avg	OBP	Slg
2001	161	619	121	184	31	4	49	125	20	72	107	.297	.372	.598
Career	1039	3742	621	1066	239	23	192	600	120	368	738	.285	.353	.515

Where He Hits the Ball

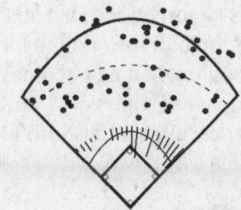
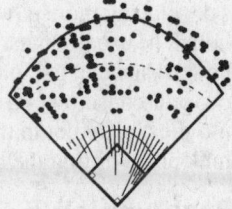

Vs. LHP   Vs. RHP

2001 Situational Stats

	AB	H	HR	RBI	Avg		AB	H	HR	RBI	Avg
Home	299	91	19	51	.304	LHP	171	51	10	27	.298
Road	320	93	30	74	.291	RHP	448	133	39	98	.297
First Half	336	97	20	64	.289	Sc Pos	145	48	10	69	.331
Scnd Half	283	87	29	61	.307	Clutch	99	29	6	17	.293

2001 Rankings (National League)

- 2nd in cleanup slugging percentage (.619)
- 3rd in errors in right field (6)
- 4th in home runs, games played and lowest fielding percentage in right field (.981)
- Led the Dodgers in home runs, at-bats, runs scored, hits, doubles, total bases (370), RBI, times on base (261), strikeouts, pitches seen (2,500), plate appearances (701), games played, slugging percentage, HR frequency (12.6 ABs per HR), stolen-base percentage (83.3), fewest GDPs per GDP situation (6.1%), batting average vs. righthanded pitchers, cleanup slugging percentage (.619), highest percentage of extra bases taken as a runner (61.7) and slugging percentage vs. righthanded pitchers (.616)

Mark Grudzielanek

2001 Season

Mark Grudzielanek was hitting .311 and on pace for 20 homers when he sprained his left ankle and went on the disabled list on June 12th. Though he came back just over two weeks later, the injury continued to hobble him throughout the rest of the campaign. Normally a very consistent offensive player, Grudzielanek ran out of steam down the stretch and hit only .215 from August 26 on.

Hitting

Grudzielanek is a real slasher at the plate. He is at his best when he sits back on the ball and drives it to right field. Not the most patient hitter, he looks for a fastball at every point in the count and can be fooled by breaking stuff outside the strike zone. He is developing more power as he moves into his 30s, though he usually must pull the ball to send it over the wall and can get into trouble when he becomes too pull-conscious. Grudzielanek fits very well into the No. 2 spot in the order, as it forces him to think about hitting the ball the other way.

Baserunning & Defense

No longer the guy who went 33-for-40 as a thief back in 1996, Grudzielanek is seldom asked to run by the Dodgers. When he is healthy, however, he retains good tactical speed and almost always will get two bases on hits to the outfield. He is not the headiest baserunner and will run himself into outs on occasion. Now entering just his third year as a second sacker, he may be a bit underrated defensively. While he does not have the softest hands in the world, Grudzielanek is very athletic and has a serviceable range to his glove side. He has a shortstop's arm and can gun his way out of trouble.

2002 Outlook

Grudzielanek is signed through 2003 and his contract would be hard to move even if the club were so inclined. When healthy, he has the potential to hit .300 and is showing signs of developing enough power to hit 15-20 balls out of the yard. Grudzielanek's value would rise if the team could just find a decent leadoff guy.

Position: 2B
Bats: R **Throws:** R
Ht: 6' 1" **Wt:** 185

Opening Day Age: 31
Born: 6/30/70 in Milwaukee, WI
ML Seasons: 7
Pronunciation: gress-uh-LAWN-ick

Overall Statistics

	G	AB	R	H	D	T	HR	RBI	SB	BB	SO	Avg	OBP	Slg
2001	133	539	83	146	21	3	13	55	4	28	83	.271	.317	.393
Career	947	3808	520	1081	200	24	48	332	106	193	508	.284	.328	.387

Where He Hits the Ball

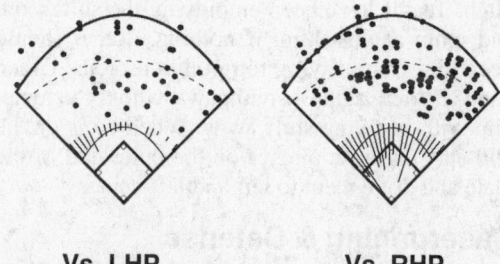

Vs. LHP   **Vs. RHP**

2001 Situational Stats

	AB	H	HR	RBI	Avg		AB	H	HR	RBI	Avg
Home	265	65	8	29	.245	LHP	122	36	6	14	.295
Road	274	81	5	26	.296	RHP	417	110	7	41	.264
First Half	267	80	8	35	.300	Sc Pos	90	30	1	35	.333
Scnd Half	272	66	5	20	.243	Clutch	81	24	3	12	.296

2001 Rankings (National League)

- 6th in errors at second base (10) and fielding percentage at second base (.984)
- Led the Dodgers in singles, hit by pitch (11) and highest groundball-flyball ratio (1.5)

Eric Karros

Position: 1B
Bats: R **Throws:** R
Ht: 6' 4" **Wt:** 226

Opening Day Age: 34
Born: 11/4/67 in Hackensack, NJ
ML Seasons: 11
Pronunciation: CARE-ose

2001 Season

Eric Karros strained his back in late February, but still managed to answer the opening bell. Though his only stint on the disabled list was for three weeks around Memorial Day, the first sacker never looked completely healthy. He had to sit out occasional games and even was benched at times, so Karros ended up with his fewest number of games played in seven years. After producing at last 30 homers and 100 RBI in five of the previous six campaigns, he did not hit a single longball after September 1.

Hitting

Karros is a heady ballplayer who makes adjustments from at-bat to at-bat, so pitchers must alter their strategies. He is the rare righthanded hitter who likes the ball down and in, but he also can take fastballs out over the plate and drive them the other way. Once he is behind in the count, Karros is fed a steady diet of breaking stuff on or just off the outside corner, and he will whiff on those or send meek grounders to the shortstop. When he is in a groove, he sends that pitch back through the box.

Baserunning & Defense

Already slow, the bad back made Karros even slower. That said, he knows when to pick his spots and will seldom run the club out of an inning. Karros' biggest liability in the field is a lack of mobility; he is unable to get down on hard-hit bouncers as well as throws in the dirt. His hands are not the softest, either. To his credit, he starts the double play as well as any righthanded first baseman.

2002 Outlook

The all-time Dodgers' home-run leader has one more year on his contract and will be the club's first baseman this season. Should Karros be able to get completely healthy and become a middle-of-the-lineup force once again, it would be a huge boost for the team. After all, look how far the Dodgers got last season despite getting such a small contribution from one of their acknowledged team leaders.

Overall Statistics

	G	AB	R	H	D	T	HR	RBI	SB	BB	SO	Avg	OBP	Slg
2001	121	438	42	103	22	0	15	63	3	41	101	.235	.303	.388
Career	1459	5478	700	1466	276	9	257	903	53	480	1031	.268	.326	.462

Where He Hits the Ball

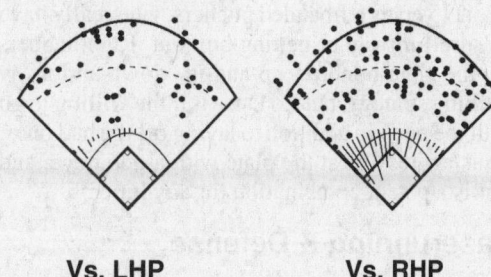

Vs. LHP   Vs. RHP

2001 Situational Stats

	AB	H	HR	RBI	Avg		AB	H	HR	RBI	Avg
Home	201	47	7	23	.234	LHP	94	24	6	17	.255
Road	237	56	8	40	.236	RHP	344	79	9	46	.230
First Half	214	54	8	36	.252	Sc Pos	123	32	2	45	.260
Scnd Half	224	49	7	27	.219	Clutch	66	15	2	15	.227

2001 Rankings (National League)

- 2nd in fielding percentage at first base (.996) and lowest batting average on an 0-2 count (.040)
- 6th in lowest batting average vs. righthanded pitchers and lowest batting average on the road
- 9th in assists at first base (71)
- 10th in lowest on-base percentage vs. righthanded pitchers (.299)
- Led the Dodgers in batting average with the bases loaded (.412)

Paul Lo Duca

2001 Season

Buried for eight years in the Dodgers' farm system, Paul Lo Duca came out of spring training with half of the catching job. He promptly took full control of the position, however, by hitting .382 over the first two months of the season. Showing surprising power, he split his time between the leadoff and No. 5 spots in the order as manager Jim Tracy kept finding ways to keep him in the lineup. Though Lo Duca slowed down the stretch, he was clearly one of the most valuable members of the squad.

Hitting

Lo Duca loves high fastballs out over the plate and can take them out to any part of the park, showing amazing power to right field for a guy his size. He hit .411 versus lefthanded pitchers, who really have no sure-fire way of getting him out. Righthanders try the time-honored up-and-in, down-and-away pitching strategy, but Lo Duca is quite willing to go with the pitch in addition to laying off the bad ones. He is aggressive at the plate with a good eye, and that is a potent combination for any hitter.

Baserunning & Defense

The years of squatting have slowed him a bit, but the 29-year-old Lo Duca still is at least an average baserunner. He is quite agile behind the plate, moving well in both directions to block balls in the dirt. Lo Duca also has a strong and accurate throwing arm and gunned down 38.5 percent of opposing basestealers. He also handled himself quite well in both the outfield and at first base, though he obviously is a bit vertically-challenged to play the latter position on a regular basis.

2002 Outlook

While it might be optimistic to expect Lo Duca to match his numbers from last season, he is a lifetime .315 hitter in the minors and has all the confidence in the world. Having waited so long to get his shot, he confounded opponents' scouting reports by adjusting as the season progressed and hit .317 or higher in every month until September. Lo Duca has emerged as a clear fan favorite and should be a vocal team leader over the next few seasons.

Position: C/1B
Bats: R **Throws:** R
Ht: 5'10" **Wt:** 185

Opening Day Age: 29
Born: 4/12/72 in Brooklyn, NY
ML Seasons: 4

Overall Statistics

	G	AB	R	H	D	T	HR	RBI	SB	BB	SO	Avg	OBP	Slg
2001	125	460	71	147	28	0	25	90	2	39	30	.320	.374	.543
Career	201	634	90	189	32	0	30	110	3	55	48	.298	.355	.491

Where He Hits the Ball

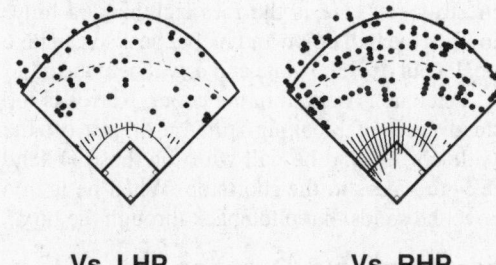

Vs. LHP   **Vs. RHP**

2001 Situational Stats

	AB	H	HR	RBI	Avg		AB	H	HR	RBI	Avg
Home	218	73	11	40	.335	LHP	112	46	7	28	.411
Road	242	74	14	50	.306	RHP	348	101	18	62	.290
First Half	205	71	14	45	.346	Sc Pos	103	39	7	66	.379
Scnd Half	255	76	11	45	.298	Clutch	70	19	4	16	.271

2001 Rankings (National League)

- 1st in batting average vs. lefthanded pitchers
- 2nd in on-base percentage for a leadoff hitter (.378)
- 4th in highest percentage of runners caught stealing as a catcher (38.5)
- 5th in batting average with runners in scoring position
- 6th in slugging percentage vs. lefthanded pitchers (.679)
- Led the Dodgers in batting average, sacrifice flies (9), lowest percentage of swings that missed (8.9), highest percentage of swings put into play (53.6), batting average with runners in scoring position, on-base percentage for a leadoff hitter (.378) and batting average with two strikes (.242)

Chan Ho Park

2001 Season

Chan Ho Park had a superb first half last season, and it looked as if he finally was on the cusp of pulling it all together. However, the pressure of a pennant race as well as impending free agency seemed to get the best of the young Korean, and he was just a .500 pitcher down the stretch. As always, he did his best work in pitcher-friendly Dodger Stadium, where his career record now stands at 42-24 with a 2.98 ERA.

Pitching

Many pitchers would make deals with the devil to have Park's stuff. He routinely hits 92-93 MPH with his fastball, and his curveball just freezes people. When he does not have a good feel for the curve early in the game, however, he tends to give up on it too quickly. While his slider is decent, he hangs it. . . and those balls often leave the yard. His changeup remains a work in progress that could become a valuable weapon, especially against lefties. Park's biggest problem is in his head. He does not handle adversity very well and has a tendency to mope when things go wrong.

Defense & Hitting

Park often tries to do too much when the ball is hit in his direction. He is particularly overzealous on bunts and soft rollers to the third-base side. He has a quick power move and does not lose anything when he uses a more compact delivery to the plate. Park fancies himself as a power hitter and takes a wild swing, so when he does connect, he can put a charge into it. He is also a pretty good bunter and runs well.

2002 Outlook

Scott Boras began his negotiations in the newspapers by throwing out an annual salary proposal of $20 million for his young would-be ace. When the 28-year-old lugged down the stretch, however, his agent blamed the club. Let the buyer beware: Park has a lifetime ERA of 4.74 outside of Chavez Ravine, and who knows how he will react when he discovers that personal catcher Chad Kreuter may not be tagging along?

Position: SP
Bats: R **Throws:** R
Ht: 6' 2" **Wt:** 204

Opening Day Age: 28
Born: 6/30/73 in Kong Ju City, Korea
ML Seasons: 8

Overall Statistics

	W	L	Pct.	ERA	G	GS	Sv	IP	H	BB	SO	HR	Ratio
2001	15	11	.577	3.50	36	35	0	234.0	183	91	218	23	1.17
Career	80	54	.597	3.80	221	176	0	1183.2	1001	560	1098	124	1.32

How Often He Throws Strikes

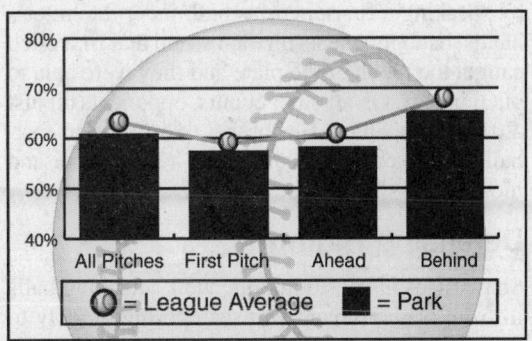

2001 Situational Stats

	W	L	ERA	Sv	IP		AB	H	HR	RBI	Avg
Home	10	4	2.36	0	126.0	LHB	392	90	16	45	.230
Road	5	7	4.83	0	108.0	RHB	455	93	7	40	.204
First Half	8	5	2.80	0	131.2	Sc Pos	173	34	5	62	.197
Scnd Half	7	6	4.40	0	102.1	Clutch	77	21	2	9	.273

2001 Rankings (National League)

- 1st in games started, hit batsmen (20) and balks (3)
- 3rd in innings pitched, strikeouts, pitches thrown (3,689) and lowest batting average allowed (.216)
- Led the Dodgers in ERA, sacrifice bunts (7), wins, losses, complete games (2), innings pitched, hits allowed, batters faced (981), walks allowed, strikeouts, pitches thrown (3,689), lowest batting average allowed (.216), lowest slugging percentage allowed (.358), lowest on-base percentage allowed (.305), lowest ERA at home, lowest ERA on the road, lowest batting average allowed with runners in scoring position and most strikeouts per nine innings (8.4)

Jeff Shaw

2001 Season

From the middle of April to early June, Jeff Shaw ran off a string of 15 straight saves without blowing one. Manager Jim Tracy already had summoned Shaw 42 times from the bullpen by the All-Star break, however, and the 35-year-old wore down in the second half. He posted a 7.59 ERA in August, but then found his second wind and finished the year on a strong note by converting his last four save chances.

Pitching

Shaw is not the prototypical closer. His fastball tops out at 90 MPH on a good day, so he must rely on guile and great command. He likes to get ahead by sneaking a first-pitch fastball under the hitter's hands, but oppoenents hit .364 when that first pitch caught too much of the plate and they were able to put it in play. On all other counts, opponents hit just .201 against Shaw. He throws two different fastballs, a sinker and a cutter, and relied more and more on his slider as the year moved along.

Defense & Hitting

Shaw fields his position quite well, attacking balls in front of the mound and scampering quickly to cover first base on grounders hit to the right side. Unlike most closers, he pays attention to the running game. Though his pickoff move is only fair, Shaw will use it quite often to keep runners close. Since he also gets rid of the ball quickly to the plate, opponents attempted just three steals off him all season. He has not made a plate appearance since joining the Dodgers in 1998.

2002 Outlook

Shaw was seriously considering retiring as the 2001 season drew to a close, no doubt frustrated by the team's failure to reach the postseason as well as the cascades of boos that rained down upon him from the home crowd down the stretch. While the Dodgers knew it would not be easy to replace Shaw's 43 saves, they decided not to pick up his $7.05 million option for 2002. If he does decide to stay in the game for another year, look for him to find work with Cincinnati or possibly a contender by next spring.

Position: RP
Bats: R **Throws:** R
Ht: 6' 2" **Wt:** 200

Opening Day Age: 35
Born: 7/7/66 in Washington Courthouse, OH
ML Seasons: 12

Overall Statistics

	W	L	Pct.	ERA	G	GS	Sv	IP	H	BB	SO	HR	Ratio
2001	3	5	.375	3.62	77	0	43	74.2	63	18	58	10	1.08
Career	34	54	.386	3.54	633	19	203	848.0	821	234	545	91	1.24

How Often He Throws Strikes

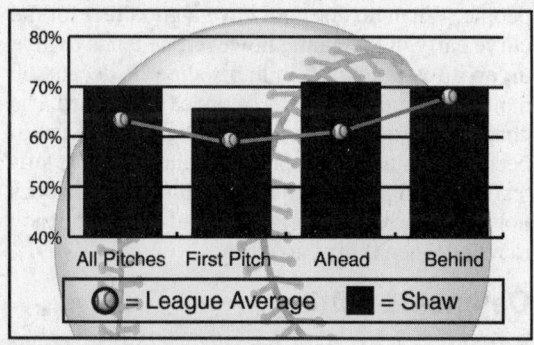

2001 Situational Stats

	W	L	ERA	Sv	IP		AB	H	HR	RBI	Avg
Home	3	4	3.09	23	46.2	LHB	130	25	1	7	.192
Road	0	1	4.50	20	28.0	RHB	148	38	9	25	.257
First Half	3	2	3.07	24	41.0	Sc Pos	60	13	3	23	.217
Scnd Half	0	3	4.28	19	33.2	Clutch	202	44	6	25	.218

2001 Rankings (National League)

- 1st in save opportunities (52) and blown saves (9)
- 2nd in saves and games finished (66)
- 4th in lowest batting average allowed vs. lefthanded batters
- 5th in fewest baserunners allowed per nine innings in relief (10.0)
- 7th in lowest save percentage (82.7)
- Led the Dodgers in games pitched, saves, games finished (66), save opportunities (52), lowest batting average allowed vs. lefthanded batters, save percentage (82.7), blown saves (9), lowest batting average allowed in relief (.227) and fewest baserunners allowed per nine innings in relief (10.0)

Gary Sheffield

2001 Season

After torching Dodgers management as spring training was about to begin, Gary Sheffield settled down and just played baseball. He got off to a decent start, then sprained a ligament in his left index finger in late May, and the painful injury lingered throughout the rest of the season. Despite that and an odd fainting spell that put him in the hospital for a night, Sheffield had a great couple of months after the break. However, he hit just .203 with no homers and just two RBI during a crucial 16-game stretch in September and early October when the Dodgers' pennant hopes died.

Hitting

Sheffield has a lightning-quick bat and wags it menacingly over his head as he awaits the pitch. He crushes high fastballs and that is the one area where he will expand the strike zone when he sees one that he likes. Otherwise, he has a great eye and often will question close pitches that are called strikes. Though he has enough power to reach either gap, almost all of Sheffield's home runs go between dead center and the left-field foul pole. In fact, more managers are employing a shift against him these days, but he has enough bat control to confound teams by grounding singles through the right side.

Baserunning & Defense

Sheffield can motor pretty well, especially when making the turn, and is a 68 percent basestealer over the course of his career. He does not get good jumps in the outfield and almost always will err on the side of caution on balls that drop in front of him. Sheffield has a good arm and was second in the league with 17 assists, including several that gunned down guys at the plate.

2002 Outlook

Sheffield almost was traded in the midst of the chaos he created last spring, but the offers were not sufficient and he performed well for the Dodgers. It would not be a surprise, however, if those trade talks resumed this winter. Sheffield is one of the best righthanded hitters in the game and regardless of his attitude, he never gives away an at-bat.

Position: LF
Bats: R **Throws:** R
Ht: 5'11" **Wt:** 205

Opening Day Age: 33
Born: 11/18/68 in Tampa, FL
ML Seasons: 14

Overall Statistics

	G	AB	R	H	D	T	HR	RBI	SB	BB	SO	Avg	OBP	Slg
2001	143	515	98	160	28	2	36	100	10	94	67	.311	.417	.583
Career	1592	5661	982	1668	293	21	315	1016	170	952	688	.295	.399	.521

Where He Hits the Ball

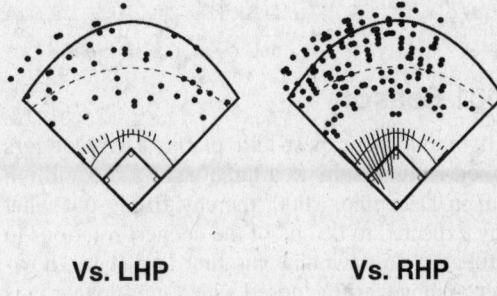

Vs. LHP   **Vs. RHP**

2001 Situational Stats

	AB	H	HR	RBI	Avg		AB	H	HR	RBI	Avg
Home	243	76	16	39	.313	LHP	107	40	10	27	.374
Road	272	84	20	61	.309	RHP	408	120	26	73	.294
First Half	248	71	18	44	.286	Sc Pos	125	38	7	61	.304
Scnd Half	267	89	18	56	.333	Clutch	83	29	9	19	.349

2001 Rankings (National League)

- 2nd in assists in left field (17)
- 4th in cleanup slugging percentage (.604), slugging percentage vs. lefthanded pitchers (.720) and lowest fielding percentage in left field (.972)
- 5th in batting average vs. lefthanded pitchers and on-base percentage vs. lefthanded pitchers (.457)
- Led the Dodgers in walks, on-base percentage, highest percentage of pitches taken (58.6), batting average in the clutch, batting average on a 3-1 count (.563), batting average on an 0-2 count (.290), slugging percentage vs. lefthanded pitchers (.720), on-base percentage vs. lefthanded pitchers (.457), on-base percentage vs. righthanded pitchers (.407), batting average at home and batting average on the road

Andy Ashby

Position: SP
Bats: R **Throws:** R
Ht: 6' 5" **Wt:** 202

Opening Day Age: 34
Born: 7/11/67 in
Kansas City, MO
ML Seasons: 11

Overall Statistics

	W	L	Pct.	ERA	G	GS	Sv	IP	H	BB	SO	HR	Ratio
2001	2	0	1.000	3.86	2	2	0	11.2	14	1	7	2	1.29
Career	86	87	.497	4.10	256	243	1	1554.0	1587	458	1023	177	1.32

2001 Situational Stats

	W	L	ERA	Sv	IP		AB	H	HR	RBI	Avg
Home	1	0	5.40	0	6.2	LHB	32	11	2	5	.344
Road	1	0	1.80	0	5.0	RHB	16	3	0	0	.188
First Half	2	0	3.86	0	11.2	Sc Pos	10	2	0	2	.200
Scnd Half	0	0	-	0	0.0	Clutch	3	1	0	2	.333

2001 Season

Talk about your best-laid plans. The Dodgers signed Andy Ashby to a three-year, $22.5 million deal in December 2000, thereby filling out what they expected to be one of the deepest rotations in baseball. After winning his first two starts, however, Ashby was diagnosed with a muscle tear in is right elbow and was lost for the season.

Pitching, Defense & Hitting

Ashby makes his living with hard sinking stuff. His two-seamed fastball might only reach the lower 90s, but it tails down and in on righthanded hitters. His slider breaks the same way in the other direction and he also will mix in a change and a splitter. While not a strikeout ace, Ashby has maintained a 2.2 strikeout-walk ratio over his career. Using a rather complex delivery, he tries to keep runners close by throwing over frequently, but opposing basestealers have maintained a 72 percent success rate over his career. He defends his position rather aggressively and can hold his own with the bat.

2002 Outlook

The Dodgers expect Ashby to be fully recovered by Opening Day, as the elbow required no reconstruction, only the re-attachment of a muscle. Since he never had relied too much on velocity, it would not be a surprise to see him come back strong in '02.

Giovanni Carrara

Position: RP
Bats: R **Throws:** R
Ht: 6' 2" **Wt:** 210

Opening Day Age: 34
Born: 3/4/68 in Edo
Anzoategui, VZ
ML Seasons: 5

Overall Statistics

	W	L	Pct.	ERA	G	GS	Sv	IP	H	BB	SO	HR	Ratio
2001	6	1	.857	3.16	47	3	0	85.1	73	24	70	12	1.14
Career	9	8	.529	6.03	88	17	0	195.2	226	91	140	42	1.62

2001 Situational Stats

	W	L	ERA	Sv	IP		AB	H	HR	RBI	Avg
Home	1	1	3.04	0	50.1	LHB	147	38	8	19	.259
Road	5	0	3.34	0	35.0	RHB	169	35	4	13	.207
First Half	1	1	3.51	0	33.1	Sc Pos	69	15	1	16	.217
Scnd Half	5	0	2.94	0	52.0	Clutch	75	20	1	4	.267

2001 Season

Signed to a minor league contract prior to spring training, Giovanni Carrara was called up in May and evolved into one of the most valuable members of the Dodgers' pitching staff. He was the ultimate staff saver, making three spot starts as well as relieving on back-to-back days six different times. No matter how he was used, Carrara was effective.

Pitching, Defense & Hitting

While Carrara does not wow anyone with his stuff, he can reach 90 MPH with his two-seamed fastball and gets good sinking action with the four-seamer. Mixing in a decent slider, he relies on his fine control and effectively uses all areas of the strike zone. Having been almost exclusively a starter during his previous 11 pro seasons, he exhibited a rubber arm when used in several multi-inning appearances. Carrara is just a fair fielder and he does not have a good pickoff move. He logged his first three major league hits last year in 12 at-bats.

2002 Outlook

After never pitching more than 50 innings in any big league season, Carrara opened some eyes last year. In fact, he could help more than a few clubs as a regular member of their rotation. With all of the question marks on the LA staff, the team may think long and hard before letting him get away.

Darren Dreifort

Position: SP
Bats: R **Throws:** R
Ht: 6' 2" **Wt:** 211

Opening Day Age: 29
Born: 5/3/72 in Wichita, KS
ML Seasons: 7
Pronunciation: DRY-fort

Overall Statistics

	W	L	Pct.	ERA	G	GS	Sv	IP	H	BB	SO	HR	Ratio
2001	4	7	.364	5.13	16	16	0	94.2	89	47	91	11	1.44
Career	43	52	.453	4.38	204	103	10	761.2	725	328	672	79	1.38

2001 Situational Stats

	W	L	ERA	Sv	IP		AB	H	HR	RBI	Avg
Home	2	3	5.14	0	49.0	LHB	163	48	7	36	.294
Road	2	4	5.12	0	45.2	RHB	191	41	4	24	.215
First Half	4	7	5.13	0	94.2	Sc Pos	90	29	2	44	.322
Scnd Half	0	0	-	0	0.0	Clutch	20	5	1	4	.250

2001 Season

After signing a huge five-year contract in December 2000, Darren Dreifort got off to an erratic start last season. He rattled off a series of solid outings in May, but it soon became obvious that something was bothering him. The righthander finally had to be shut down at the end of June with a torn ligament in his pitching elbow.

Pitching, Defense & Hitting

Dreifort's fastball has even more late tailing action than that of his more celebrated teammate, Kevin Brown, and he can (or could) routinely reach the low to mid-90s. His other main pitch is a nasty slider that is just a few ticks slower. Dreifort gets into trouble when he gets behind in the count, then lets up a bit to throw a strike. He also struggles with men on base. He is just an average fielder and his throws often handcuff infielders. Dreifort has homered in each of the past four seasons but also has struck out at least 20 times each year.

2002 Outlook

Dreifort faces a task that never has been done before: rehabbing a second ligament transfer surgery. He may not pitch in 2002, or ever again for that matter. He is seen as a real gamer, but he tends to fall apart in tough situations and has made just 10 career starts after September 1.

Eric Gagne

Position: SP
Bats: R **Throws:** R
Ht: 6' 2" **Wt:** 195

Opening Day Age: 26
Born: 1/7/76 in Montreal, PQ, Canada
ML Seasons: 3
Pronunciation: gan-YAY

Overall Statistics

	W	L	Pct.	ERA	G	GS	Sv	IP	H	BB	SO	HR	Ratio
2001	6	7	.462	4.75	33	24	0	151.2	144	46	130	24	1.25
Career	11	14	.440	4.61	58	48	0	283.0	268	121	239	47	1.37

2001 Situational Stats

	W	L	ERA	Sv	IP		AB	H	HR	RBI	Avg
Home	2	4	3.69	0	70.2	LHB	277	71	11	46	.256
Road	4	3	5.67	0	81.0	RHB	296	73	13	45	.247
First Half	1	4	5.42	0	78.0	Sc Pos	138	33	8	66	.239
Scnd Half	5	3	4.03	0	73.2	Clutch	31	9	1	5	.290

2001 Season

Last season almost was a carbon-copy of the 2000 campaign for Eric Gagne. He came out of the spring as a member of the rotation, only to put up a 6.05 ERA over his first 12 starts. After two trips to the minors, he eventually pitched his way back to the big league staff. Down the stretch, he served as a long reliever and did quite well in that role.

Pitching, Defense & Hitting

Gagne's fastball is deceptively quick, often reaching 94 MPH. He gets a lot of movement on his cutter and owns a world-class curveball. At this point, he needs to fine-tune his command and learn to challenge hitters. Like many young hurlers, he tries to nibble too much before coming in with something fat when behind in the count. Gagne handles the glove well. He keeps the running game in check with a compact delivery and not only has recorded six sacrifices in each of the past two seasons, but also smacked his first homer last year.

2002 Outlook

The Dodgers may have to learn to live with the fact that Gagne is a slow starter. He lost the confidence of Jim Tracy and pitching coach Jim Colborn, however, and that might not be easy to win back. Still, with all the injuries to the rotation, Gagne will be given every opportunity once again to win a spot.

Tom Goodwin

Position: CF
Bats: L **Throws:** R
Ht: 6' 1" **Wt:** 175

Opening Day Age: 33
Born: 7/27/68 in
Fresno, CA
ML Seasons: 11

Overall Statistics

	G	AB	R	H	D	T	HR	RBI	SB	BB	SO	Avg	OBP	Slg
2001	105	286	51	66	8	5	4	22	22	23	58	.231	.286	.336
Career	1046	3416	576	919	102	37	22	252	329	332	580	.269	.335	.340

2001 Situational Stats

	AB	H	HR	RBI	Avg		AB	H	HR	RBI	Avg
Home	130	28	1	10	.215	LHP	32	8	1	4	.250
Road	156	38	3	12	.244	RHP	254	58	3	18	.228
First Half	223	55	3	17	.247	Sc Pos	44	13	0	16	.295
Scnd Half	63	11	1	5	.175	Clutch	40	9	0	4	.225

2001 Season

Expected to fill the leadoff spot for the Dodgers, Tom Goodwin had a .276 on-base percentage after the season's first two months. That and Marquis Grissom's hot start sent the speedy centerfielder to the pine. After a short stint on the disabled list with a strained right hamstring, Goodwin collected just 41 at-bats from August 9 to the end of the season.

Hitting, Baserunning & Defense

Not only is the lefty-swinging Goodwin overwhelmed by the hardest throwers in the league, but he also is clueless against any breaking pitch. He worked very hard on his bunting game in the spring, but he was not able to master the craft and seldom tried to lay one down during the regular season. On the rare occasion that he gets on base, Goodwin is a fine basestealer. In the outfield, he gets decent jumps and can run down balls to either gap but his arm is below average.

2002 Outlook

Acquired at the trading deadline in 2000, Goodwin has hit just .239 with the Dodgers and has found himself at the end of Jim Tracy's bench. Though he is signed for one more year, it would not be a surprise to see the club simply eat his contract and send Goodwin packing. If he stays in LA, it would be as a defensive replacement and pinch-runner.

Marquis Grissom

Position: CF/LF
Bats: R **Throws:** R
Ht: 5'11" **Wt:** 188

Opening Day Age: 34
Born: 4/17/67 in
Atlanta, GA
ML Seasons: 13
Pronunciation:
mar-KEESE
Nickname: Grip

Overall Statistics

	G	AB	R	H	D	T	HR	RBI	SB	BB	SO	Avg	OBP	Slg
2001	135	448	56	99	17	1	21	60	7	16	107	.221	.250	.404
Career	1716	6646	962	1794	302	47	166	723	409	467	989	.270	.318	.404

2001 Situational Stats

	AB	H	HR	RBI	Avg		AB	H	HR	RBI	Avg
Home	231	51	9	27	.221	LHP	134	34	8	17	.254
Road	217	48	12	33	.221	RHP	314	65	13	43	.207
First Half	236	62	15	43	.263	Sc Pos	107	26	5	40	.243
Scnd Half	212	37	6	17	.175	Clutch	90	15	1	10	.167

2001 Season

Acquired at the start of spring training for perennial malcontent Devon White, Marquis Grissom was a breath of fresh air in the Dodgers' clubhouse. The good times lasted through April and May, as he hit .299 and pounded out 10 home runs. From June 1 on, however, Grissom hit just .190.

Hitting, Baserunning & Defense

Proudly proclaiming that walks aren't a part of his game, Grissom will take a wild cut anytime, anywhere. When opposing pitchers make a mistake and actually leave a ball somewhere near the plate, he has enough sock to pull it out of the park. Though Grissom no longer is a prolific basestealer, he still moves well and runs the bases like he does everything else: aggressively. Though he has lost a bit in the outfield, he gets decent jumps and can run some balls down. His arm is average at best.

2002 Outlook

Grissom has another year on his contract, so he will remain a Dodger this season. The club would like him to become a fourth outfielder. The 13-year veteran is a stand-up guy and his value to the club stretches beyond the lines. In fact, his most valuable contribution may be in his ability to keep close friend Gary Sheffield in good spirits and focused on performing up to his capabilities.

Matt Herges

Position: RP
Bats: L **Throws:** R
Ht: 6' 0" **Wt:** 200

Opening Day Age: 32
Born: 4/1/70 in
Champaign, IL
ML Seasons: 3
Pronunciation:
hur-GESS

Overall Statistics

	W	L	Pct.	ERA	G	GS	Sv	IP	H	BB	SO	HR	Ratio
2001	9	8	.529	3.44	75	0	1	99.1	97	46	76	8	1.44
Career	20	13	.606	3.38	151	4	2	234.1	221	94	169	20	1.34

2001 Situational Stats

	W	L	ERA	Sv	IP		AB	H	HR	RBI	Avg
Home	6	2	2.72	0	53.0	LHB	168	47	6	24	.280
Road	3	6	4.27	1	46.1	RHB	206	50	2	23	.243
First Half	7	6	3.43	0	57.2	Sc Pos	93	26	1	35	.280
Scnd Half	2	2	3.46	1	41.2	Clutch	214	61	2	29	.285

2001 Season

Matt Herges was a victim of his own success last year. He showed so much rubber-armed effectiveness early in the season that manager Jim Tracy kept calling his number. He appeared in 15 of the team's 27 games in June. Naturally, the 31-year-old wore down in the dog days, though he actually got his second wind starting in August.

Pitching, Defense & Hitting

Herges has a compact delivery, so his 93-MPH fastball gets right in on the hitter. He also owns a knee-buckling curveball, and when he can throw that pitch for strikes, he is a tough customer. Herges can field his position adequately and keeps runners close with a quick little move. Opposing runners were just 3-for-10 in stolen-base attempts in 2001. Though he doesn't get many chances to hit, the middle reliever banged out four hits in nine at-bats.

2002 Outlook

After toiling for eight seasons in the minors, Herges is making up for lost time. He has logged 210 innings over the last two seasons, a workload that could prove to be damaging should it continue. There is talk of making him the closer after the team declined to pick up the option on Jeff Shaw, as Herges seems to have both the pitching arsenal and the makeup to succeed in almost any role.

Chad Kreuter

Position: C
Bats: B **Throws:** R
Ht: 6' 2" **Wt:** 200

Opening Day Age: 37
Born: 8/26/64 in
Greenbrae, CA
ML Seasons: 14
Pronunciation:
CREW-ter

Overall Statistics

	G	AB	R	H	D	T	HR	RBI	SB	BB	SO	Avg	OBP	Slg
2001	73	191	21	41	11	1	6	17	0	41	52	.215	.355	.377
Career	896	2392	281	566	117	8	52	262	4	348	560	.237	.336	.357

2001 Situational Stats

	AB	H	HR	RBI	Avg		AB	H	HR	RBI	Avg
Home	80	16	4	11	.200	LHP	52	10	3	6	.192
Road	111	25	2	6	.225	RHP	139	31	3	11	.223
First Half	130	33	2	8	.254	Sc Pos	36	5	2	10	.139
Scnd Half	61	8	4	9	.131	Clutch	37	8	1	2	.216

2001 Season

Expected to garner half of the playing time behind the plate for the Dodgers, Chad Kreuter's 2001 season was done in by the phenomenon known as Paul Lo Duca. The veteran's role eventually was reduced to that of Chan Ho Park's personal catcher. It was difficult for him to find a rhythm either behind or at the plate.

Hitting, Baserunning & Defense

Kreuter is an extremely patient hitter who will take a walk in almost any situation. A switch-hitter, he looks a bit more comfortable from the left side. While he has enough power from either side to yank one out, Kreuter can be overmatched by the harder throwers and flails helplessly at most breaking pitches. He is fundamentally sound behind the slab. He moves well to block balls in the dirt and while he does not possess a gun, Kreuter keeps the running game in check with a quick release.

2002 Outlook

Though he is signed through 2002, Kreuter's value to the Dodgers will suffer greatly should Park take his services elsewhere. The team that ultimately takes on the volatile Korean hurler would be well-advised to try to acquire his caddy as well. Kreuter is not a bad guy to have around; he knows his role and seems happy to be a part of the big league fun.

Los Angeles

Luke Prokopec

Position: SP
Bats: L **Throws:** R
Ht: 5'11" **Wt:** 166

Opening Day Age: 24
Born: 2/23/78 in Blackwood, Australia
ML Seasons: 2
Pronunciation: prok-a-peck

Overall Statistics

	W	L	Pct.	ERA	G	GS	Sv	IP	H	BB	SO	HR	Ratio
2001	8	7	.533	4.88	29	22	0	138.1	146	40	91	27	1.34
Career	9	8	.529	4.63	34	25	0	159.1	165	49	103	29	1.34

2001 Situational Stats

	W	L	ERA	Sv	IP		AB	H	HR	RBI	Avg
Home	5	4	5.05	0	66.0	LHB	249	58	14	30	.233
Road	3	3	4.73	0	72.1	RHB	296	88	13	43	.297
First Half	6	4	4.18	0	90.1	Sc Pos	119	33	0	39	.277
Scnd Half	2	3	6.19	0	48.0	Clutch	26	7	3	5	.269

2001 Season

Luke Prokopec went 6-1 with a 3.33 ERA over the first two months last season and allowed more than three earned runs in only four of his first 16 starts. Things fell apart in the second half, partly due to a recurring blister that eventually sent him to the disabled list in August. Upon his return, the young Aussie worked out of the bullpen.

Pitching, Defense & Hitting

Prokopec has a good fastball that tops out in the low 90s. He uses two breaking pitches, both a slider and a curve, and a changeup that still needs some work. While his stuff is not quite top-notch, he has excellent command and knows how to take advantage of all parts of the strike zone. As might be expected of a converted outfielder, Prokopec fields his position quite well. He also can handle the bat, as proven by his .194 average last season with seven sacrifices.

2002 Outlook

Having pitched for just four-plus professional seasons now, Prokopec is quite raw. On top of that, he skipped Triple-A after his impressive spring last year. He's got the savvy and the guts to make it in the bigs, and his on-the-job training will continue in Toronto after the Dodgers dealt him in the four-player trade that netted Paul Quantrill.

Mike Trombley

Position: RP
Bats: R **Throws:** R
Ht: 6' 2" **Wt:** 204

Opening Day Age: 34
Born: 4/14/67 in Springfield, MA
ML Seasons: 10
Pronunciation: TROM-blee

Overall Statistics

	W	L	Pct.	ERA	G	GS	Sv	IP	H	BB	SO	HR	Ratio
2001	3	8	.273	4.38	69	0	6	78.0	65	37	72	9	1.31
Career	37	46	.446	4.42	504	36	44	791.2	790	318	669	112	1.40

2001 Situational Stats

	W	L	ERA	Sv	IP		AB	H	HR	RBI	Avg
Home	1	6	4.85	3	42.2	LHB	113	26	3	17	.230
Road	2	2	3.82	3	35.1	RHB	170	39	6	23	.229
First Half	2	2	3.40	3	47.2	Sc Pos	81	23	1	32	.284
Scnd Half	1	6	5.93	0	30.1	Clutch	131	35	6	25	.267

2001 Season

Desperate for some experienced arms in their bullpen, the Dodgers acquired Mike Trombley from Baltimore at the deadline. They quickly discovered why he had come so cheaply. Trombley allowed runs in five of his first nine appearances with LA and put up a 6.56 ERA after the trade.

Pitching, Defense & Hitting

Trombley relies on one pitch: a good split-fingered fastball. So it is crucial that he get ahead in the count. He held opponents to a .129 average after a first-pitch strike last season, but when the count started 1-0, they hit .302. His fastball tops out in the mid-80s and he's got a sloppy breaking pitch that is very hittable if left out over the plate. He has not made an error in the last six seasons, but he isn't particularly good at holding runners. Trombley has struck out in his only two plate appearances and never has laid down a sacrifice.

2002 Outlook

For whatever reason, Trombley did not make the transition to the Senior Circuit. Still, he recorded 24 saves as recently as 1999 and has averaged more than 80 innings over the last seven seasons. He is expected to be part of the Dodgers' bullpen mix this year, and with LA deciding not to pick up its option on Jeff Shaw, he could earn a few saves.

Other Los Angeles Dodgers

Bruce Aven (**Pos**: LF, **Age**: 30, **Bats**: R)

	G	AB	R	H	D	T	HR	RBI	SB	BB	SO	Avg	OBP	Slg
2001	21	24	3	8	2	0	1	2	0	0	5	.333	.385	.542
Career	252	592	84	164	33	2	20	103	5	53	131	.277	.344	.441

Aven showed power and speed early in his career, but injuries and lack of playing time have curbed his output. He became a free agent in October. 2002 Outlook: C

Hiram Bocachica (**Pos**: 2B, **Age**: 26, **Bats**: R)

	G	AB	R	H	D	T	HR	RBI	SB	BB	SO	Avg	OBP	Slg
2001	75	133	15	31	11	1	2	9	4	9	33	.233	.287	.376
Career	83	143	17	34	11	1	2	9	4	9	35	.238	.288	.371

Bocachica is the Dodgers' second baseman of the future, but probably needs another year of seasoning. He has shown some power and decent speed. 2002 Outlook: B

Tim Bogar (**Pos**: 1B, **Age**: 35, **Bats**: R)

	G	AB	R	H	D	T	HR	RBI	SB	BB	SO	Avg	OBP	Slg
2001	12	15	4	5	2	0	2	2	0	2	1	.333	.412	.867
Career	701	1516	180	345	69	9	24	161	13	143	272	.228	.298	.332

Hamstring, foot and ankle problems limited Bogar to just 28 games between Los Angeles and Triple-A Las Vegas in 2001. His career .298 OBP and .332 slugging mark are signs the end is near. 2002 Outlook: C

Jeff Branson (**Pos**: 2B, **Age**: 35, **Bats**: L)

	G	AB	R	H	D	T	HR	RBI	SB	BB	SO	Avg	OBP	Slg
2001	13	21	3	6	0	0	0	0	0	0	4	.286	.286	.286
Career	694	1555	173	383	72	11	34	156	9	122	312	.246	.300	.372

After playing seven years in the majors with the Reds and Indians, Branson has spent the bulk of the last two seasons in Triple-A. He is a below-average hitter with little power or speed. 2002 Outlook: C

McKay Christensen (**Pos**: CF, **Age**: 26, **Bats**: L)

	G	AB	R	H	D	T	HR	RBI	SB	BB	SO	Avg	OBP	Slg
2001	35	53	7	17	2	0	1	7	3	3	12	.321	.400	.415
Career	95	125	21	31	3	0	2	14	6	9	25	.248	.319	.320

The White Sox traded Christensen to the Dodgers for minor league pitcher Wade Parrish in July. He enjoyed his hottest major league stretch in July, but cooled in August. 2002 Outlook: C

Chris Donnels (**Pos**: 3B, **Age**: 35, **Bats**: L)

	G	AB	R	H	D	T	HR	RBI	SB	BB	SO	Avg	OBP	Slg
2001	66	88	8	15	2	0	3	8	0	12	25	.170	.277	.295
Career	376	718	78	167	32	4	14	70	5	93	151	.233	.320	.347

Donnels historically has been a selective hitter, posting a career .410 OBP in the minors. He also has displayed some power, cranking 27 homers at Triple-A in 2000. Could win a bench spot in 2002. 2002 Outlook: C

Dave Hansen (**Pos**: 1B/3B, **Age**: 33, **Bats**: L)

	G	AB	R	H	D	T	HR	RBI	SB	BB	SO	Avg	OBP	Slg
2001	92	140	13	33	10	0	2	20	0	32	29	.236	.371	.350
Career	878	1357	139	359	64	5	27	167	2	216	245	.265	.365	.379

Hansen had a chance to start at third base to begin the 2001 season, but was sidelined for the first month by a broken hand. The Dodgers have exercised his option and will use him off the bench. 2002 Outlook: B

Phil Hiatt (**Pos**: 3B, **Age**: 32, **Bats**: R)

	G	AB	R	H	D	T	HR	RBI	SB	BB	SO	Avg	OBP	Slg
2001	30	50	6	12	3	0	2	6	0	3	19	.240	.283	.420
Career	170	422	50	91	21	2	13	55	7	30	149	.216	.278	.367

After struggling with the Dodgers for the first month of last season, Hiatt prospered at Triple-A. He batted .330 and belted 44 homers, giving him 80 the last two Triple-A seasons. 2002 Outlook: C

Brian Johnson (**Pos**: C, **Age**: 34, **Bats**: R)

	G	AB	R	H	D	T	HR	RBI	SB	BB	SO	Avg	OBP	Slg
2001	3	4	0	1	0	0	0	1	0	0	1	.250	.250	.250
Career	471	1415	132	351	60	6	49	196	1	80	268	.248	.291	.403

Johnson hit .301 with six home runs in 48 games with Triple-A Las Vegas in 2001. He became a free agent, but isn't likely to catch on as a reserve catcher with another team. 2002 Outlook: C

Terry Mulholland (**Pos**: LHP, **Age**: 39)

	W	L	Pct.	ERA	G	GS	Sv	IP	H	BB	SO	HR	Ratio
2001	1	1	.500	4.66	41	4	0	65.2	78	17	42	12	1.45
Career	113	125	.475	4.30	510	311	5	2212.1	2384	572	1166	237	1.34

The Dodgers acquired Mulholland from the Pirates in a deal at the trading deadline. As is the norm with the lefthander, he spent most of the year in the bullpen, but also got four spot starts. He's an extremely versatile pitcher. 2002 Outlook: B

Gregg Olson (**Pos**: RHP, **Age**: 35)

	W	L	Pct.	ERA	G	GS	Sv	IP	H	BB	SO	HR	Ratio
2001	0	1	.000	8.03	28	0	0	24.2	26	20	24	4	1.86
Career	40	39	.506	3.46	622	0	217	672.0	598	330	588	46	1.38

Olson was released by the Dodgers halfway through the 2001 season after posting an 8.03 ERA. Considering his struggles with injury throughout his career, catching on with another team might be difficult. 2002 Outlook: D

Jesse Orosco (**Pos**: LHP, **Age**: 44)

	W	L	Pct.	ERA	G	GS	Sv	IP	H	BB	SO	HR	Ratio
2001	0	1	.000	3.94	35	0	0	16.0	17	7	21	3	1.50
Career	84	76	.525	3.04	1131	4	141	1234.1	990	548	1128	105	1.25

Orosco posted a respectable ERA in 2001, but was not used extensively by the Dodgers. He pitched in 35 games, lasting a total of just 16 innings. The 44-year-old re-signed with the Dodgers, inking a minor league contract. 2002 Outlook: C

Angel Pena (**Pos**: C, **Age**: 27, **Bats**: R)

	G	AB	R	H	D	T	HR	RBI	SB	BB	SO	Avg	OBP	Slg
2001	22	54	3	11	1	0	1	2	0	1	17	.204	.214	.278
Career	71	187	18	39	7	0	5	23	0	13	47	.209	.256	.326

Pena has great potential, but never has prospered at the major league level. He hit .313 with 16 homers in 53 games in Triple-A in 2001. He could win a backup job behind Paul Lo Duca at catcher. 2002 Outlook: C

Jeff Reboulet (Pos: SS/2B, Age: 37, Bats: R)

	G	AB	R	H	D	T	HR	RBI	SB	BB	SO	Avg	OBP	Slg
2001	94	214	35	57	15	2	3	22	0	33	48	.266	.367	.397
Career	887	1920	270	463	87	4	17	175	20	259	341	.241	.334	.317

Reboulet was a competent option off the bench for the Dodgers in 2001. He hit .266 as an utilityman. He has not become an everyday player because of his struggles with the glove. His option was picked up for another year, and he will remain a solid reserve. 2002 Outlook: B

Al Reyes (Pos: RHP, Age: 30)

	W	L	Pct.	ERA	G	GS	Sv	IP	H	BB	SO	HR	Ratio
2001	2	1	.667	3.86	19	0	1	25.2	28	13	23	3	1.60
Career	15	8	.652	4.22	192	0	3	236.2	207	126	225	31	1.41

Reyes has allowed batters to hit just .235 against him in his career. However, with the bases loaded, opponents have batted .500. He declined an assignment late in the season and became a free agent. 2002 Outlook: C

Dennis Springer (Pos: RHP, Age: 37)

	W	L	Pct.	ERA	G	GS	Sv	IP	H	BB	SO	HR	Ratio
2001	1	1	.500	3.32	4	3	0	19.0	19	2	7	3	1.11
Career	24	47	.338	5.17	129	98	1	654.0	701	256	295	108	1.46

Springer pitched OK in 2001, but might have a hard time finding a job in 2002. The knuckleballer declined an assignment by the Dodgers and became a free agent. 2002 Outlook: C

Jeff Williams (Pos: LHP, Age: 29)

	W	L	Pct.	ERA	G	GS	Sv	IP	H	BB	SO	HR	Ratio
2001	2	1	.667	6.29	15	1	0	24.1	26	17	9	5	1.77
Career	4	1	.800	6.61	27	4	0	47.2	50	34	19	8	1.76

Williams has enjoyed success in the minors as a starter, posting a 3.97 ERA last season. However, he has struggled with his control as a reliever in the majors. 2002 Outlook: C

Los Angeles Dodgers Minor League Prospects

Organization Overview:

The Dodgers haven't won a division title since 1995, their longest streak without a first-place finish since a seven-year skid between 1967 and 1973. Perhaps just as telling, Los Angeles hasn't boasted a Rookie of the Year for the past five seasons, after monopolizing the award between 1992 and 1996. With a seemingly unlimited budget, the Dodgers in recent years have been willing to pay the price to acquire players like Kevin Brown and Shawn Green. Perhaps LA is due for a reinvigoration from within its system. The Dodgers' Double-A affiliate in Jacksonville produced the best record in the Southern League and shared the championship. Their Gulf Coast League outfit boasted the top record in that circuit. The Dodgers continue to mine their share of talent in the Caribbean, and they have a number of fine arms rising from the lower levels of the organization.

Willy Aybar

Position: 3B   **Opening Day Age:** 19
Bats: B **Throws:** R   **Born:** 3/9/83 in Bani, DR
Ht: 6' 0" **Wt:** 175

Recent Statistics

	G	AB	R	H	D	T	HR	RBI	SB	BB	SO	Avg
2000 R Great Falls	70	266	39	70	15	1	4	49	5	36	45	.263
2001 A Wilmington	120	431	45	102	25	2	4	48	7	43	64	.237
2001 A Vero Beach	2	7	0	2	0	0	0	0	0	1	2	.286

Just as it had done with Adrian Beltre, LA signed Aybar out of the Dominican Republic at a very young age. They both play third base, and the Dodgers say Aybar's actions at the position are similar to Beltre's. However, while Aybar hit four home runs in the South Atlantic League at age 18 last season, Beltre pounded 26 in Class-A at the same age. Still, Aybar possesses projectible power and a nice swing from both sides of the plate. Signed to a $1.4 million bonus in 2000, he is raw. The Dodgers were impressed enough by his ability to call him up to the Florida State League late last season, where he hit a home run in the playoffs. He won't leave his teens until 2003, and Aybar might need a full year at high Class-A.

Chin-Feng Chen

Position: OF-DH   **Opening Day Age:** 24
Bats: R **Throws:** R   **Born:** 10/28/77 in Tainan
Ht: 6' 1" **Wt:** 189   City, Taiwan

Recent Statistics

	G	AB	R	H	D	T	HR	RBI	SB	BB	SO	Avg
2000 AA San Antonio	133	516	66	143	27	3	6	67	23	61	131	.277
2001 A Vero Beach	62	235	38	63	15	3	5	41	2	28	56	.268
2001 AA Jacksonville	66	224	47	70	16	2	17	50	5	41	65	.313
2001 MLE	66	215	41	61	13	1	14	44	3	30	69	.284

Chen's performance at Double-A last year confirmed his status as a top prospect. The Dodgers had signed him out of Taiwan at age 21 in 1999. And Chen made a strong

minor league debut that season by clubbing 31 homers and stealing 31 bases in the California League. But his production suffered for the next year and a half, in part because of a shoulder injury that required surgery following his 2000 campaign. He rehabbed at Vero Beach last spring, going through the paces there, but then took off after his promotion to Jacksonville. He again demonstrated the power and run producing ability that offers such promise. He's likely headed to Triple-A in 2002, where maintaining his health will be one objective.

Ben Diggins

Position: P   **Opening Day Age:** 22
Bats: R **Throws:** R   **Born:** 6/13/79 in Leota,
Ht: 6' 7" **Wt:** 230   KS

Recent Statistics

	W	L	ERA	G	GS	Sv	IP	H	R	BB	SO	HR
2001 A Wilmington	7	6	3.58	21	21	0	105.2	88	49	48	79	5

Diggins drew a lot of interest as both a pitcher and hitter when he played in high school. The Cardinals chose him with a supplemental first-round pick in 1998, but he decided to attend Arizona instead. After going 10-4 in 2000, the Dodgers made him the 17th overall selection that June. He made his professional debut last season, starting off slowly at Wilmington. He was hampered by a hamstring injury in May and experienced a drop in velocity. But the velocity returned in July and in one game he pitched seven innings of a combined no-hitter. His mid-90s fastball can touch 98 MPH, and he shows a steady changeup. At 6-foot-7, Diggins is an intimidating presence. The Dodgers also like his tenacity. He'll probably work at Vero Beach or Double-A this year.

Koyie Hill

Position: C   **Opening Day Age:** 23
Bats: B **Throws:** R   **Born:** 3/9/79 in Tulsa, OK
Ht: 6' 0" **Wt:** 190

Recent Statistics

	G	AB	R	H	D	T	HR	RBI	SB	BB	SO	Avg
2000 A Yakima	64	251	26	65	13	1	2	29	0	25	47	.259
2001 A Wilmington	134	498	65	150	20	2	8	79	21	49	82	.301

Hill played third base at Wichita State and led the Missouri Valley Conference in hits in 2000. But the Dodgers chose him in the fourth round that June with the idea of shifting him from the hot corner to behind the plate. They had worked him out at catcher prior to the draft and liked what they saw. Hill possesses the arm strength and soft hands to handle the position. In addition, he appears to have the kind of attitude that will help him make the transition. The Dodgers say he's a "baseball rat" who loves playing the game. He's a line-drive hitter with gap power. Although he batted .300 at Class-A last season, he might be able to improve his performance against breaking pitches.

Jorge Nunez

Position: SS
Bats: R **Throws:** R
Ht: 5' 10" **Wt:** 158

Opening Day Age: 24
Born: 3/3/78 in Villa
Mella, DR

Recent Statistics

	G	AB	R	H	D	T	HR	RBI	SB	BB	SO	Avg
2000 A Vero Beach	128	534	86	154	17	8	4	39	54	38	104	.288
2000 AAA Albuquerque	1	3	0	0	0	0	0	0	0	0	0	.000
2001 AA Jacksnville	123	473	63	123	15	2	4	28	44	33	88	.260
2001 MLE	123	458	55	108	12	1	3	24	33	24	94	.236

The Dodgers acquired Nunez from the Blue Jays in the deal that involved Shawn Green and Raul Mondesi. Nunez has plenty of speed and hasn't been particularly reluctant to demonstrate it. He stole over 50 bases in both 1999 and 2000, before pacing the Southern League with 44 swipes last season. His speed also comes in handy at shortstop, where he features a plus arm. In addition, he seemed to gain a measure of reliability last year. After committing 58 errors at Vero Beach in 2000, he reduced that sum to 30 in Double-A. On offense, he hits the ball all over the field but could stand to take a few more walks and strike out less often.

Ricardo Rodriguez

Position: P
Bats: R **Throws:** R
Ht: 6' 3" **Wt:** 195

Opening Day Age: 22
Born: 5/21/79 in
Guayubin, DR

Recent Statistics

	W	L	ERA	G	GS	Sv	IP	H	R	BB	SO	HR
2000 R Great Falls	10	3	1.88	15	15	0	95.2	66	32	23	129	2
2001 A Vero Beach	14	6	3.21	26	26	0	154.1	133	67	60	154	13

Rodriguez signed with the Dodgers in 1996 and spent the next three years in the Dominican Summer League. He finally worked stateside in 2000 and dominated batters in the Rookie-level Pioneer League. He then jumped to high Class-A in 2001 and hardly missed a beat, leading the Florida State League in wins and strikeouts. For his effort, Rodriguez was named the Dodgers' Minor League Pitcher of the Year. He has a solid arm and plus stuff. He throws his fastball in the low 90s and mixes in a slider and changeup. Even though he's only a year removed from Rookie ball, the Dodgers think Rodriguez might be in Los Angeles by 2003, if not by the end of this season.

Jose Rojas

Position: P
Bats: R **Throws:** R
Ht: 5' 10" **Wt:** 160

Opening Day Age: 20
Born: 3/20/82 in San
Pedro De Macoris, DR

Recent Statistics

	W	L	ERA	G	GS	Sv	IP	H	R	BB	SO	HR
2000 A Yakima	4	4	3.25	13	9	1	52.2	45	26	19	47	3
2001 A Wilmington	10	3	2.12	24	23	0	135.2	107	42	42	116	7
2001 A Vero Beach	0	0	6.00	1	0	0	3.0	3	2	1	3	0

Rojas is yet another undrafted free agent that the Dodgers signed out of the Dominican Republic. He excelled at age 19 in Class-A last season, leading the South Atlantic League with a 2.12 ERA. He even pitched in high Class-A late in the campaign. He has consistently posted strikeout-walk ratios of nearly 3:1 over the past two years. While he has a little experience as a reliever and saved a game in 2000, he's a good starting prospect. Rojas is on the small side, especially for a righthander, but the Dodgers say his ability supersedes his size. The thing that stands out about him is his arm speed. He is a projectable hurler with a low-90s fastball. He also throws a slider and a changeup, though he needs to tighten the rotation on the slider. He'll likely begin this season at Vero Beach.

Joe Thurston

Position: 2B
Bats: L **Throws:** R
Ht: 5' 11" **Wt:** 175

Opening Day Age: 22
Born: 9/29/79 in
Fairfield, CA

Recent Statistics

	G	AB	R	H	D	T	HR	RBI	SB	BB	SO	Avg
2000 A San Berndno	138	551	97	167	31	8	4	70	43	56	61	.303
2001 AA Jacksnville	134	544	80	145	25	7	7	46	20	48	65	.267
2001 MLE	134	526	70	127	21	4	6	40	14	35	69	.241

The Dodgers grabbed Thurston in the fourth round of the 1999 draft. He was named the Dodgers' Minor League Player of the Year in 2000, when he batted .303 and led the California League in hits. While his stats weren't quite as impressive last season, he was handling the jump to Double-A at age 21. Although he doesn't have one particular tool that stands out, Thurston is a solid, all-around player who is nicknamed "Joey Ballgame." He's a spray hitter who gets on base and can be used at the top of the order. He uses his brains as much as his average speed on the basepaths. With Jorge Nunez joining him at Jacksonville last season, Thurston shifted from shortstop to second base.

Others to Watch

Luke Allen (23) has a long swing but possesses some power potential. On defense, he struggled with his feet at third base. But his arm is a gun and he moved to the outfield last season. . . The Dodgers picked lefthander **Steve Colyer** (23) with a supplemental second-round choice in 1998 and signed him as a draft-and-follow. He's got a plus-arm, but his walk totals have been rather high and he's spent the past three years in high Class-A. . . Righthander **Joel Hanrahan** (20) was drafted in the second round in 2000. He has a tremendous feel for pitching and good stuff. His slider is a plus-pitch. . . While **Brennan King** (21) has endured injuries, he's a baseball nut with a great swing. He is solid defensively at third base. . . Outfielder **Lamont Matthews** (23) spent most of last season back at high Class-A Vero Beach. But he batted .307 and continued to draw a lot of walks. He reduced his swing, has heart and still is considered a prospect. . . **Shane Victorino** (21) is a great runner and stole 47 bases in the Sally League. He returned to the outfield after gaining versatility by playing second base in 2000.

Miller Park

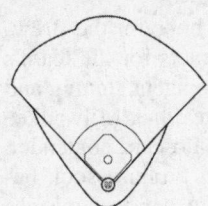

Offense

There were several slugfests early on at Miller Park, and the stadium quickly was labeled a bandbox. That may have been premature—for the season as a whole, the park barely inflated scoring at all, yielding a few extra home runs but hardly affecting any other offensive totals. Hitters complain that in day games the glare sometimes makes it tough to pick up the ball during the middle innings.

Defense

The park's limited foul territory, especially down the first base line, is forgiving for corner infielders with limited mobility. Corner outfielders need strong throwing arms when digging balls out of the deep corners. The relatively short power alleys help hide a center fielder's lack of range.

Who It Helps the Most

The short alleys turned several of Richie Sexson's doubles into homers. Of his 45 longballs last year, 28 were blasted during home games. Geoff Jenkins found he could reach the fences in both alleys and posted a slugging percentage 103 points higher at Miller Park than on the road. Raul Casanova also seemed to benefit from the hitting environment.

Who It Hurts the Most

Jeromy Burnitz, an extreme pull hitter, often found himself hitting the ball to the most unforgiving part of the park. He hit just .219 during home games, compared to .281 on the road. Jeffrey Hammonds, for whatever reason, hit poorly at Miller Park in the few games he played, and Jose Hernandez seemed to lose a few home runs to the park. Curtis Leskanic allowed eight of his 11 home runs there, and Jamey Wright had more than his share of problems in home games, too.

Rookies & Newcomers

Ruben Quevedo, who pitched poorly at Miller Park last year and gives up tons of flyballs, might see a lot of balls disappear over the walls in the alleys. The park reduced strikeouts a bit last season, but Nick Neugebauer has shown he can whiff batters just about anywhere, at least when his shoulder is healthy.

Dimensions: LF-344, LCF-371, CF-400, RCF-374, RF-345

Capacity: 42,500

Elevation: 635 feet

Surface: Grass

Foul Territory: Small

Park Factors

2001 Season

	Home Games			Away Games			Index
	Brewers	Opp	Total	Brewers	Opp	Total	
G	72	72	144	75	75	150	—
Avg	.257	.267	.262	.243	.264	.253	104
AB	2391	2495	4886	2584	2473	5057	101
R	341	357	698	334	372	706	103
H	615	666	1281	628	652	1280	104
2B	117	132	249	137	138	275	94
3B	13	14	27	16	21	37	76
HR	92	94	186	93	76	169	114
BB	213	307	520	238	306	544	99
SO	614	465	1079	658	488	1146	97
E	41	42	83	48	33	81	107
E-Infield	36	34	70	38	25	63	116
LHB-Avg	.270	.280	.275	.256	.249	.253	109
LHB-HR	41	44	85	40	30	70	133
RHB-Avg	.250	.259	.254	.235	.274	.253	100
RHB-HR	51	50	101	53	46	99	102

1999-2000 (County Stadium)

	Home Games			Away Games			Index
	Brewers	Opp	Total	Brewers	Opp	Total	
G	147	147	294	148	148	296	—
Avg	.247	.275	.262	.265	.276	.270	97
AB	4897	5244	10141	5185	4988	10173	100
R	655	777	1432	746	773	1519	95
H	1212	1440	2652	1372	1376	2748	97
2B	243	238	481	293	252	545	89
3B	26	23	49	24	39	63	78
HR	137	163	300	167	189	356	85
BB	582	602	1184	584	622	1206	98
SO	942	872	1814	1136	912	2048	89
E	109	114	223	107	101	208	108
E-Infield	95	88	183	82	79	161	114
LHB-Avg	.245	.273	.260	.274	.276	.275	94
LHB-HR	70	62	132	101	57	158	82
RHB-Avg	.249	.276	.263	.259	.276	.267	98
RHB-HR	67	101	168	66	132	198	86

2001 Rankings (National League)

- Second-highest LHB home-run factor
- Third-highest batting-average factor

Davey Lopes

2001 Season

Last year began with so much hope for the Brewers: a new ballpark, new contracts for the team's marquee players, a notable free agent signing and a rookie Olympic hero. By late June, Milwaukee was 38-34 and looked like a wild-card contender. But what began with so much promise soon became an unmitigated disaster. A wave of injuries swept over the club, and Davey Lopes could do little but watch helplessly as his team posted the National Leagues' worst record over the second half.

Offense

Lopes is on record as a proponent of the running game, but simply lacks the personnel to employ it. Only two other National League teams stole fewer bases than the Brewers last season. As a way of staying out of the double play, he used the hit-and-run more often. He also resorted to sending runners after two were out. He still emphasizes pure speed over on-base skills at the top of the order.

Pitching & Defense

Lopes refuses to let certain hitters beat him; his Brewers led the majors in intentional walks given for the second straight year. He calls more pitch-outs than average, and is fairly good at catching runners in motion. He continued to show an ability to find a pitcher's proper role, getting good results out of Ray King and Mike DeJean. Brewers relievers made 489 appearances in 2001. Only the Expos, with 491, made more.

2002 Outlook

It's a little unfair to hold Lopes responsible for the injury bug that swept the club last year. Nevertheless, he could take the fall if the club stumbles out of the chute this season. Milwaukee hasn't posted a winning record since 1992. The Miller Park honeymoon soon will be over, and the danger is that the fans will stop coming if the team keeps losing and the front office doesn't try to shake things up.

Born: 5/03/45 in East Providence, RI

Playing Experience: 1972-1987, LA, Oak, ChC, Hou

Managerial Experience: 2 seasons

Manager Statistics

Year	Team, Lg	W	L	Pct	GB	Finish
2001	Milwaukee, NL	68	94	.420	25.0	4th Central
2 Seasons		141	183	.434	—	—

2001 Starting Pitchers by Days Rest

	<=3	4	5	6+
Brewers Starts	2	86	40	22
Brewers ERA	3.38	5.21	4.11	5.79
NL Avg Starts	1	80	47	24
NL ERA	5.03	4.43	4.53	4.28

2001 Situational Stats

	Davey Lopes	NL Average
Hit & Run Success %	35.4	35.1
Stolen Base Success %	64.7	66.5
Platoon Pct.	50.7	51.5
Defensive Subs	14	20
High-Pitch Outings	3	7
Quick/Slow Hooks	25/14	19/14
Sacrifice Attempts	82	87

2001 Rankings (National League)

- 1st in intentional walks (71) and relief appearances (489)
- 2nd in quick hooks
- 3rd in starts on three days rest

Ronnie Belliard

Position: 2B
Bats: R **Throws:** R
Ht: 5' 8" **Wt:** 180

Opening Day Age: 26
Born: 4/7/75 in Bronx, NY
ML Seasons: 4
Pronunciation:
BELL-ee-yard

2001 Season

For the second straight year, the Brewers were looking for Ron Belliard to build upon his fine rookie season of 1999. And once again, he performed competently but fell a bit short of expectations. Belliard ran hot and cold in the first half of the campaign, and got going in July after being promoted to the leadoff spot. He delivered six of his 11 home runs over roughly a two-week span following the All-Star break. However, a severely sprained ankle in August wiped out almost all of the final two months of his season.

Hitting

Since Belliard runs well, makes decent contact and has a good batting eye, the Brewers have hoped that he would develop into a top-of-the-order hitter. But his table-setting skills have stagnated. However, last year—perhaps in response to his new surroundings—Belliard pulled the ball more often and boosted his power numbers. It will boost his value if he develops in one direction or the other, since at present he is not ideally suited to any particular offensive role. He uses the whole field and does a good job protecting the plate with two strikes.

Baserunning & Defense

Belliard runs well enough to steal bases, but doesn't try that often. That and the fact that he appears to carry extra weight are understandable sources of frustration. He had his best year in the field last year, cutting down on the careless errors that sometimes dogged him in the past. His pivot is smooth and he has all the tools to play second base well.

2002 Outlook

This will be a key season for Belliard. Though he's played well all-around and remains capable of becoming a Ray Durham-type player, some question Belliard's conditioning and effort. He may need to change that impression in order to remain the Brewers' second baseman beyond 2002.

Overall Statistics

	G	AB	R	H	D	T	HR	RBI	SB	BB	SO	Avg	OBP	Slg
2001	101	364	69	96	30	3	11	36	5	35	65	.264	.335	.453
Career	385	1397	213	382	89	16	27	148	16	181	208	.273	.357	.418

Where He Hits the Ball

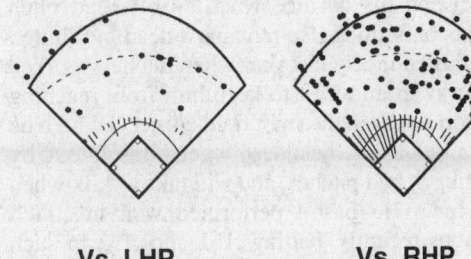

Vs. LHP   **Vs. RHP**

2001 Situational Stats

	AB	H	HR	RBI	Avg		AB	H	HR	RBI	Avg
Home	202	53	7	22	.262	LHP	67	19	5	9	.284
Road	162	43	4	14	.265	RHP	297	77	6	27	.259
First Half	263	69	4	22	.262	Sc Pos	61	19	0	23	.311
Scnd Half	101	27	7	14	.267	Clutch	50	10	0	1	.200

2001 Rankings (National League)

- 3rd in batting average on a 3-2 count (.462)
- 8th in lowest batting average on an 0-2 count (.079)
- 10th in on-base percentage for a leadoff hitter (.348) and highest percentage of extra bases taken as a runner (57.5)
- Led the Brewers in highest percentage of extra bases taken as a runner (57.5)

Milwaukee

Jeromy Burnitz

2001 Season

After a tumultuous 2000 in which Jeromy Burnitz' future in Milwaukee was very much up in the air, the slugger put such questions to rest by signing a lucrative two-year extension prior to last season. At the time, it seemed the franchise might be on the upturn. But by the end of the year, Burnitz may have regretted signing the deal. Though he put up his usual power numbers, he was helpless to prevent the club from crashing and burning in the second half.

Hitting

Burnitz isn't shy about going for the pump. His all-or-nothing uppercut can put a charge into anyone's fastball but can leave him struggling to keep his bat and his balance when an offspeed pitch disrupts his timing. He remains a dead pull hitter, but adjusted nicely last year when pitchers worked him away in an effort to keep him from reaching the short porch in the right field corner. Though he strikes out a lot, he doesn't get himself out by swinging at bad pitches, and will take a walk when given one. He hasn't performed well in clutch situations recently, batting .161 and .173 in such cases the past two years.

Baserunning & Defense

An underappreciated defender, Burnitz is an asset in right field with good range and a strong, accurate arm. He's nailed 25 baserunners over the past two seasons. After stealing 20 bases in 1997, Burnitz' total since then is also 20. He ran less often in 2001 as the club played to fit its new, more power-friendly ballpark.

2002 Outlook

Reportedly the Mets pursued Burnitz heavily during the offseason, hoping to trade for a slugger rather than pay the going rate in the free-agent market. If he's not moved, Burnitz will remain a fixture in the middle of Milwaukee's batting order. He'll likely continue to contribute his share of longballs while hoping that his teammates can stay healthy.

Position: RF
Bats: L **Throws:** R
Ht: 6' 0" **Wt:** 205

Opening Day Age: 32
Born: 4/15/69 in Westminster, CA
ML Seasons: 9
Pronunciation: ber-NITS

Overall Statistics

	G	AB	R	H	D	T	HR	RBI	SB	BB	SO	Avg	OBP	Slg
2001	154	562	104	141	32	4	34	100	0	80	150	.251	.347	.504
Career	993	3309	576	852	188	23	188	604	48	509	822	.257	.362	.499

Where He Hits the Ball

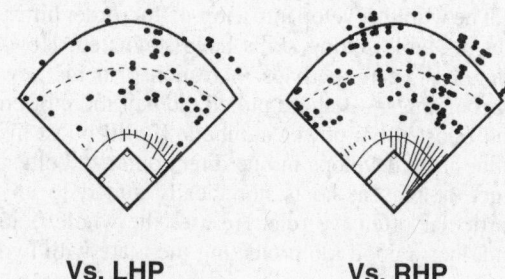

Vs. LHP   **Vs. RHP**

2001 Situational Stats

	AB	H	HR	RBI	Avg		AB	H	HR	RBI	Avg
Home	274	60	16	47	.219	LHP	161	36	9	29	.224
Road	288	81	18	53	.281	RHP	401	105	25	71	.262
First Half	284	70	18	61	.246	Sc Pos	135	37	6	61	.274
Scnd Half	278	71	16	39	.255	Clutch	75	13	3	8	.173

2001 Rankings (National League)

- 2nd in assists in right field (14) and lowest batting average at home
- 3rd in errors in right field (6), lowest batting average vs. lefthanded pitchers and lowest fielding percentage in right field (.981)
- 4th in lowest on-base percentage vs. lefthanded pitchers (.288)
- 6th in strikeouts
- Led the Brewers in runs scored, doubles, triples, caught stealing (4), walks, intentional walks (9), on-base percentage, most pitches seen per plate appearance (4.00), batting average on a 3-1 count (.526), on-base percentage vs. righthanded pitchers (.369) and batting average on the road

Jeff D'Amico

2001 Season

Jeff D'Amico, who went from oblivion to the edge of stardom in 2000, made the return trip last season. A compressed nerve in his pitching arm sent him to the disabled list in April, and when rehab failed, surgery was required. Oddly enough, though D'Amico had a lengthy list of previous arm problems, this injury was completely unrelated and quite rare for a pitcher. He returned to the rotation in September but never approached top form.

Pitching

When healthy, D'Amico's biggest weapon is his excellent command. By spotting his high-80s fastball on the corners and changing speeds with his slow curve and changeup, he is able to throw strikes and stay ahead in the count without getting hit hard by either lefthanded or righthanded hitters. Last year proved, however, that his stuff is inadequate when he lacks his good command and falls behind. Being a flyball pitcher, he can be vulnerable to the longball. He surrendered more than two home runs per nine innings in 2001.

Defense & Hitting

Though he lacks a good pickoff move, D'Amico varies his delivery and controls the running game exceptionally well for a big man. Despite his size, he never appears uncoordinated and fields his position well. He has yet to commit an error in the majors. But he's hopeless with the bat and didn't even lay down a single successful sacrifice last year. Still, three of his five career hits have resulted in extra bases.

2002 Outlook

D'Amico became a free agent over the winter and the Brewers—a club with chronic injury problems—may decide not to bring him back. Last year's injury isn't expected to recur or have long-term effects. So D'Amico quite possibly could return to his 2000 level if he's able to stay healthy. Unfortunately, he has yet to prove he can do that for a full season.

Position: SP
Bats: R **Throws:** R
Ht: 6' 7" **Wt:** 250

Opening Day Age: 26
Born: 12/27/75 in St. Petersburg, FL
ML Seasons: 5
Pronunciation: duh-MEEK-oh

Overall Statistics

	W	L	Pct.	ERA	G	GS	Sv	IP	H	BB	SO	HR	Ratio
2001	2	4	.333	6.08	10	10	0	47.1	60	16	32	11	1.61
Career	29	24	.547	4.23	74	73	0	432.1	431	136	281	71	1.31

How Often He Throws Strikes

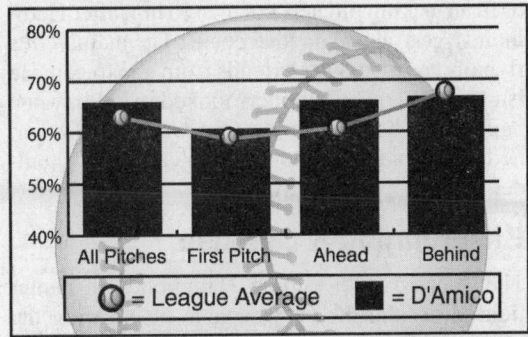

2001 Situational Stats

	W	L	ERA	Sv	IP		AB	H	HR	RBI	Avg
Home	1	0	5.19	0	17.1	LHB	75	25	5	15	.333
Road	1	4	6.60	0	30.0	RHB	121	35	6	21	.289
First Half	1	1	4.76	0	22.2	Sc Pos	57	18	6	28	.316
Scnd Half	1	3	7.30	0	24.2	Clutch	3	2	1	1	.667

2001 Rankings (National League)

- Did not rank near the top or bottom in any category

Jeffrey Hammonds

2001 Season

It was something of a shock when the Brewers shelled out big bucks for free-agent outfielder Jeffrey Hammonds last winter. It was a bit less shocking, given Hammonds' and the Brewers' histories, when he proved unable to stay healthy. A strained right shoulder—an injury that had troubled him late in the 2000 season—began bothering him again in mid-May and ended his 2001 campaign a few weeks later.

Hitting

Hammonds is an aggressive hitter and is especially dangerous on the first pitch. His free-swinging ways prevent him from working the count, though, or from making pitchers come in to him after Hammonds gets ahead in the count. He mainly hits flyballs and his power extends from gap to gap. He isn't as good as his numbers looked in 2000, when he naturally benefited from Coors Field. However, he isn't as bad as he looked last year, when shoulder pain hampered his swing.

Baserunning & Defense

The concern with putting Hammonds in center field is not that he isn't capable of covering the position, but rather that all the running will cause his past knee and leg problems to resurface. It's still an open question as to how his legs will hold up to a full season in center. The shallow gaps in Milwaukee's park help prevent Hammond's below-average arm from being overexposed. He has good speed and will swipe an occasional base when a righthander is on the mound.

2002 Outlook

Hammonds' inability to stay healthy always has been his fatal flaw. It's hoped that last summer's shoulder surgery to repair torn cartilage in his shoulder will enable him to beat the odds and avoid injuries this season. The Brewers are paying him a lot of money, so he'll be the regular center fielder if he's physically able. He certainly can be a valuable player when healthy.

Position: CF
Bats: R **Throws:** R
Ht: 6' 0" **Wt:** 200

Opening Day Age: 31
Born: 3/5/71 in Scotch Plains, NJ
ML Seasons: 9

Overall Statistics

	G	AB	R	H	D	T	HR	RBI	SB	BB	SO	Avg	OBP	Slg
2001	49	174	20	43	11	1	6	21	5	14	42	.247	.314	.425
Career	730	2325	389	650	128	12	94	362	61	207	456	.280	.341	.466

Where He Hits the Ball

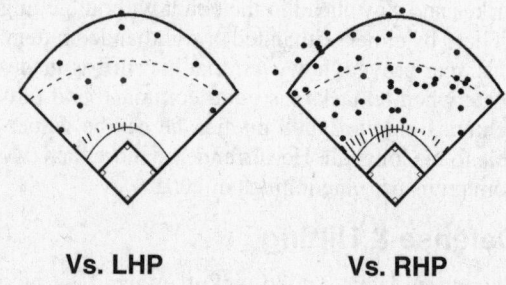

Vs. LHP   **Vs. RHP**

2001 Situational Stats

	AB	H	HR	RBI	Avg		AB	H	HR	RBI	Avg
Home	88	19	3	11	.216	LHP	38	9	0	2	.237
Road	86	24	3	10	.279	RHP	136	34	6	19	.250
First Half	174	43	6	21	.247	Sc Pos	31	11	1	16	.355
Scnd Half	0	0	0	0	-	Clutch	26	6	1	5	.231

2001 Rankings (National League)

- Did not rank near the top or bottom in any category

Jimmy Haynes

2001 Season

You'd never know it from his ugly won-lost record, but the eternally enigmatic Jimmy Haynes actually made real progress in 2001. A strained oblique muscle in late August cut into his season and resulted in a few disastrous outings after he was rushed back in late September. Before that setback, Haynes had reduced his walks, boosted his strikeout rate by nearly half and shaved nearly a full run off his ERA from the previous year. His poor record was largely the fault of his teammates, who usually gave him few runs to work with.

Pitching

Haynes always has had an impressive arsenal, with a low-90s fastball, a sinking two-seamer, an overhand curve and a splitter that he uses as a changeup. His improvement last year resulted from falling behind less often, and from getting more groundballs by relying more heavily on his two-seamer. Haynes is at his best during his first trip through the order and tends to run out of gas when asked to pitch deep into the game. He remains frustratingly inconsistent from start to start.

Defense & Hitting

Haynes lacks a good move to first but keeps runners close by throwing over often. He's fairly quick to the plate, though opposing runners still managed to swipe 12 bases in 18 attempts. He fielded his position without an error last season. He's also quick off the mound and covers first base adeptly. Haynes handles the bat about as well as the average pitcher. He showed progress in 2001 by not striking out as much as he did the year before.

2002 Outlook

Though it's clear Haynes never will attain the heights that once were envisioned for him, he seemed to be developing into a useful middle-of-the-rotation starter last year. With better run support and a better team behind him, he could win several more games this season compared to 2001.

Position: SP
Bats: R **Throws:** R
Ht: 6' 4" **Wt:** 203

Opening Day Age: 29
Born: 9/5/72 in LaGrange, GA
ML Seasons: 7

Overall Statistics

	W	L	Pct.	ERA	G	GS	Sv	IP	H	BB	SO	HR	Ratio
2001	8	17	.320	4.85	31	29	0	172.2	182	78	112	20	1.51
Career	46	64	.418	5.48	170	147	1	894.2	1004	456	579	110	1.63

How Often He Throws Strikes

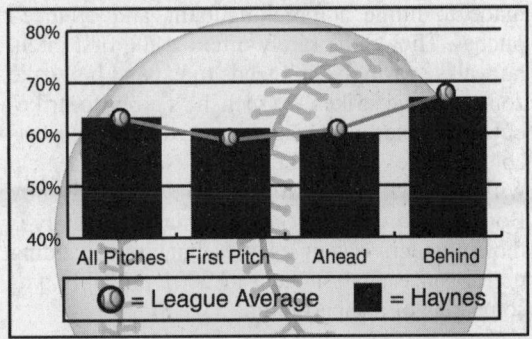

= League Average   = Haynes

2001 Situational Stats

	W	L	ERA	Sv	IP		AB	H	HR	RBI	Avg
Home	4	8	4.93	0	80.1	LHB	247	64	11	35	.259
Road	4	9	4.78	0	92.1	RHB	405	118	9	54	.291
First Half	6	10	4.81	0	116.0	Sc Pos	150	37	5	65	.247
Scnd Half	2	7	4.92	0	56.2	Clutch	26	7	1	5	.269

2001 Rankings (National League)

- 1st in fielding percentage at pitcher (1.000)
- 2nd in losses
- 3rd in lowest winning percentage
- 4th in least run support per nine innings (3.8)
- 6th in lowest strikeout-walk ratio (1.4) and highest on-base percentage allowed (.356)
- 7th in highest walks per nine innings (4.1)
- Led the Brewers in ERA, losses, wild pitches (8), stolen bases allowed (12), highest strikeout-walk ratio (1.4), lowest slugging percentage allowed (.440), lowest on-base percentage allowed (.356), fewest pitches thrown per batter (3.58), fewest home runs allowed per nine innings (1.04) and fewest walks per nine innings (4.1)

Jose Hernandez

Position: SS
Bats: R **Throws:** R
Ht: 6' 1" **Wt:** 180

Opening Day Age: 32
Born: 7/14/69 in Vega Alta, PR
ML Seasons: 10
Pronunciation: her-NAN-dezz

2001 Season

It was a season of redemption for Jose Hernandez, who had been a colossal flop as a free agent acquisition at third base the year before. Mark Loretta's early-season injury allowed Hernandez to return to shortstop, his natural position. He had one of his best offensive campaigns and avoided the fielding slumps that had plagued him in the past, fielding so well that Loretta never had a chance to win his job back.

Hitting

Hernandez has very good power to the opposite field, and does his best hitting when he stays back on the ball and drives it the other way. He can be made to lunge at breaking balls and offspeed pitches. Though he rarely offers at the first pitch, he walks sparingly, and tends to expand his strike zone with two strikes. As such, he's prone to strikeouts and sometimes struggles to maintain a respectable average. In fact, he led the National League with 185 whiffs in 2001—four shy of Bobby Bonds' major league record. Hernandez usually is more productive against lefties, but his outstanding performance against them in 2001 probably was something of an aberration.

Baserunning & Defense

While his straight-ahead speed is rather ordinary and he isn't much of a basestealer, Hernandez has very good first-step quickness and decent range at shortstop. Better footwork improved the consistency of his throws and allowed him to show off his strong arm. He can play several other positions but appears to have broken out of his utility role for the time being.

2002 Outlook

Only Rich Aurilia hit more homers among National League shortstops than Hernandez last year. Hernandez heads into 2002 as the Brewers' regular at the position, and it probably will take an injury or a massive slump for him to cede the job back to Loretta. Despite Hernandez' obvious weaknesses, the Brewers probably will be delighted if he continues to supply decent power and play quality defense.

Overall Statistics

	G	AB	R	H	D	T	HR	RBI	SB	BB	SO	Avg	OBP	Slg
2001	152	542	67	135	26	2	25	78	5	39	185	.249	.300	.443
Career	1021	2977	421	743	128	26	109	394	32	234	865	.250	.306	.420

Where He Hits the Ball

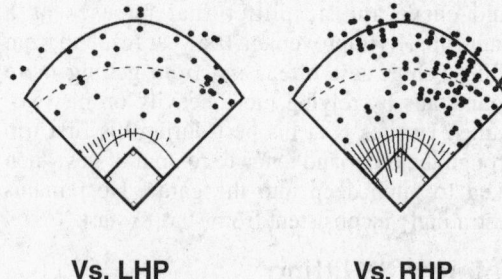

Vs. LHP   **Vs. RHP**

2001 Situational Stats

	AB	H	HR	RBI	Avg		AB	H	HR	RBI	Avg
Home	258	60	9	35	.233	LHP	109	37	11	26	.339
Road	284	75	16	43	.264	RHP	433	98	14	52	.226
First Half	298	80	17	45	.268	Sc Pos	127	37	6	55	.291
Scnd Half	244	55	8	33	.225	Clutch	77	18	2	9	.234

2001 Rankings (National League)

- 1st in strikeouts
- 2nd in lowest on-base percentage vs. righthanded pitchers (.271)
- 3rd in highest percentage of swings that missed (32.6) and lowest batting average vs. righthanded pitchers
- 5th in fielding percentage at shortstop (.972), lowest on-base percentage and lowest percentage of swings put into play (33.0)
- 7th in lowest batting average at home
- Led the Brewers in caught stealing (4), strikeouts, highest groundball-flyball ratio (1.4), batting average with runners in scoring position and lowest percentage of swings on the first pitch (27.3)

Geoff Jenkins

Position: LF
Bats: L **Throws:** R
Ht: 6' 1" **Wt:** 204

Opening Day Age: 27
Born: 7/21/74 in Olympia, WA
ML Seasons: 4

2001 Season

Coming off two fine seasons in a row, Geoff Jenkins was rewarded with a four-year contract in spring training. He then broke from the gate with a monster April, batting .348 with nine home runs that month. But he hurt his right shoulder May 1 while trying to avoid a collision in the outfield, and rarely was healthy or productive the rest of the year. Later, a bruised hand and a torn muscle in his thumb caused him to miss time and hampered him when he did play. He hit only .235 after the initial shoulder injury.

Hitting

When healthy, Jenkins has tremendous bat speed and can turn around anyone's fastball. He has good power to all fields and drives outside pitches to left. Naturally, pitchers try to upset his timing or get him to chase breaking balls in the dirt. Despite his physical maladies last year, he made real progress against southpaws. He pulled the ball more often against them and generated the best batting average versus lefties of his major league career.

Baserunning & Defense

Jenkins has good range in the outfield. He goes all-out for everything he can reach—and for many balls he can't. In fact, his only weakness is an instinctive inability to lay back and play a ball on the safe hop when there's the slimmest chance to dive for it. He has a fine arm, although his throwing was hampered by his various ailments last year. He has fairly good speed and attempts an occasional steal, usually with good success.

2002 Outlook

For a player who's had shoulder problems in the past, Jenkins' lingering pain last year was a cause for legitimate concern. He reportedly had surgery in late November, and the Brewers can only cross their fingers that he'll be back at full strength this spring—and that he'll be able to remain that way throughout the campaign. If healthy, Jenkins could put up even bigger numbers than he has in the past.

Overall Statistics

	G	AB	R	H	D	T	HR	RBI	SB	BB	SO	Avg	OBP	Slg
2001	105	397	60	105	21	1	20	63	4	36	120	.264	.334	.474
Career	459	1618	263	460	112	9	84	267	21	124	403	.284	.345	.520

Where He Hits the Ball

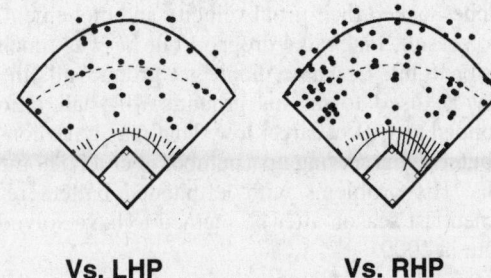

Vs. LHP   **Vs. RHP**

2001 Situational Stats

	AB	H	HR	RBI	Avg		AB	H	HR	RBI	Avg
Home	198	55	11	36	.278	LHP	114	36	6	21	.316
Road	199	50	9	27	.251	RHP	283	69	14	42	.244
First Half	245	68	13	41	.278	Sc Pos	105	30	5	43	.286
Scnd Half	152	37	7	22	.243	Clutch	51	8	1	3	.157

2001 Rankings (National League)

- 1st in lowest batting average on a 3-1 count (0.000)
- 2nd in lowest percentage of swings put into play (30.9)
- 3rd in lowest batting average in the clutch
- 4th in assists in left field (8) and highest percentage of swings that missed (31.9)
- 5th in lowest percentage of pitches taken (44.0)
- 10th in errors in left field (3)
- Led the Brewers in sacrifice flies (5) and batting average vs. lefthanded pitchers

Curtis Leskanic

2001 Season

Nothing seemed to go right for the Brewers last season, and Curtis Leskanic personified their ill fortune as much as anyone else on the club. He came into the year as the incumbent closer for the first time in his career, but eroded his standing with diminished velocity and several rocky outings early on. His save chances virtually dried up in the second half. Late in the season he was diagnosed with a partially torn labrum and rotator cuff, and he underwent surgery in early October.

Pitching

A healthy Leskanic throws a moving fastball in the low-90s, as well as a hard slider. He is tough to hit but sometimes fights his control. Last year his pitches lacked their usual velocity and movement. As a result, his walks dropped but he was much easier to hit. Leskanic didn't get groundballs the way he used to, as his groundball-flyball ratio dropped to 1.01, a career low. That may have contributed to his serving up a number of crucial home runs. His problems with lefthanded batters returned last season after he seemed to have solved them in 2000.

Defense & Hitting

Leskanic is tough to run on for a righthander. In the field, he's committed at least two errors in two of the past three seasons. Four of his seven career hits have gone for extra bases, but he rarely gets the chance to prove his power is anything more than a fluke.

2002 Outlook

Coming off surgery, Leskanic is very much a question mark heading into 2002. Even if healthy, he could be supplanted as the closer by Chad Fox. In any case, the Brewers are hoping that Leskanic will be back to full strength by the start of the season and will be able to contribute either as a closer or setup man.

Position: RP
Bats: R **Throws:** R
Ht: 6' 0" **Wt:** 186

Opening Day Age: 33
Born: 4/2/68 in Homestead, PA
ML Seasons: 9
Pronunciation: les-CAN-ik

Overall Statistics

	W	L	Pct.	ERA	G	GS	Sv	IP	H	BB	SO	HR	Ratio
2001	2	6	.250	3.63	70	0	17	69.1	63	31	64	11	1.36
Career	42	29	.592	4.48	499	11	49	616.2	593	303	554	70	1.45

How Often He Throws Strikes

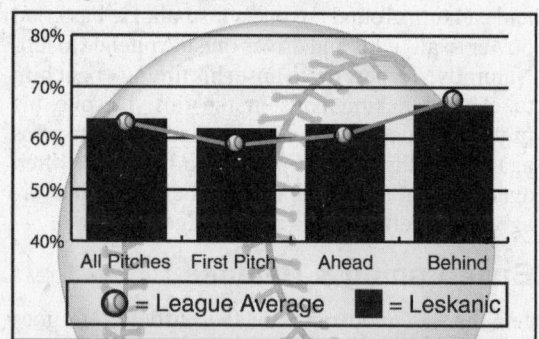

= League Average = Leskanic

2001 Situational Stats

	W	L	ERA	Sv	IP		AB	H	HR	RBI	Avg
Home	1	2	4.50	10	36.0	LHB	102	28	2	9	.275
Road	1	4	2.70	7	33.1	RHB	159	35	9	21	.220
First Half	2	4	3.54	11	40.2	Sc Pos	70	11	2	19	.157
Scnd Half	0	2	3.77	6	28.2	Clutch	130	39	5	22	.300

2001 Rankings (National League)

- 1st in lowest save percentage (70.8)
- 2nd in blown saves (7)
- 4th in relief losses (6) and lowest batting average allowed in relief with runners in scoring position (.157)
- 5th in games finished (58)
- Led the Brewers in saves, games finished (58), save opportunities (24), save percentage (70.8), blown saves (7) and relief losses (6)

Mark Loretta

2001 Season

The 2001 campaign was a bitter pill to swallow for Mark Loretta. He came in hoping to enjoy his first full, healthy season as the Brewers' regular shortstop, but suffered a torn thumb ligament in March. While he was out, Jose Hernandez moved to short and took away Loretta's job. When Loretta returned in May, he had to play his way back into shape while rotating between second and third base. Though he kept his average up, he showed some rust both at the plate and in the field. A broken leg then ended his season in late September.

Hitting

An excellent contact hitter, Loretta has been a consistent .280-.290 batsman for much of his big league career. He sprays line drives from foul line to foul line and is especially tough with two strikes. He occasionally tried to muscle up in 2000, but last year seemed content just to put the ball in play. He's a good bunter and hit-and-run man. Though he's patient, he rarely fails to put the ball in play and draws relatively few walks as a result.

Baserunning & Defense

Loretta's versatility is one of his greatest assets. He's a capable fielder at all the infield positions—even first base. Although his range is just average at shortstop, he makes up for it with his incredibly sure hands and accurate arm. He had some rough moments at third base last year but still is capable of playing the position. He is not a fast baserunner.

2002 Outlook

It isn't clear exactly how Loretta will fit in this season. However, he's being paid like a full-timer and the club likely will try to get its money's worth out of him, one way or another. It seems unlikely he'll win back the shortstop job as long as Jose Hernandez is healthy. Loretta should continue to see most of his playing time at second and third base.

Position: 2B/3B
Bats: R **Throws:** R
Ht: 6' 0" **Wt:** 180

Opening Day Age: 30
Born: 8/14/71 in Santa Monica, CA
ML Seasons: 7

Overall Statistics

	G	AB	R	H	D	T	HR	RBI	SB	BB	SO	Avg	OBP	Slg
2001	102	384	40	111	14	2	2	29	1	28	46	.289	.346	.352
Career	710	2379	326	693	121	13	27	253	22	224	272	.291	.356	.387

Where He Hits the Ball

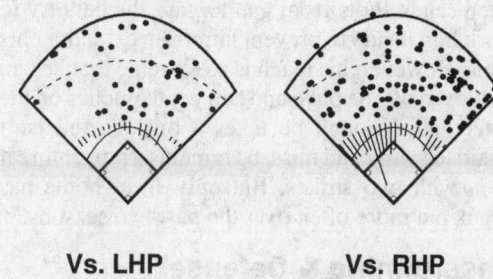

Vs. LHP   **Vs. RHP**

2001 Situational Stats

	AB	H	HR	RBI	Avg		AB	H	HR	RBI	Avg
Home	176	54	0	12	.307	LHP	96	30	0	6	.313
Road	208	57	2	17	.274	RHP	288	81	2	23	.281
First Half	162	45	0	10	.278	Sc Pos	84	24	0	22	.286
Scnd Half	222	66	2	19	.297	Clutch	56	16	0	6	.286

2001 Rankings (National League)

- 9th in lowest percentage of swings that missed (10.2)
- Led the Brewers in singles, sacrifice bunts (7), bunts in play (15), highest percentage of pitches taken (57.7), lowest percentage of swings that missed (10.2), highest percentage of swings put into play (50.7), batting average on an 0-2 count (.216), batting average on a 3-2 count (.321) and batting average with two strikes (.247)

Richie Sexson

2001 Season

Richie Sexson came into 2001 as the cornerstone of the Brewers' rebuilding project. And while the club's efforts seemingly ran into disaster at every turn, Sexson had as good a year as anyone could have expected, tying the team record for home runs. In addition, his 125 RBI fell just one shy of Milwaukee's single-season record. And his 327 total bases were the most by a Brewer since 1983. The only downside was that Sexson did the bulk of his hitting in the second half, after the Brewers already had fallen well out of contention.

Hitting

Sexson has monstrous power. He can hit the ball out to any part of the ballpark, though he most often sends shots from gap to gap. Pitchers try to work him inside to prevent him from extending his arms. However, his reach is so extreme that he can be moved off the plate and still get to pitches on the outer half. Though he takes a big cut and isn't afraid to swing and miss, he remains a power threat even with two strikes. But only Jim Thome has struck out more often over the past two seasons.

Baserunning & Defense

Sexson is a hugely underrated glove man. He simply excels at every facet of defense, from diving for smashes down the line, to digging out throws, to making strong relays from short right field. He'll be a Gold Glove candidate as soon as his reputation catches up with his performance. With big, loping strides, he seems slower than he really is.

2002 Outlook

Now 27 years old, Sexson has come into his own as a first-rate power hitter. He signed a four-year contract with Milwaukee last February, a deal that runs through 2004. The Brewers expect him to be their first baseman and cleanup hitter for years to come, and there's no reason to think otherwise.

Position: 1B
Bats: R **Throws:** R
Ht: 6' 7" **Wt:** 225

Opening Day Age: 27
Born: 12/29/74 in Portland, OR
ML Seasons: 5
Pronunciation: SECKS-un

Overall Statistics

	G	AB	R	H	D	T	HR	RBI	SB	BB	SO	Avg	OBP	Slg
2001	158	598	94	162	24	3	45	125	2	60	178	.271	.342	.547
Career	494	1799	284	487	85	12	117	367	8	159	498	.271	.334	.526

Where He Hits the Ball

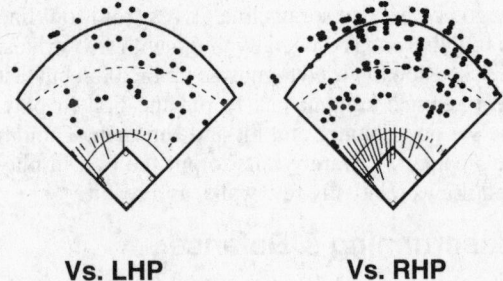

Vs. LHP   **Vs. RHP**

2001 Situational Stats

	AB	H	HR	RBI	Avg		AB	H	HR	RBI	Avg
Home	289	77	28	68	.266	LHP	139	41	11	28	.295
Road	309	85	17	57	.275	RHP	459	121	34	97	.264
First Half	315	79	18	56	.251	Sc Pos	148	40	10	73	.270
Scnd Half	283	83	27	69	.293	Clutch	76	22	2	10	.289

2001 Rankings (National League)

- 2nd in strikeouts and assists at first base (129)
- 3rd in lowest percentage of swings put into play (32.9)
- Led the Brewers in batting average, home runs, at-bats, hits, total bases (327), RBI, caught stealing (4), times on base (228), GDPs (20), pitches seen (2,608), plate appearances (667), games played, slugging percentage, HR frequency (13.3 ABs per HR), batting average in the clutch, batting average vs. righthanded pitchers, cleanup slugging percentage (.558), slugging percentage vs. lefthanded pitchers (.583), slugging percentage vs. righthanded pitchers (.536), on-base percentage vs. lefthanded pitchers (.384) and batting average at home

Ben Sheets

2001 Season

Ben Sheets followed up his Olympic success of 2000 by getting off to a great start in his first season in the majors. His record stood at 10-4 through the end of June and he was named the club's sole All-Star. But he dropped five straight decisions in July and early August before landing on the disabled list with shoulder tendinitis. He came back late in the year and proved that his arm was sound. He still finished with a winning record—a respectable accomplishment for a rookie on a 94-loss club—but his season could have been much better.

Pitching

Sheets has great stuff. He features a fastball in the low to mid-90s and a hard overhand curve. When he's on, he keeps the ball down and shows good command for a pitcher his age. He walked just 2.85 opponents per nine innings in the bigs in 2001. He often was hit hard after reaching the 75-pitch mark. Lefthanded batters gave him problems in 2001, but that might have been an aberration, since it wasn't the case when he worked in the minors the year before.

Defense & Hitting

Fielding comes naturally to Sheets, who also is careful to keep runners close. However, he is arguably the worst hitter in the majors. He struck out in more than two-thirds of his at-bats, managed only three hits and laid down just two sacrifices.

2002 Outlook

Sheets has all the makings of a quality starting pitcher. He was Milwaukee's top pick in the 1999 draft, pitched a complete-game shutout in the Gold Medal game of the 2000 Olympics, and made it to Milwaukee at age 22 last season. Barring a recurrence of his shoulder woes, he should be able to build upon last year's experience in the majors and take another step toward becoming the ace that the Brewers envision him to be some day.

Position: SP
Bats: R **Throws:** R
Ht: 6' 1" **Wt:** 195

Opening Day Age: 23
Born: 7/18/78 in St. Amant, LA
ML Seasons: 1

Overall Statistics

	W	L	Pct.	ERA	G	GS	Sv	IP	H	BB	SO	HR	Ratio
2001	11	10	.524	4.76	25	25	0	151.1	166	48	94	23	1.41
Career	11	10	.524	4.76	25	25	0	151.1	166	48	94	23	1.41

How Often He Throws Strikes

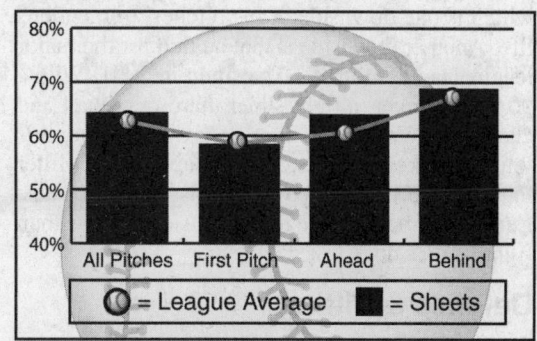

⊙ = League Average   ▮ = Sheets

2001 Situational Stats

	W	L	ERA	Sv	IP		AB	H	HR	RBI	Avg
Home	6	7	4.63	0	93.1	LHB	256	83	16	47	.324
Road	5	3	4.97	0	58.0	RHB	331	83	7	33	.251
First Half	10	5	3.59	0	100.1	Sc Pos	113	38	3	50	.336
Scnd Half	1	5	7.06	0	51.0	Clutch	19	4	1	2	.211

2001 Rankings (National League)

- 2nd in wins among rookies
- 3rd in losses among rookies
- 5th in highest batting average allowed vs. lefthanded batters
- 7th in highest ERA at home
- Led the Brewers in wins, winning percentage, most GDPs induced per GDP situation (14.3%), lowest ERA at home and lowest batting average allowed vs. righthanded batters

Milwaukee

Jamey Wright

2001 Season

Jamey Wright seemed to be putting it all together last season, only to see it all come apart. He was the club's best starter over the first half of the campaign and boasted an 8-5 record and 3.06 ERA through July 14. But he went 3-7 with a fat 7.22 ERA the rest of the way. While the truth is that he really didn't pitch as well as he seemed to in the first half or as badly as he appeared to in the second, his slide was alarming nonetheless.

Pitching

Wright's pitches have so much movement that he's tough to hit even when he's behind in the count. However, he often finds himself in that situation, which is one downside of his pitches' tremendous life. Another downside is that he tied for the major league lead by hitting 20 batsmen in 2001. With a 90-MPH sinker, a tight slider, hard curveball and changeup, Wright gets tons of groundballs and is tough to take deep—except, apparently, at Miller Park, where he allowed 17 of his 26 home runs. Lefthanded batters find him no easier to solve than righthanders do.

Defense & Hitting

Wright's non-pitching skills are among the best of any pitcher in baseball. He can hit: He batted .194, the best of any pitcher on the club with more than 20 at-bats, and he even was used as a pinch-hitter. He can field: he handled more chances than any Brewers pitcher and fielded all but one cleanly. And he can stop the running game; few righthanders have a better pickoff move. He was the only Brewers hurler to pick off a runner last year, nailing five of them.

2002 Outlook

Wright underwent arthroscopic surgery to remove a bone spur from his right elbow in October, and he is expected to be ready in time for spring training. Despite the procedure and his second-half collapse, he once again will enter 2002 as one of the Brewers' top starters. Now 27, he's established himself as a serviceable starter, but isn't likely to go much beyond that level.

Position: SP
Bats: R **Throws:** R
Ht: 6' 5" **Wt:** 221

Opening Day Age: 27
Born: 12/24/74 in Oklahoma City, OK
ML Seasons: 6

Overall Statistics

	W	L	Pct.	ERA	G	GS	Sv	IP	H	BB	SO	HR	Ratio
2001	11	12	.478	4.90	33	33	0	194.2	201	98	129	26	1.54
Career	43	54	.443	5.15	151	149	0	901.0	1006	447	464	99	1.61

How Often He Throws Strikes

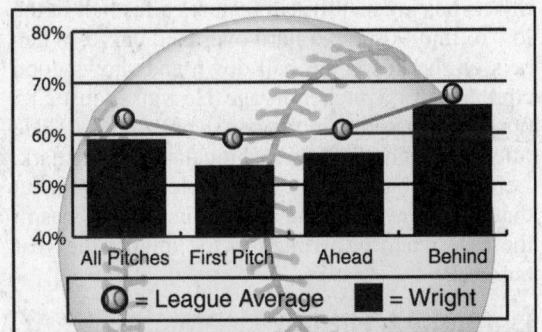

= League Average   = Wright

2001 Situational Stats

	W	L	ERA	Sv	IP		AB	H	HR	RBI	Avg
Home	7	7	5.53	0	107.1	LHB	312	81	11	40	.260
Road	4	5	4.12	0	87.1	RHB	426	120	15	59	.282
First Half	8	5	3.26	0	102.0	Sc Pos	182	41	5	67	.225
Scnd Half	3	7	6.70	0	92.2	Clutch	44	12	1	4	.273

2001 Rankings (National League)

- 1st in hit batsmen (20) and highest on-base percentage allowed (.370)
- Led the Brewers in wins, games started, innings pitched, hits allowed, batters faced (868), walks allowed, strikeouts, pitches thrown (3,190), pickoff throws (155), runners caught stealing (8), GDPs induced (26), lowest batting average allowed (.272), highest groundball-flyball ratio allowed (1.9), lowest stolen-base percentage allowed (57.9), most GDPs induced per GDP situation (14.3%), lowest ERA on the road, most run support per nine innings (5.7), lowest batting average allowed with runners in scoring position, most GDPs induced per nine innings (1.2) and most strikeouts per nine innings (6.0)

Henry Blanco

Position: C
Bats: R **Throws:** R
Ht: 5'11" **Wt:** 170

Opening Day Age: 30
Born: 8/29/71 in Caracas, VZ
ML Seasons: 4
Pronunciation: BLAHN-ko

Overall Statistics

	G	AB	R	H	D	T	HR	RBI	SB	BB	SO	Avg	OBP	Slg
2001	104	314	33	66	18	3	6	31	3	34	72	.210	.290	.344
Career	288	866	93	196	54	6	20	91	4	104	171	.226	.309	.372

2001 Situational Stats

	AB	H	HR	RBI	Avg		AB	H	HR	RBI	Avg
Home	157	33	4	11	.210	LHP	73	12	1	10	.164
Road	157	33	2	20	.210	RHP	241	54	5	21	.224
First Half	173	35	2	13	.202	Sc Pos	82	15	0	24	.183
Scnd Half	141	31	4	18	.220	Clutch	36	6	0	1	.167

2001 Season

While Henry Blanco last year solidified his status as one of the top defensive catchers in the game, he also reaffirmed that he's all leather and no stick. Even his stellar defense was insufficient to make up for his anemic bat, and his status as the Brewers' No.1 catcher was slowly slipping away before Raul Casanova got hurt.

Hitting, Baserunning & Defense

Blanco takes a power hitter's approach at the plate, trying to pull everything in the air. He doesn't make good contact, however, and pitchers know they can put him away when they need to. Coming off a shoulder injury, his throws weren't quite as strong in 2001. But his pegs still were as strong and accurate as any major league catcher's. Blanco also is respected both for his ability to block balls in the dirt and to call a game. He stole three bases in four attempts last season, purely through the element of surprise.

2002 Outlook

Blanco and Raul Casanova likely will continue to fight each other for playing time behind the plate. But Blanco may find himself with a smaller share of the job if Casanova keeps outhitting him by such a substantial margin.

Raul Casanova

Position: C
Bats: B **Throws:** R
Ht: 6' 0" **Wt:** 195

Opening Day Age: 29
Born: 8/23/72 in Humacao, PR
ML Seasons: 5

Overall Statistics

	G	AB	R	H	D	T	HR	RBI	SB	BB	SO	Avg	OBP	Slg
2001	71	192	21	50	10	0	11	33	0	12	29	.260	.303	.484
Career	299	854	78	203	36	4	27	105	2	75	153	.238	.304	.384

2001 Situational Stats

	AB	H	HR	RBI	Avg		AB	H	HR	RBI	Avg
Home	92	26	7	21	.283	LHP	15	5	1	4	.333
Road	100	24	4	12	.240	RHP	177	45	10	29	.254
First Half	136	40	9	29	.294	Sc Pos	52	14	2	19	.269
Scnd Half	56	10	2	4	.179	Clutch	42	5	1	5	.119

2001 Season

Last year Raul Casanova built on the gains he'd made the previous season, when he established himself as the Brewers' backup catcher. This time around, the switch-hitting receiver showed a much more effective approach at the plate while also making strides defensively. He took over a bigger share of the catching chores before a knee injury ended his season in mid-August.

Hitting, Baserunning & Defense

Casanova, who'd been more of a spray hitter in the past, pulled the ball and got better lift on it last year. His power numbers benefited, as his 11 home runs were a career high in the big leagues. Despite better numbers from the right side in 2001, he seems to be equally skilled from either side of the plate. He gets almost all of his at-bats as a lefthanded batter. His arm is known neither for its strength nor its accuracy, but his throwing was less of a liability in 2001. He's strictly a station-to-station baserunner.

2002 Outlook

If Casanova comes to camp fully recovered, as expected, he's positioned himself well to increase his playing time. He probably won't ever be a regular or a good defensive catcher. But his bat will make him useful. The Brewers re-signed him to a one-year, $850,000 contract in mid-December.

Mike DeJean

Position: RP
Bats: R **Throws:** R
Ht: 6' 2" **Wt:** 212

Opening Day Age: 31
Born: 9/28/70 in Baton Rouge, LA
ML Seasons: 5
Pronunciation: DAY-zshonn

Chad Fox

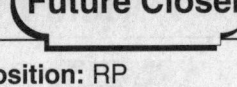

Position: RP
Bats: R **Throws:** R
Ht: 6' 3" **Wt:** 190

Opening Day Age: 31
Born: 9/3/70 in Coronado, CA
ML Seasons: 4

Overall Statistics

	W	L	Pct.	ERA	G	GS	Sv	IP	H	BB	SO	HR	Ratio
2001	4	2	.667	2.77	75	0	2	84.1	75	39	68	4	1.35
Career	18	11	.621	4.41	299	1	6	340.2	364	149	198	34	1.51

2001 Situational Stats

	W	L	ERA	Sv	IP		AB	H	HR	RBI	Avg
Home	3	0	2.47	1	47.1	LHB	132	30	1	20	.227
Road	1	2	3.16	1	37.0	RHB	186	45	3	19	.242
First Half	3	1	1.93	1	46.2	Sc Pos	95	19	0	31	.200
Scnd Half	1	1	3.82	1	37.2	Clutch	98	27	1	15	.276

Overall Statistics

	W	L	Pct.	ERA	G	GS	Sv	IP	H	BB	SO	HR	Ratio
2001	5	2	.714	1.89	65	0	2	66.2	44	36	80	6	1.20
Career	6	7	.462	3.25	150	0	2	157.2	135	76	184	15	1.34

2001 Situational Stats

	W	L	ERA	Sv	IP		AB	H	HR	RBI	Avg
Home	3	0	1.78	2	35.1	LHB	101	16	3	9	.158
Road	2	2	2.01	0	31.1	RHB	142	28	3	13	.197
First Half	2	1	1.59	0	34.0	Sc Pos	70	9	1	16	.129
Scnd Half	3	1	2.20	2	32.2	Clutch	116	19	2	5	.164

2001 Season

The Brewers' tumultuous season obscured the fine work of setup man Mike DeJean. Obtained in a trade from Colorado early last April, DeJean soon became a key component of Milwaukee's bullpen and thrived on the frequent work. After four years of pitching for the Rockies, he set career highs in games, innings and strikeouts.

Pitching, Defense & Hitting

DeJean has good stuff, with a low-90s fastball, hard splitter and occasional slider. Getting out of Coors Field undoubtedly helped his ERA, but another key to his improvement last year was pitching inside more effectively. Plus, the Brewers quickly learned that he's at his best in the first 30 pitches or so. They used him accordingly. DeJean gets groundballs and is adept at gloving his share of them. He doesn't pay much attention to baserunners, however, and can be an easy mark for those looking to run. He's a very poor hitter.

2002 Outlook

The Brewers seemed to figure out how to get the best from DeJean last year, and there's no reason he can't continue to thrive. He's expected to be one of their primary setup men again this season. He has signed a two-year deal with Milwaukee that's good through 2003, with an option for 2004.

2001 Season

The Brewers' most surprising and inspirational performer last year was Chad Fox. He had missed most of the previous two seasons after undergoing Tommy John surgery—for the *second* time—in 1999 and breaking his elbow in 2000. Fox not only returned to health, but also became the most effective member of Milwaukee's bullpen.

Pitching, Defense & Hitting

Fox' hard, darting slider is one of the most unhittable pitches in any short reliever's arsenal. With that weapon and a 90-MPH fastball, he needs little else to contain lefthanded and righthanded batters. Early last year, the Brewers were understandably cautious about using Fox on consecutive days, but he held up fine and was being used as needed by May. He can be run on, since his slider is tough for a catcher to catch and throw. Fox is a reliable fielder but can't do a thing with the bat. He has no hits and one successful sacrifice bunt in his big league career.

2002 Outlook

There is uncertainty over Curtis Leskanic's readiness to start the season. Fox will be first in line to take over as the Brewers' closer if needed. If Fox' elbow holds up, he ought to keeping blowing hitters away.

Tyler Houston

Position: 3B
Bats: L **Throws:** R
Ht: 6' 1" **Wt:** 210

Opening Day Age: 31
Born: 1/17/71 in Long Beach, CA
ML Seasons: 6

Overall Statistics

	G	AB	R	H	D	T	HR	RBI	SB	BB	SO	Avg	OBP	Slg
2001	75	235	36	68	7	0	12	38	0	18	62	.289	.343	.472
Career	535	1388	156	362	58	3	54	199	9	97	327	.261	.309	.424

2001 Situational Stats

	AB	H	HR	RBI	Avg		AB	H	HR	RBI	Avg
Home	111	33	6	21	.297	LHP	25	7	2	5	.280
Road	124	35	6	17	.282	RHP	210	61	10	33	.290
First Half	218	66	12	36	.303	Sc Pos	51	20	4	27	.392
Scnd Half	17	2	0	2	.118	Clutch	38	7	3	4	.184

2001 Season

Tyler Houston was one of the main beneficiaries when Mark Loretta hurt his thumb last spring. With Jose Hernandez sliding over to short, Houston became part of a third base platoon and quickly solidified his position there. Playing regularly against righthanders, Houston was one of the Brewers' best hitters until a stress reduction in his right foot virtually ended his season in mid-July.

Hitting, Baserunning & Defense

Houston is an aggressive hitter who's most dangerous on the first pitch. A pull hitter, he has a knack for hitting it through the hole on the right side when a runner is on first base. He hasn't had the chance to prove he can hit lefties. He'd found use in the past as a backup catcher and corner infielder, but he shelved his catcher's gear last year and played third base almost exclusively. He's adequate there, with average range and a passable arm. His speed is below average.

2002 Outlook

Houston has another season remaining on the two-year contract he signed before the 2001 campaign. He'll be looking to reclaim his platoon job at third this year. However, if all of the Brewers' infielders are healthy, the presence of Mark Loretta might eat into Houston's playing time.

Ray King

Position: RP
Bats: L **Throws:** L
Ht: 6' 1" **Wt:** 230

Opening Day Age: 28
Born: 1/15/74 in Chicago, IL
ML Seasons: 3

Overall Statistics

	W	L	Pct.	ERA	G	GS	Sv	IP	H	BB	SO	HR	Ratio
2001	0	4	.000	3.60	82	0	1	55.0	49	25	49	5	1.35
Career	3	6	.333	3.15	128	0	1	94.1	78	45	73	8	1.30

2001 Situational Stats

	W	L	ERA	Sv	IP		AB	H	HR	RBI	Avg
Home	0	2	2.93	0	30.2	LHB	105	22	1	17	.210
Road	0	2	4.44	1	24.1	RHB	98	27	4	17	.276
First Half	0	1	3.41	1	31.2	Sc Pos	70	19	2	29	.271
Scnd Half	0	3	3.86	0	23.1	Clutch	74	23	3	20	.311

2001 Season

Ray King didn't duplicate his phenomenal ERA from the year before, but what he did do was more than good enough for the Brewers. He was their only southpaw in the bullpen for most of the season, and they called on him time and again to come in and face a key lefthanded batter or two. He performed that duty quite well, limiting lefthanded swingers to a .210 average overall.

Pitching, Defense & Hitting

King comes at hitters with a 90-MPH fastball, a sinker and a slider. He does a good job of keeping the ball down and getting groundballs. He handles lefthanded batters well but rarely is asked to stay in and face the tough righthanded hitters. Baserunners got a better read on King's delivery last year and stole five bases against him without being caught. He hasn't shown himself to be anything more or less than an adequate fielder. He's gone hitless in three career at-bats.

2002 Outlook

King has value as a southpaw who can retire lefthanded hitters and pitch every other day. His 82 games pitched last season were the most ever by a Milwaukee southpaw. He is sure to continue as the Brewers' lefty specialist.

Milwaukee

Allen Levrault

Position: SP/RP
Bats: R **Throws:** R
Ht: 6' 3" **Wt:** 230

Opening Day Age: 24
Born: 8/15/77 in Fall River, MA
ML Seasons: 2
Pronunciation: LEV-ralt

Overall Statistics

	W	L	Pct.	ERA	G	GS	Sv	IP	H	BB	SO	HR	Ratio
2001	6	10	.375	6.06	32	20	0	130.2	146	59	80	27	1.57
Career	6	11	.353	5.93	37	21	0	142.2	156	66	89	27	1.56

2001 Situational Stats

	W	L	ERA	Sv	IP		AB	H	HR	RBI	Avg
Home	4	5	5.95	0	62.0	LHB	222	60	10	27	.270
Road	2	5	6.16	0	68.2	RHB	298	86	17	52	.289
First Half	3	3	5.18	0	57.1	Sc Pos	119	34	5	51	.286
Scnd Half	3	7	6.75	0	73.1	Clutch	2	1	0	0	.500

2001 Season

Allen Levrault made his major league debut in 2000 and appeared in five games for the Brewers that year. He received a longer opportunity to show what he could do in the big leagues last season but didn't seem ready for it. He was called up for the second time in the season in early May and inserted into the rotation a few weeks later due to a rash of injuries. Levrault had some decent games but rarely went more than five innings. He melted down completely in August and September, losing his rotation spot.

Pitching, Defense & Hitting

Levrault's stuff is borderline. His 90-MPH fastball is straight and hittable, his curveball and slider are inconsistent and his command is often shaky. He leaves the ball up too frequently, and last year he served up home runs at an alarming rate. With two errors in 22 career chances, he's no more than ordinary in the field. He seems to be an especially weak hitter, though a competent bunter. He gives basestealers little pause.

2002 Outlook

Levrault was thrust into a prominent role last year only out of necessity. Even taking into account that he was a rookie pitcher on a bad team in a hitters' park, there is little reason to expect much from him.

Luis Lopez

Position: 3B/SS/2B
Bats: B **Throws:** R
Ht: 5'11" **Wt:** 166

Opening Day Age: 31
Born: 9/4/70 in Cidra, PR
ML Seasons: 8
Pronunciation: LOE-pezz

Overall Statistics

	G	AB	R	H	D	T	HR	RBI	SB	BB	SO	Avg	OBP	Slg
2001	92	222	22	60	8	3	4	18	0	14	44	.270	.326	.387
Career	590	1388	153	345	71	7	19	131	9	91	296	.249	.304	.351

2001 Situational Stats

	AB	H	HR	RBI	Avg		AB	H	HR	RBI	Avg
Home	102	24	2	7	.235	LHP	38	7	0	4	.184
Road	120	36	2	11	.300	RHP	184	53	4	14	.288
First Half	80	18	1	5	.225	Sc Pos	44	11	2	15	.250
Scnd Half	142	42	3	13	.296	Clutch	32	8	0	1	.250

2001 Season

Milwaukee rewarded its top utility infielder, Luis Lopez, with a two-year deal after the 2000 season. He responded with another creditable performance in 2001. He provided flexibility for Davey Lopes' bench and filled in when injuries opened holes on the infield. He wound up starting at least nine times at second base, third base and shortstop.

Hitting, Baserunning & Defense

Though he performed much better against righthanders in 2001, the switch-hitting Lopez isn't much of a threat from either side of the plate. He sprays the ball around just enough to keep his average respectable. He's impatient and rarely draws a walk. While his power isn't exceptional, he will contribute an occasional extra-base hit. Lopez fared poorly as a pinch-hitter last year and hasn't distinguished himself in that capacity. He has adequate range and hands for any infield position. His arm is best suited to second base, but he gets rid of the ball quickly enough to get by at third. Though he's built like a basestealer, he doesn't run like one.

2002 Outlook

While Lopez has gone as far as his skills will take him, he fills his role quite adequately. He likely will continue as the Brewers' utility infielder for at least another year.

Ruben Quevedo

Position: SP
Bats: R **Throws:** R
Ht: 6' 1" **Wt:** 245

Opening Day Age: 23
Born: 1/5/79 in
Valencia Carabobo, VZ
ML Seasons: 2
Pronunciation:
keh-VAY-doh

Overall Statistics

	W	L	Pct.	ERA	G	GS	Sv	IP	H	BB	SO	HR	Ratio
2001	4	5	.444	4.61	10	10	0	56.2	56	30	60	9	1.52
Career	7	15	.318	6.35	31	25	0	144.2	152	84	125	30	1.63

2001 Situational Stats

	W	L	ERA	Sv	IP		AB	H	HR	RBI	Avg
Home	1	3	6.75	0	20.0	LHB	102	28	6	17	.275
Road	3	2	3.44	0	36.2	RHB	116	28	3	11	.241
First Half	0	0	-	0	0.0	Sc Pos	58	11	3	20	.190
Scnd Half	4	5	4.61	0	56.2	Clutch	13	4	0	1	.308

2001 Season

After young righthander Ruben Quevedo pitched his way out of the Cubs' plans with a disastrous debut season in 2000, he returned to Triple-A in 2001 and turned things around. The Brewers acquired him in the David Weathers deal at the trading deadline and immediately inserted him into their rotation. He performed rather well there before tiring at the end.

Pitching, Defense & Hitting

Quevedo, who has a decent fastball, slider, curve and changeup, likes to work up in the zone. As such, he is an extreme flyball pitcher and gives up more than his share of doubles and home runs. In fact, more than half of his hits allowed last year were of the extra-base variety. He did a decent job hitting and bunting last year, which represented a big improvement over the year before. He's a sure-handed but immobile fielder. Opposing basestealers succeeded on only three of six attempts in 2001.

2002 Outlook

It's hard to know what the Brewers have in Quevedo. Although he's listed as 23 years of age, he's already been traded twice and thrown a lot of pitches the past two years. Plus, he's in poor shape. He'll likely open this season in the rotation, but what he does beyond that is anyone's guess.

Devon White

Position: CF/LF
Bats: B **Throws:** R
Ht: 6' 2" **Wt:** 190

Opening Day Age: 39
Born: 12/29/62 in
Kingston, Jamaica
ML Seasons: 17
Nickname: Devo

Overall Statistics

	G	AB	R	H	D	T	HR	RBI	SB	BB	SO	Avg	OBP	Slg
2001	126	390	52	108	25	2	14	47	18	28	95	.277	.343	.459
Career	1941	7344	1125	1934	378	71	208	846	346	541	1526	.263	.319	.419

2001 Situational Stats

	AB	H	HR	RBI	Avg		AB	H	HR	RBI	Avg
Home	178	53	6	23	.298	LHP	88	24	2	16	.273
Road	212	55	8	24	.259	RHP	302	84	12	31	.278
First Half	184	52	9	32	.283	Sc Pos	72	18	4	36	.250
Scnd Half	206	56	5	15	.272	Clutch	67	13	1	3	.194

2001 Season

Frustrated at his lack of playing time in Los Angeles, Devon White lobbied for a trade and was dealt to Milwaukee over the winter. At first, his prospects for a return to full-time play seemed no better with the Brewers. But injuries to Geoff Jenkins and Jeffrey Hammonds enabled the 38-year-old to play semi-regularly and enjoy one of his better seasons in recent years.

Hitting, Baserunning & Defense

After having his production from the left side deteriorate over the past few seasons, the switch-hitting White brought his lefthanded swing back on par with that of his natural side last season. He has power, but not enough to be a run producer. Furthermore, he runs well and hits for a decent average, but lacks the on-base skills to be a top-flight leadoff man. He did rebound from a poor season on the bases to steal 18 bags in 21 tries last year. White still possesses the range to play a decent center field. His poor arm is his only weakness afield.

2002 Outlook

The Brewers did not exercise their 2002 option on White, making him a free agent. He has the skills to remain a useful fourth outfielder for another season or two, so he could wind up with his fifth different team in the past six years.

Other Milwaukee Brewers

Kevin Brown (Pos: C, Age: 28, Bats: R)

	G	AB	R	H	D	T	HR	RBI	SB	BB	SO	Avg	OBP	Slg
2001	17	43	7	9	0	1	4	12	0	2	18	.209	.261	.535
Career	83	188	30	48	12	2	7	31	0	14	59	.255	.313	.452

Brown was having a career season with Triple-A Syracuse, batting .335 in 2000 before he was acquired by the Brewers. His average has dropped to .234 over the last season and a half with Triple-A Indianapolis. He became a free agent in October and signed a minor league pact with Tampa Bay. 2002 Outlook: C

Mike Buddie (Pos: RHP, Age: 31)

	W	L	Pct.	ERA	G	GS	Sv	IP	H	BB	SO	HR	Ratio
2001	0	1	.000	3.89	31	0	2	41.2	34	17	22	2	1.22
Career	4	2	.667	4.73	62	2	2	91.1	91	31	48	8	1.34

Buddie split last season between Milwaukee and Triple-A Indianapolis, posting respectable numbers at both levels. He missed a month of the season with an ankle injury. He should win a middle relief spot in 2002. 2002 Outlook: B

Lou Collier (Pos: 3B/LF/CF, Age: 28, Bats: R)

	G	AB	R	H	D	T	HR	RBI	SB	BB	SO	Avg	OBP	Slg
2001	50	127	19	32	8	1	2	14	5	17	30	.252	.340	.378
Career	266	665	79	161	31	7	7	74	11	69	147	.242	.316	.341

Collier started his professional career as a shortstop, but the Brewers have been trying to groom him into an outfielder since claiming him off waivers from Pittsburgh late in 1998. He showed some power, hitting 14 homers at Triple-A in 2001. 2002 Outlook: C

Mike Coolbaugh (Pos: 3B, Age: 29, Bats: R)

	G	AB	R	H	D	T	HR	RBI	SB	BB	SO	Avg	OBP	Slg
2001	39	70	10	14	6	0	2	7	0	5	16	.200	.273	.371
Career	39	70	10	14	6	0	2	7	0	5	16	.200	.273	.371

Coolbaugh has some pop in his bat, but is not consistent enough to break into the everyday lineup for the Brewers. The third baseman, who debuted in the majors in 2001, signed with the Cards in the fall. 2002 Outlook: C

Rocky Coppinger (Pos: RHP, Age: 28)

	W	L	Pct.	ERA	G	GS	Sv	IP	H	BB	SO	HR	Ratio
2001	1	0	1.000	6.75	8	3	0	22.2	24	15	15	5	1.72
Career	17	11	.607	5.47	82	32	0	241.2	247	140	210	48	1.60

Coppinger returned last year after missing all of 2000 with elbow problems. He was impressive in Triple-A, posting a 1.97 ERA in 77.2 innings. He signed a minor league deal with the A's in November. 2002 Outlook: C

Will Cunnane (Pos: RHP, Age: 27)

	W	L	Pct.	ERA	G	GS	Sv	IP	H	BB	SO	HR	Ratio
2001	0	3	.000	5.40	31	1	0	51.2	66	22	37	6	1.70
Career	9	8	.529	5.35	139	12	0	215.1	253	105	173	28	1.66

Despite mostly starting in the minors, Cunnane has struggled as a starter in the majors. In 12 career starts, he has an 8.54 ERA, compared to 4.34 in 127 relief outings. He became a free agent in October. 2002 Outlook: C

Valerio de los Santos (Pos: LHP, Age: 26)

	W	L	Pct.	ERA	G	GS	Sv	IP	H	BB	SO	HR	Ratio
2001	0	0	-	9.00	1	0	0	1.0	1	1	1	0	2.00
Career	2	4	.333	4.82	87	2	0	104.2	96	43	94	20	1.33

De los Santos appeared in just one game last season before undergoing Tommy John surgery on his pitching elbow in April. He should be able to return by the middle of 2002, likely as a middle reliever. 2002 Outlook: C

Angel Echevarria (Pos: LF, Age: 30, Bats: R)

	G	AB	R	H	D	T	HR	RBI	SB	BB	SO	Avg	OBP	Slg
2001	75	133	12	34	11	0	5	13	0	8	29	.256	.310	.451
Career	278	445	56	122	25	0	18	69	1	38	87	.274	.341	.452

Echevarria was another reserve outfielder available to the Brewers in 2001. He received some playing time when Geoff Jenkins was out with injury. He's a career .346 hitter at home, compared to .206 on the road. He became a free agent after refusing a minor league assignment in October. 2002 Outlook: C

Gus Gandarillas (Pos: RHP, Age: 30)

	W	L	Pct.	ERA	G	GS	Sv	IP	H	BB	SO	HR	Ratio
2001	0	0	-	5.49	16	0	0	19.2	25	10	7	2	1.78
Career	0	0	-	5.49	16	0	0	19.2	25	10	7	2	1.78

Gandarillas was another player to make his major league debut with the Brewers druing the 2001 season. He liked home cooking, posting a 1.08 ERA at Miller Park in his brief stay with Milwaukee. 2002 Outlook: C

Brandon Kolb (Pos: RHP, Age: 28)

	W	L	Pct.	ERA	G	GS	Sv	IP	H	BB	SO	HR	Ratio
2001	0	0	-	13.03	10	0	0	9.2	16	8	8	6	2.48
Career	0	1	.000	7.99	21	0	0	23.2	32	19	20	6	2.15

Kolb is a durable reliever who has appeared in more than 50 games in each of the last two seasons. With a mid-90s sinker, Kolb has the potential to be successful in the majors. He signed a minor league contract with Cincinnati in November. 2002 Outlook: C

Mark Leiter (Pos: RHP, Age: 38)

	W	L	Pct.	ERA	G	GS	Sv	IP	H	BB	SO	HR	Ratio
2001	2	1	.667	3.75	20	3	0	36.0	32	8	26	6	1.11
Career	65	73	.471	4.57	335	149	26	1184.1	1205	424	892	155	1.38

After missing the better part of two seasons with shoulder problems, Leiter returned in 2001, only to sit out a bulk of the season with a biceps injury. The Brewers declined the option on his contract for the 2002 season. 2002 Outlook: C

Jesse Levis (Pos: C, Age: 33, Bats: L)

	G	AB	R	H	D	T	HR	RBI	SB	BB	SO	Avg	OBP	Slg
2001	12	33	6	8	2	0	0	3	0	3	7	.242	.306	.303
Career	319	654	66	167	23	1	3	60	2	76	66	.255	.336	.307

Levis has been a pro since 1989, splitting the majority of his time between the Indians' and Brewers' farm systems. He has hit nearly .300 in the minors for his career. His small stature limits his power. 2002 Outlook: C

James Mouton (Pos: CF/LF, **Age**: 33, **Bats**: R)

	G	AB	R	H	D	T	HR	RBI	SB	BB	SO	Avg	OBP	Slg
2001	75	138	20	34	8	0	2	10	7	11	40	.246	.329	.348
Career	723	1570	223	386	75	7	18	147	109	174	338	.246	.328	.337

Mouton is a solid bench player with enough speed to be a consistent threat to steal bases. However, a career .246 batting average has limited his opportunities. He became a free agent in November and will help a team in a reserve role. 2002 Outlook: C

Lance Painter (Pos: LHP, **Age**: 34)

	W	L	Pct.	ERA	G	GS	Sv	IP	H	BB	SO	HR	Ratio
2001	1	1	.500	6.52	23	0	0	29.0	38	18	20	7	1.93
Career	25	17	.595	5.23	292	28	3	432.0	479	171	320	63	1.50

Painter signed with the Brewers after being let go by the Blue Jays halfway through the 2001 season. He improved his numbers in Milwaukee before partially tearing a ligament in his pitching elbow. The 34-year-old became a free agent in November. 2002 Outlook: C

Elvis Pena (Pos: 2B, **Age**: 25, **Bats**: B)

	G	AB	R	H	D	T	HR	RBI	SB	BB	SO	Avg	OBP	Slg
2001	15	40	5	9	2	0	0	6	2	6	6	.225	.333	.275
Career	25	49	6	12	3	0	0	7	3	7	7	.245	.345	.306

Pena was acquired from Colorado last spring. He showed some promise at the Double-A level, batting over .300 with 69 steals from 1999-2000. He may need another year or two in the minors. 2002 Outlook: C

Robert Perez (Pos: CF, **Age**: 32, **Bats**: R)

	G	AB	R	H	D	T	HR	RBI	SB	BB	SO	Avg	OBP	Slg
2001	8	20	1	4	1	0	0	0	0	1	7	.200	.238	.250
Career	221	497	49	126	19	1	8	44	3	11	74	.254	.271	.344

The Brewers picked up Perez in June after the Yankees released him. He hit .326 at Triple-A with 10 homers and 43 RBI in 56 games. He signed another minor league deal with Milwaukee in November. 2002 Outlook: C

Kyle Peterson (Pos: RHP, **Age**: 25)

	W	L	Pct.	ERA	G	GS	Sv	IP	H	BB	SO	HR	Ratio
2001	1	2	.333	5.52	3	2	0	14.2	19	4	12	3	1.57
Career	5	9	.357	4.71	20	14	0	91.2	106	29	46	6	1.47

Peterson, a former first-round pick, has struggled since undergoing shoulder surgery almost two years ago. The righthander, who is not overpowering, had ERAs above

5.50 at both Milwaukee and Triple-A in 2001. 2002 Outlook: C

Paul Rigdon (Pos: RHP, **Age**: 26)

	W	L	Pct.	ERA	G	GS	Sv	IP	H	BB	SO	HR	Ratio
2001	3	5	.375	5.79	15	15	0	79.1	86	46	49	13	1.66
Career	8	10	.444	5.45	32	31	0	166.2	175	81	112	31	1.54

Rigdon posted a 3-5 record and a 5.79 ERA in 15 starts in 2001 before going down with an elbow injury mid-season. He had scar tissue and bone spurs removed from his pitching elbow in August. He should be ready for 2002. 2002 Outlook: B

Alex Sanchez (Pos: CF, **Age**: 25, **Bats**: L)

	G	AB	R	H	D	T	HR	RBI	SB	BB	SO	Avg	OBP	Slg
2001	30	68	7	14	3	2	0	4	6	5	13	.206	.260	.309
Career	30	68	7	14	3	2	0	4	6	5	13	.206	.260	.309

Sanchez is another young prospect in a saturated Milwaukee outfield. He doesn't possess the power of the current starters, but can make up for it with his speed. He stole 92 bases in Class-A during the 1997 season. 2002 Outlook: C

Mac Suzuki (Pos: RHP, **Age**: 26)

	W	L	Pct.	ERA	G	GS	Sv	IP	H	BB	SO	HR	Ratio
2001	5	12	.294	5.86	33	19	0	118.1	122	73	89	20	1.65
Career	16	29	.356	5.57	110	66	0	444.2	477	248	312	65	1.63

Coming off shoulder surgery, Suzuki struggled with Kansas City, Colorado and Milwaukee in 2001, before finally being released by the Brewers in October. In November he signed a minor league deal with KC, where he started 2001. 2002 Outlook: C

Mark Sweeney (Pos: LF, **Age**: 32, **Bats**: L)

	G	AB	R	H	D	T	HR	RBI	SB	BB	SO	Avg	OBP	Slg
2001	48	89	9	23	3	1	3	11	2	12	23	.258	.347	.416
Career	528	796	94	207	38	4	15	97	9	117	163	.260	.355	.374

Sweeney has proven to be a quality pinch-hitter throughout his career, but has struggled over the last two seasons. In addition to playing the outfield, Sweeney also has spent some time at first base. The Brewers re-signed him to a one-year, $515,000 deal in mid-December. 2002 Outlook: B

Milwaukee Brewers Minor League Prospects

Organization Overview:

Though the Brewers finished 26 games under .500 last season, they still enjoyed a couple of positive developments. First, they moved into Miller Park and set a franchise attendance record. Second, potential No. 1 starter Ben Sheets got his feet wet in the big leagues and shared the team lead with 11 wins. For a club that hasn't had a pitcher win more than 16 games since 1992, Sheets' arrival could be a turning point. Furthermore, the light seemed to click on for Nick Neugebauer in 2001 and he should contend for a starting job this spring. He has the potential to be even better than Sheets. And if Ruben Quevedo develops, the Brewers could boast three legitimate starters who enter this season at age 23 or less. The news isn't quite as sanguine regarding Milwaukee's position prospects, as none should be expected to make an impact in the near term.

Daryl Clark

Position: 3B　　**Opening Day Age:** 22
Bats: L **Throws:** R　　**Born:** 9/25/79 in
Ht: 6' 2"　**Wt:** 205　　Nuremburg, Germany

Recent Statistics

	G	AB	R	H	D	THR	RBI	SB	BB	SO	Avg
2000 R Ogden	64	218	54	74	12	4	15	64	5	67	53	.339
2001 A Beloit	133	501	76	142	24	2	21	92	4	61	135	.283

Clark waited until the 17th round to be taken in the 2000 draft. But he hit extremely well in the Pioneer League that summer. In addition to generating a high average and lots of power, he walked 67 times in 64 games. The result was an on-base percentage approaching .500. Although he wasn't as devastating in the Midwest League last year, he still led Beloit in home runs, RBI and runs scored. Perhaps the biggest concern about Clark is his defense. After spending time at first and third base in 2000, he worked exclusively at the hot corner last year and committed a boatload of errors—47, to be exact. He'll most likely be at high Class-A High Desert in 2002.

Cristian Guerrero

Position: OF　　**Opening Day Age:** 20
Bats: R **Throws:** R　　**Born:** 4/12/81 in Bani,
Ht: 6' 5"　**Wt:** 200　　DR

Recent Statistics

	G	AB	R	H	D	THR	RBI	SB	BB	SO	Avg
2000 A Beloit	15	55	5	9	4	0	2	8	1	1	18	.164
2000 R Ogden	66	255	56	87	14	4	12	54	24	37	42	.341
2001 A High Desert	85	327	50	102	18	2	7	41	22	18	79	.312

Like his cousin, Vladimir Guerrero, Cristian was signed as a teenager out of the Dominican Republic. Cristian reached high Class-A last year at age 20, but missed a chunk of the season with a broken foot. Nevertheless, he continued to show the ability to hit for average and decent power. Although he's a big guy at 6-foot-5, Guer-

rero has the ability to steal bases, topping 20 swipes for the past three years. His arm is solid and he should be able to handle right field as he advances. Although his frame suggests the potential for more power, Guerrero's strikeout-walk ratio has suffered at stops above rookie ball. The Brewers think he can jump to Double-A in '02, but he is young and may take some time developing.

Bill Hall

Position: SS　　**Opening Day Age:** 22
Bats: R **Throws:** R　　**Born:** 12/28/79 in
Ht: 6' 0"　**Wt:** 175　　Nettleton, MS

Recent Statistics

	G	AB	R	H	D	THR	RBI	SB	BB	SO	Avg
2000 A Beloit	130	470	57	123	30	6	3	41	10	18	127	.262
2001 A High Desert	89	346	61	105	21	6	15	51	18	22	78	.303
2001 AA Huntsville	41	160	14	41	8	1	3	14	5	5	46	.256

The Brewers selected Hall out of a Mississippi high school in 1998. His offensive game really seemed to take off at High Desert last season, though part of his success may have been due to the environment he was hitting in. Still, he reached Double-A, played well in the Arizona Fall League and showed an intriguing combination of power and speed overall. Hall's running ability helps him in the field, where he flashes good range at shortstop. However, he's not the most reliable of defenders and has committed his share of errors. Also, his plate discipline could use some work, as he's struck out at least 124 times each of the past two seasons and hasn't walked nearly enough to compensate. Added to the Brewers' 40-man roster, Hall may need more time at Double-A.

Ben Hendrickson

Position: P　　**Opening Day Age:** 21
Bats: R **Throws:** R　　**Born:** 2/4/81 in St.
Ht: 6' 3"　**Wt:** 185　　Cloud, MN

Recent Statistics

	W	L	ERA	G	GS	Sv	IP	H	R	BB	SO	HR
2000 R Ogden	4	3	5.68	13	7	1	50.2	50	37	29	48	7
2001 A Beloit	8	9	2.84	25	25	0	133.1	122	58	72	133	3

Hendrickson was drafted in the 10th round in 1999 but didn't pitch his first game in the Brewers system until the following season. Since then, he's averaged roughly one strikeout per inning. Although his 2001 record wasn't remarkable, Hendrickson's ERA ranked fifth in the Midwest League. And his curveball was rated the best breaking pitch in the circuit in a *Baseball America* poll of league managers. His fastball can reach up to 94 MPH, though it usually resides in the 90-91 MPH range. He's also working on a changeup. He has some room to grow and possibly get stronger. His control will need some attention, as he's walked nearly five batters per nine innings as a pro. Hendrickson probably will be at high Class-A High Desert this season.

Kade Johnson

Position: C   **Opening Day Age:** 23
Bats: R **Throws:** R   **Born:** 9/28/78 in
Ht: 6' 1" **Wt:** 205   Baytown, TX

Recent Statistics

	G	AB	R	H	D	T	HR	RBI	SB	BB	SO	Avg
2000 R Ogden	28	98	16	31	7	0	10	35	2	14	20	.316
2001 A High Desert	101	370	57	94	21	1	21	67	9	35	118	.254

The Brewers grabbed Johnson with their second-round pick in 1999. He had demonstrated very good power at an Oklahoma junior college that season, clubbing 38 home runs. He then blasted 10 homers in 28 games at his first professional stop in the Pioneer League and continued to show longball prowess last year. He underwent shoulder surgery in 2000, which limited his ability to work behind the plate. But Johnson spent more time catching last season and his arm appears to be strong enough to handle the receiving chores. Even if it isn't, his bat looks like it might be good enough to keep him in the lineup if he's switched to another position.

Dave Krynzel

Position: OF   **Opening Day Age:** 20
Bats: L **Throws:** L   **Born:** 11/7/81 in Dayton,
Ht: 6' 1" **Wt:** 180   OH

Recent Statistics

	G	AB	R	H	D	T	HR	RBI	SB	BB	SO	Avg
2000 R Ogden	34	131	25	47	8	3	1	29	8	16	23	.359
2001 A Beloit	35	141	22	43	1	1	1	19	11	9	28	.305
2001 A High Desert	89	383	65	106	19	5	5	33	34	27	122	.277

Krynzel was the 11th overall selection of the 2000 draft. He debuted that summer in very impressive fashion in the Pioneer League. Encouraged by his performance, the Brewers pushed him to the Midwest League last spring, where he again topped .300, albeit with very little power. He then was bumped up to high Class-A. Krynzel is fast and plays a good center field. He stole 45 bases overall last year, tying for the Brewers' minor league lead. However, his strikeout rate got a little out of hand in the California League, and he could stand to draw more walks. Krynzel's stats are somewhat reminiscent of Chad Green's, a failed No. 1 pick for Milwaukee. The Brewers hope Krynzel turns out better.

Jose Mieses

Position: P   **Opening Day Age:** 22
Bats: R **Throws:** R   **Born:** 10/14/79 in Santo
Ht: 6' 1" **Wt:** 180   Domingo, DR

Recent Statistics

	W	L	ERA	G	GS	Sv	IP	H	R	BB	SO	HR
2000 A Beloit	13	6	2.53	21	21	0	135.0	107	43	37	132	8
2000 A Mudville	4	1	2.65	6	6	0	34.0	25	11	18	40	1
2001 AA Huntsville	0	0	2.22	5	4	0	24.1	21	7	3	35	2
2001 AAA Indianapolis	0	3	6.08	3	3	0	13.1	23	12	7	13	4
2001 R Brewers	0	1	0.00	2	2	0	4.1	3	1	1	5	0
2001 R Ogden	0	1	27.00	1	1	0	1.0	3	3	1	2	0

Mieses enjoyed a tremendous season in 2000, when he led Brewers minor leaguers with 17 wins between two levels. He then got off to a very good start in Double-A last year and soon was promoted to Triple-A. Unfortunately, a back injury sidelined him for much of the campaign and he later underwent shoulder surgery. Mieses doesn't throw that hard and his fastball and curveball are just ordinary. However, he's able to succeed by employing a palmball and exhibiting good poise and command. He was signed by the Brewers out of the Dominican Republic at age 17 in 1996, so he's still fairly young. He needs to show he can stay healthy, but Mieses looked like he was breezing through Milwaukee's system before the injuries hit him last year.

Nick Neugebauer

Position: P   **Opening Day Age:** 21
Bats: R **Throws:** R   **Born:** 7/15/80 in
Ht: 6' 3" **Wt:** 225   Riverside, CA

Recent Statistics

	W	L	ERA	G	GS	Sv	IP	H	R	BB	SO	HR
2001 AA Huntsville	5	6	3.46	21	21	0	106.2	94	46	52	149	6
2001 AAA Indianapolis	2	1	1.50	4	4	0	24.0	10	5	9	26	1
2001 NL Milwaukee	1	1	7.50	2	2	0	6.0	6	5	6	11	1

Neugebauer's control took a quantum leap forward in 2001. He had always displayed a terrific arm after being selected in the second round of the 1998 draft. However, while he fanned nearly 13 batters per nine innings in his first two pro seasons, he also walked more than a batter per inning. But he certainly seemed to turn a corner last year. Instead of throwing in the high 90s, he took a little off and still produced velocity in the mid-90s. He maintained a very high strikeout rate and was able to cut his walk rate in half. His breaking ball is a slurve and he's also working on a changeup. Neugebauer underwent shoulder surgery late last season but is expected to be ready this spring. He should compete for a spot in Milwaukee's rotation and has a chance to be truly dominant.

Others to Watch

Righthander **Matt Childers'** (23) stats were ugly at High Desert last season. But he boasts a fastball that can touch 95 MPH and the Brewers reportedly like him. . . Shortstop **J.J. Hardy** (19) was a No. 2 pick in 2001. He obviously has a long way to go before he sniffs the big leagues, but his defense could be special. . . Righthander **Mike Jones** (18) was chosen in the first round of last year's draft. *Baseball America* named him the No. 1 prospect in the Midwest League. . . Righthanded reliever **Brian Mallette's** (27) velocity has increased into the low 90s. He'll likely compete for a bullpen role in Milwaukee this season. . . Like Mallette, outfielder/first baseman **Jim Rushford** (28) is no spring chicken. But his .354 average last year led all full-season hitters. He spent a number of years playing in independent leagues. . . First baseman **Billy Scott** (22) also played the outfield last season. He was the Brewers' No. 8 selection in 2000 after leading the Pac-10 in batting average that year and in home runs and RBI the year before.

Olympic Stadium

Offense

Olympic Stadium has played to the hitter's favor, especially over the past few years. It boasts a generous amount of foul territory and the speedy turf can mean a fair number of groundball hits. With high outfield walls, the park may turn some homers into doubles, but the fast artificial turf also helps boost doubles while having the opposite effect on triples. The turf also tilts the balance in basestealers' favor.

Defense

Speed is a must in the outfield, where keeping balls from going to the wall is a major responsibility. The infielders must be fearless and sure-handed, since the beat-up carpet never slows down a groundball and sends many of them bouncing in unpredictable directions.

Who It Helps the Most

With fast turf and plenty of bumps and seams, the park helps hitters who hit the ball hard. A well-hit liner can split the gaps and go to the wall, or take a bad hop and elude a fielder. No one hits the ball harder than Vladimir Guerrero, and he routinely puts up good numbers at home. Jose Vidro and Geoff Blum also benefit. Tony Armas Jr. has pitched much better here than on the road during each of his two major league seasons.

Who It Hurts the Most

Peter Bergeron, who might outrun more softly hit balls on a grass field, has hit for a lower average here each of the last two years. Scott Strickland, Graeme Lloyd and Britt Reames have pitched better on the road during their limited time with the Expos.

Rookies & Newcomers

Brad Wilkerson could get a little boost from the park and produce a lot of doubles once he gets his feet on the ground. Fernando Tatis might have problems staying healthy on the turf. If he plays, he might produce a few less homers and a few more doubles.

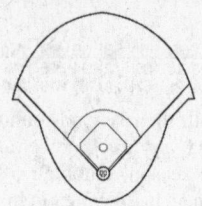

Dimensions: LF-325, LCF-375, CF-404, RCF-375, RF-325

Capacity: 46,620

Elevation: 90 feet

Surface: Turf

Foul Territory: Large

Park Factors

2001 Season

	Home Games			Away Games			
	Expos	Opp	Total	Expos	Opp	Total	Index
G	72	72	144	72	72	144	—
Avg	.258	.267	.263	.242	.271	.256	102
AB	2355	2543	4898	2417	2353	4770	103
R	308	384	692	273	327	600	115
H	607	679	1286	586	637	1223	105
2B	165	152	317	122	121	243	127
3B	8	7	15	17	16	33	44
HR	54	92	146	55	74	129	110
BB	215	225	440	203	232	435	99
SO	472	511	983	484	486	970	99
E	53	47	100	46	50	96	104
E-Infield	42	37	79	39	42	81	98
LHB-Avg	.235	.293	.264	.238	.281	.259	102
LHB-HR	18	32	50	27	35	62	82
RHB-Avg	.274	.250	.261	.246	.263	.255	103
RHB-HR	36	60	96	28	39	67	136

1999-2001

	Home Games			Away Games			
	Expos	Opp	Total	Expos	Opp	Total	Index
G	216	216	432	216	216	432	—
Avg	.266	.272	.269	.257	.276	.266	101
AB	7191	7628	14819	7478	7214	14692	101
R	975	1188	2163	914	1100	2014	107
H	1910	2078	3988	1920	1991	3911	102
2B	469	436	905	377	392	769	117
3B	42	41	83	58	45	103	80
HR	204	243	447	211	218	429	103
BB	618	717	1335	614	750	1364	97
SO	1276	1476	2752	1429	1373	2802	97
E	190	154	344	179	156	335	103
E-Infield	145	127	272	142	128	270	101
LHB-Avg	.264	.297	.282	.246	.288	.267	105
LHB-HR	62	102	164	80	99	179	93
RHB-Avg	.267	.255	.261	.263	.268	.265	98
RHB-HR	142	141	283	131	119	250	110

2001 Rankings (National League)

- Highest double factor
- Third-highest run factor
- Third-highest hit factor
- Third-highest RHB home-run factor
- Lowest triple factor
- Third-lowest LHB home-run factor

Jeff Torborg

2001 Season

Jeff Torborg was the surprise choice to take over the Expos when Felipe Alou was fired two months into the 2001 season. Torborg hadn't managed since 1993, and he was called into a difficult situation—replacing a popular manager on a team with limited talent, limited means and virtually nonexistent fan support. He stayed the course with the players he inherited and made few sweeping changes except for some alterations to the batting order. The team responded only slightly to the change in terms of wins and losses, as the team went 21-32 (.396) under Alou and 47-62 (.431) under Torborg.

Offense

Torborg, who played for the Dodgers during the 1960s, always has stressed speed and contact hitting over power. This never was more evident than when he installed Orlando Cabrera as the cleanup hitter, a move that ended up working. . . against all odds. Torborg turned everyone loose on the bases, even Vladimir Guerrero, but he did not call for the sacrifice or hit-and-run excessively. He worked Brad Wilkerson into the lineup carefully, trying hard to avoid overexposing him.

Pitching & Defense

Inserting an unproven pitcher never has fazed Torborg. He was quite willing to do so with Tomo Ohka, Troy Mattes and Matt Blank. Torborg also makes aggressive use of his bullpen, and Graeme Lloyd and Scott Strickland got plenty of work. He likes to have multiple lefties in the bullpen to give him ammunition for late-inning maneuvering. His preference for speed and defense might have helped Peter Bergeron hold onto his job.

2002 Outlook

As of presstime, the Expos' status for 2002 and beyond is up in the air. Even if the club remains operational and located in Montreal this season, Torborg may be piloting a franchise in a holding pattern, which could be a very frustrating endeavor. The best he might be able to do is be patient and try to develop what young talent he has, while hoping the team is able to retain what few superstars still occupy the roster.

Born: 11/26/41 in Plainfield, New Jersey

Playing Experience: 1964-1973, LA, Ana

Managerial Experience: 9 seasons

Manager Statistics

Year	Team, Lg	W	L	Pct	GB	Finish
2001	Montreal, NL	47	62	.431	20.0	5th East
9 Seasons		539	613	.468	—	—

2001 Starting Pitchers by Days Rest

	<=3	4	5	6+
Expos Starts	2	58	17	28
Expos ERA	4.91	4.80	3.49	5.20
NL Avg Starts	1	80	47	24
NL ERA	5.03	4.43	4.53	4.28

2001 Situational Stats

	Jeff Torborg*	NL Average
Hit & Run Success %	25.0	35.1
Stolen Base Success %	64.6	66.5
Platoon Pct.	62.1	51.5
Defensive Subs	3	20
High-Pitch Outings	5	7
Quick/Slow Hooks	19/10	19/14
Sacrifice Attempts	52	87

* Torborg managed the Expos for 109 games

2001 Rankings (National League)

- 3rd in steals of third base (18) and starts on three days rest

Tony Armas Jr.

Position: SP
Bats: R **Throws:** R
Ht: 6' 4" **Wt:** 205

Opening Day Age: 23
Born: 4/29/78 in Puerto Piritu, VZ
ML Seasons: 3
Pronunciation: ar-MUS

2001 Season

Young Tony Armas Jr. had an encouraging season last year, despite his 9-14 record. In his first full season in a major league rotation, he pitched through several minor injuries and made 34 starts, only one less than the National League leaders. Though he won only two games after the All-Star break, he pitched fairly well all year. He has yet to register a complete game in the majors, but 16 of his starts were quality outings last year.

Pitching

Armas has a lot of weapons at his command, including a low-90s fastball, a hard curve, a splitter, slider and changeup. He is very tough on righthanded hitters, but he needs to refine his approach to lefthanded batters, who still give him trouble. He showed better stamina last season, but he still has room for improvement in that area. He worked into the eighth inning just three times in 2001. Walks occasionally are a problem, though he's made slow progress in that regard as well, and it's expected that he'll continue to make gains as he hones his command and learns to trust his stuff.

Defense & Hitting

Armas is regarded as a fairly good fielder, but he committed three errors in 2001. He throws to first often, but it wasn't until he added a slide step last year that he truly got the running game under control; he didn't permit a single stolen base after the All-Star break. His hitting and bunting improved from awful to below-average last season.

2002 Outlook

Armas is at the point that Javier Vazquez was at two years ago, and he very well could develop into the same caliber of pitcher as his teammate. Armas will be the Expos' No. 2 starter in 2002, and look for him to take another small step forward this season as he continues to mature.

Overall Statistics

	W	L	Pct.	ERA	G	GS	Sv	IP	H	BB	SO	HR	Ratio
2001	9	14	.391	4.03	34	34	0	196.2	180	91	176	18	1.38
Career	16	24	.400	4.08	52	52	0	297.2	262	143	237	28	1.36

How Often He Throws Strikes

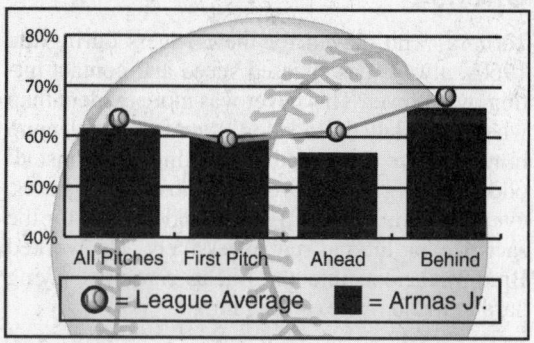

2001 Situational Stats

	W	L	ERA	Sv	IP		AB	H	HR	RBI	Avg
Home	5	5	3.21	0	109.1	LHB	324	89	9	39	.275
Road	4	9	5.05	0	87.1	RHB	405	91	9	51	.225
First Half	7	8	3.91	0	112.2	Sc Pos	169	43	7	66	.254
Scnd Half	2	6	4.18	0	84.0	Clutch	31	6	0	1	.194

2001 Rankings (National League)

- 4th in games started, most pitches thrown per batter (3.92) and lowest fielding percentage at pitcher (.921)
- 5th in walks allowed and errors at pitcher (3)
- 6th in highest walks per nine innings (4.2)
- 7th in losses and wild pitches (9)
- Led the Expos in losses, games started, walks allowed, hit batsmen (10), wild pitches (9), pick-off throws (134), runners caught stealing (6), lowest stolen-base percentage allowed (66.7), lowest ERA at home, lowest batting average allowed vs. righthanded batters, lowest batting average allowed with runners in scoring position and fewest home runs allowed per nine innings (.82)

Michael Barrett

Position: C
Bats: R **Throws:** R
Ht: 6' 2" **Wt:** 200

Opening Day Age: 25
Born: 10/22/76 in Atlanta, GA
ML Seasons: 4

2001 Season

Though his offensive numbers were nothing special, Michael Barrett's 2001 season was a million times better than the previous one, when he was repeatedly flip-flopped between two positions and lost all confidence. Last year, the Expos committed to keeping him behind the plate, and he didn't play an inning of third base. He got off to a painfully slow start *at* the plate, but battled through it and won praise for his work *behind* the plate.

Hitting

It's beginning to look like Barrett never will develop the home-run power the Expos envisioned. His level stroke produces line drives to all fields, but he never has learned to lift or pull the ball. In fact, he hit fewer flyballs than ever last year as he worked to bring up his average after his early-season slump. He tends to hit defensively, and rarely attacks the ball even when ahead in the count. An impatient hitter who makes good contact, he does not rack up high walk or strikeout totals.

Baserunning & Defense

In his first full year behind the plate, Barrett showed considerable improvement and worked well with the young Montreal pitchers. His battery-mates appreciate his quick reflexes and ability to keep balls in the dirt from going to the screen. He has an OK arm and can be a decent thrower as he hones his footwork, but he has a long ways to go before he earns the respect of opposing basestealers. He nabbed just 15 percent of would-be thieves in 2001. He has decent speed but runs conservatively.

2002 Outlook

It looks like Barrett will be the type of player who will make his biggest contributions behind the plate rather than at it, though he will need to show marked improvement against the running game. That would be fine with the Expos, who will continue to bat him near the bottom of the order and ask him to keep his attention focused on his pitch-calling and defensive duties.

Overall Statistics

	G	AB	R	H	D	T	HR	RBI	SB	BB	SO	Avg	OBP	Slg
2001	132	472	42	118	33	2	6	38	2	25	54	.250	.289	.367
Career	355	1199	126	310	82	6	16	114	2	83	134	.259	.309	.377

Where He Hits the Ball

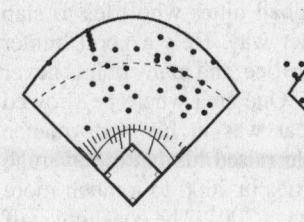

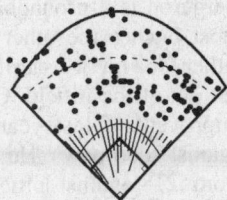

Vs. LHP   **Vs. RHP**

2001 Situational Stats

	AB	H	HR	RBI	Avg		AB	H	HR	RBI	Avg
Home	226	54	3	14	.239	LHP	122	31	0	5	.254
Road	246	64	3	24	.260	RHP	350	87	6	33	.249
First Half	256	62	4	18	.242	Sc Pos	117	24	0	28	.205
Scnd Half	216	56	2	20	.259	Clutch	73	17	1	5	.233

2001 Rankings (National League)

- 1st in lowest on-base percentage vs. lefthanded pitchers (.266) and lowest percentage of runners caught stealing as a catcher (15.2)
- 2nd in lowest on-base percentage
- 5th in lowest batting average with runners in scoring position
- 6th in highest groundball-flyball ratio (2.0)
- 7th in errors at catcher (7)
- Led the Expos in highest groundball-flyball ratio (2.0) and highest percentage of swings put into play (53.5)

Montreal

Peter Bergeron

2001 Season

In 2001, Peter Bergeron failed to carry over the momentum from the strong September of his rookie season. He began the year as the starting center fielder, but fell into a such a deep funk that he was dispatched to Triple-A Ottawa for two months. He didn't perform much better in the minors, but was recalled in late June anyway. He got hot for a month but then went into a tailspin that lasted the rest of the season, even though he continued to start in center field and lead off more often than not. His final .211 batting average was the lowest in the National League among hitters with at least 375 at-bats.

Hitting

Bergeron is a groundball hitter who tries to slap most pitches the other way. He's a good bunter either for a hit or a sacrifice, and many of hits never get out of the infield. One area where he showed improvement last year was in his performance against southpaws. He raised his batting average from .218 against lefties in 2000 to a much more respectable .250 figure in 2001. The coaching staff repeatedly changed the plate approach it wanted him to take, so it hardly was surprising that he often looked lost at the plate.

Baserunning & Defense

Bergeron is a fine defensive center fielder, with decent range and instincts and an accurate throwing arm. He reads balls well off the bat and committed only one error all season while chipping in with six assists. Though he has enough speed to steal bases, he hasn't yet learned to read pitchers or pick his spots.

2002 Outlook

As disappointing as the 2001 campaign was, Bergeron remains in the Expos' plans. They have few other options in center field, and manager Jeff Torborg always has stressed speed and defense. Bergeron likely will be given every opportunity to grow into a useful player, but he must be given the chance to decide on an approach at the plate. Then he must stick with it.

Position: CF
Bats: L **Throws:** R
Ht: 6' 0" **Wt:** 185

Opening Day Age: 24
Born: 11/9/77 in Greenfield, MA
ML Seasons: 3
Pronunciation: BERR-jer-ron

Overall Statistics

	G	AB	R	H	D	T	HR	RBI	SB	BB	SO	Avg	OBP	Slg
2001	102	375	53	79	11	4	3	16	10	28	87	.211	.275	.285
Career	266	938	145	217	38	11	8	48	21	95	192	.231	.305	.321

Where He Hits the Ball

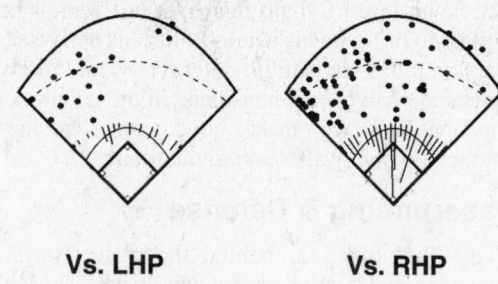

Vs. LHP   **Vs. RHP**

2001 Situational Stats

	AB	H	HR	RBI	Avg		AB	H	HR	RBI	Avg
Home	190	36	1	10	.189	LHP	80	20	1	2	.250
Road	185	43	2	6	.232	RHP	295	59	2	14	.200
First Half	121	29	1	5	.240	Sc Pos	68	14	0	13	.206
Scnd Half	254	50	2	11	.197	Clutch	44	6	0	1	.136

2001 Rankings (National League)

- 1st in lowest batting average in the clutch
- 4th in lowest on-base percentage for a leadoff hitter (.297)
- 6th in assists in center field (6)
- Led the Expos in bunts in play (20) and fewest GDPs per GDP situation (10.0%)

Orlando Cabrera

Position: SS
Bats: R **Throws:** R
Ht: 5'10" **Wt:** 175

Opening Day Age: 27
Born: 11/2/74 in Cartagena, Colombia
ML Seasons: 5
Pronunciation: kah-bray-RAH

2001 Season

Orlando Cabrera did it all last year, driving in 96 runs while splitting the year between the leadoff, cleanup and No. 5 spots in the order. He also played all 162 games and won his first Gold Glove. He came to camp bigger and stronger, intent on changing his image as a no-hit, good-field shortstop. Cabrera hit leadoff early on, but he really got going after an unexpected move to the heart of the order in June. For his efforts, he was voted the club's MVP, beating out Vladimir Guerrero and Javier Vazquez.

Hitting

Cabrera's added strength enabled him to drive pitches with more authority last year. This seemed to help his confidence, as he attacked the ball more and was less defensive than in the past. Most of his improvement came at the expense of righthanded pitchers, who had given him fits in prior seasons. He isn't a true middle-of-the-order hitter, though he admittedly did hit like one in the second half. He made more of an effort to take walks last year, but he'll never be considered a patient hitter. Still, he continued to keep his strikeout totals in check.

Baserunning & Defense

The fact that Cabrera was able to win a Gold Glove while playing on Olympic Stadium's aged, uneven carpet frankly was stunning. His range and ability to snare bad hops put him among the elite at his position. His .986 fielding percentage was the fifth-best mark in the major leagues among players with at least 100 games at short in 2001. Last year marked the first time he was given the green light on the basepaths, and he put his above-average speed to good use.

2002 Outlook

Though he took a giant step forward last year, Cabrera may need to develop his power a bit further in order to solidify his offensive role. He isn't likely to remain the cleanup hitter, but he could contribute a slot or two lower down in the order. Besides, with the way he flashes the leather, any continued progress that he makes at the plate is a bonus.

Overall Statistics

	G	AB	R	H	D	T	HR	RBI	SB	BB	SO	Avg	OBP	Slg
2001	162	626	64	173	41	6	14	96	19	43	54	.276	.324	.428
Career	486	1709	207	447	105	17	38	214	32	105	150	.262	.306	.410

Where He Hits the Ball

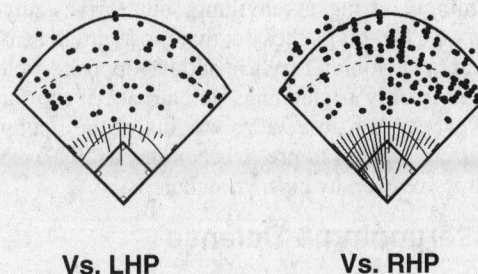

Vs. LHP   **Vs. RHP**

2001 Situational Stats

	AB	H	HR	RBI	Avg		AB	H	HR	RBI	Avg
Home	307	87	7	49	.283	LHP	153	41	4	26	.268
Road	319	86	7	47	.270	RHP	473	132	10	70	.279
First Half	341	85	5	42	.249	Sc Pos	169	55	1	78	.325
Scnd Half	285	88	9	54	.309	Clutch	95	27	2	27	.284

2001 Rankings (National League)

- 1st in games played and fielding percentage at shortstop (.986)
- 5th in at-bats
- 8th in lowest on-base percentage for a leadoff hitter (.310)
- 9th in lowest on-base percentage vs. lefthanded pitchers (.324)
- 10th in doubles
- Led the Expos in at-bats, singles, triples, sacrifice flies (7), plate appearances (684), games played, stolen-base percentage (73.1), batting average with runners in scoring position and on-base percentage for a leadoff hitter (.310)
- Led NL shortstops in RBI

2001 Season

Though he didn't match his numbers from either of the previous two campaigns, Vladimir Guerrero had another big year in 2001. He topped .300-30-100 for the fourth consecutive season, and even added basestealing to his game. His 37 swipes were a new career mark by a wide margin, and placed him third in the National League in that category. He tailed off over the last two months as the Expos wound down another irrelevant season.

Hitting

Any opponent who feeds Guerrero a first-pitch fastball is asking for trouble. He's one of the most aggressive hitters in baseball, and annually places among the leaders in first-pitch home runs. He'll seemingly swing at anything, but thrives anyhow—he can hit pitches out that most hitters can't touch (and wouldn't try to), and his opposite-field power is truly frightening. He can take it too far, however. When Jose Vidro was out of the lineup, Guerrero seemed to press, becoming wildly over-aggressive even by his own standards.

Baserunning & Defense

Former Expos manager Felipe Alou restrained Guerrero's baserunning out of fear he'd get hurt. Last year, after Alou was fired, Guerrero ran wild and became better at it as the year went on. The element of surprise was part of it; he stole third nine times, second-most in the National League. He's the same in the field as he is at the plate: aggressive—sometimes too much so; instinctive; and gifted. His throwing arm is among the best in the game.

2002 Outlook

It might be fair to ask whether there was any connection between Guerrero's basestealing and his late-season fade. Manager Jeff Torborg seems to be a big proponent of the running game, however, so for better or for worse, it probably will continue. Expos fans will hold their collective breath every time he takes off on a steal attempt, hoping that the overall physical toll won't prevent him from matching his offensive numbers from years past.

Position: RF
Bats: R **Throws:** R
Ht: 6' 3" **Wt:** 205

Opening Day Age: 26
Born: 2/9/76 in Nizao Bani, DR
ML Seasons: 6
Pronunciation: guh-RAR-oh
Nickname: Miqueas

Overall Statistics

	G	AB	R	H	D	T	HR	RBI	SB	BB	SO	Avg	OBP	Slg
2001	159	599	107	184	45	4	34	108	37	60	88	.307	.377	.566
Career	731	2755	464	879	169	29	170	512	74	234	361	.319	.378	.587

Where He Hits the Ball

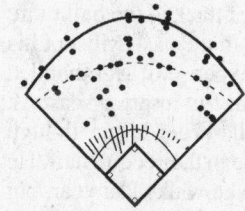
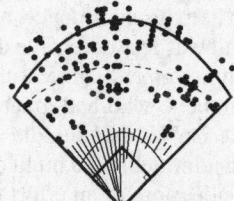

Vs. LHP   **Vs. RHP**

2001 Situational Stats

	AB	H	HR	RBI	Avg		AB	H	HR	RBI	Avg
Home	299	101	21	70	.338	LHP	135	43	8	27	.319
Road	300	83	13	38	.277	RHP	464	141	26	81	.304
First Half	327	107	21	67	.327	Sc Pos	148	46	10	75	.311
Scnd Half	272	77	13	41	.283	Clutch	86	26	4	11	.302

2001 Rankings (National League)

- 1st in errors in right field (12), assists in right field (15), GDPs (24) and lowest fielding percentage in right field (.965)
- Led the Expos in home runs, runs scored, hits, doubles, total bases (339), RBI, stolen bases, caught stealing (16), intentional walks (24), times on base (253), slugging percentage, on-base percentage, HR frequency (17.6 ABs per HR), steals of third (9), cleanup slugging percentage (.556), highest percentage of extra bases taken as a runner (56.1), slugging percentage vs. lefthanded pitchers (.607), slugging percentage vs. righthanded pitchers (.554) and on-base percentage vs. lefthanded pitchers (.420)

Graeme Lloyd

2001 Season

After missing all of 2000 with surgery for a torn labrum, lefthander Graeme Lloyd made a strong comeback over the first half of last season. As a setup man and middle reliever, he was one of the most frequently used pitchers over the first half of the campaign. He took 46 appearances and a fine 2.34 ERA into the All-Star break, but wore down under the heavy use and was hit hard in the second half. Though he earned 11 holds, he finished with his highest ERA since 1995.

Pitching

Despite the fact that Lloyd is one of the taller pitchers around at 6-foot-7, he relies on fine command rather than velocity. He features a low-90s two-seamer, a cutter and a sweeping slider, and he is very good at keeping the ball down and getting groundballs. Sometimes he's around the plate too much, however, and he can get burned on first-pitch fastballs. When they made contact with his first offering last year, opposing hitters batted .415 off Lloyd. Strictly a specialist earlier in his career, he's learned to combat righthanded hitters well enough to fill a larger role. He's capable of working several days in a row, especially if he held to a few batters at a time.

Defense & Hitting

With long arms and monstrous strides, Lloyd covers a lot of ground in the middle of the infield and is reliable with the glove. He has a good pickoff move and nailed a couple of runners last year, but his leg kick still gives baserunners a decent jump. Opposing thieves were 9-for-10 with Lloyd on the mound in 2001.

2002 Outlook

There have to be concerns after Lloyd's heavy workload and second-half dive. The only other season he made nearly as many appearances was in 1999, and he missed all of the following year. He'll remain an important component of the Expos' bullpen if healthy.

Position: RP
Bats: L **Throws:** L
Ht: 6' 7" **Wt:** 225

Opening Day Age: 34
Born: 4/9/67 in Geelong, Victoria, Australia
ML Seasons: 8
Pronunciation: gram

Overall Statistics

	W	L	Pct.	ERA	G	GS	Sv	IP	H	BB	SO	HR	Ratio
2001	9	5	.643	4.35	84	0	1	70.1	74	21	44	6	1.35
Career	25	27	.481	3.74	450	0	12	428.1	425	128	242	43	1.29

How Often He Throws Strikes

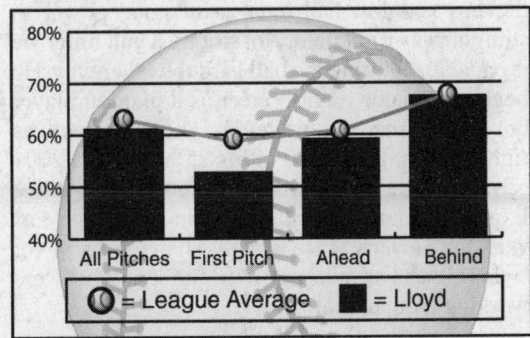

○ = League Average ■ = Lloyd

2001 Situational Stats

	W	L	ERA	Sv	IP		AB	H	HR	RBI	Avg
Home	4	4	5.84	1	37.0	LHB	103	26	3	17	.252
Road	5	1	2.70	0	33.1	RHB	169	48	3	18	.284
First Half	7	1	2.34	1	42.1	Sc Pos	75	21	0	26	.280
Scnd Half	2	4	7.39	0	28.0	Clutch	113	33	4	19	.292

2001 Rankings (National League)

- 1st in relief wins (9)
- 2nd in games pitched
- 4th in fewest strikeouts per nine innings in relief (5.6)
- 7th in highest batting average allowed in relief (.272)
- 10th in relief losses (5) and highest relief ERA (4.35)
- Led the Expos in games pitched and relief wins (9)

Lee Stevens

2001 Season

Lee Stevens' second season in Montreal brought mixed results. Though he set career highs in games played, doubles, homers and RBI, his average slipped 20 points and his strikeouts climbed. His 157 whiffs was the fourth-highest total in the National League last year. When Vladimir Guerrero was bumped up from the cleanup spot to the No. 3 spot in June, Stevens was elevated from fifth to cleanup, but his middling average and frequent strikeouts caused him to be dropped back to the five-hole in favor of the less powerful Orlando Cabrera.

Hitting

Stevens is a low-ball hitter with good power to straightaway right field. Not strictly a pull hitter, he is capable of hitting the ball hard the other way. He began his major league career as a platoon player but has learned to hit lefties about as well as righthanders, though 20 of his 25 homers in 2001 came off righties. The hitters following him in the Expos' batting order offered little protection last year, but Stevens has to bear his share of blame for swinging at bad pitches from pitchers who were working around him.

Baserunning & Defense

The aging turf at Olympic Stadium is a nightmare, especially for corner infielders, so Stevens can't be blamed entirely for becoming a little gun-shy, especially after two bad hops nearly decapitated him early in the year. He didn't move as aggressively this year, though he still scooped throws well and made accurate tosses. He's a non-factor on the bases; he's been caught twice for every successful stolen-base attempt in his career (8-for-24).

2002 Outlook

Stevens is going into the last year of his contract, and it's possible the Expos will try to move him. His salary is quite reasonable for other clubs but represents a big chunk of payroll for Montreal, a team fighting for survival. He'll remain useful wherever he ends up, but his strikeouts are hard to swallow from someone who hits just 20-25 homers a season.

Position: 1B
Bats: L **Throws:** L
Ht: 6' 4" **Wt:** 235

Opening Day Age: 34
Born: 7/10/67 in Kansas City, MO
ML Seasons: 9

Overall Statistics

	G	AB	R	H	D	T	HR	RBI	SB	BB	SO	Avg	OBP	Slg
2001	152	542	77	133	35	1	25	95	2	74	157	.245	.338	.452
Career	896	2974	390	774	172	13	129	474	8	291	743	.260	.326	.457

Where He Hits the Ball

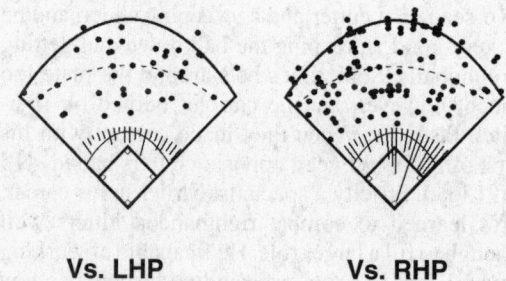

Vs. LHP   **Vs. RHP**

2001 Situational Stats

	AB	H	HR	RBI	Avg		AB	H	HR	RBI	Avg
Home	256	65	12	48	.254	LHP	152	37	5	28	.243
Road	286	68	13	47	.238	RHP	390	96	20	67	.246
First Half	319	79	14	59	.248	Sc Pos	147	41	6	72	.279
Scnd Half	223	54	11	36	.242	Clutch	79	19	3	14	.241

2001 Rankings (National League)

- 1st in errors at first base (19) and lowest fielding percentage at first base (.986)
- 3rd in lowest cleanup slugging percentage (.417)
- 4th in strikeouts and lowest percentage of swings put into play (33.0)
- 6th in assists at first base (92), lowest batting average, lowest batting average vs. lefthanded pitchers and lowest percentage of extra bases taken as a runner (34.5)
- Led the Expos in sacrifice flies (7), walks, strikeouts, pitches seen (2,430) and batting average with the bases loaded (.444)

Scott Strickland

2001 Season

Scott Strickland finally became the Expos' closer last August. He'd positioned himself for the opportunity by continuing to pitch well in a setup role, compiling a 3.71 ERA in 49 games through the end of July. After Ugueth Urbina was dealt at the trading deadline, Strickland took over the bulk of the closer's duties and converted nine of 11 save opportunities. By season's end, he had allowed just eight of 38 inherited runners to score (21 percent).

Pitching

The only thing that might prevent Strickland from being a top closer is that he simply can't deal with lefthanded hitters. His fastball-slider combination is murder on righties, who are forced to chase his slider once he gets ahead in the count. He needs a second pitch for lefties, however. After being handled carefully in 2000 because of an apparent shoulder problem, Strickland was called upon to work on consecutive days more often last year, especially late in the season, and he seemed to emerge no worse for the wear. He posted a 2.89 ERA with no days rest.

Defense & Hitting

So many baserunners try to take advantage of Strickland's high leg kick that he'll occasionally catch one leaning just by chance. The rest of the time, they run almost at will. Montreal catchers did not throw out a single one of the 18 opponents who attempted a stolen base on his watch. Strickland has made more than his share of errors in his limited chances in the field, and he's gone hitless with four strikeouts in five major league at-bats.

2002 Outlook

Strickland will open the season as the Expos' closer and could be in line for a good season. There could be some bumps along the way, however, if opposing managers make it a habit of greeting him with lefthanded pinch-hitters. On the other hand, if he's able to add a new pitch, he could become one of the top short men in the game.

Position: RP
Bats: R **Throws:** R
Ht: 5'11" **Wt:** 180

Opening Day Age: 25
Born: 4/26/76 in Houston, TX
ML Seasons: 3

Overall Statistics

	W	L	Pct.	ERA	G	GS	Sv	IP	H	BB	SO	HR	Ratio
2001	2	6	.250	3.21	77	0	9	81.1	67	41	85	9	1.33
Career	6	10	.375	3.30	143	0	18	147.1	120	68	156	15	1.28

How Often He Throws Strikes

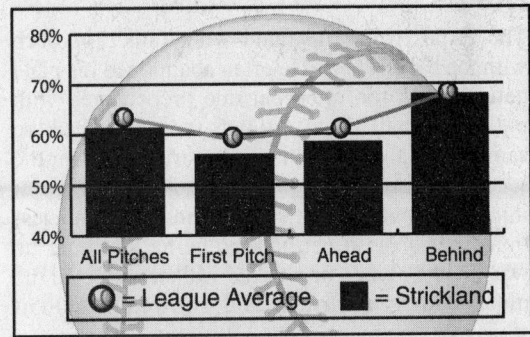

⊙ = League Average ■ = Strickland

2001 Situational Stats

	W	L	ERA	Sv	IP		AB	H	HR	RBI	Avg
Home	1	4	4.58	3	39.1	LHB	117	32	3	15	.274
Road	1	2	1.93	6	42.0	RHB	185	35	6	17	.189
First Half	1	4	3.57	0	45.1	Sc Pos	102	18	2	23	.176
Scnd Half	1	2	2.75	9	36.0	Clutch	143	33	3	16	.231

2001 Rankings (National League)

- 4th in relief losses (6)
- 7th in lowest percentage of inherited runners scored (21.1)
- 9th in relief innings (81.1) and lowest batting average allowed in relief with runners in scoring position (.176)
- 10th in games pitched
- Led the Expos in holds (12), lowest percentage of inherited runners scored (21.1), blown saves (3), relief losses (6), relief innings (81.1), relief ERA (3.21), lowest batting average allowed in relief (.222) and most strikeouts per nine innings in relief (9.4)

Fernando Tatis

Position: 3B
Bats: R **Throws:** R
Ht: 5'10" **Wt:** 170

Opening Day Age: 27
Born: 1/1/75 in San Pedro de Macoris, DR
ML Seasons: 5
Pronunciation: TAH-tece

2001 Season

When the Expos traded Dustin Hermanson and Steve Kline for Fernando Tatis in December 2000, it looked like a potential steal. Tatis was a young-ster who'd had a big year in 1999 and had been on his way to an even bigger one in 2000 before tearing a groin muscle. During 2001, however, the Cardinals' willingness to part with him became more understandable. He refused to keep the Expos apprised of his rehab progress over the winter, and limped into camp. Between the groin and several other nagging injuries, he never was 100 percent, and chronic patellar tendinitis in his left knee fi-nally ended his season in June.

Hitting

The Expos were frustrated with Tatis' approach with the bat last year. He often abandoned his plate patience and too often became preoccupied with pulling the ball. The Cardinals reportedly had the same complaints with him as he struggled over the second half of 2000. So, even taking his recent injuries into account, it's very much an open ques-tion whether he'll get back to being the hitter he was in 1999, when he worked walks, protected the plate with two strikes and showed excellent straightaway power.

Baserunning & Defense

Tatis has above-average speed and instincts on the bases when healthy, but he didn't attempt a single steal last year. In '99, he stole 21 bases. He's also regarded as a fine defensive third baseman with good hands, a strong arm and above-average range. But much like his offense, his performance on defense has slipped to well below average over the last year and a half.

2002 Outlook

It's clear that Tatis has All-Star talent. However, it's anything but clear whether he'll play like an All-Star again. Surrounded by health issues and other questions, he very much needs to show that he's healthy, motivated and willing to be more patient this year. The hope is that he is fully recovered from August knee surgery by spring, but this time the Expos want to closely monitor his rehab.

Overall Statistics

	G	AB	R	H	D	T	HR	RBI	SB	BB	SO	Avg	OBP	Slg
2001	41	145	20	37	9	0	2	11	0	16	43	.255	.339	.359
Career	496	1761	281	483	103	7	73	269	39	205	430	.274	.359	.465

Where He Hits the Ball

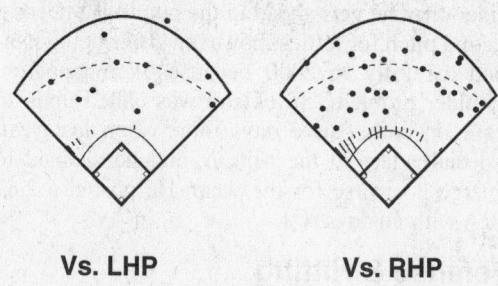

Vs. LHP   **Vs. RHP**

2001 Situational Stats

	AB	H	HR	RBI	Avg		AB	H	HR	RBI	Avg
Home	59	15	0	6	.254	LHP	34	8	1	4	.235
Road	86	22	2	5	.256	RHP	111	29	1	7	.261
First Half	145	37	2	11	.255	Sc Pos	32	8	0	9	.250
Scnd Half	0	0	0	0	-	Clutch	15	6	0	0	.400

2001 Rankings (National League)

- Did not rank near the top or bottom in any cate-gory

Mike Thurman

2001 Season

The 2000 season was a lost year for starting pitcher Mike Thurman, and 2001 almost was too. He struggled over the first two months, and then suffered a hairline fracture of the thumb on his pitching hand when he fouled a ball off that hand in late May. He missed a month, then continued to struggle in July. He turned it around in August, however, and went 3-1 with a 3.44 ERA over his last six starts.

Pitching

Thurman throws a sinker, curve and changeup, but he isn't an extreme groundballer. He worked on throwing his change more often last year to lefthanded hitters, who responded by hitting him harder than ever. He must have good command to get by but his control wavers. He had 50 walks and eight wild pitches last season. Stamina never has been Thurman's strength, but conditioning was more of a problem than ever last year, as batters found him much easier to solve after his first time through the order.

Defense & Hitting

Thurman has a weak move to first and isn't particularly quick to the plate; all 17 baserunners who tried to steal against him last year were successful, which is consistent with his career norms. He's an otherwise competent fielder, but is the worst hitter in the major leaguers, hands down. He went 1-for-42 last year and struck out in almost two-thirds of his at-bats, and now is 4-for-131 in his career (.031).

2002 Outlook

Though Thurman remains capable of putting together a string of decent starts, he's not a good bet to keep it up for an entire season. He also will continue to be a drag on any bullpen, as he averaged just 5.1 innings per start in 2001. He might hold onto his spot in the Montreal rotation, but it will be tough for him to win many games, especially with the lack of offense supporting him.

Position: SP
Bats: R **Throws:** R
Ht: 6' 5" **Wt:** 210

Opening Day Age: 28
Born: 7/22/73 in Corvallis, OR
ML Seasons: 5

Overall Statistics

	W	L	Pct.	ERA	G	GS	Sv	IP	H	BB	SO	HR	Ratio
2001	9	11	.450	5.33	28	26	0	147.0	172	50	96	21	1.51
Career	25	36	.410	5.04	93	85	0	460.2	492	178	273	57	1.45

How Often He Throws Strikes

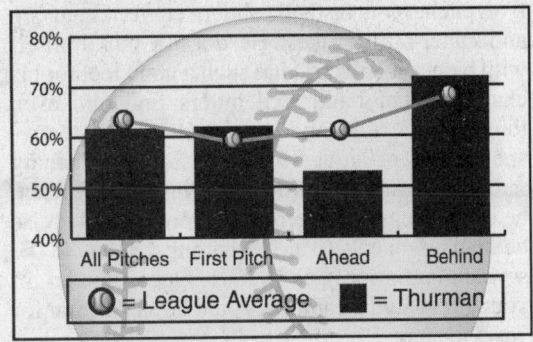

= League Average = Thurman

2001 Situational Stats

	W	L	ERA	Sv	IP		AB	H	HR	RBI	Avg
Home	4	5	4.30	0	67.0	LHB	254	87	11	39	.343
Road	5	6	6.19	0	80.0	RHB	331	85	10	42	.257
First Half	4	5	5.68	0	71.1	Sc Pos	166	44	4	61	.265
Scnd Half	5	6	5.00	0	75.2	Clutch	18	3	0	1	.167

2001 Rankings (National League)

- 2nd in highest batting average allowed vs. lefthanded batters
- 9th in wild pitches (8) and stolen bases allowed (17)
- Led the Expos in stolen bases allowed (17)

Javier Vazquez

2001 Season

Following up his strong late-season performance from 2000, Javier Vazquez took another huge step forward last year. He was on his way to possibly the first 20-win season by an Expos pitcher in 23 years when he was beaned in mid-September. At the time, he was baseball's hottest pitcher, and had been named the National League Pitcher of the Month for August. The beaning ended his season, but he finished with brilliant totals nonetheless, winning 16 games and posting a 3.42 ERA for a last-place club.

Pitching

With a maturity beyond his years, Vazquez throws five pitches—a fastball, slider, curve, changeup and cutter—for strikes. He doesn't hurt himself with bases on balls and has such a good feel for his changeup that lefthanded hitters find him even tougher than righthanded ones. He carries the re- sponsibility of an ace well, consistently pitching into the late innings without wearing down. In fact, he seems to get stronger as the game wears on, as he held opponents to a .186 batting average in the seventh inning or later in 2001. One of the bright young stars in the game, he could be an All-Star for years to come.

Defense & Hitting

Vazquez played errorless ball for the third time in four seasons while snaring everything that came his way in the middle of the infield. He's always been tough to run on, and when he added a slide step in the second half, stolen-base attempts against him nearly disappeared. Few pitchers aid their own cause at the plate as much as Vazquez. He annually ranks among the leaders in pitchers' batting average, and is one of the best bunters in the majors, position players included.

2002 Outlook

Vazquez is only 25 and could keep improving. But even if he stays right at the level that he currently has established, he's as good a bet to win 20 this year as anyone—even on a team that gives him as little help as the Expos.

Position: SP
Bats: R **Throws:** R
Ht: 6' 2" **Wt:** 195

Opening Day Age: 25
Born: 7/25/76 in Ponce, PR
ML Seasons: 4
Pronunciation: VAS-kez

Overall Statistics

	W	L	Pct.	ERA	G	GS	Sv	IP	H	BB	SO	HR	Ratio
2001	16	11	.593	3.42	32	32	0	223.2	197	44	208	24	1.08
Career	41	43	.488	4.51	124	123	0	768.1	794	225	656	99	1.33

How Often He Throws Strikes

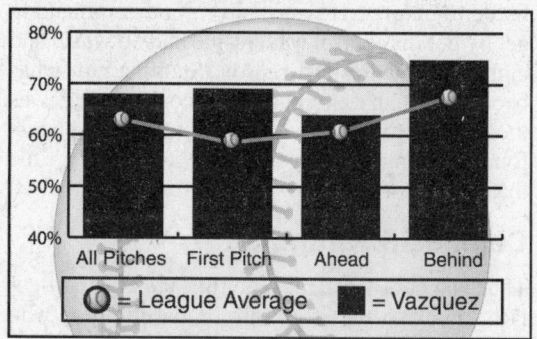

○ = League Average   ■ = Vazquez

2001 Situational Stats

	W	L	ERA	Sv	IP		AB	H	HR	RBI	Avg
Home	7	7	3.90	0	120.0	LHB	368	81	14	38	.220
Road	9	4	2.86	0	103.2	RHB	472	116	10	43	.246
First Half	7	9	4.93	0	122.1	Sc Pos	148	43	4	53	.291
Scnd Half	9	2	1.60	0	101.1	Clutch	67	13	2	5	.194

2001 Rankings (National League)

- 1st in shutouts (3) and fielding percentage at pitcher (1.000)
- Led the Expos in ERA, sacrifice bunts (16), wins, complete games (5), innings pitched, hits al- lowed, batters faced (898), home runs allowed, strikeouts, pitches thrown (3,372), GDPs in- duced (20), winning percentage, highest strike- out-walk ratio (4.7), lowest batting average allowed (.235), lowest slugging percentage al- lowed (.374), lowest on-base percentage allowed (.274), highest groundball-flyball ratio allowed (1.3), fewest pitches thrown per batter (3.76), lowest batting average allowed vs. lefthanded batters, most strikeouts per nine innings (8.4) and fewest walks per nine innings (1.8)

Jose Vidro

Position: 2B
Bats: B **Throws:** R
Ht: 5'11" **Wt:** 190

Opening Day Age: 27
Born: 8/27/74 in
Mayaguez, PR
ML Seasons: 5
Pronunciation:
VEE-drow

2001 Season

A couple of serious injuries kept Jose Vidro from duplicating his super 2000 season last year, though he finished with terrific numbers nonetheless. The first malady, a torn muscle in his left forearm in May, sidelined him for three weeks but seemed to have no lingering effects. The second was much more serious: a concussion as the result of a beaning in early August. He returned two days later, but soon was forced to sit for 10 days. After returning, he hit .283 the rest of the way, but went homerless over his last 29 games.

Hitting

Vidro is a line-drive hitter who makes excellent contact from either side of the plate. Few hitters remain as dangerous with two strikes. Though he's aggressive and rarely walks, his ability to hit for average with lots of doubles makes him well suited to his accustomed No. 2 spot in the lineup, as does his ability to shoot the ball through the hole on the right side. The switch-hitting Vidro swatted lefties at a .348 clip last year, and he now owns a .309 career mark versus southpaws.

Baserunning & Defense

Vidro has become such a capable fielder that it's hard to imagine it was only two years ago that the Expos brought in Mickey Morandini to challenge him for the second-base job. Vidro doesn't have the quickest first step and doesn't tend to make acrobatic plays, but he positions himself well and catches what he gets to. His strong arm allows him to play deep, which enhances his range, and he's capable on the pivot. He doesn't have the speed to steal bases.

2002 Outlook

All Vidro needs to do in 2002 is avoid the injuries that plagued him last year. He's in his prime and should put up another fine season if healthy. His presence in the lineup again should help take some pressure off the bat of Vladimir Guerrero.

Overall Statistics

	G	AB	R	H	D	T	HR	RBI	SB	BB	SO	Avg	OBP	Slg
2001	124	486	82	155	34	1	15	59	4	31	49	.319	.371	.486
Career	567	1960	293	592	154	6	53	250	12	147	222	.302	.355	.468

Where He Hits the Ball

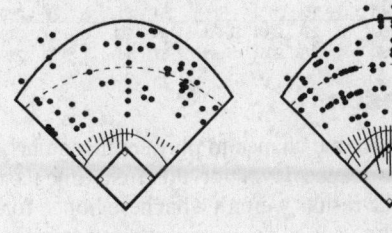

Vs. LHP   **Vs. RHP**

2001 Situational Stats

	AB	H	HR	RBI	Avg		AB	H	HR	RBI	Avg
Home	246	84	6	28	.341	LHP	135	47	3	16	.348
Road	240	71	9	31	.296	RHP	351	108	12	43	.308
First Half	268	87	11	36	.325	Sc Pos	113	36	4	40	.319
Scnd Half	218	68	4	23	.312	Clutch	68	32	2	7	.471

2001 Rankings (National League)

- 1st in batting average in the clutch
- 4th in lowest fielding percentage at second base (.983)
- Led the Expos in batting average, hit by pitch (10), lowest percentage of swings that missed (11.6), batting average vs. lefthanded pitchers, batting average vs. righthanded pitchers, batting average on a 3-1 count (.667), batting average on an 0-2 count (.225), on-base percentage vs. righthanded pitchers (.367), batting average at home, batting average on the road, batting average on a 3-2 count (.260) and batting average with two strikes (.261)
- Led NL second basemen in batting average

Geoff Blum

Position: 3B/LF/2B/1B
Bats: B **Throws:** R
Ht: 6' 3" **Wt:** 195

Opening Day Age: 28
Born: 4/26/73 in
Redwood City, CA
ML Seasons: 3

Overall Statistics

	G	AB	R	H	D	T	HR	RBI	SB	BB	SO	Avg	OBP	Slg
2001	148	453	57	107	25	0	9	50	9	43	94	.236	.313	.351
Career	317	929	118	236	52	4	28	113	11	86	179	.254	.323	.409

2001 Situational Stats

	AB	H	HR	RBI	Avg		AB	H	HR	RBI	Avg
Home	234	60	6	34	.256	LHP	99	26	4	11	.263
Road	219	47	3	16	.215	RHP	354	81	5	39	.229
First Half	210	50	5	23	.238	Sc Pos	109	26	3	39	.239
Scnd Half	243	57	4	27	.235	Clutch	67	16	1	8	.239

2001 Season

Geoff Blum got the chance to play semi-regularly at the major league level for the first time last season, but the results weren't what he'd hoped for. He opened the year as the starter at an unfamiliar position, left field, but wound up seeing a lot more time at third base after Fernando Tatis went down. He also saw time at second, as well as first base and shortstop, and performed well as a pinch-hitter.

Hitting, Baserunning & Defense

Blum is a good fastball hitter with a quick bat from either side of the plate, though he's shown a little more power hitting righthanded. He rarely swings at the first pitch, only putting such offerings in play 45 times in 453 total at-bats in 2001. He has the hands and arm strength to play anywhere on the infield, though his unimpressive range makes him best suited for the hot corner. To his credit, he played errorless ball in the outfield, though his inexperience there sometimes was evident. Despite average speed, he did a little basestealing last year.

2002 Outlook

Blum won't go into camp with a starting job, but he'll continue to get plenty of at-bats between several different positions. If nothing else, he's versatile, shows doubles power at the big league level and comes at the right price for the Expos.

Mike Mordecai

Position: 3B/2B
Bats: R **Throws:** R
Ht: 5'10" **Wt:** 185

Opening Day Age: 34
Born: 12/13/67 in
Birmingham, AL
ML Seasons: 8
Pronunciation:
more-dah-KYE

Overall Statistics

	G	AB	R	H	D	T	HR	RBI	SB	BB	SO	Avg	OBP	Slg
2001	96	254	28	71	17	2	3	32	2	19	53	.280	.330	.398
Career	564	1036	120	258	60	7	21	108	8	85	194	.249	.306	.381

2001 Situational Stats

	AB	H	HR	RBI	Avg		AB	H	HR	RBI	Avg
Home	121	29	1	14	.240	LHP	115	36	3	20	.313
Road	133	42	2	18	.316	RHP	139	35	0	12	.252
First Half	123	32	2	18	.260	Sc Pos	64	19	0	27	.297
Scnd Half	131	39	1	14	.298	Clutch	45	10	0	3	.222

2001 Season

Versatile Mike Mordecai enjoyed his second fine season in a row last year while reaching a personal high with 254 at-bats. He filled in at second base when Jose Vidro was injured and often started at third base against lefthanders after Fernando Tatis went down. He reached the .280 mark in batting average for the second consecutive campaign.

Hitting, Baserunning & Defense

Mordecai is a spray hitter who lines most of his hits over or through the infield. He's neither patient nor powerful, though he occasionally splits a gap for a double. His ability to play all the infield positions well is what keeps him in the majors, and his willingness to serve as the club's emergency catcher hasn't hurt either. He has decent range and excellent hands at any spot. His best position is second base, where his smooth pivot is an asset. One thing he hasn't done well at all over the course of his career is pinch-hit—he is just 19 of 142 (.134) in that role for his career.

2002 Outlook

Mordecai likely is to be back in his familiar role for the Expos in 2002. However, he probably won't get quite an many at-bats again unless there continues to be major injuries on the infield.

Guillermo Mota

Position: RP
Bats: R **Throws:** R
Ht: 6' 4" **Wt:** 205

Opening Day Age: 28
Born: 7/25/73 in San
Pedro de Macoris, DR
ML Seasons: 3
Pronunciation: mo-TAH

Overall Statistics

	W	L	Pct.	ERA	G	GS	Sv	IP	H	BB	SO	HR	Ratio
2001	1	3	.250	5.26	53	0	0	49.2	51	18	31	9	1.39
Career	4	8	.333	4.47	133	0	0	135.0	132	55	82	17	1.39

2001 Situational Stats

	W	L	ERA	Sv	IP		AB	H	HR	RBI	Avg
Home	1	2	7.25	0	22.1	LHB	71	22	4	11	.310
Road	0	1	3.62	0	27.1	RHB	117	29	5	23	.248
First Half	1	1	4.39	0	41.0	Sc Pos	60	19	4	29	.317
Scnd Half	0	2	9.35	0	8.2	Clutch	48	12	2	9	.250

2001 Season

One has to wonder if arriving a month late to spring camp may have helped ruin Guillermo Mota's season. The hard-throwing setup man was one of the club's busiest and most effective relievers over the first three months of the season, but he came down with a sore shoulder in July and was shut down. He was activated in September but never regained his effectiveness. In 11 appearances in September and October, his ERA was a robust 10.57.

Pitching, Defense & Hitting

Five years after being converted from shortstop to the mound, Mota still has a mid-90s fastball and little else. His slider and changeup are inconsistent, and his heater is straight enough to be hittable, despite its velocity. Opposing big league hitters have socked him at a .334 pace over his career. With several years of experience as an infielder, Mota is both an above-average hitter and fielder for a pitcher. Though he has a good pickoff move, he didn't pay attention to runners last year as well as he had in the past.

2002 Outlook

Considering his lively fastball, Mota could come around quickly if he ever masters a second pitch. Until that happens, he'll likely continue to run hot and cold, especially when asked to face lefties.

Tomokazu Ohka

Position: SP
Bats: R **Throws:** R
Ht: 6' 1" **Wt:** 180

Opening Day Age: 26
Born: 3/18/76 in Kyoto,
Japan
ML Seasons: 3
Pronunciation:
TOE-mo-KAH-zoo
OH-kah

Overall Statistics

	W	L	Pct.	ERA	G	GS	Sv	IP	H	BB	SO	HR	Ratio
2001	3	9	.250	5.47	22	21	0	107.0	134	29	68	15	1.52
Career	7	17	.292	4.66	43	35	0	189.1	225	61	116	24	1.51

2001 Situational Stats

	W	L	ERA	Sv	IP		AB	H	HR	RBI	Avg
Home	1	6	6.09	0	57.2	LHB	178	54	3	23	.303
Road	2	3	4.74	0	49.1	RHB	255	80	12	38	.314
First Half	2	4	4.95	0	43.2	Sc Pos	102	31	3	46	.304
Scnd Half	1	5	5.83	0	63.1	Clutch	4	3	0	1	.750

2001 Season

The Red Sox seemed to sour on Tomo Ohka in a hurry last year. He'd pitched decently as a rookie in 2000, and posted solid numbers for Boston last April. After two bad outings in May, however, they shipped him to Triple-A. He was recalled in July but again pitched poorly, so they dealt him to Montreal at the deadline as part of the Ugueth Urbina deal. Ohka was consistently mediocre for the Expos for the rest of the season, and he ended up with a 3-9 record for the two clubs.

Pitching, Defense & Hitting

Location is the key for Ohka, who mixes a good curve and changeup with an average fastball. His fastball has some late sink, but it also hangs too often (15 home runs allowed in 2001) and won't get much higher than 90 MPH. He has little stamina and usually lasts only five or six innings. Ohka has a good pickoff move, is very tough to run on and fields his position well. His batting experience is limited, but he was decent at the plate last year.

2002 Outlook

With the health of Carl Pavano and the stamina of Mike Thurman both in question, Ohka likely will open the year in the Expos' rotation. He probably won't pitch a lot of innings or win a lot of games, but he could be a solid back-of-the-rotation starter.

Montreal

Carl Pavano

Position: SP
Bats: R **Throws:** R
Ht: 6' 5" **Wt:** 230

Opening Day Age: 26
Born: 1/8/76 in New Britain, CT
ML Seasons: 4

Overall Statistics

	W	L	Pct.	ERA	G	GS	Sv	IP	H	BB	SO	HR	Ratio
2001	1	6	.143	6.33	8	8	0	42.2	59	16	36	7	1.76
Career	21	27	.438	4.54	66	64	0	378.1	395	128	253	41	1.38

2001 Situational Stats

	W	L	ERA	Sv	IP		AB	H	HR	RBI	Avg
Home	1	3	5.48	0	23.0	LHB	73	28	3	14	.384
Road	0	3	7.32	0	19.2	RHB	105	31	4	15	.295
First Half	0	0	-	0	0.0	Sc Pos	49	16	2	22	.327
Scnd Half	1	6	6.33	0	42.2	Clutch	4	1	1	1	.250

2001 Season

Carl Pavano was in the midst of a breakthrough season in 2000 until a sore elbow required surgery. He entered 2001 as a major question mark, and when the soreness returned in the spring, Tommy John surgery was mentioned as a possibility. He didn't return until August and was pounded mercilessly in his first two starts. He executed a stunning turnaround, however, pitching well in his final four starts to end the season on an encouraging note.

Pitching, Defense & Hitting

A healthy Pavano has good command and works in and out with a low-90s fastball, slider and changeup. Lefthanded hitters have given him problems in each of the last two years, hitting him at a .333 clip over that span. Arm problems have plagued him during his entire four-year tenure in Montreal, and he has yet to work as many as 140 innings in a season in an Expos uniform. He's an acceptable fielder and was more effective at combating the running game after improving his slide step last year. He's a below-average hitter.

2002 Outlook

As always, health will be the key for Pavano. If he comes to camp ready to go, he'll likely open the season in the starting rotation. The question is then whether his elbow will allow him to stay there.

Britt Reames

Position: RP/SP
Bats: R **Throws:** R
Ht: 5'11" **Wt:** 175

Opening Day Age: 28
Born: 8/19/73 in Seneca, SC
ML Seasons: 2
Pronunciation: REEMS

Overall Statistics

	W	L	Pct.	ERA	G	GS	Sv	IP	H	BB	SO	HR	Ratio
2001	4	8	.333	5.59	41	13	0	95.0	101	48	86	16	1.57
Career	6	9	.400	4.78	49	20	0	135.2	131	71	117	20	1.49

2001 Situational Stats

	W	L	ERA	Sv	IP		AB	H	HR	RBI	Avg
Home	1	5	7.46	0	50.2	LHB	145	43	5	24	.297
Road	3	3	3.45	0	44.1	RHB	225	58	11	40	.258
First Half	2	8	6.33	0	58.1	Sc Pos	93	29	4	47	.312
Scnd Half	2	0	4.42	0	36.2	Clutch	53	13	3	7	.245

2001 Season

Things weren't so easy for Britt Reames the second time around. The righthander, who looked so sharp in eight late-season appearances for the Cardinals in 2000, opened last year in the Expos' rotation. He pitched well in April but hit the skids in May and found himself back in Triple-A by June. Recalled after the All-Star break, he pitched decently out of the bullpen for the rest of the year.

Pitching, Defense & Hitting

Reames, who missed the 1997 and '98 seasons after undergoing Tommy John surgery, depends on his command of his out pitch: a hard curveball. When he misses with it, his low-90s fastball and changeup aren't enough to get the job done. He has one of the best pickoff moves of any righthander in the game, and hung five baserunners out to dry last year. He's also a skilled and athletic fielder. He doesn't seem to be much a hitter, though he did homer and draw four walks last year.

2002 Outlook

Reames probably will open the season in middle relief. He could return to the rotation at some point, especially if other Montreal candidates for starter such as Carl Pavano, Mike Thurman and Tomo Ohka falter. In either case, Reames is capable of pitching a lot better than he did last year.

Mark Smith

Position: LF
Bats: R **Throws:** R
Ht: 6' 3" **Wt:** 225

Opening Day Age: 31
Born: 5/7/70 in Pasadena, CA
ML Seasons: 7

Overall Statistics

	G	AB	R	H	D	T	HR	RBI	SB	BB	SO	Avg	OBP	Slg
2001	80	194	28	47	13	1	6	18	0	23	38	.242	.326	.412
Career	381	896	117	218	47	3	29	120	15	93	198	.243	.319	.400

2001 Situational Stats

	AB	H	HR	RBI	Avg		AB	H	HR	RBI	Avg
Home	97	28	3	11	.289	LHP	91	25	3	12	.275
Road	97	19	3	7	.196	RHP	103	22	3	6	.214
First Half	81	23	2	6	.284	Sc Pos	49	9	1	12	.184
Scnd Half	113	24	4	12	.212	Clutch	29	9	1	1	.310

2001 Season

With the Expos' hodgepodge of left fielders, Mark Smith actually made more starts there than anyone last year. He manned left semi-regularly in June, July and August, and often served as a pinch-hitter. The club gave him an opportunity to show he had the power they were looking for, but he came up a little short. He hit 12 home runs in pro ball last year, but six of those shots came at Triple-A Ottawa.

Hitting, Baserunning & Defense

Smith has decent power, but not quite enough to be able to stick in the big leagues on that one tool alone. He tries to jerk the ball down the line and produces a fair share of flyballs. Oddly, he always had struggled against lefthanders, until last year that is, when he hit .275 against southpaws and just .214 against righties. His recent track record as a pinch-hitter is rather unspectacular. Though he made four starts in center field last year, that isn't his role; he's a thick-legged outfielder with average speed who can get by in the corners. He has done a good job of picking his spots as a basestealer, but those spots are few and far between.

2002 Outlook

The Expos are not expected to bring Smith back this year. He might be able to latch on with a team looking for a pinch-hitter and fifth outfielder.

Scott Stewart

Position: RP
Bats: R **Throws:** L
Ht: 6' 2" **Wt:** 225

Opening Day Age: 26
Born: 8/14/75 in Stoughton, MA
ML Seasons: 1

Overall Statistics

	W	L	Pct.	ERA	G	GS	Sv	IP	H	BB	SO	HR	Ratio
2001	3	1	.750	3.78	62	0	3	47.2	43	13	39	5	1.17
Career	3	1	.750	3.78	62	0	3	47.2	43	13	39	5	1.17

2001 Situational Stats

	W	L	ERA	Sv	IP		AB	H	HR	RBI	Avg
Home	1	1	4.18	1	23.2	LHB	70	20	4	15	.286
Road	2	0	3.38	2	24.0	RHB	107	23	1	9	.215
First Half	0	0	5.19	0	26.0	Sc Pos	50	15	1	18	.300
Scnd Half	3	1	2.08	3	21.2	Clutch	48	12	2	4	.250

2001 Season

The Expos' biggest surprise in 2001 was lefty Scott Stewart, who had been picked up over the winter as a minor league free agent. He opened 2001 with eight scoreless appearances before hitting the skids and going on the disabled list in mid-May with a sore shoulder. He returned in June—minus a few pounds—and was one of Montreal's most effective relievers the rest of the way. His 62 relief appearances ranked third on the club behind Graeme Lloyd (84) and Scott Strickland (77).

Pitching, Defense & Hitting

Stewart throws a sinking fastball in the high-80s, a slider and a cutter. He works in and out and mixes his pitches well. Though he's a lefty, he's been tougher on righthanded hitters in each of the last three years, which obviously makes him ill-suited to be a lefty specialist. He fielded his position capably but hasn't yet swung a bat in the majors. He held runners well and had only two stolen bases attempted against him in 47.2 innings.

2002 Outlook

It will be surprising if Stewart continues to pitch as well as last year, though he could remain a useful part of the bullpen. He picked up three saves in 2001, and may be in line for a few opportunities in 2002 if Strickland falters as the club's stopper.

Brad Wilkerson

Position: LF
Bats: L **Throws:** L
Ht: 6' 0" **Wt:** 200

Opening Day Age: 24
Born: 6/1/77 in Daviess, KY
ML Seasons: 1

Overall Statistics

	G	AB	R	H	D	T	HR	RBI	SB	BB	SO	Avg	OBP	Slg
2001	47	117	11	24	7	2	1	5	2	17	41	.205	.304	.325
Career	47	117	11	24	7	2	1	5	2	17	41	.205	.304	.325

2001 Situational Stats

	AB	H	HR	RBI	Avg		AB	H	HR	RBI	Avg
Home	65	13	1	3	.200	LHP	8	1	0	0	.125
Road	52	11	0	2	.212	RHP	109	23	1	5	.211
First Half	0	0	0	0	-	Sc Pos	21	1	0	3	.048
Scnd Half	117	24	1	5	.205	Clutch	17	6	0	1	.353

2001 Season

Brad Wilkerson's 2001 season got off to a late start due to offseason shoulder surgery. He returned to the field in May and hit very well in Triple-A before getting the call to Montreal in July. He saw sporadic action in left field against righthanded pitching, but never hit for the power or average he had displayed in the minors.

Hitting, Baserunning & Defense

Though he hasn't yet shown it in the majors, Wilkerson is a good doubles hitter with developing home-run power who's capable of hitting for a fairly good average. Though he strikes out a lot, he's very patient and knows how to work a walk. While his big league batting average was a paltry .205, he managed to get his on-base percentage over the .300 mark. Wilkerson is stretched to cover center field, as he did on the 2000 Olympic Team, but he has more than enough range for left. He used to have a very strong arm but it wasn't always evident last year. He isn't much of a basestealer.

2002 Outlook

The Expos affirmed their commitment to Wilkerson by dealing Milton Bradley at the deadline last year. Wilkerson has the inside track on the left-field job and very well could establish himself as a productive big league hitter in 2002.

Masato Yoshii

Position: RP/SP
Bats: R **Throws:** R
Ht: 6' 2" **Wt:** 210

Opening Day Age: 36
Born: 4/20/65 in Osaka, Japan
ML Seasons: 4
Pronunciation: mah-SAH-to yo-SHE

Overall Statistics

	W	L	Pct.	ERA	G	GS	Sv	IP	H	BB	SO	HR	Ratio
2001	4	7	.364	4.78	42	11	0	113.0	127	26	63	18	1.35
Career	28	38	.424	4.73	131	98	0	626.0	662	190	373	97	1.36

2001 Situational Stats

	W	L	ERA	Sv	IP		AB	H	HR	RBI	Avg
Home	3	1	4.53	0	47.2	LHB	194	54	7	32	.278
Road	1	6	4.96	0	65.1	RHB	261	73	11	33	.280
First Half	2	5	4.27	0	65.1	Sc Pos	112	36	5	49	.321
Scnd Half	2	2	5.48	0	47.2	Clutch	31	10	2	4	.323

2001 Season

The Rockies released veteran Masato Yoshii at the end of spring training, and the Expos picked him up a few weeks later. He pitched well for Montreal out of the bullpen at first, and he was promoted to the starting rotation in late May. He was inconsistent as a starter, however, and worked mostly in long relief in the second half, with indifferent results. He was 2-7 with a 5.56 ERA as a starter.

Pitching, Defense & Hitting

Yoshii is a control pitcher who changes speeds and works up and down with an average fastball and slider. He lacks stamina and rarely is good for more than 75 pitches. His major handicap as a starter is that he performs best when given five or more days of rest, as he had been given back in Japan. Generally a reliable fielder, he committed three errors last year. Basestealers were successful in all 13 attempts against him, and he's nothing special at the plate.

2002 Outlook

The Expos don't consider Yoshii a big part of their plans, so they may choose to non-tender him. He'll likely land elsewhere as a long reliever and spot starter if he's willing to work for less money, but he will turn 37 in April and now has been pitching as a pro in Japan and America for 17 years.

Other Montreal Expos

Matt Blank (Pos: LHP, Age: 25)

	W	L	Pct.	ERA	G	GS	Sv	IP	H	BB	SO	HR	Ratio
2001	2	2	.500	5.16	5	4	0	22.2	23	13	11	5	1.59
Career	2	3	.400	5.15	18	4	0	36.2	35	18	15	6	1.45

Considering how "friendly" Blank was to opposing hitters, the Expos may have been just as happy with Matt LeBlanc. The 25-year-old lefty surrendered more than two home runs per nine innings as a starter. 2002 Outlook: C

Darwin Cubillan (Pos: RHP, Age: 27)

	W	L	Pct.	ERA	G	GS	Sv	IP	H	BB	SO	HR	Ratio
2001	0	0	-	4.10	29	0	0	26.1	31	12	19	1	1.63
Career	1	0	1.000	7.09	49	0	0	59.2	83	37	46	10	2.01

Cubillan came to the Expos in a trade with Texas last May, in exchange for Mike Johnson. Lefthanded hitters have batted .351 and .333 against Cubillan the past two seasons. 2002 Outlook: C

Tomas de la Rosa (Pos: SS, Age: 24, Bats: R)

	G	AB	R	H	D	T	HR	RBI	SB	BB	SO	Avg	OBP	Slg
2001	1	1	0	0	0	0	0	0	0	0	0	.000	.000	.000
Career	33	67	7	19	3	1	2	9	2	7	11	.284	.360	.448

After playing in 32 games for the Expos in 2000, de la Rosa spent most of last year back in Triple-A. His offense isn't anything special, even for a guy who plays shortstop. 2002 Outlook: C

Rob Ducey (Pos: LF, Age: 36, Bats: L)

	G	AB	R	H	D	T	HR	RBI	SB	BB	SO	Avg	OBP	Slg
2001	57	73	10	17	3	0	3	12	0	16	25	.233	.374	.397
Career	703	1279	190	309	78	13	31	146	22	166	346	.242	.331	.396

Ducey opened last season on the disabled list, was released by the Phillies in June, then tore his Achilles in July and missed the rest of the campaign. He became a free agent in November and could be nearing the end of the line. 2002 Outlook: C

Joey Eischen (Pos: LHP, Age: 31)

	W	L	Pct.	ERA	G	GS	Sv	IP	H	BB	SO	HR	Ratio
2001	0	1	.000	4.85	24	0	0	29.2	29	16	19	4	1.52
Career	1	3	.250	4.49	95	0	0	120.1	129	62	88	12	1.59

Eischen was effective at Triple-A Ottawa before sticking with Montreal for most of the second half of the season last year. He handled lefthanded hitters pretty well, and the Expos have re-signed him for this season. 2002 Outlook: B

Hideki Irabu (Pos: RHP, Age: 32)

	W	L	Pct.	ERA	G	GS	Sv	IP	H	BB	SO	HR	Ratio
2001	0	2	.000	4.86	3	3	0	16.2	22	3	18	3	1.50
Career	31	27	.534	5.09	88	78	0	467.0	496	159	375	80	1.40

Irabu's two-year odyssey with Montreal resulted in 14 starts, two wins and a 6.69 ERA. If that's not enough, it also featured persistent injuries and reported drinking problems before starts, which led to his release last September. 2002 Outlook: C

Mike Johnson (Pos: RHP, Age: 26)

	W	L	Pct.	ERA	G	GS	Sv	IP	H	BB	SO	HR	Ratio
2001	0	0	-	4.76	10	0	0	11.1	13	4	10	3	1.50
Career	7	14	.333	6.85	81	32	2	218.0	254	103	147	47	1.64

Johnson opened last year in the Expos' bullpen and wasn't as bad as he had been previously, but he was sent to the minors at the end of April. Then he was traded to Texas a few weeks later. The Rangers never recalled him from Triple-A. 2002 Outlook: C

Terry Jones (Pos: CF/LF, Age: 31, Bats: B)

	G	AB	R	H	D	T	HR	RBI	SB	BB	SO	Avg	OBP	Slg
2001	30	77	8	20	5	0	0	2	3	2	11	.260	.278	.325
Career	227	530	78	128	21	5	1	34	27	36	106	.242	.289	.306

Hamstring troubles were a constant companion for Jones last season. Since he has little to offer offensively outside of his wheels, he can't afford those kinds of problems. 2002 Outlook: C

Randy Knorr (Pos: C, Age: 33, Bats: R)

	G	AB	R	H	D	T	HR	RBI	SB	BB	SO	Avg	OBP	Slg
2001	34	91	13	20	2	0	3	10	0	8	22	.220	.287	.341
Career	253	676	82	153	27	3	24	88	0	47	161	.226	.278	.382

Knorr hit three homers in his first three games last April but still couldn't earn much playing time. He's toiled for five different organizations over the past four seasons. That number looks to be on the rise, as he became a free agent in November. 2002 Outlook: C

Felipe Lira (Pos: RHP, Age: 29)

	W	L	Pct.	ERA	G	GS	Sv	IP	H	BB	SO	HR	Ratio
2001	0	0	-	12.60	4	0	0	5.0	11	2	3	1	2.60
Career	26	46	.361	5.32	163	79	1	577.1	656	222	348	84	1.52

Lira surrendered at least two runs in three of his four appearances with Montreal. A 2.08 ERA in 42 games at Triple-A Ottawa wasn't enough to save him from getting released, but the Phillies signed him last August. 2002 Outlook: C

Sandy Martinez (Pos: C, Age: 29, Bats: L)

	G	AB	R	H	D	T	HR	RBI	SB	BB	SO	Avg	OBP	Slg
2001	1	1	0	0	0	0	0	0	0	0	0	.000	.000	.000
Career	214	558	39	130	32	4	6	51	1	37	144	.233	.286	.337

Martinez missed almost all of 2001 due to a torn ligament in his throwing elbow. For a guy whose arm was one of his best assets, that can't be good. He was scuffling for a job even before the injury. 2002 Outlook: C

Troy Mattes (Pos: RHP, Age: 26)

	W	L	Pct.	ERA	G	GS	Sv	IP	H	BB	SO	HR	Ratio
2001	3	3	.500	6.00	8	8	0	45.0	51	21	26	9	1.60
Career	3	3	.500	6.00	8	8	0	45.0	51	21	26	9	1.60

Mattes reached the majors last season, eight years after getting taken in the 16th round of the 1993 draft. He fashioned a 1.89 ERA in his first three starts with the Expos, but posted a 9.00 ERA in his five starts thereafter. 2002 Outlook: C

Montreal

Ryan Minor (**Pos**: 3B, **Age**: 28, **Bats**: R)

	G	AB	R	H	D	T	HR	RBI	SB	BB	SO	Avg	OBP	Slg
2001	55	95	10	15	2	0	2	13	0	9	31	.158	.234	.242
Career	142	317	30	56	11	0	5	27	1	20	97	.177	.228	.259

Minor once was touted as the successor to Cal Ripken, but Baltimore traded him to Montreal a year ago. He's struggled mightily in the majors, and Seattle claimed him off waivers in November. 2002 Outlook: C

Bobby Munoz (**Pos**: RHP, **Age**: 34)

	W	L	Pct.	ERA	G	GS	Sv	IP	H	BB	SO	HR	Ratio
2001	0	4	.000	5.14	15	7	0	42.0	53	21	21	6	1.76
Career	11	22	.333	5.17	100	38	1	278.1	324	119	153	30	1.59

Munoz saw his first action in the majors since 1998 when he was called up in mid-July. He allowed a .341 average in seven starts but was better in relief. 2002 Outlook: C

Chris Peters (**Pos**: LHP, **Age**: 30)

	W	L	Pct.	ERA	G	GS	Sv	IP	H	BB	SO	HR	Ratio
2001	2	4	.333	7.55	13	6	0	31.0	47	15	14	7	2.00
Career	19	25	.432	4.81	136	49	2	379.2	420	157	224	54	1.52

Peters passed through four organizations in the span of about seven months last year. The Expos were team No. 2 in that group. He had injury problems the previous few years, so health could be an issue. 2002 Outlook: C

Curtis Pride (**Pos**: LF, **Age**: 33, **Bats**: L)

	G	AB	R	H	D	T	HR	RBI	SB	BB	SO	Avg	OBP	Slg
2001	36	76	8	19	3	1	1	9	3	9	22	.250	.345	.355
Career	349	706	118	181	33	12	18	76	28	79	186	.256	.335	.414

Pride was back in the organization with which he made his major league debut in 1993. He can be admired for his persistence in overcoming obstacles, but isn't likely to be more than a spare part. 2002 Outlook: C

Bob Scanlan (**Pos**: RHP, **Age**: 35)

	W	L	Pct.	ERA	G	GS	Sv	IP	H	BB	SO	HR	Ratio
2001	0	0	-	7.86	18	0	0	26.1	37	14	5	0	1.94
Career	20	34	.370	4.63	290	39	17	536.2	583	209	245	41	1.48

The Expos signed Scanlan to a minor league contract last December and had the privilege of seeing him post dreadful numbers for them. He's saved 58 games at Triple-A over the past two seasons, however. He opted for free agency in November. 2002 Outlook: C

Brian Schneider (**Pos**: C, **Age**: 25, **Bats**: L)

	G	AB	R	H	D	T	HR	RBI	SB	BB	SO	Avg	OBP	Slg
2001	27	41	4	13	3	0	1	6	0	6	3	.317	.396	.463
Career	72	156	10	40	9	0	1	17	0	13	27	.256	.310	.333

Schneider was chosen by the Expos in the fifth round of the 1995 draft and reached Montreal in 2000. He did nothing wrong in last year's stint, and could be in the mix for a backup job this season. 2002 Outlook: B

Fernando Seguignol (**Pos**: 1B, **Age**: 27, **Bats**: B)

	G	AB	R	H	D	T	HR	RBI	SB	BB	SO	Avg	OBP	Slg
2001	46	50	0	7	2	0	0	5	0	2	17	.140	.185	.180
Career	173	359	42	90	23	0	17	40	0	19	111	.251	.305	.457

After four years of getting yanked between Triple-A and the majors, Seguignol became a free agent last October. Now age 27, his opportunity to emerge as a power threat may have passed him by. 2002 Outlook: C

Anthony Telford (**Pos**: RHP, **Age**: 36)

	W	L	Pct.	ERA	G	GS	Sv	IP	H	BB	SO	HR	Ratio
2001	0	1	.000	10.29	8	0	0	7.0	14	5	5	2	2.71
Career	20	24	.455	4.04	313	9	7	431.2	445	161	312	45	1.40

After averaging 71 games and 12 holds per year for the Expos between 1997 and 2000, Telford underwent arthroscopic surgery on his rotator cuff and then spent most of last season in Triple-A. He signed with Texas in November. 2002 Outlook: C

Andy Tracy (**Pos**: 3B, **Age**: 28, **Bats**: L)

	G	AB	R	H	D	T	HR	RBI	SB	BB	SO	Avg	OBP	Slg
2001	38	55	4	6	1	0	2	8	0	6	26	.109	.190	.236
Career	121	247	33	56	9	1	13	40	1	28	87	.227	.306	.429

Tracy did some good things when he got a chance to play in 2000. But his .109 average last year was the worst by any position player with 50 or more at-bats. He was 2-for-27 (.074) with runners on base. 2002 Outlook: C

Montreal Expos Minor League Prospects

Organization Overview:

While it may not have been able to compete with big-market clubs on the field, Montreal still has managed to gain some satisfaction by its seemingly continual pipeline of prospects. Vladimir Guerrero, Jose Vidro and Javier Vazquez are testaments to the Expos' ability to find and develop talent. Unfortunately, it appears the pipeline may not be as plentiful as it once was. Michael Barrett and Peter Bergeron have emerged slower than some might have hoped, while Milton Bradley has been dealt to Cleveland. Nevertheless, Montreal still has a few nuggets in its system. Although he wasn't very impressive in his big league trial in 2001, Brad Wilkerson could start in Montreal's outfield in '02. A couple hurlers (Donnie Bridges, Justin Wayne) have high ceilings and might contribute this year. And there's decent lefthanded pitching and up-the-middle prospects moving up the ladder.

Donnie Bridges

Position: P **Opening Day Age:** 23
Bats: R **Throws:** R **Born:** 12/10/78 in
Ht: 6' 4" **Wt:** 220 Hattiesburg, MS

Recent Statistics

	W	L	ERA	G	GS	Sv	IP	H	R	BB	SO	HR
2000 A Jupiter	5	5	3.19	11	11	0	73.1	58	29	20	66	0
2000 AA Harrisburg	11	7	2.39	19	19	0	128.0	104	39	49	84	5
2001 R Expos	0	1	8.44	2	2	0	5.1	2	6	5	9	0
2001 A Jupiter	0	1	6.75	1	1	0	4.0	7	6	3	2	0
2001 AA Harrisburg	1	2	3.24	3	3	0	16.2	14	10	13	14	2
2001 AAA Ottawa	3	5	7.48	13	13	0	55.1	60	50	43	49	11

Bridges emerged as one of the minor's best pitching prospects in 2000, when he won 16 games and compiled a 2.68 ERA between two levels. But he worked more than 200 innings, which may have contributed to his problems in 2001. Not only did he slump to four wins and a 6.64 ERA, he also had to be shut down for a while due to shoulder trouble. His injuries weren't considered serious, and the Expos will have him in big league camp this spring. Bridges throws a hard, sinking, 94-MPH fastball and excellent curveball. He has worked on his changeup for the past year and a half, making him a more complete pitcher.

Scott Hodges

Position: 3B **Opening Day Age:** 23
Bats: L **Throws:** R **Born:** 12/26/78 in
Ht: 6' 0" **Wt:** 190 Louisville, KY

Recent Statistics

	G	AB	R	H	D	T	HR	RBI	SB	BB	SO	Avg
2000 A Jupiter	111	422	75	129	32	1	14	83	8	49	66	.306
2000 AA Harrisburg	6	17	2	3	0	0	1	5	1	2	4	.176
2001 AA Harrisburg	85	305	30	84	11	2	5	32	3	25	56	.275
2001 MLE	85	298	26	77	10	1	4	28	2	18	59	.258

The Expos were busy on draft day in 1997. After grabbing Bridges with their own first-round pick, they se-lected Hodges with the second of seven supplemental choices prior to Round 2. Taken out of a Kentucky high school, Hodges enjoyed a breakthrough campaign in 2000, batting over .300 and exhibiting increased power. He wasn't as potent in 2001, but that probably had more to do with an illness than anything else. He reportedly suffered from an intestinal inflammation that caused him to lose weight and miss over a month of the campaign. Though he hasn't slugged more than 15 homers in any season, he has topped 30 doubles a couple times.

Luke Lockwood

Position: P **Opening Day Age:** 20
Bats: L **Throws:** L **Born:** 7/21/81 in
Ht: 6' 3" **Wt:** 170 Riverside, CA

Recent Statistics

	W	L	ERA	G	GS	Sv	IP	H	R	BB	SO	HR
2000 A Jupiter	0	1	10.93	3	3	0	14.0	24	17	5	2	3
2000 A Vermont	1	0	2.25	2	2	0	12.0	12	3	1	8	1
2000 A Cape Fear	2	4	4.50	9	9	0	48.0	49	32	20	33	3
2001 A Clinton	5	10	2.70	26	26	0	163.1	152	78	49	114	8

Although Lockwood lost twice as many games as he won last season, his 2.70 ERA ranked second in the Midwest League. Montreal selected him in the eighth round out of a California high school in 1999, and he didn't turn 20 until last July. The Expos say he's wise beyond his years. He throws the three basic pitches (fastball, curveball, changeup) and has excellent command. While his fastball sits in the 86-90 MPH range, his velocity could improve as he fills out. He needs to work on the sharpness and depth of his breaking ball. He's a bit on the lean side, so the Expos have monitored his innings and are willing to be patient with him.

Brandon Phillips

Position: SS **Opening Day Age:** 20
Bats: R **Throws:** R **Born:** 6/28/81 in
Ht: 5' 11" **Wt:** 185 Raleigh, NC

Recent Statistics

	G	AB	R	H	D	T	HR	RBI	SB	BB	SO	Avg
2000 A Cape Fear	126	484	74	117	17	8	11	72	23	38	97	.242
2001 A Jupiter	55	194	36	55	12	2	4	23	17	38	45	.284
2001 AA Harrisburg	67	265	35	79	19	0	7	36	13	12	42	.298
2001 MLE	67	258	30	72	18	0	6	31	9	8	44	.279

The Expos chose Phillips in the second round in 1999. He's made rapid progress through their system, reaching Double-A before turning 20 last June. Phillips is a good athlete with a dash of flash and flair. No one questions his tools. He has shown the ability to play shortstop and make the tough plays, while his bat is good enough that he could advance even if shifted to another position. He has hit for average and power, and has enough speed to have stolen 30 bases last season. But after demonstrating a bit more patience in the Florida State League, Phillips' walk rate deteriorated when he got to Harrisburg.

Montreal

Wilkin Ruan

Position: OF | **Opening Day Age:** 22
Bats: R **Throws:** R | **Born:** 11/18/79 in
Ht: 6' 0" **Wt:** 170 | Ramon Santana, DR

Recent Statistics

	G	AB	R	H	D	T	HR	RBI	SB	BB	SO	Avg
2000 A Cape Fear	134	574	95	165	29	10	0	51	64	24	75	.287
2001 A Jupiter	72	293	41	83	8	2	2	26	25	10	35	.283
2001 AA Harrisburg	30	117	14	29	7	0	0	6	6	3	18	.248

Ruan is one of the fastest players in the Expos' system. He complements his speed with true center-fielder instincts and a strong, accurate arm. A native of the Dominican Republic, he signed with Montreal before turning 17 years of age. After two seasons in the South Atlantic League, Ruan performed well at Jupiter and earned a promotion to Double-A in 2001. He broke a finger in the Futures Game and seemed a little overmatched at Harrisburg. He boasts the wheels and linedrive swing to be a factor near the top of an order, but his walk rate always has been poor. Not surprisingly, the Expos would like him to develop more patience.

Grady Sizemore

Position: OF | **Opening Day Age:** 19
Bats: L **Throws:** L | **Born:** 8/2/82 in Seattle,
Ht: 6' 2" **Wt:** 200 | WA

Recent Statistics

	G	AB	R	H	D	T	HR	RBI	SB	BB	SO	Avg
2000 R Expos	55	205	31	60	8	3	1	14	16	23	24	.293
2001 A Clinton	123	451	64	121	16	4	2	61	32	81	92	.268

Sizemore is an exceptional athlete and it took a $2 million contract to have him walk away from a scholarship to play quarterback at Washington. Hailing from the northwest, Sizemore may not possess as much baseball experience as some other prospects. The Expos say he is a quick learner and pushed him to the Midwest League in 2001. After a rough first half, he came on in the second. He hasn't yet demonstrated much power, though that could emerge. He has shown plate discipline and speed, however. The Expos would like him to be a bit more aggressive and to improve his pitch recognition.

T.J. Tucker

Position: P | **Opening Day Age:** 23
Bats: R **Throws:** R | **Born:** 8/20/78 in
Ht: 6' 3" **Wt:** 245 | Clearwater, FL

Recent Statistics

	W	L	ERA	G	GS	Sv	IP	H	R	BB	SO	HR
2000 AA Harrisburg	2	1	3.60	8	8	0	45.0	33	19	17	24	7
2001 AA Harrisburg	5	5	3.73	13	13	0	82.0	77	38	37	57	10
2001 AAA Ottawa	3	5	3.11	14	14	0	84.0	68	42	33	63	11

Tucker jumped from Double-A to the majors in 2000, but strained his forearm and made only two starts for Montreal before landing on the disabled list that June. He returned to the minors in 2001, and the Expos say he was throwing well by the end of the campaign. He was healthy enough to log 166 innings, a career high. A supplemental first-round draft pick in 1997, Tucker works with an 89-95 MPH fastball, curveball and changeup. The offspeed pitch has gotten better. It isn't out of the question that Tucker could compete for a rotation spot this spring or at some point during 2002.

Justin Wayne

Position: P | **Opening Day Age:** 22
Bats: R **Throws:** R | **Born:** 4/16/79 in
Ht: 6' 3" **Wt:** 200 | Honolulu, HI

Recent Statistics

	W	L	ERA	G	GS	Sv	IP	H	R	BB	SO	HR
2000 A Jupiter	0	3	5.81	5	5	0	26.1	26	22	11	24	2
2001 A Jupiter	2	3	3.02	8	7	0	41.2	31	16	9	35	0
2001 AA Harrisburg	9	2	2.62	14	14	0	92.2	87	28	34	70	4

The Expos selected Wayne with the fifth pick of the 2000 draft and signed him to a contract that included a bonus approaching $3 million. He excelled in his first full professional season and wound up being named the Expos' Minor League Pitcher of the Year. Wayne throws four pitches for strikes and draws compliments for his command, intensity and focus. Although his 87-92 MPH fastball won't light up the radar gun, its sinking action makes it effective. He also features a plus slider and changeup. He's a hurler who already knows how to pitch to situations. While the Expos would like him to perfect his location, Wayne looks like he's on the fast track.

Others to Watch

Righthander **Ron Chiavacci** (24) has good stuff, including an 88-93 MPH fastball and excellent breaking ball. He's an aggressive competitor who will struggle at times with location. He worked in the Arizona Fall League after striking out 161 batters last season. . . **Josh Girdley** (21), Montreal's top pick in 1999, was bothered by injuries and worked in only six games last year. But the Expos say he has a big arm and a superlative breaking pitch, a 78-80 MPH power curve. . . **Eric Good** (21), a No. 2 selection in 1998, came within four innings of qualifying as the Florida State League's ERA leader last season. He has an excellent breaking pitch and some deception. . . Like Girdley and Good, **Cliff Lee** (23) is another intriguing lefthander. Lee possesses one of the best and quickest arms in the Expos' system. His breaking ball is nasty and his pitches feature late explosion. Opposing hitters don't come away with many good swings against him. . . Speedy second baseman **Henry Mateo** (25) has stolen 95 bases over the past two seasons. He has a chance to stick as a backup with Montreal in 2002, especially if he proves he can handle the outfield . . . The Expos acquired lefthander **Rich Rundles** (20) in the Ugueth Urbina deal last July. Rundles compiled an extraordinary 114-13 strikeout-walk ratio at Class-A between the two organizations. . . After struggling with injuries in 2000, outfielder **Matt Watson** (23) captured his second batting title in three years by hitting .330 in the FSL. He's a smart, aggressive hitter with gap power.

Shea Stadium

Offense

The Mets ranked 15th in the National League in batting average last year, but Shea Stadium played only a minor role. New York batted 14 points lower and slugged 17 fewer homers at home. The differences are normal at Shea, for the ball doesn't carry well and the hitting background is considered the worst in the majors. The symmetrical park also features a deep center field at 410 feet, which is farther than most of the game's newer facilities.

Defense

Few teams are slower afoot than the Mets, who play on one of the league's slowest surfaces. While center field is fairly deep, the moderate power alleys (378 feet) do not require a burner in center. The toughest challenges for fielders are the horrible lights during night games and the constant roar of planes at nearby LaGuardia Airport.

Who It Helps the Most

Shea Stadium, the third-oldest park in the league, always has been known as a pitcher's park. Little was done to alter that reputation in 2001, when the Mets' hurlers posted a 3.72 ERA at home compared to 4.46 on the road. Al Leiter thrives at Shea, going 8-3 at home last year, compared to 3-8 with an ERA 1.22 higher away from Flushing. Glendon Rusch's ERA was 1.70 lower at home, and Bruce Chen's home ERA was more than half his road norm (3.32 to 7.06) while with the Mets.

Who It Hurts the Most

Power hitters from either side of the plate are affected at Shea. The open area beyond the fences can make would-be homers to left field little more than noisy outs. Mike Piazza traditionally has been affected more than any Met, though his home batting average was better than his road mark (.304 to .297) last year for the first time in his career in a full season.

Rookies & Newcomers

The Mets would love to acquire a veteran power hitter, preferably one who hits from the left side. But it's more likely that a righthanded slugger will be available, perhaps free agent Juan Gonzalez or the Dodgers' Gary Sheffield.

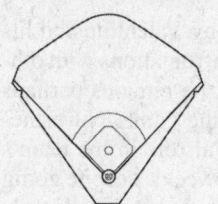

Dimensions: LF-338, LCF-378, CF-410, RCF-378, RF-338

Capacity: 56,516

Elevation: 20 feet

Surface: Grass

Foul Territory: Average

Park Factors

2001 Season

	Home Games			Away Games			
	Mets	Opp	Total	Mets	Opp	Total	Index
G	72	72	144	72	72	144	—
Avg	.244	.253	.249	.254	.271	.262	95
AB	2370	2530	4900	2480	2404	4884	100
R	267	314	581	302	340	642	90
H	578	641	1219	629	652	1281	95
2B	116	119	235	130	131	261	90
3B	9	17	26	8	12	20	130
HR	57	85	142	71	87	158	90
BB	238	197	435	244	191	435	100
SO	459	575	1034	491	479	970	106
E	48	60	108	41	49	90	120
E-Infield	40	46	86	34	39	73	118
LHB-Avg	.241	.248	.245	.232	.270	.252	97
LHB-HR	16	28	44	20	32	52	67
RHB-Avg	.245	.256	.251	.264	.272	.268	94
RHB-HR	41	57	98	51	55	106	91

1999-2001

	Home Games			Away Games			
	Mets	Opp	Total	Mets	Opp	Total	Index
G	215	215	430	216	216	432	—
Avg	.258	.247	.252	.270	.262	.266	95
AB	7062	7436	14498	7534	7175	14709	99
R	961	913	1874	1074	1021	2095	90
H	1819	1840	3659	2036	1880	3916	94
2B	346	371	717	418	397	815	89
3B	15	50	65	28	59	87	76
HR	209	210	419	251	247	498	85
BB	821	711	1532	900	704	1604	97
SO	1327	1690	3017	1431	1445	2876	106
E	137	164	301	118	156	274	110
E-Infield	111	132	243	99	130	229	107
LHB-Avg	.260	.245	.252	.259	.267	.263	96
LHB-HR	61	60	121	72	88	160	79
RHB-Avg	.256	.249	.253	.276	.259	.268	94
RHB-HR	148	150	298	179	159	338	88

2001 Rankings (National League)

- Second-highest error factor
- Third-highest infield-error factor
- Third-lowest RHB batting-average factor

Bobby Valentine

2001 Season

Little changed regarding Bobby Valentine and his massive ego. Although his confrontations with others were minimal last season, he remains perhaps the most disliked skipper in the game. Nevertheless, Valentine played a crucial role in his team's comeback during the final six weeks, despite going to battle with a popgun offense that ranked 15th in batting average in the National League.

Offense

Valentine knows his personnel as well as any manager. Not only did he have few big hitters at his disposal, the Mets' overall speed was only a hair faster than an ailing turtle. That lethal combination forced Valentine to post 97 different lineups in the team's first 105 games and to manage even more conservatively than normal. Few skippers employ the bunt less often. He gave extra playing time to productive reserves such as Joe McEwing, Desi Relaford and Tsuyoshi Shinjo, moves that helped offset disappointing efforts from Robin Ventura and Edgardo Alfonzo. Valentine also uses pinch-hitters frequently.

Pitching & Defense

Valentine does a solid job getting the most out of his starting pitchers. His dealings with Steve Trachsel, which included an 18-day stint in the minors, enabled the veteran to get back on track. Valentine also had patience with Glendon Rusch, yet was not rewarded for it. The manager tries to find different roles for pitchers in hopes of allowing them to contribute. That approach resulted in productive seasons from rookies Dicky Gonzalez, Jerrod Riggan and Grant Roberts. Valentine also insists on having a strong defensive team, which enabled New York to stay in the hunt despite its anemic offense.

2002 Outlook

Valentine knows that his team needs another big hitter to protect Mike Piazza and will lobby hard to add punch to the lineup. He is not afraid to make major alterations and has supreme confidence that his approach is the right one. Given his track record in New York, Valentine should keep the Mets in contention again in 2002.

Born: 5/13/50 in Stamford, CT

Playing Experience: 1969-1979, LA, Ana, SD, NYM, Sea

Managerial Experience: 14 seasons

Manager Statistics

Year	Team, Lg	W	L	Pct	GB	Finish
2001	New York, NL	82	80	.506	6.0	3rd East
14 Seasons		1042	986	.514	—	—

2001 Starting Pitchers by Days Rest

	<=3	4	5	6+
Mets Starts	1	71	64	19
Mets ERA	1.59	4.27	4.04	2.72
NL Avg Starts	1	80	47	24
NL ERA	5.03	4.43	4.53	4.28

2001 Situational Stats

	Bobby Valentine	NL Average
Hit & Run Success %	34.4	35.1
Stolen Base Success %	57.9	66.5
Platoon Pct.	43.3	51.5
Defensive Subs	34	20
High-Pitch Outings	7	7
Quick/Slow Hooks	9/11	19/14
Sacrifice Attempts	66	87

2001 Rankings (National League)

- 1st in sacrifice-bunt percentage (89.4%), squeeze plays (12), pitchouts with a runner moving (18) and starting lineups used (144)
- 2nd in hit-and-run attempts (128), pitchouts (76) and defensive substitutions

Edgardo Alfonzo

2001 Season

Edgardo Alfonzo emerged as a premier second baseman in 1999 and 2000. But chronic back problems landed him on the disabled list last year and ruined the first two-thirds of his year. He bounced back during the season's final seven weeks and played a key role in New York's late surge. Still, Alfonzo finished 53 points below his previous career average. He also drove in about half as many runs as he had in each of the previous two years.

Hitting

Alfonzo's ailing back prevented him from completing his swing with the proper follow-through and kept him from driving the ball. He tried to compensate for the pain, and the Mets believe he was concerned about hurting his back even further before doctors convinced him such a scenario was unlikely. Once he relaxed, Alfonzo displayed his impressive knowledge of the strike zone. When healthy, his quick wrists enable him to pull low and inside pitches, while his natural strength allows him to go the opposite way on offerings higher in the strike zone or on the outer half of the plate. Alfonzo struggled versus lefthanded pitchers last year, after batting .298 against them in 2000.

Baserunning & Defense

Through all of his discomfort, Alfonzo remained productive with the leather, committing just seven errors in 1,026 innings. He has soft hands and is the Mets' most consistent infielder. He makes all the routine plays as well as the occasional spectacular one to his left. Alfonzo's arm remains one of the game's strongest at his position. His speed dropped from marginal to slow last year due to his back. But he is an intelligent baserunner who rounds the bases better than many faster players.

2002 Outlook

While Alfonzo is only 28, the Mets are concerned his back problems may hinder him for the rest of his career. Healthy or not, Alfonzo moves back to third base in 2002, after the Mets acquired All-Star second baseman Roberto Alomar in a trade with Cleveland. Alfonzo didn't want to make the move, but he knows adding Alomar will help the Mets contend for the National League East crown.

New York (NL)

Position: 2B
Bats: R **Throws:** R
Ht: 5'11" **Wt:** 187

Opening Day Age: 28
Born: 11/8/73 in St. Teresa, VZ
ML Seasons: 7

Overall Statistics

	G	AB	R	H	D	T	HR	RBI	SB	BB	SO	Avg	OBP	Slg
2001	124	457	64	111	22	0	17	49	5	51	62	.243	.322	.403
Career	951	3407	536	985	186	14	104	482	39	396	443	.289	.363	.443

Where He Hits the Ball

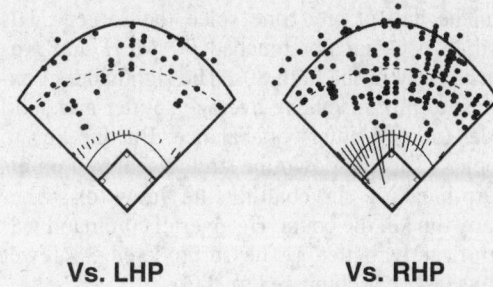

Vs. LHP   **Vs. RHP**

2001 Situational Stats

	AB	H	HR	RBI	Avg		AB	H	HR	RBI	Avg
Home	218	50	6	22	.229	LHP	90	19	2	8	.211
Road	239	61	11	27	.255	RHP	367	92	15	41	.251
First Half	219	51	9	25	.233	Sc Pos	108	27	4	33	.250
Scnd Half	238	60	8	24	.252	Clutch	63	12	1	10	.190

2001 Rankings (National League)

- 2nd in fielding percentage at second base (.987) and lowest groundball-flyball ratio (0.6)
- 3rd in lowest percentage of swings on the first pitch (14.2) and lowest batting average with the bases loaded (.100)
- 4th in lowest batting average at home
- 5th in lowest batting average
- 6th in most pitches seen per plate appearance (4.09)
- Led the Mets in sacrifice flies (5) and highest percentage of extra bases taken as a runner (46.5)

Kevin Appier

2001 Season

Kevin Appier signed as a free agent last winter and stepped into the Mets rotation as a solid No. 2 starter behind Al Leiter. Appier played a key role in New York's late-season playoff push by winning his last six decisions and going undefeated in his last 12 starts. Despite receiving little run support, he enjoyed success by ranking among the National League's top 15 starters in ERA, strikeouts and opponents' batting average.

Pitching

Appier underwent surgery on his pitching shoulder in the spring of 1998. Always one of the game's more aggressive pitchers, he showed more confidence during the final two months of last season than he had at any time since the surgery. His fastball occasionally touched 90 MPH and was consistently in the high 80s. The righthander continued to mix his above-average splitter and solid slider to keep hitters off-balance. But the key to Appier's success down the stretch centered on his sharp-breaking curveball that he threw for strikes at any time in the count. His overall command was significantly better, as he surrendered 38 fewer walks last year compared to 2000.

Defense & Hitting

Appier never has been better than an average fielder. His lack of quickness is evident when he has to charge balls hit in front of the mound or when he must cover first base. Although he spent his first 11 seasons in the American League, Appier was not the Mets' worst hitter, which actually isn't saying much considering the presence of Leiter and Glendon Rusch.

Outlook

The Mets needed pitching help when Mike Hampton bolted via free agency after the 2000 campaign. Appier went a long way toward filling the void. He pitched more than 195 innings for the third straight year and reached double digits in victories for the ninth time. If the Mets can provide more offense, the 34-year-old should reach at least 15 wins for the sixth time in his career.

Position: SP
Bats: R **Throws:** R
Ht: 6' 2" **Wt:** 200

Opening Day Age: 34
Born: 12/6/67 in Lancaster, CA
ML Seasons: 13
Pronunciation: APE-ee-er

Overall Statistics

	W	L	Pct.	ERA	G	GS	Sv	IP	H	BB	SO	HR	Ratio
2001	11	10	.524	3.57	33	33	0	206.2	181	64	172	22	1.19
Career	147	115	.561	3.63	357	345	0	2291.1	2107	823	1805	188	1.28

How Often He Throws Strikes

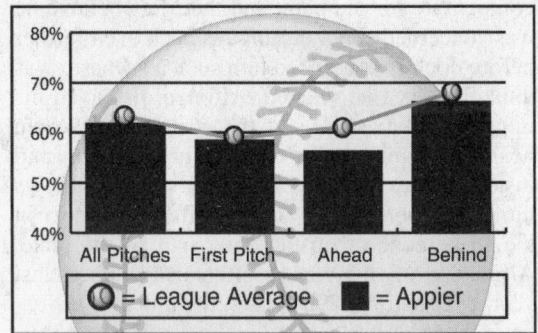

2001 Situational Stats

	W	L	ERA	Sv	IP		AB	H	HR	RBI	Avg
Home	4	5	3.62	0	104.1	LHB	360	87	14	50	.242
Road	7	5	3.52	0	102.1	RHB	404	94	8	33	.233
First Half	5	8	3.86	0	112.0	Sc Pos	162	45	4	64	.278
Scnd Half	6	2	3.23	0	94.2	Clutch	64	13	0	5	.203

2001 Rankings (National League)

- 2nd in wild pitches (12)
- 4th in stolen bases allowed (22)
- 5th in hit batsmen (15)
- 7th in least run support per nine innings (4.1) and lowest fielding percentage at pitcher (.941))
- Led the Mets in wins, games started, innings pitched, batters faced (856), walks allowed, hit batsmen (15), strikeouts, wild pitches (12), pitches thrown (3,292), stolen bases allowed (22), runners caught stealing (8), winning percentage, lowest batting average allowed (.237), lowest slugging percentage allowed (.390), lowest stolen-base percentage allowed (73.3), lowest ERA on the road and lowest batting average allowed vs. righthanded batters

Armando Benitez

2001 Season

For the second straight year, Armando Benitez re-wrote the Mets' record book by establishing the team mark for saves in a season. That effort, combined with only three blown saves, enabled the hard-throwing righthander to earn the Rolaids Relief Man Award for the National League. His effectiveness coincided with the Mets' late-season push for the playoffs. Benitez posted 17 straight saves before suffering another high-profile meltdown during two critical games against Atlanta.

Pitching

Few pitchers are more effective than Benitez when he has everything in sync. At his best, he throws a fastball in the 97-99 MPH range, along with a devastating slider and a split-finger fastball that can make him unhittable. What hampers him, however, is a tendency to become infatuated with his four-seam heater. When his fastball has trouble finding the strike zone and he gets behind in the count, Benitez will start to place the pitch, thereby reducing its velocity to a hittable 94-96 MPH. And once he gets hit, his psyche tends to become shaken, resulting in home runs.

Defense & Hitting

Most of Benitez's fielding chances come on one-hoppers back to the mound after he's thrown his splitter. He has shown consistent hands on such plays and on dribblers in front of him. He has enough athleticism to cover first base with relative ease, and he continues to do a decent job holding runners. His hitting ability is rarely seen over the course of the season.

2002 Outlook

Some scouts believe that Benitez isn't among the elite closers after watching him struggle during important games once again. In fact, Benitez has allowed seven home runs in 28 career postseason appearances. He is not as effective when he works in more than two consecutive games, which has led some observers within the organization to push for John Franco to get the call in such situations. Even if that scenario becomes a reality, Benitez remains the primary closer with another shot at a 40-save season.

Position: RP
Bats: R **Throws:** R
Ht: 6' 4" **Wt:** 229

Opening Day Age: 29
Born: 11/3/72 in Ramon Santana, DR
ML Seasons: 8
Pronunciation: buh-NEE-tezz

Overall Statistics

	W	L	Pct.	ERA	G	GS	Sv	IP	H	BB	SO	HR	Ratio
2001	6	4	.600	3.77	73	0	43	76.1	59	40	93	12	1.30
Career	25	27	.481	3.16	433	0	143	444.0	287	248	610	53	1.20

How Often He Throws Strikes

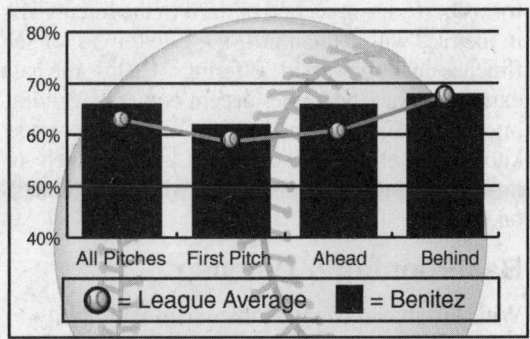

2001 Situational Stats

	W	L	ERA	Sv	IP		AB	H	HR	RBI	Avg
Home	5	2	3.10	20	40.2	LHB	113	24	4	11	.212
Road	1	2	4.54	23	35.2	RHB	163	35	8	21	.215
First Half	3	3	3.40	18	39.2	Sc Pos	66	14	5	24	.212
Scnd Half	3	1	4.17	25	36.2	Clutch	194	39	7	23	.201

2001 Rankings (National League)

- 1st in first batter efficiency (.123)
- 2nd in saves and save percentage (93.5)
- 3rd in save opportunities (46) and games finished (64)
- 6th in most strikeouts per nine innings in relief (11.0) and relief wins (6)
- 8th in lowest batting average allowed vs. lefthanded batters
- Led the Mets in games pitched, saves, games finished (64), save opportunities (46), lowest batting average allowed vs. lefthanded batters, save percentage (93.5), first batter efficiency (.123), relief wins (6), relief innings (76.1), lowest batting average allowed in relief (.214) and most strikeouts per nine innings in relief (11.0)

Matt Lawton

Position: RF
Bats: L **Throws:** R
Ht: 5'10" **Wt:** 186

Opening Day Age: 30
Born: 11/3/71 in Gulfport, MS
ML Seasons: 7

2001 Season

After spending his first six big league seasons with Minnesota, Matt Lawton joined the Mets at the trading deadline last year. The right fielder had gotten off to a slow start with the Twins and was batting .248 through May 19. He then caught fire and improved his average to .293 by the time he was dealt. The Mets' 10th leadoff hitter in 2001, Lawton struggled in his new role and batted just .241 at the top of New York's lineup.

Hitting

Lawton is not a pure leadoff man, but he was the best option that the Twins and Mets had last year. He is an above-average contact hitter who performs best batting second or third in the lineup. Hit in the face with a pitch in 1999, Lawton no longer flinches on high or inside offerings. He hits the ball extremely hard, possesses decent power by driving pitches consistently in the gaps, and has a good knowledge of the strike zone. Lawton excels in hit-and-run situations as well as when the game is on the line.

Baserunning & Defense

With his above-average athleticism and ability to get quick jumps on flyballs, Lawton can play all three outfield positions. He thrives in right field, where his strong and accurate arm upgrades any defense. He also has good range and does an excellent job cutting off balls hit in the right-center field gap. He uses his plus speed in the field and on the basepaths, where he is an above-average basestealer and routinely takes the extra base.

2002 Outlook

Lawton may have been guilty of putting too much pressure on himself after joining the Mets last summer. He also had difficulty making the adjustments to the National League and did not look comfortable atop New York's lineup. Lawton returns to the comfort of the American League Central in 2002, but he'll be wearing a Cleveland uniform after the Mets shipped him to the Indians in the Roberto Alomar trade. Lawton, who signed a four-year, $27 million deal shortly after the trade, should replace Kenny Lofton at the top of the Tribe's order.

Overall Statistics

	G	AB	R	H	D	T	HR	RBI	SB	BB	SO	Avg	OBP	Slg
2001	151	559	95	155	36	1	13	64	29	85	80	.277	.382	.415
Career	819	2855	447	784	174	14	75	397	106	430	369	.275	.378	.424

Where He Hits the Ball

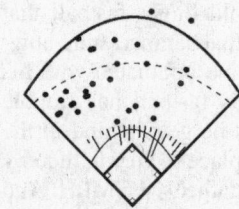

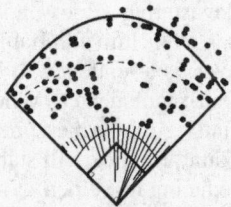

Vs. LHP   **Vs. RHP**

2001 Situational Stats

	AB	H	HR	RBI	Avg		AB	H	HR	RBI	Avg
Home	270	77	5	34	.285	LHP	123	30	1	12	.244
Road	289	78	8	30	.270	RHP	436	125	12	52	.287
First Half	317	103	10	50	.325	Sc Pos	131	39	1	49	.298
Scnd Half	242	52	3	14	.215	Clutch	88	29	5	16	.330

2001 Rankings (National League)
- Led the Mets in steals of third (3)

Al Leiter

2001 Season

The numbers do not reveal how effective Al Leiter was in the second half. He had been on the disabled list from April 21 to May 18 due to a strained elbow ligament, which limited his effectiveness throughout the first half. But the southpaw bounced back to go 7-3 with a 3.09 ERA after the All-Star break. He finished eighth in the National League with a 3.31 ERA.

Pitching

Leiter's bothersome elbow kept him from throwing his cutter as well as he would have liked. When healthy, he throws one of the game's heaviest pitches with a cutter that tails in on the fists to righthanded hitters. While his best offering to lefthanders is a fastball that runs up and in, Leiter's ailing elbow enabled lefties to average .254 last year after batting just .119 in 2000. He possesses an above-average changeup that he uses primarily on the outside half of the plate. He remains as strong as anyone deep into games, averaging a team-high 104.4 pitches per start.

Defense & Hitting

Few pitchers throw over to first base more often than Leiter. His approach was more effective last year, as he permitted 17 stolen bases compared to 22 in 2000. Leiter has good hands that allow him to field his position well, but he is no better than average at covering first base due to the long stride in his delivery. He also did little to improve his reputation as one of the game's poorest hitters, even though he hit the first triple of his career. His .065 batting average ranked fourth worst among pitchers.

2002 Outlook

Leiter has hinted that the 2002 season could be his last. However, the 36-year-old added that he would sign a new contract provided he continues to pitch well and inks a deal with the Mets. If he can pitch the way he did when healthy in 2001, look for Leiter to have an even better season and continue to serve as the team's ace for the foreseeable future.

Position: SP
Bats: L **Throws:** L
Ht: 6' 3" **Wt:** 220

Opening Day Age: 36
Born: 10/23/65 in Toms River, NJ
ML Seasons: 15
Pronunciation: LIGHTER

Overall Statistics

	W	L	Pct.	ERA	G	GS	Sv	IP	H	BB	SO	HR	Ratio
2001	11	11	.500	3.31	29	29	0	187.1	178	46	142	18	1.20
Career	117	90	.565	3.69	293	263	2	1690.0	1490	805	1449	131	1.36

How Often He Throws Strikes

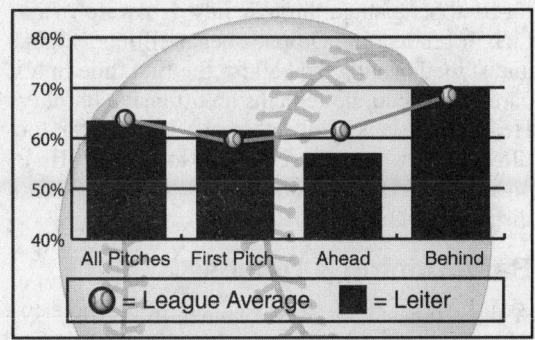

2001 Situational Stats

	W	L	ERA	Sv	IP		AB	H	HR	RBI	Avg
Home	8	3	2.72	0	96.0	LHB	114	29	2	11	.254
Road	3	8	3.94	0	91.1	RHB	593	149	16	67	.251
First Half	4	8	3.59	0	85.1	Sc Pos	156	36	3	56	.231
Scnd Half	7	3	3.09	0	102.0	Clutch	55	11	2	4	.200

2001 Rankings (National League)

- 3rd in pickoff throws (177)
- 4th in balks (2)
- 5th in most pitches thrown per batter (3.92) and lowest fielding percentage at pitcher (.933)
- 7th in highest stolen-base percentage allowed (77.3)
- Led the Mets in ERA, wins, balks (2), pickoff throws (177), GDPs induced (17), lowest on-base percentage allowed (.299), most GDPs induced per GDP situation (14.3%), lowest ERA at home, most run support per nine innings (4.1), lowest batting average allowed with runners in scoring position, fewest home runs allowed per nine innings (.86) and most GDPs induced per nine innings (0.8)

Rey Ordonez

2001 Season

After missing the last four months of the 2000 campaign with a broken arm, Rey Ordonez appeared lost during the first half of 2001. His bat was anemic and his defense was tentative before he hit his stride around midseason. Ordonez batted .290 during July and carried that momentum through the final two months to finish with a batting average four points above his career norm.

Hitting

Ordonez entered last season as a classic all-glove, no-hit shortstop. He lived up to the reputation during the first half, going the entire month of June without an extra-base hit and generating a .271 on-base percentage through July 1. Aware of his lack of production, Ordonez began lifting weights and started driving the ball for the first time in his career. Even so, he remains an offensive liability. He seldom walks, fails to make contact far too often and is too aggressive for a No. 8 hitter. He is an above-average bunter, yet rarely has a chance to display that ability.

Baserunning & Defense

A three-time Gold Glove winner from 1997-99, Ordonez did not display his typical defensive flair until late last season. A sore right shoulder may have been to blame, yet he was inconsistent on routine plays and made few spectacular efforts that had garnered a reputation earlier in his career. He has good hands and possesses outstanding quickness. That does not mean Ordonez has good speed, for he is no better than an average baserunner with just 26 steals in 46 career attempts.

2002 Outlook

The Mets placed Ordonez on irrevocable waivers at midseason but found no takers due to his large contract, which does not expire until after the 2003 season. Unless the Mets decide to eat the deal, they realize they're stuck with Ordonez, thereby giving him another full-time shot at the starting job. He needs to return to his Gold Glove ways while maintaining his second-half hitting progress from 2001 in order to remain in New York's plans.

Position: SS
Bats: R **Throws:** R
Ht: 5' 9" **Wt:** 159

Opening Day Age: 29
Born: 11/11/72 in Havana, Cuba
ML Seasons: 6
Pronunciation: RAY or-DOAN-yez

Overall Statistics

	G	AB	R	H	D	T	HR	RBI	SB	BB	SO	Avg	OBP	Slg
2001	149	461	31	114	24	4	3	44	3	34	43	.247	.299	.336
Career	772	2477	222	603	90	15	7	218	26	163	267	.243	.290	.300

Where He Hits the Ball

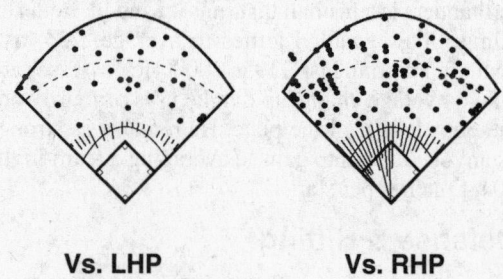

Vs. LHP   **Vs. RHP**

2001 Situational Stats

	AB	H	HR	RBI	Avg		AB	H	HR	RBI	Avg
Home	226	59	0	25	.261	LHP	88	23	1	7	.261
Road	235	55	3	19	.234	RHP	373	91	2	37	.244
First Half	254	56	0	23	.220	Sc Pos	137	33	0	37	.241
Scnd Half	207	58	3	21	.280	Clutch	66	17	0	6	.258

2001 Rankings (National League)

- 1st in lowest slugging percentage
- 2nd in fielding percentage at shortstop (.980)
- 4th in highest groundball-flyball ratio (2.1) and lowest on-base percentage
- 5th in lowest HR frequency (153.7 ABs per HR), lowest slugging percentage vs. righthanded pitchers (.335), lowest on-base percentage vs. righthanded pitchers (.287) and lowest batting average on the road
- Led the Mets in triples, sacrifice bunts (7), highest groundball-flyball ratio (2.1), lowest percentage of swings that missed (13.6), highest percentage of swings put into play (55.5) and batting average on an 0-2 count (.308)

Jay Payton

2001 Season

Jay Payton got off to an impressive start and was hitting .315 before injuries reared their head once again. The outfielder suffered a severely torn right hamstring and was placed on the disabled list from May 8 to June 26. He struggled to find his rhythm upon his return and lost his starting job in center field. He was hitting the ball hard in September, but concluded the season by suffering a non-displaced fracture of the fifth metacarpal bone in his left hand. The injury required two months to heal.

Hitting

Payton is a solid yet streaky line-drive hitter who has good power and the ability to drive the ball in the gaps. He has a short, quick swing, and he uses his strong, thick legs to generate power. His hamstring injury left him vulnerable to sliders, which proved to be his downfall during July. One of the hardest workers on the team, Payton is a fixture in the batting cage and can be seen working on his swing in the dugout between innings. The Mets believe he has the ability to hit 20 home runs annually if he can remain healthy.

Baserunning & Defense

Payton is a solid center fielder who gets good jumps on balls hit over his head and in the gaps because of his impressive quickness. After undergoing several elbow surgeries while in the minor leagues, Payton's arm is not particularly strong. But he throws accurately and to the right base. His speed is above average and he is a good baserunner. Unlike most center fielders, he is not a basestealing threat, succeeding on just four of seven attempts last year.

2002 Outlook

A late surge opened the door for Payton to remain the Mets' center fielder. Some sentiment exists in New York's front office to deal the injury-prone Payton, but the Mets don't have anyone to replace him as an everyday player. If he could stay healthy for an entire season, Payton would solidify his hold on the starting job.

Position: CF
Bats: R **Throws:** R
Ht: 5'10" **Wt:** 185

Opening Day Age: 29
Born: 11/22/72 in Zanesville, OH
ML Seasons: 4

Overall Statistics

	G	AB	R	H	D	T	HR	RBI	SB	BB	SO	Avg	OBP	Slg
2001	104	361	44	92	16	1	8	34	4	18	52	.255	.298	.371
Career	281	879	110	243	41	2	25	97	10	49	118	.276	.318	.413

Where He Hits the Ball

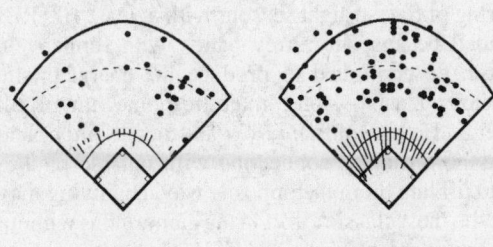

Vs. LHP   **Vs. RHP**

2001 Situational Stats

	AB	H	HR	RBI	Avg		AB	H	HR	RBI	Avg
Home	167	40	6	15	.240	LHP	69	18	2	7	.261
Road	194	52	2	19	.268	RHP	292	74	6	27	.253
First Half	161	42	3	13	.261	Sc Pos	103	19	0	24	.184
Scnd Half	200	50	5	21	.250	Clutch	68	19	1	7	.279

2001 Rankings (National League)

- 3rd in lowest batting average with runners in scoring position
- 6th in assists in center field (6)
- 7th in errors in center field (4)

Mike Piazza

2001 Season

Considering what he endured, an asterisk should be placed next to Mike Piazza's name last season. Despite having no protection in the Mets' lineup, Piazza once again shouldered the load with aplomb. In between nursing more minor ailments than an urgent care center, he put together an outstanding second half. He hit at least 30 home runs for the seventh straight season and batted .300 for the ninth consecutive campaign.

Hitting

Most hitters in Piazza's predicament last year would have struggled by trying to do too much. Not Piazza, who continued to prove he is one of the most dangerous hitters in the game. Although his string of five straight seasons with at least 100 RBI ended because he rarely batted with runners on base, he continued to produce his characteristic "Piazza blasts"—long, majestic home runs to all fields. He can pull any low and inside pitch, and has no difficulty connecting with outside pitches and driving them the opposite way. His swing may be the most classic effort in the game and is without question among the most productive.

Baserunning & Defense

Talk of moving Piazza from catcher to first base remains just that. The Mets realize that Piazza's reactions are a little slow behind the plate and that he consistently ranks last among National League receivers in retiring basestealers. Still, he does an adequate job of blocking balls, works well with pitchers and calls a decent game. He also is a warrior and among the game's most fierce competitors who answers the bell virtually every night. Years of squatting have robbed Piazza of his average speed, thereby making him a conservative baserunner.

2002 Outlook

Piazza produced one of the more unheralded performances of last season. Until the wear and tear becomes unbearable, he will remain the best offensive catcher in the game's history. If the Mets hope to turn things around in 2002, Piazza will have to be the central figure while serving as the team's primary backstop and No. 3 hitter.

Position: C
Bats: R **Throws:** R
Ht: 6' 3" **Wt:** 215

Opening Day Age: 33
Born: 9/4/68 in Norristown, PA
ML Seasons: 10
Pronunciation: pee-AH-zuh

Overall Statistics

	G	AB	R	H	D	T	HR	RBI	SB	BB	SO	Avg	OBP	Slg
2001	141	503	81	151	29	0	36	94	0	67	87	.300	.384	.573
Career	1258	4638	782	1507	228	4	314	975	17	506	719	.325	.391	.579

Where He Hits the Ball

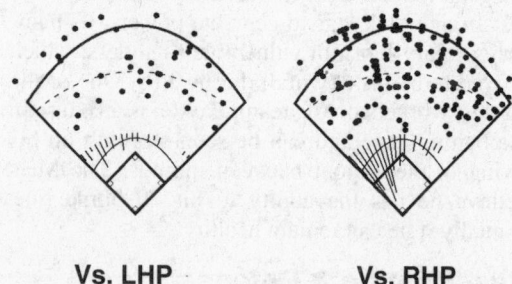

Vs. LHP   **Vs. RHP**

2001 Situational Stats

	AB	H	HR	RBI	Avg		AB	H	HR	RBI	Avg
Home	230	70	16	41	.304	LHP	99	32	8	24	.323
Road	273	81	20	53	.297	RHP	404	119	28	70	.295
First Half	279	77	21	48	.276	Sc Pos	124	32	5	51	.258
Scnd Half	224	74	15	46	.330	Clutch	80	25	6	15	.313

2001 Rankings (National League)

- 2nd in lowest percentage of runners caught stealing as a catcher (16.2)
- Led the Mets in batting average, home runs, runs scored, hits, doubles, total bases (288), RBI, intentional walks (19), times on base (220), GDPs (20), slugging percentage, on-base percentage, HR frequency (14.0 ABs per HR), batting average vs. righthanded pitchers, batting average on a 3-1 count (.533), cleanup slugging percentage (.518), slugging percentage vs. righthanded pitchers (.559), on-base percentage vs. righthanded pitchers (.366), batting average at home and batting average on the road
- Led NL catchers in batting average, home runs and RBI

Glendon Rusch

Position: SP
Bats: L **Throws:** L
Ht: 6' 1" **Wt:** 200

Opening Day Age: 27
Born: 11/7/74 in Seattle, WA
ML Seasons: 5
Pronunciation: RUSH

2001 Season

After a promising showing in 2000, Glendon Rusch had the poorest season of any Mets' starter and failed to bolster the bottom of the team's rotation. Except for a complete-game victory over Florida on September 7, the lefthander was ineffective from early August through the end of the schedule. He also maintained his streaky ways by posting a 2.58 ERA in July, only to record a 6.45 ERA in August.

Pitching

No National League starter received less run support (3.3 runs per nine innings) than Rusch. Yet the fact remains that he simply didn't pitch well last year. When he's in a groove, Rusch has a lively upper-80s fastball that sets up his other pitches and allows him to record solid strikeout totals for a finesse hurler. His struggles last year centered on his lack of command with his curveball, changeup and cutter. That forced him to try to place his fastball, a pitch hitters could sit on, resulting in an opponents' batting average of .299 or better by swingers from both sides of the plate. He also left numerous pitches up in the strike zone, leading to 23 home runs.

Defense & Hitting

Rusch remains one of the weaker fielders among moundsmen, particularly in regards to nailing lead runners on short hits. He doesn't hold runners on first base well for a lefty, was called for two balks and surrendered 13 stolen bases last year. In addition, Rusch doesn't help himself at the plate. His .056 batting average ranked third worst among pitchers.

2002 Outlook

Rusch was considered prime trade bait last July but wound up staying in New York. The Mets were shopping him again over the offseason after becoming disenchanted with him. Consistency from start to start, not to mention season to season, has plagued the 27-year-old throughout his career. However, considering his age and the dearth of quality southpaw starters, Rusch will be given every opportunity to work at the game's top level.

Overall Statistics

	W	L	Pct.	ERA	G	GS	Sv	IP	H	BB	SO	HR	Ratio
2001	8	12	.400	4.63	33	33	0	179.0	216	43	156	23	1.45
Career	31	48	.392	5.00	127	114	1	699.2	817	192	527	92	1.44

How Often He Throws Strikes

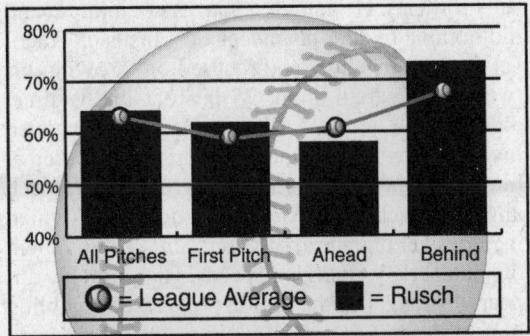

2001 Situational Stats

	W	L	ERA	Sv	IP		AB	H	HR	RBI	Avg
Home	4	8	3.80	0	92.1	LHB	120	36	3	13	.300
Road	4	4	5.50	0	86.2	RHB	598	180	20	78	.301
First Half	4	5	5.00	0	93.2	Sc Pos	159	50	3	64	.314
Scnd Half	4	7	4.22	0	85.1	Clutch	29	10	2	4	.345

2001 Rankings (National League)

- 1st in least run support per nine innings (3.3) and lowest fielding percentage at pitcher (.875)
- 2nd in highest batting average allowed (.301)
- 3rd in most pitches thrown per batter (3.93)
- 4th in balks (2)
- 5th in highest stolen-base percentage allowed (81.3)
- 6th in highest strikeout-walk ratio (3.6), highest ERA on the road and highest batting average allowed with runners in scoring position
- Led the Mets in games started, hits allowed, balks (2), highest strikeout-walk ratio (3.6), most strikeouts per nine innings (7.8) and fewest walks per nine innings (2.2)

Steve Trachsel

2001 Season

After going a combined 16-33 over the two previous seasons, Steve Trachsel appeared headed for another disappointing campaign in 2001. Saddled with a 1-6 record and 8.24 ERA in his first eight starts, he was demoted to the minor leagues for the first time since 1996. And yet, after being one of the National League's worst pitchers during the first half, Trachsel was among its best after the All-Star break. The righthander went 9-3 in his final 14 starts while working seven or more innings in 12 of those outings.

Pitching

A three-start stint at Triple-A helped reverse Trachsel's fortunes. He admitted he was not injured, and did nothing to alter his mechanics. Instead, Trachsel ditched his cutter and focused on throwing his two-seam fastball about 75 percent of the time, along with a decent curveball. He also quickened his tempo on the mound and started to challenge hitters more often. The more aggressive approach allowed Trachsel to do what he does best, which includes getting ahead of hitters and keeping them off-balance by changing speeds. His arm also appeared stronger as the season progressed, enabling him to throw his fastball close to 90 MPH, some 3-4 MPH faster than earlier in the year.

Defense & Hitting

Trachsel has always helped himself by fielding his position as well as any pitcher. He has above-average quickness and does an outstanding job of covering first base. But basestealers had more success than ever against Trachsel, resulting in 22 swipes after only 10 in 2000. He is a marginal hitter, though capable of dropping down a bunt.

2002 Outlook

The Mets hope Trachsel is ready to settle down as the team's No. 3 starter. Just 31 years of age, he is a savvy pitcher who is particularly tough against lefthanded hitters. If he can continue to make the necessary adjustments the way he did in 2001, he should be a solid fit behind Al Leiter and Kevin Appier in the New York rotation.

Position: SP
Bats: R **Throws:** R
Ht: 6' 4" **Wt:** 205

Opening Day Age: 31
Born: 10/31/70 in Oxnard, CA
ML Seasons: 9
Pronunciation: track-s'l

Overall Statistics

	W	L	Pct.	ERA	G	GS	Sv	IP	H	BB	SO	HR	Ratio
2001	11	13	.458	4.46	28	28	0	173.2	168	47	144	28	1.24
Career	79	97	.449	4.42	249	248	0	1520.2	1559	533	1083	223	1.38

How Often He Throws Strikes

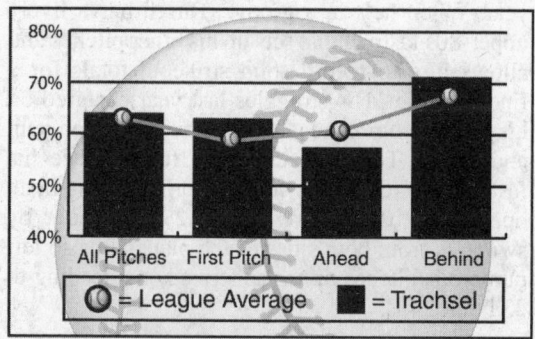

2001 Situational Stats

	W	L	ERA	Sv	IP		AB	H	HR	RBI	Avg
Home	7	6	4.00	0	92.1	LHB	302	70	12	33	.232
Road	4	7	4.98	0	81.1	RHB	359	98	16	47	.273
First Half	2	10	6.72	0	75.0	Sc Pos	132	33	8	57	.250
Scnd Half	9	3	2.74	0	98.2	Clutch	37	11	1	5	.297

2001 Rankings (National League)

- 3rd in highest stolen-base percentage allowed (88.0)
- 4th in stolen bases allowed (22)
- 5th in least run support per nine innings (3.8)
- 6th in most home runs allowed per nine innings (1.45)
- 10th in pickoff throws (129), highest strikeout-walk ratio (3.1) and lowest on-base percentage allowed (.304)
- Led the Mets in wins, losses, home runs allowed, stolen bases allowed (22), highest groundball-flyball ratio allowed (1.3) and fewest pitches thrown per batter (3.74)

Robin Ventura

2001 Season

Robin Ventura struggled for the second straight season and endured a miserable campaign. However, the third baseman wasn't coming off shoulder surgery last year, as he was in 2000. Still, while he never missed any significant activity, he battled minor ailments to his hamstring, hip, shoulder and hand. His batting average finished 36 points lower than his career norm coming into the 2001 season, and his RBI total fell short of his usual production.

Hitting

Ventura put together a decent power surge in late May and early June before falling apart shortly thereafter. After hitting 17 homers in the first half, he batted .203 and homered just four times following the All-Star break. Opposing scouts believe Ventura became his own worst enemy by trying to overcompensate from a mental standpoint, causing him to become mired even further in his slump. The surprising aspect involved his inability to move runners up as well as drive the ball when he extended his arms on pitches out over the plate, a trait that used to mean certain power.

Baserunning & Defense

While National League managers still consider Ventura one of the better third basemen in the circuit, no one argues that the six-time Gold Glover's defense has slipped over the past couple years. After committing 17 errors in 2000, he made 16 miscues last season. The 34-year-old has lost a step and now has below-average speed. He remains an intelligent baserunner, but his ability to get around the bases is nothing special.

2002 Outlook

Trade rumors were rampant last July before Ventura's disappointing production caused would-be suitors to look elsewhere for help. Yet the Mets found a good fit with the Yankees during the off-season, shipping Ventura to the Bronx for David Justice. Ventura should have a few more prime seasons ahead of him, and that gives top prospect Drew Henson enough time to develop in the minor leagues.

Position: 3B
Bats: L **Throws:** R
Ht: 6' 1" **Wt:** 198

Opening Day Age: 34
Born: 7/14/67 in Santa Maria, CA
ML Seasons: 13

Overall Statistics

	G	AB	R	H	D	T	HR	RBI	SB	BB	SO	Avg	OBP	Slg
2001	142	456	70	108	20	0	21	61	2	88	101	.237	.359	.419
Career	1698	6055	877	1638	300	13	248	1006	21	905	960	.271	.364	.447

Where He Hits the Ball

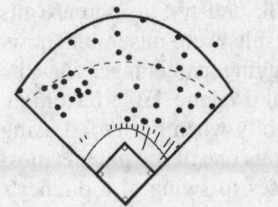 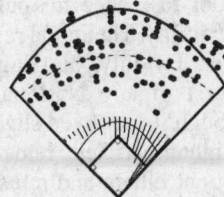

Vs. LHP   **Vs. RHP**

2001 Situational Stats

	AB	H	HR	RBI	Avg		AB	H	HR	RBI	Avg
Home	236	58	9	32	.246	LHP	96	26	2	15	.271
Road	220	50	12	29	.227	RHP	360	82	19	46	.228
First Half	274	71	17	41	.259	Sc Pos	123	29	3	39	.236
Scnd Half	182	37	4	20	.203	Clutch	67	15	5	16	.224

2001 Rankings (National League)

- 1st in lowest cleanup slugging percentage (.376) and lowest percentage of extra bases taken as a runner (27.9)
- 3rd in lowest batting average and lowest batting average on the road
- 4th in lowest batting average vs. righthanded pitchers
- 5th in errors at third base (16) and fielding percentage at third base (.957)
- Led the Mets in walks

Todd Zeile

2001 Season

Bone spurs in his right elbow and an inability to drive the ball resulted in Todd Zeile's most frustrating season since 1992. While his .266 batting average equaled his National League norm and was just two points under his career mark coming into 2001, Zeile's 10 home runs and 62 RBIs were far below his previous standards. Whenever the Mets' offensive shortcomings were discussed, Zeile and Robin Ventura were the first names mentioned.

Hitting

Although Zeile's elbow hurt, he was baffled about his inability to lift pitches, even when he made solid contact on the inner half of the plate with his quick swing. He quit lifting weights in June in order to reduce his bulk and try to increase his flexibility. The initial results were miserable, however. By July, his slugging percentage was the worst of any National League first baseman, though it improved slightly when he started using a lighter bat. Zeile remains one of the game's most patient hitters and refuses to swing at a pitcher's initial offering. In addition to leading the team with the most pitches seen per plate appearance (4.18), he hit .309 on 0-1 counts and .313 on 1-0 counts.

Baserunning & Defense

The 36-year-old Zeile appeared to lose a step last year. While he tripled once and succeeded on his only stolen base attempt, he seemed to take an extra half-second or more between the bags. A former catcher and third baseman, Zeile has good hands but is not particularly quick around first base. He also has difficulty chasing down fly balls hit behind him in foul territory.

2002 Outlook

Zeile, who had bone spurs surgically removed in November, proved again last year that his bat cannot be expected to carry an offense. The Mets lack a true power hitter other than Mike Piazza, which hurts Zeile as much as anyone on the team. Considering his declining production and effectiveness in several areas, Zeile is on the verge of becoming a part-time player who fills in at the corner positions, possibly as soon as 2002. He will be healthy by the time camp opens in February.

Position: 1B
Bats: R **Throws:** R
Ht: 6' 1" **Wt:** 200

Opening Day Age: 36
Born: 9/9/65 in Van Nuys, CA
ML Seasons: 13
Pronunciation: ZEAL

Overall Statistics

	G	AB	R	H	D	T	HR	RBI	SB	BB	SO	Avg	OBP	Slg
2001	151	531	66	141	25	1	10	62	1	73	102	.266	.359	.373
Career	1777	6420	855	1717	348	21	215	946	51	801	1050	.267	.349	.429

Where He Hits the Ball

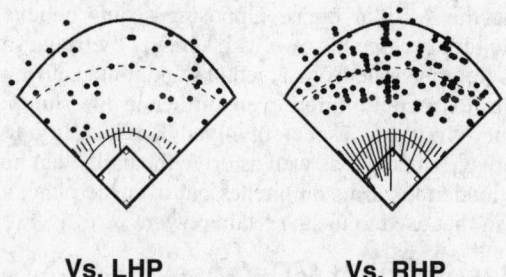

Vs. LHP   **Vs. RHP**

2001 Situational Stats

	AB	H	HR	RBI	Avg		AB	H	HR	RBI	Avg
Home	253	69	4	31	.273	LHP	104	30	5	13	.288
Road	278	72	6	31	.259	RHP	427	111	5	49	.260
First Half	309	85	6	40	.275	Sc Pos	142	45	3	53	.317
Scnd Half	222	56	4	22	.252	Clutch	90	24	4	12	.267

2001 Rankings (National League)

- 1st in lowest percentage of swings on the first pitch (11.8)
- 2nd in most pitches seen per plate appearance (4.18)
- 3rd in errors at first base (11), highest percentage of pitches taken (63.7) and lowest fielding percentage at first base (.992)
- 5th in assists at first base (112)
- Led the Mets in at-bats, singles, times on base (220), strikeouts, pitches seen (2,556), plate appearances (612), games played, most pitches seen per plate appearance (4.18), highest percentage of pitches taken (63.7) and batting average with runners in scoring position

Benny Agbayani

Position: LF
Bats: R **Throws:** R
Ht: 6' 0" **Wt:** 225

Opening Day Age: 30
Born: 12/28/71 in Honolulu, HI
ML Seasons: 4
Pronunciation:
ag-by-YAWN-ee
Nickname: The Hawaiian Punch

Overall Statistics

	G	AB	R	H	D	T	HR	RBI	SB	BB	SO	Avg	OBP	Slg
2001	91	296	28	82	14	2	6	27	4	36	73	.277	.364	.399
Career	322	937	130	264	52	6	35	129	15	123	206	.282	.372	.462

2001 Situational Stats

	AB	H	HR	RBI	Avg		AB	H	HR	RBI	Avg
Home	146	36	4	14	.247	LHP	72	24	3	9	.333
Road	150	46	2	13	.307	RHP	224	58	3	18	.259
First Half	203	54	4	17	.266	Sc Pos	59	17	1	22	.288
Scnd Half	93	28	2	10	.301	Clutch	45	16	0	5	.356

2001 Season

Benny Agbayani encountered one hurdle after another last season. A fractured left wrist washed out most of his April. Lower back pain then hindered his efforts in late May and early June. Finally, surgery to have a hook removed from the hamate bone in his right hand landed him on the disabled list after September 2. By then, Agbayani was the the odd man out in the crowded Mets outfield.

Hitting, Baserunning & Defense

The Mets were discouraged by Agbayani's performance last year after watching him excel as a regular reserve in 2000. He feasts on low fastballs from lefthanders, but has the ability to hit all kinds of pitches and use the entire field. New York was concerned about his decrease in power as well as his rate of one strikeout for every 4.05 at-bats. His defense, inconsistent at both corner outfield positions, also faltered. His baserunning and overall speed cannot be considered strengths.

2002 Outlook

Agbayani was placed on waivers by the Mets and claimed by the Giants in August, but a deal could not be worked out. That doesn't bode well for Agbayani, who is expected to lose playing time as the Mets retool. If he stays, Agbayani appears to be no more than the fifth outfielder.

Bruce Chen

Position: SP
Bats: B **Throws:** L
Ht: 6' 2" **Wt:** 210

Opening Day Age: 24
Born: 6/19/77 in Panama City, Panama
ML Seasons: 4

Overall Statistics

	W	L	Pct.	ERA	G	GS	Sv	IP	H	BB	SO	HR	Ratio
2001	7	7	.500	4.87	27	27	0	146.0	146	59	126	29	1.40
Career	18	13	.581	4.30	84	53	0	351.1	323	141	300	61	1.32

2001 Situational Stats

	W	L	ERA	Sv	IP		AB	H	HR	RBI	Avg
Home	4	4	3.51	0	74.1	LHB	90	25	5	12	.278
Road	3	3	6.28	0	71.2	RHB	473	121	24	69	.256
First Half	4	5	5.00	0	86.1	Sc Pos	114	27	7	50	.237
Scnd Half	3	2	4.68	0	59.2	Clutch	21	6	0	2	.286

2001 Season

Bruce Chen joined his third major league team in 13 months when he was traded to the Mets from Philadelphia for Turk Wendell and Dennis Cook in late July. After losing his starting job in the Phillies' rotation, Chen showed flashes of brilliance with New York. He finished with his second straight seven-win season.

Pitching, Defense & Hitting

As a prospect in Atlanta's organization, Chen reminded several observers of a poor man's Tom Glavine. Chen is extremely intelligent and has great stuff. His 88-90 MPH fastball has above-average movement, but he tends to leave it high in the zone, resulting in 29 homers last year. He is inconsistent with the placement and has difficulty throwing his curveball for strikes when struggling. The lefthander is marginal at holding runners on first, but fields his position well thanks to good athleticism. A decent hitter in the minors, he has not shown the same ability in the big leagues.

2002 Outlook

Chen is the leading candidate to become the No. 5 starter in the Mets' rotation. He never earned the role in Atlanta and lost it in Philadelphia. However, New York is confident he can begin to reach his potential with a few minor adjustments.

John Franco

Position: RP
Bats: L **Throws:** L
Ht: 5'10" **Wt:** 185

Opening Day Age: 41
Born: 9/17/60 in Brooklyn, NY
ML Seasons: 18

Overall Statistics

	W	L	Pct.	ERA	G	GS	Sv	IP	H	BB	SO	HR	Ratio
2001	6	2	.750	4.05	58	0	2	53.1	55	19	50	8	1.39
Career	88	76	.537	2.75	998	0	422	1150.1	1062	449	907	70	1.31

2001 Situational Stats

	W	L	ERA	Sv	IP		AB	H	HR	RBI	Avg
Home	1	1	5.26	2	25.2	LHB	55	13	1	10	.236
Road	5	1	2.93	0	27.2	RHB	153	42	7	20	.275
First Half	4	1	3.21	2	33.2	Sc Pos	54	14	2	22	.259
Scnd Half	2	1	5.49	0	19.2	Clutch	150	40	6	22	.267

2001 Season

John Franco did another solid job serving as the Mets' eighth-inning setup man. A bout with tendinitis in his left elbow limited him to nine games after August 15. The condition required a late September cortisone shot. Nevertheless, the 41-year-old southpaw is two outings shy of becoming the seventh pitcher in history to appear in 1,000 games.

Pitching, Defense & Hitting

Franco succeeds by mixing his lively fastball, sharp changeup and a slider that acts like a cutter. His heater may not have the velocity it once had, but the low-90s pitch changes hitting planes in the strike zone. He uses his slider to work the inside and outside parts of the plate, before his darting changeup registers the strikeout or weak groundball. No pitcher has more guile than Franco, who almost never hurts himself with his glove. He rarely is called upon to hit.

2002 Outlook

There is sentiment within the Mets' ranks to give Franco more save opportunities. Closer Armando Benitez has trouble bouncing back from tough outings and pitching more than two consecutive days. Franco maintains a closer's mentality, but he will start slowly in the spring after a December procedure to remove scar tissue from his elbow.

Lenny Harris

Position: 3B
Bats: L **Throws:** R
Ht: 5'10" **Wt:** 220

Opening Day Age: 37
Born: 10/28/64 in Miami, FL
ML Seasons: 14

Overall Statistics

	G	AB	R	H	D	T	HR	RBI	SB	BB	SO	Avg	OBP	Slg
2001	110	135	12	30	5	1	0	9	3	8	9	.222	.266	.274
Career	1531	3417	411	925	141	19	31	314	126	239	280	.271	.319	.350

2001 Situational Stats

	AB	H	HR	RBI	Avg		AB	H	HR	RBI	Avg
Home	66	15	0	4	.227	LHP	2	0	0	0	.000
Road	69	15	0	5	.217	RHP	133	30	0	9	.226
First Half	91	20	0	6	.220	Sc Pos	29	7	0	8	.241
Scnd Half	44	10	0	3	.227	Clutch	46	13	0	8	.283

2001 Season

Lenny Harris enjoyed a record-breaking campaign. He broke Rusty Staub's team mark of 81 pinch-hit at-bats in a single season, and set the new standard for career pinch-hits by overtaking Manny Mota's record of 150. In addition to topping the major leagues with 21 pinch-hits last year, Harris is the only player in history to post three straight seasons with at least 15 pinch-hits.

Hitting, Baserunning & Defense

Harris remains an excellent low-ball hitter, particularly against righthanded pitchers. Even so, last year's .222 average was his lowest since 1995. He continues to have above-average speed at age 37, and would lead the Mets in stolen bases if he were a regular. A versatile defender, Harris played at least one game last season at first, second and third base, in addition to the two corner outfield positions. However, his glovework is no better than average anywhere in the infield.

2002 Outlook

Harris is a perfect fit for a Bobby Valentine-managed team. Valentine uses his bench liberally, with Harris getting the nod for 110 games last year. Signed through the 2002 season, Harris should continue to serve as an excellent pinch-hitter and a key player for double switches.

Joe McEwing

Position: LF/3B/RF/SS
Bats: R **Throws:** R
Ht: 5'11" **Wt:** 170

Opening Day Age: 29
Born: 10/19/72 in Bristol, PA
ML Seasons: 4
Nickname: Super Joe

Overall Statistics

	G	AB	R	H	D	T	HR	RBI	SB	BB	SO	Avg	OBP	Slg
2001	116	283	41	80	17	3	8	30	8	17	57	.283	.342	.449
Career	365	969	131	259	60	8	19	94	18	64	176	.267	.321	.405

2001 Situational Stats

	AB	H	HR	RBI	Avg		AB	H	HR	RBI	Avg
Home	135	34	3	14	.252	LHP	92	23	4	13	.250
Road	148	46	5	16	.311	RHP	191	57	4	17	.298
First Half	126	38	5	12	.302	Sc Pos	55	9	0	18	.164
Scnd Half	157	42	3	18	.268	Clutch	58	16	4	8	.276

2001 Season

Joe McEwing joined Desi Relaford as two of the more valuable Mets last year. McEwing was a strong utilityman, playing at least two games at every position except pitcher and catcher. He committed just three errors in 602 innings. He also served as the Mets' leadoff hitter for 20 straight games at midseason before Matt Lawton was acquired in late July. McEwing posted a career-high batting average of .283.

Hitting, Baserunning & Defense

McEwing is an aggressive hitter with surprising power for his size. He can turn on any fastball but tends to slump against breaking balls when not playing on a regular basis. Though not blessed with outstanding speed, he reads the ball off the bat very well and does an excellent job on the basepaths. His best positions are third and second base, but he is a capable corner outfielder. His hands, arm and range are good enough to handle shortstop when needed.

2002 Outlook

After getting off to a sluggish start with the Mets in 2000, McEwing found a home in the Big Apple last season. While he may never be a full-time starter, his versatility and productive stick will land him on the field more often than not.

Desi Relaford

Traded To GIANTS

Position: 2B/SS/3B
Bats: B **Throws:** R
Ht: 5' 9" **Wt:** 174

Opening Day Age: 28
Born: 9/16/73 in Valdosta, GA
ML Seasons: 6

Overall Statistics

	G	AB	R	H	D	T	HR	RBI	SB	BB	SO	Avg	OBP	Slg
2001	120	301	43	91	27	0	8	36	13	27	65	.302	.364	.472
Career	485	1494	179	365	80	10	19	156	43	162	272	.244	.326	.349

2001 Situational Stats

	AB	H	HR	RBI	Avg		AB	H	HR	RBI	Avg
Home	141	38	4	12	.270	LHP	50	12	1	3	.240
Road	160	53	4	24	.331	RHP	251	79	7	33	.315
First Half	176	52	4	17	.295	Sc Pos	63	16	0	24	.254
Scnd Half	125	39	4	19	.312	Clutch	64	23	2	6	.359

2001 Season

Desi Relaford helped offset poor years by Edgardo Alfonzo, Robin Ventura and Rey Ordonez by splitting time between three positions and emerging as one of the game's best backup infielders. Relaford also had his best season at the plate, with career highs in batting average, doubles and home runs.

Hitting, Baserunning & Defense

The Phillies' starting shortstop in 1998, Relaford has good hands and range, and above-average quickness with an explosive first step. He also has a hose for an arm, as evidenced by the 91-MPH fastball he displayed during a one-inning pitching performance on May 17. For the first time in his career, Relaford showed the ability to make adjustments at the plate. He has scaled back his uppercut swing in order to make more contact, yet maintains plenty of strength to drive the ball into the gaps. Relaford also is the fastest baserunner on the team and paced the Mets in stolen bases last year.

2002 Outlook

Relaford is a selfless team player who manager Bobby Valentine liked having on the roster. Still, the Mets dealt him to the Giants in the Shawn Estes trade. He may get some time at third base.

Jerrod Riggan

Position: RP
Bats: R **Throws:** R
Ht: 6' 4" **Wt:** 185

Opening Day Age: 27
Born: 5/16/74 in Brewster, WA
ML Seasons: 2

Overall Statistics

	W	L	Pct.	ERA	G	GS	Sv	IP	H	BB	SO	HR	Ratio
2001	3	3	.500	3.40	35	0	0	47.2	42	24	41	5	1.38
Career	3	3	.500	3.26	36	0	0	49.2	45	24	42	5	1.39

2001 Situational Stats

	W	L	ERA	Sv	IP		AB	H	HR	RBI	Avg
Home	1	1	2.70	0	20.0	LHB	76	21	2	9	.276
Road	2	2	3.90	0	27.2	RHB	97	21	3	15	.216
First Half	0	0	4.71	0	21.0	Sc Pos	51	11	1	19	.216
Scnd Half	3	3	2.36	0	26.2	Clutch	61	14	4	10	.230

2001 Season

Jerrod Riggan made five trips between New York and Triple-A last year before earning the seventh-inning setup role after Turk Wendell was traded to Philadelphia. Riggan struggled while pitching primarily in mopup situations early in the campaign, but saved 13 games in the minors. When manager Bobby Valentine expanded his role late in the season, Riggan thrived in several pressure situations.

Pitching, Defense & Hitting

Riggan employs a moving fastball in the 91-93 MPH range, a hard slider, sharp split-finger fastball and good changeup. The slider is his best pitch, which enables him to work effectively against lefthanded batters. His splitter helped limit righties to a .216 average. An average fielder, Riggan is only mediocre at holding runners. His bat has yet to make an impact in the majors.

2002 Outlook

No reliever in the Mets' organization has been more impressive over the past two years than Riggan. He established himself in the majors last year, and he becomes a key player in the Cleveland pen after being dealt in the Roberto Alomar trade.

Grant Roberts

Position: RP
Bats: R **Throws:** R
Ht: 6' 3" **Wt:** 205

Opening Day Age: 24
Born: 9/13/77 in El Cajon, CA
ML Seasons: 2

Overall Statistics

	W	L	Pct.	ERA	G	GS	Sv	IP	H	BB	SO	HR	Ratio
2001	1	0	1.000	3.81	16	0	0	26.0	24	8	29	2	1.23
Career	1	0	1.000	5.45	20	1	0	33.0	35	12	35	2	1.42

2001 Situational Stats

	W	L	ERA	Sv	IP		AB	H	HR	RBI	Avg
Home	1	0	3.00	0	12.0	LHB	34	11	1	5	.324
Road	0	0	4.50	0	14.0	RHB	66	13	1	8	.197
First Half	0	0	0.00	0	3.1	Sc Pos	33	8	1	12	.242
Scnd Half	1	0	4.37	0	22.2	Clutch	12	2	0	2	.167

2001 Season

Difficulties at Triple-A prevented Grant Roberts from making the jump to New York when injuries hit the Mets' rotation in May. Considered one of the organization's top prospects entering the campaign, Roberts reached the majors shortly thereafter and showed promise in 16 relief appearances.

Pitching, Defense & Hitting

Roberts' strength is a 93-94 MPH fastball with excellent movement that can be overpowering. Since he has an inconsistent release point on his curveball and slider, Roberts struggles with command, causing him to ditch those offerings when the going gets tough. As a result, he becomes a one-pitch pitcher, preventing him from starting and enabling hitters to sit on his heater. Roberts also tends to leave his pitches up in the strike zone, which can lead to constant danger. Above-average athleticism makes him a decent fielder, though the jury is still out regarding his hitting ability.

2002 Outlook

The Mets were encouraged by Roberts' new-found maturity last year. Depending on the adjustments he makes in spring training, and how well he recovers from offseason tendinitis, Roberts could be the Mets' fifth starter, rejoin the bullpen or continue to hone his skills at Triple-A.

Tsuyoshi Shinjo

Traded To GIANTS

Position: CF/LF/RF
Bats: R **Throws:** R
Ht: 6' 1" **Wt:** 185

Opening Day Age: 30
Born: 1/28/72 in
Fukuoka, Japan
ML Seasons: 1
Pronunciation:
t-yo-she sin-joe

Overall Statistics

	G	AB	R	H	D	T	HR	RBI	SB	BB	SO	Avg	OBP	Slg
2001	123	400	46	107	23	1	10	56	4	25	70	.268	.320	.405
Career	123	400	46	107	23	1	10	56	4	25	70	.268	.320	.405

2001 Situational Stats

	AB	H	HR	RBI	Avg		AB	H	HR	RBI	Avg
Home	178	43	4	16	.242	LHP	82	25	1	8	.305
Road	222	64	6	40	.288	RHP	318	82	9	48	.258
First Half	196	55	5	32	.281	Sc Pos	100	26	3	46	.260
Scnd Half	204	52	5	24	.255	Clutch	73	20	3	14	.274

2001 Season

Ichiro Suzuki wasn't the only Japanese veteran to make an impact in the majors last year. Unlike his heralded countryman, Tsuyoshi Shinjo quietly starred as the Mets' fourth outfielder while ranking high on the club in home runs and RBI. He succeeded despite playing much of the second half with a strained quadriceps muscle that landed him on the disabled list from June 20 to July 16.

Hitting, Baserunning & Defense

Shinjo has extra-base power, is capable of pulling the ball for home runs and shows excellent knowledge of the strike zone. His approach consists of anticipating the fastball and adjusting to offspeed stuff. Bobby Valentine was impressed enough to place Shinjo in the cleanup spot for most of the final month. The quick-footed outfielder won the equivalent of seven Gold Gloves as a center fielder in Japan. He emerged as the Mets' best defensive outfielder, making numerous spectacular catches and displaying a strong, accurate arm.

2002 Outlook

While it's debatable if Shinjo can handle an everyday job, the Giants stepped forward and traded Shawn Estes to get him. They are looking for center-field options other than Marvin Benard.

Rick White

Position: RP
Bats: R **Throws:** R
Ht: 6' 4" **Wt:** 230

Opening Day Age: 33
Born: 12/23/68 in
Springfield, OH
ML Seasons: 6

Overall Statistics

	W	L	Pct.	ERA	G	GS	Sv	IP	H	BB	SO	HR	Ratio
2001	4	5	.444	3.88	55	0	2	69.2	71	17	51	7	1.26
Career	22	31	.415	3.93	280	18	11	476.1	497	151	305	44	1.36

2001 Situational Stats

	W	L	ERA	Sv	IP		AB	H	HR	RBI	Avg
Home	1	3	4.00	1	36.0	LHB	107	29	4	16	.271
Road	3	2	3.74	1	33.2	RHB	169	42	3	23	.249
First Half	2	1	4.32	1	33.1	Sc Pos	75	19	2	30	.253
Scnd Half	2	4	3.47	1	36.1	Clutch	107	31	4	19	.290

2001 Season

Rick White stepped up as the Mets' righthanded setup man after Turk Wendell was shipped to Philadelphia at the trading deadline. White endured two early-season stints on the disabled list with a strained rotator cuff but got stronger as the campaign progressed. By the end of the year, he was one of Bobby Valentine's most consistent pitchers.

Pitching, Defense & Hitting

White showed he could handle the setup role and bounce back quickly after Valentine began limiting the righthander's outings to a maximum of two innings. That approach enabled White to throw his entire repertoire, including a four-seam fastball in the 92-MPH range, a sharp slider and a decent changeup, curveball and splitter. He loves to challenge hitters and is not afraid to pitch inside, which shouldn't be surprising considering he's a former bar bouncer. He also is a decent fielder and holds runners well for a righthander. A lack of experience has contributed to his development as a poor hitter.

2002 Outlook

White has outlasted his competition in New York and is ready to accept the righthanded setup job full-time. He has enjoyed three straight solid major league seasons and seems to have found his niche, which should lead to more success in 2002.

Other New York Mets

Mark Corey (**Pos**: RHP, **Age**: 27)

	W	L	Pct.	ERA	G	GS	Sv	IP	H	BB	SO	HR	Ratio
2001	0	0	-	16.20	2	0	0	1.2	5	3	3	0	4.80
Career	0	0	-	16.20	2	0	0	1.2	5	3	3	0	4.80

Mostly a starter in the minors, Corey pitched well in his first real chance to close last year, saving 27 games. He deserves a crack at a middle relief job. 2002 Outlook: C

Dicky Gonzalez (**Pos**: RHP, **Age**: 23)

	W	L	Pct.	ERA	G	GS	Sv	IP	H	BB	SO	HR	Ratio
2001	3	2	.600	4.88	16	7	0	59.0	72	17	31	4	1.51
Career	3	2	.600	4.88	16	7	0	59.0	72	17	31	4	1.51

Gonzalez has been successful in the minors. He might be in the mix for a rotation spot, but he pitched much better out of the bullpen last year. 2002 Outlook: B

Darryl Hamilton (**Pos**: LF/CF, **Age**: 37, **Bats**: L)

	G	AB	R	H	D	T	HR	RBI	SB	BB	SO	Avg	OBP	Slg
2001	52	126	15	27	7	1	1	5	3	19	20	.214	.322	.310
Career	1328	4577	707	1333	204	37	51	454	163	493	494	.291	.360	.385

Hamilton had an eventful season, suffering neck, shoulder, knee and toe woes, disagreeing with Bobby Valentine, gaining his release and signing with Colorado. His days as a full-timer probably are over. 2002 Outlook: C

Brett Hinchliffe (**Pos**: RHP, **Age**: 27)

	W	L	Pct.	ERA	G	GS	Sv	IP	H	BB	SO	HR	Ratio
2001	0	1	.000	36.00	1	1	0	2.0	9	1	2	2	5.00
Career	0	5	.000	10.22	14	5	0	34.1	51	23	16	12	2.16

Hinchliffe made one horrible start for the Mets before he was banished to Triple-A. His career ratio of 3.15 home runs per nine innings is the highest for anyone with at least 30 innings. 2002 Outlook: C

Mark Johnson (**Pos**: 1B/LF, **Age**: 34, **Bats**: L)

	G	AB	R	H	D	T	HR	RBI	SB	BB	SO	Avg	OBP	Slg
2001	71	118	17	30	6	1	6	23	0	16	31	.254	.338	.475
Career	386	937	137	222	46	2	37	133	12	145	254	.237	.342	.409

Johnson hasn't collected a hit off a lefthanded major league pitcher since 1997, but he occasionally can connect against righties. While he batted under .200 at Shea last year, he was over .300 on the road. 2002 Outlook: C

Tom Martin (**Pos**: LHP, **Age**: 31)

	W	L	Pct.	ERA	G	GS	Sv	IP	H	BB	SO	HR	Ratio
2001	1	0	1.000	10.06	14	0	0	17.0	23	10	12	4	1.94
Career	8	5	.615	5.32	120	0	2	130.1	149	63	86	14	1.63

Cleveland traded Martin to the Mets last January, but he missed much of the season due to a strained rotator cuff. He was ineffective when he was able to pitch, and became a free agent. 2002 Outlook: C

C.J. Nitkowski (**Pos**: LHP, **Age**: 29)

	W	L	Pct.	ERA	G	GS	Sv	IP	H	BB	SO	HR	Ratio
2001	1	3	.250	4.94	61	0	0	51.0	54	34	42	7	1.73
Career	16	30	.348	5.37	270	44	3	419.1	446	224	300	53	1.60

After posting a 10.67 ERA for the Tigers last July and August, Nitkowski was traded to the Mets for a player to be named. He wasn't as effective against lefthanded batters as he had been previously. The lefty became a free agent in October. 2002 Outlook: C

Timo Perez (**Pos**: RF, **Age**: 24, **Bats**: L)

	G	AB	R	H	D	T	HR	RBI	SB	BB	SO	Avg	OBP	Slg
2001	85	239	26	59	9	1	5	22	1	12	25	.247	.287	.356
Career	109	288	37	73	13	2	6	25	2	15	30	.253	.295	.375

After playing well during a late-season callup in 2000, Perez spent much of the second half of last season at Triple-A. He broke the hamate bone in his right hand in winter ball and may start slowly. 2002 Outlook: B

Jorge Toca (**Pos**: 1B, **Age**: 27, **Bats**: R)

	G	AB	R	H	D	T	HR	RBI	SB	BB	SO	Avg	OBP	Slg
2001	13	17	3	3	0	0	0	1	0	0	8	.176	.176	.176
Career	25	27	4	7	1	0	0	5	0	0	11	.259	.259	.296

Toca, a Cuban, debuted very strongly in his first minor league season in 1999. But he hasn't hit for as much average or power the past couple years, and now must be considered a long shot. 2002 Outlook: C

Jorge Velandia (**Pos**: SS, **Age**: 27, **Bats**: R)

	G	AB	R	H	D	T	HR	RBI	SB	BB	SO	Avg	OBP	Slg
2001	9	9	1	0	0	0	0	0	0	2	1	.000	.182	.000
Career	127	121	7	16	4	0	0	4	2	7	30	.132	.192	.165

Velandia reached Triple-A at age 20 in 1995, but hasn't managed to carve out much time in the majors. He has more errors (1) than hits (0) in 24 games since joining the Mets in August of 2000. 2002 Outlook: C

Pete Walker (**Pos**: RHP, **Age**: 32)

	W	L	Pct.	ERA	G	GS	Sv	IP	H	BB	SO	HR	Ratio
2001	0	0	-	2.70	2	0	0	6.2	6	0	4	0	0.90
Career	1	0	1.000	6.07	19	0	0	29.2	40	12	12	4	1.75

Walker originally was drafted by the Mets in 1990 and rejoined them after his release from Colorado last year. He was effective in 26 minor league starts in 2001, and the Mets inked him to a minor league contract. 2002 Outlook: C

Donne Wall (**Pos**: RHP, **Age**: 34)

	W	L	Pct.	ERA	G	GS	Sv	IP	H	BB	SO	HR	Ratio
2001	0	4	.000	4.85	32	0	0	42.2	51	17	31	8	1.59
Career	31	28	.525	4.09	217	37	2	453.0	451	148	309	59	1.32

The Mets appear to have gotten the worst of the deal that sent Bubba Trammell to the Padres for Wall. While Trammell drove in 92 runs for San Diego, Wall went winless and then became a free agent. 2002 Outlook: B

Vance Wilson (**Pos**: C, **Age**: 29, **Bats**: R)

	G	AB	R	H	D	T	HR	RBI	SB	BB	SO	Avg	OBP	Slg
2001	32	57	3	17	3	0	0	6	0	2	16	.298	.339	.351
Career	37	61	3	17	3	0	0	6	0	2	18	.279	.318	.328

Wilson got called up last summer when Mike Piazza was hurt, and wound up sticking with the Mets the rest of the way. He has a decent chance of keeping the backup role again this season. 2002 Outlook: B

New York Mets Minor League Prospects

Organization Overview:

A year after making it to the World Series, the Mets struggled to finish two games over .500 in 2001. But they and the Braves and Giants are the only National League teams to finish with winning records each of the past five seasons. Although the Mets are a veteran team, they feel they have more talent in their farm system than many people think. They say they have a handful of genuine first-division players rising through the ranks, with enough depth behind them to either help the big club or to use in trades. They used a couple of of prospects in the deal to obtain Roberto Alomar. The strength of the system is in its pitching. The Mets have used their top pick on hurlers each of the past three drafts. New York also has tried to concentrate on finding talent in the lower parts of the draft in recent years, but the organization may be a bit thin in corner infield prospects.

Eric Cammack

Position: P
Bats: R **Throws:** R
Ht: 6' 1" **Wt:** 185
Opening Day Age: 26
Born: 8/14/75 in
Nederland, TX

Recent Statistics

	W	L	ERA	G	GS	Sv	IP	H	R	BB	SO	HR
2000 AAA Norfolk	6	2	1.70	47	0	9	63.2	38	14	31	67	2

Cammack has generated tremendous ratios throughout his minor league career. He's struck out nearly 12 batters per nine innings as a pro. His hits allowed rate of 4.8 per nine innings is even more impressive. Not bad for a 13th-round pick in the 1997 draft. He had a chance to stick in the bigs last year but missed the campaign due to elbow problems. His fastball isn't exceptional, as it resides in the low 90s. He also throws a slider and curveball and has some deception. His command isn't great and he tends to go to 3-2 counts a lot. His control looks like it got away from him when he worked in eight games with the Mets in 2000. Nevertheless, he again has a shot at claiming a spot in the team's bullpen if he's healthy.

Jaime Cerda

Position: P
Bats: L **Throws:** L
Ht: 6' 0" **Wt:** 175
Opening Day Age: 23
Born: 10/26/78 in
Fresno, CA

Recent Statistics

	W	L	ERA	G	GS	Sv	IP	H	R	BB	SO	HR
2000 A Pittsfield	4	1	0.57	20	1	5	47.0	33	6	6	51	0
2001 A St. Lucie	2	1	0.97	28	0	6	55.2	40	8	12	56	3
2001 AA Binghamton	1	0	3.10	12	0	3	20.1	17	7	6	22	1
2001 AAA Norfolk	0	0	3.86	3	0	0	4.2	2	2	4	4	0

Cerda was a 23rd-round pick out of Fresno Community College in 1998. But he didn't make his professional debut until 2000, when he posted a great ERA and strikeout-walk ratio in the New York-Penn League. He then made up for lost time by pitching at three levels last season, finishing at Triple-A. The Mets say he made as much progress as anybody in their system. They also were happy with the way he responded the more he was challenged. He compares to John Franco in terms of size. Cerda is lefthander with a funky delivery and deception. He works with a 90-94 MPH fastball, changeup and slider. The slider is particularly effective versus lefthanded hitters. Considering his experience above Class-A still is fairly limited, Cerda probably is headed back to the minors this year.

Aaron Heilman

Position: P
Bats: R **Throws:** R
Ht: 6' 5" **Wt:** 220
Opening Day Age: 23
Born: 11/12/78 in
Logansport, IN

Recent Statistics

	W	L	ERA	G	GS	Sv	IP	H	R	BB	SO	HR
2001 A St. Lucie	0	1	2.35	7	7	0	38.1	26	11	13	39	0

Using one of the picks they had obtained when the Rockies signed Mike Hampton, the Mets grabbed Heilman with the 18th overall choice in last year's draft. Heilman is a fairly mature hurler, having spent four years at Notre Dame after failing to sign with Minnesota as a supplemental pick in 2000. He began his professional career by pitching well in high Class-A, before standing out in instructional league. He pitches off a 90-92 MPH fastball that can touch 94 MPH and features heavy life and natural sink. He also throws a splitter, slider and changeup. The Mets would like him to gain consistency with the slider and to work on the change, since the splitter will tend to put more strain on his elbow.

Neal Musser

Position: P
Bats: L **Throws:** L
Ht: 6' 2" **Wt:** 185
Opening Day Age: 21
Born: 8/25/80 in
Lafayette, IN

Recent Statistics

	W	L	ERA	G	GS	Sv	IP	H	R	BB	SO	HR
2000 R Kingsport	3	2	2.10	7	7	0	34.1	33	10	6	21	1
2001 A Capital City	7	4	2.84	17	17	0	95.0	86	38	18	98	3
2001 A St. Lucie	3	4	3.55	9	9	0	45.2	45	24	19	40	2

Musser was selected in the second round of the 1999 draft out of an Indiana high school. Although he compiled a 2.06 ERA over his first two professional seasons, he worked in only seven games in 2000. The Mets say he gained weight and added muscle, but that his body just wasn't ready for the change. Musser dropped the weight, is now wiry strong, and the results were evident in 2001. He has made progress and knows how to pitch. He loves to throw inside, especially for someone so young. The lefthander works with an 87-91 MPH fastball, changeup and curveball. The breaking ball probably ranks as his third pitch, and he could improve its consistency. Musser figures to begin 2002 in St. Lucie or Double-A.

Jose Reyes

Position: SS
Bats: B **Throws:** R
Ht: 6' 0" **Wt:** 160

Opening Day Age: 18
Born: 6/11/83 in Villa
Gonzalez, Santiago, DR

Recent Statistics

	G	AB	R	H	D	T	HR	RBI	SB	BB	SO	Avg
2000 R Kingsport	49	132	22	33	3	3	0	8	10	20	37	.250
2001 A Capital Cty	108	407	71	125	22	15	5	48	30	18	71	.307

Reyes may be the Mets' best young defensive infielder since Rey Ordonez. Reyes isn't as flashy at shortstop as Ordonez, but he opened last season as a 17-year-old in the South Atlantic League and more than held his own. Reyes committed just 18 errors, a very respectable total. He also ranked fifth in the circuit with a .307 batting average. He hit a modest five home runs and the Mets say they aren't looking for power from him, but Reyes added 22 doubles and 15 triples. In addition, he runs well and can steal bases. While high Class-A is the next logical step, he may reach Double-A this season. He possibly could replace Ordonez in a couple years.

Jae Weong Seo

Position: P
Bats: R **Throws:** R
Ht: 6' 1" **Wt:** 215

Opening Day Age: 24
Born: 5/24/77 in Kwanju,
South Korea

Recent Statistics

	W	L	ERA	G	GS	Sv	IP	H	R	BB	SO	HR
2001 A St. Lucie	2	3	3.55	6	5	0	25.1	21	11	6	19	2
2001 AA Binghamton	5	1	1.94	12	10	0	60.1	44	14	11	47	3
2001 AAA Norfolk	2	2	3.42	9	9	0	47.1	53	18	6	25	4

After missing most of the previous two seasons following Tommy John surgery, Seo managed to work in 133 innings between three levels in 2001. The Mets were careful with him early in the year, holding Seo to a strict pitch count. When they sent him to the Arizona Fall League after the season and tendinitis became an issue, he started just one game there. But he should be fine. A native of Korea, Seo's velocity hasn't completely returned. His fastball was usually 86-89 MPH last season, though he could reach his previous form of 89-92 in spurts. He also throws a curveball and slider and succeeds with great command and control. The Mets hope he can stay healthy and keep pitching.

Pat Strange

Position: P
Bats: R **Throws:** R
Ht: 6' 5" **Wt:** 243

Opening Day Age: 21
Born: 8/23/80 in
Springfield, MA

Recent Statistics

	W	L	ERA	G	GS	Sv	IP	H	R	BB	SO	HR
2000 A St. Lucie	10	1	3.58	19	13	0	88.0	78	48	32	77	4
2000 AA Binghamton	4	3	4.55	10	10	0	55.1	62	30	30	36	2
2001 AA Binghamton	11	6	4.87	26	24	0	153.1	171	94	52	106	18
2001 AAA Norfolk	1	0	0.00	1	1	0	6.0	4	0	1	6	0

Strange struggled in the first half of last season as one of the younger players in Double-A. He was bothered by a ligament in his middle finger, which affected his out pitch, a cut change. The problem made him use his slider and circle change more often, which may make him a better pitcher in the long run. And he did pitch better when the cut change returned last year. Strange doesn't have conventional mechanics and throws from a three-quarters arm slot. That helps give his 89-93 MPH fastball decent life. He is slated for Triple-A, where he might work on his slider and command of all his pitches.

Adam Walker

Position: P
Bats: L **Throws:** L
Ht: 6' 7" **Wt:** 205

Opening Day Age: 25
Born: 5/28/76 in
Albuquerque, NM

Recent Statistics

	W	L	ERA	G	GS	Sv	IP	H	R	BB	SO	HR
2000 A Piedmont	6	1	2.05	8	8	0	48.1	37	11	14	50	1
2000 A Clearwater	9	8	3.08	18	17	0	114.0	116	50	39	87	6
2001 AA Reading	7	4	1.88	15	15	0	91.0	50	22	28	81	2
2001 AA Binghamton	0	0	0.00	2	2	0	4.0	3	0	2	7	0

The Mets acquired Walker in the same deal that netted Bruce Chen for Dennis Cook and Turk Wendell last July. Walker has been successful since getting selected in the 27th round of the 1997 draft. But he really seemed to blossom in Double-A last year. At 84-87 MPH, his fastball is below average. However, he throws on a good downward plane and with nice deception. He also works with a curveball, slider and changeup. Walker had been throwing across his body, raising injury concerns. The Mets tried to move the landing point of his front foot a few inches farther from the first-base side. He threw at least 130 pitches a few times last season and developed tendinitis, but an MRI revealed nothing major.

Others to Watch

Righthander **Jeremy Griffiths** (24) went 9-8 between two levels in 2001, peaking at Double-A Binghamton. He was chosen by the Mets in the third round of the '99 draft. . . **Angel Pagan** (20) may be the fastest player in the Mets' system. He's hit .322 as a pro and has a chance to be an exceptional center fielder and stolen-base threat. A switch-hitter whose natural side is the right, he's trying to get better plate discipline but has very little power. . . **Jason Phillips** (25) had been considered a nice catch-and-throw receiver. But he's filling out and now driving the ball at the plate. He has a chance to compete at catcher if Mike Piazza ever moves to first base. . . The Mets acquired righthander **Saul Rivera** (24) off waivers from the Twins. His slider is his out pitch. His fastball is 91-94 MPH and has some sink, but is inconsistent. He needs to work on his command. . . Outfielder **Robert Stratton** (24) still needs to work on making contact, especially against breaking balls. He struck out over 200 times last year, but also stroked 30 doubles and 30 homers. . . Righthander **Tyler Yates** (24) has the stuff to be a closer, but it didn't show until he emerged at high Class-A Modesto in 2000. Over recent seasons, Yates' velocity has jumped from 89-91 MPH to 96-97 MPH. He also features a power slider. The Mets obtained him as part of the package for David Justice this offseason.

Veterans Stadium

Offense

The Vet had slightly tilted towards being a hitters' park in recent years, but that wasn't the case in 2001. The most likely reason for the change was the installation of the NexTurf artificial surface. The surface was much more grass-like than the moonscape the Phillies had played on. It measurably slowed groundballs through the infield and line drives through the outfield. The surface still is conducive to the speed game so instrumental to Philadelphia's offense. Hitters pick up the ball well, especially at night.

Defense

The NexTurf surface afforded fielders true hops, and infielders were able to cover more ground because of its relative softness. Scott Rolen heartily endorsed the new "grass," and his back was able to handle a much heavier workload. While it's not real grass, it's safe to say that the Phils have addressed one of the many reasons Philadelphia was an undesirable destination for many free agents.

Who It Helps the Most

The Phillies love to run, and the surface enables players like Jimmy Rollins, Doug Glanville, Bobby Abreu, Scott Rolen and Marlon Anderson to get untracked quickly. Groundball pitchers like Omar Daal, Brandon Duckworth, Vicente Padilla and David Coggin now have a much better chance of succeeding on the slower NexTurf surface.

Who It Hurts the Most

While the dimensions of the park are fair, a flyball pitcher who locates the ball poorly can be hurt. Randy Wolf and Robert Person must therefore hit their spots to succeed at home. Person rose to the occasion by going 12-2 with a 3.69 ERA at the Vet. Very slow players' weaknesses are magnified.

Rookies & Newcomers

The Phillies consider themselves contenders, so newcomers in 2002 likely will be free agents or trade acquisitions rather than rookies. One exception might be Marlon Byrd, who could contend for the center-field job in the spring. While not a prototypical defensive center fielder, the bulky Byrd is a gap-hitter whose skills should play well at home.

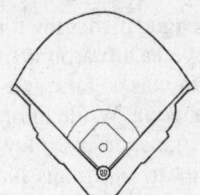

Dimensions: LF-330, LCF-371, CF-408, RCF-371, RF-330

Capacity: 62,418

Elevation: 20 feet

Surface: Turf

Foul Territory: Large

Park Factors

2001 Season

	Home Games			Away Games			
---	Phillies	Opp	Total	Phillies	Opp	Total	Index
G	72	72	144	72	72	144	—
Avg	.253	.249	.251	.268	.270	.269	93
AB	2342	2473	4815	2513	2382	4895	98
R	319	295	614	337	340	677	91
H	593	616	1209	673	644	1317	92
2B	127	149	276	130	144	274	102
3B	15	14	29	12	17	29	102
HR	71	69	140	72	75	147	97
BB	246	233	479	243	231	474	103
SO	487	519	1006	511	454	965	106
E	30	44	74	52	58	110	67
E-Infield	27	39	66	36	47	83	80
LHB-Avg	.244	.258	.250	.276	.272	.274	91
LHB-HR	35	25	60	31	18	49	117
RHB-Avg	.262	.244	.252	.260	.270	.265	95
RHB-HR	36	44	80	41	57	98	87

1999-2001

	Home Games			Away Games			
---	Phillies	Opp	Total	Phillies	Opp	Total	Index
G	216	216	432	216	216	432	—
Avg	.264	.256	.260	.260	.274	.267	97
AB	7205	7492	14697	7473	7134	14607	101
R	1030	1050	2080	960	1081	2041	102
H	1901	1921	3822	1940	1956	3896	98
2B	414	468	882	358	394	752	117
3B	57	44	101	45	41	86	117
HR	199	257	456	205	255	460	99
BB	824	842	1666	758	740	1498	111
SO	1500	1617	3117	1452	1295	2747	113
E	103	128	231	156	163	319	72
E-Infield	90	107	197	119	131	250	79
LHB-Avg	.271	.255	.263	.260	.284	.271	97
LHB-HR	86	94	180	65	75	140	122
RHB-Avg	.259	.257	.258	.259	.269	.264	98
RHB-HR	113	163	276	140	180	320	88

2001 Rankings (National League)

- Lowest error factor
- Lowest infield-error factor
- Third-lowest LHB batting-average factor

Larry Bowa

2001 Season

Larry Bowa returned to major league managing for the first time since 1988, and keyed a turnaround of the long-dormant Phillies. Bowa was a stark, necessary departure from Terry Francona. While Francona was a laid-back "players' manager" with few rules, Bowa expected his troops to do things his way every time. He did inspire quite a bit of hatred within the clubhouse, most of which faded with the club's success. However, a growing rift with Scott Rolen threatened to prevent a long-term contract agreement, making an offseason trade possible.

Offense

Bowa prefers to play a set everyday lineup, and tailors his approach to his team's strengths and weaknesses. On this club, that means efficient and effective utilization of the club's speed. The Phillies ran the bases exceptionally well last season, leading the league with 153 stolen bases and a success rate of 76.5 percent. Bowa's demanding nature extends to his coaching staff. Batting coach and longtime friend Richie Hebner was let go at season's end, paying the price for the Phils' inability to capitalize on hitters' counts and their penchant for taking called third strikes.

Pitching & Defense

Bowa doesn't live and die by pitch counts; he will ride a starting pitcher as long as he's throwing well. He likes to stick with clearly defined bullpen roles as much as possible, but doesn't tolerate poor pitch location in any situation. Bowa expects good defense from everyday players, as he dislikes making moves simply for late-inning defensive purposes.

2002 Outlook

The Phillies learned how to win in 2001, taking the Braves to the last weekend. However, the resolution of the Scott Rolen issue will, to a large extent, determine the course of the franchise in 2002 and beyond. If Bowa is handed the same team he had last year, plus a key free agent or two, he will drive them to win now. Ditto if a Rolen trade returns a mother lode of major league talent. If not, wins might be tough to come by and the clubhouse bickering could consume Bowa and/or those above him.

Born: 12/06/45 in Sacramento, CA

Playing Experience: 1970-1985, Phi, ChC, NYM

Managerial Experience: 3 seasons

Manager Statistics

Year	Team, Lg	W	L	Pct	GB	Finish
2001	Philadelphia, NL	86	76	.531	2.0	2nd East
3 Seasons		167	203	.451	—	—

2001 Starting Pitchers by Days Rest

	<=3	4	5	6+
Phillies Starts	0	72	58	23
Phillies ERA	—	4.33	4.07	4.27
NL Avg Starts	1	80	47	24
NL ERA	5.03	4.43	4.53	4.28

2001 Situational Stats

	Larry Bowa	NL Average
Hit & Run Success %	29.3	35.1
Stolen Base Success %	76.5	66.5
Platoon Pct.	59.3	51.5
Defensive Subs	5	20
High-Pitch Outings	6	7
Quick/Slow Hooks	21/12	19/14
Sacrifice Attempts	87	87

2001 Rankings (National League)

- 1st in stolen base attempts (200), stolen-base percentage, steals of second base (123), steals of third base (30) and double steals (11)
- 2nd in mid-inning pitching changes (182), first-batter platoon percentage and one-batter pitcher appearances (57)
- 3rd in fewest caught stealings of third base (3)

Bobby Abreu

Position: RF
Bats: L **Throws:** R
Ht: 6' 0"   **Wt:** 197

Opening Day Age: 28
Born: 3/11/74 in Aragua, VZ
ML Seasons: 6
Pronunciation: ah-BRAY-you

2001 Season

Bobby Abreu didn't bat .300 for the first time since 1997 last season. But that's as close as one can come to finding a negative about his campaign. Abreu combined on-base ability, power and speed and became the first 30-30 player in Phillies history. He managed to put up stellar all-around numbers despite still not solving the mystery of lefthanded pitchers, against whom he batted just .258 with one homer. He played 162 games and has logged over 150 contests in all four seasons with Philadelphia.

Hitting

Abreu is two different hitters, depending upon whether he's facing a lefty or righty. He's a monster versus righthanders. He works the count and looks for fastballs to pull for distance, although he can and will drive the ball the other way with authority. Against southpaws, he's content to hit the ball to left for singles and the occasional gapper. If he learns to pull the ball for power against lefties, watch out. Though he has a good eye, he swings from the heels and strikes out often. He sacrificed some average for power last season, hitting the ball in the air much more often than in previous years.

Baserunning & Defense

Abreu regressed a bit in these areas in 2001. Although he stole 36 bases, a career high, his 72 percent success rate was his lowest in three years. He also made more baserunning mistakes than in recent seasons. While he retains an above-average throwing arm, Abreu's range dropped somewhat in 2001. His errors doubled from four to eight, and some were of the half-hearted variety.

2002 Outlook

Abreu is primed for even greater things this year. He has worked hard to make himself a passable offensive player against lefthanders, and could put up Coors Field numbers once he learns to take them deep. He's also playing for a new deal. His contract expires after 2002, and the Phillies' inevitable long-term offer will be based upon his performance this season. A .300 average and 40-plus homers can't be ruled out.

Overall Statistics

	G	AB	R	H	D	T	HR	RBI	SB	BB	SO	Avg	OBP	Slg
2001	162	588	118	170	48	4	31	110	36	106	137	.289	.393	.543
Career	693	2417	430	742	165	33	96	383	117	422	550	.307	.408	.522

Where He Hits the Ball

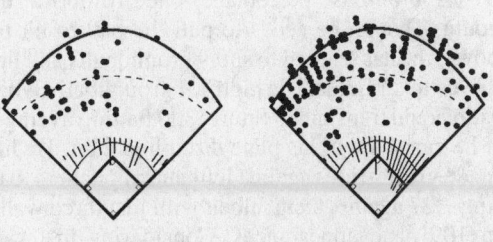

Vs. LHP	Vs. RHP

2001 Situational Stats

	AB	H	HR	RBI	Avg		AB	H	HR	RBI	Avg
Home	283	74	13	51	.261	LHP	159	41	1	24	.258
Road	305	96	18	59	.315	RHP	429	129	30	86	.301
First Half	315	89	17	62	.283	Scd Pos	141	38	7	73	.270
Scnd Half	273	81	14	48	.297	Clutch	89	27	3	13	.303

2001 Rankings (National League)

- 1st in pitches seen (2,896) and games played
- Led the Phillies in home runs, runs scored, doubles, total bases (319), RBI, caught stealing (14), walks, intentional walks (11), times on base (277), slugging percentage, on-base percentage, HR frequency (19.0 ABs per HR), most pitches seen per plate appearance (4.11), highest percentage of pitches taken (63.1), batting average vs. righthanded pitchers, cleanup slugging percentage (.494), slugging percentage vs. righthanded pitchers (.608), on-base percentage vs. righthanded pitchers (.404), batting average on the road and lowest percentage of swings on the first pitch (16.1)

Marlon Anderson

2001 Season

Marlon Anderson may have been the most pleasant surprise in the Phillies' breakthrough season. He struggled with the bat early in the year as the club raced to a 35-18 start. But it was Anderson who kept the club afloat in the summer months as his teammates slumped. Anderson batted .317, .317, and .353 in June, July and August, respectively. He was effective in a variety of diverse offensive roles, batting in seven different slots in the order.

Hitting

Anderson is an aggressive hitter who often looks for fastballs early in the count. He batted .381 when putting the first pitch in play, but struggled mightily (.236 on-base percentage) once behind in the count. Though he needs to pull the ball to hit for power, he has learned to spray groundballs and line drives to all fields. His high 1.9 groundball-flyball ratio could translate to future .300 batting averages if he can sharpen his plate discipline a bit. He has made great strides against lefthanded pitchers, batting .327 against them, albeit with just three walks in 109 plate appearances. Considering his walk rate, Anderson is best suited for the sixth or seventh spots in the order.

Baserunning & Defense

Anderson does nothing in a fundamentally perfect manner. Though his raw speed is well above average, he is not a particularly aggressive baserunner, and his basestealing technique leaves much to be desired. He often appears to be off-balance defensively, and his arm strength is average at best. However, he studies hitters diligently, and positions himself well enough to make more than his share of plays at second base.

2002 Outlook

For the first time, Anderson is assured of a full-time job entering spring training. If he responds with the same hunger he showed in 2001, he could at least maintain last year's numbers. The Phillies are about to start paying some serious money to their core players, and will need less expensive performers like Anderson to continue to improve.

Position: 2B
Bats: L **Throws:** R
Ht: 5'11" **Wt:** 198

Opening Day Age: 28
Born: 1/6/74 in Montgomery, AL
ML Seasons: 4

Overall Statistics

	G	AB	R	H	D	T	HR	RBI	SB	BB	SO	Avg	OBP	Slg
2001	147	522	69	153	30	2	11	61	8	35	74	.293	.337	.421
Career	334	1179	131	318	67	7	18	134	25	72	163	.270	.312	.384

Where He Hits the Ball

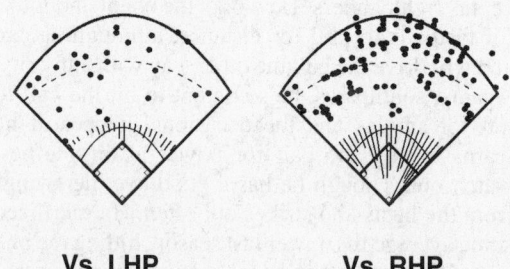

Vs. LHP   **Vs. RHP**

2001 Situational Stats

	AB	H	HR	RBI	Avg		AB	H	HR	RBI	Avg
Home	269	76	7	28	.283	LHP	101	33	1	13	.327
Road	253	77	4	33	.304	RHP	421	120	10	48	.285
First Half	266	71	8	42	.267	Sc Pos	129	36	0	41	.279
Scnd Half	256	82	3	19	.320	Clutch	88	30	5	17	.341

2001 Rankings (National League)

- 2nd in errors at second base (12)
- 3rd in lowest fielding percentage at second base (.982)
- 7th in highest groundball-flyball ratio (1.9)
- 9th in bunts in play (22)
- Led the Phillies in batting average, sacrifice bunts (10), highest groundball-flyball ratio (1.9), batting average in the clutch and batting average on a 3-2 count (.276)

Pat Burrell

Position: LF
Bats: R **Throws:** R
Ht: 6' 4" **Wt:** 225

Opening Day Age: 25
Born: 10/10/76 in Eureka Springs, AR
ML Seasons: 2
Pronunciation: BURL
Nickname: Pat The Bat

2001 Season

Last season was a key stage in the learning process for future big-time slugger Pat Burrell. On occasion, he showed flashes of his scary upside—just ask Armando Benitez, whom Burrell dented for three homers and two walks in six appearances. On the downside, Burrell was rumored headed to the minors as late as July, as his batting approach routinely broke down when he fell behind in the count. He also was benched for several key games in late September, as another slump sapped him of his confidence.

Hitting

Burrell has a natural power stroke that is capable of generating tremendous power from foul line to foul line. He takes a mighty cut and likely will always be a 100-strikeout guy. However, he simply must improve his hefty strikeout rate to reach his potential. Burrell does have a solid concept of the strike zone for his age, drawing a reasonable number of walks. When he's slumping, he has a tendency to pull his head off the pitch in an extreme manner, especially against righthanders (136 whiffs in 482 plate appearances). Once he learns to consistently stay on the ball, his overall numbers will explode. He mauls southpaws, producing a .602 slugging percentage against them in 2001.

Baserunning & Defense

While Burrell is by no means fast, he's worked hard to improve his flexibility. As a result, he isn't a baseclogger. Defensively, his range is adequate, but he possesses a cannon arm (National League-leading 18 assists) and sound instincts. Burrell also has experience at both infield corners, and could fill short-term voids at those positions if needed.

2002 Outlook

Burrell is on the brink of a major boost in production. Few players hit the ball as hard. He simply needs to put it in play more often, especially against righthanders. The flaws in his batting mechanics and approach are obvious and correctable. As Burrell's strikeout and walk numbers move toward each other, meeting at around 100, he will evolve into a .280 hitter with at least 40 homers. This could be his breakthrough season.

Overall Statistics

	G	AB	R	H	D	T	HR	RBI	SB	BB	SO	Avg	OBP	Slg
2001	155	539	70	139	29	2	27	89	2	70	162	.258	.346	.469
Career	266	947	127	245	56	3	45	168	2	133	301	.259	.352	.467

Where He Hits the Ball

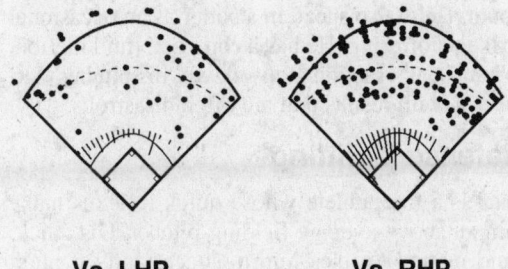

Vs. LHP   **Vs. RHP**

2001 Situational Stats

	AB	H	HR	RBI	Avg		AB	H	HR	RBI	Avg
Home	263	61	10	44	.232	LHP	113	30	9	25	.265
Road	276	78	17	45	.283	RHP	426	109	18	64	.256
First Half	306	85	9	44	.278	Sc Pos	152	39	7	58	.257
Scnd Half	233	54	18	45	.232	Clutch	104	28	3	16	.269

2001 Rankings (National League)

- 1st in assists in left field (18)
- 2nd in errors in left field (7)
- 3rd in strikeouts and lowest fielding percentage in left field (.972)
- Led the Phillies in strikeouts and slugging percentage vs. lefthanded pitchers (.602)

Omar Daal

Position: SP
Bats: L **Throws:** L
Ht: 6' 3" **Wt:** 195

Opening Day Age: 30
Born: 3/1/72 in
Maracaibo, VZ
ML Seasons: 9
Pronunciation: DOLL

2001 Season

Omar Daal's season was quite a roller coaster ride, which at least was an improvement over his night-marish, 19-loss campaign of 2000. Daal was one of the National League's best starters through April and May, and even outdueled Pedro Martinez on June 9. But he posted a 7.53 ERA in June overall, a 5.72 ERA in August, and was skipped in the rotation for a key start in late September.

Pitching

Daal relies on placement and variation of speed to achieve success, as his raw stuff leaves much to be desired. His fastball rarely tops 85 MPH, but it can be used as a strikeout pitch when he effectively utilizes his curveball and changeup early in the count. He'll also sneak in a slider as an occasional strikeout offering. He has a compact, fluid motion. When Daal's motion slows down, his pitches flat-ten out, with results that are often disastrous.

Defense & Hitting

Daal is a fine athlete whose quick reflexes make him an above-average fielding pitcher. His quick, fluid motion enables him to successfully contain the running game. He has allowed just five steals in 11 attempts over the past two seasons. He also helps himself out quite a bit with the bat. He batted .236 last season and is a .203 career hitter. He bunts quite well and can be counted on to put the ball in play on the occasional hit-and-run.

2002 Outlook

The Phillies held a $4.5 million option on Daal for 2002, which they exercised in early November. Philadelphia then turned around and dealt him to the Dodgers for minor league pitchers Eric Junge and Jesus Cordero. The Phillies obviously were happy with the young starting pitchers who audi-tioned in the second half of 2001, and the team needed the cash saved on Daal to dangle in front of cornerstone Scott Rolen and to address other club shortcomings. Daal will find a place in the LA starting rotation, where he should prove that 2001—not his 4-19 record the year before—was an accurate barometer of his true ability.

Overall Statistics

	W	L	Pct.	ERA	G	GS	Sv	IP	H	BB	SO	HR	Ratio
2001	13	7	.650	4.46	32	32	0	185.2	199	56	107	26	1.37
Career	53	58	.477	4.48	334	124	1	943.2	974	357	648	109	1.41

How Often He Throws Strikes

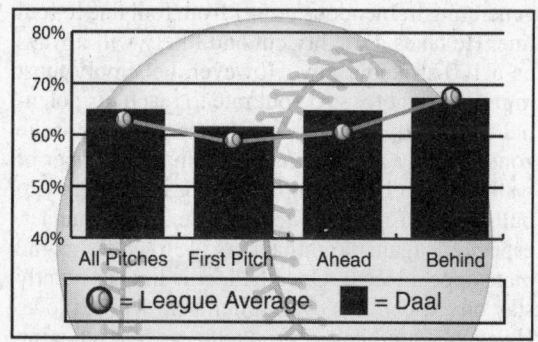

= League Average   ■ = Daal

2001 Situational Stats

	W	L	ERA	Sv	IP		AB	H	HR	RBI	Avg
Home	7	5	4.35	0	93.0	LHB	126	27	4	12	.214
Road	6	2	4.56	0	92.2	RHB	602	172	22	74	.286
First Half	9	2	4.69	0	103.2	Sc Pos	151	42	2	49	.278
Scnd Half	4	5	4.17	0	82.0	Clutch	33	8	0	1	.242

2001 Rankings (National League)

- 1st in balks (3)
- 5th in most GDPs induced per nine innings (1.1)
- 6th in fewest strikeouts per nine innings (5.2)
- 7th in GDPs induced (22)
- 8th in highest slugging percentage allowed (.462)
- 9th in most run support per nine innings (5.8)
- 10th in fewest pitches thrown per batter (3.55) and highest ERA at home
- Led the Phillies in hits allowed, pickoff throws (100), GDPs induced (22), highest groundball-flyball ratio allowed (1.2), lowest stolen-base percentage allowed (60.0), fewest pitches thrown per batter (3.55), most run support per nine innings (5.8), most GDPs induced per nine innings (1.1) and fewest walks per nine innings (2.7)

Doug Glanville

2001 Season

Doug Glanville's utter lack of on-base skills would make him a subpar offensive player at any position and at any spot in the order. But for an outfielder and top-of-the-lineup fixture, his .285 on-base percentage last season was beyond unacceptable. His performance against righthanders was particularly noteworthy, as he walked just 10 times in 533 plate appearances against them.

Hitting

Glanville appears to have no plan at the plate, and if he does, it's not a good one. He seems to possess an uncanny knack for swinging at balls and taking strikes, without regard to the game situation. For a player with only modest extra-base power, Glanville hits too many flyballs and pulls the ball too often. He's hit one homer to the right of center field in his entire career. He would be best served by batting sixth or seventh in the order, where he could be a decent RBI guy if he slightly enhanced his plate discipline.

Baserunning & Defense

All of Glanville's modest value is in these areas. He is a high-percentage basestealer with sound baserunning instincts. If anything, he could be a bit more aggressive on the bases. His defensive style changed for the better in 2001. He played much shallower, and the singles he saved far outnumbered the additional extra-base hits he yielded. Outside of Andruw Jones and possibly Gary Matthews Jr., no National League center fielder covers as much ground. His arm strength is only average.

2002 Outlook

The Phillies need more players who can reach base and need to cut some salary corners to land a top pitcher. They could accomplish both goals by dispatching Glanville and inserting promising rookie Marlon Byrd in center field in 2002. However, the Phils always have focused on Glanville's few positives and underestimated his glaring deficiencies. Don't expect Glanville at age 31 to learn new tricks, though he still has a limited run ahead of him as a big league starter.

Position: CF
Bats: R **Throws:** R
Ht: 6' 2" **Wt:** 172

Opening Day Age: 31
Born: 8/25/70 in Hackensack, NJ
ML Seasons: 6

Overall Statistics

	G	AB	R	H	D	T	HR	RBI	SB	BB	SO	Avg	OBP	Slg
2001	153	634	74	166	24	3	14	55	28	19	91	.262	.285	.375
Career	810	3134	459	896	144	28	46	274	137	167	395	.286	.323	.394

Where He Hits the Ball

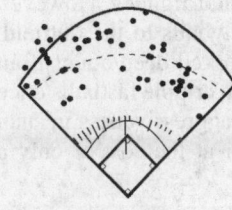
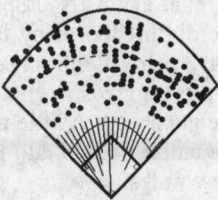

Vs. LHP **Vs. RHP**

2001 Situational Stats

	AB	H	HR	RBI	Avg		AB	H	HR	RBI	Avg
Home	306	87	6	28	.284	LHP	131	38	5	14	.290
Road	328	79	8	27	.241	RHP	503	128	9	41	.254
First Half	357	99	11	33	.277	Sc Pos	135	33	1	40	.244
Scnd Half	277	67	3	22	.242	Clutch	102	21	1	9	.206

2001 Rankings (National League)

- 1st in lowest on-base percentage and lowest on-base percentage vs. righthanded pitchers (.270)
- 2nd in lowest on-base percentage for a leadoff hitter (.288)
- 3rd in at-bats and fielding percentage in center field (.991)
- 4th in assists in center field (8) and steals of third (7)
- 6th in singles
- Led the Phillies in singles and sacrifice bunts (10)

Travis Lee

2001 Season

Travis Lee had a steady season in his first full year with the Phillies. He posted career highs in doubles, RBI and runs scored. He also provided some of the club's most exciting moments. Four last-inning home runs all made the highlight reels. As in years past, however, Lee tired down the stretch. He hit only five of his 20 homers after July 31.

Hitting

Lee was basically a dead-pull hitter entering 2001, but learned to use the entire field as last season progressed. This more refined approach enabled him to handle lefthanded pitchers much better than in previous seasons. His batting average, on-base percentage and slugging percentage were quite similar against southpaws and righties. However, he did lift too many lazy flyballs to the outfield. Like many Phillies, Lee worked deep counts, but wasn't aggressive enough on cripple fastballs once he got ahead. A little more aggressiveness in such situations would add power at the cost of only a few walks.

Baserunning & Defense

Lee moves quite well for a big man, but succeeded on only three of seven stolen base attempts after previously going 33-for-38 in his career. Of course, the Phillies are looking to him for RBI in his current role, not table-setting skills. He is an exceptional defender, covering a lot of ground for his position, scooping balls out of the dirt well, and turning the 3-6-3 double play expertly.

2002 Outlook

Lee appears to be a slightly souped-up version of former Phillie Rico Brogna. Though that's not close to what was expected of Lee after being a draft loophole bonus baby, it does represent substantial progress since his acquisition in the Curt Schilling deal. Lee is capable of raising his offensive numbers a little bit across the board, but doesn't look like a budding star. If the Phillies are unable to lock up Scott Rolen for the long haul, they might need to substantially upgrade at Lee's position, making him potential trade bait.

Position: 1B
Bats: L **Throws:** L
Ht: 6' 3" **Wt:** 214

Opening Day Age: 26
Born: 5/26/75 in San Diego, CA
ML Seasons: 4

Overall Statistics

	G	AB	R	H	D	T	HR	RBI	SB	BB	SO	Avg	OBP	Slg
2001	157	555	75	143	34	2	20	90	3	71	109	.258	.341	.434
Career	551	1896	256	478	94	7	60	266	36	261	361	.252	.342	.404

Where He Hits the Ball

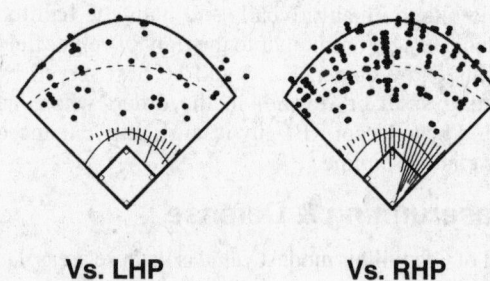

Vs. LHP   **Vs. RHP**

2001 Situational Stats

	AB	H	HR	RBI	Avg		AB	H	HR	RBI	Avg
Home	280	72	11	45	.257	LHP	132	35	6	28	.265
Road	275	71	9	45	.258	RHP	423	108	14	62	.255
First Half	302	84	14	53	.278	Sc Pos	155	40	6	70	.258
Scnd Half	253	59	6	37	.233	Clutch	92	24	4	13	.261

2001 Rankings (National League)

- 3rd in fielding percentage at first base (.996) and lowest percentage of extra bases taken as a runner (31.5)
- 6th in batting average on a 3-1 count (.706)
- 8th in sacrifice flies (9) and assists at first base (75)
- 9th in errors at first base (6)
- Led the Phillies in GDPs (15), batting average on a 3-1 count (.706) and batting average on an 0-2 count (.231)

Mike Lieberthal

Position: C
Bats: R **Throws:** R
Ht: 6' 0" **Wt:** 190

Opening Day Age: 30
Born: 1/18/72 in Glendale, CA
ML Seasons: 8
Pronunciation: LEE-ber-thal

2001 Season

Mike Lieberthal suffered a season-ending knee injury on May 12. Before then, he had gotten off to a very slow start at the plate. He had only two homers in 121 at-bats and hit just .186 against righties. Lieberthal's defensive ability (only nine steals allowed in 284 innings) and game-calling skills were greatly missed by the Phillies' young pitching staff.

Hitting

For a catcher, Lieberthal possesses a sound all-around offensive game. He is a flyball hitter whose 0.68 groundball-flyball ratio is not conducive to hitting for a high average. He generally will make contact and hit the ball where it's pitched. In his better offensive seasons, he has aggressively pounced on middle-in fastballs when ahead in the count. That was not the case in his abbreviated 2001 season, when too often he settled for the pitcher's pitch after working the count. Lieberthal mauls lefthanded pitching—he batted .350 and .417 against them in 2000 and 2001, respectively.

Baserunning & Defense

While Lieberthal never has been a basestealer, he always had gotten around the bases well for a catcher. The cumulative effect of the hip, ankle and knee injuries of recent seasons is likely to take its toll and limit his workload going forward. Lieberthal's defensive skills rank among the best—and most underrated—at his position. Few runners even bother trying to steal against him, and he consistently throws out a relatively high percentage of those who do. Lieberthal has developed into a mature veteran presence and handles young pitchers well.

2002 Outlook

Lieberthal is playing for his standard of living in 2002, as the Phillies hold a $7.25 million club option for the 2003 campaign. His health obviously is key, but Lieberthal's workload is likely to be scaled back compared to previous seasons, even in the absence of injury. Expect him to provide 15-20 homers and a batting average around .260 in about 110 games. He also should add the defense and intangibles the Phils so sorely need to take them to the next level.

Overall Statistics

	G	AB	R	H	D	T	HR	RBI	SB	BB	SO	Avg	OBP	Slg
2001	34	121	21	28	8	0	2	11	0	12	21	.231	.316	.347
Career	597	2080	286	556	126	6	84	332	7	175	320	.267	.330	.455

Where He Hits the Ball

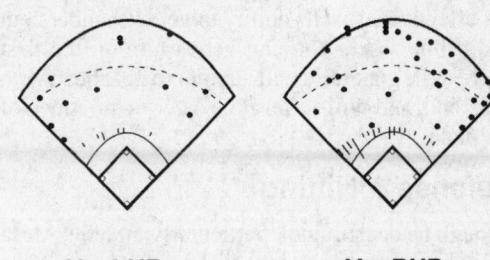

Vs. LHP   **Vs. RHP**

2001 Situational Stats

	AB	H	HR	RBI	Avg		AB	H	HR	RBI	Avg
Home	53	13	0	5	.245	LHP	24	10	0	4	.417
Road	68	15	2	6	.221	RHP	97	18	2	7	.186
First Half	121	28	2	11	.231	Sc Pos	30	7	0	7	.233
Scnd Half	0	0	0	0	-	Clutch	18	5	0	4	.278

2001 Rankings (National League)

- Did not rank near the top or bottom in any category

Jose Mesa

2001 Season

Those who predicted that Jose Mesa would be the free agent bust of 2001 had to eat crow, when he surprisingly emerged as one of the most consistent closers in the National League. His control was the best he's had since his salad days with the Indians in the mid-90s, as he consistently kept the ball low and in the ballpark. He didn't allow a single earned run in July or August, when the Phillies stayed afloat in the NL East.

Pitching

Mesa comes after you with hard stuff; his best offerings are his mid-90s fastball and hard slider. He needs to keep the ball down in the strike zone and was able to do so after several years of declining effectiveness. His ability to get lefthanders out is a prime asset. You can get to him on the first pitch, as he generally will attempt to get ahead with a fastball, and will suffer if he catches too much of the plate.

Defense & Hitting

Though he doesn't look particularly athletic, Mesa fields his position quite well. His range is passable, and he hasn't made an error since 1999. He gets the ball to the plate quickly for a power pitcher. He totally shut down the running game last season, permitting no steals in three attempts. He's batted exactly once—drawing a walk—in his 13 major league seasons.

2002 Outlook

As well as Mesa pitched in 2001, the downward trend he experienced the previous three years in the American League can't be ignored. He evokes memories of former Phillies closer Al Holland. As long as Holland was throwing in the mid-90s and hitting his spots, things were fine. However, the second he lost a tick of velocity and began to place the ball poorly, the decline was swift and gruesome. Expect Mesa's number of bad days to increase a bit in 2002, though he should retain the closer's job, record 30 or so saves and compile around a 4.00 ERA.

Position: RP
Bats: R **Throws:** R
Ht: 6' 3" **Wt:** 225

Opening Day Age: 35
Born: 5/22/66 in Azua, DR
ML Seasons: 13
Pronunciation: MAY-sa
Nickname: Joe Table

Overall Statistics

	W	L	Pct.	ERA	G	GS	Sv	IP	H	BB	SO	HR	Ratio
2001	3	3	.500	2.34	71	0	42	69.1	65	20	59	4	1.23
Career	61	78	.439	4.30	627	95	180	1166.0	1228	474	787	108	1.46

How Often He Throws Strikes

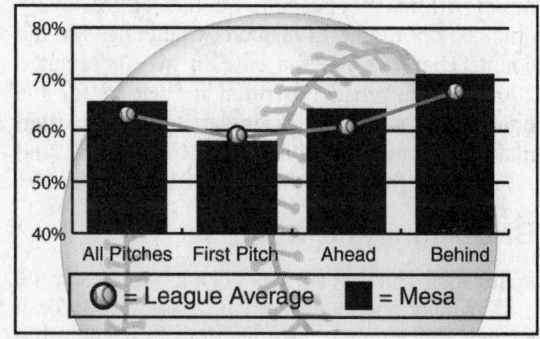

= League Average   ■ = Mesa

2001 Situational Stats

	W	L	ERA	Sv	IP		AB	H	HR	RBI	Avg
Home	2	3	3.48	21	41.1	LHB	127	30	1	8	.236
Road	1	0	0.64	21	28.0	RHB	137	35	3	12	.255
First Half	1	1	3.08	24	38.0	Sc Pos	57	11	1	16	.193
Scnd Half	2	2	1.44	18	31.1	Clutch	186	40	3	11	.215

2001 Rankings (National League)
- 3rd in save opportunities (46)
- 4th in save percentage (91.3) and games finished (59)
- 5th in saves, relief ERA (2.34) and lowest batting average allowed in relief with runners on base (.180)
- 6th in worst first batter efficiency (.339)
- Led the Phillies in games pitched, saves, games finished (59), save opportunities (46), save percentage (91.3), relief innings (69.1), relief ERA (2.34), most strikeouts per nine innings in relief (7.7), and fewest baserunners allowed per nine innings in relief (11.3)

Robert Person

Position: SP
Bats: R **Throws:** R
Ht: 6' 0" **Wt:** 194

Opening Day Age: 32
Born: 10/6/69 in St. Louis, MO
ML Seasons: 7

2001 Season

Veteran Robert Person emerged as the ace of Philadelphia's young pitching staff in the second half of last season. He went 9-2 with a 3.41 ERA after the All-Star break, keeping the club in the pennant race while it was playing under .500 overall. As the season progressed, Person began to get ahead of hitters with more regularity, kept more reasonable pitch counts and lasted deeper into games. His stuff was nasty as usual, making him quite difficult to hit.

Pitching

Person is a straight-ahead, power pitcher who is learning to pitch relatively late in life. His fastball reaches the mid-90s, and his arsenal also includes a sharp slider, splitter, curveball and changeup. He held hitters to a .234 average last season, displaying the best command of his career. When Person places his fastball well early in the count, his slider and splitter can emerge as additional strikeout pitches. He is an extreme flyball pitcher whose mistakes often leave the park. He maintains his velocity deep into games and held opponents to a .125 average after the 105th pitch last season.

Defense & Hitting

Person is just an adequate fielder, as his delivery often leaves him out of position on balls hit back through the middle. He also is quite slow to the plate, giving basestealers opportunities to take liberties. Offensively, he is a low average hitter (.122 career) who takes a massive cut and occasionally hits paydirt (two homers in 2001).

2002 Outlook

Person is being counted upon to carry a 200-inning load for the Phillies. His improved ability to get ahead of hitters and retire them early in the count is encouraging. He might not be an ace pitcher for a playoff caliber club, but plenty of playoff teams would love to have him as their No. 2 or 3 starter. If the Phils can ink an ace or develop Randy Wolf into one, Person in the two-hole could make the team a dangerous postseason force in the next few seasons.

Overall Statistics

	W	L	Pct.	ERA	G	GS	Sv	IP	H	BB	SO	HR	Ratio
2001	15	7	.682	4.19	33	33	0	208.1	179	80	183	34	1.24
Career	47	37	.560	4.51	183	119	8	798.0	723	379	702	116	1.38

How Often He Throws Strikes

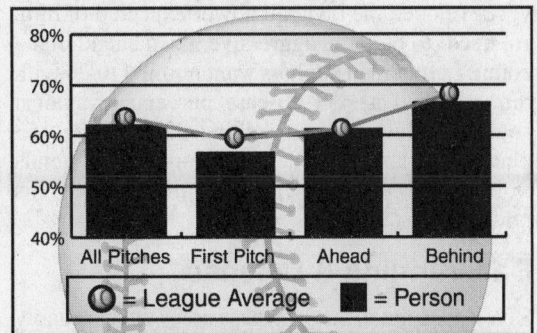

◎ = League Average   ■ = Person

2001 Situational Stats

	W	L	ERA	Sv	IP		AB	H	HR	RBI	Avg
Home	12	2	3.69	0	114.2	LHB	340	80	17	37	.235
Road	3	5	4.80	0	93.2	RHB	425	99	17	50	.233
First Half	6	5	4.92	0	108.0	Sc Pos	152	33	7	52	.217
Scnd Half	9	2	3.41	0	100.1	Clutch	56	12	2	4	.214

2001 Rankings (National League)

- 1st in fielding percentage at pitcher (1.000) and lowest groundball-flyball ratio allowed (0.6)
- 3rd in wild pitches (10)
- 5th in home runs allowed and most home runs allowed per nine innings (1.47)
- Led the Phillies in wins, games started, innings pitched, batters faced (867), home runs allowed, walks allowed, strikeouts, wild pitches (10), pitches thrown (3,315), stolen bases allowed (14), runners caught stealing (6), winning percentage, lowest batting average allowed (.234), lowest on-base percentage allowed (.311), lowest ERA at home, lowest batting average allowed vs. righthanded batters and lowest batting average allowed with runners in scoring position

Scott Rolen

2001 Season

Franchise linchpin Scott Rolen hit only eight homers before the All-Star break, and his lack of production drew the public wrath of manager Larry Bowa and front office member Dallas Green. Rolen exploded with the bat shortly after the Green incident, going 10-for-15 with three homers in one stretch. Hampered by back woes in the past, he carried a heavier workload in 2001, though he was hobbled late in the year by a sprained ankle. His final numbers were in line with career norms.

Hitting

Rolen works the count and hits the ball to all fields with authority. An extreme flyball hitter, he hasn't yet developed the longball power expected of him. He needs to be more aggressive when ahead in the count. Lefthanded pitchers want nothing to do with him—he had a .458 on-base percentage against southpaws last season, walking 32 times in 153 plate appearances. While his batting average tends to be fairly consistent from month to month, his power comes in spurts.

Baserunning & Defense

Rolen adds much more in these areas than arguably any other corner infielder in the game. He is athletic enough to have been recruited as a point guard by Kentucky and Georgia, and complements his plus speed with a nuanced reckless abandon on the bases. Defensively, he is a shortstop playing third base. He compares favorably to Mike Schmidt at a similar stage in development, and gets to balls that Brooks Robinson never dreamed of reaching. Rolen's arm strength is at the top of the scale.

2002 Outlook

Rolen's long-term future is up in the air. He is eligible to become a free agent at the end of 2002, and in November he said he wanted to test the free-agent waters. This makes a trade between now and July 31 a strong possibility. The Phillies will go to the ends of the earth to attempt to persuade him to stay. That's a wise approach, as Rolen is a good bet to become a perennial All-Star over the next decade.

Position: 3B
Bats: R **Throws:** R
Ht: 6' 4" **Wt:** 226

Opening Day Age: 26
Born: 4/4/75 in Jasper, IN
ML Seasons: 6
Pronunciation: ROH-len

Overall Statistics

	G	AB	R	H	D	T	HR	RBI	SB	BB	SO	Avg	OBP	Slg
2001	151	554	96	160	39	1	25	107	16	74	127	.289	.378	.498
Career	744	2750	481	783	186	15	133	493	66	374	646	.285	.375	.508

Where He Hits the Ball

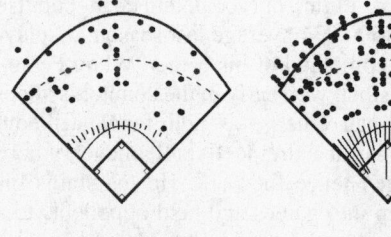

Vs. LHP   **Vs. RHP**

2001 Situational Stats

	AB	H	HR	RBI	Avg			AB	H	HR	RBI	Avg
Home	277	83	12	58	.300		LHP	113	32	4	21	.283
Road	277	77	13	49	.278		RHP	441	128	21	86	.290
First Half	309	86	8	52	.278		Sc Pos	157	55	4	79	.350
Scnd Half	245	74	17	55	.302		Clutch	94	28	6	20	.298

2001 Rankings (National League)

- 2nd in sacrifice flies (12)
- 3rd in fielding percentage at third base (.973)
- 4th in on-base percentage vs. lefthanded pitchers (.458)
- 5th in lowest groundball-flyball ratio (0.7)
- 7th in hit by pitch (13), errors at third base (12) and lowest cleanup slugging percentage (.471)
- Led the Phillies in sacrifice flies (12), hit by pitch (13), batting average with runners in scoring position, batting average with the bases loaded (.400), on-base percentage vs. lefthanded pitchers (.458) and batting average at home

Jimmy Rollins

2001 Season

In most seasons, Jimmy Rollins would have been a prime Rookie of the Year candidate. Instead, Albert Pujols' amazing year allowed Rollins to perform admirably while staying under the opposition's radar. Rollins led the National League in steals, swiping 35 in a row during one stretch. He reached double figures in doubles, triples and homers, and was a steadying force defensively. He avoided major slumps and was Philadelphia's only All-Star.

Hitting

Though small in stature, Rollins can pack a wallop. The switch-hitter lines the ball with authority to all fields, occasionally pouncing on mistake fastballs and pulling the ball for distance. He still has a ways to go to become a quality leadoff man, however. Last year's 1.06 groundball-flyball ratio was much too low, and was largely due to his penchant for chasing fastballs up in the strike zone, resulting in too many strikeouts and lazy popups. Rollins takes more pitches and makes more consistent contact from the right side. He always has been one of the youngest players at each level. It will be interesting to see how good his numbers are once he fully matures and figures out the strike zone.

Baserunning & Defense

Rollins is one of the best—and fastest—baserunners in the game. There is no wasted motion in his stride, making any gapper a potential triple. His basestealing technique is exceedingly advanced for his age. He reads pitchers well, innately senses game situations and gets good jumps. While his defensive range isn't remarkable, his consistency and dependability afield are. Rollins simply doesn't make throwing errors and his tosses usually hit the first baseman squarely in the chest.

2002 Outlook

Rollins is a huge part of the Phillies' future. He's an exciting and productive player who's already good and getting better. He's also the most likely of the Phils' young nucleus to eventually emerge as a galvanizing team leader. Look for Rollins to edge his on-base percentage to around the .350 level in 2002, which only will be scratching the surface of what he eventually can accomplish.

Position: SS
Bats: B **Throws:** R
Ht: 5' 8" **Wt:** 160

Opening Day Age: 23
Born: 11/27/78 in Oakland, CA
ML Seasons: 2

Philadelphia

Overall Statistics

	G	AB	R	H	D	T	HR	RBI	SB	BB	SO	Avg	OBP	Slg
2001	158	656	97	180	29	12	14	54	46	48	108	.274	.323	.419
Career	172	709	102	197	30	13	14	59	49	50	115	.278	.325	.416

Where He Hits the Ball

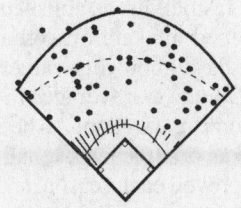
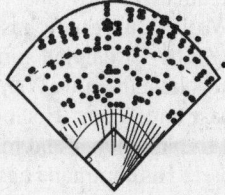

Vs. LHP   **Vs. RHP**

2001 Situational Stats

	AB	H	HR	RBI	Avg		AB	H	HR	RBI	Avg
Home	327	87	8	32	.266	LHP	148	47	3	12	.318
Road	329	93	6	22	.283	RHP	508	133	11	42	.262
First Half	360	98	8	38	.272	Sc Pos	123	32	2	36	.260
Scnd Half	296	82	6	16	.277	Clutch	102	31	2	11	.304

2001 Rankings (National League)

- 1st in at-bats, triples and stolen bases
- 2nd in plate appearances (720)
- 3rd in batting average among rookies, home runs among rookies, RBI among rookies, fielding percentage at shortstop (.979) and steals of third (8)
- Led the Phillies in hits, singles, plate appearances (720), stolen-base percentage (85.2), bunts in play (23), lowest percentage of swings that missed (16.4), highest percentage of swings put into play (48.4), steals of third (8), fewest GDPs per GDP situation (4.6%), batting average vs. lefthanded pitchers, on-base percentage for a leadoff hitter (.346), highest percentage of extra bases taken as a runner (57.1) and batting average with two strikes (.221)

Randy Wolf

2001 Season

Randy Wolf experienced his share of highs and lows last season. He was downright miserable in April (1-4, 6.46) and June (0-5, 7.71). But for the rest of the campaign, he produced a scintillating 9-2 record, compiled a 2.10 ERA, and allowed only 79 hits in 111 innings. He landed on the disabled list for a month beginning in early August due to a sprained left ankle, but was the Phillies best hurler down the stretch, pitching a one-hitter in late September.

Pitching

Wolf features a 90 MPH fastball that he bores in on the hands of righthanded batters, plus a changeup that serves as a second legitimate strikeout pitch against righties once his fastball is established. Wolf's curveball has helped make him lethal against lefthanded hitters throughout his career; he's held them to .209, .227 and .171 averages the past three years. His location is paramount, as he's a flyball pitcher and mistakes often leave the ballpark. His command has improved each season, and his 2001 average of just 15.9 pitches per inning serves notice that he may have many complete games in his near future.

Defense & Hitting

Wolf is a solid athlete who fields his position well and effectively contains the running game. He's allowed just seven stolen bases over the past two seasons. He's a scrappy hitter who regularly sprays line drives to the opposite field and has a .197 career average. The guess here is that he goes yard for the first time in the next year or two.

2002 Outlook

Wolf appears poised for a major breakthrough. Toss out last April and June, and he was as good as any pitcher in the majors. Still only 25 years old, Wolf is farther along the learning curve than most hurlers his age. A 15-17 win season certainly seems within reach, and Wolf seems the best suited of Philadelphia's younger starting pitchers to challenge Robert Person for staff ace status in the near term.

Position: SP
Bats: L **Throws:** L
Ht: 6' 0" **Wt:** 194

Opening Day Age: 25
Born: 8/22/76 in Canoga Park, CA
ML Seasons: 3

Overall Statistics

	W	L	Pct.	ERA	G	GS	Sv	IP	H	BB	SO	HR	Ratio
2001	10	11	.476	3.70	28	25	0	163.0	150	51	152	15	1.23
Career	27	29	.482	4.44	82	78	0	491.0	486	201	428	60	1.40

How Often He Throws Strikes

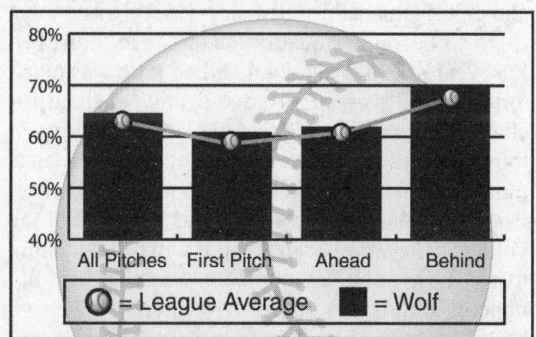

○ = League Average   ■ = Wolf

2001 Situational Stats

	W	L	ERA	Sv	IP		AB	H	HR	RBI	Avg
Home	3	4	3.30	0	62.2	LHB	123	21	2	10	.171
Road	7	7	3.95	0	100.1	RHB	482	129	13	63	.268
First Half	5	9	4.84	0	93.0	Sc Pos	130	34	0	51	.262
Scnd Half	5	2	2.19	0	70.0	Clutch	17	2	0	0	.118

2001 Rankings (National League)

- 2nd in lowest batting average allowed vs. lefthanded batters
- 3rd in shutouts (2) and lowest groundball-flyball ratio allowed (0.8)
- 4th in complete games (4) and most strikeouts per nine innings (8.4)
- Led the Phillies in ERA, losses, complete games (4), shutouts (2), hit batsmen (10), highest strikeout-walk ratio (3.0), lowest slugging percentage allowed (.397), lowest ERA on the road, lowest batting average allowed vs. lefthanded batters, fewest home runs allowed per nine innings (.83) and most strikeouts per nine innings (8.4)

Ricky Bottalico

Position: RP
Bats: L **Throws:** R
Ht: 6' 1" **Wt:** 215

Opening Day Age: 32
Born: 8/26/69 in New Britain, CT
ML Seasons: 8
Pronunciation: bo-TAL-e-koh

Overall Statistics

	W	L	Pct.	ERA	G	GS	Sv	IP	H	BB	SO	HR	Ratio
2001	3	4	.429	3.90	66	0	3	67.0	58	25	57	11	1.24
Career	27	35	.435	4.00	430	0	114	488.2	428	248	459	58	1.38

2001 Situational Stats

	W	L	ERA	Sv	IP		AB	H	HR	RBI	Avg
Home	2	1	3.47	1	36.1	LHB	85	24	3	12	.282
Road	1	3	4.40	2	30.2	RHB	156	34	8	32	.218
First Half	2	4	3.98	2	40.2	Sc Pos	61	14	3	33	.230
Scnd Half	1	0	3.76	1	26.1	Clutch	139	31	7	23	.223

2001 Season

Ricky Bottalico was another controversial addition to last season's Phillies bullpen. But he was surprisingly effective for much of the year. He served as a lights-out setup man in the early going, before a 6.33 ERA between June and August raised his mark closer to his recent career norms.

Pitching, Defense & Hitting

Bottalico is an aggressive hurler who goes after hitters with a low-90s fastball, a sharp slider and a changeup most often used as a waste pitch. While his control was better last season, his location within the zone left much to be desired. He's a flyball pitcher whose mistakes are hit a country mile. Bottalico lacks a true out pitch against lefthanded batters, limiting him to a strict setup role. He has quick reflexes in the field, holds runners well, and is a converted catcher who gets good licks at the plate in his rare opportunities.

2002 Outlook

Although he became a free agent at the end of last season, Bottalico likely showed the Phils enough to be asked back. Performance aside, he's the type of feisty battler who manager Larry Bowa likes. Bottalico likely will compete with Turk Wendell for the primary righty setup slot, and could serve as closer insurance if Jose Mesa falters.

Dave Coggin

Position: SP
Bats: R **Throws:** R
Ht: 6' 4" **Wt:** 195

Opening Day Age: 25
Born: 10/30/76 in Covina, CA
ML Seasons: 2

Overall Statistics

	W	L	Pct.	ERA	G	GS	Sv	IP	H	BB	SO	HR	Ratio
2001	6	7	.462	4.17	17	17	0	95.0	99	39	62	7	1.45
Career	8	7	.533	4.43	22	22	0	122.0	134	51	79	9	1.52

2001 Situational Stats

	W	L	ERA	Sv	IP		AB	H	HR	RBI	Avg
Home	2	3	4.04	0	49.0	LHB	153	42	1	10	.275
Road	4	4	4.30	0	46.0	RHB	211	57	6	29	.270
First Half	1	0	4.63	0	11.2	Sc Pos	90	26	3	33	.289
Scnd Half	5	7	4.10	0	83.1	Clutch	22	8	0	3	.364

2001 Season

David Coggin was called up in late June to replace Amaury Telemaco in the Phillies' rotation. More often than not, Coggin kept the team in the games he pitched. One notable exception was a key September start against the Mets, when he didn't retire a single batter. He also had a maddening habit of allowing hitters to reach base after retiring the first two batters of an inning.

Pitching, Defense & Hitting

Coggin has a diverse four-pitch repertoire, featuring a low-90s fastball, plus a curveball, slider and changeup. Though the pedigreed former top pick has good stuff and solid command, he lacks a true strikeout pitch. A highly recruited quarterback in high school, Coggin is a fine athlete who fields his position well. He also shuts down the running game well for a righthander. He's a terrible hitter who has difficulty simply putting the ball in play.

2002 Outlook

Coggin will be in the mix competing for the fourth or fifth starter role this season. If he could hone one of his pitches into a strikeout offering via mechanical tweaking, his stock would make a major move upwards. He has shown no signs of doing so, however, so he'll likely remain just an adequate innings-eater.

Dennis Cook

Position: RP
Bats: L **Throws:** L
Ht: 6' 3" **Wt:** 190

Opening Day Age: 39
Born: 10/4/62 in
Lamarque, TX
ML Seasons: 14

Overall Statistics

	W	L	Pct.	ERA	G	GS	Sv	IP	H	BB	SO	HR	Ratio
2001	1	1	.500	4.53	62	0	0	45.2	43	14	38	8	1.25
Career	63	45	.583	3.93	628	71	9	987.2	929	380	726	128	1.33

2001 Situational Stats

	W	L	ERA	Sv	IP		AB	H	HR	RBI	Avg
Home	0	1	8.69	0	19.2	LHB	79	17	3	10	.215
Road	1	0	1.38	0	26.0	RHB	95	26	5	12	.274
First Half	1	1	4.88	0	31.1	Sc Pos	50	10	2	13	.200
Scnd Half	0	0	3.77	0	14.1	Clutch	73	21	4	12	.288

2001 Season

Dennis Cook was traded from the Mets to the Phillies in a four-player swap last July 27. He was more effective as a Met, posting a 4.25 ERA before the trade, compared to a 5.59 mark afterward. Cook also had to return home for personal reasons for an extended period in August.

Pitching, Defense & Hitting

Cook is a sinker/slider hurler who has fashioned his ability to retire lefthanders and pitch on multiple consecutive days into a long career. His role has diminished the last couple seasons as his command within the strike zone has wavered. He held lefties to a .215 mark in 2001, but righties touched him for five homers in only 95 at-bats. He was hit hard pitching behind in the count, when opponents could sit on Cook's now-mediocre fastball. He is a fine athlete who fields his position well. He's a .264 career hitter, though he has no hits since 1997.

2002 Outlook

Cook faces an uncertain future with the Phillies. His contract expired after last season, and while the Phils remain a bit short on the left side of their bullpen, they may look for younger, less expensive options. It's very possible that Cook's reasonably successful career as a situational lefty has reached its end.

Rheal Cormier

Position: RP
Bats: L **Throws:** L
Ht: 5'10" **Wt:** 187

Opening Day Age: 34
Born: 4/23/67 in
Moncton, NB, Canada
ML Seasons: 10
Pronunciation: ree-AL
cor-MEE-ay
Nickname: Frenchy

Overall Statistics

	W	L	Pct.	ERA	G	GS	Sv	IP	H	BB	SO	HR	Ratio
2001	5	6	.455	4.21	60	0	1	51.1	49	17	37	5	1.29
Career	48	48	.500	4.18	353	108	1	897.2	955	200	544	89	1.29

2001 Situational Stats

	W	L	ERA	Sv	IP		AB	H	HR	RBI	Avg
Home	2	0	2.77	0	26.0	LHB	68	20	2	12	.294
Road	3	6	5.68	1	25.1	RHB	130	29	3	10	.223
First Half	5	1	2.64	1	30.2	Sc Pos	50	16	0	15	.320
Scnd Half	0	5	6.53	0	20.2	Clutch	117	30	3	16	.256

2001 Season

The Phillies inked Rheal Cormier to a three-year, $8.75 million contract prior to last season. He was effective throughout the first half before physically hitting the wall, posting a 6.53 ERA after the break. That's when he yielded four homers in 78 at-bats, including a couple of walkoff backbreakers.

Pitching, Defense & Hitting

Cormier features a 90-MPH sinking fastball, a slider and a splitter. He needs to locate all his pitches on the low edges of the strike zone to be effective. He's an extreme groundball pitcher—his 2.05 groundball-flyball ratio last season was consistent with his career norms. Though often brought in to retire lefthanded batters, he yielded a .294 average against them in 2001. He doesn't control the running game that well for a southpaw, and has just one at-bat since 1997.

2002 Outlook

The Phillies are financially committed to Cormier for two more seasons and were expected to say goodbye to Dennis Cook and Eddie Oropesa, their other two bullpen lefties. Now 35 years old, Cormier is a fairly durable, though hittable, situational lefty who will throw more than his share of double-play balls. The Phils would like to see him haul a slightly heavier workload in 2002.

Brandon Duckworth

Position: SP
Bats: B **Throws:** R
Ht: 6' 2" **Wt:** 185

Opening Day Age: 26
Born: 1/23/76 in Salt
Lake City, UT
ML Seasons: 1

Overall Statistics

	W	L	Pct.	ERA	G	GS	Sv	IP	H	BB	SO	HR	Ratio
2001	3	2	.600	3.52	11	11	0	69.0	57	29	40	2	1.25
Career	3	2	.600	3.52	11	11	0	69.0	57	29	40	2	1.25

2001 Situational Stats

	W	L	ERA	Sv	IP		AB	H	HR	RBI	Avg
Home	2	0	2.03	0	40.0	LHB	90	23	1	10	.256
Road	1	2	5.59	0	29.0	RHB	154	34	1	15	.221
First Half	0	0	-	0	0.0	Sc Pos	49	17	1	23	.347
Scnd Half	3	2	3.52	0	69.0	Clutch	19	7	0	2	.368

2001 Season

Brandon Duckworth was the Phillies' Minor League Pitcher of the Year in 2000, and he duplicated the feat last season. His 13-2 record and 2.63 ERA was enough to be named Triple-A Player of the Year by *Baseball America*. He kept the Phillies in all but the last game he started after his recall.

Pitching, Defense & Hitting

Duckworth overmatched minor leaguers by mixing a 90-MPH fastball, hard overhand curve and deceptive changeup, throwing all three for quality strikes on any count. He became less of a strikeout pitcher in the majors, when hitters spoiled many of his offerings. His walk rate increased, and he showed a tendency to nibble early in games. He handles the running game exceptionally well for a righthander. Duckworth was erratic defensively, sometimes squeezing the ball too tightly on throws to first. He is a solid hitter, batting .227 as a rookie.

2002 Outlook

While Duckworth looks like a legitimate major league starter, it would be unfair to expect him to match his gaudy minor league numbers. Bear in mind that he's already 26. Look for Duckworth to quickly move toward becoming a reliable seven-inning starter who will win consistently if given decent run support.

Johnny Estrada

Position: C
Bats: B **Throws:** R
Ht: 5'11" **Wt:** 195

Opening Day Age: 25
Born: 6/27/76 in
Hayward, CA
ML Seasons: 1

Overall Statistics

	G	AB	R	H	D	T	HR	RBI	SB	BB	SO	Avg	OBP	Slg
2001	89	298	26	68	15	0	8	37	0	16	32	.228	.273	.359
Career	89	298	26	68	15	0	8	37	0	16	32	.228	.273	.359

2001 Situational Stats

	AB	H	HR	RBI	Avg		AB	H	HR	RBI	Avg
Home	154	35	7	18	.227	LHP	55	12	3	7	.218
Road	144	33	1	19	.229	RHP	243	56	5	30	.230
First Half	145	39	3	22	.269	Sc Pos	64	19	2	30	.297
Scnd Half	153	29	5	15	.190	Clutch	48	9	2	4	.188

2001 Season

Johnny Estrada handled most of the Phillies' starting catcher duties after Mike Lieberthal went down with a knee injury on May 12. After a fast start in the majors, Estrada's averaged steadily dropped, and he ended the season in a 19-for-105 (.181) skid.

Hitting, Baserunning & Defense

Estrada puts the ball in play fairly consistently and has sneaky power. However, he has two major offensive limitations. First, his plate discipline is very poor. Second, his foot speed is utterly lacking, which is compounded by his tendency to hit groundballs. The switch-hitter has a slightly more disciplined approach from the left side and a little more power from the right. His technical defensive skills are fine. Estrada's arm is strong and he moves well behind the plate.

2002 Outlook

The Phillies feel quite comfortable with Estrada as Lieberthal's backup. However, Estrada has a lot of work to do to become more than a career second-stringer. Major league pitchers will continue to expose the massive holes in his offensive game unless he develops a modicum of plate discipline. A reasonably productive .250 average in 200 at-bats should be expected this season.

Vicente Padilla

Position: RP
Bats: R **Throws:** R
Ht: 6' 2" **Wt:** 200

Opening Day Age: 24
Born: 9/27/77 in Chinandega, Nicaragua
ML Seasons: 3
Pronunciation: pa-DEE-ya

Overall Statistics

	W	L	Pct.	ERA	G	GS	Sv	IP	H	BB	SO	HR	Ratio
2001	3	1	.750	4.24	23	0	0	34.0	36	12	29	1	1.41
Career	7	9	.438	4.24	83	0	2	102.0	115	43	80	5	1.55

2001 Situational Stats

	W	L	ERA	Sv	IP		AB	H	HR	RBI	Avg
Home	1	1	3.31	0	16.1	LHB	39	12	1	10	.308
Road	2	0	5.09	0	17.2	RHB	93	24	0	13	.258
First Half	3	1	4.50	0	26.0	Sc Pos	48	17	1	22	.354
Scnd Half	0	0	3.38	0	8.0	Clutch	15	1	0	0	.067

2001 Season

Vicente Padilla began last season as a long reliever with Philadelphia, but was dispatched to Triple-A in early summer. He was used as a starter after the demotion and was a revelation in that role. He went 7-0 with a 2.42 ERA in the minors, giving him a chance for a major league rotation berth in 2002.

Pitching, Defense & Hitting

Padilla features a mid-90s fastball and a power curveball, and mixes in the occasional changeup. When he maintains a consistent release point, his pitches have sharp downward movement. Padilla occasionally will drop down to a sidearm release to catch righties off guard. Development of the changeup is important to his performance versus lefthanded batters. He sometimes gets caught between his two release points, flattening out the movement on his pitches and making him quite hittable. He's not a particularly athletic defender, and can be run on. He handles the bat well.

2002 Outlook

Padilla will be given an opportunity for a starting job in spring training. The keys will be his ability to develop secondary pitches and to keep lefties off balance. A return to setup relief is a reasonable fallback position. Expect Padilla to begin delivering on his promise and to be a key asset in 2002.

Cliff Politte

Position: RP
Bats: R **Throws:** R
Ht: 5'11" **Wt:** 185

Opening Day Age: 28
Born: 2/27/74 in St. Louis, MO
ML Seasons: 4
Pronunciation: po-LEET

Overall Statistics

	W	L	Pct.	ERA	G	GS	Sv	IP	H	BB	SO	HR	Ratio
2001	2	3	.400	2.42	23	0	0	26.0	24	8	23	2	1.23
Career	9	9	.500	4.58	56	16	0	139.2	143	68	110	18	1.51

2001 Situational Stats

	W	L	ERA	Sv	IP		AB	H	HR	RBI	Avg
Home	0	1	1.42	0	12.2	LHB	26	6	0	2	.231
Road	2	2	3.38	0	13.1	RHB	70	18	2	8	.257
First Half	0	0	0.00	0	0.2	Sc Pos	23	5	0	8	.217
Scnd Half	2	3	2.49	0	25.1	Clutch	37	8	2	2	.216

2001 Season

After losing a spring training battle for the fifth starter slot, Cliff Politte opened the regular season on the 60-day disabled list with a stress reaction in his pitching arm. But when he returned to Philadelphia in July, he pitched the best baseball of his brief big league career. He showed surprising power and control in a variety of relief roles and allowed no extra-base hits to lefthanded hitters in 26 at-bats.

Pitching, Defense & Hitting

Politte once was a promising starting pitcher prospect, using four pitches to handle hitters in the low minor leagues. But he has had more success in the majors after narrowing his repertoire and relying more heavily on his slider and low-90s fastball. He is an erratic fielder who made two errors in only 10 chances last season. He's a poor hitter, striking out in 13 of 31 career at-bats and hitting just .097.

2002 Outlook

Politte sits on the fringe of the Phillies' 2002 plans. But his success in limited action last year earns him a chance to make the club this spring. When he's hitting his spots, he's a tough customer for both lefties and righties. Don't be surprised if he makes a stern run for the Phillies' first or second righthanded setup role.

Jose Santiago

Position: RP
Bats: R **Throws:** R
Ht: 6' 3" **Wt:** 215

Opening Day Age: 27
Born: 11/5/74 in
Fajardo, PR
ML Seasons: 5
Pronunciation:
SAWN-tea-ah-go

Overall Statistics

	W	L	Pct.	ERA	G	GS	Sv	IP	H	BB	SO	HR	Ratio
2001	4	6	.400	4.61	73	0	0	91.2	106	22	43	5	1.40
Career	15	16	.484	4.11	158	0	4	214.2	233	64	105	19	1.38

2001 Situational Stats

	W	L	ERA	Sv	IP		AB	H	HR	RBI	Avg
Home	2	4	4.97	0	54.1	LHB	145	51	3	26	.352
Road	2	2	4.10	0	37.1	RHB	218	55	2	29	.252
First Half	2	3	5.65	0	51.0	Sc Pos	112	36	2	48	.321
Scnd Half	2	3	3.32	0	40.2	Clutch	138	41	2	19	.297

2001 Season

The Phillies acquired Jose Santiago from the Royals on June 5 in exchange for Paul Byrd. Santiago quickly became a workhorse in Philadelphia's bullpen. He was quite sharp from the time of the trade through the end of July, notching an 18-2 strikeout-walk ratio, before fading to a 10-11 mark the rest of the way.

Pitching, Defense & Hitting

Santiago features a slider and a straight, low-90s heater that he sinks onto the low edges of the strike zone with some regularity. He can be hit hard when he's not painting the corners. An extreme ground-ball pitcher without a strikeout pitch, he's averaged fewer than 4.5 whiffs per nine innings for his career. Lefties enjoyed great success against him last season (.352 average). He's a decent fielder who handles the running game only adequately. He struck out in all three of his 2001 at-bats.

2002 Outlook

Santiago figures to be a bit player in the Phillies' 2002 bullpen plans. His abilities to take the ball on consecutive days and induce groundballs are his primary strengths. The Phils or any other potential employer would be wise to limit his exposure to lefthanded hitters, however. Santiago lives squarely on the major league fringe.

Turk Wendell

Position: RP
Bats: L **Throws:** R
Ht: 6' 2" **Wt:** 205

Opening Day Age: 34
Born: 5/19/67 in
Pittsfield, MA
ML Seasons: 9
Pronunciation:
WENN-dull

Overall Statistics

	W	L	Pct.	ERA	G	GS	Sv	IP	H	BB	SO	HR	Ratio
2001	4	5	.444	4.43	70	0	1	67.0	63	34	56	12	1.45
Career	33	30	.524	3.90	484	6	32	565.0	508	284	477	63	1.40

2001 Situational Stats

	W	L	ERA	Sv	IP		AB	H	HR	RBI	Avg
Home	4	0	3.89	1	34.2	LHB	95	28	6	17	.295
Road	0	5	5.01	0	32.1	RHB	158	35	6	28	.222
First Half	3	3	4.19	1	43.0	Sc Pos	76	17	2	30	.224
Scnd Half	1	2	4.88	0	24.0	Clutch	88	25	6	20	.284

2001 Season

The Phillies were looking for some veteran leadership when they acquired Turk Wendell and Dennis Cook last July 27. But Wendell was downright awful with Philadelphia, where he posted a 7.47 ERA. He allowed 33 baserunners in 15.2 innings, and on multiple occasions confronted booing fans after being pulled from games. He was shut down for part of September with a tender elbow.

Pitching, Defense & Hitting

Wendell combines an upper-80s fastball with a sharp slider, and must expertly vary speed and location in order to succeed. He always has been a flyball pitcher. In his heyday, he generated plenty of movement on his pitches and would get away with mistakes up in the strike zone. Those days could be over. Wendell's defensive range is solid, but he doesn't control the running game very well. He's absolutely clueless as a batter.

2002 Outlook

Wendell is signed through 2003 and the Phillies likely will give him a full shot at regaining his previous form. In the intermediate term, look for him to retain the ability to pitch on consecutive days, albeit with less success than pre-2001. Phillies fans can take comfort in the fact that Wendell is not as bad as he appeared late last season.

Chris Brock (Pos: RHP, **Age**: 32)

	W	L	Pct.	ERA	G	GS	Sv	IP	H	BB	SO	HR	Ratio
2001	3	0	1.000	4.13	24	0	0	32.2	35	15	26	6	1.53
Career	16	16	.500	4.82	126	30	1	291.0	309	123	206	50	1.48

Even though Brock reportedly had signed a two-year deal with the Phillies in January 2001, the 31-year-old didn't make it through the middle of June before being designated for assignment. He was traded to Baltimore in mid-December. 2002 Outlook: C

Felipe Crespo (Pos: 1B, **Age**: 29, **Bats**: B)

	G	AB	R	H	D	T	HR	RBI	SB	BB	SO	Avg	OBP	Slg
2001	73	107	9	20	4	1	4	15	1	11	34	.187	.266	.355
Career	262	445	46	109	22	4	10	68	9	50	101	.245	.330	.380

The Giants sent Crespo to the Phillies last July in exchange for Wayne Gomes. Crespo had missed a month earlier in the year with a foot injury and his average plummeted in 2001. He can switch-hit and play several different positions. 2002 Outlook: B

Nelson Figueroa (Pos: RHP, **Age**: 27)

	W	L	Pct.	ERA	G	GS	Sv	IP	H	BB	SO	HR	Ratio
2001	4	5	.444	3.94	19	13	0	89.0	95	37	61	8	1.48
Career	4	6	.400	4.47	22	16	0	104.2	112	42	68	12	1.47

While Figueroa isn't an awesome physical specimen, he's enjoyed consistent success in the minors. He figures to compete for at least a bullpen role in 2001, and could even help out at the end of the Phillies' rotation. 2002 Outlook: B

P.J. Forbes (Pos: 2B, **Age**: 34, **Bats**: R)

	G	AB	R	H	D	T	HR	RBI	SB	BB	SO	Avg	OBP	Slg
2001	3	7	1	2	0	0	0	1	0	0	2	.286	.286	.286
Career	12	17	1	3	0	0	0	3	0	0	2	.176	.176	.176

Forbes can be commended for his persistence. Drafted in 1990, he's played 1,265 games in the minors, but only 12 in the bigs. While he had a nice season at Triple-A last year, he's a longshot to stick. 2002 Outlook: D

Brian Hunter (Pos: LF/CF, **Age**: 31, **Bats**: R)

	G	AB	R	H	D	T	HR	RBI	SB	BB	SO	Avg	OBP	Slg
2001	83	145	22	40	6	0	2	16	14	16	25	.276	.344	.359
Career	846	3048	455	805	124	24	22	208	255	221	521	.264	.313	.342

Hunter's playing time has been fading since 1997. He still has great speed and can play any outfield position, but he needs to get on base to warrant playing time. The Astros giving him a two-year deal is a surprise. 2002 Outlook: B

Kevin Jordan (Pos: 1B, **Age**: 32, **Bats**: R)

	G	AB	R	H	D	T	HR	RBI	SB	BB	SO	Avg	OBP	Slg
2001	68	113	9	27	5	0	1	13	0	14	21	.239	.323	.310
Career	560	1409	138	363	70	5	23	175	2	73	181	.258	.297	.363

While Jordan's versatility is an asset, he doesn't possess much power and has batted a meager .184 as a pinch-hitter over the past three years. He might be clinging to the 25th spot on a roster. 2002 Outlook: C

Jason Michaels (Pos: LF, **Age**: 25, **Bats**: R)

	G	AB	R	H	D	T	HR	RBI	SB	BB	SO	Avg	OBP	Slg
2001	6	6	0	1	0	0	0	1	0	0	2	.167	.167	.167
Career	6	6	0	1	0	0	0	1	0	0	2	.167	.167	.167

Michaels was taken by the Phillies in the fourth round of the 1998 draft out of Miami. He's climbed a level each season since. He showed improved power last year, though his strikeout rate rose. 2002 Outlook: C

David Newhan (Pos: 2B, **Age**: 28, **Bats**: L)

	G	AB	R	H	D	T	HR	RBI	SB	BB	SO	Avg	OBP	Slg
2001	7	6	2	2	1	0	0	1	0	1	0	.333	.375	.500
Career	63	86	17	14	3	0	3	9	2	10	24	.163	.247	.302

Newhan began last season on the Phillies' bench, but missed most of the campaign due to a shoulder injury. Philadelphia designated him for assignment in October. 2002 Outlook: C

Doug Nickle (Pos: RHP, **Age**: 27)

	W	L	Pct.	ERA	G	GS	Sv	IP	H	BB	SO	HR	Ratio
2001	0	0	-	0.00	2	0	0	2.0	1	0	1	0	0.50
Career	0	0	-	7.71	6	0	0	4.2	6	2	1	0	1.71

Nickle has a chance to work in a middle relief or setup role. He owns a 93-94 MPH fastball and a knuckle-curve that serves as his out pitch. His ERA was under two at Triple-A last year. 2002 Outlook: C

Eddie Oropesa (Pos: LHP, **Age**: 30)

	W	L	Pct.	ERA	G	GS	Sv	IP	H	BB	SO	HR	Ratio
2001	1	0	1.000	4.74	30	0	0	19.0	16	17	15	1	1.74
Career	1	0	1.000	4.74	30	0	0	19.0	16	17	15	1	1.74

Oropesa finally garnered his first look in the majors, working as a situational southpaw. Lefthanded batters went 5-for-32 (.156) against him, which sparked Arizona to sign him. 2002 Outlook: B

Tomas Perez (Pos: 2B, **Age**: 28, **Bats**: B)

	G	AB	R	H	D	T	HR	RBI	SB	BB	SO	Avg	OBP	Slg
2001	62	135	11	41	7	1	3	19	0	7	22	.304	.347	.437
Career	285	800	74	195	33	9	6	68	3	62	130	.244	.301	.330

Perez enjoyed his best offensive season in the major leagues last year. He can play three infield positions and even some outfield. Since 2000, he's batted more than one hundred points higher versus southpaws. 2002 Outlook: B

Todd Pratt (Pos: C, **Age**: 35, **Bats**: R)

	G	AB	R	H	D	T	HR	RBI	SB	BB	SO	Avg	OBP	Slg
2001	80	173	18	32	8	0	4	11	1	34	61	.185	.327	.301
Career	413	943	117	232	48	2	28	130	3	113	257	.246	.334	.390

The Mets traded Pratt to the Phillies last July, reuniting him with the team for which he debuted. After four years at .275 or better, his average nosedived last season, but could rebound. He became a free agent in early November. 2002 Outlook: B

Nick Punto (Pos: SS, Age: 24, Bats: B)

	G	AB	R	H	D	T	HR	RBI	SB	BB	SO	Avg	OBP	Slg
2001	4	5	0	2	0	0	0	0	0	0	0	.400	.400	.400
Career	4	5	0	2	0	0	0	0	0	0	0	.400	.400	.400

Punto has a decent eye and can steal a base, but his power is minimal—especially for a guy who struck out more than 100 times at Triple-A last year. 2002 Outlook: C

Amaury Telemaco (Pos: RHP, Age: 28)

	W	L	Pct.	ERA	G	GS	Sv	IP	H	BB	SO	HR	Ratio
2001	5	5	.500	5.54	24	14	0	89.1	93	32	59	15	1.40
Career	22	28	.440	5.13	162	56	0	450.2	475	160	295	73	1.41

Telemaco had started 14 games for the Phillies by June 23, but was demoted to the bullpen and then Triple-A. He became a free agent after the season. 2002 Outlook: C

Ed Vosberg (Pos: LHP, Age: 40)

	W	L	Pct.	ERA	G	GS	Sv	IP	H	BB	SO	HR	Ratio
2001	0	0	-	2.84	18	0	0	12.2	8	3	11	0	0.87
Career	10	15	.400	4.26	262	3	13	232.1	247	108	179	21	1.53

A poor man's Jesse Orosco. Now 40, Vosberg has split the past three years between the minors and majors. As long as he's willing to pursue the dream, he might find work as a situational lefty. 2002 Outlook: C

Matt Walbeck (Pos: SS, Age: 32, Bats: B)

	G	AB	R	H	D	T	HR	RBI	SB	BB	SO	Avg	OBP	Slg
2001	1	1	0	1	0	0	0	0	0	0	0	1.000	1.000	1.000
Career	596	1886	200	448	73	4	27	199	13	127	303	.238	.287	.323

After three seasons with the Angels, Walbeck signed minor league deals with the Reds and Phillies last season. But his only at-bat of 2001 didn't occur until September 30. He later became a free agent. 2002 Outlook: C

Turner Ward (Pos: SS, Age: 36, Bats: B)

	G	AB	R	H	D	T	HR	RBI	SB	BB	SO	Avg	OBP	Slg
2001	17	15	1	4	1	0	0	2	0	1	6	.267	.353	.333
Career	626	1548	210	389	73	11	39	219	33	186	247	.251	.332	.388

Ward signed a minor league deal with Philadelphia last offseason and squeaked out 17 games with the Phillies. His 15 at-bats represented the lowest total of his 12-year big league career. 2002 Outlook: C

Philadelphia Phillies Minor League Prospects

Organization Overview:

Things are looking up in Philadelphia, after the Phillies posted their first winning record since 1993 last season. They improved by 21 games over the year before and pushed the Braves for the National League East title. Even better, the Phillies succeeded with a young and talented lineup. Rookie Jimmy Rollins settled in at shortstop and enjoyed an impressive season at age 22. The pitching staff received a shot in the arm when Brandon Duckworth was called up in August, and Dave Coggin also contributed. They helped boost a solid group of other homegrown products that includes Scott Rolen, Pat Burrell and Randy Wolf. It's getting hard to break into the Phillies lineup, but outfielder Marlon Byrd, whom the Phillies consider their No. 1 prospect, possesses exciting ability and could be ready in the near future. The Phils also say Carlos Silva might be like Duckworth and move up to the big leagues by the end of the year.

Taylor Buchholz

Position: P
Bats: R **Throws:** R
Ht: 6' 4" **Wt:** 225
Opening Day Age: 20
Born: 10/13/81 in Lower Merion, PA

Recent Statistics

	W	L	ERA	G	GS	Sv	IP	H	R	BB	SO	HR
2000 R Phillies	2	3	2.25	12	7	0	44.0	46	22	14	41	2
2001 A Lakewood	9	14	3.36	28	26	0	176.2	165	83	57	136	8

Buchholz pitched at a Philadelphia area high school and was plucked in the sixth round of the 2000 draft. After signing for a nice bonus, he debuted that year with an ERA that would have ranked second in the Rookie-level Gulf Coast League if he had enough innings to qualify. The Phillies boosted Buchholz to a full-season Class-A league in 2001. He then led all Phillies minor leaguers with five complete games. Still a teenager, he worked more innings than all but one pitcher in the South Atlantic League. Buchholz throws a plus fastball that reaches 93 MPH, as well a good curveball and developing changeup. The Phillies say he really came on last summer and made significant improvement. He should be at high Class-A this season.

Marlon Byrd

Position: OF
Bats: R **Throws:** R
Ht: 6' 0" **Wt:** 225
Opening Day Age: 24
Born: 8/30/77 in Boynton Beach, FL

Recent Statistics

	G	AB	R	H	D	THR	RBI	SB	BB	SO	Avg
2000 A Piedmont	133	515	104	159	29	13	17	93	41	51	110	.309
2001 AA Reading	137	510	108	161	22	8	28	89	32	52	93	.316
2001 MLE	137	491	87	142	21	6	22	72	22	36	101	.289

When the Phillies selected Byrd out of a Georgia Junior College in 1999, they thought they were drafting a player with an impressive combination of power and speed.

He's justified that perception ever since. He continues to get better, moving up to Double-A in 2001 and nearly producing a 30-30 campaign. He's topped .300 and scored over 100 runs each of the past two seasons. His work ethic draws praise and he's a pretty good center fielder, though his arm is only average. He could still use some work on identifying breaking pitches at the plate and getting better reads in the outfield. The Phillies feel a full year of Triple-A would be beneficial, but Byrd's talent might push the timetable.

Andy Machado

Position: SS
Bats: B **Throws:** R
Ht: 5' 11" **Wt:** 165
Opening Day Age: 21
Born: 1/25/81 in Caracas, VZ

Recent Statistics

	G	AB	R	H	D	THR	RBI	SB	BB	SO	Avg
2000 A Clearwater	117	417	55	102	19	7	1	35	32	54	103	.245
2000 AA Reading	3	11	2	4	1	0	1	2	0	0	4	.364
2001 A Clearwater	82	272	49	71	5	8	5	36	23	31	66	.261
2001 AA Reading	31	101	13	15	2	0	1	8	5	12	25	.149

Machado is a Venezuelan shortstop who signed with the Phillies just before his 17th birthday in 1998. Blessed with great range and hands and a plus arm, he probably could play defense in the big leagues right now. His offense, however, isn't as advanced. After reaching Double-A as a teenager in 2000, Machado was back in the Florida State League last year, where he continued to flash his plus speed. He again stole over 20 bases, and added more triples than doubles. But he appeared overmatched when he finished the campaign at Reading. The Phillies would like him to get stronger, and Machado is expected to begin 2002 at Double-A.

Brett Myers

Position: P
Bats: R **Throws:** R
Ht: 6' 4" **Wt:** 215
Opening Day Age: 21
Born: 8/17/80 in Jacksonville, FL

Recent Statistics

	W	L	ERA	G	GS	Sv	IP	H	R	BB	SO	HR
2000 A Piedmont	13	7	3.18	27	27	0	175.1	165	78	69	140	7
2001 AA Reading	13	4	3.87	26	23	0	156.0	156	71	43	130	21

The Phillies selected Myers with the 12th overall pick in 1999 out of a Jacksonville high school. He's done nothing but win as a pro. After posting 13 victories in the South Atlantic League in 2000, Myers was bumped up to Double-A last year, where he again won 13 times. He's made great strides and displays good maturity, control and command. His fastball is 92-93 MPH but can reach 95-96 on occasion. His curveball also is a plus pitch, while his changeup is close at times to being another effective offering. Having conquered Reading, Myers' next challenge figures to be Triple-A. He might be knocking on the major league door before turning 22 in August.

Carlos Silva

Position: P

Opening Day Age: 22

Bats: R **Throws:** R

Born: 4/23/79 in Bolivar, VZ

Ht: 6' 4" **Wt:** 225

Recent Statistics

	W	L	ERA	G	GS	Sv	IP	H	R	BB	SO	HR
2000 A Clearwater	8	13	3.57	26	24	0	176.1	229	99	26	82	7
2001 AA Reading	15	8	3.90	28	28	0	180.0	197	85	27	100	20

Like Machado, Silva was born in Venezuela and signed with the Phillies as a 16-year-old. Silva competed at Double-A as a 22-year-old last season and led the Eastern League with 15 wins. He isn't a big strikeout sort of pitcher but instead features a 93-94 MPH fastball with sinking life. The heater can touch 95-96 and is joined in Silva's repertoire by an improving slider and curveball and developing changeup. He has proven durable, averaging over 170 innings the past three years. He rarely issues a free pass, but the Phillies would like him to improve his command. They also feel he needs to improve the consistency of his breaking ball.

Reggie Taylor

Position: OF

Opening Day Age: 25

Bats: L **Throws:** R

Born: 1/12/77 in Newberry, SC

Ht: 6' 1" **Wt:** 178

Recent Statistics

	G	AB	R	H	D	T	HR	RBI	SB	BB	SO	Avg
2001 AAA Scranton-WB	111	464	56	122	20	9	7	50	31	24	94	.263
2001 NL Philadelphia	5	7	1	0	0	0	0	0	0	1	1	.000
2001 MLE	111	457	50	115	20	7	6	45	24	22	100	.252

Taylor hasn't developed as many might have hoped after he was selected with the 14th overall pick in 1995. Since then, he's spent a couple seasons at almost every level, including the past two years at Triple-A. Part of the problem has been injuries, including broken hands and a sprained ankle. But he's also had trouble gaining consistency. Taylor pulls off the ball and sometimes has difficulty identifying offspeed pitches. However, he still possesses great tools and has stolen at least 22 bases every year since 1996. He has good range and the Phillies say he can play center field with anybody. After turning 25 this January, the time may have come to lower expectations. But Taylor might have value as an extra outfielder and defensive replacement.

Chase Utley

Position: 2B

Opening Day Age: 23

Bats: L **Throws:** R

Born: 12/17/78 in Pasadena, CA

Ht: 6' 1" **Wt:** 185

Recent Statistics

	G	AB	R	H	D	T	HR	RBI	SB	BB	SO	Avg
2000 A Batavia	40	153	21	47	13	1	2	22	5	18	23	.307
2001 A Clearwater	122	467	65	120	25	2	16	59	19	37	88	.257

Utley surpassed .300 in three seasons at UCLA, topping out at .382 in 2000. The Phillies chose him with the 15th overall pick that year, and he remained a .300 hitter in his professional debut in the New York-Penn League. While the average dipped a bit when he jumped to the Florida State League last season, Utley still projects as a second baseman who can hit in the middle of the order and drive in runs. He shared the team lead with 16 home runs at Clearwater. He has gap power but must avoid getting pull-conscious. His speed is average, though he can steal a base. He has made good progress defensively and should be able to stay at second base as he moves up the ladder. He figures to begin 2002 in Double-A.

Eric Valent

Position: OF

Opening Day Age: 24

Bats: L **Throws:** L

Born: 4/4/77 in La Mirada, CA

Ht: 6' 0" **Wt:** 191

Recent Statistics

	G	AB	R	H	D	T	HR	RBI	SB	BB	SO	Avg
2001 AAA Scranton-WB	117	448	65	122	30	2	21	78	0	49	105	.272
2001 NL Philadelphia	22	41	3	4	2	0	0	1	0	4	11	.098
2001 MLE	117	442	58	116	30	1	19	70	0	45	112	.262

Valent played with Chase Utley for a season at UCLA and will be remembered as the player Philadelphia drafted with the supplemental pick obtained for failing to sign J.D. Drew. Valent led the Pacific 10 with 30 homers in 1998, and he's hit at least 20 each of the past three years in the minors. He's been a pull hitter but now will go to left-center with the pitch. He has a good arm with enough instincts to play the outfield, and gained some experience at first base last season. He is not a basestealer, going the entire 2001 season without a swipe. Valent is close to being ready, but his window of opportunity may not be very good on the Phillies, considering their outfield is pretty set. He certainly didn't make a great impression during his trials with the team last year, going hitless in his final 26 major league at-bats.

Others to Watch

Righthander **Brad Baisley** (22) is listed at 6-foot-9, and the Phillies say he sometimes has gotten out of whack with his delivery. Picked in the second round in 1998, Baisley has a good breaking ball and throws his fastball 91-92 MPH. . . Righty **Yoel Hernandez** (19) is another guy the Phillies signed out of Venezuela. He worked in the South Atlantic League at age 19 last season. . . The Phillies acquired righthander **Eric Junge** (25) in the package for Omar Daal in November. Junge was an 11th-round selection in 1999 and went 10-11 at Double-A last season. . . After ranking second in the Sally League with a 2.59 ERA in 2000, righthander **Ryan Madson** (21) didn't have the same kind of success in high Class-A last year. He was a No. 9 pick in 1998. . . Righthander **Franklin Nunez** (25) averaged more than a strikeout per inning at Double-A Reading. A native of the Dominican Republic, he split his time between starting and working out of the bullpen. . . **Jorge Padilla** (22) is gaining power and has a right fielder's arm. The Phillies say his ceiling is high and that he's a middle-of-the-order hitter.

PNC Park

Offense

When designing and constructing PNC Park, the Pirates wanted the ballpark to be fair. That's how it turned out in its inaugural season, as scoring there was in the average range. However, the park proved to play a little bit bigger than expected and was among the National League's most difficult places in which to homer. PNC Park favors lefthanded hitters, with a short 320-foot porch down the right field line. Conversely, long drives often die in left field and particularly in left-center.

Defense

Many visiting players complained early in the season about the PNC Park infield. They felt the grass was too high and the dirt was too hard. While it is only 320 feet down the right field line and 325 to left, the fence juts out in a hurry in both gaps. That places a premium on having a center fielder who can cover ground.

Who It Helps the Most

The park definitely tilts in favor of lefthanders. It is tailor made for Pirates left fielder Brian Giles, who hit .338 at home last year. Utility player Rob Mackowiak also had a huge home/road split, batting .319 at home and .204 on the road. The high grass and deep dimensions in left-center helped southpaw Jimmy Anderson, whose ERA was nearly two runs lower at home.

Who It Hurts the Most

Righthanded hitters struggle at PNC Park. Catcher Jason Kendall insisted the new park cost him at least 10 home runs, as he hit three at home and seven on the road. Third baseman Aramis Ramirez hit .325 on the road as opposed to .275 at home.

Rookies & Newcomers

The Pirates' top three prospects are righthanded—catcher J.R. House and pitchers Bobby Bradley and John VanBenschoten. How PNC Park affects them remains to be seen. However, the Pirates are definitely leaning toward the left when taking players in the amateur draft or trading for prospects.

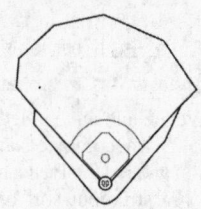

Dimensions: LF-325, LCF-389, CF-399, RCF-375, RF-320

Capacity: 37,898

Elevation: 730 feet

Surface: Grass

Foul Territory: Small

Park Factors

2001 Season

| | Home Games | | | Away Games | | | |
	Pirates	Opp	Total	Pirates	Opp	Total	Index
G	75	75	150	72	72	144	—
Avg	.257	.265	.261	.233	.281	.257	102
AB	2489	2626	5115	2408	2363	4771	103
R	322	400	722	263	391	654	106
H	639	697	1336	562	663	1225	105
2B	133	149	282	103	139	242	109
3B	10	12	22	12	19	31	66
HR	70	73	143	76	79	155	86
BB	215	265	480	208	244	452	99
SO	467	432	899	550	399	949	88
E	69	67	136	54	55	109	120
E-Infield	53	59	112	45	47	92	117
LHB-Avg	.261	.279	.270	.235	.309	.271	100
LHB-HR	29	33	62	25	30	55	100
RHB-Avg	.254	.257	.256	.232	.265	.249	103
RHB-HR	41	40	81	51	49	100	78

1999-2000 (Three Rivers Stadium)

| | Home Games | | | Away Games | | | |
	Pirates	Opp	Total	Pirates	Opp	Total	Index
G	147	147	294	146	146	292	—
Avg	.261	.259	.260	.261	.278	.269	97
AB	4889	5106	9995	5128	4947	10075	99
R	715	731	1446	687	779	1466	98
H	1277	1325	2602	1338	1377	2715	95
2B	292	280	572	254	281	535	108
3B	38	25	63	28	37	65	98
HR	152	152	304	140	139	279	110
BB	509	588	1097	526	629	1155	96
SO	1013	1051	2064	1021	901	1922	108
E	120	123	243	133	95	228	106
E-Infield	102	101	203	108	76	184	110
LHB-Avg	.276	.270	.273	.266	.300	.282	97
LHB-HR	80	64	144	69	61	130	115
RHB-Avg	.251	.253	.252	.257	.266	.261	97
RHB-HR	72	88	160	71	78	149	106

2001 Rankings (National League)

- Third-highest error factor
- Second-lowest home-run factor
- Second-lowest strikeout factor
- Third-lowest triple factor
- Third-lowest RHB home-run factor

Lloyd McClendon

2001 Season

After four years as the Pirates' hitting coach, Lloyd McClendon took over managing duties from the fired Gene Lamont prior to last season . The Pirates moved into PNC Park, their new multi-million dollar home, with great optimism. But their 62-100 record tied Tampa Bay for the worst mark in the major leagues. The Pirates had 17 different players go on the disabled list and couldn't recover from a 19-41 start that cost General Manager Cam Bonifay his job. However, the fiery McClendon kept his team playing hard until the end.

Offense

McClendon is hamstrung by the fact that the Pirates possess neither great power nor speed. He tried to force the issue on the bases last year with plenty of hit-and-run plays in an effort to generate offense. However, the Pirates too often ran themselves into outs. McClendon was inconsistent with his use of young players, allowing Jack Wilson to bat .223 but limiting the use of power-hitting rookie Craig Wilson.

Pitching & Defense

McClendon believes the Pirates' best hope of returning to prominence is through pitching and defense. He did a good job of handling Pittsburgh's young pitching staff last year. He was extremely cognizant of pitch counts and always erred on the side of caution in removing his starters. That was a welcome change from previous regimes that seemed intent on burning out every young hurler who came to the majors. McClendon stresses defense and will sacrifice offense to get a better glove man in the lineup.

2002 Outlook

It is hard to imagine the Pirates getting significantly better this season, as the farm system is barren at the upper levels and owner Kevin McClatchy isn't willing to significantly increase the $52 million payroll. McClendon has two years left on his three-year contract and McClatchy is solidly behind him. However, if the Pirates get off to another bad start, new general manager Dave Littlefield could get an itch to bring in his own manager.

Born: 1/11/59 in Gary, IN

Playing Experience: 1987-1994, Cin, ChC, Pit

Managerial Experience: 1 season

Manager Statistics

Year	Team, Lg	W	L	Pct	GB	Finish
2001	Pittsburgh, NL	62	100	.383	31.0	6th Central
1 Season		62	100	.383	—	—

2001 Starting Pitchers by Days Rest

	<=3	4	5	6+
Pirates Starts	0	75	55	21
Pirates ERA	—	5.04	5.63	5.55
NL Avg Starts	1	80	47	24
NL ERA	5.03	4.43	4.53	4.28

2001 Situational Stats

	Lloyd McClendon	NL Average
Hit & Run Success %	28.4	35.1
Stolen Base Success %	56.0	66.5
Platoon Pct.	51.4	51.5
Defensive Subs	32	20
High-Pitch Outings	2	7
Quick/Slow Hooks	27/19	19/14
Sacrifice Attempts	83	87

2001 Rankings (National League)

- 1st in hit-and-run attempts (148) and quick hooks
- 2nd in slow hooks
- 3rd in pitchouts (52), intentional walks (49) and defensive substitutions

Jimmy Anderson

2001 Season

Jimmy Anderson's 17 losses were the most by a Pirates pitcher since Jose DeLeon went 2-19 in 1985. However, Anderson prevented the season from being a total disaster by going 3-1 with a 2.49 ERA in his last six starts. Until then, he was 6-16 and on course to become the major league's first 20-game loser since Oakland's Brian Kingman in 1980.

Pitching

Anderson lacks overpowering stuff and has to be fine in order to be effective. His best pitch is a sinker that usually resides in the mid-80s. When it has good movement, it produces plenty of ground-ball outs on PNC Park's high grass. Although Anderson also throws a decent slider, the key for him is having command of his changeup, since it provides something to keep hitters off balance. Anderson has a tendency to get into more than his share of jams because he often lacks concentration. He then has a hard time extracting himself from tough situations because he lacks a strikeout pitch.

Defense & Hitting

For someone with a roly-poly physique, Anderson gets off the mound well but tends to rush his throws. Although he has the advantage of being lefthanded, he is absolutely horrible at holding men on base and teams continually put runners in motion. The Pirates have tried to speed up Anderson's delivery, but he has never taken well to the changes. He can handle the bat and drop down a bunt.

2002 Outlook

Anderson's strong finish last season will give him another shot at the starting rotation. While Pirates manager Lloyd McClendon thinks Anderson can be something special, few others share that opinion. Anderson seems to be no better than a No. 4 starter and someone who can fill out a rotation on a second-division club. He must make progress this season or he'll be gone, since he'll become eligible for arbitration at the end of the year.

Position: SP
Bats: L **Throws:** L
Ht: 6' 1" **Wt:** 207

Opening Day Age: 26
Born: 1/22/76 in Portsmouth, VA
ML Seasons: 3

Overall Statistics

	W	L	Pct.	ERA	G	GS	Sv	IP	H	BB	SO	HR	Ratio
2001	9	17	.346	5.10	34	34	0	206.1	232	83	89	15	1.53
Career	16	29	.356	5.07	74	64	0	379.2	426	157	175	30	1.54

How Often He Throws Strikes

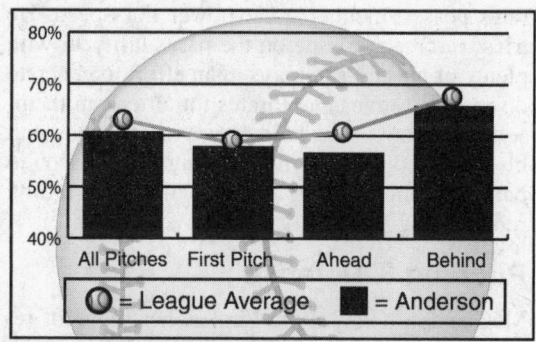

2001 Situational Stats

	W	L	ERA	Sv	IP		AB	H	HR	RBI	Avg
Home	6	8	4.26	0	118.1	LHB	142	46	4	23	.324
Road	3	9	6.24	0	88.0	RHB	666	186	11	83	.279
First Half	4	8	5.03	0	107.1	Sc Pos	214	60	4	86	.280
Scnd Half	5	9	5.18	0	99.0	Clutch	36	14	0	2	.389

2001 Rankings (National League)

- 1st in stolen bases allowed (33), GDPs induced (29), highest groundball-flyball ratio allowed (2.5), lowest strikeout-walk ratio (1.1), highest stolen-base percentage allowed (89.2) and highest ERA on the road
- 2nd in losses, pickoff throws (178) and fewest strikeouts per nine innings (3.9)
- Led the Pirates in losses, games started, hits allowed, batters faced (922), walks allowed, hit batsmen (11), pitches thrown (3,130), pickoff throws (178), lowest slugging percentage allowed (.402), most run support per nine innings (4.1), fewest home runs allowed per nine innings (.65) and most GDPs induced per nine innings (1.3)

Derek Bell

Position: RF
Bats: R **Throws:** R
Ht: 6' 2" **Wt:** 215

Opening Day Age: 33
Born: 12/11/68 in
Tampa, FL
ML Seasons: 11

2001 Season

In December of 2000, the Pirates signed free agent Derek Bell to a two-year, $9.75 million contract. The deal raised some eyebrows, since he had hit just .187 for the Mets after the All-Star break that season. As many predicted, Bell turned out to be a bust in 2001. He battled a strained left knee and strained right hamstring, landed on the disabled list twice, and didn't play for Pittsburgh after July 3. Bell went to Triple-A for a rehabilitation assignment in late August, hit a homer in his last game, and then mysteriously was never activated.

Hitting

Bell's bat has slowed to the point where he can't even catch up to mediocre fastballs, especially high in the strike zone. He's always had a weakness with breaking balls low and away, and pitchers exploited that flaw more than ever last year. Bell is a notorious streak hitter who sprays line drives to all fields when hot. Even in an awful season, he showed his ability to have a hot stretch by batting .310 with a .524 on-base percentage in his last 10 Pirates games.

Baserunning & Defense

Bell plays the game hard and is aggressive on the bases. Leg injuries have robbed him of speed and he now must pick his spots to take chances. Bell is an adequate corner outfielder with enough arm to play right field. He tends to be better going back on balls than coming in, and is a step slow when getting to shots in the gap.

2002 Outlook

With a .179 batting average since August 1, 2000, Bell looks like a player near the end of the line. The Pirates owe him $4 million this year and a $750,000 buyout in 2003, as they won't exercise their $5 million option for that season. That's a lot of money to eat for a small-market club. But the Pirates have little choice, since no one is likely to trade for him.

Overall Statistics

	G	AB	R	H	D	T	HR	RBI	SB	BB	SO	Avg	OBP	Slg
2001	46	156	14	27	3	0	5	13	0	25	38	.173	.287	.288
Career	1210	4578	642	1262	232	15	134	668	170	377	955	.276	.336	.421

Where He Hits the Ball

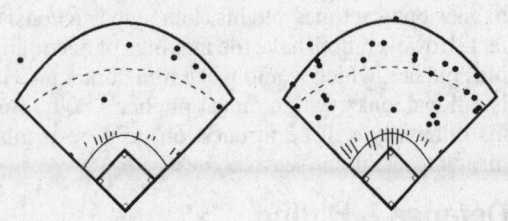

Vs. LHP   **Vs. RHP**

2001 Situational Stats

	AB	H	HR	RBI	Avg		AB	H	HR	RBI	Avg
Home	72	12	4	9	.167	LHP	30	5	1	5	.167
Road	84	15	1	4	.179	RHP	126	22	4	8	.175
First Half	156	27	5	13	.173	Sc Pos	38	6	1	8	.158
Scnd Half	0	0	0	0	-	Clutch	22	4	0	1	.182

2001 Rankings (National League)

- 2nd in lowest batting average on a 3-2 count (.048)

Pittsburgh

Kris Benson

Position: SP
Bats: R **Throws:** R
Ht: 6' 4" **Wt:** 200

Opening Day Age: 27
Born: 11/7/74 in Superior, WI
ML Seasons: 2

2001 Season

After pitching a combined five shutout innings in his first two starts of the exhibition season last March, Kris Benson seemed poised for a breakthrough year. However, he hurt his elbow March 10 while working against Minnesota in a Grapefruit League game. He never pitched in a regular season contest and eventually underwent reconstructive elbow surgery on May 22.

Pitching

Benson has the stuff to be a No. 1 starter, provided he recovers from last year's surgery. He throws hard, as his fastball routinely hits 95 MPH with outstanding movement. He also has a good hard slider with a sharp break. Benson's curveball tends to get sloppy at times and his changeup is inconsistent. However, both have the makings of becoming plus pitches, which would make him dominant. He is tall and lanky with an ideal pitcher's body. But his durability will be in question until he begins throwing again this season.

Defense & Hitting

Benson is adequate defensively, though he can be a tad slow coming off the mound to charge bunts or cover first base. He pays close attention to runners and has a fairly deceptive move to first. While Benson isn't a great hitter, he also isn't a total zero. He usually can get a bunt down when needed.

2002 Outlook

Benson obviously is a question mark coming into the 2002 campaign. He was able to start playing catch by the end of last season and was slated to throw off a mound in December. The Pirates felt his rehabilitation was ahead of schedule and he had no setbacks going into the winter. If all goes according to plan, Benson will go on a minor league injury rehabilitation assignment in April and join the Pirates' rotation sometime in early May. However, keep in mind that Benson had serious surgery. It wouldn't be fair to expect him to totally regain his form until 2003.

Overall Statistics

	W	L	Pct.	ERA	G	GS	Sv	IP	H	BB	SO	HR	Ratio
2001					Did Not Play								
Career	21	26	.447	3.95	63	63	0	414.1	390	169	323	40	1.35

How Often He Throws Strikes

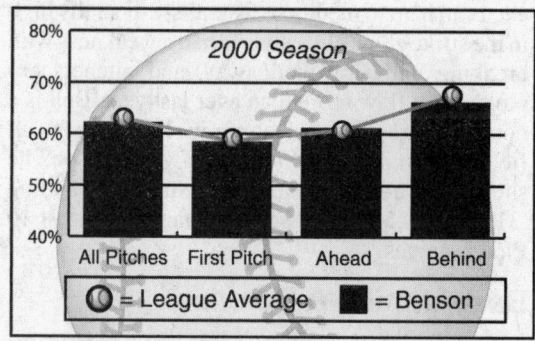

2000 Season

◯ = League Average ■ = Benson

2001 Situational Stats

	W	L	ERA	Sv	IP		AB	H	HR	RBI	Avg
Home	—	—	—	—	—	LHB	—	—	—	—	—
Road	—	—	—	—	—	RHB	—	—	—	—	—
First Half	—	—	—	—	—	Sc Pos	—	—	—	—	—
Scnd Half	—	—	—	—	—	Clutch	—	—	—	—	—

2001 Rankings (National League)

- Did not rank near the top or bottom in any category

Adrian Brown

2001 Season

Adrian Brown began last season as the Pirates' center fielder and leadoff hitter. But a torn labrum in his right shoulder limited him to only eight games. He went on the disabled list retroactive to April 12 and then had arthroscopic surgery in mid-May. Brown made injury rehabilitation assignments to Class-A Lynchburg and short-season Williamsport in late August and early September. However, his shoulder still was too painful to allow him to play in the major leagues.

Hitting

Brown has made great strides since arriving in the major leagues in 1997. He no longer is completely fooled by breaking balls. While he primarily remains a fastball hitter, Brown now can fight off curveballs and sliders better, and no longer is befuddled by changeups. He's willing to do the things necessary for a leadoff man to succeed, as he'll take pitches, hit the ball on the ground and bunt. He is a natural righthanded hitter, but has improved greatly from the left side in recent years. Earlier in his career, the Pirates nearly had Brown abandon switch-hitting.

Baserunning & Defense

Brown has good speed and utilizes it well. He picks his spots to steal and always is looking to go from first to third or second to home on singles, and from first to home on doubles. Brown plays all three outfield positions well. He is a natural center fielder and his range is above average. However, his strong arm enables him to play right field if needed.

2002 Outlook

Despite setbacks in his rehab last year, Brown is expected to be 100 percent when spring training begins. He won't automatically be given back his center-field job, since the Pirates also like the potential of Gary Matthews Jr., who was claimed on waivers from the Chicago Cubs last August. Remember, however, that Brown has beaten long odds throughout his career, considering he was the Pirates' 48th-round pick in the 1992 amateur draft.

Position: CF
Bats: B **Throws:** R
Ht: 6' 0" **Wt:** 185

Opening Day Age: 28
Born: 2/7/74 in McComb, MS
ML Seasons: 5

Overall Statistics

	G	AB	R	H	D	T	HR	RBI	SB	BB	SO	Avg	OBP	Slg
2001	8	31	3	6	0	0	1	2	2	3	3	.194	.265	.290
Career	317	864	138	235	33	6	10	62	32	87	112	.272	.341	.359

Where He Hits the Ball

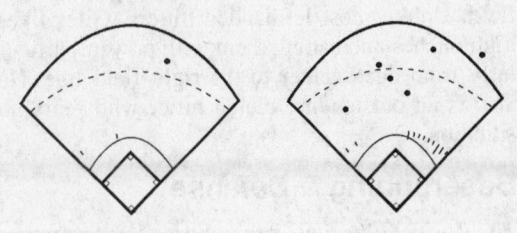

Vs. LHP   **Vs. RHP**

2001 Situational Stats

	AB	H	HR	RBI	Avg		AB	H	HR	RBI	Avg
Home	8	1	0	0	.125	LHP	3	0	0	0	.000
Road	23	5	1	2	.217	RHP	28	6	1	2	.214
First Half	31	6	1	2	.194	Sc Pos	6	1	1	2	.167
Scnd Half	0	0	0	0	-	Clutch	4	2	0	0	.500

2001 Rankings (National League)

- Did not rank near the top or bottom in any category

Brian Giles

2001 Season

Brian Giles produced another fine season for the Pirates, playing in his second straight All-Star Game and again proving he is one of the top offensive players in the National League. He established career highs in games, hits, at-bats, runs scored and stolen bases while tying career highs in doubles and triples. Giles' 116 runs were the most by a Pirate since Ralph Kiner scored 124 times in 1951.

Hitting

Giles is one of the best all-around hitters in the game. He can hit for both power and average while drawing a good number of walks. He has a compact stroke with no glaring holes. He can turn on the inside pitch and take the outside pitch to right field. Unlike most lefthanded hitters, Giles likes high pitches and can hit them with power, particularly from dead center to the right field line. He also is an outstanding clutch hitter who fears no situation.

Baserunning & Defense

The stocky Giles runs with a short, choppy motion that looks like something out of an old black-and-white film. However, he moves well, has good instincts and will steal the occasional base. He has wound up playing center field in parts of the past five years because of injuries and ineffectiveness by others. Giles has done an adequate job in center, though his best spot is left field, where his average range and arm are more than acceptable.

2002 Outlook

Acquiring Giles from Cleveland in a trade for Ricardo Rincon following the 1998 season was the best move ever made by former Pirates general manager Cam Bonifay. Giles has blossomed into a star and is the Pirates' best player. While Pittsburgh has a lot of work to do in order to become competitive again, Giles is someone to build around. They have him signed through 2005 and will count on him to help raise the franchise out of the ashes.

Position: LF/CF
Bats: L **Throws:** L
Ht: 5'10" **Wt:** 200

Opening Day Age: 31
Born: 1/20/71 in El Cajon, CA
ML Seasons: 7
Pronunciation: JYLES

Overall Statistics

	G	AB	R	H	D	T	HR	RBI	SB	BB	SO	Avg	OBP	Slg
2001	160	576	116	178	37	7	37	95	13	90	67	.309	.404	.590
Career	756	2513	486	761	155	21	150	490	51	454	355	.303	.409	.560

Where He Hits the Ball

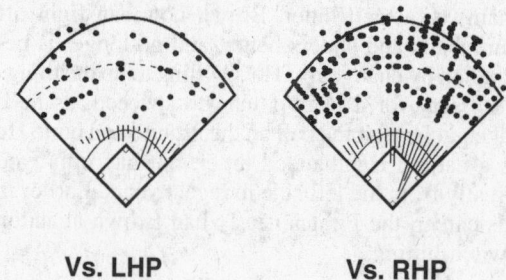

Vs. LHP **Vs. RHP**

2001 Situational Stats

	AB	H	HR	RBI	Avg		AB	H	HR	RBI	Avg
Home	296	100	18	52	.338	LHP	135	36	4	16	.267
Road	280	78	19	43	.279	RHP	441	142	33	79	.322
First Half	325	109	21	55	.335	Sc Pos	135	42	10	63	.311
Scnd Half	251	69	16	40	.275	Clutch	67	24	6	13	.358

2001 Rankings (National League)

- 1st in lowest fielding percentage in left field (.967)
- Led the Pirates in batting average, home runs, runs scored, triples, total bases (340), walks, intentional walks (14), times on base (272), plate appearances (674), games played, slugging percentage, on-base percentage, HR frequency (15.6 ABs per HR), lowest percentage of swings that missed (9.4), batting average in the clutch, batting average vs. righthanded pitchers, cleanup slugging percentage (.584), slugging percentage vs. righthanded pitchers (.642), on-base percentage vs. righthanded pitchers (.419), batting average at home, batting average on a 3-2 count (.290) and batting average with two strikes (.230)

Jason Kendall

2001 Season

Jason Kendall's 2001 batting average was the worst of his six years in the major leagues, 48 points below his career mark. He tore a ligament in his left thumb on April 9 in the opener at PNC Park, but he played through the injury all year and set a personal high with 157 games. After playing nothing but catcher in his first five seasons, Kendall made 27 starts in the outfield last year.

Hitting

The thumb injury had an obvious affect on Kendall's hitting, as he wasn't able to spray line drives to all fields like usual. He is at his best when he uses the whole field. Perhaps trying to justify the six-year, $60 million contract extension he signed in November 2000, Kendall tried to pull too many pitches out of the park last year. He has spent his career shuttling between the top and middle of the order. His talents are best suited for leadoff, though his lack of plate discipline in 2001 is a concern.

Baserunning & Defense

Kendall, one of the fastest catchers in baseball history, lost half a step last season. He was thrown out more times than he succeeded during stolen-base attempts. That stat perhaps measures the residual effect of Kendall's severe ankle dislocation in 1999. His defense also slipped as he had trouble blocking errant pitches. His throwing is below average and he falls into the bad habit of wrapping his hand behind his head. He is shaky in the outfield, but that's normal for a novice at the position.

2002 Outlook

Kendall's drop-off in 2001 likely was an aberration, since he is too young to go into decline. The thumb injury required reconstructive surgery just days after the regular season was over, but he is expected to make a full recovery and should be at full speed in time for spring training. Pittsburgh will leave him behind the plate in 2002, though the organization has eventual designs on switching him to second base or center field because of his fine athletic ability. The Pirates would love to see Kendall make the conversion to second like Craig Biggio. However, Kendall is cool to that idea.

Position: C/LF/RF
Bats: R **Throws:** R
Ht: 6' 0" **Wt:** 195

Opening Day Age: 27
Born: 6/26/74 in San Diego, CA
ML Seasons: 6

Overall Statistics

	G	AB	R	H	D	T	HR	RBI	SB	BB	SO	Avg	OBP	Slg
2001	157	606	84	161	22	2	10	53	13	44	48	.266	.335	.358
Career	810	2900	477	881	170	23	55	318	106	296	293	.304	.389	.435

Where He Hits the Ball

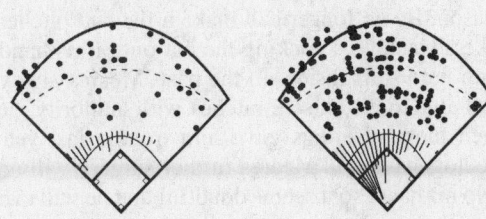

Vs. LHP   **Vs. RHP**

2001 Situational Stats

	AB	H	HR	RBI	Avg		AB	H	HR	RBI	Avg
Home	293	87	3	28	.297	LHP	111	31	4	15	.279
Road	313	74	7	25	.236	RHP	495	130	6	38	.263
First Half	339	87	4	32	.257	Sc Pos	110	28	2	41	.255
Scnd Half	267	74	6	21	.277	Clutch	78	20	1	9	.256

2001 Rankings (National League)

- 1st in errors at catcher (12), lowest stolen-base percentage (48.1) and lowest fielding percentage at catcher (.985)
- 2nd in lowest percentage of swings on the first pitch (13.1)
- 3rd in hit by pitch (20)
- Led the Pirates in at-bats, singles, caught stealing (14), hit by pitch (20), GDPs (18), pitches seen (2,520), highest groundball-flyball ratio (1.2), highest percentage of pitches taken (60.1), highest percentage of swings put into play (55.6), on-base percentage for a leadoff hitter (.330), highest percentage of extra bases taken as a runner (56.3) and lowest percentage of swings on the first pitch (13.1)

Pat Meares

Position: 2B
Bats: R **Throws:** R
Ht: 6' 0" **Wt:** 187

Opening Day Age: 33
Born: 9/6/68 in Salina, KS
ML Seasons: 9
Pronunciation: MEERS

2001 Season

The Pirates converted Pat Meares from shortstop to second base in spring training to open a spot in the lineup for rookie Jack Wilson. However, Meares went on to have the worst season of his nine-year career, producing personal lows in batting average, on-base percentage and slugging percentage. He particularly struggled late in the campaign. He finished on a 13-for-82 (.159) skid after sitting out a month with a sprained left ankle.

Hitting

Meares has progressively lost strength in his left hand since 1999 surgery that repaired torn tendons in his wrist and little finger. While he did deliver 13 homers in 2000, the hand really deteriorated last season. He no longer can make a fist and pitchers take advantage, knocking the bat out of his hands with hard stuff inside. In the past, Meares always was able to hit outside pitches with authority, but even those offerings gave him trouble last year. Doctors have told Meares further surgery will not help his hand, so it seems doubtful that he will ever again be an effective hitter.

Baserunning & Defense

Meares never has been much of a basestealer and was strictly a station-to-station runner in 2001, when he was bothered by knee and ankle injuries. His range has declined sharply in recent years and even the move from shortstop to second base couldn't hide that. He does have a good arm, particularly for a second sacker. But he has trouble making the double play pivot at his new position.

2002 Outlook

The Pirates are in a tough spot with Meares. Although he has two years and $7.5 million left on a contract he signed in April 1999, his days of being a regular are over. With seemingly no trade market, the Pirates may wind up releasing Meares and eating his salary, hoping they can get most of their money back through an insurance settlement.

Overall Statistics

	G	AB	R	H	D	T	HR	RBI	SB	BB	SO	Avg	OBP	Slg
2001	87	270	27	57	11	1	4	25	0	10	45	.211	.244	.304
Career	982	3287	401	849	157	24	58	382	43	150	588	.258	.299	.374

Where He Hits the Ball

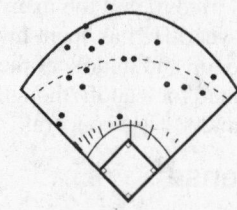
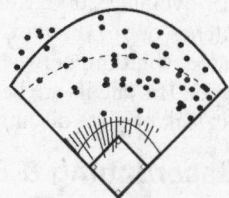

Vs. LHP   **Vs. RHP**

2001 Situational Stats

	AB	H	HR	RBI	Avg		AB	H	HR	RBI	Avg
Home	133	30	2	16	.226	LHP	61	12	1	6	.197
Road	137	27	2	9	.197	RHP	209	45	3	19	.215
First Half	188	44	3	16	.234	Sc Pos	74	16	3	23	.216
Scnd Half	82	13	1	9	.159	Clutch	39	6	1	5	.154

2001 Rankings (National League)
- 6th in errors at second base (10)

Aramis Ramirez

2001 Season

After splitting the previous three seasons between the majors and Triple-A, Aramis Ramirez broke through in his first full year in the big leagues. He set career highs in every offensive category. His club-leading 112 RBI were the most by a Pirates third baseman since Pie Traynor delivered 119 in 1930. Furthermore, Ramirez' 34 homers were one short of the club record by a third baseman, set by Frank Thomas in 1958. Ramirez also did a good job of getting his pudgy body into shape, going from 228 pounds at the start of the campaign to 210 by the end.

Hitting

Ramirez emerged as one of the top clutch hitters in the National League last season. He batted .379 with runners in scoring position, prompting Pirates manager Lloyd McClendon to predict a future RBI title. Ramirez loves to hit in pressure situations. He became successful in them last year because of his willingness to use the whole field. He is a good breaking ball hitter and particularly likes the ball from the middle of the plate out, where he can extend his arms. He can be given trouble by pitches on the hands and also needs to sharpen his batting eye. Unlike most young hitters, falling behind in the count doesn't faze Ramirez.

Baserunning & Defense

Ramirez is a slow runner who will steal an occasional base but primarily goes station to station. He is a below-average fielder, though he has an extremely strong arm. He charges balls well but doesn't have good lateral movement. While Ramirez has a plus arm, he tends to get lazy with his footwork and sails throws from time to time.

2002 Outlook

Ramirez established himself as a rising star last season and there is no reason to think he can't build upon that success. He still needs some polish, particularly with his plate discipline and defense. There also is some concern about Ramirez' attitude, as his ego is rather large.

Position: 3B
Bats: R **Throws:** R
Ht: 6' 1" **Wt:** 219

Opening Day Age: 23
Born: 6/25/78 in Santo Domingo, DR
ML Seasons: 4
Pronunciation: ah-RAH-mis

Overall Statistics

	G	AB	R	H	D	T	HR	RBI	SB	BB	SO	Avg	OBP	Slg
2001	158	603	83	181	40	0	34	112	5	40	100	.300	.350	.536
Career	321	1164	127	315	66	4	46	178	5	74	217	.271	.321	.453

Where He Hits the Ball

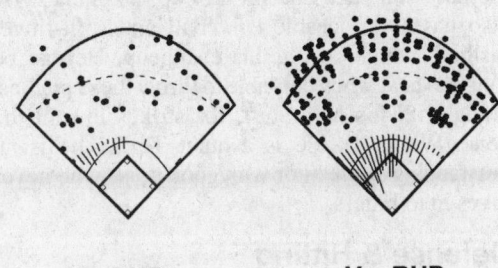

Vs. LHP   **Vs. RHP**

2001 Situational Stats

	AB	H	HR	RBI	Avg		AB	H	HR	RBI	Avg
Home	298	82	16	55	.275	LHP	111	33	4	19	.297
Road	305	99	18	57	.325	RHP	492	148	30	93	.301
First Half	322	95	16	59	.295	Sc Pos	145	55	9	76	.379
Scnd Half	281	86	18	53	.306	Clutch	89	26	6	17	.292

2001 Rankings (National League)

- 2nd in errors at third base (25) and lowest fielding percentage at third base (.945)
- 3rd in batting average with runners in scoring position
- 5th in batting average on the road and lowest cleanup slugging percentage (.458)
- Led the Pirates in hits, doubles, RBI, batting average with runners in scoring position, batting average with the bases loaded (.500), batting average vs. lefthanded pitchers, batting average on an 0-2 count (.288), slugging percentage vs. lefthanded pitchers (.486), on-base percentage vs. lefthanded pitchers (.373) and batting average on the road

Todd Ritchie

2001 Season

Todd Ritchie endured the worst start of any pitcher in the Pirates' 115-year history. He lost his first eight decisions before finally gaining his first victory on June 12. Ritchie turned it around after that, winning 11 of his next 15 decisions before losing his final three outings. He also set career highs in starts, complete games, shutouts and innings pitched while tying his career high for strikeouts.

Pitching

Ritchie has a good power arsenal with a fastball that regularly hits 92-93 MPH and a hard slider with good bite, though it can be inconsistent. However, he gets in trouble when he relies strictly on the hard stuff and doesn't mix up his pitches. He also has a serviceable curveball and split-finger fastball, which acts as his changeup. He can be tough to beat when he's able to throw those pitches, along with his hard stuff, for strikes low in the zone. While Ritchie is a quiet Texan, he is an outstanding competitor with good poise who never gives in to hitters.

Defense & Hitting

Ritchie is a good athlete who fields his position well and makes good decisions. Unlike most of the Pirates, he pays attention to baserunners and has a decent pickoff move. Ritchie knows how to handle the bat. While he isn't a home run threat, he can put the ball in play and also is reliable in bunt situations.

2002 Outlook

Ritchie was asked to be the Pirates' No. 1 starter last year when Kris Benson missed the entire season following reconstructive elbow surgery. Though Ritchie was the closest thing the Pirates had to an ace on their injury-depleted pitching staff in 2001, he was traded at the winter meetings to the Chicago White Sox along with minor league catcher Lee Evans for righthanders Josh Fogg, Sean Lowe and Kip Wells. The White Sox plan to have Ritchie help anchor a young starting rotation. Chicago general manager Ken Williams believes Ritchie can consistently win 15-18 games a season, but that may be a little ambitious.

Position: SP
Bats: R **Throws:** R
Ht: 6' 3" **Wt:** 222

Opening Day Age: 30
Born: 11/7/71 in Portsmouth, VA
ML Seasons: 5

Overall Statistics

	W	L	Pct.	ERA	G	GS	Sv	IP	H	BB	SO	HR	Ratio
2001	11	15	.423	4.47	33	33	0	207.1	211	52	124	23	1.27
Career	37	35	.514	4.37	149	90	0	665.1	705	194	420	78	1.35

How Often He Throws Strikes

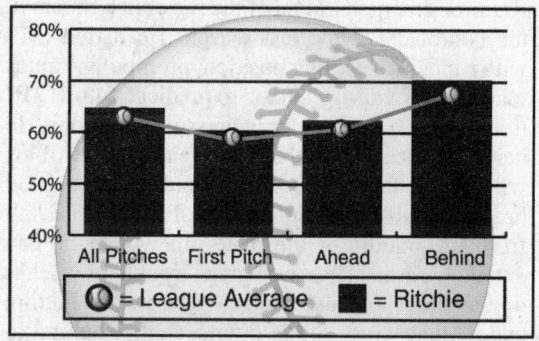

= League Average   = Ritchie

2001 Situational Stats

	W	L	ERA	Sv	IP		AB	H	HR	RBI	Avg
Home	8	4	3.47	0	109.0	LHB	378	108	13	60	.286
Road	3	11	5.58	0	98.1	RHB	436	103	10	44	.236
First Half	5	9	4.07	0	115.0	Sc Pos	177	49	4	70	.277
Scnd Half	6	6	4.97	0	92.1	Clutch	48	13	1	5	.271

2001 Rankings (National League)

- 3rd in shutouts (2), fewest pitches thrown per batter (3.39) and least run support per nine innings (3.7)
- Led the Pirates in ERA, wins, complete games (4), shutouts (2), innings pitched, home runs allowed, strikeouts, winning percentage, highest strikeout-walk ratio (2.4), lowest batting average allowed (.259), lowest on-base percentage allowed (.308), fewest pitches thrown per batter (3.39), lowest ERA at home, lowest ERA on the road, lowest batting average allowed vs. righthanded batters, lowest batting average allowed with runners in scoring position, most strikeouts per nine innings (5.4) and fewest walks per nine innings (2.3)

Dave Williams

2001 Season

Dave Williams made a quick rise through the Pirates' farm system. He went 5-2 with a 2.61 ERA in nine games at Double-A and then 1-1 with a 3.38 ERA in two starts at Triple-A. His minor league performance helped earn a callup to Pittsburgh on June 5. Williams began in the Pirates' bullpen before moving into the starting rotation after just four relief appearances. He finished up strong, going 2-2 with a 2.54 ERA in his last eight starts and allowing three earned runs or fewer in 10 of his final 11 outings.

Pitching

Williams has a lot of moxie for a young pitcher, enabling him to get hitters out despite not having overpowering stuff. Although his fastball rarely touches 90 MPH, it looks quicker because of his deceptive motion. He also throws a decent changeup, and his big breaking curveball is effective against both righthanded and lefthanded hitters when he keeps it in the strike zone. Stamina was a problem for Williams last year, as he tended to hit a wall after 75 pitches, allowing a .350 batting average after that point. He also falls into the habit of trying to overthrow in tight situations.

Defense & Hitting

Williams does the little things well. He is good at fielding his position, and is very alert in getting off the mound quickly and throwing to the right base. Williams also has a good pickoff move that slows down the running game. He isn't a zero at the plate, as he is a reliable bunter and occasionally can put a charge into the ball.

2002 Outlook

Williams should be able to build on a good rookie season. His lack of a strikeout pitch last year is a bit of a concern. However, he led all minor leaguers with 201 strikeouts at Class-A Hickory in 2000, giving hope he will get better with experience. Williams should settle in as a solid middle-of-the-rotation starter.

Position: SP
Bats: L **Throws:** L
Ht: 6' 2" **Wt:** 205

Opening Day Age: 23
Born: 3/12/79 in Anchorage, AK
ML Seasons: 1

Overall Statistics

	W	L	Pct.	ERA	G	GS	Sv	IP	H	BB	SO	HR	Ratio
2001	3	7	.300	3.71	22	18	0	114.0	100	45	57	15	1.27
Career	3	7	.300	3.71	22	18	0	114.0	100	45	57	15	1.27

How Often He Throws Strikes

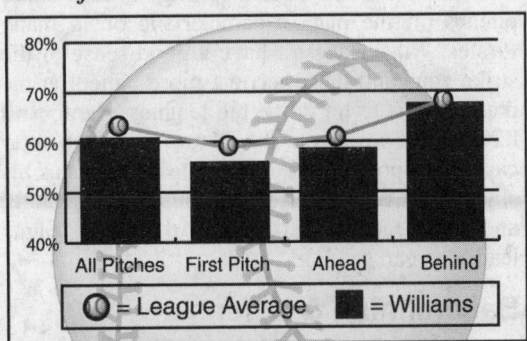

◯ = League Average   ■ = Williams

2001 Situational Stats

	W	L	ERA	Sv	IP		AB	H	HR	RBI	Avg
Home	2	3	4.06	0	51.0	LHB	106	27	2	15	.255
Road	1	4	3.43	0	63.0	RHB	303	73	13	39	.241
First Half	1	1	3.58	0	27.2	Sc Pos	71	22	3	36	.310
Scnd Half	2	6	3.75	0	86.1	Clutch	9	3	1	2	.333

2001 Rankings (National League)

- 7th in runners caught stealing (9)
- Led the Pirates in runners caught stealing (9)

Jack Wilson

2001 Season

Although he had never played above Double-A, Jack Wilson won the starting shortstop job in spring training, as the Pirates moved veteran Pat Meares to second base to open a spot. Wilson then hit .155 and made eight errors in 19 games before being sent to Triple-A on May 5. He returned to the majors for good five weeks later, after batting .369 at Nashville. He faded badly down the stretch for the Pirates, with his average falling from .273 on July 13 to its final level of .223.

Hitting

Wilson struggled in the second half of his rookie season, as hurlers began getting him to chase pitches off the plate. Characteristic of so many Pirates, Wilson doesn't have a good sense of the strike zone and must become more patient at the plate if he is to hit in the big leagues. He doesn't have a lot of power, but should turn into a gap hitter capable of popping 10 home runs per year as his slight body fills out. He is an outstanding bunter and his 17 sacrifice hits tied for the major league lead last year.

Baserunning & Defense

While Wilson isn't a burner, he runs well enough to pose problems on the bases. But defense is his calling card. He has good range, particularly to his right, an above-average throwing arm and great instincts. The ebullient Wilson also has a flair for making the spectacular play. He tends to get lazy with his throws at times, but maturity should solve that problem.

2002 Outlook

Although Wilson's rookie year finished on a downer, there still is much to like about him. He should emerge as one of the best defensive short-stops in the league this season, perhaps eventually winning a Gold Glove. His minor league history indicates he can become a competent hitter, and maybe a little more.

Position: SS
Bats: R **Throws:** R
Ht: 5'10" **Wt:** 170

Opening Day Age: 24
Born: 12/29/77 in Westlake Village, CA
ML Seasons: 1

Overall Statistics

	G	AB	R	H	D	T	HR	RBI	SB	BB	SO	Avg	OBP	Slg
2001	108	390	44	87	17	1	3	25	1	16	70	.223	.255	.295
Career	108	390	44	87	17	1	3	25	1	16	70	.223	.255	.295

Where He Hits the Ball

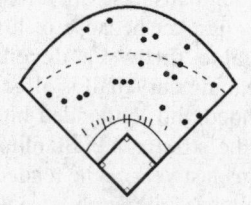
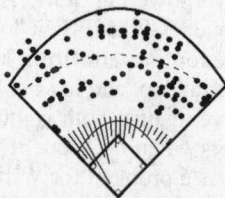

Vs. LHP   **Vs. RHP**

2001 Situational Stats

	AB	H	HR	RBI	Avg		AB	H	HR	RBI	Avg
Home	191	42	0	15	.220	LHP	59	13	0	2	.220
Road	199	45	3	10	.226	RHP	331	74	3	23	.224
First Half	135	36	2	14	.267	Sc Pos	70	18	0	20	.257
Scnd Half	255	51	1	11	.200	Clutch	47	13	1	6	.277

2001 Rankings (National League)

- 1st in sacrifice bunts (17)
- 5th in bunts in play (25)
- 9th in errors at shortstop (16)
- 10th in fewest GDPs per GDP situation (5.6%)
- Led the Pirates in sacrifice bunts (17), bunts in play (25) and fewest GDPs per GDP situation (5.6%)

Kevin Young

2001 Season

Young endured his second substandard season in a row as the Pirates' starting first baseman. He produced his lowest home-run and RBI totals since he was a reserve in 1996. His batting average, which fluctuated from month to month, wound up as his worst since 1995. He really swooned in May, when he had just 11 hits in 76 at-bats (.145) and drove in just six runs.

Hitting

While Young always has had a long swing, his bat was slower than ever last season. He experiences significant problems with inside pitches. He also can be made to chase high fastballs up and away, though his best power comes on pitches on the outer half of the plate. He has completely lost his plate patience over the past two seasons and is in big trouble when he falls behind in the count.

Baserunning & Defense

Young has lost much of his speed since having right knee surgery following the 1999 season. He still has good base running instincts, however, and will steal a base if the opposition doesn't pay attention. After making a combined 40 errors in 1999 and 2000, Young's defense returned to an above-average level last season as the Pirates moved from turf to grass. He doesn't have great range but is surehanded and adept at stretching for and digging out bad throws.

2002 Outlook

Young has two years and $12 million left on his four-year, $23.5 million contract. The Pirates are stuck with Young, as he has no trade value. So he will be back as their first baseman. He has become a large target of fan abuse in Pittsburgh, but in fairness, has been beset by injury and personal tragedies the past two years. Young is a hard worker and it's not out of the question to think he can improve offensively. Still, it's doubtful that he can get back to the 100-RBI level of 1998 and 1999.

Position: 1B
Bats: R **Throws:** R
Ht: 6' 3" **Wt:** 222

Opening Day Age: 32
Born: 6/16/69 in Alpena, MI
ML Seasons: 10

Overall Statistics

	G	AB	R	H	D	T	HR	RBI	SB	BB	SO	Avg	OBP	Slg
2001	142	449	53	104	33	0	14	65	15	42	119	.232	.310	.399
Career	1007	3345	468	875	205	16	126	548	78	274	756	.262	.324	.445

Where He Hits the Ball

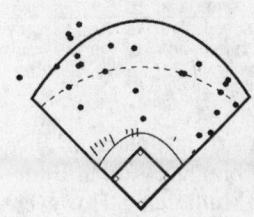 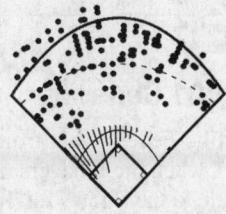

Vs. LHP **Vs. RHP**

2001 Situational Stats

	AB	H	HR	RBI	Avg		AB	H	HR	RBI	Avg
Home	222	63	7	35	.284	LHP	74	20	3	9	.270
Road	227	41	7	30	.181	RHP	375	84	11	56	.224
First Half	237	52	7	31	.219	Sc Pos	110	23	1	36	.209
Scnd Half	212	52	7	34	.245	Clutch	80	21	4	16	.263

2001 Rankings (National League)

- 1st in lowest batting average, lowest batting average on a 3-1 count (0.000) and lowest batting average on the road
- 2nd in lowest batting average vs. righthanded pitchers
- 4th in most pitches seen per plate appearance (4.11), lowest groundball-flyball ratio (0.7) and lowest stolen-base percentage (57.7)
- 6th in fielding percentage at first base (.994)
- 7th in lowest on-base percentage vs. righthanded pitchers (.294)
- Led the Pirates in sacrifice flies (5), stolen bases, strikeouts, stolen-base percentage (57.7), most pitches seen per plate appearance (4.11) and batting average with the bases loaded (.500)

Mike Fetters

Position: RP
Bats: R **Throws:** R
Ht: 6' 4" **Wt:** 226

Opening Day Age: 37
Born: 12/19/64 in Van Nuys, CA
ML Seasons: 13

Overall Statistics

	W	L	Pct.	ERA	G	GS	Sv	IP	H	BB	SO	HR	Ratio
2001	3	2	.600	5.51	54	0	9	47.1	49	26	37	7	1.58
Career	28	37	.431	3.73	527	6	99	637.0	621	299	450	56	1.44

2001 Situational Stats

	W	L	ERA	Sv	IP		AB	H	HR	RBI	Avg
Home	2	1	6.53	4	20.2	LHB	85	21	5	17	.247
Road	1	1	4.73	5	26.2	RHB	104	28	2	17	.269
First Half	2	1	6.46	1	23.2	Sc Pos	73	18	4	30	.247
Scnd Half	1	1	4.56	8	23.2	Clutch	104	22	3	15	.212

2001 Season

Mike Fetters went from first to last place on July 31 when the Dodgers dealt him and Adrian Burnside to the Pirates for Terry Mulholland. However, the trade enabled Fetters to close on a regular basis for the first time since 1996. He converted eight of nine save opportunities for Pittsburgh.

Pitching, Defense & Hitting

Fetters no longer can blow hitters away. But he has a very good split-finger fastball that darts down and away from lefthanded batters. He also throws a sinker and slider, and is quite effective when he keeps the ball low in the strike zone. Fetters struggles with his control and often falls behind in the count, but finds a way to get outs. He has a history of elbow problems, which makes it tough to use him on consecutive days. From the neck up, Fetters looks like an NFL lineman. Still, he has good agility and fields his position well. He never has batted in his 13-year big league career.

2002 Outlook

Fetters filed a formal trade demand in November, so he can become a free agent if the Pirates don't trade him by March 15. Fetters isn't a top-flight closer anymore, but his professionalism and upbeat attitude still are pluses, especially if he were to be a part of a young pitching staff.

Rob Mackowiak

Position: RF/2B/LF
Bats: L **Throws:** R
Ht: 5'10" **Wt:** 168

Opening Day Age: 25
Born: 6/20/76 in Oak Lawn, IL
ML Seasons: 1

Overall Statistics

	G	AB	R	H	D	T	HR	RBI	SB	BB	SO	Avg	OBP	Slg
2001	83	214	30	57	15	2	4	21	4	15	52	.266	.319	.411
Career	83	214	30	57	15	2	4	21	4	15	52	.266	.319	.411

2001 Situational Stats

	AB	H	HR	RBI	Avg		AB	H	HR	RBI	Avg
Home	116	37	3	12	.319	LHP	6	1	0	1	.167
Road	98	20	1	9	.204	RHP	208	56	4	20	.269
First Half	98	28	2	12	.286	Sc Pos	50	11	0	13	.220
Scnd Half	116	29	2	9	.250	Clutch	29	9	1	5	.310

2001 Season

Rob Mackowiak did not go to spring training with the Pirates but wound up spending the majority of the season with the club. His contract was purchased from Triple-A on May 18 after he had hit .288 with three home runs and 10 RBI in 23 games. Mackowiak was versatile for the Pirates, making 31 starts in right field, 19 at second base and six in left field.

Hitting, Baserunning & Defense

Mackowiak is a line drive hitter with decent power to the gaps. He is a much better hitter when he gets ahead in the count because he is susceptible to being finished off by pitchers with good changeups and breaking balls. Mackowiak won't steal a lot of bases but has decent speed. Although he mainly played second base in the minor leagues, his range has been found wanting in the majors. He is an acceptable corner outfielder, where his strong arm is a plus.

2002 Outlook

Mackowiak isn't quite good enough to be a regular in the big leagues. However, he could forge a long career as a utility player, since he bats lefthanded and can play every position on the field.

Josias Manzanillo

Position: RP
Bats: R **Throws:** R
Ht: 6' 0" **Wt:** 205

Opening Day Age: 34
Born: 10/16/67 in San Pedro de Macoris, DR
ML Seasons: 8
Pronunciation:
hose-EYE-ess
man-zah-NEE-oh

Overall Statistics

	W	L	Pct.	ERA	G	GS	Sv	IP	H	BB	SO	HR	Ratio
2001	3	2	.600	3.39	71	0	2	79.2	60	26	80	4	1.08
Career	10	10	.500	4.12	219	1	5	286.0	251	129	257	28	1.33

2001 Situational Stats

	W	L	ERA	Sv	IP		AB	H	HR	RBI	Avg
Home	2	0	2.83	1	41.1	LHB	106	30	2	16	.283
Road	1	2	3.99	1	38.1	RHB	179	30	2	30	.168
First Half	2	2	3.61	0	47.1	Sc Pos	89	25	2	44	.281
Scnd Half	1	0	3.06	2	32.1	Clutch	95	16	1	14	.168

2001 Season

Josias Manzanillo enjoyed the finest season of his long journeyman career. He set career highs in nearly every pitching category while primarily serving as a middle and setup reliever for the Pirates. He posted a 2.22 ERA in his last 41 appearances.

Pitching, Defense & Hitting

Manzanillo is a power pitcher who goes right after hitters and is hard to pick up because of a high leg kick. He has a live fastball that reaches 94 MPH and usually sits around 91-92 MPH. The heater sets up a sharp slider that serves as Manzanillo's strikeout pitch. Though he began his professional career in 1983 at age 15 and has had elbow and shoulder surgeries, he can work on consecutive days and pitch more than one inning an appearance. He is quick off the mound and fields his position well. He is 1-for-11 as a major league hitter.

2002 Outlook

Manzanillo became a free agent at the end of last season. The timing was perfect, since he had his best year. While the Pirates need a closer, they feel he is too hyper for that role and is better served as a setup man. However, some team might take a flyer on his power arm and try him as a closer.

Gary Matthews Jr.

Position: CF/LF
Bats: B **Throws:** R
Ht: 6' 3" **Wt:** 210

Opening Day Age: 27
Born: 8/25/74 in San Francisco, CA
ML Seasons: 3

Overall Statistics

	G	AB	R	H	D	T	HR	RBI	SB	BB	SO	Avg	OBP	Slg
2001	152	405	63	92	15	2	14	44	8	60	100	.227	.328	.378
Career	255	599	91	130	16	4	18	65	13	84	137	.217	.315	.347

2001 Situational Stats

	AB	H	HR	RBI	Avg		AB	H	HR	RBI	Avg
Home	201	43	4	20	.214	LHP	108	26	6	18	.241
Road	204	49	10	24	.240	RHP	297	66	8	26	.222
First Half	216	53	9	28	.245	Sc Pos	96	23	2	27	.240
Scnd Half	189	39	5	16	.206	Clutch	80	23	4	13	.288

2001 Season

Gary Matthews Jr. began his first full season in the major leagues as a reserve outfielder with the Chicago Cubs. He was lost to the Pirates on an August 10 waiver claim. He then started 40 games in center field over the final two months of the campaign.

Hitting, Baserunning & Defense

Matthews is an intriguing hitter because of his raw power. However, Matthews has plenty of holes in his swing and a serious problem recognizing breaking balls. He is somewhat of paradox as he draws his fair share of walks but also strikes out a lot on wild swings. Matthews has more power as a righthanded batter and makes better contact from the left side. But many believe he would be better served by giving up switch-hitting and batting exclusively from the right side. He has good speed on the bases. He also covers a lot of ground in center field and has a strong arm, though he occasionally gets bad jumps.

2002 Outlook

Matthews has plenty of ability but never has showed consistency. He piqued the Pirates' curiosity enough late last season that they will let him compete with Adrian Brown for the starting center-field job in spring training.

Tony McKnight

Position: SP
Bats: L **Throws:** R
Ht: 6' 5" **Wt:** 205

Opening Day Age: 24
Born: 6/29/77 in Texarkana, AR
ML Seasons: 2

Overall Statistics

	W	L	Pct.	ERA	G	GS	Sv	IP	H	BB	SO	HR	Ratio
2001	3	6	.333	4.95	15	15	0	87.1	109	24	46	19	1.52
Career	7	7	.500	4.63	21	21	0	122.1	144	33	69	23	1.45

2001 Situational Stats

	W	L	ERA	Sv	IP		AB	H	HR	RBI	Avg
Home	2	2	4.17	0	49.2	LHB	156	43	8	20	.276
Road	1	4	5.97	0	37.2	RHB	204	66	11	26	.324
First Half	0	0	4.91	0	11.0	Sc Pos	104	21	5	30	.202
Scnd Half	3	6	4.95	0	76.1	Clutch	15	3	0	0	.200

2001 Season

After getting passed in the Houston organization by such fine young pitchers as Wade Miller, Roy Oswalt and Tim Redding, Tony McKnight was traded to the Pirates last July 31 for Mike Williams. McKnight immediately moved into the Pirates' rotation but went only 2-6 with a 5.19 ERA over 12 starts.

Pitching, Defense & Hitting

While McKnight is a four-pitch pitcher, nothing in his repertoire is dominant. His fastball usually sits around 88 MPH with decent sinking action, though he occasionally will crank it up to 93. He also has a curveball, which can be a good pitch when he doesn't hang it, to go along with a slider and changeup. McKnight is OK as a fielder but doesn't do a good job of holding runners. His lifetime mark at the plate is 0-for-37, which speaks for itself.

2002 Outlook

McKnight will get a chance to make the Pirates' rotation this season. He has decent stuff but is not a lock after fading down the stretch in 2001. He could be a decent starter in the middle or at the end of a rotation once he figures out how to pitch at the major league level.

Warren Morris

Position: 2B
Bats: L **Throws:** R
Ht: 5'11" **Wt:** 179

Opening Day Age: 28
Born: 1/11/74 in Alexandria, LA
ML Seasons: 3

Overall Statistics

	G	AB	R	H	D	T	HR	RBI	SB	BB	SO	Avg	OBP	Slg
2001	48	103	6	21	6	0	2	11	2	3	9	.204	.239	.320
Career	339	1142	139	305	57	5	20	127	12	127	175	.267	.341	.378

2001 Situational Stats

	AB	H	HR	RBI	Avg		AB	H	HR	RBI	Avg
Home	62	17	2	10	.274	LHP	10	3	0	0	.300
Road	41	4	0	1	.098	RHP	93	18	2	11	.194
First Half	16	2	0	1	.125	Sc Pos	27	6	0	9	.222
Scnd Half	87	19	2	10	.218	Clutch	15	2	0	1	.133

2001 Season

After spending the previous two seasons as the Pirates' starting second baseman, Warren Morris began last year at Triple-A. He returned to the majors for a nine-game stint in May and was recalled for good on July 20, after batting .305 with five homers and 40 RBI in 57 games at Nashville. He went on the DL for a couple of weeks at the end of August to have surgery on his left big toe, and finished the year with just 103 big league at-bats.

Hitting, Baserunning & Defense

Morris hit well enough in 1999 to finish third in the National League Rookie of the Year voting. However, pitchers have caught on to his tendency to pull everything and mostly have fed him offspeed pitches on the outside corner the past two years. He's an average runner who has had fewer stolen bases than caught stealings in every season in the majors. He is surehanded and turns the double play well, but his poor range has cost him playing time.

2002 Outlook

It said a lot when the Pirates played the pedestrian Pat Meares ahead of Morris at second base last year. Pittsburgh clearly is down on Morris and feels he no longer can handle the position on a regular basis. While he is too young and talented to give up on, Morris desperately needs a change of scenery.

Abraham Nunez

Position: 2B/SS
Bats: B **Throws:** R
Ht: 5'11" **Wt:** 185

Opening Day Age: 26
Born: 3/16/76 in Santo Domingo, DR
ML Seasons: 5
Pronunciation: NOON-yez

Overall Statistics

	G	AB	R	H	D	T	HR	RBI	SB	BB	SO	Avg	OBP	Slg
2001	115	301	30	79	11	4	1	21	8	28	53	.262	.326	.336
Career	288	743	74	175	24	6	3	54	22	79	145	.236	.311	.296

2001 Situational Stats

	AB	H	HR	RBI	Avg		AB	H	HR	RBI	Avg
Home	134	31	0	5	.231	LHP	37	11	0	3	.297
Road	167	48	1	16	.287	RHP	264	68	1	18	.258
First Half	183	47	0	16	.257	Sc Pos	65	13	0	20	.200
Scnd Half	118	32	1	5	.271	Clutch	50	13	0	9	.260

2001 Season

Abraham Nunez was among the Pirates' final cuts of last spring training. He then was driving from Florida to Triple-A Nashville when he was called to Pittsburgh to take the roster spot of Mike Benjamin, who needed elbow surgery. Nunez wound up spending his first full season in the major leagues as a reserve, though he sat out the final month with a strained right hamstring.

Hitting, Baserunning & Defense

Nunez put on 12 pounds of muscle before last season and the extra strength enabled him to finally handle major league pitching. In the past, the slight Nunez could be overpowered by even average fastballs. He still has problems with offspeed stuff, especially from the left side, and can be made to chase bad pitches. He has good speed and runs the bases well. Though his range is not outstanding, Nunez is a fine defender at shortstop and second base with good hands and a good arm.

2002 Outlook

After shuttling between the majors and minors since 1997, Nunez appears to be in the big leagues to stay. He doesn't hit enough to be a regular, but does enough things to forge a career as a top-notch backup.

Armando Rios

Position: RF/LF
Bats: L **Throws:** L
Ht: 5' 9" **Wt:** 185

Opening Day Age: 30
Born: 9/13/71 in Santurce, PR
ML Seasons: 4

Overall Statistics

	G	AB	R	H	D	T	HR	RBI	SB	BB	SO	Avg	OBP	Slg
2001	95	319	38	83	17	3	14	50	3	36	74	.260	.332	.464
Career	294	709	111	198	41	8	33	132	13	94	154	.279	.361	.499

2001 Situational Stats

	AB	H	HR	RBI	Avg		AB	H	HR	RBI	Avg
Home	170	37	3	15	.218	LHP	46	15	3	7	.326
Road	149	46	11	35	.309	RHP	273	68	11	43	.249
First Half	275	71	12	45	.258	Sc Pos	94	25	4	36	.266
Scnd Half	44	12	2	5	.273	Clutch	45	11	1	7	.244

2001 Season

Pittsburgh acquired Armando Rios and righthander Ryan Vogelsong from San Francisco in a July 30 trade for Jason Schmidt and John Vander Wal. Rios was installed as the Pirates' starting right fielder, but tore his left ACL two days later and had season ending reconstructive surgery. Rios had hit .287 in his final two months with the Giants after batting .235 through May.

Hitting, Baserunning & Defense

Rios has good power but is an all or nothing hitter. While he crushes fastballs over the middle of the plate, he is susceptible to breaking balls and off-speed pitches, particularly away. Rios has a pronounced uppercut swing and limited strike-zone judgment, depressing his batting average and on-base percentage. He has adequate speed and doesn't clog the basis. Although Rios has played center field in the past, he is better suited to the corners as he lacks range but possesses a good arm.

2002 Outlook

The Pirates desperately need a right fielder with some pop. So Rios will get a chance to earn playing time this season if he can make a full recovery from his knee surgery by February or March. However, he still has holes in his game even with a healthy knee, and probably fits better as a fourth outfielder.

Scott Sauerbeck

Position: RP
Bats: R **Throws:** L
Ht: 6' 3" **Wt:** 197

Opening Day Age: 30
Born: 11/9/71 in Cincinnati, OH
ML Seasons: 3

Overall Statistics

	W	L	Pct.	ERA	G	GS	Sv	IP	H	BB	SO	HR	Ratio
2001	2	2	.500	5.60	70	0	2	62.2	61	40	79	4	1.61
Career	11	7	.611	3.84	210	0	5	206.0	190	139	217	14	1.60

2001 Situational Stats

	W	L	ERA	Sv	IP		AB	H	HR	RBI	Avg
Home	0	0	4.24	1	34.0	LHB	92	25	2	15	.272
Road	2	2	7.22	1	28.2	RHB	145	36	2	19	.248
First Half	1	2	5.82	1	34.0	Sc Pos	76	22	3	32	.289
Scnd Half	1	0	5.34	1	28.2	Clutch	99	22	0	9	.222

2001 Season

The Pirates signed Scott Sauerbeck to a three-year, $2.4 million contract on March 5 last season. The timing was a little more than two years after the Pirates stole him from the New York Mets in the Rule 5 Draft. Ironically, Sauerbeck then had his worst season as a middle reliever, posting the highest ERA of his career. However, he did go through a stretch of 18 appearances in August and September during which his ERA was a sparkling 1.56.

Pitching, Defense & Hitting

Sauerbeck lives and dies with his curveball. He throws the curve at different speeds and from various arm angles. Normally, it is a very tough pitch for lefthanded hitters to handle, though they batted .272 against him last year. While Sauerbeck also has an adequate fastball and changeup, those pitches are primarily for show. He does a decent job with the glove but rarely ever bats as a late-inning reliever.

2002 Outlook

Sauerbeck figures to be the Pirates' top bullpen southpaw for a fourth straight season. There has been some sentiment within the organization to convert him into a starter. However, that doesn't seem like a good idea, since Sauerbeck has only one above-average pitch.

Craig Wilson

Position: 1B/RF/C
Bats: R **Throws:** R
Ht: 6' 2" **Wt:** 217

Opening Day Age: 25
Born: 11/30/76 in Fountain Valley, CA
ML Seasons: 1

Overall Statistics

	G	AB	R	H	D	T	HR	RBI	SB	BB	SO	Avg	OBP	Slg
2001	88	158	27	49	3	1	13	32	3	15	53	.310	.390	.589
Career	88	158	27	49	3	1	13	32	3	15	53	.310	.390	.589

2001 Situational Stats

	AB	H	HR	RBI	Avg		AB	H	HR	RBI	Avg
Home	81	23	8	18	.284	LHP	45	17	4	8	.378
Road	77	26	5	14	.338	RHP	113	32	9	24	.283
First Half	48	15	6	9	.313	Sc Pos	42	15	3	20	.357
Scnd Half	110	34	7	23	.309	Clutch	37	9	3	5	.243

2001 Season

Craig Wilson began the season in Triple-A but was recalled April 17. He wound up belting seven pinch-hit home runs to tie the major league record set by Los Angeles' Dave Hansen in 2000. Wilson made 17 starts at first base, 11 in right field and four at catcher.

Hitting, Baserunning & Defense

Wilson possesses outstanding power to all fields with a short stroke that doesn't require much maintenance. He also has the ability to hit for average, though he tends to strike out too much. He is a dead fastball hitter who can be fooled by good breaking pitches, especially down and away. A slightly below-average runner, Wilson makes good decisions and doesn't clog the bases. He came to the big leagues with a reputation as a poor defensive player. But he was adequate last year at first base and in right field, though he needs some polish behind the plate.

2002 Outlook

The Pirates lack power and need to find ways to get Wilson's bat into the lineup. He ranked fourth on the team last year in home runs despite getting fewer than 200 plate appearances. Wilson went to the Dominican Republic to play winter ball, where he was to work on his fielding.

Other Pittsburgh Pirates

Bronson Arroyo (Pos: RHP, Age: 25)

	W	L	Pct.	ERA	G	GS	Sv	IP	H	BB	SO	HR	Ratio
2001	5	7	.417	5.09	24	13	0	88.1	99	34	39	12	1.51
Career	7	13	.350	5.68	44	25	0	160.0	187	70	89	22	1.61

Arroyo is not dominating, but has a wide range of pitches that keeps opposing batters off balance. He was used as a starter and as a reliever in 2001 and should challenge for a starting spot in the Pirates' rotation in 2002. 2002 Outlook: B

Andy Barkett (Pos: LF, Age: 27, Bats: L)

	G	AB	R	H	D	T	HR	RBI	SB	BB	SO	Avg	OBP	Slg
2001	17	46	5	14	2	0	1	3	1	4	7	.304	.373	.413
Career	17	46	5	14	2	0	1	3	1	4	7	.304	.373	.413

Barkett struggled in the minors the last two years after posting some solid numbers in 1998 and 1999. He hit .304 in 46 at-bats with the Pirates. He's a longshot to make the team as a lefty off the bench. 2002 Outlook: C

Joe Beimel (Pos: LHP, Age: 24)

	W	L	Pct.	ERA	G	GS	Sv	IP	H	BB	SO	HR	Ratio
2001	7	11	.389	5.23	42	15	0	115.1	131	49	58	12	1.56
Career	7	11	.389	5.23	42	15	0	115.1	131	49	58	12	1.56

Because of numerous injuries to the Pirates' pitching staff, Beimel spent the entire 2001 season, his rookie campaign, with Pittsburgh. He split time between starting and relief. With more seasoning, he may be a full-time starter eventually. 2002 Outlook: B

Luis Figueroa (Pos: 2B, Age: 28, Bats: B)

	G	AB	R	H	D	T	HR	RBI	SB	BB	SO	Avg	OBP	Slg
2001	4	2	0	0	0	0	0	0	0	0	0	.000	.000	.000
Career	4	2	0	0	0	0	0	0	0	0	0	.000	.000	.000

Figueroa was let go by the Pirates after hitting .300 at Triple-A last season. The Mets claimed the second baseman off waivers and assigned him to their Triple-A club. Light hitter, but solid on defense. 2002 Outlook: C

Chad Hermansen (Pos: RF, Age: 24, Bats: R)

	G	AB	R	H	D	T	HR	RBI	SB	BB	SO	Avg	OBP	Slg
2001	22	55	5	9	1	0	2	5	0	1	18	.164	.179	.291
Career	74	223	22	43	8	1	5	14	2	14	74	.193	.243	.305

Hermansen, considered one of the top prospects in the Pirates' system, was supposed to be Pittsburgh's center fielder of the future. However, he has struggled to hit above .240 in Triple-A over the last two years. 2002 Outlook: C

Alex Hernandez (Pos: RF, Age: 24, Bats: L)

	G	AB	R	H	D	T	HR	RBI	SB	BB	SO	Avg	OBP	Slg
2001	7	11	0	1	0	0	0	0	0	0	2	.091	.091	.091
Career	27	71	4	13	3	0	1	5	1	0	15	.183	.183	.268

Hernandez missed two months last season with a stress fracture in his back. He has improved at the plate, batting .299 in the minors over the last two seasons. He still needs to be more selective and possibly could serve as a lefty bat off the bench. 2002 Outlook: C

Adam Hyzdu (Pos: RF, Age: 30, Bats: R)

	G	AB	R	H	D	T	HR	RBI	SB	BB	SO	Avg	OBP	Slg
2001	51	72	7	15	1	0	5	9	0	4	18	.208	.260	.431
Career	63	90	9	22	3	0	6	13	0	4	22	.244	.284	.478

Hyzdu got his first legitimate opportunity to display his skills in the majors last season. Even though he showed some power, he struggled at the plate, hitting just over .200 with Pittsburgh. 2002 Outlook: C

Mike Lincoln (Pos: RHP, Age: 26)

	W	L	Pct.	ERA	G	GS	Sv	IP	H	BB	SO	HR	Ratio
2001	2	1	.667	2.68	31	0	0	40.1	34	11	24	3	1.12
Career	5	14	.263	6.23	57	19	0	137.1	172	50	66	24	1.62

After struggling as a starter with the Twins, Lincoln seemed to find his niche, posting solid numbers as a reliever with the Pirates last season. For his career, he has an 8.42 ERA as a starter, and a 2.83 ERA in relief. 2002 Outlook: B

Rich Loiselle (Pos: RHP, Age: 30)

	W	L	Pct.	ERA	G	GS	Sv	IP	H	BB	SO	HR	Ratio
2001	0	1	.000	11.50	18	0	1	18.0	28	17	9	3	2.50
Career	9	18	.333	4.38	202	3	49	224.0	241	124	178	22	1.63

Loiselle declined assignment to the minors and became a free agent in October. However, the Pirates may look to re-sign him for next season. He doesn't have enough control to be a closer, so he likely is stuck as a middle man. 2002 Outlook: C

Mendy Lopez (Pos: 2B, Age: 27, Bats: R)

	G	AB	R	H	D	T	HR	RBI	SB	BB	SO	Avg	OBP	Slg
2001	32	58	8	14	3	1	1	7	0	6	20	.241	.318	.379
Career	117	287	28	72	13	4	2	25	5	19	66	.251	.302	.345

Lopez started the 2001 season with the Astros, but was waived and picked up by the Pirates. He is a decent hitter with some pop for a middle infielder. The 27-year-old re-signed by agreeing to a minor league contract in December. 2002 Outlook: C

Damaso Marte (Pos: LHP, Age: 27)

	W	L	Pct.	ERA	G	GS	Sv	IP	H	BB	SO	HR	Ratio
2001	0	1	.000	4.71	23	0	0	36.1	34	12	39	5	1.27
Career	0	2	.000	5.60	28	0	0	45.0	50	18	42	8	1.51

The Pirates acquired Marte from the New York Yankees in exchange for Enrique Wilson in June. He missed most of the 2000 season with injury, but came back to post respectable numbers in 2001. 2002 Outlook: C

Ramon Martinez (Pos: RHP, Age: 34)

	W	L	Pct.	ERA	G	GS	Sv	IP	H	BB	SO	HR	Ratio
2001	0	2	.000	8.62	4	4	0	15.2	16	16	9	4	2.04
Career	135	88	.605	3.67	301	297	0	1895.2	1691	795	1427	170	1.31

Martinez asked to be released by the Dodgers prior to last season after finding out he would not be in the team's starting rotation. He then signed with Pittsburgh two weeks later. After four games with the Pirates, he retired. 2002 Outlook: D

Omar Olivares (Pos: RHP, **Age**: 34)

	W	L	Pct.	ERA	G	GS	Sv	IP	H	BB	SO	HR	Ratio
2001	6	9	.400	6.55	45	12	1	110.0	123	42	69	17	1.50
Career	77	86	.472	4.67	349	229	4	1591.2	1678	685	853	159	1.48

The A's dealt Olivares to the Pirates in March. He began the season in the Pirates' starting rotation, but once his ERA ballooned to 7.21, he was moved to relief. He likely will stay in relief with an occasional spot start. 2002 Outlook: B

Keith Osik (Pos: C, **Age**: 33, **Bats**: R)

	G	AB	R	H	D	T	HR	RBI	SB	BB	SO	Avg	OBP	Slg
2001	56	120	9	25	4	0	2	13	1	13	24	.208	.299	.292
Career	304	753	68	181	40	4	9	76	6	74	124	.240	.318	.340

Osik isn't the greatest offensive catcher in the league, but he can hold his own on defense. He also can play 1B, 2B, 3B and OF. He should see more at-bats if Jason Kendall continues to log time in the outfield. 2002 Outlook: B

Tike Redman (Pos: CF, **Age**: 25, **Bats**: L)

	G	AB	R	H	D	T	HR	RBI	SB	BB	SO	Avg	OBP	Slg
2001	37	125	8	28	4	1	1	4	3	4	25	.224	.246	.296
Career	46	143	10	34	5	1	2	5	4	5	32	.238	.262	.329

The Pirates used Redman as their leadoff hitter because of his speed, but a .246 on-base percentage did not keep him there long. He lacked patience at the plate, posting a 25-4 K-BB ratio. Also needs work defensively. 2002 Outlook: B

Jose Silva (Pos: RHP, **Age**: 28)

	W	L	Pct.	ERA	G	GS	Sv	IP	H	BB	SO	HR	Ratio
2001	3	3	.500	6.75	26	0	0	32.0	35	9	23	6	1.38
Career	24	28	.462	5.48	142	53	4	404.0	482	144	292	44	1.55

Silva missed almost four months of the season in 2001 after he was hit by an Andruw Jones liner, breaking a bone in his left leg. He has the potential to be a closer in the majors, but injuries and poor control get in the way. 2002 Outlook: B

Billy Taylor (Pos: RHP, **Age**: 40)

	W	L	Pct.	ERA	G	GS	Sv	IP	H	BB	SO	HR	Ratio
2001	0	0	-	4.50	1	0	0	2.0	2	0	3	1	1.00
Career	16	28	.364	4.21	317	0	100	324.2	314	133	307	27	1.38

Taylor spent four seasons as Oakland's closer, but at the age of 40, it is highly doubtful that he will return to that

role. The righthander appeared in just 21 games last season between Pittsburgh and Triple-A Nashville. 2002 Outlook: D

Ryan Vogelsong (Pos: RHP, **Age**: 24)

	W	L	Pct.	ERA	G	GS	Sv	IP	H	BB	SO	HR	Ratio
2001	0	5	.000	6.75	15	2	0	34.2	39	20	24	6	1.70
Career	0	5	.000	5.75	19	2	0	40.2	43	22	30	6	1.60

Vogelsong started the season in the bullpen for the Giants. He then was dealt to the Pirates, joining their starting rotation. The righthander needed elbow surgery after just two starts and likely will miss all of 2002. 2002 Outlook: D

John Wehner (Pos: 1B, **Age**: 34, **Bats**: R)

	G	AB	R	H	D	T	HR	RBI	SB	BB	SO	Avg	OBP	Slg
2001	43	51	3	10	1	0	0	2	2	10	12	.196	.328	.216
Career	461	804	99	200	33	4	4	54	15	73	136	.249	.311	.315

Wehner can play every position on the field, which probably is why he has stuck around so long. He has spent only one season in his 14-year pro career exclusively in the majors. Time in the minors is inevitable. 2002 Outlook: C

Don Wengert (Pos: RHP, **Age**: 32)

	W	L	Pct.	ERA	G	GS	Sv	IP	H	BB	SO	HR	Ratio
2001	0	2	.000	12.38	4	4	0	16.0	33	6	4	2	2.44
Career	14	32	.304	6.01	160	48	3	438.2	569	157	226	73	1.66

Wengert has bounced around the league, playing for six different teams in seven major league seasons. The Pirates used him exclusively as a starter last year. Lasted just 16 innings in four starts with Pittsburgh in 2001. 2002 Outlook: C

Marc Wilkins (Pos: RHP, **Age**: 31)

	W	L	Pct.	ERA	G	GS	Sv	IP	H	BB	SO	HR	Ratio
2001	0	1	.000	6.75	14	0	0	17.1	22	8	11	2	1.73
Career	19	14	.576	4.28	245	2	3	294.2	278	155	218	23	1.47

Wilkins is not going to eat up many innings. He also is not going to overpower opposing hitters. The righthander struck out just 24 batters in 32 games with Triple-A Nashville last season, posting a 4.75 ERA. 2002 Outlook: C

Pittsburgh Pirates Minor League Prospects

Organization Overview:

The Pirates may have opened last season in spanking new PNC Park, but the team itself looked like the same old outfit that has not posted a winning record since 1992. Pittsburgh lost 100 times, a National League high, ranking near the bottom in almost every phase of the game. Although the Pirates could use an infusion of talent from within their system, five of their six affiliates finished at least six games below .500. The notable exception was in Williamsport, where the Crosscutters shared the New York-Penn League championship. By extension, the Pirates' best prospects probably are a year or so away from contributing in Pittsburgh. Nevertheless, the organization possesses a solid base of righthanded pitching. It has some intriguing two-way outfield prospects. And few teams can match the Pirates' catching talent and depth.

Tony Alvarez

Position: OF **Opening Day Age:** 22
Bats: R **Throws:** R **Born:** 5/10/79 in
Ht: 6' 1" **Wt:** 202 Caracas, VZ

Recent Statistics

	G	AB	R	H	D	T	HR	RBI	SB	BB	SO	Avg
2000 A Hickory	118	442	75	126	25	4	15	77	52	39	93	.285
2001 A Lynchburg	25	93	10	32	4	0	2	11	7	7	11	.344
2001 AA Altoona	67	254	34	81	16	1	6	25	17	9	30	.319
2001 MLE	67	247	30	74	15	0	5	22	13	6	31	.300

Alvarez is a fan favorite, displaying a tremendous zest and flair for the game. The Pirates say he's the kind of guy who can play on Astroturf but still get mud on his uniform. He's strong yet acrobatic, and does things that are unconventional but effective. After winning MVP honors in the New York-Penn League in 1999, Alvarez moved from third base to the outfield. He stole 52 bases in 2000, before batting well over .300 at two stops in 2001. His walk rate declined in Double-A before he returned to Venezuela in August to attend to his ailing father. The Pirates would like him to cut his swing a bit.

Bobby Bradley

Position: P **Opening Day Age:** 21
Bats: R **Throws:** R **Born:** 12/15/80 in West
Ht: 6' 1" **Wt:** 164 Palm Beach, FL

Recent Statistics

	W	L	ERA	G	GS	Sv	IP	H	R	BB	SO	HR
2000 A Hickory	8	2	2.29	14	14	0	82.2	62	31	21	118	3
2001 A Lynchburg	1	2	3.12	9	9	0	49.0	44	23	20	46	3

The biggest question surrounding Bradley concerns his health and durability, not his talent. The Pirates signed him to a huge bonus after choosing him eighth overall in 1999. But he's thrown just 162.2 innings over his first three pro seasons. A sprained elbow ligament forced him to miss much of 2000. He then made only nine starts in

2001 before undergoing surgery to remove bone chips and shave a bone spur in his elbow in June. He's the complete package when healthy, with outstanding command, a great curveball and a developing changeup. Unfortunately, he underwent a second elbow surgery in mid-October and may be lost for most or all of 2002. Until he gains experience and shows he can remain in a rotation, Bradley has to be viewed with skepticism.

Sean Burnett

Position: P **Opening Day Age:** 19
Bats: L **Throws:** L **Born:** 9/17/82 in
Ht: 6' 1" **Wt:** 172 Dunedin, FL

Recent Statistics

	W	L	ERA	G	GS	Sv	IP	H	R	BB	SO	HR
2000 R Pirates	2	1	4.06	8	6	0	31.0	31	17	3	24	0
2001 A Hickory	11	8	2.62	26	26	0	161.1	164	63	33	134	11

Burnett already was linked to Bradley, since they hail from the same Florida high school. Their link was strengthened when Pittsburgh selected them with first-round picks in successive years. Burnett worked in the South Atlantic League last season at age 18 and was named the Pirates' Minor League Pitcher of the Year. While his fastball isn't considered anything special, the Pirates say the only thing he really needs to work on is tightening his curveball. If he can maintain his great control, he should continue to thrive despite not being overpowering. His strikeout rate has been respectable as a pro, and he's averaged fewer than two walks per nine innings. He may compete for a spot in Double-A this season, even though he won't turn 20 until September.

J.R. House

Position: C **Opening Day Age:** 22
Bats: R **Throws:** R **Born:** 11/11/79 in
Ht: 6' 1" **Wt:** 202 Charleston, WV

Recent Statistics

	G	AB	R	H	D	T	HR	RBI	SB	BB	SO	Avg
2000 A Hickory	110	420	78	146	29	1	23	90	1	46	91	.348
2001 AA Altoona	112	426	51	110	25	1	11	56	1	37	103	.258
2001 MLE	112	417	45	101	23	0	9	50	0	28	108	.242

Superficially, House's campaign was a statistical disappointment. His average dipped by nearly 100 points, while his homers were sliced in half from the year before. However, he had been pushed to Double-A at age 21, and his stamina was stretched by his continued flirtation with college football. He devoted a couple hours per day to football workouts before making the decision to stick with baseball full-time. He opened the season slowly, caught fire, then showed signs of fatigue when his bat seemed to drag in August. While he has improved defensively, he faces some competition in Pittsburgh's system. The Pirates expect House to rebound this season and demonstrate more power.

Nate McLouth

Position: OF
Bats: L **Throws:** R
Ht: 5' 11" **Wt:** 170

Opening Day Age: 20
Born: 10/28/81 in Muskegon, MI

Recent Statistics

	G	AB	R	H	D	THR	RBI	SB	BB	SO	Avg
2001 A Hickory	96	351	59	100	17	5	12	54	21	43	54	.285

The Pirates selected McLouth in the 25th round from a Michigan high school in 2000. Although he didn't make his professional debut until last season, he showed that he might have been a draft day steal. He more than held his own at age 19 in the South Atlantic League, flashing a tantalizing combination of power and speed. He's a tablesetter with pop, as evidenced by his 34 extra-base hits. He isn't reluctant to take a walk or steal a base, helping him lead Hickory in runs scored. He may have worn down as the season progressed, but he should move up to high Class-A or better in 2002.

Ian Oquendo

Position: P
Bats: R **Throws:** R
Ht: 5' 11" **Wt:** 160

Opening Day Age: 20
Born: 10/30/81 in Dover, DE

Recent Statistics

	W	L	ERA	G	GS	Sv	IP	H	R	BB	SO	HR
2000 R Pirates	1	0	2.35	4	0	0	7.2	5	2	1	8	1
2001 R Pirates	3	0	0.47	3	3	0	19.0	12	2	5	13	0
2001 A Williamsprt	7	0	1.39	10	9	0	64.2	55	16	10	56	2

Oquendo breezed through two levels in 2001, and he has yet to lose a game as a professional. He isn't particularly imposing at his size, but his wiry build, loose arm and big hands help him rush his fastball up to 94 MPH. His great strikeout-walk rate gives some indication of his precocious pitching sense, while his 1.39 ERA ranked second in the New York-Penn League. He didn't turn 20 years of age until after the season, and the Pirates say the more he pitches the better he should get. If he can continue to limit walks and home runs, he figures to enjoy success. Although he may need to add a layer of maturity, it isn't out of the question that he could fight for a spot in Double-A this season.

Justin Reid

Position: P
Bats: R **Throws:** R
Ht: 6' 6" **Wt:** 200

Opening Day Age: 24
Born: 6/30/77 in Lakewood, CA

Recent Statistics

	W	L	ERA	G	GS	Sv	IP	H	R	BB	SO	HR
2000 A Hickory	9	8	3.02	27	22	3	170.0	146	82	30	176	12
2001 A Lynchburg	2	4	2.25	8	8	0	56.0	50	15	6	48	4
2001 AA Altoona	5	5	2.54	17	16	0	110.0	104	38	14	70	5

Reid's size may convey a deceiving impression. Although he's 6-foot-6 and delivers a fastball with good movement, his velocity isn't overpowering and he might be a little short in terms of tools. At the same time, his large frame hasn't adversely affected his control, which is exceptional. Reid's 2.54 ERA would have ranked fourth in the Eastern League had he worked a few more innings. A fourth-round pick in 1999, he's handled at least 166 total innings each of the past two years. While he is aggressive with his stuff, he throws lots of strikes and is economical with his pitches. He does a good job of locating his slider and has been able to succeed with two pitches, but probably needs to improve his changeup to flourish at higher levels.

John VanBenschoten

Position: P-DH
Bats: R **Throws:** R
Ht: 6' 4" **Wt:** 215

Opening Day Age: 21
Born: 4/14/80 in San Diego, CA

Recent Statistics

	W	L	ERA	G	GS	Sv	IP	H	R	BB	SO	HR
2001 A Williamsport	0	2	3.51	9	9	0	25.2	23	11	10	19	0

Although he batted .443 and led NCAA Division I with 31 homers last season, the Pirates drafted VanBenschoten with the eighth overall pick with the intention to use him as a pitcher. Based on the early returns, Pittsburgh is pleased with its decision. VanBenschoten isn't a novice on the mound, having doubled as a pitcher in college. He boasts nice size and features a plus slider, curveball and developing changeup. He adhered to a 75-pitch limit and didn't post overwhelming statistics after signing with the Pirates. While Pittsburgh is encouraged by his initial professional exposure, VanBenschoten likely will require plenty of innings and possibly a couple of years before he reaches the majors.

Others to Watch

While catcher **Humberto Cota** (23) is only nine months older and played at a higher level than J.R. House in 2001, he probably will have to fight to stay ahead of House in the Pirates' plans. Cota features the better throwing arm. He's more of a contact hitter, though he muscled up for 22 doubles and 14 homers in Triple-A last year. . . **Ryan Doumit** (20) is another catcher to keep an eye on. He hurt his back and missed a chunk of 2001. But he's a switch-hitter with the best defensive skills in the system. . . The Pirates obtained lefty **Adrian Burnside** (25) from the Dodgers last July. A native of Australia, he pitched well at Double-A in 2001, striking out 99 in 100 innings. . . Righthander **Josh Fogg** (25) has a great feel for pitching and mixes his stuff well. He throws a sinking fastball that has good life, an above-average changeup and a slider. He split time between starting and relief in the White Sox' system last year and was traded to the Pirates in December. . . Righthander **Jeffery Sharber** (20), a fifth-round choice in 2000, pushed his way to the South Atlantic League as a teenager. His above-average fastball and curveball, and good pitching sense helped him post a 1.56 ERA with 76 strikeouts in 63.1 innings. . . Although **Edwin Yan** (20) has very good tools, he shifted from short to second in low Class-A last year. He's raw and may never be more than a singles hitter, but he stole 56 bases in 2001.

Busch Stadium

Offense

There are few ballparks that are fairer than Busch Stadium. The power alleys are reachable and home runs have increased in recent years. However, there aren't many cheap homers in St. Louis. The addition of grass a few years ago has made the infield less of an offensive weapon than it was when it was covered by artificial turf. However, the hot Missouri summer keeps the infield surface hard.

Defense

St. Louis has several strikeout pitchers in its rotation, which helps during hot weather when the ball tends to fly at Busch. The Cards have outfielders with exceptional range in Jim Edmonds and J.D. Drew. They're needed in an outfield featuring larger-than-average gaps. Busch also has a decent amount of foul territory to aid getting popouts.

Who It Helps the Most

Edmonds' career has turned around since coming to St. Louis, where he can hit home runs to the opposite field. Young players like Drew and Albert Pujols have learned to be more complete hitters because they don't have any quirky dimensions at which to aim. Strikeout/flyball pitchers like Woody Williams also enjoy pitching in Busch. Matt Morris went 15-2 with a 1.62 ERA at home last season, compared to 7-6 with an ERA over five on the road.

Who It Hurts the Most

Because cheap home runs are rare, lighter hitters such as Placido Polanco and Edgar Renteria can't hope to generate much power at home. And though St. Louis fans are among the best in baseball, they can be rough on disappointments. Such was the case with Andy Benes last year.

Rookies & Newcomers

After Pujols made such a huge splash in 2001, he could be the Cardinals' new hero following the departure of Mark McGwire. Most players consider St. Louis among the best places to play in baseball. The atmosphere at Busch is a big selling point as the Cardinals pursue free-agent options.

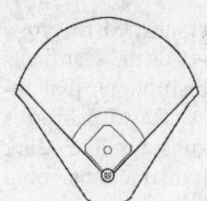

Dimensions: LF-330, LCF-372, CF-402, RCF-372, RF-330

Capacity: 49,814

Elevation: 535 feet

Surface: Grass

Foul Territory: Large

Park Factors

2001 Season

	Home Games			Away Games			
	Cardinals	Opp	Total	Cardinals	Opp	Total	Index
G	73	73	146	74	74	148	—
Avg	.282	.244	.263	.257	.269	.263	100
AB	2389	2459	4848	2561	2443	5004	98
R	395	280	675	352	338	690	99
H	673	600	1273	659	657	1316	98
2B	128	112	240	127	150	277	89
3B	18	9	27	12	11	23	121
HR	88	86	174	94	93	187	96
BB	239	245	484	247	231	478	105
SO	457	531	988	542	455	997	102
E	47	60	107	52	48	100	108
E-Infield	37	41	78	40	40	80	99
LHB-Avg	.283	.246	.265	.282	.265	.274	97
LHB-HR	43	38	81	40	40	80	111
RHB-Avg	.281	.243	.261	.240	.272	.256	102
RHB-HR	45	48	93	54	53	107	86

1999-2001

	Home Games			Away Games			
	Cardinals	Opp	Total	Cardinals	Opp	Total	Index
G	219	219	438	221	221	442	—
Avg	.271	.257	.264	.261	.269	.265	100
AB	7237	7532	14769	7690	7309	14999	99
R	1152	1036	2188	1130	1027	2157	102
H	1964	1939	3903	2008	1965	3973	99
2B	337	404	741	406	407	813	93
3B	42	30	72	38	45	83	88
HR	300	255	555	273	249	522	108
BB	867	855	1722	807	783	1590	110
SO	1495	1536	3031	1741	1372	3113	99
E	172	166	338	152	171	323	106
E-Infield	140	124	264	117	140	257	104
LHB-Avg	.283	.259	.271	.275	.268	.272	100
LHB-HR	119	102	221	105	96	201	117
RHB-Avg	.265	.256	.261	.253	.269	.261	100
RHB-HR	181	153	334	168	153	321	103

2001 Rankings (National League)
- Third-lowest double factor

St. Louis

Tony La Russa

2001 Season

As if the future Hall of Famer needed to prove anything else, Tony La Russa kept the Cardinals together through a series of disruptions that included Rick Ankiel's problems, Ray Lankford's sulking and key injuries to mainstays like Mark McGwire and J.D. Drew. Such distractions could have been enough to derail other teams. Instead, the Redbirds got hot in the final six weeks of the campaign and rolled to a second straight playoff berth. St. Louis fell short of the division title on the season's final weekend. That one stumble forced them to meet eventual World Champion Arizona in the Division Series.

Offense

La Russa always will look for opportunities to force the action with hit-and-run plays and by putting runners in motion. He's always been a master at utilizing his bench and keeping his reserve players sharp. Due to injuries, La Russa juggled lineups all season. He employed rookie Albert Pujols in four different positions, for example. La Russa also doesn't hesitate to sit a slumping regular.

Pitching & Defense

Though he often infuriates critics with his penchant for micro-managing late-inning bullpen moves, La Russa doesn't appear reluctant to ride his starting pitchers. The Cardinals had four of the league's top innings-eaters in their rotation. At the same time, he wasn't afraid to insert a rookie (Bud Smith) into the heat of the pennant race. Lacking an Eckersley-like closer, La Russa will vary who his closer might be. Seven different Cardinals relievers earned saves last year.

2002 Outlook

La Russa's focus and legendary intensity remain unswerving. He and general manager Walt Jocketty have one of the best front office relationships in the game. The result is that the Cardinals boast a nucleus of players that ranks among the best in baseball. They also have excellent clubhouse chemistry that has been carefully nurtured by La Russa. He should be managing in pennant races as long as he wants to keep wearing the Cardinals' uniform.

Born: 10/04/44 in Tampa, FL

Playing Experience: 1963-1973, Oak, Atl, ChC

Managerial Experience: 23 seasons

Manager Statistics

Year	Team, Lg	W	L	Pct	GB	Finish
2001	St. Louis, NL	93	69	.574	—	1st Central
23 Seasons		1827	1647	.525	—	—

2001 Starting Pitchers by Days Rest

	<=3	4	5	6+
Cardinals Starts	0	84	49	21
Cardinals ERA	—	3.54	4.46	3.28
NL Avg Starts	1	80	47	24
NL ERA	5.03	4.43	4.53	4.28

2001 Situational Stats

	Tony La Russa	NL Average
Hit & Run Success %	55.1	35.1
Stolen Base Success %	72.2	66.5
Platoon Pct.	47.1	51.5
Defensive Subs	13	20
High-Pitch Outings	7	7
Quick/Slow Hooks	21/13	19/14
Sacrifice Attempts	102	87

2001 Rankings (National League)

- 1st in hit-and-run success percentage, mid-inning pitching changes (209), first-batter platoon percentage, one-batter pitcher appearances (60) and 2+ pitching changes in low-scoring games (46)
- 2nd in steals of home plate (1), fewest caught stealings of second base (27) and relief appearances (485)
- 3rd in stolen-base percentage, sacrifice bunt attempts, sacrifice-bunt percentage (88.2%), squeeze plays (9) and hit-and-run attempts (118)

J.D. Drew

2001 Season

Buoyed by a torrid start, J.D. Drew was poised for the breakout season many had expected from him ever since he was considered the top player in the country as an amateur. He hit .366 in May and had swatted 18 homers by the end of that month. However, the injury bug once again bit him. A broken right hand courtesy of an errant David Wells pitch eliminated virtually a third of Drew's season. After he returned from his extended stint on the DL, back problems slowed him for two more weeks. Even so, he easily set career highs in most categories while compiling an on-base percentage over .400.

Hitting

As Drew has started adding muscle, he also has begun to reduce his strikeouts and learn to hit the ball where it's pitched more often. As a result, he has grown into a .300 hitter with 40-homer potential. He still will try to pull too many pitches and can be tied up with hard stuff directed in on his hands. But he is fighting off more of those inside pitches. He can be an extra-base machine when he's able to get his arms extended on either the hard stuff or breaking pitches. Drew also has become more willing to take a walk and hangs in much better against lefthanded pitching.

Baserunning & Defense

Drew is the total package. He has good straight-line speed and will be an increasingly dangerous basestealer as he continues to improve his ability to get jumps. Right field is where he appears best suited defensively. His range is exceptional and his arm has gotten better as he's improved the quickness of his release.

2002 Outlook

With Mark McGwire now out of the picture, the Cardinals need Drew to step up into a leadership role. Drew has grown immensely as both a player and teammate the past two seasons. He possesses all the ingredients to be a major star and to remain a key part of the Cardinals' foundation over the next several years.

Position: RF/CF
Bats: L **Throws:** R
Ht: 6' 1" **Wt:** 195

Opening Day Age: 26
Born: 11/20/75 in Valdosta, GA
ML Seasons: 4

Overall Statistics

	G	AB	R	H	D	T	HR	RBI	SB	BB	SO	Avg	OBP	Slg
2001	109	375	80	121	18	5	27	73	13	57	75	.323	.414	.613
Career	362	1186	234	345	54	14	63	182	49	178	261	.291	.388	.519

Where He Hits the Ball

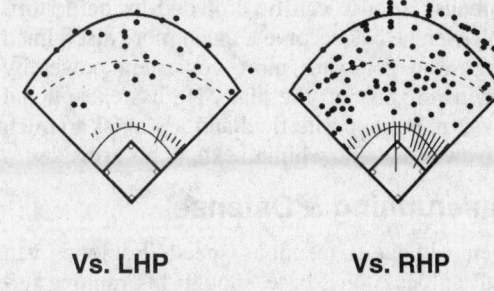

Vs. LHP   **Vs. RHP**

2001 Situational Stats

	AB	H	HR	RBI	Avg		AB	H	HR	RBI	Avg
Home	174	58	15	37	.333	LHP	83	24	3	17	.289
Road	201	63	12	36	.313	RHP	292	97	24	56	.332
First Half	218	72	21	49	.330	Sc Pos	98	33	5	42	.337
Scnd Half	157	49	6	24	.312	Clutch	36	12	3	8	.333

2001 Rankings (National League)

- 1st in batting average on a 3-1 count (.778)
- 7th in errors in right field (5)
- Led the Cardinals in fewest GDPs per GDP situation (6.1%) and batting average on a 3-1 count (.778)

St. Louis

Jim Edmonds

2001 Season

Jim Edmonds got off to a torrid start last April and was batting .411 through May 1. But bothered by assorted physical problems, he struggled for much of the next three months. However, like so many other Cardinals, Edmonds came on strong down the stretch to finish with one of his best all-around seasons. He swatted at least 30 homers for the second straight year and reached .300 for the third time in his nine big league seasons. His 110 RBI represented a career best, and he won another Gold Glove.

Hitting

Edmonds always will have a lot of strikeouts because of his big swing and his vulnerability to high fastballs. He also can be crowded by hard stuff. However, he has become a much more disciplined hitter who generates more consistent power by moving slightly off the plate. He has exceptional power to the opposite field and it's a risk to pitch him away and allow him to extend his arms.

Baserunning & Defense

Even without tremendous speed, Edmonds can steal an occasional base, though his running has been limited by knee and back troubles. At times, he tends to coast out of the batter's box and will coast himself out a chance at more doubles and triples. He has few equals in center field, where he gets a great jump and has an accurate arm with a quick release. He also shows a fearless ability to either dive for balls in front of him or time his progress going back to make over-the-shoulder catches.

2002 Outlook

Edmonds is only 31 years of age and, if he maintains his intensity, can be a star for several years to come. He particularly impressed the Cardinals last year by turning around what looked to be a lackluster season. He will remain a top run producer as long as there is a good lineup around him.

Position: CF
Bats: L **Throws:** L
Ht: 6' 1" **Wt:** 212

Opening Day Age: 31
Born: 6/27/70 in Fullerton, CA
ML Seasons: 9
Pronunciation: ED-muns

Overall Statistics

	G	AB	R	H	D	T	HR	RBI	SB	BB	SO	Avg	OBP	Slg
2001	150	500	95	152	38	1	30	110	5	93	136	.304	.410	.564
Career	1011	3669	688	1075	224	13	193	626	41	470	861	.293	.374	.519

Where He Hits the Ball

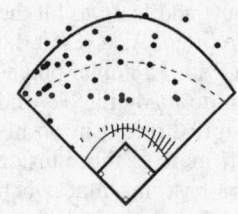

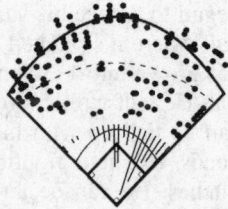

Vs. LHP **Vs. RHP**

2001 Situational Stats

	AB	H	HR	RBI	Avg		AB	H	HR	RBI	Avg
Home	246	77	16	61	.313	LHP	122	30	3	19	.246
Road	254	75	14	49	.295	RHP	378	122	27	91	.323
First Half	257	75	13	48	.292	Sc Pos	137	46	8	75	.336
Scnd Half	243	77	17	62	.317	Clutch	61	16	1	7	.262

2001 Rankings (National League)

- 1st in assists in center field (12)
- 3rd in lowest fielding percentage in center field (.982)
- 4th in batting average on a 3-1 count (.737) and errors in center field (6)
- 6th in sacrifice flies (10)
- Led the Cardinals in sacrifice flies (10), walks, intentional walks (12), strikeouts, on-base percentage, most pitches seen per plate appearance (4.08), highest percentage of pitches taken (61.0), batting average with the bases loaded (.500), on-base percentage vs. righthanded pitchers (.428) and lowest percentage of swings on the first pitch (25.6)
- Led NL center fielders in RBI

Dustin Hermanson

2001 Season

The Cardinals acquired Dustin Hermanson along with Steve Kline from the Expos last December, in exchange for Fernando Tatis and Britt Reames. By midseason, while Tatis was out for the year due to knee surgery, Hermanson was fitting well into the Cardinals' rotation. He finished the year strong, winning six of his last 11 decisions. He didn't miss a start all year and hurled just under 200 innings.

Pitching

Pitching coach Dave Duncan worked with Hermanson on mechanics, something with which Hermanson has always struggled. Hermanson began finding a more consistent release point, which helped both his command and the movement of his 90-92 MPH fastball and slider. He also began getting more outs with both his cutter and changeup, which helped him greatly improve his effectiveness against lefthanded hitters. His control remains the greatest obstacle to becoming a big winner. But late in the season, he finally began showing signs of reducing his always-high walk totals and pitch counts.

Defense & Hitting

Hermanson has a very good pickoff move. With the help of catcher Mike Matheny, he allowed only seven stolen bases last year with a success rate of only 50 percent. He is just an average fielding pitcher. With a career average under .100, Hermanson usually is incapable of helping himself with the bat. He collected just one hit after July 15 last season.

2002 Outlook

In a deep St. Louis rotation, Hermanson was perfectly situated as a fourth or fifth starter. Now he looks like a No. 2 starter after the Red Sox traded three minor leaguers to line him up behind Pedro Martinez. Like so many other pitchers, Hermanson just may be entering his prime as he nears 30 years of age. If he picks up where he left off, it's possible he'll become a consistent 15-17 game winner for a Boston club that generally stays competitive in the American League East.

Position: SP
Bats: R **Throws:** R
Ht: 6' 2" **Wt:** 200

Opening Day Age: 29
Born: 12/21/72 in Springfield, OH
ML Seasons: 7

Overall Statistics

	W	L	Pct.	ERA	G	GS	Sv	IP	H	BB	SO	HR	Ratio
2001	14	13	.519	4.45	33	33	0	192.1	195	73	123	34	1.39
Career	61	61	.500	4.22	203	155	4	997.1	996	365	682	127	1.36

How Often He Throws Strikes

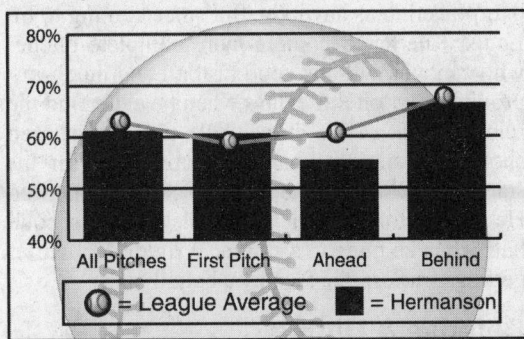

○ = League Average   ■ = Hermanson

2001 Situational Stats

	W	L	ERA	Sv	IP		AB	H	HR	RBI	Avg
Home	8	7	4.46	0	103.0	LHB	304	84	21	48	.276
Road	6	6	4.43	0	89.1	RHB	436	111	13	45	.255
First Half	6	7	5.19	0	102.1	Sc Pos	176	40	4	54	.227
Scnd Half	8	6	3.60	0	90.0	Clutch	40	15	5	8	.375

2001 Rankings (National League)

- 3rd in most home runs allowed per nine innings (1.59)
- 5th in home runs allowed and highest slugging percentage allowed (.481)
- 9th in most pitches thrown per batter (3.83) and highest ERA at home
- 10th in lowest stolen-base percentage allowed (50.0)
- Led the Cardinals in losses, home runs allowed, walks allowed, wild pitches (6), pickoff throws (77), runners caught stealing (7) and lowest batting average allowed (.264)

St. Louis

Darryl Kile

2001 Season

For the second straight year, Darryl Kile was the guts of the Cardinals' pitching staff. In some ways, he pitched better than he had in 2000, when he became a 20-game winner. He led the club in innings last season, and could have possibly won a half-dozen more than the 16 victories he wound up earning. Kile was a true staff leader, never missing a turn and working at least six innings in all but five starts.

Pitching

Kile will always be defined by his curveball, a 12-to-6 breaking ball that is among the best in baseball. When he has his best curve, he can be as overpowering as anybody. But since coming to St. Louis, Kile has become a more complete pitcher who can win with his good fastball and much-improved cutter on those days when he can't find the release point of his curve. Kile also has started showing a straight change. He prepares for his starts as well as anyone and is a great competitor. He set the tone for the Cardinals' strong second half when he hung in a start at Wrigley Field after getting struck in the face by a batted ball.

Defense & Hitting

As part of his stepping up in all areas, Kile has improved his attention to holding runners. Though he has a slow delivery home and an ordinary pick-off move, he will slow down the game to freeze runners, who last year stole only four bases against him. Kile also is no longer an automatic out. He homered last year and can help himself when he gets the ball in play.

2002 Outlook

There are few better deals than the Cardinals owning the durable Kile for at least the next two seasons at a reasonable $6 million per year. He is among the game's most valuable top-of-the-rotation hurlers. Now 33 years of age, he still has the ability to produce 80 wins over the next five years.

Position: SP
Bats: R **Throws:** R
Ht: 6' 5" **Wt:** 212

Opening Day Age: 33
Born: 12/2/68 in
Garden Grove, CA
ML Seasons: 11

Overall Statistics

	W	L	Pct.	ERA	G	GS	Sv	IP	H	BB	SO	HR	Ratio
2001	16	11	.593	3.09	34	34	0	227.1	228	65	179	22	1.29
Career	128	115	.527	4.14	345	317	0	2080.2	2053	890	1618	205	1.41

How Often He Throws Strikes

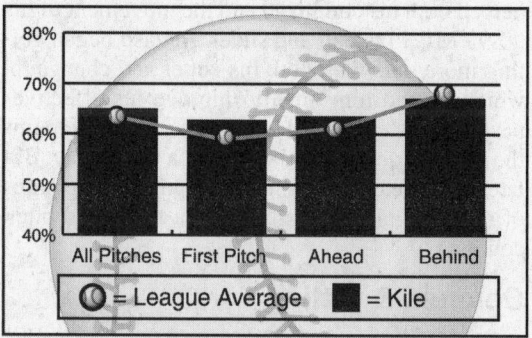

2001 Situational Stats

	W	L	ERA	Sv	IP		AB	H	HR	RBI	Avg
Home	7	5	2.68	0	104.0	LHB	380	106	11	41	.279
Road	9	6	3.43	0	123.1	RHB	482	122	11	32	.253
First Half	9	6	3.35	0	123.2	Sc Pos	186	39	3	44	.210
Scnd Half	7	5	2.78	0	103.2	Clutch	49	15	1	3	.306

2001 Rankings (National League)

- 4th in games started
- 5th in ERA, lowest stolen-base percentage allowed (36.4) and lowest batting average allowed with runners in scoring position
- 6th in innings pitched, hits allowed and batters faced (956)
- Led the Cardinals in ERA, games started, innings pitched, hits allowed, batters faced (956), wild pitches (6), pitches thrown (3,377), runners caught stealing (7), GDPs induced (20), lowest stolen-base percentage allowed (36.4), fewest pitches thrown per batter (3.53), lowest ERA on the road, lowest batting average allowed with runners in scoring position and most GDPs induced per nine innings (0.8)

Steve Kline

2001 Season

With the possible exception of Matt Morris and Darryl Kile, probably no Cardinals pitcher was more valuable than lefthander Steve Kline last season. Kline had arrived via a trade with Montreal, and ended up being St. Louis' most reliable reliever. For the third straight year, he led all National League pitchers in appearances. He also compiled a career-best 1.80 ERA and converted nine of 10 saves opportunities when used as a closer late in the season.

Pitching

Kline keeps virtually everything down in the strike zone with his heavy sinker and hard slider. His consistency down in the zone extends even to those rare occasions when he's wild, because when he does miss, he almost always misses low. That makes him tough against both lefthanded and righthanded batters. It also means a lot of groundballs and few extra-base hits. He allowed just three home runs last year and was scored on in only 11 of his 89 appearances. If he's not asked to get more than three or four outs, Kline has proven he can handle a heavy workload, averaging over 80 appearances the past four seasons.

Defense & Hitting

Kline holds runners well, employing a slide step in running situations. He also is quick coming home with his delivery. He fields his position well and has good instincts coming off the mound. He's made only 10 plate appearances in his big league career, but earned his first hit last season.

2002 Outlook

St. Louis could not have expected any more than it got from Kline. He fit right in on a staff full of gamers and picked up the slack when closer Dave Veres was injured. The Cardinals ideally would like to keep the durable lefty in a specialist and setup role, and that seemed more likely after they signed Oakland closer Jason Isringhausen to a four-year deal.

Position: RP
Bats: B **Throws:** L
Ht: 6' 1" **Wt:** 215

Opening Day Age: 29
Born: 8/22/72 in Sunbury, PA
ML Seasons: 5

Overall Statistics

	W	L	Pct.	ERA	G	GS	Sv	IP	H	BB	SO	HR	Ratio
2001	3	3	.500	1.80	89	0	9	75.0	53	29	54	3	1.09
Career	18	22	.450	3.41	378	1	24	351.1	332	153	300	33	1.38

How Often He Throws Strikes

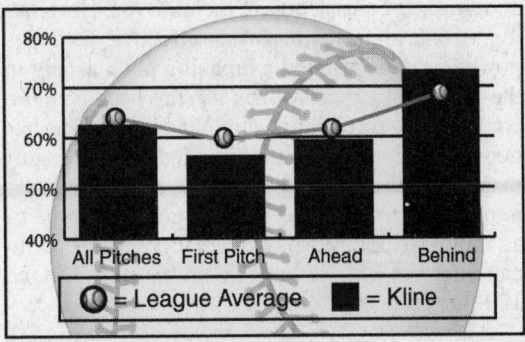

2001 Situational Stats

	W	L	ERA	Sv	IP		AB	H	HR	RBI	Avg
Home	2	1	1.26	6	43.0	LHB	101	15	0	10	.149
Road	1	2	2.53	3	32.0	RHB	160	38	3	14	.238
First Half	1	3	2.45	2	40.1	Sc Pos	76	17	0	18	.224
Scnd Half	2	0	1.04	7	34.2	Clutch	123	30	0	11	.244

2001 Rankings (National League)

- 1st in games pitched
- 2nd in relief ERA (1.80)
- 8th in lowest batting average allowed in relief (.203)
- 9th in fewest baserunners allowed per nine innings in relief (10.3)
- Led the Cardinals in games pitched, holds (17), lowest percentage of inherited runners scored (23.4), relief innings (75.0), relief ERA (1.80), lowest batting average allowed in relief (.203) and fewest baserunners allowed per nine innings in relief (10.3)

St. Louis

623

Matt Morris

Position: SP
Bats: R **Throws:** R
Ht: 6' 5" **Wt:** 210

Opening Day Age: 27
Born: 8/9/74 in Middletown, NY
ML Seasons: 4

2001 Season

Healthy and back in the starting rotation, Matt Morris realized his promise as one of baseball's best starting pitchers. Morris recorded a decision in all but four of his 34 starts, and was darn near unbeatable at Busch Stadium. He wound up tying Curt Schilling for the most wins in the National League while also ranking among the leaders in numerous other categories. His 22 victories were the most by a Cardinals hurler since Bob Gibson won 23 in 1970.

Pitching

Few pitchers have Morris' array of weapons. He can ride his four-seam fastball up in the strike zone and throw it consistently in the mid-90s. His sinking, two-seam fastball is just as effective, while his power curve is as good a breaking pitch as any in the National League. Morris also has become more confident in throwing a straight change. He has good control of all his offerings, and his heavy stuff makes home runs against him rare. As he continues to mature physically, he will become even more of an innings-eater. Morris is a great competitor who can pitch out of trouble and hold his stuff into the 120-pitch range.

Defense & Hitting

Morris does not hold runners well and his delivery is fairly slow, which can lead to stolen bases. But he's a good athlete on the mound, and he isn't a bad hitter, either. He led Cardinals pitchers with 10 hits and five RBI last season.

2002 Outlook

Stardom has been predicted for Morris almost from the time he was chosen with the 12th overall pick in the 1995 draft. An elbow injury may have delayed his progress and wiped out his 1999 season, but Morris indeed has arrived. His performance last year was not an aberration. If he can stay healthy, he should remain as one of the league's elite pitchers for years to come.

Overall Statistics

	W	L	Pct.	ERA	G	GS	Sv	IP	H	BB	SO	HR	Ratio
2001	22	8	.733	3.16	34	34	0	216.1	218	54	185	13	1.26
Career	44	25	.638	3.09	115	84	4	600.0	580	182	447	36	1.27

How Often He Throws Strikes

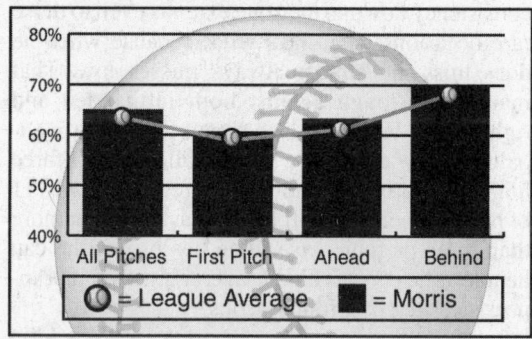

2001 Situational Stats

	W	L	ERA	Sv	IP		AB	H	HR	RBI	Avg
Home	15	2	1.62	0	122.0	LHB	358	85	7	29	.237
Road	7	6	5.15	0	94.1	RHB	465	133	6	50	.286
First Half	10	5	3.23	0	114.1	Sc Pos	188	48	5	64	.255
Scnd Half	12	3	3.09	0	102.0	Clutch	66	22	1	8	.333

2001 Rankings (National League)

- 1st in wins and lowest ERA at home
- 3rd in highest groundball-flyball ratio allowed (2.0), most run support per nine innings (6.4) and fewest home runs allowed per nine innings (.54)
- Led the Cardinals in games started, hit batsmen (13), strikeouts, stolen bases allowed (11), winning percentage, highest strikeout-walk ratio (3.4), lowest slugging percentage allowed (.372), lowest on-base percentage allowed (.318), highest groundball-flyball ratio allowed (2.0), lowest batting average allowed vs. lefthanded batters, most run support per nine innings (6.4), fewest home runs allowed per nine innings (.54), most strikeouts per nine innings (7.7) and fewest walks per nine innings (2.2)

Placido Polanco

2001 Season

The ripple effect from Mark McGwire's knee injury gave Placido Polanco the chance to play every day in the big leagues for the first time. And the young infielder took advantage of the opportunity. He settled into the No. 2 spot in the Cardinals lineup, hit over .300 and played outstanding defense at third base.

Hitting

Polanco is a tough out, someone who puts the ball in play virtually all the time. He's difficult to strike out because he can fight off hard stuff with his short stroke and is a good breaking-ball hitter. However, he's a slap hitter who doesn't possess the strength or swing to lift many pitches for power. He also doesn't draw very many walks. As a result, his .300 batting average was a soft .300. Only 33 of his hits went for extra-bases, and he worked just 25 free passes in over 600 plate appearances. In addition, he wasn't consistent in clutch situations.

Baserunning & Defense

Though not a burner, Polanco gets good jumps and has a quick first step, which allows him to be a high-percentage basestealer if used properly. He has great hands in the field. While his arm strength is only average, he is very accurate and has a quick release. His range is probably best at second base, though Polanco performs very well at both third base and shortstop. The Cardinals also think he could fill in as an emergency left fielder if needed.

2002 Outlook

As well as Polanco has performed, he is sort of a "tweener." His lack of power makes it difficult to justify playing him every day at third base, a traditional power position, yet the Cardinals will be without Craig Paquette, who better fits the mold but signed with Detroit. Right now, the Cardinals don't have an opening in the middle of their infield, where Polanco's offensive abilities are best suited. However, his versatility and ability to get on base make him a valuable commodity, whether Polanco is stationed at third or playing a utility role.

Position: 3B/SS/2B
Bats: R **Throws:** R
Ht: 5'10" **Wt:** 168

Opening Day Age: 26
Born: 10/10/75 in Santo Domingo, DR
ML Seasons: 4
Pronunciation:
pluh-SEE-doh
poh-LAHNK-oh

Overall Statistics

	G	AB	R	H	D	T	HR	RBI	SB	BB	SO	Avg	OBP	Slg
2001	144	564	87	173	26	4	3	38	12	25	43	.307	.342	.383
Career	395	1221	171	365	50	12	10	107	19	61	102	.299	.335	.384

Where He Hits the Ball

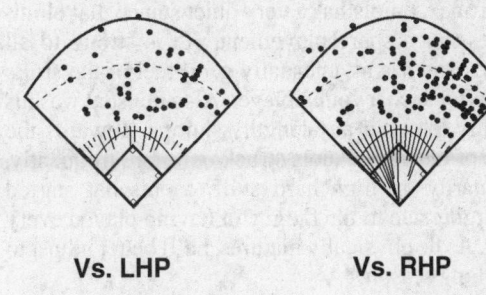

Vs. LHP   **Vs. RHP**

2001 Situational Stats

	AB	H	HR	RBI	Avg		AB	H	HR	RBI	Avg
Home	293	95	1	20	.324	LHP	143	50	0	10	.350
Road	271	78	2	18	.288	RHP	421	123	3	28	.292
First Half	268	90	0	17	.336	Sc Pos	119	30	1	32	.252
Scnd Half	296	83	3	21	.280	Clutch	63	18	0	5	.286

2001 Rankings (National League)
- 3rd in singles, highest groundball-flyball ratio (2.3), GDPs (22) and lowest HR frequency (188.0 ABs per HR)
- 5th in most GDPs per GDP situation (19.8%)
- 6th in batting average vs. lefthanded pitchers and fewest pitches seen per plate appearance (3.21)
- 7th in lowest percentage of swings that missed (9.1) and highest percentage of swings put into play (55.0)
- 8th in sacrifice bunts (14)
- Led the Cardinals in sacrifice bunts (14), GDPs (22), highest groundball-flyball ratio (2.3) and batting average vs. lefthanded pitchers

2001 Season

Albert Pujols wasn't just the unanimous winner of the National League Rookie of the Year Award. He produced one of the best rookies seasons *ever* and was one of the league's half-dozen most valuable players. Pujols set an NL record for RBI by a rookie and fell one homer shy of tying the league's rookie mark in that category. He accomplished all this while keeping his average in the .320s or above virtually the entire season. What made it all the more impressive was that Pujols managed to be an offensive force while starting at four different positions over the course of the campaign.

Hitting

Pujols reminds many scouts of a bigger Edgar Martinez. Pujols has a very quiet stance that eliminates much spare movement. He is strong to all fields and has an unusually good feel of the strike zone for such a young player. Also unusual was his ability to avoid any lengthy slumps. Towards the end of the year, Pujols struck out more frequently, primarily on high hard stuff, as his bat started dragging due to the fatigue of having played every day. As he physically matures, he'll better adjust to the long season.

Baserunning & Defense

Pujols is a below-average basestealer for whom the stolen base will never be a weapon, but he is very aggressive advancing on hits. His most experience on defense has come at third base, where he has a great arm and Gold Glove potential. But he still is prone to erratic play. He played well at first base and boasts the kind of arm that can handle right field. However, Pujols' range in the outfield is better suited for left.

2002 Outlook

Once they make their offseason moves, the Cardinals hope to settle on one position for Pujols and avoid moving him around the diamond. However, he has a veteran's mentality and should be a superstar for years to come, no matter how he is used in the field. With Mark McGwire now retired, the Cardinals will count on Pujols to remain a vital offensive cog.

Position: 3B/1B/LF/RF
Bats: R **Throws:** R
Ht: 6' 3" **Wt:** 210

Opening Day Age: 22
Born: 1/16/80 in Santo Domingo, DR
ML Seasons: 1

Overall Statistics

	G	AB	R	H	D	T	HR	RBI	SB	BB	SO	Avg	OBP	Slg
2001	161	590	112	194	47	4	37	130	1	69	93	.329	.403	.610
Career	161	590	112	194	47	4	37	130	1	69	93	.329	.403	.610

Where He Hits the Ball

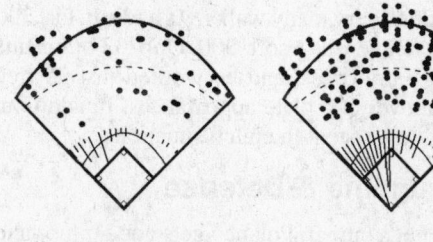

Vs. LHP **Vs. RHP**

2001 Situational Stats

	AB	H	HR	RBI	Avg		AB	H	HR	RBI	Avg
Home	291	103	18	64	.354	LHP	122	34	8	22	.279
Road	299	91	19	66	.304	RHP	468	160	29	108	.342
First Half	313	101	21	66	.323	Sc Pos	174	54	10	93	.310
Scnd Half	277	93	16	64	.336	Clutch	79	24	4	16	.304

2001 Rankings (National League)

- 1st in batting average among rookies, home runs among rookies and RBI among rookies
- 2nd in batting average vs. righthanded pitchers
- 4th in batting average with two strikes (.268)
- Led the Cardinals in batting average, home runs, runs scored, hits, doubles, total bases (360), RBI, times on base (272), pitches seen (2,716), games played, slugging percentage, HR frequency (15.9 ABs per HR), batting average vs. righthanded pitchers, cleanup slugging percentage (.595), highest percentage of extra bases taken as a runner (60.4), slugging percentage vs. lefthanded pitchers (.557), slugging percentage vs. righthanded pitchers (.624), batting average at home and batting average with two strikes (.268)

Edgar Renteria

2001 Season

While Edgar Renteria's production fell in most areas last year, it could have been much worse for the Cardinals shortstop. His average barely stayed over .200 through the first third of the season. But a strong second half when he generated several key hits largely salvaged his campaign. He batted better than .300 in both August and September.

Hitting

After generating 49 extra-base hits in both 1999 and 2000, Renteria fell victim to trying to lift too many balls last season. His swing plane widened, causing both his bat speed and plate coverage to slip. He became very vulnerable to hard stuff and hit too many pitches in the air. Renteria is at his best when his swing is more compact and when he's thinking about hitting line drives to all fields. He is a good fastball hitter and has shown signs of improving against offspeed pitches. He drew a career-high 63 bases on balls in 2000, but his walk rate declined last season. He often looks to swing early in the count.

Baserunning & Defense

Renteria possesses good speed and uses very good baserunning judgment. Depending on where he bats in the order, Renteria picks his spot to run and has become a high-percentage basestealer. His range, throwing ability and hands are as good as any shortstop. However, he has a tendency to occasionally take his batting problems onto the field. He makes too many errors due to lack of concentration or sloppy throwing mechanics.

2002 Outlook

For much of last season, St. Louis' brain trust was privately questioning its decision to give Renteria a long-term contract, and there were many trade rumors involving him. However, his good finish eased some of the concern. Renteria has only begun to mature both physically and emotionally. Considering he doesn't turn 27 until this August, he has the ability to be one of the National League's best all-around shortstops over the next few years.

Position: SS
Bats: R **Throws:** R
Ht: 6' 1" **Wt:** 180

Opening Day Age: 26
Born: 8/7/75 in Barranquilla, Colombia
ML Seasons: 6
Pronunciation: ren-ter-REE-uh

Overall Statistics

	G	AB	R	H	D	T	HR	RBI	SB	BB	SO	Avg	OBP	Slg
2001	141	493	54	128	19	3	10	57	17	39	73	.260	.314	.371
Career	838	3205	477	895	144	14	49	310	164	281	486	.279	.337	.379

Where He Hits the Ball

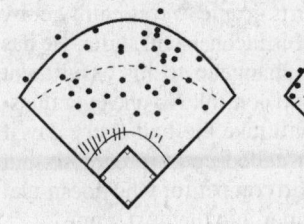
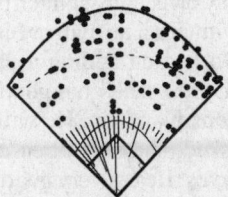

Vs. LHP   **Vs. RHP**

2001 Situational Stats

	AB	H	HR	RBI	Avg		AB	H	HR	RBI	Avg
Home	234	63	3	24	.269	LHP	98	32	3	17	.327
Road	259	65	7	33	.251	RHP	395	96	7	40	.243
First Half	246	58	5	28	.236	Sc Pos	114	30	3	49	.263
Scnd Half	247	70	5	29	.283	Clutch	63	18	0	7	.286

2001 Rankings (National League)

- 2nd in errors at shortstop (24)
- 3rd in lowest fielding percentage at shortstop (.961)
- 6th in lowest on-base percentage vs. righthanded pitchers (.292)
- 8th in stolen-base percentage (81.0)
- Led the Cardinals in stolen bases and stolen-base percentage (81.0)

Dave Veres

2001 Season

After saving 31 and 29 games the previous two years, Dave Veres was considered the Cardinals' closer entering 2001. But his hold on the job slipped as the season went on. His save total wound up nearly cut in half from the year before, while his earned run average rose by nearly a run. He also was hampered by back troubles in July and by a strained hamstring late in the campaign, and didn't garner any save opportunities after August 18.

Pitching

Veres often has to struggle to maintain the proper release point of his split-finger fastball. When everything is in gear, his splitter can produce strikeouts and groundballs. However, on those days when his splitter is erratic, Veres can't get by with just a fastball or his inconsistent slider. He has worked on adding a changeup to his assortment and he usually has good control. No one ever questions his effort. He will take the ball every day if asked, and he's often called upon to earn six-out saves. He is a very good competitor who doesn't let a bad performance linger into the next game.

Defense & Hitting

Unlike many relievers, Veres is a complete pitcher. However, after going errorless during his two years with Colorado, he's committed five miscues the past two seasons. He holds runners well, though he is fairly slow in his delivery home. He allowed just one stolen base in 2001. On the rare instances when he's called upon to bat, Veres can lay down a bunt or make contact.

2002 Outlook

St. Louis signed Oakland closer Jason Isringhausen over the winter. Even with Veres out as the main closer, he will remain an important part of the Cardinals' bullpen mix. He will provide greater value if he can limit the kind of damage that lefthanded batters inflicted last season.

Position: RP
Bats: R **Throws:** R
Ht: 6' 2" **Wt:** 220

Opening Day Age: 35
Born: 10/19/66 in Montgomery, AL
ML Seasons: 8
Pronunciation: VEERZ

Overall Statistics

	W	L	Pct.	ERA	G	GS	Sv	IP	H	BB	SO	HR	Ratio
2001	3	2	.600	3.70	71	0	15	65.2	57	28	61	12	1.29
Career	29	26	.527	3.36	503	0	90	578.2	558	213	523	62	1.33

How Often He Throws Strikes

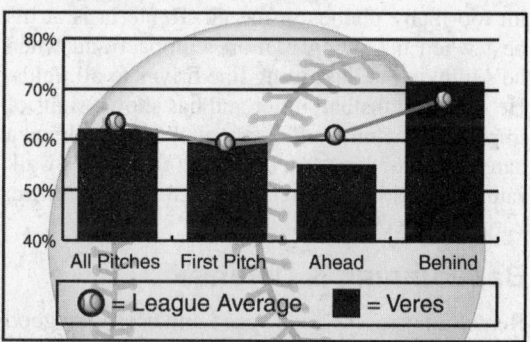

2001 Situational Stats

	W	L	ERA	Sv	IP		AB	H	HR	RBI	Avg
Home	1	1	4.50	8	34.0	LHB	93	22	7	10	.237
Road	2	1	2.84	7	31.2	RHB	153	35	5	16	.229
First Half	0	1	3.31	11	35.1	Sc Pos	64	11	3	16	.172
Scnd Half	3	1	4.15	4	30.1	Clutch	119	28	5	14	.235

2001 Rankings (National League)

- 7th in lowest batting average allowed in relief with runners in scoring position (.172)
- Led the Cardinals in saves, games finished (44), wild pitches (6), save opportunities (19), blown saves (4) and most strikeouts per nine innings in relief (8.4)

Fernando Vina

2001 Season

Fernando Vina put to rest the notion that he couldn't hold up for an entire season by having the best all-around year of his career. He was one of the Cardinals' most valuable players, logging 154 games on his way to hitting .300. He scored 95 runs and posted career-highs in homers and RBI. In addition, he won a Gold Glove for his defensive play at second base.

Hitting

Few hitters put the ball in play more consistently than Vina. He is tough to both strike out and walk. The lack of base on balls is the one flaw in his otherwise complete leadoff hitter's package. However, he is one of the best at "stealing" first base by allowing pitches to just graze him while at the plate. He is a good fastball hitter who can fight off breaking stuff to the opposite field. Vina also is an adept bunter and mixes in very underrated gap power, which last year produced 47 extra-base hits. He hits lefthanded and righthanded pitching equally well.

Baserunning & Defense

Vina is someone who possesses more quickness than exceptional speed. As a result, he is an inconsistent basestealer. Even though he gets great jumps, a good throw still can beat him. Defensively, he's a premier second baseman. Though he may not quite have Alomar-esque range, Vina does have a strong and accurate arm, fearless diving ability and great hands. And no one hangs in better on the double play.

2002 Outlook

Like so many other modern players who hit their prime in their 30s due to improved conditioning, Vina's best years may be ahead of him. He is one of the game's best second basemen and he also brings to the table a leadoff skill that is increasingly rare. He can be a premier player for St. Louis into the foreseeable future.

Position: 2B
Bats: L **Throws:** R
Ht: 5' 9" **Wt:** 174

Opening Day Age: 32
Born: 4/16/69 in Sacramento, CA
ML Seasons: 9
Pronunciation: VEEN-yah

Overall Statistics

	G	AB	R	H	D	T	HR	RBI	SB	BB	SO	Avg	OBP	Slg
2001	154	631	95	191	30	8	9	56	17	32	35	.303	.357	.418
Career	908	3244	496	937	146	40	35	259	93	224	223	.289	.356	.391

Where He Hits the Ball

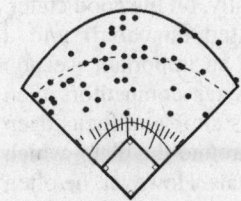
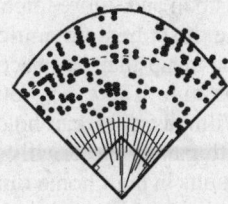

Vs. LHP   **Vs. RHP**

2001 Situational Stats

	AB	H	HR	RBI	Avg		AB	H	HR	RBI	Avg
Home	314	90	5	35	.287	LHP	130	41	2	16	.315
Road	317	101	4	21	.319	RHP	501	150	7	40	.299
First Half	339	102	3	33	.301	Sc Pos	119	37	2	46	.311
Scnd Half	292	89	6	23	.305	Clutch	73	23	1	11	.315

2001 Rankings (National League)

- 1st in fielding percentage at second base (.987) and fewest pitches seen per plate appearance (3.18)
- 2nd in singles, hit by pitch (22) and bunts in play (34)
- Led the Cardinals in at-bats, singles, triples, stolen bases, caught stealing (7), hit by pitch (22), plate appearances (690), bunts in play (34), lowest percentage of swings that missed (7.7), highest percentage of swings put into play (56.0), steals of third (3), batting average in the clutch, on-base percentage for a leadoff hitter (.356), on-base percentage vs. lefthanded pitchers (.390) and batting average on the road

Woody Williams

2001 Season

Few General Managers have made more good trades over the last few years than Cardinals GM Walt Jocketty. And none of his moves were better than last summer's acquisition of Woody Williams. After coming from San Diego in exchange for the benched Ray Lankford, Williams was one of baseball's best starters down the stretch. He went 7-1 in 11 St. Louis starts, with three complete games and a 2.28 earned run average. He also came up big in the playoffs versus Arizona.

Pitching

A year removed from surgery to remove an aneurysm near his right armpit, Williams rehabbed himself into great shape. He's added 2-4 MPH on his fastball and, more importantly, on his good cutter. He also has an underrated curveball and a changeup that has become an important weapon for him. There are few better competitors than Williams, who can hold his stuff and focus deep into games. He usually is around the plate, which results in high home run totals. However, he often limits the damage done by the longballs because he controls his walks and pitches well with men on base.

Defense & Hitting

Williams is slow coming to the plate and lacks a good pickoff move. As a result, he is very vulnerable to basestealers. But he is a fundamentally sound defensive player. Williams has made himself one of the top hitting pitchers in the National League. His career average is over .200, and he delivered five doubles and seven RBI in 2001.

2002 Outlook

In Williams, St. Louis added another character player to its starting rotation. A relatively late bloomer, Williams didn't record his 10th major league victory until he was 30 years of age. But he's won at least 10 games each of the past four seasons. He fits in perfectly with the Cardinals. There's every expectation that he can match or even improve upon the 15 wins he registered between two teams in 2001.

Position: SP
Bats: R **Throws:** R
Ht: 6' 0" **Wt:** 195

Opening Day Age: 35
Born: 8/19/66 in Houston, TX
ML Seasons: 9

Overall Statistics

	W	L	Pct.	ERA	G	GS	Sv	IP	H	BB	SO	HR	Ratio
2001	15	9	.625	4.05	34	34	0	220.0	224	56	154	35	1.27
Career	65	63	.508	4.20	256	166	0	1209.2	1178	434	841	179	1.33

How Often He Throws Strikes

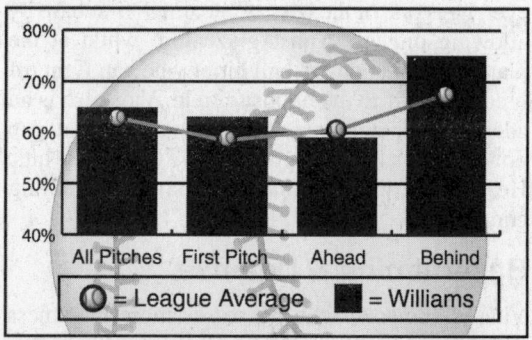

2001 Situational Stats

	W	L	ERA	Sv	IP		AB	H	HR	RBI	Avg
Home	5	4	3.59	0	95.1	LHB	374	94	16	47	.251
Road	10	5	4.40	0	124.2	RHB	463	130	19	53	.281
First Half	6	6	5.04	0	121.1	Sc Pos	162	43	6	63	.265
Scnd Half	9	3	2.83	0	98.2	Clutch	48	14	2	4	.292

2001 Rankings (National League)

- 1st in errors at pitcher (4)
- 3rd in lowest fielding percentage at pitcher (.907)
- 4th in games started (34), home runs allowed (35) and most run support per nine innings (6.0)
- 7th in complete games (3), pitches thrown (3,498) and most home runs allowed per nine innings (1.43)
- 8th in hits allowed (224)
- 9th in innings pitched (220.0)
- 10th in batters faced (922)
- Led the Cardinals in complete games (3) and most GDPs induced per GDP situation (21.4%)

Rick Ankiel

Position: SP
Bats: L **Throws:** L
Ht: 6' 1" **Wt:** 210

Opening Day Age: 22
Born: 7/19/79 in Fort Pierce, FL
ML Seasons: 3
Pronunciation: ann-KEEL

Overall Statistics

	W	L	Pct.	ERA	G	GS	Sv	IP	H	BB	SO	HR	Ratio
2001	1	2	.333	7.13	6	6	0	24.0	25	25	27	7	2.08
Career	12	10	.545	3.84	46	41	0	232.0	188	129	260	30	1.37

2001 Situational Stats

	W	L	ERA	Sv	IP		AB	H	HR	RBI	Avg
Home	0	1	7.30	0	12.1	LHB	9	3	0	1	.333
Road	1	1	6.94	0	11.2	RHB	82	22	7	16	.268
First Half	1	2	7.13	0	24.0	Sc Pos	35	3	1	9	.086
Scnd Half	0	0	-	0	0.0	Clutch	0	0	0	0	-

2001 Season

Rick Ankiel's comeback from the inexplicable wildness that emerged at the end of 2000 lasted six tortured starts in St. Louis. He worked a total of 24 innings in those outings, during which time he was hit hard and battled his lack of control. The Cardinals shut Ankiel down for a bit before dispatching him to a Rookie-level league, where they hoped he could enjoy success and regain some of his previous form. That he did, striking out more than 16 batters per nine innings in the Appalachian League.

Pitching, Defense & Hitting

Ankiel's problem has never been physical. His stuff is awesome, and includes a high-90s fastball that can explode up in the zone or sink. He also has a big-time curveball and effective changeup. Still, it all comes down to Ankiel's not unraveling. With maturity, he should be a good fielder. He already may be the best hitting pitcher in baseball, nailing 10 homers in the minors last season.

2002 Outlook

By adding to the depth of their starting rotation, the Cardinals can be patient with Ankiel. Remember, he's still just 22, roughly two years younger than Roy Oswalt. If Ankiel indeed can overcome Steve Blass Disease, St. Louis will have one of the game's best young pitchers.

Andy Benes

Position: SP
Bats: R **Throws:** R
Ht: 6' 6" **Wt:** 245

Opening Day Age: 34
Born: 8/20/67 in Evansville, IN
ML Seasons: 13
Pronunciation: BENN-ess
Nickname: Big Train, Rain Man

Overall Statistics

	W	L	Pct.	ERA	G	GS	Sv	IP	H	BB	SO	HR	Ratio
2001	7	7	.500	7.38	27	19	0	107.1	122	61	78	30	1.70
Career	150	135	.526	4.02	385	370	1	2408.1	2297	858	1936	279	1.31

2001 Situational Stats

	W	L	ERA	Sv	IP		AB	H	HR	RBI	Avg
Home	6	2	5.71	0	63.0	LHB	185	53	13	35	.286
Road	1	5	9.74	0	44.1	RHB	241	69	17	48	.286
First Half	6	6	6.95	0	89.1	Sc Pos	93	30	3	48	.323
Scnd Half	1	1	9.50	0	18.0	Clutch	16	7	3	5	.438

2001 Season

After posting double-digit victory totals in 10 of the previous 11 seasons, Andy Benes opened his 2001 campaign by allowing 10 runs at Coors Field on April 4. It didn't get a whole lot better thereafter, and by midseason, Benes had pitched himself out of the Cardinals' starting rotation. He ended up with the worst ERA of his career. He also allowed 30 homers in just 107.1 innings, the second highest rate in history (minimum 100 innings).

Pitching, Defense & Hitting

The story of Benes' career slide begins with his inability to consistently change speeds. His velocity has slipped into the upper 80s and he has lost the release point on his slider, making him exceptionally vulnerable to the home run. Benes always has been an average fielder. He is slow to the plate and can be run on. He occasionally helps himself with the bat, as his three extra-base hits last season ranked second among Cardinal hurlers.

2002 Outlook

Benes has become a very marginal commodity. His market value has plummeted to the point where St. Louis can't give him away. Although he's signed for this season, his only chance to help the Cardinals' staff would seem to be as a long reliever.

St. Louis

Luther Hackman

Position: RP
Bats: R **Throws:** R
Ht: 6' 4" **Wt:** 195

Opening Day Age: 27
Born: 10/10/74 in Columbus, MS
ML Seasons: 3

Overall Statistics

	W	L	Pct.	ERA	G	GS	Sv	IP	H	BB	SO	HR	Ratio
2001	1	2	.333	4.29	35	0	1	35.2	28	14	24	7	1.18
Career	2	4	.333	6.46	41	3	1	54.1	58	30	34	12	1.62

2001 Situational Stats

	W	L	ERA	Sv	IP		AB	H	HR	RBI	Avg
Home	0	0	4.82	0	18.2	LHB	39	12	3	5	.308
Road	1	2	3.71	1	17.0	RHB	93	16	4	10	.172
First Half	0	0	5.06	0	5.1	Sc Pos	43	4	1	6	.093
Scnd Half	1	2	4.15	1	30.1	Clutch	38	7	1	4	.184

2001 Season

Luther Hackman opened last season on the disabled list due to a sore right elbow. He returned to the minors when he was able to pitch, but was called up to St. Louis by the end of June. He then settled in to do a solid job in middle relief with the Cardinals. He allowed only one of 20 inherited runners to score.

Pitching, Defense & Hitting

Hackman throws a cutter in the low 90s and also a sinker. He can be tough to hit when he is ahead in the count. However, he doesn't have consistent command, nor has he yet developed a serviceable offspeed pitch. Hackman has a slow delivery but holds runners well. He does an adequate job of fielding his position. He has handled the bat fairly well in limited chances.

2002 Outlook

Last year was Hackman's first full season as a reliever. He had been a starter while working in the Colorado organization and initially in the Cardinals' system. But he has a good arm and showed enough last season to be considered a candidate for a middle-relief job in 2002.

Eli Marrero

Position: C
Bats: R **Throws:** R
Ht: 6' 1" **Wt:** 180

Opening Day Age: 28
Born: 11/17/73 in Havana, Cuba
ML Seasons: 5
Pronunciation: muh-RARE-oh

Overall Statistics

	G	AB	R	H	D	T	HR	RBI	SB	BB	SO	Avg	OBP	Slg
2001	86	203	37	54	11	3	6	23	6	15	36	.266	.312	.438
Career	353	921	122	211	47	6	23	101	32	72	163	.229	.285	.368

2001 Situational Stats

	AB	H	HR	RBI	Avg		AB	H	HR	RBI	Avg
Home	100	31	2	15	.310	LHP	43	11	2	2	.256
Road	103	23	4	8	.223	RHP	160	43	4	21	.269
First Half	93	26	3	8	.280	Sc Pos	55	15	0	16	.273
Scnd Half	110	28	3	15	.255	Clutch	30	7	1	2	.233

2001 Season

Though he shared playing time behind the plate with Mike Matheny last season, Eli Marrero revived much of the promise he had lost when struggling through the previous two campaigns. Marrero's .266 batting average represented a career high in the big leagues, as did his 37 runs scored. He was the Cardinals' semi-regular catcher for much of the second half.

Hitting, Baserunning & Defense

Marrero has worked on shortening his stroke and has begun using the whole field more effectively. He is a good fastball hitter, is showing better patience, and is doing a decent job of laying off breaking balls early in the count. He is one of the better running catchers in baseball and always has stolen a handful of bases with the Cardinals. Manager Tony La Russa often has used Marrero in a pinch-running capacity. Marrero has good catching skills and a quick, strong throwing arm that at times can be erratic.

2002 Outlook

Marrero gives St. Louis a solid presence as a reserve catcher, and he also has experience at first base and the outfield. The Cardinals signed Mike DiFelice, hoping to free up Marrero for more playing time at first and the outfield corners.

Mike Matheny

Position: C
Bats: R **Throws:** R
Ht: 6' 3" **Wt:** 205

Opening Day Age: 31
Born: 9/22/70 in Reynoldsburg, OH
ML Seasons: 8
Pronunciation: ma-THEEN-ee

Overall Statistics

	G	AB	R	H	D	T	HR	RBI	SB	BB	SO	Avg	OBP	Slg
2001	121	381	40	83	12	0	7	42	0	28	76	.218	.276	.304
Career	751	2133	199	498	96	5	35	234	6	129	461	.233	.285	.332

2001 Situational Stats

	AB	H	HR	RBI	Avg		AB	H	HR	RBI	Avg
Home	191	43	4	24	.225	LHP	76	14	4	14	.184
Road	190	40	3	18	.211	RHP	305	69	3	28	.226
First Half	216	52	3	20	.241	Sc Pos	86	21	1	32	.244
Scnd Half	165	31	4	22	.188	Clutch	39	10	0	3	.256

2001 Season

Mike Matheny enjoyed arguably his finest offensive season in 2000, and the Cardinals signed him to a three-year contract extension last April. But he struggled at the plate in 2001 and began losing playing time to Eli Marrero. Nevertheless, Matheny remained valuable to the Cards with his Gold Glove play behind the plate.

Hitting, Baserunning & Defense

National League pitchers have begun hammering Matheny with hard stuff on the inner half and he's had trouble adjusting. He can pull mistakes for power; his seven home runs last season were the second most of his big league career. When he's swinging well, he can put the ball in play to the opposite field. He is no threat to run. Matheny's strength is his defense at catcher, where he's the complete package. He shuts down the opposition's running game, handles pitchers well and has excellent skills in blocking balls.

2002 Outlook

St. Louis should have the kind of lineup that can carry a weaker bat, and the team's pitching staff values Matheny's catching ability. However, he needs to get his average back into the .240 range if he wants to stay in the lineup every day.

Craig Paquette

Position: 3B/LF/RF/1B
Bats: R **Throws:** R
Ht: 6' 0" **Wt:** 190

Opening Day Age: 33
Born: 3/28/69 in Long Beach, CA
ML Seasons: 9
Pronunciation: pah-KET

Overall Statistics

	G	AB	R	H	D	T	HR	RBI	SB	BB	SO	Avg	OBP	Slg
2001	123	340	47	96	17	0	15	64	3	18	67	.282	.326	.465
Career	731	2306	282	566	114	9	95	357	26	110	562	.245	.281	.426

2001 Situational Stats

	AB	H	HR	RBI	Avg		AB	H	HR	RBI	Avg
Home	168	53	8	32	.315	LHP	93	29	3	16	.312
Road	172	43	7	32	.250	RHP	247	67	12	48	.271
First Half	153	37	7	24	.242	Sc Pos	94	35	2	44	.372
Scnd Half	187	59	8	40	.316	Clutch	41	10	2	10	.244

2001 Season

Craig Paquette solidified his spot as one of the best utility players in the National League. He started at five different positions while batting .282 overall. He hit 15 homers for a second straight year and drove in 64 runs, his most since 1996. He was particularly effective with runners on base, when he batted .353 with a .561 slugging percentage.

Hitting, Baserunning & Defense

Few pitchers can get a fastball by Paquette, who zones in on the inside part of the plate and looks to drive the ball in a fastball count. He has worked on shortening his stroke, which has helped him go to the opposite field with breaking stuff away. But he always has drawn few walks, as his career on-base percentage might indicate. Paquette is a serviceable outfielder and an above-average third baseman, where he has good hands and acceptable range. He possesses average speed and rarely tries to steal.

2002 Outlook

One of Tony La Russa's favorite players, Paquette was signed away by the Tigers when he was offered a two-year deal. He can be trusted to do the job whenever asked, and he will get time at both the infield and outfield corners. Paquette is a dangerous bat to use against lefthanded pitching.

St. Louis

Bud Smith 2001 No-Hitter

Position: SP
Bats: L **Throws:** L
Ht: 6' 0" **Wt:** 170

Opening Day Age: 22
Born: 10/23/79 in Torrance, CA
ML Seasons: 1

Overall Statistics

	W	L	Pct.	ERA	G	GS	Sv	IP	H	BB	SO	HR	Ratio
2001	6	3	.667	3.83	16	14	0	84.2	79	24	59	12	1.22
Career	6	3	.667	3.83	16	14	0	84.2	79	24	59	12	1.22

2001 Situational Stats

	W	L	ERA	Sv	IP		AB	H	HR	RBI	Avg
Home	3	1	3.64	0	47.0	LHB	78	23	1	10	.295
Road	3	2	4.06	0	37.2	RHB	238	56	11	28	.235
First Half	1	0	3.52	0	7.2	Sc Pos	68	14	1	20	.206
Scnd Half	5	3	3.86	0	77.0	Clutch	10	1	1	1	.100

2001 Season

Bud Smith completed a rapid rise through the Cardinals' organization. Drafted in 1998, he arrived ahead of schedule in the majors, making his debut last June and playing a big role after the All-Star break. He provided a substantial upgrade over veteran Andy Benes in the team's rotation. Smith ended up winning six of his 14 starts and made history by throwing a no-hitter on September 3.

Pitching, Defense & Hitting

Although Smith doesn't light up radar guns, his fastball touches 90 MPH and he has excellent command, which helps him set up a very good curveball and outstanding changeup. The change actually makes him more effective against righthanded hitters. Smith is an outstanding athlete but needs to learn how to hold runners better. He swings the bat very well.

2002 Outlook

With four solid veteran righthanders around him in the rotation, Smith is perfectly positioned to be an effective part of the Cardinals' staff. His stuff is not eye-popping, but he's been a winner throughout his young career and should be a solid double-figure winner for St. Louis. While phenom Rick Ankiel has struggled, Smith looks to be a nice consolation.

Gene Stechschulte

Position: RP
Bats: R **Throws:** R
Ht: 6' 5" **Wt:** 210

Opening Day Age: 28
Born: 8/12/73 in Lima, OH
ML Seasons: 2

Overall Statistics

	W	L	Pct.	ERA	G	GS	Sv	IP	H	BB	SO	HR	Ratio
2001	1	5	.167	3.86	67	0	6	70.0	71	30	51	10	1.44
Career	2	5	.286	4.52	87	0	6	95.2	95	47	63	16	1.48

2001 Situational Stats

	W	L	ERA	Sv	IP		AB	H	HR	RBI	Avg
Home	1	2	3.03	5	35.2	LHB	80	22	1	5	.275
Road	0	3	4.72	1	34.1	RHB	180	49	9	34	.272
First Half	0	4	3.61	2	42.1	Sc Pos	62	20	3	29	.323
Scnd Half	1	1	4.23	4	27.2	Clutch	101	23	3	14	.228

2001 Season

In his first full big league season, Gene Stechschulte pitched himself into an important role in the Cardinals' bullpen as a late-inning setup man and occasional closer. He finished third on the club in appearances, ranked second with 13 holds, and earned his first six saves in the majors.

Pitching, Defense & Hitting

A successful closer in the minors, the jury is out on whether Stechschulte has the out pitch to be employed in the same role in the big leagues. He has added velocity over the last couple of years and his heavy sinker now touches the low 90s. However, his slider is erratic and he can't pitch from behind in the count. He falls off the mound, which puts him in poor fielding position. He also is fairly easy to run on. He had two hits in three at-bats last season, including a home run.

2002 Outlook

St. Louis said it might give Stechschulte a chance to close, but the Jason Isringhausen signing leaves him with middle-relief duties for which his stuff is better suited. In any case, his ability to pitch on consecutive days or fill a variety of roles may help him remain a useful contributor in the Redbirds' bullpen.

Garrett Stephenson

Position: SP
Bats: R **Throws:** R
Ht: 6' 5" **Wt:** 208

Opening Day Age: 30
Born: 1/2/72 in Takoma Park, MD
ML Seasons: 5

Overall Statistics

	W	L	Pct.	ERA	G	GS	Sv	IP	H	BB	SO	HR	Ratio
2001					Did Not Play								
Career	30	21	.588	4.44	79	67	0	432.0	447	152	283	57	1.39

2001 Situational Stats

	W	L	ERA	Sv	IP		AB	H	HR	RBI	Avg
Home	—	—	—	—	—	LHB	—	—	—	—	—
Road	—	—	—	—	—	RHB	—	—	—	—	—
First Half	—	—	—	—	—	Sc Pos	—	—	—	—	—
Scnd Half	—	—	—	—	—	Clutch	—	—	—	—	—

2001 Season

Garrett Stephenson was one of the Cardinals' most important pitchers in 2000, when he ranked second on the staff with 16 wins. But an elbow injury suffered in the playoffs that year eventually resulted in surgery, which sidelined him for all of 2001. He had only begun a throwing program by the end of the season.

Pitching, Defense & Hitting

Even when at his best, Stephenson never knocked anyone's eyes out with his stuff. He relied on a good sense of the strike zone, changing speeds and moving the ball in and out while keeping it down in the zone. Stephenson cannot survive if he is consistently falling behind in the count and is forced to throw predictable fastballs. He has a good move to first base and fields his position well. He is not a particularly good hitter. His career average is .073 (9-for-124), and he's scored just one run in 152 plate appearances.

2002 Outlook

St. Louis hopes Stephenson will be ready to take on a regular workload when spring training begins. If he is healthy and shows the kind of effectiveness that he did in 2000, Stephenson provides depth for the Cardinals, either for their own staff or in the form of trade material.

Mike Timlin

Position: RP
Bats: R **Throws:** R
Ht: 6' 4" **Wt:** 210

Opening Day Age: 36
Born: 3/10/66 in Midland, TX
ML Seasons: 11
Pronunciation: TIM-lin

Overall Statistics

	W	L	Pct.	ERA	G	GS	Sv	IP	H	BB	SO	HR	Ratio
2001	4	5	.444	4.09	67	0	3	72.2	78	19	47	6	1.33
Career	41	45	.477	3.65	592	3	114	698.2	671	265	549	59	1.34

2001 Situational Stats

	W	L	ERA	Sv	IP		AB	H	HR	RBI	Avg
Home	3	1	1.87	0	43.1	LHB	91	29	4	17	.319
Road	1	4	7.36	3	29.1	RHB	191	49	2	12	.257
First Half	3	4	3.51	2	48.2	Sc Pos	59	16	0	19	.271
Scnd Half	1	1	5.25	1	24.0	Clutch	117	31	2	12	.265

2001 Season

Mike Timlin was one of four Cardinals relievers who appeared in over 60 games last season. He served largely a setup man, though he did get seven save opportunities, four of which he blew. He tore a knee ligament and went on the disabled list in late July, a period that coincided with a general drop in effectiveness. He allowed a .243 average before the All-Star break, and a .333 mark thereafter.

Pitching, Defense & Hitting

Timlin throws in the low to mid-90s with sinking movement. He also has what can at times be an overpowering slider. However, the slider too often is inconsistent, as is his overall command. Those are two reasons why lefthanded hitters batted over .300 against him. He does a good job holding runners and fields his position adequately. Timlin has had only one at-bat in his career.

2002 Outlook

Timlin's ability to take the ball regularly makes him a useful part of any bullpen. He has worked at least 60 games each of the past five seasons. He can be used in a variety of roles and figures to remain especially valuable when spotted against righthanded hitters.

St. Louis

Other St. Louis Cardinals

Alan Benes (**Pos**: RHP, **Age**: 30)

	W	L	Pct.	ERA	G	GS	Sv	IP	H	BB	SO	HR	Ratio
2001	2	0	1.000	7.36	9	1	0	14.2	14	12	10	5	1.77
Career	27	23	.540	4.42	101	59	0	431.1	414	194	349	54	1.41

Benes has had moderate success in the minors as a starter, but has struggled in the majors as a reliever. He's lost velocity due to shoulder problems. 2002 Outlook: C

Bobby Bonilla (**Pos**: 1B, **Age**: 39, **Bats**: B)

	G	AB	R	H	D	T	HR	RBI	SB	BB	SO	Avg	OBP	Slg
2001	93	174	17	37	7	0	5	21	1	23	53	.213	.308	.339
Career	2113	7213	1084	2010	408	61	287	1173	45	912	1204	.279	.358	.472

Bonilla will be 39 this season and his years as an everyday player are well behind him. The switch-hitter became a free agent in November. 2002 Outlook: C

Miguel Cairo (**Pos**: 3B/2B, **Age**: 27, **Bats**: R)

	G	AB	R	H	D	T	HR	RBI	SB	BB	SO	Avg	OBP	Slg
2001	93	156	25	46	8	1	3	16	2	18	23	.295	.366	.417
Career	507	1567	196	432	70	13	12	134	71	99	159	.276	.323	.360

Cairo was picked up by the Cardinals off waivers from the Cubs in August. The utilityman doesn't have much power, but has some speed, stealing 28 bases in 2000. Cairo hit .333 as a reserve in St. Louis. 2002 Outlook: B

Stubby Clapp (**Pos**: 2B, **Age**: 29, **Bats**: B)

	G	AB	R	H	D	T	HR	RBI	SB	BB	SO	Avg	OBP	Slg
2001	23	25	0	5	2	0	0	1	0	1	7	.200	.231	.280
Career	23	25	0	5	2	0	0	1	0	1	7	.200	.231	.280

Clapp struggled with strikeouts over his first few seasons as a pro. He was more disciplined last season, and as a result, raised his batting average at Triple-A to .304. He has little power and moderate speed. 2002 Outlook: C

Mike James (**Pos**: RHP, **Age**: 34)

	W	L	Pct.	ERA	G	GS	Sv	IP	H	BB	SO	HR	Ratio
2001	1	2	.333	5.21	40	0	0	38.0	43	17	26	5	1.58
Career	16	14	.533	3.60	275	0	11	302.2	273	144	237	28	1.38

After overcoming elbow problems, James was limited to 40 games in 2001 by tendinitis in his throwing shoulder. He missed two months with the injury, and then became a free agent in November. 2002 Outlook: C

Jason Karnuth (**Pos**: RHP, **Age**: 25)

	W	L	Pct.	ERA	G	GS	Sv	IP	H	BB	SO	HR	Ratio
2001	0	0	-	1.80	4	0	0	5.0	6	4	1	1	2.00
Career	0	0	-	1.80	4	0	0	5.0	6	4	1	1	2.00

Karnuth is not an overpowering pitcher and has some control problems. However, he pitched well in a short stint with the Cardinals early in 2001. 2002 Outlook: C

T.J. Mathews (**Pos**: RHP, **Age**: 32)

	W	L	Pct.	ERA	G	GS	Sv	IP	H	BB	SO	HR	Ratio
2001	1	1	.500	4.30	30	0	1	37.2	39	12	29	4	1.35
Career	32	26	.552	3.84	350	0	16	417.0	387	159	344	47	1.31

Mathews was signed by the Cards last July after being designated for assignment by the A's. The reliever appeared in 30 games between the two teams, with much better numbers in St. Louis. He opted for free agency in November. 2002 Outlook: B

Mike Matthews (**Pos**: LHP, **Age**: 28)

	W	L	Pct.	ERA	G	GS	Sv	IP	H	BB	SO	HR	Ratio
2001	3	4	.429	3.24	51	10	1	89.0	74	33	72	11	1.20
Career	3	4	.429	4.03	65	10	1	98.1	89	43	80	13	1.34

Matthews appeared in 65 games for St. Louis since 2000, including 10 starts. He fared better in relief, posting a 3.00 ERA compared to 5.13 as a starter. Lefties have hit just .150 against him. 2002 Outlook: B

Keith McDonald (**Pos**: C, **Age**: 29, **Bats**: R)

	G	AB	R	H	D	T	HR	RBI	SB	BB	SO	Avg	OBP	Slg
2001	2	2	0	0	0	0	0	0	0	0	1	.000	.000	.000
Career	8	9	3	3	0	0	3	5	0	2	2	.333	.455	1.333

Not really known as a power hitter, McDonald has cranked three home runs in nine career at-bats in the major leagues. He has spent the last four years in Triple-A, batting nearly .280. A possible third catcher for St. Louis. 2002 Outlook: C

Mark McGwire (**Pos**: 1B, **Age**: 38, **Bats**: R)

	G	AB	R	H	D	T	HR	RBI	SB	BB	SO	Avg	OBP	Slg
2001	97	299	48	56	4	0	29	64	0	56	118	.187	.316	.492
Career	1874	6187	1167	1626	252	6	583	1414	12	1317	1596	.263	.394	.588

In a year when his single-season home-run record was being shattered, knee problems helped reduce McGwire to clubbing taters, walking or striking out. He decided to call it quits 17 homers shy of 600. 2002 Outlook: D

Kerry Robinson (**Pos**: LF/CF/RF, **Age**: 28, **Bats**: L)

	G	AB	R	H	D	T	HR	RBI	SB	BB	SO	Avg	OBP	Slg
2001	114	186	34	53	6	1	1	15	11	12	20	.285	.330	.344
Career	125	190	38	53	6	1	1	15	11	12	22	.279	.324	.337

Robinson is a consistent hitter who almost always puts the ball in play. He struck out just 20 times in 186 at-bats. His downfalls are his lack of power and lack of a strong arm in the outfield. 2002 Outlook: C

Larry Sutton (**Pos**: 1B, **Age**: 31, **Bats**: L)

	G	AB	R	H	D	T	HR	RBI	SB	BB	SO	Avg	OBP	Slg
2001	33	42	3	5	1	0	1	3	0	1	10	.119	.140	.214
Career	237	548	60	132	23	2	11	74	4	53	92	.241	.307	.350

Sutton was traded to the Twins after filling in for the injured Mark McGwire at first base for St. Louis. Sutton, who also can play outfield, has shown some power, but not consistently. Disciplined hitter. 2002 Outlook: C

Jeff Tabaka (**Pos**: LHP, **Age**: 38)

	W	L	Pct.	ERA	G	GS	Sv	IP	H	BB	SO	HR	Ratio
2001	0	0	-	7.36	8	0	0	3.2	6	1	3	1	1.91
Career	6	5	.545	4.31	139	0	2	148.1	131	82	119	16	1.44

Tabaka started in the minors in 1986 and has made only 139 appearances in the majors in his career. Elbow problems have limited his production over the last few years. Despite a 2.60 ERA in Triple-A in 2001, the lefty was released by the Cardinals in November. 2002 Outlook: D

St. Louis Cardinals Minor League Prospects

Organization Overview:

The Cardinals are an interesting organization. Not one of their affiliates finished more than a handful of games below .500 last season. You'll have a hard time finding many upper-echelon gems in their system. And many of their best pitching prospects were stricken with serious arm injuries in 2001. Yet over the past few years, that same system has been able to pump out players who have either contributed with the Cardinals or been used as trade bait. Albert Pujols jumped to the majors at age 21 and was named the National League's Rookie of the Year in 2001. Bud Smith threw a no-hitter in his 11th big league start. And over the past couple years, prospects have been included in trade packages that have landed players the caliber of Jim Edmonds, Darryl Kile and Dustin Hermanson. Someone could surprise this season, but the minor league pipeline now seems fairly dry.

Shaun Boyd

Position: 2B   **Opening Day Age:** 20
Bats: R **Throws:** R   **Born:** 8/15/81 in Corona,
Ht: 5' 10" **Wt:** 175   CA

Recent Statistics

	G	AB	R	H	D	THR	RBI	SB	BB	SO	Avg
2000 R Johnson Cty	43	152	15	40	9	0	2	15	6	10	22	.263
2001 A Peoria	81	277	42	78	12	2	5	27	20	33	42	.282

The Cardinals used the first of two No. 1 picks in 2000 to select Boyd with the 13th choice overall. Although he hasn't posted fabulous numbers in his first two professional seasons, the Cardinals say Boyd has made great strides at the plate. He has gap power and uses the whole field. Last year's walk and strikeout rates indicate that he could have fairly decent control of the strike zone. He may be only an average runner, but still stole 20 bases in the Midwest League last year. His defensive game looks like it still needs some work. After playing the outfield in 2000, he switched to second base at Peoria. His arm may be a bit short but he does have good quickness.

Luis Garcia

Position: 1B   **Opening Day Age:** 23
Bats: R **Throws:** R   **Born:** 11/5/78 in
Ht: 6' 4" **Wt:** 184   Guadalajara, Mexico

Recent Statistics

	G	AB	R	H	D	THR	RBI	SB	BB	SO	Avg
2000 A Augusta	128	493	72	128	27	5	20	77	8	51	112	.260
2001 A Sarasota	65	267	38	81	14	1	12	44	2	18	61	.303
2001 AA Trenton	63	229	35	71	20	1	14	45	0	28	68	.310
2001 MLE	63	221	28	63	19	0	10	36	0	19	73	.285

Garcia was signed by the Red Sox as a pitcher in 1996, but an arm injury quickly ended his career on the mound. He went to the Dominican Summer League in 1998 as a hitter, didn't show much, and found himself on loan to Monterrey of the Mexican League in '99. Garcia sur- prised the Red Sox by stroking 20 homers at Class-A Augusta in 2000. Then he batted .306-26-89 and slugged .540 between high Class-A Sarasota and Double-A Trenton last summer. The Cardinals obtained him in the package for Dustin Hermanson in December. Garcia can hit the fastball, recognizes the breaking ball and has shown some inclination to draw walks. He is a decent defender and has some experience in the outfield.

Jimmy Journell

Position: P   **Opening Day Age:** 24
Bats: R **Throws:** R   **Born:** 12/29/77 in
Ht: 6' 4" **Wt:** 205   Springfield, OH

Recent Statistics

	W	L	ERA	G	GS	Sv	IP	H	R	BB	SO	HR
2000 A New Jersey	1	0	1.97	13	1	0	32.0	12	12	24	39	0
2001 A Potomac	14	6	2.50	26	26	0	151.0	121	54	42	156	8
2001 AA New Haven	1	0	0.00	1	1	0	7.0	0	0	3	6	0

St. Louis grabbed Journell in the fourth round of the 1999 draft. Although he was the fifth hurler taken overall by the Cardinals that year, he now may be the best pitching prospect in their entire minor league system. He throws a plus fastball that can reach 97 MPH and usually resides at 94-95 MPH. He also has a power slider that got better as last season progressed, as well as a good changeup. He needs to use his other stuff more often and gain consistency. He has had injury problems in the past and hadn't pitched that much professionally until last season, when he led the Carolina League in ERA. The Cardinals want him to face better hitters, which he'll probably do in Double-A this year.

Jeremy Lambert

Position: P   **Opening Day Age:** 23
Bats: R **Throws:** R   **Born:** 1/10/79 in Salt
Ht: 6' 1" **Wt:** 195   Lake City, UT

Recent Statistics

	W	L	ERA	G	GS	Sv	IP	H	R	BB	SO	HR
2000 A Potomac	0	0	4.40	16	3	0	28.2	30	17	7	28	1
2000 AA Arkansas	0	2	3.83	39	0	3	47.0	41	27	28	63	1
2001 AA New Haven	2	2	2.97	31	0	14	33.1	32	17	17	48	4
2001 AAA Memphis	5	1	3.23	28	0	3	30.2	23	14	8	39	7

Lambert signed with the Cardinals as a 16th-round pick out of a Utah high school in 1997. He reached Triple-A last season at age 22. He is not an overpowering sort, with a fastball that resides in the 87-90 MPH range. But he possesses a good understanding of how to pitch, features some deception in his delivery and can be effective when he keeps the ball down. He complements the fastball with a slider and a changeup, helping him strike out 12.2 batters per nine innings in 2001. It was his first lengthy shot at closing and he led New Haven in saves in roughly half a season there. He can get in trouble, how- ever, if he gets his pitches up in the zone. He likely is ticketed for Triple-A this year.

Scotty Layfield

Position: P **Opening Day Age:** 25
Bats: R **Throws:** R **Born:** 9/13/76 in
Ht: 6' 2" **Wt:** 205 Americas, GA

Recent Statistics

	W	L	ERA	G	GS	Sv	IP	H	R	BB	SO	HR
2000 A Peoria	2	4	5.13	53	0	15	54.1	65	46	40	50	4
2001 A Potomac	1	2	1.84	47	0	31	53.2	36	13	18	66	1

Layfield hasn't attracted much attention in the past. He pitched collegiately at Valdosta State and wasn't selected until the 20th round of the 1999 draft. And he hadn't shown much in the minors until last season, when the Cardinals say he kind of jumped up on them. He led the organization with 31 saves in 2001 and St. Louis has added Layfield to its 40-man roster. He has a power arm and works with a plus fastball and slider. He is a physical specimen and the Redbirds actually have had to tone down his weight work. His velocity has increased by four MPH and his fastball now travels between 90-94 MPH. Even though he turned 25 last September and has yet to pitch above Class-A, the Cardinals are excited by Layfield's progress.

Chris Narveson

Position: P **Opening Day Age:** 20
Bats: L **Throws:** L **Born:** 12/20/81 in
Ht: 6' 3" **Wt:** 180 Englewood, CO

Recent Statistics

	W	L	ERA	G	GS	Sv	IP	H	R	BB	SO	HR
2000 R Johnson Cty	2	4	3.27	12	12	0	55.0	57	33	25	63	7
2001 A Peoria	3	3	1.98	8	8	0	50.0	32	14	11	53	3
2001 A Potomac	4	3	2.57	11	11	0	66.2	52	22	13	53	4

Injuries wreaked havoc with many of the Cardinals' top pitching prospects last season, and Narveson couldn't escape the scourge. He hurt his elbow and had Tommy John surgery in August. Before going under the knife, Narveson had compiled great numbers at two stops in Class-A, where he demonstrated impressive maturity while working at age 19. Drafted in the second round out of a North Carolina high school in 2000, Narveson possesses great mound presence and decent command of all three of his pitches—an 87-91 MPH fastball, curveball and changeup. The Cardinals hope he can be back throwing off a mound in spring training, though it may be a bit longer before he pitches in a full-season league.

Bill Ortega

Position: OF **Opening Day Age:** 26
Bats: R **Throws:** R **Born:** 7/24/75 in
Ht: 6' 4" **Wt:** 205 Havana, Cuba

Recent Statistics

	G	AB	R	H	D	T	HR	RBI	SB	BB	SO	Avg
2001 AAA Memphis	134	495	55	142	26	4	6	62	6	40	74	.287
2001 NL St. Louis	5	5	0	1	0	0	0	0	0	0	1	.200
2001 MLE	134	477	44	124	23	2	4	50	4	32	77	.260

Ortega signed with the Cardinals as an undrafted free agent in early 1997. Although he hit OK during his first season at Triple-A Memphis last season, he didn't enjoy quite the success he had the previous two years, when he topped .300. He also didn't show a great deal of power, something the Cardinals would like to see more of from him, especially when you consider how Ortega looks physically. He is an outstanding athlete and has made great strides in the outfield. While he can handle center field, he profiles best in right. Already 26 years of age, he isn't a tremendous prospect, but he has a chance to play in the big leagues this season.

Nick Stocks

Position: P **Opening Day Age:** 23
Bats: R **Throws:** R **Born:** 8/27/78 in Tampa,
Ht: 6' 2" **Wt:** 185 FL

Recent Statistics

	W	L	ERA	G	GS	Sv	IP	H	R	BB	SO	HR
2000 A Peoria	10	10	3.78	25	24	0	150.0	133	88	52	118	4
2001 AA New Haven	2	12	5.16	16	15	0	82.0	89	52	33	63	10

Stocks is one Cardinals prospect who had Tommy John surgery before he joined the organization. Stocks bounced back well enough from the procedure that the Cardinals chose him with a supplemental first-round pick in 1999. Pitching for Florida State that season, he had led the Atlantic Coast Conference with 139 strikeouts while sharing the league lead with 13 wins. Stocks didn't enjoy nearly the same type of success at Double-A in 2001, where he also suffered back pain. His out pitch is a big curveball, which he uses along with an 89-94 MPH fastball and fair changeup. He may need to get away from a strikeout mentality and work on his approach with hitters. He could be back at Double-A in 2002, though Triple-A also is a possibility.

Others to Watch

Covelli Crisp (22) ranked third in the Carolina League with a .306 average. He will try to make the shift to center field, though his arm may not be strong enough. . . Some evaluators are big on righthander **Michael Crudale's** (25) arm. His stuff isn't necessarily electric, but he does possess a 90-93 MPH fastball, a slurvy kind of slider and a changeup. That combination has helped him strike out roughly one man per inning during his professional career. . . Righthander **Chad Hutchinson** (25) may have finally given up after walking over a batter per inning at Triple-A last year. A standout quarterback in college, he reportedly was considering taking a shot at the NFL. . . Outfielder **Christopher Morris** (22) led the minor leagues with 111 stolen bases in 2001. He also draws a lot of walks, but has very little power. . . Righthander **Josh Pearce** (24) was a second-round supplemental pick in 1999. He hasn't walked many hitters and won 10 games between Double- and Triple-A last season. . . **Luis Saturria's** (25) batting average plummeted at Triple-A Memphis. He has occasional power, can play any outfield position, and may stick as a spare part for the Cardinals.

Qualcomm Stadium

Offense

Qualcomm Stadium strongly favors pitchers. There is an above-average amount of foul territory around the infield, and ever since they enclosed the outfield in 1998 to accommodate the Super Bowl, the ball carries very poorly. The ball *does* carry better in day games, but the mound and hitters' background are in the glaring Southern California sun while the plate is covered in shadows, making pitches disappear halfway to the plate.

Defense

Left field at Qualcomm is a very difficult place to play. The sun is the problem in day games, and the light standards are so low that the glare interferes with all but the most towering flyballs at night. The hardness of the infield soil is uneven, making for some interesting hops. The bullpens, which are in play, are just off the outfield corners and partially hidden from home plate by a section of the stands that juts out just short of the foul line.

Who It Helps the Most

Just about any pitcher will find the confines of the Q friendly. Bobby Jones probably was the greatest beneficiary of home cooking, with an ERA of nearly two runs less at home, and Kevin Jarvis also fared significantly better in San Diego than on the road. Rookie Brian Lawrence pitched better on the road, though that is likely to change as he gets used to taking advantage of his home park.

Who It Hurts the Most

Before the changes to the outfield stands, Qualcomm actually was a good place for home-run hitters, righthanders in particular. Ever since then, it's been tough on all hitters. Everyone but Tony Gwynn, Phil Nevin and Mark Kotsay saw an appreciable drop in batting average at home in 2001.

Rookies & Newcomers

Qualcomm's run-suppressing ways should help young hurlers like Brett Tomko, Brett Jodie and Jason Middlebrook gain confidence. D'Angelo Jimenez struggled at home, but his plate discipline helped offset any dip in slugging. Sean Burroughs' power may not yet show, but he looks like he can hit just about anywhere.

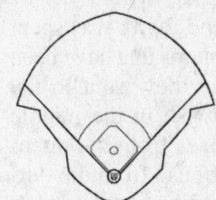

Dimensions: LF-327, LCF-370, CF-405, RCF-370, RF-330

Capacity: 46,510

Elevation: 20 feet

Surface: Grass

Foul Territory: Large

Park Factors

2001 Season

| | Home Games | | | Away Games | | | |
	Padres	Opp	Total	Padres	Opp	Total	Index
G	72	72	144	75	75	150	—
Avg	.227	.253	.241	.271	.283	.277	87
AB	2334	2535	4869	2645	2576	5221	97
R	278	344	622	437	384	821	79
H	530	641	1171	716	728	1444	84
2B	102	110	212	152	154	306	74
3B	14	14	28	11	17	28	107
HR	56	98	154	89	102	191	86
BB	292	217	509	325	222	547	100
SO	581	514	1095	589	469	1058	111
E	77	38	115	54	62	116	103
E-Infield	72	32	104	43	48	91	119
LHB-Avg	.249	.262	.255	.287	.275	.281	91
LHB-HR	26	50	76	36	44	80	99
RHB-Avg	.209	.246	.229	.258	.288	.273	84
RHB-HR	30	48	78	53	58	111	77

1999-2001

| | Home Games | | | Away Games | | | |
	Padres	Opp	Total	Padres	Opp	Total	Index
G	218	218	436	223	223	446	—
Avg	.250	.249	.249	.258	.282	.270	92
AB	7196	7603	14799	7737	7575	15312	99
R	942	994	1936	1135	1214	2349	84
H	1797	1893	3690	1994	2135	4129	91
2B	331	328	659	413	404	817	83
3B	42	31	73	36	49	85	89
HR	186	259	445	249	291	540	85
BB	850	693	1543	864	807	1671	96
SO	1619	1542	3161	1665	1376	3041	108
E	211	143	354	172	163	335	108
E-Infield	192	117	309	144	134	278	114
LHB-Avg	.267	.251	.258	.274	.291	.283	91
LHB-HR	68	105	173	81	118	199	85
RHB-Avg	.238	.248	.243	.247	.275	.261	93
RHB-HR	118	154	272	168	173	341	86

2001 Rankings (National League)
- Second-highest strikeout factor
- Second-highest infield-error factor
- Lowest batting-average factor
- Lowest run factor
- Lowest hit factor
- Lowest double factor
- Lowest RHB batting-average factor
- Second-lowest LHB batting-average factor
- Second-lowest RHB home-run factor

San Diego

Bruce Bochy

2001 Season

Last season, much like 1999 and 2000, was spent trying to solve three major problems that have been plaguing the Padres ever since they went to the World Series in '98: poor defense in the middle infield, inconsistent performances from the pitching staff and below-average offense from the outfield. GM Kevin Towers acquired a good number of players this year, leaving Bochy with his hands full trying to fit together the pieces of the Padres' puzzle. Their final 79-83 record in the competitive NL West suggests he did a decent job.

Offense

Bochy is willing to try anything on offense in order to keep the opposition guessing. It's not uncommon for him to use his resources inefficiently, such as using a pinch-hitter to sacrifice bunt. He also has a predilection for fiddling with the batting order—not since his first year as manager has he used fewer than 110 different starting lineups in a season. In his favor, Bochy is perhaps the ultimate player's manager. He is very loyal, patient, open and honest with his players, and they return an uncommonly strong devotion to him. The result is that he gets a supreme team effort.

Defense & Pitching

Bochy usually is very conscientious regarding workloads and pitch counts. He also does a good job of instilling confidence in his pitchers, giving his starters ample opportunity to work themselves out of jams, and his relievers a chance to redeem themselves at the first opportunity. Bochy's teams are not particularly sound fundamentally speaking, so errors and questionable defensive decisions seem to plague them year after year.

2002 Outlook

San Diego has assembled its most talented team since the '98 NL champs. Yet Bochy faces some interesting challenges: how to work top prospect Sean Burroughs into the mix, how to maximize the middle-infield production of youngsters D'Angelo Jimenez and Ramon Vazquez and how to incorporate several quality pitching prospects into the rotation as they are ready. His faith in his players could be rewarded with a run at the division title.

Born: 4/16/55 in Landes de Bussac, France

Playing Experience: 1978-1987, Hou, NYM, SD

Managerial Experience: 7 seasons

Manager Statistics

Year	Team, Lg	W	L	Pct	GB	Finish
2001	San Diego, NL	79	83	.488	13.0	4th West
7 Seasons		564	552	.505	—	—

2001 Starting Pitchers by Days Rest

	<=3	4	5	6+
Padres Starts	0	74	59	18
Padres ERA	—	4.98	4.62	3.88
NL Avg Starts	1	80	47	24
NL ERA	5.03	4.43	4.53	4.28

2001 Situational Stats

	Bruce Bochy	NL Average
Hit & Run Success %	36.1	35.1
Stolen Base Success %	74.6	66.5
Platoon Pct.	60.0	51.5
Defensive Subs	27	20
High-Pitch Outings	6	7
Quick/Slow Hooks	14/15	19/14
Sacrifice Attempts	43	87

2001 Rankings (National League)
- 1st in saves with over 1 inning pitched (10)
- 2nd in stolen-base percentage, steals of second base (111) and double steals (10)
- 3rd in stolen base attempts (173), steals of third base (18), fewest caught stealings of third base (3) and slow hooks

Ben Davis

2001 Season

Ben Davis got off to a rough start in spring training but was able to win the starting catching job in San Diego by the end of April. Once entrenched behind the plate, he hit .276 and slugged .408 for the first three months of the campaign. He tired badly in the second half, though he managed to finish the season with the most homers by a Padres catcher since 1991.

Hitting

Davis' power is developing, so 15-20 homers a year is not out of the question in the near future. He has shortened his swing, but he still strikes out at a fairly high rate. His walk rate made a huge jump, however, a strong positive indicator for a player who has yet to reach his offensive potential. Davis may be more prone to second-half slumps than other catchers as the grind of working behind the plate is especially hard on a player as tall and lanky as he is. As he gains more body mass and experience with age, those splits should become less pronounced.

Baserunning & Defense

Davis isn't particularly fast, but his long strides allow him to take an extra base on well-hit balls and occasionally steal a base. He has a strong arm, and only inconsistent footwork prevents him from dominating the running game from behind the plate. His work as a receiver—blocking balls in the dirt, framing pitches and calling a game—in 2001 improved significantly over the previous campaign.

2002 Outlook

Davis moves on to Seattle after being traded in a six-player deal in December. He will continue to develop into one of the better defensive backstops in the major leagues under the tutelage of Mariners catcher Dan Wilson. If his walk rate improves even further, he could become a very good offensive player, as well. Another key to his continued success will be his conditioning, as he does not want to make a habit of second-half drop-offs.

Position: C
Bats: B **Throws:** R
Ht: 6' 4" **Wt:** 215

Opening Day Age: 25
Born: 3/10/77 in Chester, PA
ML Seasons: 4

Overall Statistics

	G	AB	R	H	D	T	HR	RBI	SB	BB	SO	Avg	OBP	Slg
2001	138	448	56	107	20	0	11	57	4	66	112	.239	.337	.357
Career	258	845	97	201	40	1	19	101	7	105	217	.238	.322	.355

Where He Hits the Ball

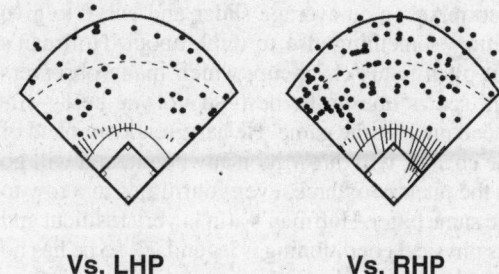

Vs. LHP   **Vs. RHP**

2001 Situational Stats

	AB	H	HR	RBI	Avg		AB	H	HR	RBI	Avg
Home	214	49	3	22	.229	LHP	108	26	5	16	.241
Road	234	58	8	35	.248	RHP	340	81	6	41	.238
First Half	250	69	7	39	.276	Sc Pos	117	32	3	49	.274
Scnd Half	198	38	4	18	.192	Clutch	78	18	1	6	.231

2001 Rankings (National League)
- 3rd in lowest fielding percentage at catcher (.990)
- 4th in errors at catcher (9) and lowest batting average

San Diego

Trevor Hoffman

2001 Season

Trevor Hoffman bounced back after a subpar 2000 season to save 43 games in 46 chances in 2001. He had a rough stretch at the end of May and all of June, giving up 15 hits and 10 earned runs in 9.2 innings, but he finished the year an a strong note, posting a 2.48 ERA after the All-Star break. Hoffman's walks and home-run rate were up over previous campaigns, perhaps an indicator that hitters are beginning to look for his changeup exclusively.

Pitching

Hoffman has a reputation of having a mid-90s fastball, but the fact is that he rarely tops 90 MPH anymore. Most of his fastballs run around 87-89 MPH with his location usually just off the plate. He also mixes in an average slider and curve to give batters something else to think about. Hoffman's out pitch is his changeup, which many observers still see as one of the best—if not *the* best—off-speed pitch in the game. He has great command of the change, will throw it on any count, and will go to the pitch two, three, even four times in a row to the same hitter. Hoffman's arm is very resilient and his physical conditioning is legendary, so he has no trouble pitching more than an inning at a time or several days in a row.

Defense & Hitting

Hoffman is a decent fielder for a reliever. Even with his high leg kick, he gets in a good position to field after delivering the ball. He has been charged with just one error in his nine-year career. His high leg kick does not help deter the running game, but he's rarely in a position where opponents are attempting to steal on him. Hoffman rarely gets a chance to hit, but when he does, he takes aggressive swings and usually gets the bat on the ball.

2002 Outlook

Hoffman, who now is the longest-tenured of any of the current Padres, is 34 years old. Whether the increase in walks and homers is a sign of aging, or just a statistical hiccup in a great career, he still has enough guile to remain one of the better closers in baseball through the last two years of his current contract.

Position: RP
Bats: R **Throws:** R
Ht: 6' 0" **Wt:** 215

Opening Day Age: 34
Born: 10/13/67 in Bellflower, CA
ML Seasons: 9

Overall Statistics

	W	L	Pct.	ERA	G	GS	Sv	IP	H	BB	SO	HR	Ratio
2001	3	4	.429	3.43	62	0	43	60.1	48	21	63	10	1.14
Career	43	39	.524	2.79	571	0	314	641.2	474	196	728	63	1.04

How Often He Throws Strikes

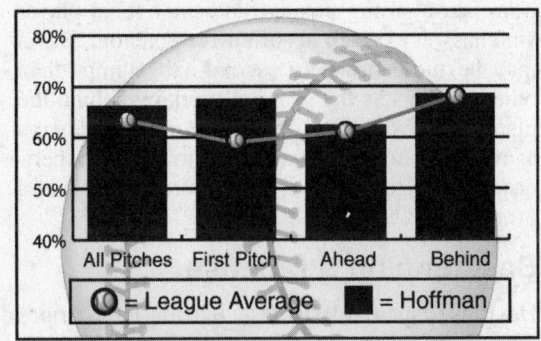

= League Average   ■ = Hoffman

2001 Situational Stats

	W	L	ERA	Sv	IP		AB	H	HR	RBI	Avg
Home	3	4	3.64	19	29.2	LHB	98	21	5	9	.214
Road	0	0	3.23	24	30.2	RHB	124	27	5	22	.218
First Half	2	3	4.31	18	31.1	Sc Pos	52	13	1	20	.250
Scnd Half	1	1	2.48	25	29.0	Clutch	177	37	6	24	.209

2001 Rankings (National League)

- 2nd in saves and save percentage (93.5)
- 3rd in save opportunities (46)
- 4th in lowest percentage of inherited runners scored (20.6)
- 7th in games finished (55)
- Led the Padres in games pitched, saves, games finished (55), save opportunities (46), save percentage (93.5), lowest percentage of inherited runners scored (20.6), first batter efficiency (.241), relief losses (4), relief innings (60.1), lowest batting average allowed in relief (.216), most strikeouts per nine innings in relief (9.4) and fewest baserunners allowed per nine innings in relief (10.4)

Kevin Jarvis

Position: SP
Bats: L **Throws:** R
Ht: 6' 2" **Wt:** 200

Opening Day Age: 32
Born: 8/1/69 in Lexington, KY
ML Seasons: 7

2001 Season

Kevin Jarvis was the Padres' biggest surprise in 2001, leading the team in wins, strikeouts and fewest baserunners per nine innings among the starters with at least 100 innings pitched. Formerly a journeyman long reliever/fifth starter, Jarvis was signed last winter as a free agent after a fairly pedestrian year in Colorado. In fact, it wasn't until he threw a seven-hit, 10-strikeout shutout against the Phillies on April 26 that he showed he could be a productive regular starter. From that game on, he was 12-9 with a 4.40 ERA.

Pitching

Jarvis is not overpowering. He throws an 89-90 MPH fastball and mixes in a decent slider, curve and change. He is very aggressive with his pitch selection, throwing strikes down in the zone and daring the hitters to swing. The upside to this strategy is that he doesn't walk many hitters and more often than not gets opponents to hit the ball on the ground. The downside is that when he doesn't keep the ball down, he gives up a lot of extra-base hits. He allowed 37 home runs—tied for second most in the majors.

Defense & Hitting

Merely an average fielder off the mound, Jarvis nevertheless holds baserunners very well. At the plate, he's certainly no automatic out. He hit a respectable .180 in 2001, and among pitchers he was second in RBI with 10, and tied for first in walks (five).

2002 Outlook

Jarvis blossomed into a solid middle-of-the-rotation starter in 2001. The Padres would like to lock him into a multiyear deal, but he pitched well enough last year to earn a substantial raise, something San Diego probably can't afford. Should he stay in Southern California, he will be counted on heavily as San Diego heads into the '02 campaign without the services of Adam Eaton, who will spend most of the upcoming season rehabbing from Tommy John surgery. At the very least, the Padres need Jarvis to continue to be a serviceable innings-eater until their collection of talented young pitchers is ready for the majors.

Overall Statistics

	W	L	Pct.	ERA	G	GS	Sv	IP	H	BB	SO	HR	Ratio
2001	12	11	.522	4.79	32	32	0	193.1	189	49	133	37	1.23
Career	27	34	.443	5.91	141	91	1	607.1	719	197	358	120	1.51

How Often He Throws Strikes

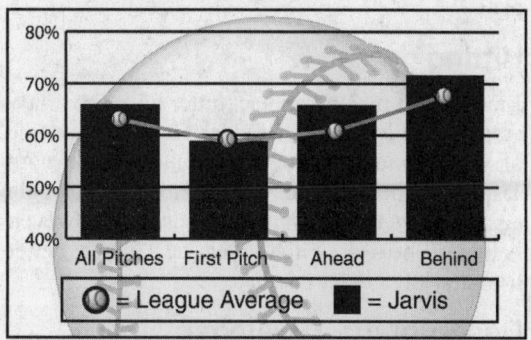

= League Average   = Jarvis

2001 Situational Stats

	W	L	ERA	Sv	IP		AB	H	HR	RBI	Avg
Home	6	5	4.17	0	101.1	LHB	319	82	19	48	.257
Road	6	6	5.48	0	92.0	RHB	425	107	18	46	.252
First Half	5	7	4.98	0	106.2	Sc Pos	152	37	7	52	.243
Scnd Half	7	4	4.57	0	86.2	Clutch	23	6	0	1	.261

2001 Rankings (National League)

- 1st in home runs allowed and most home runs allowed per nine innings (1.72)
- Led the Padres in ERA, sacrifice bunts (5), wins, walks allowed, strikeouts, runners caught stealing (8), winning percentage, lowest batting average allowed (.254), lowest slugging percentage allowed (.485), lowest on-base percentage allowed (.303), lowest stolen-base percentage allowed (50.0), fewest pitches thrown per batter (3.54), lowest ERA at home, lowest ERA on the road, lowest batting average allowed vs. lefthanded batters, most run support per nine innings (5.8), lowest batting average allowed with runners in scoring position and most strikeouts per nine innings (6.2)

D'Angelo Jimenez

2001 Season

With Derek Jeter entrenched at shortstop and the bullpen thinning from free-agent defections, the Yankees dangled highly touted shortstop prospect D'Angelo Jimenez to general managers around the league in hopes of procuring a top-flight reliever. The Expos got the first shot, offering to send closer Ugueth Urbina to the Bronx in exchange for Jimenez. But the deal fell through when Urbina failed his Yankees physical. Four days later, Jimenez was a Padre, traded for reliever Jay Witasick, who was in the midst of a breakthrough year. Jimenez had an unusual rookie season in that whenever he got hot at the plate, he struggled in the field, and whenever he played flawless defense, he struggled at the plate.

Hitting

Jimenez is a patient, contact hitter with above-average power for a middle fielder. He is just a couple of years removed from a 15-homer season with Triple-A Columbus in 1999. He will struggle against pitchers who change speeds well, however. Although he's a switch-hitter, he's much better from the left side of the plate.

Baserunning & Defense

Jimenez has above-average speed, but his basestealing skills are not polished enough to take advantage of it. He has decent range at short. He has the potential to become a very good shortstop with better positioning and footwork.

2002 Outlook

Jimenez missed almost all of the 2000 season due to a neck fracture he suffered in an offseason car accident. So it remains to be seen if his inconsistent defense in 2001 was due to the layoff, fatigue, rookie jitters or perhaps permanent lingering effects from the injury. If he plays up to the level he displayed as a 21-year-old in Triple-A ball in 1999, he'll be a key component of San Diego's middle infield. Jimenez now looks like the starting second baseman for 2002, as the Padres traded for Seattle shortstop prospect Ramon Vazquez during the offseason.

Position: SS
Bats: B **Throws:** R
Ht: 6' 0" **Wt:** 194

Opening Day Age: 24
Born: 12/21/77 in Santo Domingo, Dominican Republic
ML Seasons: 2
Pronunciation: HIM-en-ez

Overall Statistics

	G	AB	R	H	D	T	HR	RBI	SB	BB	SO	Avg	OBP	Slg
2001	86	308	45	85	19	0	3	33	2	39	68	.276	.355	.367
Career	93	328	48	93	21	0	3	37	2	42	72	.284	.363	.375

Where He Hits the Ball

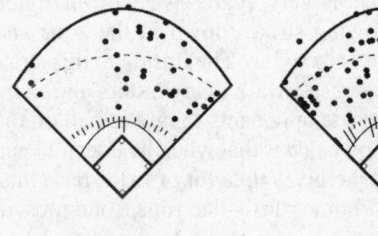

Vs. LHP　　　**Vs. RHP**

2001 Situational Stats

	AB	H	HR	RBI	Avg		AB	H	HR	RBI	Avg
Home	140	34	2	12	.243	LHP	87	21	0	9	.241
Road	168	51	1	21	.304	RHP	221	64	3	24	.290
First Half	41	11	1	6	.268	Sc Pos	72	21	0	28	.292
Scnd Half	267	74	2	27	.277	Clutch	40	13	0	8	.325

2001 Rankings (National League)

- 2nd in batting average among rookies
- 5th in errors at shortstop (21)

Bobby Jones

Position: SP
Bats: R **Throws:** R
Ht: 6' 4" **Wt:** 225

Opening Day Age: 32
Born: 2/10/70 in
Fresno, CA
ML Seasons: 9

2001 Season

For the first two months of the season, Bobby Jones was the victim of terrible luck. Heading into the last week in May, he had an ERA of 2.67, but his record stood at 2-6. Shoddy defense and a lack of run support were the primary culprits. Unfortunately for Jones, the season went from bad to worse. Over the last four months of the campaign, he was hit very hard, giving up 178 hits in 120.2 innings and posting an ERA of 6.34. Only Bruce Bochy's hook in the third inning of a September 27 contest at Coors prevented him from becoming the first 20-game loser since Brian Kingman in 1980.

Pitching

Jones has a wide repertoire of pitches, the best of which is a big-breaking curve. He mixes in a fastball in the mid-80s that he can cut to either side of the plate or sink down in the zone, and he changes speeds well with all his pitches. Jones works quickly and has good control, inducing plenty of grounders. However, because he's not overpowering, when he doesn't hit his spots, he gives up a lot of hard-hit line drives and more than his fair share of home runs.

Defense & Hitting

Jones is a good fielder but does not hold runners particularly well. Even with strong arms like Wiki Gonzalez and Ben Davis behind the plate, basestealers were thrown out just 26.7 percent of the time on Jones' watch. His overall hitting skills are meager, and he's just an average bunter.

2002 Outlook

With Adam Eaton sidelined for most if not all of the 2002 season after undergoing Tommy John surgery in August, Jones may be called upon to be the temporary ace of the Padres' staff. While his stuff might not warrant anything more than a No. 3 or 4 label, his knowledge and savvy will be invaluable to an organization that has a number of very promising young pitchers on the way.

Overall Statistics

	W	L	Pct.	ERA	G	GS	Sv	IP	H	BB	SO	HR	Ratio
2001	8	19	.296	5.12	33	33	0	195.0	250	38	113	37	1.48
Career	82	75	.522	4.27	226	223	0	1410.2	1505	391	827	174	1.34

How Often He Throws Strikes

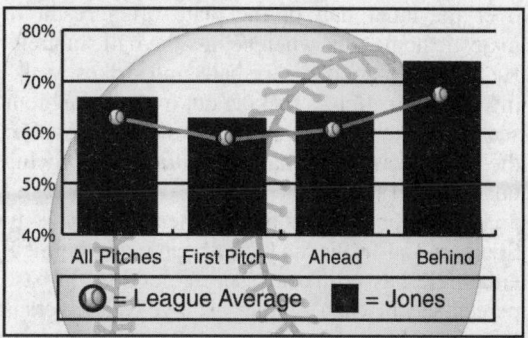

2001 Situational Stats

	W	L	ERA	Sv	IP		AB	H	HR	RBI	Avg
Home	3	11	4.20	0	100.2	LHB	310	87	15	49	.281
Road	5	8	6.11	0	94.1	RHB	510	163	22	78	.320
First Half	4	12	4.02	0	116.1	Sc Pos	211	60	9	84	.284
Scnd Half	4	7	6.75	0	78.2	Clutch	35	11	1	4	.314

2001 Rankings (National League)

- 1st in losses, home runs allowed, fielding percentage at pitcher (1.000), lowest winning percentage, highest batting average allowed (.305) and highest slugging percentage allowed (.506)
- Led the Padres in games started, innings pitched, hits allowed, batters faced (880), pitches thrown (3,129), pickoff throws (133), stolen bases allowed (22), runners caught stealing (8), highest strikeout-walk ratio (3.0), highest groundball-flyball ratio allowed (1.3), fewest home runs allowed per nine innings (1.71) and fewest walks per nine innings (1.8)

Ryan Klesko

2001 Season

Ryan Klesko followed up a solid 2000 season with an even better 2001 campaign. The difference was due to an improved Padres lineup that afforded him more opportunities on a daily basis. Klesko also proved that his stolen-base explosion in 2000 was no fluke, as he swiped 23 sacks again in '01 to finish tied for second on the team. Last May was perhaps his best month as a professional: he hit 11 homers, drove in 40 runs and stole 10 bases without being caught.

Hitting

Klesko has a long swing, but he has terrific bat speed and covers the plate well. Fastballs left up over the inner half of the plate often result in majestic home runs when he hits the ball squarely. He also has a good eye for balls and strikes, walking nearly as often as striking out over the last four seasons. When Klesko was dealt to the Padres after the 1999 season, he had a reputation for being unable to hit lefthanded pitchers. While he hasn't exactly torched southpaws since his move to Southern California, he hasn't been overwhelmed, either. He has posted a respectable .344 on-base percentage in each of the last two years versus lefties.

Baserunning & Defense

While he's no threat to win a Gold Glove, Klesko has improved his defense at first base to the point where he's no longer too much of a liability there. He has a good arm and adequate range around the bag. On the basepaths, Klesko has become a legitimate basestealing threat, not only with the number of stolen bases, but also with a surprisingly good success rate.

2002 Outlook

With Sean Burroughs expected to take over at third and Phil Nevin moving to first in 2002, Klesko once again will be roaming the outfield, most likely in right. Klesko clearly is more comfortable at first, but he is a good enough athlete and has a strong enough arm to make the change successfully. He is signed through 2004, so he should have plenty of time to become comfortable with Qualcomm's challenging outfield.

Position: 1B
Bats: L **Throws:** L
Ht: 6' 3" **Wt:** 220

Opening Day Age: 30
Born: 6/12/71 in Westminster, CA
ML Seasons: 10

Overall Statistics

	G	AB	R	H	D	T	HR	RBI	SB	BB	SO	Avg	OBP	Slg
2001	146	538	105	154	34	6	30	113	23	88	89	.286	.384	.539
Career	1083	3463	567	978	207	26	195	655	72	480	693	.282	.369	.526

Where He Hits the Ball

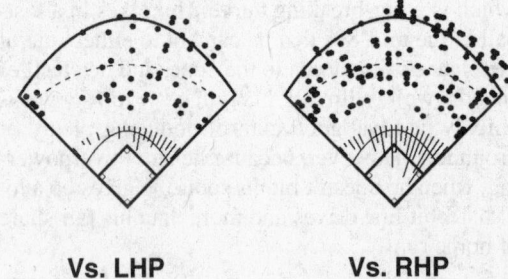

Vs. LHP   **Vs. RHP**

2001 Situational Stats

	AB	H	HR	RBI	Avg		AB	H	HR	RBI	Avg
Home	256	62	15	52	.242	LHP	164	42	4	20	.256
Road	282	92	15	61	.326	RHP	374	112	26	93	.299
First Half	313	93	17	75	.297	Sc Pos	135	45	8	83	.333
Scnd Half	225	61	13	38	.271	Clutch	78	22	5	20	.282

2001 Rankings (National League)

- 2nd in lowest fielding percentage at first base (.991)
- 3rd in errors at first base (11)
- Led the Padres in runs scored, doubles, triples, sacrifice flies (9), walks, intentional walks (7), times on base (245), GDPs (16), plate appearances (638), stolen-base percentage (85.2), steals of third (6), batting average with runners in scoring position, batting average in the clutch, batting average vs. righthanded pitchers, slugging percentage vs. righthanded pitchers (.596), on-base percentage vs. righthanded pitchers (.400), batting average on the road, batting average on a 3-2 count (.345) and batting average with two strikes (.253)

Mark Kotsay

2001 Season

The Padres acquired Mark Kotsay and Cesar Crespo from the Marlins in spring training in exchange for the enigmatic Matt Clement, utility outfielder Eric Owens and minor league righthander Omar Ortiz. Kotsay spent much of the first month of the season on the bench nursing a strained quadriceps. Once healthy, he put his all-around skills on display, hitting for power, stealing bases and playing fundamentally sound defense. In his final at-bat against Florida on August 25, he sprained his right hand, an injury that eventually consigned him mainly to pinch-running duties for the last three weeks of the season.

Hitting

Kotsay has a keen eye at the plate, walking nearly as often as he strikes out. He has good line-drive power that might develop into a few more home runs with a little uppercut to his swing. He makes contact on better than 90 percent of his swings, gets on base and drives the ball to all fields, skills which make him an ideal No. 2 hitter. He eventually may move down in the lineup, as his talent suggests a hitter capable of hitting 40 doubles and 20 homers a season.

Baserunning & Defense

Kotsay has above-average speed and very good baserunning instincts. In the outfield, he's one of the best in the game. He gets great jumps off the bat and always takes the most direct route to flyballs. His body and health are afterthoughts if it means stealing a hit. He also has a strong, accurate arm that has accounted for 57 outfield assists in the last four years.

2002 Outlook

Kotsay signed a two-year, $7.5 million contract extension with the Padres in May 2001 and will open 2002 as their starting center fielder. Injuries camouflaged a pretty encouraging year in which he posted a career high in on-base percentage, and nearly equaled a career best in slugging. A breakout season is in the very near future if he can stay healthy.

Position: CF
Bats: L **Throws:** L
Ht: 6' 0" **Wt:** 190

Opening Day Age: 26
Born: 12/2/75 in Whittier, CA
ML Seasons: 5
Pronunciation: COT-say

Overall Statistics

	G	AB	R	H	D	T	HR	RBI	SB	BB	SO	Avg	OBP	Slg
2001	119	406	67	118	29	1	10	58	13	48	58	.291	.366	.441
Career	587	2061	288	581	109	23	41	237	52	157	222	.282	.331	.417

Where He Hits the Ball

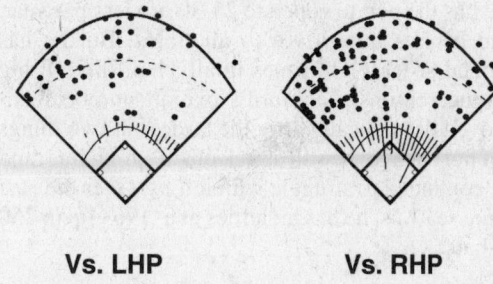

Vs. LHP   **Vs. RHP**

2001 Situational Stats

	AB	H	HR	RBI	Avg		AB	H	HR	RBI	Avg
Home	180	57	3	21	.317	LHP	107	23	2	20	.215
Road	226	61	7	37	.270	RHP	299	95	8	38	.318
First Half	255	75	6	34	.294	Sc Pos	99	31	3	46	.313
Scnd Half	151	43	4	24	.285	Clutch	55	13	0	4	.236

2001 Rankings (National League)
- 1st in batting average on an 0-2 count (.357)
- 7th in errors in center field (4)
- Led the Padres in batting average on an 0-2 count (.357)

Ray Lankford

2001 Season

Following a disappointing 2000 season, the Cardinals' braintrust decided to platoon Ray Lankford to begin the 2001 campaign. Lankford continued to struggle at the plate with strikeouts and in the dugout with Tony La Russa, and he was dealt to the Padres in exchange for Woody Williams at the beginning of August. Lankford's career may have been saved by the deal. After a few conversations with Tony Gwynn, he showed signs of breaking out of his nearly two-year funk and finished with a .288 batting average in 40 games in San Diego.

Hitting

Lankford has a quick but long swing that gives him good power but also makes him prone to strikeouts. He has the pop to generate 25-30 homers per year, and he hits line drives to all fields. But he has fanned at least 110 times in all 11 of his full big league seasons. Lankford's overall numbers improved dramatically after the trade, but two things did not change: he still struck out at a high rate, and he continued to struggle with lefties. Over the past three seasons, he has hit lefties at a .196 clip in 250 at-bats.

Baserunning & Defense

Knee problems have slowed Lankford from his 40-steal days with the Cardinals, but he is capable of taking an extra base and swiping 20 or more bags. Because the Padres aren't stocked with an excessive amount of power, Lankford should continue to get the green light to steal; in his 40 games with the San Diego in 2001, he swiped six bases without being caught. In left field, he reads the ball off the bat well and has enough speed to run down misreads. His arm is average but accurate.

2002 Outlook

Lankford's immediate future with the Padres is anything but certain. If he remains with the club in 2002, he likely will be platooned in left with either Mike Colangelo or Bubba Trammell—unless he somehow proves he can hit lefties this spring. Ryan Klesko's move to the outfield could further eat into Lankford's playing time.

Position: LF/CF
Bats: L **Throws:** L
Ht: 5'11" **Wt:** 200

Opening Day Age: 34
Born: 6/5/67 in Modesto, CA
ML Seasons: 12

Overall Statistics

	G	AB	R	H	D	T	HR	RBI	SB	BB	SO	Avg	OBP	Slg
2001	131	389	58	98	28	4	19	58	10	62	145	.252	.358	.491
Career	1528	5342	912	1464	335	52	226	826	254	769	1434	.274	.366	.483

Where He Hits the Ball

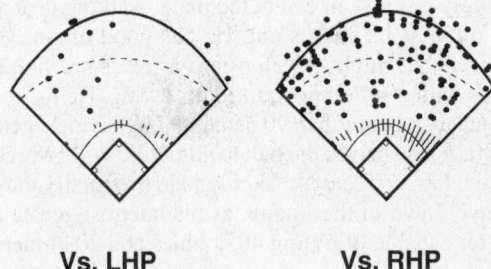

Vs. LHP   **Vs. RHP**

2001 Situational Stats

	AB	H	HR	RBI	Avg		AB	H	HR	RBI	Avg
Home	190	42	10	30	.221	LHP	62	12	3	7	.194
Road	199	56	9	28	.281	RHP	327	86	16	51	.263
First Half	228	54	14	35	.237	Sc Pos	92	22	4	34	.239
Scnd Half	161	44	5	23	.273	Clutch	48	9	2	7	.188

2001 Rankings (National League)

- 1st in highest percentage of swings that missed (34.1) and lowest percentage of swings put into play (30.2)
- 5th in errors in left field (6)
- 8th in strikeouts (145)
- 10th in assists in left field (6)

Brian Lawrence

2001 Season

Brian Lawrence opened the season in Triple-A, but he shuttled back and forth to the Padres' bullpen for the first three months of the season. He got his first start on June 23, a four-hit gem over 7.1 innings against the Dodgers. He made another solid start before being optioned back to the minors when Sterling Hitchcock was activated from the 60-day disabled list at the beginning of July. Lawrence was called up several times to make spot starts, but it wasn't until the beginning of August, after Hitchcock and Woody Williams were traded, that he got a regular turn in the rotation. Once he became a regular starter, Lawrence held the opposition to two earned runs or less in 10 of his final 13 starts. He finished first in ERA among all San Diego starters with at least 15 starts.

Pitching

Like teammate Brian Tollberg, Lawrence does not light up a radar gun. He throws a high-80s fastball that he can sink or cut, and he mixes in a decent changeup. However, his out pitch is a sharp, late-breaking slider. He works quickly and efficiently, using both sides of the plate and spotting his pitches very well. He fared much better against righthanded hitters last year, and surrendered just one righthanded home run in 242 at-bats.

Defense & Hitting

Lawrence does an acceptable job of holding runners on even though he doesn't have a great move to first. He's a sure-handed fielder, but he tends to rush his throws, which led to his four errors this season. Lawrence is not a good hitter but does a decent job of getting bunts down.

2002 Outlook

Lawrence has the fewest question marks of any of the Padres' starters opening the 2002 season. He doesn't look like a strong candidate for a sophomore jinx, as he pitched reasonably well facing teams a second and third time last year. With better run support, he could be a surprise win producer in the middle of the San Diego rotation.

Position: SP/RP
Bats: R **Throws:** R
Ht: 6' 2" **Wt:** 195

Opening Day Age: 25
Born: 5/14/76 in Fort Collins, CO
ML Seasons: 1

Overall Statistics

	W	L	Pct.	ERA	G	GS	Sv	IP	H	BB	SO	HR	Ratio
2001	5	5	.500	3.45	27	15	0	114.2	107	34	84	10	1.23
Career	5	5	.500	3.45	27	15	0	114.2	107	34	84	10	1.23

How Often He Throws Strikes

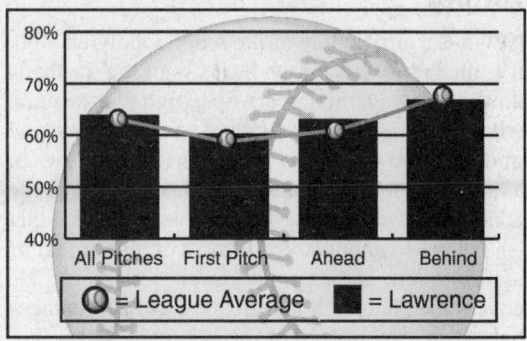

2001 Situational Stats

	W	L	ERA	Sv	IP		AB	H	HR	RBI	Avg
Home	0	4	4.07	0	59.2	LHB	196	55	9	26	.281
Road	5	1	2.78	0	55.0	RHB	242	52	1	23	.215
First Half	1	0	4.31	0	31.1	Sc Pos	103	27	2	36	.262
Scnd Half	4	5	3.13	0	83.1	Clutch	26	4	0	0	.154

2001 Rankings (National League)
- 1st in errors at pitcher (4)
- 9th in lowest batting average allowed vs. righthanded batters
- Led the Padres in lowest batting average allowed vs. righthanded batters

Phil Nevin

Position: 3B
Bats: R **Throws:** R
Ht: 6' 2" **Wt:** 231

Opening Day Age: 31
Born: 1/19/71 in
Fullerton, CA
ML Seasons: 7

2001 Season

The year began on somewhat of a down note for Phil Nevin, as he was traded in January to the Brewers on the condition that Jeromy Burnitz sign a long-term deal with the Padres. Burnitz rejected the offer, keeping Nevin in San Diego for another year, a development the Padres no doubt are ecstatic about in retrospect. Among all major league third baseman, Nevin tied for the lead in homers, finished first in RBI, third in on-base percentage and second in slugging percentage. He also led the majors with four grand slams and drove in five or more runs in five different games. On October 6, he had the first three-homer game of his career.

Hitting

Nevin is a terrific low-strike hitter. Oddly enough, it's pitchers who throw heavy sinking fastballs down and away, mixing it with a high four-seamer, who give him the most trouble. Leave a low strike middle-in, however, and it'll depart the premises in a hurry. He doesn't handle good fastballs up in the zone very well, but he'll mash any mistake that isn't elevated enough. While most of his home runs are hit to left, he has good power to all fields. He covers the plate well and his on-base percentages have increased in each of the last three years.

Baserunning & Defense

Nevin is not fast, but he's a smart baserunner and no one breaks up a potential double play with more enthusiasm. On defense, he has average range but awkward footwork, which leads to too many misplays. His glovework is average, but he makes up for it with strong and accurate throws across the diamond.

2002 Outlook

The Padres worked with Nevin and inked him to a four-year, $34 million extension in late November. He plays hard and, along with Trevor Hoffman, is one of the emotional leaders of this team. The Padres have contacted former San Diego first baseman Wally Joyner to work with Nevin this offseason at first, so that Sean Burroughs can play third.

Overall Statistics

	G	AB	R	H	D	T	HR	RBI	SB	BB	SO	Avg	OBP	Slg
2001	149	546	97	167	31	0	41	126	4	71	147	.306	.388	.588
Career	673	2231	323	609	125	4	123	412	9	249	564	.273	.349	.498

Where He Hits the Ball

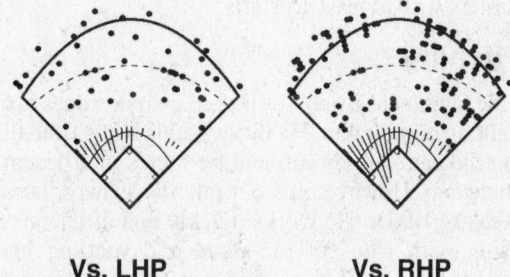

Vs. LHP   **Vs. RHP**

2001 Situational Stats

	AB	H	HR	RBI	Avg		AB	H	HR	RBI	Avg
Home	265	81	19	55	.306	LHP	155	51	9	27	.329
Road	281	86	22	71	.306	RHP	391	116	32	99	.297
First Half	297	92	21	72	.310	Sc Pos	161	48	12	86	.298
Scnd Half	249	75	20	54	.301	Clutch	72	17	4	14	.236

2001 Rankings (National League)

- 1st in errors at third base (27) and lowest fielding percentage at third base (.930)
- Led the Padres in batting average, home runs, at-bats, hits, singles, total bases (321), RBI, slugging percentage, on-base percentage, HR frequency (13.3 ABs per HR), highest groundball-flyball ratio (1.2), most pitches seen per plate appearance (4.06), batting average with the bases loaded (.524), batting average vs. lefthanded pitchers, cleanup slugging percentage (.594), slugging percentage vs. lefthanded pitchers (.581), on-base percentage vs. lefthanded pitchers (.416), batting average at home and lowest percentage of swings on the first pitch (30.0)
- Led NL third basemen in home runs and RBI

Brian Tollberg

2001 Season

Brian Tollberg earned a spot in the Padres' rotation last year with a fine rookie campaign in 2000. But the signings of Bobby Jones and Kevin Jarvis, and the emergence of Adam Eaton, pushed Tollberg to the bottom of the starting staff to open 2001. Despite that setback, he was San Diego's best and most consistent starter in April. The run of quality outings ended when he broke the middle finger on his pitching hand in a May 6 start against the Reds. The injury sidelined him for two months, and he was not nearly as effective after his return. He posted an ERA that was nearly one and a half runs higher in the second half.

Pitching

Because he lacks exciting stuff, Tollberg has been overlooked his entire career. He throws a fastball that rarely reaches 90 MPH and mixes in a nice curve and changeup. He pitches quickly and aggressively, using pinpoint control to induce groundballs nearly two-thirds of the time. He also is a very efficient hurler, and he went at least six innings in 13 of his 19 starts. Tollberg never threw more than 104 pitches in any of those outings.

Defense & Hitting

Tollberg has a good move to first base and does a solid job of holding runners close to the bag. His quick, compact delivery gives the catcher enough time to throw out would-be thieves even on breaking pitches. Opposing basestealers were successful on just four of eight attempts against Tollberg last year. He occasionally hurts himself with his fielding, however, and he already has three errors in his two big league campaigns. He's not a good hitter overall, but he's a very good bunter.

2002 Outlook

The Padres are hoping that Tollberg's second-half struggle was merely a lingering effect from his finger injury. If he pitches in spring training as well as he did to open 2001, he'll begin 2002 as one of the Padres' top two starters. The elbow injury to Eaton only increases Tollberg's value to a young San Diego staff.

Position: SP
Bats: R **Throws:** R
Ht: 6' 3" **Wt:** 195

Opening Day Age: 29
Born: 9/16/72 in Tampa, FL
ML Seasons: 2

Overall Statistics

	W	L	Pct.	ERA	G	GS	Sv	IP	H	BB	SO	HR	Ratio
2001	10	4	.714	4.30	19	19	0	117.1	133	25	71	15	1.35
Career	14	9	.609	3.94	38	38	0	235.1	259	60	147	28	1.36

How Often He Throws Strikes

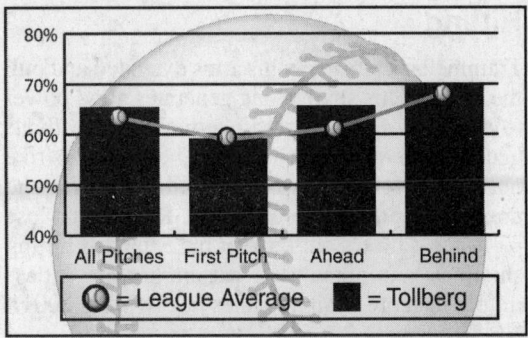

2001 Situational Stats

	W	L	ERA	Sv	IP		AB	H	HR	RBI	Avg
Home	3	1	4.37	0	45.1	LHB	195	55	7	20	.282
Road	7	3	4.25	0	72.0	RHB	269	78	8	32	.290
First Half	3	2	3.32	0	38.0	Sc Pos	114	29	3	36	.254
Scnd Half	7	2	4.76	0	79.1	Clutch	22	10	0	3	.455

2001 Rankings (National League)

- Led the Padres in sacrifice bunts (5)

San Diego

Bubba Trammell

2001 Season

The Padres traded reliever Donne Wall to the Mets for little used Bubba Trammell after the 2000 campaign. Trammell had displayed very good power in the minors but never was given much of an opportunity to show it with the Tigers, Devil Rays or Mets. However, he was so confident in his ability to hit that he told GM Kevin Towers he would play for free if he would be promised 500 at-bats. His reasoning was that he'd hit well enough to make up any back salary in arbitration and, judging from the contract the Padres just gave him, he wasn't far off. Trammell turned out to be one of the biggest steals of the 2001 season, providing some much-needed sock in the middle of the Padres' batting order.

Hitting

Trammell prefers to get his arms extended and pull the ball, but his short swing generates good power to all fields. Pitchers with overpowering fastballs generally give him trouble, but he doesn't strike out excessively for someone with his power and draws a decent number of walks. He still can lose patience at times, but he kept his extended hitting slumps to a minimum last season; he went hitless in four or more straight games just twice in 2001.

Baserunning & Defense

Trammell is basically a station-to-station runner. It is a rare occasion when he is asked to steal a base. Contrary to his reputation as a poor fielder, he showed acceptable range and an average arm playing both corner outfield positions. He has trouble reading the ball off the bat on line drives and still takes awkward routes on occasion, but overall he has proven to be a better defender than originally advertised.

2002 Outlook

Trammell signed a three-year, $8.75 million contract extension at the end of September, with a club option for a fourth year. Unless San Diego moves Ray Lankford, Trammell likely will split time between left and right, playing against lefties and giving both Ryan Klesko and Lankford days off. He'll still get around 500 at-bats, especially with the playing-time voids left behind by Tony Gwynn and Rickey Henderson.

Position: RF/LF
Bats: R **Throws:** R
Ht: 6' 2" **Wt:** 220

Opening Day Age: 30
Born: 11/6/71 in Knoxville, TN
ML Seasons: 5
Pronunciation: TRAM-mull

Overall Statistics

	G	AB	R	H	D	T	HR	RBI	SB	BB	SO	Avg	OBP	Slg
2001	142	490	66	128	20	3	25	92	2	48	78	.261	.330	.467
Career	429	1340	185	360	75	6	65	224	9	151	244	.269	.344	.479

Where He Hits the Ball

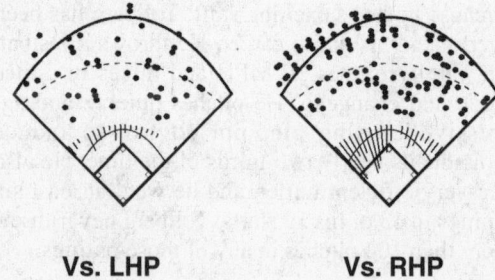

Vs. LHP   **Vs. RHP**

2001 Situational Stats

	AB	H	HR	RBI	Avg		AB	H	HR	RBI	Avg
Home	243	53	11	35	.218	LHP	129	36	4	20	.279
Road	247	75	14	57	.304	RHP	361	92	21	72	.255
First Half	245	60	14	53	.245	Sc Pos	143	42	8	68	.294
Scnd Half	245	68	11	39	.278	Clutch	72	19	6	17	.264

2001 Rankings (National League)

- 1st in lowest batting average at home
- 8th in errors in right field (4)
- 10th in lowest groundball-flyball ratio (0.8)
- Led the Padres in highest percentage of swings put into play (45.0)

Mike Colangelo

Signed By
ATHLETICS

Position: LF/CF
Bats: R **Throws:** R
Ht: 6' 1" **Wt:** 185

Opening Day Age: 25
Born: 10/22/76 in Teaneck, NJ
ML Seasons: 2

Overall Statistics

	G	AB	R	H	D	T	HR	RBI	SB	BB	SO	Avg	OBP	Slg
2001	50	91	10	22	3	3	2	8	0	8	30	.242	.310	.407
Career	51	93	10	23	3	3	2	8	0	9	30	.247	.320	.409

2001 Situational Stats

	AB	H	HR	RBI	Avg		AB	H	HR	RBI	Avg
Home	46	13	1	6	.283	LHP	57	19	2	7	.333
Road	45	9	1	2	.200	RHP	34	3	0	1	.088
First Half	62	17	1	7	.274	Sc Pos	23	4	0	4	.174
Scnd Half	29	5	1	1	.172	Clutch	15	6	1	2	.400

2001 Season

Mike Colangelo brought a reputation for being a fine hitter but very injury prone. Fortunately for the Padres, his first season with them showed more of the former than the latter. He had few starts as the team's fifth option in the outfield, but he was highly productive when he did get the call. He was especially effective against lefties, hitting .333 with a .561 slugging percentage against them.

Hitting, Baserunning & Defense

Colangelo is a very confident hitter, especially for a guy with only 749 professional at-bats. He's particularly productive when ahead in the count, but his game plan breaks down when he falls behind, as his aggressive approach only digs him into a deeper hole. His speed is good enough to steal an occasional base, and he has a good feel for taking extra bases on well-hit balls. He has adequate range in the outfield and an average arm.

2002 Outlook

Colangelo seems fully recovered from March 2000 surgery to repair a torn labrum in his right shoulder, an injury that wiped out his entire 2000 campaign. He signed a minor league deal with the A's and could be a productive part-time player.

Cesar Crespo

Position: 2B/CF
Bats: B **Throws:** R
Ht: 5'11" **Wt:** 170

Opening Day Age: 22
Born: 5/23/79 in Rio Piedras, Puerto Rico
ML Seasons: 1

Overall Statistics

	G	AB	R	H	D	T	HR	RBI	SB	BB	SO	Avg	OBP	Slg
2001	55	153	27	32	6	0	4	12	6	25	50	.209	.320	.327
Career	55	153	27	32	6	0	4	12	6	25	50	.209	.320	.327

2001 Situational Stats

	AB	H	HR	RBI	Avg		AB	H	HR	RBI	Avg
Home	85	16	0	0	.188	LHP	25	4	0	1	.160
Road	68	16	4	12	.235	RHP	128	28	4	11	.219
First Half	85	19	1	5	.224	Sc Pos	34	5	0	6	.147
Scnd Half	68	13	3	7	.191	Clutch	23	2	0	0	.087

2001 Season

GM Kevin Towers singled out Cesar Crespo as an important component in the deal that brought Mark Kotsay to the Padres. The switch-hitting second baseman shuttled between Triple-A and the majors for much of the season, but he came up to stay at the end of August. His season did not end memorably, however. He hit just .191 down the stretch, striking out 26 times in his final 68 at-bats.

Hitting, Baserunning & Defense

Crespo has excellent bat speed and above-average power for a middle infielder. While he strikes out quite a bit, he does draw an encouraging number of walks. That moderate degree of discipline, combined with his blazing speed and good baserunning instincts, make him a potentially formidable leadoff hitter. His defense at the keystone is not spectacular, but he is surehanded. He has a strong enough arm to play third base, shortstop or right field, and he saw action in all three of those spots at Triple-A.

2002 Outlook

Crespo's versatility makes him a perfect utility man, capable of playing the middle infield or the outfield without any appreciable drop-off on defense. He's still quite young, so another stint in Triple-A is not out of the question.

San Diego

Mike Darr

Position: RF/CF
Bats: L **Throws:** R
Ht: 6' 3" **Wt:** 205

Opening Day Age: 26
Born: 3/21/76 in
Corona, CA
ML Seasons: 3

Overall Statistics

	G	AB	R	H	D	T	HR	RBI	SB	BB	SO	Avg	OBP	Slg
2001	105	289	36	80	13	1	2	34	6	39	72	.277	.363	.349
Career	188	542	63	148	28	5	5	67	17	67	135	.273	.353	.371

2001 Situational Stats

	AB	H	HR	RBI	Avg		AB	H	HR	RBI	Avg
Home	151	40	2	18	.265	LHP	73	24	0	10	.329
Road	138	40	0	16	.290	RHP	216	56	2	24	.259
First Half	189	56	0	25	.296	Sc Pos	81	21	0	29	.259
Scnd Half	100	24	2	9	.240	Clutch	44	12	2	6	.273

2001 Season

Mike Darr began the season as the Padres' fourth outfielder, but injuries limited his effectiveness and playing time. A slight muscle tear in his elbow at the end of August reduced him to an occasional pinch-hitting appearance for the remainder of the season. Darr finished with just two home runs. However, he made his longballs count: a two-run, game-winner against the Mets, and a pinch-hit, walk-off 10th-inning rope against the Giants.

Hitting, Baserunning & Defense

When he's healthy Darr's quick level swing generates blistering line drives. He rarely pulls the ball down the right-field line, but instead prefers to go to center and left. Darr has above-average speed and is a very smart baserunner. He does not steal bases for volume, but he picks his spots well. He's a potential Gold Glove right fielder, possessing good range and a strong arm.

2002 Outlook

With Ray Lankford, Bubba Trammell and Mark Kotsay on board, and Ryan Klesko also targeted for the outfield, the Padres again will use Darr as a utility outfielder and hope that he can stay healthy. San Diego also would like to see him flash a little more of the modest pop that he demonstrated in his last four full years in the minors.

Jeremy Fikac

Position: RP
Bats: R **Throws:** R
Ht: 6' 2" **Wt:** 185

Opening Day Age: 26
Born: 4/8/75 in Shiner, TX
ML Seasons: 1
Pronunciation:
fee-kotch

Overall Statistics

	W	L	Pct.	ERA	G	GS	Sv	IP	H	BB	SO	HR	Ratio
2001	2	0	1.000	1.37	23	0	0	26.1	15	5	19	2	0.76
Career	2	0	1.000	1.37	23	0	0	26.1	15	5	19	2	0.76

2001 Situational Stats

	W	L	ERA	Sv	IP		AB	H	HR	RBI	Avg
Home	1	0	2.19	0	12.1	LHB	27	0	0	0	.000
Road	1	0	0.64	0	14.0	RHB	64	15	2	8	.234
First Half	0	0	-	0	0.0	Sc Pos	26	4	1	7	.154
Scnd Half	2	0	1.37	0	26.1	Clutch	50	10	1	4	.200

2001 Season

Jeremy Fikac was called up in August after a stellar season spent primarily at Double-A. He finished 6-0 with 18 saves and an ERA of 1.97, and was the winning pitcher in the Southern League All-Star Game. His results in the big leagues weren't that different. Major league batters hit just .165 against him, and he allowed the opposition to reach first base in only nine of his 23 outings.

Pitching, Defense & Hitting

Fikac works quickly and efficiently, throwing a 90-MPH fastball, a sharp-breaking slider and a changeup for strikes. He also has a curve that he'll show. However, like Trevor Hoffman, his out pitch is his change. He showed no adverse affects from working several days in a row, even after throwing more than an inning an outing. Primarily a third baseman in college, Fikac fields his position well and probably hits better than the average pitcher.

2002 Outlook

Fikac will be Hoffman's primary setup man in 2002. He is developing into one of the better relievers in the National League. Bruce Bochy will not hesitate to give him save opportunities when Hoffman needs a day off. Fikac also could be an intriguing alternative at closer when Hoffman's current contract runs out at the end of 2003.

Wiki Gonzalez

Position: C
Bats: R **Throws:** R
Ht: 5'11" **Wt:** 203

Opening Day Age: 27
Born: 5/17/74 in
Aragua, Venezuela
ML Seasons: 3
Pronunciation:
WICK-ee

Overall Statistics

	G	AB	R	H	D	T	HR	RBI	SB	BB	SO	Avg	OBP	Slg
2001	64	160	16	44	6	0	8	27	2	11	28	.275	.335	.463
Career	189	527	48	131	23	2	16	69	3	42	67	.249	.313	.391

2001 Situational Stats

	AB	H	HR	RBI	Avg		AB	H	HR	RBI	Avg
Home	80	18	5	12	.225	LHP	58	20	5	16	.345
Road	80	26	3	15	.325	RHP	102	24	3	11	.235
First Half	72	21	5	17	.292	Sc Pos	52	15	3	20	.288
Scnd Half	88	23	3	10	.261	Clutch	27	5	0	2	.185

2001 Season

Wiki Gonzalez had a surprisingly productive year for the Padres as Ben Davis' backup at catcher. The stocky receiver set career highs in batting average, on-base percentage and slugging percentage despite getting 124 fewer at-bats than he did in 2000. He even stole two bases.

Hitting, Baserunning & Defense

Gonzalez, who has good power for a catcher, simply crushed lefties in 2001. He's very aggressive at the plate, swinging at the first pitch he can get his bat on. As such, he doesn't draw many walks—just 42 in 527 career big league at-bats. However, he doesn't strike out much either, and he hits into fewer double plays than expected. Gonzalez is an agile receiver with a strong arm and quick release, and is fearless when it comes to blocking the plate. He nabbed 37 percent of would-be thieves, but he did allow six passed balls.

2002 Outlook

Gonzalez arguably was the best backup catcher in baseball in 2001. His status changes in 2002 after Davis was shipped to Seattle in a trade that netted 38-year-old catcher Tom Lampkin. Gonzalez should get many more opportunities to produce as the primary catcher in 2002.

Rickey Henderson (Hall of Famer)

Position: LF
Bats: R **Throws:** L
Ht: 5'10" **Wt:** 190

Opening Day Age: 43
Born: 12/25/58 in
Chicago, IL
ML Seasons: 23

Overall Statistics

	G	AB	R	H	D	T	HR	RBI	SB	BB	SO	Avg	OBP	Slg
2001	123	379	70	86	17	3	8	42	25	81	84	.227	.366	.351
Career	2979	10710	2248	3000	503	65	290	1094	1395	2141	1631	.280	.402	.420

2001 Situational Stats

	AB	H	HR	RBI	Avg		AB	H	HR	RBI	Avg
Home	182	36	2	12	.198	LHP	124	26	2	18	.210
Road	197	50	6	30	.254	RHP	255	60	6	24	.235
First Half	220	49	5	21	.223	Sc Pos	77	20	1	31	.260
Scnd Half	159	37	3	21	.233	Clutch	52	10	0	4	.192

2001 Season

Rickey Henderson opened the spring without a contract before accepting a minor league deal with the Padres. Despite turning 42 and struggling though all but May and September, he was able to post the sixth-best on-base percentage of any regular leadoff hitter in the National League. He also was able to achieve several notable milestones: he broke Babe Ruth's major league record for career walks and Ty Cobb's major league record for most career runs scored. He also got his 3,000th hit.

Hitting, Baserunning & Defense

Henderson's bat speed has slowed to a point where he can't get around on good fastballs inside. He catches up to mistakes, however, and his eye at the plate is unwavering. He walked 81 times, though it was the first time since 1981 that he failed to post at least as many walks as strikeouts (84). He's still a threat on the basepaths, swiping 25 bags in 32 attempts last year. Despite his speed, a weak arm and limited range make him a liability in the field.

2002 Outlook

While he's only a shadow of the offensive force he once was, Henderson can be a useful player as long as he has minimal exposure to playing the field. His problem will be finding a team that wants to put a 43-year-old DH into the leadoff spot.

Damian Jackson

Position: 2B
Bats: R **Throws:** R
Ht: 5'11" **Wt:** 185

Opening Day Age: 28
Born: 8/16/73 in Los Angeles, CA
ML Seasons: 6

Overall Statistics

	G	AB	R	H	D	T	HR	RBI	SB	BB	SO	Avg	OBP	Slg
2001	122	440	67	106	21	6	4	38	23	44	128	.241	.316	.343
Career	431	1382	205	335	77	15	20	124	89	170	357	.242	.329	.363

2001 Situational Stats

	AB	H	HR	RBI	Avg		AB	H	HR	RBI	Avg
Home	219	51	1	15	.233	LHP	113	36	1	12	.319
Road	221	55	3	23	.249	RHP	327	70	3	26	.214
First Half	196	54	1	17	.276	Sc Pos	97	22	2	31	.227
Scnd Half	244	52	3	21	.213	Clutch	51	8	0	2	.157

2001 Season

As was the case in the previous two seasons, 2001 was another roller-coaster year for Damian Jackson. An errant A.J. Burnett fastball during his no-hit performance broke Jackson's right thumb, sending him to the disabled list for more than a month. Once he returned, his hitting went through its usual cycle of very good and then very bad streaks.

Hitting, Baserunning & Defense

Jackson has the power and speed to hit lots of doubles and triples but has yet to put it all together for a full season. His walk rate took a big step back this year and his strikeout rate increased. In the field, he's always had terrific range, and the move to second base appears to have cured his struggles with errors.

2002 Outlook

Jackson wants to be the starting second baseman for the Padres next season, but now he would have to displace highly regarded D'Angelo Jimenez. The Padres acquired rookie shortstop Ramon Vazquez in December, and Jackson looks like the odd man out in the infield. A utility role is likely.

David Lundquist

Position: RP
Bats: R **Throws:** R
Ht: 6' 2" **Wt:** 200

Opening Day Age: 28
Born: 6/4/73 in Beverly, MA
ML Seasons: 2

Overall Statistics

	W	L	Pct.	ERA	G	GS	Sv	IP	H	BB	SO	HR	Ratio
2001	0	1	.000	5.95	17	0	0	19.2	20	7	19	1	1.37
Career	1	2	.333	7.34	34	0	0	41.2	48	19	37	4	1.61

2001 Situational Stats

	W	L	ERA	Sv	IP		AB	H	HR	RBI	Avg
Home	0	0	2.70	0	6.2	LHB	29	7	0	4	.241
Road	0	1	7.62	0	13.0	RHB	48	13	1	8	.271
First Half	0	0	-	0	0.0	Sc Pos	19	6	1	12	.316
Scnd Half	0	1	5.95	0	19.2	Clutch	7	1	0	0	.143

2001 Season

After nine years, 12 different teams and an assortment of injuries, David Lundquist finally was healthy enough to show what he could do in the majors. Other than one outing in Colorado in which he allowed five earned runs in a third of an inning, Lundquist pitched very well down the stretch, striking out 19 hitters in 19 innings while allowing only 28 baserunners.

Pitching, Defense & Hitting

Lundquist features a fastball that reaches as high as 95 MPH, which he likes to throw up in the zone. He mixes it with an average slider and change. Like many hard-throwing righthanders, he has difficulty fielding balls hit to his right. However, his delivery is quick to home; baserunners were unsuccessful in both of their attempts against him. Lundquist has yet to log a major league at-bat.

2002 Outlook

Lundquist will join Jeremy Fikac and Tom Davey as the Padres' short-relief men from the right side, setting up closer Trevor Hoffman. And while that role may not be glamorous, Lundquist likely will be ecstatic to be on a major league Opening Day roster for just the second time in 10 professional seasons.

Jose Antonio Nunez

Position: RP
Bats: L **Throws:** L
Ht: 6' 2" **Wt:** 165

Opening Day Age: 23
Born: 3/14/79 in Monte Cristy, Dominican Republic
ML Seasons: 1
Pronunciation: noon-yez

Overall Statistics

	W	L	Pct.	ERA	G	GS	Sv	IP	H	BB	SO	HR	Ratio
2001	4	2	.667	4.58	62	0	0	59.0	62	25	60	7	1.47
Career	4	2	.667	4.58	62	0	0	59.0	62	25	60	7	1.47

2001 Situational Stats

	W	L	ERA	Sv	IP		AB	H	HR	RBI	Avg
Home	2	2	5.27	0	27.1	LHB	116	28	4	12	.241
Road	2	0	3.98	0	31.2	RHB	116	34	3	20	.293
First Half	1	2	7.80	0	30.0	Sc Pos	69	15	2	24	.217
Scnd Half	3	0	1.24	0	29.0	Clutch	69	18	1	6	.261

2001 Season

The Padres claimed Jose Antonio Nunez off waivers from the Dodgers after LA released the Rule 5 draftee following a disastrous outing in a 20-1 loss in Chicago. Nunez provided solid relief work, finishing with 11 holds, good for second on the team. He also struck out 49 hitters in 51.2 innings and posted an ERA of 3.31 with San Diego.

Pitching, Defense & Hitting

Nunez mixes a high-80s fastball with a big, sweeping slider, reminiscent of Tony Fossas. Don't be fooled by his lack of true heat, however, as he struck out 9.4 batters per nine innings in three seasons in the low minors. Nunez is an adequate fielder, but he has surprising trouble holding runners—big league basestealers were successful on eight of nine attempts against him in 2001. He rarely will bat as a reliever and it's probably better that way.

2002 Outlook

For the past five years, the Padres have been searching for a lefthanded reliever. With Nunez and Kevin Walker, who'll miss most of 2002 recovering from Tommy John surgery, they finally may have found a long-term answer. With Walker sidelined, Nunez will be the primary lefthanded setup man for the Padres this season.

Wascar Serrano

Traded To MARINERS

Position: RP
Bats: R **Throws:** R
Ht: 6' 2" **Wt:** 178

Opening Day Age: 23
Born: 6/2/78 in Santo Domingo, Dominican Republic
ML Seasons: 1
Pronunciation: WASS-car SAIR-on-noe

Overall Statistics

	W	L	Pct.	ERA	G	GS	Sv	IP	H	BB	SO	HR	Ratio
2001	3	3	.500	6.56	20	5	0	46.2	60	21	39	7	1.74
Career	3	3	.500	6.56	20	5	0	46.2	60	21	39	7	1.74

2001 Situational Stats

	W	L	ERA	Sv	IP		AB	H	HR	RBI	Avg
Home	2	2	4.41	0	32.2	LHB	75	25	2	12	.333
Road	1	1	11.57	0	14.0	RHB	117	35	5	20	.299
First Half	2	2	5.34	0	28.2	Sc Pos	67	19	1	23	.284
Scnd Half	1	1	8.50	0	18.0	Clutch	9	2	1	2	.222

2001 Season

Wascar Serrano opened the season at Triple-A. He was called up on May 10 after Brian Tollberg went on the disabled list. Serrano got the loss in his major league debut on May 12 against the Marlins despite allowing only one earned run. It just so happened that his opponent that night, A.J. Burnett, topped his effort by throwing a no-hitter. After five uneven starts, Serrano moved to the bullpen, where he struggled the rest of the season.

Pitching, Defense & Hitting

Serrano throws two fastballs—one a mid-90s four-seamer and the other a low-90s sinking two-seamer. He also works in an improving changeup and a breaking pitch that's somewhere between a slider and a slurve. He has quick feet and hands and is one of the Padres' better fielding pitchers. He's a decent bunter but provides little else with the bat.

2002 Outlook

Serrano had struggled initially each time he'd been promoted, only to make adjustments the following year and finish on a strong note. That may be good news for the Mariners, who acquired the second-year man in a six-player deal with San Diego. He may get more Triple-A seasoning in 2002, as the Mariners' staff is much deeper than the Padres.

San Diego

Alex Arias (**Pos**: 3B/1B/2B/SS, **Age**: 34, **Bats**: R)

	G	AB	R	H	D	T	HR	RBI	SB	BB	SO	Avg	OBP	Slg
2001	70	137	19	31	9	0	2	12	1	17	22	.226	.312	.336
Career	769	1766	203	470	84	6	18	196	10	180	209	.266	.339	.351

Arias' success with the Phils in '98 and '99 are a distant memory. Still, he played all four infield spots last year, and he takes his utility skills to Seattle. 2002 Outlook: C

Emil Brown (**Pos**: CF, **Age**: 27, **Bats**: R)

	G	AB	R	H	D	T	HR	RBI	SB	BB	SO	Avg	OBP	Slg
2001	74	137	21	26	4	1	3	13	12	16	49	.190	.284	.299
Career	209	404	52	81	13	2	8	38	20	38	129	.200	.289	.302

The Padres acquired Brown in July, but there wasn't room for him in the outfield. They waived him after he went 1-for-14. After parts of five seasons in the majors, he's at the Mendoza Line for his career. 2002 Outlook: C

Tom Davey (**Pos**: RHP, **Age**: 28)

	W	L	Pct.	ERA	G	GS	Sv	IP	H	BB	SO	HR	Ratio
2001	2	4	.333	4.50	39	0	0	38.0	41	17	37	3	1.53
Career	6	6	.500	4.20	95	0	1	115.2	115	59	102	8	1.50

Davey was showing signs of being a serviceable reliever until arm troubles late in July sidetracked his season. He could be in the bullpen mix. 2002 Outlook: B

Adam Eaton (**Pos**: RHP, **Age**: 24)

	W	L	Pct.	ERA	G	GS	Sv	IP	H	BB	SO	HR	Ratio
2001	8	5	.615	4.32	17	17	0	116.2	108	40	109	20	1.27
Career	15	9	.625	4.22	39	39	0	251.2	242	101	199	34	1.36

Eaton impressed with a solid rookie season in 2000, but elbow pain interrupted his 2001 campaign in July. He had Tommy John surgery and will be out all year. 2002 Outlook: D

Tony Gwynn (**Pos**: RF, **Age**: 41, **Bats**: L)

	G	AB	R	H	D	T	HR	RBI	SB	BB	SO	Avg	OBP	Slg
2001	71	102	5	33	9	1	1	17	1	10	9	.324	.384	.461
Career	2440	9288	1383	3141	543	85	135	1138	319	790	434	.338	.388	.459

Even when he was hurt or used sparingly in his last two seasons, Gwynn batted well above .300. His Hall of Fame career ends with a .338 average and .388 on-base percentage. Cooperstown or bust. 2002 Outlook: D

Junior Herndon (**Pos**: RHP, **Age**: 23)

	W	L	Pct.	ERA	G	GS	Sv	IP	H	BB	SO	HR	Ratio
2001	2	6	.250	6.33	12	8	0	42.2	55	25	14	5	1.88
Career	2	6	.250	6.33	12	8	0	42.2	55	25	14	5	1.88

Herndon is a Padres prospect who hasn't had much success in the high minors. His walk rate is too high and he does not dominate hitters. More Triple-A time probably is in his future. 2002 Outlook: C

Brett Jodie (**Pos**: RHP, **Age**: 25)

	W	L	Pct.	ERA	G	GS	Sv	IP	H	BB	SO	HR	Ratio
2001	0	2	.000	6.39	8	3	0	25.1	26	13	13	10	1.54
Career	0	2	.000	6.39	8	3	0	25.1	26	13	13	10	1.54

Jodie was a Yankees prospect who was acquired for Sterling Hitchcock in July. Jodie was 13-5 in the minors

in 2000 and 10-4 (3.01) at Triple-A Columbus before the deal. Big league hitters fared significantly better against him after 45 pitches, which could prompt a move to long relief. 2002 Outlook: B

David Lee (**Pos**: RHP, **Age**: 29)

	W	L	Pct.	ERA	G	GS	Sv	IP	H	BB	SO	HR	Ratio
2001	1	0	1.000	3.70	41	0	0	48.2	52	27	42	6	1.62
Career	4	2	.667	4.09	84	0	1	103.1	105	62	86	13	1.62

Lee was inconsistent and gave up a lot of walks in his first season in the San Diego bullpen. Escaping Colorado can't hurt, and he may be useful if he isn't pushed aside by more promising younger hurlers. 2002 Outlook: B

Carlton Loewer (**Pos**: RHP, **Age**: 28)

	W	L	Pct.	ERA	G	GS	Sv	IP	H	BB	SO	HR	Ratio
2001	0	2	.000	24.92	2	2	0	4.1	13	3	1	2	3.69
Career	9	16	.360	6.06	43	36	0	216.2	267	68	107	29	1.55

A minor prospect with the Phils, Loewer was dealt to San Diego for Andy Ashby in 1999. He broke his leg while hunting and endured rotator cuff surgery since the trade. His chance may have passed him by. 2002 Outlook: C

Dave Magadan (**Pos**: 3B, **Age**: 39, **Bats**: L)

	G	AB	R	H	D	T	HR	RBI	SB	BB	SO	Avg	OBP	Slg
2001	91	128	12	32	7	0	1	12	0	12	20	.250	.317	.328
Career	1582	4159	516	1197	218	13	42	495	11	718	546	.288	.390	.377

No matter how few plate appearances Magadan has made in a season, he's managed to hit for a respectable average and very good OBP. He retired after a less effective 2001 at age 38. 2002 Outlook: D

Dave Maurer (**Pos**: LHP, **Age**: 27)

	W	L	Pct.	ERA	G	GS	Sv	IP	H	BB	SO	HR	Ratio
2001	0	0	-	10.80	3	0	0	5.0	8	4	4	1	2.40
Career	1	0	1.000	5.49	17	0	0	19.2	23	9	17	3	1.63

Maurer fared well in his major league debut in 2000 but wasn't the same pitcher last April. He moved on and played Triple-A ball in the Reds' and A's systems before the season was over. 2002 Outlook: C

Chuck McElroy (**Pos**: LHP, **Age**: 34)

	W	L	Pct.	ERA	G	GS	Sv	IP	H	BB	SO	HR	Ratio
2001	2	3	.400	5.28	49	5	0	75.0	87	46	47	14	1.77
Career	38	30	.559	3.90	654	7	17	739.1	724	362	604	66	1.47

McElroy's last productive season was with the Rockies in 1998, and his ERA has been near 5.00 ever since. He did limit righthanders to a .234 average in 2001, so the lefty should get another chance. 2002 Outlook: C

Rodney Myers (**Pos**: RHP, **Age**: 32)

	W	L	Pct.	ERA	G	GS	Sv	IP	H	BB	SO	HR	Ratio
2001	1	2	.333	5.32	37	0	1	47.1	53	20	29	6	1.54
Career	6	4	.600	4.99	148	1	1	207.1	225	96	144	26	1.55

Myers endured shoulder pain following shoulder surgery performed in 2000. He wasn't very effective in 2001 and younger relievers came up and did the job. 2002 Outlook: C

Jimmy Osting (**Pos**: LHP, **Age**: 24)

	W	L	Pct.	ERA	G	GS	Sv	IP	H	BB	SO	HR	Ratio
2001	0	0	-	0.00	3	0	0	2.0	1	2	3	0	1.50
Career	0	0	-	0.00	3	0	0	2.0	1	2	3	0	1.50

An Atlanta prospect who had Tommy John surgery as a minor leaguer, Osting is a soft-tossing lefty who could have a future as a situational reliever. He hasn't had success at the Triple-A level yet. 2002 Outlook: C

Santiago Perez (**Pos**: CF, **Age**: 26, **Bats**: B)

	G	AB	R	H	D	T	HR	RBI	SB	BB	SO	Avg	OBP	Slg
2001	43	81	13	16	1	0	0	4	5	15	29	.198	.320	.210
Career	67	133	21	25	3	0	0	6	9	23	38	.188	.308	.211

Perez, a one-time prospect, was dealt from Milwaukee to San Diego in December 2000. He batted .306 in April with 11 walks for a .468 OBP. Then he crashed and burned. He signed a minor league deal with Texas in November. 2002 Outlook: C

Adam Riggs (**Pos**: 2B, **Age**: 29, **Bats**: R)

	G	AB	R	H	D	T	HR	RBI	SB	BB	SO	Avg	OBP	Slg
2001	12	36	2	7	1	0	0	1	1	2	8	.194	.237	.222
Career	21	56	5	11	2	0	0	2	2	6	11	.196	.274	.232

Riggs is a second baseman who has shown some pop in five Triple-A seasons. He didn't hit enough in his short stay to displace Damian Jackson, and he signed a minor league contract with Detroit in the fall. 2002 Outlook: C

Kevin Walker (**Pos**: LHP, **Age**: 25)

	W	L	Pct.	ERA	G	GS	Sv	IP	H	BB	SO	HR	Ratio
2001	0	0	-	3.00	16	0	0	12.0	5	8	17	0	1.08
Career	7	1	.875	4.00	86	0	0	78.2	54	46	73	5	1.27

Walker enjoyed a promising rookie season in 2000, and he got off to a solid start last spring. Then elbow troubles surfaced and Walker had Tommy John surgery in early August. Look for him again in 2003. 2002 Outlook: D

Rick Wilkins (**Pos**: C, **Age**: 34, **Bats**: L)

	G	AB	R	H	D	T	HR	RBI	SB	BB	SO	Avg	OBP	Slg
2001	12	22	3	4	1	0	1	8	0	2	8	.182	.250	.364
Career	720	2114	280	515	95	7	81	275	9	278	571	.244	.332	.410

Wilkins is following the Benito Santiago career path, having played for seven teams in the last six years. But he's never going to start again. He declined a Triple-A assignment and became a free agent. 2002 Outlook: C

Kevin Witt (**Pos**: 1B, **Age**: 26, **Bats**: L)

	G	AB	R	H	D	T	HR	RBI	SB	BB	SO	Avg	OBP	Slg
2001	14	27	5	5	0	0	2	5	0	2	7	.185	.233	.407
Career	34	68	8	13	1	0	3	10	0	4	19	.191	.233	.338

Originally a power prospect with Toronto, Witt has averaged 26 homers a season in the high minors the last five years. If he could tame his strikeout-walk ratio, the Padres might give him a chance. 2002 Outlook: C

San Diego

San Diego Padres Minor League Prospects

Organization Overview:

Even with the tragic loss of Gerik Baxter, few organizations can match the Padres' collection of legitimate pitching prospects. Through the draft and through trades, GM Kevin Towers has amassed quality arms at every level. Lake Elsinore, the Padres' California League affiliate, was named *Baseball America*'s Minor League Team of the Year after winning 91 games largely on the strength of its pitching. The organization is thin on positional prospects, except at third base, where it has an impractical abundance. This year's draft class added to the logjam, as Towers selected Tulane third baseman Jake Gautreau, USF third baseman Taggert Bozied and Matt Harrington, a high school pitching phenom who held out a year after being drafted by Colorado in 2000.

Sean Burroughs

Position: 3B   **Opening Day Age:** 21
Bats: L **Throws:** R   **Born:** 9/12/80 in Atlanta,
Ht: 6' 2" **Wt:** 200   GA

Recent Statistics

	G	AB	R	H	D	T	HR	RBI	SB	BB	SO	Avg
2000 AA Mobile	108	392	46	114	29	4	2	42	6	58	45	.291
2001 AAA Portland	104	394	60	127	28	1	9	55	9	37	54	.322
2001 MLE	104	380	54	113	24	0	7	49	6	32	57	.297

Burroughs has been in the limelight practically all his life. He's the son of former AL MVP Jeff Burroughs. He was the star of two championship Little League World Series teams, one of the most heavily recruited high school players ever and a hitting star for the gold medal winning U.S. team in the 2000 Olympics. For the last three years, he's been a sensation in the minors—hitting line drives to all fields, drawing walks as often as striking out and showing solid defensive skills at third. The only knock on his game so far has been a lack of home-run power, but that may be changing. San Diego is optimistic that he's ready for the major leagues, even though he just turned 21. Barring a disastrous spring, he likely will open the season as the Padres' third baseman, with Phil Nevin moving to first and Ryan Klesko moving to right field.

Ben Howard

Position: P   **Opening Day Age:** 23
Bats: R **Throws:** R   **Born:** 1/15/79 in
Ht: 6' 2" **Wt:** 190   Danville, IL

Recent Statistics

	W	L	ERA	G	GS	Sv	IP	H	R	BB	SO	HR
2000 A Rancho Cuca	5	11	6.37	32	19	0	107.1	88	87	111	150	8
2001 A Lk Elsinore	8	2	2.83	18	18	0	101.2	86	37	32	107	4
2001 AA Mobile	2	0	2.40	7	5	0	30.0	17	9	15	29	3

Howard came into this season as a talented but very wild pitcher. In 2000, he struck out 150 batters in 107.1 innings but also walked 111. In 2001, Lake Elsinore pitching coach Darren Balsley changed Howard's arm angle and the results were dramatic. He still struck out batters at a very high rate but he walked just 47 hitters between high Class-A and Double-A. The 23-year-old features a moving fastball that reaches the mid-90s and a good slider. His offspeed stuff needs work if he's going to succeed as a starter in the majors. He'll probably begin 2002 at Double-A, but he could be called up to work out of the pen in San Diego later in the year.

Jason Middlebrook

Position: P   **Opening Day Age:** 26
Bats: R **Throws:** R   **Born:** 6/26/75 in
Ht: 6' 3" **Wt:** 215   Jackson, MI

Recent Statistics

	W	L	ERA	G	GS	Sv	IP	H	R	BB	SO	HR
2001 AA Mobile	3	0	1.20	10	9	0	52.2	36	10	9	51	1
2001 AAA Portland	7	4	3.29	15	15	0	90.1	86	34	23	66	5
2001 NL San Diego	2	1	5.12	4	3	0	19.1	18	11	10	10	6

Middlebrook was one of the most highly touted amateurs in baseball after a phenomenal freshman season at Stanford. However, elbow troubles the following year dropped him from a sure first-rounder to the Pads' ninth-round pick. His elbow and shoulder have troubled him throughout his minor league career, but he continues to show glimpses of the form that earned him high regards in college. His first big league start was memorable, dueling Kevin Brown for six innings and earning the win. Middlebrook also took away some not-so-good memories from the 2001 season: Barry Bonds was 3-for-3 against him with three homers (Nos. 65, 66 and 68) and a pair of walks. Middlebrook's fastball tops out at 94 MPH, and he mixes in an above-average slider and change. In 2002, he will compete for a spot in the San Diego rotation.

Xavier Nady

Position: 1B   **Opening Day Age:** 23
Bats: R **Throws:** R   **Born:** 11/14/78 in
Ht: 6' 1" **Wt:** 185   Carmel, CA

Recent Statistics

	G	AB	R	H	D	T	HR	RBI	SB	BB	SO	Avg
2001 A Lk Elsinore	137	524	96	158	38	1	26	100	6	62	109	.302

Nady was considered one of the most talented players in the 2000 draft, but fell to the Padres in the second round because of signability concerns. After a protracted negotiation, he was inked in time to get his first pro at-bat in the majors. This year, the Pads assigned him to Lake Elsinore in the high Class-A California League, where he tied for the league lead in home runs and walked away with MVP honors. Surgery to reconstruct Nady's elbow has shelved a plan to move him to second base next year, and left field is a more likely long-term destination. Until his elbow is fully healed, he'll probably play in Lake Elsinore, where he can be the team's full-time DH.

Jake Peavy

Position: P
Bats: R **Throws:** R
Ht: 6' 1" **Wt:** 180

Opening Day Age: 20
Born: 5/31/81 in Mobile, AL

Recent Statistics

	W	L	ERA	G	GS	Sv	IP	H	R	BB	SO	HR
2000 A Fort Wayne	13	8	2.90	26	25	0	133.2	107	61	53	164	6
2001 A Lk Elsinore	7	5	3.08	19	19	0	105.1	76	41	33	144	6
2001 AA Mobile	2	1	2.57	5	5	0	28.0	19	8	12	44	3

Peavy has been a star in the making ever since the Padres selected him in the 15th round of the 1999 draft. He's dominated every level in which he's pitched. He throws three above-average pitches—a 92-MPH fastball, a late-breaking slider and a surprisingly good changeup—and has terrific control. He strikes out batters more than four times as often as he walks them. He also averages nearly 13 Ks per nine innings. Peavy likely will begin 2002 with a refresher stint at Double-A, but he could move up quickly. He'll be in the Padres' rotation no later than 2003, when they open their new ballpark.

Mark Phillips

Position: P
Bats: L **Throws:** L
Ht: 6' 3" **Wt:** 205

Opening Day Age: 20
Born: 12/30/81 in Hanover, PA

Recent Statistics

	W	L	ERA	G	GS	Sv	IP	H	R	BB	SO	HR
2000 R Idaho Falls	1	1	5.35	10	10	0	37.0	35	30	24	37	2
2001 A Eugene	3	1	3.74	4	4	0	21.2	16	10	9	19	1
2001 A Fort Wayne	4	1	2.64	5	5	0	30.2	19	11	14	27	1
2001 A Lk Elsinore	2	1	2.57	5	5	0	28.0	19	8	14	34	0

Phillips was the Padres' first-round draft pick in 2000. The 20-year-old lefty has a moving fastball that's consistently in the low 90s and a biting curve he throws as hard as a slider. The 2001 campaign got off to an inauspicious start, however, as Phillips came to spring training out of shape, forcing the Padres to place him in extended spring training. To his credit, he took that as a reminder that he shouldn't take his talents or his career so lightly. After nine starts between the short-season Northwest League and the Class-A Midwest League, he was promoted to high Class-A. While his control and changeup still need work, there's no question that he has the potential to become a terrific major league starter. With a strong spring, he'll likely begin 2002 in Double-A.

Dennis Tankersley

Position: P
Bats: R **Throws:** R
Ht: 6' 2" **Wt:** 185

Opening Day Age: 23
Born: 2/24/79 in Troy, MO

Recent Statistics

	W	L	ERA	G	GS	Sv	IP	H	R	BB	SO	HR
2000 A Augusta	5	3	4.06	15	15	0	75.1	73	41	32	74	4
2000 A Fort Wayne	5	2	2.85	12	12	0	66.1	48	25	25	87	5
2001 A Lk Elsinore	5	1	0.52	9	8	0	52.1	29	5	12	68	1
2001 AA Mobile	4	1	2.07	13	13	0	69.2	44	23	24	89	6
2001 AAA Portland	1	2	6.91	3	3	0	14.1	16	13	8	16	2

When the Pads traded Ed Sprague to the Red Sox in 2000 for shortstop Cesar Saba, they asked for a throw-in arm to seal the deal. Tankersley was the throw-in. Ever since the trade, Tankersley has been one of the most dominating pitchers in the minors. His mix of a low to mid-90s sinking fastball and a nasty slider has drawn comparisons to Kevin Brown and Dave Stieb. He also has very good control for a pitcher who throws as hard as he does. In 2001, he dominated two levels on his way to finishing the year in Triple-A. A tired arm shut him down after three starts in Triple-A, however. While he'll probably pick up right there to start 2002, there's a strong possibility he'll be in the Padres' rotation by the end of the year.

Ramon Vazquez

Position: SS
Bats: L **Throws:** R
Ht: 5' 11" **Wt:** 170

Opening Day Age: 25
Born: 8/21/76 in Aibonito, PR

Recent Statistics

	G	AB	R	H	D	THR	RBI	SB	BB	SO	Avg
2001 AAA Tacoma	127	466	85	140	28	1	10	79	9	76	84	.300
2001 AL Seattle	17	35	5	8	0	0	0	4	0	0	3	.229
2001 MLE	127	448	73	122	24	0	8	68	6	66	89	.272

A 27th-round pick of the Mariners in 1995, Vazquez has made steady progress over the years, displaying solid instincts and a good feel for the game. Defensively he's sound, with good range and a strong arm. He doesn't run well for a middle infielder, but he compensates with his instinctual play. He's always drawn walks and hit for a decent average, but he came to camp stronger last spring and set career highs in average, runs, doubles, homers, RBI and slugging at Triple-A Tacoma in 2001. He's played some third base in winter ball, and he also can play second. Seattle dealt Vazquez to the Padres in a six-player swap in December, and he has a chance to be the starting shortstop in San Diego this season.

Others to Watch

Lefty **Eric Cyr** (23) didn't get as much press as Dennis Tankersley, Jacob Peavy or Mark Phillips, but he was just as dominating, striking out 131 California League batters at Lake Elsinore in 100.2 innings. . . **Kevin Eberwein** (25), who moved from third to first to accommodate Sean Burroughs, still is slugging and waiting for his chance at the majors. Ankle surgery and a broken hand limited his playing time in 2001, but the Padres continue to be intrigued with his power. . . Outfielder **Kory DeHaan** (25), a Rule 5 pickup from the Pirates, showed he wasn't ready for the majors in 2000. However, he displayed good power and excellent plate discipline while splitting time between three minor league levels in 2001. . . Due to questions about his defense and an organizational overstock of third basemen, sweet-swinging **Jake Gautreau** (22) may be moved to the outfield. He had a .517 slugging percentage in 178 at-bats in low-A Eugene. . . **Donaldo Mendez** (23), selected out of the Houston organization in the 2001 Rule 5 draft, is a brilliant defensive shortstop who clearly was over-matched at the plate against major league pitching.

Pacific Bell Park

Offense

In its second year of existence, Pacific Bell Park strengthened its growing reputation as a pitchers' haven, Barry Bonds' presence to the contrary. Only 8.6 runs per game were scored there, the fourth-lowest average in the majors. Despite the cozy 309-foot distance down the right-field line, the 25-foot-high barrier in right field has limited drives into McCovey Cove. The yawning expanse in center field and the sizable alleys created by Pac Bell's asymmetrical contours favor gap-to-gap hitters.

Defense

Though the Giants' fielding worsened this year, they committed 10 fewer errors at home than on the road, owing partly to Pac Bell's superior playing surface. The roomy center field became a stage for Calvin Murray, a rangy fielder who regularly made highlight-film catches. Caroms off the high right-field wall, along with balls ricocheting around the wall's arches, prove challenging.

Who It Helps the Most

Most Giants pitchers find a way to capitalize on Pac Bell. Their home ERA of 3.79 clashed with their 4.60 ERA on the road. Jason Schmidt went 4-0 with a 2.42 ERA in four Pac Bell starts. Very few hitters enjoyed a home-field advantage. That select group included Rich Aurilia and Shawon Dunston.

Who It Hurts the Most

Lefthanded pull hitters such as J.T. Snow and John Vander Wal were dreadful at Pac Bell. Same with Marvin Benard, another lefthanded batter who doesn't pull as much. Despite being lefthanded, reliever Aaron Fultz posted a 5.14 ERA at Pac Bell, more than a run higher than his road figure.

Rookies & Newcomers

The Giants know that Pac Bell almost automatically can improve most pitchers, young and old alike. But they have to be a little confused about the effect it has on hitters, given the fluctuations of Snow and Jeff Kent from 2000 to 2001. What's certain is that incoming lefthanded batters must not be seduced by the inviting right-field wall.

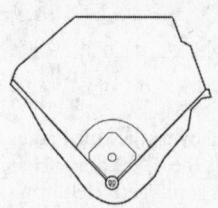

Dimensions: LF-339, LCF-364, CF-399, RCF-421, RF-309

Capacity: 41,341

Elevation: 0 feet

Surface: Grass

Foul Territory: Average

Park Factors

2001 Season

	Home Games			Away Games			Index
	Giants	Opp	Total	Giants	Opp	Total	
G	75	75	150	72	72	144	—
Avg	.256	.253	.255	.282	.270	.276	92
AB	2523	2642	5165	2600	2425	5025	99
R	330	336	666	412	371	783	82
H	647	669	1316	732	654	1386	91
2B	142	140	282	141	124	265	104
3B	23	24	47	15	18	33	139
HR	90	48	138	129	86	215	62
BB	301	260	561	279	276	555	98
SO	472	524	996	527	468	995	97
E	52	37	89	54	47	101	85
E-Infield	42	32	74	38	38	76	93
LHB-Avg	.241	.259	.251	.301	.295	.298	84
LHB-HR	48	12	60	66	34	100	57
RHB-Avg	.265	.249	.257	.272	.253	.263	98
RHB-HR	42	36	78	63	52	115	67

2000 Season

	Home Games			Away Games			Index
	Giants	Opp	Total	Giants	Opp	Total	
G	72	72	144	75	75	150	—
Avg	.281	.244	.263	.270	.280	.275	95
AB	2356	2416	4772	2634	2526	5160	96
R	407	265	672	426	405	831	84
H	663	590	1253	712	707	1419	92
2B	127	107	234	142	129	271	93
3B	24	11	35	18	26	44	86
HR	99	54	153	100	81	181	91
BB	304	251	555	353	307	660	91
SO	404	475	879	539	507	1046	91
E	30	37	67	58	54	112	62
E-Infield	28	29	57	42	46	88	67
LHB-Avg	.271	.235	.255	.275	.279	.277	92
LHB-HR	39	16	55	50	28	78	77
RHB-Avg	.290	.249	.267	.267	.280	.274	98
RHB-HR	60	38	98	50	53	103	102

2001 Rankings (National League)

- Lowest home-run factor
- Lowest LHB batting-average factor
- Lowest LHB home-run factor
- Lowest RHB home-run factor
- Second-lowest batting-average factor
- Second-lowest hit factor
- Second-lowest error factor
- Third-lowest run factor

Dusty Baker

2001 Season

Dusty Baker now boasts baseball's second-longest active continuous tenure, trailing only Atlanta's Bobby Cox. Baker's reputation has grown tremendously through this stretch. One former Giant said that Baker does something every day to make each player feel like a part of the team. Baker accomplishes that by maintaining a relaxed atmosphere and defining each player's role so clearly that he knows he'll be used when the situation calls.

Offense

Baker's elevation of Rich Aurilia into the No. 2 spot gave the Giants a jolt. Even with Barry Bonds' record home-run output, San Francisco needed every bit of Aurilia's increased production. Baker was prompted to mix and match, trying to play who was hottest. Often Baker's decisions were platoon-oriented, but not always. Though Baker did what he could, he ultimately was frustrated, as the Giants led the league in runners left on base (1,242) and posted the NL's fourth-worst average with runners in scoring position (.252).

Pitching & Defense

Once the Giants' starting pitchers proved more capable of working deep into games, Baker simply let them. Still, he was second-guessed for juggling his rotation in the season's final week to have Russ Ortiz pitch a series finale in Houston and Shawn Estes face Los Angeles. Ortiz won his game, but Estes lasted two-thirds of an inning in an 11-10 Giants loss that eliminated them from the playoffs. Though the Giants' fielding galled Baker, he substituted liberally to strengthen his defense, usually finishing games with infielder Ramon Martinez and center fielder Calvin Murray in the lineup.

2002 Outlook

Unfortunately for Giants fans, the worrisome speculation about Baker's managerial future that dampened the end of the 2000 season soon will resume, since his contract expires at the end of this year. Baker might be tiring of the club's payroll constraints and criticism surrounding his lack of postseason success. The only thing that's certain is that Baker once again will squeeze maximum effort and production from the Giants in 2002.

Born: 6/15/49 in Riverside, CA

Playing Experience: 1968-1986, Atl, LA, SF, Oak

Managerial Experience: 9 seasons

Manager Statistics

Year	Team, Lg	W	L	Pct	GB	Finish
2001	San Francisco, NL	90	72	.556	2.0	2nd West
9 Seasons		745	649	.534	—	—

2001 Starting Pitchers by Days Rest

	<=3	4	5	6+
Giants Starts	3	78	55	19
Giants ERA	2.21	4.19	4.26	4.31
NL Avg Starts	1	80	47	24
NL ERA	5.03	4.43	4.53	4.28

2001 Situational Stats

	Dusty Baker	NL Average
Hit & Run Success %	46.9	35.1
Stolen Base Success %	57.6	66.5
Platoon Pct.	48.3	51.5
Defensive Subs	19	20
High-Pitch Outings	10	7
Quick/Slow Hooks	19/15	19/14
Sacrifice Attempts	95	87

2001 Rankings (National League)

- 2nd in hit-and-run success percentage, starts with over 120 pitches (10) and starts on three days rest
- 3rd in slow hooks

Rich Aurilia

2001 Season

Previously regarded as an overachiever, Rich Aurilia enjoyed the type of year that's associated with elite shortstops such as Alex Rodriguez. He became only the third Giant to reach the 200-hit level, joining Willie Mays (200, 1958) and Bobby Bonds (200, 1970). Elevated into the second spot in the batting order, Aurilia raised his game as well, so much so that he received consideration in the lower end of the National League MVP balloting. Though his batting average dropped significantly after the All-Star break, he more than doubled his home-run output in the second half.

Hitting

An enthusiastic high-ball hitter, Aurilia may have capitalized on the elevated strike zone more than any other player in the majors. He probably saw more fastballs while batting in front of Barry Bonds, since pitchers were loathe to walk anybody before the record-setting slugger came to bat. But give Aurilia some credit; when he got his pitch, he rarely missed it. Though he shows definite pull tendencies, he can be productive shooting for the gaps. He'll chase sliders down and off the plate, and given his tendencies it's not surprising that he'll reach for fastballs on two-strike counts.

Baserunning & Defense

Aurilia's range is average at best, and nobody raves about his arm. But he compensates with intelligent positioning. Refusing to cruise on his offensive ability, he remained more than willing to attempt diving stops. Now that Aurilia's 30 years old, some experts wonder how long he'll maintain enough physical resiliency and elasticity to play shortstop. With mediocre speed, he never has been a threat to steal, but he knows what he's doing on the bases.

2002 Outlook

In another of general manager Brian Sabean's shrewd moves, the Giants signed Aurilia to a three-year contract extension in December 2000. Though Aurilia may have trouble matching last year's numbers, so would almost anyone else. Even a "regression" to his pre-2001 standards—around 20 home runs and 80 RBI—would leave him in the upper echelon of NL shortstops.

Position: SS
Bats: R **Throws:** R
Ht: 6' 1" **Wt:** 185

Opening Day Age: 30
Born: 9/2/71 in Brooklyn, NY
ML Seasons: 7
Pronunciation: uh-REEL-yuh
Nickname: Dickie

Overall Statistics

	G	AB	R	H	D	T	HR	RBI	SB	BB	SO	Avg	OBP	Slg
2001	156	636	114	206	37	5	37	97	1	47	83	.324	.369	.572
Career	731	2555	350	724	129	11	98	354	13	209	375	.283	.337	.458

Where He Hits the Ball

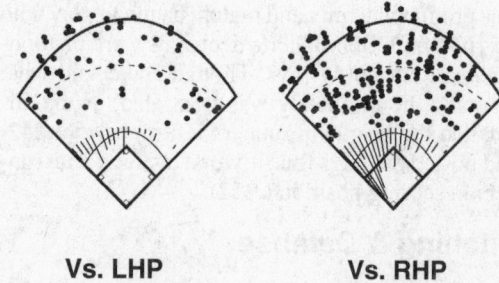

Vs. LHP   **Vs. RHP**

2001 Situational Stats

	AB	H	HR	RBI	Avg		AB	H	HR	RBI	Avg
Home	305	107	15	46	.351	LHP	143	46	12	26	.322
Road	331	99	22	51	.299	RHP	493	160	25	71	.325
First Half	337	120	12	38	.356	Sc Pos	137	36	6	48	.263
Scnd Half	299	86	25	59	.288	Clutch	97	21	6	13	.216

2001 Rankings (National League)

- 1st in hits
- 2nd in at-bats
- 4th in singles and fielding percentage at shortstop (.975)
- 6th in total bases (364) and batting average at home
- 7th in slugging percentage vs. lefthanded pitchers (.650)
- Led the Giants in at-bats, hits, singles, batting average vs. lefthanded pitchers, batting average at home, batting average on a 3-2 count (.305) and batting average with two strikes (.226)
- Led NL shortstops in batting average, home runs and RBI

Barry Bonds

2001 Season

Time will render the ultimate judgment on Barry Bonds' wondrous 2001 season. The horror of the September 11 terrorist attacks diverted attention from Bonds' successful pursuit of the single-season home-run record. The fact that Bonds broke the record in a West Coast night game further thrust his accomplishments into the background. While true aficionados appreciate Bonds' feats, others will need to absorb the impact of his prodigious record-shattering, MVP accomplishments in retrospect.

Hitting

Bonds' compact, uppercut swing, combined with his otherworldly bat speed, almost automatically produces home runs when he gets a pitch he wants. Always a finicky hitter, he actually became *more* selective, as he drew a major league-record 177 walks. But he was just as attentive as he was patient, hitting 23 homers on the first or second pitch. Bonds improved drastically against lefthanders after hitting just .230 against them in 2000. Pitchers found him susceptible to fastballs up and in or below his hands, and neutralized him by changing speeds and eye levels with their deliveries.

Baserunning & Defense

Bonds remains a respected outfielder, though he'll probably never regain the proficiency that enabled him to win eight Gold Glove Awards. While his range and arm strength have decreased, his hands and throwing accuracy are top-notch. He quickly became an expert at playing caroms off Pacific Bell Park's left-field wall and corner. No longer a 40-40 threat, Bonds stole 13 bases in 2001. Already history's only player with at least 400 career home runs and 400 stolen bases, Bonds needs just 16 of the latter to carve out his very own 500-500 niche.

2002 Outlook

Bonds will turn 38 this season, an age that's inevitably accompanied by athletic decline. Though it's dangerous to predict that Bonds will be an exception, bear in mind that he will be stimulated by the prospect of hitting his 600th career home run and catching his godfather, Willie Mays (660 homers), after that. Bonds is a good bet to keep slugging for another two or three years.

Position: LF
Bats: L **Throws:** L
Ht: 6' 2" **Wt:** 210

Opening Day Age: 37
Born: 7/24/64 in Riverside, CA
ML Seasons: 16
Nickname: BB

Overall Statistics

	G	AB	R	H	D	T	HR	RBI	SB	BB	SO	Avg	OBP	Slg
2001	153	476	129	156	32	2	73	137	13	177	93	.328	.515	.863
Career	2296	7932	1713	2313	483	71	567	1542	484	1724	1282	.292	.419	.585

Where He Hits the Ball

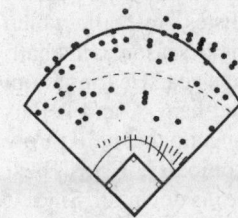 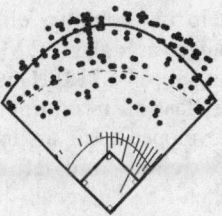

Vs. LHP   **Vs. RHP**

2001 Situational Stats

	AB	H	HR	RBI	Avg		AB	H	HR	RBI	Avg
Home	224	75	37	71	.335	LHP	141	44	17	34	.312
Road	252	81	36	66	.321	RHP	335	112	56	103	.334
First Half	259	79	39	73	.305	Sc Pos	89	34	13	59	.382
Scnd Half	217	77	34	64	.355	Clutch	70	22	10	14	.314

2001 Rankings (National League)

- 1st in home runs, walks, times on base (342), slugging percentage, on-base percentage, HR frequency (6.5 ABs per HR), slugging percentage vs. righthanded pitchers (.910), on-base percentage vs. righthanded pitchers (.526) and lowest groundball-flyball ratio (0.6)
- Led the Giants in batting average, runs scored, total bases (411), RBI, stolen bases, most pitches seen per plate appearance (3.84), highest percentage of pitches taken (65.7), batting average with runners in scoring position, batting average in the clutch, batting average on the road and lowest percentage of swings on the first pitch (25.7)
- Led NL left fielders in batting average and home runs

Shawn Estes

2001 Season

Known for his erratic performances, Shawn Estes frustrated the Giants for the final time. He briefly led the league in ERA early in 2001, and built a 7-2 record with a 2.90 ERA through June. Then came a series of poor performances, exacerbated by a sprained left ankle. Estes recovered and turned in a couple of encouraging late-season efforts. But the final note he struck was woefully off-key: a two-thirds inning, five-run outing against Los Angeles in an 11-10 loss on October 5 that eliminated the Giants from the postseason.

Pitching

Once capable of blowing the ball by hitters, Estes now must rely on finesse. His ankle injury didn't help his velocity, either. Estes' fastball, which ranged as high as 92 MPH in the season's first half, hit only 84-87 MPH later in the year. He tries to run his fastball in on righthanded batters, and he has developed a fair sinking changeup that he'll throw to righties and lefties. Ironically, Estes' best pitch—his curveball—can be his downfall. Since it breaks straight down, a top-to-bottom movement that few other lefthanders possess, he has to throw it over the plate to get a called strike. Shaving off a corner is difficult for him. One scout theorized that some umpires are so bamboozled by Estes' unique break that they're too stunned to call strikes.

Defense & Hitting

Estes committed a career-high three errors last year, weakening his shaky equilibrium on the mound. He's fairly adept at holding runners on first base. Estes' hitting, previously respectable, suffered with the rest of his game last season (.071 after a .206 year in 2000).

2002 Outlook

It would have been a major surprise if Estes had begun 2002 with San Francisco. The Giants lost patience with his erratic pitching, and they dealt him to the Mets for Tsuyoshi Shinjo and Desi Relaford. Estes and his still-tantalizing potential join a Mets rotation that already has five solid arms. The Mets probably aren't done trading yet.

Position: SP
Bats: R **Throws:** L
Ht: 6' 2" **Wt:** 195

Opening Day Age: 29
Born: 2/18/73 in San Bernardino, CA
ML Seasons: 7
Pronunciation: EST-us
Nickname: Buck

Overall Statistics

	W	L	Pct.	ERA	G	GS	Sv	IP	H	BB	SO	HR	Ratio
2001	9	8	.529	4.02	27	27	0	159.0	151	77	109	11	1.43
Career	64	50	.561	4.25	160	160	0	990.0	945	521	795	74	1.48

How Often He Throws Strikes

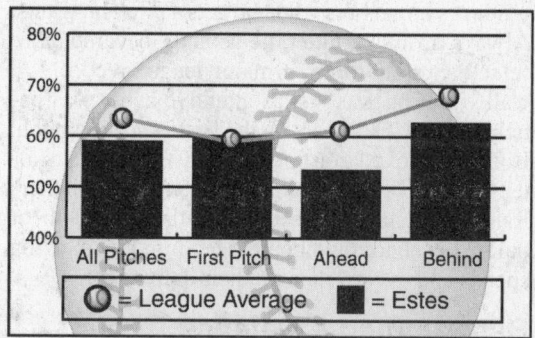

○ = League Average   ■ = Estes

2001 Situational Stats

	W	L	ERA	Sv	IP		AB	H	HR	RBI	Avg
Home	7	2	3.15	0	91.1	LHB	154	35	2	12	.227
Road	2	6	5.19	0	67.2	RHB	443	116	9	51	.262
First Half	7	3	3.51	0	100.0	Sc Pos	154	37	1	43	.240
Scnd Half	2	5	4.88	0	59.0	Clutch	36	3	0	0	.083

2001 Rankings (National League)

- 3rd in wild pitches (10)
- 4th in balks (2)
- 5th in errors at pitcher (3)
- Led the Giants in hit batsmen (5), wild pitches (10) and balks (2)

Livan Hernandez

2001 Season

The Giants kept giving Livan Hernandez the ball in 2001, and he gave them heartache in return. They thought he had emerged as a legitimate staff ace in 2000, when he won 17 games and the Division Series opener against New York. But last year his ERA rose by nearly a run and a half as he posted his third sub-.500 record in four seasons.

Pitching

Hernandez' power-pitching days officially are a thing of the past. Rarely does he push his fastball into the 91-92 MPH range. His motion is so languid that he can slip an 87-MPH fastball by an unsuspecting hitter, but that's an increasingly rare occurrence. When Hernandez lacks command, he gets pounded. He prefers to change speeds with his slider, changeup and curveball, which he does more artfully than most pitchers. While the slider is a favored tool against righthanded hitters, he's liable to throw his change to lefties or righties.

Defense & Hitting

Hernandez' excellent hand-eye coordination also helps him field his position adroitly. He has committed two errors in 147 career games, none since joining the Giants in 1999. Now the proud owner of a .243 lifetime average, maybe Hernandez can switch from pitching to hitting full-time. He put together a streak of eight consecutive hits last year while batting .296 and now has exceeded 20 hits for two years in a row.

2002 Outlook

The notion of trading Hernandez would have been unthinkable a year ago. It's now an extremely viable option. Some insiders believe he doesn't pitch effectively unless he changes scenery every so often. Despite his fluctuating performances, he'd be easy to trade, since his value is locked in by a contract that runs through 2003 with a club option for 2004. All this could be moot if Hernandez doesn't maintain his precise pitch location or regain a little of the steam on his fastball. Maybe winning 10-12 games while pitching 200-plus innings each year is his destiny. Certainly, he could do worse.

Position: SP
Bats: R **Throws:** R
Ht: 6' 2" **Wt:** 222

Opening Day Age: 27
Born: 2/20/75 in Villa Clara, Cuba
ML Seasons: 6
Pronunciation:
lee-VAHN her-NAN-dezz

Overall Statistics

	W	L	Pct.	ERA	G	GS	Sv	IP	H	BB	SO	HR	Ratio
2001	13	15	.464	5.24	34	34	0	226.2	266	85	138	24	1.55
Career	57	53	.518	4.43	148	147	0	1000.0	1096	378	683	111	1.47

How Often He Throws Strikes

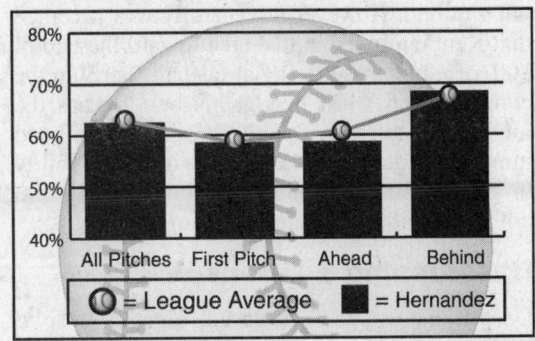

2001 Situational Stats

	W	L	ERA	Sv	IP		AB	H	HR	RBI	Avg
Home	6	9	5.13	0	124.2	LHB	425	127	10	67	.299
Road	7	6	5.38	0	102.0	RHB	470	139	14	67	.296
First Half	6	11	6.07	0	126.0	Sc Pos	226	80	4	101	.354
Scnd Half	7	4	4.20	0	100.2	Clutch	82	22	3	10	.268

2001 Rankings (National League)

- 1st in hits allowed, fielding percentage at pitcher (1.000) and highest batting average allowed with runners in scoring position
- 2nd in batters faced (1,008)
- 3rd in highest batting average allowed (.297)
- 4th in losses, games started, pitches thrown (3,684) and highest ERA
- 5th in pickoff throws (144)
- 6th in highest ERA at home
- Led the Giants in losses, games started, complete games (2), innings pitched, batters faced (1,008), pitches thrown (3,684), pickoff throws (144), highest groundball-flyball ratio allowed (1.3) and fewest pitches thrown per batter (3.65)

San Francisco

Jeff Kent

2001 Season

Entering the 2001 season as the reigning National League MVP, Jeff Kent endured a subpar campaign by his standards. He managed to exceed 100 RBI for the fifth consecutive season, but his home-run output dropped by one-third and his batting average with runners in scoring position plummeted 75 points. Still, Kent drove in 21 runs in the season's final month while opponents absolutely refused to pitch to Barry Bonds, proving he still had the knack for the big hit.

Hitting

Scouts thought Kent lacked patience at the plate in situations when opponents would walk Bonds to pitch to him. However, it generally was accepted that Kent improved in that area toward the end of 2001. He prefers to swing at fastballs early in the count, though when he's at his best he has the intelligence to sit on a pitcher's breaking ball and jump on it when it comes. Because of Kent's ability to adjust, any pitcher thinking about getting him out with a slider had better set it up astutely.

Baserunning & Defense

Despite having average speed, Kent is a solid baserunner fundamentally, more than capable of seizing upon an opponent's defensive mistake. Never flashy defensively, he has made himself into a decent second baseman, quickening his release on throws after having to go to his right for a ball. His overall consistency helps obscure his lack of above-average tools. Kent may not possess the athleticism of a Pokey Reese, but he is handy enough to fill in at first base when the Giants need help there.

2002 Outlook

Even with Bonds' record-setting feats and Rich Aurilia's emergence, Kent remains vital to San Francisco's success. Since Kent will be eligible for free agency after the 2002 season, incentive should not be an issue. While his age will prompt potential suitors to question his future productivity, he's poised to receive a substantial increase from the $6 million he'll earn this year. The Giants will be more than happy to benefit from Kent's attempts to hike his value.

Position: 2B/1B
Bats: R **Throws:** R
Ht: 6' 1" **Wt:** 205

Opening Day Age: 34
Born: 3/7/68 in Bellflower, CA
ML Seasons: 10

Overall Statistics

	G	AB	R	H	D	T	HR	RBI	SB	BB	SO	Avg	OBP	Slg
2001	159	607	84	181	49	6	22	106	7	65	96	.298	.369	.507
Career	1350	4936	764	1409	323	31	216	899	68	452	973	.285	.351	.495

Where He Hits the Ball

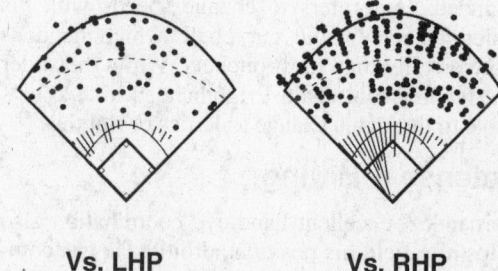

Vs. LHP   Vs. RHP

2001 Situational Stats

	AB	H	HR	RBI	Avg		AB	H	HR	RBI	Avg
Home	286	83	8	45	.290	LHP	129	38	3	22	.295
Road	321	98	14	61	.305	RHP	478	143	19	84	.299
First Half	327	97	12	64	.297	Sc Pos	168	45	6	82	.268
Scnd Half	280	84	10	42	.300	Clutch	89	24	2	10	.270

2001 Rankings (National League)

- 1st in sacrifice flies (13)
- 3rd in doubles and fielding percentage at second base (.987)
- 5th in batting average with the bases loaded (.526)
- 8th in errors at second base (9)
- 9th in plate appearances (696)
- Led the Giants in doubles, triples, sacrifice flies (13), hit by pitch (11), strikeouts, plate appearances (696), games played, batting average with the bases loaded (.526), cleanup slugging percentage (.524) and highest percentage of extra bases taken as a runner (51.9)
- Led NL second basemen in home runs and RBI

Robb Nen

2001 Season

While bolstering his reputation as one of the game's most dominating closers, Robb Nen also maintained his curious statistical pattern of alternating 3.00-plus ERA seasons with sub-2.00 ERA campaigns. Though he recorded a 3.01 ERA last year after posting a 1.50 mark in 2000, he still reached a single-season career high in saves. Though the Giants took pains to keep Nen fresh, they received a strong reminder that he also needs regular work to stay sharp. He lost two crucial games immediately after the weeklong break precipitated by the September 11 terrorist attacks.

Pitching

Though Nen is said to be a good student of hitters, he doesn't bother with trying to out-think opponents. Everybody knows he's going to throw something hard—whether it's his fastball, which ranges between 94-98 MPH; a cut fastball at 91-94 MPH; or a slider that hovers between 87-92 MPH. Nen's slider can be devastating, especially to lefthanders. Though his odd toe-tap in the middle of his delivery has become familiar, it still can disrupt a hitter's timing. Hard throwers with somewhat violent deliveries such as Nen can't maintain their command every outing, which is why he occasionally lights up the scoreboard as well as the radar gun.

Defense & Hitting

Opponents steal Nen blind. His slow delivery makes him easy to run on. Then again, since Nen allowed only 9.27 hits and walks per nine innings last year, simply reaching base against him is an extreme challenge. As a closer with 13 career at-bats, Nen is a non-factor offensively.

2002 Outlook

Nen's immediate future could be intriguing. Even some of history's most formidable closers lost their effectiveness almost overnight. Nen's almost imperceptible slippage last year should prompt the Giants to monitor him carefully. His nine-inning rates of strikeouts decreased from 12.55 to 10.78, while his hits allowed rose from 5.05 to 6.72. Moreover, this will be a year of decision for Nen, who must weigh player options for 2003 and 2004 after his contract expires at the end of this year.

Position: RP
Bats: R **Throws:** R
Ht: 6' 5" **Wt:** 215

Opening Day Age: 32
Born: 11/28/69 in San Pedro, CA
ML Seasons: 9

Overall Statistics

	W	L	Pct.	ERA	G	GS	Sv	IP	H	BB	SO	HR	Ratio
2001	4	5	.444	3.01	79	0	45	77.2	58	22	93	6	1.03
Career	39	40	.494	3.07	575	4	271	641.1	543	240	712	49	1.22

How Often He Throws Strikes

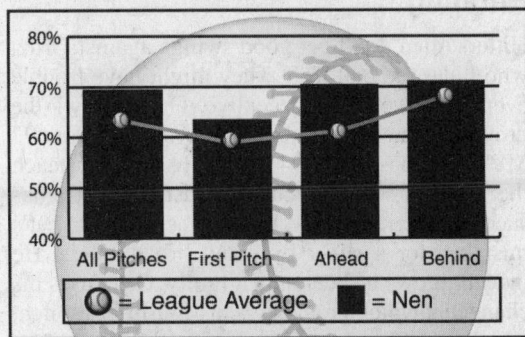

2001 Situational Stats

	W	L	ERA	Sv	IP		AB	H	HR	RBI	Avg
Home	4	2	2.56	27	45.2	LHB	150	36	2	16	.240
Road	0	3	3.66	18	32.0	RHB	136	22	4	12	.162
First Half	2	2	3.09	26	43.2	Sc Pos	74	16	2	22	.216
Scnd Half	2	3	2.91	19	34.0	Clutch	212	47	4	25	.222

2001 Rankings (National League)

- 1st in save opportunities (52), saves and games finished (71)
- 2nd in fewest baserunners allowed per nine innings in relief (9.4) and blown saves (7)
- 7th in games pitched, save percentage (86.5) and lowest batting average allowed in relief (.203)
- Led the Giants in saves, games finished (71), stolen bases allowed (17), save opportunities (52), save percentage (86.5), first batter efficiency (.192), blown saves (7), relief losses (5) and most strikeouts per nine innings in relief (10.8)

San Francisco

Russ Ortiz

2001 Season

Aside from Barry Bonds' home-run binge, Russ Ortiz' improvement was one of the brightest aspects of the Giants' year. He posted career bests in ERA, innings pitched and strikeouts while substantially cutting down his walks and home runs allowed. Ortiz was particularly efficient in the latter category, permitting only 13 longballs after coughing up 28 in 2000. That helped San Francisco yield a National League-low 145 homers. Ortiz won 49 games from 1999-2001, the most victories by any Giants hurler in a three-year span since Hall of Famers Juan Marichal and Gaylord Perry anchored the rotation in the late 1960s and early '70s.

Pitching

Hitters often don't get good swings against Ortiz, who hides the ball well. They might have trouble even if he were less deceptive. Ortiz throws the proverbial "heavy" fastball that averages about 92 MPH and tops out at 94 MPH. He also can reach the low 90s when he cuts his fastball. Ortiz has succeeded with a hard-breaking curveball that's mistaken for a slider by many broadcasters. He indeed throws a slider, albeit rarely. Ortiz uses his changeup, which probably is his fourth-best pitch, mostly to lefties. Interestingly, after hitting 13 batters in 1999-2000, Ortiz didn't even nick one last year. Yet he still relies on pitching inside.

Defense & Hitting

Ortiz moves nimbly around the mound, abetting his efforts to become a complete pitcher. He participated in four double plays, second-most on the Giants' staff. Ortiz also helps himself at the plate, as his .205 career batting average and NL-high six doubles in 2001 demonstrate.

2002 Outlook

With pitching as fragile as it is, the Giants can be heartened by Ortiz' sound health and relatively steady performances since he joined the rotation full-time three years ago. In short, he's not Shawn Estes or Livan Hernandez. Given Ortiz' youth, he could be poised to become a legitimate staff ace with just a little more polish. Contract status won't be a distraction, since he is signed through 2003 with a club option for 2004.

Position: SP
Bats: R **Throws:** R
Ht: 6' 1" **Wt:** 210

Opening Day Age: 27
Born: 6/5/74 in Encino, CA
ML Seasons: 4
Pronunciation: OR-teez

Overall Statistics

	W	L	Pct.	ERA	G	GS	Sv	IP	H	BB	SO	HR	Ratio
2001	17	9	.654	3.29	33	33	0	218.2	187	91	169	13	1.27
Career	53	34	.609	4.13	121	111	0	710.1	658	374	575	76	1.45

How Often He Throws Strikes

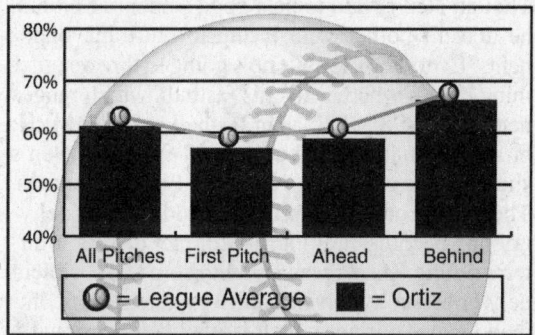

= League Average   = Ortiz

2001 Situational Stats

	W	L	ERA	Sv	IP		AB	H	HR	RBI	Avg
Home	8	3	2.49	0	108.1	LHB	393	108	7	44	.275
Road	9	6	4.08	0	110.1	RHB	413	79	6	33	.191
First Half	9	5	3.28	0	112.1	Sc Pos	177	42	4	59	.237
Scnd Half	8	4	3.30	0	106.1	Clutch	72	19	3	9	.264

2001 Rankings (National League)

- 2nd in fewest home runs allowed per nine innings (.54)
- 3rd in lowest slugging percentage allowed (.328)
- Led the Giants in ERA, wins, walks allowed, strikeouts, winning percentage, highest strikeout-walk ratio (1.9), lowest batting average allowed (.232), lowest slugging percentage allowed (.328), lowest on-base percentage allowed (.309), lowest ERA at home, lowest ERA on the road, lowest batting average allowed vs. righthanded batters, most run support per nine innings (5.7), lowest batting average allowed with runners in scoring position, fewest home runs allowed per nine innings (.54) and most strikeouts per nine innings (7.0)

Kirk Rueter

2001 Season

The most revealing example of Kirk Rueter's value to the Giants emerged in last season's final days, when manager Dusty Baker realigned his starting rotation. Baker's adjustment guaranteed that Rueter would pitch the regular-season finale. This reflected Baker's trust in Rueter, who conceivably could have been pitching to preserve the team's postseason hopes. Once again, Rueter's hits allowed exceeded his innings pitched, and his strikeout total was unimpressive. Yet he again finished with a winning record.

Pitching

Rueter accomplishes what might be thought impossible—he works aggressively with soft stuff. Though his fastball rarely breaks 86 MPH, he'll test righthanded hitters with his cutter, daring them to pull it. He's liable to toss his changeup on consecutive pitches, even while risking that opponents will adjust to the speed. In short, Rueter will throw any pitch on any count toward any location. He is adept at coaxing groundballs with his sinking fastball and plunging curveball, so hitters try to force him to elevate his deliveries and hope that they'll catch too much of the strike zone. Speaking of the strike zone, Rueter struggled early last season to cope with the renewed emphasis on the high strike and on not calling pitches off the corners. Like any capable veteran, he adjusted.

Defense & Hitting

Rueter is remarkably handy. Helped by a smooth slide-step delivery and pickoff move, he's difficult to run on. Blessed with good hands, he participated in 11 double plays last year. At the plate, Rueter struck out just five times in 58 at-bats while hitting a respectable .172, with a team-high 10 sacrifices.

2002 Outlook

Since 1997, Rueter's first full year with San Francisco, he has displayed the consistency of a metronome: 13-6, 16-9, 15-10, 11-9 and 14-12. The Giants will be content to leave him alone, return him to the No. 2 or 3 slot in the starting rotation and let him do his thing. He has two years left on a three-year, $15.6 million deal, making him a truly low-maintenance performer.

Position: SP
Bats: L **Throws:** L
Ht: 6' 2" **Wt:** 205

Opening Day Age: 31
Born: 12/1/70 in Centralia, IL
ML Seasons: 9
Pronunciation: REE-ter
Nickname: Woody

Overall Statistics

	W	L	Pct.	ERA	G	GS	Sv	IP	H	BB	SO	HR	Ratio
2001	14	12	.538	4.42	34	34	0	195.1	213	66	83	25	1.43
Career	95	60	.613	4.20	227	225	0	1269.2	1362	368	620	151	1.36

How Often He Throws Strikes

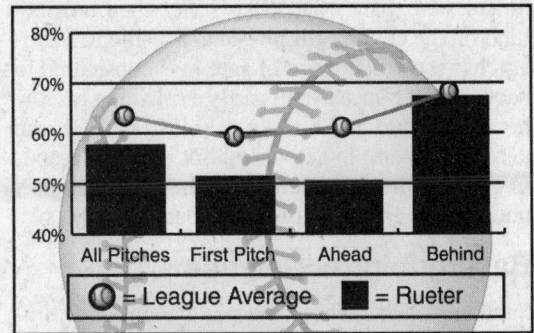

= League Average   = Rueter

2001 Situational Stats

	W	L	ERA	Sv	IP		AB	H	HR	RBI	Avg
Home	5	6	4.33	0	87.1	LHB	176	49	6	22	.278
Road	9	6	4.50	0	108.0	RHB	577	164	19	70	.284
First Half	8	6	4.88	0	103.1	Sc Pos	170	44	2	57	.259
Scnd Half	6	6	3.91	0	92.0	Clutch	15	5	1	2	.333

2001 Rankings (National League)

- 1st in most GDPs induced per nine innings (1.3), fielding percentage at pitcher (1.000) and fewest strikeouts per nine innings (3.8)
- 3rd in GDPs induced (28), lowest stolen-base percentage allowed (25.0) and lowest strikeout-walk ratio (1.3)
- 4th in games started
- 7th in runners caught stealing (9) and highest slugging percentage allowed (.465)
- Led the Giants in sacrifice bunts (10), games started, home runs allowed, runners caught stealing (9), GDPs induced (28), lowest stolen-base percentage allowed (25.0) and fewest walks per nine innings (3.0)

San Francisco

Benito Santiago

2001 Season

Players couldn't understand why Benito Santiago remained unsigned as a free agent until late spring training. While observers saw a well-worn 36-year-old, his peers saw a canny veteran blessed with the body of a much younger man. The players were right. Unhappy with their catching depth, the Giants signed Santiago in March, and he proceeded to play himself into everyday status by late May. He appeared in 133 games, his most since 1996.

Hitting

Santiago remained an incurable early-count hitter, putting the first or second pitch in play on more than 40 percent of his at-bats. More than most hitters, he expands his strike zone when he's behind on the count. Still physically resilient, Santiago has shown one sign of age: he's considered to have a "slider-speed" bat, partly explaining his low home-run total and his second-half fade. He can tattoo down-and-in deliveries, but pitches up-and-in give him trouble. Deft at handling the bat, he's not afraid to try to bunt for a hit occasionally.

Baserunning & Defense

Santiago's skill behind the plate thoroughly impressed the Giants. Though his arm strength has dwindled to average, his polished technique enabled him to throw out 35 of 101 runners attempting to steal. His quick release is further streamlined when he unleashes his signature throw from his knees. Ignore Santiago's total of eight passed balls, which tied for fourth-most in the league. He was efficient at blocking pitches as he dealt with a staff full of hard throwers with wicked movement.

2002 Outlook

Lacking any glittering catching prospects in the organization, the Giants negotiated a two-year contract with Santiago. Unless Edwards Guzman or Yorvit Torrealba suddenly blossoms, Santiago will far surpass the 100-game plateau again this year if his body holds up. Age and the rigors of playing the sport's most demanding position inevitably will erode Santiago, so the Giants will eye his performance anxiously as 2002 progresses.

Position: C
Bats: R **Throws:** R
Ht: 6' 1" **Wt:** 195

Opening Day Age: 37
Born: 3/9/65 in Ponce, PR
ML Seasons: 16
Pronunciation: sahn-tee-AH-go

Overall Statistics

	G	AB	R	H	D	T	HR	RBI	SB	BB	SO	Avg	OBP	Slg
2001	133	477	39	125	25	4	6	45	5	23	78	.262	.295	.369
Career	1689	5874	630	1531	267	33	184	767	86	366	1093	.261	.305	.411

Where He Hits the Ball

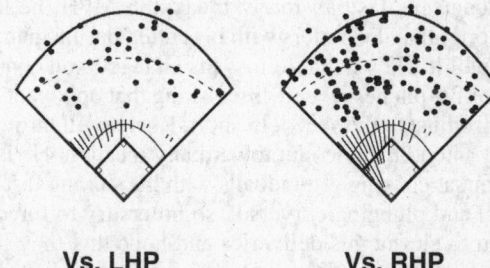

Vs. LHP   **Vs. RHP**

2001 Situational Stats

	AB	H	HR	RBI	Avg		AB	H	HR	RBI	Avg
Home	228	56	3	21	.246	LHP	117	30	1	7	.256
Road	249	69	3	24	.277	RHP	360	95	5	38	.264
First Half	237	68	3	26	.287	Sc Pos	118	30	0	38	.254
Scnd Half	240	57	3	19	.238	Clutch	81	20	0	6	.247

2001 Rankings (National League)

- 3rd in lowest on-base percentage and lowest on-base percentage vs. lefthanded pitchers (.288)
- 4th in fielding percentage at catcher (.994) and highest percentage of swings on the first pitch (45.9)
- Led the Giants in GDPs (19), highest groundball-flyball ratio (1.4) and steals of third (2)

Jason Schmidt

2001 Season

Last year may not have been a breakthrough for Jason Schmidt, but it may have represented a turn-around. Having undergone surgery to repair a frayed rotator cuff in his pitching shoulder in August 2000, he silenced the post-operation doubts by winning seven of eight decisions with the Giants after they acquired him from Pittsburgh with John Vander Wal for outfielder Armando Rios and pitching prospect Ryan Vogelsong. Schmidt's 13 wins and 4.07 ERA overall tied career bests.

Pitching

Schmidt long has been known for his impressive stuff, though he doesn't always show it right away. Scouts have noticed that he'll begin games throwing his fastball in the high 80s, turn it up to 91 MPH, then blow it by hitters at 92-94 MPH. Maybe this isn't an ideal approach, but it lent the impression that Schmidt had command of his stuff and possessed the confidence to pace himself. He complements his lively fastball with a hard slider that he'll often use for an out pitch. He'll mix in an occasional curve or changeup, but neither really plays an integral role in his plan.

Defense & Hitting

Schmidt has acquired a reputation for shoddy defense, but he has committed zero errors during the last two seasons. He improved his hitting, batting .163 last year with two home runs after entering the season with an .082 career average. Sacrifice bunting still can challenge Schmidt, who had six sac bunts last year after recording 12 in 1998 and '99.

2002 Outlook

Thriving down the stretch for the Giants propelled Schmidt nicely into free agency. He expressed a desire to stay in San Francisco, and in December he agreed to a four-year, $31 million deal with the Giants. It's widely believed that Schmidt, who never flourished in Pittsburgh under expectations that he should be a No. 1 starter, might benefit from being on a staff such as San Francisco's, where he wouldn't be regarded as the rotation's center of attention. Schmidt said he took less money to return.

Position: SP
Bats: R **Throws:** R
Ht: 6' 5" **Wt:** 213

Opening Day Age: 29
Born: 1/29/73 in Lewiston, ID
ML Seasons: 7

Overall Statistics

	W	L	Pct.	ERA	G	GS	Sv	IP	H	BB	SO	HR	Ratio
2001	13	7	.650	4.07	25	25	0	150.1	138	61	142	13	1.32
Career	56	54	.509	4.50	162	153	0	949.2	984	405	728	95	1.46

How Often He Throws Strikes

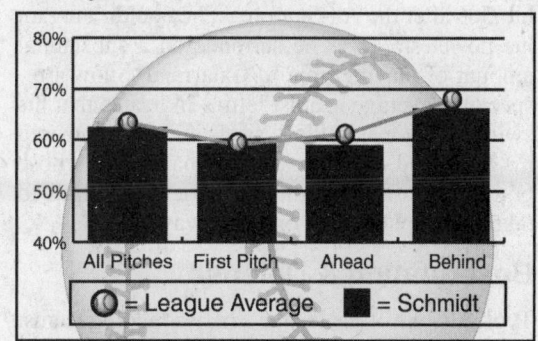

2001 Situational Stats

	W	L	ERA	Sv	IP		AB	H	HR	RBI	Avg
Home	6	4	3.95	0	70.2	LHB	238	67	8	29	.282
Road	7	3	4.18	0	79.2	RHB	327	71	5	34	.217
First Half	5	4	5.52	0	62.0	Sc Pos	132	39	2	46	.295
Scnd Half	8	3	3.06	0	88.1	Clutch	18	6	1	2	.333

2001 Rankings (National League)
- 9th in wild pitches (8)
- 10th in lowest batting average allowed vs. righthanded batters (.217) and highest batting average allowed with runners in scoring position (.295)

J.T. Snow

2001 Season

After averaging 22 homers and 94 RBI from 1997-2000 with San Francisco, J.T. Snow staggered through a miserable season, posting his worst offensive numbers since he split 1994 between Triple-A Vancouver and the Angels. Snow's sudden drop was precipitated by a series of ailments: bruised ribs, sore groin muscles in both legs and a flu attack. The Giants felt compelled to acquire Andres Galarraga at midseason to bolster their offensive production from first base.

Hitting

Snow never fully recovered from a slow start. He batted .201 through June. Though he managed to hit .306 after the All-Star break, he couldn't regain his power stroke as he surrendered a substantial amount of playing time to Galarraga. Snow's respectable average against lefties indicates that his swing isn't gone, just lost, as his injuries hampered his bat speed. A proficient low-ball hitter whose power is mostly to right-center field, he tends to take higher pitches the opposite way.

Baserunning & Defense

Typically one of the league's better fielding teams, the Giants ranked 12th in that category last year. Part of that decline stemmed from Snow's woes, since he either wasn't available or able to save his fellow infielders from throwing errors, as he did so often while winning Gold Glove Awards from 1995-2000. He remains slick around the first-base bag and strong-armed, prompting his appearance late in several games that Galarraga started. Never renowned for his speed, Snow became even more stationary on the bases due to his injuries.

2002 Outlook

The Giants can't afford to keep both Snow and Galarraga, though Snow would be virtually impossible to trade, since he's due about $12 million on a contract that extends through 2003. Unless general manager Brian Sabean, who artfully has kept the Giants competitive, can upgrade first base without exceeding the payroll budget, San Francisco must hope that Snow can recover his pre-2001 form.

Position: 1B
Bats: L **Throws:** L
Ht: 6' 2" **Wt:** 205

Opening Day Age: 34
Born: 2/26/68 in Long Beach, CA
ML Seasons: 10
Nickname: Snowball

Overall Statistics

	G	AB	R	H	D	T	HR	RBI	SB	BB	SO	Avg	OBP	Slg
2001	101	285	43	70	12	1	8	34	0	55	81	.246	.371	.379
Career	1207	4132	596	1092	200	11	159	669	14	548	867	.264	.351	.433

Where He Hits the Ball

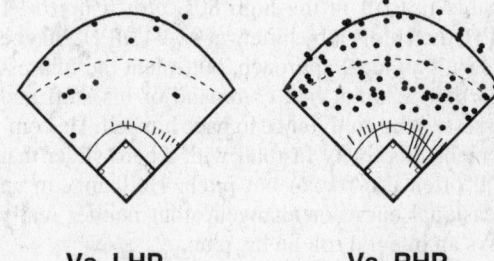

Vs. LHP   Vs. RHP

2001 Situational Stats

	AB	H	HR	RBI	Avg		AB	H	HR	RBI	Avg
Home	142	26	3	13	.183	LHP	49	15	1	7	.306
Road	143	44	5	21	.308	RHP	236	55	7	27	.233
First Half	164	33	5	15	.201	Sc Pos	77	13	1	25	.169
Scnd Half	121	37	3	19	.306	Clutch	36	9	2	6	.250

2001 Rankings (National League)

- 1st in lowest batting average with runners in scoring position

John Vander Wal

2001 Season

Though John Vander Wal's production slipped from his 2000 level, it could have been worse. Vander Wal thought he had secured a starting job in Pittsburgh with a strong 2000, but the Pirates' ill-advised acquisition of Derek Bell cut into his playing time. Vander Wal played frequently for Pittsburgh after it became apparent that Bell's health and skills had declined, but that didn't last. San Francisco then obtained Vander Wal and pitcher Jason Schmidt on July 30 for Ryan Vogelsong and Armando Rios. From then on, Vander Wal played semi-regularly, platooning in right field with Shawon Dunston and Eric Davis.

Hitting

Vander Wal prefers low pitches, which he likes to spray into the gaps, though he has some power when he pulls the ball. His "pull" swing also produces a lot of groundballs. He tends to use more of the field when he hits the ball in the air. Vander Wal's an excellent fastball hitter, though pitchers have succeeded at crowding him. His ability to handle the hard stuff accounts for his proficiency as a pinch hitter.

Baserunning & Defense

If Vander Wal were a better defensive player, he wouldn't have spent most of his career as a reserve. He's difficult to take the extra base on when he charges batted balls, but opponents can run on him when he has to move laterally to make a play. Mechanically, Vander Wal is a sound baserunner who's nevertheless prone to occasional poor decisions between first and third base that will lead to a crucial out. After stealing 11 bases in 2000, Vander Wal added eight last year.

2002 Outlook

Vander Wal must fully shake the tendinitis in his left elbow, which hampered his hitting late in the season. The Yankees believed he would be fine when they dealt Jay Witasick to acquire him. New York probably will use him in a platoon, much like the Giants did. If so, Vander Wal would get most of the at-bats while sharing right field with Shane Spencer.

Position: RF/LF/1B
Bats: L **Throws:** L
Ht: 6' 2" **Wt:** 197

Opening Day Age: 35
Born: 4/29/66 in Grand Rapids, MI
ML Seasons: 11

Overall Statistics

	G	AB	R	H	D	T	HR	RBI	SB	BB	SO	Avg	OBP	Slg
2001	146	452	58	122	28	4	14	70	8	68	122	.270	.364	.442
Career	1129	2154	292	570	126	16	75	361	36	312	516	.265	.357	.442

Where He Hits the Ball

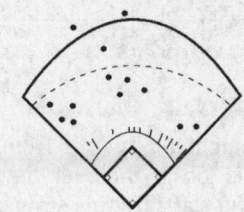
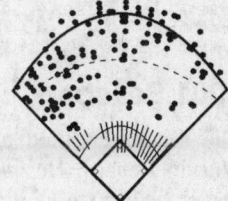

Vs. LHP   **Vs. RHP**

2001 Situational Stats

	AB	H	HR	RBI	Avg		AB	H	HR	RBI	Avg
Home	222	50	6	32	.225	LHP	54	16	0	15	.296
Road	230	72	8	38	.313	RHP	398	106	14	55	.266
First Half	257	72	10	48	.280	Sc Pos	126	33	2	53	.262
Scnd Half	195	50	4	22	.256	Clutch	57	18	0	8	.316

2001 Rankings (National League)

- 3rd in lowest batting average at home (.225)
- 5th in lowest percentage of extra bases taken as a runner (32.6)
- 9th in most pitches seen per plate appearance (4.05)

Marvin Benard

Position: CF/RF/LF
Bats: L **Throws:** L
Ht: 5' 9" **Wt:** 185

Opening Day Age: 32
Born: 1/20/70 in Bluefields, Nicaragua
ML Seasons: 7
Pronunciation: buh-NARD

Overall Statistics

	G	AB	R	H	D	T	HR	RBI	SB	BB	SO	Avg	OBP	Slg
2001	129	392	70	104	19	2	15	44	10	29	66	.265	.320	.439
Career	780	2436	420	666	126	18	53	243	99	254	419	.273	.347	.405

2001 Situational Stats

	AB	H	HR	RBI	Avg		AB	H	HR	RBI	Avg
Home	196	48	3	19	.245	LHP	41	16	1	6	.390
Road	196	56	12	25	.286	RHP	351	88	14	38	.251
First Half	214	45	5	22	.210	Sc Pos	79	23	2	27	.291
Scnd Half	178	59	10	22	.331	Clutch	61	13	3	9	.213

2001 Season

The Giants endured an enigmatic season from Marvin Benard. He lost his job as the everyday center fielder with a dreadful start. But his strong finish left San Francisco wondering why he can't sustain that kind of performance year-round.

Hitting, Baserunning & Defense

Benard likes to jump on pitches early in the count. He'll expand his strike zone when he's behind, even to the point of chasing neck-high fastballs. He remains a decent bunter and became a threat last year as a pinch-hitter. Benard has a average arm and often takes poor routes to flyballs, shortcomings he tries to mask with determination and hustle. Late in games in which they led, the Giants frequently moved Benard out of center field for Calvin Murray, a superior defender. Benard is a capable basestealer.

2002 Outlook

Center field was one area the Giants were hoping to upgrade during the offseason, but in trade talks, teams want no part of Benard's three-year, $11.1 million contract, which runs through 2003. The Giants traded for a new center-field option when they acquired Tsuyoshi Shinjo from the Mets. Benard would be better as a fourth outfielder.

Brian Boehringer

Position: RP
Bats: B **Throws:** R
Ht: 6' 2" **Wt:** 190

Opening Day Age: 32
Born: 1/8/70 in St. Louis, MO
ML Seasons: 7
Pronunciation: BOH-ring-irr

Overall Statistics

	W	L	Pct.	ERA	G	GS	Sv	IP	H	BB	SO	HR	Ratio
2001	0	4	.000	3.65	51	0	2	69.0	67	29	60	7	1.39
Career	16	23	.410	4.36	203	21	2	367.1	366	194	300	46	1.52

2001 Situational Stats

	W	L	ERA	Sv	IP		AB	H	HR	RBI	Avg
Home	0	1	4.88	0	24.0	LHB	94	31	4	21	.330
Road	0	3	3.00	2	45.0	RHB	177	36	3	23	.203
First Half	0	2	3.35	1	37.2	Sc Pos	83	27	3	38	.325
Scnd Half	0	2	4.02	1	31.1	Clutch	51	11	2	10	.216

2001 Season

After suffering shoulder problems in 1999 and 2000, Brian Boehringer needed to prove he could remain healthy. He did just that in 2001, making 29 appearances for San Francisco after coming over from the Yankees in a July 4 trade. The well-traveled Boehringer appeared primarily in middle innings to neutralize opposing righthanded hitters.

Pitching, Defense & Hitting

Boehringer works aggressively to both sides of the plate with a fastball that averages 92 MPH and a slider that hits 85 MPH. But that's about all he has. He doesn't cut his fastball and rarely uses his changeup. He'd probably be more effective if he could develop a split-finger delivery to take a hitter's mind off his fastball and slider. A pro since 1991, Boehringer has developed a good pickoff move and a decent slide-step delivery. He also fields his position well but has hit poorly in his limited opportunities (.067 lifetime).

2002 Outlook

Middle relievers of Boehringer's ilk are almost interchangeable, as harsh as that may sound. Given his effectiveness against righties, the Giants may try to retain him and at least keep him around through spring training, or until a better alternative comes along.

Jason Christiansen

Position: RP
Bats: R **Throws:** L
Ht: 6' 5" **Wt:** 241

Opening Day Age: 32
Born: 9/21/69 in
Omaha, NE
ML Seasons: 7

Overall Statistics

	W	L	Pct.	ERA	G	GS	Sv	IP	H	BB	SO	HR	Ratio
2001	2	1	.667	3.22	55	0	3	36.1	29	15	31	5	1.21
Career	17	21	.447	4.07	354	0	13	321.0	289	161	318	26	1.40

2001 Situational Stats

	W	L	ERA	Sv	IP		AB	H	HR	RBI	Avg
Home	1	0	3.52	3	15.1	LHB	59	15	2	9	.254
Road	1	1	3.00	0	21.0	RHB	70	14	3	13	.200
First Half	1	0	3.68	1	14.2	Sc Pos	41	11	3	20	.268
Scnd Half	1	1	2.91	2	21.2	Clutch	41	7	2	8	.171

2001 Season

Acquired from St. Louis on July 31 for two minor league pitchers, Jason Christiansen adapted well to his new team. His 1.59 ERA with the Giants was nearly one-third of what it was with the Cards. Used occasionally as a closer in St. Louis, Christiansen strictly was a middle man in San Francisco.

Pitching, Defense & Hitting

Christiansen threw harder before his shoulder surgery in October 2000. Since he now lacks overpowering velocity (topping out at 90 MPH), he'll cut almost every fastball he throws, particularly as he tries to crowd righties. His slider, which travels at 82-84 MPH, is tough on lefthanded batters. Nevertheless, he actually fared better against righties than lefties after joining San Francisco. Christiansen has a serviceable pickoff move. He never batted for the Giants and rarely did for his previous teams, so he's no factor at the plate.

2002 Outlook

After last season ended, the Giants specifically cited Christiansen as a player they'd like to retain. They then signed him to a three-year, $6.8 million extension in early December with a club option for 2005. Despite his lack of success against lefties last year for the Giants, he will be looked upon to get the tough lefthanded hitters out in 2002.

Shawon Dunston

Position: RF/CF/LF
Bats: R **Throws:** R
Ht: 6' 1" **Wt:** 180

Opening Day Age: 39
Born: 3/21/63 in
Brooklyn, NY
ML Seasons: 17
Pronunciation: SHAWN

Overall Statistics

	G	AB	R	H	D	T	HR	RBI	SB	BB	SO	Avg	OBP	Slg
2001	88	186	26	52	10	3	9	25	3	2	32	.280	.293	.511
Career	1742	5780	729	1563	287	62	149	659	211	200	967	.270	.297	.419

2001 Situational Stats

	AB	H	HR	RBI	Avg		AB	H	HR	RBI	Avg
Home	83	24	3	7	.289	LHP	88	28	6	17	.318
Road	103	28	6	18	.272	RHP	98	24	3	8	.245
First Half	116	32	3	10	.276	Sc Pos	47	11	1	14	.234
Scnd Half	70	20	6	15	.286	Clutch	42	10	2	5	.238

2001 Season

Settling in for his third tour of duty with San Francisco, Shawon Dunston was more valuable to the Giants than ever. He platooned in right field—sharing starts against lefties with Eric Davis—and received occasional playing time in center. He made most of his hits count, recording a .511 slugging percentage. Dunston also capitalized on his savvy as a pinch-hitter.

Hitting, Baserunning & Defense

Still a good fastball hitter, Dunston will try to put the ball in play early in the count. He likes the ball low but will chase the high fastball, and he's especially susceptible to breaking pitches with two strikes. Though Dunston always has been a gap-to-gap hitter, his ability to drive the ball over the wall must now be recognized. He runs well enough to take the extra base and steal on occasion. No longer an infielder, Dunston has decent outfield instincts and a solid throwing arm.

2002 Outlook

The Giants were thrilled when Dunston exercised his $1.15 million player option for 2002, which probably will be his last season in the majors. Dunston continues to prove his value not only on the field, but also in the clubhouse.

San Francisco

Pedro Feliz

Position: 3B
Bats: R **Throws:** R
Ht: 6' 1" **Wt:** 180

Opening Day Age: 24
Born: 4/27/77 in Azua, DR
ML Seasons: 2

Overall Statistics

	G	AB	R	H	D	T	HR	RBI	SB	BB	SO	Avg	OBP	Slg
2001	94	220	23	50	9	1	7	22	2	10	50	.227	.264	.373
Career	102	227	24	52	9	1	7	22	2	10	51	.229	.264	.370

2001 Situational Stats

	AB	H	HR	RBI	Avg		AB	H	HR	RBI	Avg
Home	106	24	3	10	.226	LHP	58	23	3	13	.397
Road	114	26	4	12	.228	RHP	162	27	4	9	.167
First Half	107	22	3	11	.206	Sc Pos	49	9	1	16	.184
Scnd Half	113	28	4	11	.248	Clutch	37	9	0	6	.243

2001 Season

Pedro Feliz wasn't a complete disaster in his rookie season, but he left plenty of room for improvement. Impressed with Feliz' hitting credentials, the Giants hoped he could establish himself at third base. They even released veteran third baseman Russ Davis on June 22. But Feliz wasn't ready. He showed promise in July, hitting .347, but that was offset by a woeful .114 in the season's final month.

Hitting, Baserunning & Defense

Feliz must tighten up his swing if he's to fulfill his potential. Like a lot of young players, he flails at breaking balls and low fastballs and will panic on two-strike counts. He has the ability to turn on an inside fastball and drive it a long way. Defensively, Feliz has a strong arm with decent accuracy. His only throwing flaw is a mildly slow release. He has above-average range to his left and should only improve with more experience. Feliz has decent speed, though he's not much of a threat to steal.

2002 Outlook

The Giants are willing to give Feliz a chance to assert himself. However, there seems to be more faith in him within the organization than outside of it. Except for Ramon Martinez, who's strictly a utilityman, there are no obvious alternatives to Feliz, so he desperately needs to blossom.

Andres Galarraga

Position: 1B/DH
Bats: R **Throws:** R
Ht: 6' 3" **Wt:** 250

Opening Day Age: 40
Born: 6/18/61 in Caracas, VZ
ML Seasons: 16
Pronunciation: ON-dress Gahl-la-RAH-ga
Nickname: Big Cat

Overall Statistics

	G	AB	R	H	D	T	HR	RBI	SB	BB	SO	Avg	OBP	Slg
2001	121	399	50	102	28	1	17	69	1	31	117	.256	.326	.459
Career	2036	7522	1128	2172	417	32	377	1341	125	534	1858	.289	.347	.503

2001 Situational Stats

	AB	H	HR	RBI	Avg		AB	H	HR	RBI	Avg
Home	189	49	8	31	.259	LHP	112	30	7	24	.268
Road	210	53	9	38	.252	RHP	287	72	10	45	.251
First Half	223	52	8	30	.233	Sc Pos	121	36	4	51	.298
Scnd Half	176	50	9	39	.284	Clutch	64	14	6	15	.219

2001 Season

A July 24 trade that brought Andres Galarraga to the Giants from Texas rejuvenated the Big Cat. His batting average in San Francisco was 53 points higher than it had been in Texas, while his slugging percentage was 89 points higher. He also exceeded his Rangers RBI total by one despite playing 23 fewer games in San Francisco.

Hitting, Baserunning & Defense

Galarraga still vigorously chases pitches early in the count. He's a decent breaking-ball hitter and he'll devour a pitcher's mistakes. But he has begun to struggle with inside fastballs, especially since he likes to dive toward pitches over the plate as he strides. Once a sneaky basestealer, Galarraga has become a station-to-station runner. Defensively, the former Gold Glover has lost some of his quickness afield and doesn't react to balls as well as he once did, though his hands remain above-average.

2002 Outlook

The Giants wrestled with the issue over whether to pick up Galarraga's 2002 option, since they're saddled with J.T. Snow's contract through 2003. They weren't prepared to keep both players and declined Galarraga's option. While he's no longer an everyday player, he remains extremely valuable in a platoon or part-time role.

Ramon Martinez

Position: 3B/2B/SS
Bats: R **Throws:** R
Ht: 6' 1" **Wt:** 187

Opening Day Age: 29
Born: 10/10/72 in Philadelphia, PA
ML Seasons: 4

Overall Statistics

	G	AB	R	H	D	T	HR	RBI	SB	BB	SO	Avg	OBP	Slg
2001	128	391	48	99	18	3	5	37	1	38	52	.253	.323	.353
Career	296	743	103	200	38	5	16	81	5	71	93	.269	.335	.398

2001 Situational Stats

	AB	H	HR	RBI	Avg		AB	H	HR	RBI	Avg
Home	186	44	1	13	.237	LHP	82	24	0	6	.293
Road	205	55	4	24	.268	RHP	309	75	5	31	.243
First Half	186	49	3	17	.263	Sc Pos	82	25	0	30	.305
Scnd Half	205	50	2	20	.244	Clutch	72	14	0	5	.194

2001 Season

Ramon Martinez continued to play an increasingly important role with the Giants, reaching a career high in games played while more than doubling the number of at-bats he had between 1998-2000. He started 63 games at third base, 26 at second and 16 at shortstop as San Francisco's top utility infielder.

Hitting, Baserunning & Defense

Though Martinez suffered a drop from the .287 career average he took into last season, he showed a knack for responding with men in scoring position. He was 9-for-15 with runners on third base and less than two outs and went 4-for-4 with the bases loaded. Martinez tends to look for fastballs from the middle of the plate in. Some scouts don't think he has an overly quick bat, but he's capable of spraying hits into the gaps. Martinez is an average baserunner but a below-average basestealer. Like most utility infielders, he has acceptable defensive tools but is not flashy.

2002 Outlook

Martinez will be eligible for arbitration for the first time, but as a part-time player his salary shouldn't skyrocket. With Jeff Kent approaching his middle 30s and third base still a question mark, the Giants need Martinez as insurance against injury or ineffectiveness.

Calvin Murray

Position: CF
Bats: R **Throws:** R
Ht: 5'11" **Wt:** 190

Opening Day Age: 30
Born: 7/30/71 in Dallas, TX
ML Seasons: 3
Pronunciation: MUR-ee

Overall Statistics

	G	AB	R	H	D	T	HR	RBI	SB	BB	SO	Avg	OBP	Slg
2001	106	326	54	80	14	2	6	25	8	32	57	.245	.319	.356
Career	229	539	90	132	28	3	8	52	18	63	94	.245	.330	.353

2001 Situational Stats

	AB	H	HR	RBI	Avg		AB	H	HR	RBI	Avg
Home	140	30	3	10	.214	LHP	84	20	1	6	.238
Road	186	50	3	15	.269	RHP	242	60	5	19	.248
First Half	140	41	4	16	.293	Sc Pos	72	20	3	22	.278
Scnd Half	186	39	2	9	.210	Clutch	51	10	1	2	.196

2001 Season

While receiving the most extensive playing time of his brief major league career, Calvin Murray left the Giants hoping that his skills can continue to develop. He definitely possesses the proverbial tools. If he could hit nearly as well as he plays center field, San Francisco might have another All-Star in its lineup.

Hitting, Baserunning & Defense

Murray lacks decent coverage of pitches on the outer third of the plate. That, along with his slightly uppercut swing, accounts for the excess of flyballs he hits. With his speed, he should be trying to hit more grounders. Nobody would blame him for trying to steal more often, either. In center field, Murray is an absolute gem. He has superb range, takes good routes to balls and owns an average arm.

2002 Outlook

At age 30 and after nine professional seasons, Murray is running out of chances to figure out what to do with his swing. The Giants would love to pick up an established center fielder/leadoff hitter, but their payroll limitations may not allow that. Whatever happens, Murray likely will be destined for fourth-outfielder status unless he sharpens his stroke.

San Francisco

Felix Rodriguez

Tough on Lefties

Position: RP
Bats: R **Throws:** R
Ht: 6' 1" **Wt:** 190

Opening Day Age: 29
Born: 12/5/72 in
Montecristi, DR
ML Seasons: 6

Overall Statistics

	W	L	Pct.	ERA	G	GS	Sv	IP	H	BB	SO	HR	Ratio
2001	9	1	.900	1.68	80	0	0	80.1	53	27	91	5	1.00
Career	16	9	.640	3.34	283	1	8	329.0	288	160	316	25	1.36

2001 Situational Stats

	W	L	ERA	Sv	IP		AB	H	HR	RBI	Avg
Home	5	0	0.91	0	39.2	LHB	113	17	2	8	.150
Road	4	1	2.43	0	40.2	RHB	169	36	3	13	.213
First Half	4	1	1.87	0	43.1	Sc Pos	47	10	1	16	.213
Scnd Half	5	0	1.46	0	37.0	Clutch	218	40	3	13	.183

2001 Season

For the second year in a row, Felix Rodriguez teamed with Robb Nen to force opponents to beat the Giants in seven innings. The setup artist limited opponents to a career-low .188 batting average while posting a career-best 9-1 record and 1.68 ERA. Though Rodriguez reached a personal high in appearances, he didn't fade in the second half.

Pitching, Defense & Hitting

There's no mystery to Rodriguez' approach. He either gets you with a fastball that can reach 98 MPH, or you get him. His slider is somewhat flat, but it can look befuddling amid a steady stream of his fastballs. Rodriguez has excellent control, but his tendency to run up deep counts occasionally gets him in trouble. Rodriguez has decent hands, but he rarely has to use them to field because of the strikeouts and flyballs he coaxes. He never batted last year, freezing his lifetime average at .154.

2002 Outlook

Rodriguez signed a complex multiyear extension with San Francisco prior to the start of the 2001 season, which pays him at a setup reliever's rate if he stays in his current role, and gives him a higher salary if he becomes the closer. The latter might not happen as long as Nen is around, but Rodriguez definitely has the stuff to pitch the ninth inning.

Tim Worrell

Position: RP
Bats: R **Throws:** R
Ht: 6' 4" **Wt:** 231

Opening Day Age: 34
Born: 7/5/67 in
Pasadena, CA
ML Seasons: 9
Pronunciation:
wor-RELL

Overall Statistics

	W	L	Pct.	ERA	G	GS	Sv	IP	H	BB	SO	HR	Ratio
2001	2	5	.286	3.45	73	0	0	78.1	71	33	63	4	1.33
Career	27	43	.386	4.19	371	49	7	676.0	672	268	523	72	1.39

2001 Situational Stats

	W	L	ERA	Sv	IP		AB	H	HR	RBI	Avg
Home	1	4	2.75	0	36.0	LHB	125	31	2	17	.248
Road	1	1	4.04	0	42.1	RHB	171	40	2	27	.234
First Half	1	2	3.51	0	48.2	Sc Pos	88	23	0	39	.261
Scnd Half	1	3	3.34	0	29.2	Clutch	117	28	2	17	.239

2001 Season

After pitching for six different teams, Tim Worrell may have found a niche with the Giants. He established personal highs in appearances and relief innings in 2001 while working as a middle man, often as the first righthander out of the bullpen. Worrell's ERA rose by almost a run from his mark in 2000, but it still was lower than his career figure.

Pitching, Defense & Hitting

Worrell likes to throw his slider to righthanded hitters and a split-finger that resembles a changeup to lefthanders. He doesn't have an especially deceptive arm angle, so he must change speeds against lefties to disrupt their timing. Worrell's fastball can hit 91 MPH, while his slider hovers around 83-86 MPH. Worrell's velocity and movement—or lack thereof—forces him to aim for the corners and the lower perimeter of the zone. Worrell slipped a bit defensively last year, committing two errors. He's a lifetime .110 hitter.

2002 Outlook

Signed through this year with a club option for 2003, Worrell should be low maintenance. His salary and role are equally established. Unless a phenom or offseason acquisition emerges and forces his way into San Francisco's veteran-laden bullpen, Worrell's status appears safe for another year.

Other San Francisco Giants

Eric Davis (**Pos**: RF, **Age**: 39, **Bats**: R)

	G	AB	R	H	D	T	HR	RBI	SB	BB	SO	Avg	OBP	Slg
2001	74	156	17	32	7	3	4	22	1	13	38	.205	.269	.365
Career	1626	5321	938	1430	239	26	282	934	349	740	1398	.269	.359	.482

Davis, who is set to retire, didn't do much in his swan song except show some pop versus lefthanders. The inspirational outfielder leaves the game after 18 years and 282 homers. 2002 Outlook: D

Russ Davis (**Pos**: 3B, **Age**: 32, **Bats**: R)

	G	AB	R	H	D	T	HR	RBI	SB	BB	SO	Avg	OBP	Slg
2001	53	167	16	43	13	1	7	17	1	17	49	.257	.326	.473
Career	612	1980	261	508	108	6	84	276	16	146	503	.257	.310	.444

Davis' lack of success against righthanded pitching and his mediocre fielding forced his release in June. He didn't resurface the rest of the summer. 2002 Outlook: D

Aaron Fultz (**Pos**: LHP, **Age**: 28)

	W	L	Pct.	ERA	G	GS	Sv	IP	H	BB	SO	HR	Ratio
2001	3	1	.750	4.56	66	0	1	71.0	70	21	67	9	1.28
Career	8	3	.727	4.62	124	0	2	140.1	137	49	129	17	1.33

In 2001, Fultz nearly matched the 2000 numbers of his major league debut. He was at his best in June and July, but didn't turn the big corner. Still, he was effective against lefthanded hitters. 2002 Outlook: B

Mark Gardner (**Pos**: RHP, **Age**: 40)

	W	L	Pct.	ERA	G	GS	Sv	IP	H	BB	SO	HR	Ratio
2001	5	5	.500	5.40	23	15	0	91.2	93	34	53	17	1.39
Career	99	93	.516	4.56	345	275	1	1764.2	1752	628	1256	237	1.35

A shoulder strain sidelined Gardner for much of the second half. He will be 40 in the spring and has had poor seasons in two of the last three years with the Giants. He became a free agent in November. 2002 Outlook: C

Wayne Gomes (**Pos**: RHP, **Age**: 29)

	W	L	Pct.	ERA	G	GS	Sv	IP	H	BB	SO	HR	Ratio
2001	6	3	.667	5.29	55	0	1	63.0	72	29	52	7	1.60
Career	29	21	.580	4.60	301	0	28	346.2	353	179	269	31	1.53

The Giants acquired Gomes for the stretch run, but he didn't provide relief. He posted an 8.06 ERA and .344 batting average allowed during the second half. The Giants obviously were not impressed and released him in early December. 2002 Outlook: C

Edwards Guzman (**Pos**: C, **Age**: 25, **Bats**: L)

	G	AB	R	H	D	T	HR	RBI	SB	BB	SO	Avg	OBP	Slg
2001	61	115	8	28	6	0	3	7	0	5	16	.243	.273	.374
Career	75	130	8	28	6	0	3	7	0	5	20	.215	.243	.331

The backup catching job was open and Guzman had a hot streak at Triple-A Fresno, but the contact hitter didn't show much at the plate. The 25-year-old lefty did hit .271 from August on and made just one error behind the plate for the season. 2002 Outlook: C

Ryan Jensen (**Pos**: RHP, **Age**: 26)

	W	L	Pct.	ERA	G	GS	Sv	IP	H	BB	SO	HR	Ratio
2001	1	2	.333	4.25	10	7	0	42.1	44	25	26	5	1.63
Career	1	2	.333	4.25	10	7	0	42.1	44	25	26	5	1.63

In 2001, Jensen was an effective starter at Triple-A Fresno for the first time in three seasons. He was solid in three July starts with the Giants but faded and worked out of the pen, where he struggled. 2002 Outlook: C

Jalal Leach (**Pos**: RF, **Age**: 33, **Bats**: L)

	G	AB	R	H	D	T	HR	RBI	SB	BB	SO	Avg	OBP	Slg
2001	8	10	0	1	0	0	0	1	0	2	3	.100	.250	.100
Career	8	10	0	1	0	0	0	1	0	2	3	.100	.250	.100

Leach got his first taste of the majors in his 12th minor league season. He's been playing Triple-A ball since 1994, and that's his likely destination in 2002. It definitely won't be in San Francisco, as he was released at the end of November. 2002 Outlook: C

Damon Minor (**Pos**: 1B, **Age**: 28, **Bats**: L)

	G	AB	R	H	D	T	HR	RBI	SB	BB	SO	Avg	OBP	Slg
2001	19	45	3	7	1	0	3	0	0	3	8	.156	.208	.178
Career	29	54	6	11	1	0	3	9	0	5	9	.204	.271	.389

Minor has hit 54 homers in two Triple-A seasons, plus three more in nine trips during his first cup of coffee in 2000. He failed miserably to build on that when he got a chance in 2001. 2002 Outlook: C

Dante Powell (**Pos**: LF, **Age**: 28, **Bats**: R)

	G	AB	R	H	D	T	HR	RBI	SB	BB	SO	Avg	OBP	Slg
2001	13	6	5	2	0	0	0	0	0	0	0	.333	.333	.333
Career	70	74	19	20	4	0	2	5	3	9	17	.270	.349	.405

Powell's days as a prospect are over, but he hit a career-high 22 homers at Triple-A Fresno in 2001. His 122-34 strikeout-walk ratio there will temper any enthusiasm. He was released in late November. 2002 Outlook: C

Yorvit Torrealba (**Pos**: C, **Age**: 23, **Bats**: R)

	G	AB	R	H	D	T	HR	RBI	SB	BB	SO	Avg	OBP	Slg
2001	3	4	0	2	0	1	0	2	0	0	0	.500	.500	1.000
Career	3	4	0	2	0	1	0	2	0	0	0	.500	.500	1.000

Torrealba hasn't shown much patience or power in seven minor league seasons, but he got his first taste of the bigs in 2001. His catching skills are his best ticket to a second chance. 2002 Outlook: C

Chad Zerbe (**Pos**: LHP, **Age**: 29)

	W	L	Pct.	ERA	G	GS	Sv	IP	H	BB	SO	HR	Ratio
2001	3	0	1.000	3.92	27	1	0	39.0	41	10	22	3	1.31
Career	3	0	1.000	4.00	31	1	0	45.0	47	11	27	4	1.29

Zerbe enjoyed success in the high minors the last two seasons, and he was very good in San Francisco in April and May. Then he struggled. Righties against him: .215. Lefties: .396. Go figure. 2002 Outlook: B

San Francisco Giants Minor League Prospects

Organization Overview:

Although they may not have much to show for it, the Giants have been one of the most successful teams in the National League over the past five seasons. They've won at least 86 games each year, but have managed just one victory in two playoff appearances during that span. The big concern now is whether the Giants will be able to afford keeping Barry Bonds. Their farm system probably would be better prepared trying to replace a pitcher. San Francisco has used its top draft pick on a hurler in six of the past seven drafts, and pitching appears to be the organization's strength. Kurt Ainsworth has a decent shot at cracking the starting staff this season, while others like Jerome Williams and Felix Diaz figure to follow in the future. Tony Torcato may be the position player with the best chance of contributing in 2002, especially if an outfielder departs.

Kurt Ainsworth

Position: P
Bats: R **Throws:** R
Ht: 6' 3" **Wt:** 185
Opening Day Age: 23
Born: 9/9/78 in Baton Rouge, LA

Recent Statistics

	W	L	ERA	G	GS	Sv	IP	H	R	BB	SO	HR
2001 AAA Fresno	10	9	5.07	27	26	0	149.0	139	91	54	157	22
2001 NL San Francisco	0	0	13.50	2	0	0	2.0	3	3	2	3	1

Ainsworth was San Francisco's top pick in the 1999 draft. He struggled early last season, trying to be too fine with his good stuff. But he was better in the second half, when he went right after hitters, stayed ahead in the count and made pitches of quality. Although his overall ERA at Triple-A wasn't impressive, the Giants still consider Ainsworth their top pitching prospect. His delivery is solid and he has an idea of what to do on the mound. There's no weak link in his pitch arsenal, which includes a 93-MPH fastball, slider, curveball and changeup. He has experience working in big games, winning twice at the 2000 Olympics. Ainsworth should contend for a spot in the Giants' rotation this season.

Boof Bonser

Position: P
Bats: R **Throws:** R
Ht: 6' 4" **Wt:** 230
Opening Day Age: 20
Born: 10/14/81 in St. Petersburg, FL

Recent Statistics

	W	L	ERA	G	GS	Sv	IP	H	R	BB	SO	HR
2000 A Salem-Keizr	1	4	6.00	10	9	0	33.0	21	23	29	41	2
2001 A Hagerstown	16	4	2.49	27	27	0	134.0	91	40	61	178	7

Bonser was one of the South Atlantic League's most dominant hurlers in 2001, when he led the circuit in wins and finished second in strikeouts. He overmatched many hitters with a quality 95-MPH fastball, and he's also starting to improve his curveball and changeup. Bonser

is a tough competitor and demonstrates fine stamina. The Giants say his last pitch in a game often is as hard as his first. They selected him in the first round of the 2000 draft out of a Florida high school. He should move up to high Class-A this season at age 20, where he can work on improving his command, secondary pitches and ability to hold runners. He has a great arm and appears to have a great future.

Felix Diaz

Position: P
Bats: R **Throws:** R
Ht: 6' 1" **Wt:** 165
Opening Day Age: 20
Born: 7/27/81 in Las Mata De Farfan, DR

Recent Statistics

	W	L	ERA	G	GS	Sv	IP	H	R	BB	SO	HR
2000 R Giants	3	4	4.16	11	11	0	62.2	56	35	16	58	0
2000 A Salem-Keizr	0	1	8.10	3	0	0	3.1	6	6	1	2	2
2001 A Hagerstown	1	4	3.66	15	12	0	51.2	49	27	16	56	4

Bothered by tenderness under his armpit, Diaz managed to pitch in just 15 games last season. But the problem was considered to be minor, and the Giants say Diaz pitched "lights out" during the instructional league. He also enjoyed success in the Arizona Fall League and has been placed on San Francisco's 40-man roster. Diaz does a good job directing his fastball to a specific location, working the ball in and out as well as up and down in the zone. His straight change is described as a plus-plus pitch. He also has a good idea with his slider, though his curveball may be a little too slow. All he really needs is experience, which he'll hope to find at Double-A in 2002. The Dominican righthander is on a quick pace.

Lance Niekro

Position: 3B
Bats: R **Throws:** R
Ht: 6' 3" **Wt:** 210
Opening Day Age: 23
Born: 1/29/79 in Winter Haven, FL

Recent Statistics

	G	AB	R	H	D	T	HR	RBI	SB	BB	SO	Avg
2000 A Salem-Keizr	49	196	27	71	14	4	5	44	2	11	25	.362
2001 A San Jose	42	163	18	47	11	0	3	34	4	4	14	.288

Lance is part of the famous Niekro family; his father is Joe and his uncle is Phil. But Lance doesn't pitch. Instead, he may be the best righthanded hitter in San Francisco's minor league system. He has a nice swing, with power from left- to right-center field. He has shown that he can be a good RBI man and projects as a guy who could hit in the middle of the batting order. While Niekro has soft hands and the Giants like what they've seen from him at third, he may wind up at another position. His 2001 season was cut short by shoulder surgery, but he was back working as a designated hitter in instructional league. Niekro is expected to be 100 percent this season and play at Double-A. But he probably won't finish there.

Cody Ransom

Position: SS **Opening Day Age:** 26
Bats: R **Throws:** R **Born:** 2/17/76 in Mesa,
Ht: 6' 2" **Wt:** 190 AZ

Recent Statistics

	G	AB	R	H	D	T	HR	RBI	SB	BB	SO	Avg
2001 AAA Fresno	134	469	77	113	21	6	23	78	17	44	137	.241
2001 NL San Francisco	9	7	1	0	0	0	0	0	0	0	5	.000
2001 MLE	134	451	57	95	18	4	16	58	11	32	142	.211

Ransom may not make as much contact as you'd like, as he chases too many pitches. That defect contributed to his striking out more than 130 times for the second straight season in 2001. Nevertheless, he did boost his average 41 points from the year before and led Fresno with 78 RBI. He also slugged 23 homers, not a bad total for someone who has been described as an acrobatic shortstop. In fact, Ransom's defense is better than his offense. He has good range, soft hands and a decent arm. His speed also is better than average. Ransom now has more than 1,500 at-bats in the minor leagues. But he faces a tough task trying to unseat Rich Aurilia.

Erick Threets

Position: P **Opening Day Age:** 20
Bats: L **Throws:** L **Born:** 11/4/81 in
Ht: 6' 5" **Wt:** 220 Hayward, CA

Recent Statistics

	W	L	ERA	G	GS	Sv	IP	H	R	BB	SO	HR
2001 A San Jose	0	10	4.25	14	14	0	59.1	49	34	40	60	2
2001 A Hagerstown	2	0	0.75	12	0	1	24.0	13	3	9	32	1

To appreciate Threets' potential, you shouldn't look at his winless record in the California League last season. Instead, consider the rate with which the big lefthander fires his fastball, which has been clocked in triple digits. He reached 102 MPH at least three times in instructional league, so Threets clearly is an exceptional talent. He had been a mid-90s sidearmer when the Giants chose him in the seventh round in 2000. But they have gotten him to make adjustments with his delivery and to throw more on top. He was on an 80-pitch limit as a starter last year. The Giants can control his success more when he's used out of the bullpen, but Threets might return to the rotation. He has tremendous upside and could come quickly.

Tony Torcato

Position: OF-DH **Opening Day Age:** 22
Bats: L **Throws:** R **Born:** 10/25/79 in
Ht: 6' 1" **Wt:** 195 Woodland, CA

Recent Statistics

	G	AB	R	H	D	T	HR	RBI	SB	BB	SO	Avg
2000 A San Jose	119	490	77	159	37	2	7	88	19	41	62	.324
2000 AA Shreveport	2	8	1	4	0	0	0	2	0	0	1	.500
2001 A San Jose	67	258	38	88	21	2	2	47	9	17	40	.341
2001 AA Shreveport	36	147	13	43	9	1	1	23	0	9	15	.293
2001 AAA Fresno	35	150	20	48	8	1	2	8	0	2	20	.320
2001 MLE	71	284	26	78	14	0	1	26	0	7	35	.275

Torcato may be the best hitter in San Francisco's minor league system. He is a pure hitter who consistently has hit for a good average since being selected with the Giants' top pick in 1998. He may not be a patient hitter, but he still can take pitches low and away to left field. He also hasn't shown much home-run power, but the Giants think that eventually could come. Although Torcato has had arm problems in the past, his arm felt terrific last year when he moved from third base to the outfield. He is an average runner who likely projects to left, though right field isn't out of the question. It's also possible that he could see action in San Francisco's outfield this season.

Jerome Williams

Position: P **Opening Day Age:** 20
Bats: R **Throws:** R **Born:** 12/4/81 in
Ht: 6' 3" **Wt:** 190 Honolulu, HI

Recent Statistics

	W	L	ERA	G	GS	Sv	IP	H	R	BB	SO	HR
2000 A San Jose	7	6	2.94	23	19	0	125.2	89	53	48	115	6
2001 AA Shreveport	9	7	3.95	23	23	0	130.0	116	69	34	84	14

The Giants grabbed Williams out of a Honolulu high school with a supplemental first-round pick in 1999. He moved up to Double-A last year while still only a teenager. A lot of pitchers do what they can, but Williams does what he wants. He throws a 93-95 MPH fastball with good location, particularly for someone his age. His repertoire also includes a slurvy kind of slider, a changeup and a hard curveball with which he'll take velocity on and off. Although he's a fine athlete, Williams watches hitters and succeeds with good feel. He might need to work on pitching to certain game situations and not getting hurt with his third or fourth pitch. But he isn't far from competing for a big league job.

Others to Watch

Righthander **Luke Anderson** (23), a No. 18 pick in 2000, saved 30 games at San Jose last season. He struck out 76 and walked only 13. . . **Nelson Castro** (25) showed off his excellent speed by leading the Texas League with 38 stolen bases. Claimed off waivers from the Angels a couple years ago, he could be a utility guy for the Giants this season. . . **Todd Linden** (21) is a switch-hitting outfielder with great power from both sides of the plate. He has a big swing that makes hard contact. After getting drafted last June and impressing in the instructional league, he may play at Double-A in 2002. . . Drafted 29th overall in 1998, outfielder **Arturo McDowell** (22) is a tools player who has yet to hit for much average or power. The Giants think both skills will develop, however. . . **Sean McGowan** (24) was a No. 3 pick in 1999 after leading the Big East with 25 homers and a .430 batting average that year. He's continued to hit for a nice average as a pro, reaching Triple-A in 2001. . . Outfielder **Carlos Valderrama** (24), a native of Venezuela, missed much of last season after hurting his shoulder. He is an exciting player with a plus arm, plus speed (54 stolen bases in 2000) and spurts of power. He should be in Triple-A this year.

2001 American League Leaders

Batters

Batting Average
minimum 502 PA

Ichiro Suzuki	**.350**
Jason Giambi	.342
Roberto Alomar	.336

Home Runs

Alex Rodriguez	**52**
Jim Thome	49
Rafael Palmeiro	47

Runs Batted In

Bret Boone	**141**
Juan Gonzalez	140
Alex Rodriguez	135

Games Played

4 players tied with	**162**

At-Bats

Ichiro Suzuki	**692**
Garret Anderson	672
Johnny Damon	644

Runs Scored

Alex Rodriguez	**133**
Ichiro Suzuki	127
Bret Boone	118

Hits

Ichiro Suzuki	**242**
Bret Boone	206
Shannon Stewart	202

Singles

Ichiro Suzuki	**192**
Shannon Stewart	139
David Eckstein	134

Doubles

Jason Giambi	**47**
Mike Sweeney	46
Shannon Stewart	44

Triples

Cristian Guzman	**14**
Roberto Alomar	12
Carlos Beltran	12

Stolen Bases

Ichiro Suzuki	**56**
Roger Cedeno	55
Alfonso Soriano	43

Caught Stealing

Roger Cedeno	**15**
Alfonso Soriano	14
Ichiro Suzuki	14

Walks

Jason Giambi	**129**
Carlos Delgado	111
Jim Thome	111

Intentional Walks

Manny Ramirez	**25**
Jason Giambi	24
Carlos Delgado	22

Hit by Pitch

David Eckstein	**21**
Frank Menechino	19
3 players tied with	16

Strikeouts

Jim Thome	**185**
Ben Grieve	159
Troy Glaus	158

GDP

John Olerud	**21**
Paul O'Neill	20
3 players tied with	18

Sacrifice Hits

David Eckstein	**16**
Omar Vizquel	15
Chris Singleton	14

Sacrifice Flies

Juan Gonzalez	**16**
Bret Boone	13
Mike Cameron	13

Plate Appearances

Ichiro Suzuki	**738**
Alex Rodriguez	732
Johnny Damon	719

Times on Base

Jason Giambi	**320**
Alex Rodriguez	292
Carlos Delgado	287

Total Bases

Alex Rodriguez	**393**
Bret Boone	360
Jason Giambi	343

Slugging Percentage
minimum 502 PA

Jason Giambi	**.660**
Jim Thome	.624
Alex Rodriguez	.622

Slugging vs. LHP
minimum 125 PA

Bret Boone	**.715**
Magglio Ordonez	.709
Juan Gonzalez	.675

Slugging vs. RHP
minimum 377 PA

Jim Thome	**.716**
Jason Giambi	.707
Alex Rodriguez	.626

Cleanup Slugging
minimum 150 PA

Manny Ramirez	**.607**
Juan Gonzalez	.590
Rafael Palmeiro	.568

On-Base Percentage
minimum 502 PA

Jason Giambi	**.477**
Edgar Martinez	.423
Jim Thome	.416

OBP vs. LHP
minimum 125 PA

Bret Boone	**.497**
Manny Ramirez	.462
Raul Mondesi	.453

OBP vs. RHP
minimum 377 PA

Jason Giambi	**.491**
Jim Thome	.445
Roberto Alomar	.437

Leadoff Hitters OBP
minimum 150 PA

Frank Catalanotto	**.398**
Luis Rivas	.392
Ichiro Suzuki	.382

AB per HR
minimum 502 PA

Jim Thome	**10.7**
Alex Rodriguez	12.2
Rafael Palmeiro	12.8

Ground/Fly Ratio
minimum 502 PA

Ichiro Suzuki	**2.63**
Roger Cedeno	2.52
Ben Grieve	2.13

% Extra Bases Taken
minimum 40 Opp to Advance

Mike Cameron	**77.4**
David Eckstein	72.4
Ray Durham	61.7

% Runs/Time on Base
minimum 502 PA

Kenny Lofton	**49.5**
Miguel Tejada	48.2
Johnny Damon	46.8

SB Success %
minimum 20 SB Attempts

Carlos Beltran	**96.9**
Derek Jeter	90.0
Paul O'Neill	88.0

Steals of Third

Ichiro Suzuki	**14**
Alfonso Soriano	11
Roberto Alomar	8

AVG Scoring Position
minimum 100 PA

Ichiro Suzuki	**.449**
Roberto Alomar	.424
Jeff Conine	.400

AVG Late & Close
minimum 50 PA

Cristian Guzman	**.467**
Jacque Jones	.423
Ichiro Suzuki	.400

AVG Bases Loaded
minimum 10 PA

Shane Halter	**.714**
Corey Koskie	.636
2 players tied with	.583

GDP/GDP Opp
minimum 50 PA

Russell Branyan	**0.02**
Carl Everett	0.03
Al Martin	0.03

AVG vs. LHP
minimum 125 PA

Bret Boone	**.444**
Jeff Conine	.376
Juan Gonzalez	.368

AVG vs. RHP
minimum 377 PA

Ichiro Suzuki	**.362**
Roberto Alomar	.356
Jason Giambi	.347

AVG at Home
minimum 251 PA

Alex Rodriguez	**.361**
Shannon Stewart	.351
Jason Giambi	.349

AVG on the Road
minimum 251 PA

Ichiro Suzuki	**.356**
Magglio Ordonez	.349
Roberto Alomar	.345

Pitchers

AVG on 3-1 Count
minimum 10 PA

Chris Stynes	**.778**
4 players tied with	.750

AVG with Two Strikes
minimum 150 PA

Matt Lawton	**.294**
Bret Boone	.271
Jason Giambi	.271

AVG on 0-2 Count
minimum 20 PA

David Eckstein	**.351**
John Flaherty	.333
Randall Simon	.320

AVG on Full Count
minimum 40 PA

Mike Bordick	**.429**
Brian Roberts	.419
2 players tied with	.400

Pitches Seen

Alex Rodriguez	**2881**
Troy Glaus	2853
Ray Durham	2822

Pitches per PA
minimum 502 PA

Jim Thome	**4.16**
Jose Valentin	4.14
Trot Nixon	4.14

% Pitches Taken
minimum 1500 Pitches

Frank Menechino	**65.9**
Mark McLemore	65.5
Edgar Martinez	65.3

% Swings that Missed
minimum 1500 Pitches Seen

David Eckstein	**8.1**
Chuck Knoblauch	8.2
Omar Vizquel	8.8

% Swings Put in Play
minimum 1500 Pitches Seen

Ichiro Suzuki	**54.8**
John Olerud	53.7
Einar Diaz	53.5

Bunts in Play

Chris Singleton	**37**
David Eckstein	33
Melvin Mora	33

Earned Run Average
minimum 162 IP

Freddy Garcia	**3.05**
Mike Mussina	3.15
Joe Mays	3.16

Wins

Mark Mulder	**21**
Roger Clemens	20
Jamie Moyer	20

Losses

Jose Mercedes	**17**
Chad Durbin	16
Jeff Weaver	16

Won-Lost Percentage
minimum 15 decisions

Roger Clemens	**.870**
Paul Abbott	.810
C.C. Sabathia	.773

Games

Paul Quantrill	**80**
Mike Stanton	76
Jason Grimsley	73

Games Started

Tim Hudson	**35**
Barry Zito	**35**
9 players tied with	34

Complete Games

Steve W. Sparks	**8**
Mark Mulder	6
Brad Radke	6

Shutouts

Mark Mulder	**4**
Freddy Garcia	3
Mike Mussina	3

Games Finished

Keith Foulke	**69**
Mariano Rivera	66
Kazuhiro Sasaki	63

Innings Pitched

Freddy Garcia	**238.2**
Tim Hudson	235.0
Joe Mays	233.2

Hits Allowed

Rick Helling	**256**
Steve W. Sparks	244
Esteban Loaiza	239

Batters Faced

Jeff Weaver	**985**
Steve W. Sparks	982
Tim Hudson	980

Runs Allowed

Rick Helling	**134**
Jose Mercedes	125
Scott Schoeneweis	122

Earned Runs Allowed

Rick Helling	**124**
Jose Mercedes	119
Scott Schoeneweis	116

Home Runs Allowed

Rick Helling	**38**
Eric Milton	35
Ryan Rupe	30

Walks Allowed

Hideo Nomo	**96**
C.C. Sabathia	95
Bartolo Colon	90

Hit Batsmen

Tim Wakefield	**18**
Chris Carpenter	16
2 players tied with	14

Strikeouts

Hideo Nomo	**220**
Mike Mussina	214
Roger Clemens	213

Wild Pitches

Roger Clemens	**14**
Kip Wells	**14**
Dan Reichert	12

Balks

Chris Michalak	**6**
Mark Buehrle	5
3 players tied with	3

Run Support per 9 IP
minimum 162 IP

Paul Abbott	**7.79**
Roger Clemens	6.58
Aaron Sele	6.57

Baserunners per 9 IP
minimum 162 IP

Mike Mussina	**9.8**
Mark Buehrle	9.9
Freddy Garcia	10.3

Opposition AVG
minimum 162 IP

Freddy Garcia	**.225**
C.C. Sabathia	.228
Barry Zito	.230

Opposition SLG
minimum 162 IP

Freddy Garcia	**.344**
Barry Zito	.345
Mark Mulder	.349

Opposition OBP
minimum 162 IP

Mike Mussina	**.274**
Mark Buehrle	.279
Freddy Garcia	.283

Home Runs per 9 IP
minimum 162 IP

Freddy Garcia	**0.60**
Mark Mulder	0.63
Andy Pettitte	0.63

Strikeouts per 9 IP
minimum 162 IP

Hideo Nomo	**10.00**
Roger Clemens	8.70
Barry Zito	8.61

Walks per 9 IP
minimum 162 IP

Brad Radke	**1.0**
Mike Mussina	1.7
Andy Pettitte	1.8

K/BB Ratio
minimum 162 IP

Brad Radke	**5.27**
Mike Mussina	5.10
Andy Pettitte	4.00

Steals Allowed

Hideo Nomo	**52**
Roger Clemens	34
Jason Johnson	34

Caught Stealing Off

Jason Johnson	**19**
C.C. Sabathia	15
2 players tied with	13

SB % Allowed
minimum 162 IP

Rick Helling	**35.0**
Doug Davis	35.3
Mike Mussina	40.9

GDPs Induced

Mark Mulder	**26**
3 players tied with	25

GDPs per 9 IP
minimum 162 IP

Chad Durbin	**1.2**
Scott Schoeneweis	1.1
Chris Carpenter	1.0

GDP/GDP Opp
minimum 30 BFP

Danny Patterson	**0.28**
Bob File	0.26
Paul Quantrill	0.21

Ground/Fly Ratio Off
minimum 162 IP

Tim Hudson	**2.3**
Mark Mulder	1.9
Scott Schoeneweis	1.8

AVG Allowed Sc Pos		Blown Saves		Fielding		
minimum 125 BFP				**Errors by Pitcher**		
Joe Mays	**.202**	**LaTroy Hawkins**	**9**	**Ramon Ortiz**	**6**	
Kelvim Escobar	.204	**Jason Isringhausen**	**9**	Tim Hudson	5	
Joe Kennedy	.214	**Esteban Yan**	**9**	5 players tied with	4	

Pitches Thrown

		Save Opportunities		Errors by Catcher	
Bartolo Colon	3650	**Mariano Rivera**	57	**Ramon Hernandez**	11
Jeff Weaver	3619	Kazuhiro Sasaki	52	**Jorge Posada**	11
Roger Clemens	3604	Keith Foulke	45	2 players tied with	10

Pitches per Batter

minimum 162 IP		**Save Percentage**		**Errors by First Base**	
Brad Radke	**3.45**	minimum 20 SvOp		**Mike Sweeney**	12
Ramon Ortiz	3.46	**Keith Foulke**	93.3	Brian Daubach	11
Scott Schoeneweis	3.49	Troy Percival	92.9	Jason Giambi	11
		Matt Anderson	91.7		

Pickoff Throws

		Holds		Errors by Second Base	
Paul Wilson	180	**Arthur Rhodes**	32	**Jerry Hairston Jr.**	19
Tim Hudson	178	Jason Grimsley	26	**Alfonso Soriano**	19
Mark Mulder	172	Jeff Nelson	26	2 players tied with	15

ERA at Home

minimum 81 IP		**Relief Innings**		**Errors by Third Base**	
Mark Mulder	**2.69**	**Pat Mahomes**	92.1	**Scott Brosius**	22
Jamie Moyer	2.77	Ramiro Mendoza	91.0	Troy Glaus	19
Jason Johnson	2.97	Paul Quantrill	83.0	2 players tied with	18

ERA on the Road

minimum 81 IP		**Relief AVG Allowed**		**Errors by Shortstop**	
Joe Mays	**3.00**	minimum 50 relief IP		**Cristian Guzman**	21
Jarrod Washburn	3.02	**Jeff Nelson**	**.136**	Miguel Tejada	20
Freddy Garcia	3.09	Troy Percival	.187	Alex Rodriguez	18
		Arthur Rhodes	.189		

AVG vs. LHB

minimum 125 BFP		**Relief Runners/9 IP**		**Errors by Left Field**	
Cory Bailey	**.164**	minimum 50 relief IP		**Bobby Higginson**	8
Troy Percival	.176	**Arthur Rhodes**	7.8	**Carlos Lee**	8
Pat Hentgen	.178	Mariano Rivera	8.3	3 players tied with	5
		Kazuhiro Sasaki	8.5		

AVG vs. RHB

minimum 225 BFP		**Relief Strikeouts/9 IP**		**Errors by Center Field**	
Freddy Garcia	**.205**	minimum 50 relief IP		**Mike Cameron**	6
Kelvim Escobar	.206	**Jeff Nelson**	12.1	**Kenny Lofton**	6
C.C. Sabathia	.223	Paul Shuey	11.6	3 players tied with	5
		Troy Percival	11.1		

Relief ERA

minimum 50 relief IP		**% Inh Runners Scored**		**Errors by Right Field**	
Arthur Rhodes	**1.72**	minimum 30 inh runners		**Raul Mondesi**	8
Al Levine	2.11	**Jeff Nelson**	13.2	Roger Cedeno	7
Keith Foulke	2.33	Ramiro Mendoza	15.2	Jermaine Dye	6
		Danny Patterson	16.1		

Relief Wins

		1st Batter AVG		% CS by Catchers	
Paul Quantrill	11	minimum 40 relief first BFP		minimum 70 SB Attempts	
Mike Stanton	9	**Danys Baez**	.103	**Einar Diaz**	35.4
4 players tied with	8	Jeff Nelson	.107	Doug Mirabelli	34.4
		Keith Foulke	.136	Ramon Hernandez	25.2

Relief Losses

Al Levine	10
Derek Lowe	10
Keith Foulke	9

Saves

Mariano Rivera	50
Kazuhiro Sasaki	45
Keith Foulke	42

2001 National League Leaders

Batters

Batting Average
minimum 502 PA

Larry Walker	.350
Todd Helton	.336
Moises Alou	.331

Home Runs

Barry Bonds	73
Sammy Sosa	64
Luis Gonzalez	57

Runs Batted In

Sammy Sosa	160
Todd Helton	146
Luis Gonzalez	142

Games Played

Bobby Abreu	162
Orlando Cabrera	162
Luis Gonzalez	162

At-Bats

Jimmy Rollins	656
Rich Aurilia	636
Doug Glanville	634

Runs Scored

Sammy Sosa	146
Todd Helton	132
Barry Bonds	129

Hits

Rich Aurilia	206
Juan Pierre	202
Luis Gonzalez	198

Singles

Juan Pierre	163
Fernando Vina	144
Placido Polanco	140

Doubles

Lance Berkman	55
Todd Helton	54
Jeff Kent	49

Triples

Jimmy Rollins	12
Juan Pierre	11
Juan Uribe	11

Stolen Bases

Juan Pierre	46
Jimmy Rollins	46
Vladimir Guerrero	37

Caught Stealing

Juan Pierre	17
Luis Castillo	16
Vladimir Guerrero	16

Walks

Barry Bonds	177
Sammy Sosa	116
2 players tied with	106

Intentional Walks

Sammy Sosa	37
Barry Bonds	35
2 players tied with	24

Hit by Pitch

Craig Biggio	28
Fernando Vina	22
Jason Kendall	20

Strikeouts

Jose Hernandez	185
Richie Sexson	178
Pat Burrell	162

GDP

Vladimir Guerrero	24
Ron Coomer	23
2 players tied with	22

Sacrifice Hits

Tom Glavine	17
Ricky Gutierrez	17
Jack Wilson	17

Sacrifice Flies

Jeff Kent	13
Scott Rolen	12
Sammy Sosa	12

Plate Appearances

Luis Gonzalez	728
Jimmy Rollins	720
2 players tied with	717

Times on Base

Barry Bonds	342
Luis Gonzalez	312
Sammy Sosa	311

Total Bases

Sammy Sosa	425
Luis Gonzalez	419
Barry Bonds	411

Slugging Percentage
minimum 502 PA

Barry Bonds	.863
Sammy Sosa	.737
Luis Gonzalez	.688

Slugging vs. LHP
minimum 125 PA

Sammy Sosa	.882
Barry Bonds	.752
Larry Walker	.750

Slugging vs. RHP
minimum 377 PA

Barry Bonds	.910
Todd Helton	.758
Luis Gonzalez	.716

Cleanup Slugging
minimum 150 PA

Todd Helton	.722
Shawn Green	.619
Chipper Jones	.614

On-Base Percentage
minimum 502 PA

Barry Bonds	.515
Larry Walker	.449
Sammy Sosa	.437

OBP vs. LHP
minimum 125 PA

Sammy Sosa	.569
Barry Bonds	.487
Chipper Jones	.462

OBP vs. RHP
minimum 377 PA

Barry Bonds	.526
Todd Helton	.453
Larry Walker	.452

Leadoff Hitters OBP
minimum 150 PA

Craig Biggio	.378
Paul Lo Duca	.378
Craig Counsell	.377

AB per HR
minimum 502 PA

Barry Bonds	6.5
Sammy Sosa	9.0
Luis Gonzalez	10.7

Ground/Fly Ratio
minimum 502 PA

Juan Pierre	2.77
Luis Castillo	2.59
Placido Polanco	2.31

% Extra Bases Taken
minimum 40 Opp to Advance

Brian Jordan	71.2
Jeff Cirillo	69.4
Juan Pierre	69.2

% Runs/Time on Base
minimum 502 PA

Cliff Floyd	50.2
Julio Lugo	50.0
Andruw Jones	48.1

SB Success %
minimum 20 SB Attempts

Pokey Reese	86.2
Cliff Floyd	85.7
Devon White	85.7

Steals of Third

Juan Pierre	14
Vladimir Guerrero	9
Jimmy Rollins	8

AVG Scoring Position
minimum 100 PA

Craig Biggio	.388
Barry Bonds	.382
Aramis Ramirez	.379

AVG Late & Close
minimum 50 PA

Jose Vidro	.471
Matt Williams	.419
Moises Alou	.395

AVG Bases Loaded
minimum 10 PA

Devon White	.700
Sammy Sosa	.667
Tsuyoshi Shinjo	.583

GDP/GDP Opp
minimum 50 PA

Erubiel Durazo	0.02
Reggie Sanders	0.02
Barry Bonds	0.03

AVG vs. LHP
minimum 125 PA

Paul Lo Duca	.411
Sammy Sosa	.387
Larry Walker	.378

AVG vs. RHP
minimum 377 PA

Todd Helton	.354
Albert Pujols	.342
Larry Walker	.338

AVG at Home
minimum 251 PA

Larry Walker	.406
Todd Helton	.384
Jeff Cirillo	.362

AVG on the Road
minimum 251 PA

Chipper Jones	.349
Sean Casey	.339
Lance Berkman	.327

Pitchers

AVG on 3-1 Count
minimum 10 PA

J.D. Drew	**.778**
Cesar Crespo	.750
Brent Mayne	.750

AVG with Two Strikes
minimum 150 PA

Juan Pierre	**.325**
Mark Grace	.294
Todd Helton	.273

AVG on 0-2 Count
minimum 20 PA

Mark Kotsay	**.357**
Mike Lowell	.343
Tony Womack	.342

AVG on Full Count
minimum 40 PA

Dave Martinez	**.526**
Juan Pierre	.500
Ronnie Belliard	.462

Pitches Seen

Bobby Abreu	**2896**
Jeff Bagwell	2890
Todd Helton	2824

Pitches per PA
minimum 502 PA

Jay Bell	**4.27**
Todd Zeile	4.18
Luis Castillo	4.13

% Pitches Taken
minimum 1500 Pitches Seen

Rickey Henderson	**66.6**
Barry Bonds	65.7
Todd Zeile	63.7

% Swings that Missed
minimum 1500 Pitches Seen

Juan Pierre	**5.8**
Luis Castillo	6.5
Fernando Vina	7.7

% Swings Put in Play
minimum 1500 Pitches Seen

Eric Young	**58.5**
Juan Pierre	56.3
Fernando Vina	56.0

Bunts in Play

Juan Pierre	**55**
Fernando Vina	34
2 players tied with	32

Earned Run Average
minimum 162 IP

Randy Johnson	**2.49**
Curt Schilling	2.98
John Burkett	3.04

Wins

Matt Morris	**22**
Curt Schilling	**22**
Randy Johnson	21

Losses

Bobby J. Jones	**19**
Jimmy Anderson	17
Jimmy Haynes	17

Won-Lost Percentage
minimum 15 decisions

Roy Oswalt	**.824**
Curt Schilling	.786
Randy Johnson	.778

Games

Steve Kline	**89**
Graeme Lloyd	84
2 players tied with	82

Games Started

Tom Glavine	**35**
Chan Ho Park	**35**
Curt Schilling	**35**

Complete Games

Curt Schilling	**6**
Jon Lieber	5
Javier Vazquez	5

Shutouts

Greg Maddux	**3**
Javier Vazquez	**3**
4 players tied with	2

Games Finished

Robb Nen	**71**
Jeff Shaw	66
Armando Benitez	64

Innings Pitched

Curt Schilling	**256.2**
Randy Johnson	249.2
Chan Ho Park	234.0

Hits Allowed

Livan Hernandez	**266**
Bobby J. Jones	250
Curt Schilling	237

Batters Faced

Curt Schilling	**1021**
Livan Hernandez	1008
Randy Johnson	994

Runs Allowed

Livan Hernandez	**143**
Mike Hampton	138
Bobby J. Jones	137

Earned Runs Allowed

Livan Hernandez	**132**
Mike Hampton	122
Jimmy Anderson	117

Home Runs Allowed

Kevin Jarvis	**37**
Bobby J. Jones	**37**
Curt Schilling	**37**

Walks Allowed

Ryan Dempster	**112**
Jamey Wright	98
Tom Glavine	97

Hit Batsmen

Chan Ho Park	**20**
Jamey Wright	**20**
Randy Johnson	18

Strikeouts

Randy Johnson	**372**
Curt Schilling	293
Chan Ho Park	218

Wild Pitches

Matt Clement	**15**
Kevin Appier	12
4 players tied with	10

Balks

Omar Daal	**3**
Chan Ho Park	**3**
Odalis Perez	**3**

Run Support per 9 IP
minimum 162 IP

Mike Hampton	**7.09**
Denny Neagle	6.91
Matt Morris	6.41

Baserunners per 9 IP
minimum 162 IP

Curt Schilling	**9.7**
Randy Johnson	9.7
Greg Maddux	9.8

Opposition AVG
minimum 162 IP

Kerry Wood	**.202**
Randy Johnson	.203
Chan Ho Park	.216

Opposition SLG
minimum 162 IP

Randy Johnson	**.309**
Kerry Wood	.315
Russ Ortiz	.328

Opposition OBP
minimum 162 IP

Curt Schilling	**.273**
Randy Johnson	.274
Javier Vazquez	.274

Home Runs per 9 IP
minimum 162 IP

Terry Adams	**0.49**
Russ Ortiz	0.54
Matt Morris	0.54

Strikeouts per 9 IP
minimum 162 IP

Randy Johnson	**13.41**
Kerry Wood	11.20
Curt Schilling	10.27

Walks per 9 IP
minimum 162 IP

Greg Maddux	**1.0**
Curt Schilling	1.4
Jon Lieber	1.6

K/BB Ratio
minimum 162 IP

Curt Schilling	**7.51**
Greg Maddux	6.41
Randy Johnson	5.24

Steals Allowed

Jimmy Anderson	**33**
Miguel Batista	24
Greg Maddux	24

Caught Stealing Off

Elmer Dessens	**15**
Randy Johnson	**15**
Greg Maddux	14

SB % Allowed
minimum 162 IP

Mike Hampton	**16.7**
Jon Lieber	22.2
Kirk Rueter	25.0

GDPs Induced

Jimmy Anderson	**29**
Mike Hampton	**29**
Kirk Rueter	28

GDPs per 9 IP
minimum 162 IP

Kirk Rueter	**1.3**
Mike Hampton	1.3
Jimmy Anderson	1.3

GDP/GDP Opp
minimum 30 BFP

Albie Lopez	**0.22**
Armando Reynoso	0.21
Junior Herndon	0.21

Ground/Fly Ratio Off
minimum 162 IP

Jimmy Anderson	**2.5**
Terry Adams	2.3
Matt Morris	2.0

AVG Allowed Sc Pos
minimum 125 BFP

Randy Johnson	**.178**
Scott Sullivan	.185
Chan Ho Park	.197

Pitches Thrown

Randy Johnson	**4076**
Curt Schilling	3709
Chan Ho Park	3689

Pitches per Batter
minimum 162 IP

Greg Maddux	**3.18**
Shane Reynolds	3.30
Todd Ritchie	3.39

Pickoff Throws

John Burkett	**244**
Jimmy Anderson	178
Al Leiter	177

ERA at Home
minimum 81 IP

Matt Morris	**1.62**
Roy Oswalt	2.15
Brad Penny	2.27

ERA on the Road
minimum 81 IP

Randy Johnson	**2.43**
John Burkett	2.58
Curt Schilling	2.82

AVG vs. LHB
minimum 125 BFP

Felix Rodriguez	**.150**
Randy Wolf	.171
John Thomson	.177

AVG vs. RHB
minimum 225 BFP

Octavio Dotel	**.178**
Kevin Brown	.184
Russ Ortiz	.190

Relief ERA
minimum 50 relief IP

Felix Rodriguez	**1.68**
Steve Kline	1.80
Chad Fox	1.89

Relief Wins

Matt Herges	**9**
Graeme Lloyd	**9**
Felix Rodriguez	**9**

Relief Losses

Matt Herges	**8**
Jim Brower	7
Gabe White	7

Saves

Robb Nen	**45**
3 players tied with	43

Blown Saves

Jeff Shaw	**9**
4 players tied with	7

Save Opportunities

Robb Nen	**52**
Jeff Shaw	**52**
3 players tied with	46

Save Percentage
minimum 20 SvOp

Billy Wagner	**95.1**
Armando Benitez	93.5
Trevor Hoffman	93.5

Holds

Felix Rodriguez	**32**
Mike Remlinger	31
Jeff Fassero	25

Relief Innings

Scott Sullivan	**103.1**
Matt Herges	99.1
Byung-Hyun Kim	98.0

Relief AVG Allowed
minimum 50 relief IP

Byung-Hyun Kim	**.173**
Chad Fox	.181
Octavio Dotel	.182

Relief Runners/9 IP
minimum 50 relief IP

Felix Rodriguez	**9.1**
Robb Nen	9.4
Octavio Dotel	9.6

Relief Strikeouts/9 IP
minimum 50 relief IP

Octavio Dotel	**13.7**
Kyle Farnsworth	11.7
2 players tied with	11.3

% Inh Runners Scored
minimum 30 inh runners

Dennis Cook	**18.2**
Dave Weathers	**18.2**
Aaron Fultz	18.6

1st Batter AVG
minimum 40 relief first BFP

Armando Benitez	**.123**
Scott Sullivan	.125
Billy Wagner	.138

Fielding

Errors by Pitcher

4 players tied with	4

Errors by Catcher

Jason Kendall	**12**
Kelly Stinnett	**12**
Javy Lopez	10

Errors by First Base

Lee Stevens	**19**
Jeff Bagwell	12
2 players tied with	11

Errors by Second Base

Luis Castillo	**13**
Marlon Anderson	12
Eric Young	12

Errors by Third Base

Phil Nevin	**27**
Aramis Ramirez	25
Aaron Boone	19

Errors by Shortstop

Alex Gonzalez	**26**
Edgar Renteria	24
2 players tied with	22

Errors by Left Field

Cliff Floyd	**8**
3 players tied with	7

Errors by Center Field

Juan Pierre	**8**
Marvin Benard	7
Gary Matthews Jr.	7

Errors by Right Field

Vladimir Guerrero	**12**
Bobby Abreu	8
4 players tied with	6

% CS by Catchers
minimum 70 SB Attempts

Henry Blanco	**42.3**
Brad Ausmus	40.0
Charles Johnson	39.5

Stars, Bums and Sleepers: Who's Who in 2002

Can anyone follow in the footsteps of American League MVP, Rookie of the Year and Gold Glove winner Ichiro Suzuki, one of our sleeper picks for 2001? It's unlikely that this trifecta ever will be reached again, but we present our choices for sleepers to watch in 2002—and more—in this section of the book.

Some of our other sleepers for 2001 were Lance Berkman, Mark Buehrle, Robert Fick, Frank Menechino, Juan Pierre, Joel Pineiro, Luke Prokopec, Aramis Ramirez, Luis Rivas, Jimmy Rollins and Alfonso Soriano. The system we use to project a future brighter than a player's past performance is the creation of Bill James, who introduced his forecasting methods in *The Bill James Baseball Abstract*. Over the years, Bill and STATS founder John Dewan have refined the system, combining advice from our scouts and staff experts.

The system is used to project more than just sleepers. The following pages also are dedicated to predicting players in decline and those we can expect consistent performance from in 2002. There are some general truths that go into these projections. Younger players are inclined to improve and older guys tend to decline. Age 27 is when we can expect peak performance and career years from major league hitters. Players who enjoy an unexpectedly good year commonly fail to repeat their success, while those who experience a dropoff in their numbers often rebound.

Each player position in this section is broken into four groups: Expect a Better Year, Look for Consistency, Production Will Drop and Sleepers. Players are placed into these groups based on 2001 performance only.

We take a different approach with Sleepers. The statistics we show here combine major and minor league totals, and we factored in projected playing time for 2002 when we made our decisions late in 2001. Not all of our picks will demonstrate the budding promise of Ichiro or Berkman, but a number of them will emerge this season.

Major leaguers are considered at their most common position in 2001, with a few adjustments for anticipated positional changes. Then we look at their career trends. Using the complex formula refined by Bill and John, forecasts are generated based on complete careers. That way an unusually good or bad 2001 season isn't the primary determinant of a projection.

When appropriate, minor league numbers also are factored into the system. Bill found that minor league performance, when properly adjusted, is just as reliable as major league performance in making big league projections.

Of course, there are factors outside of our control. While we evaluate teams' positional battles in estimating playing time, spring-training results and injuries will alter the picture for many players. We also concede that pitchers are full of surprises. For every five hitters who perform consistently, there may be just one pitcher who's as reliable.

Catcher

Expect A Better Year

| | 2001 Statistics | | | |
	Avg	HR	RBI	SB
Mike Piazza	.300	36	94	0
Ivan Rodriguez	.308	25	65	10
Jason Kendall	.266	10	53	13
Javy Lopez	.267	17	66	1
Ramon Hernandez	.254	15	60	1
Mike Lieberthal	.231	2	11	0
Jason Varitek	.293	7	25	0
Ben Petrick	.240	12	48	4
Wiki Gonzalez	.266	8	28	2
Brad Ausmus	.232	5	34	4
Michael Barrett	.250	6	38	2
Bobby Estalella	.241	14	52	0
Jason LaRue	.236	12	43	3
Darrin Fletcher	.226	11	56	0
Henry Blanco	.210	6	31	3
Todd Hundley	.187	12	31	0
Brook Fordyce	.209	5	19	1

Look for Consistency

| | 2001 Statistics | | | |
	Avg	HR	RBI	SB
Jorge Posada	.277	22	95	2
Charles Johnson	.259	18	75	0
Einar Diaz	.277	4	56	1
Ben Davis	.239	11	57	4
Damian Miller	.271	13	47	0
A.J. Pierzynski	.289	7	55	1
Dan Wilson	.265	10	42	3
Raul Casanova	.260	11	33	0
Scott Hatteberg	.245	3	25	1
Brent Mayne	.285	2	40	1
Ben Molina	.271	6	45	0
Sandy Alomar Jr.	.245	4	21	1
Chad Kreuter	.215	6	17	0
Eli Marrero	.266	6	23	6
Mark L. Johnson	.260	9	42	4
John Flaherty	.238	4	29	1
Joe Girardi	.253	3	25	0

Production Will Drop

| | 2001 Statistics | | | |
	Avg	HR	RBI	SB
Paul Lo Duca	.320	25	90	2
Benito Santiago	.262	6	45	5
Mike Redmond	.312	4	14	0
Gregg Zaun	.320	6	18	1
Mike Matheny	.218	7	42	0

Sleepers

| | 2001 Statistics (includes minor leagues) | | | |
	Avg	HR	RBI	SB
Toby Hall	.323	23	102	3
Josh Phelps	.285	31	98	4
Craig A. Wilson	.305	14	35	3
Brandon Inge	.210	3	34	2
Corky Miller	.292	19	77	4
Josh Paul	.271	7	32	6
Gary Bennett	.263	4	24	0

First Base

Expect A Better Year

| | 2001 Statistics | | | |
	Avg	HR	RBI	SB
Frank Thomas	.221	4	10	0
Sean Casey	.310	13	89	3
Tony Clark	.287	16	75	0
Chris Richard	.265	15	61	11
Eric Karros	.235	15	63	3
Erubiel Durazo	.269	13	39	0
J.T. Snow	.246	8	34	0

Look for Consistency

| | 2001 Statistics | | | |
	Avg	HR	RBI	SB
Todd Helton	.336	49	146	7
Jeff Bagwell	.288	39	130	11
Carlos Delgado	.279	39	102	3
Rafael Palmeiro	.273	47	123	1
Mike Sweeney	.304	29	99	10
Ryan Klesko	.286	30	113	23
Richie Sexson	.271	45	125	2
Paul Konerko	.282	32	99	1
John Olerud	.302	21	95	3
Brian Daubach	.263	22	71	1
Derrek Lee	.282	21	75	4
Mark Grace	.298	15	78	1
Travis Lee	.258	20	90	3
Robert Fick	.272	19	61	0
Lee Stevens	.245	25	95	2

	Avg	HR	RBI	SB
Kevin Young	.232	14	65	15
Matt Stairs	.250	17	61	2
Todd Zeile	.266	10	62	1
David Segui	.301	10	46	1
Ron Coomer	.261	8	53	0
Shawn Wooten	.312	8	32	2
Randall Simon	.305	6	37	0
Dave McCarty	.250	7	26	0

Production Will Drop

| | 2001 Statistics | | | |
	Avg	HR	RBI	SB
Jason Giambi	.342	38	120	2
Jim Thome	.291	49	124	0
Tino Martinez	.280	34	113	1
Fred McGriff	.306	31	102	1
Doug Mientkiewicz	.306	15	74	2
Kevin Millar	.314	20	85	0
Andres Galarraga	.256	17	69	1
Scott Spiezio	.271	13	54	5

Sleepers

| | 2001 Statistics (includes minor leagues) | | | |
	Avg	HR	RBI	SB
Julio Zuleta	.270	13	53	3
Carlos Pena	.284	26	86	11
Nick Johnson	.246	20	57	9
Hee Seop Choi	.229	13	45	5

Second Base

Expect A Better Year

	2001 Statistics			
	Avg	HR	RBI	SB
Edgardo Alfonzo	.243	17	49	5
Jose Vidro	.319	15	59	4
Ronnie Belliard	.264	11	36	5
Luis Castillo	.263	2	45	33
Adam Kennedy	.270	6	40	12
Carlos Febles	.236	8	25	5
Michael Young	.249	11	49	3
Pokey Reese	.224	9	40	25
Jerry Hairston Jr.	.233	8	47	29
Quilvio Veras	.252	3	25	7
Warren Morris	.204	2	11	2

Look for Consistency

	2001 Statistics			
	Avg	HR	RBI	SB
Jeff Kent	.298	22	106	7
Ray Durham	.267	20	65	23
Todd Walker	.296	17	75	1
Alfonso Soriano	.268	18	73	43
Marlon Anderson	.293	11	61	8
Damion Easley	.250	11	65	10
Mark Grudzielanek	.271	13	55	4
Jay Bell	.248	13	46	0
Homer Bush	.306	3	27	13
David Eckstein	.285	4	41	29
Eric Young	.279	6	42	31
Frank Menechino	.242	12	60	2
Randy Velarde	.278	9	32	6
Luis Rivas	.266	7	47	31
Jose Offerman	.267	9	49	5
Craig Counsell	.275	4	38	6
Damian Jackson	.241	4	38	23
Russ Johnson	.294	4	33	2
Denny Hocking	.251	3	25	6
Tony Graffanino	.303	2	15	4
Junior Spivey	.258	5	21	3

Production Will Drop

	2001 Statistics			
	Avg	HR	RBI	SB
Roberto Alomar	.336	20	100	30
Bret Boone	.331	37	141	5
Craig Biggio	.292	20	70	7
Fernando Vina	.303	9	56	17
Frank Catalanotto	.330	11	54	15
Mark McLemore	.286	5	57	39
Luis Alicea	.274	4	32	8

Sleepers

	2001 Statistics (includes minor leagues)			
	Avg	HR	RBI	SB
Jose Ortiz	.257	20	77	11
Marcus Giles	.298	15	75	15
Esteban German	.311	10	44	48
Brent Abernathy	.284	9	56	19

Third Base

Expect A Better Year

	2001 Statistics			
	Avg	HR	RBI	SB
Tony Batista	.238	25	87	5
Adrian Beltre	.265	13	60	13
Joe Randa	.253	13	83	3
Robin Ventura	.237	21	61	2
Dean Palmer	.222	11	40	4
Travis Fryman	.263	3	38	1
Fernando Tatis	.255	2	11	0
Matt Williams	.275	16	65	1
Bill Mueller	.295	6	23	1
Russell Branyan	.232	20	54	1
Aubrey Huff	.254	11	55	1
Mike Lamb	.302	12	75	2
John Valentin	.200	1	5	0
Russ Davis	.257	7	17	1
Hiram Bocachica	.233	2	9	4
Enrique Wilson	.211	2	20	0

Look for Consistency

	2001 Statistics			
	Avg	HR	RBI	SB
Chipper Jones	.330	38	102	9
Troy Glaus	.250	41	108	10
Scott Rolen	.289	25	107	16
Eric Chavez	.288	32	114	8
Aramis Ramirez	.300	34	112	5
Jeff Cirillo	.313	17	83	12
Corey Koskie	.276	26	103	27
Mike Lowell	.283	18	100	1
David Bell	.260	15	64	2

	2001 Statistics			
	Avg	HR	RBI	SB
Aaron Boone	.294	14	62	6
Chris Stynes	.280	8	33	4
Greg Norton	.267	13	40	1
Tyler Houston	.289	12	38	0
Ken Caminiti	.228	15	41	0
Herbert Perry	.256	7	32	2
Wes Helms	.222	10	36	1

Production Will Drop

	2001 Statistics			
	Avg	HR	RBI	SB
Albert Pujols	.329	37	130	1
Phil Nevin	.306	41	126	4
Jeff Conine	.311	14	97	12
Vinny Castilla	.260	25	91	1
Placido Polanco	.307	3	38	12
Shane Halter	.284	12	65	3
Craig Paquette	.282	15	64	3
Jose Macias	.268	8	51	21
Shea Hillenbrand	.263	12	49	3

Sleepers

	2001 Statistics (includes minor leagues)			
	Avg	HR	RBI	SB
Hank Blalock	.352	18	108	10
D'Angelo Jimenez	.270	8	52	7
Morgan Ensberg	.310	23	61	6
Sean Burroughs	.322	9	55	9
Joe Crede	.271	17	72	3
Luis Lopez	.303	13	83	1
Chris Truby	.280	20	94	11

Shortstop

Expect A Better Year

| | 2001 Statistics | | | |
	Avg	HR	RBI	SB
Nomar Garciaparra	.289	4	8	0
Edgar Renteria	.260	10	57	17
Rafael Furcal	.275	4	30	22
Deivi Cruz	.256	7	52	4
Barry Larkin	.256	2	17	3
Omar Vizquel	.255	2	50	13
Ramon E. Martinez	.253	5	37	1
Mike Bordick	.249	7	30	9
Mark Loretta	.289	2	29	1
Alex Cora	.217	4	29	0
Jack Wilson	.223	3	25	1
Dave Berg	.242	4	16	0

Look for Consistency

| | 2001 Statistics | | | |
	Avg	HR	RBI	SB
Alex Rodriguez	.318	52	135	18
Miguel Tejada	.267	31	113	11
Derek Jeter	.311	21	74	27
Jimmy Rollins	.274	14	54	46
Alex S. Gonzalez	.253	17	76	18
Julio Lugo	.263	10	37	12
Jose Valentin	.258	28	68	9
Neifi Perez	.279	8	59	9
Tony Womack	.266	3	30	28
Royce Clayton	.263	9	60	10
Alex Gonzalez	.250	9	48	2
Mike Lansing	.250	8	34	3
Carlos Guillen	.259	5	53	4
Chris Gomez	.259	8	43	4
Abraham Nunez	.262	1	21	8
Rey Ordonez	.247	3	44	3

Production Will Drop

| | 2001 Statistics | | | |
	Avg	HR	RBI	SB
Rich Aurilia	.324	37	97	1
Orlando Cabrera	.276	14	96	19
Cristian Guzman	.302	10	51	25
Jose Hernandez	.249	25	78	5
Ricky Gutierrez	.290	10	66	4
Rey Sanchez	.281	0	37	11
Benji Gil	.296	8	39	3
Desi Relaford	.302	8	36	13

Sleepers

| | 2001 Statistics (includes minor leagues) | | | |
	Avg	HR	RBI	SB
Juan Uribe	.303	15	102	15
Felipe Lopez	.267	23	71	21
Wilson Betemit	.304	12	62	15
Cesar Izturis	.286	4	44	32
Ramon Vazquez	.295	10	83	9

Left Field

Expect A Better Year

| | 2001 Statistics | | | |
	Avg	HR	RBI	SB
Johnny Damon	.256	9	49	27
Pat Burrell	.258	27	89	2
Carlos Lee	.269	24	84	17
Geoff Jenkins	.264	20	63	4
Mark Quinn	.269	17	60	9
David Justice	.241	18	51	1
Jacque Jones	.276	14	49	12
Chuck Knoblauch	.250	9	44	38
Rusty Greer	.273	7	29	1
Troy O'Leary	.240	13	50	1
Benny Agbayani	.277	6	27	4
Al Martin	.240	7	42	9
Steve Cox	.256	13	54	2
Ricky Ledee	.231	2	36	3
Wil Cordero	.250	4	21	0

Look for Consistency

| | 2001 Statistics | | | |
	Avg	HR	RBI	SB
Lance Berkman	.331	34	126	7
Brian Giles	.309	37	95	13
Gary Sheffield	.311	36	100	10
Shannon Stewart	.316	12	60	27
Garret Anderson	.289	28	123	13
Rondell White	.307	17	50	1
Bobby Higginson	.277	17	71	20
Bubba Trammell	.261	25	92	2
Dmitri Young	.302	21	69	8
Greg Vaughn	.233	24	82	11
Ray Lankford	.252	19	58	10
Todd Hollandsworth	.368	6	19	5

		Avg	HR	RBI	SB
B.J. Surhoff		.271	10	58	9
Randy Winn		.273	6	50	12
Geoff Blum		.236	9	50	9
Tsuyoshi Shinjo		.268	10	56	4
Ron Gant		.258	10	35	5
Jason Tyner		.280	0	21	31
Joe McEwing		.283	8	30	8
Terry Shumpert		.289	4	24	14
Delino DeShields		.234	5	37	23
Shane Spencer		.258	10	46	4

Production Will Drop

| | 2001 Statistics | | | |
	Avg	HR	RBI	SB
Barry Bonds	.328	73	137	13
Luis Gonzalez	.325	57	142	1
Cliff Floyd	.317	31	103	18
Marty Cordova	.301	20	69	0
Rickey Henderson	.227	8	42	25
Stan Javier	.292	4	33	11

Sleepers

| | 2001 Statistics (includes minor leagues) | | | |
	Avg	HR	RBI	SB
Adam Dunn	.305	51	127	15
Jason Lane	.316	38	124	10
Jack Cust	.279	27	79	6
Dee Brown	.249	9	46	5
Aaron Rowand	.294	20	68	13
Brad Wilkerson	.247	13	54	14
Bobby Kielty	.279	14	64	8
Mario Encarnacion	.287	14	46	6

Center Field

Expect A Better Year

| | 2001 Statistics | | | |
	Avg	HR	RBI	SB
Andruw Jones	.251	34	104	11
Ken Griffey Jr.	.286	22	65	2
Richard Hidalgo	.275	19	80	3
Darin Erstad	.258	9	63	24
Gabe Kapler	.267	17	72	23
Carl Everett	.257	14	58	9
Jay Payton	.260	8	34	4
Kenny Lofton	.261	14	66	16
Juan Encarnacion	.242	12	52	9
Jeffrey Hammonds	.247	6	21	5
Peter Bergeron	.211	3	16	10
Tom Goodwin	.231	4	22	22
Gerald Williams	.201	4	19	13

Look for Consistency

| | 2001 Statistics | | | |
	Avg	HR	RBI	SB
Bernie Williams	.307	26	94	11
Mike Cameron	.267	25	110	34
Carlos Beltran	.306	24	101	31
J.D. Drew	.323	27	73	13
Preston Wilson	.274	23	71	20
Juan Pierre	.327	2	55	46
Terrence Long	.283	12	85	9
Doug Glanville	.262	14	55	28
Torii Hunter	.261	27	92	9
Steve Finley	.275	14	73	11
Mark Kotsay	.291	10	58	13
Marvin Benard	.265	15	44	10
Chris Singleton	.298	7	45	12
Marquis Grissom	.221	21	60	7
Gary Matthews Jr.	.227	14	44	8
Ruben Rivera	.255	10	34	6
Calvin Murray	.245	6	25	8

Production Will Drop

| | 2001 Statistics | | | |
	Avg	HR	RBI	SB
Jim Edmonds	.304	30	110	5
Jose Cruz	.274	34	88	32
Michael Tucker	.252	12	61	16
Devon White	.277	14	47	18
Melvin Mora	.250	7	48	11
Jolbert Cabrera	.261	1	38	10

Sleepers

| | 2001 Statistics (includes minor leagues) | | | |
	Avg	HR	RBI	SB
Marlon Byrd	.316	28	89	32
Joe Borchard	.295	27	98	5
Vernon Wells	.287	13	58	20
Alex Escobar	.260	15	60	19
Milton Bradley	.244	8	47	31
Corey Patterson	.245	11	46	23

Right Field

Expect A Better Year

| | 2001 Statistics | | | |
	Avg	HR	RBI	SB
Vladimir Guerrero	.307	34	108	37
Jermaine Dye	.282	26	106	9
Raul Mondesi	.252	27	84	30
Ben Grieve	.264	11	72	7
Tim Salmon	.227	17	49	9
Jeremy Giambi	.283	12	57	0
Daryle Ward	.263	9	39	0
Brady Anderson	.202	8	45	12
Danny Bautista	.302	5	26	3
Eric Owens	.253	5	28	8
Mike Darr	.277	2	34	6
Jose Guillen	.274	3	11	2
Wendell Magee	.222	5	18	3
Derek Bell	.173	5	13	0
Brian Buchanan	.274	10	32	1

Look for Consistency

| | 2001 Statistics | | | |
	Avg	HR	RBI	SB
Manny Ramirez	.306	41	125	0
Bobby Abreu	.289	31	110	36
Magglio Ordonez	.305	31	113	25
Ichiro Suzuki	.350	8	69	56
Jeromy Burnitz	.251	34	100	0
John Vander Wal	.270	14	70	8
Matt Lawton	.277	13	64	29
Roger Cedeno	.293	6	48	55
Armando Rios	.260	14	50	3
Dante Bichette	.286	12	49	2
David Dellucci	.276	10	40	2
Chad Allen	.274	5	21	3
Dave Martinez	.287	2	20	3

Production Will Drop

| | 2001 Statistics | | | |
	Avg	HR	RBI	SB
Sammy Sosa	.328	64	160	0
Larry Walker	.350	38	123	14
Shawn Green	.297	49	125	20
Juan Gonzalez	.325	35	140	1
Moises Alou	.331	27	108	5
Trot Nixon	.280	27	88	7
Brian Jordan	.295	25	97	3
Ellis Burks	.280	28	74	5
Reggie Sanders	.263	33	90	14
Alex Ochoa	.276	8	52	17
Ruben Sierra	.291	23	67	2
Raul Ibanez	.280	13	54	0

Sleepers

| | 2001 Statistics (includes minor leagues) | | | |
	Avg	HR	RBI	SB
Adam Piatt	.251	2	23	2
Jeff Liefer	.265	24	60	3
Timo Perez	.297	11	41	16
Brady Clark	.264	8	36	10

Designated Hitter

Expect A Better Year

	2001 Statistics			
	Avg	HR	RBI	SB
Brad Fullmer	.274	18	83	5
David Ortiz	.234	18	48	1
Olmedo Saenz	.220	9	32	0

Production Will Drop

	2001 Statistics			
	Avg	HR	RBI	SB
Jose Canseco	.258	16	49	2

Look for Consistency

	2001 Statistics			
	Avg	HR	RBI	SB
Edgar Martinez	.306	23	116	4
Mike Kinkade	.275	4	16	2

Starting Pitchers

Expect A Better Year

	2001 Statistics				
	W	L	ERA	Sv	Ratio
Pedro Martinez	7	3	2.39	0	0.93
Kevin Brown	10	4	2.65	0	1.14
Dennis Springer	1	1	3.32	0	1.11
Pat Hentgen	2	3	3.47	0	1.12
Josh Towers	8	10	4.49	0	1.29
Kevin Millwood	7	7	4.31	0	1.33
Andy Ashby	2	0	3.86	0	1.29
Matt Wise	1	4	4.38	0	1.32
David Wells	5	7	4.47	0	1.40
Pedro Astacio	8	14	5.09	0	1.39
Sidney Ponson	5	10	4.94	0	1.43
Mike Hampton	14	13	5.41	0	1.58
Brian Anderson	4	9	5.20	0	1.39
Darren Dreifort	4	7	5.13	0	1.44
Francisco Cordero	0	1	3.86	0	2.14
Bret Saberhagen	1	3	4.46	0	1.08
Shawn Chacon	6	10	5.06	0	1.52
Chuck Finley	8	7	5.54	0	1.46
Jose Lima	6	12	5.54	0	1.42
Jose Mercedes	8	17	5.82	0	1.53
Gil Heredia	7	8	5.58	0	1.58
Jeff D'Amico	3	4	5.60	0	1.48
Scott Elarton	4	11	7.05	0	1.56
Carl Pavano	4	8	4.79	0	1.44
Robert Ellis	6	5	5.77	0	1.52
Bryan Rekar	3	13	5.89	0	1.51
Kent Bottenfield	2	6	7.08	1	1.54
Dave Burba	10	10	6.21	0	1.61
Kenny Rogers	5	7	6.19	0	1.65
Charles Nagy	5	6	6.40	0	1.73
Andy Benes	7	7	7.38	0	1.70
Brian Bohanon	5	8	7.14	0	1.79
Jim Parque	0	3	8.04	0	1.64
Brian Reith	0	7	7.81	0	1.79
Travis Harper	0	2	7.71	0	2.57
Brian Powell	0	1	18.00	0	2.67

Look for Consistency

	2001 Statistics				
	W	L	ERA	Sv	Ratio
Randy Johnson	21	6	2.49	0	1.01
Roy Oswalt	14	3	2.73	0	1.06
Greg Maddux	17	11	3.05	0	1.06
Mike Mussina	17	11	3.15	0	1.07
Mark Buehrle	16	8	3.29	0	1.07
Matt Morris	22	8	3.16	0	1.26
Freddy Garcia	18	6	3.05	0	1.12
Tim Hudson	18	9	3.37	0	1.22
Roger Clemens	20	3	3.51	0	1.26
Chan Ho Park	15	11	3.50	0	1.17
Darryl Kile	16	11	3.09	0	1.29
Russ Ortiz	17	9	3.29	0	1.27
Barry Zito	17	8	3.49	0	1.23
Al Leiter	11	11	3.31	0	1.20
Brad Radke	15	11	3.94	0	1.15

Look for Consistency (continued)

Aaron Sele	15	5	3.60	0	1.24
Kerry Wood	12	6	3.36	0	1.26
Kevin Appier	11	10	3.57	0	1.19
Brad Penny	10	10	3.69	0	1.16
Randy Wolf	10	11	3.70	0	1.23
Tom Glavine	16	7	3.57	0	1.41
Rick Reed	12	12	4.05	0	1.20
Woody Williams	15	9	4.05	0	1.27
Robert Person	15	7	4.19	0	1.24
Andy Pettitte	15	10	3.99	0	1.32
Jarrod Washburn	11	10	3.77	0	1.29
Brian Lawrence	5	5	3.45	0	1.23
Eric Milton	15	7	4.32	0	1.28
Jeff Weaver	13	16	4.08	0	1.32
Jason Schmidt	13	7	4.07	0	1.32
C.C. Sabathia	17	5	4.39	0	1.35
Paul Abbott	17	4	4.25	0	1.42
Bartolo Colon	14	12	4.09	0	1.39
Shane Reynolds	14	11	4.34	0	1.34
Frank Castillo	10	9	4.21	0	1.27
Todd Ritchie	11	15	4.47	0	1.27
Terry Adams	12	8	4.33	0	1.36
Hideo Nomo	13	10	4.50	0	1.35
Adam Eaton	8	5	4.32	0	1.27
Dustin Hermanson	14	13	4.45	0	1.39
Chris Carpenter	11	11	4.09	0	1.41
Tony Armas Jr.	9	14	4.03	0	1.38
Omar Daal	13	7	4.46	0	1.37
Brian Tollberg	10	4	4.30	0	1.35
Kirk Rueter	14	12	4.42	0	1.43
Shawn Estes	9	8	4.02	0	1.43
Elmer Dessens	10	14	4.48	0	1.35
Jeff Suppan	10	14	4.37	0	1.38
Kip Wells	10	11	4.79	0	1.54
Kevin Tapani	9	14	4.49	0	1.34
Ismael Valdes	9	13	4.45	0	1.39
Eric Gagne	6	7	4.75	0	1.25
James Baldwin	10	11	4.42	0	1.45
Ben Sheets	11	10	4.76	0	1.41
Dave Coggin	6	7	4.17	0	1.45
Luke Prokopec	8	7	4.88	0	1.34
John Halama	10	7	4.73	0	1.43
David Cone	9	7	4.31	0	1.51
Julian Tavarez	10	9	4.52	0	1.49
Paul Byrd	6	7	4.44	0	1.41
Glendon Rusch	8	12	4.63	0	1.45
Ryan Dempster	15	12	4.94	0	1.56
Chris Michalak	8	9	4.41	1	1.55
Bruce Chen	7	7	4.87	0	1.40
Albie Lopez	9	19	4.81	0	1.46
Esteban Loaiza	11	11	5.02	0	1.47
Paul Wilson	8	9	4.88	0	1.43
Chuck Smith	5	5	4.70	0	1.41
Rick Helling	12	11	5.17	0	1.48
Pat Rapp	5	12	4.76	0	1.41
Jamey Wright	11	12	4.90	0	1.54
Rick Bauer	0	5	4.64	0	1.33
Scott Schoeneweis	10	11	5.08	0	1.48

Look for Consistency (continued)

	W	L	ERA	Sv	Ratio
Jimmy Haynes	8	17	4.85	0	1.51
Livan Hernandez	13	15	5.24	0	1.55
Bobby J. Jones	8	19	5.12	0	1.48
Matt Clement	9	10	5.05	0	1.52
Chris Reitsma	7	15	5.29	0	1.42
Jimmy Anderson	9	17	5.10	0	1.53
Paxton Crawford	3	0	4.75	0	1.47
Odalis Perez	7	8	4.91	0	1.54
Denny Neagle	9	8	5.38	0	1.48
Mike Thurman	9	11	5.33	0	1.51
Mark Gardner	5	5	5.40	0	1.39
Bronson Arroyo	5	7	5.09	0	1.51
Amaury Telemaco	5	5	5.54	0	1.40
Tony McKnight	3	6	4.95	0	1.52
Tomokazu Ohka	3	9	5.47	0	1.52
Dan Reichert	8	8	5.63	0	1.61
Sterling Hitchcock	6	5	5.63	0	1.56
Matt Blank	2	2	5.16	0	1.59
Darren Oliver	11	11	6.02	0	1.65
Dave Mlicki	11	11	6.17	0	1.65
Allen Levrault	6	10	6.06	0	1.57
Chris Holt	7	9	5.77	0	1.68
Ryan Rupe	5	12	6.59	0	1.46
Mac Suzuki	5	12	5.86	0	1.65
J.C. Romero	1	4	6.23	0	1.46
Joey Hamilton	6	10	5.93	0	1.70
Paul Rigdon	3	5	5.79	0	1.66
Jason Grilli	2	2	6.07	0	1.54
Rob Bell	5	10	6.67	0	1.60
Randy Keisler	1	2	6.22	0	1.70
Aaron Myette	4	5	7.14	0	1.62
Osvaldo Fernandez	5	6	6.92	0	1.71
Tim Drew	0	2	7.97	0	1.91

Production Will Drop

	W	L	ERA	Sv	Ratio
	2001 Statistics				
Curt Schilling	22	6	2.98	0	1.08
Joel Pineiro	6	2	2.03	0	0.94
Jamie Moyer	20	6	3.43	0	1.10
Mark Mulder	21	8	3.45	0	1.16
Joe Mays	17	13	3.16	0	1.15
Javier Vazquez	16	11	3.42	0	1.08
Jon Lieber	20	6	3.80	0	1.15
John Burkett	12	12	3.04	0	1.17
Wade Miller	16	8	3.40	0	1.22
Cory Lidle	13	6	3.59	0	1.15
Roy Halladay	5	3	3.16	0	1.16
Steve W. Sparks	14	9	3.65	0	1.33
A.J. Burnett	11	12	4.05	0	1.32
Adrian Hernandez	0	3	3.68	0	1.14
John Thomson	4	5	4.04	0	1.16
Steve Trachsel	11	13	4.46	0	1.24
Erik Hiljus	5	0	3.41	0	1.38
Jon Garland	6	7	3.69	1	1.52
Jason Bere	11	11	4.31	0	1.32
Kevin Jarvis	12	11	4.79	0	1.23
Jason Johnson	10	12	4.09	0	1.38
Ramon Ortiz	13	11	4.36	0	1.43
Calvin Maduro	5	6	4.23	0	1.27

Production Will Drop (continued)

	W	L	ERA	Sv	Ratio
Tanyon Sturtze	11	12	4.42	1	1.43
Nelson Figueroa	4	5	3.94	0	1.48
Doug Davis	11	10	4.45	0	1.55
Chad Durbin	9	16	4.93	0	1.45
Bobby Witt	4	1	4.78	0	1.41
Ruben Quevedo	4	5	4.61	0	1.52
Kris Wilson	6	5	5.19	1	1.50
Rocky Biddle	7	8	5.39	0	1.47
Ted Lilly	5	6	5.37	0	1.47
Denny Stark	1	1	9.20	0	1.70

Sleepers

	2001 Statistics (includes minor leagues)				
	W	L	ERA	Sv	Ratio
Carlos Hernandez	13	3	3.39	0	1.29
Josh Beckett	16	3	1.54	0	0.86
Juan Cruz	12	7	3.80	0	1.35
Bud Smith	14	8	3.22	0	1.27
Brandon Duckworth	16	4	2.92	0	1.13
Dave Williams	9	10	3.34	0	1.18
Brandon Lyon	15	7	3.88	0	1.17
Joe Kennedy	13	8	3.12	0	1.15
Lance Davis	15	6	4.02	0	1.37
Orlando Hernandez	5	7	4.26	0	1.32
Casey Fossum	6	9	3.39	0	1.20
Jason Jennings	13	9	4.45	0	1.43
Mike MacDougal	9	9	4.68	0	1.52
Jesus Sanchez	8	5	3.90	0	1.34
Steve Parris	4	6	4.49	0	1.53
Jose Acevedo	9	11	4.66	0	1.31
Mark Redman	2	7	4.81	0	1.51
Chris George	15	11	4.33	0	1.33
Ryan Jensen	12	4	3.70	0	1.35
Jason Middlebrook	12	5	2.83	0	1.12
Kyle Lohse	11	10	4.26	0	1.30
Tim Redding	17	4	3.67	0	1.17
Sean Douglass	10	10	3.70	0	1.39
Nick Bierbrodt	11	8	3.98	0	1.44
Adam Pettyjohn	6	14	4.33	0	1.36
Kyle Peterson	3	12	5.69	0	1.48
Armando Reynoso	1	6	5.54	0	1.51
Troy Mattes	8	8	4.45	0	1.41
Dan Wright	12	10	3.77	0	1.35
Brian Meadows	7	11	6.43	0	1.60
Pete Harnisch	1	4	6.81	0	1.91
Junior Herndon	11	11	5.05	0	1.58
Jaret Wright	5	3	5.15	0	1.52
Ryan Glynn	3	11	6.70	0	1.70
Rick Ankiel	6	7	3.26	0	1.12
Kurt Ainsworth	10	9	5.19	0	1.31
Adam Johnson	7	9	4.79	0	1.35
Nick Neugebauer	8	8	3.29	0	1.30
Nate Cornejo	20	7	3.62	0	1.37
Brad Thomas	10	5	2.85	0	1.11
Carlton Loewer	5	7	4.55	0	1.42
Brett Hinchliffe	3	3	4.09	0	1.52
Joe Borowski	8	8	3.06	1	1.09

Relief Pitchers

Expect A Better Year

	W	L	ERA	Sv	Ratio
	2001 Statistics				
Danny Graves	6	5	4.15	32	1.26
Steve Karsay	3	5	2.35	8	1.11
Danys Baez	5	3	2.50	0	1.07
John Smoltz	3	3	3.36	10	1.07
Bret Prinz	4	1	2.63	9	1.27
Derek Lowe	5	10	3.53	24	1.44
Octavio Dotel	7	5	2.66	2	1.20
John Riedling	1	1	2.41	0	1.07
Buddy Groom	1	4	3.55	11	1.11
Billy Koch	2	5	4.80	36	1.47
Kevin Walker	0	0	3.00	0	1.08

Expect A Better Year (continued)

	W	L	ERA	Sv	Ratio
John Frascatore	1	0	2.20	0	1.22
Dave Veres	3	2	3.70	15	1.29
Mike Remlinger	3	3	2.76	1	1.20
Curtis Leskanic	2	6	3.63	17	1.36
Rudy Seanez	0	2	2.75	1	1.17
Jason Grimsley	1	5	3.02	0	1.23
Rich Garces	6	1	3.90	1	1.19
Jim Mecir	2	8	3.43	3	1.27
Kerry Ligtenberg	3	3	2.97	1	1.34
Ricky Bottalico	3	5	3.75	3	1.21
Matt Mantei	0	0	2.57	2	1.43
Grant Roberts	1	0	3.81	0	1.23
Tim Wakefield	9	12	3.90	3	1.36

Name	W	L	ERA	Sv	Ratio
Juan Moreno	3	3	3.92	0	1.21
Mike Trombley	3	8	4.38	6	1.31
Mike Timlin	4	5	4.09	3	1.33
Dennis Cook	1	1	4.63	0	1.29
T.J. Mathews	2	2	3.59	5	1.29
Graeme Lloyd	9	5	4.35	1	1.35
John Franco	6	2	4.05	2	1.39
Victor Santos	2	2	3.30	0	1.45
Mike Jackson	5	3	4.70	4	1.30
Tim Spooneybarger	0	1	2.25	0	1.75
Carlos Almanzar	0	1	3.38	0	1.50
Terry Mulholland	1	3	4.63	0	1.49
Todd Jones	5	5	4.24	13	1.71
Bob Wells	8	5	5.11	2	1.31
Bob Howry	4	5	4.69	5	1.46
Turk Wendell	4	5	4.43	1	1.45
Masato Yoshii	4	7	4.78	0	1.35
Chris Brock	3	0	4.13	0	1.53
Dan Miceli	2	5	4.80	1	1.40
Mike Holtz	1	2	4.86	0	1.49
LaTroy Hawkins	1	5	5.96	28	1.91
C.J. Nitkowski	1	3	4.85	0	1.71
Marc Valdes	10	11	4.68	2	1.39
John Wasdin	3	2	5.11	0	1.49
Guillermo Mota	1	3	5.26	0	1.39
Juan Acevedo	2	5	4.18	0	1.71
Hipolito Pichardo	2	1	4.93	0	1.50
Anthony Telford	3	7	5.11	1	1.42
Wayne Gomes	6	3	5.18	1	1.61
Pete Schourek	1	5	5.30	0	1.71
Travis Miller	1	4	4.81	0	1.52
Steve Woodard	3	3	5.20	0	1.51
Joey Eischen	0	1	4.85	0	1.52
Courtney Duncan	3	3	5.06	0	1.57
Donne Wall	0	4	4.85	0	1.59
Mike James	1	2	5.21	0	1.58
Mark Lukasiewicz	0	2	6.04	0	1.34
Luis Pineda	0	1	4.91	0	1.64
Brett Tomko	3	1	5.19	0	1.64
Scott Sauerbeck	2	2	5.60	2	1.61
Ron Villone	6	10	5.89	0	1.62
Gabe White	1	7	6.25	0	1.42
Jose Silva	3	3	6.75	0	1.38
Bobby Munoz	0	4	5.14	0	1.76
Doug Henry	2	2	6.07	0	1.59
Alan Embree	2	4	6.53	1	1.42
Rocky Coppinger	9	1	3.05	4	1.23
Scott Radinsky	2	3	4.87	4	1.33
Lance Painter	2	2	5.13	0	1.75
Brett Jodie	0	2	6.39	0	1.54
Kelly Wunsch	2	1	7.66	0	1.34
Felix Heredia	2	2	6.17	0	1.74
Alan Mills	1	1	6.00	1	1.56
Willie Blair	5	7	4.69	0	1.33
Tony Cogan	0	4	5.84	0	1.82
Mark Petkovsek	1	2	6.69	0	1.71
Manny Aybar	2	1	6.35	0	1.99
Bobby Chouinard	0	0	8.22	0	1.43
Brian Rose	0	3	7.45	0	1.90
Chris Peters	2	4	7.55	0	2.00
Gregg Olson	0	1	8.03	0	1.86
Joe Slusarski	0	1	9.00	0	1.81
V. de los Santos	0	0	9.00	0	2.00
Trey Moore	0	0	11.25	0	2.25
Bryce Florie	0	1	11.42	0	2.19
Frank Rodriguez	0	0	11.42	0	2.42
Felipe Lira	0	0	12.60	0	2.60
Horacio Estrada	1	1	14.54	0	2.08
Kevin Beirne	0	0	12.86	0	2.71
Wilfredo Rodriguez	0	0	15.00	0	2.33
Antonio Osuna	0	0	20.77	0	2.31

Look for Consistency

	W	L	ERA	Sv	Ratio
			2001 Statistics		
Mariano Rivera	4	6	2.34	50	0.90
Keith Foulke	4	9	2.33	42	0.98
Troy Percival	4	2	2.65	39	0.99
Robb Nen	4	5	3.01	45	1.03
Kazuhiro Sasaki	0	4	3.24	45	0.88
Jason Isringhausen	4	3	2.65	34	1.08

Name	W	L	ERA	Sv	Ratio
Billy Wagner	2	5	2.73	39	1.02
Jeff Shaw	3	5	3.62	43	1.08
Trevor Hoffman	3	4	3.43	43	1.14
Armando Benitez	6	4	3.77	43	1.30
Byung-Hyun Kim	5	6	2.94	19	1.04
Flash Gordon	1	2	3.38	27	1.06
Antonio Alfonseca	4	4	3.06	28	1.35
Jeff Nelson	4	3	2.76	4	1.13
Chad Fox	5	2	1.89	2	1.20
Ugueth Urbina	2	2	3.64	24	1.23
Roberto Hernandez	5	6	4.12	28	1.40
Mike Williams	6	4	3.80	22	1.48
Bob File	5	3	3.27	0	1.16
Scott Strickland	2	6	3.21	9	1.33
Kelvim Escobar	6	8	3.50	0	1.15
Todd Van Poppel	4	1	2.52	0	1.35
John Rocker	5	9	4.32	23	1.49
Scott Sullivan	7	1	3.31	0	1.26
Scott Stewart	3	1	3.78	3	1.17
Paul Shuey	5	3	2.82	2	1.45
Ron Mahay	0	0	2.61	0	1.40
Pedro Borbon	2	4	3.71	0	1.13
Jesus Colome	2	3	3.33	0	1.27
Jason Marquis	5	6	3.48	0	1.33
Mike Fyhrie	0	2	3.15	0	1.30
Rick White	4	5	3.88	2	1.26
Tim Worrell	2	5	3.45	0	1.33
Greg Swindell	2	6	4.53	2	1.10
Jerrod Riggan	3	3	3.40	0	1.38
Justin Speier	6	3	4.58	0	1.19
S. Hasegawa	5	6	4.04	0	1.29
Mike Myers	2	3	3.60	0	1.40
Vic Darensbourg	1	2	4.25	1	1.27
Aaron Fultz	3	1	4.56	1	1.28
Scott MacRae	0	1	4.02	0	1.31
Lou Pote	2	0	4.15	0	1.38
Jose Paniagua	4	3	4.36	3	1.47
Vicente Padilla	3	1	4.24	0	1.41
Damaso Marte	0	1	4.71	0	1.27
Jose Santiago	4	6	4.61	0	1.40
Jesse Orosco	0	1	3.94	0	1.50
Hector Carrasco	4	3	4.64	1	1.45
Darwin Cubillan	0	0	4.10	0	1.63
Matt Ginter	1	0	5.22	0	1.21
Jose Antonio Nunez	4	2	4.58	0	1.47
David Lee	1	0	3.70	0	1.62
Mike Morgan	1	0	4.17	0	1.63
Tom Davey	2	4	4.50	0	1.53
Armando Almanza	2	2	4.83	0	1.46
Mike Fetters	3	2	5.51	9	1.58
Todd Erdos	0	0	4.96	0	1.41
Johan Santana	1	0	4.74	0	1.51
Joe Beimel	7	11	5.23	0	1.56
Troy Brohawn	2	3	4.93	1	1.58
Dennys Reyes	2	6	4.92	0	1.62
Rodney Myers	1	2	5.32	0	1.54
Pat Mahomes	7	6	5.70	0	1.58
Britt Reames	4	8	5.59	0	1.57
David Lundquist	0	1	5.95	0	1.37
Jeff Brantley	0	1	5.14	0	1.67
Omar Olivares	6	9	6.55	1	1.50
Mike Judd	1	1	5.28	0	1.69
Chuck McElroy	2	3	5.28	0	1.77
Will Cunnane	0	3	5.40	0	1.70
J.D. Smart	1	2	6.46	0	1.50
Dave Borkowski	0	2	6.37	0	1.52
Russ Springer	0	0	7.13	1	1.36
Adam Bernero	0	0	7.30	0	1.38
John Parrish	1	2	6.14	0	1.77
Sun-Woo Kim	0	2	5.83	0	1.80
Jeff Williams	2	1	6.29	0	1.77
Ryan Kohlmeier	1	2	7.30	6	1.65
Marc Wilkins	0	1	6.75	0	1.73
Heath Murray	1	7	6.54	0	1.93
Mike Mohler	0	0	7.24	0	1.68
Alan Benes	2	0	7.36	0	1.77
Matt Whiteside	0	1	7.16	0	1.84
Tim Crabtree	0	5	6.56	4	2.19
Dan Wheeler	1	0	8.66	0	1.98
Tom Martin	1	0	10.06	0	1.94

Production Will Drop

	W	L	ERA	Sv	Ratio
			2001 Statistics		

Name	W	L	ERA	Sv	Ratio
Jose Mesa	3	3	2.34	42	1.23
Jeff Zimmerman	4	4	2.40	28	0.90
Bob Wickman	5	0	2.39	32	1.11
Arthur Rhodes	8	0	1.72	3	0.85
Felix Rodriguez	9	1	1.68	0	1.00
Steve Kline	3	3	1.80	9	1.09
Eddie Guardado	7	1	3.51	12	1.05
Chad Fox	5	2	1.89	2	1.20
Esteban Yan	4	6	3.90	22	1.20
Dave Weathers	4	5	2.41	4	1.15
Paul Quantrill	11	2	3.04	2	1.18
Norm Charlton	4	3	3.02	1	0.99
Al Levine	8	10	2.38	2	1.31
Jeff Fassero	4	4	3.42	12	1.21
Kyle Farnsworth	4	6	2.74	2	1.15
Ramiro Mendoza	8	4	3.75	6	1.11
Mike Lincoln	2	1	2.68	0	1.12
Mike Magnante	3	1	2.77	0	1.14
Vladimir Nunez	4	5	2.74	0	1.18
Mike Stanton	9	4	2.58	0	1.36
Giovanni Carrara	6	1	3.16	0	1.14
Cliff Politte	2	3	2.42	0	1.23
Jose Cabrera	7	4	2.88	2	1.30
Danny Patterson	5	4	3.06	1	1.18
Miguel Batista	11	8	3.36	0	1.24
Josias Manzanillo	3	2	3.39	2	1.08
Ricardo Rincon	2	1	2.83	2	1.20
Rolando Arrojo	5	4	3.48	5	1.19
Sean Lowe	9	4	3.61	3	1.22
David Riske	2	0	1.98	1	1.39
Jose Jimenez	6	1	4.09	17	1.42
Mike DeJean	4	2	2.77	1	1.35
Matt Anderson	3	1	4.82	22	1.32
Jason Christiansen	2	1	3.22	3	1.21
Chad Bradford	2	1	2.70	1	1.28
Mike Matthews	3	4	3.24	1	1.20
Jay Powell	5	3	3.24	7	1.41
Jeff Tam	2	4	3.01	3	1.30
Rod Beck	6	4	3.90	6	1.30
Mark Leiter	2	1	3.75	0	1.11
Jay Witasick	8	2	3.30	1	1.41
Jack Cressend	3	2	3.67	0	1.17
Randy Choate	3	1	3.35	0	1.26
Braden Looper	3	3	3.55	3	1.31
Ryan Franklin	5	1	3.56	0	1.28
Matt Herges	9	8	3.44	1	1.44
Dan Plesac	4	5	3.57	1	1.28
Steve Reed	3	3	3.55	1	1.29
Nelson Cruz	3	3	4.15	2	1.17
Ben Weber	6	2	3.42	0	1.42
Mike Buddie	0	1	3.89	2	1.22
Jim Brower	7	10	3.97	1	1.38
Rheal Cormier	5	6	4.21	1	1.29
Chad Zerbe	3	0	3.92	0	1.31
Ray King	0	4	3.60	1	1.35

Production Will Drop (continued)

Name	W	L	ERA	Sv	Ratio
Luther Hackman	1	2	4.29	1	1.18
Gene Stechschulte	1	5	3.86	6	1.44
Scott Eyre	1	2	3.45	2	1.40
Brian Boehringer	0	4	3.65	2	1.39
Mark Guthrie	6	2	4.47	1	1.32
Mike Venafro	5	5	4.80	4	1.37
Willis Roberts	9	10	4.91	6	1.49
Pasqual Coco	1	0	4.40	0	1.26
Mark Wohlers	4	1	4.26	0	1.39
Erik Sabel	3	2	4.38	0	1.34
Gary Glover	5	5	4.93	0	1.30
B.J. Ryan	2	4	4.25	2	1.45
Blake Stein	7	8	4.74	1	1.46
Jeff Wallace	0	3	3.40	0	1.59
Rich Rodriguez	2	2	4.15	0	1.49
Kane Davis	2	4	4.35	0	1.43
Luis Vizcaino	2	1	4.66	1	1.36
Al Reyes	2	1	3.86	1	1.60
Hector Mercado	3	2	4.08	0	1.60
Chris Nichting	0	3	4.46	1	1.49
Matt DeWitt	0	2	3.79	0	1.68
Doug Creek	2	5	4.31	0	1.60
Rusty Meacham	1	3	5.60	0	1.39
Ricky Bones	4	4	5.06	0	1.63
Jake Westbrook	4	4	5.85	0	1.56
Matt Perisho	2	3	5.72	0	1.73
Todd Belitz	1	1	7.71	0	1.29

Sleepers

2001 Statistics (includes minor leagues)

Name	W	L	ERA	Sv	Ratio
Jeremy Fikac	8	0	1.84	18	0.99
Victor Zambrano	7	4	2.76	14	1.15
Scott Chiasson	4	5	1.91	34	1.01
Travis Phelps	4	2	2.78	5	1.15
Ryan Drese	11	10	3.58	0	1.18
Cory Bailey	2	1	3.03	1	1.25
Jorge Julio	2	3	3.27	19	1.29
Dicky Gonzalez	9	7	3.77	0	1.32
Lorenzo Barcelo	2	0	4.85	0	1.50
Chad Paronto	4	6	4.73	1	1.59
Eddie Oropesa	2	1	3.47	0	1.49
Bobby Seay	3	6	6.03	0	1.61
Wascar Serrano	9	8	5.21	0	1.53
Mike Bacsik	13	6	3.37	0	1.14
Justin Duchscherer	14	7	3.26	0	1.09
Toby Borland	7	4	2.67	3	1.17
Carlos Zambrano	11	7	4.43	0	1.33
Ken Vining	2	3	3.93	4	1.44
Mark Corey	9	4	1.96	27	1.21
Joe Nelson	1	2	2.81	8	1.10
Josh Fogg	4	7	4.50	4	1.34

STATS' Top 50 Prospects

STATS ranks the top 50 prospects in baseball below. Only players who haven't exceeded major league rookie limits of 130 at-bats and 50 innings pitched were considered. The ages listed are as of Opening Day (April 1, 2002).

Hitters	Pos	Age	2000 Levels	G	Avg	HR	RBI	SB	OBP	SLG
2. Hank Blalock, Tex	3B	21	AA/A+	131	.352	18	108	10	.424	.550
3. Wilson Betemit, Atl	SS	20	Majors/AA/A+	139	.304	12	62	15	.350	.446
4. Carlos Pena, Tex	1B	23	Majors/AAA	141	.284	26	86	11	.403	.544
5. Sean Burroughs, SD	3B	21	AAA	104	.322	9	55	9	.386	.467
6. Joe Borchard, CWS	OF	23	AA	133	.295	27	98	5	.384	.509
7. Marlon Byrd, Phi	OF	24	AA	137	.316	28	89	32	.386	.555
10. Angel Berroa, KC	SS	22	Majors/AA/A+	146	.304	14	71	27	.373	.480
12. Brandon Phillips, Mon	SS	20	AA/A+	122	.292	11	59	30	.372	.440
13. Austin Kearns, Cin	OF	21	AA/R	65	.261	6	40	7	.352	.419
14. Mike Cuddyer, Min	3B-1B	23	Majors/AA	149	.298	30	88	6	.392	.552
15. Nick Johnson, NYY	1B	23	Majors/AAA	133	.246	20	57	9	.393	.439
17. Joe Mauer, Min	C	18	R+	32	.400	0	14	4	.492	.491
19. Josh Phelps, Tor	C	23	Majors/AA	144	.285	31	98	4	.400	.548
22. Josh Hamilton, TB	OF	20	AA/A	27	.200	1	6	2	.250	.290
23. Jack Cust, Ari	OF	23	Majors/AAA	138	.279	27	79	6	.417	.525
24. Juan Rivera, NYY	OF	23	Majors/AAA/AA	135	.320	28	98	9	.358	.553
25. Mark Teixeira, Tex	3B	21			Did Not Play					
26. Chris Snelling, Sea	OF	20	A+	114	.336	7	73	12	.418	.491
27. Bobby Hill, ChC	2B	23	AA/R	60	.298	3	22	21	.395	.385
30. Carl Crawford, TB	OF	20	AA	132	.274	4	51	36	.323	.352
31. Alex Escobar, NYM	OF	23	Majors/AAA	129	.260	15	60	19	.318	.427
34. Jose Reyes, NYM	SS	18	A	108	.307	5	48	30	.337	.472
35. John Buck, Hou	C	21	A	122	.275	22	73	4	.345	.483
36. Xavier Nady, SD	1B	23	A+	137	.302	26	100	6	.381	.527
38. Orlando Hudson, Tor	2B	24	AAA/AA	139	.306	8	79	19	.382	.470
39. Antonio Perez, Sea	SS	20	AA	5	.143	0	0	0	.143	.143
41. Omar Infante, Det	SS	20	AA	132	.302	2	62	27	.355	.367
42. Joe Crede, CWS	3B	23	Majors/AAA	141	.271	17	72	3	.341	.446
43. Jason Lane, Hou	OF	25	AA	137	.316	38	124	14	.407	.608
46. Esteban German, Oak	2B	23	AAA/AA	130	.311	10	44	48	.427	.443
47. Ramon Vazquez, Sea	SS	25	Majors/AAA	144	.295	10	83	9	.387	.415
48. J.R. House, Pit	C	22	AA	112	.258	11	56	1	.323	.399
49. Hee Seop Choi, ChC	1B	23	AAA	77	.229	13	45	5	.313	.417

Pitchers	Pos	Age	2000 Levels	W	L	ERA	IP	H	BB	SO
1. Josh Beckett, Fla	RHP	21	Majors/AA/A+	16	3	1.54	164.0	96	45	227
8. Nick Neugebauer, Mil	RHP	21	Majors/AAA/AA	8	8	3.29	136.2	110	67	186
9. Juan Cruz, ChC	RHP	21	Majors/AA	12	7	3.80	166.0	147	77	176
11. Mark Prior, ChC	RHP	21			Did Not Play					
16. Dennis Tankersley, SD	RHP	23	AAA/AA/A+	10	4	1.98	136.1	89	44	173
18. Ryan Anderson, Sea	LHP	22			Did Not Play—Injured					
20. Carlos Hernandez, Hou	LHP	21	Majors/AA	13	3	3.39	156.2	126	76	184
21. Jake Peavy, SD	RHP	20	AA/A+	9	6	2.97	133.1	95	45	188
28. Jon Rauch, CWS	RHP	23	AAA	1	3	5.79	28.0	28	7	27
29. Rafael Soriano, Sea	RHP	22	AA/A+	8	5	2.82	137.1	83	53	151
32. Kurt Ainsworth, SF	RHP	23	Majors/AAA	10	9	5.19	151.0	142	56	160
33. Corwin Malone, CWS	LHP	21	AA/A+/A	13	5	1.98	168.1	116	66	177
37. Ty Howington, Cin	LHP	21	AA/A+/A	8	5	2.30	117.1	84	53	129
40. Adam Johnson, Min	RHP	22	Majors/AAA/AA	7	9	4.79	161.2	156	62	152
44. Jerome Williams, SF	RHP	20	AA	9	7	3.95	130.0	116	34	84
45. Brett Myers, Phi	RHP	21	AA	13	4	3.87	156.0	156	43	130
50. Mario Ramos, Oak	LHP	24	AAA/AA	16	4	3.10	174.0	145	55	150

700

About STATS, Inc.

STATS, Inc., a News Corporation company, is affiliated with—and is the official statistics provider to—FOX Sports. STATS collects and disseminates most, if not all, of the information found within these pages, in addition to the statistics you might find on your favorite website. STATS, Inc. is the nation's leading sports information and statistical analysis company, providing detailed sports services for a wide array of consumer and commercial clients.

As one of the elite companies in sports, STATS provides the most detailed, up-to-the-minute sports information to professional teams, print and broadcast media, software developers and interactive service providers around the country. STATS' network of trained sports reporters records the details of more than 3,800 sporting events across the four major sports annually. Some of our major clients include FOX Sports, the Associated Press, Lycos, *The Sporting News*, ESPN.com, Yahoo!, Electronic Arts, MSNBC, SONY, Topps and WGN Sports.

STATS Publishing, a division of STATS, Inc., produces 10 pro sports annuals, including the *Major League Handbook*, *The Scouting Notebook*, the *Pro Football Handbook*, the *Pro Basketball Handbook* and the *Hockey Handbook*. The annuals now are available in an e-book format on our website (www.stats.com), as well as the traditional book form. In 1998, we introduced two baseball encyclopedias, the *All-Time Major League Handbook* (second edition updated through 1999) and the *All-Time Baseball Sourcebook*. Together they combine for more than 5,000 pages of baseball history. We added the *Pro Football Sourcebook* as an annual in 2000. Also, original articles by STATS authors appear three times per week in the Insider section of ESPN.com. All of our publications and additional editorial content deliver STATS' expertise to fans, scouts, general managers and media across the country.

In addition, STATS Fantasy Sports is at the forefront of the fantasy sports industry. We develop fantasy baseball, football, basketball, hockey, golf and auto racing games for a host of sites. We also feature the first historical baseball simulation game created specifically for the Internet—Diamond Legends. No matter what time of year, STATS Fantasy Sports has a fantasy game to keep even the most passionate sports fan satisfied.

Information technology has grown by leaps and bounds in the last decade. STATS will continue to be at the forefront as a supplier of the most up-to-date, in-depth sports information available.

For more information on our products, or on joining our reporter network, contact us via:

Internet — www.stats.com
          http://biz.stats.com

Toll Free in the USA at 1-800-63-STATS (1-800-637-8287)

Outside the USA at 1-847-470-8798

Or write to:

STATS, Inc.
8130 Lehigh Ave.
Morton Grove, IL 60053

Index

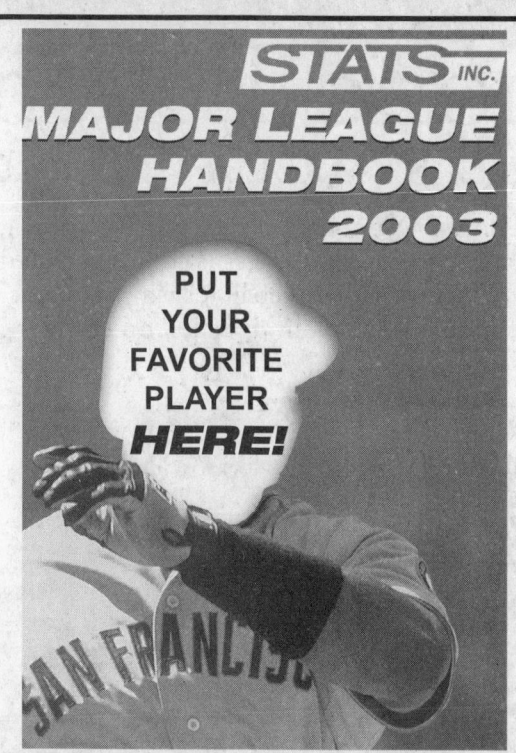
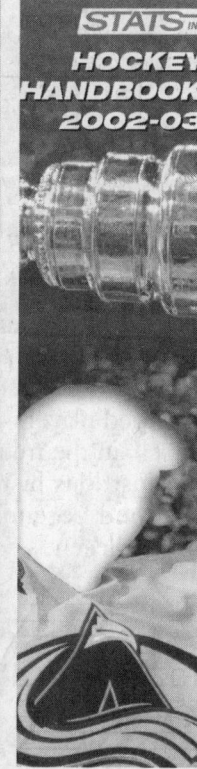